International Literature in English
Essays on the Major Writers

Garland Reference Library of the Humanities (Vol. 1159)

INTERNATIONAL LITERATURE IN ENGLISH

ESSAYS ON THE MAJOR WRITERS

Edited by

ROBERT L. ROSS

THE EDWARD A. CLARK CENTER FOR AUSTRALIAN STUDIES
THE UNIVERSITY OF TEXAS AT AUSTIN

GARLAND PUBLISHING, INC.
1991
NEW YORK & LONDON

Library of Congress Cataloging–in–Publication Data

International literature in English : essays on the major writers / edited by Robert L. Ross.
    p.   cm. — (Garland reference library of the humanities; vol. 1159)
    Includes bibliographical references and index.
    ISBN 0–8240–3437–6
    1. Commonwealth of Nations literature (English)—History and criticism. 2. English
literature—Foreign countries—History and criticism. 3. Decolonization in literature. 4.
Colonies in literature. I. Ross, Robert L. II. Series.
PR9080.I57   1991   90-24468
820.9˝9171241—dc20   CIP

Excerpts from *The Arkansas Testament,* copyright © 1987 by Derek Walcott; *The Collected Poems, 1948–1984,* copyright © 1986 by Derek Walcott; *Dream on Monkey Mountain and Other Plays,* copyright © 1970 by Derek Walcott; *Three Plays,* copyright © 1986 by Derek Walcott. Reprinted by permission of Farrar, Straus and Giroux, Inc.

Quotations from "Panther and Peacock," "I am the Captain of my Soul," "Clair de Lune," "Triste, Triste," "Fido's Paw is Bleeding," "The Lion's Bride," "A Valediction," "A Feline Requiem," "Schrodinger's Cat Preaches to the Mice," "Reflections," "Carapace," by Gwen Harwood from *Selected Poems.* Copyright © Gwen Harwood, 1975, 1985, 1990. Reprinted by permission of Collins, Angus & Robertson.

Quotations from "Bora Ring," "Country Town," "Nigger's Leap, New England," "South of My Days," "Our Love So Natural," "Australia 1970," "The Vision," by Judith Wright from *Collected Poems, 1942–1970*, copyright © Judith Wright 1946, 1953, 1970, 1971; "Two Dream Times," by Judith Wright from *Alive: Poems 1971–1972,* copyright © Judith Wright, 1973; "Brief Notes on Canberra," "Unpacking Books," by Judith Wright from *Fourth Quarter and Other Poems,* copyright © Judith Wright, 1976; "Rockpool," by Judith Wright from *Phantom Dwelling,* copyright © Judith Wright, 1985. Reprinted by permission of Collins, Angus & Robertson.

Quotations from "Conch Shell," "Conversation," "The Faa-Samoa is Perfect, They sd," "Flying Fox," "Master Fortune," "Stranger on the Plateau," by Albert Wendt from *Inside Us the Dead,* copyright © Albert Wendt, 1976; "Shamans of Visions," by Albert Wendt from *Shamans of Visions,* copyright © Albert Wendt, 1984. Reprinted by permission of the author.

Excerpts from *The Vernacular Republic: Selected Poems,* copyright © 1982 by Les A. Murray; *The Daylight Moon and Other Poems,* copyright © 1988 by Les A. Murray. Reprinted by permission of Persea Books, Inc.

Design by Julie Threlkeld

Printed on acid-free, 250-year-life paper
Manufactured in the United States of America

Contents

Preface

> But before Father could explain more, about beauty and emotion
> and inspiration and imagination, Mother took the book and said it
> was her turn now and too much theory she did not want to listen
> to, it was confusing and did not make as much sense as reading
> the stories, she would read them her way and Father could read
> them his.
>
> —Rohinton Mistry, "Swimming Lessons"

This collection of biographical sketches, essays, and bibliographical materials is intended as an introduction to the riches of a literature in English that comes not from the familiar sources, Great Britain and the United States, but from all corners of the world where English may be the first, second, third, or tenth language. This writing has often been relegated to a literary limbo, sometimes even in its own country, half accepted and half known. But that situation is changing radically as literature in English becomes truly international—so much so that some observers have predicted that eventually British and American writing will be absorbed into this body and no longer enjoy a privileged place, their days of assumed superiority ended. While once the literary capitals were London and New York, today they reach out to include Delhi, Sydney, Nairobi, Johannesburg, Auckland, Toronto, Lagos, and so on. The emergence and slow but sure recognition of international literature in English does not herald the fading of British and American writing. Instead the writing from abroad enriches the very literature that, in the first place, provided the language, the traditions, the text for a creative expansion comparable to the Roman Empire's dispersion of Latin. Not that international writing in English comprises a sort of carbon copy of the mother literature. Far from it. The major writers, represented here, have built and reversed, negated and revised, re-formed and altered that on which they drew.

Except in larger libraries, critical material on this literature still remains scant; if available at all it is often limited to surveys, digests, reviews, plot summaries. Although there is a handful of scholarly journals devoted to the study of international writing, they are often not widely available. The major literary journals—those on most library shelves—rarely include material on writers other than American and British or those from Western Europe. For example, the century-old *Publication of the Modern Language Association* (*PMLA*) published its first such article in 1987. Hence the need for a book that addresses this work in a thoroughly developed manner.

The writers and their work are arranged thematically so that they might first be apprehended as part of a larger scene, then as representatives of their particular country. Each is accorded a short biographical sketch that specifies the place of birth. Not that that means much: A writer considered African, for instance, might have lived in London for the past several years; another may be claimed by both Great Britain and the West Indies; someone still called an Indian novelist could have become an American citizen. Often in the past the aspiring writer from a colonial background found it necessary to go to London to fulfill literary ambitions and to be assured of recognition. Many of these authors still lead peripatetic lives, several having now made connections in the United States. Living in the so-called metropolis though—whether London or New York—no longer seems a necessity but rather a matter of choice or circumstances—such as political exile. There are those who stayed at home to write and succeeded.

The heart of each entry is the essay itself. Focused directly on the writer's work, some offer a survey in order to explore major themes; some take up a single work, usually one widely known as illustrative of the entire body; others examine technique, biographical relationships, the writer's overall development, or the historical setting. None has been published previously.

The development of what is being called postcolonial critical theory has started to play an important role in the study of international English writing. While taking into consideration some of the inherent critical problems this literature raises, these essays set out not to propose how to treat the literature but to treat it. After all, before critical theory can have much significance the literature itself need be known thoroughly. Many of the discussions, of course, do rely in part on contemporary feminist thinking, the incipient postcolonial discourse, tenets of postmodernism, principles of comparative studies, linguistics, intertextuality, and so on; but they wear their theory modestly.

The list of the writer's work that follows the essay does not supply publishers' names, considering the flux of international publishing: companies going in and out of business and absorbing one another; new editions appearing and disappearing; books coming out in one country under one imprint, elsewhere under another, sometimes even with different titles. These lists are not always exhaustive, for many writers have published uncollected poems, fiction, and articles in newspapers and journals; when one of the articles is considered especially significant, it is listed and described. The annotated entries under "Selected Critical Readings" supply information on specialized articles and comprehensive book-length studies. As well, these entries and the introductory note introducing them provide information on the writer's critical reception and reputation.

Fiction dominates, which has been the case in overseas reception. Possibly fiction travels better than poetry and drama.

Some might argue that those who appear are not the only major writers of international literature in English. True enough. Others, while not questioning the appropriateness of most, might well insist that a few are not major at all. The criteria for selection rested primarily on international reputation and publication abroad, but in some instances the historical place of a particular author was taken into consideration. With some of the newer writers who have not published all that much, the selection was made on the basis of what could be considered their future importance.

The critics preparing the entries are as international as the literature they discuss. Many take up writers from their own countries while some address those from other places and other cultures. They carry impressive credentials, many having published books and articles on the figures they are treating as well as work on the other writers included.

This collection offers an uncommon wealth of criticism, which attests to the fact that a field once considered a little less than scholarly has come of age.

(Source of quotation: p. 246. Mistry, Rohinton. "Swimming Lessons." From *Swimming Lessons and Other Stories from Firozsha Baag.* Boston: Houghton Mifflin, 1989. 229–50.)

Acknowledgments

International Literature in English is in itself an international collaborative effort. Each of the entries was prepared as a labor of love by critics from every part of the world. As editor I am deeply indebted to them, as will be the readers of this book in the years to come.

The capabilities of word processing simplified editing and preparing the manuscript. I am most appreciative of the assistance given by Cedric Tung, who with great skill converted mysterious computer disks from far corners of the world and scanned endless manuscript pages.

Several colleagues were helpful in making arrangements with contributors and in some cases suggesting writers who should be included. I am especially grateful to those who assisted in these areas: Rudolf Bader, Reed Way Dasenbrock, Rodney Edgecombe, Yasmine Gooneratne, Feroza Jussawalla, Bernth Lindfors, J.A. Wainwright.

And I appreciate the support of this project by The Edward A. Clark Center for Australian Studies at The University of Texas at Austin.

Introduction

THE ACT AND ART OF DECOLONIZATION

The East was too strident, too dissonant, too austere, too raw; it had to be muted, toned down, tarted up—its music larded with familiar rhythms, its literature wrenched into shapes recognized by Western tradition, its dances made palatable by an infusion of known idioms, its people taught to genuflect before understatement, before a measure of acceptance came. Undilute East had always been too much for the West; and soulful East always came lapdog fashion to the West, mutely asking to be not too little and not too much, but just right.

—Kamala Markandaya, *Possession*

The once powerful British Empire left many a legacy behind. One of its more constructive and most lasting contributions was the English language and the literature that resulted. From the outset colonizers wrote: at first travel books about the strange lands they settled; then poetry and fiction and drama that played on their exotic surroundings even while they imitated English forms and often apologized for the excesses of Empire. The writing, published at first in England, later in the colonies, was not taken all that seriously but more often considered a minor appendage to the genuine literature of Great Britain.

By the end of the nineteenth century, though, the colonials and then the colonized started to develop their own distinctive literature—in Africa, India, Australia, in New Zealand, Canada, the West Indies, and so on. No longer content to remain in the shadows of British literature, this writing incorporated indigenous materials, stressed the unique nature of colonial society, and reached toward a national identity apart from that bestowed by the Empire. While drawing from the established text handed to it, the literature introduced all manner of invigorating themes, characters, setting, conflict; it incorporated untried usage of the English language and developed fresh stylistic devices. So a new English literature emerged, especially as Empire faded after the World Wars and Independence came.

How to treat a literature in English that belongs neither to England nor the United States, still what many consider the bastions of English-language writing? What to call this body of writing? In the past it was described as "literature of the dominions," "colonial," "Commonwealth"; once the Empire crumbled, "postcolonial," then "Third World" became fashionable, followed by "the new literatures in English."

Ironically, the official name adopted by the Modern Language Association tells what it is not: "English Literature Other than British and American." To name this writing and to treat it, this collection relies on "international literature in English." Such a title calls up no outdated political connections, promotes no critical theory, carries no connotation of "Other." It allows the critic to stress both a literary work's unique national quality and its place in a world literature, to determine its debt to a non-Western tradition as well as its intertextuality, to apply both internal and external critical standards, and to examine the larger meaning.

Although the essays were written independently—directed only by editorial guidelines more concerned with form than content, a commonality emerges time and again. This is not say that the collection forms a melting pot to break down the differences and make bland the variety, thus validating Kamala Markandaya's cogent observation that literature from faraway places need be "wrenched into shapes recognized by Western tradition." Such may have been true once but no more as these essays prove. The writing in English from around the world no longer finds it necessary to mold itself into the pre-set form of an imposed tradition. For these writers have constructed their own molds, apart from the old shapes, but a part of the larger shape international literature in English has taken.

Nevertheless, there emerges a commonality amid the divergence. And that commonality is the preoccupation with colonialism—or perhaps more accurately with decolonization, whether actual or metaphorical. The entries discussing the rich "art of decolonization" are arranged under "the acts of decolonization." Such an arrangement is not intended to foreclose on the obvious overlapping of the myriad concerns arising from these acts: the decolonization of history, patriarchy, boundaries, self, and art. For these are the convergent themes.

Decolonization through the act and art of writing has enlarged literature in English. The project has brought about a literature at times confrontational as it rewrites history and subverts established patriarchy, in other instances reconciliatory as it brings together disparate cultures. It is a literature intent on the destruction of boundaries, original in the journey to selfhood, and inventive in new ways of seeing. It at once explores strange physical terrain and the familiar territory of the mind.

(Source of quotation: p. 116. Markandaya, Kamala. *Possession.* New York: John Day, 1963.)

INTERNATIONAL LITERATURE IN ENGLISH

Essays on the Major Writers

I. Decolonizing History

Writing to decolonize colonial history came early. Olive Schreiner, whom many consider the first significant international writer in English, published *The Story of an African Farm* in 1883. Discussing her work, Gerald Monsman points out that "all of Schreiner's fiction anticipates those disruptions of colonial expansion addressed by contemporary third world protest literature." Monsman goes on to suggest that this white South African writer sets out as well to decolonize patriarchy through her feminist perspective, boundaries through her aversion to racialism and imperial expansion, self through her handling of the alienated individual, art through her inventive use of native materials. To some extent, the work of Olive Schreiner serves to introduce those common themes that have emerged and diverged in international literature.

The rewriting of colonial history came later to the indigenous peoples whose lands had been usurped by settler societies. J.J. Healy discusses the work of the Australian Aboriginal writer Colin Johnson/Mudrooroo Narogin in this light, finding that the act of changing his name from the Anglo-Saxon to the Aboriginal symbolized this "imaginative movement across cultural boundaries." Such is the thrust of the essays on two Maori writers from New Zealand, Nan Albinski's on the work of Witi Ihimaera and Margery Fee's on that of Keri Hulme. Albinski notes that while Ihimaera's earlier work re-creates the Maori past sympathetically, often lovingly, the more recent fiction has become "strongly confrontational" in its handling of the conflicts between the Maori and Pakeha worlds. Fee calls Hulme's *The Bone People* a "part of postcolonial discursive formation evolving worldwide to counter not only the 'truths' that drove the imperialism of nineteenth century, but also those that drive the centers of power in the twentieth." Likewise Jean-Pierre Durix in discussing the Samoan writer Albert Wendt concludes that he "aims to rewrite the history of his island," and to do so in his own way.

In 1935 Mulk Raj Anand published *Untouchable*, the first major novel by an Indian writer—not a Britisher writing about India. This fictional protest against imperialism is perhaps one of the purest examples of literary decolonization, as Shyam Asnani points out in his discussion of it along with the two similar books that followed soon after, *Coolie* and *Two Leaves and a Bud*. While some now consider Anand more of a propagandist than artist, Asnani argues that his books will endure as testaments to "a renewal of the human spirit." Similarly, Feroza Jussawalla sees R.K. Narayan's *Swami and Friends*, which appeared the same year as Anand's book, as a work of protest. Although Narayan is more often thought of today as a writer of gentle social comedies about South Indian life, Jussawalla insists that the "sweet mangos" have turned to "malt vinegar." She views Narayan as being acutely concerned with postcolonial social and political events, which he satirizes even while accepting them as part of "the cycle of history."

There are no comparable indigenous novels from Africa during the 1930s. Instead the African novels, the major ones appearing first in the late 1950s, condemned the Empire as it was fading, or after the fact, then name it the source for the malaise of the once-colonized and the ills of the newly independent countries. G.D. Killam, in his study of Chinua Achebe, strikes a chord that resounds through much of this writing: ". . . to set the record of Nigeria's (and by implication Africa's) encounter with colonial history straight, to write about his own people and for his own people." Similarly, Ayi Kwei Armah, according to Rudolf Bader's discussion, moves away from a focus on the isolated individual to the larger community as he endeavors to record the past, present, and future of Africa, its "beauty, hope, and community . . . from the earliest migrations . . . through slavery and colonialism to the present perils... of the modern world."

Once African countries gained independence, writers like Ngugi wa Thiong'o and Nuruddin Farah were determined to rewrite neocolonialism. The euphoria of independence gone, the new nations all too often were headed by corrupt governments so that the people had often exchanged white colonial masters for black puppets. As G.D. Killam points out, Ngugi is a committed political writer in whose work is embedded a strong social purpose, so much so that Ngugi has described himself as writing down the "barrel of a pen." His scathing representations of Kenya do not limit themselves to that country alone, but inculcate the ironic dimensions affecting much of postcolonial Africa. Rosemary Colmer, in her discussion of Farah, talks about the "territories of pain" experienced by his colonized characters—modern day Somalis living under a harsh regime—as they search for an identity that has eluded or been denied them. For they too often discover, as does one of the characters in Farah's novel *Sardines*, that "In this century, the African is a guest whether in Africa or elsewhere." Both Ngugi and Farah live in exile.

West Indian George Lamming creates what Rudolf Bader calls "the paradigm of colonialism," attempting to free his characters (and his readers) of its effects on "individual consciousness." Bader quotes Lamming's own wish for readership: "My greatest pleasure would be to know that the cane-cutters and the laboring class read and understood *In the Castle of My Skin*." Reed Way Dasenbrock in discussing another West Indian writer says that Earl Lovelace has "unobtrusively decolonized himself" in his fictional quest for a postcolonial Caribbean identity that is no longer dependent on England or, more recently, on the United States.

Whereas the novel may have in some quarters evolved into a higher form invoking personal and communal rather than political decolonization, it has not yet reached that stage in South Africa. Although other South Africans wrote about race and colonialism after Olive Schreiner, it was not until 1948 that Alan Paton's *Cry, the Beloved Country* appeared. The novel spoke so forcefully and eloquently on the monstrosity of racialism that almost overnight it caught the world's imagination. Published at the same time the Afrikaner National Party came into power and introduced apartheid, the novel is not so much a condemnation of a single country's inhumanity as it is a testament to universal humaneness. Jonathan Paton, commenting on his father's writing, sees at work in *Cry, the Beloved Country* a Christian ethic calling for "comfort in desolation." Although, as the younger Paton admits, his father did not fulfill the promise the first novel held, this book has become a classic in the literature, still widely read and admired. Alan Paton did go on to write a series of important histories about the beleaguered country he loved so much.

Two other white South African novelists have gained international recognition as well, Nadine Gordimer and André Brink, both of whom have concentrated on rewriting the colonial dilemma that worsened as the years went by. Rowland Smith describes Gordimer's fiction as a "life-long scrutiny of the roles open to whites" in an apartheid society and treats her use of irony to delineate the peculiar part white South Africans with conscience have played in the freedom struggle. Brink, on the other hand, is especially interesting because he originally wrote in Afrikaans—the language of the official "tribe," then in English and often translated his work from one to the other. Anthony Hassall concludes in his essay on Brink's fiction that it "has worked variations" on a single story: "The black struggle for independence and human dignity, for the right to love and freedom, continues, and no escalation of white repression seems likely to break its spirit."

On the surface it may seem odd that those most widely recognized for their handling of racialism in South Africa are white, and therefore privileged. But the political structure hardly encouraged black writers, many of whom left the country and directed their energies toward political independence. However, Cecil Abrahams's discussion of the most important but not the only South African black writer, Alex La Guma, shows how La Guma, who died in exile, managed both to write lasting fiction and, in his own words, to "dedicate all my energies to ensure the betterment of all my people."

Another kind of historical decolonizing takes place in the work of the Australian poet Judith Wright, according to Bruce Bennett's discussion of a "vision" he describes as "ecological" and one "relevant" for today. Calling Wright both an artist and a moralist, Bennett traces the poet's overriding concern with the desolation of the land's original inhabitants and the land itself. It is a story of the Empire that could be told many times over.

So for those who write to decolonize history the past is theirs to restructure, the present to record, the future to imagine.

Olive Schreiner

Olive Emilie Albertina Schreiner, named after three siblings who died in infancy, was born at Wittenberg Mission Station, Cape Colony, South Africa, on 24 March 1855, the ninth of twelve children. Being raised on mission outposts and being many years old before she saw a town must have intensified Schreiner's proclivity for introspective brooding if not her "self-willed and impetuous" disposition. Her father, Gottlob, was a dreamy, impractical, German-born missionary, who lost his post for violating trading regulations. Schreiner described him as a man "with his Bible in his pocket and his head in the clouds, and his heart with Christ." Rebecca Lyndall, Schreiner's mother, was the daughter of an English clergyman; she was both repressed (Schreiner's image for her was "a grand piano kept permanently locked up and used as a common dining table") and repressive ("for generations my ancestors have been strict Puritans"). She undoubtedly instilled in the young Olive, or as she was then called, Emilie, the corrosive sense of inadequacy that became the psychological basis for the fictionalized autobiographical account of Undine's and Waldo's suffering in two of her novels.

The financial disintegration of the family and Schreiner's years of traveling back and forth among the households of friends and relatives—fourteen places in thirteen years, including living in a tent in the diamond fields, followed by her succession of posts as a governess on the remote farms of the Karoo, introduced her to the social, sexual, and educational difficulties of women. Except for some maternal instruction, Schreiner, unlike her brothers, was self-educated. Additionally, the shock of her little sister Ellie's death led her to question accepted religious beliefs, much to her pioneering missionary family's dismay. She outrageously may have retaliated against their religious harassment, turning the tables on their biblical literalism by insisting that the Sermon on the Mount be applied *au pied de la lettre*.

Schreiner left the Cape for England in 1881, still in the process of writing out her fair copy of *An African Farm*, her major work on it probably having been done from 1876 to 1880, coinciding roughly with her time as a governess. Self-educated in the great humanistic books, with a kind of haphazard minor in political/economic theory, through precocious reading of Herbert Spenser, J.S. Mill, Charles Darwin, R.W. Emerson, Thomas Carlyle, and Goethe, among many others, her intention in traveling to London had been to study for the medical profession. But her virulent asthma and the success in 1883 of her novel (for which the publisher's reader had been George Meredith) confirmed her in a literary career. Her circle of progressive intellectual friends and quirky paramours included Eleanor Marx, Havelock Ellis, George Moore, and Arthur Symons, among others.

To recover her emotional stability and to fight her dependency on narcotics, she traveled to Italy, returning in 1889 to South Africa with a considerable reputation, and settling for her health in the isolated village of Matjesfontein. Growing dumpier and more asthmatic, Schreiner also became progressively more mercurial, eccentric, and hysterical. She met and in 1894 married Samuel Cron Cronwright, a gentleman farmer and businessman. They briefly experienced the breadbaking bliss of domesticity before the death of their only child in infancy (carried around with her for years in a little white coffin, according to her husband) and ensuing marital stress resulted in prolonged separations.

Feeding the insatiable maw of urgent political causes and social concerns—*pro* feminism, socialism, pacifism; *contra* sexism, racism, imperialism, sadism, she fought a losing battle with deep-seated blockages to finish her fictional *magnum opus*, *From Man to Man*, on which she labored sporadically for more than forty years. Initially an admirer and close personal friend of Cecil Rhodes, Schreiner's sympathy with the natives and Boers led her to publish in 1897 *Trooper Peter Halket of Mashonaland*, a political novel sharply critical of Rhodes's native policy—less a "policy," according to the book, than simple extermination. In 1899 she published *An English South African's View of the Situation*, a pro-Boer essay. Her treatise on equal rights for women, *Women and Labour*, and her personal confession of pacifist beliefs, "The Dawn of Civilization" (begun during the First World War), followed in 1911 and 1921. She spent the War years in England apart from her husband and returned to South Africa as an invalid only to die there a few months later on 10 December 1920. Her unfinished novel, *From Man to Man*, dedicated to her little sister Ellie who had died so early, was edited by her husband and published in 1926; the autobiographically revealing *Undine* was released by him three years later.

A CHILD ON THE FARM

A little-remarked-upon sentence taken from Alexis de Tocqueville and affixed by Schreiner as an epigraph to her first published novel, *The Story of an African Farm*, suggests how central the figure of the child is to her political and social thinking:

> We must see the first images which the external world casts upon
> the dark mirror of his mind; or must hear the first words which
> awaken the sleeping powers of thought, and stand by his earliest
> efforts, if we would understand the prejudices, the habits, and the
> passions that will rule his life. The entire man is, so to speak, to be
> found in the cradle of the child.

Schreiner is primarily a writer interested in the relationship between early experiences and later development, and her fictional and intellectual prose has a strongly psychological and sociological cast. Although the child's world anticipates with great fidelity the personality of the mature adult, including religious orientation and sociopolitical choices in future life, many of Schreiner's most effectively portrayed children never or barely reach maturity. In particular, five children in Schreiner's fiction are highly reflective of her major concerns: Jannita in "Dream Life and Real Life: A Little African Story," Undine Bock in *Undine*, Lyndall and Waldo in *The Story of an African Farm*, and Rebekah in Schreiner's unfinished novel, *From Man to Man*. Sensitive and living on isolated farms, they are marginalized in various degrees, from outright victimization to benign neglect. With the exception of Rebekah, who as an adult transforms the African farm into an embodiment of her independent femaleness, the children who remain on or return to the farm never find a *modus vivendi* that successfully combines their social and psychic identities.

Schreiner's world is a different milieu from William Wordsworth's joyous natural order where "Heaven lies about us in our infancy." Wordsworth's Romantic celebration of the child "trailing clouds of glory" has become for Schreiner, as it had become earlier for Dickens, an orphanhood reflective of a deep alienation from society and nature. The African farm is a microcosm of colonial society, and the child on the farm epitomizes both the power of a crushing colonial/patriarchal structure (not only for children, but for all victims of gender, class, race) and the distorted self-image acquired by all those outside the social system. Yet if Dickens's children have been stripped of Wordsworth's inner hints of a divine reality, at least they ultimately find their way back into the social structure through a process of initiation/education, much as did Tom Jones in an earlier era. Schreiner's youngsters, on the other hand, often are denied the opportunities to apply to their advantage the lessons of experience; their isolation typifies the condition of all victims who are stifled to the end. Rebelling against authoritarian religion or against adult or patriarchal power, the child is both victimized and sometimes warped by her (or his) uneven struggle.

Schreiner stated in the Dedication to the volume in which her "Dream Life and Real Life" was reprinted that this story was "one of the first I ever made," and several of her most characteristic concerns in later years are fully present here. Her lifelong concern with the political issue of power, with those who are victims and those who victimize, is strongly foregrounded in this story; and the work was meant to shift her readers' political values and attitudes toward societal relationships. Though perhaps the pathos of little Jannita's death embodies a sentimentality that Schreiner later avoided or, at least, tempered with ironic interludes in her longer works, the motif of self-sacrifice epitomizes the author's moral and ethical world view. This and all of Schreiner's fiction anticipates those disruptions of colonial expansion addressed by contemporary third world protest literature.

Jannita, an orphan who only dreams of a parent's love, is charged with minding goats on the isolated farm of a tyrannical Afrikaner who indifferently starves and maltreats her. The status of Jannita as an indentured servant was nearly comparable to that of Schreiner herself, living as an adjunct to the Afrikaner households on the dry Karoo tablelands, though in practice Jannita's situation is even more closely aligned with the *de facto* enslavement of the natives by the settlers. As Jannita dozes, one of the goats she is minding is stolen by her fellow goatherd, Dirk the Hottentot, and is slaughtered and eaten by him and his two companions, a Bushman and an English railway worker. Dirk, who cozens Jannita and then supplies his whip to the Boer to thrash her for alleged negligence, projects his own oppressed and rejected state onto Jannita. And because the logical result of colonialism is to turn all its victims brutish, Dirk also desires to revenge himself on this second-rate imperialist. Unknown to the farmer, Dirk, the Bushman and the Navvy have been planning to murder these Boers because of greed and, on the Bushman's part, revenge for the destruction of his family by the settlers.

Clearly, the salient trait of Jannita's character is her radical innocence in an evil world. She cannot even defend herself with a white lie when asked by the sadistic farmer if she fell asleep minding the sheep. Perhaps she somehow escapes the "deadly sickness" of lies because, like Waldo's father Otto in *An African Farm*, she may be in the world but she is not of it. Although Jannita has a certain moral superiority by virtue of her status as child, the world subjects her to an isolation and frustrated longing for some parental love and final meaning that is incompatible with its religious, social, and political conditions. The father that she had originally fantasized as carrying her "away, away!" and the wild springbuck that actually fled "Away, away!" become the embodiments of her desire to seek freedom from her forced labor, a desire that is both a pragmatic response to maltreatment and a reflection of the human need everywhere to escape a spiritually stifling existence. So Jannita flees along the river to a natural enclosure beside the river among the rocks, a place filled with "a glorious soft green light." Nourishing kippersol trees surround the spot. Like the mellow light at the end of *An African Farm* that combines the harsh sunlight and the soft moonlight, this magical glow and beatific happiness is not quite earthly. But such mystic places and moments are frequently shot through with ambiguity. Schreiner's trees, often child sized, may indeed preside over spiritual vision; but dwarfed or stunted, they also testify to a lack of nourishment, constraint, and death. This derives from the fact already noted that personal vision pitted against either sociopolitical injustice or the original sin of the human heart cannot hope to have an immediate, broadly revitalizing response. Schreiner here is describing the political impotence of her own liberalism, caught between the claims of the abused natives and the powerful forces of the opposing colonial society, though the added irony of Jannita's story is that her moral concern is for the tyrant himself.

In contrast to the Bushman's desire for revenge, Jannita remains selflessly loyal to the Dutch family and runs to warn them of the plan she has overheard. Too late to arrive at the homestead before the murderers, she cries "Master, master, wake." The Boer is warned, though selfishly he supposes he has heard a jackal at his sheep; but Jannita is killed by the trio of human jackals and buried in an isolated grave. The story's major irony and theological crux is that the Boer, who like a petty imperialist tyrannizes over both the child and the natives, is not killed by the hate he has generated. Rather, Jannita dies as a sacrificial lamb in the guilty farmer's stead, anticipating in this respect at least one other Schreiner hero, Peter Halket, who follows his conscience to a martyr's death. Had the child succeeded in winning acceptance into the family circle by warning the farmer without herself being caught by the murderers, Schreiner's story simply would have become a stale cliché. In *An African Farm*, young Lyndall observes that only "made-up" stories turn out happily, but that reality is never so nice; similarly, Rebekah in "The Child's Day" had a favorite alphabet-book picture she looked at whenever "she wanted to make up stories. She had made one long story about it: how people were not kind to Peter and he had no one to love him but his pig, and how they both ran away together by that far-off road that went over the hill, and saw all the beautiful things on the other side." But waiting for the dreaming Rebekah is a real cobra in the orchard.

Schreiner's fiction clearly models itself on the truth of a harsher reality that cannot be imagined away. Yet the horror one feels at little Jannita's barbaric death, prefigured in the butchered goat from her flock (the child's hair is "silky" like that of her goats and, presumably, she is killed with the same bowie knife), is not meant to ironize her morality; rather, it is Schreiner's way of leading the reader to seek relief by identifying some inner victory for the child. At the end of the narrative, the moon that has been gradually waxing full throughout the action bestows a benediction on the child's final resting place; its radiance on the river's willows, emblems of mourning, and on the natural shelter ready for the inhabitant who never returns, breaks a supernatural light over that desolation, as if some invisible *pietà* has come to pass.

Potentially answering to the absence of love and the litany of embittered acts that feed upon others would be a nourishing paternal or maternal presence. But for the children in Schreiner's fiction who typically are without father or mother, that sustenance must come from nature itself. Yet because the farm that by definition should be a place of physical nourishment is the site of spiritual impoverishment, only outside its sphere does Jannita find healing for her hand cut by the whip of her master: "She listened and smiled, and pressed closer to the rock that took care of her. She pressed the palm of her hand against it. When you have no one to love you, you love the dumb things very much." For Jannita the "rock" is her father—*petr*- is the Greek root for both "father" and "rock," a pun that Schreiner would have been familiar with through Christ's weighty but witty assertion that he will build his church on the rock of Peter's confession. Precisely for this reason the cut hand against the rock of faith becomes a religious image for healing through Christ's stripes, Jannita's cuts ultimately doubling those of her redeemer. Certainly the absent father, parodied in the tyrannical Boer and ideally present in the child's dreams, becomes truly manifest only through Jannita's death. This must be understood in the light of Schreiner's intensely evangelical missionary upbringing in which the innocent child, by imitating the sacrifice of Christ who died for the guilty, makes manifest the Father of All. It may not be fashionable in some political circles to recognize the longstanding link between social activism and evangelical Christianity, but on the South African frontier in the nineteenth century the only force confronting the maxim gun was the Gospel. But sadly, Schreiner often seems to deny any material improvement for the specific moment in time; conquest is in the future and for humanity as a whole.

The heading of the first chapter of *Undine* describes the novel's eponymous heroine as "A Queer Little Child," epitomizing the feeling of difference from the social environment that all the other children also experience. This aching sense of alienation is allegorically described in Schreiner's short piece, "The Winged Butterfly" (the soul as breath is frequently figured as a butterfly), where wings transform the creeping caterpillar into a thing of beauty but separate it from more ordinary insects. Unable to bridge the gap between its winged state and that of its earth-bound companions, the butterfly dies of a broken heart. So, too, the child Undine, whose soul is more lovely than those around, finds her family and friends to be like the bitter, narrow conformist companions of the butterfly. Throughout, Undine is isolated and, in self-defeating response, seeks out physical, emotional, and spiritual seclusion—all the while longing for a love that does not destroy her independence. Inevitably, her infatuation with the cold-hearted Albert Blair runs a downward course described by the chapter headings: "Beautiful Snow," "Trodden Snow," "Melted Snow."

Even as a child, Undine senses that the masculine power-figure embodies sexual domination (one of the parallels between racial, class, and gender exploitation under colonialism). Thus, Undine's rejection of the male often is couched in negative and covertly sexual imagery. Her grandfather, whose chapel preaches a wrath-and-damnation gospel, resembles "ox hides . . . and he was so tall and thin . . . I never could see him rise . . . without having recalled to my mind the image of an earthworm creeping out of the ground, which unfolds and unfolds itself to unimagined lengths. He had more resemblance to the skin than to the earthworm, however; for he was mentally as ossified and incapable of growth as an ox hide under the sun. . . . In those days I had not eaten of the tree of knowledge." The incipient phallicism of the unfolding worm becomes explicit in the imagery of the worm-in-the-rose describing her cousin, the Reverend Mr. Jonathan Barnacles, in whose home Undine later lives:

> She hung as far from his reach as the rose that hangs in the topmost branch of a bush is from the worm that creeps up and down on the rotten leaves below. He hated her, and yet he loved her with a love that had grown with her opening beauty and her softening figure, as the worm grows while the rose bud swells.

The already-married Barnacles had been trying to seduce Undine; she vehemently rejects him, and "as he shuffled through the doorway he dropped one green slipper on the mat." Playing the part of Potiphar's wife, however, Barnacles writes to the one man Undine loves, permanently alienating him. Although the slipper recalls the shirt of the biblical Joseph, this seems to have been an actual episode in Schreiner's own adolescence when she resided in the home of the Reverend Mr. Zadoc Robinson. Years later she disclosed to Havelock Ellis, her friend (the sexologist, a kind of Anglo-Saxon Freud): "Yes, all that part of Undine is exactly autobiography. Old Rob. did leave his slipper. It is all true, but it isn't art, any more than a diary is."

Both in her personal experience and fictionally, Schreiner found the guardians of morality to be hypocritical; real beauty, moral or physical, is broken on the wheel of an institutionalized conformity. Even—perhaps especially—Undine's sole object of love, Albert Blair, requires this conformity from the butterfly:

> A woman to be womanly should have nothing striking or peculiar about her; she should shun all extremes in manners and modes of expression; she should have no strong views on any question, especially when they differ from those of her surroundings; she should not be too reserved in her manners, and still less too affable and undignified. There is between all extremes a happy mediate, and there a woman should always be found. Men may turn to one side or the other; woman never must.

In contrast to the crushing conformity of Albert's submissive ideal, which would do credit to Browning's Duke of Ferrara, is the young girl's basic desire to know and understand her surroundings without constraint. Undine must eat of the tree of knowledge and become an outcast; and her first words in the novel, addressed to Socrates, her monkey, are: "I wish we knew." This aspiration ironically is interrupted by the call to prayers. There, as Undine tries to listen to the words meant for God, she hears another voice:

> "Tick, tick," cried the inexorable old clock, "what good have you ever done? . . . Undine tried to listen to the prayer again, and she caught these words: "Thousands, O Lord, are going to destruction every moment."
>
> "Yes, yes, yes," said the clock, "tick, tick, hell, hell, going, going going, thousands, thousands, thousands, tick, tick, tick, tick." . . . She felt as though she were being suffocated.

In contrast to this narrow dogmatism with its message of predestination is the largeness of nature, including the mystical rocks among which Jannita had found solace:

> How peacefully the great round stones lay resting on each other. Through that subtle sympathy which binds together all things, and to stumps and rocks gives a speech which even we can understand, the night spoke to the child the sweet words of comfort which she had looked for in vain in the brown Testament.

For Schreiner, divine power inheres especially in nature, an insight not unlike that voiced in the 1877 sonnets of her contemporary, G. M. Hopkins: "The world is charged with the grandeur of God." But, as in Hopkins's "Wreck of the Deutschland" or later sonnets, nature for Schreiner also can have something of a divided or ambiguous identity—like the Great Mother that Walter Pater in "Hippolytus Veiled" had described as both nurturing her young and yet a huntress too, her maternity defined by "the arrow of death on the string." Thus the novel had begun with Undine and her monkey contemplating the stars; and it ends with Undine, according to the chapter heading, dying "Alone with the Stars." The stars teach her—in a phrase that strikingly anticipates Wallace Stevens's "Death is the mother of beauty"—that "the thing which you call death is the father of all life and beauty. Till life goes, till blood flows, no higher life can come." Only at her death when she is no longer subject to temporal determinants does Undine hear in the male voice the ideal acceptance that butterflies never have: "she heard in the dim delicious confusion the voice . . . 'My little girl, my own little girl—Undine,' it said over and over, and the soft tears of gladness filled her eyes, and in delicious dreamy darkness it seemed as though his arms were close around her."

If Jannita's death had been an embrace of guilt and atonement, Undine's death is a more Wordsworthian acceptance of and return to the forces of nature, "Rolled round in earth's diurnal course,/With rocks, and stones, and trees." Though renewal is necessarily a function of a ceaseless interplay between womb and tomb (Tennyson's "Eternal process moving on"), Schreiner's nature is frequently a harsh desert with ferocious sun and precious little water, and those child-sized trees indicate a maternal/paternal nourishment imperfectly received until the bitter end. The child's wistful desire to know is realized finally in her having learned not how to live but how to die. This is also evident in *An African Farm* where little Waldo finds in the prickly-pear on the summit of the "kopje" a reflection of his own alienation: "With his swollen eyes he sat there on a flat stone at the very top of the 'kopje': and the tree, with every one of its wicked leaves, blinked, and blinked, and blinked at him." Suppliant in the opening scene with its "thorny arms" and "fleshy leaves," the prickly-pear in the moonlight becomes a sinister expression of what Waldo takes to be his own isolated inner self; and the child loathes this apocalyptic manifestation of his lost self.

In contradistinction to this spiritual darkness and specifically juxtaposed with a suspended pocket watch relentlessly ticking in absolute darkness (an image cannibalized from the *Undine* manuscript), the softly beautiful moonlight in the novel's opening scene bathes the farm as Lyndall briefly awakens. Moon and watch, hung aloft silver and round, both tell time; but whereas the moonlight lovingly hides the children's flaws, Waldo's watch-as-moon emphasizes human defects and epitomizes a constrained, patriarchal version of nature and divinity. The ticking watch recalls Dickens's *Dombey and Son* (read by Schreiner, according to her husband's biography, during the period surrounding the composition of *Undine* and *An African Farm*) in which the power of civilization to grind and crush is epitomized in Mr. Dombey's ticking watch and in the remorseless clock at Dr. Blimber's Academy. Additionally, Undine's image of "the great world machine that grinds on so mysteriously with its ever-jarring, never-resting wheels flying around forever," possibly echoes Thomas Carlyle's image of the world as an engine, "rolling on, in its dead indifference, to grind me limb from limb" (*Sartor Resartus*). Schreiner constructs a parallel here between the punishing patriarchal God and the forgiving and maternal moon, that ancient mythical mother of the night who is the spirit of feeling, imagination, and intuition, those free-ranging, nonrational forces—although the "almost oppressive beauty" of the moon's light suggests a surfeit that threatens to suffocate or drown the child.

The god of the watch, driving Waldo to grovel in the dirt (it is a hunter or hunting watch, meaning that it has a cover to protect the crystal from field accidents, but also implying that its temporal ethos seeks to pursue and slay) looks forward to such cruel events as Waldo beaten on the fuel house floor by the overseer Blenkins or the black ox whipped to the ground and knifed by the transport rider—helpless animal like helpless child. The image of the ox Schreiner herself witnessed and described in "The Dawn of Civilization": "Three times I had seen an ox striving to pull a heavily loaded waggon up a hill, the blood and foam streaming from its mouth and nostrils as it struggled, and I had seen it fall dead, under the lash." Like the Boer who whips Jannita, Blenkins relishes using the parental rod on Waldo; ironically, Waldo is whipped not for the intellectual nourishment he found in the attic's books but, in a parody of Adam's punishment, for his supposed eating of dried peaches there: "'Waldo, answer me as you would your own father, in whose place I now stand to you: have you, or have you not, did you, or did you not, eat of the peaches in the loft? . . . Chasten thy son while there is hope,' said Bonaparte, 'and let not thy soul spare for his crying.' Those are God's words. I shall act as father to you, Waldo. I think we had better have your naked back.'" If Blenkins parodies male domination, Tant' Sannie parodies matriarchal power, barely able to reproduce her kind but ruling her husbands and family with an iron fist and enjoying an almost tribal sense of family and community—she knows precisely who is related to whom, as her disquisition to Piet indicates. Her immensity testifies to the palpable materiality of her life. Displaying a deep-seated suspicion of change, she is bereft, in Waldo's sense, of any yearning to understand and is blind to nature.

For the children, their true parents are absent; those mothers and fathers who are present are parodies of authority. Significantly, Waldo's artistic mentor, the Bushman, the sole exception to the children's alienation even from the natives who suffer the identical dispossession, is exterminated by the settlers. The lives of boy and girl are complementary instances, as Schreiner herself had experienced it, of the colonial hostility both to creativity and to the dispossessed. Both children (Lyndall is only seventeen) forfeit their creations—Lyndall has a baby and Waldo invents a sheep-shearing machine: The identical nine-month span is clearly deliberate. In a parallel to Schreiner's own doubts, both Waldo and Lyndall early on have been stripped of those conventional religious beliefs that upheld the colonial system; questors who seek what cannot be found—knowledge, beauty, love—the children seem under a malign enchantment. Like Undine, Lyndall is a sprite of the potentially restorative but also treacherous, mirage-like water and moonlight, both their lives ironically blighted, stunted in the very environment of growth, the farm. Although Lyndall dies looking at her image in the mirror, locked within herself and unable to construct a bridge back to any life-giving reality, Waldo ultimately finds in nature a parent, coming to terms with the death of his actual father and transcending his childhood desire for a literal epiphany of the divine Father:

> Only . . . when the old hope is dead, when the old desire is crushed, then the Divine compensation of Nature is made manifest. She shows herself to you. So near she draws to you, that the blood seems to flow from her to you, through a still uncut cord: you feel the throb of her life. . . . When that day comes, . . . when the very thirst for knowledge through long-continued thwarting has grown dull . . . Nature enfolds you.

Here the yellow sunlight that flows out to bathe in its golden unity the yellow chicks and flowers combines perfectly the dreaming feminine moon and the waking masculine sun, a loving-fierce cosmic androgyny more satisfying than either the harsh dazzling sunlight or the oppressive glut of moonlight that threatens to drown the child. Waldo, as if a celebrant in some ritual purification, washes his hands in this healing and nourishing light that hides defects and dissolution as lovingly as does the moon goddess.

This authorial solution to the child's political and existential powerlessness—that is, the momentary naturalization of Waldo's dream within actuality—connects with an acceptance of limitations to produce in "The Child's Day" what at least one early commentator on Schreiner's work described as the summit of her achievement. Much of little Rebekah's story in this introductory section (Schreiner called it a "prelude") to the unfinished novel, *From Man to Man*, transpires in a context not of parental absence but of momentary neglect. On the day her mother delivers twins, one living and one stillborn, little Rebekah must fend for herself owing to her parents' inattention. Unlike the predicament of Jannita, Undine, or Waldo and Lyndall, the parental vacuum here is not psychologically unhealthy; and, were one to conjecture, one might say that Rebekah's situation is possibly closer to Schreiner's actual experience than that of any other fictional child. Like Undine, Rebekah is repeatedly called "a strange child"; and like the other children, she seeks some place that can accommodate her as she is. Here the child's tyrant is the native servant, merely comically despotic; much to Rebekah's irritation, old Ayah constantly scolds her as "a wicked, naughty child"—a gruff but protectively-meant expression of patriarchal values. The temporality of this child's "day" is clearly marked by references to the passage of clock time and contrasts with the boundless knowledge that will last the child a lifetime, an antithesis not unlike that between Waldo's ticking watch and the moon's ancient rhythms. But the fateful ticking of the clock in *Undine* and *An African Farm* here reappears less as the voice of predestination than as the emblem of the human condition, of time and mortality. When envisioning a more ideal order of existence, Rebekah says to her imaginary child: "If you should wake in the night, my baby . . . and hear anything, don't be afraid: just call to me. I'll be close by. And if you hear the clock ticking, *don't* think it means any of those dreadful things—it doesn't. I'll stop it if it makes you sad." It was precisely the impossibility of stopping the grinding of this "world machine" that drove Undine and Waldo to despair. Rebekah only imagines she can stop time, but unlike the other children, she ultimately will employ her fallenness against itself to accomplish new work. Although her imaginary child is no more real than the stillborn twin she had desired for a playmate, both anticipate her later binding the cultures together by adopting the child of her husband and the black servant girl.

A similar amelioration of the farm's harsh conditions occurs in Rebekah's desire to know, comparable to Undine's thirst for a knowledge but not answered here only in prayerful words of damnation:

> She watched the tallow candle fixedly. . . . She held up her hand and let the light shine through her fingers; the hand made a long dark shadow on the wall to the left of the room. Why was the shadow so much longer than the hand, she wondered, and why did it fall just where it did? . . . If only one were grown up, one would know all about these things! . . . Perhaps, even grown-up people didn't know all. Perhaps only God knew what lights and shadows were!

Though the desire for knowledge is a function of her fall (the "dark shadow"), the tentative "perhaps only" (the phrase is the novel's subtitle) is unproductive of either Undine's or Waldo's unmitigated anguish. In the "Preface" to *An African Farm*

Schreiner had observed that human life is a play without a name and that "If there sits a spectator who knows, he sits so high that the players in the gaslight cannot hear his breathing." Less significant for Rebekah than justifying the ways of God to man is, as the title suggests, charity from man to man. What occurs to Rebekah is not only an awakening to her mortality but a discovery of how to bring her fantasies into productive contact with real, though painfully imperfect, life. In short, the movement in this story is from death to birth; and Schreiner is writing here a modern, autobiographical account of a fall from innocence and the reacquisition of a paradise within.

In this realistic parable, the nurturiant aspects of nature are balanced with and not overwhelmed by a darker knowledge of guilt and death. There is a Tree of Knowledge in this orchard and even a snake, a cobra, that reproaches Rebekah much as Waldo's prickly-pear had accused him: "it was almost as if *she herself* were a snake, and had gone krinkle! krinkle! krinkle! over the grass. She had a sense of all the world being abandonedly wicked." Particularly effective is the manner in which the mother's anguish in bringing forth a child contextualizes Rebekah's foretaste of her fallen condition as she comes to experience the human meaning of life and death: "in sorrow thou shalt bring forth children; and thy desire shall be to thy husband, and he shall rule over thee" (Genesis 3:16). In much of the novel that follows, we watch Rebekah attempt to sort out the latter part of this original curse. In contrast to the still-born baby that will "never open its eyes again," the living Rebekah must inevitably have her eyes opened in Adam and Eve's manner (Genesis 3:7). Ayah, of course, is the comic voice of the patriarchal God asking if Rebekah has, as it were, "eaten of the tree"; her role is analogous to that of Blenkins in *An African Farm*; and Ayah's also is the primly Victorian articulation of Rebekah's dawning awareness of her "nakedness," her openness to sin: "And get your face washed and your hair done, and tell Mietje to put you on a clean dress and white pinafore." Although until now the child had been quite content within her farm world, fantasy intervenes to take her to an imaginary island that is really an enlarged version of the "little island a few feet wide with water flowing all around," across from which young Olive herself had sat watching as the sun began to rise. Including a little house "as high in proportion to her as grown-up people's houses are in proportion to them," Rebekah's isle shares qualities both with Jannita's house among the large stones and, because Rebekah's "was covered with books from the floor to the ceiling," with the loft and its trunk of books in Tant' Sannie's house to which Waldo fed his mind. But because Rebekah's island is purely her invention, it has a utopian exemption from pain, guilt, unloveliness, and isolation. Knowledge, whether of good and evil or of mathematical and scientific facts, is not yet here a product of her fall.

Rebekah's dream ends with a visionary scene so powerful it remained with her almost as if part of her actual experience: "A spasm of delight thrilled up the spine of the child under the pear tree. When a full-grown woman, long years afterwards she could always recall that island, the little house, the bricks, the wonderful light over earth and sky, and the swans swimming on the still water." Though this is a vision about to be shattered by the snake in the grass, in later years Rebekah is able to attain an independent *modus vivendi*, finding both a physical means of support and a psychological equilibrium between sorrow and joy. At the price of lost dreams and the acceptance of an imperfect reality, nurturiant strength now becomes an essential constituent of her personality. In "The Child's Day" we last see her protectively entwined with her sister when Ayah comes to remove baby Bertie from Rebekah's cot: "But when she turned down the cover she found the hands of the sisters so interlocked, and the arm of the elder sister so closely round the younger, that she could not remove it without awakening both." Though theirs is a world of "deep shadows," Rebekah and baby Bertie sleep "well." Here the "dark shadow" of the candlelight on the wall returns not as the primal curse but as the context in which the bonds of sisterhood and love are forged. Surely in this last scene Schreiner's reader may say with assurance that the entire woman—the already nurturing personality—is found in the cradle of the child. Yet something of the tragic quality of Schreiner's vision is also evident to the reader of her fiction, inasmuch as only one of the bright and hopeful children here discussed attains an adult identity and vocation, bears children, and directly aids and serves the next generation.

OLIVE SCHREINER'S PUBLISHED WORK

Works of Imagination

The Story of an African Farm, 1883
Dreams, 1890
Dream Life and Real Life, 1893
Trooper Peter Halket of Mashonaland, 1897
Stories, Dreams, Allegories, 1923
From Man to Man; or, Perhaps Only, 1927
Undine, 1929

Polemical Writings

The Political Situation, 1896
> An attack (written in collaboration with her husband) on Rhodes's barbarous native policy and the methods used to open the land above the Limpopo; excellent background for her political novel, *Trooper Peter.*

An English South African's View of the Situation: Words in Season, 1899
> An anti-war pamphlet at the outbreak of the Anglo-Boer War; regards unscrupulous British leaders like Rhodes who embodied British expansionism as betraying freedom and oppressing of the brave Boers.

A Letter on the Jew, 1906
> A pamphlet that denounced anti-semitic prejudice in South Africa and elsewhere and that singled out the historic Jewish contribution to ethics and religion as preeminent.

Closer Union, 1909
> A pamphlet supporting a federal union for South Africa, with a one-man-one-vote franchise: "no distinction of race or colour should be made between South Africans."

Women and Labour, 1911
> A feminist analysis of the economic exploitation of women and a plea for an enhanced understanding of the role women should play in society as equal partners with men: "Give us labour and the training which fits for labour!"

Thoughts on South Africa, 1923
> A series of historical and political essays devoted to the different South African ethnic groups and their interrelated strengths and limitations—English, Boers, Natives, and Coloreds.

SELECTED CRITICAL READINGS

Olive Schreiner was the first South African writer to gain a significant reputation abroad, and the influence of her thought and craft on such later writers as Alan Paton, Doris Lessing, and Nadine Gordimer has been substantial; both her advice to the novelist to "paint what lies before him" and the polemical cast of her writing stand at the fountainhead of much South African fiction. But apart from valuable biographical and feminist analyses of her life and thought, there has been as yet no book-length study of her specifically artistic accomplishment (narrative patterns such as the story within a story, imagery, satiric/stylistic techniques), nor have the interrelationships and ambiguities in her compositional chronology been resolved. The forthcoming publication of the Schreiner-Ellis correspondence will provide an important new source of data but despite numerous reprints (facsimile or otherwise), a scholarly edition of her works is not even on the horizon. The future of Schreiner scholarship may lie in all those interrelationships, outward from her autobiographical impulse to the other texts of her era, inward from the links between her style and topics to the depths of her psyche—both to those patterns of her consciousness that are fixed and to those that undergo development.

Berkman, Joyce Avrech. *The Healing Imagination of Olive Schreiner: Beyond South African Colonialism.* Amherst: U of Massachusetts P, 1989. An intellectual biography with a feminist perspective, placing Schreiner's life within her socio-political context; caught in a colonial culture, her struggle (with its contradictions and limitations) to heal the maladies of her times is impressively documented with both known and previously undiscovered sources.

Clayton, Cherry, editor. *Olive Schreiner.* Johannesburg: McGraw-Hill, 1983. A collection appearing on the centenary of *An African Farm* that includes contemporaneous reviews, extracts (of Schreiner and others) from journals/letters bearing on her literary background, and a spectrum of critical opinion (both reprints and original essays) on the artistic worth and theoretical relevance of her fiction and polemical prose. Biographical and bibliographical data included.

Cronwright Schreiner, Samuel Cron. *The Life of Olive Schreiner.* London: Unwin, 1924. Although it questions little and ignores much, its anecdotes about Schreiner's neurotic behavior are an invaluable primary source, making this more than just an early tribute; Schreiner's husband may have lacked any consistent interpretation, but he perceived her difficulties—and clearly was irritated with her a good deal more than he can admit to himself.

DuPlessis, Rachel Blau. "The Rupture of Story and *The Story of an African Farm.*" *Writing Beyond the Ending: Narrative Strategies of Twentieth-Century Women Writers.* Bloomington: Indiana UP, 1985. 20–30. Argues that Schreiner's transvaluation of the novelistic conventions of poetic justice, spiritual quest or education, and romantic union or hierogamy undermine all available narrative possibilities, discrediting the ideologies (scripts of feminine abasement) on which these patterns draw. Schreiner believed "conventional gender roles repress human growth and social progress," but her women are caught and unable to escape this trap.

First, Ruth, and Ann Scott. *Olive Schreiner.* New York: Schocken, 1980. Both feminist and neo-Marxist—feminist in its concern with Schreiner's response to nineteenth-century sexual stereotypes and neo-Marxist in its emphasis upon the whole cultural framework of Schreiner's life (political, religious, medical, psychological, as well as literary)—this biography is neither doctrinaire nor reductive, though the authors rely on a psychoanalytic framework to contain their feminist-political-economic analysis. They stress Schreiner's unhappiness and chronic ill-health, which they see as symbolic of a failure to establish an adequate sense of self by breaking out of the specific social-patriarchal-historical structures in which she found herself enmeshed.

Gray, Stephen. "An Approach to Schreiner's Realism in *The Story of an African Farm.*" *Standpunte* 31 (1978): 38–49. Places Schreiner's novel within the "contours of realist fiction in Southern Africa," suggesting the need for translingual comparisons among works in the liberal-realistic tradition. This tradition emerges in the novel's persona, especially in "the *differences* between the author's life and the novel's life"; facile, stereotypical biographical criticism is of less value than critical definition of what kind of an artist she was.

Marcus, Jane. "Olive Schreiner: Cartographer of the Spirit: A Review Article." *The Minnesota Review* n.s. 12 (1979): 58–66. Contrasts irony and allegory as instruments in "the literature of dissent," noting how Schreiner uses allegory "to restore the myth of female power."

Marquard, Jean. "Olive Schreiner's 'Prelude': The Child as Artist." *English Studies in Africa* 22 (1979): 1–11. Symbol and allegory are not an artistic escape from harsh social and psychological truth but an interpretation of them; the creative individual spirit enables author and characters to deal with the real, fallen world.

Monsman, Gerald. "Patterns of Narration and Characterization in Schreiner's *The Story of an African Farm.*" *English Literature in Transition* 28 (1985): 253–70. Defends the novel's philosophical, stylistic, imagistic, and structural coherence as differing from nineteenth-century conventions of dramatic continuity and closure and resembling modern works in which there is a breakdown of mimetic assumptions and an avoidance of determinate categories.

————. "The Idea of 'Story' in Olive Schreiner's *Story of an African Farm.*" *Texas Studies in Literature and Language* 27 (1985): 249–69. Narrative pushes at the limits of fictional form, replacing the unilinear cause and effect of conventional plot with a coherent structure of inverted parallels, ironic juxtapositions, discursive genres (dream, letter, allegory, confession, polemic), and a correspondingly discontinuous chronology.

————. "Olive Schreiner: Literature and the Politics of Power." *Texas Studies in Literature and Language* 30 (1988): 583–610. Explores in terms of landscape imagery the parallel between imperialism/colonialism and sexual exploitation, relating this to Schreiner's attack upon all hierarchies of power, all categories of limitation, even those of narrative closure.

Paxton, Nancy L. "*The Story of an African Farm* and the Dynamic of Woman-to-Woman Influence." *Texas Studies in Literature and Language* 30 (1988): 562–82. Argues that Schreiner is indebted to George Eliot's criticism of sexist assumptions in Spenser and Darwin: "Eliot dramatized the value of women's labor, demonstrated the historical contributions to culture made by women who defied the restrictive social conventions defining femininity, and represented, in her own person, the intellectual and artistic power a woman writer could claim even when she refused the roles of wife and mother that evolutionary science defined as her duty to her race."

Pechey, Graham. "*The Story of an African Farm*: Colonial History and the Discontinuous Text." *Critical Arts: A Journal of Media Studies* 3 (1983): 65–78. Character, plot, and style each reflect a discontinuous mode that exists also between Parts I and II of the novel; the story's pre-industrial setting teeters on the edge of society's political and ideological transformation, a moment when cultural diversity ("co-existing social formations") resisted reduction to English language and English economic power.

Showalter, Elaine. *A Literature of Their Own: British Women Novelists from Bronte to Lessing*. Princeton: Princeton UP, 1977. Pages 196–203 express one of the harshest current negative judgments on Schreiner's fiction: "The labors of construction and plotting were beyond her; . . . the novels are depressing and claustrophobic, [and] she was not a productive or self-disciplined writer." Schreiner nevertheless is seen as important as a first-wave feminist theorist.

Smith, Malvern van Wyk, and Don Maclennan, editors. *Olive Schreiner and After: Essays on South African Literature in Honour of Guy Butler*. Cape Town: David Philip, 1983. The Schreiner essays in this *festschrift* (in Part One) cover her reputation, fictional accomplishments, and political sympathies, including essays by authors Paton and Gordimer; particular attention is paid to her political/feminist impact.

Wilson, Elaine. "Pervasive Symbolism in *The Story of an African Farm*." *English Studies in Africa* 14 (1971): 179–88. Schreiner is a poet in prose and the symbol of sleep is pervasive behind the narrative realism, its actual and metaphoric meanings summarizing the main themes of the novel—the lack of questioning, escape, consolation, or insight.

— GERALD MONSMAN

Colin Johnson/
Mudrooroo Narogin

Colin Johnson/Mudrooroo Narogin was born at Narrogin in the southwestern part of Western Australia, 21 August 1938. He changed his name to Mudrooroo Narogin during the Australian Bicentennial Year of 1988 as a protest against the European occupation of Australia and as a reaffirmation of his own tribal (Bibbulman) identity. Like many young part-Aborigines, he was brought up in an orphanage in conformity with the aggressive assimilationist policies of a state government that enforced the separation of these children from their Aboriginal relations.

He left Western Australia for Melbourne in 1958. He was already writing by that time. He won a competition run by the journal *Westerly* with a play, "The Delinks," in 1959. His first novel, *Wild Cat Falling*, was published in 1965.

He spent most of the next ten years outside Australia, traveling in Asia, Europe, and North America. Seven of these years he spent in India, studying Buddhism and becoming a Buddhist monk.

After returning to Australia, he took up in 1976 a position with the Aboriginal Research Centre at Monash University, studied at Melbourne University, received an M.A. degree, and taught at Koorie College. He subsequently taught Aboriginal Literature at Murdoch University and at the University of Queensland. He was also National Coordinator for the Aboriginal Writers Oral Literature and Dramatists Association.

AN IMAGINATIVE MOVEMENT ACROSS CULTURAL BOUNDARIES

Australian Aborigines, who number about 1 percent of the Australian population, have a tragic history of extermination, reorganization, marginalization, and institutional control. For most of the last 200 years they have been on the receiving and outside edge of a dominant colonial society, which, when it did not destroy them outright in the process of settlement, pursued a policy of protection when it felt the remnant survivors were part of a dying race, and a policy of selective assimilation when they did not die. It was not until 1967 that Aborigines were admitted to citizenship within the Australian State. They then gained rights, and since that time they have sought to exercise them, often in the face of political and social intransigence on the part of the majority society.

Colin Johnson/Mudrooroo Narogin has been part of this history: the one that Aborigines underwent before 1967 and the one that they have been trying to shape more actively since them.

His novel, *Wild Cat Falling*, published in 1965, captured the anomie of a young Aboriginal in the Melbourne of the late 1950s and early 1960s, who had drifted to that city from a country town in Western Australia. He would have been a representative part of a migration that saw many Aborigines moving into the metropolitan areas of Australia from the fringes of country towns in the postwar years, except that he was also young enough to be part of the youth counterculture of the period, and alert enough to be attentive, in a reflective way, to what he saw and what he felt. It was as if Johnson had floated away from the fixities— historical and social—of his Aboriginal, Western Australian background, moving as a nomadic voice/eye through the different institutions and compartments—black and white— of Melbourne life. This quality of imaginative movement across cultural boundaries and the art of writing fiction itself were acts of considerable courage.

Colin Johnson had no model within Aboriginal horizons for writing a novel. David Unaipon had been writing legendary tales in isolation since the late twenties, but there were few young Aborigines of Colin Johnson's background who were reading Sartre, Camus, and Robbe-Grillet, listening to jazz, and shaping this world into the words, images, and episodes of a novel. It was the kind of novel that could have been written, not by Ralph Ellison himself, but by the invisible protagonist of *Invisible Man*.

What I propose to do in this essay is to look at *Wild Cat Falling* as the founding breakthrough novel that would fund and worry Johnson's career into reflective creativity for the next twenty-five years. I shall then consider the outline of that career, paying special attention to the notion of Aboriginality.

There is a loner quality to *Wild Cat Falling*. It is the preface to a career that did not then know that it was going to be a career. It remains a reacting, expressive book open very much to the landscape of idiom that swirled around Melbourne at the time. If we wanted to get the life-moment, life-history dimension of this landscape we could look at A.E. Manning's *The Bodgie*, a report produced in 1958, the year that Mary Durack was seeing Colin Johnson off from the Perth railway station. What was striking about the Bodgie phenomenon as a youth culture, in Manning's accounts of individual lives, was its misfit/driftage feature. It was not a coherent culture of political rejection (as in the Angry Young Man phase of British social and dramatic life in the fifties), nor was it as orchestrated or as confidently enacted as the Beat Movement in the United States. It certainly had little affiliation with the solidified counterculture of the sixties. The Bodgie option for a certain age/class group in Melbourne was no doubt a preface to subsequent developments, and it had strands that fed into similar groups in other parts of the Western world. But in the Melbourne of Colin Johnson it had an unformed, limbo quality of emotional withdrawal/dissent about it.

That is why I speak about it in terms of a landscape of *idiom*. Idiom at this stage, maybe at this age, is more important than ideology. *Affective* relationship to people, places, institutions is what matters. Affect/sensibility precedes ideology. It contains, in an inchoate, dispersed way, a trace of the ideological, and it may firm itself into the full bloom. In the coffee houses of Melbourne it was a plant that had not yet grown; in the pages of Daniel Bell's *The End of Ideology* it was a plant that had withered. Essentially, in the Bodgie world of *Wild Cat Falling*, we are confronted with a primacy of atmosphere, an allegiance of tone and generation.

Even when the narrator leaves the working class bodgies to move into the middle class student lounges of the University of Melbourne, we are still in an atmosphere of tone and generation, one in which Beckett and Aboriginal welfare are part of a ritualized choreography of concern. Johnson picks up on the mannerisms of engagement that make up the world of the students. He has a good ear and a caustic eye—ones that distrust the seen and the heard, although they use the textures of both to locate the moods/shapes of his own self, his own Aboriginal world.

It is the way he listens/watches himself *through* the filter/mirror of his hearing/ seeing others that is of interest about *Wild Cat Falling*. From a landscape of idiom, affect, tone, which remains in an important way, pre-ideological, he steals an interesting set of shapes that had for nearly two hundred years in Australia remained invisible: the color black, the country black, the predicament black, in a very white difficult Australia. *Wild Cat Falling* is not yet the color purple. But it was an act of speaking, the discovery of a voice. It was, looking back nearly twenty-five years, the beginning of something momentous. From its groping integrities, a new literature would emerge in Australia. *Wild Cat Falling* was a first fiction, a very significant performance in the expressive emergence of any culture. It dealt with the frictions between black and white groups in Australia, masked somewhat by the youthful alliances against authority. It was a fiction that dealt with contact in an *urban* environment, which served at the time to mask the fact of *contact*, a feature that most white Australians would have placed in the outback and probably in the nineteenth century. The novel was, then, a first fiction of contemporary contact, with the added value that it was the *inside narrative*—Melville's term for *Billy Budd*— of contact as, in phenomenological terms, lived experience. What I would also suggest is that *Wild Cat Falling* was written from within the liminalities of an undergone, but not fully comprehended, experience of contact.

We can read it now in a retrospect of comprehension, one that can take advantage of what has happened in Australia since then, of what Colin Johnson has gone on to achieve. I am not sure that *Wild Cat Falling* has been much looked at in terms of its own contemporary apprehensions or our subsequent knowledge of the world that came after it, and came after it in a way that never quite fitted it. It has remained an isolated book abandoned even by Johnson himself. This is Johnson writing in 1983:

> I think my poems in the *Song Circle of Jackie* are much closer to Aboriginal culture than my novels. The problem with *Wild Cat* and *Sandawara* is that they are alienated novels. They lack a basic underpinning of community and this is why I didn't give them as examples (of what Aboriginal novels should be). But in Thelwell's book [*The Harder They Come*, by Jamaican novelist Michael M. Thelwell], the community is always present, and Wendt's book (Albert Wendt, Samoan novelist, poet, scholar), too, and this is what Aboriginal novels should be aiming for, I think, to have the

> feeling of community; not existing in isolation, bourgeois isolation,
> as an individual. (Davis and Hodge 31)

The young man who had trailed away from Perth in 1958 was very much less certain. He was then, in the opening words of Mary Durack's foreword to *Wild Cat Falling*, "a long, lonely streak of a youth in black jeans, black shirt and flapping overcoat, playing down his apprehension of the big strange city on the other side of the continent" (v). *Wild Cat Falling* is not, under any definition, bourgeois isolation, nor can it be said to have grown from either a perspective or an aesthetic of individualism. An enormous confidence of community has since emerged politically and culturally in Aboriginal Australia, one that, naturally enough, has its own ideological and literary aspirations. It would be a great pity if *Wild Cat Falling* were pigeonholed.

It could have had as its preface, and perhaps still should have, Richard Wright's account of the origin of *Native Son* in his essay "How Bigger Was Born." It does retain the textures and the trials of how Colin Johnson as an Aboriginal author was born, of the conditions—Jim Crow too—under which Aboriginal Australians did, do, live. Wright pointed out how his physical removal from the South to Chicago freed him from the daily pressure of the Southern environment. Moving from Perth to Melbourne did something similar for Johnson. But for both of them the act of writing about who, where, and what they were, was personally cathartic and culturally reconstitutive. "I was able," said Wright, "to come into possession of my own feelings" (Miller 282). Let us look then, briefly, at *Wild Cat Falling* as an act of possession, re-possession, looking at it as a contact fiction in which the frictions of actual contact are being rehearsed from its inside edge.

There is the narrator, the young Aboriginal caught in late adolescence between a Bodgie subculture and a fallout of Beckett. What we notice is the presence of character as speaking subject, as voice tracked somewhere between a soliloquy and a dialogue, although there seems to be little contact with an existing social and historical world or with other persons. Just a swirl of voice that curls away from the self toward something/someone else as gesture before returning to source. Voice as a loping, looping curve around image and feeling. *Wild Cat Falling* is the fiction of a writer who was spending his wages "on jazz, folksong and blues and his time reading science fiction, poetry, Hindu philosophy and plays" (Preface *Wild Cat Falling* xv), who was, as he said to Mary Durack, being influenced by Sartre, Robbe-Grillet, Beckett.

But if there is self-consciousness in the way he deploys references to Beckett or rehearses the language of a beat culture, it is a self-consciousness that we meet again, with powerful authenticity in Keri Hulme's portrait of Kerewin Holmes in her tower of allusions, *The Bone People* (1983). And if his character, in a haze of alcohol, says to the woman at his side, "All things are alien from me. I am rejected and I stand utterly alone. Nothing is mine or belongs to me and I belong nowhere in this world or the next " (92), it is a mood and a phrasing that could have come from the anomic world of Wole Soyinka's *The Interpreters*, in which a postcolonial West African generation rehearsed their own and Soyinka's sense of the world as void. The rehearsal of mode, the deployment of mood have, in *Wild Cat Falling*, a genuineness of their own, one which accommodates posture without becoming artificial. Certainly, Beckett is invoked as icon when the narrator first acquires *Waiting for Godot*, but in this firstfiction, prisonfiction of Aboriginal Australia, this is no more strained than the famous performance of *Waiting for Godot* was in San Quentin Prison. Johnson, too, manages to capture in the pores of his language, the boredom and the monotony of waiting, of being outside of life, blocked into the world as prison, repression. But the text that defers to Godot is hypnotized by it, particularly by the following lines:

> All the dead voices.
> They make a noise like wings.
> Like leaves.
> Like sand.
> Like leaves. (84)

These lines fascinate Johnson, who can, like many readers of Beckett, almost hear the taste of the words. In *Wild Cat Falling* they are an oasis of peace in a world which, for the narrator, is a barrage of emotion: rage, anger, despair, frustration.

At one point in the novel, the narrator finds himself looking at an exhibition of Australian art. He cannot relate to it. "But then, I suppose I'm not what they call Australian. I'm just an odd species of native fauna cross-bred with the migrant flotsam of a goldfield" (69).

The narrator of *Wild Cat Falling* carries hatred in sacks heavy with memory; self-contempt in the Noongah environment of Western Australia—orphanage, prison, poverty, stealing, humiliation. But these memories *are* the shape of the fringedwelling frontier that Aboriginal Australians have lived on for most of the post-contact period, although by replacing the word "frontier" with the word "fringe" white Australians have kept the clear frame of history/pioneer settlement for themselves, leaving, in the marginal neutralized notion of fringe, a devalorized nowhere space for Aborigines, trapped in a culture of poverty. The voice of Robert Bropho's oral narrative *Fringedweller* (1980) is, however, a voice from a frontier that comes from ways of life and forms of culture that have been continuous and evolving since the first killing fallout of the Swan River settlement in 1828. This much is graphically clear from Lois Tilbrook's *Nyungar Tradition: Glimpses of Aborigines of South-West Australia 1829–1914*. Again, we can see the way in which Sally Morgan's bestselling autobiography, *My Place* (1987), as a courageous act of recovery, provides contexts of social and personal history, which, if available to the young narrator or to the young writer of *Wild Cat Falling* would have lessened the desolation/isolation of the book. Almost everything in that world of the early sixties in Perth and Melbourne was blurred for the protagonist. He wanted himself to mean and his environment to have meaning. But whatever was understood by white Australian historians then to be Australian history was not Colin Johnson's history; whatever the going definitions of Australian society were, they did not include Aboriginal, part-Aboriginal young men like Colin Johnson. So, the narrator of *Wild Cat Falling* carries memories of his own isolate life, without any socially-given consolations; he has to make meaning out of the drifting *bricolage* of experiences.

The narrator watches, looks, listens. And apprehension precedes comprehension. Apprehensive is the best adjective to describe him—like a deer poised for both attention and flight at the same time, like a wolf loping gingerly across the thin ice of a frozen lake. He *listens*—an incredibly tensed verb here—to a conversation going on in a university lounge on the Aboriginal Question; "What is the best sociological solution to the difficulties at the Aboriginal settlement at Austral Grove?" (73). He *watches*, again the intensity, the borders of a white society that is so economically dominant as to constitute another society, one that is both zoned and patrolled. The narrator crisscrosses those borders as a petty criminal, as an outsider. From his own perspective, he lives in a police state in which authority controls his every move. These are not the metaphorical, metaphysical miseries of Kafka. They are the concrete detail of life on the Aboriginal side of the fence. Johnson captures with bitter precision the voices, the faces, the teachers, the judges, the probation officers, the policemen.

The tensions of the book belong, then, not so much to the plot, as to the feelings that range through it and break into the text page after page. One could sum them up under the heading of alienation and exclusion, but each of these conditions, as a complication of feelings, has a thousand faces, moods, facets. They have, of course, the generalized elements of alienation that have been thematized into our understanding of Camus and onto our models of adolescent behavior. But in *Wild Cat Falling* these feelings retain the integrity of being black—Aboriginal responses to white Australia of being black; Aboriginal responses to being black; Aboriginal in a different, black Australia. Having been written out of white Australia, the narrator sets out to write himself into another Australia, one whose contours become *just* visible at the end.

Meanwhile, there is the haunting absence of lost Aboriginal lives:

> All the dead voices.
> They make a noise like wings.
> Like leaves.
> Like sand.
> Like leaves. (84)

Alan Schneider, the American theater director, takes a comment that Samuel Beckett had made about James Joyce but applies it to Beckett: "Sam is basically not writing about something, he is writing something" (244). The words that the narrator of *Wild Cat Falling* takes from Beckett are basically not *about* the narrator, not *about* the Aborigines. They *are* his live voice, *their* dead voices given life by the lostness of *his* voice searching for himself and them in the present moment of the text.

The book is filled with devastation through which emotions are being expressed, weighed, sorted out. The word *vastation* would be in order. Behind the real physical space of isolation we get the spiritual spaces of emptiness. The deeps in which the narrator finds himself have an orphaned, abandoned texture to them that call to mind the lines from Hopkins's "The Wreck of the Deutschland": "the widow-making unchilding unfathering deeps." He does, out of sheer shame and confusion, abandon his own mother who has, out of a similar shame and confusion, abandoned her own people, her own self.

We can see how Beckett and the Bodgies fit in. One was the current intellectual marker for the figure of man alone in a hostile world from which belief and meaning had departed. The other was the marker in that time, for that generation, of the outsider. Johnson responded to the accent of truth that each of these markers, in spite of the element of kitsch and mannerism attached to them, reflected. He bent them in his own direction. He redeemed from them, as twin sites, the feeling of the world as shape, the shape of the world as feeling.

The writing and publishing of *Wild Cat Falling* was the most important act of Johnson's life to that point, and that novel would become the anchor marker for his career up to and beyond his publication of *Doin Wildcat* in 1988. A close reading of this first novel must constitute the base for any serious consideration of him as the major Aboriginal writer of what turned out to be an emergence of Aboriginal literature.

His departure from Australia for Asia and Europe was symptomatic of the difficulties that faced an Aboriginal writer in 1965 and symbolic of the grasp that he came to have of himself and his black culture, a grasp that had strengthened as a result of writing the novel. Leaving Australia was a deliberate act. His going abroad again reminds us of the narrator of Ellison's *Invisible Man* climbing into his manhole to keep his sanity and his self visible and intact until that future moment when he could surface without fear or camouflage. Buddhism and travel were Johnson's way of keeping the lights on, maintaining the definitions. The two figures who come to mind as having pursued a similar route in Black American literature, apart from Ellison, are Jean Toomer and his Quaker Christianity and Malcolm X in Islam/ Mecca. Johnson's interest in Buddhism was deep, necessary, and connected to his search as an Aboriginal in Australia for a contempt-free, liberating space of belief.

The surprising feature of his subsequent career is the limited creative use to which he put this contact with Buddhism. He spoke briefly about Kundalini yoga and its symbolism of sexuality in the first interview after his return in 1974 and gives the impression that one of his early intentions was to harness his Indian experiences to fiction. But he did not so in any extensive way. We can see traces of address to human sexuality in a physical/ideological/metaphysical sense in *Doctor Wooreddy's Prescription for Enduring the Ending of the World*, which recall his remarks on Kundalini yoga, but by that stage it is more likely that he had fallen under the influence of Ronald M. Berndt's *Three Faces of Love: Traditional Aboriginal Song Poetry* (1976), a book dealing with three song cycles from northeastern Arnhem Land.

When Johnson returned from his manhole of exile, he was no longer alone. A new day had dawned, for much had happened in Aboriginal Australia. In 1965 Charles Perkins, Ted Noffs, and Jim Spigelman had organized a freedom ride bus tour through the towns of northern New South Wales and exposed the systematic discrimination practiced against the Aboriginal population. In 1966 the Gurindji walked off the Wave Hill pastoral station in protest against the delay in paying Aborigines equal wages. By 1963 the Yirrkala settlement in Arnhem Land was protesting the operations of the Nabalco bauxite company on their land. Land rights and discrimination were coming to the fore in Australian politics, fanned rather than quelled by the granting of citizenship to Aboriginal Australians in the Referendum of 1967. The most dramatic, symbolic gesture of this phase of heightened Aboriginal activity was the erection of a tent embassy on the lawns of Parliament House in Canberra on 26 January 1972. For the first time Aborigines, in a pan-Aboriginal sense, abandoned the definitions and the sites that had been imposed on them by Australian society. The consequences were almost immediate. The tent lasted for six months before the police tore it down, but by the time it was dismantled Aborigines had gained the sympathy and, to the extent that was possible, the imagination of Gough Whitlam and a Labor Party that was soon to become the government. In February 1973 the government appointed Justice A.E. Woodward to head a Commission examining all aspects of Aboriginal land rights. By the time he submitted his Report in 1974, there had been a quite massive rehearsal of Aboriginal affairs in black and white Australia (Broome 160–201). The deep, complicit silences of 1964 were so far in the past that the isolation of *Wild Cat Falling* struck Colin Johnson as dated.

I have already quoted his statement that it was a bourgeois book and from the platform of his new activism it may well have lost, in his eyes, the fragilities of apprehension and voice that still, in my view, attach to the novel.

What Johnson did was to make contact with his people—the writers, dramatists, activists like Kath Walker, Kevin Gilbert, Jack Davis, Bruce McGuinness, Denis Walker, Lionel Fogarty. He also made contact with white Australians interested in Aboriginal matters, like Catherine and Ronald Berndt, Stephen Muecke, Hugh Webb. Johnson entered the debate in Aboriginal Australia, participated in the debate on Aboriginal Australia that white Australians were conducting in the universities, and set about inserting the difficulties and the possibilities of those debates into fiction, poetry, and criticism.

The pan-Aboriginal impulse, which had expressed itself most graphically in the tent embassy episode, presented the dispersed urban, rural, and tribal Aboriginal groups with the task of constructing not just a common front before the government and the mining companies but a common sense of who they were. They had to deal with the politics and the poetics of identity. This 1 per cent of the overall population was split into different constituencies. An Aborigine on tribal land in Central Australia was quite different from an urban Aborigine in Sydney with no memory or experience of an intact Aboriginal culture. The main ideological project that Johnson walked back into was the construction of a new Aboriginality. Jones and Hill-Burnet describe this as an emergent ethnogenesis in which Aborigines were constructing organizations, ideas, attitudes to explain themselves to themselves in order to strengthen their hand in their dealings with white Australia. "The process of ethnic formation," they wrote, "may indeed begin with a single individual, or a small set of individuals who begin acting in accordance with the new categories" (Howard 216).

All of Johnson's subsequent work would be written under this developing conception of Aboriginality. It would be the canopy under which he would write and think, the ground on which he would sort out his relation to himself, to Aboriginal history, to white society. The kind of attention he brought to the subjects he handled were always marked by this intention: to put the past and present of Australian Aborigines in contact with each other.

Long Live Sandawara, published in 1979, set out to bring the Aboriginal youth culture of Perth in the 1970s into a fruitful fictional relationship with a heroic Aboriginal warrior in the Kimberleys who resisted the whites in the 1890s. *Doctor Wooreddy's Prescription for Enduring the Ending of the World* took as its retrieval task the rewriting, from an Aboriginal perspective, of the events that led to the destruction of the Tasmanian Aborigines in the first half of the nineteenth century. *The Song Circle of Jacky* registered Johnson's attempt to recast his poetry into the forms of traditional Aboriginal culture, just as *Dalwurra* was "inspired by the eastern Arnhem land song genre, *Manikay*, which may be defined as a clan song series alluding to ancestral beings" (7). What the project of Aboriginality meant for Johnson in literary terms was the practice of new cultural and literary categories, ones embedded in the resounding integrity of fully Aboriginal worlds. The song cycles from Arnhem land were forms for him to work with artistically, but they were also representational frames that enabled him to re-address his own travels in India and Britain as a kind of retrospective wandering Aboriginality. He visits his own past just as deliberately as he sends his language back to Wooreddy's dying world, bringing the optics of Aboriginality to bear on both. He was doing what he said the Aboriginal writer must do: create a distinct cultural space occupied totally by Aborigines, living through Aboriginal eyes, in Aboriginal forms, on Aboriginal ground, unintimidated, unwounded by European/white pressure, presence, power, knowledge.

This is not an easy space for an Aboriginal writer to open up. For one thing the recorders, whether they are anthropologists, historians, missionaries, are and have been white, and the institutions in which they work and store this knowledge—universities, museums, art galleries—are also white. The road to Sandawara was paved, among other oral sources, by Ion Idriess, the popular white Australian novelist who wrote a historical fiction on this subject, *Outlaws of the Leopolds*; the road to Wooreddy by contemporary historians like Plomley and Turnbull and the diary of George Augustus Robinson; the road to Arnhem land song cycles by the anthropological work of Ronald and Catherine Berndt. Johnson has been critical of editorial interventions by whites in the life histories that have emerged as an important portion of Aboriginal literature in the seventies and eighties (Davis and Hodge 23–25). He also feels that his own novel *Wild Cat Falling* suffered from interventionist editorial attentions. The distinct cultural space that he wants for the Aboriginal writer writing under the sign of Aboriginality is not one, interestingly enough, that, in his view, many of the most important Aboriginal writers have produced. *Writing from the Fringe*, appearing in 1990, spells out his views of his fellow Aboriginal authors. Archie Weller, the novelist and short story writer, is too pessimistic and models his short stories on standard English and received literary forms; Jack Davis, the dramatist, in his early work was too distant from his people, and in his editing of the Aboriginal journal *Identity* too attentive to a white audience. He is harsh toward what he calls the literature of the assimilationist period of the sixties, produced by himself and Kath Walker. He is critical of the formal conservatism that went along with the protest poetry in the seventies of Kevin Gilbert, the poet, dramatist, and foremost cultural/political commentator in Aboriginal Australia. He is unsympathetic to the most recent autobiographical work of Sally Carter and Glenyse Walker for adhering to an integrationist multicultural notion of Australia and writing a phase of Aboriginal literature that he calls a literature of understanding, one that speaks for itself but is designed to be overheard by other Australians. He is uneasy with an Aboriginal drama that seems to him to be flirting with a post-separatist sense of itself, although his preface to Jack Davis's most recent play, *Barungin* (1989), admits this most distinguished of Aboriginal playwrights back into the fold of Aboriginality (xii).

All of these caveats of unease give us a clearer sense of the space he has proposed for his own work. He is hoping to create/construct what he already believes to exist, but that must be brought to articulate, visible expression if a transfigured Aboriginal reality is to live again in Australia. He calls this underlying feature "the metatext of Aboriginality" (58).

We can see what he is getting at from the titles of his articles. He wants to eradicate the white forms/Aboriginal content syndrome in favor of what he sees in Lionel Fogarty's poetry, a guerrilla response to standard English, one which breaks standard syntax into the distinctive linguistic forms of his own Aboriginality. Johnson had championed the oral presentation of Robert Bropho's *Fringedweller* as soon as it appeared and it is clear that he sees Fogarty's poetry as the next step after Bropho toward a conscious aesthetics of Aboriginality. In *Writing from the Fringe*, he examines Fogarty's texts as a means of getting to the metatext—this boils down to a structuralist analysis—and describes the total body of Fogarty's output in this way: "Single texts may be compared to the artifacts discovered in an archaeological excavation with the five volumes being the earth, and the metatext being the culture which left these artifacts to be covered by the earth" (58).

Apart from the obscurities of this statement, it is clear that Aboriginality is locked inevitably into the territory of theory/text/metatext. It is this trinity of interdependent items, in which the postmodern and the postcolonial have been recruited to support the opening into new Aboriginal cultural space, that most characterizes his latest work, particularly the pre-text, post-text explications that become an integral part of the main texts of *Dalwurra* and his bicentennial gift poem, "Sunlight Spreadeagles Perth in Blackness."

It often seems that Narogin's drive toward the *independence* of Aboriginal realities within white Australia has been excessively *dependent* upon, indeed driven by European theory. Structuralism, semiotics, discourse theory are now everywhere present in his thinking, to the extent that in his course on Aboriginal literature at the University of Queensland in 1989, he provided a diagram that reinterpreted *Wild Cat Falling* within the reader response/semiotic frames of Author/Text/Reader, Messenger/Message/Receiver. Deconstruction has become routine in Narogin's address to whatever he reads, and he brings a gaze of suspicion to bear on anything that comes from white Australia, not excluding, as we have seen, his own early work. Aboriginality as horizontal prospect and as present politics also has a retrospective aspect.

There are ironies and ambiguities in Narogin's working through the cruxes of Aboriginality/ethnogenesis. But the difficulties persist only as long as we fail to see the Aborigines as an indigenous people caught inside a majority settler state. This is the position of many First Nations in what is often referred to as the Fourth World. Narogin may well be one of the most exploratory and reflective writers of these intensely pressured groups, in which persistent domination by the State is matched only by the poverty that goes along with the domination. Aborigines are so heavily implicated in the cultural, social, and institutional forms of mainstream Australian society that thinking about themselves is often a question of sorting through the saturations of contact. Extricating a core of Aboriginal values from what has been, historically, a devastation of implication, cannot be achieved by an innocent eye of indignation. The native writer in this situation cannot be nonreflective. Trinh T. Minh-ha has spoken of this in her book, *Woman, Native, Other*:

> A subversion of the colonizer's ability to represent colonized cultures—can only radically challenge the established power relations when it carries with it a tightly critical relation with the colonizer's most confident characteristic discourses. (71)

Johnson/Narogin will use structuralism to get to the metatext of Aboriginality or semiotics to undermine standard white Australian readings of Aboriginal writing, which tend to be attached to ideologically given, stereotyped assumptions about both Aborigines and literature itself and assumptions about Australian society. Postmodernism, as a heightened consciousness of method and assumption, is a means to a Fourth World end; it is a pedagogy not of the oppressed, as Paolo Freire would have it, nor *for* the oppressed, which is the use to which Freire is sometimes put, but *from* the oppressed.

Foucault, Barthes, Bakhtin, the reflections of Deleuze and Guattari in Stephen Muecke, are simply tracks to this dreaming space of a new-old Aboriginality. Nothing that would impede this task is allowed any shrift. Even Stephen Muecke—whose shared production with Paddy Roe and Krim Benterrak, *Reading the Country* (1984), remains central to any consideration of European/Aboriginal discourse in contemporary Australia, and who has been an influence on how Johnson-on-the-way-to-becoming-Narogin read his own culture—is sacrificed quite brutally. *Reading the Country* was a collaboration between a white Australian with a theorized eye, a Moroccan-Australian painter, and a distinguished Aboriginal storyteller from the Pilbara district of Western Australia. When it appeared it was so revolutionary—graphically, imaginatively, intellectually—for Australian literature that it received much attention but little commentary. Johnson welcomed it in 1984. By 1990, the Bicentennial, his name-change, and an enlarged political and moral sense of what Aboriginality was had sharpened his pen. It does not matter now how faithfully or carefully noninterventionist Muecke was with his tape-recorder before Roe, no matter how genuine an atmosphere of trust emerged between Muecke and Roe, the Aboriginal presence in the book is attended, mediated, framed by the country/culture of Muecke's sophisticated postmodern literacies, which overread/override everything not bearing its imprint. Narogin writes:

> Paddy Roe is reduced to language, or discourse as heard through the ears of a European. Kriol or Aboriginal English becomes an interesting artifact which may be measured and deciphered using the methods of European criticism. In *Reading the Country* this has been pushed to such an extreme that Paddy Roe's discourse becomes imprisoned between slabs of academic prose resembling nothing more than the walls of a prison. (151)

When the high incidence of Aboriginal deaths in Australian prisons—an issue that came to prominence in the eighties—is attached to this observation, the dismissal is brutal. Any reading of Aboriginal territory that would appropriate it for anything other than itself is, in this defense of Aboriginality, a taking of that territory, not unlike mining and ranching, in Aboriginal country.

Narogin's favorite postmodernist quotation is from Roland Barthes's essay, "The Death of the Author" in *Image-Music-Text*, which advances the notion "that a text is not a line of words releasing a single 'theological' meaning (the 'message' of the Author-God) but a multidimensional space in which a variety of writings, none of them original, blend and clash. The text is a tissue of quotations drawn from the innumerable centres of cultures" (quoted in *Writing from the Fringe* 181). The attraction of this piece of Barthes as manifesto and aesthetic is understandable. After all, the whole debate on Aboriginality in the seventies emerged from the unilateral, quite theological, imposition by white Australians on all Aborigines— living, dead, tribal, urban—of a single umbrella term, Aborigine, with a very distinctive bias of content.

In a war of definitions in which the government favored the image of a traditional intact Aboriginal—an Aranda warrior, male, isolate, dignified against a backdrop that could be infinity or Central Australia—as the dominant legitimized sign of Aboriginality, these multidimensional spaces in which innumerable centers of cultures—Pintubi, Worora, French—touch, interact, speak, are of enormous value to Narogin. There were always dangers, of course, that Aborigines would be induced into projecting a counter-ideology of Aboriginality in response to the leveling definitions they encountered from white Australia, and Johnson/Narogin, working very much with his own energies on the *aesthetics* of Aboriginality, has watched himself closely. He has understood a Fourth World insight that Trinh T. Minh-ha captured with precision and humor: "Trying to find the other by defining otherness, or by explaining the other through laws and generalities is, as Zen says, like beating the moon with a pole or scratching an itching foot from the outside of a shoe" (Minh-ha 76).

Another interesting feature of his fascination with this passage of Barthes may relate, in its death of the author feature, to his own passage from Colin Johnson to Mudrooroo Narogin, at once a willed death and a willed birth, acts of culture within a culture. There is no doubt that the older Johnson who returned from India had outgrown the young man who had written *Wild Cat Falling*. He may have concluded in 1965 that "I now find myself oriented to the Aboriginal people and am for the first time definitely committed to race" (*Wild Cat Falling* xv), but compared to the possibilities of orientation and commitment that became available to him in the period surrounding *Long Live Sandawara* and *Doctor Wooreddy* this compact of identity was fragile. Johnson was then weighting his sense of who he was and what he wanted to become into the mythologies/memories of an Aboriginal world that had come into the range of his feelings but that still eluded his knowledge. The relation of this symbolic avowal of his Aboriginal roots first to white Australia, as the dominant society, and then to Buddhism, as an access route to humankind as a whole, remained yet to be explored. The kind of books that Johnson would write would always depend on the kind of Aboriginal author he felt he was or should be. This, in turn, touched on his sense of personal identity, which, in turn, touched on the social and cultural community within which he moved in a primary way. We can see in the process of his career a loosening of reference/dependence from white interpretations of society and history in Australia to an understanding of black Australia, but this transfer of reference cultures was one that needed, in the emergent contexts of Aboriginal identities, to be continuously negotiated and constructed and created. Neither as person nor as author could Johnson maintain the singular, "theological" fiction of being, for the duration of his career, the author of *Wild Cat Falling*. Paradoxically, both black and white Australians have been inclined to invest him with this kind of founding authority, an investment that he has always sought to dodge, deny, interrogate.

Johnson's life has been a dying of authors and a re-shaping of selves. This is what his concern with Aboriginality has been all about. The Barthes quotation gave Johnson a formula of release from the ascriptive, the prescriptive, the restrictive horizons that often surround minority cultures in majority settings. Barthes provides a permit for Johnson to go, to know, to act whenever he needs to become the full possibility that, as an Aboriginal writer, he wishes to become. There is a cunning and necessity to this concept that we can detect in those non-European peoples, who have been, in Eric Wolf's ironic words, without "history":

> In the rough and tumble of social interaction, groups are known to exploit the ambiguities of inherited forms, to impart new evaluations or valences to them, to borrow forms more expressive of their interests, or to create wholly new forms to answer the changed circumstance. (387)

This captures the rationale for the different centers, cultures, discourses that mark Johnson's work. His borrowings have been a burrowing to open up new public and private Aboriginal space, in which nothing from anywhere, Arnhem Land or Paris, postmodern or premodern, is refused, in which the creative impulse is always at work to re-fuse this diversity/difference of source into Aboriginal resonance. The final move in the strategies, of which Barthes and Wolf speak, has been the shift of this highly conscious form of attention from cultural and textual matters to the name of the author himself.

"Colin Johnson" as a signifier of identity, waiting for the logic of Aboriginality to descend upon it, fits what Wolf calls the ambiguity of an inherited European form. Johnson had been through these ambiguities in connection with the forms of his poetry/fictions, trying to "Aboriginalize" them as mode and mood as well as content. Now he turned Barthes's "The Death of the Author" on himself, ending up as Mudrooroo Narogin.

How did he arrive at this decision? He has given us an explanation that associates his decision with that of Kath Walker to jettison her Anglo-Australian name.

> During the coming together of the tribes in January 1988 in Sydney, I spoke to Oodgeroo, and she explained to me that her name Oodgeroo means *paperbark* and that as creative writers our totem, or dreaming should be the paperbark tree. This seemed logical as the paperbark tree or whitefella name *maleleuca*, or my country name, Mudrooroo, has always had an important place in Aboriginal life in that it has been used for *Myas*, roofing materials, for bandages and for drawings. And so, this has become our *Dreaming*, or our secondary totem, or our functional dreaming. Thus Kath Walker has taken, or changed her whitefella name to Oodgeroo Nunaccul, and I have changed my name to Mudrooroo Narogin. Kath Walker's last name refers to her tribal name, the Nunaccul tribe of Stradbroke Island, but in regard to my last name it refers to my place of birth in Western Australia. I have used a place in that it is difficult to isolate the particular name of the tribe which owns that part of Western Australia, as we have coalesced into one people, the Nyungar and possibly one tribe, the Bibbulman which I think refers more to the Swan River basin than to my area. (Rutherford 36)

This places his decision in a specific context of, time, place, person: January 1988, Sydney, Oodgeroo. But "Colin Johnson" had been hanging heavy on him for some time. It was clearly a name embedded in a white, non-Aboriginal text, the full extent of which remained hidden from him when he began in the beginning to speak through the unnamed protagonist of *Wild Cat Falling.* Knowing was part of his task then; naming, names would come later. And when they came they did so in the form of other persons, other places, and other times: The Kimberleys/Sandawara, Van Diemen's Land/Wooreddy. This took him through the seventies to the early eighties, when he began to re-direct an increasing sense of the cultural fields and forms that surrounded Sandawara and Wooreddy back onto his own lives. *The Song Circle of Jacky* did this as late as 1986, but the cover name, Colin Johnson, still held. *Dalwurra* intensified this process. It represented a naming of himself but in the name and under the sign of the black bittern as a dreaming ancestral being. He is shifting his literature from the heroic to the totemic, transforming it, by design, into functional dreaming. At the beginning of the Bicentennial year he found himself on the threshold of a new self-designation. The poem cycle acknowledges a double authorial reference: Colin Johnson [Mudrooroo Narogin]. His Aboriginal name has broken into print, hovering still in a bracket of subordination. *Dalwurra* came with the white editorial and critical editing of the Australian scholar, Veronica Brady, a practice of Aboriginal promotion/ demotion that he would condemn throughout the body of Aboriginal productions in

Writing from the Fringe. It was not until the publication of *Doin Wildcat* in 1988 that Mudrooroo Narogin took over the script of naming, sending "Colin Johnson" into the territory of "previously known as."

Doin Wildcat is his most freestanding work to date, standing on a ground of Aboriginality he has cleared himself and taking for its subject those authors and selves who had previously done service for the man who had now become Mudrooroo Narogin. He was digging, as Paddy Roe said in another context, to find the black soil inside. Johnson had shared the Aboriginal ethnogenesis of his community from the seventies on but had brought to it an agenda and a subjectivity that was distinctively his own. Eventually, that agenda would snag on a name that he needed to get outside of to grasp the full extent to which it had eclipsed and compromised a whole life. When he attached the chosen designation of Mudrooroo Narogin to *Doin Wildcat*, eluding for the first time the imposed Anglo-Australian name of Colin Johnson, he was able to see the scars and constraints that had accompanied the most intense listening/watching of *Wild Cat Falling*, as well as that traumatic experience of having a film made by an American director out of the site of his youth and in the vulnerable aftermath of an exile that had not worked.

Doin Wildcat is a very special site in Aboriginal literature and in the life/work of Mudrooroo Narogin. Although it collapses Narogin's Aboriginal consciousness back onto the most highly tensed moments of his career (1965/novel; 1975/film; 1988/novelscript), it still maintains the alluvial integrity of affect and feeling that marked those points in time. He attends to how he was who he was; he listens, using a language spoken by other Aborigines not just written by himself, to who he is becoming. It is a following of tracks back through twenty-five years, a block of decades that has seen more cultural, ideological, and emotional expression from the Aboriginal community that at any point since the destruction of the tribes. *Doin Wildcat* is the archaeology of the terror, humiliation, and resistance that have flowed through the patrolled lost lives of many Aborigines. It speaks for Narogin, but for the Wooreddys and Sandawaras and Truganinis as well.

In April 1979 the National Aboriginal Conference brought up the question of negotiations between the Aboriginal peoples and the Australian government and the possibility of shaping these negotiations around the idea of a treaty. They used the Yolngu word "Makarrata" to describe it. It means "the end of the dispute and the resumption of normal relations," or "coming together after a long struggle" (Ryan 399). "Makarrata" is designed here to address black and white groups in Australia, but the Yolngu word may also, in the context of Colin Johnson/Mudrooroo Narogin, be brought to bear on matters of consequence internal to black Australia. Aboriginality, not least in the innovative way Johnson/Narogin has pursued it, has had its continuous Makarrata dimension. When we put the texts of *Wild Cat Falling* and *Doin Wildcat* together, when we see the way *Doin Wildcat* absorbs the Aboriginality he has been exploring and the postmodernism he has been exploiting and doing so inside the Aboriginal vernacular that Bropho and Thelwell spoke to him of, then we begin to understand Narogin and *Doin Wildcat* as speaking to the coming together after a long struggle of a writer, a culture, a people, a body of work.

WORKS CITED

Benterrak, Krim, Stephen Muecke, and Paddy Roe. *Reading the Country*. Fremantle: Fremantle Arts Centre Press, 1984.

Berndt, Ronald M. *Traditional Faces of Love, Traditional Aboriginal Song-Poetry*. Melbourne: Nelson, 1976.

Broome, Richard. *Aboriginal Australians, Black Response to White Dominance 1788–1980*. Sydney: George Allen and Unwin, 1982.

Davis, Jack, and Bob Hodges, editors. *Aboriginal Writing Today*. Canberra: Australian Institute of Aboriginal Studies, 1985.

Jones, D., and J. Hill-Burnet. "The Political Context of Ethnogenesis: An Australian Example." *Aboriginal Power in Australian Society*. St. Lucia: U of Queensland P, 1982. 214–46.

Manning, A.E. *The Bodgie. A Study in Psychological Abnormality*. Sydney: Angus & Robertson, 1958.

Minh-ha, Trinh T. *Woman, Native, Other: Writing Postcoloniality and Feminism*. Bloomington: Indiana UP, 1989.

Ryan, Lyndall. "Aboriginals and Islanders." *From Fraser to Hawke: Australian Public Policy in the 1980's*. Melbourne: Longman Cheshire, 1989. 394–408.

Rutherford, Anna, editor. *Aboriginal Culture Today*. Aarhus: Dangaroo Press, 1988.

Schneider, Alan. "Working with Beckett." *On Beckett*. Edited by S.E. Gontarski. New York: Grove Press, 1986. 236–54.

Wolf, E. *Europe and the People Without History*. Berkeley: U of California P, 1982.

Wright, Richard. "How Bigger Was Born." *Backgrounds to Blackamerican Literature*. Scranton: Chandler Publishing Co., 1971. 197–217.

ABORIGINAL WRITERS MENTIONED

Bropho, Robert. *Fringedweller*. Sydney: Alternative Publishing Co-operative, 1980.

Davis, Jack. *Barungin*. Sydney: Currency Press, 1989.

Fogarty, Lionel. *Ngutji*. Spring Hill, Queensland: Cheryl Buchanan, 1984.

Gilbert, Kevin. *People Are Legends*. St. Lucia: U of Queensland P, 1978.

———. *Because a White Man'll Never Do It*. Sydney: Angus & Robertson, 1973.

Morgan, Sally. *My Place*. Fremantle: Fremantle Arts Centre Press, 1987.

Walker, Kath. *My People. A Kath Walker Collection*. Brisbane: Jacaranda Press, 1970.

Ward, Glenyse. *Wandering Girl*. Broome: Magabala Books, 1987.

Weller, Archie. *Going Home. Stories*. Sydney: Allen and Unwin, 1986.

COLIN JOHNSON'S/MUDROOROO NAROGIN'S PUBLISHED WORK

AS COLIN JOHNSON

Novels

Wild Cat Falling, 1965
Long Live Sandawara, 1979
Doctor Wooreddy's Prescription for Enduring the Ending of the World, 1983

Poetry

The Song Circle of Jacky and Selected Poems, 1986

History

Before the Invasion. Aboriginal Life to 1788 (with Colin Bourke and Isobel White), 1980

Criticism

"White Forms, Aboriginal Content." In *Aboriginal Writing Today*. Edited by Jack Davis and Bob Hodge.

Canberra: Australian Institute of Aboriginal Studies, 1985. 21–33.
Says that Aboriginal fiction belongs to "Fourth World Literature," which indigenous minorities produce. Argues that literature can help to forge an Aboriginal identity.

As Mudrooroo Narogin

Fiction

Doin Wildcat. A Novel "Koori" Script as Constructed by Mudrooroo Narogin, 1988

Poetry

Dalwurra. The Black Bittern: A Poem Cycle, 1988

Criticism

"Paperbark." *Aboriginal Culture Today.* Edited by Anna Rutherford. Aarhus: Dangaroo Press, 1988. 36–49.
Discusses the reason for changing his name and presents his most recent theories on Aboriginal writing.
Writing from the Fringe. A Study of Modern Australian Literature. Melbourne: Hyland House, 1990.
Approaches Aboriginal writing, in part, from current European literary theory. Presents a kind of manifesto for Aboriginal literature.

Selected Critical Readings

The amount of criticism on Aboriginal writing has been scant in the past, but recently it seems to be catching up with the writing, if not outpacing it at times. Generally considered the major Aboriginal writer, Colin Johnson/Mudrooroo Narogin has received a large part of the attention. The critical interest is not limited to Australia, for European and North American critics have also addressed this new field of Australian writing. Some efforts at comparative studies with Afro-American, Native American, and African literature have been made; this seems a likely field of pursuit in the future as well as the study of a theoretical basis of Aboriginal writing.

Arthur, Kateryna. "Fiction and the Rewriting of History: A Reading of Colin Johnson." *Westerly* 30.1 (1985): 55–60. Discusses how white writers and historians have excluded Aboriginal art and oral storytelling. Argues that work such as that of Johnson will be instrumental in erasing the errors in white-written texts

Cotter, Michael. "'Perth or the Bush?': Sense of Place in the Novels of Colin Johnson." *A Sense of Place in the New Literatures in English.* St. Lucia: U of Queensland P, 1986. 97–111. Shows that Johnson's *Wild Cat Falling* and *Long Live Sandawara* contain a disparity of place: one part their urban setting; the other part, the mythological bush.

Diamond, Anne. "Colin Johnson's Lyric Dispossessions: Written in English, Lived Elsewhere." *Meanjin* 46 (1987): 230–34. Notes how the poetry in *The Song Circle of Jacky* "shapes the landscape of dispossession and denial." Contends that Johnson's use of substandard grammatical forms makes "English speak against itself."

Healy, J.J. "'The True Life in Our History': Aboriginal Literature in Australia." *Antipodes* 2 (1988): 79–85. Discusses a number of Aboriginal writers, including Johnson/Narogin; concludes that these writers "are writing both themselves and a new Australia into visibility."

Nelson, Emmanuel S. "Connecting with the Dreamtime: The Novels of Colin Johnson." *Southerly* 46 (1986): 337–43. Discusses Johnson in connection with other postcolonial writers, noting that he—in this tradition—has redeemed the Aborigine from his defeat, degradation, and humiliation in the past and has helped to reshape white consciousness.

———. "Black America and the Australian Aboriginal Literary Consciousness." *Westerly* 30.4 (1985): 43–54. Traces the impact of Black American thought and literature on the awakening of Aboriginal consciousness, citing *Wild Cat Falling* to show how it uses the blues and incorporates Black American views. (Also discusses Jack Davis's and Kath Walker's work.)

———, editor. *Connections: Essays on Black Literatures*. Canberra: Aboriginal Studies Press, 1988. Contains a series of essays on various aspects of Aboriginal literature, including a discussion of Johnson's/Narogin's short fiction, by Adam Shoemaker.

———. "Literature against History. An Approach to Aboriginal Writing." *World Literature Today* 64 (1990): 30–34. Surveys Australian Aboriginal writing in an introductory vein, pointing out that "preoccupation with versions of history . . . manifests itself with special urgency" in Aboriginal literature. Discusses Johnson/Narogin, along with others.

Shoemaker, Adam. "Sex and Violence in the Black Australian Novel." *Westerly* 29.1 (1984): 45–57. Discusses *Doctor Wooreddy* alongside Faith Bandler's *Wacvie* and Archie Weller's *The Day of the Dog*, showing that the novels' sexual and cultural violence most likely stems from the effects of white culture.

Tiffin, Chris. "Look to the New-Found Dreaming: Identity and Technique in Australian Aboriginal Writing." *Journal of Commonwealth Literature* 20.1 (1985): 156–70. Discusses the work of Johnson, Kath Walker, Lionel Fogarty, Jack Davis, and others, to illustrate how they handle the themes concerning urbanized Aboriginal writers. Notes that most Aboriginal writing is "overtly political" and bears little resemblance to traditional Aboriginal "orature."

Interviews:

With Bruce Bennett and Laurie Lockwood. *Westerly* No. 3 (1975): 33–37.
With Eckhard Breitinger. *Studies in Commonwealth Literature*, 1985: 11–14.

— J.J. HEALY

Witi Ihimaera

The life of Witi Ihimaera, born in 1944 in New Zealand, reflects many of the tensions during that country's postwar years. His ancestry is "mostly Maori," he has said, "but there's a Scottish whaler and some Irish blood in my past"; and his name reflects this dual inheritance. "Ihimaera" is the Maori pronunciation of Ishmael, the name taken by his great-grandfather, but, as Ihimaera has noted, " . . . another generation of Europeans was unable to pronounce Ihimaera, and so they rendered the name as Smiler." His parents are Mormons, and he spent some time at a Mormon college. Like many of his characters, he was raised in a rural town and village; English, not Maori, was his language, and only one of his novels has been translated into Maori. His move to the city in the 1960s was at the time of a Maori exodus from the countryside. In 1970 he married a Pakeha (a New Zealander of European origin), and their daughters have both Maori and English names.

Ihimaera attributes the inception of his career as a writer to the spur given by an essayist's remark on the absence of Maori novelists. What followed was not one career but two, for after reading Ihimaera's first book, the then Prime Minister of New Zealand decided to offer the young Maori writer a place in the Ministry of Foreign Affairs. This sequence of random—or fictive —events led to an impressive range of "firsts" for which Ihimaera was particularly well qualified.

A compulsive storyteller, Ihimaera scribbled ideas for stories on the wall and the wallpaper; he later took a B.A. in literature. Subsequently he was a journalist, first on a newspaper, then with the Post Office. In 1970 he began to publish short stories in a variety of New Zealand magazines and journals, including English-language Maori publications. After a third prize in the national Wattie Award in 1973, he was the winner in 1974 and 1986, and in 1987 joint winner of the Commonwealth Writers' Prize for South-East Asia and the Pacific. In 1975 he held the Burns Fellowship at Otago University, Dunedin, New Zealand, in 1982 the Writer's Fellowship at his old university, Victoria University of Wellington.

Ihimaera's diplomatic career began in 1976 and has included overseas postings to Australia and the United States, where he was New Zealand Consul in New York. Late in 1989 he took a year's leave, returning from Washington to New Zealand to work on another novel and the libretti of two operas.

A gap of nearly ten years separates Ihimaera's publishing history into two parts, a gap during which he co-edited with D.S. Long an anthology of Maori writing, *Into the World of Light* (1982), and reworked his second novel, *Whanau*, as an opera: *Waituhi, The Life of the Village*. In "Maori Life and Literature" he describes this break as a time of reassessment, his response to the changing political reality of race relations in New Zealand. It was also a period when he himself was involved in this changing reality, both as a protester and an initiating organizer of Maori cultural councils. The anthology that he coedited during this period aimed to draw other Maori writers "into the light," and it included work by many Maori writers sharply critical of social injustice, a theme of his own later writing.

While his career has been one of striking individual achievement, he has lived through rapidly changing times for both New Zealand cultures—Maori and Pakeha, and his work has been a barometer of this change.

GLIMPSES OF CHILDHOOD

Beginning with his first publication in 1970, Witi Ihimaera's direction as a writer has closely paralleled that of written Maori literature. Nineteen-seventy was also the year of the anthology edited by Margaret Orbell, *Contemporary Maori Writing*, the first volume by Maori writers. Maori literature of this period had much in common; it was, as Ihimaera has called it, "the pastoral tradition of written Maori literature," lyrical and elegiac but lacking "anger or political thought,"—constraints he attributes to all New Zealand writing of the period:

> . . . nor, I think, did the authors of *Contemporary Maori Writing* ever have any objective in mind than to provide glimpses of childhood; of a time in the 1940s and 1950s when the emotional values and *aroha* (love and sympathy for one another), *whanaungatanga* (kinship and family responsibility) and *manaakitanga* (reciprocal assistance to one another) were intact. ("Maori Life and Literature" 50–51)

Newly fledged writers, the beginning of a culture's literature, denial of conflict— together the images are of naivety and innocence. Maori literature of the early 1970s abounds with such images, and Ihimaera has described his first published collection of short stories, *Pounamu, Pounamu*, as his "Songs of Innocence," an apt definition also for his early novels. Here Romantic images of childhood abound. His characters live in a "'hard case,' hugger mugger Eden, rough as guts but lovable" (Beatson 22), sustained by *aroha, whanaungatanga, manaakitanga*. Within this world, Ihimaera's children have the timelessness of innocence as forever new, but they also share a very time-specific presence within Maori culture and the extended Maori family. Perhaps the best analogy to this combination of the universal and the specific is with the Dylan Thomas of "Fern Hill" and the early chapters of *Portrait of the Artist as Young Dog*.

But 1975 brought change to New Zealand. Beatson defines this as the watershed year (12), and it was also one for Ihimaera, who felt that need for writing "landscapes of the heart" had passed as political reality hardened ("Maori Life and Literature" 52–53). His next published work, again a collection of short stories, *The New Net Goes Fishing*, he has termed his "Songs of Experience"; and as this suggests, they include glimpses of a childhood lifted from that Eden and placed in a different world—one of violent and disruptive change. Children have continued to play a significant role in his later, more confrontational fiction, a direction taken by Maori writers as a whole. By tracing the figure of the child, we can see clearly the path that has been followed not only by Ihimaera, but by Maori writers generally.

While the European-derived values or customs of the Pakeha constitute a threat to Maori culture in Ihimaera's early fiction, it is slow and erosive, not confrontational. Sometimes these values are subsumed under Maori culture and are thus changed. In an Easter hockey competition, for instance ("Beginning of the Tournament," *Pounamu, Pounamu*), harsh competition is dampened—"The game is important, but it's meeting together that's more important" (12)—and the after game celebration includes traditional Maori action songs. The tournament is permeated with "Maoriness" to such an extent that it must be explained to a first-time Pakeha participant. Instances of such cross-cultural adaptations abound, like the playing of cards on the casket at the *tangi* (the three-day ritual ceremonial of death and burial) of an inveterate card player, who has died, laughing, at the game. These are small ways of incorporation, allowing Maori values to remain transcendent, although against a background of the drift to the cities and life on the fringe. Larger questions of land ownership, economic deprivation, and racial discrimination are left alone.

The children of these stories remain secure, for their parents have not made the decision to move to the city. *Pounamu, Pounamu* does include one story of a family's departure, "In Search of the Emerald City," which takes them no farther than farewells and departure, leaving them at the edge of the village, Waituhi. This pastoral world is not free from sorrow; death frequently appears, but it is a natural event, and within traditional rituals it is understood and transcended, binding community even more closely together.

Of the many stories told from a child's perspective in *Pounamu, Pounamu,* "One Summer Morning" stands out, a moving and rib-tickling elegy for the passing of childhood as experienced by a young Maori boy, Hema, now at puberty. It follows his actions and reflections between his 5.30 a.m. rising and breakfast, as he farewells innocence in a conscious rite of passage. The story concludes with his father's acknowledgement of Hema's physical maturity; he agrees that Hema should change from short to long trousers. Hema's thoughts alternate between lingering remembrances of his childhood on the family farm, and his racing enthusiasm and pride in signs of maturity, which he sees in terms of a magic adult world of sex and motorbikes.

"This place is where I, Hema Tipene, have lived all my years as a kid. It has been a happy time. Now that I am a man, I am sorry to leave those times behind" (87). The symbols of maturity are all Pakeha, not traditional Maori; and Hema's sexual fantasies are fed by American movies. The story could be read as a parable of a cultural Maori rite of passage from a Golden Age of the past to a future in which Pakeha values dominate. But Hema's fantasies do not include leaving the land; his is a movement in time, not place. Security and continuity of place are ensured, above all within the essential "Maoriness" of the world of the farm, and so the sense of displacement is contained. Although the parents are the only members of the family who speak the Maori language, a break in culture is not foreseen. Permission from the father is crucial to gaining his coveted long trousers, and there is further continuity in the realism of the cost of those long trousers, which is far from his movie-inspired fantasies. His father reminds him: "I expect you to act like a man." The narrator describes the boy's reactions to his father's exhortation: "Gosh, he'll have to get up at five every morning now! And as he goes down the steps of the back verandah, the vision of being a man becomes suddenly appalling" (103–04).

The world of his childhood is described in lyrical terms that cast a glow over the garden of the farm. Formerly of a different kind, a European-style garden with tennis courts, it has been neglected for the more serious work of farming, and nature has asserted itself:

> Everything grows wild now. The leaves from the trees fall in autumn. The grass grows wild beneath the trees. The flowers wither in winter. Fruit falls and remains to rot on the ground. And yet, everything is right somehow. . . . The soil is nurtured by the fallen leaves and fruit, the grass tufts up to be eaten by the sheep and horses, and although the flowers die they come up again, the next year. There is some strange purpose here which does not need our help. We have beauty without cultivating it. Or maybe we're just lazy. (85)

The suggestion of the stereotype of shiftlessness begs refutation after the lyricism of the passage, with its evocation of an Eden untended. The subsequent pages overwhelm it completely, by detailing the hard work associated with the farm: shearing, scrub cutting, and, a delightful image of rural childhood—the docking season, where the young children trail behind catching the docked lambs' tails to cook and eat them on the spot (87). Together the association of the wild garden and the hard work of the farm create the "hugger mugger Eden," in which Hema will take his own natural place as a young man.

Balanced against Hema as the lyrical child of this Eden is the rambunctious Hema, who listens to his friends' sexual boasting, tries to make sense of the changes in his body, and daydreams in the milking shed of a love scene, straight out of a Hollywood romance, with "a skinny, tall Pakeha girl called Claudia Petrie" (96). The comic overtones are increased by the name's sly reference to the substance of Hema's recent (first) wet dream—a Roman epic which stars "Claudia" (81):

> Kiss me as you never have before . . . she cries. And he does as she commands. . . . Right smack bang on the bristled behind of Queenie who kicks him back into the sad, sad world of reality. (97)

Hema's is a world of contradictions, but they are firmly held within the familiarity of the family and the farm; his future may hold something other than the world of his wildest fantasies, but these too are known and understood, in spite of his grumbles.

In other stories of this period, kinship brings responsibility to rest on the shoulders of the child. "The Child" (*Pounamu, Pounamu*) and an important narrative strand of the novel *Whanau* depict the relationship between child and grandparent, which is very important in Maori culture. In each, the grandparent is old, frail, and dependent on the child's loving care. The grandmother in "The Child" is "a child too, in an old woman's body" (107). Her grandson finds her dead on their beach after school one day and, not knowing death, gives as his response one that comes perfectly from a child's understanding: "Her mind had wandered far away, and my Nanny, she had wandered after it" (113). The response to the impending death in *Whanau* is quite different. Here Pene, the child, "runs away" with his grandfather during a family conflict over whether the old man should be taken away for medical care by his daughter in the city or kept at home. In the rainy night, the old man is drawn to the village meeting house, where "shadows wait, where people sing" (167). The love and strength of the child pulls him away from these voices calling to

> . . . the warmth of the village hearth before the flame began to grow cold. . . . To family aroha, but more than that, village aroha. Family together, before the great family began to splinter apart. (168)

His actions contribute to a return to that time of "village aroha," as the searchers for child and old man forget family or community conflicts and join for one purpose. Although the undercurrents of tension are merely submerged, the spiritual link between child and grandparent, the only people able to hear the otherworldly voices, extends to the whole village. The flame of the hearth is not cold while the child exists to return it to life.

The novel *Tangi* describes the remembrance of childhood as a passage through a son's mourning for his father and his rebirth into a new maturity. His father's *tangi* (the Maori three day ritual of mourning for the dead, which includes burial and communal feasting) is a "homecalling" from the city for the eldest son. The past he evokes is a another secure, rural childhood. The ritual of the *tangi*, according to Ihimaera, is a force in the *te taura tangata*, "the rope of man," which emphasizes "continuing transmission" (Wilkinson 100, 105), both through the gathering that reinforces the community *aroha* and through acknowledgement of emotional continuity with the one who has died. An important narrative thread, alternating with remembrances of childhood and the ritual proceedings of the *tangi*, is the story of creation, of the separation of the Mother (Earth) and the Father (Sky) that allows their children to emerge into the light. This resolution of the paradox of renewal, which unites "the time of separation and the dawning of the first day" (204), has special meaning for the son. For him, as for Hema of "One Summer Morning," the journey through childhood leads to emancipation, in this case, to an understanding of his own grief, and the willing acceptance of his guardianship of younger brother and sister.

After 1975 comes the change from such transmissions of culture. Peter Beatson characterizes the important events of the period: the Great Maori Land March; the beginning of economic recession; the consequences of the Maori exodus from the land that occurred in the twenty years after the war (a figure set as high as 85%); the election of the National Party, which was to support sporting contacts with South Africa, thus raising the question of racism in a foreign context that was then transferred to the domestic (12). Ihimaera talks of a change in race relations as

". . . a hardening of attitudes on both sides. Of inflexibility. Of infighting." ("Maori Life and Literature" 52–53). Certainly his comments on his writing had changed from 1973: "We're all in this *waka* [canoe] together" ("Te Taha Maori" 6), to the statement concerning his controversial 1986 novel, *The Matriarch*, whose Pakeha characters are limited to victims or shadowy bit players: "If you want them to hurt, you don't write about the massacre of the Maori people, you write about the massacre of European people. . . . My business is to make European people cry" (Interview with Murphy).

The title of Witi Ihimaera's second collection of short stories, *The New Net Goes Fishing* (the first with an English title) is a Maori proverb, and serves as an epigraph to the book: "The old net is cast aside, the new net goes fishing. A new generation takes the place of the old." Beston points to an ambivalence in the title, which was also used as a section heading to Ihimaera's *Maori*, where "it specifically means that the Maori are now coming into their own and insist on their rights. . . . The new net that will bring in a rich harvest is the resurgence of Maori identity and of *Maoritanga*, the Maori way of doing things" (22). This proverb, and that of Wellington as the Emerald City, are the controlling metaphors of *The New Net*. The title of Ihimaera's first collection of stories, *Pounamu, Pounamu*, is the Maori name for greenstone, "our most prized possession," which Ihimaera describes: "It's such a beautiful, luminous, glowing stone and I've always used it to symbolize Maori culture, while I use hard, brittle, glittering emeralds to symbolize the attractions of Pakeha culture" (Wilkinson 106). Maori writer Patricia Grace uses a similar metaphor in her *Electric City and Other Stories* (1987), developing a confusion of the pronunciation of electricity into a metaphor for Pakeha urban life: "Electric City . . . And you always have to pay" (39).

Where security and continuity of traditional Maori values in some measure balance cultural erosion in Ihimaera's earlier fiction, the stories in *The New Net Goes Fishing* bring us into an urban world where change is swift and disconcerting and where dislocation replaces security. In some stories the child is a helpless witness to its elders' loss of direction. In others those who have succeeded search in their pasts for the child they have lost; in only one, "The House with the Sugarbag Windows," is this past the source of strength that it is in *Tangi*. For others, succeeding in a culture where the two-story brick house, the two-car garage are symbols of success, there is regret for the security and continuity of the other world. But the stories in the collection are more of loss than gain, for these urban "Songs of Experience" depict more alienation than triumph. In "Big Brother, Little Sister," two urban babes run from their deserted mother's abusive lover. As they try to find the way back to their grandmother in the country, they are trapped in the harsh, glittering sterility of the Emerald City "a maze for them, with no way out" (Sharkey 63):

> Then the lights turned green and the traffic leapt through the intersection. . . . Emerald lights were strung across the dead facade of the Winter Show Building. . . . A star burst across the sky. The lights of the city tightened round them. (13, 26)

Although *The New Net* includes several stories of young radical Maoris, "Clenched Fist" and "Tent on the Home Ground," the most successful in this collection are those that employ central images rather than rhetoric to bear the weight of meaning.

"The Seahorse and the Reef," told by a child, poignantly relates the effect on a Maori community of the pollution caused by the release of effluent into the sea. The child observes his father's reaction: his "fists were clenched and his eyes were angry. . . . First the land, and now our food" (188). But it is more than their food. The pollution casually, impersonally destroys the Sunday community gathering of urban Maoris, poisons the sea, their friend to which the father apologizes: "We have lost our aroha for you and our respect for your life" (188). And the children's seahorse is left "searching frantically for clean and crystal waters" (189).

This collection is framed by two stories that establish the Emerald City theme: "Yellow Brick Road" (arrival in Wellington of the family who left Waituhi in "In Search of the Emerald City" in *Pounamu, Pounamu*) and "Return from Oz" (a generation later, the father, now a grandfather, returns). "Return from Oz" ends the book on a note of hope. This family, symbolic of the great exodus, has fared better than most of the people depicted in the other stories, or at least the narrative shows neither their brushes with racism nor the cost of their success in Pakeha terms. The father of the final story is the child, Matiu, narrator of the first; he is now a lawyer, with a Pakeha wife. His son, Christopher, has a Pakeha name and has learned some Maori at school (a reflection of changed educational policy in New Zealand schools, with their "language nests" that followed adoption of Maori as one of New Zealand's official languages in 1974). He cherishes his grandfather and respects what he has to teach; his final words show that this "new net" seems likely to hold: "For yes, Grandfather, I will come to see you often. No matter where you are, I will come. It is not too late, e pa" (200). Sure of his place in urban, Pakeha culture, holding the bridge to Maori culture, his life is enriched by the old ties of cross-generational affinity.

But this glimmer of hope in "Return from Oz" does not signal an end to Ihimaera's greater commitment to writing about the "inflexibility" in New Zealand society. Nowhere is this better illustrated than in a comparison of a very early story, "Halcyon" (1971), with its substantially revised form published in 1989 as "The Halcyon Summer" (*Dear Miss Mansfield*). In this volume of responses to, and variations on, the stories of Katherine Mansfield, "The Halcyon Summer" is paired with her "At the Bay," yet the dialogue here is less between Ihimaera and Mansfield, than between the early and the later Ihimaera. Characterization, setting, time, and theme have been completely rethought, injecting a new political consciousness into his earlier pastoral world, including direct confrontation between Maori/Pakeha. By loosing a serpent into this "hugger mugger Eden," Ihimaera shows that while *aroha* may have been intact in the 1940s and 1950s, these decades held much more conflict than was acknowledged in the past.

The 1971 "Halcyon" is a seven-year-old boy's tale of a holiday at his grandmother's house. Here he is introduced to Maori ways, the rough and tumble of a large family, an open air life by the sea. This first Tama learns to swim and ride, goes to church and observes from the fringe a weekend-long drinking party that is without a sign of violence. He learns something of his Maori inheritance, which stays with him but does not affect his life other than as a memory of the perfect "summer solstice." The second Tama leaves changed irrevocably, for in the 1989 story the fictional elements lead to a very different end as this Tama is pulled into history. The opening sentence marks the time as 1950, a time of passage in New Zealand history, the end of an age of assimilation: "It was the year that Sir Apirana Ngata died" (156); Ngata was founder of the Maori Land Councils, proponent (as his knighthood implies) of working within the Pakeha system, not radical confrontation. So the story portends the birth of more abrasive attitudes, although these were not to surface until the late 1970s.

The next sentence confirms this shift by introducing a reason for Tama's holiday. "That summer the children's parents decided to go to the Empire Games in Auckland." The parents return at story's end to learn of a threat to family land that has been developing while they have been observers at the "Empire Games," an interesting metaphor for the role of the Maori in New Zealand history. Young Tama knows that "Something was happening at the edge of childhood. It was just around the corner, and, whatever it was, it would forever change all their lives" (179). While he cannot understand it fully, his parents do and are politicized by it. His father, seeing the well-oiled gun being readied for the arrival of the Pakeha in two days time, "looked grim and almost afraid" (179), and the parents plan to return for the fight but without the children.

This new Tama, another childish witness to dislocation, is an eleven-year-old, and narrative viewpoint has been changed from first to third person to allow authorial comment. He is more sexually curious about his older girl cousins (though not yet at puberty, like Hema of "One Summer Morning") and at an age where he has to fight his male cousins to prove himself. The first Tama's childhood pleasures in play are repeated in an abbreviated form for the second Tama, but the sheer joy of childhood has been replaced by fuller induction into the "Maoriness" of this new life. By implication he comes to these lessons alienated from his birthright, and his summer lessons go far beyond gathering shellfish from the rocks. Against a background of threatened—and ill understood—violence, he must discover some things that Christopher of "Return from Oz" has already learned. Tama's other language, for instance, is French, not Maori; he is clearly a child of the culturally repressive 1950s, not the 1980s.

Furthermore, what he is learning is now under threat of disruption—not erosion, but violent disruption; although he may not understand this fully, he can understand enough to wish to be involved. When his grandparents leave to visit other Maori communities along the coast, when kinsmen increasingly hold meetings at their house, Tama is excluded. "The Halcyon Summer" depicts the beginning of a battle over land—a theme fully developed in Patricia Grace's novel *Potiki* (1986), but because it is presented through the eyes of an eleven-year-old, the cause stays remote. Intrusive visits of authority represented by the white policeman are reminders of legal conflict and add a constant threat to the earlier simple pastoral lyric, expressed in talk such as "We may have lost the case in court . . . but no one's going to move us off. . . . Maori Affairs is appealing the decision for us" (160, 166). The visit to town is no longer just to see movies, socialize, shop, and go to church; the adults now have "business with Maori Affairs" (171). Omitted are the weekend drinking party and the visit to church. Instead, distraught at the danger of losing her land, the grandmother "drinking her troubles away" becomes a staggering, monstrous figure: "'Fuggen hell,' she swore, 'blimmen hell'" (176). In the earlier story, it is a teenage girl cousin who gets drunk, scandalizing the grandmother, who represents the sober, responsible Maori woman. This breakdown is portrayed as a response to the strain the grandmother carries, as chief organizer against Pakeha authority. The grandfather calls her "the one who keeps us all together" (168), and it is she who teaches Tama of *aroha, whanaungatanga, manaakitanga*: "Whenever you need us, all you have to do is call. And whenever you are needed, you must come" (170).

The political significance of these changes in dealing with the past is obvious. But the future is also dealt with differently in 1989. The 1971 story ends with Tama's adult voice confessing the alienation to come, from which the story was written:

> I never saw Nanny again. I never even went to her tangi. . . . You see, I grew older. I spread my wings and flew from city to city, year after year after year. Sometimes, I found a haven, a small niche from the wind. Most times I have been happy. Yet . . . ("Te Taha Maori" 69)

In the story's revision, the future is only foreshadowed: "for some reason his vision became all blurry as if, after the long summer, rain had finally come to the Coast" (180). The induction of Tama into Maori culture and his readiness to learn mark him, too, as a "new net." However, the urgency and potential violence, which are a background to his new learning and which differ from the ease of Christopher's Maori associations in "Return from Oz," are portents of further storms to come.

Of the other stories in *Dear Miss Mansfield*, children are central figures in over half, some Maori, some Pakeha. Maori life is the central theme of many of these, with the exception of "The Cicada" in which Aroha, a country girl at school in Wellington fights her racist peers, and a grandmother reveals her shame at dropping an unbearable burden of *whanaungatanga* as a child in "A Contemporary Kezia."

Between *The New Net Goes Fishing* and *Dear Miss Mansfield* Ihimaera published two novels. They are extraordinarily dissimilar, though the core of both again is the child/grandparent relationship, worth examining in its changing manifestations. Circumstances surrounding the birth and childhood of Kahu, the girl in the later novel, reveal her to be associated with the legendary hero depicted in *The Whale Rider*. But her grandfather ignores these circumstances, seeking a spiritual heir and refusing to accept a woman as leader. Kahu's own whale ride passes into the realm of the supernatural, confronts and overcomes his prejudice, and confirms her role. Written for Ihimaera's daughters, this small, engaging fable does not have the contentiousness of *The Matriarch*. The incidents of racism in *The Whale Rider* are displaced onto New Guinea society; while in New Zealand, Maori and Pakeha conservationists cooperate in a climactic scene, salvaging beached whales. The sexual chauvinism of the grandfather may parallel racial chauvinism, but with natural and supernatural evidence to quell it, his minority attitude has no chance of success.

Ihimaera's contentious epic novel, *The Matriarch*, has an equally troubled child/grandparent relationship as the central thread of a far more complex structure. The perspective of the child is again reclaimed through memory, revealing between this grandson and his imperious, sensual, and often violent grandmother a situation that is not capable of the resolution of *The Whale Rider*. When compared with the earlier grandparents, the matriarch seems like someone from a different race entirely. Her patrician heritage along with her determination to force her grandson to learn from her—not the greenstone warmth and luminosity, but the elements of fighting and a Machiavellian hand with opponents, her association with the supernatural, and her superciliousness towards those without her strength make this quite a different novel from those preceding it. The narrator's search to remember his past, particularly an incident on the marae at Wellington where Maori and Prime Minister meet and where his grandmother confronts not the Pakeha but other Maori, is the novel's linchpin within several other time frames. These include a chronological history of New Zealand, beginning not with the arrival of the Pakeha but with the creation as well as a linear reclamation of events from his childhood and his quest undertaken in the watershed years of 1974 and 1975. The past is substantiated through his own memories and those of his elders.

Strongly confrontational in its historical context, *The Matriarch* is an original work in many ways. It is, with Pat Baker's *Behind the Tattooed Face* (1975), one of the few books that confronts received Pakeha history with a Maori-based version of events. Through the operatic references to Verdi, connections with Venice, and liberal use of Italian in the text, it connects the Maori struggle with the Risorgimento. In the contemporary sections, it attempts to give a picture of *Maoritanga*, of *aroha* continuing within the family. The historical elements of the novel are firmer than the personal, which throughout remain the most troubling—partly through the figure of the matriarch itself, partly through the relationship with the child who is faced with demands beyond his comprehension (and this includes the supernatural), partly because of the seductive appeal of the matriarch. One of the most troubling aspects is that this child does not carry the Romantic associations of childhood but is instead drawn so firmly into the orbit of the matriarch that the innocence directing the childhood figure for good or ill through the social context evolves into complicity with an unreliable force. He is tutored in power games and internecine struggles within the Maori community. Here is Ihimaera's most striking break with the past, and the point that New Zealanders, both Maori and Pakeha, have found most objectionable.

Ihimaera's publications of the last five years are diverse; little, it seems, can be foretold of his future direction. His next work is to be called "Tiana," which will be a sequel to *The Matriarch* and will focus on the narrator's mother. He has described this as a work of "dark, derelict, subterranean, subway culture centred round people with no chances," citing as his model the American novel *Last Exit to Brooklyn* (Interview in *Evening Post*). Nothing, it seems, could be further from the world of the greenstone. But in whatever guise, it is certain that the figure of a child will carry the tenor of the work and remain evocative of the shifting moods of the New Zealand Maori.

WORKS CITED

Beatson, Peter. *The Healing Tongue. Themes in Contemporary Maori Literature.* Palmerston North: Studies in New Zealand Art and Society, 1989.

Beston, John B. "An Interview with Witi Ihimaera." *World Literature Written in English* 16 (1977): 115–25.

Corballis, Richard. "A Bibliography of Works By and About Witi Ihimaera." *Span* 18 (1984): 89–101.

Grace, Patricia. *Electric City and Other Stories.* Auckland: Penguin, 1987.

Ihimaera, Witi. "Halcyon." *Te Ao Hou* 69 (1971): 14–23, 42–52.

———. "Maori Life and Literature: A Sensory Perception." *New Zealand Through the Arts: Past and Present.* Wellington: The Friends of the Turnbull Library, 1982. 45–55.

———. "Te Taha Maori (the Maori Side) Belongs to Us All." *New Zealand Bookworld* 2 (1973): 3–6.

———. "Interview." *Evening Post* (Wellington), 1 Sept. 1989. (Page number unavailable)

Murphy, Roy. "Interview with Witi Ihimaera." *Dominion Sunday Times* 7 June 1987. (Page number unavailable)

Orbell, Margaret, editor. *Contemporary Maori Writing.* Wellington: A.H. & A.W. Reed, 1970.

Sharkey, Michael. Review, *The New Net Goes Fishing. New Literatures Review* 9 (1981): 60–64.

Wilkinson, Jane. "Witi Ihimaera. Interview." *Kunapipi* 7.1 (1985): 98–110.

WITI IHIMAERA'S PUBLISHED WORK

Novels

Tangi, 1973
Whanau, 1974
The Matriarch, 1986
The Whale Rider, 1987

Short Story Collections

Pounamu, Pounamu, 1972
The New Net Goes Fishing, 1977
Dear Miss Mansfield, 1989

Opera

Waituhi, The Life of the Village, 1985

History

Maori, 1975

> Introduction to Maori culture and history, and a frank discussion of contemporary race relations. Critical of the "one-way process" of integration requiring change only of the Maori. Written for the Ministry of Foreign Affairs and published by the New Zealand government.

SELECTED CRITICAL READINGS

Most critical articles on Witi Ihimaera's fiction have discussed his earliest works, rather than taking a synoptic view. Initial New Zealand responses were often ambivalent toward the first Maori novelist: encouraging rather than critical, though wary of his "sentimentality." International critics and reviewers are now finding this quality acceptable, even, in some instances, a sign of sophistication. *The Matriarch* remains the most contentious of his works, assailed in New Zealand on a variety of cultural and literary grounds and as yet receiving little international attention. Its sequel, *Tiana* is sure to attract attention, which will solidify assessments of the 1986 novel. Comparative studies of Ihimaera and Pacific and African writers are now adding breadth to the texture of criticism, though generally these, too, have been limited to the earlier works.

Albinski, Nan Bowman. "Broken Houses: The Indigenous Novelists." *The Commonwealth Novel since 1960.* London: Macmillan, 1991. Examines theme of cultural dislocation in novels by Aboriginal Mudrooroo Narogin (Colin Johnson), Canadian Metis writer Beatrice Culleton, and Ihimaera. Looks at the mythic and supernatural elements of *The Matriarch.* Concludes that Ihimaera's atypical concentration on Maori-Maori conflict within the novel distorts its effectiveness in dealing with the theme discussed.

Beckmann, Susan. "Language as Cultural Identity in Achebe, Ihimaera, Laurence and Atwood." *World Literature Written in English* 20 (1981): 117–84. Compares Achebe's parallels of loss of language and loss of culture with Ihimaera's bicultural combinations of Maori and English, particularly in *Tangi.* Also discusses Laurence's Metis and Scottish characters and Atwood's Canadians resisting the American idiom.

Beston, John B. "Witi Ihimaera, Maori Novelist in a Changing World." *Commonwealth, Essays and Studies* 3 (1977–78): 19–28. Comments on Ihimaera's scrupulous fairness in dealing with Maori/Pakeha relations. Finds his work vibrant and optimistic, its expression of emotion associated with traditional Maori beliefs healthy; considers that accusations of "sentimentality" stem from Pakeha repression.

Corballis, Richard, and Simon Garrett. *Introducing Witi Ihimaera.* Auckland: Longman Paul, 1982. Particularly useful for the non-New Zealand reader. Detailed discussion of short stories, many uncollected, especially significance of revisions. Considers Ihimaera's narrative construction his main strength.

Dasenbrock, Reed Way. "Intelligibility and Meaningfulness in Multicultural Literature in English." *PMLA* 102 (1987): 10–19. Includes Ihimaera with Narayan, Kingston, Anaya as a multicultural writer who uses language to confront monocultural readers with cultural diversity. Examines Ihimaera's use of Maori language in *Tangi* and its effect on non-Maori readers. Considers that accusations of sentimentality reveal success of this confrontation.

Garrett, Simon. "A Maori Place in New Zealand Writing: Recovery and Discovery in the Novels of Witi Ihimaera." *A Sense of Place in the New Literatures in English.* St. Lucia: U of Queensland P, 1986. 112–22. Argues for Ihimaera's sophisticated use of advanced narrative skills derived from two cultures: Maori oral literature, with its similarities to Old English, and New Zealand literature, particularly that of Katherine Mansfield.

Isernhagen, Hartwig. "Witi Ihimaera's Fiction: From Indigenous Myth to Late Modernist City Myth?" *World Literature Written in English* 24 (1984): 189–200. Compares Wendt's transformational, historical use of myth to that of Grace, which is spiritual and personal. Locates Ihimaera between the two. Sees role of traditional myth in *Whanau* as a stabilizing social, communal force. Identifies modernist influence on *The New Net Goes Fishing*, where traditional myths are ineffectual.

Murton, Brian J. "Waituhi: A Place in Maori New Zealand." *New Zealand Geographer* 35.1 (1979): 24–33. Useful cultural background on role of Waituhi in Ihimaera's fiction, describing the traditional significance of place to Maori communities and its contemporary political implications.

Nightingale, Peggy. "All Any Man with a Club Can Do." *Myth and Metaphor.* Adelaide: Centre for Research in the New Literatures in English, 1982. 53–70. Contrasts Wendt's ironical vision of the dualities of darkness and light that underlie conflicting European-Samoan value systems with Ihimaera's more optimistic reading of the outcome of social change. For Ihimaera, a more coherent tradition offers a source of strength to those who retain contact with the past. Notes that definitive images for Wendt are the setting sun, isolation; for Ihimaera, the rainbow, symbol of hope.

Ojinmah, Umelo Reubens. *Witi Ihimaera and the Bicultural Vision.* Otago, New Zealand: U of Otago P, 1990. Compares Ihimaera and Achebe.

Pearson, Bill. "Witi Ihimaera and Patricia Grace." *Critical Essays on the New Zealand Short Story.* Auckland: Heinemann, 1982. 166–84. Describes the dominant modes of Ihimaera's stories as "comedy, elegy and lyricism." Dismisses charges of naivety. Finds similarities between the elegiac in *Tangi* and Old English poetry. Little direct comparison with Grace, though deems her characterization superior.

Poananga, Atareta. "*The Matriarch*: Tahia Wahine Toa (Trample on Strong Women)." *Broadsheet* Dec. 1986: 24–28; Jan.-Feb. 1987: 24–29. Lengthy review article on *The Matriarch*, which condemns Ihimaera's sexism and "Uncle Tomism"; charges him with perpetuating stereotypes of violent Maori women and misrepresenting women's roles in traditional Maori culture.

Simms, Norman. "Maori Literature in English: Prose Writers. Part Two: Witi Ihimaera." *Pacific Quarterly (Moana): An International Review of Arts and Ideas* 3 (1978): 336–48. Stresses Maori literature's need for a poet. Accuses Ihimaera of sentimentality and superficiality, lack of rigor, and "shirking real issues." Considers style acceptable but tone lamentable.

Tiffin, Chris. "Mates, Mum, and Maui: The Theme of Maturity in Three Antipodean Novels." *Awakened Conscience: Studies in Commonwealth Literature.* New Delhi: Sterling, 1978. 127–45. Discusses search for identity in coming-of-age novels: Stow and Wendt define necessity of repudiating early ties; Ihimaera emphasizes importance of their continuation. Praises Ihimaera as "superb stylist."

Wynn, Graeme C. "Tradition and Change in Recent Maori Fiction: The Writings of Witi Ihimaera." *International Fiction Review* 2 (1975): 127–31. Examines Ihimaera's role in reaffirming traditional Maori values under change and acting as interpreter to non-Maori readers.

—NAN BOWMAN ALBINSKI

Keri Hulme

In 1985, Keri Hulme's winning of the Booker-McConnell Prize for her novel *The Bone People* brought her to international attention.

She was born in Christchurch, New Zealand, on 9 March 1947. Her father, a carpenter, was a first-generation New Zealander of wholly English descent from Lancashire. He died when Hulme was 11; her mother—of Orkney Scots and Kai Tahu descent—supported six children by working as a clerk and credit manager, then shop owner and manager.

Hulme spent her childhood between Christchurch, where she went to school, and Moeraki, about 200 miles to the south, where she spent holidays with her mother's family. She began an Honors Law degree at the University of Canterbury, Christchurch, in 1967, but left after the fourth term. She subsequently worked at a variety of jobs, including short-order cook, television director, postal worker, census enumerator, agricultural and factory worker, and fisher.

In 1972, she began writing full time. She has been Writer-in-Residence at Otago University, Dunedin (1978), the University of Canterbury (1985), and the University of New South Wales, Sydney, Australia (1990). She has been a member of the Literary Fund Advisory Committee (1985–89) and is on the Indecent Publications Tribunal (1985–90).

She has won many prizes for her writing, including the Bank of New Zealand-New Zealand Women's Writers Katherine Mansfield Award in 1975 for the short story "Hooks and Feelers"; the Maori Trust Fund prize (for writing in English), 1977; the ICI Writing Bursary, 1982; the New Zealand Writing Bursary, 1983; and, for *The Bone People*, the Mobil Pegasus Award for Maori Writers and the New Zealand Book of the Year Award for fiction, 1984, as well as the Booker-McConnell Prize.

She now lives in Okarito, a village along the west coast of New Zealand's South Island. A book of her poetry, "Strands," is forthcoming from Auckland University Press and her work in progress is a novel called "Bait."

INVENTING NEW ANCESTORS FOR AOTEAROA

The plot of Keri Hulme's *The Bone People* is implausible, even melodramatic. A straightforward account of events would lurch from those typical of the marvelous—a strange child found after a shipwreck becomes the catalyst for a relationship that, it is implied, will change a whole nation, to those of soap opera—his foster father beats him viciously, eventually leaving him in a coma but is finally forgiven—then to those of myth, in which man, woman, and child together prove to be the fulfilment of a prophecy. The story is not told straightforwardly, however, but in dense, witty, and often poetic language laid out in a highly purposeful and sophisticated structure. The story cannot, ultimately, be told straightforwardly because the text is attempting to rework the old stories that govern the way New Zealanders—both Maori (indigenous New Zealanders) and Pakeha (New Zealanders of European origin)—think about their country. The new story set in its place is of the bone people who incorporate a variegated ancestry, and who may, in turn, become the spiritual ancestors of a transformed land.

A shifting series of narrative frames is established by allusions to a range of literary works from *Robinson Crusoe* to *The Lord of the Rings* and to a range of popular narrative conventions. At the simplest level, the function of these frames is to keep the reader reading. The desire to discover more about Simon's mysterious origins, for example, drives one to read on as Kerewin undertakes a case reminiscent of a Sherlock Holmes story. But the expected neat unfolding of the solution never occurs although most of its parts are available, because Simon's past proves irrelevant either to his survival or to the future. Hulme lays out the openings to some of the most powerful fantasies, or "master narratives," of Western culture, not just to entice readers but to undermine these narratives' pervasive power, usually by dropping, reshaping, or awkwardly rushing their conclusions. Among the most powerful of these narratives are the fantasies of the self-sufficient individual, of empire, of limitless riches, of the transforming power of heterosexual romance, and of superhuman strength.

Fantasies of escape to desert islands where the individual can prove his self-sufficiency and impose his individual will are part of Western culture, and as Kerewin Holmes picks up Simon's sandal at the beginning of *The Bone People* we find ourselves in the midst of that particular fantasy: "She frowns. She doesn't like children, doesn't like people, and has discouraged anyone from coming on her land." Then she goes home to her well-equipped tower, and we find ourselves in the related fantasy of the isolated intellectual or writer, alone in the library, completely self-sufficient: "There is just about everything in her library" (15). She even says to herself "Gimme something escapist . . ." (16), but as she looks for it, she catches sight of Simon. He will prevent any escape, dragging her out of her individualism and into both the local Pakeha community and his extended Maori foster family. But it is a long struggle: Even when she knows she may be dying, Kerewin refuses all offers of assistance, insisting against considerable evidence to the contrary that no one cares whether she dies alone or not.

Simon is Friday to Kerewin's Robinson Crusoe, his worn sandal and footprints on the beach echoing a literary encounter that has become emblematic of imperial-colonial relations. Later, when he teaches her "his" language, she describes his opening gesture as "an amerindian opening parley" (23). The encounter, between a handicapped European child and a part-Maori, becomes analogous to the encounter between the European and the Indigene but in reverse. Hulme's reversal here indicates her desire to rework the subordination of Maori by Pakeha that followed this national originary encounter. Further, her Friday is not a submissive servant but a willful child whom she will eventually adopt.

The fantasy of winning a million dollars appears here strongly enough to have led critics to say the novel is a species of wish-fulfillment. Kerewin Holmes has it all: She has won a lottery, built her dream tower, and can devote herself to the upper middle-class pleasures of gourmet cooking, bibelot collecting, interior decoration, and wine connoisseurship. Further, she is an artist, an Aikido expert, and indeed, as Lawrence Jones notes, "omnicompetent . . . a kind of superwoman" (203). Kerewin puts it differently: "'Really I'm just a brilliant amateur. In everything,' she adds sourly" (55). Given Hulme's intention to highlight the value of Maori culture, it makes sense to have such a heroine. The point is that the main character must be shown to "have it all" and to remain dissatisfied, because "all" in the Pakeha sense is not enough. Significantly, the lottery win that permitted her to build the Tower was succeeded by the loss of her artistic talent, by depression and self-loathing.

Enter Simon's handsome Maori foster father, Joe, a widower, to set up what appears to be the beginning of the perfect romance: ". . . in a flood of sensation she is aware of the rustle of the man's felted wool coat, the breadth of his shoulders contrasted with the child's bone-thinness; the blackness of his long straight hair; the half-wonderment, half-weariness of his face. And the fact that he is exactly as tall as herself" (54). But as we discover, Kerewin is "a neuter" (266), uninterested in the kind of sexual and romantic consummation commonly used to end novels.

In raising the issue of violence, Hulme critiques Western society's smug faith in physical technique and prowess as a solution to problems. Kerewin is a faster and better fighter than a man. Because of our immersion in and acceptance of cultural forms filled with violence, we find it easy to be caught up in its excitement: "She is screaming with delight inside herself, trembling with dark joy. Fight. Fight. Fight" (190). Because she uses her power to stop Joe in the act of hitting Simon, what she does seems justified. However, after she has "stood gloating a minute," she is felled by a pain that she later compares to Seppuku—Japanese ritual suicide by disembowelment (192–93).

The allusion is a clue to how her violence should be interpreted. Mastery of Aikido means one defuses violence, not only without using violence but also preferably without drawing attention to one's intervention. Aiki, as Kerewin explains to Joe, "is not a technique to fight with . . . it is the way to reconcile the world, and make human beings one family" (199). As Joe observes, she "picked up the techniques, but not the spirit of it." Later he asks her, "Did you wonder whether that pain might be a consequence of sort of misusing knowledge?" (200), a suggestion she disregards. Thus her violence turns upon her in the form of an apparently malignant growth that nearly kills her. Her physical and mental suffering is a critique of the belief in technique without spiritual insight: one of Western society's greatest errors. Nor does her physical ability save Simon from Joe, because although she could have stopped his final beating, she has lost her temper over a stolen knife and a broken guitar and "hopes his father knocks him sillier than he is now" (307).

No one, of course, is tempted to justify Joe's violence, except Joe in moments of rage or self-pity. But he does use two common strategies to excuse it. He blames the victim (". . . he's trying to start a fight, and he'll keep on stirring until he gets one" [189]) or rationalizes it as a "lesson" ("I'm sorry to have to hit you so hard, but you've got to learn to do as I say" [136]). What happens to both him and Kerewin shows the ironic truth behind the hackneyed phrase "this hurts me more than it hurts you." Both use violence to assert self. As a result, their violence recoils on them. Some critics have voiced concern that Joe's forgiveness amounts to an apology for child beating. But to treat the violent with violence does not solve the problem, nor can they be excluded from a society that institutionalizes violence in everything from children's toys to international policy. Hulme does not try simply to dismiss the human tendency to use violence rather than reason or love, for peace can only be achieved out of a constant struggle with violence. It, like all the other tendencies that interfere with social harmony, will not just vanish because writers refrain from dealing with it explicitly in novels.

These powerful stories-cum-collective fantasies cannot be dismissed; they must be told in order to be undermined and revised. Hulme has written a novel that is intended to change New Zealand, to rewrite it into a place where Maori and Pakeha can not only live together but also evolve a distinctive culture that takes in the best of world civilization while retaining its heart in the traditions of the Maori past, in the land and the surrounding sea. This requires a shift in the colonial view of New Zealand as an under-populated sheep pasture on the edge of nowhere to one that sees it as the center of a new cultural experiment. Yet this shift is just that; it cannot be a wholesale abandonment of all that has gone before. However, the narratives that uphold individualism, imperialism, racism, materialism, sexism, and violence all would preclude the successful achievement of community that is pictured at the novel's conclusion. Those images and stereotypes that insist on rigid differences and all-or-nothing responses are part of both Maori and Pakeha culture. These must be dismantled if what is best in each culture is to survive to form a new community.

The three main characters frequently suffer from being taken for what they are not. Nor are they immune to taking others the wrong way. Because Simon cannot speak, people assume he is retarded. Kerewin's first reaction to his handicap is to classify him as "one of the maimed, the contaminating..." (17). And her first sight of Joe is in a bar, telling some "rambling, drunken anecdote." Her response is stereotyped: "I'd believe the poor effing fella's short of words. Or thought. Or maybe just intellectual energy" (12). Then, expecting an encounter with Simon's father and basing her expectations on Simon's appearance, she again stereotypes: "She longs for the Gillayley father to arrive and carry off his offspring, right now. A loud and boisterous Viking type she'd bet, from the child's colouring. Yer rowdy Aryan barbarian, face like a broken crag, tall as a door, and thick all the way through" (28). In both cases she is proven wrong. Even after she has spent hours with him, Joe's story of his childhood forces her to stay up "rearranging the picture she had built in her mind of what Joe is, until it is daylight.... Very disturbing. You just get someone neatly arranged in a slot that appears to fit them, and they wriggle on their pins and spoil it all" (231). Joe, too, has been guilty of denying difference. Reflecting on his near-fatal beating of Simon, he thinks, "I wanted him as ordinarily complex and normally simple as one of Piri's rowdies. I resented his difference, and therefore, I tried to make him as tame and malleable as possible, so I could show myself [in him]." He continues, thinking of Kerewin: "I was trying to make her fit my idea of what a friend, a partner was. I could see only the one way" (381). Kerewin, because of her appearance and because she is not obviously heterosexual, is automatically assumed to be a lesbian. All three, from one extreme perspective, are summed up by a fat carpenter in a bar as "stinkin' leslies and Mahries and that bloody little freak" (247). In opposition to this sort of intolerance, Hulme works in a world where categories are fluid, where the socially constructed divisions among people are shown as just that, constructs that assist the process of exclusion so conducive to the exercise of authoritarian power.

Buildings become symbolic of the novel's attempt to soften rigid categories. The tower represents the fantasy of self-sufficient individualism (Dale 415), which must be torn down not only physically, with a sledge-hammer, but ideologically, with Kerewin's "brainy nails" (7). Significantly, a central symbol of community, the *tricephalos*, rises out of the tower's ashes like the phoenix on the signet ring that is Simon's inheritance from his father. Then, after her recovery, Kerewin undertakes the rebuilding of the Maori meeting house at Moerangi practically single-handedly. Once the symbol of Western culture is demolished and the symbol of Maori culture rebuilt—that is, some balance restored, she moves to another possibility. The new building she constructs for her new family stands on the foundations of the old tower and takes the spiral shape typical of the decorations of the meeting house—and, doubtless also significantly, of the chambered nautilus, a beautiful-shelled sea creature that evolved 600 million years ago and survives today. Filled with treasures from all cultures, this structure represents Kerewin's new ideal of commensalism (sharing the same table), an ideal that takes from both Pakeha and Maori cultures but points to the need to build something new out of the strengths of both.

The spiral shape of the novel, which is filled with echoes of literature from all cultures and eras, is analogous. Hulme's prefatory explanation for her difficulties in having *The Bone People* published pick up on some of the novel's themes: " . . . the first three publishers turned it down on the grounds, among others, that it was too large, too unwieldy, too *different* when compared with the normal shape of a novel." That a feminist collective finally undertook publication somehow seems fitting for a work that celebrates a tolerant collectivity. Noting that her editor "respected . . . oddities," a word that is repeated through the book, she continues: "To those used to one standard, this book may offer a taste passing strange, like the original mouthful of kina roe. Persist. Kina can become a favourite food."

The *tricephalos*, the three-fold relationship that fulfils the prophecy that a "digger, or stranger, or broken man" (338) would come to preserve and awaken the Mauri, or life principle, of Aotearoa (the Maori name for New Zealand) further resists the contemporary emphasis on the individual. Although some, including Hulme herself, have resisted drawing any connection between this odd trio and the Holy Family, its echoes—the foster father called Joseph, the virgin "mother," the all-forgiving, suffering child of mysterious origins—do reinforce the novel's message at the mythic level (Dale 419-21). Together they are the bone people, described in the epigraph as the "heart and muscles and mind of something perilous and new": Presumably Simon is the heart, Joe the muscles, and Kerewin the mind. Although none of them is able to function alone, this inability is not depicted as a failure of psychological development but as natural. As Hulme says in an interview: "You can't ever be alone: the air you breathe is full of other people, other beings—and all their breathing— and you yourself are a knit and weaving of a thousand generations" (*Contemporary*

Authors 212). Each has lost family: Simon his parents and foster mothers, Joe his father, wife and son to death, and mother to madness, Kerewin her entire family to her own perverse inability to realize that they will forgive her. As a result all are given to terrible depression, insecurity, and self-loathing and share the tendency to turn to drink or violence to deal with these feelings. Dale notes that ". . . all three of them bore physical scars from an earlier time . . . and all three undergo suffering. All three travel close to death and return having in various ways worked out their own salvations, in each case with the aid of a 'helper'" (419). Although each one is, as events prove, intelligent and self-reliant, without the love and trust of the others each is blighted, unable to flower.

Their interdependence begins the moment Simon walks into Kerewin's tower and hides in the library, here symbolic of the human mind and the Western culture it encloses, and is discovered just as Kerewin is looking for a fantasy by Tolkein: "In the window, standing stiff and straight like some weird saint in a stained gold window, is a child. A thin shockheaded person haloed in hair, shrouded in the dying sunlight" (16). The echo here is not of Middle Earth, but of the Byzantium of that other Tower-dweller, W.B. Yeats:

> O sages standing in God's holy fire
> As in the gold mosaic of a wall,
> Come from the holy fire, perne in a gyre,
> And be the singing-masters of my soul.
> ("Sailing to Byzantium")

Oblivious to the iconology, Kerewin orders Simon down, and like Tolkien's Gollum, "half-skidding half-slithering down to the chest, splayed like a lizard on a wall," he comes down. She thinks, in quick succession that he is "nasty," "gnomish," and "unnatural" (16), and later, a "small evil buddha" (21). The combination of the malign and the numinous persists, as Simon reels between sweetness and violence.

From Simon's point of view here is a fairy-tale tower inhabited by a peculiar creature—he cannot tell whether she is a man or a woman—who may, he hopes, help prevent Joe from beating him. Kerewin desperately needs a "singing-master" to inspire a spiritual transformation: "Estranged from my family, bereft of my art, hollow of soul, I am a rock in the desert" (289). The Prologue, which celebrates the reunion of Simon, Joe, and Kerewin at the end of the novel, says of Simon that "he is the singer," even though he is mute. At a more mundane level, she needs a family and Simon needs a mother. In a poem "He Hoha" [What a Fuss], Hulme writes the story of the encounter from the perspective of the body, aging toward infertility, but invaded by a "cuckoo child" (263):

> He turned full to face me, with a cry to come home—
> do you know the language of silence, can you read eyes?
>
> When I think of my other bones, I bleed inside,
> and he won't go, the cuckoo-child.

It is not born; it is not live; it is not dead;
it haunts all my singing, lingers greyly, hates and hurts
and hopes impossible things.

Here are several allusions to the novel's title: the "other bones" are her blood relations, her family, with whom she has quarreled, but also the Maori part of her. Simon seems to invade like a cuckoo. (Cuckoos lay their eggs in those of other, usually smaller birds; the chick hatches, pushes the natural chicks out, and is fed by the coopted adoptive parents). But, in fact, he does not displace another child and ultimately returns Kerewin to her family and to her art. He forces her out of her too comfortable "nest" of a tower and coopts her into the adult responsibility of emotional commitment she has been avoiding. At another level the poem is about Keri Hulme's "haunting" by her fictional character. Simon eventually becomes Kerewin's adoptive son, but he is never just an ordinary child. He is as much symbol as "real" because of his extraordinary powers: He can see people's auras (93), has visions of the "old people" (251), and captures the sound of silence in his music hutches.

The surface of the text generally is resolutely realistic—at least, once Kerewin's eccentric running commentary to herself is accepted. The fantastic events are embedded in the daily workings of society, where accounts of the local policemen, mailmen, bus drivers, doctors, teachers, merchants, and bartenders serve to ground what otherwise might simply fail to convince us to suspend our disbelief. Even Joe's encounter with the Kaumatua and the "little god" is told in a way that integrates the natural and the supernatural, rather than splitting them apart. And this is the everyday world of a specific place, New Zealand. The fictional setting is mapped over the real geography with loving precision. Just as Hulme has barely disguised her own name in that of her heroine, so Whangaroa, the name of the fictional town in Westland where most of the novel is set sounds like Whataroa, the name of the nearest town to Okarito, where Hulme now lives; the name Moerangi, where the holiday scenes are set sounds like Moeraki, the name of the place on the east coast where Hulme spent her childhood holidays. However, as Hulme notes, "the land isn't a static thing that I can happily describe as '*slightly weathered glacial outwash gravel and till, quaternary formation*'" but best known through "living referents, ghostly referents, referents who—or which—have wept, do bleed, will be ecstatic" ("Okarito" 1). Hulme refuses to allow the novel to lift off from the real world, ultimately, because it is the real world she is interested in changing. The novel is not intended simply to divert but to present a close allegory of the changes necessary to transform a colonial-minded and potentially racially-split New Zealand into a creative and harmonious Aotearoa.

The novel is one of a group of postcolonial writings that might be termed "nation-building novels": novels that attempt to rewrite their author's nation, often showing ways to reunite a nation split along cultural lines. For example, just as Hulme's novel tackles the Maori-Pakeha split, so Salman Rushdie's *Midnight's Children* tackles the complex racial, religious, and political splits of India, while Margaret Laurence's *The Diviners* attempts to overcome the divisions among French-speaking, English-speaking, and native people in Canada. These novels vary in the explicitness with which they deal with political issues, but nonetheless share many features, the result of rewriting the ideology of nationalism at a metaphorical level. Primary among these features is the use of a family, or a version of family, to represent the nation. Some others are the theme of adoption, the use of children as symbols of change, and an emphasis on the importance both of remembering and then of transcending the past. The central characters of all three novels are adopted (to be precise, Saleem is a changeling), a way of resisting those forms of nationalism that stress blood ties and "racial purity." Thus the point is made that although people cannot change their biology, its importance is negligible. Adopted children learn the language and culture of their adoptive parents, whatever their genetic background. Similarly, all people can and many do change their cultural attitudes. Children are of course most likely to undertake these changes and in their flexibility and potential symbolize the future. Thus, they recur in novels of this kind. Finally, the past cannot be ignored, because it is the source of the emotions that evoke the desire for the evolution of a harmonious national unity. Memory is double edged, however, because it revives thoughts of oppression and violence that may erupt again in the present. As with Joe's violence, "It's past, but we live with it forever" (444).

The Bone People is part of a postcolonial discursive formation evolving worldwide to counter not only the "truths" that drove the imperialism of nineteenth-century but also those that drive the centers of power in the twentieth. The literary texts in this formation are worked out separately, in different corners of the world, by writers familiar, perhaps all too familiar, with American popular culture and the British literary canon but unfamiliar with each other's political or cultural context. It will reward much careful study, preferably of the sort that, while comparing it to other works sharing its concerns, refuses to ignore the differences that mark it as written by a part-Maori woman from New Zealand in the late twentieth century.

Works Cited

Dale, Judith. *"the bone people*: (Not) Having It Both Ways." *Landfall* 39 (1985): 413–28.

"Hulme, Keri." *Contemporary Authors*. Detroit: Gale, 1989. 125: 209–15.

Hulme, Keri. *The Bone People*. Auckland: Spiral Collective, 1984. (Baton Rouge: Louisiana State UP, 1985)

———. "Okarito and Moeraki." *Te Whenua Te Iwi/The Land and the People*. Ed. Jock Phillips. Wellington: Allen and Unwin/Port Nicholson Press, 1987. 1–9.

Jones, Lawrence. "Modernism, Myth and Post-Modernism: Keri Hulme and C. K. Stead." *Barbed Wire and Mirrors: Essays on New Zealand Prose*. Dunedin: U of Otago P, 1987. 201–07.

Keri Hulme's Published Work

Novel

The Bone People, 1983

Short Story Collections

Lost Possessions, 1985
Te Kaihau: The Windeater, 1986

Poetry

The Silences Between (Moeraki Conversations), 1982

SELECTED CRITICAL READINGS

Because Hulme has only been known outside New Zealand since 1985, little criticism exists. Many of the articles on Hulme have appeared in small journals, difficult to find outside their places of publication. Although it certainly can bear intense analysis in isolation, *The Bone People* begs to be placed in comparative contexts—for example, those of New Zealand writing, especially by Maori writers such as Patricia Grace and Witi Ihimaera, of postcolonial writing, of feminist writing, and of writing by indigenous minorities in settler nations like Australia, the United States, and Canada. Many works of Latin American literature also have similar "nation building" perspectives.

Dale, Judith. *"the bone people:* (Not) Having It Both Ways." *Landfall* 39 (1985): 413–28. Examines the contradictions in the novel's presentation of individualism (despite the obvious intention to promote community, Kerewin is the novel's controlling consciousness and will be a community leader), of Simon's suffering (especially its gratuitousness and, thus, its Christian reverberations), and of homosexuality ("there is a clear impulse . . . to link male sexuality, homosexuality. . . as disgusting, and violence" 425). Compares the novel briefly with Alice Walker's *The Color Purple.*

During, Simon. "Postmodernism or Postcolonialism?" *Landfall* 39 (1985): 366–80. An important theoretical study that has stimulated much debate. During argues that the collapse of the historical master narratives makes it impossible simply to reassert, as he sees Hulme doing, modernist solutions to postcolonial problems: "Maori culture is absorbed and controlled by [the novel's] profoundly Occidental narratives. And the text's index—which is not at all external to the work—finishes this appropriation of the precolonial by translating the Maori words into English and thus allowing them no otherness within its Europeanising apparatus" (374). Concludes that Hulme's attempt to resurrect the failed master narratives of identity guarantees that "unwillingly, blindly [the novel] enters into the postmodern condition" (373–74).

Fee, Margery. "Why C.K. Stead didn't like Keri Hulme's *the bone people:* Who can write as Other?" *Australian and New Zealand Studies in Canada* 1 (Spring 1989): 11–32. Uses Stead's critique of Hulme as a springboard for an attempt to deal with the ethical problems involved when a majority group member speaks about, for, or as a minority group member. Considers the legitimacy of the concept of "membership" in such groups. Sets the novel into the context of criticism of fiction written by African, Aboriginal, and Amerindian writers. Deals with Hulme's undermining of Western ideology.

Gaffney, Carmel. "Making the Net Whole: Design in Keri Hulme's *The Bone People.*" *Southerly* 46 (1986): 293–302. Unlike many other critics, Gaffney separates Kerewin Holmes from Keri Hulme: "Not a few of Kerewin's self-validating Romantic experiences that make 'the net whole' cause us to respond skeptically, and this seems to be Hulme's intention" (294). Although generally positive about the novel, Gaffney is uneasy about the validity of the mystical events and the sketchy connections between the main characters' psychological needs and the Maori past.

Jones, Lawrence. "Modernism, Myth and Post-Modernism: Keri Hulme and C.K. Stead." *Barbed Wire and Mirrors: Essays on New Zealand Prose*. Dunedin: U of Otago P, 1987. 201–07. Despite the title, does not compare Hulme and Stead, but sets *The Bone People* and Stead's *All Visitors Ashore* (1984) into the contemporary debate in New Zealand about postmodernism and postcolonialism. Also provides a commentary on and evaluation of *The Bone People*.

Prentice, Chris. "Re-writing Their Stories, Renaming Themselves: Post-Colonialism and Feminism in the Fictions of Keri Hulme and Audrey Thomas." *Span* 23 (1986): 68–80. The analogy of colonization—of Canadians, Africans, and New Zealanders by the imperial power, of Maori and Native Canadian by white New Zealanders and Canadians, of women by men—is used to show how both Hulme and Thomas undermine the dichotomies of the dominant discourse, beginning with the Self-Other dichotomy: "Keri Hulme combines the Maori and the Pakeha, the Western and the Eastern, in patterns which defy rigid boundaries" (74).

Stead, C. K. "Keri Hulme's 'The Bone People,' and the Pegasus Award for Maori Literature." *Ariel* 16 (1985): 101–08. Argues that the novel should not have won the Pegasus Award because it is not a Maori work, and gives his definition of Maori. Feels the novel has been over-praised because it is fashionably female and Maori. Although partly negative, makes perceptive comments about the novel's structure and appeal. (This piece was also published as a Letter to the Editor of the *London Review of Books*, 5 Dec. 1985; the responses to it are varied and interesting: see 19 Dec. 1985 and 23 Jan 1986 issues; see Fee's response, annotated above.)

Webby, Elizabeth. "Spiralling to Success." *Meanjin* 44 (1985): 15–25. Mainly a personal account of Webby's introduction to Hulme. Brief history of the difficulties in publishing *The Bone People* and a discussion of the importance of *Maoritanga* ("Maoriness") in Hulme's other works.

— MARGERY FEE

Albert Wendt

Born in Samoa, 27 October 1939, the son of a Samoan family, which included a German great-grandfather, Albert Wendt is probably the best-known writer in the South Pacific. Sent to New Plymouth Boys' High School in New Zealand in 1952 on a scholarship, he soon became acquainted with another tradition and culture, that of the *papalagi* (Samoan word for people of European descent), which, whether he liked it or not, became one of the major components of his rich and complex personality. After studying at Ardmore Teachers' College near Auckland, he graduated with a master's degree in history from Victoria University in Wellington, New Zealand.

Because Samoan literary tradition was more oral than written, Wendt had always admired the craft of storytellers like his grandmother, who could capture the attention of countless children with her tales. He was also encouraged in his artistic vocation by the example of Robert Louis Stevenson, the Scotsman who chose to spend the last years of his life on Wendt's native island and whose *Beach at Falesa*, despite the limitations of his nineteenth-century European outlook, constitutes the first really affectionate written inquiry into Samoan life. Through Stevenson's stories echo the myth of the "South Seas Paradise," which exerted such a powerful attraction on Paul Gauguin or Blaise Cendrars; they also include an implicit indictment of the callous European outlook on Polynesia. Among the writers who impressed him most, Wendt cites J.K. Baxter and Maurice Shadbolt, two important New Zealand literary figures of his time. Dylan Thomas's Rabelaisian adventure with language and J.K. Baxter's plunge into Maori culture during the second half of his life provided new openings for the young Samoan artist. Maurice Duggan, one of the most sophisticated prose stylists in New Zealand, was one of Wendt's great favorites. In an interview in *World Literature Written in English* (1977), the author evokes the impact that Duggan's "Mandarin prose" in *Immanuel's Land* had on him. In the same interview, he also admits to being influenced by William Faulkner's attempt to create the fictional history of a whole region.

With his wife Jenny, Wendt returned to Samoa in 1965 to teach at Samoa College, whose principal he became in 1969. Although basically a novelist and a poet, Wendt has also written (unpublished) plays, notably "Comes the Revolution," performed at the first South Pacific Arts Festival in 1972, and "The Contract," performed at the Schools' Drama Festival in Apia the same year.

In 1974 he took up an appointment as Senior Lecturer in English at the University of the South Pacific in Fiji, where he became a promoter of the arts in the region somewhat in the manner of Ulli Beier in Nigeria and Papua New Guinea. While in

Fiji, Wendt worked very closely with *Mana,* a magazine of creative and critical writing. In the Mana Publications series produced at the University of the South Pacific, he edited in 1975 collections of poems from Fiji, Western Samoa, the New Hebrides (now Vanuatu), and the Solomons.

In 1977, Wendt returned home to set up the University of the South Pacific center in Samoa. This attempt at decentralization was made possible by the use of modern systems of communication such as satellite television, whereby programs and lectures were broadcast all over the region. Wendt continued his promotion of the arts through his editing of *Lali* (1980), a major anthology of writing from the Pacific. After another stay in Fiji from 1982 to 1988, the author took up a professorship of Pacific studies at the University of Auckland, a particularly appropriate appointment in a city reputed for having the largest Polynesian population in the world.

THE ATTEMPT "TO SNARE THE VOID AND GIVE IT WORD"

Albert Wendt's first published story, "Tagata, the Man who Searched for the Freedom Tree," in 1963, shows the author's fondness for picaresque characters and his interest in experimenting with unusual narrative voices. The Samoan "pidgin" he uses there does away with articles, omits the auxiliary "to be," dispenses with inflections for the plural, introduces infinitives with "for to," and uses a simplified form of the present for all tenses. Samoan word sequences and patterns are freely "transliterated" into a version of English that remains perfectly understandable to a non-Samoan speaker. Tagata, the trickster hero of the story, manages to cheat his way through life and, though eventually defeated by fate, puts up a brave fight.

Sons for the Return Home, Wendt's first published novel, in 1973, appears traditional in style and language. The plot contains the usual ingredients of the culture-clash theme frequently encountered in the first generation of novelists from the Third World: The hero, a young Samoan brought up in New Zealand by parents who dream of returning home, falls in love with a New Zealand *papalagi* girl whom he meets at the university. Though their mutual involvement increases, they discover in each other a number of prejudices that taint their relationship. For one thing, the girl tends to assume that every Samoan male is a sexual expert. In moments of crisis, he readily loads her with all the sins that *papalagi* ever committed against his people. Similarly, the boy's mother considers white people weak, badly educated, destructive, and perverted. Maori and immigrant groups from other Pacific islands are also the butt of Samoan mockery. The allegorical value of the novel is stressed by the main characters' lack of proper names; they appear throughout as merely "he" or "she." In this rich-white-girl-meets-poor-immigrant-boy idyll, the mothers play the parts of the villains: Through her silent disapproval, the girl's mother blackmails her daughter into not marrying her friend; the Samoan mother is certain that the girl, though likeable, will not make a proper wife for her son because she will never fit in Samoa. The fathers, on the contrary, show far more understanding.

Though sexually satisfied in their relationship, the young couple still remain foreign to each other in their minds. The situation improves when they take a camping trip together and go into the country where they visit the site of the girl's ancestors' first settlement in New Zealand. Through this evocation, a whole history of *pakeha* (Maori word for New Zealanders of European descent) conquest of the land unfolds, with its callous destruction of the primeval forest and desecration of sacred burial grounds. As the family prospered, a family business empire, which is still in the hands of the girl's father, was founded in the city. Progressing further into the heartland, the young couple reach the "desert road," a plateau of lava and dust near the major volcanic range of the North Island. Amid this scenery, which contains all the features of Wendt's archetypal landscape, the young man holds forth about the Polynesian epic of Maui, whom he reinterprets as a tragic Camus-like challenger of the gods who is eventually destroyed by his own daring in his ultimate attempt to penetrate Hine nui te Po, the goddess of darkness.

This love story is doomed from the beginning. Secretly encouraged by the boy's mother, the girl, who has discovered that she is pregnant, goes to Australia to have an abortion. The boy later feels distressed that he has been an accomplice in this killing of his baby. As the girl decides to spend some time in Britain, the boy goes home to Samoa with his parents only to realize that his mother's constant idealization of the ancestral land bears little relationship with reality; he suffers from the heat, lack of hygiene, and from the promiscuity of communal living in the open *fale* (Samoan traditional house). He sadly watches his mother acting as the typical returned immigrant, who feels obliged to display the symbols of *papalagi* prosperity in front of bemused and admiring relatives.

After an unsuccessful escape to Alpia where he relives a parody of the individualist life he enjoyed in Wellington, the boy returns to the village to discover his grandfather's grave, which everybody had hidden from him. As he clears the vegetation off the boulders, a secret strand of his inheritance is revealed to him. Later, on overcoming his father's reluctance to discuss the subject, he finds a deep affinity with that ancestor who always sought truth and clarity whatever the cost to himself or his family. A traditional healer, he tried to help his wife to abort her fourth child, whom he mistakenly thought was not his, and killed her in the process. Though no absolute solace to the boy, this discovery reveals a tragic form of filiation.

The first part of the novel alternates Wellington scenes and memories of an earlier life in Samoa or the journey to New Zealand. This narrative structure mirrors the two poles between which the protagonist feels torn. In the last scene on a plane traveling back to New Zealand, he flees Samoan life, which he cannot endure. Yet in mid-air between two islands and two worlds, his future seems uncertain. The concluding paragraph brings together an evocation of Camus's *Sisyphus Myth* and the traditional story of Maui's doomed attempt to penetrate the death goddess. Like Sisyphus, the boy intensely enjoys the beauty of being alive despite the absurdity of existence.

According to Wendt, the stories collected in *Flying-Fox in a Freedom Tree* are "modern fables, as opposed to the realism of *Sons for the Return Home*" (Interview 156). A good number of the stories were written before the novel, but, for marketing reasons, Longman Paul preferred to bring out *Sons for the Return Home* first. Mauga, the hero of "A Descendant of the Mountain," has just lost his wife who died in a flu epidemic brought by white sailors. Mauga relives the first time he met her, a tempting creature on the edge of the pool where he always bathed and which he considered his own. Now that she is dead, he sits there looking emptily at the water.

Timu, his son, intrudes on the scene and wonders why his father, the powerful chief, appears so weak. Taking possession of himself again, Mauga breaks the image in the pool by throwing a stone that brings mud to the surface. This simple tale contains in undertones the tragedy of the meeting of two civilizations, one unwittingly bringing death to the other. But it also stages a typically Samoan drama by showing the tragic consequences of a code of honor according to which a courageous and respectable man must never show his grief and distress.

The strictness of the traditional ethic eventually destroys Tala, the anti-hero of "A Resurrection," a Samoan version of a theme later treated by Gabriel García Márquez in *Chronicle of a Death Foretold*. Tala seeks refuge in the priesthood, having failed to wash in blood the honor of his sister, who was raped by a neighbor. The interest of this story revolves around the narrator's ambiguous attitude towards the conflict between Christian morality and the need to keep intact the honor of the *aiga* (extended family). But a principle applies in the private domain too, as we see with "Declarations of Independence," in which Paovale is killed by his wife because she suspects he is having an affair with a Chinese secretary in his office.

As in *Sons for the Return Home*, the plight of the returned immigrant looms large in "The Coming of the Whiteman." Peilua, a man whom his compatriots considered a "brilliant scholar," has been deported from New Zealand, a shameful situation better kept hidden. Still he manages to remain a source of wonder to most people because of the imported objects he keeps in his suitcase. But once he loses this distinction, he becomes a nobody: His woman leaves him; he is beaten unconscious by louts and ends up in a wheelchair. Once again the narrator's position towards Peilua wavers between satire and sympathy. The final remark suggests a tragic interpretation of the protagonist: "The true son of the Vaipe died in New Zealand, killed by a woman who didn't love him. A whiteman was deported to the Vaipe. We crucified him" (83).

Many characters in *Flying-Fox in a Freedom Tree* have rebelled against the prevailing code, a mixture of traditional loyalty to the clan and "modern" puritan capitalistic principles. The young boy hero of "The Cross of Soot" spends his time with convicts from the neighboring penal settlement. In "Pint-Size Devil on a Thoroughbred," despite his wife's protests, the first-person narrator takes in Pili, a distant uncle and a famous hanger-on who constantly gets into trouble with the law. In a very clever metafictional trick, the narrator regrets not being the author of the parodic "Ballad of Pili the Kid," which celebrates the feats of the popular ruffian on the local radio. In an ironical twist, the author roots Pili's noncomformity in tradition by drawing a parallel between Pili and the narrator's own grandfather, who was a law unto himself.

In *Flying-Fox in a Freedom Tree*, Wendt pursues the linguistic experiments initiated in "Tagata, the Man Who Searched for the Freedom Tree." The first person narrators of "Virgin-Wise—The Last Confession of Humble Man Who Is Man Got Religion" and of "Captain Full—The Strongest Man Who Got Allthing Strong Men Got" express themselves in Wendt's half-serious, half-parodic version of pidgin. The hero of "Captain Full" proves absolutely cynical and does not hesitate to cheat his way through prosperity and respectability, even if this entails abandoning old friends and earning his living as a pimp.

The world of *Flying-Fox in a Freedom Tree* is dominated by two main sets of values. Although a Samoanized version of the Christian faith prevails, in a continuation of the old tradition the church goes hand in hand with secular powers. The stories are built so as to point out the hypocrisy of rich and powerful people who, though they outwardly place God above everything, behave just as they please. Weber's view of the protestant ethic with its respect for God, power, and money, is naturally superimposed on the ancient values of a highly competitive society based on the authority of the *matai* (head of an *aiga*), who ruled almost absolutely over his extended family, whose financial prosperity and prestige he was supposed to guarantee. In modern society, the social barriers that restricted the *matais*' temptations to tyrannize everybody have disappeared, and they can claim the best of both worlds. Such characters appear as despicable frauds when the stories are told from the point of view of a son who challenges all authority, abandons most Christian principles, and just tries to outdo others at the power game. Sometimes the lawless heroes behave in an absurdly self-destructive way just for the sake of living in style, a feeling that might well be seen as a perversion of the old sense of honor.

The protagonist of *Pouliuli*, Wendt's next novel, has been described as a Pacific version of *King Lear*. One morning Faleasa Osovae, a most influential seventy-six-year-old *matai* in Malaelua, wakes up to find that he really despises the social and religious ideals for which he has lived so far. He starts shocking people into satisfying his whims by judiciously provoking the violent bouts of nausea he has had since the decisive morning. He plays at being possessed by the spirit of his dead mother and delights in insulting Filemoni, their respected pastor who has come to offer his help. Faleasa enjoys seeing everybody trying to humor him and delights in his newly-gained freedom of speech. Sau, a friend whom he had always trusted, suddenly shows a less pleasant side of himself now that he thinks that the old chief is unable to hear him. Faleasa trusts only Lemigao, a man who, because he has a club foot and never knew his father, has been the butt of much jeering in the village. The old *matai* explains that, up to then, he has been an easy prey for all the greedy appetites of his *aiga*. But he is now convinced that what people commonly call insanity is the only form of sanity, and he begs Lemigao's support to pursue his search for individual freedom to its logical conclusion.

The main narration is interspersed with flashbacks about Faleasa's past relationship with his father, a ruthless tyrant and womanizer, who taught Faleasa never to show any weakness. Faleasa has chosen as his successor, Moaula, his favorite son and a very strong if sometimes reckless man. After informing him that he is only pretending to be mad, Faleasa warns him that Felefele, his mother, is plotting to obtain the *matai* title for his brother Elefane. By making the rounds of the important men in his *aiga* and reminding them of all they owe him, Faleasa gets them to vote for Moaula.

After two chapters, which describe the characters' encounter with missionaries in 1921 and with American troops during the war, the narration rejoins the main strand: Faleasa manipulates public opinion into getting Filemoni banished from the village on a charge of misusing church funds. He obtains the same sentence for Sau by spreading rumors about his alleged incestuous relationship with a niece. Still Faleasa is trapped by his own game, and his family no longer respects him. The mythological character of Pili provides him with a representation of his own plight;

in the old tale, Pili, an ugly lizard, has been dropped onto earth by his father Tagaloaalagi, the supreme creator, who begot him with Sina, a mortal woman. Thanks to the help of three friends, Tausamitele (Insatiable Appetite), Lelemalosi (Strong Flight), and Pouliuli (Darkness), he goes up to the Ninth Heaven and after going through different trials set by his father, blackmails Tagaloaalagi into turning him back into a good-looking young man. He also extorts from him a live ember, a fishing net, and a war club, which he brings back to earth, thus making him the most powerful man in Samoa. Unfortunately, when he grows older, his children, like Faleasa's, fight over his inheritance and begin to ignore him. So he vanishes from Malaelua and people claim that he has been swallowed by his friend Pouliuli. Faleasa feels that, like Pili, he has jumped into a living darkness. In an attempt to make sense of his situation, the hero also remembers the crazy old man, whom his father welcomed into his *fale* as an honored guest after his son had found him lying on the church steps. Faleasa's last and fatal trick is to undo Malaga, the MP whom he had elected, a man he now hates for his corruption. The trick turns into a tragedy on the night of the election when the defeated Malaga comes back with some of his supporters to seek revenge on Faleasa. Moaula, who has won the mandate, interposes himself with his cutlass and kills two of Malaga's men while defending his father. As Moaula is condemned to life imprisonment, Elefane is elected to his vacant seat and Faleasa is left to wander insanely like the old crazy man found on the church steps.

Leaves of the Banyan Tree, a Samoan family saga, extends through several decades until the post-Independence period. The original manuscript of this novel, which the author started in 1963, was about twice the size of the finished product, published in 1979, and was revised and rewritten many times. The title story of *Flying-Fox in a Freedom Tree* constitutes the central "book" of the novel. It is framed by the life story of Tauilopepe, a Samoan village *matai*, who gains power and success through putting the members of his *aiga* to work in "Leaves of the Banyan Tree," his own plantation. He wins precedence over Malo, his rival, by seducing his wife and manipulating the council into having him banished. Having secured the cooperation of the church by his generous donations, nothing can hamper his social and financial ambitions. And yet Pepe, his son, starts associating with the worst rascals in town. He befriends Tagata, whose father owns the market, and together they start living off the gullibility of tourists and end up setting fire to the Protestant Church Hall and breaking into Tauilopepe's store, an episode that leads to their arrest. The "trial of the native son" is a supreme humiliation for Tauilopepe, especially as Pepe regrets nothing and publicly declares his rejection of what he sees as the corrupt religion and ethic epitomized by his father. In the third "book" entitled "Funerals and Heirs," after Pepe has died of tuberculosis, the old man decides that Lalolagi, Pepe's son, will inherit his estate. But after studying in New Zealand, the grandson becomes a parody of the callous rich boy who has no concern for his social responsibilities. In a *coup de théâtre*, Galupo, a mysterious character, turns up in the village and declares he is the illegitimate son that Tauilopepe had with Moa, Malo's wife. A clever trickster, he ingratiates himself with everybody, and, when the powerful *matai* dies of a heart attack, he blackmails his solicitor into rewriting Tauilopepe's will in his favor.

This enigmatic ending leaves the reader in doubt as to whether this arch-manipulator is to be admired. Wendt certainly offers a gallery of such tricksters: Besides Tagata and Pepe, characters reminiscent of some of the earlier short stories, Taifau, one of Tauilopepe's most trusted assistants, plays a major part in the plot. First described as a coward, Taifau influences politics with his satirical songs that people take up and spread, thus giving his words an anonymous and therefore even more powerful base. This ribald character who lies easily also has "a talent for being human" (324). Rarely pushing himself to the forefront, he expertly flatters people in order to obtain what he wants. Despite his central position as a "respectable" citizen, Tauilopepe himself is a transgressor who failed his father when he was expelled from missionary school for sexual and financial misdemeanors.

Most of the characters share with the gifted writer a talent for creating a world out of words. Tagata, who ends up hanging himself from a mango tree is likened to a flying-fox, the Samoan fruit-bat that has hair like other mammals, perches with its head down and can fly like a bird. This animal epitomizes the rebellious artist, a Promethean figure who belongs to the earth but who can rise above the surface and turn reality upside down.

Through the manipulation of others, Galupo believes that he can fashion not only other people's worlds but also his own. He sees society divided into himself and what he calls "Other-Worlders." In a bold assertion worthy of a post-Nietzschean character, he declares, "I am the product of my own imagination" (412). At the end of the novel, Galup seems all-powerful. But his fate may eventually be seen as tragic because he can only face the "darkness," a notion inscribed in his name—"Galupo" means "wave of darkness." Most characters are eventually defeated; but they generally seek to brave it out with style, for panache is all that is left to those who have lost all belief in metaphysical justifications for life.

The central "book" contrasts with the other two in its experiment with various narrative voices, which are humorously called "English-style," "Vaipe-style" (the version of pidgin spoken in the popular quarters of Apia), and "my style," a supposed synthesis of all. In this kaleidoscopic organization, each voice carries with it a certain set of cultural preconceptions and limitations. "English-style" alone cannot adequately account for everyday Samoan experience. "Vaipe-style" remains limited and not always consistent (perhaps on purpose to show the common people's frustratingly imperfect mastery of expression). Yet the dominating style in the novel is transparent to a non-Samoan speaker, thus perhaps belying the discordant accents of the second "book." Still the tension between these disparate voices remains one of the dominant forces in Wendt's fiction as well as in his poetry.

The Birth and Death of the Miracle Man contains stories such as "A Talent," which deals with the old theme of the trickster, or "Justice," another variation on the "trial of the native son." The mood in this collection is definitely more tragic. The title story tells of a major crisis in the life of a teacher who, like Faleasa in *Pouliuli,* suddenly questions the principles on which his life was based. Still the enigmatic dénouement might suggest a partial acceptance of a compromise. "Elena's Son" tells about a young man's discovery of the family's skeleton in the cupboard. Narrated in the first person in the "Vaipe-style," it derives its particular strength from the contrast between the gravity of the truth uncovered and the apparent equanimity that the protagonist keeps throughout. A tentative, though reluctant, repossession of one's father's past also forms the core of "The Balloonfish and the Armadillo," a *tour de force* narrated in the second person. One feels that, like Salman Rushdie in *The Satanic Verses*, the author has come to a stage when he can go beyond the son's rebellion against the principles represented by the father. More serene, because he has accepted the unavoidable, he can view himself as a father contemplating his children, a situation examined with lucidity and affection in "Birthdays," a story that ends with a "love letter to my daughter Mele."

One can feel Wendt moving in new directions; some pieces, which explore similar themes or even include the same characters, may prefigure novels to come. Perhaps we have the germs of a South Pacific *Things Fall Apart* in "Prospecting" and "Daughter of the Mango Season," which go back to the 1890s, when the ways of the first *papalagi* traders and missionaries in Samoa crossed those of local villagers. The power, but also the loneliness of the teacher, is sensitively treated in "Crocodile" and "Hamlet." "I Will Be Our Saviour from the Bad Smell," a humorous fantasy, tells of a Samoan village that wakes up one morning to discover that it is pervaded with a terrible stench. The protagonist's picaresque initiatives lead to the discovery that the smell's outer limits have an egg-shape and the phenomenon centers on the local church—an obvious quip at the tyranny of religion in the Pacific.

It is evident that Wendt has a moral concern in his writing. But this cannot be reduced to a number of simple recipes. The author's complex and sometimes contradictory relays in the narration should be a reminder that any implicit criticism is usually tainted with irony. Fundamentalist Christian principles are ridiculed. Yet Wendt believes that the Christian church has had a positive influence in Samoa. When he laughs at the new Westernized elites, he remains aware that he too belongs to that category. In his interview in *World Literature Written in English*, he stated what could well be his position at the end of the 1970s: "Basically I believe that a novelist is a moralist. . . . But I like to use humor to make a moral point. . . . I don't want to change things: I just want to grip people" (155).

Wendt does grip his readers with the force of his complex images. And he perhaps achieves this aim nowhere better than in his poetry, and particularly in his first collection, *Inside Us the Dead*, published in 1976. A journey to lava fields triggers off a meditation on man's absurd condition and yet on the necessity for him to continue watching out for the flimsiest sign of hope. In "Stranger on the Plateau," the protagonist rediscovers his native land after a long absence. An anonymous voice informs him

> That the journey to self
> is towards the innermost
> galaxy of the heart,
> a generation's trek across
> the lava plains of the mind
> under the leopard sun of the eye

Return to the world of men,
the frail mountain orchid
in your hand.

The title poem, which often reminds the reader of Derek Walcott's "Another Life," successively takes up the different strands of the author's ancestry. It starts with the Polynesians emerging "from the sea's eye like turtles/scuttling to beach their eggs," and the missionaries "the Sky-Piercers terrible as moonlight/in black and winged ships breaking/from the sun's yoke through/the turtle-shell of sky/into these reefs." The German great-grandfather came "too late/for a fortune, reaped a brood/of 'half-castes' and then fled/for the last atoll and a whisky death." Memories of a mother who died when the narrator was twelve emerge like "flamboyant/blooms scattered across/pitted lava field under/the moon's scaffold." A Promethean engineer of a brother who wanted to be "feet in iron, head/in the rainbow, rewinding/the moon" was brought back from the cold climates in "an oak box polished to see/your face in" after his car "had slipped off/an ordinary/highway built/for ordinary mortals,/car buckling in, like/a cannibal flower, to womb/him in/death" (13). In "Conch Shell," the poet feels helpless and dreams "of a priest without hands" when his daughter asks him to blow the conch that sits on his bookshelf and was used once "to snare the void and give it word."

Wendt exposes nationalist stereotypes about young independent nations in "Master Future," whose protagonist "struts down/in the street,/in black jeans, got/two bob for the movie/Tarzan in the Promised Land." He playfully mixes cultural references in "Flying Fox," a poem about the famous fruit-bat whom the narrator promises to catch and eat for stealing the mangoes and pawpaw on his plantation: "I'll be chewing Batman,/Count Dracula, and all superstitions/about vampires." He ridicules clichés about Samoan "authenticity" in "The Faa-Samoa is Perfect, They sd": "you're too fiapalagi, they sd,/you even have a palagi wife,/what do you know about/our way of life?/i drink it every day, i sd,/give me some more alofa/on the rocks." The volume also includes more intimate poems like "For Sina" or "Conversation," in which the artist quotes his daughter commenting on the wind "licking/its wounds and panting/and wagging its tail;/it had eyes as large/as mine."

Shaman of Visions contains a number of lyrical pieces about the poet's everyday existence at home or brief poems composed during his journeys abroad. Maturity has taught the creator to accept the inevitable confrontation with "Darkness." Yet the abandoned models and utopias of youth loom large like figures of lost lovers, whom irony and sarcasm cannot quite erase from the mind. The whole collection probes the artist's endless hand-to-hand fight with language for "in words in the silence/before Tagaloaalagi created the dawn of solitude./We measure ourselves against our words."

Wendt is still in the midst of his most creative period. Though he obviously aims to rewrite the history of his island to place his region on the literary map of the world, it would be wrong to reduce his works to a slightly modified form of history or anthropology. Wendt is acutely aware of the power and ambiguities of language, especially in cross-cultural situations. Exploring the past is not an excuse for reclaiming a lost paradise, which never existed anyway. Wendt rewrites old myths to see how tradition can still cast a meaningful light on the present. Acutely aware that Christianity, the English language, and economic dependence on richer nations are part and parcel of Samoan experience today, he accepts this multiple heritage and probes its contradictory consequences, questioning stereotypes, and unmasking hypocrisy.

While offering an often cynical picture of present-day Samoa, Wendt juggles with various registers: a master of humor, irony, and parody, he usually leaves the reader undecided about the level at which his words are meant to be interpreted. Playing on different moods, cultural references, and modes of metafiction, he, too, is a trickster with language. The stridency and protest in Wendt's earlier works is counterbalanced by more roundness, tolerance, and intimacy in his later fiction. But this takes away nothing from the author's particularly sharp dissection of deception and false appearances, especially when it concerns his own attitudes.

Endlessly probing the frontiers of darkness with his pen, the artist knows that he does not possess Maui's capacity to slow down the course of the sun. But, like his protagonist walking through the lava fields of Savaii, he relentlessly scatters his words, like clumps of miraculous flowers round the arid boulders of absurdity.

WORK CITED

Beston, J.B. and R.M. "An Interview with Albert Wendt." *World Literature Written in English* 16 (1977): 152–62.

ALBERT WENDT'S PUBLISHED WORK

Novels

Sons for the Return Home, 1973
Pouliuli, 1976
Leaves of the Banyan Tree, 1979

Short Story Collections

Flying-Fox in a Freedom Tree, 1974
The Birth and Death of the Miracle Man, 1986

Poetry

Inside Us the Dead: Poems 1961 to 1975, 1976
Shaman of Visions, 1984

Anthologies edited by Albert Wendt

Some Modern Poetry from Fiji, 1975
Some Modern Poetry from Western Samoa, 1975
Some Modern Poetry from the New Hebrides, 1975
Some Modern Poetry from The Solomons, 1975
Lali, A Pacific Anthology, 1980

SELECTED CRITICAL READINGS

The attention paid to this highly original writer has been limited mainly to Europe and New Zealand. More critical work, though, will likely emerge as general interest develops concerning cross-cultural traits and postcolonial themes.

Arvidson, K.O. "The Emergence of Polynesian Literature." *World Literature Written in English* 14 (1975): 91–116. Provides a general survey of this emergent literature, with some attention to Wendt's work.

Echos du Commonwealth No. 8 (1981). Special Albert Wendt issue. Besides "Prospecting," a story by Wendt, and a primary and secondary bibliography up to the date of publication, the volume contains the following essays: Carole Durix, "Networks and Itineraries in Albert Wendt's Poetry"; Maryvonne Nedeljkovic, "Albert Wendt—In Between Two Cultures"; Subramani, "Oral Forms in Wendt's Fiction"; Jacqueline Bardolph, "Narrative Voices, Narrative Personae in *Flying-Fox in a Freedom Tree*"; Jean-Pierre Durix, "Power in *Leaves of the Banyan Tree*."

Robinson, Roger. "Albert Wendt: An Assessment." *Landfall* (1980): 275–89. Surveys Wendt's accomplishment to date.

Subramani. *South Pacific Literature, From Myth to Fabulation.* Suva: U of the South Pacific, 1985. This pioneering introductory study includes a perceptive chapter entitled "Wendt's Crippled Cosmos" (117–150), a survey of Wendt's main themes and techniques.

—JEAN-PIERRE DURIX

Mulk Raj Anand

Born in Peshawar, India, 12 December 1905, Mulk Raj Anand is the son of a soldier in the Punjab. Educated at the University of Punjab, he went on to receive a Ph.D. in 1929 at University College, London.

After spending several years in Europe—during which he taught in Geneva, studied at Cambridge, joined a Marxist workers' study circle, and fought with the Republicans in the Spanish Civil War—he returned to India. He was active in India's long struggle for independence and was closely associated with Gandhi's circle. In 1949 he married Shirin Vajifdar, a classical dancer; they have one daughter, and live in Bombay.

He has taught at various Indian universities and was the first Tagore Professor of Art and Literature at Panjab University, Chandigarh. Long involved with Indian cultural life, he has edited the journal *Marg*, operated a publishing house, and promoted various cultural foundations. He served for a time as the cultural advisor to the Prime Minister of India and organized numerous international cultural conferences. He also has helped rural people build roads, open new schools, and improve hygiene in the village Khandala near Bombay.

Anand's first novel, *Untouchable*, was completed in Gandhi's Sabarmati Ashram in Ahmedabad, then rejected by 19 London publishers. The twentieth agreed to publish the book only if E.M. Forster would write a preface, which he did. The book appeared first in 1935, then again in 1970 in a revised form. Still in print, translated into many languages, it has sold innumerable copies the world over.

Anand has received many awards, including the Leverhulme Fellowship, 1940–42; World Peace Council Prize, 1952; Padma Bhushan Award, 1968; and the Sahitya Academy Award, 1947.

OF CRUSHED HUMANITY

Contemporary critical opinion on Mulk Raj Anand concludes that he is the most "committed" and "propagandistic" of writers, that he champions the cause of the downtrodden and underprivileged, and that he overtly exhibits Marxist tendencies by denouncing the rich as exploiters of the poor. Regretting the critical neglect that Anand has suffered in India and the English-speaking West, C.D. Narasimhaiah holds that Anand

> . . . has not had his share of praise from the serious literary critic. He has been dubbed a social propagandist without being read, and

unfortunately the titles of his novels have had a good deal to do with the prevalent prejudice. It is good to remember that all art is, in a sense, propaganda, and it is the treatment that should decide. The social concerns and artistic preoccupations seem to take hold of Anand by turns, and where the two fuse, as in *Untouchable*, the novel is safe and its course is one of absorbing human interest. (89)

Whether or not various critical pronouncements characterize Anand's work as propaganda, problem fiction, or tales with doctrinaire ends, his numerous novels and collections of short stories make a significant contribution to international literature in English through their thematic content as well as their aesthetic form.

One of the reasons why Anand as a novelist has not been properly evaluated by many critics—Indian and Western alike—may be that most of these critics have studied and taught British and American authors and have a tendency to judge the works of an Indian-English novelist by the norms and criteria set by Western critics for their own literature, which is determined by a different social milieu and different life responses. What is, therefore, required is the reappraisal of "our critical values with reference to the literature produced in India" (Singh iii), keeping in view the Indian sensibility with a broader and more balanced perspective of the relation of literature to life. Since the Indian-English novelist faces a unique challenge of "using the English language in a way that will be distinctively Indian and still remain English" (Mukherjee 170), the techniques must perforce differ from those employed by Western writers just as the Indian writer's "essentially Indian ethos must colour everything he writes, when he is not merely playing the sedulous ape to his Western masters but actually lives and acts as a kind of a literary Adam in a new world of writing" (Naik 153). Conscious of this unique task of the Indian novelist in English, Anand himself warns his readers and critics against accepting the novel of the West in its totality, noting that the Indian-English novelist has to "reveal the new consciousness of our old-age people, in all its miscellaneousness, through the imaginative portrayal of human life that is the novel" ("A Note on Henry James" 7). The critic of Indian literature in English, therefore, must evolve new instruments for evaluation; he must devise new tests—a new internalist criticism—that measure the degrees of achievement between challenge and response.

Anand's powerful imagination has fused the philosophies and the ideals of the Orient and the Occident into what has been called a rare assimilation of the "introvert-extrovert centres of experience" (Singh ii). The fact that he has created a whole living myriad world in his fiction is perhaps the chief accomplishment of Anand as a novelist. One can discern the overwhelming impact of Tolstoy and Balzac in his comprehensive grasp of life; and of Tagore, Dostoevsky, and Joyce in his analysis of moral and psychological motivation.

Another salient feature of Anand's imaginative art appears again and again when he writes of crushed humanity. To Jack Lindsay goes the credit of tracing and bringing into light the "elements of deep human feeling and large-scale vision" (2) that form the essential ingredients of Anand's art. His absorbing interest in people at various levels and his attempt to get into his prism the whole variegated life of India perhaps make for panoramic structures. But, after all, Anand has always sought to capture the kaleidoscopic range of contemporary India. The untouchables and coolies, the sadhus and the maharajas, the destitution in the villages and the abject poverty in the cities, the temple and the mosque: All these characters, objects, incidents have been patterned in appropriate modes to reveal the complex of forces impinging upon the consciousness of his characters. Further, his knowledge of the people he writes about is too concrete and full to be reduced to abstract idealism and types. He has known, seen, and felt fully and intimately the rural life of the Punjab, the villagers groaning under abject poverty, the village life being sucked dry by the parasites and priests. That is why the sweeper, the peasant, the coolie, the plantation-laborer, the city-drudge, the soldier, despite their thwarted purposes, have been made the central characters of his representative novels. In the preface to the second edition of *Two Leaves and a Bud*, Anand writes about his choice of characters:

> All these heroes as other men and women, who had emerged in my novels and short stories, were dear to me because they were the reflections of the real people I had known during my childhood and youth. And I was only repaying the debt of gratitude I owed them for much of the inspiration they had given me to mature into manhood, when I began to interpret their lives in my writing. They were not mere phantoms. . . . They were the flesh of my flesh and blood of my blood, and obsessed me in the way in which certain human beings obsess an artist's soul. And I was doing no more than what a writer does when he seeks to interpret the truth from the realities of his life. (1)

Despite hostile criticism, Anand would not mind his novels being called "a literature of protest," for they set out to expose social ills and surpass mere intellectual exercises in Marxism. The roots of protest lay embedded in Anand's childhood when he cursed God for singling out his cousin Kaushalya to die in infancy. Later, the young Anand could not compromise with his father's subservience to the British and his mother's blind faith in ritualistic observance and superstitions. It was again the profound and unflinching sense of justice that compelled him to raise his voice against human bondage, against social repression and religious hypocrisy. A committed humanist, Anand does not indulge in diatribe but makes a constructive protest, heralds a revolt, and wages a creative battle to bring about a new society.

Anand resembles Prem Chand, who wrote in Hindi, and Sarat Chandra, writing in Bengali, both of them passionately concerned with the hardships of the villagers, their poverty, squalor, and backwardness. Anand—as he describes it in his own words—became "the fiery voice of the people, who through his own torments, urges and exaltations, by realizing the pains, frustrations and aspirations of others and by cultivating his incipient powers of expression, transmuted in art all feelings, all thought, all experience" ("Pigeon Indian" 246). The Indian life he depicts in his novels is that of the waifs, the disinherited, the lowly, and the lost. It would be unfair to put labels on his genuine, compassionate humanistic concerns, notwithstanding the fact that the proletariat in him protested against the colossus of manmade laws, the scheme of cruelty and exploitation, the decadent and perverted orthodoxy of his times. He took upon himself the task of attacking social wrongs, well realizing, as he has said, that "this struggle requires the courage to say the unmentionable things, the unconventional truths, the recognition of our civilization" ("A Note on Modern Indian Fiction" 57). Through each of his novels, Anand impresses on his readers the need to recognize fundamental principles of human existence and to exercise vigilance against the real enemies of freedom. He advocates the need to help raise the untouchables, the peasants, the serfs, the coolies, and the oppressed to a level of human dignity and self-awareness and to shake them free of ignorance, apathy, and despair.

Anand's first three novels—*Untouchable, Coolie, Two Leaves and a Bud*—take up the wretchedness of the poor and their struggle for a better life. The scope of this essay is limited to the discussion of the protest element in these novels, as they evince his odyssey away from what he called a "Bloomsbury literary consciousness" to another world "whose denizens have always been considered 'vulgar' and unfit" for literature ("Why I Write" 7). In the context of Indian writing in English, Anand's work breaks new ground and represents a departure from the tradition of previous novels in which the ordinary folk had been excluded. His subsequent novels largely provide a variation on the same theme and delineate the plight of the ever-burdened Bakhas, Munoos, and Gangus—the main characters in these first three books—who are balked at every step in their aspirations for a better life.

As a matter of fact, all great literature is protest literature and the level of imaginative excellence in a writer depends upon his comprehensive awareness of the sources of evil. The writer pinpoints the maladies that afflict the society and reveals his insight into the roots of suffering. He makes concrete his perception of the human predicament and sensitizes his readers to the horror. Then the misery and disaster caused by evil in the body-politic lead to revulsion and revolt.

In *Untouchable*, which was published in 1935, eighteen-year-old Bakha—like his father Lakha, a sweeper, a cleaner of toilets—is an outcast. Anand focuses on "untouchability" and the treatment of latrine cleaners condemned to isolation because they handle excrement by narrating a single day's events in Bakha's life. Sturdy and genial, Bakha lives and works in the army camp, pathetically aspiring to be as much like the sahibs as possible and playing hockey with their children. But early on the fateful day, he touches a Brahmin by accident and is reviled for making the Brahmin unclean. He then undergoes further shocks: He is abused and slapped for polluting a merchant; he is chased out of a temple by the priest who has been trying to molest his sister; he receives a shower of abuse for polluting an injured child in his attempt to help him. Finally, he cries out in anguish: "I only get abuse and derision wherever I go. Pollution, pollution. I do nothing else but pollute people" (96). For a moment he stands aghast, possessed by rebellion. But this momentary rage and revolt soon evaporate when he finds that he is still too much bound to his low caste status. His anger and fury can only make him realize that rebellion would lead to futility. So during his moment of strength the slave in him asserts itself, and he lapses back "wild with torture, biting his lips, ruminating his grievances" (161). He walks about frustrated and highly disappointed but encounters three people who seem to make a difference. First, he sees Colonel Hutchinson, the Salvationist, with his shield of casteless society and salvation for all; then Gandhi with his strong dislike for untouchability as the greatest blot on Hinduism and his belief that untouchables are in fact the Harijans—"the children of God"; finally Bakha meets the poet Iqbal Nath Sarshar with his new machine (the flush toilet) that "will clean dung without anyone having to handle it" (171). All three encounters raise temporary hope in Bakha; and each, significant in its own way, forms an integral part of the novel. Colonel Hutchinson's friendly offer for salvation astonishes Bakha at the moment of his crisis, when he is plagued with a sense of isolation and humiliation by high caste people. Gandhi's exposition, in effect, reaffirms his faith in his job, which he decides to continue without qualms. And the encounter with the poet opens up new and exciting possibilities.

E.M. Forster must have foreseen the adverse criticism the conclusion of the novel would invite, so he defended it in his preface:

> Some readers may find this closing section of the book too valuable and sophisticated, in comparison with the clear observation which has preceded it, but it is an integral part of the author's scheme. It is the necessary climax, and it has mounted up with triple effect. Bakha returns to his father and his wretched bed, thinking now of the Mahatma, now of the Machine. His Indian day is over and the next day will be like it, but on the surface of the earth, if not in the depths of the sky, a change is at hand. (8)

Despite Forster's cogent defense, some critics have found the conclusion unsatisfactory for various reasons. K.R.S. Iyengar argues that Bakha's returning home and being roundly scolded by his father for idling away the afternoon, then driven out of the house, should really be the end of the story (337–38). Taking a cue from Iyengar, Paul Verghese complains that the three solutions result from Anand's desire to be a social reformer at the expense of his novelistic art (131). R.S. Singh, misreading the purport of the encounters, comments that Bakha's future will simply repeat itself (42). William Walsh believes that of the three solutions suggested the flush toilet is most favored by Anand (7). C.D. Narasimhaiah, mistaking the encounters for solutions, objects: "Why didn't the novelist hint at the evils of machinery? What would happen to Bakha when the machine took his place? . . . That Anand does not seem to see" (69–70). H.M. Williams thinks what he considers Anand's promotion of scientific materialism "a curious anti-climax" (36). The fact, however, is that Anand has offered neither solutions nor his own preferences. He has only suggested a choice of possibilities. It is in this section of the novel that we see Bakha endowed with a constructive and imaginative bent of mind, sorting out the different possibilities and integrating his own being in the process. That is why we find him returning to his father, to the old world of filth, but looking to his father with positive faith and hope. The dénouement, therefore, with Bakha's vague hope that he might "find the poet on the way back and ask him about his machine" (174), is not only integral to the scheme of the novel but lends significance to the central form of the narrative as well.

The novel is a forthright condemnation of a system that has for ages subverted human dignity and warped the individual, a condemnation of the caste system that seizes Indian life in its grip, so that people have come to accept a stratified society based on ideas of high and low, thus mocking those very scriptures chanted on all auspicious occasions. Bakha is a prototype of millions of untouchables in India, representing the anguish, misery, and frustration of those considered low caste. Of course, there is no easy solution to the problems of caste and its inherent poverty, ignorance, backwardness, and superstition. Fifty-five years after Anand's novel was published and forty-three years after Independence, the problem still remains. As an Indian I can say despite the fact that the Indian Constitution has made it a crime to practice untouchability, we still witness Anand's Sohinis and Golabos waiting at the village well, some standing up, bending over, joining their palms in beggary, others twisting their lips in various attitudes of servile appeal and abject humility as they remain on the ground. We still have the residential areas of the high-caste Hindus through which untouchables are forbidden to take their marriage processions, hotels where low-caste people are not allowed the use of utensils meant for other customers. We still witness the shameful scenes of untouchables being murdered by villagers for daring to grow their moustaches upwards, when local tradition demands that they grow them downwards to signify their low status in the caste hierarchy.

In *Coolie*, which appeared a year after *Untouchable*, Anand again shows his concern for the neglected, despised, and maltreated poor. The central character is Munoo, a poor orphan boy from the hills, innocent, underfed, and ill-treated by his aunt. He leaves his native village to find work and to see the world, but the very first encounter with reality shatters his dreams. Employed in the house of a bank clerk, Munoon, with his inborn naive gaiety, amuses and entertains the employer's daughter by dancing like a monkey for her; but the vindictive housewife interferes and makes him aware of his lowly position: "He had no right to join the laughter of his superiors. He was to be a slave, a servant who should do the work, all the odd jobs, someone to be abused, even beaten" (34).

Constant abuse and the rage of his mistress send him fleeing. He next works in a primitive pickle factory in Daulatpur, where the dispute between the two partners leaves him unshielded and helpless. So he moves on, but exasperated with the frantic competition and cunning among his fellow coolies, he fails as a market porter. The satire here becomes more general, directed not at one or two examples of vice and folly but at man's inhumanity to his fellow man. The generous but feckless Prabha, Munoo's protector and surrogate father, is betrayed by a paranoid foreman, harried by an absurd retired judge called Sir Todar Mal—a Dickensian grotesque who emerges with considerable comic power. This deprivation and injustice drive Munoo to still another adventure. With the help of a circus elephant driver, he goes to Bombay. Before he is thrown into the city's sea of humanity, the elephant driver tells him, almost like a prophet: "The bigger a city is, the more cruel it is to the sons of Adam" (177). In Bombay he starts working in the British-owned Sir George White Cotton Mills and is brutally exploited along with other factory workers. The squalid lives of the workers and their families are described vividly. Wage cuts and exploitation lead finally to a labor strike, which ultimately turns into a Hindu-Muslim riot. Shocked and bewildered, Munoo steals out of the clashing crowd but is struck by Mrs. Mainwaring's car and then transported to Shimla to work as a page and rickshaw puller for Mrs. Mainwaring, an indolent, extremely neurotic, and somewhat nymphomaniac European memsahib. In Shimla, overwork and under-nourishment gradually fret away his health until he dies of consumption.

Anand's indictment is directed against Indian society as a whole, a society that breeds such cruelty and causes Munoo's downfall. This economic exploitation of the proletariat by a few is described by one of the characters in *Coolie*:

> There are only two kinds of people in the world: the rich and the poor and between the two there is no connection. The rich and the powerful, the magnificent and the glorious, whose opulence is built on robbery and theft and open warfare, are honoured and admired by the whole world and by themselves. You, the poor and the humble, you the meek and the gentle, . . . are swindled out of your rights, and broken in body and soul. You are respected by no one and you do not respect yourselves. (265–66)

In spite of its relentless account of suffering, the book does hold a certain charm, which stems from Munoo's innocence, his naive warm-heartedness, his love and ability for comradeship, his irrepressible curiosity and zest for life. The Bombay toiling, suffering, starving masses are at once vivid and realistic, among whom Munoo, an insignificant part of the millions of ill-fed, half-naked workers, is nothing more than a speck. And it is precisely for this reason that the story does not end in Bombay. Anand transports his hero to the mountain resort of Shimla where he regains his identity, even though he dies from mistreatment. *Coolie* has been de-scribed as a "cosmic painting of the lives of thousands of orphans, coolies, boy-servants, factory-workers and rickshaw-pullers, their health running down 'through the hour-glass of time'" (Karmanadham 53). Deeply moved by the poverty and innocence of India's masses, Anand wanted to write an angry, bitter book, a book to sear the conscience. He succeeded.

Two Leaves and a Bud, which appeared a year after *Coolie*, describes the con-dition of laborers in tea gardens, where Indian coolies work as near slaves alongside their wives and children. The central character, Gangu, tempted by false promises, is transported to Assam with his wife and daughter to work in a British-owned tea plantation. The coolies there are treated like beasts, and their wives and daughters are subjected to the lust of white sahibs like Reggie Hunt. Then some of the coolies, shaking off their docility, approach the authorities for fair treatment, but this is mistaken for rebellion. The army is summoned, airplanes gun down the terror-stricken coolies, grinding them once more into submission, and order is restored.

Gangu feels bewildered, lonely, and lost when his wife Sajani dies of malaria. In his efforts to borrow money for her funeral expenses, he is kicked out of the plantation owner's house, beaten, and abused. He comes back to Buta, the Garden Sardar who had brought him to the tea plantation on fabulous promises, and says:

> "The Sahib will not give me a loan. . . . I have just been. He beat
> me for coming out of quarantine. Oh, friend Buta Ram, if only I had

known things were going to turn out this way I wouldn't have come here." And he took his hand to his eyes to wipe the tears that had welled up in them with the reproach against the Sardar that he had suppressed into self-pity. (118)

Gangu, with cold passivity, tender loyalties, compassion and depth of suffering—all symbolic of the Indian peasantry—is by now able to watch the rain wash away the meager harvest of his paddy with an almost imperturbable calm, as if in this moment of despair, he has somehow been purged. Hopelessly embedded in the coils of a system that can only throttle him, Gangu has learned to accept the rigors of his life with complete resignation and stoical serenity:

> And, as in the old days in his village, so now he plodded on like an ox all day, knowing all in his crude bovine way, grasping the distinction between himself and his masters, conscious even of the days when he was young and had kicked against the pricks and the proddings of the rod, of the hate, the fear and the sorrow he had known, but detached and forgetful in the Nirvanic bliss of emptiness where the good and evil of fortune seemed the equally just retribution, omniscient Providence, of whom Siva and Vishnu and Krishna were the supreme incarnations. (237)

The novel ends with the murder of Gangu in his attempt to rescue his daughter from the lustful Reggie Hunt. The white jury that tries the case ironically finds Hunt not guilty of murder by one vote and not guilty of culpable homicide by a majority.

Dr. Havre, the character who seems to speak for Anand, holds an idealistic dream of some kind of revolution and recognizes imperialism as an egregious form of exploitation. To him a socio-political revolution is the only way to emancipate the masses. He tries to protect the coolies and encourages them to resist the injustice and indignities they undergo at the hands of British planters and rich Indian businessmen; Anand, speaking through Dr. Havre, can easily be seen as angry that the millions of India suffer so:

> "Is it because the festering swamps of the tropics breed disease and that they cannot check the tribulations of destiny? Certainly it seemed to me so, at first—that fate had here conspired with the seasons to obliterate everything capriciously. . . . But why didn't it occur to anyone—the simple, obvious thing that people don't need Marx to realize here. The black coolies clear the forests, plant the fields, toil and garner the harvest, while all the money-grubbing, slave-driving, soulless managers and directors draw their salaries and dividends and build up monopolies. Therein lies the necessity of revolution in this country." (122–23)

Anand has been criticized for his biased views against the British, and this novel, according to H.M. Williams, is on one level "a crude piece of propaganda portraying the British as vicious and absurd" (38). Admitting that the novel is not as good as his earlier ones, Anand still defends it in a preface to a later edition:

> I do not think that it is one of the best of my early novels. It is perhaps better written, and technically, it is more complex than *Untouchable* or *Coolie* because I tried to evoke in it in varying moods of the beautiful Eastern Indian Landscape and felt the passions with an intensity which owed not a little to the fact that it was a real story which I was writing in thinly veiled fiction. But I confess that, as I got into the book, I was biased in favour of my Indian characters and tended to caricature the Englishmen and English women who play such a vital part in this book. . . . And the truth has to be told about the relations of the blacks and whites, unpalatable as it might be, even as the disease of serfdom had to be analysed in Russia before it could be eradicated. And if in so doing, one's art spills over into an amorphous passion, then, well, that should be forgiven in an age which so often excuses cynicism and contempt and even violence on the other side. (vii)

Able, spirited, and bold as this defense is, it does not answer all the doubts and questions. For example, in his over-enthusiastic defiance of exploitation, Anand has Gangu brood in an intellectual manner, which is not only untrue to his character but also sounds like a crude piece of propaganda inartistically thrust into the character's mouth:

> "I have always said it and I say it now again that, though the earth is bought and sold and confiscated, God never meant that to happen, for He does not like some persons to have a comfortable living and the others to suffer from dire poverty. He has created land enough to maintain all men and yet many die of hunger and most live under a heavy burden of poverty all their lives, as if the earth were made for a few and not for all men." (247–48)

Although such lapses occur, they never infiltrate the total artistic effect, for the crude part of overt propaganda is made subservient to the human content. Anand has, therefore, ably withstood the attack of the critics, whom he reminds in his preface that "the catharsis of the book lies ultimately in the pity, the compassion and understanding of an artist and not in his partiality" (vii).

The indirect criticism in his novels of the rigidity and self-centeredness of the high castes gives place finally to a more frontal attack on the illogical injustices of society as a whole. The protagonists' protest in these novels is at three levels: In *Untouchable*, it is against the tyranny of the caste system; in *Coolie*, it is against the capitalists' treatment of workers; in *Two Leaves and a Bud*, it is against colonial exploitation. Yet this does not mean that the books comprise little more than dissertations on socio-ethical problems; rather they offer illuminating documents of human behavior. Through them Anand has pointed out social conflicts and ills, not because he champions any abstract social theory, but because he has seen these conflicts and ills in his own surroundings. Anand always urges for a broader outlook, more tolerance, more understanding and benevolence, more self-sacrifice. He stresses that intolerance, greed, and egoism lie at the root of all social and personal problems.

Anand, through his fiction, has been able to live the experiences of other people and thereby discover what silent passions burst in their hearts, what sorrows possess them, where they want to go, and how they grapple with their destinies. He has tried in this way to express his love for the suffering masses and has ignored those who call his preoccupation with outcasts, disinherited peasants, and eternally wronged women as a morbid, sentimental preoccupation with "ignorant people" (Anand *Apology* 138–39).

Anand's protagonists are profoundly conscious of their position in society. But in their struggle against social and economic exploitation, they display their sensitivity to love and sympathy as well as to hatred and suffering. Men of integrity, active and hardworking, continue their struggle, thus symbolizing their faith in humankind's potential. This essential aspect of Anand's humanist creed is derived from European Hellenism rather than from "the traditional attitude of India," which in this context Anand says "has been essentially nonhuman" (*Apology* 95).

Anand is indeed a forerunner in the writing of Indian protest fiction. But he cannot be dismissed as a mere propagandist, for he expresses unbounding faith in a renewal of the human spirit.

WORKS CITED

Anand, Mulk Raj. *Apology for Heroism.* Bombay: Kutub Popular, 1946.

———. *Coolie.* Delhi: Orient Paperbacks, 1970.

———. "Pigeon Indian." *Studies in Australian and Indian Literatures.* Delhi: Indian Council for Cultural Relations, 1971. 240–50.

———. "A Note on Henry James and the Art of Fiction in India." *Commonwealth Quarterly* 12 (1978): 1–14.

———. "A Note on Modern Indian Fiction." *Indian Literature* 8 (1965): 50–61.

———. *Two Leaves and a Bud.* Bombay: Kutub Popular, 1951. (With author's preface)

———. *Untouchable.* Bombay: Kutub Popular, 1970. (With 1935 preface by E.M. Forster)

———. "Why I Write?" *Perspectives on Mulk Raj Anand.* Ghaziabad: Vimal Prakashan, 1978. 1–12.

———. "The Writer's Role in National Integration." *Indian Literature* 5 (1962): 52–61.

Iyengar, K.R.S. *Indian Writing in English.* Bombay: Asia Publishing House, 1973.

Karmanadham, K. "The Novels of Mulk Raj Anand." *Triveni* 36 (1967): 50–61.

Lindsay, Jack. "Mulk Raj Anand." *Kakatiya Journal of English Studies* 2 (1977): 1–12.

Mukherjee, Meenakshi. *The Twice Born Fiction.* Delhi: Heinemann, 1971.

Naik, M.K. *Mulk Raj Anand.* Delhi: Heinemann, 1973.

Narasimhaiah, C.D. "Mulk Raj Anand." *Journal of Commonwealth Literature* 5 (1968): 81–92.

———. *The Writer's Gandhi.* Patiala: Panjabi University, 1967.

Singh, R.S. *Indian Novel in English.* Delhi: Heinemann, 1977.

Singh, Satyanarain. "Editorial" in Mulk Raj Anand Special Number. *Kakatiya Journal of English Studies* 2 (1977): iii.

Verghese, C. Paul. *Problems of the Indian Creative Writer in English.* Bombay: Somaiya Publications, 1970.

Walsh, William. *Commonwealth Literature.* London: Oxford, 1973.

Williams, H.M. *Indo-Anglian Literature, 1800–1970: A Survey.* Delhi: Orient Longman, 1976.

MULK RAJ ANAND'S PUBLISHED WORK

Novels

Untouchable, 1935 (Revised edition, 1970)
Coolie, 1936 (Revised edition, 1972)
Two Leaves and a Bud, 1937
The Village, 1939
Lament on the Death of a Master of Arts, 1939
Across the Black Waters, 1940
The Sword and the Sickle, 1942
The Big Heart, 1945 (Revised edition, 1980)
Seven Summers: The Story of an Indian Childhood, 1951
Private Life of an Indian Prince, 1953 (Revised edition, 1970)
The Old Woman and the Cow, 1960 (Published as *Gauri*, 1976)
The Road, 1961
Death of a Hero, 1963
Morning Face, 1968
Confession of a Lover, 1976
The Bubble, 1984

Short Story Collections

The Lost Child and Other Stories, 1934
The Barber's Trade Union and Other Stories, 1944
The Tractor and the Corn Goddess and Other Stories, 1947
Reflections on the Golden Bed, 1947
The Power of Darkness and Other Stories, 1958
Lajwanti and Other Stories, 1966
Between Tears and Laughter, 1973
Selected Short Stories of Mulk Raj Anand, 1977

Children's Books

Indian Fairy Tales: Retold, 1946
The Story of Man, 1952
Aesop's Fables, 1960
More Indian Fairy Tales, 1961
The Story of Chacha Nehru, 1965
Folk Tales of Punjab, 1974

Art Criticism

Persian Painting, 1930
The Hindu View of Art, 1957
Kama Kala: Some Notes on the Philosophical Basis of Hindu Erotic Sculpture, 1962
The Third Eye: A Lecture on the Appreciation of Art, 1966
Indian Ivories, 1970
Album of Indian Paintings, 1973

Literary Criticism

The Golden Breath: Studies in Five Poets of the New India, 1933
Homage to Tagore, 1946
The Indian Theatre, 1950
The Volcano: Some Comments on the Development of Rabindranath Tagore's Aesthetic Theories, 1968

Roots and Flowers: Two Lectures on the Metamorphosis of Technique and Content in the Indian-English Novel, 1972

History and Commentary

Letters on India, 1942
Apology for Heroism: An Essay in Search of Faith, 1946
On Education, 1947
The King-Emperor's English; or, The Role of the English Language in the Free India, 1948
Lines Written to an Indian Air: Essays, 1949
Is There a Contemporary Indian Civilisation?, 1963
The Humanism of M.K. Gandhi: Three Lectures, 1967
Delhi, Agra, Sikri, 1968
The Humanism of Jawaharlal Nehru, 1978
The Humanism of Rabindranath Tagore, 1979

Reminiscences

Conversations in Bloomsbury, 1981
Pilpali Sahab: The Story of a Childhood under the Raj, 1985

Letters

Author to Critic: The Letters of Mulk Raj Anand (edited by Saros Cowasjee), 1973

SELECTED CRITICAL READINGS

The fiction of Mulk Raj Anand has received wide critical attention, both in India and abroad. To some degree, his reputation as a novelist rests on his first two books, *Untouchable* and *Coolie*; at least those are the works that have most often been the subject of critical essays, whereas numerous full-length studies have addressed his impressive number of novels and short stories. Most often considered a writer espousing a cause, Anand has in recent times been neglected as more sophisticated fiction in English has appeared in India. Still, he holds a special place in Indian literature as a key figure not only in the development of the protest novel in India but in the emergence of a strong tradition in English-language writing. For that reason it is likely that interest in Anand will continue, the emphasis perhaps shifting away from the social reality to the art itself. Like Zola and Balzac, Anand has been the secretary to Indian life over the past fifty years. More attention should also be given to his nonfictional writing, especially his criticism of English-language literature in India.

Berry, Margaret. *Mulk Raj Anand: The Man and the Novelist.* Amsterdam-Maarsen: Oriental Press, 1971. Discusses both the novels and short stories. Argues that Anand has often failed to disengage himself from the political, thus regrets that Anand with his "considerable talents and energies should so early and so long have operated in the restrictive climate of a doctrinaire aesthetic."

Contemporary Indian Literature 5 (1965). Special Mulk Raj Anand Issue. Contains articles by several scholars, commemorating Anand's sixtieth birthday.

Cowasjee, Saros. *So Many Freedoms: A Study of the Major Fiction of Mulk Raj Anand.* Delhi: Oxford UP, 1977. Points out that even though Anand shows passionate concern with society's betterment and revolution, none of his heroes attain victory. Attends to all of the novels, giving an especially full treatment of the Trilogy: *The Village, Across the Black Waters,* and *The Sword and the Sickle.*

Dommergues, André. "An Interpretation of Mulk Raj Anand's *Untouchable.*" *Commonwealth Essays and Studies* 8 (1985): 14–21. Discusses the book in the light of the workings of the caste system and the way Anand treats the character caught up in so cruel a social system.

Jha, Ramā. "Mulk Raj Anand: The Champion of Gandhian Humanism." *Gandhian Thought and Indo-Anglian Novelists.* Delhi: Chanakya Publications, 1983. 55–85. Argues that Anand has been consistently preoccupied with themes that are an essential part of Gandhian thought. Considers Anand as directly inspired by Gandhi. Discusses the fiction in this light, showing how it remains concerned with the basic elements of Gandhian values.

Kulshrestha, Chirantan. "The Hero As Survivor: Reflections on Anand's *Untouchable.*" *World Literature Written in English* 19 (1980): 84–91. Admits to Anand's limitations as a creative writer, but argues that Anand's humanity saved *Untouchable* and *Coolie* from their "stylistic clumsiness" and causes them to continue to be read and admired.

Naik, M.K. *Mulk Raj Anand.* New York: Humanities Press, 1973. Offers a full discussion of the fiction, including the short stories, and acknowledges both the doctrinaire and artistic aspects, while praising him for his substantial achievement. Describes Anand as "a banyan, august and many-branched, in the field of Indo-Anglian writing."

Pontes, Hilda. "A Select Checklist of Critical Responses to Mulk Raj Anand's *Untouchable.*" *Journal of Commonwealth Literature* 23.1 (1988): 189–98. A useful and intriguing study of the international response to Anand's first novel.

———. "The Education of a Rebel: Mulk Raj Anand." *Literary Half Yearly* 27 (1986): 311–52. A largely biographical article, which reveals interesting details about Anand's life.

Robertson, R.T. "*Untouchable* as an Archetypal Novel." *World Literature Written in English* 14 (1975): 339–46. Proposes that certain archetypal figures emerge in the early stages of "Commonwealth literature," and sees *Untouchable* as the best example so far "of the archetype of the conflict between society and the individual who is trying to free himself from it."

Sharma, K.K., editor. *Perspectives on Mulk Raj Anand.* Atlantic Highlands, NJ: Humanities Press, 1978. (First published in India by Vimal Prakasham) A collection of essays that address various aspects of Anand's fiction and other work. Includes Anand's essay, "Why I Write?"

Sinha, Krishna Nandan. *Mulk Raj Anand.* Boston: Twayne, 1972. Surveys the fiction, partially within a biographical and historical framework. Admires Anand's ability as an "authentic interpreter" of human experience and "His vision of the vast human concourse." Believes that Anand is "perhaps the foremost and most significant novelist of today's India."

—SHYAM ASNANI

R. K. Narayan

Rasipuram Krishnaswami Narayan was born in Madras, India, 10 October 1906. Since Narayan does not like to give interviews or write about himself, the principal source of information about him remains *My Days*, his 1974 biographical account that covers his life and writing career to that time. More recent information is hard to gain. *My Days* chronicles his schooling and education as well as the story of his wife's death from typhoid in 1939. This story is also poignantly recorded in *The English Teacher* or *Grateful to Life and Death*. He has one daughter.

Although born and raised in Madras, Narayan has spent most of his life in Mysore, a South Indian city, where he was educated at Maharaja's College. It is South India that serves as the setting for his fiction; his imaginary town of Malgudi in his novels and short stories has been compared to Faulkner's Yoknapatawpha Country.

During 1956 he spent time in California on a Rockefeller Foundation grant, where he wrote *The Guide*. Since then he has traveled in the United States frequently, and has lectured at various institutions, including Vassar College in 1983 and the University of Texas at Austin in 1989. He has received the Padma Bhushan, India's highest literary award.

When "Sweet Mangoes" Turn to "Malt Vinegar"

This essay derives its title from William Walsh's 1962 article on R. K. Narayan entitled "Sweet Mangoes and Malt Vinegar: The Novels of R. K. Narayan." Walsh begins by saying:

> It is odd at a time when we are beginning to pay attention to Commonwealth writers . . . that a writer of the character and maturity of R.K. Narayan should hardly have been noticed at all! It is true that some of the more obvious motives directing us to these writers probably do not operate in respect of Narayan. His themes are not particularly contemporary, fashionable or provocative. Except for Gandhi's "Quit India" campaign in *Waiting for the Mahatma*, and even here the interest isn't primarily political; politics, especially racial politics, figure very little in his work. (121)

That Narayan is unconcerned with politics and history is an oft repeated criticism. In fact, in reading Narayan's work, it may seem as though the twists and turns of an individual's fortune interest him more than that of whole nations or groups of people.

In fact, C.D. Narasimhaiah has likened Narayan's work to Jane Austen's. Perhaps the appropriate metaphor here is one that Walsh borrows from Narayan's novel *Mr. Sampath* or *The Printer of Malgudi*—that of a four-inch bit of sandalwood where the carving shows an exquisitely poised Nataraj trampling a demon. Srinivas prays to the idol "to illumine his mind" (Walsh 128). For Narayan, the ray that illumines his mind is that the demon the Nataraj is trampling represents India under oppression—political oppression and illusory oppression, the oppression of the *maya* that fails to let Indian creativity and Indianness triumph in the manner that Nataraj does. For Walsh is mistaken when he lists the following as Narayan's only subjects:

> The detail suggests, surely and economically, the special flavour of Malgudi, a blend of Oriental and pre-1914 British, like an Edwardian mixture of sweet mangoes and malt vinegar—a wedding with its horoscopes and gold-edged, elegantly printed invitation cards, tiny shops with the shopkeeper hunched on the counter selling plantains, betel leaves, snuff and English biscuits: the casuarina and the post office Savings Bank: the brasspots and the volumes of Milton and Carlyle: the shaved head and the ochre robes of the sanyasi and the Mssr. Binn's catalogue of cricket bats. (128–29)

Walsh fails to read what these odd mixtures of sweet mangoes and cricket bats mean in the context of Narayan's fictional Malgudi. Are they just setting and background? Exotica perhaps? Or do they in fact fulfill the purpose of alerting the reader to cultures and nations in conflict? Critics such as Walsh, Narasimhaiah, Y. V. Kantak, and Uma Parameswaran have altogether too facilely dismissed Narayan's work as a "one-stringed instrument fashioned out of bamboo and coconut shells" (Parameswaran 57). There are in fact many strings to Narayan's fictional instrument, and when played differently it produces varied tunes.

In this essay, I intend to argue that under the rather simplistic veneer of each of the Malgudi stories rages a response to politics and to contemporary events—a response that most readers are likely to overlook in their habitual way of reading Narayan as a creator of comedies of manners and mores. Narayan's themes are very similar to those of several contemporary and overtly political writers in the international literature in English: nationhood, postcolonialism, the hybridization of contemporary man by the process Salman Rushdie has called "migration" and "metamorphoses" (52). But, in Narayan's work, these themes are intertwined with his and his readers' interests in perennial issues of character, humankind's hope, and fate. It is Narayan's particularly sensitive treatment of individuals that makes one embrace these miniature tales of South India, often in preference to the sprawl of a Rushdie or an Amitav Ghosh or a Vikram Seth novel, because their works are often peopled by stereotypes and caricatures that supposedly represent the postcolonial world instead of the distinct individuals who make up Malgudi. No reader identifies with a "Gibreel Farishta" in *Satanic Verses* (1988) or even with "the Rawul" in Ruth Prawer Jhabvala's *Three Continents* (1988). But in the day and the age of Ivan Boesky, readers either in India or the West identify with Margayya, the greedy hero of *The Financial Expert*, even as they are alerted to the politics and history that give rise to a character like Margayya. It is this intertwining of the political and the historical with the fate of an individual that makes Narayan's work of continuing interest.

Of all of Narayan's novels, his first, *Swami and Friends*—published in 1935 at the time of the burgeoning of the Independence movement—most effectively embodies the sense of decolonization. It tells how children internalize the "colonial oppressors" and eventually develop a sense of their race in relation to their history. The homes of Indians in the civil and cantonment lines, the club, cricket, and Mssr. Binn's catalog of cricket bats all become symbols through which Narayan expresses ambiguous feelings towards the acculturation processes to which Indian children were subjected. Swami's maturation process leads not just to an adolescent's awareness of himself but to a political awareness of "self" as embodied in what begins to mean "home" to him versus the "other," the British and the westernized India.

As the novel opens, Narayan details the colonial endeavor of making "nurture stick on nature." All the Indian children go to Albert Mission School or to the Board School where they are taught in the true fashion of Macaulay, who had argued in his Minute of 1835: "We have to educate a people who cannot at present be educated by means of their mother tongue. . . . The claims of our own language it is hardly necessary to recapitulate." Swami's father, the true British-loving Indian, believed in the power of English education; and in the novel we see the acculturation process that Swami undergoes as the boys learn their alphabet. For that matter, in his autobiography, *My Days*, Narayan details how boys like himself actually learned the alphabet:

> A is for Apple Pie, B bit it and C cut it. When the boys ask what an apple pie is, the teacher tells them it is something they eat in England. When they ask if it is like "our Mango," he tells them not to be foolish. (58)

In "When India Was a Colony," Narayan wrote:

> The school textbooks were all British manufactured at one time, compiled by Englishmen, published by British firms and shipped to India on P. and O. steamers. From a child's primer with "A was an apple" or "Baa, Baa, Black Sheep" to college physics by Dexter and Garlick, algebra by Ross and logarithm tables compiled by Clark, not a single Indian name was on any book either as author or publisher. Indian history was written by British historians—extremely well documented and researched but not always impartial. History had to serve its purpose: Everything was made subservient to the glory of the Union Jack. Latter-day Indian scholars presented a contrary picture. The Black Hole of Calcutta never existed. Various Muslim rulers who invaded and proselytized with fire and sword were proved to have protected and endowed Hindu temples. When I mentioned this aspect to a distinguished British historian some years

ago in London, he brushed aside my observation with: "I'm sorry, Indians are without a sense of history. Indians are temperamentally nonhistorical." (104)

With *Swami and Friends*, however, we see a greater questioning of the coloniz-ers' missionary zeal. When *Swami and Friends* opens, the young Swami is getting ready to go off to classes at the Albert Mission School, which his father has picked with great care because he wants Swami to have an English education in order to get a secure government position in the Indian Civil Service, like his own. One of the first classes he must attend is "Scripture" where Mr. Ebenezer asks: "'Oh, wretched idiots!. . . Why do you worship dirty, lifeless, wooden idols and stone images?" Mr. Ebenezer further provokes the boys' ire by asking, "'Did our Jesus practice dark tricks on those around him?'" Angry, Swaminathan (the boy's full name) gets up and asks: "'If he did not, why was he crucified?'" This response, of course, results in a terrible row (3–4). For Narayan, the fictional event had its source in an autobiographical event, which he describes in *My Days*:

> Even in the classroom, this was a routine procedure. I studied in a mission school and the daily Scripture class proved a torment. Our Scripture master, though a native, was so devout a convert that he would spend the first 10 minutes calling Krishna a lecher and thief full of devilment. How could one ever pray to him while Jesus was waiting there to save us? His voice quavered at the thought of his God. Once, incensed by his remarks, I put the question, "If Jesus were a real God, why did he not kill the bad men?" which made the teacher so angry that he screamed, "Stand up on the bench, you idiot." (104)

The whole metaphor of Swami and his friends' immersion in cricket internalizes the values of the colonizer. According to the standard set, the boys who play cricket are the ones who know about justice and fair play, because to play cricket is to be like the white man, to be superior. These values are completely internalized by Swami and his friends, particularly Rajam, the district police superintendent's son. Through playing cricket and obtaining the right British education, one gained entrance to "the club"—not just the club where one goes for tea and cucumber sandwiches but that of the Indian Civil Service. Such are the values inculcated in the boys of the Albert Mission school.

But Swami soon begins to see the sham of these values; he has been expelled from the school because of his outburst against Christianity and must now go to the Indian Board School. His friends, especially Rajam whom he admires so much because of his English cricket goods, remain at the Albert Mission School; ironically, Swami stays on the cricket team that had challenged the Board School to play in a tournament with the Mission boys. The cricket match looms large in Swami's consciousness, especially considering that he has to play for his old friend Rajam. But now his loyalties are split, and, caving in under the pressure, he runs away from the whole experience. Rajam, however, does not care about Swami when he disappears before the all important cricket match in which they are going to lick the "local" boys. So Swami realizes that he is dispensable, valuable only when he can fulfill a need. Rajam's attitude toward his one-time friend typifies the way the British had trained the Anglicized Indians to treat their non-Westernized countrymen; Rajam and his father are emblematic of "the solid core of Anglophilia" the British had created. One of the principles the Indian Civil Service manual taught the "Brown Sahib" was not to be too familiar with anyone, even his own countryman. The image Narayan offers of British rule in India is that of the Kheddah "where wild elephants are hemmed in and driven into stockades by trained ones" ("When India" 96). Through this experience it is not just Swami, the young hero of the novel, who gains enlightenment but also his father who comes to an awareness of himself through Rajam's father's behavior. The discovery of themselves as essentially Indian proves to be the essential knowledge these "colonial Adams" gain and serves as the focus of the novel.

Political knowledge, then, comprises an important component of Swami's initiation process. One day going to the Board School, Swami finds himself joining a political protest and destroying ink-pots at the Albert Mission School. But something else happens to Swami who had in the political protest heard someone say:

> "Just think a while. . . . England is no bigger than our Madras Presidency and is inhabited by a handful of white rogues and is thousands of miles away. Yet we bow in homage before the Englishman! . . . Let every Indian spit on England and the quantity of saliva will be enough to drown England."

Later Swami asks his friend Mani:

> "Is it true?"
> "Which?"
> "Spitting and drowning the Europeans."
> "Must be, otherwise do you think the fellow would suggest it?"
> "Then why not do it? It is easy."
> "Europeans will shoot us, they have no heart," said Mani. (95)

Eventually Rajam's father is transferred out of town. As a parting gift to Rajam, Swami gives him "the only book that he respected: It was a neat tiny volume of Andersen's *Fairy Tales* that his father had bought in Madras years ago for him. He could never get through the book to his satisfaction. There were too many unknown unpronounceable English words in it" (181). With this symbolic action, Swami has taken leave of Rajam who had literally become the oppressing western half of his consciousness. Thus, by the end of *Swami and Friends*, we see that the sweet mangoes the Edwardians so cherished had turned to bitter malt vinegar as the very acculturated Indians whom the British treasured had evolved into nationalists.

K.R. Srinivasa Iyengar quotes Narayan from an article titled "The Fiction Writer in India," in which Narayan remarked: ". . . during the period of nationalist agitation, the subject matter of fiction became inescapably political. . . . The mood of comedy, the sensitivity to atmosphere, the probing of psychological factors, the crisis in the individual soul and its resolution, and above all the detached observation, which constitute the stuff of fiction, were forced into the background" (Iyengar 360). Although in this statement Narayan may be separating *Swami and Friends* from his other novels, it is interesting to note that while Narayan prizes detached observation, his own was not always entirely so.

Only after some painful personal experiences did Narayan metamorphose into the detached, ironic observer, the authorial voice that distantly gives us the nationalistic commentary of the later novels. In *The Bachelor of Arts* and *The English Teacher*, we have the depiction of the common man in India, an emphasis almost Marxist. Krishna and his wife Sushila are the very archetypes of India's common people, neither the wealthy aristocrats of Paul Scott nor the Harrow boys of some of Jhabvala's fiction nor Narayan's own characters aspiring to fame in the British Civil Service but an ordinary man and his wife soon to be thwarted by what they cannot afford. The houses that Krishna and his wife will go to look at are not those situated on the neat civil lines but ones with an "infected latrine" through which Sushila catches typhoid. In *Study of Representative Indo-English Novelists*, Uma Parmeswaran proposes that the blunt depiction of this autobiographical event is an attempt at self-therapy (54). But could it be instead a criticism of a government that allowed the rich to live in comfort while the poor perished of unchecked diseases? Like Lopahin in *The Cherry Orchard*, is Narayan a pragmatist crying out for a change in a world that would not grant health and happiness to all? Just as Chekhov's work carries the implicit political message of the 1861 serf uprising, Narayan's work holds the hope of a better life after Independence.

But Narayan's rationalistic dreams are soon to be dashed and smashed. The figure who arrives on the scene to save India is not one in whom Narayan can place his faith. The revered Mahatma of *Waiting for the Mahatma*, who emerges from the flames of the burning cloth of Swami's cricket cap in *Swami and Friends*, turns out to be a toothless little man who visits in rich people's homes, calling to himself little "sweeper boys" whom he eventually teaches to spit orange pips. Narayan's own disappointment with the political leader expresses a Beckett-like irony and alienation. If the Mahatma could only attract mindless individuals like Sriram, who in turn is only attracted by the good-looking Bharati, who is always at the side of the Mahatma, then perhaps all was not as it should be.

The sense of the futility of Indians governing themselves, however, is captured in the last group of Malgudi novels. It is interesting that Narayan invests the novels with this sense despite his insistence that Malgudi is fixed in time within the 1930s. It is the new government of India moving without direction, a young country with no firm administration, that gives birth to saints and sinners alike. Raju, the fake sannyasi of *The Guide*, Margayya in *The Financial Expert*, the crooked astrologer under his banyan tree outside the city government offices in *Astrologer's Day* are all manifestations of a government unable to govern, going full tilt, for instance, toward a family planning program from which, metaphorically, the only escape is to jump up in a tree and hide, as Daisy does in *The Painter of Signs*. This is Narayan's way of chronicling the history of post-Independence India.

What is interesting and most important to note, however, is that Narayan maintains his authorial stance as the pragmatic and detached observer. Never does one get the impression that the author is "situated" with "positional superiority." Here the question of representation is paramount, for Narayan never seems to *represent* or create representations of his characters from an outsider's point of view. In this way he is again very much like Jane Austen. The people of Malgudi are his friends, his sisters and brothers and cousins. Their faults and foibles generate not from "the soil of India," as suggested by Iyengar who wrote of Narayan's characters: "The soil of India doubtless breeds every type of idealist and eccentric, waif and vagabond" (369). Narayan would not agree with Iyengar; if he did, he would be sitting in judgment over his own people and thereby forfeiting his role of the detached observer for that of the interested party. Instead Narayan means to show that his characters are caught up in the wheel of history, which the more it turns around, the more it returns. The poverty and oppression stay or reappear in post-colonial India, and the characters remain pawns in the hands of a historical fate that continues to make them subjects of greed and passion. In this depiction, Narayan is very different from Rushdie; while Rushdie writes of the same chaotic conditions in *Midnight's Children,* he finds specific villains to satirize and caricature. After all, he portrays Mrs. Gandhi in the same light as General Dyer, showing that both share similar nihilistic instincts towards Indians. In another example, the handling of the family planning movement in *Midnight's Children* differs vastly from Narayan's treatment in *The Painter of Signs,* where he chooses to depict the movement only as a foible soon to pass amid the turmoil of politics and history. This contrast is important because Narayan's reader does not come away with a negative image of India or Indians, as well he might after reading Rushdie. For, as Edward Said points out in *Orientalism,* when an image begins "to gravitate about its own madness," then the power of negative representation can result in the biases and prejudices that cause individuals' nihilistic instincts to come to the forefront (27).

Narayan knows that the assigning of blame, even if through the instrument of satire, is a futile attempt because as the cycle of history turns, social events repeat themselves. For instance, with the coming of American economic imperialism to India, we see in *The Vendor of Sweets* the return of the "memsahib" unable to understand Jagan the father-in-law, and the Western educated son with his desire for material goods. But like the cycle of Anglo-India, the cycle of American interest in India will soon pass away too. In fact, much of this sense of the cyclical history and politics of India is conveyed in Narayan's indictment of industry's interest in India: "... a minor modern version of such historical globe trotters as Hannibal, Alexander, Napoleon and heaven knows who else, who moved their hordes and elaborate engines of destruction across continents. Their Indian-oriented counterpart today carries an elaborate load of equipment of a different type—to set up his camp in a strange land, to create illusions of his choice" ("When India" 94). Narayan knows that he does not wish to battle the tiger or to capture it, or to cage it, because he and the tiger may be "family friends." Thus it is that Narayan, like the Sadhu of *A Tiger for Malgudi,* has tamed the tiger of politics and history, which follows in the wake of his characters' footsteps.

Still, defending Narayan is a daunting job, especially since he once said in an interview, "Save me from my champions" (Graubard 234). In fact, it seems that Narayan's refusal to "champion" his cause through his "champions" may well lead to the dismissal of his work from the now forming canon of what is considered international literature in English, with its emphasis on colonialism, neocolonialism, postcolonialism, decolonization, and the myriad of subjects suggested by those terms. But then, Narayan would undoubtedly say, "Even that will pass away."

WORKS CITED

Graubard, Stephen. "An Interview with R. R. Narayan." *Daedalus* (1989): 233–37.

Iyengar, K.R.S. *Indian Writing in English*. 2nd ed. Bombay: Asia Publishing, 1973.

Narayan, R.K. "When India Was a Colony." *New York Times Magazine* 16 Sept. 1984: 94–97.

Parameswaran, Uma. *A Study of Representative Indo-English Novelists*. New Delhi: Vikas, 1976.

Rushdie, Salman. "A Pen Against the Sword: In Good Faith." *Newsweek* 12 Feb. 1990: 52–57.

Said, Edward. *Orientalism*. New York: Vintage Books, 1979.

Walsh, William. "Sweet Mangoes and Malt Vinegar: The Novels of R. K. Narayan." *Indo-English Literature: A Collection of Critical Essays*. Ghaziabad: Vimal Prakashan, 1977. 121–40.

R.K. NARAYAN'S PUBLISHED WORK

Novels

Swami and Friends, 1935
The Bachelor of Arts, 1937
The Dark Room, 1938
The English Teacher (also known as *Grateful to Life and Death*), 1945
Mr. Sampath (also known as *The Printer of Malgudi*), 1949
The Financial Expert, 1952
Waiting for the Mahatma, 1955
The Guide, 1958
The Man-Eater of Malgudi, 1961
The Sweet Vendor (also known as *The Vendor of Sweets*), 1967
The Painter of Signs, 1976
A Tiger for Malgudi, 1982
Talkative Man, 1987
The World of Nagaraj, 1990

Short Story Collections

Malgudi Days, 1941
Dodu and Other Stories, 1943
Cyclone and Other Stories, 1944
An Astrologer's Day and Other Stories, 1947
Lawley Road, 1956
A Horse and Two Goats, 1970

Memoirs

My Days, 1974
My Dateless Diary, 1960 (travel journal)

Mythology

Gods, Demons and Others, 1965
The Ramayana, 1972
The Mahabharata, 1978

Essays

Next Sunday, 1960
A Writer's Nightmare (Selected Essays 1958–88), 1988 (Includes "When India Was a Colony," published in *New York Times Magazine*, 16 Sept. 1984)

SELECTED CRITICAL READINGS

R.K. Narayan has unfortunately not received extensive international critical attention. He has been reviewed widely in the United States and in India, but there have not been very many critical essays written on the fiction outside of India. Even then much of the criticism on Narayan so far consists largely of plot summaries and descriptions of his novels. Further studies of his technique as well as on his political implications would be welcome.

Dasenbrock, Reed Way. "Intelligibility and Meaningfulness in Multicultural Literature in English." *PMLA* 102 (1987): 10–19. Takes a critical-theoretical approach to Narayan's work, comparing it to that of American writers Rudolfo Anaya and Maxine Hong Kingston and New Zealand writer Witi Ihimaera.

Journal of Indian Writing in English 11.1 (1983). Special issue on R.K. Narayan. Contains a reception history of all Narayan's novels and short stories up to *A Horse and Two Goats*. Lists and annotates every review of a Narayan novel from an American newspaper or magazine.

Jussawalla, Feroza. *Family Quarrels: Towards a Criticism of Indian Writing in English.* New York: Peter Lang, 1985. 70–84. Applies sociolinguistic criteria in a study of Narayan's Indian-English style.

Naipaul, V.S. *India: A Wounded Civilization.* 1977. New York: Penguin, 1983. 18–54. Basing his comments in part on talks with Narayan, Naipaul discusses several of the novels, placing them in the context of Indian civilization.

Parameswaran, Uma. *A Study of Representative Indo-English Novelists.* New Delhi: Vikas, 1976. Offers a detailed and thorough essay on Narayan as a "native genius." Discusses his reception by critics and applies Wayne Booth's critical criteria to the novels.

Ram, Atma, editor. *Perspectives on R.K. Narayan.* Ghaziabad: Vimal Prakashan, 1981. Contains 20 essays on various aspects of the fiction, in an attempt to "redress Narayan's neglect" as a major novelist. Includes primary and secondary bibliographical material.

Sundaram, P.S. *R.K. Narayan.* Delhi: Arnold Heinemann, 1973 (Revised Version. Delhi: B. R. Publishing Corporation, 1988). Provides a comprehensive survey of Narayan's work.

Walsh, William. "Sweet Mangos and Malt Vinegar: The Novels of R.K. Narayan." *Indo-English Literature: A Collection of Critical Essays.* Ghaziabad: Vimal Prakashan, 1977: 121–40 (Originally appeared in *Listener* 1 March 1962). Sees Narayan as a recorder of Indian ways, a talented storyteller who dwells on the peculiarities of Indian life and people. Does not consider Narayan typical of the postcolonial writer interested in politics.

— FEROZA JUSSAWALLA

Chinua Achebe

Chinua Achebe was born 16 November 1930, in the village of Ogidi, Eastern Nigeria. His father was a catechist for the Church Missionary Society and Achebe's primary education was in the society's school in his village. He was eight when he began to learn English and fourteen when he went to the Government College at Unuahia, one of the best schools in West Africa. He matriculated in 1948 to the recently founded University College, Ibadan, as a member of the first class. Although he intended to study medicine, he soon switched to literary studies, prompted by a reading of Joyce Cary's depiction of Nigeria and the Nigerian character in *Mister Johnson* (1939). He graduated in 1953, taught for a year, and then embarked on a twelve-year career as a Talks Producer for the Nigerian Broadcasting Corporation, where he was promoted to head of his department.

In 1957 he went to London to attend the British Broadcasting Corporation Staff School. One of his teachers was the novelist and literary critic, Gilbert Phelps, who recognized the unique quality of *Things Fall Apart* and recommended it for publication. So on its first try the book, which has become a twentieth-century classic, went safely into print. Achebe has remarked that he never had the experience of being a struggling artist.

No Longer at Ease, Arrow of God, and *A Man of the People* followed in quick succession, the latter published only a few days before the first military coup d'état in Nigeria. Achebe resigned his post as Director of External Broadcasting when, as a prelude to civil war, massacres of Igbo people took place in Northern Nigeria in 1966. He returned to Eastern Nigeria, and when Biafra declared its independence from Nigeria in 1967 (and with the outbreak of Civil War), Achebe traveled widely in his quest for help for the Biafran cause.

When hostilities ceased he accepted teaching appointments in Nigeria and the United States. He has been awarded honorary degrees in the United Kingdom, the United States, and Canada. He has twice received the Nigerian National Merit Award, the only Nigerian to be so honored.

Since *A Man of the People* appeared, he has published poetry, collections of short stories, essays, and another novel, all of which place him in the forefront of contemporary writers.

A Different Order of Reality

Chinua Achebe is arguably the most discussed African writer of his generation. Ten critical books and more than a hundred articles have already appeared, paying tribute to his novelistic technique and linguistic inventiveness. *Things Fall Apart*, his first novel, has become a classic in its own time, read and discussed throughout the anglophone world and elsewhere through translation into some forty foreign languages. Sales are estimated to be in excess of three million copies. His other novels, short stories, poetry, critical essays, and political commentary are equally respected.

Achebe is a master of the craft of fiction; he has renewed the form by locating it in a new and unexplored locale and extended the capability of English. His control of language is absolute, and his range of usage exactly appropriate to the multiplicity of his interests. Nothing is out of place in his imaginative work.

Things Fall Apart first received attention, however, because of the social purposes he assigned to it and to himself as a writer. The novel was published in 1958, two years before Nigerian independence and a period of excitement and optimism. Achebe understood the necessity of showing his countrymen how the strength of their own culture could assist in the task of nation building, a strength that had been, if not lost, greatly diminished through the imposition of an alien culture. As he wrote at the time in "The Novelist as Teacher":

> . . . as far as I am concerned the fundamental theme must first be disposed of. This theme—put quite simply—is that African people did not hear of culture for the first time from Europeans; that their societies were not mindless but frequently had a philosophy of great depth and value and beauty, that they had poetry and, above all, they had dignity. It is this dignity that African people all but lost during the colonial period, and it is this that they must now regain. (162)

Interested in stories and storytelling from his youth, Achebe committed himself to being a writer when he encountered Joyce Cary's novel, *Mister Johnson*, as an undergraduate at University College, Ibadan:

> [Cary] was in this country as an Administrative Officer during the First World War and he wrote this novel called *Mister Johnson*, which is quite famous, and I feel that it's not—in spite of this man's ability, in spite of his sympathy and understanding, he could not get under the skin of his African. They just did not communicate. And I felt if a good writer could make this mess perhaps we ought to try our hand. (Whitelaw)

Achebe's purpose was to set the record of Nigeria's (and by extension Africa's) encounter with colonial history straight, to write about his own people and for his own people. His five novels to date form a continuum over some 100 years of Igbo civilization. The novels record an imaginative history of a segment of a major group of people in what eventually became Nigeria as seen from the perspective of a Christian Igboman.

Given Achebe's purposes as an artist—his duty to art and the social purposes he means it to serve—one can say that his is a distinctly Igbo sensibility (whatever correspondences one might identify between his sensibility and that of artists in other places and cultures). His art reflects in all of its variety the endless permutations of the essential duality of Igbo life. The connection between this world view and artistic irony is of course apparent, for Achebe's art is essentially an art of irony, from the simple to the profound. What makes Achebe's irony different from that of writers from purely literary cultures is that while their uses of irony are cultivated, his is instinctive, generating as it does out of the substance of the culture from which it is inseparable.

And while Achebe conceived his role as partly that of "teacher"—"perhaps what I write is applied art as distinct from pure. But who cares?"—he is not a "preacher":

> I'm very fully aware and fully conscious of the dangers of idealization. . . . I bend over backwards to paint in all the unsavoury, all the unfavourable aspects of that culture. Because what I think I am is a kind of witness and I think I would not be doing justice to my cause if I could be faulted on the matter of truth. ("Novelist as Teacher" 162)

Achebe describes *Things Fall Apart* as "an act of atonement with my past, the ritual return and homage of a prodigal son." The novel tells the tragic story of the rise and fall of Okonkwo and the equally tragic story of the disintegration of Igbo culture, symbolized by the agrarian society of Umuofia under the relentless encroachments of British Christian Imperialism. Okonkwo embodies the qualities most valued by his people (even if in an exaggerated form)—energy, a strong sense of purpose, a sense of communal cooperativeness, which at the same time are marked by a strong sense of individuality. Both Okonkwo and his society also display a degree of rigidity and inflexibility that ultimately account for their destruction. In portraying the complexities of the psychological makeup of Okonkwo and of the mores of the clan, Achebe shows the civility, dignity, and orderliness of the society and the rigidity that made it impossible for the clan to adapt to the inevitable changes wrought by the more powerful and imported culture. *Things Fall Apart* is therefore both an apostrophe to and a lament for the past and a fictional evocation of the inevitability of historical change.

The meaning of the book is sustained by the consummate control Achebe exercises over his materials in an English appropriate to all the moods and modes of the story. In the novel Achebe demonstrates his thesis that

> The price of a world language must be prepared to pay is submission to many different kinds of use. The African writer should aim to use English in a way that brings out his message best without altering the language to the extent that its value as a medium for international exchange will be lost. He should aim at fashioning out an English which is at once universal and able to carry his peculiar experience. ("The African Writer" 61)

Things Fall Apart (and *Arrow of God*) is an account of colonial history from the point of view of the colonized rather than the colonizer. The perspective is African ontology instead of Eurocentric historiography. That ontology consists of a novel that explores the philosophical principles of an African community, unique and autonomous at the outset. The discussion, direct and inferred, does not have the depth of the third novel, *Arrow of God*—and it was for that reason Achebe says he returned to the theme in his third book.

Achebe's second novel, *No Longer at Ease*, is set in modern Nigeria in the days immediately before political independence from British colonial rule. The novel reveals the changes to Nigerian society that resulted from foreign intervention, the extent to which things have fallen apart. The nature of these changes unfolds through the experiences, actions, and beliefs of Obi Okonkwo, the grandson of the hero of *Things Fall Apart.* In *No Longer at Ease* Obi's professional, social, and moral decline arise from and run parallel to a confusion of values in modern Nigerian society. Obi is a highly individualized character who may nevertheless be understood to represent young Nigerians of his generation. Obi's is the tragic story of a modern man: His values are shaped by his links with his Igbo culture as revealed by his mother; but they are contorted by his formal, alien education overseas—he has a B.A., Honors in English, from London University. The novel also tells the tragic story of a modern state, for through Obi's experiences Achebe provides a record, transmuted by his personal vision of, on the one hand, the nature of "modernity"— in terms of its social, political, and economic implications—derived through colonial rule as Nigerians have accommodated themselves to these, and, on the other hand, the price Nigerians have paid for this kind of modernity.

Obi is not an admirable character; his distanced, literary, and supercilious responses to events in his community, both the traditional society of his village and to his "European" job in the capital city, are smug and callow. His flaw is that he has no moral reserves to deal with the calamities he brings down on his own head. Yet his experiences testify to the oppressive weight of doubt, guilt, and regret that the colonial experience has occasioned in Nigeria.

Achebe returns to the past in his third novel, *Arrow of God.* Here he creates a world much like that of Oknokwo's, but a more dynamic world, evoked in comprehensive detail, one redolent with the complexities of daily domestic, social, political, and religious living but further complicated by the religious and political proscriptions that the colonial force has introduced into Igbo society and institutionalized. *Arrow of God* "goes back to the past, not as remotely as [*Things Fall Apart*] because I've learned to think that my first book is no longer adequate. I've learned a lot more about these particular people . . . my ancestors" ("Interview" 20). The dynamics of the life lived by the people of Umuaro are rendered with vivid detail, displaying the tragedy of Ezeulu, Chief Priest of Ulu and the spiritual and political leader of his people.

The novel is a meditation on the nature and uses of power, and on the responsibility of the person who wields it. Ezeulu becomes engaged in a struggle for power with both the people of his village and the Officers of the British Political Service. Always sensitive to the source of his power, Ezeulu is forced to try to reconcile the contending impulses in his own nature to serve as the protecting deity of his own people and to gain greater personal power by pushing his authority to its very limits. Out of this attempt to reconcile these contending impulses his tragedy arises.

Achebe has said, in a statement adumbrating the widest and most profound implications of the story he has been telling, that

> In the society we have been looking at in the story you do not do things in the name of the son but in the name of father. The legitimacy is with the elders, the ancestors, with tradition and age. We now have a new dispensation in which youth and inexperience gain a new legitimacy. This is something new and different. Wisdom belongs to the elders, but the new wisdom is going to the young people. They are going to go to school, to go to church, and will tell their fathers what it is. This almost amounts to turning the world upside down. I think that Ezeulu himself sensed it coming; he had some kind of psychic vision. This was confirmed the first time he was interviewed by the English administrator Clarke, and Ezeulu looked up and the image in his mind was that of a puppy, something unfinished, half-baked, too young; and yet there was authority. Now this reversal itself is tied up with the colonial situation. There is no other situation in the world where power resides with inexperience and young people. A young man would not approach the seat of power in England, but in the colonial situation he is given power and he can order a chief around. In a very deep sense this reversal is the quintessence of colonialism. It is a loss of independence. (Serumaga 1)

The consequences of the loss of predictable political power at the village level are one thing, at the national level quite another. And it is to this latter reality that Achebe turns in his fourth novel, *A Man of the People*, which is set in the post-colonial period in an independent African country. The governance of the country lies, nominally, in the hands of the people, and it is the quality of the leadership and the response of the people to that leadership that concerns Achebe. There is no collective will in the people. Nor is there responsible leadership. Moreover, the collective voice manifest at the village level and through which collective agreement is articulated, as we have seen in *Things Fall Apart* and *Arrow of God*, no longer exists.

Whereas the novels set in the past displayed a society in which a balance between collective religious observance and individual monetary pursuits was achieved, contemporary society is revealed as devoid of religious concerns. Only a vestige remains of the religious beliefs that kept the acquisitiveness of the society in check. Concerning this loss Achebe has written:

> A man's position in society was usually determined by his wealth. All four titles in my village were taken—not given—and each had its own price. But in those days wealth meant the strength of your

arm. No one became rich by swindling the community or stealing government money. In fact a man who was guilty of theft immediately lost all his titles. Today we have kept the materialism and thrown away the spirituality which should keep it in check. ("The Role of the Writer" 160)

So in *A Man of the People* there reigns an atmosphere of unrestrained acquisitiveness in the midst of political corruption, where there is no national voice but only a confusion of competing village voices, an atmosphere where every man tries to acquire as large a piece of the national financial pie as possible and by whatever means are the most effective. The narrator is a politically disaffected university graduate who cynically describes the evils around him even as he participates in them. By presenting Odili as an anti-hero, Achebe is able to display the public and private motives that inform political action.

The novel is open ended, for an impasse in the political system has been reached, and military intervention is plainly not a solution to the problems of public governance. Achebe has, in another context, said of military coups:

> There's no question at all that the military intervention was popular. It was a great relief because we had almost come to an impasse. The whole point of constitutional government is that the rules must be obeyed, must be followed. And the basic rule of this is that there is the possibility of change through elections. Now when the electoral process is abused and manipulated you really don't have any other recourse but perhaps violence or something like a military coup.
>
> I don't think they [the military] will stay in power forever, in fact I don't think they'll be there unduly long because Nigerians are highly political. And it's up to the military, the people who are in power now, to do whatever they have to do as quickly as possible and create the possibility for return to civilian government. This is the ultimate hope. (Gzowski)

But by the time *Anthills of the Savannah* appeared in 1986, twenty years after *A Man of the People*, the ultimate hope had not been realized. The novel is set in the West African country of Kangan, which to all intents and purposes is Nigeria. *A Man of the People* ended with a military coup; and *Anthills of the Savannah* ends with yet another military coup. So history goes on repeating itself, a measure of how far the country is from solving its political problems. Achebe examines the consequences of military rule, finding military leadership not much better than the Nanga-ism of the regime it replaced. In fact it is worse: Political chaos has been replaced by a dictatorship; cynical self-interest has been replaced by megalomania. *Anthills of the Savannah* elaborates and adumbrates many of the problems Achebe identified in his political pamphlet, *The Trouble with Nigeria*.

Kangan, is ruled by a military governor and a cabinet of civilian ministers, is a regime that can take no credit for its accomplishments. As one of the characters in the novel muses:

It can't be the massive corruption though its scale and pervasiveness are truly intolerable; it isn't the subservience to foreign manipulation, degrading as it is; it isn't even this second-class hand-me-down capitalism, ludicrous and doomed; . . . nor is it the damnable shooting of striking railway-workers and demonstrating students and the banning thereafter of independent unions and cooperatives. It is the failure of our rulers to establish vital inner links with the poor and dispossessed of this country, with the bruised heart that throbs painfully at the core of the national being. (141)

In barest outline, *Anthills of the Savannah*—complex, resourceful, demanding in structure and ideas, told from a multiplicity of viewpoints, contemporary in setting yet mindful of the relevance of historical tradition—tells the tragic story of three boyhood friends against the background of a society in chaos: Sam, His Excellency and would-be President for Life; Ikem Osodi, poet and editor of *The National Gazette*; and Chris Oriko, Minister of Information. For Achebe the trouble with Kangan is leadership. In fact, *The Trouble with Nigeria* provides a gloss on the novel (or the reverse). Admitting that external factors have a bearing on the nation's problems, one of the characters says that "to blame all these things on imperialism and international capitalism as our modish radicals want us to do is, in my view, sheer cant and humbug" (159). Nor is the leadership problem to be solved by a "democratic dictatorship of the proletariat," because if the proletariat is composed of workers and students, as Iken is informed at a public meeting at the university, then no two bodies have been more derelict than workers and students in their commitment to public and civil causes.

Achebe examines the writer's role in affecting this solution, for *Anthills of the Savannah* is a novel about "story." Its persistent references to the role of "story" and the "storyteller" exemplify the claims that Achebe makes for art in his essays "The Truth of Fiction" and "What Has Literature Got to Do with It?":

> . . . stories serve the purpose of consolidating whatever gains a people or their leaders have made or imagine they have made in their existential journey through the world; but they also serve to sanction change when it can no longer be denied. At such critical moments new versions of old stories or entirely fresh ones tend to be brought into being to mediate the changes and sometimes to consecrate opportunistic defections into more honourable rites of passage. ("What Has Literature" 112)

Anthills of the Savannah aims at giving the story back to the people, at reclaiming the art of storytelling in a society where oral wisdom is in danger of dying out because of the increasing development of the modern technocratic society and where the communal—and public—act of storytelling is yielding to the private form of the printed word. This novel reveals that the two distinct forms can meet, can assist in closing the gap between the educated and uneducated (the use of "pidgin" in the novel promotes this cause as well), so that story is once more capable of fulfilling its traditional role.

Morning Yet on Creation Day contains fifteen essays, written between 1962 and 1973, on various literary and political subjects. The collection is divided into two parts, the first containing eight essays on the role of the African writer in his society, the second containing essays more personal in nature although with a public application in the conclusions drawn. Of special interest is the essay on "'Chi' in Igbo Cosmology," because it throws light on the "chi"—a man's personal god—in Achebe's first and third novels. This volume has been superseded by *Hopes and Impediments*, published in 1988, which retains some of the essays of the earlier volume and adds essays and addresses from the intervening years. Of special note are "The Truth of Fiction" and "What Has Literature Got to Do with It?" (the latter Achebe's address on receiving the Nigerian National Merit Award).

Achebe has been recognized at home and abroad with honorary degrees and visiting academic appointments and has been involved in literary activities both in Nigeria and overseas. He has continued to comment on the political life of Nigeria in the press and various journals, and the question of what kind of leadership would best serve the country remains the center of his concern. During 1983 in the face of an impending federal election, he published *The Trouble with Nigeria*, which expounds the thesis that the trouble is simply a failure of leadership:

> There is nothing basically wrong with the Nigerian character, Nigerian land or climate or water or air or anything else. The Nigerian problem is the unwillingness or inability of its leaders to rise to the responsibility, to the challenge of personal example which are the hallmarks of true leadership. (1)

Before the election was held the military intervened, and it has been suggested that Achebe's words in part prompted this action. Whatever the truth of these assertions, he says of the book:

> You must remember that the book we are talking about was actually published before the election. It was intended to be a kind of warning. We are now looking at it as a postmortem, but it was not initially intended to be that. At that point in time I was appealing to this generation of educated Nigerians, the young Nigerians, to get out of the rut, not to follow what I call the "old performers" . . . those [who] have by and large decided that it would perhaps take too long to set up their own political structures and that perhaps the quickest thing would be to make use of existing structures through the old masters of the game, and so perhaps change the system from the inside. Now I think we must think again. (Gzowski)

Achebe continues to be involved in the quest to determine a just system of governance for Nigerians and to advocate the role of literature in serving society's needs. Achebe was recently awarded the Nigerian National Merit Award for the second time, and in his acceptance speech—"What Has Literature Got to Do with It?"—he acknowledges that the goal of a developing nation like Nigeria is, of course, development or, one should say, "modernization," and that literature is central in the quest of achieving this goal:

> Literature, whether handed down by word of mouth or in print, gives us a second handle on reality; enabling us to encounter in the safe manageable dimensions of make-believe the very same threats to integrity that may assail the psyche in real life; and at the same time providing through the self-discovery which it imparts, a veritable weapon for coping with these threats whether they are found within our problematic and incoherent selves or in the world around us. What better preparation can a people desire as they begin their journey into the strange revolutionary world of modernization? ("What Has Literature" 117)

Flaubert, in one of his letters to Turgenev, said that there was nothing new for the writer to say, but there had to be new ways of saying the old things. Such is not the case with Achebe. The old things that were said about Africa over a long period, things predicated on denigrating racial assumptions, were not worth saying again; indeed they had to be refuted. Achebe has new things to say, important things to say. And he has found a new way of saying them. He sets the record of history straight, for no one can still think about Africa in the terms that applied before his first novel. He restores his people's faith in themselves and provides a context by which his people can "articulate their values and define their goals in relation to the cold, alien world around them" ("What Has Literature" 117).

Achebe dominates the African novel and holds a central place in contemporary literature, because he more than any of his peers, reflectively and unobtrusively, has modified the traditions of fiction, derived forms distinctively his own for the purpose of envisaging and conveying experience that is deeply convincing. Deceptive profundity, discriminating insight, mental and moral fastidiousness, elegance and lucidity: These are the hallmarks of Achebe's art.

WORKS CITED

Achebe, Chinua. "The African Writer and the English Language." *Morning Yet on Creation Day.* London: Heinemann, 1975.

———. *Anthills of the Savannah.* London: Heinemann, 1986.

———. "Interview with Lewis Nkosi." *Africa Report* (July 1964): 20.

———. "The Novelist as Teacher." *New Statesman* (January 1965): 162.

———. "The Role of the Writer in the New Nation." *Nigeria Magazine* (June 1964): 160.

———. *The Trouble with Nigeria.* Enugu: Fourth Dimension Publishing Co, 1983.

———. "What Has Literature Got to Do with It?" *Hopes and Impediments.* London: Heinemann, 1988.

Gzowski, Peter. Unpublished interview with Chinua Achebe, Canadian Broadcasting Corp., 23 June 1985.

Serumaga, Robert. Interview with Chinua Achebe. London: Transcription Centre, 1971.

Whitelaw, Marjorie. Unpublished interview with Chinua Achebe. Nigerian Broadcasting Corp., 23 May 1962.

CHINUA ACHEBE'S PUBLISHED WORK

Novels

Things Fall Apart, 1958
No Longer at Ease, 1960
Arrow of God, 1964
A Man of the People, 1966
Anthills of the Savannah, 1987

Short Story Collections

The Sacrificial Egg and Other Stories, 1962
Girls at War and Other Stories, 1972

Poetry

Beware Soul Brother and Other Poems, 1971 (Revised and enlarged, published as *Christmas in Biafra and Other Poems*, 1973)

Commentary and Essays

Morning Yet on Creation Day: Essays, 1975
The Trouble with Nigeria, 1983
Hopes and Impediments, 1988

Children's Books

Chike and the River, 1966
How the Leopard Got His Claws (with John Iroaganachi), 1972

SELECTED CRITICAL READINGS

Criticism and commentary on Achebe's writing, his critical reputation, and literary and other influences are so extensive that it is impossible to represent the vast body of work here. The basic studies still prove useful. Readers are directed to entries on Achebe and his writing in three bibliographies edited by Bernth Lindfors: *Black African Literature in English: 1977–1981*; *Black African Literature in English: A Guide to Information Sources*; *Black African Literature in English, 1982–1986* (see General Bibliography). Readers will also want to consult *Chinua Achebe: A Bio-Bibliography* (Nsukka, February 1990). This work was written and compiled by the staff of the Nnamdi Zaikiwe Library at the University of Nigeria on the occasion of Chinua Achebe's Sixtieth Birthday in 1990. It is the most comprehensive listing of Achebe's publications in various world languages together with exhaustive listing of critical materials.

Carroll, David. *Chinua Achebe*. New York: Twayne, 1970. Considers Achebe's achievement through detailed analysis of the novels and short stories to the time of *A Man of the People*.

Colmer, Rosemary. "The Start of Weeping Is Always Hard: The Ironic Structure of *No Longer at Ease*." *Literary Half-Yearly* 21 (1980): 121–35. Praised by Achebe for its comprehensive discussion of this novel.

Irele, Abiola. "The Tragic Conflict in Achebe's Novels." *Black Orpheus* 17 (1965): 24–32. Rpt. *Introduction to African Literature*. Evanston: Northwestern University Press, 1967: 167–78. Discusses Achebe's fiction in terms of its relationship to tragic theory.

Iyasere, Solomon O. "Narrative Techniques in *Things Fall Apart*." *New Letters* 40.3 (1974): 73–93. Comprehensive analysis of the various narrative voices in the novel.

Killam, G.D. *The Novels of Chinua Achebe*. New York: Africana Publishing Co., 1969. (Rev. *The Writings of Chinua Achebe*, 1977.) First systematic study of Achebe's writing, discussing the novels, short stories, poetry, and essays in order of their publication.

Lindfors, Bernth. "The Palm Oil with Which Achebe's Words Are Eaten." *African Literature Today* 1 (1968): 3–18. Rpt. *Folklore in Nigerian Literature*. New York: Africana Publishing, 1973: 73–93. Landmark study of Achebe's use of proverbial materials in fiction.

Maxwell, D.E.S. "Landscape and Theme." *Commonwealth Literature: Unity and Diversity in a Common Culture*. London: Heinemann, 1965. 82–89. On *Things Fall Apart* and Randolph Stow's *To the Islands*. Concentrates on the disjunction between place and language in the two novels, establishing a model for comparative postcolonial literary theory.

Ravenscroft, Arthur. *Chinua Achebe*. Essex: Longmans, Green, 1969. Brief but thorough appreciation and critical commentary of Achebe's first four novels.

Wren, Robert. *Achebe's World: The Historical and Cultural Contexts of the Novels of Chinua Achebe*. Washington, D.C.: Three Continents Press, 1980. Detailed study of the oral and written sources of Achebe's first four novels within their historical and cultural settings.

—G.D. KILLAM

Ayi Kwei Armah

A yi Kwei Armah was born in Sekondi Takoradi, Ghana, 1939; he belongs to the Fante tribe of the Akan people. He was first educated at Achimota College near Accra. In 1959, he won a scholarship, which took him to the United States, first to Groton School, Massachusetts, then to Harvard University and Columbia University.

At Harvard, he started as a student of literature; however, he got bored reading novels, decided to study social sciences instead, and graduated with a B.A. in that field. Under the influence of American black activism and the civil rights marches of the early 1960s, he cut short his education and went to Algeria in 1963, where he worked for the magazine *Révolution Africaine*. He then wanted to volunteer for revolutionary action in Southern Africa. Soon realizing the romantic nature of his hasty decision, he returned to the Western world, where he began to write essays under the ideological influence of Frantz Fanon and Amil Cabral.

Although in 1964 Armah returned to Ghana, where he worked as a scriptwriter for Ghana television, he did not remain there for long. From 1967 to 1968 he was editor of the magazine *Jeune Afrique* in Paris. Between 1968 and 1970 he was back in the United States, where he was again influenced by various American myths of race and sex, which were to become a major issue in his third novel, *Why Are We So Blest?* In 1968, he published his first novel, *The Beautyful Ones Are Not Yet Born*. Though he published another four novels up to 1978, this first novel has remained his best-known work. His short stories basically employ parts of the larger themes of his novels.

Over the past twenty years or so, Armah has lived and worked as a translator, essayist, novelist, short story writer, teacher, and university professor in many different places between Dar-es-Salaam and Massachusetts and from Lesotho to Wisconsin, most recently in Senegal. He has acquired an international reputation as one of Africa's most provocative writers.

His most recent essays explore the practical implications of some of the polemics contained in his novels. So far, however, he has not returned to the creative form of the novel.

A Vision of Past, Present, and Future

One of the fundamental issues in the critical discussion of Armah's novels concerns the reconciliation between what seem to be extremely different approaches to the art of the novel in the African context. For many critics, there is a radical difference of theme and narrative technique between Armah's first three novels and his last two "historical" novels. Robert Fraser, for example, writes that in the early novels there is "a morbid and sterile preoccupation with the harrowing position of the artist figure isolated in an unsympathetic environment" that stems from the European Romantic tradition, but he notes a considerable change in the two most recent novels:

> The artist figure disappears, or is merged in a wider professional group or guild. Simultaneously the emphasis on the re-creation of individual states of mind recedes, to the extent that Armah can now be regarded pre-eminently as the craftsman of the plural voice, the communal consciousness, the racial memory. (x)

This marked shift from an individual protagonist to what is generally felt to be a plural voice—an ethnic community or group consciousness—has been received with varying reactions by Armah's critics. Not everyone agrees with Rand Bishop when he writes:

> The impact of this fourth novel [*Two Thousand Seasons*], I predict, will be immense, once its form is fully appreciated and its message is widely disseminated. Taken together with the fifth work, *The Healers*, this pair of novels represents an exciting new development that sets Armah apart from the rest of his contemporaries. (532–33)

Whatever the respective critics' reactions, the first three novels are thought to trace the plight of one or two characters in a community that contradicts the values they represent, while the last two novels tell long and rhetorically impressive stories "built around the striving for unity by a whole group of people" (Gikandi 73).

Yet certain themes and narrative devices clearly run through all of Armah's novels, and thematically and technically connect his earlier and his later works. First of all, his *oeuvre* constitutes a complete vision of the past, the present, and the future, each novel functioning as a piece within the whole cosmic puzzle: The first three novels examine the present, *Two Thousand Seasons* reviews the past, and *The Healers* offers a prospect of a possible future. Thus, in a way, all five novels together can be seen as one great work, one "heightened form of the historical novel" (Fraser 104). So they are not merely a series of isolated attempts "but rather parts of a very grand scheme, the full dimensions of which are only gradually becoming apparent" (Bishop 537). Another aspect, which shows the interrelatedness of the five novels, is Armah's preoccupation with the symbolic relationship between men of art and men of power.

On the whole, one can observe the unity throughout Armah's work in three areas: theme and metaphor, characterization, and narrative technique. In regard to the question of theme and metaphor, one finds that Armah remains remarkably consistent throughout his work, which shows his preoccupation with patterns of evolution, cyclical metaphors, and political commitment. These general tendencies, however, may take different shapes in each of the novels, as becomes particularly clear in the variations of the general metaphoric pattern of the cycle through the five books:

> In each book the commanding metaphor is quite different, in fact:
> the ingestion-evacuation circuit in the first; fragmentation, coupled
> with selective blindness and returning ghosts, in the second;
> Promethean deliverance in the third; the ongoing, cyclical course of
> water and the seasons, in opposition to the changeless blank of the
> desert, in the fourth; the restorative healing of wounds—personal,
> national and racial—in the fifth. (Wright 14)

Thus, according to Wright, one can call the intellectual shape of Armah's metaphors recurrent, rather than the symbols themselves.

The great unifying force within Armah's work is the theme of Africa: Africa in its socio-economic, cultural and political plight, particularly the theme of the tensions and conflicts between indigenous values and outside influences. In spite of Chinua Achebe's early attacks (*Morning Yet on Creation Day* 25–26) and Charles Larson's allegations to the effect that Armah seems to regard himself "as a novelist only incidentally African" (258), which Armah himself has contradicted, the Africanness of Armah's writing must become evident for any careful reader. This Africanness not only appears in Armah's fresh use of the English language, it also forms the prerequisite for a number of further characteristics of his novels in the domain of theme and metaphor.

Armah's treatment of society can be called characteristically African. Once the interpretation of his writing is stripped of its reliance on non-African thinkers from Karl Marx to Frantz Fanon, it becomes obvious that the novels are all concerned with a specifically African representation of social instruments, social powers, and human relationships within society. One of the recurrent themes in this context has already been mentioned: the relationship between men of art and men of power, whether in the shape of "the man" and his former schoolmate Koomson in *The Beautyful Ones Are Not Yet Born* or of the healer Densu and the general Asamoa Nkwanta in *The Healers*. This relationship can be seen as yet another expression of the African principle of reciprocity, as advocated in *Two Thousand Seasons* as "our way, the way," and as employed as an ordering principle by Armah himself. These African characteristics are not what Achebe calls "props" (204), but clearly they are alternatives to Western ways of approaching similar social issues. For example, the social effectiveness of the healers is unthinkable in a European or North American context. The same can be shown for the depiction of suffering as a communal experience, from *The Beautyful Ones Are Not Yet Born* and *Fragments*, where this experience may be felt by the community but only recognized and acknowledged by a few elect, to *The Healers*, where it is seen as a social disease to be cured by the protagonist Densu and his comrades, and most effectively in *Two Thousand Seasons*, where the individual recedes behind all communal concerns. It is this depiction of suffering that really is the "true test of Armah's attitude to the African past" (Izevbaye 247).

Another unifying theme in Armah's novels is heralded by his consistent use of images of journeying, as well as by his preoccupation with water imagery. This is the theme of hope and hopelessness, the dialectics of human victory and defeat on an ontological level. The theme is thrust upon the reader's consciousness in *The Beautyful Ones Are Not Yet Born*:

> As he turned along the road to go home, the man felt completely apart from all that was taking place. He would like to know about it, but there would be plenty of time for it, and he was not burdened with any hopes that new things, really new things, were as yet ready to come out. Someday in the long future a new life would maybe flower in the country, but when it came, it would not choose as its instruments the same people who had made a habit of killing new flowers. The future goodness may come eventually, but before then where were the things in the present which would prepare the way for it? (159–60)

This passage is closely connected with the symbolic image of the flower painted on the back of the bus, which the man sees on the following day: the flower containing the slogan that is the title of the novel. The slogan, in turn, leads us back to the sentence, "Someday in the long future a new life would maybe flower in the country"; and together, in the sphere where "not yet" and "maybe" meet, they comprise the dialectics of hope and hopelessness.

The theme runs through all of Armah's novels and seems to gain even more strength in his later works; it surely lies behind one of the symbolic tales in *The Healers*:

> A story reached Kumase from Ejiso. A year back a woman, barren till that time, had inexplicably conceived. The ninth month came and went, and the tenth, and the eleventh. The pregnancy continued to grow, but yielded no child. Then when a precise year had passed, a child was born to the woman, exactly in the blind middle of the night. As if there hadn't been enough wonders already, this strange night-child commenced to talk as soon as he had freed his head from his mother's womb. The child spoke like an old man, one who had eaten barrels of pepper and salt in a long life:
>
> "What a place you have brought me to, my mother. And what a time you have brought me into, my mother. But, my mother, why have you brought me here at a time like this? Did I tell you this was where I wanted to come? The home I'm coming from is peaceful. I'm going back there, my mother. You here will never see me again."
>
> With that the wonderful child disappeared. The mother, dazed by so many unbelievable events and words, crawled outside the house, intending to call back the child. She could find no trace of him. In defeat she returned to her house. But she could not recognize the place she had left just a moment before. The whole

house was covered with grass and thick bush, as if for two seasons
no human being had lived there. (246)

The theme of pregnancy is naturally connected with the general theme of hope.
When the child is born at last—a victory of life—he is disappointed with the world
as he finds it, already disillusioned by the barrels of pepper and salt of life, and he
leaves the world again, thus completing the natural cycle of birth and death. The
mother, on the other hand, tries to find her lost child and, in defeat, returns to her
house. The covering of the house by grass and bush may encapsulate both hope and
hopelessness in the future. For while this event may be interpreted as an image of
the hopeless destruction of human civilization by the forces of nature, it can also be
read to suggest a new beginning in harmony with the victorious inevitability of
nature.

What has already been discussed under the aspect of theme and metaphor may
be extended to character and narrative technique, as some examples have already
indicated. While the various protagonists and their fellow characters might be
critically examined and eventually be found to lack credibility—such as Modin in
Why Are We So Blest?—or individuality—such as Abena in *Two Thousand Seasons*
or Densu in *The Healers*, they nevertheless leave very strong impressions in the
reader's memory and engage compassion to a considerable degree. If they might not
fully satisfy reader expectations based upon the European Romantic tradition of plot-
and-character-oriented narrative, it ought to be remembered that there is no
obligation for them to do so. They serve other functions. Armah's art does indeed
make use of individual characterization, perhaps most impressively in the character
of Baako in *Fragments*, but in most cases character is only meant to support and
illustrate the central messages of hope and hopelessness, of victory and defeat, and
of reciprocity, viewed under a specifically political perspective. Armah's art is a case
of *littérature engagée* displacing art for art's sake and still remaining art. As Gareth
Griffiths writes with reference to *The Beautyful Ones Are Not Yet Born*: "No
character in the novel is allowed to rise above the confusion and impenetrability of
the action" (225). It is this subordination of character under the astringent needs of
the message that makes Armah a truly political writer with a deterministic
commitment. Under this artistic principle, the differences in the relative treatment
of individual characters between the earlier and the later novels are mere variations
of such subordination. Traditional European criteria for the assessment of character
disappear behind this larger principle and become irrelevant. The best proof lies in
the figure of "the man" in *The Beautyful Ones Are Not Yet Born*: a figure lacking
many of the qualities that make a convincing literary character in the European
tradition, a figure even lacking a name, but nevertheless a most memorable
individual, a human being who invites the reader to participate in his thoughts and
feelings, decidedly not an Everyman figure. This man bridges the difference between
the individual and the community and personifies the dichotomy of the concrete and
the symbolic. The figure of Densu in *The Healers* is not his opposite but his generic
relative.

In the question of narrative technique, the five novels offer, not two opposing, but
five concurrent variations of the same central issues of beauty, hope, and community

in the face of various phases of African history from the earliest migrations of the Akan people, through slavery and colonialism to the present perils of the materialistic and political temptations of the modern world and possible paths to be taken by future African communities. This basic pattern is then approached from five different angles. What is subject to a variation of narrative technique is the time span covered, the social and individual entries to and exits from the central issue, and the narrative perspective—the "I" of the beholder.

The supposed deviations between the earlier and the later novels prove to be based on a superficial inspection and do not stand up to closer scrutiny. The differences confirmed by an analysis of theme and metaphor, of character, and of narrative technique are not differences in kind but in degree; essentially, they are rich variations of a central idea underscored by changes in mood and technical approach. *Two Thousand Seasons* and *The Healers* are as imaginative, as rewarding, and as serious as the earlier novels. They are all politically and philosophically honest and therefore true.

WORKS CITED

Achebe, Chinua. *Morning Yet on Creation Day.* London: Heinemann, 1975.
———. "The Novelist as Teacher." *Commonwealth Literature.* London, Heinemann, 1965. 202–05.
Armah, Ayi Kwei. *The Beautyful Ones Are Not Yet Born.* London: Heinemann, 1975.
———. *Fragments.* London: Heinemann, 1983.
———. *The Healers.* London: Heinemann, 1979.
———. *Two Thousand Seasons.* London: Heinemann, 1979.
———. *Why Are We So Blest?* London: Heinemann, 1974.
———. "Larsony, or Fiction as Criticism of Fiction." *Asemka* 4 (September 1976): 1–14.
Bishop, Rand. "The Beautyful Ones Are Born: Armah's First Five Novels." *World Literature Written in English* 21 (1982): 531–37.
Fraser, Robert. *The Novels of Ayi Kwei Armah: A Study in Polemical Fiction.* London: Heinemann, 1980.
Gikandi, Simon. *Reading the African Novel.* London: James Currey, 1987.
Griffiths, Gareth. "Structure and Image in Armah's *The Beautyful Ones Are Not Yet Born.*" *Ghanaian Literatures.* New York: Greenwood, 1988. 225–40.
Izevbaye, D. S. "Ayi Kwei Armah and the 'I' of the Beholder." *Ghanaian Literatures.* New York: Greenwood, 1988. 241–52.
Larson, Charles. *The Emergence of African Fiction.* 2nd ed. London: Macmillan, 1978.
Lazarus, Neil. "Pessimism of the Intellect, Optimism of the Will: A Reading of Ayi Kwei Armah's *The Beautyful Ones Are Not Yet Born.*" *Research in African Literatures* 18 (1987): 137–75.

AYI KWEI ARMAH'S PUBLISHED WORK

Novels

The Beautyful Ones Are Not Yet Born, 1968 (Translated into Swahili as *Wema Hawajazaliwa*, 1976)
Fragments, 1970
Why Are We So Blest?, 1972
Two Thousand Seasons, 1973
The Healers, 1978

Short Stories

"Contact." *The New African* 4 (December 1965): 244–46, 248.
"Asemka." *Okyeame* 3 (1966): 28–32.
"Yaw Manu's Charm." *Atlantic* (May 1968): 89–95.
"An African Fable." *Présence Africaine* 68 (1968): 192–96.

"The Offal Kind." *Harper's Magazine* (Jan. 1969): 79–84.
"Halfway to Nirvana." *West Africa* (24 Sept. 1984): 1947–48.

SELECTED CRITICAL READINGS

Ayi Kwei Armah published five novels between 1968 and 1978 and has not published another since. Even after the publication of Armah's fifth and final novel to date, extensive criticism has focused on his first novel, but there has been a steady increase in articles concerned with any one of his novels, with his entire *oeuvre*, or with his work in relation to other African writers. There are two book-length studies examining Armah's work, one by Robert Fraser (1980) and a longer and more comprehensive one by Derek Wright (1989), the most eminent critic of Armah's. Due to the considerable number of articles and because many were published in journals not easily available, the following list represents a selection of the most relevant and accessible criticism. The most comprehensive and up-to-date bibliography of secondary material appears in Wright's book.

Amuta, Chidi. "The Contemporary African Artist in Armah's Novels." *World Literature Written in English* 21 (1982): 467–76. Interprets the visionary artist figures in Armah's five novels, beginning with the latest two novels. Justifies this with reference to the role of the artist in contemporary African society. Finds that, in the social and metaphysical totality depicted in *Two Thousand Seasons* and *The Healers*, art is implicit and integral to the rituals of everyday life, whereas the contemporary African reality of the first three novels makes the artist's life an epic quest for relevance. Sees a cardinal contradiction in Armah's visionary protagonists.

Bishop, Rand. "The Beautyful Ones Are Born: Armah's First Five Novels." *World Literature Written in English* 21 (1982): 531–37. Reviews Robert Fraser's book but gives separate interpretation of Armah's novels. Finds The *Healers* the least satisfying of the five novels because of the breakdown of formal control expressed by the excessive recounting of dreams and by the failure to resolve the dual plot. Praises Fraser for demonstrating the interrelatedness of Armah's novels, which are seen as forming a great scheme.

Booth, James. "*Why Are We So Blest?* and the Limits of Metaphor." *Journal of Commonwealth Literature* 15.1 (1980): 50–64. Investigates the inherent racism in Armah's third novel: The characters are found to play their preordained parts in a macabre and morbid drama dictated by their race. Places this novel in Chinua Achebe's category of malignant fiction, because it seems to elevate its case history into a universal metaphor of relations between white and black. Stresses the metaphoric power of the end of the novel, which leads to the even more clearly negative definition of Africanness in Armah's next novel.

Chetin, Sara. "Armah's Women." *Kunapipi* 6.3 (1984): 47–56. Examines the female characters in *Fragments*, who all have some strength and appear to want to save Baako from his misery. Finds that Armah seems unable to see women as anything apart from healers and destroyers. Concludes that Armah, like the other male writers from Africa, merely perpetuates specific male stereotypes of women and presents distortions of femaleness.

Collins, Harold R. "The Ironic Imagery of Armah's *The Beautyful Ones Are Not Yet Born*: The Putrescent Vision." *World Literature Written in English* 20 (1971): 37–50. Argues that the prevailing critical impression of Armah's first novel being full of Ghanaian excrement, filth, and stench on every page does not stand up to closer scrutiny. Employs Northrop Frye's concept of the ironic mode to the novel's excremental imagery. Also finds qualifying elements of beauty to compensate for the ugliness in the novel. Concludes that the chosen mode of fiction justifies the conspicuous images of nastiness.

Colmer, Rosemary. "The Human and the Divine: Fragments and *Why Are We So Blest?*" *Kunapipi* 2.2 (1980): 77–90. Traces the plots and major images in Armah's second and third novels. Asserts that both novels are strongly influenced by Frantz Fanon's studies. Finds that the central images of *Fragments* involve the idea of communication between the mundane and the divine realms, and those of *Why Are We So Blest?* depend on the dividing line between the human and the divine.

Fraser, Robert. "The American Background in *Why Are We So Blest?*" *African Literature Today* 9 (1978): 39–46. Explores the American connections at work in Armah's third novel, particularly the ill-advised alliance between Modin and Aimee. Finds a harsh undercurrent in the dialectic that forces the characters into irreconcilable camps leading to segregation. Traces influences of Frantz Fanon and the Black Muslim Movement, comparing Armah to James Baldwin.

———. *The Novels of Ayi Kwei Armah: A Study in Polemical Fiction.* London: Heinemann, 1980. Introduces Armah's five novels chronologically and examines in particular the developments in theme and narrative technique from an early preoccupation with the artist figure in the European Romantic tradition to an increasing use of the plural voice. Presents Armah's indebtedness to Frantz Fanon's theories of neo-colonialism and the inferiority feelings of colonized peoples. Concludes that Armah's work attempts to fulfill the difficult task of the novel couched in the English language in postcolonial Africa by introducing a heightened form of the historical novel, but Armah pays too high a qualitative price for the dogmatic thrust in his last novels.

Gikandi, Simon. "The Parabolical Narrative: Character and Consciousness in the Novels of Camara Laye and Ayi Kwei Armah." *Reading the African Novel.* London: James Currey, 1987. 1–40. Compares Armah and Laye by showing the effectiveness of the latter's private mythology and the former's historical myths as instruments of interpreting the African experience. Underscores the functionality of the dramatic and narrative devices that both novelists utilize. Examines in particular the narrative voice in *Two Thousand Seasons* and the relation between history and character in *The Healers.*

———. "The Subjective Narrative: Exile and Alienation in the Novels of Wole Soyinka and the Early Ayi Kwei Armah." *Reading the African Novel.* London: James Currey, 1987. 72–110. Compares Armah and Soyinka as novelists who are both opposed to alienation on an ideological level but who tend to confront it nakedly in their works. Asserts that they are not formalists but among the most stylish prose writers in Africa today, using form as an integral part of value and meaning. Examines in particular the themes of loneliness and isolation in Armah's first novel, illusion and experience in his second, and the consciousness of failure in the third.

Goldie, Terry. "A Connection of Images: The Structure of Symbols in *The Beautyful Ones Are Not Yet Born.*" *Kunapipi* 1.1 (1979): 94–107. Examines the dominant imagery in Armah's first novel: images of communication and journeying, images of numbness and sleep, images of light and dark, images of excrement and filth, and images of the sea. Finds that these image patterns lead to the major thematic concerns of hope and hopelessness and of victory and defeat, which are finally brought together into a meaningful whole in the last pages.

Griffiths, Gareth. "Structure and Image in Armah's *The Beautyful Ones Are Not Yet Born.*" *Studies in Black Literature* 2 (1971): 1–9. Rept. in *Ghanaian Literatures.* New York, 1988. 225–40. Traces the imagery and its employment as the main structuring device in Armah's first novel, arguing that no character in the novel is allowed to rise above the confusion and impenetrability of the action. Asserts that the interest of the book lies firmly in the existential rather than the political dimension. Pinpoints the predominant metaphor as one of ingestion, digestion, and excretion, linked to the theme of corruption and bribery. Examines three distinct sections of the novel, with chapter six as pivotal.

Izevbaye, D. S. "Ayi Kwei Armah and the 'I' of the Beholder." *A Celebration of Black and African Writing.* Oxford: Oxford UP, 1975. 232–44. Reprinted in *Ghanaian Literatures.* New York: Greenwood, 1988. 241–52. Investigates the theme of beauty and its connection with the eye of the beholder as a central issue in Armah's first four novels. Distinguishes between an active, external beauty whose power makes the beholder's eye a mere receiver of impressions and a passive ideal beauty hidden in nature, thus challenging the beholder's ability to penetrate the object to the beauty beyond.

Johnson, Joyce. "The Promethean 'Factor' in Ayi Kwei Armah's *Fragments* and *Why Are We So Blest?*" *World Literature Written in English* 21 (1982): 497–510. Explores the myth of Prometheus as used by Armah in his second and third novels for the depiction of the attempt of a conscientious intellectual to dissociate himself from the new political elite in order to serve the interests of the people. Finds that Armah's interpretation of the myth differs from the traditional Western one, Armah's futile Promethean hero being merely the vector of a foreign culture.

Kibera, Leonard. "Pessimism and the African Novelist: Ayi Kwei Armah's *The Beautyful Ones Are Not Yet Born.*" *Journal of Commonwealth Literature* 14.1 (1979): 64–72. Argues that Armah's first novel presents the African world as static, unfeeling, and pessimistic. Finds that the novel is not a moral fable in which the good could remain good or even triumphant but, as in Frantz Fanon's work, man is defined by that which he hates. Concludes that the novel lacks development and significant plot.

Lazarus, Neil. "Pessimism of the Intellect, Optimism of the Will: A Reading of Ayi Kwei Armah's *The Beautyful Ones Are Not Yet Born.*" *Research in African Literatures* 18 (1987): 137–75. Argues convincingly that *The Beautyful Ones Are Not Yet Born* depends for its effect upon the reciprocity of its ordering categories, with the glorious future of the "beautyful ones" already being found implicitly in the degradation of the real world as presented through the protagonist's experience. Relegates the alleged pessimism of the novel into a position of relativity by appreciating the potency of the titular "not yet."

Lobb, Edward. "Armah's *Fragments* and the Vision of the Whole." *Ariel* 10.1 (1979): 25–38. Interprets the structure of Armah's second novel and the relation of images and themes within this structure. Finds that the novel is based on the principles of ambiguity and contradiction and that it reflects the problem of developing a viewpoint that will encompass reality without plunging the viewer into despair.

McEwan, Neil. "Independence: Soyinka, Achebe, Armah." *Africa and the Novel* London: Macmillan, 1983. 61–101. Discusses Achebe's attack on Armah's first novel as "a sick book." Argues that the book's subject is poverty and its temptations and that it is mainly concerned with a state of mind. Concludes that, whereas Achebe and Soyinka offer more complete and satisfying modern African worlds, Armah's narrower and more painful work is no less African and no less modern.

Petersen, Kirsten Holst. "Loss and Frustration: An Analysis of A. K. Armah's *Fragments*." *Kunapipi* 1.1 (1979): 53–65. Analyzes the broken time sequence of *Fragments* as the clue to the significance of the main metaphor of the novel: the contrast between, and the overlapping of, the circular and the linear principle—two areas corresponding to two world views, the traditional African and the modern Western outlook respectively. Interprets the book's use of the cargo cult and of Frantz Fanon's theories.

Priebe, Richard. "Escaping the Nightmare of History: The Development of a Mythic Consciousness in West African Literature." *Ariel* 4.2 (1973): 55–67. Places Armah, together with Wole Soyinka and Kofi Awoonor, in a mainstream mode of African literature that can be traced to Amos Tutuola. Finds that these writers, despite their apparent differences, have much in common in their use of myth, demonic and apocalyptic imagery, and language.

Sekyi-Otu, Ato. "'Toward Anoa . . . Not Back to Anoa': The Grammar of Revolutionary Homecoming in *Two Thousand Seasons*." *Research in African Literatures* 18 (1987): 192–214. Examines the strategic use of language in *Two Thousand Seasons* and argues that the novel ought not to be read as a teleological narrative governed by an allegorical scheme analogous to the "messianic triad" of "Origin, Fall, and Redemption." Contests the dominant interpretation of the "concluding" action of the narrative as presenting an apocalyptic vision of a final reconciliation.

Wright, Derek. "Orality in the African Historical Novel: Yambo Ouologuem's *Bound to Violence* and Ayi Kwei Armah's *Two Thousand Seasons*." *Journal of Commonwealth Literature* 23.1 (1988): 91–101. With references to Ouologuem's novel, focuses on the aspect of simulated orality, interpreting *Two Thousand Seasons* as an innovative, pseudo-oral narrative, a simulated exercise, a literary affectation imitating the griot's didactic communal narrative and straining to reproduce an illusion of orality. Finds that Armah's scriptural chant suffers from a kind of hermetic banality, a rhetorical stutter that repeats but reveals little and exhorts without enlightening and that Armah does not so much as record history as re-invent it.

_____. *Ayi Kwei Armah's Africa: The Sources of His Fiction.* London: Hans Zell, 1989. Offers a detailed and comprehensive interpretation of Armah's work to date. Answers the charges made by Chinua Achebe and his disciples on the (lack of) authenticity and Africanness of Armah's language and social vision. Shows how Armah exposes the Westernized corruption of traditional family values not only in Nkrumah's Ghana but in West African society in general. Analyzes Armah's short stories, essays, and novels and demonstrates the ritual background and the Akan sources of his fiction. Places an emphasis on the discontinuity of Armah's literary career and exposes the decline in performance Armah has moved away from his earlier awareness of the delimited value of traditional culture. Argues that Armah's choice of an alternative genre in his later novels also means a loss of subtlety and complexity in both symbolism and characterization.

—RUDOLF BADER

Ngugi wa Thiong'o

Ngugi wa Thiong'o (christened James Ngugi) was born in Kamarithu, Kenya, 5 January 1938. He was educated at Gukuyu Karig'a School, Alliance High School, and Makerere University College, Kampala, Uganda. During his student days he wrote *The Black Hermit*, a play in celebration of Uganda's independence, and in his final college year he was editor of the student literary magazine, *Penpoint*.

In 1964 he worked for *The Sunday Nation* newspaper in Nairobi before entering Leeds University in England. In 1968 he was appointed lecturer in the Department of English, University College, Nairobi, but resigned in 1969 in protest against government interference with academic freedom. In the same year he entered Northwestern University in the United States. He remained there until 1971, when he returned to Nairobi as a lecturer in the Department of Literature at the University of Nairobi. In 1972 he became Acting Head of the Department.

On 31 December 1977, he was placed in detention by Kenyan police and was released on 12 December 1978. Since then he has lived in exile, mostly in London.

WRITING DOWN THE BARREL OF A PEN

Ngugi's writing proceeds from the conviction that there is, in his words, "no room for 'art for art's sake,'" that "the very act of writing is a social act." He goes on to say that "As a writer one tries to see the factors that impinge on a human being . . . the kind of social structure that breeds the various kinds of conflicts and tensions we have in this society and how we can transform the structure so that some of the conflicts might be eliminated" (*Writers* x). Ngugi's career has followed along the lines suggested in these words, for social purpose has always guided the writing of his novels and plays, first in English and then, as this purpose sharpened, in the Gikuyu language. His fiction traces the evolution of modern Kenya from its pre-colonial beginnings to the present, from the alienating effects of British Christian Imperial annexation to the betrayal of the Kenyan people by a small *comprador* class of Kenyans who thrive in cynical association with overseas financial interests.

Ngugi's reputation as a writer derives principally from his fiction. But to understand the full weight and depth of his literary achievement, one ought also to read the nonfiction—*Homecoming, Writers in Politics, Detained, Barrel of a Pen*, and *Decolonising the Mind*—as a gloss on the imaginative work.

The River Between is Ngugi's first novel (although published after *Weep Not Child*, 1964), and initiates a sequence of novels that fit loosely together to trace the history of Kenya from the period of the first colonial incursions. It tells the story of a rivalry between two Kikuyu villages—the villagers of Kameno who retain their traditional culture and religious beliefs and those who live on Makuyu ridge and are Christians. The enmity of the two groups is focused on the antagonism between Joshua, the leader of the Christians and a fierce, unswerving convert to the faith, and Kabonyi, who is equally zealous in protecting traditional faith from foreign corruption. To further the conflict, the Christian missionaries have arrived to preach their gospel and have established western-style schools that challenge traditional authority; and the British colonial government has introduced severe taxes, which set into motion the progressive alienation of the Kikuyu from their land. Poised between these groups is Waiyaki, the novel's protagonist, who seeks through his particular blend of Kikuyu and Christian religion the reconciliation of the opposing elements. He believes his father's enjoinder that he is "the son who shall arrive among the clan" whose "duty shall be to save the people" (*River Between* 20). He founds a series of Kikuyu Independent Schools to promote education among his people. But his single-minded enthusiasm for his quest blinds him to the political realities of the confrontation between the villages, between Christians led by Joshua and the tribalists led by Kabonyi. Moreover, by falling in love with Nyambura, the daughter of Joshua, he ends all hope of reconciling the two fierce ideologues, Joshua and Kabonyi. Ultimately, he and Nyambura are repudiated by their people and condemned to die.

Through the novel, Ngugi shows the effects of tribalism, racialism, and religious factionalism, which have their origins in the colonial policy of divide and rule, and he dramatizes the effect of these antagonisms on the sensibilities of individuals and their relationships. He depicts, as well, the beginnings of resistance to colonial rule by Kenyans, as they quickly recognize the deleterious effect of foreign intrusion on their society. Finally, Ngugi begins here an examination of the Christian myth and message in light of its analogies with the Kikuyu creation myth; this theme, in constantly transmuted or revised form, remains a dominant element throughout his writing.

The theme is further elaborated in Ngugi's first published novel, *Weep Not, Child.* Here, too, Ngugi explores the correspondences between the Kikuyu and Christian religions, and seeks a reconciliation through education in the messianic role that the book's hero, Njoroge, conceives for himself. The novel is set in Kenya before and during the War of Independence. Against this background of armed struggle, the young Njoroge's conviction that the future for his family and the village "rested not only on a hope for sound education but also on the belief in a God of love and mercy, who long ago walked the earth with Gikuyu and Mumbi, or Adam and Eve" (55) is subsumed by the struggle and ultimately destroyed. Ngugi reveals the physical and psychological violence experienced by all the participants in the struggle for Independence, conveyed principally through the experiences of Njoroge. His story runs parallel to and eventually intersects with the larger events of the adult world. At the close of the novel, Njoroge's messianic dream lies in ruins, his father and brother are dead, and his home is destroyed. He is saved from suicide by his mother, the only remaining member of his family.

A Grain of Wheat, a novel of astonishing complexity and craftsmanship, elaborates further the Independence struggle. In a narrative that moves quickly and easily back and forth between time periods, Ngugi encapsulates the historical processes that led to the Independence struggle, revealing the struggle in a vivid textual present by invoking a variety of technical devices—narration, interior monologues, dialogue, recollections, and anecdotes. And while he is at pains to provide an authentic fictional record of this crucial period in Kenya's history, Ngugi is equally interested in the fragility of human life and personal relationships.

The novel, set in Kenya in the four days leading up to the country's Independence celebrations, dramatizes and relays the actions, thoughts, and sufferings of four principal characters—Mugo, Mumbi, Gikonyo, and Karanja—as they have cause to review their lives in light of the coming Independence and especially in light of their recollections of Mumbi's brother Kihika, a renowned freedom fighter and a boyhood friend of the men. Through Kihika and the manner in which he uses a familiarity with Christian teaching to turn the arguments of the Christians against themselves, Ngugi explores further his conviction that Christian doctrine was used to lead the people away from the land and to seduce them into accepting European policies.

The political theme of the novel is balanced by various personal relationships that center on the betrayal of people and of ideals. First, it traces the betrayal of Kihika by Mugo, the most prominent figure in the book because he is the most guilt-ridden. Mugo, during the Independence struggle, betrays Kihika to the colonial authorities in a fit of jealousy, then lives out his guilt until he finally makes a public confession at the Uhuru Day celebrations at Independence, thereby achieving a cleansing release and, ironically, saving the life of Karanja, an apostate of the Independence cause and former colonial servant thought to be Kihika's betrayer. The novel tells, too, of Gikonya's betrayal of the Independence struggle for the love of Mumbi who, on hearing of his release from prison, gives herself to Karanja, an act of treachery in the eyes of Gikonya. He bears the pain of this betrayal in his heart until Mugo unwittingly but silently acts as confessor to both himself and Mumbi; and they, after Mugo's confession and their recognition of the weight of guilt he has born, find that they can start to come to terms with their own limitations. Mugo, paradoxically, is the closest Ngugi comes to creating the messiah who carries his people's burden of guilt. Joseph Conrad's influence on Ngugi has been frequently noted, and it is nowhere more apparent than in *A Grain of Wheat*, where the sources of individual guilt are revealed gradually, then followed by expiation of various kinds.

As with Ngugi's earlier novels (and those that follow), an end forecasts a beginning. General R's confused questioning—"I know even now that this war is not ended. We get Uhuru today. Tomorrow we shall ask: Where is the land? Where is the food? Where are the schools?" (191–92)—suggests at the end of *A Grain of Wheat* the development of a political context in which Kenyan will be pitted against Kenyan.

In 1967, in a comment that bridges the gap between *A Grain of Wheat* and *Petals of Blood*, and anticipates the subject matter of *Devil on a Cross*, *I Will Marry When I Want* (Ngaahika Ndeenda), and *Matagari*, Ngugi said:

> Colonisation has three stages. The first is one of acceptance . . . the second stage is . . . [one] of rivalry and challenge. The coloured people begin to challenge the assumptions of the coloniser. . . . Then

you come to the third stage where the coloniser realizes the game is up. So he quickly makes arrangements with the nationalist elite and gives them independence. But for the peasants who are really the base of the whole struggle, this is not real independence but a realisation that they are still exploited and the struggle has got to start all over again. (Marcuson iii)

Petals of Blood is the culminating point in the themes Ngugi has examined in his previous fiction. As well, it is his last piece of imaginative writing in English; the novels that follow, *Devil on a Cross* and *Matagari*, were published first in Gikuyu and subsequently in English translations done by Ngugi, as was the play *Ngaahika Ndeenda*. About his decision to abandon English as the primary language for his imaginative writing Ngugi said:

In my previous books, and to some extent *Petals of Blood*, I was writing about peasants of Kenya and their experience of History. But the language I used (English) excluded them as a target-audience.

. . .

I would like to be able to continue to write for the consumption of ordinary people in a language they can understand. As for content, I would like to continue to articulate their aspirations for a better quality of life. (*Detained* 98)

In *Petals of Blood*, Ngugi's themes are religion, both tribal and Christian; education, both formal and informal; the alienation of the Kikuyu from their land, both as an historical process of colonialism and a continuing process through the actions of the Kenyan bourgeoise entrepreneurs; the struggle for Independence and the price paid to achieve it; the nature and cost of modernity as this coincides with the emergence of a Kenyan middle class; the need for a new independence struggle to be fostered by the peasants and workers of Kenya. The latter group is the audience Ngugi wants to reach, for his appeal is to them. Judging from the fact that his books have been banned and he has been forced to spend the past dozen years in exile, it would appear his appeal has been understood, at least by the authorities.

Petals of Blood, like *A Grain of Wheat*, tells the interconnected stories of four principal characters—Wanja, Karega, Munira, and Abdulla—from the time of Independence almost up to the present; in the process it reveals their relationships with a host of other characters in Nairobi and in Ilmorog. Ilmorog is depicted as a typical rural village emerging into a New Ilmorog, which represents the worst excesses of modern development resulting from the creation of a class structure more insidious than that fostered by the British colonizers but which is its predictable apotheosis.

Ngugi castigates relentlessly and furiously the cynical political posturing and heartless commercialism of modern Kenya's politicians, who are the inheritors of the political machinations of Jomo Kenyatta (the father of Kenyan independence) in the last stages of his apostasy, as Ngugi describes it in *Detained* and *Writers in Politics*. The Marxist rhetoric of Ngugi's indictment is humanized by his compassionate understanding and depiction of the lives of the people, first as peasants and then as workers, who are made victims of a remorseless and soulless capitalism. The novel ends with a passionate plea to the peasants and workers to rise in unified militant protest against their oppressors.

The narrative unfolds in the form of a crime-thriller, opening with the murder of three industrial and economic leaders of the new Kenya—Kimeria, Mzigo, and Chui—and the arrest of four principal suspects—Munira, Karega, Abdulla, and Wanja. The narrative shifts backwards and forwards in time, as it did in *A Grain of Wheat,* and adopts a variety of narrative and temporal perspectives. The present-day action takes place over ten days; but the lives of the principal characters are revealed over a twelve year span, thus expanding the sweep of the frame by moving through Kenya's history from colonial times to the present.

Ngugi creates two basic groups—the exploiters and the exploited—and through his castigation of the former—Chui, Mzigo, Kimeria and the debased M.P. Nderi wa Rieri—asserts his faith in the potential of the latter—Karega, the young Joseph, foster child to Abdulla, and the as yet (and perhaps appropriately) faceless peasants and workers—to build the just society. The novel also celebrates the glory of the sacrifices made by the survivors of the Independence struggle.

In between the publication of *Petals of Blood* and *Devil on a Cross,* Ngugi with a namesake, Ngugi wa Mirii, collaborated in the writing and producing of the play *I Will Marry When I Want (Ngaahika Ndeenda).* He had earlier collaborated with a colleague, Micere Mugo, in writing and producing *The Trial of Dedan Kimathi,* which enjoyed a popular success in Nairobi. The earlier play seeks to restore to its proper place in Kenyan history the reputation of Dedan Kimathi, the Mau Mau general despised by the British because he was so successful in the struggle against their rule. The play intends as well to show to a younger generation of Kenyans the debt they owe to Kimathi and his fellow freedom fighters. And it is a call to arms to the exploited masses in contemporary Kenya, as it castigates the Kenyan capitalist system for its seduction of the innocent masses and reveals a special scorn for Christianity as an agent of capitalist collusion. In the present, the historical Kimathi continues as a revolutionary leader, a voice to inspire the suppressed.

In the latter respect *The Trial of Dedan Kimathi* resembles *I Will Marry When I Want (Ngaahika Ndeenda).* This play exposes the exploitation of simple folk—here represented by the laborer Kiguunda (a former freedom fighter), his wife Wangeei, and daughter Gatoni—by foreign capitalists in league with the Kenyan entrepreneurial class represented by Kioi, a wealthy businessman, his wife Jezebel, and their son John Muhuumi. When a marriage between Gatoni and John Muhuumi is arranged and when money is needed for a proper Christian wedding, Kiguunda mortgages his land. But the wedding fails to take place once Gatoni is found pregnant by John Muhuumi and he rejects her; the bank then forecloses on the land, Kiguunda's only valuable possession, and he is left with the worthless trappings of modern clothing and furniture. Here again Christianity serves as the agent of capitalist exploitation, and authors are relentless in exposing its duplicity and hypocrisy.

Ngugi's writing develops logically and systematically, and in *Devil on a Cross* he takes up where *Petals of Blood* left off (as he did in the case of *A Grain of Wheat* and *Petals of Blood*). In this translation of his first Gikuyu novel, *Caitani Mutharabaina,*

Ngugi tells the story of Wariinga, a victim of the brutality of Kenyan neo-colonialism and male sexism, of her survival and her eventual triumph over both the social world in which she is forced to operate and over her recurrent nightmare vision of the crucified Devil on the Cross being removed by black men who acquire a measure of his exploitative cunning. The ambiguity and irresoluteness of Ngugi's responses to Christianity, along with his fury over the betrayal of the inherent redemptive potential in the Christian religion, create a containing metaphor for the novel. In this version, it is the Devil who returns to earth to offer guidance and redemption and the kind of commercialized, secularized heaven the contemporary world demands. The Christian myth is challenged most forcefully in the novel when Gatuiria says to Wariinga ". . . it doesn't really matter if the devil exists or if he's merely a certain image of the world"; and the ambiguity between good and evil is specified by The Voice that speaks to Wariinga:

> . . . the nature of God is the image of the good we do here on Earth.
> The nature of Satan is the image of all the evil we do here on earth.
> The question is: what are evil actions and what are good actions?
> (97)

Wariinga becomes Ngugi's armed avenger when she assassinates her fiance's father, her first seducer and the epitome of the malevolent forces behind modern capitalism.

Running parallel to the realistic plot that records Wariinga's encounters is the comic and satiric horror of the scenes devoted to the Devil's Feast. Swiftian in its abundance of invention and invective, the Devil's Feast is held to decide who is the greatest exploiter of the people, judged not only by methods currently practiced but also by proposals put forward for greater, more ruthless exploitation in the future. The contestant-exploiters go from one excess to greater excesses—making proposals for selling citizens land on which to grow their foodstuffs and bottled air for them to breathe; for tiny "birds-nests" for houses that would turn the people into nomads; for gaining total control of human organs so the elite may preserve their lives at the expense of the multitude; for sedating the people through programs of religion, education, and false culture in order to have their blood and sweat drawn from them and sold on the market—a suggestion that The Voice tells Wariinga is derived from the Christian celebration of the body and the blood of Christ. But the contestants are eventually forced to flee the cave when the workers and peasants descend on them. The scene, Ngugi tells us, is emblematic of the struggle of interest groups in Kenya:

> Until democratic-minded Kenyans, workers, peasants, students, progressive intellectuals and others, unite on the most minimum basis of a patriotic opposition to imperialist foreign domination of our economy, politics and culture, things will not get better but worse, no matter who sits on the throne of power. No country can consider itself politically independent for as long as its economy and culture are dominated by foreign interests. (*Detained* xv)

In *Matagari*, Ngugi's most recent novel ". . . la lutta continuua" [the struggle continues]. Translated from the original Gikuyu—Ngugi dedicates the novel "to all those committed to the development of the languages of all the African peoples"— the book follows from and displays the same political commitment and ideology as *Devil on the Cross* and the nonfiction political books, *Detained, Writers in Politics, Barrel of a Pen,* and *Decolonising the Mind,* which were written in English.

Ngugi tells his "Reader/Listener" that the story is imaginary in its actions, characters, and country; that it has no fixed time, no fixed space, and that it "does not demarcate time in terms of seconds or minutes or hours or days" (*Matagari* ix). These last two admonishments are appropriate because action in the novel moves with a fluidity through time and space appropriate to myth and/or legend. For this is the mythic story of the legendary Matagari, an embodiment of the virtues, the values, and the moral purity of the downtrodden masses he seeks to inspire. While it is true to say that the story is imaginary in its actions and characters, it is less so to say that the country is not real. Whatever analogies readers discern between what goes on in the novel's imaginary land and other places, the country is plainly Kenya; so, for that matter, are the characters—in name, in circumstances, in language, and especially in the historical circumstances that account for the present action of the novel.

Above all, Ngugi takes up his quest for a society based on Truth and Justice for all, for equity and fair return to those who create the wealth of the society. What he wants, therefore, is a reversal of the situation in contemporary Kenya: a society wherein a privileged few—the *comprador* bourgeoisie in league with international capitalists—exploit and oppress the workers and peasants and repudiate those who fought and won the War of Independence.

Matagari—his full name is Matagari wa Njiruungi, "he who survived the bullets"—is the embodiment of that struggle. He returns from the forest, buries his weapons, puts on the belt of peace, and moves through the country seeking his family—that is, the free Kenyan people. Only when he finds them will he return to his home. Along the way he meets the dispossessed: children forced to live in used car dumps, union leaders harassed by the security police and sometimes murdered by them, young women forced into prostitution, and so on. Ranged against these victims of the system are the wealthy few: the heirs of the white colonists, those Kenyans now grown rich through collusion, the black politicians who preach a doctrine of truth and justice that is blatantly self-serving. Ngugi also offers variant treatment on themes familiar in his writing, such as the apostasy of the Christian church in alleviating the suffering of the needy and the failure of western education to achieve the same necessary end.

In this novel, Ngugi exploits the Christian legend in varied ways, for the biblical story provides the containing metaphor of the book. Matagari is a modern-day Jesus who suffers the little children to come unto him, but even though the people want a savior, they, like those who looked for the militant savior of Biblical times, fail to recognize him when he moves among them. When Matagari is arrested, he is jailed with ten detainees who are equated with the Apostles of Jesus. These are people who in their various roles as teacher, student, and union worker ought to work for the benefit of society. Indeed they have tried and that is why they are in prison; but they recant when pressure is put on them and then reverse their stand at the further recognition of Matagari's legendary and magical power. The biblical allusions or coordinates are sustained throughout the scenes in prison. For example, one among the prisoners is an informer, a Judas figure. In another instance, when Matagari produces food and drink for the hungry prisoners, his sharing is recognized as a last supper by the drunkard who says: "This is my body, which I give to you. Do this unto one another until the Second Coming. He then took the cup, and after blessing it he said: And this cup is a testament of the covenant we entered with one another with our blood. Do this until our kingdom comes, through the will of the people!" When Matagari and the others are mysteriously set free from prison, their experience is compared to the biblical account of Saint Paul's prison escape. Finally, as he departs, Matagari tells them: "You will see me again after only three days" (57).

Ngugi's familiar use of Biblical materials is evident in all his writing and proceeds from the naive faith of the young Njoroge in *Weep Not, Child* through to what some might construe as blasphemy in *Devil on a Cross.* Is Ngugi using the biblical analogies to attack a religion that betrayed him? Or can he serve his rhetorical purposes better by basing his story on familiar materials and therefore persuade his readers?

Whether or not there is ambiguity in his use of biblical materials, there is no ambiguity in his dealing with Settler Williams, a partner in exploitation with John Boy, Jr.—both directors of three international banking and finance institutions whose acronyms are AICI, ACIO, and BUI, when translated from the Gikuyu mean "The Real Thieves." The third member of the trio is the Minister of Truth and Justice, who describes himself as "An African Anglophile and Proud of It," and who preaches, surrounded by armed guards and toadies in the form of academicians and ministers of the church, a doctrine called "Parrotry." His daily admonishments to the populace are published in the sole national newspaper, *The Daily Parrot.* According to the Minister, the true patriots in the Independence struggle were the collaborators with the colonialists, and it is their postcolonial liaisons that account for the current affluent state of the country.

The Swiftian ironies are familiar to readers of *Devil on a Cross.* While they appear obvious and heavy handed as literary devices, there is no way of knowing how the audience at which they are aimed receives them, except to cite the author himself in his "Note on the English Edition" of *Matagari*:

> The novel was published in the Gikuyu-language original in Kenya in October 1986. By January 1987, intelligence reports had it that peasants in Central Kenya were whispering and talking about a man called Matagari who was roaming the whole country making demands about truth and justice. There were orders for his immediate arrest, but police discovered that Matagari was only a fictional character in a book of the same name. In February 1987, the police raided all the bookshops and seized every copy of the novel.
>
> Matagari, the fictional hero, and the novel, his only habitation, have been effectively banned in Kenya. With the publication of the

English edition, they have joined their author in exile. (*Matagari* viii)

Ngugi is a serious and passionately committed writer, unflinching in his message and undeviating in the conveyance of it. His powerful attack on neocolonialism provides a metaphor for other countries where the economic disparity between rich and poor, foisted on an uneducated class in need of the kind of education this book provides, is untenable, where the people stand in need of a champion—a Matagari. Ngugi's faith in the reformist possibilities of the oppressed—the ordinary people— is unequivocal. His hope for the future is unshakeable: "There is no night so dark that it does not end in dawn." And his stance is militant: "Justice for the oppressed comes from a sharpened spear" (Matagari 131).

WORKS CITED

Ngugi wa Thiong'o. *Detained: A Writer's Prison Diary*. London: Heinemann, 1981.
———. *Devil on a Cross*. London: Heinemann, 1982.
———. *A Grain of Wheat*. London: Heinemann, 1967.
———. *Matagari*. London: Heinemann, 1987.
———. *The River Between*. London: Heinemann, 1965.
———. *Weep Not, Child*. London: Heinemann, 1964.
———. *Writers in Politics*. London: Heinemann, 1981.
Marcuson, Alan, and others. "James Ngugi Interviewed at Leeds University." *CulEA* 31 (1967): i–v.

NGUGI WA THIONG'O'S PUBLISHED WORK

Novels

Weep Not, Child, 1964
The River Between, 1965
A Grain of Wheat, 1967
Petals of Blood, 1977
Devil on a Cross (*Caitani Mutharabaina*), 1982
Matagari, 1987

Plays

The Trial of Dedan Kimathi (with Micere Mugo), 1977
I Will Marry When I Want (*Ngaahika Ndeenda*) (with Ngugi wa Mirii), 1982

Political Commentary

Detained: A Writer's Prison Diary, 1981
Writers in Politics, 1981
Barrel of a Pen: Resistance to Oppression in Neo-Colonial Kenya, 1983
Decolonising the Mind: The Politics of Language in African Literature, 1986

SELECTED CRITICAL READINGS

The most comprehensive source of information about Ngugi's writing is *Black African Literature in English*, edited in three volumes by Bernth Lindfors. Needless to say, the critical response to Ngugi's writing is extensive. That listed below constitutes some of the most accessible and basic material.

Cochrane, Judith. "Women as Guardians of the Tribe in Ngugi's Novels." *ACLALS Bulletin* 4 (1977): 1–11. First article to pay specific attention to the role of women in Ngugi's early fiction; still a reliable guide to those values that inform subsequent presentations.

Cook, David, and Michael Okenimpke. *Ngugi wa Thiong'o: An Explanation of His Writing.* London: Heinemann, 1982. First literary biography of Ngugi, offering a comprehensive exegesis of the text in relation to the author's life.

Durix, J.P. "Politics in *Petals of Blood.*" *Echos du Commonwealth* 6 (1980–81): 98–115. Comprehensive discussion of the function of politics in Ngugi's epic novel.

Killam, G.D. *An Introduction to the Writings of Ngugi.* London: Heinemann, 1980. Discussion of Ngugi's fiction to the publication of *Petals of Blood*, tracing literary and biographical influences in relation to the fiction, plays, and short stories.

————. "Ngugi wa Thiong'o." *The Writing of East and Central Africa.* London: Heinemann, 1964. 123–43. Places Ngugi's writing in the context of the development of East and Central African writing. (Also contains essays on Ugandan, Tanzanian, Zambian, Mauritian, and Zimbabwean writing)

Nazareth, Peter. "Imperialism, Race and Class: A Literary Illustration of the Ideas of *Homecoming* by Ngugi wa Thiong'o." *Joliso* 1.1 (1973): 25–34. Considers the development of Ngugi's literary and political beliefs in light of the essays in his first volume of criticism.

Robson, C.B. *Ngugi wa Thiong'o.* London: Macmillan, 1979. First book-length study of Ngugi's writing, covering all aspects of his work.

Sekyi-Otu, Ato. "The Refusal of Agency: The Founding Narrative and Waiyaki's Tragedy in *The River Between.*" *Research in African Literatures* 16 (1985): 157–78. Considers the seminal position in the Ngugi canon of his first and least discussed novel.

Sharma, G.N. "Ngugi's Christian Vision: Theme and Pattern in *A Grain of Wheat.*" *African Literature Today* 10 (1979): 167–76; "Ngugi's Apocalypse, Marxism, Christianity and African Utopianism in *Petals of Blood.*" *World Literature Written in English* 18 (1979): 302–14. Sharma's two articles address the effect of Ngugi's concern with reconciling beliefs of his Christian upbringing with the postulates of Marxism in advancing the idea of a just African society.

Sicherman, Carol M. "Ngugi wa Thiong'o and the Writing of Kenyan History." *Research in African Literatures* 20 (1989): 347–70. Traces in detail the development of Ngugi's understanding of "the role of history in African literature and of his own role in the rewriting of Kenyan history."

—G.D. KILLAM

Nuruddin Farah

N uruddin Farah was born in 1945 in Baidoa, Italian Somaliland. He was born in a period of rapid change, which would see national boundaries redrawn, new political movements ascendant, and the public repudiation of the tribal loyalties that still, in fact, surreptitiously control political life. On 1 July 1960 the British and Italian Somali territories were united to form Somalia; Somali people live also in Djibouti, northern Kenya, and the Ogaden. Farah is deeply interested in recent Somali history and in contemporary politics. His first novel is set on the eve of Independence, his fifth harks back to Somali resistance to the Italian colonists, and his most recent takes place against the background of the conflict in Ethiopia.

Farah is familiar with Somali literary traditions, which are exclusively oral, since the Somali language had no accepted script until the early 1970s. At the time he began writing, at about eighteen, Farah had little choice but to write in a foreign language. He is multilingual, and might have chosen to write in Arabic or Italian, but the major part of his published writing has been in English. He attributes his decision to write in English to the fact that English-script typewriters were more readily available than Arabic-script ones: "I had lots of things to say and *language* did not matter; what mattered was the practicality of putting things down on paper." He says he feels "comfortable" using English. In any case, as Jacqueline Bardolph suggests in "Un cas singulier: Nuruddin Farah, écrivain somali" ("A Curious Instance: Nuruddin Farah, Somali Writer"): "Une écriture à la fois poétique et politique, qui rappelle aux gouvernants quelle est la loi juste, est dans le droit fil de la tradition litteraire somalie" ("Writing at once poetic and political, reminding the people in power of what is just, is in the mainstream of Somali literary heritage") (63). Extracts from his works are reported to circulate underground in Somalia, in Somali translation. His first published work, written at eighteen or nineteen, was a novella, *Why Dead So Soon?*, but much of his early writing was for the theater.

After working for the Department of Education, Farah left Somalia to study literature and philosophy at the University of Chandigarh (India), where he wrote plays and the novel *From a Crooked Rib*. Its final page attests that he began writing on 19 March 1968 and finished on 15 April.

Farah returned from the University of Chandigarh to Somalia, where, in October 1969, Major-General Siyad Barre staged a "bloodless" coup and began a regime of "scientific socialism," with Soviet backing. Farah was deeply disturbed by the nature of the regime and by the developing national cult of the President as "Father" of the nation, no less than by the repressive methods through which the government silenced opposition. His writing from this period on becomes highly critical of the

Siyad Barre government, which he sees as representative of all African dictatorships. Censors suppressed the serialization of a novel he wrote in Somali soon after the government decreed the use of an official script.

For a time Farah taught at the National University of Somalia and was involved in theater in Somalia, before traveling to Britain to do graduate work in theater. His second novel, *A Naked Needle*, was written in Mogadiscio in 1972, and its troubled central character bears the same name as Farah's young son.

When *A Naked Needle* was published in 1976, Farah was still in Europe. In an interview with Tom Smith for the New York Public Radio Book Show, he tells of telephoning from Rome to his brothers in Somalia to give details of his plane flight home, only to be told that it would be "wise not to return." The Minister for Justice subsequently confirmed that if Farah set foot in Somalia he would be given thirty years in jail. He has expressed his interest in returning to live in Somalia, but the increasingly critical tone of his writing has guaranteed him fifteen years of exile. *A Naked Needle* was followed by a trilogy collectively entitled *Variations on the Theme of an African Dictatorship*. His work focuses on what makes dictatorships in Africa survive, and the way in which the patriarchies and matriarchies of the old order are "woven into the current tyrannies of dictatorship."

He has held positions at the Universities of London, Essex, Jos, and Bayreuth, but lives principally in Italy, although he continues to write in English rather than Italian.

TERRITORIES OF PAIN

Nuruddin Farah is a writer who is acutely aware of his position as a political critic writing in a colonial language about a homeland from which the circumstances of his life have frequently removed him. Indeed, the central metaphor of his novel *Sardines* is that of guest and host, with the journalist Medina pondering whether her foreign education in an alien ideology has not rendered her a guest in her own land and therefore disqualified her from criticizing what she finds there, while in a later novel, *Maps*, the question of personal identity is inseparable from the question of national identity. For Farah rejoices in his identity as a Somali writer, and his works are intensely focused on the state of the Somali nation, within Somalia and beyond its borders. Here is no exile turning back in memory to a lost land, but a writer passionately engaged with Somalia today.

In each novel, he takes up a different set of issues and explores them through the consciousness of a single central character (or, in *Sardines*, a group). In his realization of these characters lies much of his achievement in the novels, for each is fully invested with the turns of thought, mannerisms, and obsession that individualize them, so that the issues addressed in each novel are colored by their focalization. Thus the views expressed through the angry young man of the 1970s in *A Naked Needle* are a far cry from the concerns of the confused schoolboy of the 1980s in *Maps* or the meditations of the devout elderly man in *Close Sesame*.

He is a highly conscious stylist, particularly in the later novels, where a dense interwoven texture of motifs carries much of the moral judgement and links character, motive, and action on a recognizable verbal level. The verbal richness enables Farah to open up areas of nonlogical connection that would not be available in a more literal style, and that are vital in conveying the levels of interplay between personal and political structures or between the emotional and the rational.

In his first novel, *From a Crooked Rib*, set in 1959 on the eve of Independence, Farah takes as his central character an ignorant nomad girl who flees from an unwelcome arranged marriage to the city. Ebla's ignorance is not simply a lack of knowledge about town life but, more importantly, a lack of self-knowledge. Her new experiences force her to question her ideas about life as well as the assumptions made by those around her. Having made the one bold choice in her life and escaped from the authority of her family, Ebla blunders from one arranged match to the next, until within a very few weeks she has accumulated four "husbands" simultaneously. The first two matches, to which her word was carried by a male relative but without her true consent, do not bother her, but she angrily comments on the Somali view of women, which reduces her to trade goods bartered by the men of her own family for their own gain in cash or kind. The third match is the one into which she enters willingly, but a month later, and without a divorce, she marries again. This time she is a little concerned about the legality of the union and begins to be disturbed at the hectic pace her life has assumed:

> Ebla thought maybe this kind of going from one hand to another would come to an end one day. She never regretted doing anything. The suggestion to marry Tiffo was Asha's, the one to marry Awill was the widow's, the one to get engaged to an old man in the country (she had even forgotten his name now) was her grandfather's. It was always someone else's suggestions that she either accepted or rejected. One is fed with suggestions all through one's life, starting from the time one comes into this world and ending when one dies. "Do this; do that; don't do this; don't do that"—this is life. But it is a life that has been poisoned, the potion has been fed to us, like medicine. This is the medicine we live on, the medicine we eat and drink, but do we realize it? (128–29)

The fact that Ebla can give voice to these thoughts signals that she is on the verge of discovering a more active involvement with her fate.

When one of her husbands is having trouble with his first wife, she defiantly flings at him the announcement that he is not her only husband: "You have another wife and I have another husband. We are even: you are a man and I am a woman, so we are equal. You need me and I need you. We are equal" (145). Her Somali merchant husband naturally rejects such ridiculous claims—"We are not equal. You are a woman and you are inferior to me"—and this leads Ebla to ponder at length over the relative values of men and women, and their possible relations to one another. She even holds an audible debate in male and female voices while gazing in her mirror. She comes to recognize that she alone is morally responsible for her own actions; but the novel ends ambiguously with Ebla not yet having chosen whether to accept inferiority and live by deceit or to insist on honest equality in her relations with Awill, the husband of her choice. That the decision is to be put off until the following day suggests that deceit may be the chosen way.

The novel closes, suggestively, a month before Independence. It is possible to see, in Ebla's history and options, the choices confronting the new nation, and her indecision does not augur well for the future. Interestingly, Farah refers later in *Maps* to a Somali poetic tradition of describing Somalia as a beautiful woman who "has made it her habit to betray her man, the Somali" by accepting all the advances made by other men (98).

From a Crooked Rib was written at great speed while Farah was studying at the University of Chandigarh. On his return to Somalia he became a secondary school teacher (he had formerly, like Awill, worked in the Ministry of Education), and the central character in his second novel, *A Naked Needle*, is on the verge of resigning from his teaching job. Nevertheless, it would be a mistake to see this character as a self-portrait, for much that identifies Koschin's voice is absent from Farah's other novels.

A Naked Needle takes place over twenty-four hours in the life of Koschin, as he anticipates the arrival in Somalia of Nancy, a British woman who is unexpectedly taking him up on his promise to marry her. The first part of the novel is a mental diatribe, addressed to Nancy, against women in general and foreign wives in particular; in the fourth "movement" of the six-part novel, he takes her on a long walk around the city, accompanied by his monologue on everything from the paucity of bookshops to the habits of Egyptian émigrés. In the final section of the novel they attend a party given by people for whom he has little regard and a good deal of contempt. Each of these scenes provides an opportunity for Koschin to castigate those elements of his society that do not conform to his revolutionary ideals. The entire novel is a savage condemnation of modern Somali city life through the person of Koschin.

Koschin is full of nationalist fervor, but he is also deeply disturbed by the relations between men and women around him, and at times his tone is hysterically misogynist. By removing him from the teaching job for which he claims a vocation, Farah avoids presenting any situation in which Koschin might gain sympathy or appear to act to any effect. Even his resignation from the teaching job is contemplated, not completed, though word of it has already spread by that evening to the party guests. He accuses, but does not act; he appears in his relations with Nancy to be falling into those very errors that he has identified in the behavior of his friends.

The critique of life in Mogadiscio presented through Koschin is strong but not tightly focused. Neo-colonialism, tribalism, philistinism, mixed-race marriages, sexual exploitation, and corruption are jumbled together in an amorphous tangle of issues. This is the angry cry of the frustrated idealist, whose first taste of reality is too bitter to swallow. Koschin is irritated by so much in his environment that his criticisms come to seem a constant petty carping against a life that does not suit him; in particular, the negative portraits of people met by chance reveal a determinedly jaundiced view:

The women's bottoms collide with each other as he pulls the car
door to, and down his weight descends on the extended meatmats
of the women, although he is not in the least prepared to risk
inviting the rancour of the veiled owls. Up his weight rises and
lands, all in one piece, again on the edge of the space-barricading
bottom of the big bertha next to him. No grunts from her, no
complaint, and it seems as if she doesn't even mind. . . . She begins
rattling away with her companion, who, glancing at her from that
fleshy distance, Koschin imagines must be suffering from mumps,
because of the swelling in her salivary glands. And the mouth of the
woman next to him opens and closes with the speed of an
unshackled two-hundred-words-per-minute speech, and she yawns,
smiting her fat hand across her mouth. Her teeth, Koschin thinks,
are faultlessly ugly, tobacco-tarnished and what have you. Her hair
on the nape is kinky, and she wears a blouse on top of her guntino
robe. Her hands look crippled, as if contradicting the supreme
hugeness of the rest of her body. (43)

The gratuitous wealth of descriptive detail lavished on this nameless woman belies
her total insignificance in the novel but is of a piece with the view of Somalia, which
can impel Koschin to provide this potted history:

My!! Mogadiscio, Koschin thinks, the slaughterhouse turned city.
The Slit-eyed from the east, because of his interest in incense and
myrrh, itinerated his way into the interior of what was then the
Puntland. The Greasy-bum, to say the least, bargained with the
tribesmen and chieftains and settled for more than half a century,
guaranteeing that he would keep peace among the tribesmen.
Before them all, before the Slit-eyed and the Greasy-bum to
Mogadiscio came the Oily Onion-eaters. Not to forget, of course,
the Airy Bastard who belted the natives by the hundreds, concocting
the story (for the world outside) that if he left, nothing would be
there for anyone to own, that they would feed upon one another.
Then the Lousy Servile approached from another angle, through
another channel (they are much more mine than they are yours),
and forged history, and earned himself a name as the producer of
the best Chocolate-coloured in Negroland. . . .
Mogadiscio. Mogadixo. Magaldisho. Muugdisho. Its populace:
gangsters with no gang, a town with no treasure, no history beyond
what Davidson gives it in his most authenticated narrative as blood-
suckers in Berbera. People with no purity. Donkey-man damned to
the last degree, that is what we all are, not on this side of darkness,
neither on the other, unacceptable to everybody on the face of this
earth. (20–21)

The novel is, essentially, a series of set-pieces of rant like this, undercut by Farah's scrupulous recognition of his character's ineffectuality. Koschin is a teacher who does not teach, a lover who does not love, an orator whose audience is imaginary through most of the novel. His friends' marriages with European women horrify him, but he is about to launch into such a marriage himself, acting as deceitfully as those whose deceptions he reviles. He inflicts the tour of the sights of Mogadiscio, plus accompanying lecture, on Nancy because he is reluctant to show her the dirty, cockroach-infested room where he lives. The grand speeches about the false materialism of others are a cover up for his embarrassment about his own living quarters and what he has made of his life in Mogadiscio. Even his grand gesture of resignation from his job in protest against the principal's exploitation of a girl student is undercut, first by the department's regulations about telephoned resignations being unacceptable and then by the principal's bland self-assurance in the face of his accusations. Koschin utters truths unpalatably; in self-knowledge, however, he lags behind even Ebla.

A Naked Needle was written in 1972, only three years after the coup, later redefined as a revolution, which ushered in the military regime led by Major General Mohamed Siyad Barre. Koschin's idealism is in sympathy with the revolution and some of its avowed aims, and his anger is directed at those he sees as falling away from those ideals. Farah's next novel was the first in a trilogy that deals in a quieter but much bleaker way with the aftermath of the revolution as it hardens into a military dictatorship that summarily stifles the least breath of protest. Koschin reappears as an incidental character, whose imprisonment and torture are mentioned in each volume of the trilogy.

Farah's title for the trilogy, *Variations on the Theme of an African Dictatorship*, summarizes the common element. The three novels—*Sweet and Sour Milk, Sardines*, and *Close Sesame*—concern a group of young Somalis who agree to unite to resist the tyranny of the government. Some die for their principles, some betray their friends, some lie low, some attempt an assassination. In each novel the list of those destroyed by the regime grows longer; in the third novel the father of one conspirator finds and reads the whole list of the original group. By the end of the novel only two are free: One is the traitor, the other is banned from publishing her work.

Sweet and Sour Milk opens with the death of Soyaan, one of the opponents of the regime. His twin brother, Loyaan, an apolitical dentist from a regional town, resents the fact that the publicity machine of the state replaces his brother's dying cry to him with "Labour is Honour," later to be elaborated on his tomb into the almost blasphemous sentiment, "Labour is honour and there is no General but our General." While his sister Ladan wants to know the reason why her brother died, Loyaan is at first more concerned with the reason the state wants Soyaan to live again in this false form. There are even plans to name a street in his honor. This annexation of his twin's name and falsification of his existence disturbs Loyaan, not least because he has sometimes been mistaken for his brother, and his own photograph erroneously appears with Soyaan's death notice and fake last words in the paper. Loyaan sets out to reconstruct for himself the truth of his brother's last days and death.

The quest reveals to him, as it does to the reader, the nature of the government under which he is living. No dissent is permitted; any criticism, however oblique and poetic, is dangerous. Although tribalism has been renounced, it still governs all political relations, and the state is run by a tight clique of the General's kinsmen. Power is absolute and those who do not cooperate are coerced or consigned to detention; a doctor tells of midnight visits to tend torture victims and mentions the Russian colleague whose complicity extends to giving mysterious injections to those under interrogation. Loyaan's search exposes him to the unsuspected realities of life: Bureaucrats can redefine one's existence by moving a file from one office to another; an affair with the former mistress of a government minister may bring death.

Loyaan's father Keynaan has been dismissed when one of his victims died under torture, and he has been required to marry his victim's widow in compensation. His unswerving loyalty to the government is now rewarded when he is reinstated, and as head of the family he is required to mimic the General's paternalistic authority and restrain Loyaan from pursuing his enquiries. Soyaan's death is an "embarrassment" to those whom Loyaan approaches, and the publicity campaign, which Keynaan supports, to establish him as a hero of the revolution he opposed is even more "embarrassing," but eventually Loyaan himself becomes enough of an embarrassment to require attention—he is told he is to be shipped off to Belgrade, nominally to a consular post but in reality to an exile under guard.

Soyaan does indeed live again but not in the street name honoring the lie. His newborn half-brother, son of the torture victim's widow who dies at his birth, is given his name, suggesting that his spirit of rebellion will persist into the next generation.

Certainly it persists into the next novel, albeit in a very subdued form. *Sardines* is about two others in the group of dissidents, Medina and her husband Samater. He has been won over by the regime and has become a minister. She was briefly the editor of the daily paper, but since she used this elevation to remove the General's picture and his speeches from the pages of the paper, she was lucky to last three days in the job, luckier still not to find herself in jail. Instead, she is banned from publishing anything, and she subsequently limits her subversive activities to altering a single phrase in her unpublished translation of an Ibo folk tale. The story, from Chinua Achebe, concerns the tortoise who was a guest of the sky people and cheated his companions of their share of the feast by renaming himself "All of You," so that anything prepared "for all of you" became his portion. Medina replaces "all of you" with "He": a clear reference to General Siyad. The story is another example of the pervasive use in this novel of the metaphor of the overreaching guest. In a more concrete action, though, she is able to maneuver her husband out of the government.

The novel centers largely on the relations between mothers and their offspring, particularly their daughters. Ebla reappears, now the mother of a young athlete who plans to defect in public protest against the regime but is too disorganized to train properly for the international event that will provide her with her grandstand and in the end is upstaged by the arrest of her main competitors for writing political graffiti. Medina has a young daughter whose political and moral education is her chief care; and a young friend also has a daughter, conceived of a rape that was a political reprisal against the victim's father. This group of mothers and daughters illustrates many of the ways in which the patriarchal tyranny of the family victimizes women and enables parallels to be drawn between such domestic despotism and the military dictatorship. Each of the adult women in this central group has vowed to reject the authoritarian model of the family and to rear her child in rational affection, not just blind obedience, though her influence on her child may be no less overwhelming. These are women who dissent from the prevailing ideology of their society, in politics as well as in domestic life, and while their own practices may break with the norms of the past, there is an ever-present danger that defying the authoritarian framework of their society will bring down its wrath on their heads.

Medina engineers a situation in which her husband will be forced to recognize and reject the insufferable meddling of his mother from which she, a guest in her own home, has hitherto protected him. But Samater's rebellion against his family authority is read as a rebellion against all authority and cannot be condoned.

While *Sweet and Sour Milk* was a reconstruction of a past life of dissent, which led to the dawning of a new political consciousness in Loyaan, *Sardines* deals with restraint, the frustration of political action, and the fear of the consequences of action. Medina cannot publish; Sagal cannot defect; Amina cannot prosecute her rapists. Yet, if nothing is gained, nothing is lost either, and a new generation is being reared to reason and to love and to reject tyranny.

The central character of *Close Sesame* is the most contemplative of any in the trilogy, and yet this novel contains the deepest political commitment and the most violent political action. Deeriye is the father of Mursal, one of the original group of conspirators. He is old, ill, a hero of yesteryear who is now largely discounted by his family. Here is no patriarch but an elderly man experiencing the loving tyranny of grown children who know what is best for their father and who hound him with loving enquiries after his health.

Deeriye is a former dissident who has spent most of his life in detention but is now sickly, a devout old dreamer who is no longer able to sit through a political meeting without nodding off to sleep, so that he cannot be sure what he heard and what he dreamed in the course of the meeting. His most rewarding discussions are with his dead wife, who returns to chat with him in the half hour before he wakes in the morning. Excluded from the political movement for which his son is willing to die, coddled and cosetted and moved from house to house for his own good but without his own volition, the old man becomes simultaneously an observer and a participant in political life. Treachery is as pervasive among Deeriye's aged cronies at the tea shop as it is among the next generation of political plotters. What the bustling, confident young do not realize, as they organize everything for the good of their old father or the good of the nation, is that the doddering old man at his devotions or lost in a dream of the past can judge as truly and see as clearly as they do. He can, with the benefit of his greater experience, see the pattern of contemporary events unfolding in a replica of the events of long ago, when he was first taken into detention. Nor is he above learning from the young, with their talk of the *lex talionis*, an eye for an eye, as he demonstrates when his son is killed and he seeks blood vengeance.

Yet Deeriye is not idealized as the voice of traditional wisdom. His political commitment has removed him from the pains and joys of real life, which he is only belatedly beginning to experience. While his clan starved as a result of a retaliatory slaughter of their livestock by the colonial government, he was well fed in prison. While his children grew up and found their own way to political commitment, he was far away in jail. His periods of detention come to seem less like martyrdom and more insulations from real life. Only in age does he begin to know how to love and care for a child, his grandson Samawade, and to value the political education of a child as a worthy task to undertake; but age brings also its own terrors until he dares not walk outside the house for fear of a young boy throwing stones. His interpretations of events are influenced not only by his experience of the past but also by the mystical slant of his piety. His prophetic dreams and conversations with his dead wife are as important to him as what goes on in the real world around him.

After Mursal's death, he embarks on a mission of vengeance, which is pitiful in its misguided heroism. He has always been a pacifist and has never used a gun, but he borrows a military uniform, takes his son's gun, and tries to assassinate the General. He pulls out his rosary instead and is shot down by the guards. The pathos of Deeriye's death only reinforces the tragedy of all the deaths that have preceded his. The "Variations on the Theme of an African Dictatorship" come to seem only variations of the failure of dissent. Farah insists on the value of political commitment, but under the reign of Siyad, those who act on their consciences do not live long.

Throughout the trilogy, the next generation is important. Although the roll of the dead lengthens, there is always another, a brother or even a father, to take up the task; and always the next generation is growing up, developing their own political consciousness, and emerging freer than their parents from the bonds of tradition.

With *Maps*, his sixth novel, Farah moves away from the group of characters who have inhabited the earlier novels. *Maps* is the first/second/third-person story of a young boy from the Ogaden who comes to Mogadiscio at the age of seven and of his relations with Misra, the Ethiopian woman who raises him in the Ogaden, and with the Somali couple, Hilaal and Salaado, who educate him in the city.

National identity and personal identity are interlinked in a challenging way in this novel. Askar's mother has died at his birth, and his ideas of birth and death, of being and becoming, are colored by this, as they are by his identification of Misra with the world, with all that which constitutes the "other." As he is learning to talk, he points to Misra when told to point to the earth. Yet he is also an extension of her *soma*, her third leg or third breast, as he sleeps wrapped in her body. Only with his circumcision, the ritual end of infancy, is he separated from her, and the separation brings on a crisis of identity:

> I don't know what curses I shouted or uttered. All I can tell you is
> that I woke up, my body wet with sweat, my throat aching from
> crying and saying again and again and again, "Who am I? Who am
> I? Where am I? Where am I? Who am I?" (93)

As a young boy, Askar draws maps on his skin so that self and location become one. But maps, he learns, are not necessarily truths. The Ogaden, where he was born, has been part of Ethiopia and part of Somalia. "Ethiopia" and "Somalia" are themselves names for concepts abstracted from the mapmaking process, terms that express different kinds of reality, since all Somalis constitute Somalia, whereas Ethiopia is a foreign term for an aggregate nation.

Shortly after his circumcision he is separated from Misra and crosses the imaginary line between Ethiopia and Somalia to live with Hilaal and Salaado in Mogadiscio. In Somalia, he needs papers to prove his identity as a Somali and a citizen of Somalia. Like the maps that write geography, the papers write his identity, and the written form outweighs any other:

> Looking at the photograph and, under it, like a caption, my name, I began to see myself in images carved out of the letters which my name comprised. It meant that I had a *foglio famiglia* and that I wasn't just a refugee from the Ogaden. It is unfair, I thought to myself, that Misra wasn't even given a mention on my identity card. Now I discarded my earlier belief that this was because she was Oromo and I, Somali. Perhaps, I concluded, it was because our relationship dates back to before my coming to Mogadiscio and before—goes back to before I myself acquired the Somali identity in written form. I reminded myself that Misra belonged to my "non-literate" past—by which I mean that she belonged to a past in which I spoke, but did not write or read in, Somali. . . .
>
> I confess, I did think that I was expected, from that moment onwards, to perceive myself in the identity created for me. (164–65)

There are written truths that outweigh known truths, but there are also believed truths that are more powerful still. The stories of Askar's birth carry mythic force even when factually disproved; other stories, like the tales of Misra's treachery, may not be true but carry enough weight to bring about her death. Her identity as an Ethiopian among a Somali community assures her neighbors of her identity as the traitor who betrayed a camp of 600 fighting men.

Askar, coming to manhood in the city and faced with the choice of university or a training camp with the Western Liberation Front is faced as well with a visit from Misra. Barely secure yet in his own identity, he avoids as far as he can any dealings with this mother/not mother, traitor/not traitor, Somali/Ethiopian whose body was the first thing he learned to distinguish from his own.

Farah's concern with the relative weightings to be given to personal loyalties and political ones underlies most of his novels. He consistently rejects tribalism and the domination of the autocratic family head, but he places a high value on supportive, nonrestrictive affection within the immediate family; at the same time, political commitment is an imperative, and political action desirable. The first novel is the only one in which the political dimension is subsumed to the personal, but the personal dimension is never absent. Indeed, for the characters, though never for the reader, the minutiae of daily life within the family often threaten to obscure the larger issues. In the trilogy particularly, Farah presents with sympathy the scrambling, chaotic life of a political activist who is also a family member, where a puppet show put on by the children takes precedence over a political meeting, and a co-

conspirator's last visit before his violent death is an unwelcome interruption to a family game of cards. But puppet show and card game themselves become metaphors for the political games being played at a higher level, with which the characters are choosing to engage.

As a stylist, Farah is richly inventive. In his recognition that the structure of family life may mirror in miniature the structures of the state and society permits the dominance of an unfit few and oppresses the many (and Farah is critical particularly of the social victimization of Somali women), he is making an incomparably valuable literary contribution to social consciousness. As a political critic, he makes vitriolic attacks through the mouths of his characters, and those characters are widely varied and intimately realized. He can see and present with sympathy many ways of reacting to society and to the state; hence the perceived need for a trilogy of *Variations*. Samater colluding with the powerful or Deeriye setting out to avenge his son is portrayed with compelling intelligence and a sympathy that does not preclude moral judgment—just as Askar tells his own life in *Maps*:

> As he told the story yet again, time grew like a tree, with more branches and far more falling leaves than the tree which is on the face of the moon. In the process he became the defendant. He was at one and the same time, the plaintiff and the juror. Finally . . . his different personae . . . act as judge, as audience and as witness. (246)

WORKS CITED

Farah, Nuruddin. *From a Crooked Rib*. London: Heinemann, 1970.
———. *Maps*. London: Pan Books, 1986.
———. *A Naked Needle*. London: Heinemann, 1976.
———. *Sweet and Sour Milk*. London: Allison and Busby, 1979.

NURUDDIN FARAH'S PUBLISHED WORK

From a Crooked Rib, 1970
A Naked Needle, 1976
Trilogy: *Sweet and Sour Milk*, 1979; *Sardines*, 1981; *Close Sesame*, 1983
Maps, 1986

SELECTED CRITICAL READINGS

Early critics of Farah's writing were surprised and delighted by his use of a female protagonist in *From a Crooked Rib*, for not many male writers from Africa have chosen to employ such a voice. Critics commenting on the second and third novels have dealt with them on the whole as literature of political protest and as expressions of that same angrily ambivalent rejection of a corrupt *nouvelle bourgeoisie* that may be found in the works of other African writers such as Ouologuem or Armah. After Farah turned, in *Sardines*, to a female focalizer once more, some critics picked up his use of the female voice to comment on broader political structures that reproduce at a national level the tyrannies and repressions of the family unit. In the light of the two novels following *Sardines*, this would appear to be a line of discussion that would repay more attention. With a couple of exceptions (given in the list that follows), surprisingly little has been written about his wordplay or his richly evocative use of elaborate extended metaphor.

Adam, Ian. "The Murder of Soyaan Keynaan." *World Literature Written in English* 26 (1986): 203–21. Treats the structural relation between *Sweet and Sour Milk* and the detective story.

_____. "Nuruddin Farah and James Joyce: Some Issues of Intertextuality." *World Literature Written in English* 24 (1984): 34–42. Compares principally *A Naked Needle* with *A Portrait of the Artist as a Young Man.*

Cochrane, Judith. "The Theme of Sacrifice in the Novels of Nuruddin Farah." *World Literature Written in English* 18 (1979): 69–77. Deals with the victimization of women in *From a Crooked Rib* and Somalia in *A Naked Needle.*

Ewen, D.R. "Nuruddin Farah." *The Writing of East and Central Africa.* Ed. G.D. Killam. London: Heinemann, 1984: 192–201. Discusses the early novels; especially good on Farah's wordplay; includes material from an unpublished interview.

———. "Nuruddin Farah: *Sweet and Sour Milk.*" *World Literature Written in English* 20 (1981): 221–24. Review.

Okonkwo, Juliet I. "Nuruddin Farah and the Changing Roles of Women." *World Literature Today* 58 (1984): 215–21. Picks up Kirsten Holst Petersen's point about Farah's feminism; deals with the first four novels.

———. "Nuruddin Farah and the Politics of Somalia." *Présence Africaine* 132 (1984): 44–53. Addresses *Sweet and Sour Milk* and *Sardines*; contains comparisons with Armah, Ngugi, Soyinka.

Petersen, Kirsten Holst. "The Personal and the Political: The Case of Nuruddin Farah." *Ariel* 12.3 (1981): 93–101. Stresses political commitment in the first four novels; draws comparisons with Armah and Ngugi.

Stratton, Florence. "The Novels of Nuruddin Farah." *World Literature Written in English* 25 (1985): 16–30. Discusses tyranny in the family and in society as it is depicted in the first four novels.

Walmesley, Anne. "Nuruddin Farah and Somalia." *Index on Censorship* 10.2 (1981): 17–19. Provides an interesting sidelight on the reception of Farah's works in Somalia; followed by an extract from *Sweet and Sour Milk.*

Journal of Commonwealth Literature 24.1 (Spring 1989). Contains a colloquium of papers on Farah's work, addressing it from a variety of approaches.

— ROSEMARY COLMER

George Lamming

George Lamming was born in Barbados on 8 June 1927 and through his childhood and adolescence, he witnessed the beginnings of trade unionism, the Bridgetown riots, the growth of political consciousness among working class people, and the awareness that led to the independence movements of the 1950s. At school, he was influenced by Frank Collymore, who was his English master and the editor of the magazine *Bim*, the most important voice of Caribbean poets at that time.

In 1946 he went to Trinidad, where, especially through his work for *Bim*, he came into contact with a number of Trinidadian and other Caribbean writers. In 1950, he left Trinidad for England with the conscious intention of becoming a poet, thinking of London as "the literary Mecca." As it turned out, he gave up writing poetry after the publication of his first novel. He was reasonably successful as a young writer in England, publishing no less than four novels plus a book of essays by 1960. He received a Guggenheim Fellowship for his first novel in 1954 and the Somerset Maugham Award in 1957.

Between 1954 and 1958, Lamming traveled widely in Europe, the United States, and the Caribbean. In 1956 he addressed in Paris the First Congress of Negro Writers and Artists, arguing that the black consciousness being partly defined in terms of confrontation against white otherness, which makes understanding impossible, is part of the contemporary human condition. In 1956, Lamming also returned to the Caribbean, where he witnessed the vodun ceremonies in Haiti. In these ceremonies, he found a suitable metaphor for communication between the present and a buried past.

Between 1950 and 1962, Lamming regularly produced radio programs for the overseas service of the BBC. In 1962 he was awarded a Canada Council Fellowship. He continued traveling throughout the world from the base of his London flat through the 1960s and 1970s, lecturing at universities in North America, Europe, and Africa. In 1976 he was awarded a Commonwealth Foundation grant. Recently he received an honorary doctorate from the University of the West Indies. He also returned to Barbados to work on a new novel, which, according to his most eminent critic, Ian Munro, is to be about the 1930s in the Caribbean.

CHARACTERIZATION AND THE COLONIAL MYTH

Many readers find George Lamming's novels difficult. David West has observed: "Lamming realizes that he is a difficult writer, that he is not for everyone. He wants to be read slowly and carefully, and deserves to be. He offers his themes to those who can appreciate them" (82).

There are several reasons for this general assessment. The most obvious one stems from Lamming's dual allegiance to the English language and to the socio-cultural tensions in the Caribbean, which finds expression in his preoccupation with the theme of the colonial condition through the means of the Prospero-Caliban metaphor drawn from Shakespeare's *The Tempest* (an idea he develops in *The Pleasures of Exile*). Another reason lies in Lamming's poetic style, which favors complex sentence structure and extended symbolic allusions. But the single aspect of Lamming's novels that may pose the greatest challenge is his idiosyncratic art of characterization.

After all, the characters in Lamming's novels are not primarily individuals but representatives of ideas or concepts, even personifications of socio-cultural conflicts. Their significance within the larger scheme is more evident than is their individuality as fictional beings with a credibility and appeal to compassion. As Ian Munro describes this quality:

> Lamming's works are all symbolic to some degree: his characters frequently embody themes and act out roles appropriate to their place in the symbolic scheme. The importance of ideas in Lamming's work has led to accusations of "tendentiousness" and "lifelessness" by some critics and reviewers, while others have been more willing to accept the *donné* of the work, that the political goals and issues of the novel ultimately bulk larger than the individual life of its characters. (*Sourcebook* 271)

Other West Indian writers, including V. S. Naipaul and Wilson Harris, have commented on the effects of the lack of individuality in Lamming's characters. Certainly, the tendency to associate his characters with ideas so intensely is not always admired. *In the Castle of My Skin*, for example, may be viewed less as a story about the development of G. and more as a "dissection of the colonial hierarchy" (Paquet 16); in *Water with Berries* the portrayal of character is recognized as being subservient to the "historical equation" (Tiffin "Freedom" 91). With reference to *Of Age and Innocence*, Sandra Pouchet Paquet observes very accurately:

> Lamming offers a detailed social analysis based on specific relationships between representative, and therefore typical, characters, and between these characters and their environment. Individual characters carry the weight of the social milieu they inhabit, and personal relationships the weight of historical conflicts and alliances. (64)

Such could be said of the characters and relationships in all of Lamming's novels. The questions therefore arise: What are the main effects of such a handling of character? And what consequences does it have for the experience of the reader?

The most outstanding effect is probably the shift of the reader's attention from a concern for individuals and their fate to a social concern embracing the entire community depicted, possibly even the whole of humanity. This social concern may not be so obvious in Lamming's first novel, *In the Castle of My Skin*, though it is already there, but it emerges quite strongly in the second novel, *The Emigrants*, which depicts the consequences of the colonial myth concerning England's alleged superiority. The myth, as Lamming himself points out, develops in the West Indies from the earliest stages of education: "It begins with the fact of England's supremacy in taste and judgment: a fact which can only have meaning and weight by a calculated cutting down to size of all non-England. The first to be cut down is the colonial himself" (*The Pleasures of Exile* 27). In *The Emigrants*, this is illustrated through the numerous discussions among the West Indians on the ship en route to England. Although they come from different Caribbean islands, their common desire to reach England unites them as a group, so that their individual identities are granted less importance. This subordination is not only achieved by impersonal labels like "the Barbadian" or "the Strange Man," but it is also a consequence of the shift of the narrative perspective, which is effected by the transformation of the initial artist-narrator into Collis, a minor member of the group, "a young poet whose experience cannot easily be separated from that of the other emigrants" (Munro *West Indian Literature* 130). However, the lack of individual concern becomes most obvious in parts two and three of *The Emigrants*, when the group is no longer together after their ship has reached England. Once they disperse, the reader witnesses their disintegration, yet their individual concerns still do not assume any importance. With the exception of Collis, Tornado, Higgins, and Dickson, one can hardly remember their names or any individual characteristics when they reappear after an absence of more than a dozen pages or so. Indeed, some seem interchangeable. Their individual experiences become "typified"; they themselves become stereotyped; and they form part of the masses in England. Ian Munro correctly observes:

> Their dilemma is typified by Dickson, a respectable schoolteacher from Barbados, who forms a liaison with an Englishwoman, and then discovers that she is curious about him only as a stereotyped sexual object, the black male. The episode shatters his concept of himself as a "black Englishman." In various ways, each of the emigrants undergoes a similar experience of disillusionment and loss of identity, including Collis, whose ambitions for a writing career are reduced to doing liner notes for record albums. He makes his living as a factory worker, at which he is unlucky and incompetent. His alienation from people is expressed in a tendency to see them as objects. (*West Indian Literature* 131)

The second effect of this method of characterization is in fact an immediate consequence of the first: The colonial paradigm becomes more clearly visible once the characters are submerged. As Kirsten Holst Petersen points out:

> His purpose is not to probe the individual mind for its own sake, but rather to give an imaginative insight into the growth of West Indian

sensibility and through that to offer an interpretation of West Indian history. He is thus concerned with the problems of a community rather than an individual, and in this way his books could perhaps be said to resemble the second (and much ignored) part of *Pilgrim's Progress*. This is particularly the case in *Natives of My Person*. (283)

And what are these problems of the community envisaged in Lamming's novels if not the colonial paradigm with special reference to the condition of the West Indian mind? The several levels on which the colonial paradigm can be observed in its effect upon individual consciousness include the colonial attitudes already in the minds of the colonizers (equally heavily, though differently, affected as the colonized)—as dramatized in *Natives of My Person*, the colonial thought patterns at work in pre-independence, early post-independence, and young nationalist Caribbean society—as illustrated in *In the Castle of My Skin*, *Of Age and Innocence*, and *Season of Adventure*, and the colonial confrontation in the colonizer's own society—as developed on a communal basis in *The Emigrants* and elaborated on a more symbolic level in *Water with Berries*. This emphasis makes Lamming's novels more didactic than entertaining, more *utile* than *dulce*.

The paradigmatic nature of many of Lamming's later characters is introduced in the character of Mr Slime in *In the Castle of My Skin*. As Ngugi wa Thiong'o has pointed out:

> Mr Slime's strength lies in his ability to harmonize these warring views [on the course of history and the poor people's role in it] into a vision embodying people's deepest aspirations. To the villagers he is a new Moses leading them to a Jerusalem where they can have better houses and permanently own their plots of land; hence they are ready to endure thirst and hunger across the desert. (122)

Knowing very little of the affairs in the world outside their village, the people have no choice but to trust Mr Slime. He represents a type of profiteer, who manages to persuade the people of his honest intentions. It is only Trumper, familiar with such types oppressing and cheating the black workers in the United States (himself a type of a different cast), who can recognize the paradigmatic nature of Mr Slime; he expresses his opinion when change comes to the unprepared villagers, and it becomes clear that Slime's schemes are responsible for sending Pa to the almshouse:

> "The Alms House," said Trumper. "'Tis a place he would never ever go on his own accord in this life. He wus too decent, Pa. Slime couldn't look Pa in the face if it's a question o' dignity we talkin' 'bout. But that's life. 'Tis the way o' the world, an' in a world o' Slimes there ain't no way out for those who don't know how to be slimy." (286)

So the name of this first representative of Lamming's leader-figure types is symbolic and paradigmatic, representing "the rising power of a new, indigenous middle class"

(Munro *Sourcebook* 266) whose "slimy" aspects are even more drastically exposed in *Season of Adventure.*

There is a third effect of this method of characterization, and here the real challenge begins. Considering that concern for individuals is comparatively weak in Lamming's novels, one may gradually lose interest in what happens to the characters, whose names one cannot remember very well anyway. Because the novels are not naturalistic accounts of events and character, the concept of plot is therefore put to the test in new and daring ways. One of the most striking aspects is the open-endedness of the narratives. But Lamming himself insists that "there is really no closing of the drama" (Kent 88) because he sees his work as movements in a continuing process. This thematic interconnectedness with changing characters and open-endedness contributes to the further separation of human and function in his characters—most clearly observed in *Water with Berries* and *Natives of My Person.* Helen Tiffin has shown how this aspect works in *Water with Berries;* she observes that in the character of Teeton human and function are separated when he rejects everything and everybody that he has formerly lived for and believed in: his American rescue, his wife, and his revolutionary comrades. As for the other characters, Tiffin notes: "After rejecting Nicole so violently, Roger, like Derek, disintegrates from person into stereotype" ("Tyranny" 47). In *Natives of My Person,* it is most obviously the crew of the ship *Reconnaissance* who are merely personified functions, which is signalled by the namelessness of some of their number and particularly of their officers, who are called Steward, Boatswain, Surgeon, and Priest throughout. Those who are allowed a real name all have foreign names like Pierre, Ivan, or Pinteados, and the leader is merely called the Commandant. Tiffin has noted that "This separation of man and function indicates the degree to which personality tends to disintegrate in the struggle for power, fame or fortune" ("Tyranny" 40).

The disintegration of character is perhaps most readily acceptable in the case of *Natives of My Person,* because Lamming reveals the quasi-allegorical framework of the entire journey and thus directs the reader's expectations accordingly. In his subsequent novels, however, the idiosyncratic and experimental treatment of character calls for a new reader commitment. Simply put, the traditional reader looking for a good story will be disappointed.

In an interview published in 1972, George Lamming was asked what kind of reading public he has in mind for his work. After admitting that he has never read any of his own books from cover to cover, he arrives at the central problem:

> I hope it does not seem to contain an element of arrogance to say that a book like *In the Castle of My Skin* seems to be a book that is relevant to intelligent and sensitive reading in any part of the English-speaking world, for the reason that the kind of theme, the internal and external drama I am concerned with, is a very universal drama.
>
> I know that there is an accusation by critics that I am a bit difficult. This means that I have to be read more slowly than would be the case with some writers, which I think is a good thing. I would have no objection to the reading taking the pace of a page a

day—I mean, once one had the assurance that you finished it. Within the context of the Caribbean, what has hurt somewhat is that I am in fact cut off because of the lack of training in reading at a mass level of society. My greatest pleasure would be to know that the cane-cutters and the laboring class read and understood *In the Castle of My Skin*; that would be infinitely more pleasing to me than the verdict of whoever is known as the most sensitive and perceptive critic. (Munro and Sander 11)

So the most important criteria are some understanding of the universal drama that Lamming's first novel unfolds. If this requirement is extended to Lamming's entire *oeuvre*, it means that those who recognize the paradigm of colonialism—the universal drama that unfolds in all his novels—and who read the works slowly, intelligently, and sensitively can understand them. It follows that someone familiar with the various implications of colonialism, particularly with the West Indian experience, is bound to gain more by the reading of Lamming's novels than will an uniformed reader.

It seems obvious then that the concern for the greater questions behind the narrative must sustain the interest. Indeed, those with a sound theoretical background in the literature in English that grew out of colonialism and/or West Indian history would certainly find all of Lamming's novels richly rewarding. But are such readers not limited? Lamming wants an audience that takes as much pleasure in the development and the variation of abstract ideas as in the fate of fictional characters. Whether such an audience can be found "at a mass level of society" is probably an open question—and not only in the Caribbean.

WORKS CITED

Kent, George E. "A Conversation with George Lamming." *Black World* 22.5 (1973): 4–14, 88–97.

Lamming, George. *In the Castle of My Skin*. New York: Schocken Books, 1983.

———. *The Pleasures of Exile*. London: Allison & Busby, 1984.

Munro, Ian. "George Lamming." *West Indian Literature*. London: Macmillan, 1979. 126–43.

———. "George Lamming." *Fifty Caribbean Writers: A Bio-Bibliographical Critical Sourcebook*. Westport: Greenwood, 1986. 264–75.

——— and Reinhard Sander, editors. "Interview with George Lamming." *Kas-Kas: Interviews with Three Caribbean Writers in Texas*. Austin: African and Afro-American Research Institute, 1972. 5–21.

Ngugi wa Thiong'o. "George Lamming's *In the Castle of My Skin*." *Homecoming: Essays on African and Caribbean Literature, Culture and Politics*. New York: Lawrence Hall, 1972. 110–26.

Paquet, Sandra Pouchet. *The Novels of George Lamming*. London: Heinemann, 1982.

Petersen, Kirsten Holst. "Time, Timelessness, and the Journey Metaphor in George Lamming's *In the Castle of My Skin* and *Natives of My Person*." *Commonwealth Writers Overseas*. Brussels: Didier, 1976. 283–88.

Tiffin, Helen. "Freedom after the Fall: Renaissance and Disillusion in *Water with Berries* and *Guerrillas*." *Individual and Community in Commonwealth Literature*. Malta: UP, 1979. 90–98.

———. "The Tyranny of History: George Lamming's *Natives of My Person* and *Water with Berries*." *Ariel* 10.4 (1979): 37–52.

GEORGE LAMMING'S PUBLISHED WORK

Novels

In the Castle of My Skin, 1953
The Emigrants, 1954
Of Age and Innocence, 1958
Season of Adventure, 1960
Water with Berries, 1971
Natives of My Person, 1971

Criticism

The Pleasures of Exile, 1960. Rpt. 1984.

> Collection of ten essays. Treats the predicament of the writer-in-exile, raising questions about the cultural and political identity of a society and its writers emerging from the colonial condition. Interprets Shakespeare's *The Tempest* as a political allegory and applies it to postcolonial societies. The author claims full kinship with his slave ancestry and identifies himself, ironically, with both Caliban and Prospero.

SELECTED CRITICAL READINGS

In accordance with George Lamming's uneven rhythm of publication, academic criticism of his work has followed an irregular pattern, with the early reviews in the 1950s hailing him as a promising young writer, the articles published in the 1960s attempting to grasp the problems posed by his first five books, and only the studies written after 1972 approaching the full extent of Lamming's scope and revealing the development between his first and second phase of publication. Lamming's poetry and short prose, much of which was written for and mostly broadcast by the Caribbean and Colonial Service of the BBC from London but never completely anthologized, is not only inaccessible but, according to the few critical comments available, mostly experimental, imitative, and of rather poor quality. Thus academic criticism, with very few exceptions, deals with his six novels and his book of essays, *The Pleasures of Exile.* Although Lamming reveals an extreme preoccupation with style, little critical light has so far been shed on this aspect of his work. The overwhelming majority of critics discuss his political commitment and his literary treatment of the colonial condition. A descriptive bibliography of criticism and reviews on Lamming's work, by Arturo Maldonado Diaz, was published in the *Journal of Commonwealth Literature* (16.2, 1982: 165–73). *Critical Perspectives on George Lamming,* edited by Anthony Boxill, is forthcoming.

Aiyejina, Funso. "The Backward Glance: Lamming's *Season of Adventure* and Williams' *Other Leopards.*" *African Literature Today* 14 (1984): 118–26. Focuses on the awareness of the African heritage in these two novels and demonstrates how Lamming's use of a virile image of Africa in the thought and behavior patterns of Afro-West Indians as a significant factor in their psyche culminates in self-discovery and self-awareness. Concludes that, in both novels, the West Indian may relate to Africa and the African as an ancestor figure, an alter ego, and a compatriot in man's struggle within time and space.

Barthold, Bonnie J. "George Lamming, *In the Castle of My Skin.*" *Black Time: Fiction of Africa, the Caribbean, and the United States.* New Haven: Yale UP, 1981. 150–57. Interprets Lamming's first novel in view of the tradition of the *Bildungsroman.* Shows how the novel presents a world in a state of flux and how G's growth in three stages from the stability of childhood to the uncertainties of being a man coincides with a duality of time that mimes the historic antagonism between myth and history. Finds that, by the conclusion of the novel, myth has given place to dispossession.

Baugh, Edward. "Cuckoo and Culture: *In the Castle of My Skin.*" *Ariel* 8.3 (1977): 23–33. Focuses on the description of the food prepared by the protagonist's mother in Lamming's first novel and shows that this scene embodies vital concerns of the novel by symbolizing certain values (or lack of values) in the kind of society depicted and in human life generally: values attached to the concepts of tradition, community, self-respect, creativity, and work.

Cartey, Wilfred. "Lamming and the Search for Freedom." *New World Quarterly* 3.1 & 2 (1967): 121–28. Shows that history, in Lamming's books, becomes not a mere chronicle of events but a series of continuous images not severed by static memory but woven together through recollection and intuitive penetration.

Kom, Ambroise. "*In the Castle of My Skin*: George Lamming and the Colonial Caribbean." *World Literature Written in English* 18 (1979): 406–20. Examines the structure of the social milieu during colonization depicted in Lamming's first novel and explores the nature of the changes that affect the village community as well as the emerging social order. Argues that the novel employs a significant relationship between the physical and temporal setting and individual development. Compares this with other novels by black writers in the Caribbean, the United States, and Africa.

———. "Londres des Nègres dans *The Emigrants* et dans *Water with Berries* de George Lamming." *Etudes anglaises* 34 (1981): 44–60. Compares the different positions of London and its impact on the West Indian characters in these two novels through an analysis of the characters' aspirations, a juxtaposition of their dreams, and the author's presentation of the social reality, and an examination of the characters' social behavior patterns, concluding with an interpretation of the Prospero-Caliban allegory in the later novel.

Maes-Jelinek, Hena. "The Awakening of a West Indian Sensibility." *Der karibische Raum zwischen Selbst- und Fremdbestimmung.* Frankfurt: Peter Lang, 1984. 189–203. Sets out from Lamming's *The Pleasures of Exile*, its emphasis on Prospero's gift of language to Caliban and its pervasive inherent irony. Proceeds to explain Lamming's concept of a West Indian sensibility, which is more than mere protest against the colonizers: a deconstruction of inherited prejudices by satire and other literary means, a constant effort to know his own people, and pride in his ethnic origins. Compares Lamming's manner of awakening from the nightmare of history with those demonstrated by Edward Brathwaite, V.S. Naipaul, and Wilson Harris.

Maldonado Diaz, Arturo. "Place and Nature in George Lamming's Poetry." *Revista/Review Interamericana* 4 (1974): 402–10. Discusses five poems by Lamming and argues that they express man's oneness with nature, as man acting simultaneously and in concert with nature. Shows how, in these poems, West Indians in northern, white cities lose their place in nature and their human warmth. Finds that this makes the nature poetry of the English-speaking Caribbean distinct from the European Romantic tradition.

Munro, Ian H. "The Early Work of George Lamming: Poetry and Short Prose, 1946–1951." *Neo-African Literature and Culture: Essays in Memory of Janheinz Jahn.* Wiesbaden: Heymann, 1976. 327–45. Considers forty-one poems and six short prose works written, but mostly not published, by Lamming between 1946 and 1951. Finds that the pieces, which mainly express a rejection of West Indian society and politics and develop Lamming's poetic persona, generally suffer from a lack of objectivity, genuine feeling, or experience behind the moral statement. The early work may be only a preparation for writing the first novel, after which Lamming never returned to poetry.

———. "George Lamming." *West Indian Literature.* London: Macmillan, 1979. 126–43. Examines Lamming's work chronologically and in an introductory manner. Interprets the novels individually in view of Lamming's artistic expression of the colonial condition. Concludes that *Natives of My Person* draws together the themes of Lamming's previous work: his concern with the quest for identity and the enduring myth of colonialism, and the problem of human misunderstanding as a reflection of the distortions in relationships created by colonialism.

———. "The Theme of Exile in George Lamming's *In the Castle of My Skin.*" *World Literature Written in English* 20 (1971): 51–60. Investigates the theme of departure in Lamming's first novel, arguing that his departure implies a judgment on the relation of the artist to West Indian society. Explores the concrete relation between vision and setting in this novel. Finds significant differences between the private areas of the narrator and the demands of his society. Concludes that the whole of the novel is a preparation for the final departure.

Ngugi wa Thiong'o. "George Lamming's *In the Castle of My Skin.*" *Homecoming: Essays on African and Caribbean Literature, Culture and Politics.* New York: Lawrence Hill, 1972. 110–26. Examines Lamming's first novel as a study of colonial revolt and argues that it shows the motive forces behind this revolt and its development through three main stages: a static phase, then a phase of rebellion, and finally a phase of achievement and disillusionment with society poised on the edge of a new struggle. Asserts that the novel sharply delineates the opposition between the aspirations of the peasantry and those of the emerging native elite. Calls it one of the great novels in modern literature about colonialism.

———. "George Lamming and the Colonial Situation." *Homecoming: Essays on African and Caribbean Literature, Culture and Politics.* New York: Lawrence Hill, 1972. 127–44. Concentrates on the theme of exile as a universal experience in Lamming's novels, especially in *The Emigrants* and *Of Age and Innocence.* Sets out from Lamming's own reference to the sense of exile in *The Pleasures of Exile* and suggests that there are four uses to which he puts the word "exile" in his novels: exile from history and a past style of living, from race, from class, and from self.

Nunez-Harrell, Elizabeth. "Lamming and Naipaul: Some Criteria for Evaluating the Third World Novel." *Contemporary Literature* 19 (1978): 26–47. Compares Lamming's and Naipaul's uses of the English language within the paradox of the West Indian writer's position. Argues that for many West Indian writers the only viable alternative to Standard English is the dialect of the country. Finds that, in contrast to Naipaul, Lamming does not seem to be able to avoid adopting the British attitude towards dialects and consequently drains the language of its authenticity, leaving it barren and lifeless, merely the vehicle of his ideas. Sets this in relation to the role of the English literary tradition in view of the Caribbean consciousness, relying heavily on Wilson Harris's views.

Paquet, Sandra Pouchet. *The Novels of George Lamming.* London: Heinemann, 1982. Introduces Lamming's six novels chronologically and examines their depiction of the structure and organization of a society affected by colonization and the extent to which this shapes individual response and action. Stresses the characteristic ways in which Lamming's fiction explores the present in relation to the past and the future as well as the public responsibility of the artist within a society shaped by a colonial mentality, the political message being that both societies, the descendants of Caliban and of Prospero alike, still have to emancipate themselves from the bias of their colonial inheritance.

Petersen, Kirsten Holst. "Time, Timelessness, and the Journey Metaphor in George Lamming's *In the Castle of My Skin* and *Natives of My Person.*" *Commonwealth Writers Overseas.* Brussels: Didier, 1976. 283–88. Considers the first and latest of Lamming's novels. Applies Wilson Harris's concept of "fossil awareness" of the past to Lamming's use of time: Being concerned with community rather than the individual, these novels resemble the second part of *Pilgrim's Progress,* and Lamming's entire *oeuvre* can be understood as one long journey.

Tiffin, Helen. "The Tyranny of History: George Lamming's *Natives of My Person* and *Water with Berries.*" *Ariel* 10.4 (1979): 37–52. Approaches the thematic influence of history on Lamming's latest two novels. Argues that the personal relationships depicted, particularly those between the sexes, reflect the pattern of enslavement in its historical and political dimension, emphasizing the interlocked relationship between colonizer and colonized, from which no voyage can offer an escape.

West, David S. "Lamming's Poetic Language in *In the Castle of My Skin.*" *Literary Half-Yearly* 18 (1977): 71–83. Examines Lamming's use of language in his first novel. Demonstrates how the devices of sound, symbol, and imagery are employed to convey a wealth of suggestion in a poetic manner. Divides the devices into two categories: the skillful use of sound and rhythm and the consistent use of symbols throughout the novel. Adds a more detailed investigation of the symbol of the castle.

Interviews

With Frank Birbalsingh. *Journal of Commonwealth Literature* 23.1 (1988): 182–88.
With Ian Munro and Reinhard Sander. *Kas-Kas: Interviews with Three Caribbean Writers in Texas.* Austin: African and Afro-American Research Institute, 1972. 5–21.

— RUDOLF BADER

Earl Lovelace

E arl Lovelace is unusual among West Indian writers in that—though he was educated at Howard University and has taught at Johns Hopkins University—he has lived virtually all of his life in the West Indies, in Trinidad and Tobago. He was born in 1935 in Toco, Trinidad, and was raised in Tobago and in Trinidad's largest city, Port of Spain.

He has worked for the Trinidad Civil Service in the Forestry Department and for the Department of Agriculture. He has also worked as a journalist and now teaches at the University of the West Indies, Trinidad. His first novel, *While Gods Are Falling*, received the BP Independence Literary Award.

COMMUNITY AND CULTURE

Though Earl Lovelace has published a collection of plays and a collection of short stories, his novels constitute his major claim to critical attention. Each of his four novels stands on its own; there are no overt connections among them such as overlapping plots or characters. Yet in another sense they demand consideration together, as they form a sustained meditation on a common cluster of themes. The central question posed in all the novels is the same: How can a sense of community be realized in West Indian (or, more specifically, in Trinidadian) society with its complex stratifications and divisions resulting from its entangled history and demography? The proper verb here is "posed," not "answered," because the open-endedness and lack of finality in Lovelace's thinking must strike anyone who looks at the novels as a whole. His fiction, though concerned with social questions, is never tendentious or narrowly ideological.

Of the four novels, the first and the third, *While Gods Are Falling* and *The Dragon Can't Dance*, share a contemporary urban setting in Port of Spain, while the second and the fourth, *The Schoolmaster* and *The Wine of Astonishment*, are set in rural Trinidadian villages a generation or two ago. But the novels also group themselves another way. Lovelace's first two books, published closely together in the 1960s, tell much the same story despite their different setting, while his later two novels, also published closely together, interweave in complex and subtle ways. In the later two much more technically assured novels and Lovelace's major achievements to date, his enduring concern with community is complemented by a growing concern with culture, specifically with the popular or vernacular culture of the Caribbean. It is his ability in these two great works to tap the energies of that culture, thus making them the powerful statement and expression they are.

While Gods Are Falling is reflected through a central consciousness, Walter Castle, who is also the protagonist of the novel. Castle is a frustrated, disillusioned man, frustrated by his own failure to move ahead in the government bureaucracy in which he works, disillusioned by the condition of his country after Independence. He lives in a tenement in a Port of Spain slum, which represents a tangible image of his failure. What he wants to do (or says he wants to do) is to quit his job and return to the village in the country where he was born. Across the novel, flashbacks return to his native village and to his memories of two years spent cutting timber in an isolated part of Trinidad. These events are particularly powerful memories for him because at that time he felt part of an undivided and whole community, not isolated as he is in the Port of Spain bureaucracy and slum life. Yet another part of him recognizes that this life is not there to resume, because political organization of the woodcutters and new environmental restrictions have led to the dissolution of that community; he soon realizes that rural Trinidad faces many of the same problems as urban Trinidad. In any case he has a wife and a child to support. The solution Castle embraces is not to escape the city but to transform it. A young man, who Castle knows slightly, is falsely arrested for taking part in the murder of a man by a gang, so Castle risks his job by organizing community support for the accused. Before long virtually everyone in the tenement joins in this endeavor. Once atomization is overcome in the face of social solidarity, a genuine human community emerges. The young man is freed, and the novel ends with Castle and his wife going off to a community meeting.

While Gods Are Falling is a remarkable first novel that undoubtedly deserved the award it received, but one flaw lies in its reliance on Castle's reflections to carry the theme. On the other hand, *The Schoolmaster*, Lovelace's second novel, avoids the use of any central, reflective consciousness. It is set in the remote village of Kumaca, a village not unlike the woodcutters' community in *While Gods Are Falling*, at least in its innocence and strong sense of community. But *The Schoolmaster* tells of the loss of that innocence. The village people ask for a school and a road to link them to the rest of the island; the schoolmaster has nothing but contempt for their rural simplicity, and he quickly conspires with the shopkeeper in the village to profit from the new road by buying up the land in its path. He also rapes and impregnates a young village girl. When the schoolmaster's deeds are revealed after the girl commits suicide, he tries to leave the village; but the villagers kill him by shooting his horse, causing him to fall and break his neck. They simply tell the authorities that he died as a result of a fall from his horse. In the dénouement *The Schoolmaster* most closely resembles *While Gods Are Falling*. Although it involves a crime instead of a false accusation, in each case someone is freed from prison (or its possibility), freed from the coercive power of the state, and freed by an act of social solidarity. The community of the village—though violated by the outside world—restores itself in the end, restored not by one energetic individual—as in *While Gods Are Falling*—but by the cohesive action of the whole community.

This evocation of communal solidarity is difficult to resist emotionally, particularly given Lovelace's rich evocation of the rural setting of *The Schoolmaster*. But intellectually the resolution of Lovelace's second novel shares a weakness with *While Gods Are Falling*. The unanswered question is a simple one: What next? What will come of the admittedly fragile community of the urban populace of Port of Spain? What will happen to the re-emergent but still damaged community of Kumaca? Lovelace is too perceptive an observer not to have delineated all the tensions underneath the achievement of community at the end of each novel; and the differences in status, in economic level, and in education that caused the initial disintegration of community have not been eliminated, which makes the re-achievement of community both fragile and not completely convincing.

Lovelace has not figured out how to express this community in the form of the novel. Essays on Lovelace's work by Marjorie Thorpe and Harold Barratt have presented the search for a hero as his central theme, but Lovelace seems more interested in the search for a community without a need for a hero. In this sense, *The Schoolmaster* represents an advance over *While Gods Are Falling*, which by the choice of the (at least initially) alienated intellectual Walter Castle as protagonist, seems caught up in the very atomization it seeks to overcome. *The Schoolmaster* has no single protagonist, and in this it seems more expressive of Lovelace's social vision. Yet the tone of the narrative—written in correct, metropolitan standard English— is very much outside and above the villagers, part of the wider world that Lovelace nonetheless sees as the problem. If there is a character in the novel who could have written it, it would be the evil schoolmaster. And I think it fair to say that in neither of his first two novels has Lovelace completely overcome a gap between the kind of novel he is writing and the kind he would like to write.

This may explain the long period between the 1965 publication of *The Schoolmaster* and the 1979 publication of Lovelace's third novel, *The Dragon Can't Dance*, followed shortly in 1982 by *The Wine of Astonishment*. The latter two have successfully and triumphantly eliminated any felt gap between subject and style. They represent a tremendous breakthrough, not just in Lovelace's fiction, but also for the expressive possibilities of West Indian fiction. They may well be the most successful and powerful works of West Indian fiction in the last twenty-five years.

"'All o' we is one'" is the phrase that resounds throughout *The Dragon Can't Dance*. But far from being a straightforward evocation of community, the phrase is a complex representation of the palpable barriers to community that exist, of the ways in which "we" are not one. For the words are spoken by Miss Cleothilda, the mulatto storekeeper in the yard of a Port of Spain poor neighborhood, where the novel is set. Most of the year, Cleothilda considers herself better than her neighbors because she is lighter skinned; but as Carnival approaches, she drops her superior pose in favor of solidarity.

Carnival is the event for which most of the yard lives and during which everyone feels most alive. Philo, who Cleothilda will not let in her bed because of his dark skin, is a calypsonian who each year hopes to win the annual prize; Fisheye is a street tough or "warrior" who expresses his manhood yearly as a member of Calvary Hill's steelband; Aldrick annually masquerades as a dragon and dances through Carnival. There is more than irony in Cleothilda's words, for during the few days of Carnival "'all o' we is one'": The tensions and strains of a postcolonial society are overcome in ritual celebration that creates a sense of community rooted in local, vernacular culture.

Lovelace's development beyond his first two novels, especially *While Gods Are Falling*, is obvious. The community Lovelace had been looking for in the first novel he now perceives to have been there all along, in the popular or vernacular culture, in calypso, in steel band music, above all in Carnival. The idea is expressed indirectly through the multiple protagonists of the novel; and the style of *The Dragon Can't Dance* is in perfect keeping with this sense of community, for the earlier split between the language of the dialogue and the language of the narration has at last been overcome. There is an omniscient, third-person narrator, but his voice stays close in style, diction, and grammar to that of the characters. He seems like another person living on the Hill as he cuts the distance between the perspective of the novel and the characters.

This book would seem to accomplish all of the community-creation Lovelace sought in his earlier work, and indeed one of the themes in *The Dragon Can't Dance* is a celebration of Carnival as an image of a desirably democratic and popular West Indian society. Angelita Reyes has expertly analyzed this aspect of the novel in terms of Victor Turner's anthropological concepts of anti-structure and liminality. (Bakhtin's work on popular festivals in *Rabelais and His World* would also be useful here.) But Carnival lasts only three days: What about the rest of the year? How can the sense that "'all o' we is one'" last beyond Carnival? After all, the title of the novel is *The Dragon Can't Dance*, which serves as one expression of the barriers to the diffusion of Carnival spirit beyond its temporal limit.

Most of the novel portrays, in fact, the same kind of erosion of the community spirit traced in Lovelace's other work. After the first Carnival is depicted in all its richness, we see in successive years the communal spirit under pressure, with the three major male characters feeling this loss of spirit and reacting to it differently. The warrior Fisheye turns resolutely against the trend. The steelbands in Carnival are becoming commercialized and getting sponsors who abhor the violence associated with the warriors; therefore, Fisheye turns increasingly antagonistic toward his former fellow band members. Philo, in contrast, develops into a successful calypsonian, swimming with the tide and eventually moving from Calvary Hill out to the suburbs. Aldrick, the most attractive character, finds himself caught between these two clear-cut responses. The concrete embodiment of his dilemma is Sylvia, a beautiful young girl living in the yard, obviously attracted to him yet pursued by Guy, the rent collector. Aldrick is afraid of commitment, for it would make him complicit in the conventional society from which he has tried to stay free; but he also fears that a refusal of commitment means accepting an ineffective marginality. So Carnival may not be a viable model for social transformation as much as an escape valve for the dispossessed.

These reflections help shape Aldrick's role in the strangest event of the novel, which occurs when he, Fisheye, and a few others kidnap a policeman and declare themselves the People's Liberation Army. Their attempted revolt fails, and they are sentenced to prison, where Aldrick realizes why they did not succeed. He tells Fisheye, who does not understand, that they were only "playing mas'," playing a masquerade just as Aldrick only played the dragon in Carnival. So the theatrical nature of their revolt underscores its lack of connection with reality. After all, in the social world that governs the year except for the few days of Carnival, the dragon can't dance.

The novel's conclusion brings all these forces together. Aldrick gets out of prison, returns to the yard to see Sylvia only to be told that she is going to marry Guy, who has become a City Councillor and is in England. At about the same time, Philo realizes with a start that he has become everything he once despised. In a crucial conversation close to the end of the novel, he tells a friend about the roots of his music, which came from the Spiritual Baptist community where he was raised. Through this confession, he criticizes himself for commercializing something that belonged to the whole community. He then returns to the Hill to see Cleothilda, who tells him that Sylvia has left Guy's apartment and run away to find Aldrick. She asks him if he is leaving the island and in the very last sentence of the novel invites him into her bedroom.

The ending is richly ambivalent. Cleothilda's invitation to Philo serves as an image of the distinct crumbling of the old racism. Yet is she willing to sleep with Philo now just because he is rich and famous? Aldrick's new connection to Sylvia may be his desire to break out of his own chosen marginality, yet he is still as marginal with respect to economic structures as ever. Sylvia's and Philo's actions may be taken as a repudiation of the bourgeois respectability they were moving towards, but there are crucial differences between them. If Philo goes abroad, is not that just a further suburbanization, a further move away from his roots in the Trinidadian community? But these "what next" questions are not damaging to the novel's coherence the way similar questions were for the earlier novels, because they are questions Lovelace asks these characters and they ask themselves. The ending is triumphantly rather than awkwardly ambivalent, for Lovelace has created an ensemble of characters changing and growing in just the ways they need to.

The Dragon Can't Dance would seem to cry out for a "sequel," for a look at what happens next to these characters, but *The Wine of Astonishment* instead builds on Philo's reflection on his youth and returns to the rural Trinidad of the 1930s and 1940s. The novel is set in the village of Bonasse and narrated by Eva, the wife of a Spiritual Baptist preacher. This use of a narrator, a first for Lovelace, is perhaps even more successful than the use of a Creolized English by the omniscient narrator of *The Dragon Can't Dance*, for here Eva's dialect is dramatically perfect as well as stylistically powerful and exciting. The Spiritual Baptists were a religious community at odds with the law in colonial Trinidad, for they sang, spoke in tongues, and in general broke the English decorum of colonial Christianity in favor of what they saw as African religious practices. They were outlawed for a time in Trinidad, and *The Wine of Astonishment* tells the story of one congregation of Spiritual Baptists struggling to keep their identity with their characteristic form of worship proscribed. The community looks to the village schoolteacher, Ivan Morton, for help; again, however, education has led to acculturation, for he thinks they should stop their "heathen practices" and refuses to help. Bolo, the village warrior, in contrast, tries to resist the police when they come to arrest the congregation, but this attempt at violent resistance is as unsuccessful as Fisheye's in *The Dragon Can't Dance*. The congregation dwindles and loses its focus, while the wartime economic boom transforms the Trinidad economy, and much of the village goes off to work for the Americans. Thus this one village becomes a microcosm for the Caribbean and its cultural identity: Should they follow Ivan Morton and Anglicize themselves through education? Should they Americanize themselves through capitalism and economic development? Or can they somehow retain their own authentic identity?

At the end of the novel, the law is repealed, as the Spiritual Baptists appear so marginal that they appear to represent no threat. The congregation fervently returns to the old singing, but nothing happens: "The hymns we was singing was coming out our mouth in the Anglican and Catholic way and it wasn't like old times at all." The Spirit does not come and everyone feels crushed. But when Eva and her husband on their way home from church find a steelband playing and people dancing, they feel that "the music that those boys playing on the steelband have in it that same Spirit that we miss in our church: the same Spirit; and listening to them, my heart swell and it is like resurrection morning."

This awareness leads into *The Dragon Can't Dance* just as the end of *The Dragon* leads into *The Wine of Astonishment.* What Spiritual Baptist and steelband music have in common, that "Spirit " of which Eva speaks, is that both proceed from the people and are not imposed on them from without. Such a spirit Lovelace's fiction always celebrates, and celebrates it by style as well as subject. The novels together suggest a quiet optimism as to the ability of that spirit to survive and triumph. Its manifestations will change, but the spirit itself will not. Community is always under pressure in the world of Lovelace's fiction, but it nonetheless restores itself, primarily through culture, through the vernacular or popular culture of the West Indian people. Lovelace is one of the greatest West Indian writers today precisely because of his ability to tap the power of that culture.

All of this emphasis on community may seem to make Lovelace an exceedingly inappropriate candidate to include in this collection of essays, for one way of presenting him would be as the least international of all West Indian writers in English, content to stay on Trinidad and quite set against the internationalization of West Indian culture. But this approach would be incorrect. In the great debate over a Caribbean identity, Lovelace is clearly on the side of the indigenists: We do not need to go off to England with Ivan Morton or Guy; neither do we need to go off to America. We need to look to our own traditions. But here is a debate that runs though all of international literature in English, and Lovelace's position has clear parallels in other situations. The clearest analogy is to the debate over decolonization in African literature. But Lovelace's work is less akin to Chinweizu's fervent denunciation of anyone who does not meet his "decolonialization" standard than to the work of Ngugi, who has declared the necessity of writing in African languages and using African forms. Lovelace has no other language than English in which to write, but his embracing of Creole or dialect rather than standard English is a comparable declaration of literary independence. Perhaps one reason Lovelace's work has not received the attention it deserves is that he has unobtrusively decolonized himself rather than loudly denouncing others for not meeting some impossible standard of decolonization or indigenism.

There is one substantial problem, however. The community with which Lovelace identifies and seeks to celebrate is the black Caribbean one, another reason the reference to Africa seems appropriate. But if a broad, inclusive sense of community is to be created in a place like Trinidad, it cannot be founded purely along black and Africanist lines. Trinidad is an especially complex multicultural and multiracial society, and a sense of a Trinidadian community cannot be based exclusively on a black identity without leaving out a large part of that community. Trinidad and Guyana are distinguished from the rest of the West Indies by their large East Asian population, 32 per cent in the case of Trinidad, more than 50 per cent in Guyana. The community Lovelace celebrates must therefore coexist with other communities.

Lovelace is too good a writer not to be aware of this problem, and his awareness surfaces in *The Dragon Can't Dance*, through the East Indian character Pariag, the one Indian who lives in the yard. Although he tries to fit in with the others, all his attempts are rebuffed and eventually he stops trying. By the end of the novel, he runs his own shop, which has undercut Cleothilda's business, and he is well on his way to the same kind of atomized social success as Philo. Pariag represents the aspect of Trinidadian society that Lovelace has not quite been able to fit into his vision of community; and until he does so, his vision will seem partial and incomplete.

But perhaps Lovelace is in the same boat as everyone else: the more urgent task in the world today is to balance assertions of identity with an acceptance of difference. International writing in English is of particular importance in this regard because it is a theater in which these issues are played out, stylistically as well as thematically. And Earl Lovelace is one of the most powerful voices in that theater.

EARL LOVELACE'S PUBLISHED WORK

Novels

While Gods Are Falling, 1965
The Schoolmaster, 1968
The Dragon Can't Dance, 1979
The Wine of Astonishment, 1982

Short Story Collection

A Brief Conversion and Other Stories, 1988

Drama

Jestina's Calypso and Other Plays, 1984

SELECTED CRITICAL READINGS

Astonishingly little has been written on Earl Lovelace. The study of Caribbean literature suffers from an overly restrictive canon in which three or four writers receive the lion's share of critical attention, and Lovelace is not one of those writers. Standard works on Caribbean literature tend to ignore him: Kenneth Ramchand's 1970 study *The West Indian Novel and Its Background* does not mention Lovelace, while the foreword to the 1982 reprint acknowledges him as an important omission but does not rectify it. Critics who celebrate the popular and political aspect of Caribbean literature, such as Selwyn Cudjoe in *Resistance and Caribbean Literature* or Amon Saba Sakaana in *The Colonial Legacy in Caribbean Literature*, ought to find

Lovelace their ideal Caribbean writer; but oddly and disappointingly neither critic does more than mention his work. Hence the critical literature on Lovelace, as listed below, consists of just seven articles appearing in specialized journals in the field, primarily *World Literature Written in English* and *The Literary Half-Yearly.*

Barratt, Harold. ""Metaphor and Symbol in *The Dragon Can't Dance.*" *World Literature Written in English* 23 (1984): 405–13. Concentrates on how the Carnival setting and the implicit references to the Crucifixion help structure *The Dragon Can't Dance.*

———. "Michael Anthony and Earl Lovelace: The Search for Selfhood." *ACLALS Bulletin* 5.3 (1980): 62–73. Compares the two Trinidadian writers in terms of their sense of place and the theme of selfhood or individuation in their novels.

Cary, Norman Reed. "Salvation, Self and Solidarity in the Work of Earl Lovelace." *World Literature Written in English* 28 (1988): 103–14. Discusses the relation between the individual and society in all of Lovelace's work, probably the most comprehensive look to date.

Gowda, H. H. Anniah. "A Brief Note on the Dialect Novels of Sam Selvon and Earl Lovelace." *The Literary Half-Yearly* 27.2 (1986): 98–103. Compares the two Trinidadian novelists in terms of their use of dialect.

Reyes, Angelita. "Carnival: Ritual Dance of the Past and Present in Earl Lovelace's *The Dragon Can't Dance.*" *World Literature Written in English* 24 (1984): 107–20. Probably the most substantive essay on Lovelace's work. Relates *The Dragon Can't Dance* to Victor Turner's work on ritual and community.

Sunitha, K. T. "The Discovery of Selfhood in the Fiction of Earl Lovelace." *Subjects Worthy of Fame: Essays on Commonwealth Literature in Honour of H. H. Anniah Gowda.* Delhi: Sterling, 1989. 123–32. Similar to Barratt and Thorpe in its focus on the individual in Lovelace's work.

Thorpe, Marjorie. "In Search of the West Indian Hero: A Study of Earl Lovelace's Fiction." *Critical Issues in West Indian Literature: Selected Papers from West Indian Literature Conferences 1981–1983.* Parkersburg, Iowa: Caribbean Books, 1984. 90–100. Presents "the search for a hero-figure" as the central theme of Lovelace's four novels. Distinguishes between the true heroes, the false heroes committed to materialism, and the failed heroes who withdraw into alienation.

— REED WAY DASENBROCK

Alan Paton

Alan Stewart Paton was born in Pietermaritzburg, South Africa, 11 January 1903. He was educated at Maritzburg College and Natal University College, where he obtained a B.Sc. degree and a teacher's diploma.

After teaching at his old school, Maritzburg College, he was in 1935 appointed principal of Diepkloof Reformatory for young black delinquents. Diepkloof was situated on the outskirts of Johannesburg, close to the black township of Orlando, later to be incorporated into Soweto.

In 1948 Paton's first novel, *Cry, the Beloved Country*, was published simultaneously in the United States and Great Britain. In the same year Dr. Malan and his National Party came to power on an apartheid ticket. Paton then resigned from Diepkloof and embarked on a full-time writing career.

Paton's second novel, *Too Late the Phalarope*, was published in 1953. This was followed by a collection of short stories entitled *Debbie Go Home* (U.S. title: *Tales from a Troubled Land*), and several books on contemporary South Africa, its politics and its problems. *Hofmeyr*, the biography of a leading South African politician, was published in 1964. Soon after the death of Paton's wife, Dorrie, in 1967, he wrote a tribute to her entitled *Kontakion for You Departed*. They had two sons, David and Jonathan.

In 1969 Paton married his second wife, Anne. Four years later another biography, *Apartheid and the Archbishop*, was published. This work detailed the life of a former Anglican Archbishop of Cape Town, Geoffrey Clayton.

Paton's role as writer was often in conflict with his role as reluctant politician. He was a founding member of the Liberal Party of South Africa in 1953 and later became its president. In 1968 government legislation made the continued existence of the Liberal Party impossible, and it was disbanded. For his literary and humanitarian work Paton received several honorary doctorates from universities throughout the world, including Harvard, Yale, Edinburgh, Natal, and Witwatersrand.

Toward the end of his life Paton wrote and completed his autobiography. Part I is titled *Towards the Mountain* and was published in 1980; Part II, *Journey Continued*, completes his life story and was published less than three weeks after his death.

Alan Paton died at his home near Durban on 12 April 1988.

COMFORT IN DESOLATION

It is not easy for the son to write a critical appreciation of his father's books. It would be far easier for me to write an autobiography entitled "Son of Alan Paton," in which I would spell out both humorously and seriously the advantages and disadvantages of being the son of the great South African writer. Let me add that the disadvantages far outweigh the advantages. In this essay, I have resisted the temptation to speak of "my father" and will instead refer to him as "Alan Paton" or "Paton." However, I shall continue to write the essay in the first person, and in my comments on the various works the reader will detect a subjective, personal approach, not a detached analytical and critical style.

Cry, the Beloved Country was Alan Paton's first published novel. He had published several poems in student magazines in his youth and had attempted and abandoned at least two novels in the 1920s and early 1930s, but he did not earn the reputation of a "writer" until the publication of *Cry, the Beloved Country.* This novel gripped the imagination of the world and became a best seller overnight. In New York, Maxwell Anderson and Kurt Weill turned it into a successful musical, *Lost in the Stars*, which opened on Broadway in 1949. Soon afterward London Films produced a film of the novel, directed by Zolton Korda. Some readers in the United States and Great Britain were familiar with the works of South African poets and writers like Roy Campbell, William Plomer, and Olive Schreiner before the Second World War, but there is no doubt, as a South African critic once remarked, that *Cry, the Beloved Country* placed South Africa firmly on the international literary map.

In the introduction to *Cry, the Beloved Country*, Paton explains that although the novel is fictitious, it is largely rooted in fact—most of the events are fictional but certain events are "a compound of truth and fiction." "In these respects therefore," he writes, "the story is not true, but considered as a social record it is the plain and simple truth." Moral considerations are also important to Paton, considerations based on his Christian beliefs, even though throughout his career he was opposed to literature that was essentially didactic. Nevertheless he once stated that his aim was to write books that would "stab South Africa in the conscience." I believe that apart from narrating a gripping story, Paton is deliberately attempting to do just that in the pages of *Cry, the Beloved Country.*

Paton wrote the novel while he was away from South Africa, touring Scandinavia, Britain, and the United States, visiting reformatories and other penal institutions— he was still principal of Diepkloof Reformatory. He began the book in a lonely hotel room in Trondheim, Norway, and finished it in San Francisco. This was Paton's first lengthy visit away from his native land, and he was filled with nostalgia for his beloved country. While visiting the cathedral in Trondheim, he was deeply moved by the beauty of a large rose window. He left the cathedral filled with "strange emotions," returned to his hotel room and wrote down, almost without hesitation: "There is a lovely road that runs from Ixopo into the hills" and then completed the rest of the chapter before going out to dinner. Ixopo is a beautiful country village in Natal where Paton had met and fallen in love with his first wife, Dorrie. At the same time he had also fallen in love with the extraordinary beauty of Ixopo's rolling hills covered in grass and bracken, "lovely beyond any singing of it."

While strong feelings of nostalgia drove Paton to begin writing *Cry, the Beloved Country,* he certainly did not write a nostalgic novel. The story of the simple Zulu parson, Stephen Kumalo, and his desperate search for his son, Absalom, in the vast city of Johannesburg, arouses a wide range of emotions. The novel is indeed, as it is subtitled, "a story of comfort in desolation." It is also a story of the injustices of segregation and the white man's laws. Readers will notice I have not used the word "apartheid." Paton wrote the novel toward the end of 1946. It was only in 1948 (the year of the novel's publication) that the Afrikaner Nationalist government came into power and entrenched "apartheid." The injustices, however, of the system go back a long way, for it was in the nineteenth century that the blacks lost most of their land. By 1946 Paton had been principal of Diepkloof Reformatory for eleven years, and he had discovered the appalling consequences of migratory labor. Black men were attracted to places like Johannesburg to work in the mines and other industries, but their wives and children were not allowed to accompany them. The character of Arthur Jarvis in the novel is very much modeled on Paton himself. After Jarvis is murdered, his father spends some time in his son's study reading from a manuscript that is still incomplete. Here is one of the passages he reads:

> It was permissible when we discovered gold to bring labour to the mines. It was permissible to build compounds and to keep women and children away from the towns. It was permissible as an experiment, in the light of what we knew. But in the light of what we know now, with certain exceptions, it is no longer permissible. It is not permissible for us to go on destroying family life when we know that we are destroying it.

These views were very much Paton's own and were to lead him into a head-on clash with the Afrikaner Nationalist government in later years.

A great deal has been written about the style of *Cry, the Beloved Country,* so not much will be said about it here. The language on the whole is simple, yet profound. There are many cadences that bring to mind passages from the King James version of the Bible. Paton was a devout Christian and read and reread the Bible many times. He was also familiar with the Zulu language, and on occasion the prose imitates the style of Zulu speech rhythms. Of course, there are several other styles in the book, one of which is illustrated in the example of Arthur Jarvis's forceful indictment of migrant labor. This is often the style used by Paton in his nonfictional writing.

The central theme of the novel is, in my opinion, the theme of detribalization, of social disintegration. Before the industrial revolution began in South Africa, most black people lived in the tribal homelands, areas that had been allocated to them after they were dispossessed of most of their land. But the stretches where they lived were on the whole of poor quality, partly due to the nature of the terrain, partly due to overgrazing and ignorance of conservation methods. Paton describes that land vividly in *Cry, the Beloved Country:*

> The great red hills stand desolate, and the earth has torn away like flesh. . . . Down in the valleys women scratch the soil that is left,

and the maize hardly reaches the height of a man. They are valleys of old men and old women, of mothers and children. The men are away, the young men and the girls are away. The soil cannot keep them anymore.

The men and the women could no longer support their families and moved to the cities. Some sent money and returned home once a year to visit; but others neglected their families and found lovers. The stories of Absalom and of Gertrude and of John Kumalo are the stories of thousands upon thousands of black South Africans even today. As principal of Diepkloof Reformatory, Paton made a close study of juvenile crime in the cities and found that the root causes were the breakup of family life and the lack of a tribal support system. Overcrowded slums and unemployment contributed further to the growing crime wave.

Another theme that runs through the novel is the theme of fear, for there is fear throughout the land. At the beginning, Kumalo is afraid to open the letter from Johannesburg. He is afraid of Johannesburg. He is afraid that when people go to Johannesburg they do not come back. Later in the novel, Msimangu tells Kumalo: "It is fear that rules this land." Whites fear that blacks will rob them of their land and possessions. Blacks fear the cruelty of the white man's law. The author's voice also takes up this theme:

> Cry, the beloved country, for the unborn child that is the inheritor
> of our fear. . . . Let him not be moved when the birds of the land
> are singing, nor give too much of his heart to a mountain or a valley.
> For fear will rob him of all if he gives too much.

But the most striking illustration of the theme of fear is the remark that Msimangu makes to Kumalo about white people: "I have one great fear in my heart, that one day when they are turned to loving, they will find we are turned to hating." It is remarkable to think that Paton wrote these words in 1946. In the late 1980s the Afrikaner Nationalist government began to redress some of the wrongs of the past, but many black leaders claimed that it was doing "too little, too late." In fairness, however, it should be pointed out that in 1990 there are hundreds of thousands of black people who *do not* hate whites and who *do* seek reconciliation.

It would be wrong to conclude these comments about *Cry, the Beloved Country* on a note of destruction and fear. It is, after all, a story of *comfort* in desolation. In *Alan Paton*, Edward Callan points out the counter-theme of the need to restore: "Stephen Kumalo's physical search for his son, Absalom, and James Jarvis's intellectual search for his son, Arthur" both resulted in "an inner, spiritual awakening" (28). The reader cannot fail to see the author's optimism in the belief that restoration will follow disintegration. And the theme of fear is counter-balanced by the theme of love, rooted in Paton's Christian convictions. Until his death in 1988, he refused to give up the struggle for racial reconciliation in South Africa. For he *did* believe that one day the dawn would come "of our emancipation, from the fear of bondage and the bondage of fear."

I have devoted a considerable portion of this essay to a discussion of *Cry, the Beloved Country*, partly because it is by far the best known of Paton's works, but also because I believe it is essential reading if one is to understand the complex issues that exist in South Africa in 1990. Certain sections of the novel have become dated, but most of it remains relevant forty years later.

Paton on more than one occasion remarked that his second novel, *Too Late the Phalarope*, was a better novel than *Cry, the Beloved Country*. However, he did not go into great detail on his reasons. All he would say is that *Too Late the Phalarope* had a "better structure." I would agree with this view, but at the same time I think I can understand why the work never enjoyed the popularity of the first novel, particularly outside South Africa. One reason lies in the title of the book. The phalarope (pronounced "fallarope") is a bird found in several parts of the world, including South Africa and the United States. But it is rarely seen and is totally unknown to most people. I have met many people who have heard of the book, but who have not the slightest idea of what a phalarope is, let alone how the strange word is pronounced.

There are other problems. Many of my students have the read the book but still fail to understand the title. They fail to see that the moment of the sighting of the phalarope by Jakob van Vlaanderen and his son Pieter marks a moment of potential reconciliation between estranged father and son, for the father rests his arm on the son's shoulder. But the moment has come too late, for the terrifying process that will culminate in Pieter's arrest in terms of the Immorality Act has already been set in motion.

A problem for readers outside South Africa is the lack of understanding of the Afrikaner people and their history. A few years ago I met several people in the United States who thought that Afrikaners were black. It is possible that in 1990 the name "Afrikaner" is more widely understood, since South Africa has been much in the limelight in recent years. Paton came to know Afrikaners very well during his years at Diepkloof Reformatory, where most of his white staff were Afrikaans-speaking. He admired the Afrikaans language and was an avid reader of Afrikaans literature. But he was an implacable opponent of Afrikaner Nationalism and its apartheid ideology. *Too Late the Phalarope* is not, as some critics have suggested, anti-Afrikaner. It shows tremendous compassion for the Afrikaner while at the same time criticizing the racist laws implemented by Afrikaner nationalism.

In *Cry, the Beloved Country*, the protagonist is a Zulu parson, Stephen Kumalo. In *Too Late the Phalarope* the protagonist is an Afrikaner policeman, Pieter van Vlaanderen. Both characters undergo deep and terrible suffering and are treated with great compassion by the author. Both novels are indictments of racist legislation and the pain it causes. Both novels contain superb descriptions of the beauty of the author's native country. But there the similarities cease. *Cry, the Beloved Country* is a story of comfort in desolation. In *Too Late the Phalarope* there is very little comfort. As Callan has pointed out, the latter novel may be compared to a Greek tragedy. Once Pieter has committed the "crime" against the white Afrikaner race of having sexual intercourse with a black woman, his fate has been sealed, in spite of his attempts to repent and to persuade his wife to be less sexually inhibited. Like Oedipus, Pieter is caught in an inextricable web and his family is destroyed. The harsh society that made the "iron law" of the Immorality Act does not allow for restoration.

Too Late the Phalarope is a gripping story throughout. The narrator, Pieter's Aunt Sophie, suffers a physical deformity, and although aware of the impending tragedy, feels helpless to intervene. Paton excels in depicting Pieter's inner conflict, the sexual frustration in his marriage, his subsequent attraction for the black woman, Stephanie, and the enormous guilt he experiences each time he has intercourse with her. The deeply religious Pieter, steeped in guilt for his infidelity to his wife and even more so for breaking the "iron law" of the Afrikaner nation, prays to God for forgiveness. But his prayers are in vain, for he is arrested and sent to prison and the family of van Vlaanderen is destroyed. Old Jakob van Vlaanderen is unable to forgive his son and dies a broken man.

After *Too Late the Phalarope* Paton ceased writing novels for some time. He continued to write short stories, poems, political articles, religious works, two biographies, and two volumes of his own autobiography. I wish to comment briefly on his third and last novel, *Ah, But Your Land Is Beautiful*, appearing nearly 30 years after *Too Late the Phalarope*. In the 1970s Paton had read and found most impressive Paul Scott's *The Raj Quartet*. The mixture of fact and fiction in these four novels intrigued Paton. Around 1980 he decided that he would attempt to depict South Africa's contemporary history as Scott had done with India. He planned a trilogy: the first novel would be based on the decade of the 1950s, the second on the 1960s, the third on the 1970s, including the riots in Soweto in 1976.

Ah, But Your Land Is Beautiful, set in the 1950s, is not, in my opinion, a success. It lacks the deeply moving qualities of *Cry, the Beloved Country* as well as its compassion and messages of comfort in desolation. While it is also an indictment of racial discrimination, there is no character in the novel whose personal tragedy is depicted so vividly and terrifyingly as that of Stephen Kumalo or Pieter van Vlaanderen. The characters, on the whole, are much shallower than the characters of the earlier novels. Mansfield, the white liberal, is clearly based to some extent on the author himself. Actual historical personages such as Trevor Huddleston and Albert Lutuli also appear in the novel. I think that Paton realized he had lost the art of novel writing (while still remaining a superb writer), for he abandoned the rest of the trilogy.

Paton is so well known as the author of *Cry, the Beloved Country* that many readers are unaware that he also wrote several excellent short stories. In 1960 some of these were published in New York under the title *Tales from a Troubled Land* and in London as *Debbie Go Home*. Most of these stories are based on his experiences at Diepkloof Reformatory and are accounts of sometimes tragic, sometimes comic episodes involving inmates and staff of the reformatory. Perhaps the best of these is "Sponono," a story in which the principal and an incorrigible inmate are involved in a seemingly endless duel about the nature of forgiveness. This story was turned into a musical and enjoyed a reasonably successful run on Broadway in 1964. Paton's best story is, in my opinion, "The Hero of Currie Road," published in the collection *Knocking on the Door*. It is a story, told with pathos and humor, of the dilemma that confronts a white South African liberal in his attempts to fight against white racism on one hand and militant black nationalism, which condones violence, on the other.

It is again, to some extent, the story of Paton's own life.

The bulk of Paton's writing, which will not be discussed here, falls under the heading of nonfiction. The author became increasingly interested in the writing of biography and devoted many years of his life to the researching and writing of the biography entitled *Hofmeyr*. Jan Hofmeyr, one of South Africa's most brilliant sons, was a close friend of Paton's, and his strongly held liberal beliefs exerted a powerful influence on the author. Paton's biography tells of Hofmeyr's domination by his mother and by General Jan Smuts, South Africa's Prime Minister during the 1940s. Hofmeyr could never break free of Smuts's domination and failed in his attempts to steer South Africa in a more liberal direction; hence the American edition of this book was entitled *South African Tragedy*. Paton's second biography, less intriguing than *Hofmeyr*, was entitled *Apartheid and the Archbishop*, and is about a former Archbishop of Cape Town, Geoffrey Clayton.

For me, Paton's most moving work is *Kontakion for You Departed*, which narrates the story of the author's life with his wife Dorrie. It is an account of my mother and father's life together, and I was moved to tears when I first read it. I find it extremely painful to reread. (In the United States the book is called *For You Departed*.)

In conclusion, I shall mention briefly the two parts of Paton's autobiography. The first is called *Towards the Mountain* and tells in remarkably frank detail the story of the author's life from 1903 to 1948. The second, *Journey Continued*, is far less frank and, I think, considerably less successful. But I do find its conclusion very moving, written as it was shortly before Alan Paton's death. I should like to end by quoting the concluding lines:

> I shall not write anything more of any weight. I am grateful that life made it possible for me to pursue my writing career. I am now ready to go when I am called.

> God bless Africa
> Guard her children
> Guide her rulers
> And give her peace
> Amen.

WORK CITED

Callan, Edward. *Alan Paton, Revised Edition.* Boston: Twayne, 1982.

ALAN PATON'S PUBLISHED WORK

Novels

Cry, the Beloved Country, 1948
Too Late the Phalarope, 1953
Ah, But Your Land Is Beautiful, 1981

Short Story Collection

Tales from a Troubled Land, 1961 (British title: *Debbie Go Home*)

Plays

Lost in the Stars (with Maxwell Anderson), 1950
Sponono (with Krishna Shah), 1965

Biographies

Hofmeyr, 1964
South African Tragedy: The Life and Times of Jan Hofmeyr (abridged version of *Hofmeyr*), 1965
Apartheid and the Archbishop: The Life and Times of Geoffrey Clayton, Archbishop of Cape Town, 1973

Autobiographies

For You Departed, 1969 (British title: *Kontakion for You Departed*)
Towards the Mountain, 1980
Journey Continued, 1988

Nonfiction

South Africa in Transition (with Dan Weiner), 1956
Instrument of Thy Peace, 1968

Collected Writings

The Long View (edited by Edward Callan), 1968
Knocking on the Door: Shorter Writings of Alan Paton (edited by Colin Gardner), 1975
Save the Beloved Country (edited by Hans Strydom and David Jones), 1987

SELECTED CRITICAL READINGS

Like many writers who have gained a popular following, Alan Paton has never received extensive critical attention in academic journals, even in South Africa. His first two novels were widely and favorably reviewed in major international publications; but as the years went by and no more fiction appeared, critical interest seemed to lag, even though *Cry, the Beloved Country*, in particular, continues to be read the world over. Eventually, both the writer and his first novel became legendary to a degree, and his pivotal place in international literature in English was simply accepted but rarely commented on. The publication of articles in major international journals during the 1980s suggests that Paton's fiction has finally started to receive the serious attention it deserves. (I wish to acknowledge the use of Edward Callan's comprehensive bibliography of Paton's work and to express my thanks to Daniel Rabinowitz for his assistance in the collection of bibliographical material.)

Baker, Sheridan. "Paton's Late Phalarope." *English Studies in Africa* 3 (1960): 152–59. Critical review of Paton's technique and an examination of its shortcomings in *Too Late the Phalarope*.

Brown, Peter. "Alan Paton's *Ah, But Your Land Is Beautiful.*" *Reality* 14 (January 1982): 3. In this brief review Brown highlights the social and historical context of *Ah, But Your Land Is Beautiful.*

Callan, Edward. *Alan Paton, Revised Edition.* Boston: Twayne, 1982. Comprehensive and highly informative work on Paton's life and writings. (First edition published in 1968)

———. "Alan Paton's *Apartheid and the Archbishop:* an Allegory of the Christian Way." *English Studies in Africa* 19 (1976): 39–47. Examination of Paton's Christian humanism and the limitations of race consciousness.

Cooke, John. "A Hunger of the Soul: *Too Late the Phalarope* Reconsidered." *English Studies in Africa* 22 (1979): 37–43. Suggests that this novel embodies the psychic conflict within the Afrikaner nation toward miscegenation.

Maclennan, Don. "The South African Short Story." *English Studies in Africa* 13 (1970): 117–19. A brief appraisal of Paton's short stories that questions the transcendental quality of his religious conviction.

Morphet, Tony. "Alan Paton: The Honour of Meditation." *English in Africa* 10 (1983): 1–10. An appraisal of Paton at eighty. Commentary on the powerful emotions of fear and uncertainty that permeate his writings and that he attempted to resolve through his involvement in the Liberal Party and Anglican Church.

Moss, Rose. "Alan Paton: Bringing a Sense of the Sacred." *World Literature Today* 57 (1983): 233–37. Discusses Paton's fictional use of place, a usage at once physical, spiritual, universal, and mythical. Concludes that "the prophetic imperative he spoke in 1948 remains the imperative."

Stevens, Irma Ned. "Paton's Narrator Sophie: Justice and Mercy in *Too Late the Phalarope.*" *International Fiction Review* 8 (1981): 68–70. Argues that an appreciation and understanding of the narrator's position shows the novel's psychological truth, as well as its sociological value.

Thompson, John. "Poetic Truth in *Too Late the Phalarope.*" *English Studies in Africa* 24 (1981): 37–44. Analyzes the delicacy and complexity of human relationships as revealed in this novel.

Watson, Stephen. "*Cry, the Beloved Country* and the Failure of Liberal Vision." *English Studies in Africa* 9 (1982): 29–44. A scathing, controversial critique of this novel.

Voss, Tony. "Getting Up There Again: A Review of Alan Paton's *Knocking on the Door.*" *Reality* 8 (1976): 17–19. Sees *Knocking on the Door* as a scrutiny of Paton's liberal principles, in which an attempt is made to reconcile his Christian faith on one hand with the realities of South Africa on the other.

Watts, Nicholas H.Z. "A Study of Alan Paton's *Too Late the Phalarope.*" *Durham University Journal* 76 (1984): 249–54. Examines the novel in light of its depiction of the tragedy created by apartheid.

Interview

With Myriam Roson. *A Journal on the Teaching of English* 21 (1987): 43–47.

—JONATHAN PATON

Nadine Gordimer

The South African novelist, Nadine Gordimer, has been publishing fiction since 1937. In that year, when she was thirteen years old, a story of hers appeared in a Johannesburg newspaper. Her first book, a collection of short stories entitled *Face to Face*, appeared in Johannesburg in 1949. Since then she has produced a steady flow of fiction that reflects the social, moral, and political condition of life in South Africa. In 1953 her volume of short stories, *The Soft Voice of the Serpent*, was published in London and New York. The recognition earned by that book made her an international figure whose reputation has grown steadily and whose work has since been published and reviewed widely.

Born on 20 November 1923 to immigrant Jewish parents in Springs, a mining town on the Witwatersrand, the gold-bearing "reef" that runs through Johannesburg, she spent her childhood in that small-town setting, within commuting distance of Johannesburg. Her father was of Lithuanian extraction and worked as a watchmaker and jeweler. Her mother was of English origin. In a celebrated interview published in the *Paris Review* in 1983, Gordimer described the crucial effect of a decision by her mother to remove her from school at the age of eleven and keep her at home until the age of sixteen on the pretext of a heart condition. Not only was the young Gordimer prevented from continuing her dancing lessons, which she loved, but she was also deprived of the company of young people, visiting a private tutor for a few hours each day (after a year's complete absence from schooling) and otherwise living solely in the orbit of her parents and their friends. As a substitute for both her "acrobatic" dancing and friendship with children, she took to voracious reading and to writing. By the time she reached her mid-teens she had a completed a significant amount of juvenile writing, and she produced "adult" stories from her mid-teens on. She attended the University of the Witwatersrand for a short period as an undergraduate but left the University without taking a degree. After an unsuccessful and short-lived first marriage, she married again and has lived since then as a politically public but personally private Johannesburg figure, whose husband is himself known in the antique and art world. She has traveled extensively in Africa, Europe, and North America and makes frequent appearances as a speaker in North America.

Her status as a major world writer has been particularly secure since the publication in 1974 of her novel, *The Conservationist*, which won the Booker Prize. Gordimer's essays and articles have until recently been less well known and critically received than her short stories and novels. As she has become a more prominent analyst of the South African scene, however, her critical writing has become a focus of interest for those concerned with politics and literature in South Africa. The publication in 1988 of a collection of her essays, *The Essential Gesture*, exemplifies this growing interest in all aspects of Gordimer's work.

TRUTH, IRONY, AND COMMITMENT

Nadine Gordimer's life has been lived mainly in South Africa. In this she shares with prominent white novelists Alan Paton and J. M. Coetzee an insistence on her rooted Africanness but differs from so many other white, English-speaking writers who have chosen to leave South Africa. Together with her decision to live on in Johannesburg comes her life-long scrutiny of the roles open to whites in her apartheid-ridden home.

As the political scene has changed since the late forties, so has altered her own position. From a starting point at which she analyzed white complicity in the injustices of the regime, whatever the good intentions of her more or less well-meaning, "decent" white protagonists, she moved on to investigate the failure of liberal hopes and policies (from whites who opposed the regime) in the late fifties and early sixties. In the mid-sixties and seventies she turned to an evocation of the dead end of white "occupation" and possession, with a new interest in the psychology of her characters, whether of the occupying class or of the class who tried—with varying degrees of integrity—to alter things. With the publication of *Burger's Daughter* in 1979, she introduced a new demand for action and commitment into her analysis of the complexities of white involvement in apartheid politics. That insistence has grown stronger in her later depictions of both the present, now-violent struggle and her vision of revolutionary conflict to come. In these later works the impetus for change is in the hands of blacks, and her investigation focuses on how whites can (and do) adapt to a situation in which their role in "liberation" is secondary but nonetheless demanding.

Gordimer's later work shows an increasingly confident use of fictional form. Not only does her political emphasis become more radical from the seventies on, but her controlled variations of point of view and narrative voice also combine with structural leitmotifs in language, image, and metaphor to give her later novels extraordinary depth and resonance.

Throughout her career Gordimer has insisted on the "truth," or at least truthfulness, of her fiction. In a celebrated public address, she argued: "I remain a writer, not a public speaker; nothing I say here will be as true as my fiction" ("Living in the Interregnum" 264). The consequence of this conviction is that she attempts in all her work to present the many-sidedness of the social and political situations she examines. Judgements by the reader emerge from the often-neutral presentation of events by the narrative voice. All sides of the case have to be presented or at least alluded to. The inappropriateness of some attitudes, beliefs, or behavior informs the judgements implicit in the text, but seldom are the appropriate reactions spelled out by the author. In Gordimer's view, it is in the accuracy of her presentation and in the depth of her imaginative grasp of the events portrayed that the fictional "truth" is to be found. Propaganda and polemic are, to her, the concerns of nonfictional prose, not of imaginative writing.

Gordimer does not always live up to this conviction. She does make ex-cathedra statements from time to time in her fiction, particularly of the summational kind, in the form of choric closing comments on the action. But generally her approach is to preserve a neutral narrative stance herself, allowing the characters or events to speak for themselves. It is up to the reader to draw the inference from the drama enacted or the comments made. This technique has resulted in Gordimer's having been criticized for coldness in her early career. Her apparent detachment from her subject has been taken as a sign of her "frozen" sensibility, a product of her white observer status in the depiction of the compromises and collusions of bourgeois conscience in apartheid South Africa.

Such criticism diminished after the appearance of *The Conservationist,* which established her as a master in the control of different kinds of voice in her narrative. The austerity of her vision was still a feature of *The Conservationist,* but the richness of its texture meant that few could criticize the text itself for being detached or cold. In it the constantly shifting viewpoint incorporates the thoughts and memories of its protagonist, attitudes of a wide range of characters, black, white and Indian, snatches of dialogue both remembered and direct, as well as epigraphs from a nineteenth-century treatise on the religious beliefs of the Zulus that bind sections of the text with a superbly resonant yet oblique choric commentary.

In *A Guest of Honor,* the novel published before *The Conservationist,* Gordimer had also drawn on a wide range of experiences. Set in an independent South-Central-East African state, the novel reveals her perennial concern with the role of whites in Africa and captures not only the predicament of its protagonist, a "liberal" white returned, as guest of its political leader, to the now independent country in which he served as a sympathetic colonial officer before independence but also the tensions in the debate over postcolonial tactics and strategies in independent Africa.

A Guest of Honor won the James Tait Black Memorial Prize, but has not occasioned as much comment or interest as the Booker Prize–winning *Conservationist.* The setting itself, and the debate over socialism or neo-colonial capitalism in that non-South African setting, were less recognizably part of Gordimer's world than what was to be found in her later work. Nevertheless, *A Guest of Honor* does incorporate two elements typical of Gordimer's concerns and methods. By focusing on the protagonist's dilemma as to whether to become actively involved in political action, albeit in an independent country in which he is a "guest," she is dealing with the theme that informs almost all her writing: the role of the white person in Africa, and in particular the obligation to commitment and action. And the discussions in *A Guest of Honor* over the relative merits of the President's capitalism and his opponent's socialism demonstrate her ability to incorporate into her fiction an analysis of the "real," nonfictional political debate of the period at the same time as she creates her customarily accurate depictions of locales and customs. This ability to reproduce—in her fictional worlds—the timbre and texture of current political arguments has been crucial in her writing since then. A familiarity with the theoretical debates within the South African Communist Party and other liberation groups informs *Burger's Daughter* in particular. And in that novel, too, historical accuracy is combined with a compelling imaginative power in the creation of its protagonist's fictional, personal world.

Gordimer's later novel *A Sport of Nature* takes this process a step further. Less tightly-woven than those that preceded it, *A Sport of Nature* leads its white female protagonist from middle-class Johannesburg to several African countries, the United States, and Eastern Europe. Its cast of characters includes real historical figures involved with African politics and also includes cameo appearances from characters in other Gordimer novels. For all its variety, however, its broadly-drawn panorama of South African liberation politics—whether inside or outside the country—from the sixties to a mythical future in which independence day is celebrated in liberated Cape Town still has at its core the issue of the role of the white in that struggle. In its freakish female protagonist, a sport or aberration of nature, the novel depicts an instinctive ability to transcend the limitations of other, cerebral whites. Whereas most whites in the novel, for all their good intentions, cannot join the black power struggle as un-self-consciously or as wholeheartedly as the sensual, self-serving, and self-centered heroine, she can achieve a union both sexually and politically with powerful black political figures and is subsumed into their future. The image of linked hands, black and white, runs through *A Sport of Nature* and embodies the fusion of the races, both physical and political, that only its heroine achieves.

Both *July's People* and the novella "Something Out There" had also dealt with imagined revolutionary events. The first is set during a future armed struggle that causes its white protagonists to flee from Johannesburg under attack, and the latter describes a sabotage attack mounted on the outskirts of Johannesburg by a mixed group of white and black saboteurs. In spite of the attention Gordimer gives to verisimilitude in these works, the future conflict—convincingly portrayed—is less the center of her attention than the current reality of her world, which is reflected in the situations she predicts. In *July's People* it is the sickening complexity of the master/mistress/servant relationship itself that is revealed as the white couple seek safety in the bush village of their former servant, July, now their host and protector. While the future collapse of white military power is presupposed in the novel, the current bankruptcy of white moral suzerainty is exposed and analyzed. In "Something Out There" the myopic concerns of suburban white Johannesburgers over an ubiquitous escaped ape, which terrorizes their mundane pleasures and pursuits, mask the real threat to their security created by the sabotage group, under cover as a white couple and black servants on a rented property close to their target. While the permanent threat to settled white domesticity posed by the unseen forces "out there" is suggested in the panic caused by the at first unidentified ape's unpredictable appearances, so, too, is the obtuseness of white complacency in overlooking the real, determined threat of the professionally anonymous squad of saboteurs.

The underlying metaphor of the unseen terror "out there" in the novella becomes part of its closely-observed depiction of typical Johannesburg social pursuits, in a series of vignettes drawn from all white classes. The presence of such a powerful linking metaphor or pattern of imagery is a feature of Gordimer's later work. In *Burger's Daughter* it is the image of jail and the inevitable progression towards jail made by the protagonist, the daughter of a celebrated Johannesburg white communist who himself dies in jail. For all her need to be independent of the obligations forced on her by being her father's daughter, Rosa Burger discovers she cannot "defect" and finds a serenity similar to Lionel Burger's by returning from a private life in Europe to South Africa, the liberation struggle, and jail. The book opens with the teenage Rosa outside a jail waiting to visit her activist mother inside, and it closes with the mature Rosa in jail, but lively and girl-like in her appearance.

In *The Conservationist*, the recurring image that haunts the white protagonist's reveries on his "weekend" farm is that of the body of an anonymous black man found on his "property" and hastily buried by the police. The nameless corpse, buried in the land itself, becomes not only an autochthonous, albeit inarticulate, companion to Mehring's troubled wanderings over the surface of his farm but is also ceremoniously buried again by the black workers on the farm after being washed from its shallow grave in a flood. The closing of the novel emphasizes the difference between Mehring's inauthentic occupation of the land and the dead black man's ultimately legitimate possession of it: "they had put him away to rest, at last; he had come back. He took possession of this earth, theirs; one of them" (252).

The evocative range of this final sentence is typical of Gordimer's mature style. The slogan of the African National Congress in the 1950s, "Africa, Come Back!" or "Come Back, Africa!" is echoed in the phrase describing the corpse's return to land and people. The comradely groupiness of the pronoun "they"—by means of which the dead man assumes his rightful, but faceless, place among the faceless "people"— contrasts with the disdainful and alienated use of the same pronoun throughout the novel when the point of view is Mehring's or that of other whites. In their mouths the pronoun is part of the uncomprehending otherness associated with the low and indestructible form of life represented by farm laborers and "location." Here is Mehring, early in the novel, describing the "location" or black township close to his farm: "There's a high fence all round to keep them from getting in and out except through the location gates, but there're great big gaps where they cut the wire and come out at night. I haven't lost anything yet but an old chap, De Beer, reckons to lose a couple of head a year. In spite of his dogs. And his reputation for shooting on sight" (27). It is against practical mean-mindedness like this—the moral small change of technologically superior occupation—that the rhetorical swell of the last lines of the book creates the sense of historical inevitability.

Both these passages from *The Conservationist* show Gordimer's way of conveying judgments. Although the closing of the novel is choric, it does not embody an imposed "message" from the author. The point of view is more that of the black people on the farm than anyone else's, and it is Gordimer's knack to articulate their instincts in such a way as to make that perspective the viewpoint of history. In the earlier passage, the smugness of tone—offered without comment from the author— with which Mehring puts his weekend property in sociological context provides a chilling socio-moral context of its own.

In her early stories Gordimer uses an ironic juxtaposition of bland tone and heartless action to encapsulate an arid world of masters and servants; "race relations" in the forties and early fifties entailed mainly the exploitation or "decent" treatment of black laborers and servants by their white overlords, with the cards unquestionably in the hands of the whites. In her twenties, Gordimer produced short stories like "Ah, Woe Is Me," "The Train from Rhodesia," and "Is There Nowhere Else Where We Can Meet?" that epitomize both her technique and the themes of her early fiction. All three were first published in South African magazines between September and December 1947: "Is There . . . ?" in *Common Sense*, September 1946; "The Train" in *Trek*, September 1947; "Ah, Woe" in *Common Sense*, December 1947.

The intractability in these stories is rooted in situations examined for that very intractability. In this they differ from Gordimer's latest works, "Something Out There" and *A Sport of Nature*, which do predict successful action. Even the comparatively late *July's People*, with its ostensibly revolutionary setting, is dominated by a sense of blockage. In it the impasse between white mistress and her servant/host—the dead end entailed in her realization of the difference between the bourgeois comforts and morality she has abandoned and the stark village ethos she has entered—result in Maureen Smales' taking off in panic-stricken flight at the end of the novel without any sense in the text of what the outcome of her flight will be.

The trapped impotence revealed in the short stories of the forties is of an altogether more limited and domestic order. The white Mistress of "Ah, Woe Is Me" reacts in this way to the sobbing of her ex-maid's daughter. The maid has been let go because of illness, but the daughter has returned regularly for handouts from the former employer-family. On this particular visit she is devastated by her mother's grave illness:

> And she began to cry again, her face crumpling up, sobbing and gasping. Desperately, she rubbed at her nose with her wet arm.
> What could I do for her? What could I do?
> Here . . . I said. Here—take this, and gave her my handkerchief.
> (*Selected Stories* 34–35)

It is white obtuseness that this closing reveals. A similar sense of impotence and limitation is revealed in the other two classic stories of the forties, but the white observer in those tales, from whose point of view the narrative is fashioned, understands her own involvement in the situation and her own inability to alter it.

In "The Train from Rhodesia," the white protagonist, returning from her honeymoon, observes her callow husband beat down the price for a piece of African carving in a bartering session at one of the train's rural stops. The young man's pride at having achieved a ridiculous bargain as the train draws off leaves the young woman ashamed and alienated from him.

The protagonist in "Is There Nowhere Else Where We Can Meet?" (the title is redolent of mid-century concern) is the superficial victim in the tale. Assailed by a ragged black man as she walks in the country, the young woman fights off his attempt to snatch her purse and is horrified by his violence, otherness, and pathetic condition. As she makes her getaway, her guilt surfaces; she avoids any further action, and the text establishes that the black man is the real victim:

> Why did I fight, she thought suddenly. What did I fight for? Why didn't I give him the money and let him go? His red eyes, and the smell and those cracks in his feet, fissures, erosion. She shuddered. The cold of the morning flowed into her.

> She turned away from the gate and went down the road slowly,
> like an invalid, beginning to pick the blackjacks from her stockings.
> (*Selected Stories* 20)

Gordimer was twenty-three when this story first appeared, and General Smuts, of the United Party, was Prime Minister. The National Party had not yet won its electoral victory of 1948.

An ironic manner was still Gordimer's main stock in trade in *The Conservationist*; impasse and a bland obtuseness still the ethos of the white consciousness she reflected. The realpolitik of white power was revealed with more complexity than in the early stories, however. Mehring is often correct in his scorn for liberal posturing and bad faith, and much of *The Conservationist* is taken up with the stream of his thoughts on the subject. At the same time, his own lack of belief or magnanimity (his only cause is "development") is as arid as the drought-stricken winter landscape. Tormented as he is by doubts and irritations of all kinds, by a perplexed sensing of his own inauthenticity, the early description of the "peace" of his farm sets the unsettlingly ironic tone of the book:

> . . . you could see the farm, see the mile of willows (people
> remarked that it would have been worth buying for the willows
> alone) in the declivity between two gently rising stretches of land,
> see the Katbosrand in the distance, see the house nobody lived in.
> No one would believe (they also said) the city was only twenty-five
> miles away, and that vast location just behind you. Peace. (22)

Peace of exclusion. Not only is the house unlived-in, but that absence is an ideal. To be able to ignore both the black "location" nearby, and the gold-and-violence metropolis of Johannesburg twenty-five miles away is to ensure tranquillity. Although the viewpoint here is not Mehring's but that of the "people" who visit him, the blinkered world evoked by the description *is* Mehring's. And the flat use of the word "people"—not in any sense THE PEOPLE who inhabit the location—is typical of the flatness in his well-managed life, in which emptiness is itself a sought-after commodity.

After the Soweto rising of 1976, movement was just possible to discern on the South African scene, even if movement toward liberation was met immediately with massive state counter-movement. The tone of Gordimer's writing after *The Conservationist* is less frozen, even when she does still depict an impasse. In *Burger's Daughter*, the semi-literate, defiant pronouncements of Soweto students are incorporated into the text and offer a new perspective on change, unforeseen in the days of traditional black resistance to the white monolith.

The sense of historical inevitability that informs the closing sentences of *The Conservationist* recurs in the closing of "Something Out There," but black legitimacy is given a far more active role in the later choric passage. In it blacks are shown to be doers, not only in the pre-colonial past but also in the revolutionary present. Two of the saboteurs are known to have hidden in a disused mine-working before their power-station attack. The text establishes the correct historical context:

> The mine-working where Eddie and Vusi hid, . . . identified as belonging to the turn of the 19th century, is in fact far, far older. . . . No one knows that with the brief occupation of Vusi and Eddie, and the terrible tools that were all they had to work with, a circle was closed; because before the gold-rush prospectors of the 1890s, centuries before time was measured, here, in such units, there was an ancient mine-working out there, and metals precious to men were discovered, dug and smelted, for themselves, by black men. ("Something Out There" 203)

This is a far cry from the static situations in Gordimer's earlier writing. The tone of optimism grows from a belief in historical inevitability rather than from present reality: It must happen, it has to happen, things will improve some time. The irony that characterizes all her writing is not applied to this belief but rather to the day-to-day details of the world waiting for the big event to occur. In *A Sport of Nature* liberation itself is imagined as a Utopian event, and even here Gordimer's irony plays round all the sordid details of white and black compromise with a new, imagined political reality. What is not ironic is her belief that even in South Africa the People will eventually discover and manage the precious things of their own lives for themselves.

Her writing career chronicles, with stunning imaginative power, both the perception of that need and the role of whites in that process.

WORKS CITED

Gordimer, Nadine. *Burger's Daughter.* London: Cape, 1979.

———. *The Conservationist.* New York: Viking, 1975.

———. *A Guest of Honor.* London: Cape, 1971.

———. "Is There Nowhere Else Where We Can Meet?" *Selected Stories.* Harmondsworth: Penguin, 1978. 17–20.

———. *July's People.* London: Cape, 1981.

———. "Living in the Interregnum." *The Essential Gesture: Writing Politics and Places.* Ed. Stephen Clingman. London: Cape, 1988. 261–84.

———. *Something Out There.* London: Cape, 1984.

———. *A Sport of Nature.* London: Cape, 1987.

———. "The Train from Rhodesia." *Selected Stories.* Harmondsworth: Penguin, 1978. 50–55.

———. "Ah, Woe Is Me." *Selected Stories.* Harmondsworth: Penguin, 1978. 27–35.

NADINE GORDIMER'S PUBLISHED WORK

Novels

The Lying Days, 1953
A World of Strangers, 1958
Occasion for Loving, 1963
The Late Bourgeois World, 1966
A Guest of Honor, 1971
The Conservationist, 1974
Burger's Daughter, 1979

July's People, 1981
A Sport of Nature, 1987
My Son's Story, 1990

Short Story Collections

Face to Face, 1949
The Soft Voice of the Serpent, 1953
Six Feet of the Country, 1956
Friday's Footprint, 1960
Not for Publication, 1965
Livingstone's Companions, 1972
No Place Like: Selected Stories, 1975
Some Monday for Sure, 1976
A Soldier's Embrace, 1980
Something Out There, 1984

Essays

The Essential Gesture: Writing, Politics and Places, 1988

SELECTED CRITICAL READINGS

Nadine Gordimer's writing is receiving increasing attention. Not only are her books reviewed extensively on publication, but also there is a growing body of serious scholarship devoted to her work. Critical writing on Gordimer tends to fall into three broad categories: comment on the political content of her fiction; formalist studies; an increasing amount of work from a feminist perspective. The annotated entries that follow include only full-length books on Gordimer and special issues of journals devoted entirely to her work. There are many articles on individual works, several of them collected in *Critical Essays on Nadine Gordimer* listed below; they are not included in this bibliography, however, since all are cited in the discrete bibliographies of the full-length works listed.

Books

Clingman, Stephen. *The Novels of Nadine Gordimer: History from the Inside.* London: Allen and Unwin, 1986. The best book to date on Gordimer. Deals with the relation between her fiction and political events in South Africa. Excellent in discussing the social and cultural context in which the novels and stories were written.

Cooke, John. *The Novels of Nadine Gordimer: Private Lives/Public Landscapes.* Baton Rouge: Louisiana State UP, 1985. Discusses Gordimer's use of landscape and her "theme" of the rebellion of daughters against possessive mothers. Makes central use of the *Paris Review* interview about Gordimer's own mother keeping her at home because of her imagined heart condition.

Newman, Judie. *Nadine Gordimer.* New York: Routledge, 1988. A volume in the *Contemporary Writers* series. Discusses Gordimer's ideas in a postmodernist context, and places emphasis on the "relation of gender to genre."

Smith, Rowland, editor. *Critical Essays on Nadine Gordimer.* Boston: G. K. Hall, 1990. A selection of material already published: essays, reviews and chapters of books on Gordimer, the first dating from 1953 and the latest from 1988. A wide range of contributors, from four continents, and a wide range of approaches.

Special Issues of Journals Devoted to Gordimer

Ariel 19 (October 1988).
Salmagundi 62 (Winter 1984).

—ROWLAND SMITH

André Brink

A ndré Philippus Brink was born on 29 May 1935 in Vrede, a rural village in the Orange Free State of South Africa. His father was a magistrate and his mother a teacher. He attended Potchefstroom University, graduating with an M.A. in Afrikaans, 1958, and an M.A. in English a year later.

In 1959 Brink went to Paris, where he undertook postgraduate research in comparative literature at the Sorbonne. He was profoundly influenced by this first experience of Europe: "My postgraduate study in Paris brought me an explosive awareness of contemporary trends in European literature and resulted in . . . *Lobola vir die lewe* (*Dowry for Life*), which has since been termed a breakthrough in the modern Afrikaans novel. I later became involved in the 'Sestiger' or 'Writers of the Sixties' movement which brought about a total renewal in Afrikaans fiction by destroying all the existing taboos pertaining to sex, ethics, religion, and politics governing traditional Afrikaans fiction" (*Contemporary Authors* 104: 54).

From 1961 Brink taught at Rhodes University in Grahamstown, where he was Professor of Afrikaans and Dutch Literature. In 1968 he returned to Paris for a year, and considered settling there permanently with his close friend Breyten Breytenbach, the South African painter and poet, who was married to a Vietnamese and in exile from South Africa. The traumatic political events of that year caused Brink to rethink the relationship between the writer and society. He returned to his homeland determined to involve himself in the opposition to apartheid, and his subsequent books have explored both the temptations of exile and the compulsion to return to South Africa and to oppose its racist government. His first politically committed novel, *Kennis von die Aand* (*Looking on Darkness*), was banned in 1974, and he replied by beginning to write in English as well as Afrikaans. His work is now translated into twenty-five languages.

Brink has won many literary prizes. He is the only South African author to win the CNA Award—the major South African Literary Prize—for work in both English and Afrikaans (he has won the Award three times). Both *An Instant in the Wind* and *Rumors of Rain* were shortlisted for the Booker Prize, and he has won the Reina Prinsen Geerligs Prize, the Martin Luther King Memorial Prize, and the Prix Médicis Étranger. In 1982 the French Government awarded him the Legion d'Honneur, and in 1987 he was made Officier de l'Ordre des Arts et des Lettres.

Brink now lives in Cape Town and teaches at the University there. He has three sons and one daughter.

THE LIVES OF ADAMASTOR

In his most recent novel, *States of Emergency*, André Brink portrays a novelist academic not unlike himself, who is embroiled in the political upheavals in the Eastern Cape in 1985-86 and struggling to complete a novel entitled "The Lives of Adamastor." The title is drawn from the epic *The Lusiads*—the first European literary work to describe South Africa—in which the sixteenth-century Portuguese poet Luiz Vaz de Camões images the country as Adamastor, a Titan who rebelled against the new order of the Greek gods and was imprisoned sprawling in the oceans of the Southern Hemisphere. All of Brink's work, profoundly topical as it is, looks back to this originary image of the enduring political plight of his country and its people.

While he is fluent in a number of European languages, Brink's first language is Afrikaans, and most of his writing, which includes novels, plays, and literary criticism, is first done in that language. He came to prominence as a writer in English with the publication of his novel *Looking on Darkness* in 1974. Its Afrikaans edition, *Kennis van die Aand*, created intense controversy when it was published in South Africa in 1973 and was the first Afrikaans novel to be banned in that country. Brink responded by translating it into English and all of his subsequent novels have been published in his own English translations (and by other hands in many other languages). The South African government's ban on *Kennis van die Aand* thus succeeded only in creating a large international audience for one of its most committed and eloquent critics.

The South African poet Roy Campbell once described literature as "the result of social and racial ferment" (Gray 31); and Brink, like Alan Paton, Nadine Gordimer, J.M. Coetzee, and Athol Fugard, has been preoccupied with the political and racial turmoil that followed the assumption of power by the Afrikaners in 1948 and the consequent implementation of the political philosophy of apartheid. Brink has described the insidious development of apartheid and its threat to the language and the culture of the Afrikaner:

> For apartheid to be sanctioned as the definitive characteristic of the Afrikaner Establishment, it had to reach far beyond the domain of politics: it was not simply a political policy 'adopted' as a response to the racial situation in the country but had to be accepted as an extension of an entire value system, embracing all the territories of social experience, economics, philosophy, morality and above all religion. The Church itself had to provide the ultimate justification for the ideology.
>
> Even this was not enough: the ideology also attempted to annex the language . . . to turn Afrikaans into the language of apartheid. This development drew into the arena the writer who realized that to diminish and restrict Afrikaans in this way, as an instrument of the oppressor, went against the very essence of the language . . . the language is the living repository of . . . everything lived through in the hard process of learning not only to survive in this continent but

to survive as part of it: part of its blood and flesh and bones and guts, part of its deep and awful rhythms. . . . The dissident writer . . . appreciates the tragic possibilities inherent in the situation . . . it is not just a struggle aimed at the liberation of blacks from oppression by whites, but also a struggle for the liberation of the Afrikaner from the ideology in which he has come to negate his better self. (*Mapmakers* 18–20)

All of Brink's novels address these issues in a passionate attempt to influence the course of events in South Africa and to save what is valuable in the Afrikaner tradition from the holocaust it seems determined to bring upon itself.

Echoing Campbell, Ronald Ayling notes that "most South African writers of fiction since Olive Schreiner have been exclusively concerned with relations between the races" (91), and in *Looking on Darkness* Brink goes straight to the heart of this matter by focusing on the particularly sensitive area of sexual relations between a black man and a white woman. Brink has observed that: "Racism almost invariably goes with male chauvinism—it's why I've been fascinated in several books by the relationship between a white woman and a black man. Part of what draws them together is the common experience of oppression" (Waldren 8). *Looking on Darkness* purports to be the final testament of Joseph Malan, a Coloured university-educated actor, as he awaits execution for the murder of his white lover Jessica Thomson. It is also made clear, however, that Joseph's testament has not in fact survived: The condemned man anticipates his gaolers' censorship—and prevents his narrative implicating his friends—by flushing it down the toilet each night after it is written. He then substitutes memorized Shakespeare sonnets in which his story is ironically encoded ("everything is summarized") to deflect suspicion. Brink uses this transparently interventionist narrative method to show how the political system suppresses the stories of its victims and denies them the human sympathy that might challenge the system. His role as novelist is to speak the silence that the system enforces and so to circumvent its repressive intent.

Framed between a page of seven epigraphs in four languages at the beginning and thirteen Shakespeare sonnets—all of which are imperfectly remembered and include errors—at the end, *Looking on Darkness* is a very literary and intertextual narrative. Within this context of other writings, Joseph Malan searches for an answer to the existential question "Who am I?"— both in the classic European theatrical roles he performs and in his mother's stories of his black and mixed-race ancestors. The eight-generation history of the Malans parallels the history of South Africa though it does not participate in the events the whites use to structure their history; not even when Abraham, the only "white" member of the male line, tries to fight in the Anglo-Boer War, misses all the action, and is executed anyway. As his family saga nears its end in contemporary South Africa, Joseph comes to see it as "a journey more and more deeply into the night into ever-increasing darkness: a way of suffering which doesn't purify or purge or break through to tragic wisdom, but which remains true to its own futility . . . the darkness now is more than in the beginning" (68).

Brink has a sharp eye for the ironies as well as the cruelties of racial discrimination. In one particularly telling scene, the boy actor Joseph is told by his white friend that he cannot play the black king in the Christmas nativity play because he is not white. And later his mother spells out the lesson on the night that Joseph plays Prospero in a school production of *The Tempest*—a play that is now interpreted as a classic text of European colonialism: "You trying to get into the light, thet's what. En, we people mus' stay out, it's not our place. The Lawd made us fo' his sheddows, we his night people" (109). But despite her warnings, Joseph goes on to re-enact the futile protest of his eight generations of ancestors against a system that denies them their place in the light. He spends nine years in England learning his trade as an actor, but even his success—he eventually joins the Royal Shakespeare Company—cannot overcome his growing awareness of the emptiness and anguish of the expatriate's life and his concern that playing the classics to elite English audiences is fiddling while South Africa burns. So he returns home to assemble a makeshift company and to play to Coloured audiences, where he finds himself progressively adapting the classics to address more and more directly the local political and racial situation, and this in turn attracts escalating persecution from the Security Police.

Joseph's situation is clearly analogous to that of Brink, who also agonizes about the possibilities open to an art patronized by a white elite, many of whose members are complicit with the system. Both Joseph and Brink seek to influence a South African audience in ways that inevitably provoke suppression—which they must somehow avoid if they are to continue to be effective. *Looking on Darkness* is thus both a deliberate attempt to subvert a political system and a self-conscious work of fiction that explores the relations between literature and political activism. It brims with detail to the point of prolixity but is held together by its tragic pattern, its moral anguish, and its sustained imagery of darkness—mystical, racial, sexual, and moral— much of which is drawn from the many texts alluded to in the course of the narrative. These texts provide a depth of resonance to the specific Southern African experience that Brink portrays with intensity and blazing indignation.

Brink's next novel, *An Instant in the Wind*, is altogether sparer and simpler. It is set in the eighteenth century, and draws on the Mrs. Fraser story from colonial Australia, mythologized in Sidney Nolan's paintings and Patrick White's novel, *A Fringe of Leaves*, also published in 1976 (Hassall 3-28). *An Instant in the Wind* is essentially concerned with one man and one woman alone—except for their memories—in an almost empty continent. Adam Mantoor (the name suggests a descendant of Adamastor) and Elisabeth Larsson have both escaped from imprisonment into the unexplored interior of South Africa. Adam has been a slave and a convict on Robben Island. Elisabeth has been a woman in a masculinist society and a disappointed partner in an unhappy marriage. Despite their initial fear and reluctance, they join forces to survive and then find themselves in love. After an idyllic interlude they are drawn remorselessly back to the cruelties and betrayals of "civilization" at the magnetic Cape. Brink uses their story to explore the origins of contemporary South African society. In the conflicts and tensions of a slave colony on the tip of an unexplored continent in the eighteenth century, he seeks some explanations for the evolution of modern South Africa.

Unlike Brink's second "historical" novel, *A Chain of Voices*, which is based on actual archival records of the Slave Revolt of 1824, *An Instant in the Wind* has a fabricated frame of pseudo-historical records (Davidson 28). The deliberate artificiality of the framing devices in both *An Instant in the Wind* and *Looking on Darkness* demonstrates Brink's postmodern awareness that the literary text

> . . . is not a transparent glass through which a "world beyond" can be observed. The qualities of the glass itself—its opacity, thickness, coloration, convexity or concavity, its smoothness or otherwise—demand the attention of the spectator . . . in the final analysis it is the density of the literary experience which determines our way of looking "through" it at the world beyond. (*Mapmakers* 122)

In *A Chain of Voices*, by contrast, Brink frames the narrative with the historical "Act of Accusation" at the beginning and the "Verdict" at the end. He does, however, use a series of epigraphs, as in *Looking on Darkness*, including quotations from Engels and Barthes on the relations between the forces of history and individual freedom to choose. What happens in between these framing documents is Brink's bleak and bitter attempt to imagine, without the mediation of a narrator but through a series of eighty-four interior monologues from thirty characters involved in the Revolt, what "really" happened—or might have happened—on a Boer farm in the Cape Colony in the 1820s, when the British take over in Cape Town and rumors of slave emancipation spread. There are clear parallels with the 1980s, when apartheid, the Boers' replacement for slavery, is under worldwide attack, and the winds of political change gather strength.

Between these novels with historical settings, Brink wrote two novels with contemporary settings, depicting from widely different perspectives the dilemmas facing Afrikaners who must decide, in the light of events like the Soweto uprising of 1976, the extent of their complicity with the political system in South Africa. In the first of these, *Rumors of Rain*, Martin Mynhardt is a successful Afrikaner business executive in a world of mining and money dominated by English and Jewish South Africans. Such a character must have required almost as great a leap of imaginative sympathy on Brink's part as did his crossing of gender and race boundaries elsewhere in his fiction. Mynardt writes a first-person diary narrative in a London hotel room during an unplanned nine-day stopover between conferences. We may wonder at such a man composing a narrative that exposes so remorselessly—and in events crammed into a single, traumatic weekend—his own transparent selfishness: He successively betrays his best friend Bernard Franken—a lawyer and anti-government activist, his dying father, his wife Elise, his son Louis, his lover Bea, and his loyal black assistant Charlie Mofokeng. Although all these people close to him try to make him see that his determination to succeed in a corrupt system is destroying his humanity and all his personal ties, Mynhardt never really has any doubts, and he continues to sacrifice love to success—his "heart complaint" is more than biological. In the circumstances it seems questionable whether he would document so graphically and so persuasively arguments that he continually rejects. Brink's portrait of the ugly face of Afrikanerdom from within its own *laager* is nonetheless a powerful polemic. And Mynhardt's essay in self-scrutiny—however awkward and tentative—suggests that in the wake of Soweto the Afrikaner hegemony might begin to ponder its future.

Soweto also forms the background of *A Dry White Season*, which was largely written some years earlier, but put aside on the death of Steve Biko, which it in fact anticipated but might have seemed to exploit. Ben Du Toit, the protagonist, is another Afrikaner, a teacher of the "official" history of South Africa, like Martin Mynhardt's father. He finds his life overtaken by contemporary history when Jonathan Ngubene, the son of his school's cleaner, dies at the hands of the Security Police during the Soweto uprising, and Du Toit begins an investigation into how and why Jonathan died. Du Toit is discouraged by almost everyone in his increasingly stubborn and determined pursuit of the truth. Only the black taxi driver Stanley Makhaya, who introduces him to the "other" world of Soweto—the alternative history of South Africa—and the white Professor Bruwer encourage his quest, and even they recognize the terrible risks he runs.

Brink's method of narration in this book imitates the course of the narrative itself, with its progressive implication of Du Toit in the police state. Shortly before he is "accidentally" killed in a motor accident, Du Toit asks a former university friend, now a writer of popular fiction, to accept his notes and papers and "to use them if necessary" (13). Like his subject, the writer is slowly drawn into the experience: He reads Du Toit's diaries and papers and eventually writes a book. The reader follows the writer into Du Toit's story and is progressively confronted by a real alternative history of contemporary South Africa in place of the approved version peddled by the media and official sources.

These two Soweto novels show Brink's Afrikaner readers how they are inevitably—even if unwillingly—complicit in the brutalities of a system fighting to maintain its position of privilege. His next novel, *A Chain of Voices*, goes back to the nineteenth century, presenting an alternative history of the slave revolt of 1824 and seeking to enlist the sympathy of whites by confronting them with an imaginative re-creation of the black experience of slavery. Brink shows that the apartheid system of the 1960s formalized centuries of racial oppression in South Africa and was effectively an Afrikaner re-imposition of the slavery officially abolished in 1836 by the British.

In *The Wall of the Plague*, Brink moves out of South Africa to France. Like the London years of *Looking on Darkness*, this novel follows the diaspora of writers and intellectuals from South Africa in the early 1960s. This time the Coloured protagonist is a woman, Andrea Malgas, who has fought off the nostalgia for home that claimed Joseph Malan and resolutely disregarded the exhortations of the expatriate community that she should at least feel guilty about staying away. Andrea has built a life for herself first in England, then in France, and she means to stay there. Then she makes a research trip to Provence for her lover Paul Joubert, an expatriate Afrikaner, who wants to marry her and so commit her irrevocably to life in Europe. Like Martin Mynhardt's time in the London hotel, Andrea's trip offers her an opportunity for reassessment, a chance to consider the crucial decisions she has made, and has still to make, against the background of a medieval plague that led to the construction of a protective wall, a *cordon sanitaire*, like the wall of apartheid, like the *laager* of wagons, to save those within at the expense of those—potentially infected— without.

She is accompanied to Provence by the Xhosa activist Mandla Mqayisa, whom she initially detests but whom she comes to recognize as the voice of her country and her race calling her home. Her relationship with the white Joubert, accepted in France, would be illegal in South Africa, though marginally more acceptable than the relationship between a white woman and a black man. In the event, Brink has Andrea relinquish and even betray Joubert, both sexually with Mandla Mqayisa and also, and more damagingly, by deciding to return to South Africa.

The Wall of the Plague appears initially to be a first-person narrative by Andrea, but the ending reveals that it is in fact a re-creation, in which Joubert endeavors to understand and to come to terms with Andrea's desertion. Here Brink again puts a "writer" in his narrative as the putative "author," displacing his own role to one further remove. The reader thus experiences the seeming immediacy of a first-person narrative for most of the story, only to have that sense of immediacy framed by Joubert's confession of authorship—and of his own inability to "explain" Andrea's decision. His bewilderment problematizes the attempt of any person (writer or not) to understand and explain another person, especially if that person is of another race and/or another gender. Brink's method also qualifies the reader's sense that anything can be explained by fiction, whether it is a medieval plague, a political system like apartheid, or a single human choice like Andrea's.

In 1985 Brink published a newly translated and revised version of *File on a Diplomat*, which originally appeared in 1967 as *The Ambassador*. This early novel is also set in France, and draws on Brink's years as a postgraduate student in Paris from 1959 to 1961. Like his second period in Paris during the revolutionary year of 1968, this first period was "traumatic" (9) and deeply influenced his writing. Though its events coincide with the Sharpeville massacre, the book explores sexual transgression—it caused a good deal of outrage and attempts were made to ban it when it was first published—but it is not about race. Brink has always been interested in love as "the beginning of violence and betrayal" (*Instant* 101). *The Ambassador* charts the destruction of Paul van Heerden, the efficient South African ambassador to France, through his love for Nicolette Alford. The love story is set in a context of secret international arms deals, negotiated in a cosmopolitan city throbbing with life, and boasting a risqué underworld far removed from the narrow Calvinist provincialities of South Africa. Even in its revised form it remains a young writer's book, determined to be explicit, full of energy and youthful disillusionment, and fascinated by the city of Paris.

Brink's most recent novel, *States of Emergency*, is formally his most complex but the story is similar to that of *The Ambassador*: a love affair between a young woman and a middle-aged man of prominence. The narrative begins with a text, a manuscript sent (by "Jane Ferguson") to the narrator—a well-known writer, somewhat like André Brink—who tries unsuccessfully to have it published. Its quality is recognized, but the writer is unknown; the piece, called "A Sense of Occasion" is too short for separate publication, and the English reading public wants its South African fiction spiced with political reference. Ironically, when Jane Ferguson's father later delivers her diary to the writer, it turns out that her love affair on which her novella was based was with Chris de Villiers, a celebrated political activist, who was fleeing the country to escape the Security Police when they met.

So the original "text" is Jane Ferguson's experience with Chris de Villiers. This is partly textualized in her diary, which in turn forms the base for the novella "A Sense of Occasion," which she writes at her father's suggestion as attempted therapy after de Villiers "dies" in police custody. The therapy fails, however, and the text of "life" then imitates art when she commits suicide like the heroine of her story. In the novella the young woman warns her lover: "There are only three choices in love: freedom, or madness, or death . . . do you know what happens to a woman who goes mad? . . . she burns" (1). Jane Ferguson struggles with madness and eventually burns herself to death because the choice of freedom is denied to her.

Not only does her diary provide the political context that the literary agents and editors want "A Sense of Occasion" to have, but the writer of *States of Emergency* is himself writing a text that places both the novella and the diary squarely in the context of the political states of emergency in South Africa in 1985. He also doubles her text by constructing "Notes towards a love story," which includes the love story of Philip Malan and Melissa Lotman, which in turn appropriates and absorbs scenes, descriptions, and indeed its basic structure from "A Sense of Occasion." The name Malan also echoes Joseph Malan from *Looking on Darkness*. The text includes extensive authorial commentary and an apparatus of footnotes, cross references, reflections on theory, and narrative alternatives that may or may not be developed. These devices are very much in the manner of eighteenth-century self-conscious authors like Sterne and Fielding, but they are also overlaid with an acute postmodern awareness of the multi-dimensional nature of textuality and the multiple regressions of "reality" behind and beyond the proliferating layers of texts. Thus the reader does not know whether all the internal texts are part of the narrator's own imagined text or whether they have any extra-textual reference. This uncertainty is increased by the confessional "feel" of the Malan-Lotman story and the suspicion that the extremely elaborate fictionalizing process is a strategy to render love into text so as to make it bearable. As the first epigraph from Athol Fugard says: "The only safe place in the world is inside a story."

States of Emergency draws the reader progressively into this world inside a story, while deferring any sense of safe enclosure. The narrator, we learn, is a writer struggling with a recalcitrant novel, "The Lives of Adamastor," while the political turmoil in the country deprives him of the "inner lucidity" necessary for composition. He is concerned that a simple love story might be "socially irresponsible," as Barthes suggests (*States* 5). There is, however, the compelling example of Wagner falling in love with Mathilde Wesendonck, abandoning the *Ring* as Siegfried abandoned Brünnhilde, and writing *Tristan and Isolde* instead; and also of the Chinese love story *Returning Home* by Lin Shu-teh, condemned as "ideologically meaningless" in 1963 by correct revolutionary critics but popular nonetheless with the students.

We then watch the narrator choose a name, a role, and a character for his heroine—she becomes Melissa Lotman ("Fate-man" in Afrikaans), a postgraduate student—and then for his hero—who becomes Philip Malan ("bad year" in French), her professor of literary theory at a university in the Eastern Cape. Then there are three possible beginnings for the story, like the three possible endings of *The French*

Lieutenant's Woman, and the reader is left to contemplate them in relation to one another. The effect of this and of the metafictional complications that follow is to draw the reader tantalizingly into a maze of textuality continually deferring the "real story" the reader desires, while at the same time documenting the revolutionary political context, which both obstructs and "realizes" the telling of the stories that in turn move out of one fictional frame into another. The narrator's "real" black friend Milton Thaya, for example, becomes a character in the narrator's story and persuades the "fictional" Melissa to start a school for black children.

The constant doubling and echoing in the text begins with the title: The states of emergency are both personal and social and involve both love and politics. The echoes extend to the *Liebestod* of Tristan and Isolde, to the composer Wagner in nineteenth-century revolutionary Europe, and to the writer Lin Shu-teh in twentieth-century revolutionary China. The text parallels "reality" in crisis, as racial violence makes South African society unworkable, with "fiction" in crisis, as the heightened self-consciousness induced by literary theory makes "straight" fiction seem a simplistic cop-out. The experience of love, however, and its demand to be textualized remain as insistent as ever. And the desire of readers for love stories is increased rather than reduced in revolutionary times. Like Wagner, who eventually completed *The Twilight of the Gods,* a story that finds many echoes in *States of Emergency,* Brink eventually published his disrupted and side-tracked "novel," which had often seemed unwritable.

All of which makes *States of Emergency* very much a text for its times. While it lacks the tragic closure of the love story in *An Instant in the Wind,* it opens on to contemporary dilemmas in politics and fiction and examines the connections between them. It explores how we textualize political experience and how we fictionalize personal experience in disintegrating times. Brink has always been concerned with love as a transgressive force, with its power to deconstruct the social shelters in which we try to protect ourselves from the elemental experiences surrounding us. In this novel he is also concerned to cross the "wall" between fiction and reality, to deconstruct that convenient but falsely rigid polarity, and to confront his reader with a writer in a state of siege.

The writer of *States of Emergency* may not have been able to complete *The Lives of Adamastor,* but it is a work that André Brink has been writing all his life—the stories of those who inhabit the country that Camões portrayed as the disfigured Titan, imprisoned by the goddess Thetis for aspiring to her (forbidden) love and for rebelling against the new gods. Brink's continuing theme has been the black man of Africa loving the white woman of Europe, rebelling against the tyranny of colonial rule, and being doubly punished for his presumption. He has worked variations on this story from the eighteenth century to the present, but the myth remains essentially the same. The black struggle for independence and human dignity, for the right to love and freedom, continues, and no escalation of white repression seems likely to break its spirit.

WORKS CITED

Ayling, Ronald. "Literature of the Eastern Cape from Schreiner to Fugard." *Ariel* 16.2 (1985): 77–98.

Brink, André. *The Ambassador.* London: Fontana, 1985.

———. *A Chain of Voices.* London: Fontana, 1983.

———. *A Dry White Season.* London: Fontana, 1984.

———. *An Instant in the Wind.* London: Fontana 1983.

———. *Looking on Darkness.* London: Fontana, 1984.

———. *Mapmakers: Writing in a State of Siege.* London: Faber, 1983.

———. *Rumours of Rain.* London: Fontana, 1984.

———. *States of Emergency.* London: Faber, 1988.

———. *The Wall of the Plague.* London: Faber, 1984.

Camoens, Luis Vaz De. *The Lusiads.* Trans. William C. Atkinson. Harmondsworth: Penguin, 1952.

Davidson, Jim. "An Interview with André Brink." *Overland* 94/95 (1984): 24–30.

Gray, Stephen. *Southern African Literature: An Introduction.* London: Rex Collings, 1979.

Hassall, A.J. "The Making of a Colonial Myth: The Mrs. Fraser Story in Patrick White's *A Fringe of Leaves* and André Brink's *An Instant in the Wind.*" *Ariel* 18:3 (1987): 3–28.

Ross, Jean W. "André Brink." *Contemporary Authors.* Detroit: Gale, 1982. 104:54–59.

Waldren, Murray. "State of Siege: An Interview with André Brink." *The Weekend Australian* (23–24 September 1989): 8.

ANDRE BRINK'S PUBLISHED WORK

(Works in Afrikaans not translated into English are not listed.)

Novels

Looking on Darkness, 1974
An Instant in the Wind, 1976
Rumors of Rain, 1978
A Dry White Season, 1979
A Chain of Voices, 1982
The Wall of the Plague, 1984
The Ambassador, 1985 (new translation and revision of a novel published in 1963 in Afrikaans and in 1967 in English)
States of Emergency, 1988

Essays

Mapmakers: Writing in a State of Siege, 1983
    Collection of essays on literature and politics.

SELECTED CRITICAL READINGS

To date there has been only one book devoted to Brink's work, the collection of essays edited by Jan Senekal, and that is currently available only in Afrikaans. His English fiction has been widely reviewed and critical interest is growing, but the number of articles to date is slight.

Ayling, Ronald. "Literature of the Eastern Cape from Schreiner to Fugard." *Ariel* 16.2 (1985): 77–98. Review essay on *Olive Schreiner and After: Essays on Southern African Literature in Honour of Guy Butler* (Edited by Malvern van Wyk Smith and Don Maclennan. London: David Philip,

1983). Brink's work is "a strange omission" (92) from the volume under review; but the essay remains a useful survey of the literary, geographical, and university background of Brink.

Cope, Jack. *The Adversary Within: Dissident Writers in Afrikaans.* London: Rex Collins, 1982. An account of the Sestiger movement, in which Afrikaner writers of the 1960s sought "freedom of subject matter and the breaking down of taboos, freedom to challenge and criticise." The Afrikaner Establishment (ix) makes extensive reference to Brink's involvement in this literary and political movement.

Dussen de Kestergat, J.M. van der. "Apartheid et litterature." *Bulletin des Séances: Academie Royale des Sciences d'Outre-Mer* (Brussels) 32.4 (1986): 607–18. Argues that Brink shares with Breyten Breytenbach a deep nostalgia for the Boer tradition as well as anti-apartheid anger.

Findlay, Allan. "André Brink and the Challenge from within South Africa." *Proceedings from the Second Nordic Conference for English Studies.* Helsinki: Abo Akademi, 1984. 581–590. Reviews novels to *A Dry White Season* and includes some useful information, though critically uneven.

Hassall, A. J. "The Making of a Colonial Myth: The Mrs. Fraser Story in Patrick White's *A Fringe of Leaves* and André Brink's *An Instant in the Wind.*" *Ariel* 18.3 (1987): 3–28. Traces the origins of the two novels in Sidney Nolan's "Mrs. Fraser series of paintings," and compares the books as versions of colonial mythmaking.

JanMohamed, Abdul R. "The Economy of Manichean Allegory: The Function of Racial Difference in Colonialist Literature." *Critical Inquiry* 12.1 (1985): 59–87. Mentions *A Chain of Voices* briefly (72-3) and reductively as a novel in which the whites are stereotypically in sexual control, while the blacks lack control and need to be managed.

MacDermott, Doireann. "A Narrow Beam of Light: A Reading of Two Novels by André Brink." *World Literature Written In English* 28 (1988): 178–88. A perceptive reading of *Rumors of Rain* and *A Dry White Season* after a brief survey of Brink's career and the limited critical attention he has so far received. Argues that *Rumors of Rain* is somewhat prolix and that *A Dry White Season* is sparer and more successful.

Rich, Paul. "Tradition and Revolt in South African Fiction: The Novels of André Brink, Nadine Gordimer and J.M. Coetzee." *Journal of Southern African Studies* 9 (1982): 54–73. Compares *Rumors of Rain* with Gordimer's *The Conservationist* and Coetzee's *In the Heart of the Country* as expressions of the still essentially colonial political experience in South Africa.

Senekal, Jan, editor. *Donker Weerlig.* Cape Town: Jutalit, 1988. Collection of 13 essays, all in Afrikaans, on Brink's fiction, with some reference to his essays and plays. Discusses all of the English fiction except *States of Emergency.* Many of the essays employ structuralist or poststructuralist methodologies.

Viola, André. "André Brink and the Writer 'in a State of Siege.'" *Commonwealth* 7.2 (1985): 64–71. Brief analytical account of the narrative structures, methods, and patterns of the first five novels in the light of Brink's comments on his art in *Mapmakers.*

Zoontjens, Adrienne. "L'Apartheid, Le Racisme et Les Prix Litteraires Français." *Peuples Noirs Peuples Africains* 23 (Sept.-Oct. 1981): 136–40. Sees Brink as paternalistic, as appropriating the voice and the point of view of Southern African blacks, as a "hypocrite" (138) and, therefore, as an inappropriate recipient of "Le Prix Médicis" for *Une saison blanche et sèche.* (*A Dry White Season*).

—ANTHONY J. HASSALL

Alex La Guma

W hen Alex La Guma died suddenly of a heart attack in October 1985 in Havana, Cuba, his short stories, novels, literary and political essays, and his travel book on the Soviet Union were being read in twenty languages, and his reputation as a world literary figure was already firmly established. La Guma's beginnings were humble. The only son of a labor union leader and a cigarette factory worker, he grew up in a house where political discussion was more plentiful than food. Born into the oppressed Cape Coloured community on 20 February 1925, he left school early to become a factory worker; he soon joined the executive of the workers' committee and helped to organize a strike for better working conditions.

In 1947, La Guma joined the Young Communist League, and in 1948 he became a member of the party. The Communist Party was declared illegal in 1950, but La Guma carried on his political activities as a member of the South African Coloured Peoples Organization. In 1955, the latter group became part of the African National Congress (ANC). He served the ANC with great distinction, leading protest activities and often being detained by the apartheid regime for his activities. In 1955, he and 155 other South Africans were tried for treason. All of them were finally acquitted in 1960. From 1960 to his voluntary exit from South Africa in 1966, La Guma was either placed under house arrest or put into prison for his opposition to the apartheid system. Once outside South Africa, he served the exiled wing of the ANC in various capacities. At the time of his death, he was chief ANC representative in the Caribbean.

As a writer, La Guma began his career in journalism in 1955 with the progressive, left-wing weekly *New Age*. Most of his reports and columns dealt with the socio-economic conditions of the Cape Coloured community. It was not until 1957 that La Guma published his first creative piece. The story "Etude," later to be known as "Nocturne," demonstrated clearly the talent he possessed. After several more stories, La Guma published his first novel, *A Walk in the Night*, in 1962. At the time of his death, La Guma was writing "Crowns of Battle." In addition to his creative work, he recorded impressions of the Soviet Union in *A Soviet Journey* (1978), and he has written many essays dealing with the political and cultural contexts of South Africa.

La Guma's reputation inside South Africa is firmly established. His emphasis in his writings on the destruction of the apartheid system and the development of a nonracial democracy is at the very heart of serious South African literature. This emphasis is also a universal one, thus making La Guma's intense, human-oriented stories significant to a wider public.

DEFIANCE AND RESISTANCE

In an interview with me in London in 1978, La Guma stated his objectives both in his writing and in the conduct of his life:

> For as long as I can remember, my life has been tied up with the struggle of the oppressed people of South Africa for a better social, economic and cultural life, and for participation in a political life that is free of discrimination and which promotes a non-racial, democratic society. I grew up in a home where political discussion and action were more precious than bread. I walked into my community and country and recognized the injustice of the apartheid system. And I swore then that I would dedicate all my energies to ensure the betterment of all my people. Whether in active political action or in my creative work, this has been my lifelong aim. (Unpublished Interview)

True to his word, from as early as his first short story, "Etude" (published later as "Nocturne"), to his last novel *Time of the Butcherbird*, La Guma has preoccupied himself with the struggle of the oppressed people of South Africa to free themselves from the yoke of apartheid slavery that had been imposed on them for more than 300 years. Through his great imaginative gifts and his considerable creative skills, he succeeded, as well, to write stories and novels free of propaganda and sloganeering but filled with the wonder of dynamic characters who, in turn, embraced central and existing themes.

The very first story La Guma wrote, "Nocturne," reveals his strength in creating atmosphere, portraying character, reporting dialogue, using contrasts, and amplifying the surface meaning of the story so that the reader can suggest possible further meanings. The story deals with Harry, a member of a trio who is planning to rob a factory. While the plans of the robbery are being worked out, Harry's attention is caught by music emanating from a piano across the street. He is especially interested in "Nocturne No. 2, in E flat major, by Chopin." After he takes leave of his friends, Harry enters a drab, poverty-stricken world from where the music emanates. He is surprised that such beauty can survive among such hopeless ugliness. The music, however, is not enough of a deterrent to keep Harry from participating in the robbery; nor are the ugliness and poverty, associated with the building, reasons enough to deter the "dark and fine and delicate" (114) piano player from participating in the beautiful and uplifting world of Chopin's music. In this very first story La Guma stakes out the territory he intends to explore in all of his work. No matter how bleak the sociopolitical situation may be, no human being must succumb to it through slothful indulgence. Darkness must be replaced by light no matter how severe the struggle may be.

In La Guma's first novel, *A Walk in the Night*, he develops the theme of defiance and resistance, which escalates in each of the next four novels, until it breaks out into revolutionary action. The novel concerns itself with the social, economic, and political purpose of the Cape Coloured community. The developing consciousness of the community is depicted through the development of many major and minor characters and through the setting of District Six, the suburb of Cape Town where the action occurs. First there is Michael Adonis's gradual movement from being a law-abiding citizen to the desperate position of being a "skollie," or local thug. Second, the novel studies the development of the lives of Willieboy and the "skollies" and shows how inevitably the unfair racist system forces law-abiding people such as Adonis to join either the dissolute ranks of Willieboy or the world of underground violence and crime and the "skollies." Third, through the study of the perverse police work of Constable Raalt, the reader is given an insight into the objectives and *modus operandi* of the South African white police. Last, La Guma describes the conditions of living in District Six and demonstrates clearly why the lives of the various characters develop as they do.

To illustrate the central objective of La Guma's writing, I shall concentrate only on the first two aspects of the novel. Although Michael Adonis is aware that as a colored person his status in his country is low, he refuses, however, to accept the insults literally thrown at him by a white worker:

> That white bastard was lucky I didn't pull him up good. He had been asking for it a long time. Every time a man goes to the piss-house he starts moaning. Jesus Christ, the way he went on you'd think a man had to wet his pants rather than take a minute off. Well, he picked on me for going for a leak and I told him to go to hell. (4)

Regardless of whether or not Adonis will lose his job, La Guma believes that one must not tolerate injustice, and thus he commends Adonis's action. Adonis, on the other hand, is narrowly preoccupied with revenge, rather than with eradicating this form of injustice. When soon after this event he is crudely and without cause accosted by the white police, Adonis's need for revenge against all whites is compounded.

But Adonis does not permit himself to move beyond the pain of insult he has experienced at the hands of whites who are more powerful than he is. His "feeling of rage, frustration and violence" (12) does not dissipate when Adonis makes his contact with the wretched of the white society. Uncle Doughty, a poor white, failed Shakespearean actor, ekes out an existence in a filthy room situated in the building where Adonis lives. Uncle Doughty invites Adonis into his room to "have a drink" from a bottle of port he purchased with his "old age pension." Adonis responds angrily against both Uncle Doughty and the humiliation that whites had caused him by rejecting the old man's offer. Furthermore, Adonis blurs his vision of the white worker who had insulted him with that of the drunken, white "old bastard" and avenges himself by striking "the bony, blotched, sprouting skull" (28–29) of Uncle Doughty with the bottle of port.

Adonis's first reaction after the killing is a shocked awareness of the unpremeditated deed: "God, I didn't mean it. I didn't mean to kill the blerry old man" (29). His next reaction is to seek shelter from the law and to excuse the vile deed. Adonis's tragic irony is that throughout the story he had been humiliated by the whites and the specter of revenge had loomed strongly in his mind. But now that he has in fact received some measure of revenge, the specter of his humiliation and defeat becomes an even greater presence to contend with. If he saw himself as a haunted figure before, his conscience now makes him doubly haunted and forces him into a life he had not contemplated at the beginning of the story.

The tragedy in Adonis's behavior, as La Guma sees it, is that Adonis spurned his righteous indignation and fiery commitment to correct injustice by avenging himself on an innocent bystander, and one who is himself a victim of the apartheid system. That Adonis decides not to report his crime to an unjust system of justice is natural. But that another innocent bystander, Willieboy, is hunted down by the police for the crime and eventually killed, is condemned by La Guma. Adonis's crime against Uncle Doughty and his betrayal of the cause he set out to follow at the beginning are compounded by his decision to join hands with the "skollies." Before Uncle Doughty's death Adonis had been one of the unlucky "walkers of the night" whose entire existence was at the mercy of the white society's whims. Now, after the death, he is an aimless and haunted walker of the night whose fear finally leads him to join the true underground world of the "skollies" and the night.

The case of Willieboy, who is wrongfully accused of Uncle Doughty's death, is less tragic than that of Michael Adonis. Willieboy, unlike Adonis, is a passive victim of the apartheid system. Brought up in a poor home where his father brutally abused him and his mother, he chooses the path of least resistance, a slothful existence. When Adonis relates the incident at work to Willieboy, the latter derides those who work: "Me, I never work for no white john. Not even brown one. To hell with work. Work, work, work, where does it get you? Not me, pally" (4). Willieboy prides himself further on the fact that he is able to survive by living off the generosity of others. It is in pursuit of this aim that he is drawn to the building where Adonis and Uncle Doughty live and where Adonis has just killed Uncle Doughty.

Willieboy's aim is, first of all, to pursue Adonis and to seek a loan. When Adonis fails to respond to his knock on the door, Willieboy then decides to knock on the door of Uncle Doughty's room to ask him for money to buy marijuana. When there is no reply from the old man, Willieboy turns the knob and discovers "the dead blue-gray face" of Uncle Doughty. Willieboy's response is to slam the door and escape from the scene in the fear of being accused of the killing. But, unfortunately, he runs into one of the tenants, who recognizes him, and when she discovers Uncle Doughty's body she is convinced that Willieboy had killed the old man. Like Michael Adonis, Willieboy's hopeless but bearable life of simply walking the night of poverty in the ghetto is now transformed into a life of fear and panic as he attempts to escape the tentacles of the law.

La Guma recognizes again, as he did in the case of Adonis, that in a country where one's guilt or innocence is determined by one's skin color, Willieboy's chances of escaping the charge of murder are poor. On the other hand, La Guma does not approve of willing victims to any system of justice. Since Willieboy's fate is determined by the apartheid laws, La Guma believes that Willieboy must do everything in his power to challenge that fate rather than succumb to the system in the painful and ignoble manner in which he does. Willieboy now lives the life of a fugitive of the law, slouching along the streets by night, "keeping instinctively to the shadows." He roams the "shebeens" (illegal drinking places) where drinking and prostitution thrive and where he is able to beg. Eventually, however, the police catch up with him and he is shot.

Willieboy's life is a tragic path from an unloving home into a loveless society that finally brutalizes him to death. As one of the ghosts walking the restless night, his own being does not surface at all and his death is a relief from the mindless suffering he has endured. Willieboy's life is one of the choices that Michael Adonis has once he has lost his job, but Adonis does not choose Willieboy's passive slothfulness. Instead, he joins the "skollies," whose victims are the ghosts already victimized by a cruel and unjust system. *A Walk in the Night* flies in the face of La Guma's belief in strong, committed characters that can transform an unjust society.

In La Guma's second novel, *And a Threefold Cord*, he concedes that the individual by himself cannot fully transform a system that has given rise to so much oppression and corruption. He explains the title and objective of the novel as follows:

> The title comes as an excerpt from a biblical quotation. I think it is Ecclesiastes 4:9–12. This excerpt emphasizes the idea that the individual alone cannot survive, that he has to have somebody around him to which to cling in times of difficulty and adversity and I tried to convey the idea that loneliness of people, loneliness of individuals is one thing, but at some time or another they've got to turn away from their loneliness and try to associate with other people. And I try throughout this novel to show that while people have got their own problems, or what they believe to be their own problems, these problems are not actually entirely their own but they are shared by other people. (quoted in Abrahams *Alex La Guma* 71)

The chief character in *And a Threefold Cord* is the socio-economic and political environment of the Cape Town slum where the human action occurs. As in *A Walk in the Night*, La Guma takes us on a painstaking journey where the dreadful lives of the victims of the slum are examined at a time when the Cape winter has set in and where the rain has fallen continuously for days.

The slum has grown through sheer desperation and in stealth as the harried inhabitants are either removed forcibly from ancestral lands and property or they move away from their impoverished rural settings to the hoped-for material success of the cities. Consequently, with no municipal authorities concerned about the standard of buildings, number of occupants, electricity, sewage, and health ordinances, the slum simply grows in a haphazard manner. Everywhere in the settlement there is a decaying smell of "pulpy mould, rotten sacking, rain, cookery, chickens and the rickety latrines that leaned crazily in pools of horror liquid, like drunken men in their own regurgitation" (46). And in the winter, when life is generally harsher, "there is no evening" and "the unresisting daylight" is smothered under "its chill, dark blanket." Now the slum dwellers are forced inside their unbearably crowded space "where they crouched over sputtering oil stoves, wood braziers or old iron stones" (87).

The poverty-stricken human dwellers of the slum fend against their frustration and hopelessness by indulging themselves in cheap liquor, prostitution, family quarrels, and violence. Whereas La Guma, in an extended metaphor of a trapped fly, admits that the slum dwellers are trapped by the racist and class system of South Africa, he blames them, however, for their failure to form a community to console one another and to unite against their oppressive situation. Instead, many of them turn violently against weaker members in the slum in search of satisfaction and the rebuilding of destroyed egos. Others, such as Ben Pauls, see their condition to be God given and trust God to set things right. Again, others, such as Roman, indulge in cheap wine to forget the pain of their condition and to fire themselves up with so-called courage to commit violent acts on weaker victims. And women, such as Susie Meyer, enter into a world of cheap dreams and prostitute themselves to seek an escape from their debilitating poverty.

Charlie Pauls is the only character in the novel who is able to grasp the meaning of the slum dwellers' fate, but he does not possess the force of character to transform the environment in any significant manner. He is, however, morally and psychologically superior to the characters in *A Walk in the Night.* Although Charlie is aware that the poverty of the slum is in a large measure related to the dismal socio-economic and political system of South Africa, he does not move in any way to improve the situation. His only rebellion against the unjust system comes when he defies a raiding policeman and hits him on his "exposed jawbone" and escapes "into the jungle of shacks" (141-42). But the moment of triumph is shortlived. He must return to the settlement where the cast-offs of life reside, where poverty destroys, where family life has been obliterated, where love turns into hatred because of the overwhelming burden, where children fantasize away their lives believing they are killers and soldiers going to war, and where the game of "teckies [detectives] and burgs [criminals]" predominates. The weight of the environment and the inertia of the slum dwellers conspire against the defiant living that La Guma espouses.

In La Guma's third novel, *The Stone Country*, published in 1967, he concentrates his attention on the lives of the "over 20 percent of the non-white population" who in large part have transgressed the petty and mindless laws of apartheid. The novel, says La Guma, is based

> . . . essentially upon my own experiences and the experiences of other prisoners in South African prisons. I used the accounts and stories related by other people who have been in prison to produce the novel. Most of it is completely authentic, but, of course, from my point of view. (quoted in Abrahams *Alex La Guma* 87)

As in the first two novels, the socioeconomic and political environment of apartheid South Africa dominates. The failed characters of the first two books have now assembled in the jail houses of South Africa. The prison comprises "ragged street-corner hoodlums, shivering drunks, thugs in cheap flamboyant clothes and knowledgeable looks, murderers, robbers, housebreakers, petty criminals, rapists, loiterers and simple permit-offenders . . ." (19).

The prison is a "stone country" where guards and prisoners are "the enforced inhabitants of another country, another world" (18). The guards put great stress on keeping "everything under control" and are prepared to wield brutal authority to ensure this control. The control takes many forms, including denial of bare necessities such as blankets, refusal of meals, detention in the Isolation Block and the fearsome Hole, and the design of a system where the most brutal prisoners are permitted to mete out cruel punishment on those who show contempt for, defy, and disobey the guards' authority.

It is to this place that George Adams, a political prisoner, is brought. Like La Guma, Adams believes that no matter how oppressive a situation may be there is always some room for challenging oppression and forcing change, so the spirit of organized defiance that Adams showed outside he brings into the prison. Adams, however, observes immediately that in this "half-world" there is "an atmosphere of every-man-for-himself" and that "the strong preyed on the weak, and the strong and brutal acknowledged a sort of nebulous alliance among themselves for the terrorisation of the underlings" (37). Generally, because of the brutal regime, the prisoners accept their deprived situation and like the oppressed outside, they leave their trust in God, sing hymns, and attend the Sunday church service.

Buoyed by his own belief that "you did what you decided was the right thing, and then accepted the consequences," Adams sets out to oppose the injustice of the system and to unite the inmates so as to take common and concerted action against their oppressors. But his thinking is not supported by the prisoners. He is unable to stop Butcherboy, the prison bully, and Yusef the Turk from engaging in a brutal fight, which, through the help of the prisoner Casbah the Kid, leads to Butcherboy's death. He recognizes that the authorities have succeeded in their "divide and rule policy" and "they got us fighting each other like dogs" (74). Adams, though not defeated, is left with a deep sense of frustration. He knows that only when the oppressed are fully aware of their predicament and are prepared to work together to overthrow the yoke of the oppressor will they be able to destroy the country of stone that has until now made them prey to the lions in the den.

It is not until La Guma's last two novels, *In the Fog of the Seasons' End* and *Time of the Butcherbird*, that he is able truly to create defiant and resistant characters. Although the South Africa of these novels had become by degrees more oppressive, the socioeconomic and political conditions that La Guma railed against in the first three books were still there to obstruct the development of courageous characters. But in these books he places the emphasis on the political struggle rather than on the socioeconomic problems as he had done in the earlier work. The dedication and preface to *In the Fog of the Seasons' End* indicate clearly that the purpose of the novel is to demonstrate the rapid development of both passive and military active opposition to the racist regime of South Africa. Through the underground organizing work of the political activists, Tekwane and Beukes, and through the brutal organization of the racist police, La Guma prepares the reader for the impending and inevitable warlike situation between oppressor and oppressed, which Beukes predicts at the end of the novel. As Isaac and the other two guerrilla activists leave South Africa for military training outside the country, Beukes defiantly and triumphantly states:

... they have gone to war in the name of a suffering people. What the enemy himself has created, these will become battle-grounds, and what we see now is only the tip of an iceberg of resentment against an ignoble regime, the tortured victims of hatred and humiliation. And those who persist in hatred and humiliation must prepare. Let them prepare hard and fast—they do not have long to wait. (180–81)

In this novel La Guma shows that with constant work and determination it is possible to challenge and to defeat the "ignoble" system.

The novel provides a comprehensive view of the plethora of racist laws and practices which exists in South Africa. The municipal park that Beukes rests in labels the benches "Whites" and "Non-Whites" (12); the "open-air restaurant" adjoining the museum where Beukes will meet Isaac is reserved for "Whites Only" (8); a sign near the top of the statue of Rhodes points toward "the segregated lavatories" (12); the museum once had separate "Whites" and "Non-Whites" entrances but now begrudgingly permits "non-white" visitors on specially set aside days" (18); the beaches of South Africa are divided along racial lines, with the inferior sections being set aside for the "non-whites" (19); there are separate racial entrances to the train station, different compartments for "White" and "Non-White" passengers on the train, and "Non-Whites" are forbidden to cross the "White footbridge" (64); separate schools for white and non-white schoolchildren (83–84); and separate places for the races at the circus, with the inferior areas being reserved for the non-whites (40).

The most serious laws of apartheid that La Guma discusses in this novel are the ones that deal with the Pass book, the Group Areas, and the Migrant Labour System. The Pass law forces all blacks over the age of sixteen years to carry the hated Pass book. To demonstrate the viciousness of the Pass system, La Guma depicts a discussion between a brutal, contemptuous white South African policeman and a black man, who, although his Pass book is in order, is subjected to the terrifying situation of apartheid South Africa. The black man is humiliated by the officer's use of the derogatory denotation of "Kaffir," by his insolent and absurd questioning, by his contempt and brutality, and by the laws of the country that subject a citizen to so much indignity. Without the Pass the black man is not permitted to live in his township, to travel from one place to another, to work, and, in fact, to exist, as indicated by the policeman. But even with the Pass the black man is not permitted to have his family visit or live with him without prior permission or he stands to have "the wrath of the Devil and all his minions" (81) invoked against him. The policeman also reminds the man that he is "not allowed to leave" his job with his present employer without permission, nor can he leave his present place of abode for another without consent. Among the humiliations that spur Tekwane on to revolt against the racist system is the insult he suffers at the Pass office.

The Group Areas law ensures that where the races must share common territory this territory be rigidly divided by race and that where possible the races do not have any contact. Hence, throughout South Africa, and especially in the populated urban center, residential areas and townships are set aside for the various groups. And as is everywhere common under apartheid, the best areas are reserved for whites. Furthermore, whenever the whites require more territory, the blacks are forcibly removed from their area and placed in townships where the government-built houses have walls that peel "like diseased skin" and where the sad children stare "out over fences like shabby glove-puppets" (164). In these townships, much like in the slum of *And a Threefold Cord*, the township dwellers vent their frustrations on each other.

Migrant labor ensures that the industrial development of South Africa is supplied with a cheap and docile work force. Often, as in the case of the all-important and sensitive gold mining industry, docile black laborers from the rural areas of South Africa and from neighboring countries are recruited. These workers are sifted and graded like slabs of meat, and they are then transported like sheep and cows to their workplace. They are contracted for periods of time, housed in compounds, not permitted to have a family life, and generally treated as company slaves. Tekwane's father had been one of the miners who had died in a mine accident instead of coming home to die ignobly and poverty-stricken of pthisis.

Faced with a hostile socioeconomic and political environment, one that is further compounded by the selfishness and apathy of many of the oppressed, and a society riddled with police brutality reinforced by cohorts of "informers," Tekwane and Beukes determinedly set about making the oppressed aware of their reforming and revolutionary option. With the help of others, Tekwane and Beukes clandestinely prepare to deliver protest pamphlets that proclaim the inability of the police to quell all dissent and that urge the oppressed to ready themselves for the inevitable struggle. The success of this venture is reinforced by defiant slogans on walls in the suburbs and by the decision of some of the oppressed to be trained as "freedom fighters" outside South Africa. This determination to meet the violence-oriented police on their own battlegrounds is a necessary and an encouraging development for Beuke: "It is a good thing that we are now working for armed struggle. It gives people confidence to think that soon they might combine mass activity with military force. One does not like facing the fascist guns like sheep" (143–44). The novel ends with "Peter," "Michael," and "Paul" leaving South Africa to be trained so as to return to continue the battle in a more militant fashion. There is a certain knowledge that the foggy night with its walking ghosts is about to be burned away.

In *Time of the Butcherbird*, La Guma concentrates on the metaphor of the butcherbird, which he describes as follows:

> The title of the novel comes from African folklore. One of the riddles from the oral tradition indicates that the butcherbird represents something which not only cleanses the cattle but also cleanses the society. It does away with the wizards, the sorcerers, and those people who have a negative effect on the society. What I'm trying to say is that conscious resistance of the people heralds the time when the butcherbird will cleanse South Africa of racism, oppression, and so on. (quoted in Abrahams *Alex La Guma* 118)

Hence, when the white racists threaten to dispossess the rural black community of their ancestral lands, Mma-Tau, the militant sister of the headman Hlangeni, instructs the oppressed to disobey Hlangeni's advice of passive slothfulness and to inform the government that they do not intend to "go from this land." She then directs the people to barricade themselves and to wait for the white sergeant and his convoy of farm lorries. When the sergeant arrives, he is surprised to meet resistance. Annoyed, he "unbuttons his pistol holster," which leads a black youth to "hurl a stone at" him. The stone misses the sergeant, but his clerk panics, then runs. This action creates fear and confusion among the drivers in the convoy and they leave the scene. Red-faced and embarrassed, the sergeant wonders "who would have thought that these bloody kaffirs would start something like this?" And yet, not completely convinced by the militant action of the blacks, he views the resistance as a defeat "by a lot of baboons in jumble-sale clothing" (112). Then to confirm their determination not to permit the "ticks" to keep sucking their blood without resistance, the defiant blacks throw stones at the sergeant and his convoy.

While the sergeant returns to the town to seek reinforcements, the people move into the hills to continue their resistance. For them, the time of the butcherbird has arrived. The final three paragraphs of the novel contrast sharply with the hopelessness of the opening scene where Hlangeni and the remnant of his followers await death at the hands of the cruel white society.

As the "yellowing afternoon light puts a golden colour on the land," a "flight of birds swoop overhead towards a water-hole" (119)—the symbolism is clear; the drought of human destruction and unjust dispossession of land has ended, and now the butcherbird will smell out the sorcerer, hunt him down, and cleanse the society of his bloodsucking nature.

Albeit more personal, the act of revenge that Shilling Murile carries out against Hannes Meulen falls in line with La Guma's theme of defiance and resistance. Meulen is the descendant of three generations of Afrikaners, the dominant white racist group; he is a university graduate, a businessman, the owner of a farm, and the leader of the Afrikaners in the Karoo; and like his community he has great contempt for black people. On the occasion of his sister's wedding, he and the farm foreman, Jaap Opperman, punish Shilling and his brother, Timi, for letting out sheep from their kraal to wander around. The Afrikaners tie the two brothers to a fence, exposing them to the bitterly cold night. In the morning, Meulen discovers that Timi has died, and Shilling tries desperately to take revenge. He slashes Opperman and is imprisoned for eight years, where he plans fuller revenge.

Once out of prison, Shilling proceeds like the butcherbird to search out the "tick" Meulen. When he eventually reaches Meulen's farm, he discovers that Opperman has died and that Meulen is in town. Shilling takes one of Meulen's automatic shotguns and proceeds to the hotel where Meulen is staying. He arrives soon after the Afrikaner prayer service for rain and kills the "tick" Meulen who has plagued him and his people in the past. Once Shilling has completed his personal mission, he joins Mma-Tau in the collective resistance against the sergeant and his convoy of lorries.

At the time of La Guma's death, he was busy writing another novel of defiance, resistance, and triumph. His constant objective, namely that of transforming his own frustrated and, at times, apathetic people into defiant, resistant characters seeking change, is clearly demonstrated in the last two novels. If La Guma were alive today, he would be pleased to observe how many of the oppressed have joined the militant cause he espoused. Furthermore, he would be happy to know that his stories and novels contributed to this important transformation.

WORKS CITED

Abrahams, Cecil A. *Alex La Guma*. Boston: Twayne, 1985.

La Guma, Alex. "Nocturne," in *Quartet*. Ed. R. Rive. London: Heinemann, 1965.

———. *A Walk in the Night*. London: Heinemann, 1967.

———. *And a Threefold Cord*. Berlin: Seven Seas, 1964.

———. *The Stone Country*. London: Heinemann, 1974.

———. *In the Fog of the Seasons' End*. London: Heinemann, 1972.

———. *Time of the Butcherbird*. London: Heinemann, 1979.

ALEX LA GUMA'S PUBLISHED WORK

Novels

A Walk in the Night, 1962 (*A Walk in the Night and Other Stories*, 1967)
And a Threefold Cord, 1964
The Stone Country, 1967
In the Fog of the Seasons' End, 1972
Time of the Butcherbird, 1979

Short Stories

"Etude." *New Age* (24 January 1957): 6. Rpt. *Quartet* as "Nocturne." Ed. R. Rive. London: Heinemann, 1965. 111–16.

"Out of Darkness." *Africa South* 2.1 (October 1957): 118–22. Rpt. *Quartet*. 33–38.

"A Glass of Wine." *Black Orpheus* 7 (1960): 22–25. Rpt. *Quartet*. 91–96.

"Slipper Satin." *Black Orpheus* 8 (1960): 32–35. Rpt. *Quartet*. 67–73.

"A Matter of Taste." In *A Walk in the Night and Other Stories*. London: Heinemann, 1967. 125–30.

"At the Portagee's." *Black Orpheus* 11 (1963): 18–21. Rpt. *A Walk in the Night and Other Stories*: 108–13.

"Tattoo Marks and Nails." *Black Orpheus* 14 (1964): 48–53. Rpt. *A Walk in the Night and Other Stories*: 97–107.

"The Lemon Orchard." In *A Walk in the Night and Other Stories*. 131–36.

"Blankets." *Black Orpheus* 15 (1964): 57–58. Rpt. *African Writing Today*. Ed E. Mphahlele. Harmondsworth: Penguin, 1967: 268–73; and *A Walk in the Night and Other Stories*: 121-24.

"Coffee for the Road." In *Modern African Stories*. Ed. E. A. Komey and E. Mphahlele. London: Faber & Faber, 1964. 85–94.

"A Matter of Honour." *New African* 4.7 (1965): 167–70.

"The Gladiators." In *A Walk in the Night and Other Stories*. 114–20.

"Late Edition." *Lotus: Afro-Asian Writings* 29 (1976): 42–47.

"Thang's Bicycle." *Lotus: Afro-Asian Writings* 29 (1976): 42–47.

SELECTED CRITICAL READINGS

Critical studies dealing with Alex La Guma's work are increasing steadily and are being pursued worldwide. Since my own first full-length study of La Guma's life and work, doctoral dissertations—the basis for future books on La Guma—have been undertaken by students at many universities. Furthermore, my own present activity in ensuring that La Guma's unpublished creative and literary productions are brought into print will guarantee that many more scholars become involved in research on La Guma. Current critical work on La Guma has centered mainly on the writer's political activities and the relationship of those activities to his literary output. What is sorely needed are careful studies dealing with La Guma's use of language, descriptive literary style, and use of imagery and metaphor. In time, there will be the need for full-length studies of the short stories and each of the novels.

Abrahams, Cecil A. *Alex La Guma.* Boston: Twayne, 1985. Provides biographical material and literary analyses. (Author is La Guma's official biographer.)

———. *Essays on Literature.* Montreal: AFO Enterprises, 1989. Contains several essays dealing with La Guma's work.

———, editor. *Alex La Guma's Uncollected Work.* Trenton: Africa World Press, 1990. Contains several literary and critical pieces by La Guma not published before.

———, editor. *Critical Essays on La Guma.* Trenton: Africa World Press, 1990. Contains 10 essays by various La Guma critics.

Asein, S. O. "The Revolutionary Vision in Alex La Guma's Novels." *Lotus: Afro-Asian Writings* 24 & 25 (1975). 9–21. Argues that in La Guma's case literature cannot be divorced from the South African reality.

Coetzee, J. M. "Man's Fate in the Novels of Alex La Guma." *Studies in Black Literature* 5.1 (1974): 16–23. Examines characters in La Guma's work.

Kibera, L. "A Critical Appreciation of Alex La Guma's *In the Fog of the Seasons' End.*" *Busara* 8.1 (1976): 59–66. Deals effectively with the novel's purpose.

Obuke, J. O. "The Structure of Commitment: A Study of Alex La Guma." *Ba Shiru* 5.1 (1973): 14–20. Discusses structure of La Guma's work.

— CECIL A. ABRAHAMS

Judith Wright

J udith Wright was born in 1915 near Armidale in New South Wales, Australia, to a well-established pioneering family whose early history and treatment of Aborigines she relates in *The Generations of Men* and *The Cry for the Dead*. Her father Phillip Wright's autobiographical *Memories of a Bushwacker* (1971) describes the region called New England, where Judith Wright grew up and which has influenced much of her work.

Shortly after her mother's death in 1926, she was sent to a boarding school in Armidale and later studied Arts at the University of Sydney. In 1938–39, after her studies, she traveled through Great Britain and Europe, returning before the outbreak of war to work and write in Sydney. Due to the wartime shortage of workers, she was called back to Wallamumbi, the family property in New England, to help her father. In 1943 she moved to Brisbane, where she worked for the University of Queensland and for the new and influential literary magazine *Meanjin Papers*; while in Brisbane she met and married the philosopher J.P. McKinney (1891–1966).

In 1946, Judith Wright's first volume of poetry, *The Moving Image*, immediately established her as a major writer, and from that time she has been a prolific woman of letters and convictions. In addition to her poetry, she has written children's books and literary criticism, edited works, and given many lectures. She has also devoted much of her energy to preserving the environment and championing the rights of the Aborigines so ill-treated by her ancestors. Among many other honors, in recognition of her literary work, she was elected a foundation fellow of the Australian Academy of the Humanities in 1970.

She now lives near Mongarlowe in the mountains of southern New South Wales surrounded by the bush she has worked so hard to preserve.

An Ecological Vision

Although Judith Wright is a deeply respected figure in the Australian cultural community—and highly regarded internationally as well, her poetry and prose have gone "off the boil" for many critics and readers in recent years. This is likely to be a temporary phenomenon, for it will soon be recognized that the informing ecological vision so deeply rooted in her work since her first book of poems, *The Moving Image*, is ever more urgently relevant. As "green" movements multiply around the world, the vision of this Australian poet may indeed be seen as a guiding philosophy and an emotional set towards the world that could be accepted by utopianists and realists alike: In this process, her poetry and prose works are likely to be rediscovered by fresh eyes and minds.

While believing strongly in poetry as an art, Wright is also a moralist (Bennett 76). In her case, this connotes no fixed or inflexible program of belief and behavior but the achievement of a delicate balance among individuals, communities, and the environment, which will vary according to time and circumstance around the earth's surface. Throughout her work, from the earliest poems written and published in the 1940s to her book on the conservation of Australia's Great Barrier Reef, *The Coral Battleground*, and beyond, Wright has espoused the notion of ecology in its broadest sense, as it derives from the Greek word *oikos*, meaning "household, home, or place to live." In dealing with the organism in relation to its environment, ecology has been said to concern itself with "the economy of nature." From an anthropocentric perspective, the "ecosystem" described by ecologists can be considered as a life-support system composed of the air, earth, water, minerals, animals, and micro-organisms, which all function together—with humans, who are part of the system—and maintain the whole. Wright's various problems and questions in understanding herself and the universe, as they are posed in the *roman fleuve* of her literary and critical writings, lead her toward the totalizing concept of ecology and away from the narrow specialist categories she has perceived as a feature of contemporary industrial societies. Having chosen our *oikos*, or home territory, according to Wright, we should become active participants in achieving and maintaining an "economy of nature," although this may involve a radical break with prevailing notions of economic management. Furthermore, Wright is critical of the many contemporary artists who opt out of the ecosystem to become exiles; perhaps unfairly, she is inclined to consider the choice of exile, and its accompanying mentality, as a "sickness" and a general weakening of the system as a whole.

Few poets have managed to include the words "ecological" and "ecosystem" in a single poem. Wright has achieved this in the final section of a series of brief verse observations on Australia's capital, Canberra, in one of her later books, *Fourth Quarter*:

> Considered as an ecosystem
> Canberra is impossible.

The poem proceeds with the various deficiencies of this city when it is considered against the ideal of an active organism within an interactive environment:

> No balance between input and output;
> a monoculture community
> whose energy goes entirely into organization.
> Too little diversity
> means instability
> the scientists say.
> No fooling.
>
> Too many predators.
> Too few producers.

Too little feedback
and very few refuges for prey species.

Somehow it continues to exist
as an ecological miracle.
  ("Brief Notes on Canberra")

If the irony of this "miracle" seems to drop a little too heavily in its deliberately prosaic context, in ways reminiscent of earlier city poems such as "Typists in the Phoenix Building" (*The Other Half*) or "The City" (*Shadow*), its intent is clear enough. Behind it may be felt the continuing narratorial presence of the spirited young woman who, after traveling in Europe in 1938–39, returned during the early war years to help out at the family property, Wallamumbi, near Armidale in the New England tablelands. There she made a rediscovery of "home" and set out on the first of a series of personal pilgrimages to understand herself in relation to the environment in its regional, national, and universal manifestations.

The fundamental notion of a living ecosystem, which required of its human actors that they be conservationist in outlook and practice, was expressed in most forthright terms in Judith Wright's 1968 essay "Conservation as a Concept." At this time Wright was President and co-founder of the Wildlife Preservation Society of Queensland and a member of the Provisional Council of the Australian Conservation Foundation. Her essay relates the difficulties of reform in a country with Australia's history of development at all costs and contrasts the lack of any university course for the study of conservation and its problems in Australia compared with fifteen such programs in the United States (29). Her polemical prose was insistently persuasive in its call for human responsibility for "the maintenance of this planet and its elemental and biotic systems":

> The results of uncontrolled exploitation are obvious everywhere, in dwindling soil fertility and the consequent "march of the deserts," in the increasingly destructive catastrophes of flood, famine, drought, deforestation and extinction of exploited species, and the vanishing from the "genetic pool" of numbers of plants and animals as habitat and landscape are altered and destroyed in our short-term interests. Water-tables are being lowered, uplands stripped of protective plant and forest cover, lakes, rivers, oceans and the air itself polluted by industrial and human wastes and by the use of pesticides and herbicides, agriculture extended into dangerously marginal areas with human and natural impoverishment, mining carried on without consideration for waste-disposal, proper land-use, or future human requirements, and biotic systems radically altered without regard for, or any knowledge of, the possible consequences. (30)

Borrowing Heller's term, the "disinherited mind," Wright sought to replace it with "a new kind of creative relationship" (30). An objective understanding of issues was insufficient. Value was conferred, in Wright's view, not by ratiocination but by feeling and imagination. Thus the emergent concept of conservation and its allied science of ecology held open the possibility of a new relationship between humans and their environment:

> . . . a renewed humility and a revival of imaginative participation in a life-process which includes us, and to which we contribute our own conscious knowledge of it, as part of it, not as separate from it. (33)

As readers and critics begin to acknowledge the mobility of discursive practice within and across genres and that poetry might be considered as no more "magic" than prose, it should be easier to recognize the important links between Wright's public statements on conservation and ecology and her apparently more private discourse of poetry. But for the ecologist there is no final distinction between "inner" and "outer": A holistic notion of relations between fully functioning organisms in an ecosystem requires a world that does not close itself off into such specialisms as the inner and outer person, head and heart, or the other bifurcations that flow from analytical thought or urban industrial specialization. Certainly, in 1962, when Wright was composing some of her "inward" metaphysical verse, she still insisted that poetry had to be concerned with the issues of its time:

> But then, what are the issues? Not the obvious scarehead issues; not even perhaps the fall-out or the colour-bar or the tear-gas bombs flung over the wall, but something a good deal deeper and less temporal. A reconciliation with ourselves, perhaps?—which implies a reconciliation with the others, who are also ourselves.
>
> If that is true, poetry has a good chance of becoming once more an influential art-form—if poets take it and themselves seriously and rightly. Poetry, like the significant dream in an analysis, is a reconciling force where self and outer image can come together in understanding. Precisely, poetry only happens when being and image clash and generate a spark—that's poetry. A way of finding a difficult balance: relating inner and outer. ("Context" 37–38)

The verb "to reconcile" and the noun "reconciliation" are key words in Wright's vocabulary here and elsewhere, as is "balance." In a wildly oscillating system in which humans are the chief destructive element, the poet's creativity lies in perceiving organic solutions: in seeking out the green shoots of growth towards understanding and reconciliation in a fragile system of checks and balances.

Wright's return to the family property in the early years of World War II served as a catalyst to her consideration of environmental values. Her mother having died when she was eleven, her father, Phillip Wright, had a major influence on her outlook. As A.D. Hope has pointed out, Phillip Wright "was a conservationist and [his daughter] grew up with a passionate love of and involvement in the life of the country and all its creatures" (6). In her twenties, for instance, Wright took a close and informed interest in the problem of soil erosion, which is only beginning to be addressed seriously in many parts of Australia—and elsewhere for that matter—in the 1990s. In his sympathetic reading of Judith Wright and her work, Hope is one of the few critics to refuse a separation of Judith Wright into two people, the poet and the conservationist. Peter Abotomey presented the opposite point of view when he declared that in Wright's writing career the conservationist had become "destructive of" the poet: "The love for her country that she affirms so often in her poems means that the association with the landscape under threat and in destruction finally brings her to a standstill as a poet" (4). This point of view is typical among academic literary critics in giving primacy to poetry over other genres and in assuming the superiority of certain kinds of (non-interventionist) poetry over others. While recognizing an important distinction between art and propaganda herself, Wright has nevertheless reiterated her belief that art should have the capacity to communicate with an audience and that it should not retreat from historical actualities. In attempting this delicate balance and wrestling at times with a failing faith in poetry as a means of understanding and communicating, Wright honestly exposed the dilemmas of the talented poet who aspires to change hearts and minds.

The shadow of war hangs over Wright's work in the 1940s. However, along with the fears that were engendered by Australia's involvement in the war in the Pacific went a burgeoning nationalism. In Wright's case, she was impelled to search for roots in the landscape and history of her New England region—her "blood's country." Later, in Brisbane from 1944 to 1948, through contact with Clem Christesen, editor of *Meanjin Papers*, and others, she extended this search to a wider view of Australia as a nation in the world. As a young woman in her mid-twenties who had studied English at the University of Sydney, traveled in Europe, and worked in clerical jobs, Wright found her "homecoming" to Wallamumbi both a pleasure and a challenge; here, she began to observe, listen, read, and reconstruct the landscape, myths, and history of the New England region—and then of Australia. And she perceived clearly the postcolonial dilemma of a country such as Australia:

> The European consciousness, particularly here in Australia, was plunged suddenly, after centuries of growth inside traditions, into a totally new situation where the traditions went ludicrously astray. We have had to discover just what has happened to us, and in discovering, laboriously make the happening true. Even when it has looked from the outside as though we were merely imitating— building mock-English sandcastles—Australian writers have been occupied with something quite other; trying to find a way to make these new pressures, shapes, events mean something to a consciousness trained to expect everything to be other than it was. When East becomes North and West is under your feet, your compass spins frighteningly. To calm it, you must find yourself a new axis. ("Context" 38)

In her essay, "The Upside-Down Hut," she enlarged upon the problems for the artist and the intellectual in those stirring post-war, embryonically postcolonial times:

> Australia is still, for us, not a country but a state—or states—of mind. We do not yet speak from within her, but from outside: from the state of mind that describes, rather than expresses, its surroundings, or from the state of mind that imposes itself upon, rather than lives through, landscape and event. . . . We are caught up in the old nineteenth-century split of consciousness, the stunned shock of those who cross the seas and find themselves, as the Australian ballad puts it, in a "hut that's upside down." (30)

There are many strands in this argument, and ways of reading it, but in the personal allegory of Wright's work, it reveals a search for the *oikos* in which an individual consciousness might become an active (not merely passive) partner in the reshaping of a vital Australian environment—cultural, physical, and social. This, she believed, would contribute to the ecosystem as a whole.

Wright's agenda for change, as it developed through the 1940s and 50s, was conservative (or, more properly, conservationist) as well as reformist. Believing, as she had since her early years, in the creative imagination as more fundamental to the human species than rational intellection—a belief encouraged by her reading of the British Romantic poets, especially Wordsworth and Blake—Wright exercised it first in her "blood's country" of New England. She exercised her powers of observation and imagination in a landscape that she perceived as humanized and suffering—as humans could suffer—in the bitterly cold winters of mountainous southeastern Australia, where

> rises that tableland, high delicate outline
> of bony slopes wincing under winter,
> low trees blue-leaved and olive, outcropping granite—
> clean, lean, hungry country.
> ("South of My Days," *The Moving Image*)

The underlying ecological concept here, as elsewhere, is not detached and scientific but involves an empathetic transfer of emotions from the human consciousness to the nonhuman landscape; this landscape is not "framed" or "bracketed off" from human experience but is presented as a fellow contributor to the drama of the ecosystem—in this case, as a suffering partner under the cold skies of winter. The cozy sentimentality that can sometimes result from an easy personification of landscape is avoided by this poet's recognition that pain as well as pleasure may result from this identification.

What then is Wright's attitude to change? In keeping with her emergent view of a pattern of interdependence between humans and their natural environment, it is not surprising that she has often opposed the negative impact of urbanization and industrialization. For her, "progress" and "development" should always be reviewed in relation to an understanding of the past, which Australians often lack. Her early poem "Country Town" (*The Moving Image*) illustrates the tendency:

This is a landscape that the town creeps over;
a landscape safe with bitumen and banks.
The hostile hills are netted in with fences
and the roads lead to houses and the pictures.

The town on which this poem is based is Armidale, some 350 miles northeast of Sydney, the nearest town to the Wrights' family property. The image of Australians making themselves safe in towns ("with bitumen and banks") and fearfully fencing off nature ("the hostile hills") dramatizes Wright's concept of a European society that has failed to adapt in its consciousness or its practice to a frightening but ultimately life-giving environment. So she turns outside the tameness of towns to the wild country in her attempt to reimagine an alternative self-definition for Australians. In turning, as she did in "Country Town," to a not-so-distant nineteenth-century past populated by convicts and bushrangers, she sought anti-types to the town and city-dwellers whom she saw as tamed by place and circumstance. Her images of these outsiders in Australian society were the products of a nostalgic mythmaking, not unlike that of early Yeats or even of "Easter 1916," invoking the memories of those whose "wild" experience might be taken into the national consciousness, thereby enriching it:

Remember Thunderbolt, buried under the air-raid trenches.
Remember the bearded men singing of exile.
Remember the shepherds under their strange stars.

In the midst of war, when this poem was written, Wright was gently urging her fellow Australians to recognize their past, to develop a communal memory that would make them more fully functioning actors in the universal drama. The allusion to the biblical shepherds in the last line is forward looking, suggesting prophetic possibilities for Australians who dream dreams beyond those imposed by her metonymic country town.

The consciousness of a past from which Australians' sense of a future might spring was developed by Wright, in the first instance from sources closest to hand: the stories of her father, the diaries of her grandparents, the anecdotes of local men and women. Later, she incorporated into her outlook academic studies such as Russel Ward's *The Australian Legend* (1958), a book that traced the development of an Australian self-image or mystique and was influenced in its assumptions and methodology by Frederick Jackson Turner's American "frontier thesis" in *The Frontier in American History* (1920) and H.C. Allen's *Bush and Backwoods* (1959). Ward's version of an Australian past documented the oral traditions of convicts and itinerant bushworkers and developed from it a radical nationalist thesis, which has subsequently been criticized as masculinist, racist, and exclusivist by Australian feminist writers (Miriam Dixson, *The Real Matilda: Women and Identity in Australia, 1788 to 1975*, 1976, and Ann Summers, *Damned Whores and God's Police*, 1975) and by the New Left (Humphrey McQueen, *A New Brittania: An Argument Concerning the Social Origins of Australian Radicalism and Nationalism*, 1970, rev. 1986). Although Wright, like Ward, was interested in the ballads and oral tradition, she created her own version of an Australian literary tradition in *Preoccupations in Australian Poetry* through her selection of talismanic literary poets.

The key figures in *Preoccupations* was Australia's first major "literary" poet, Charles Harpur, the son of convict parents. Wright's reading of Harpur's work was that of both an advocate (he was a neglected figure in the Australian literary canon until Wright restored him) and a reformer of the Australian consciousness. As Australia's self-proclaimed first poet, Harpur assumed a bardic role and, as Wright quoted him, dedicated himself to dreams of a time when

> all men shall stand
> proudly beneath the fair wide roof of heaven
> as God-created equals.

Harpur's dreams of liberty and equality constituted one side of the "double aspect" that Wright saw as pervasive in "inner Australia": For the radical such as Harpur, there was a sense of liberty and scope for a new chance, but for the conservative a pervasive sense of exile prevailed. It is interesting that in her first volume of poems, *The Moving Image*, Wright presented herself in similar terms as the hybridized "double tree" of her European and Australian inheritances. While refusing to accept radical nationalist oversimplifications, the implication of her dramatized metaphors of duality is that a process of self-realization is necessary, in which the transplanted organism adapts fully to its local environment. As Susan McKernan has pointed out, Wright's particular brand of Australian nationalism had not succumbed to a simplistic jingoism, in spite of temptations to do so during wartime. When other Australian nationalists were deaf to the claims of "internationalists" or "Europeanists," Wright took their points of view into account, rejecting the polarities between radical nationalist and conservative, nationalist and internationalist, and even bush and city, "because she believed that these polarities could be reconciled in poetry" (144).

Nevertheless, a major stumbling block to a reconciled, properly ecological adaptation for European Australians, in Wright's view, was their relationship with the Aborigines—the first inhabitants of a country that the Europeans had invaded in the late eighteenth century and since then treated abominably. Against the background of what she felt was a frightening rapidity of change in Australia compared with the invasions of the Saxons and the fate of the Celts in the British Isles, she attempted to retrieve an Aboriginal past, in the first instance, within her own region and experience. The opening stanza of "Bora Ring" (*The Moving Image*) sets the tone for a finely conceived, understated elegy that links a particular piece of once sacred ground with the fate of a people:

> The song is gone; the dance
> is secret with the dancers in the earth,
> the ritual useless, and the tribal story
> lost in an alien tale.

The link between her personal experience and this elegy was recalled by Wright in an article in *Hemisphere* in 1963:

> Perhaps ten miles from the homestead (at Wallamumbi) was a paddock known as the Bora Paddock. It was a shock for me to realise, riding through it one day with my cousins, that the grass-grown ring of earth from which it took its name had been there perhaps for many centuries before my grandmother's house had been built. Yet of the tribe to which this country had once been home there was nobody left. I had scarcely seen an aboriginal in my life. (25)

Wright's admission would hardly be surprising to white Australians, who, having won the battle for dominance of Australia's "resources," have generally fenced themselves off from further contact with Aborigines.

During the course of her later work and travels, Wright has become acquainted with many Aborigines and her authorship of the prose works *The Cry for the Dead* and *We Call for a Treaty* are testimony to her concern to make reparation for the rapacious destructiveness of her own forebears and the wider Australian community. Her friendship with the popular Aboriginal poet Kath Walker (now called Oodgeroo Noonuccal) is celebrated in the poem "Two Dreamtimes" (*Alive*), but a divisive past is also recalled:

> You were one of the dark children
> I wasn't allowed to play with—
> riverbank campers, the wrong colour,
> (I couldn't turn you white.)

When a kind of reconciliation is offered, it is typically not in terms of the civilizing institutions of town and city but in an unspoiled countryside of childhood, "The easy Eden-dreamtime then/in a country of birds and trees." A proper reconciliation between the races, then, would require a capacity for adult understanding and a childlike perception of oneness with the natural world; and the shared lament of these two sister poets, one black and one white, is for a despoiled land, "the ripped length of the island beaches,/the drained paperbark swamps."

A characteristic of Wright's treatment of race relations, whether in her poetry or in her longer prose works, has been to use landmarks as symbols. Thus the poems "Nigger's Leap, New England" (*The Moving Image*) and "Myall Creek" (*The Cry for the Dead*, *We Call for a Treaty*) stand as memorials for atrocities committed by whites on blacks. But Wright is not content with static symbolism or unidimensional didacticism. "Nigger's Leap, New England," for instance, resuscitates a popular white nickname for a landmark later called Darkie Point (or Head) in deference to changing racial sensibilities and political circumstances. Wright has described the poem's genesis in the place where the original incident occurred:

> Across the valley north of the Point (Point Lookout) stands an escarpment jutting from the tableland, and dropping in sheer cliffs of hundreds of feet to the rainforest below. It is named Darkie Point. My father, one of the few who know a little of the unwritten history

of that eastern side of the tableland, stood beside me once on Point Lookout when I asked the meaning of its name. Long ago, he said, the white settlers of that region of the tableland had driven the Aborigines over its cliffs for the spearing of their cattle. . . . Long afterwards, I wrote a poem about it titled "Nigger's Leap"—another local name, disused for obvious reasons. ("Darkie Point")

As well as memorializing this place as a site of white culpability, Wright typically also notices, in a landscape of breathtaking beauty, the possibility of reconciliation. Is her assumed role of peacemaker too easily attained in spite of the facts? I do not think so. The following lines in "Nigger's Leap, New England" are characteristic:

Did we not know their blood channelled our rivers,
and the black dust our crops ate was their dust?
O all men are one man at last.

In context, the synthesizing statement in the last of these lines is less a statement of fact than of hope, which occurs against a background of historic repression and obliterated memories. In context, it seems like a single voice crying against a nighttime of brute force and chaos. The "haunted country" is an extension of a single vividly realized place and its violent associations. An idealized image of preternatural harmony between Aborigines and this place is rehearsed in an elegiac refrain: "Never from earth again the coolamon/or thin black children dancing like the shadows/of saplings in the wind." The movement is from precise location to general reflection, and the paradisaical dream is not confused with reality.

The Myall Creek massacre of 1838, which is analyzed and commented on in *The Cry for the Dead* and *We Call for a Treaty*, is also located precisely—in northwest New South Wales where it actually occurred. This precision of detail is combined with Wright's treatment of the incident as parable: ". . . there was nothing unusual about the Myall Creek murders, and certainly nothing which the squatters would have deplored. They were, as was later made clear, only the latest of a series of such incidents—none of which was to be reported or investigated" (*Cry* 50). Wright's New England, like William Faulkner's South, is a place, precisely detailed and symbolically resonant, where "the red bitter blood boils through the land." Earth, this earth, is Judith Wright's element. (By contrast, water is the element that tends to hold the imaginative attention of exiles rather than those who seek their *oikos* in a native land.) And although Wright's poetic development reveals excursions into the other elements of fire and air—especially in the 1950s and early 1960s in some of the philosophical and metaphysical poems of *The Gateway, The Two Fires*, and *Five Senses*—it is this land as metonymy for the earth as a whole that persists in her imagination in spite of human attempts to transcend or forget it. In "Australia 1970" (*Shadow*) the poet's persona applauds the signs of the earth's active fight against the destructive exploitation of humans:

I praise the scoring drought, the flying dust,
the drying creek, the furious animal,

that they oppose us still;
that we are ruined by the thing we kill.

The countervailing force to the wars, massacres, and willful destruction of fauna and flora that haunt Wright's work is a notion of natural love. Clear autobiographical references to Wright's relationship with her philosopher husband Jack McKinney are evident in many love poems ranging from *Woman to Man* to the elegies following McKinney's death in 1966 in *Shadow*. Her love poems celebrate human passion, motherhood, and the "nature" of love itself, which is not analyzed so much as wondered at:

> Our love is so natural,
> the wild animals move
> gentle and light on
> the shores of our love.
>   ("Our Love Is So Natural," *The Gateway*)

An unstrained Blakean simplicity, not to be mistaken for naivety, characterizes this opening stanza; the context of the poem as a whole contrasts this experience of "found" love with fears at the lover's absence:

> My heart crouches under,
> silent and still,
> as the avalanche gathers
> above the green hill.
>
> Our love is so natural—
> I cannot but fear.
> I would reach out and touch you.
> Why are you not here?

Like other love poems by Wright, "Our Love Is So Natural" evokes the outdoors, for it does not set the lovers apart in a lonely room filled by their burgeoning egos and aspirations, as in Donne's "The Sun Rising." The lovers' temporary separation is a springboard to the speaker's contemplation of the ecological harmony that exists when they are together:

> Bird and beast are at home
> and star lives in tree
> when we are together
> as we should be.

The rhythms and imagery here suggest an Elizabethan "music of the spheres" as much as contemporary Australia. Nor is the speaker's voice idiosyncratic, egotistical, or demanding. As Chris Wallace-Crabbe noted in a comparison of Wright's poetry with Elizabeth Bishop's, she manages to write "without a style," that is, "a recognizable series of gestures which testify . . . to the presence of a stable ego" (53). Some critics found this impersonality in apparently personal poetry a disturbing feature of Wright's development as a poet in the 1950s and 60s, but Wallace-Crabbe found it refreshing in "a period of narcissistic arts and neurasthenic judderings" (53). In terms of the ecological system, which she had discerned at work, Wright's subdued ego may be seen here not so much as a repression of self as a recognition of proper humility in the face of nature.

As a poet of love, Wright avoids the confessional mode of exploring feelings and direct reference to sexual behavior. Her reticence in this respect has been contrasted by critics such as Devindra Kohli and H.H. Anniah Gowda with Indian poet Kamala Das. In comparing poems of love and of childbirth by the two women poets, Kohli demonstrates that Wright's poems "modulate more into the intellectual than the sensuous" (44). The recurrent light and dark symbolism indicate that she was more concerned with modes of perception, understanding, and vision in poems such as "Woman to Man" and "Woman's Song" than in self-dramatizations of lovemaking or giving birth. The Indian critics find a delicate balance in Wright's verse between physical, emotional, and intellectual elements, whereas they see Das's poetry as more passionate, confessional, and fleshly.

For Wright, nothing is exclusively personal: Her emphasis on lovemaking as a procreative act, for instance, may be seen within an ecological perspective as the linking of human with animal and vegetable nature without depreciation of any of these species. Yet much of Wright's poetry of the 1950s and 60s does attempt an inward journey to a still center of personal vision. Echoes of T.S. Eliot reinforce the philosophical, quasi-religious dimension of this personal quest, which seems also to have been influenced by the philosophy of J.P. McKinney, exemplified in his *The Structure of Modern Thought* (1971). In her poem, "The Vision" (*Shadow*), written after McKinney's death and dedicated to him, Wright compares the philosopher's capacity to "move entire/into the very core of concentration," which she admired and envied, with her own poet-thinker's tendency towards distraction:

> Yes, I was jealous of your close companion,
> your angel being brother to my own,
> but you were rapt, were held, and less alone,
> given more utterly to your communion
> than I, who struggled with my own desire.

This self-admitted tendency in Wright towards what might be called peripheral vision—her struggle with distracting desire and worldly detail—may have prevented her from becoming a pure philosopher or a visionary, but it was essential to her development as a poet and prose writer. Her interest in the activity and physicality of the world, held at bay somewhat in the personal pilgrimage towards self and spirit in the poetry of her middle years—though explored at this time in some of her stories in *The Nature of Love*, which are set in Queensland where Wright was living with her husband and daughter—resurfaced in her later work. Something of the pleasure of physicality in an early poem like the "The Surfer"—"He thrust his joy against the weight of the sea"—is reawakened in memories of music and dancing in the poem "Unpacking Books" (*Fourth Quarter*) addressed to West Indian poet Derek Walcott:

> I pick you up, poet of loves and pities,
>
> and from the green Caribbean nights again you sing,
> This banjo-world have one string
> *and all men does dance to that tune.*
> Yes, yes and yes, my blood answers,
> takes up the tune and dances.

The strong rhythmic identification of Australia's leading lyricist of the postwar period with the Caribbean's major songmaker is a reminder of a little publicized campaign for the lyric that Wright carried out in the Sydney press in the mid-1960s. An open verse letter to her friend and poet A.D. Hope was published in the *Sydney Morning Herald* on 13 November 1965, which took Hope to task for his championing of "the discursive mode" in poetry. That, she argued, would be false ecology: "No: let's consult authorities/before importing any pest." Her authorities were the workers in the field and their advice was clear:

> The organ-cactus, tall John Dryden,
> that thorn-bush Alexander Pope,
> may flourish as the deserts widen,
> but give our worn-out soils no Hope.
> Come plant the Lyric everywhere!

As Vivian Smith has pointed out, Wright used her ecological analogy to good effect (13). Moreover, her campaign was successful: A resurgence of the lyric occurred among younger Australian poets in the late 1960s and 70s, and neo-Romantics such as Robert Adamson and others have testified to her influence.

Whether Wright's hyperbolic claim for the lyric as Australia's "natural" mode is acceptable or not, her use of the ecological analogy shows again how pervasive it has been in her thinking. Moreover, it is a reminder of the dominance in her vocabulary of metaphors of planting and growing. Early in her career as a poet, Wright marveled at the organic growth of natural life; for example, this sense of wonder was imaged in coral reefs in "The Builders" (*Woman to Man*): "Only those coral insects live/ that work and endure under/the breakers' cold continual thunder." Similarly, she observed, in a typical transposition from lyric to argumentative assertion: "Only those men survive/who dare to hold their love against the world?" This perception of a link between a nurturing love and natural evolutionary forces was present also in muted form behind the politics and polemic of *The Coral Battleground*: "It was easy to see that the shibboleths of [economic] growth and progress needed a balancing force, if the future was going to be lived in a world fit for humans" (3).

In Wright's view, a continual program of education, restoration and rehabilitation is necessary if the checks and balances of a finely tuned ecosystem are not to be reduced to chaos by economic expansionists. Wright's poem "The Builders" was published when she was thirty-four. In a later poem, "Rockpool" (*Phantom Dwelling*), published when Wright was seventy, the tone is more clenched, the outlook less expansively meliorist:

> My generation is dying, after long lives
> swung from war to depression to war to fatness.
> I watch the claws in the rockpool, the scuttle, the crouch—
> green humps, the biggest barnacled, eaten by seaworms.

Contemplating the "cancers"—the pun is bitter—that humans have brought to the natural world, the toughness of "devouring and mating," she also accepts the process of decay with a sense of necessity, at the ocean's edge where it all began. But the book is not all as bleak as this. A recognition exists that houses and settlements are only "phantom dwellings," but an old lyric note resurges in "Smalltown Dance" in which two countrywomen folding bedsheets demonstrate the archetypal scope of humans (especially women) to combine dreams and practical living:

> Fold
> those beckoning roads to some impossible world,
> put them away and close the cupboard door.

The young woman's optimism is now muted in old age by a recognition of limits and ends. However, "smalltown dancers" such as these women folding their sheets demonstrate a resurgent capacity in ordinary men and women to resist the destructive element and take partners in the ecological dance.

WORKS CITED

Abotomey, Peter. "Class Lecture After a Recent Visit by Judith Wright." *LiNQ* 6 (1978): 1–5.

Bennett, Bruce. "Judith Wright, Moralist." *Westerly* 21.1 (1976): 76–82.

Gowda, H.H. Anniah. "Perfected Passions: The Love Poetry of Kamala Das and Judith Wright." *The Literary Half-Yearly* 20–21 (1979): 116–30.

Hope, A.D. *Judith Wright.* Melbourne: Oxford UP, 1975.

Kohli, Devindra. "The Crystal Glance of Love: Judith Wright as a Love Poet." *Journal of Commonwealth Literature* 6 (1971): 42–52.

McKernan, Susan. *A Question of Commitment: Australian Literature in the Twenty Years After the War.* Sydney: Allen and Unwin, 1989.

Smith, Vivian. "Experiment and Renewal: A Missing Link in Modern Australian Poetry." *Southerly* 47 (1987): 3–18.

Wallace-Crabbe, Chris. "Matters of Style: Judith Wright and Elizabeth Bishop." *Westerly* 23.1 (1978): 53–57.

Wright, Judith. References to *The Moving Image* (1946), *Woman to Man* (1949), *The Gateway* (1953), *The Two Fires* (1955), *Five Senses* (1963), *The Other Half* (1966), and *Shadow* (1970): *Collected Poems 1942–1970* (Sydney: Angus & Robertson, 1971). References to later books of poems are from the following editions: *Alive: Poems 1971–72* (1973); *Fourth Quarter* (1976); and *Phantom Dwelling* (1985)—all published by Angus & Robertson, Sydney.

———. "Conservation as a Concept." *Quadrant* 12.1 (1968): 29–33.

———. "Context: Judith Wright." *The London Magazine* (February 1962): 37–38.

———. *The Coral Battleground.* Melbourne: Thomas Nelson, 1977.

———. *The Cry for the Dead.* Melbourne: Oxford UP, 1981.

———. "Darkie Point: New England National Park." *Notes and Furphies* 12 (1984): 6–7.

———. *Preoccupations in Australian Poetry.* Melbourne: Oxford UP, 1965.

———. "The Upside-Down Hut." *Australian Letters* 3.4 (1961): 30–34.

———. *We Call for a Treaty.* Sydney: Collins/Fontana, 1985.

———. "What It Means To Be a Descendant of Pioneers." *Hemisphere* 7.6 (1953): 24–27.

JUDITH WRIGHT'S PUBLISHED WORK

Poetry

The Moving Image, 1946
Woman to Man, 1949
The Gateway, 1953
The Two Fires, 1955
Australian Bird Poems, 1961
Birds: Poems, 1962
Judith Wright, 1963
Five Senses: Selected Poems, 1963; rev. 1972
City Sunrise, 1964
The Other Half, 1966
Collected Poems, 1942–1970, 1971
Alive: Poems, 1971–1972, 1973
Fourth Quarter and Other Poems, 1976
The Double Tree: Selected Poems 1942–1976, 1978
Phantom Dwelling, 1985

Short Story Collection

The Nature of Love, 1966

Children's Books

King of the Dingoes, 1958
The Day the Mountains Played, 1960
Range the Mountains High, 1962; rev. 1971
Country Towns, 1963
The River and the Road, 1966; rev. 1971

Biography and History

The Generations of Men, 1959
    An account of the author's pioneer ancestors in the early nineteenth century.
The Cry for the Dead, 1981
    Continuation of the previous book, but concentrating on the treatment of Aborigines by early pioneers.

Literary Criticism

Charles Harpur, 1963; rev. 1977
Preoccupations in Australian Poetry, 1965
Henry Lawson, 1967

Environmental Commentary

The Coral Battleground, 1977
    History of the struggle to save Australia's Great Barrier Reef from exploitation.

Aboriginal Rights

We Call for a Treaty, 1985
    Polemical account of the struggle for Aboriginal land rights.

Collection

Because I Was Invited, 1975
    Lectures on literature, Aboriginals, conservation.

Selected Articles

"Inheritance and Discovery in Australian Poetry." *Poetry Magazine* 5 (1965): 3–11.
"Landscape and Dreaming." *Daedalus* 114 (1985): 29–56.
    Recounts white settlers' exploitation of natural resources and ignorance of ecological matters, as
    they violated the Aborigines' centuries-old right to the Australian land.

DISCUSSION OF SELECTED CRITICAL READINGS

(I wish to thank Bruce McClintock for his help in preparing the bibliographical and biographical material.)

Two early books on Judith Wright are A.D. Hope's appreciative commentary on her life and writings, *Judith Wright* (Melbourne: Oxford UP, 1975), and Shirley Walker's *The Poetry of Judith Wright: A Search for Unity* (Melbourne: Edward Arnold, 1980). As her title indicates, Walker presents the work as a manifestation of Wright's continuing search for psychic and physical unity. Shirley Walker has updated her study of Wright's poetry in *Flame and Shadow* (St. Lucia: U of Queensland P, 1991). This study stresses Wright as a "lyrical poet whose images reflect yet transcend the Australian context."

Australian critics who "discovered" Judith Wright in her first two books of poems, *The Moving Image* (1946) and *Woman to Man* (1949), were at first loath to accept changes in pattern and direction of Australian poetry. Charles Higham in "Judith Wright's Vision" (*Quadrant* 5.3, 1961: 33–41) was typical in seeing the early poems as "bold, vibrant, impressive, written in a sudden blaze of invention" (35), and not untypical in asserting that "in the experience of being a mother—Judith Wright reached the highest point of her achievement" (39). Thereafter, in the 1950s, according to Higham and others, the "rot" set in and her poetry became abstract, metaphysical, and nonsensuous. However, academic critics such as G.A. Wilkes ("The Later Poetry of Judith Wright," *Southerly* 25, 1965: 163–71), H.P. Heseltine ("Wrestling with the Angel: Judith Wright's Poetry in the 1950s," *Southerly* 38, 1978: 163–71), and Terry Sturm ("Continuity and Development in the Work of Judith Wright," *Southerly* 36, 1976: 161–76) gave more sympathetic attention to changing poetic styles and preoccupations in the 1950s and 60s. Wilkes noted the shift from "the world as perceived" to "the world as starting point for reflection." Heseltine saw in certain poems of the 1950s a move from the lyric towards the dramatic and the private to the public sphere, which anticipated her later entry into politics and ecology. Commenting on continuity and development into the 1970s, Sturm observed an extension of the "range of moods" and the "development of techniques" rather than new themes, concluding that the hallmark of the later style was "a casual or understated surface texture." Vivian Smith's "Experiment and Renewal: A

Missing Link in Modern Australian Poetry" (*Southerly* 47, 1987: 3–18) gave a literary-historical dimension to Wright's poetry, by presenting her as a "defender of the lyric" and a counter-influence to the classicism of A.D. Hope.

The best articles developing international comparisons are Devindra Kohli's "The Crystal Glance of Love: Judith Wright as a Love Poet" (*Journal of Commonwealth Literature* 6.1, 1971: 42–52), which compares her with Indian poet Kamala Das; and Chris Wallace-Crabbe's "Matters of Style: Judith Wright and Elizabeth Bishop," (*Westerly* 23.1, 1978: 53–57).

The question of Wright's female perspective or feminine sensibility is discussed in Fay Zwicky's "Another Side of Paradise: A.D. Hope and Judith Wright" (*Southerly* 48, 1988: 3–21), and in Jennifer Strauss's "The Poetry of Dobson, Harwood and Wright: 'Within the Bounds of Feminine Sensibility?'" (*Meanjin* 38, 1979: 334–49). Like Leonie Kramer in "Judith Wright, Hope, McAuley" (*The Literary Criterion* 15, 1980: 83–92), Zwicky and Strauss cast doubts on the "intellectual" claims of her verse, Strauss calling it "thoughtful, but not intellectual" (347). None of these critics gives adequate attention to the nature and scope of Wright's vision.

Few critics have yet linked Wright's prose writings with her poetry. Dennis Robinson elucidates *The Generations of Men* in "Australia's 'Double Aspect' in Judith Wright's *The Generations of Men*" (*Southerly* 39, 1979: 283–97). Shirley Walker's "*The Cry for the Dead*—Judith Wright and the Aborigines" (in *The Writer's Sense of the Past*, Singapore: Singapore UP, 1987: 152–59) proposes that examining Wright's poetry in light of her prose would amplify the earlier poems concerned with Aborigines. The Aboriginal theme is also discussed in J.J. Healy's *Literature and the Aborigine in Australia* (St. Lucia: U of Queensland P, 1989). Bruce Bennett discusses Wright's literary and social criticism in *Because I Was Invited* and elsewhere in "Judith Wright, Moralist" (*Westerly* 21.1, 1976: 76–82).

Although critics in the 1980s did not generally take much interest in Wright, Andrew Taylor has attempted a postmodern perspective on the "doubleness" and "otherness" in her verse in *Reading Australian Poetry* (St. Lucia, U of Queensland P, 1987: Chapter 7); Susan McKernan has explored Wright's "commitment" as both poet and social critic in *A Question of Commitment* (Sydney: Allen and Unwin, 1987: Chapter 6).

The field remains open for rereadings in the light of contemporary conditions and the circumstances of this remarkable writer's life and work.

— BRUCE BENNETT

II. Decolonizing Patriarchy

Parallels between colonial and patriarchal society are drawn in several of the essays, which address the subjugation of women in a male-dominated world. The critics see their authors—Indian, Pakistani, African, Australian, and Canadian— as determined to decolonize patriarchy, much in the same way as Anand or Achebe set themselves to liberating the subjects of colonialism.

In this project, initiated by Olive Schreiner—particularly in the unfinished *From Man to Man*—Canadian Margaret Atwood has probably received the fullest attention. Through a close textual reading of Atwood's *Cat's Eye*, Sharon Wilson finds in the novel she calls "postmodern" a woman's search for a genuine vision that will lead to emancipation from "the restricting roles of fairy tales, comics, television, the Bible, history, and myth"; this freedom will in turn enable her to develop an identity through a vision at least bright "enough to see by."

The Australian writer Christina Stead has also been widely recognized, especially for *The Man Who Loved Children*. Phyllis Edelson addresses "gender and power" in this novel, which she considers as exemplary of all of Stead's work as it consistently "enlarges our vision of . . . sexual politics." Edelson also points out that while Stead decolonizes "the unfortunate legacy of gender roles and conditioning" she shows herself a truly international writer, not one "distinctively Australian."

Two Indian critics, Ramā Jha and Ramesh Chadha, reveal how female Indian writers in English, like their Western counterparts, have also written to free women from masculine colonization, in this case sanctioned by religion and tradition. Jha views the work of Kamala Markandaya as a reflection of Gandhian thought, therefore compelled to advocate the equality of Indian women. Markandaya's female characters, Jha argues, define the identity sought by women in postcolonial India, an identity to be marked by patriarchal decolonization as well as political. Much the same approach is taken by Chadha as she addresses Nayantara Sahgal's depiction of the male-female relationship in novels both sexually and politically sophisticated. Chadha pictures Sahgal a franker novelist than the gentler and subtler Markandaya, for Sahgal deals directly with divorce, infidelity, the double standard, religious taboos, and masculinist tradition.

Fawzia Afzal-Khan examines the work of another Asian writer, Bapsi Sidhwa, who gives women a place in history long denied them. Analyzing Sidhwa's two novels about the Partition of India after Independence, *The Bride* and *Ice-Candy-Man*, Afzal-Khan proposes that this Pakistani writer decolonizes a patriarchal history that long suppressed the role of Asian women, and in so doing demonstrates that if history were to be defined in the future by such women it might well be less violent.

Kirsten Holst Petersen shows how the African writer, Buchi Emecheta, also challenges unjust gender roles blindly accepted as tradition. Although, as Petersen notes, Emecheta's feminism—which the author herself denies—may seem mild to Westerners, it has enraged African male critics who consider her a traitor to her own culture. Petersen describes Emecheta's often autobiographical fiction as a "vigorous departure" in African literature, and calls Emecheta "a role model for her sisters" as she seeks to break feminine subjugation and searches "for new ways of social and sexual organization."

On the Canadian front, critics of Margaret Laurence and Alice Munro see their subjects determined to decolonize patriarchal society in ways more indirect than those taken by the Asian and African writers. But that difference likely stems from the subtler forms of masculinist domination practiced in predominantly Anglo-Saxon territory. Greta Coger analyzes each of Laurence's women protagonists and traces how they strive for and attain identity. Coger stresses the importance of Laurence's experiences in colonial Africa where she discovered that all women face a colonization not unlike that of the African natives. J. A. Wainwright looks at Munro's "probing, self-conscious, female narrative voices" who long to decolonize the paradoxes, oppositions, contradictions, and competitions that dominate male-female relationships. Through a discussion of the closely allied thematic-artistic texture of Munro's work, Wainwright records the recognitions she has made about a world one of her characters describes as "dull, simple, amazing and unfathomable."

Marian Arkin takes up the often neglected work of an early international English writer, Henry Handel Richardson (the pseudonym of Ethel Florence Lindesay Robertson). An Australian, Richardson spent most of her life in England, yet wrote mainly about her homeland in novels often called "naturalistic," a form thought by many today to be so archaic that her work holds little appeal for modern readers. But Arkin sets out to redeem this impressive body of fiction she insists is wrongly labeled and proposes a "new reading strategy" to rely on a "feminist framework."

The parallel of colonial and feminine subjugation has been well served as women writers from the East and the West have successfully subverted a patriarchal past.

Margaret Atwood

Internationally known Canadian novelist, poet, short-story writer, and critic, Margaret Atwood has also painted watercolors (recently published) as illustrations or book covers for particular texts, written and illustrated comic strips and children's literature, been active in feminist and human rights organizations, and served as editor at Anansi Press, on the Board of Directors of the Canadian Civil Liberties Association, and as Chairperson of the Canadian Writer's Union. She has written travel articles, libretti, scenarios, radio and television scripts, and screen plays.

Atwood was born in Ottawa, 18 November 1939, to Carl Edmund and Margaret Dorothy (Killim) Atwood from Nova Scotia. Her father, an entomologist who taught at the University of Toronto, took the family with him for field work in the wilderness of northern Quebec and Ontario. Atwood has lived in various places and has traveled widely, currently residing in Toronto with the writer Graeme Gibson and their daughter Jess.

Atwood has a B.A. with honors in English Language and Literature from Victoria College, University of Toronto (1961), where she studied with Northrop Frye and published poetry in *Canadian Forum, Alphabet, Jargon,* and *Tamarack Review.* A rare chapbook, *Double Persephone,* was published by Hawkshead Press in 1961. Atwood received an A.M. in English from Radcliffe College (1962) and worked toward a Ph.D. in Victorian literature at Radcliffe 1962-63, 1965-67 (uncompleted dissertation: "Nature and Power in the English Metaphysical Romance of the Nineteenth and Twentieth Centuries"). She wrote her first (unpublished) novel, *Up in the Air So Blue,* about 1964.

Atwood's numerous literary prizes include the E. J. Pratt Medal (1961), Governor General's Medal for *The Circle Game* (1966) and *The Handmaid's Tale* (1986), Union Poetry Prize (*Poetry* 1969), Welsh Arts Council Writer's Prize (1982), *Los Angeles Times* Fiction Award (1986), Booker Prize Shortlist (1987, 1989), Arthur C. Clarke Award for Best Science Fiction (1987), Humanist of the Year Award (1987), Canadian Club Arts and Letters Award (1989), and the Canadian Booksellers Association Author-of-the-Year Award (1989). She has also received a Guggenheim Fellowship (1981), is Fellow of the Royal Society of Canada, and has received honorary degrees from Trent and Queen's Universities, the Universities of Toronto, Waterloo, and Guelph; and Concordia, Smith, and Mount Holyoke Colleges. She has taught at Canadian, U.S., and Australian universities.

EYES AND I'S

Like the earlier *Life Before Man*, Margaret Atwood's most recent novel, *Cat's Eye*, initially seems to be a "realistic" departure from the deconstructed fantasy and romance dominant from *The Edible Woman* through *The Handmaid's Tale*. Although *Life Before Man* and *Cat's Eye* are set in contemporary Toronto and demonstrate comedy of manners traditions, on one level they are the kind of Jamesian ghost story Atwood admires. In the case of *Cat's Eye*, the protagonist's memories of her "girlfriends" and a gothic childhood and adolescence in Toronto are her ghosts. The city of Toronto, associated with poison, malice, and the spirits of the dead, even seems out to kill her. Like Atwood's earlier novels, however, *Cat's Eye* also "revisions" or transforms other fantastic intertexts (stories or works consciously or unconsciously within the main text) that influence the novel's images, structure, and themes. This time drawing on the Triple Goddess myth, the Bible, *King Lear*, and related images from movies, television, and other popular arts to focus on the child's fairy-tale journey into adulthood, Atwood again portrays a symbolically dismembered character capable of fairy-tale metamorphosis. In this case, the metamorphosis affects not only vision and the self but her (and our) conceptions of time and art. Despite the novel's apparent realism, the narrator, Elaine Risley, again enters a fabulous world of old ghosts, cruel stepsisters, deceitful witches and wizards, disappointing princes, a merciful fairy-godmother, and tests to be faced alone in an alien inner landscape. Because Elaine is a visual artist, the development of her identity or "I" is even more dependent upon the development of her vision, her "eye," than in Atwood's earlier works.

From the beginning of her career, Atwood's narrators and personas have to overcome the mirror and camera vision, with their consequent narcissism, that stand in the way of genuine vision. According to Atwood's *Murder in the Dark*, genuine vision sometimes comes through a "third-eye": "Try not to resist the third eye: it knows what it's doing. Leave it alone and it will show you that this truth is not the only truth. . . .You will reach out in any direction and you will touch the light itself. . . . You see. You see" ("Instructions for the Third Eye" 61–62). Instead of enabling genuine vision, in Atwood's early, rare *Kaleidoscopes Baroque*, illustrated with Charles Pachter's woodcuts, "an eye of mirrors" functions like a kaleidoscope: "fragments of sight/reflected back, made multiple:/bouquets of hands unfolded. . ., a cannibal/ flower of mouths grew from each face, a sun/gathered from every lightbulb" (4). In *The Circle Game* the "camera man"'s "glass eye" freezes the persona and even the clouds and the sun into a "souvenir" ("Camera" 56). In this volume's title poem, although the narrator, caught in circular games, gropes toward the other through a melting mirror, "eyes' cold blue thumbtacks" not only fix her in his "mind's continent," but anticipate the dilemma most Atwood characters face in the "room" of relationship: Like the lies of his touch and language, this kind of vision is an attempt to keep her "at a certain distance/and (at length) avoid/admitting [she is there]" (48-50). Symbolically trapped in mirror vision, split between head and body, and afraid to see either past or present, the unnamed narrator of *Surfacing* (1972) lies to readers and herself so extensively that her contradictions and revisions deconstruct or erase both the novel and her self as she creates them by telling her story. Rennie of *Bodily Harm* (1982) actually carries and uses a camera that distances her from the realities (cancer, sexism, revolution, torture) she does not want to feel. But *Surfacing's* narrator, Marian (*Edible Woman*), Joan (*Lady Oracle*), Lesje, Nate, and Elizabeth (*Life Before Man*), and Offred (*The Handmaid's Tale*) share with Rennie a tendency to freeze memory in photograph trophies and force experience into frames.

In order to free themselves from the restricting roles of fairy tales, comics, television, the Bible, history, and myth and heal their split identities, Atwood's characters and personas must recover feeling. They must use what might be called an empathetic vision, one that does not lie or refuse to see, narcissistically reflect the viewer or the viewed, diminish what is viewed, dehumanize the subject (including the self) by treating as object Other, or, like the hobgoblin's fragmented mirror in Andersen's "The Snow Queen," shrink the good in order to magnify the unpleasant or bad. In order to see rather than reflect, they must stop being mirrors and using others as mirrors. They must remove the glass eyes of mirror or camera vision that alienate them from themselves, others, and the world. Paradoxically, cameras or mirrors also contribute to characters' fairy-tale metamorphoses by leading them to the recognition that they do live in conditioned textual "frames" (of fairy tales, advertising, comic books, true romance stories, prescribed sex roles, nationality) resembling mirrors and photographs.

Atwood's earliest work also associates art with the freezing vision of mirrors or glass. If in one sense art and the artist "with gorgon touch" can freeze and even kill the natural world by creating the immortality of "a world of glass" (*Double Persephone* "Formal Garden," "Her Song" n.p.), art is also a true or distorting mirror reflecting the reader, the reader's world, and even the text. At its best, art is a lens giving not merely a reflection but a distillation or condensation ("Atwood Interview" 79). As Atwood says in "An End to Audience?" the writer is a soothsayer, "both an eye-witness and an I-witness, the one to whom personal experience happens and the one who makes experience personal for others. The writer *bears witness*, ...speak[s] the forbidden, . . . especially in times of political repression" (*Second Words* 348, 350). As a lens rather than a possibly faulty mirror, art is vision and voice, responsive and responsible.

All the major characters of Atwood's fiction and many of her personas simultaneously develop vision and identity, but in Atwood's most recent works empathetic vision is accompanied with both touch and voice: relationship or involvement and an obligation to speak out, often for those who are silenced. As long as Atwood's characters function as mirrors or cameras, they are symbolically frozen in fairy-tale towers. They are cut off from others and their vision, voice, and touch are either frozen (symbolically amputated) or freezing.

In her 1972 essay, "Ice-Women vs. Earth Mothers," Atwood discusses Canadian literature's preponderance of sinister or life-denying women, who correspond to one aspect of the Triple Goddess and demonstrate what Atwood calls the Rapunzel Syndrome. Robert Graves "divides Woman into three mythological categories or identities. First comes the elusive Diana or Maiden figure, the young girl; next the Venus figure, goddess of love, sex, and fertility; then the Hecate figure, called by Graves the Crone, goddess of the underworld" (*Survival* 199). Canada's version of the ancient Triple Goddess is "not just an Ice-Virgin-Hecate figure, but a Hecate with Venus and Diana trapped inside." This Hecate is an extension of the Grimms' Rapunzel. According to Atwood, the Rapunzel Syndrome normally has four elements: Rapunzel, the wicked witch who imprisons her, the tower she is imprisoned in, and the Rescuer. In Canada's version, Rapunzel walks around with a mouth "like [a] clenched fist." She and her tower are synonymous: "These heroines have internalized the values of their culture to such an extent that they have become their own prisons." In most cases, "the Rescuer is not much help" (209-10). Such Rapunzels recall other fairy-tale and mythic figures, like Andersen's Snow Queen and Ice Maiden and the Grimms' Girl Without Hands, who are literally or figuratively "cut off."

In *Cat's Eye*, the main Rapunzel/Snow Queen figure is the narrator, a visual artist named Elaine Risley. When she returns to Toronto for her "retrospective," where she humorously decides to wear vampire and Hecate black, she experiences the same kind of "eye problems" and transformations of vision as Atwood's other narrators and personas. She, too, makes a habit of watching herself in literal or metaphoric mirrors and framing others in mental photographs. Since she is a visual artist, she literally frames Mrs. Smeath, Cordelia, Jon, and Joseph in "eye for an eye" paintings that lead to further blindness. Because she has repressed pain by "forgetting" and by cultivating her own unfeeling glass eye, like what she imagines to be the alien vision of a cat's eye marble, she, too, is discomforted, dis/eased, by the literal and figurative amputations she notices around her. The "severed limbs" in Jon's apartment remind Elaine of the parts of her self that are missing: the eight-year-old "body," especially the vulnerable fingers and eyes, that first the "girlfriends" and then she buried in nothingness. Like other Canadian Hecates and, in a sense, all mature adults, she contains her Diana and Venus selves. Although the book's narration is retrospective and Elaine has remembered her burial and near freezing before the novel's present, Atwood withholds the scene where Elaine "sees her life entire" (398) almost until the end of the novel and restructures Elaine's life and memory as she self-consciously fragments conventional notions of both the novel and time. As the book's first section emphasizes, "If you can bend space you can bend time also, and if you knew enough and could move faster than light you could travel backwards in time and exist in two places at once" (3). When Elaine returns to her childhood home in Toronto, symbolically she (and with her the reader) is in two places and times at once. Elaine is unable to re/member until she re/views nothingness and her "death," this time meeting her "twin" Cordelia's gaze. She must return to where she and Cordelia changed places in the past: the ravine, with its bridge and the frozen river of the dead, for the snow to leave her eyes and the ice her fingers. She must not only resist the witch or Snow Queen: She must stop *being* either Rapunzel or the Snow Queen. This middle-aged "Hecate" must release the Diana self that is trapped inside.

Both the Grimm's Rapunzel and Anderson's Snow Queen embody entrapment and alienation, and both fairy tales are, at least in part, about regaining vision and relationship. The enchantress of "Rapunzel," Dame Gothel, has walled up herself and her lush garden as protection against others' hunger. When her "walls" are violated, she takes the violator's child, Rapunzel, named after the herb rampion, and creates a mirror image. She separates Rapunzel "from all the world" in a tower, with neither stairs nor door, within a forest. When Rapunzel, who spends her time singing to herself, hears a voice, she lets down her long hair and the witch climbs up. When the King's son hears her song and climbs up, Rapunzel gives no indication of loving him but thinks "he will love [her] more" than Dame Gothel and agrees to leave with him when she has woven a ladder. But the enchantress finds out, cuts off Rapunzel's hair, and exiles her again, this time in a desert. When the prince faces the witch's "wicked, venomous" gaze, he leaps from the tower and is blinded by thorns. In his aimless wanderings, he finally comes to the desert and is drawn again to Rapunzel's voice. This time, rather than being obsessed with herself, Rapunzel feels for another: Counteracting the witch's gaze, her tears "[wet] his eyes" and his vision grows "clear again" (Grimms 76). The couple and their twins, representing their no longer alienated selves, return to society and live happily.

Rather than using wall, tower, forest, and desert images, "The Snow Queen" symbolizes narcissism and amputating alienation with images of mirrors, ice, and snow. A fragment from the hobgoblin's distorting mirror pierces and almost freezes little Kay's heart. Then the glass gets into his eye, symbolically blinding him to life and nature and preparing him for the Snow Queen's abduction to her ice palace. Made of ice but alive, the Snow Queen has "eyes [that sparkle] like bright stars, but there [is] neither peace nor rest in her glance." Kay fastens his sled to her sleigh and, because she looks at him "just as if they [are] acquainted," he continues to follow her, repeating "mental arithmetic" when he becomes frightened. Her kiss penetrates to Kay's heart and makes him feel as if he is going to die, "but only for a moment; he soon seem[s] quite well again, and [does] not notice the cold around him." When she kisses Kay for the second time, he forgets Gerda, his grandmother, and home. The Snow Queen recognizes that she may "kiss [him] to death" if she continues (*Complete Andersen* 55-58). When Kay's friend, Gerda, makes her archetypal journey to rescue him, she finds him shaping words from pieces of ice in the Snow Queen's frozen lake. Enclosed by the ice palace, this lake, over which she presides, is ironically called "The Mirror of Reason." Paradoxically, each piece is already "perfect as a work of art," but Kay wants to make something of them. Cut off from nature and playing "the icy game of reason," he is an impotent artist. Because of the glass still in his eye, he thinks the figures and words he makes are "of the highest importance," but he is unable to form the one word that would make him his own master. Like Rapunzel, the prince, and most of Atwood's characters, in order to free himself from internal and external "mirrors," he needs to balance reason with feeling, in this case again through another's tears and touch. Gerda, whose vision is neither narcissistic nor icy, proves her power and her love: They return to the green world, where they realize they are grown up. The Snow Queen, now without a double, remains alone, presiding over her frozen world.

Atwood draws the "icewomen" of her Rapunzel Syndrome from both "Rapunzel" and "The Snow Queen." To the extent that Atwood's personas and characters look through glass eyes without feeling, they are internally separated. Like Dame Gothel, Rapunzel, the Snow Queen, and Kay, they also separate themselves from the world behind symbolic walls, in towers or ice palaces. In order to resist the alien Gaze or touch of the Other, guard against becoming an Other, and rescue themselves, they must remove the "glass" from their eyes: They must recognize the world and the

Other as subjects rather than objects or mirrors of themselves. Like Rapunzel, they must reach out, symbolically regrowing or thawing "amputated" or frozen parts of themselves. In order to release her own Diana-maiden self, Elaine must recognize that her "twin," Cordelia, and the world are separate from her and that she is neither everything nor nothing. Then, like Rapunzel and Kay, she can go home.

Even more than Atwood's earlier novels, *Cat's Eye* focuses on vision: in the title, in character descriptions, and in cinematic memory scenes. Since Elaine retrospectively narrates the novel, the book's vision (and through it the reader's) is hers. Because she resees continuously changing past selves as she narrates, we experience at least eight kinds of subjective "reality" in *Cat's Eye*: Elaine's "backseat" and microscope vision, her perception of the vision of others (the Other), the Nothingness of the "bad time" she "forgets," cat's eye vision, Virgin Mary vision, "tourist vision" of Toronto from British Columbia, and fairy-tale restored vision of herself, others, and the world.

Prior to the girlfriends, prior to Elaine's repression of her internal "fracture" and the accompanying experience of nothingness, Elaine presents her vision as "backseat," the innocent vision of a child being driven where her parents take her. Accompanying her family while her father does entomological field work in northern Canada, she focuses on the back of her family's ears and the quickly passing sideview from the car window, preparing her for later tourist vision. Because her family is transitory, she is not in school, and she plays only with her brother; she spends her time happily as a person rather than a gender-conditioned female. This backseat vision begins to change as she acquires a camera, reads horror comic books, learns about insect infestations, and acquires an interest in cross-section drawings, in which organisms are "cut open so you can see what's inside them" (34). Visiting her father's lab when the family settles in Toronto for his new job, Elaine begins to try microscope vision, in which, since "there isn't room for a whole arm or leg," one magnifies a part. Watching a parade of "people dressed like snowflakes . . . strangely truncated because [she's] looking down on them" from the Zoology Building, she ironically associates these snow figures with the lab and its dead or caged animals, including the mice who kill any mouse with an "alien" scent (36-37). Retrospectively aware of how she is already distancing and therefore alienating herself, Elaine analyzes these memory "pictures of the dead" (26) in order to recover the missing parts of her, the parts that fragment, are buried, and then freeze under the gaze of Cordelia and the girlfriends.

Others' visions include that of God, Elaine's parents, other fathers, Mrs. Smeath, Carol's and Cordelia's mothers, Toronto, the "girlfriends," Susie, Elaine's brother, other boys, Joseph, Jon, Ben, teachers, the women's group with its other women artists, hijackers and their "eye for an eye" vision (388), dead animals, Elaine's daughters, and Charna and other "Sub-Versions" critics and artists. Unlike *Lady Oracle*'s Joan Foster, in general Elaine feels comfortable with her immediate family, including her parents, brother, current husband, and daughters; but most other people make her feel "objectified," diminished, or unfree. To the child Elaine, the heavens are watchful and God is a faceless engine (101, 181). Mrs. Smeath is a single-breasted witch walled up in self-righteousness, and even her "bad heart" is an evil eye. Elaine would like to incinerate it with comic book "eye rays" before it sums her up and judges her with "It serves her right" (180). Although Elaine is initially comfortable with boys whose conversations are mostly silence and whose power over her "is held through [her] eyes" (237, 240), the gaze of her later "princes" is freezing and fragmenting. Rather than rescuing her, they turn her into a "fallen" woman. Instead of Elaine's healing their sight, as Rapunzel does with her prince, their gaze blurs Elaine's vision and reduces her to "fragments" (372, 316). Her art teacher Joseph, whom she ironically wishes to rescue, dreams of a Rapunzel woman wrapped totally in cellophane. Seeming to have violet eyes, this "wizzard" looks at women as "helpless flowers, or shapes to be arranged and contemplated" (318). As Elaine's Park Plaza Hotel mirror reflection confirms, after putting her into a perfume ad role, he changes her into a vacant Pre-Raphaelite woman. His touch first freezes and then erases her. Later even Toronto, unlike the Seven Dwarfs' movie backdrop of British Columbia, where Elaine "vacations" in tourist reality with her travel agent husband, is a mirror-hell she must reenter, with a limiting gaze she must stare down.

Most of all, Elaine fears the gaze of the girlfriends, this novel's "wicked stepsisters." Carol takes in Elaine's unfinished house with "incredulous glee, . . . as if she's reporting on the antics of some primitive tribe" (49). Grace's "glassy eyes" register everything Elaine does in Sunday School so that she can report to Cordelia. As Elaine's "mirror image," Cordelia is also both the deceptive Snow Queen, whose "kisses" freeze, and "Rapunzel"'s wall-erecting witch. Under the pressure of Cordelia's always "measuring" eyes, that find her "not normal" and remind her that "People are looking!" (70, 118-20), Elaine is afraid of bursting inwards, of being crushed "like mud in a fist, until [she] implode[s]." If the girlfriends were enemies, Elaine could throw snowballs and feel hatred and anger. Because they are her "best friends," she wants to please. Yielding to social conditioning, trying to become "a girl" and "be for others" instead of being herself, Elaine understands the word "implode": "It has a dull final sound to it, like a lead door closing" (142). Because Elaine uses the girlfriends (especially Cordelia) as mirrors, she sees herself as she thinks they see her. Thus, she confuses Cordelia with herself. Cordelia, like *King Lear*'s cursed and doomed third sister, makes her father angry when she talks back to him and is eventually "banished." Never able to satisfy either parent and feeling she is nothing, Cordelia hides her own insecurity by cultivating a confident "parent" image and projecting her powerlessness onto Elaine. Using "her voice for adults" and giving Elaine "a squeeze of complicity," Cordelia implies that "Everything will be all right as long as [Elaine] sit[s] still, say[s] nothing, reveal[s] nothing." Cordelia tries to do this in her family before she is silenced (evident in the rest-home slurred speech the family no longer has to hear). When asked what she has to say for herself, now and much of the time Elaine has "nothing" to say in this novel dramatizing nothingness. As Elaine explains, "Even to myself I am mute" (252). Unsurprisingly, "Cordelia's voice" (the "Little Mermaid" silenced voice Elaine associates with her negative self-concept) later precipitates Elaine's suicide attempt.

Since Elaine cannot survive as a mirror of the nothingness or void of identity Cordelia actually feels, she erases memory. The "bad time" Elaine does not want to remember is the winter vision of nothingness, her "burial," when the "stepsisters" or triple "witches"—Carol, Grace, and Cordelia—enact their own version of

"Rapunzel" and "Snow Queen" entombment: They dress Elaine like Mary Queen of Scots, "headless [and therefore visionless and voiceless] already," throw her into the backyard hole Cordelia digs, and cover it with boards and then dirt. Analogous to Marian's place of "absolute zero" or her vision of Peter the Chef's barbecue where she is missing in *Edible Woman*, Elaine's "square of darkness" is a "time-marker that separates the time before from the time after. The point at which [she loses] power." Ironically wearing a black dress and cloak, like her later vision of the Virgin Mary who saves her from freezing, Elaine has "no image of [herself] in the hole; only a black square filled with nothing, a square like a door" (253). This door resembles Atwood's many other fearful door images, like that in "Hesitations Outside the Door," where the female persona fears the amputations of entrapment in the Grimms' "Fitcher's Bird." When Cordelia later tries to remind Elaine of the hole and the time in which they both feel "a dark blank," Elaine associates Cordelia's "double-cross" with poison nightshade and again sees herself reflected in Cordelia's "mirror eyes" (her sunglasses) "in duplicate and monochrome, . . . a great deal smaller than life-size." Like Dame Gothel, Cordelia buries her alter ego in the only safe place of her own she can make, in this case a hole symbolizing void of identity. (Not wanting to remember, Elaine later wonders why she relishes scaring Cordelia by pretending to be a vampire. Later still, she refuses to rescue Cordelia from the "looney bin" rest home where Cordelia is banished.) Ironically imitating Narcissus and eradicating self, the Other, and the world, Elaine adopts Cordelia's narcissistic vision: Confusing image with reality, she accepts the image Cordelia painfully constructs to hide her void. Elaine is unable even to recognize Cordelia "behind the disguise of costume" in a play. Much later, Elaine shows her retrospective awareness of Cordelia's mask in her painting, *Half a Face*.

Under the gaze of others, Elaine, like other Atwood characters and "Rapunzel"'s prince, goes "blind": She symbolically adopts an unseeing glass eye in order to deal with her "implosion." After Elaine loses her backseat vision, adopts the gaze of the other as her own vision, experiences nothingness, and becomes moldable "mud," cat's eye vision temporarily helps her survive the metaphoric "snow and ice" so fatal in Canadian literature. Ironically, to survive the Snow Queen, Elaine adopts Snow Queen vision, thereby choosing to freeze. Trying to emulate the "power" and "vision" of the beautiful cat's eye marble, she attempts to transform the lines of her implosion into such an eye: "The eye part of it, inside its crystal sphere, is so blue, so pure. It's like something frozen in the ice." Despite the eye's apparent "purity," however, cat's eyes are distinguished from the totally clear "puries," without a hidden internal pattern. When she uses cat's eye vision to see "the way it sees," she "can look at [people's] shapes and sizes, their colours, without feeling anything else about them. [She is] alive in [her] eyes only," like the dead raven that looks at her with a "shrivelled-up eye." Resembling the pieces of the hobgoblin's mirror that penetrate little Kay's eye and heart, the cold cat's eye seems to fall out of the sky, where it replaces the sun, and to pass right into Elaine "without hurting." Biting or peeling off skin from her lips and feet, dreaming that one of her twin selves is missing and that not she but her parents are sinking through earth resembling ice, she learns to spend time outside her body:

At these times I feel blurred, as if there are two of me, one

superimposed on the other, but imperfectly. There's an edge of
transparency, and beside it a rim of solid flesh that's without feeling,
like a scar. I can see what's happening, I can hear what's being said
to me, but I don't have to pay any attention. My eyes are open but
I'm not there. I'm off to the side. (173)

Learning to contain her internal fracture, she even retains a clear, smooth,
"intact" surface, like that of a cat's eye marble. Inside her "protective" Rapunzel
tower or Snow Queen palace, an amputated and silenced Elaine is her own prison.
Looking back on this period, Elaine later does "a self-portrait of sorts" she ironically
names *Cat's Eye*. Symbolically commenting on the texts Elaine and we read, the
painting recalls both the cat's eye marble and the pier-glass in Van Eyck's *The Arnolfini
Marriage*, studied in Elaine's art class. *Cat's Eye* depicts Elaine's "half-head," an
ornately framed convex mirror reflecting a piece of the back of Elaine's younger
head, and the three girlfriends walking "against a field of snow" (408). Elaine's
mirror vision, like Van Eyck's pier-glass, reflects people who "aren't in the main
picture at all." In Van Eyck's painting, "These figures reflected in the mirror are
slightly askew, as if a different law of gravity, a different arrangement of space exists
inside, locked in, sealed up in the glass as if in a paperweight. This round mirror is
like an eye, a single eye that sees more than anyone else looking" (327). Like other
Atwood texts, *Cat's Eye* mirrors itself and its narrator, self-consciously drawing the
reader's attention to its icy eyes and split or narcissistic I's.

When "snow angel" Cordelia becomes angry and "forces" Elaine to enter the
forbidden ravine territory beneath the bridge, Elaine would possibly literally freeze
without the countering sympathetic vision of her Virgin Mary. This novel's "fairy
godmother," the Virgin is also a Venus phase of the Triple Goddess cloaked in black,
the color of the wise hag, Hecate. Significantly, this "exposed heart" vision comes
to Elaine near Easter as she is immersed in the partly frozen river of the dead,
recalling not only the rivers Styx and Lethe but the glacier pool of dissolved dead
where Andersen's Ice Maiden claims Rudy ("The Ice Maiden" 412). Imagining first
that she sees three heads, suggesting the triple goddess and coinciding with the
book's other repeated patterns of three's, and then that her head is filling with black
snow that gets in through her eyes, she sees the Virgin holding out her arms. Her
voice tells Elaine, "You can go home now. . . . It will be all right. Go home" (185,
187-89). Later Elaine does a painting about this experience: In *Unified Field Theory*,
the Virgin of Lost Things holds a glass object, a cat's eye marble "at the level of her
heart." Below the bridge is what appears to be the universe but is "the underside of
the ground" and "the land of the dead people" (408). But the snow does not leave
Elaine's eyes and she is not reborn after the vision. Although she is able to walk away
from her shadowy alter egos, feels "free," and imagines she "can see right into
them," she is "indifferent to them. There's something hard in [her], crystalline, a
kernel of glass" (193-94). For years she represses her burial and freezing, the whole
period in which she is subject to the Gaze, and even the lost cat's eye marble.

Elaine cannot re/member herself or the Other until she sees "her life entire,"
significantly in a basement where she searches through a trunk. Like *The Edible
Woman's* Marian and *Surfacing's* unnamed narrator, who have repressed the

"subgrounds" of their existence, she must penetrate layers of the past. Like *Bodily Harm*'s Rennie, she must bridge the distance between "here" and "there." The barrier between Elaine and her mother cannot be removed until, recovering the cat's eye marble in the trunk, Elaine symbolically removes the glass from her eye. Again Elaine's paintings are revealing. Later, "To bring her [mother] back to life" and eradicate her repressed "implosion," Elaine does her *Pressure Cooker* double trip- tych of her owlwise real (earth goddess) mother, who didn't "give a hoot" about what others say a woman is supposed to be. Elaine now recognizes that her mother, unlike herself, always controlled the societal "pressure cooker," even using it for her own purposes. In contrast, her still lifes of Mrs. Smeath say "I see," but, like many Atwood personas, she is "blind" until, near the end of the novel, she resees with mercy or empathy. Then Elaine recognizes that the Medusa gaze of her "stepmother/ witch" Mrs. Smeath was not self-righteous but "defeated, . . . heavy with unloved duty" (405). It is her own gaze as an artist that, Medusa-like, can freeze the Other into an unexamined past. Like "The Snow Queen"'s little Kay, who cannot find himself in the fragmented piece⁀ of his icy art, Elaine needs heart as well as head.

Finally, Elaine reenters the ⸱⸱rld of mirrors, where she is Cordelia's reflection. Replaying her frozen memory of the scene in the ravine, Elaine rescues herself from her entrapment in reflections of the past. Revisiting the frozen underworld as a wise Hecate, the Virgin of lost things, Elaine becomes her own fairy godmother. She releases Cordelia and her own Diana-maiden self from their internalized ice palace/ tower. Transcending the "difference" or gap, merging subject and object, and symbolically opening a third eye, Elaine puts her arms out to the Cordelia of her vision as her exposed-heart Virgin had to her and speaks against both of their silencings. No longer protecting herself with cat's eye vision, Elaine is able to give back to Cordelia the fear and insecurity that were always hers rather than Elaine's, recognize that her "twin," Cordelia, is the subject of her own story, and, send Cordelia "home," symbolically stepping out of her mirror image. When Elaine does that, "The snow in [her] eyes withdraws like smoke." Finally, when her projections cease and Toronto is cleared of witches and ghosts, she realizes that the landscape is "not empty" but "filled with whatever it is by itself when [she's] not looking" (419). No longer either Rapunzel or the Snow Queen, no longer using an ice/glass eye, Elaine can leave "frozen" Toronto for the west and home. Now an "I" with eyes, Elaine paradoxically sees with the transformed vision of myth and fairy tales.

This postmodern novel deconstructs its fairy-tale intertext, however. Aging Elaine, a mother with two grown daughters, is not and does not wish to be a fairy- tale princess, and she is unlikely to live "happily ever after" with her aging "prince." Aware that she and Cordelia can never "play again like children, but this time without the pain," she enviously watches two giggling old women who, like her mother, "don't give a hoot." Her vision has come at a cost. Similarly, despite the unreality of its "postcard mountains," the Canadian "watery coast" she heads for is not an American dream but where land ends in her "real life" (14). Her night is moonless and the stars, not eternal and not even where we think they are, offer "old light." "Shining out of the midst of nothing," however, now "it's enough to see by" (420–21).

WORKS CITED

"A Margaret Atwood Interview with Karla Hammond." *Concerning Poetry* 12.11 (1979): 73–81.

Atwood, Margaret. *Cat's Eye*. Toronto: McClelland and Stewart, 1988.

———. *The Circle Game*. Toronto: Anansi, 1966.

———. *Double Persephone*. 1, Market Book Series. Toronto: Hawkshead Press, 1961.

———. *Murder in the Dark*. Toronto: Coach House, 1983.

———. *Second Words: Selected Critical Prose*. Toronto: Anansi, 1982.

———. *Survival: A Thematic Guide to Canadian Literature*. Toronto: Anansi, 1972.

The Complete Hans Christian Andersen Fairy Tales. Ed. Lily Owens. New York: Avenel, 1981.

Hunt, Margaret, and James Stern, trans. *The Complete Grimm's Fairy Tales*. New York: Pantheon, 1972.

Hutcheon, Linda. "From Poetic to Narrative Structures: The Novels of Margaret Atwood." Edited by Sherrill Grace and Lorraine Weir. *Margaret Atwood: Language, Text and System*. Vancouver: U of British Columbia P, 1983. 17–31.

Sartre, Jean-Paul. *Being and Nothingness*. Trans. Hazel E. Barnes. New York: Philosophical Library, 1956.

Wilson, Sharon R. "Bluebeard's Forbidden Room: Gender Images in Margaret Atwood's Visual and Literary Art." *American Review of Canadian Studies* 16.4 (Winter 1986): 385–97.

———. "Camera Images in Margaret Atwood's Novels." *Margaret Atwood: Reflection and Reality*. Ed. Beatrice Mendez-Egle. Edinburg, Tx.: Pan American Univ., 1987. 29–57.

———. "Deconstructing Text and Self: Mirroring in Atwood's *Surfacing* and Beckett's *Molloy*." *Journal of Popular Literature* 3 (Spring/Summer 1987): 53–69.

———. "Fairy-Tale Cannibalism in *The Edible Women*." *Cooking By the Book: Food in Literature and Culture*. Ed. Mary Anne Schofield. Bowling Green: Bowling Green State UP, 1989.

———. "The Fragmented Self in *Lady Oracle*. *Commonwealth Novel in English* 1.1 (1982): 50–85.

MARGARET ATWOOD'S PUBLISHED WORK

Novels

Edible Woman, 1969
Surfacing, 1972
Lady Oracle, 1976
Life Before Man, 1979
Bodily Harm, 1981
The Handmaid's Tale, 1985
Cat's Eye, 1988

Short Story Collections

Dancing Girls, 1977
Murder in the Dark, 1982
Bluebeard's Egg, 1983

Poetry

Kaleidoscopes Baroque, 1965
The Circle Game, 1966
The Animals in That Country, 1968
The Journals of Susanna Moodie, 1970
Procedures for the Underground, 1970
Power Politics, 1971
You Are Happy, 1974
Selected Poems, 1976

Two-Headed Poems, 1978
True Stories, 1981
Interlunar, 1984
Selected Poems II: Poems Selected and New, 1976-1986, 1986

Criticism

Survival: A Thematic Guide to Canadian Literature, 1972
Second Words: Selected Critical Prose, 1982

Children's Books

Anna's Pet, 1980
Up in the Tree, 1978

Miscellaneous Nonfiction

Days of the Rebels: 1815-1840 (Canada's Illustrated Heritage, Vol. 4), 1977
The CanLit Foodbook: From Pen to Palate—A Collection of Tasty Literary Fare, 1987
Foreword to *Cambridge Guide to Literature in English,* 1988

SELECTED CRITICAL READINGS

Margaret Atwood criticism is extensive and varied. Not only the best-known Canadian writer but the one to receive the most critical attention, Atwood was first known as a poet. After *The Circle Game* (1966) received the prestigious Governor General's Award, her work was reviewed widely in Canada. Although *The Edible Woman* was written in 1965, it was not published until 1969. Feminists from the United States then began writing about this and Atwood's subsequent novel, *Surfacing* (1972). That same year, *Survival* established Atwood as one of Canada's most important literary critics. Her work has been translated into over fourteen languages. Atwood criticism is international, including all major approaches. The international Margaret Atwood Society, which meets in conjunction with the Modern Language Association and publishes a newsletter with an annual bibliography, was founded in New York City in 1984.

Carrington, Ildiko de Papp. "Margaret Atwood and Her Works." *Canadian Writers and Their Works, Fiction Series.* Vol. 9. Toronto: ECW Press, 1987. 23–116. Presents biography and discusses themes in novels.

Davey, Frank. *Margaret Atwood: A Feminist Poetics.* Toronto: Coach House, 1984. Says Atwood's poetry opposes male and female space and argues that order and language are male concepts imposed on experience. Although few feminists would recognize the approach, Davey offers distinctive if not always plausible readings of Atwood's poetry, short stories, and novels.

Davidson, Arnold and Cathy, editors. *The Art of Margaret Atwood: Essays in Criticism.* Toronto: Anansi, 1981. Examines Atwood's diversity from varied viewpoints. Discusses the Canadian and international contexts of Atwood's poetry, its double vision and female voice, the evolution of female fictional protagonists, *Dancing Girls* as a bridge between Atwood's poetry and fiction, and her criticism. This excellent anthology of mostly Canadian criticism includes articles by Annis Pratt, Clara Thomas, and George Woodcock.

Godard, Barbara. "Tales Within Tales: Margaret Atwood's Folk Narratives." *Canadian Literature* 109 (1986): 57–84. Argues that Atwood experiences a "breakthrough" in technique with *Bluebeard's Egg* by promoting Canadian oral narrative to "high culture."

Grace, Sherrill. *Violent Duality: A Study of Margaret Atwood.* Montreal: Vehicle Press, 1980. "Forgets" the biographical Margaret Atwood in order to be "an interpretative guide" to Atwood's form and theme. Argues persuasively that Atwood's works dramatize a "violent duality": the subject/object duplicity of life. First book on Atwood.

————, and Lorraine Weir, editors. *Margaret Atwood: Language, Text and System.* Vancouver: U of British Columbia P, 1983. Proposes to examine the functioning of what Tzvetan Todorov calls the author's "system," including language within individual texts, texts within the author's *oeuvre*, and that *oeuvre* within the world text, from a variety of methodologies, including hermeneutic, phenomenological, computer assisted, and anthropological. Permeated with critical terminology and difficult.

Horne, Alan. "An Annotated Bibliography (Prose)." *The Annotated Bibliography of Canada's Major Authors.* Vol. 1. Toronto: ECW Press, 1979. 13–46. Lists primary and secondary sources.

————. "An Annotated Bibliography (Poetry)." *The Annotated Bibliography of Canada's Major Authors.* Vol. 2. Toronto: ECW Press, 1980. 13–53. Lists primary (including Atwood's rare poetry volumes) and secondary sources. See Horne's "Margaret Atwood: A Checklist of Writings By and About Margaret Atwood" in Davidson, *The Art of Margaret Atwood,* 243–85.

Keith, W.J. *Introducing Margaret Atwood's The Edible Woman: A Reader's Guide.* Toronto: ECW Press, 1989. Guides beginning students with information about the author, the importance of the work, and its critical reception. Gives chapter overviews and discusses its comic facets. Very basic.

Mallinson, Jean. *Margaret Atwood and Her Works.* Toronto: ECW Press, undated [1984?]. Concentrates on Atwood's poetry (through *True Stories*) so exclusively that even this "lyric poet's" physical appearance receives more comment than her fiction. Traces a pattern of self-dramatization from absence, to theatrical presence through personae, to wary presence, to reluctant settlement. Extended essay.

McCombs, Judith. "Atwood's Fictive Portraits of the Artist: From Victim to Surfacer, from Oracle to Birth." *Women's Studies* 12.1 (1986): 69–88. In a preliminary version of her book-in-progress, sees three stages in Atwood's fictive portraits of artists: the Closed, Divided, Mirroring World ending 1977, the realistic Open World 1978–83, and, with *Interlunar,* a radical shift towards alien mysticism or a possible Other World.

———, editor. *Critical Essays on Margaret Atwood.* Boston: G. K. Hall, 1988. Reprints important, mostly Canadian, reviews and articles. Convenient for American scholars interested in the history of criticism, but reviews, sometimes inaccurate, are often dated. Good overview of Atwood criticism in introductory essay.

Mendez-Egle, Beatrice, editor. *Margaret Atwood: Reflection and Reality.* Edinburg, Tx.: Pan American UP, 1987. Despite the preface's misleading discussion of "objective reality" in Atwood's work, includes useful essays from varied (archetypal, feminist) approaches on topics including Atwood's use of magic, didactic characterization, Jungian archetype, camera images, and narration.

Onley, Gloria. "Power Politics in Bluebeard's Castle." *Poets and Critics: Essays from Canadian Literature 1966-1974.* Toronto: Oxford UP, 1974. 191–214. Perceptive and still current early discussion of Bluebeard motif.

Page, Sheila. "Supermarket Survival: A Critical Analysis of Margaret Atwood's *The Edible Woman.*" *Sphinx* 1 (1974): 9–19. Useful early discussion of eating imagery in *Edible Woman.*

Pratt, Annis. "*Surfacing* and the Rebirth Journey." *The Art of Margaret Atwood: Essays in Criticism.* Toronto: Anansi, 1981. 139–57. Reads *Surfacing* from a feminist archetypal approach developed in Pratt's *Archetypal Patterns in Women's Fiction* (Bloomington: Indiana UP, 1981).

Rigney, Barbara Hill. *Margaret Atwood.* Women Writers Series. Totowa, New Jersey: Barnes and Noble, 1987. Stresses Atwood's political and moral dimension, suggesting that she is a "radical humanist" teaching through negative example with her unheroic, failed artists. Suggests that Atwood's fiction and poems comprise one story, with significant differences between early and later works, "of the disaster which is the world." Intriguing but very brief feminist discussion, with only passing allusion to important volumes of poetry and little reference to current Atwood scholarship.

Rosenberg, Jerome H. *Margaret Atwood.* Boston: Twayne, 1984. Uses typical Twayne format, trying to emphasize Atwood's work more than her life, and attempts to place these works in their Canadian context. Comprehensive through *Second Words.*

Rubenstein, Roberta. "Escape Artists and Split Personalities" (Atwood). *Boundaries of the Self: Gender, Culture, Fiction.* Urbana: U of Illinois P, 1987. 63–122. Examines Siamese twin imagery from *The Edible Woman* to *The Handmaid's Tale* within psychological and cultural (Canadian-United States) contexts.

Sandler, Linda, editor. "Margaret Atwood: A Symposium." Special Issue. *The Malahat Review* 41 (Jan. 1977). First book-length study of Atwood. Canadian. Includes poems, fiction, and art as well as critical articles. See Atwood's "An Album of Photographs" and "Worksheets" and Sandler's "Interview with Margaret Atwood."

Van Spanckeren, Kathryn, and Jan Garden Castro, editors. *Margaret Atwood: Vision and Forms.* Carbondale: S. Illinois UP, 1988. Examines "enduring concerns" in Atwood's work, including feminism, ecology, the Gothic, and the relationship of the United States and Canada, from varied perspectives. Two essays utilize materials in the Atwood Papers at the University of Toronto. Excellent American feminist collection includes essays by Atwood, Roberta Rubenstein, Lorna Irvine, Gayle Greene, Sherrill Grace, and others. See especially Atwood's "Great Expectations" and her watercolors.

Wilson, Sharon R. "Sexual Politics in Margaret Atwood's Visual Art." *Margaret Atwood: Vision and Form.* 205–13. Publishes Atwood's watercolors, seven for the first time, and relates them to images and themes in her poetry and fiction. Based on research in the Atwood Papers at the Thomas Fisher Rare Book Library.

Interviews

With Jan Garden Castro. *River Styx* 15 (Women's Issues): 6–21.
With Graeme Gibson. *Eleven Canadian Novelists.* Toronto: Anansi, 1973.

— SHARON R. WILSON

Christina Stead

Christina Stead was born 17 July 1902 in Rockdale, a suburb of Sydney, Australia, to David Stead, a naturalist specializing in Australian fisheries, and Ellen, who died in December of 1904. In 1907 Stead's father married Ada Gibbons, and Christina as the eldest assumed much of the responsibility for the six children of this marriage.

Stead's talent as a writer was recognized at Sydney High School and Sydney Teachers' College where she wrote for and edited school magazines. After her college course work in education, she taught briefly and then became a demonstrator in psychology for the New South Wales education system.

In 1928 she left Australia for London, having saved money for five years while working at secretarial jobs and attending business courses at night. In London she got a job as a secretary to a company of grain merchants, where she met William Blake, an American writer who brought her fiction to the attention of her first publisher. She lived with Blake in Europe until 1937 when they moved to the United States. During her nine years in the States she wrote novels, worked as a scriptwriter in Hollywood, taught a workshop in the novel at New York University, and wrote literary criticism for *New Masses* and the *New York Times*.

In 1946 Christina Stead and Blake left to travel in Europe, settling near London in 1953. After a twenty-four year relationship, they were married in 1952. He was unable to get a divorce from his first wife until that time. Blake died in 1968. As a Fellow in the Creative Arts at Canberra's Australian National University, Stead visited Australia in 1969 for the first time in 40 years. She returned in 1974 to live with a brother in a Sydney suburb and was the first Australian writer to receive the Patrick White Award. She died in Sydney, 30 March 1983.

GENDER AND POWER

Critical discussion of Christina Stead's masterpiece, *The Man Who Loved Children*, begins with the substantial introduction written by Randall Jarrell for the 1965 Henry Holt edition of the novel. Jarrell recognized early and revealed skillfully in his critical essay the strengths in Stead's presentation of family relationships. He focuses on the novel's "frightening power of remembrance" (v), that capacity to bring back suppressed childhood memories. He cites Stead's presentation of "the immoderate and insensate nature of a family's private life as opposed to its public life" (vi), exploring for the reader the world of the children in this family novel, children following the battlefield trails of their parents, Henny and Sam, whose marriage has become a war.

Stead was deeply moved by Jarrell's tribute to her novel that had been largely neglected for twenty-five years after its publication. Those contemporary readers shaped by a feminist awareness, however, might consider that Jarrell misses the core of Stead's work when he values it primarily as an attempt to represent "a family in such conclusive detail" (xxii). For to find the achievement of this novel in the truth of its family dynamics is to limit its scope. *The Man Who Loved Children* goes beyond the narrative of family to wider issues—issues of gender and power in traditionally organized Western society. Uncovering the structures defined by sex in a patriarchal social life, the narrative focuses on the desperation of Henny, wife/mother, pitted against Sam, a self-absorbed demanding husband, who revels in his role as father of a large family; and it focuses on their children—particularly the eldest, Louisa—caught in the crossfire of their parents' ongoing conflict. In the process, the novel unveils each character's story of empowerment or powerlessness.

The first sentence is telling: "All the June Saturday afternoon Sam Pollit's children were on the lookout for him" (3). We do learn that the children have other connections— "Henrietta, their mother, was in town, Bonnie, their youthful aunt and general servant, had her afternoon off, and they were being minded by Louisa, their half sister" (3); but they are first identified in relation to their father. The narrative then begins to unfold the many-layered implications of his ownership. For example, on page two Henrietta opens a letter addressed to Mrs. Samuel Clemens Pollit. Children and wife are thus immediately labeled as belonging to Sam, and the novel traces the consequences of his dominance. Stead's concern, in part, is to portray middle-class marriage in western society and the damaging effects of its subordination of women. This task she accomplishes through close documentation of Henny's daily life.

When the children cluster about their mother examining her packages, asking about her purchases, she says: "Oh, leave me alone; you're worse than your father" (4). When they startle her as she daydreams, she yells: "What do you mean sneaking up on me like that, are you spying on me like your father?" (7). Their father is to Henny, superintendent, prison warden, inquisitor. It is only when Sam Pollit, husband, is absent that the subordinate, resentful Henny can sit in the most comfortable chair, tend to the cooking, drink her tea, and assume control of her home. In Sam's absence the house seems to belong to her. That is when she knits her "pattern into bonnets and booties"(15); when she delights the children with riddles; when she appears to be the self she was before marriage.

Through Henny, Stead traces the effects of confinement, of restrictions upon women. Embodying in Henny's predicament the trap in which women have been caught for centuries, Stead describes a woman married not to a man, but to a house:

> She belonged to the house and it to her. Though she was a prisoner
> in it, she possessed it. She and it were her marriage. She was
> indwelling in every board and stone of it. (7)

Henny knows each torn curtain and worn spot. But this house that she owns by right of her knowledge of it, her sweat in running it, the hours of her life she spends in it, this house is also the site of her "confined life" (7), her "life sentence" (8); she is "house jailed" (36). But the house is not hers; it is paid for by her father and her husband. Neither owner nor renter, she may inhabit and shape the spirit of the place, but the domestic economy lies in the hands of male others. She holds no real power over the context in which her life is spent. Filled with the "insult," "grudge," "miseries," "running sores," and "scabs" (7) of her marriage, the house is where she lives literally and figuratively.

The effects of her confinement are clear. Henny, tied by her large family and limited money to a house from which she makes occasional forays but never escapes, sees the world outside as threatening. Specifically she sees that outside world in which she plays no part as rife with male threat to which she or any woman might fall prey. The world itself is negative in Henny's eyes, "low down . . . filled with scandal, slander filth" (10). There is no place for her in it.

Marriage has been Henny's nemesis. Her married life with Sam, prescribed by her father and the social expectations of her class, closed down that brief and glory-filled period of seeming empowerment when she was an eligible young girl from a wealthy family. To those long past years, Henny returns for sustenance in memory and daydream. Once the lovely, slim, dark, silk-gowned young woman of her stepdaughter's early memory, she has become a "grubby," "angry," "screeching," "crying and falling in a faint" wife (34). In Henny's sympathetic identification with the mouse she chases from room to room (12), Stead suggests that Henny is a woman caught in traps on all sides. She loves her house, but knows it is her prison. She loves her children, but knows that she is their prisoner as well. "Child-chained" (36), she looks at her children and thinks ". . . I should have been better off if I'd never laid eyes on any of them" (16).

Stead thus shows her readers a powerless Henny, humiliated in all of her relationships with men. Her father failed to keep the promises of wealth, ease, and nurture he made in her childhood. Her husband controls, criticizes, and directs every aspect of her life to which he can get access. Her coarse lover, to whom she is driven for sympathy, becomes just another man from whom she must squeeze a few dollars to ease her debts. Her life belongs to others and there is no portion of self left to call her own.

This novel draws a devastating picture of middle-class wifedom, for Stead allows no way out for Henny. To have her own life in the traditional social order, she would have to have the means to pay for it. Henny, like most married women of her time, has no money that is truly her own. Untrained to manage money she runs up debts. Unequal before the law she would lose her children if she tried to leave her husband. Constantly worried about aging, as women valued mostly for their looks do worry, she compares her marriage unfavorably to prostitution: "I look like what I am, a poor old wreck. If I'd done 10 years of streetwalking, I wouldn't look so weather-beaten!" (61). The novel makes a strong case for the victimization of women in a patriarchal economic structure.

It would be difficult to find a more striking contrast to Henny, the disenfranchised female, than Sam, the socially empowered male, in whom Stead presents the figure of the patriarch. She shows in a series of dramatic scenes how much Sam loves the house, glories in his children but, unlike Henny, is confined by neither. Early in the novel he relishes having been newly appointed to a project in the Pacific. His work, his accomplishments as breadwinner, are opportunities denied to Henny. His male role as husband, father, and participant in the world of work gives him an independence, a pleasure in himself and in life that Henny and the multitude of women like her will never know. Concerned that we see this distinction, in chapter two Stead has Sam review his status in the world: "I've come a long way . . .," he says ". . . I feel free" (17). Sam, thoroughly pleased with himself, dares imagine even greater achievements, thinking, "What it must be to taste supreme power" (17).

Such thoughts are, of course, the polar opposites of Henny's ruminations on life as a prison sentence, on her unending drudgery, on her children, without whom she thinks she would be better off. But for Sam those very children are the crown of his life. Even the contemplation of his mission to the Pacific turns sweeter when he anticipates how much his children will miss him (18). Underscoring the point, Stead identifies Sam as an initiator:

> Before it was light the dooryard thrush began to drop his son. . . .
> Sam whistled to him and then nestlings fluttered, a beast fell to the
> ground, the early birds got to work, and presently, by hearty
> creaking and concerted peeping, they and Sam made the sky pale
> and flagged the daystar. (24)

Sam and Henny: polar opposites; villain and victim. Although this profile certainly can be located in *The Man Who Loved Children,* it does not constitute the whole of the novel. Complex, rich in character development, in tension and ambiguity, this novel is the masterly complement of two dimensions of Stead's concerns as a novelist. First, it is an examination of a social order; second, it is a re-creation of the fascinating contradictions that characterize the fictional individuals who live in that order. There are no stereotypes in this narrative. Nor is there a simple allegory to be found in any of Stead's works. Whatever they may represent of the plight of man and woman, Henny and Sam are always unmistakably themselves.

Sam, a sometime villain, is also presented as Sam, a magical father. Fond of children, he turns routine hours into high-spirited adventure, charming his young charges with rhyme and pun, infecting them with his energy, delighting them with his creativity. His children wait on the street for him to come home because he brings joy with him. He is the parent-companion of many a child's dream as he shares his naturalist's observations and awakens his own and the neighborhood children to the small miracles around them. His optimism is catching. He can turn getting up early in the morning into a ritual of celebration. Stead insists that we see his charm, insists that we recognize the satisfaction and pride that he takes in his children. Yet the construction of his character is strikingly complex. For example, in his very gift for language—a positive quality, a delightful aspect of his personality, and the vital legacy he passes to his writer-daughter Louisa—lies his destructive strategy for controlling others. Speaking a blend of folksy dialect, puns, and light verse, Sam Pollit invents, teases, and plays with words, performing endlessly. Never at a loss, he produces disquisitions and chants for every occasion and revels in nicknames that tell more about his power plays than about those named. For example, his docile younger daughter, he nicknames "Little Womey" (27), thus defining her role as his little woman scurrying to provide his creature comforts, or he calls her "Mouse-deer" (295), "Penthestes (chickadee)", and "Troglodytes (house wren)" (26), admirably synthesizing the attributes of woman as domestic and diminutive.

When Sam persistently woos Louisa's attention and she pretends not to hear his whistle, he calls out to "little glumpy Looloo" (22). "Glumpy", an outgrowth of glum, suggests his sympathy for her downcast state, but it is also related to "lumpy," indicating his negative appraisal of her avoidance of him. "Little Looloo" is, of course, an appeal to her dependency, which he wishes to perpetuate. In this incident, as in others, he coaxes her out of her resistance with talk—plays on pronunciations and lilting word fun. But should he find her reading what he disapproves of, she is "Loolook" (22) searching in a direction that displeases, or "Loozy" (27) when she is too lazy to rise at dawn as he does. In the misery of his warlike marriage, to seek his daughter's comfort, he will call out yearningly to "Loo-loo dirl" (133). When he is angry, she becomes "Loobeck" or worse, "Bluebeak."

Sam's exuberance with words is also a vehicle for his sexism. He values looks in women and transmits that value to his children. For example, in a Sunday morning scene, the children are ranged about Sam, who sits up in bed with magazines spread out before him. Kissing the magazine paper with illustrations of beautiful women, Sam comments derisively on the less attractive: "Not her, she's a fright, she's a holy terror. . . . This one would frighten a screech owl at midnight on Bear Mountain" (28). Contradictory, even in his sexism, Sam does possess intellectual insight into the woman's plight. Stead probes the psychological dynamic behind sexist attitudes when she demonstrates that Sam's understanding does not alter his behavior. Sam knows that women, as he says, ". . . have been brought up to the husband chase" and have been "educated in useless arts" (62). But his fantasies reveal his need to perpetuate the subordination that follows preparation for a career in "the husband chase." Sam's fantasies also often have a political construction. He imagines himself a Mormon with a family of fifty wives and children or sees himself as the director of a great camp where the girls are ensconced in the "spick and span settlement" (48) with its connotations of strictly domestic work. Many critics have noted the fascistic undertones beneath Sam's democratic rhetoric. Stead suggests in this way that the dynamics of power within the family are not far removed from those within the nation.

Sam is a many-sided character who displays both potential and limitations. He is a great player of games, but he always wants to set the rules; a great lover of children, so long as they allow him center stage and accept his domination. Because Stead is concerned to show the possibilities of this man not only as father, but also as husband, we feel the stirrings of the human. Instead of black and white, we find ambiguity, even confusion. Flashes of Sam as a young husband with dreams of a large and loving family, of Sam as the essential domestic man, believer in hearth and home, show a male protagonist with an attitude of commitment. Even in his terrible battles with Henny, Sam's dream of marriage and family as the highest good refuses to die. Before he leaves for the Pacific he begs Henny for a renewal of their love and couples his plea with the wish for another child. The potential for tenderness in Sam, the man who believes in life and love, the man with an affirmative, positive vision—Stead keeps these qualities before us. She forces us to evaluate and re-evaluate him, allowing no stability in our reading that might pigeonhole Sam, or any of the major characters, thus making any of them less lifelike.

In fact, Stead often makes it clear that Sam is an injured party. Henny's behavior to Louisa is difficult to forgive, her money management is inefficient, and she lies about her debts. Sam's kindness to his sister Bonnie and her illegitimate child is sincere and admirable, and his wish to avoid separation and keep his family together is, at least, understandable. Through Stead's skill in uncovering layer after layer of personality, thereby revealing her characters in all their lifelike contradictions, she offers the multiple perspectives needed to represent personality, which is so often composed of warring parts. Although the text readily supports a reading that sees Henny as victim, Stead also draws her as complex and no less contradictory than Sam; she emerges a full character who victimizes others as often as she is victimized. She deludes herself into believing that Sam is responsible for the failures of her life; and she provokes the worst in him during each of their encounters. Stead indeed depicts a Henny who is, in large measure, self-destructive. We are not permitted to forget that Henny did little more than wait for the world to drop "commercial fortune" (11) into her lap. When that did not happen, she retreated into solitary card games, daydreams, and tea. Her self-pity then soured into self-hatred, leaving her paralyzed. The blow that completes her defeat is economic. When Sam loses his job and the anticipated inheritance from her father does not materialize, Henny loses her beautiful home, the last remnant of her social status. It is this loss that moves her to the final step—suicide. Henny is thus not an attractive victim. Nor is her motive for suicide a noble one. Here again Stead destabilizes our reading by going for the truth of character over consistency.

This is a two-tiered narrative of unforgettable characters living their individual lives, and of these same characters as members of a society shaped by traditions that decide the parameters of their development. Henny's response to retreat is clearly a learned response, for passivity has been a trait cultivated in middle-class women like Henny for generations. The novel provokes the recognition that Henny was shaped for her fate by a social order that has prescribed both economic and psychological dependency for women. Just how far social conditioning is responsible for personality has yet to be ascertained, but in the world of Stead's texts the two become one. That is why Sam's greatest weapon against Henny is simply his male gender. His egotism, his need to subordinate others to his will, his impulse to direct and control are all well within the western tradition of the masculine. As Joan Lidoff has noted, Sam's status as a middle-class male affirms his least humanly attractive traits (30). What we would most like to change about him is reinforced by social mores and social organization. Similarly, Henny's lack of self-confidence is fed by her traditional subordinate female role as she allows herself to be pushed toward suicide. There is here a synergy of individual and social forces working toward the tragic end.

Stead makes clear that no hope lies in the traditional web of gender and power relationships ensnaring Sam and Henny. It is, rather, the next generation, represented by Louisa, that may shift some of the well-worn lines and modify a destructive imbalance of power. Louisa disavows the extremes of both parents, leaving behind her woman's heritage of powerlessness and finding a way to separate and to empower herself. The key to her separation from both her family and the outmoded social system it represents is her success in shaping her own language. Of significance are Louisa's diary, written in code to hide its contents from the prying Sam; her play about incest; her move closer to Henny as she begins to recognize Sam as their common enemy; and the displacement of Sam as her audience and mentor when she finds women (teacher and friend) who share her love of literature. Louisa revolts against Henny's destiny and Sam's domination. She is proof against the seduction, charm, and power in Sam's language, and defeats him as much in her linguistic coup as in her escape from the patriarchal home. Clearly a writer of talent, she replaces Sam as the enchanter, astonishing even herself with her imaginative flow. As the novel ends she departs for "a walk round the world" (527). She will turn her father's gift with language to her own advantage, reshaping it to her own need and ambition and thus leave behind her Henny's helplessness. Louisa sets out on her own to find or make a world where gender does not determine power.

Stead's interest in the gender/power theme may be traced through all her fiction. It forms part of her overall concern with varieties of exploitation: economic, social, familial, sexual, and personal. As in *The Man Who Loved Children*, Stead in other novels is largely concerned with the politics of interpersonal relationships, with the crossroads of the personal and the social. Her two other works that come closest in quality to *The Man Who Loved Children* are *For Love Alone* and *Cotter's England* (published in the U.S. as *Dark Places of the Heart*). In both, the question of gender and power is central. Teresa, the young heroine of *For Love Alone*, is an older Louisa. (Both novels draw heavily on Stead's own life.) As Teresa, like Louisa, separates from her family, she falls in love with a man who intellectualizes his coldness towards her. Not until she works through the fallacies of his position and his painful rejection is she free to mold her own life according to the dictates of love and creativity, dictates she holds sacred.

In *Cotter's England*, Stead investigates a partial reversal of traditional gender roles, developing a female character, Nelly Cotter, who has a compelling need to control the lives of others. Afraid to lose the security of her fragile marriage, committed to work for her own variety of socialism and the problems of the working class as she sees them, Nelly is a gifted talker and a natural leader with a somewhat confused political vision. She has Sam's fantastic energy and, perhaps, more than his share of grandiosity as she sees a world vastly improved through her personal intervention into the lives of the suffering—largely women. Although Nelly feels herself a victim of male control, she is revealed in a stunning uncovering of layers as predatory. In this fascinating study of personality, Stead again examines destructive power struggles and misunderstood human needs complicated by an unfortunate legacy of gender roles and conditioning.

Boundaries, then, remain central to Stead's fiction—boundaries of gender, economics, politics. In her own life, she crossed national boundaries, leaving Australia early to live and write in Europe and the United States. So she is not a distinctively Australian writer. Although *Seven Poor Men of Sydney*, part of *For Love Alone*, and a few of the stories in *The Salzburg Tales* have Australian settings, most of her work is set elsewhere. She is too rich and varied a writer to be capsulated by typing or labeling of her fiction, by placing it within any national boundaries. Rather, she is best seen as a leading figure among international writers in English, one who enlarges the vision of the sexual politics that shape our culture and ourselves.

WORKS CITED

Jarrell, Randall. "An Unread Book." Introduction to *The Man Who Loved Children* by Christina Stead. New York: Henry Holt and Company, 1965. v–xli.

Lidoff, Joan. *Christina Stead.* New York: Frederick Ungar, 1982.

Stead, Christina. *Dark Places of the Heart.* New York: Holt, Rhinehart & Winston, 1966.

———. *For Love Alone.* New York: Harcourt Brace Jovanovich, 1944.

———. *The Man Who Loved Children.* New York: Henry Holt and Company, 1965.

CHRISTINA STEAD'S PUBLISHED WORK

Novels

Seven Poor Men of Sydney, 1934
The Beauties and Furies, 1936
House of All Nations, 1938
The Man Who Loved Children, 1940
For Love Alone, 1944
Letty Fox: Her Luck, 1946
A Little Tea, A Little Chat, 1948
The People with the Dogs, 1952
Dark Places of the Heart, 1966 (British title: *Cotter's England,* 1967)
The Puzzleheaded Girl, Four Novellas, 1967
The Little Hotel: A Novel, 1973
Miss Herbert (The Suburban Wife), 1976
I'm Dying Laughing (unfinished novel), 1987

Short Story Collections

The Salzburg Tales, 1934
Ocean of Story, The Uncollected Stories of Christina Stead, 1985

Collection

A Christina Stead Reader (edited by Jean B. Read), 1976

SELECTED CRITICAL READINGS

Current Stead criticism often finds itself in the theoretical heart of feminist inquiry, which goes beyond analysis of individual texts to juxtapose theory and text, illuminating the one through the other. Stead's writing has been examined as well from Marxist perspectives, looking at her interest in economic exploitation; from stylistic perspectives, attempting to articulate her unique brand of realism; from psychological/sociological points of view; and from the standpoint of her use of language. It is most likely that criticism of Stead's works will continue to grow in all of these directions—and possibly others. More critical work is needed on Stead's novellas and lesser novels that merit attention in their own right and for what they reveal about her finest works.

Bader, Rudolf. "Christina Stead and the *Bildungsroman*." *World Literature Written in English* 23 (1984): 31–39. Considers Stead's work "in the literary context of the *Bildungsroman*," thus placing Stead in a European tradition.

Brydon, Diana. *Christina Stead*. New York: Barnes and Noble Books, 1987. Adopts a narrow ideological focus: Stead's marxist-socialist values and feminist concerns. Argues well within stated parameters.

Clancy, Laurie. "The Economy of Love: Christina Stead's Women." *Who Is She?* New York: St. Martin's Press, 1983. 136–49. Traces the intermingling of love and money as a key theme in Stead's work. Particularly interesting on *Letty Fox*.

Geering, R.G. *Christina Stead*. New York: Twayne, 1969. Although mechanical in presentation, offers a detailed look at the texts and provides a general introduction to her work.

Jarrell, Randall. "An Unread Book." Introduction to *The Man Who Loved Children*. New York: Holt, Rinehart & Winston, 1965. v–xli. The critical essay that brought Stead recognition. Sees the novel as a masterwork that reveals the inner dynamics of family relationships and re-creates the world of childhood.

Kiernan, Brian. "Christina Stead: *Seven Poor Men of Sydney* and *For Love Alone*." *Images of Society and Nature: Seven Essays on Australian Novels*. Melbourne: Oxford UP, 1971. Chapter 3. Close critical analysis and appreciative evaluations of both novels.

Lidoff, Joan. *Christina Stead*. New York: Ungar, 1982. The best, most inclusive critical work on Stead. Represents Stead as a critic of character and a writer of psychological insights, especially interested in uncovering egotism in both the personal and political spheres; notes that in the process Stead uncovers the profound insights into women's lives that have been investigated further by feminist writers. Offers detailed analyses of *The Man Who Loved Children* and *For Love Alone*. An overview of the other works, a biographical section, and an argument for Stead's ingenuity in developing a "Domestic Gothic Style" enrich this study.

Sheridan, Susan. *Christina Stead*. Bloomington: Indiana UP, 1988. Explores Stead's interest in women, her rejection of organized feminism, and the interaction between Stead's writing and contemporary feminist theories. Emphasizes Stead's use of language and sees in the novel a feminine version of the Oedipus story. Provides a sophisticated discussion of critical theory.

Sturm, Terry. "Christina Stead's New Realism: *The Man Who Loved Children* and *Cotter's England*." *Cunning Exiles: Studies of Modern Prose Writers*. Sydney: Angus & Robertson, 1974. 9–35. Argues for Stead as an ideological writer perfecting a new mode of realism. Strong critical discussion of *Cotter's England*.

Williams, Chris. *Christina Stead: A Life of Letters*. Melbourne: McPhee-Gribble, 1989. First full biography of Stead. Draws on unpublished letters and many interviews integrating the life with material from the novels. Readable and informative.

—PHYLLIS FAHRIE EDELSON

Kamala Markandaya

Born into a Brahmin family in South India, in 1924, Kamala Markandaya (a pseudonym for Kamala Purnaiya Taylor) has lived in England for the last thirty or so years and is not known to have visited her land of birth since the 1960s. Educated at Madras University, she began her career as a journalist for *The Hindu*, a Madras daily newspaper.

One of the foremost Indian novelists in English during the post-1947 era, Markandaya is conspicuous by her physical absence in India. Her work, however, is highly regarded in India and is prescribed for school courses. She is a unique example of an expatriate novelist capable of handling the variegated experience of Indian sociocultural and political reality and has succeeded in creating, as she says, "a literature of social concern." Her expatriate experience—with the subsequent intercultural forces at work—has afforded her a kind of objectivity and distance not otherwise possible, for even as she has withdrawn from India physically she has developed emotionally and intellectually a keen social concern for the country she left behind. In a paper presented at a 1973 seminar sponsored by the East-West Center for Cultural Interchange in Honolulu, Markandaya stressed that literature brings out "the elementary truths of human commonality" and emphasized as well that she does not consider herself a "didactic novelist," whom she described as a "poor novelist." Married to a British national, Markandaya lives in London.

THE WOMAN'S WORLD

It is not with any specific prejudice in favor of Western feminist research and the application of its conclusions to literary works that one should look at the world Kamala Markandaya creates. Of all the post-Independence Indian women writers in English, Markandaya benefits most from being examined from this perspective, for her novels bear testimony to the "female" experience of the Indian social reality. Close scrutiny of the Indian woman's world she depicts shows that her views reflect Western feminist theory. Any discussion of Markandaya's novels must also reckon with the fact that she shared with her Indian predecessors, who wrote fiction in English during the 1930s and 1940s, the potent influence of Gandhian thought. Having absorbed the liberating impact of a thinking that defined the Indian woman as an equal partner with man, Markandaya was ready to assimilate Western ideas. Her voluntary exile in England also afforded her firsthand experience of the women's liberation movement, for living in the midst of a society vibrating with a revolution in women's perceptions of themselves, Markandaya inevitably registered this new thought in her fiction. Consequently, for the first time in Indian fiction in English, Markandaya confronts the world through female eyes. From *Nectar in a Sieve* onward she makes a conscious effort to view the socio-economic, political, and spiritual reality of India through what we now understand as purely "female imagination" (Spacks).

When taking account of traditional approaches to Indian fiction in English, it may sound heretical to approach Markandaya's work from this perspective. However, considering not only her exile but also her westernized education, her formative years in an anglicized Indian family, and her career as a journalist writing on contemporary socio-cultural issues, her feminist posture should not be surprising. She shares the intellectual background drawn from a mix of the East and the West with Gandhi himself and with many of her literary predecessors—Raja Rao, R.K. Narayan, Mulk Raj Anand, and Bhabani Bhattacharya as well as with contemporary women novelists, such as Nayantara Sahgal and Santha Rama Rau.

Further, Markandaya offers neither apologies nor explanations for her exile, even though some critics consider this experience a hurdle to her realistic grasp of subject matter. Nostalgia for India, they say, makes her picture of that country a romantic one. And perhaps there is a partial truth in this criticism of her novels. Removed from the actual scene of contemporary India, Markandaya's work may, arguably, suffer from this distance. At the same time, though, this distance affords her greater objectivity in the treatment of her characters with whom she empathizes closely— the women in particular. Although not a part of the turbulent Indian scene, she registers truthfully the hopelessness of the woman's plight in modern India and takes stock of the evolving consciousness among women there.

Basically, then, her novels embody a feminine protest, one that marks a rare symbiosis of the Indian woman's plight and the Western woman's struggle. Perhaps because of this unlikely alliance, her women are shown always to handle their situations, no matter how difficult, with grace. They may appear as passive sufferers, as in the case of Rukmini in *Nectar in a Sieve*, or as targets of male domination and ego in *A Silence of Desire*, or as victims diminished by physical violence that the superficially modernized urban males perpetrate on village innocence in *Two Virgins*. But always they are survivors, and ultimately the women themselves take hold of their own circumstances. The female characters invariably emerge as rebels who question the conservative ethos around them. The more obvious examples are a village woman like Rukmini, a small town woman like Sarojini in *A Silence of Desire*, the more sophisticated Mira of *Some Inner Fury*, and the English women like Helen of *The Coffer Dams* and Caroline of *Possession*.

Markandaya's first novel, *Nectar in a Sieve*, unfolds a tale of village life. The central character, Rukmini, could be any peasant woman in village India in the 1950s. (For that matter, the situation has not changed much in the 1990s.) Markandaya invests Rukmini with a sharper sensitivity than perhaps she should rightly possess, considering her station in life and background; however, as the first expression of a novelist who has just been through the shared national experience of Gandhian idealism, it is natural that she would idealize Rukmini's character. This also explains her preoccupation with the urbanization of Indian villages and the disastrous effect on the villagers, women in particular. Rukmini's tragedy takes on the added dimension of neo-colonialism after Independence, which helped to destroy Gandhian values as they were envisioned before 1947. This theme Markandaya shares with many other novelists in India; only in her case the preoccupation acquires a sharpness and depth as she records the toll it has taken on women.

It is notable that all through the series of events that push Rukmini and Nathan to their doom, the mother figure Rukmini sustains the world around her. She appears to have transcended the limited identities of being a devoted wife and a sacrificing mother and represents instead a universal mother figure: She is the axis, the immovable affirmative force around whom all the other characters revolve. There comes a point in her life, when like a Sanyasin, she has no illusions in life and is disturbed by neither desire nor longing. Yet her support of all family members does not waver. It is also important to note that Markandaya does not show Rukmini in any emotional outbursts, however dire the situation, thus exploding the myth perpetuated by male writers for so long that a woman is childish, impulsive, and powerless to decide for herself (Shamsul 15). One instance proves her strength: Driven by the instinct for creation, Rukmini consults Dr. Kennington, who cures her of infertility; and this she does without consulting her husband. She repeats the bold step once more when she takes her daughter to Dr. Kennington to be cured of infertility as well. Even in her traditional attitude toward child bearing, Rukmini is very modern in taking sides with one of her own sex, in this case her daughter. These sound like trivial details, but in the masculinist village world she inhabits Rukmini displays through such actions a realistic grasp of what she should be doing at a particular point in her life.

Clearly, Markandaya intends to project Rukmini as a strong woman when once more she takes in stride her husband's infidelity with Kunti. Yet her response should not be interpreted as the passive acceptance of a helpless, traditional woman tolerating her husband's sexual misbehavior. Rukmini displays instead a disarming honesty in her awareness of the facts, when she says that Kunti has fire in her body so that "men burn before and after" (19). Sure of herself and the bond between her and her husband, she finds no need for belligerence, as might a typical character created by a male writer. Throughout, Rukmini faces the chaos that overtakes Indian villages once Gandhian values are destroyed by neo-colonialism after 1947. Although passive in her narration of what takes place, she is not indifferent to her circumstances. Her passivity, as Uma Parameswaran points out, ". . . does not signify absence of emotion" (73). For Rukmini has been intimately and actively involved with life, absorbing all extremes of pleasure and pain through flood and famine and personal crises. So when she narrates her experience, it seems as though everything has been run through the sieve of a woman's profound awareness, and a rare nectar emerges.

In *Some Inner Fury*, Markandaya looks back at the Indian freedom movement through Mira, the narrator and central character. The novel depicts the fury of the 1942 Quit India Movement and registers the ravages of that fury Mira faces when she loses her two brothers and her British lover. If Rukmini, who derives her power from peasant roots, is Markandaya's introduction of the traditional Hindu "Shakti" image into Indian fiction in English, then Mira confirms the "Shakti" image through different nuances. She embodies Markandaya's obsession with the vision of an educated city woman thrown into the vortex of contemporary political reality. Through Mira, Markandaya's obsession with the tangles of human relationships extend further as she probes the interaction between Indians and Britishers, one of her favorite themes. Mira is deeply involved with Richard, a British national, and faces a confusion of identities. The civil service represented by her lover upholds everything British, while Govind, her foster brother, sides with the terrorists. Although in love with Richard, she eventually parts with him in favor of India.

This is the first novel by an Indian woman on the Independence movement and the havoc it caused in individual lives. One of the characters, Kitsamy, is an anglophile who rejects everything Indian, yet with his wife Premala he is the most traditional husband. Ironically, Kitsamy imposes on her his anglophile ways and social ambitions, even as he treats her as a typical Indian wife. Torn between her duty to Kitsamy and her love for Govind, she sublimates her passion by devoting herself to working on a school building sponsored by the missionary society. Clearly, Markandaya's portrayal of Premala shows a "woman seeking influence through martyrdom," as Elaine Showalter would have it (184). But it is Premala's persistence on which Markandaya focuses, while allowing her "female imagination" full play as she stresses the traditional nature of male-female relationships that persevere even in anglicized Indian society. Premala helps to delineate the peculiarities of the Indian male who expects total obedience from *his woman*.

Mira stands in sharp contrast to Premala, for she has been brought up in a westernized Indian family where women participated in the European way of life and spoke English more fluently than their own language. In fact, Mira is the first authentic monolingual character in Indian fiction in English. Markandaya handles Mira's character superbly, showing her to be sensitive, impetuous, and in charge of her own life and mind. Because she responds so freely and openly to Richard, the parting with him may strike some readers as false. Many critics, however, see the Mira-Richard relationship as an encounter between the East and the West and as an illustration of the irreconcilable gap between the two (Riemenschneider 145). At the time of parting, Mira says:

> Soon I would go too. When the tail of the procession went through the door, I would join in, and Richard would stay behind. This was not a time for decision, for he knew I cannot stay; it was simply the time for parting. (283)

These lines may give the impression that Markandaya has Mira reject Richard, the symbol of colonial power, in favor of her patriotic feelings for India, thus verging on a melodramatic and contrived conclusion. A closer reading, though, into Mira's emotional construct and intellectual background shows that she is the only person who lives at an experiential level and accepts life with all its pain. Her thoughts are not just a repetition of the Kipling cliché that "East is East and West is West and never the twain shall meet." Although awareness of racial differences never existed between Richard and Mira in their relationship, she decides to throw her lot with India. In light of the Gandhian thought that pervaded the 1940s, Mira's painful decision constitutes a sacrificial gesture, befitting a woman of her strength who is free of self-indulgence. By showing Mira accepting her fate with equanimity, Markandaya highlights the image of an Indian woman who may choose suffering over her own selfish desire for happiness.

The thematic tension in the next novel, *A Silence of Desire*, stems from the conflict between "faith and reason" (87). The action revolves around the lives of Dandekar and his wife Sarojini, a good mother, wife, and housekeeper, again the active center of the family. Here Markandaya examines marriage in a traditional Brahmin household in which the roles for husband and wife are firmly set by centuries of tradition. Sarojini, however, disrupts this pattern, when she is drawn to the Swami, because Dandekar has little use for the religious faith central to her life; for Sarojini the gods and goddesses are living presences, while for Dandekar such faith is impossible. Ironically, in spite of his scientific and modern outlook, he holds a purely traditional view of women in society. So when Sarojini goes to visit the Swami in secret—reluctant to reveal to her husband the true reason for her absences—he accuses her of infidelity. When confronted, she only states: "The man whom I worship is a God," she said, looking at him directly. "You are very nearly right in that one thing—just that one thing" (72). The tormented Dandekar makes a painful journey to the Swami's house in the village, but when he finds Sarojini as one of the devotees he is stunned, shocked to learn that she comes to the Swami to be cured of her tumor. She tells him that his Western notions and talk of superstition meant that he did not know what lay beyond reason. Again, Markandaya has created a strong character who accepts life and its circumstances without rancor, without anger, but asserts her own womanhood.

In *Possession*, Markandaya's main character is a forceful English woman, Lady Caroline Bell, who discovers the shepherd boy Valmiki in an Indian village, and, convinced of his artistic genius, whisks him off to England and succeeds in turning him into a celebrated painter. Sadly, though, Valmiki loses his soul in the process. His involvement with Ellie and later with Annabel finally makes him aware that he must sever his ties with Caroline and return to India to recover his true self. Here Markandaya also addresses the dual themes of colonialism and colonial confrontation. For Caroline is a symbol of the British Raj in India, and Markandaya makes clear her nationalistic bias as she shows Caroline possessed by a mania to subjugate and thus to corrupt Valmiki, thereby depleting him of his spiritual strength.

Helen, in *The Coffer Dams*, provides an apter illustration of the East-West encounter in postcolonial India. Markandaya's sympathies clearly lie with Helen who cannot subscribe to her engineer husband's belief in industrializing India at any cost. For the first time a woman character in Markandaya, as Shiv K. Kumar says, is "caught existentially between moments of choices and commitments" (10). Helen, faced with the choice of asserting herself or submitting to her husband, moves out in the direction of self-affirmation to achieve a full life by living for the larger good and working with the tribal people in India.

Of the later novels, from the feminist perspective, *Two Virgins* stands out, even if some critics consider the novel to be low in merit, because "there is little attempt at plot construction . . . with stereotyped contrasts between pre- and post-independent India, village and city, traditional and modern ways, the whole thing amounting to nothing more than a documentary about village living, such as the film-director in the novel actually makes" (Joseph 19). The first part of *Two Virgins* describes the village with its different characters, the two sisters Lalitha and Saroja being the most prominent. Although told from Saroja's point of view, the novel focuses more sharply on Lalitha's fate. Village and family remain central, but Makandaya introduces a new element—the individual caught between the pulls of traditional forces and modernization. In *Two Virgins*, there is the resonance of Gandhian ideas, clearly indicating that India today is not what was envisioned during the Independence struggle. Contemporary India emerges as a kind of hodgepodge of traditional Indian and modern western cultures, a country undergoing rapid social change from within and without, where the peasantry no longer know the security of the traditional ways of life. Thus stability must come from the inner strength of the individual—male and female.

An archetypal story of the loss of innocence, the novel presents a study in contrast of two sisters: Lalitha, the elder, who is exposed to Western schooling and Saroja who attends a traditional Indian school. Lalitha is caught up in the web of urbanization when she runs away to pursue a movie career, only to become a victim of Gupta's lust and to separate herself from her family. Ironically, even as Lalitha faces calamity she shows admirable strength, refusing to return to her family and to abort her child; perhaps with this strength she will even survive the process of urbanization. On the other hand, Charles Larson says that the depiction of Saroja's evolving consciousness, obviously preferable to Lalitha's plight, is a feat often achieved in post-colonial fiction: "Saroja perceives, she changes, she grows" (147).

Of all the novels, *Two Virgins* expresses most sharply Markandaya's concern with the situation of women in modern India. The narrative embraces, beside Saroja and Lalitha, women of all age groups and different class backgrounds, including Aunt Alamelu, the widow who suffers simply because she has no husband or children; Mannikkam's wife, who bears child after child in total ignorance of birth control methods; Amma, Saroja's mother, a typically subdued Indian wife. The village is a man's world, Markandaya says, where "Women had no boltholes. There was no escape for them, they had to stand where they were and take it" (123).

The Nowhere Man, a novel about Indian emigrants in the United Kingdom, marks an exception to Markandaya's "woman's world," for the central character is a man, Srinivas. Yet brief as his wife Vasantha's appearance in the novel, she leaves behind the impression of a strong character, obstinately rooted to her Indian background and refusing to adapt to the land her husband has chosen. For one thing, she treasures a handful of Indian soil and a bottle of water from the holy river, the Ganga. At her death, the drops of the Ganga's water are sprinkled on her ashes, so in a way she has transformed the Thames into the holy river, just as she had created a little India at No. 5 Ashcroft Avenue. Markandaya often characterizes Indian women in foreign settings in this way, thereby suggesting that women are the preservers and purveyors of cultural moorings.

The Golden Honeycomb, a historical novel depicting three generations of princely life in the state of Devapur, reveals much about the role women played among Indian royalty. The tragedy of Bawaji Rao I, the people's king condemned to die in solitary confinement for his spirit of independence, paves the way for the crowning of Bawaji

Rao II. Seeds of rebellion are sown by his spirited queen, Manjula, when she insists on suckling her baby, a practice repugnant to royal custom. She perceives this restriction as an unwarranted denial of her basic human freedom. Although Bawaji Rao II, a loyalist to the British Raj, persuades his queen to accept not only his love but also his value system, she continues to harbor resentment, especially as she watches her son, the future Bawaji Rao III, grow into a British loyalist like his father. The young prince, however, falls in love with a commoner, Mohini, who takes her cue from the rebellious Queen Mother and refuses to become Bawaji Rao III's queen but agrees to be his concubine and bears him a son, the heir apparent.

Other Indian writers in English have taken up the intriguing subject matter of princely states, namely Mulk Raj Anand in *The Private Life of an Indian Prince* (1953) and Manohar Malgonkar in *The Princes* (1973). When compared to Markandaya's novel, these others are incomplete artistic reconstructions of the decline and fall of patriarchal monarchy dating back to the unrecorded history of ancient India. Further, neither work achieves the historical continuity of *The Golden Honeycomb*, which traces the origins of a patriarchal system that still affects Indian women. Markandaya's account differs in another way, for she shows the women as strong and able to hold their own in palace intrigue, while the men are effeminate good-for-nothings who beg alms from the British Resident Officer, the real head of the princely state.

Markandaya's key novels establish her ability to penetrate the female psyche, especially that of Indian women. Her characters range widely, from illiterate peasant women to westernized city women, from British women to Indian royalty. The novels explore all segments of the woman's world, from the peasant village to the Indian city to the lands beyond the Black Sea. Markandaya's peculiar strength, as William Walsh has noted, lies in "the delicate analysis of the relationship of persons, especially when they have a more developed consciousness of their problems and are attempting to grope towards some more independent existence" (19).

Of course, this discussion was not intended to suggest that Markandaya has self-consciously created a world governed by clichéd patterns of feminist fiction. Her world is an all-inclusive one—albeit a woman's world—in which she explores the tangled web of human relationships. When Markandaya "broke away into exile" (Showalter 190)—to use a feminist expression—she broke all barriers to weaving stories in the set models of Indian fiction in English such as we find in the work of Narayan, Anand, Rao, and Bhattacharya. She wrote as herself—a woman—and brought to bear her individual "female imagination" on the Indian fictional world she created.

WORKS CITED

Joseph, Margaret P. *Kamala Markandaya*. New Delhi: Heinemann, 1980.

Kumar, Shiv K. "Tradition and Change in the Novels of Kamala Markandaya." *Osmania Journal of English Studies* 7 (1969): 1–10.

Larson, Charles R. *Fiction in the Third World*. Washington, DC: Inscape Publishers, 1976.

Parameswaran, Uma. "Native Aliens and Expatriates—Kamala Markandaya and Balachandra Rajan." *Representative Indo-Anglian Novelists*. New Delhi: Vikas, 1976. 85–140.

Riemenschneider, Dieter. "British Characters in Indo-Anglian Fiction." *Aspects of Indian Writing in English*. New Delhi: Macmillan India, 1979.

Shamsul, I. *Chronicles of the Raj.* London: Macmillan, 1979.
Showalter, Elaine. *A Literature of Their Own: British Women Novelists from the Brontes to Lessing.* New York: Princeton UP, 1977.
Spacks, Patricia Meyer. *The Female Imagination.* New York: Knopf, 1975.
Walsh, William. *Commonwealth Literature.* London: Oxford UP, 1973.

KAMALA MARKANDAYA'S PUBLISHED WORK

Novels

Nectar in a Sieve, 1954
Some Inner Fury, 1955
A Silence of Desire, 1960
Possession, 1960
A Handful of Rice, 1966
The Coffer Dams, 1969
The Nowhere Man, 1972
Two Virgins, 1973
The Golden Honeycomb, 1977
Pleasure City 1983

SELECTED CRITICAL READINGS

Criticism of Kamala Markandaya's novels has increased in India, partly as a result of the women's movement. The awareness engendered by this movement has brought about a change in women's perception of themselves and consequently produced feminist literary criticism by female Indian critics. As well, Markandaya's books are on the prescribed reading list in most Indian universities, so her work has been the subject of theses and dissertations. Although in the past, Indian criticism tended to be general in its approach, there is a movement today toward concentrated studies of individual novels. In many cases, Markandaya's work is compared to other women writers, such as Anita Desai, Nayantara Sahgal, and Ruth Prawer Jhabvala. International critics have also addressed her work, which has a wide audience abroad.

Chatterji, Arundhati. "Rukmini, the Mother Figure in *Nectar in a Sieve.*" *Studies in Indian Fiction in English.* Gulbarga: JIWE, 1987. 85–92. Notes that the mother figure of Rukmini constitutes a positive image representing the "Shakti" concept. Argues that by virtue of her sacrifice and compassion, the woman in Markandaya's fiction is ultimately the winner. Concludes that the woman's centrality as a sustaining mother figure provides a key to Markandaya's attitude toward her female characters.

Gooneratne, Yasmine. "Traditional Elements in the Fiction of Kamala Markandaya, R.K. Narayan and Ruth Prawer Jhabvala." *World Literature Written in English* 15 (1981):121–33. Discusses the traditional intellectual heritage these writers inherited from the classical Indian epic and the romanticized Western image of India and shows how they replace and revitalize it with indigenous myths.

Jha, Ramā. "Kamala Markandaya: An Overview." *Perspectives on Indian Fiction in English.* New Delhi: Abhinvav, 1985. 161–73. Analyzes how Markandaya as a product of the Gandhian era portrays emancipated women seeking release from traditional taboos. Discusses how Markandaya combines her South Indian identity and expatriate status to create a world that inculcates a clear understanding of contemporary India.

Joseph, Margaret P. *Kamala Markandaya.* New Delhi: Heinemann, 1980.
Traces the process of development in Markandaya's handling of theme, character, and style. Based in part on correspondence with the author. Intended as a general introduction to Markandaya's work.

Krishnaswamy, Shanta. "Kamala Markandaya: Autonomy, Nurturance and the Sisterhood of Man." *Glimpses of Indian Women.* New Delhi: Aashish Publications, 1983. 161–235. Provides a detailed discussion of the varied women characters in Markandaya's fiction. Argues that the author's goal throughout her work is to establish autonomy for the individual, nurturance for the family, and feeling for the human community. Underlines Markandaya's ability to create a literature of concern amid a realistic world in which women are pitted against socio-economic inequality.

Larson, Charles. "Revolt and Rebirth: Cultural Renewal." *The Novel in the Third World.* Washington, DC: Inscape Publishers, 1986. 143–75. Analyzes *Two Virgins* to show how cultural renewal begins within the native culture itself—its basic foundations are the village and the family. Examines how Markandaya's focus on the feminine viewpoint leads to an evolving consciousness in her female characters. Discusses the impact of Indian urbanization and industrialization on women. Concludes that Markandaya's achievement lies in her ability to write novels that bridge the gap between East and West.

Parameswaran, Uma. "Native Aliens and Expatriates—Kamala Markandaya and Balachandra Rajan." *Representative Indo-Anglian Novelists.* New Delhi: Vikas, 1976. 85–140. Agrees that Markandaya is one of the major Indian novelists in English but argues that her perspective on the Indian social reality is that of an alien. Illustrates how she falls short of other Indian novelists' work in English and suggests that she tends to romanticize India.

Prasad, Madhusudan, editor. *Perspectives on Kamala Markandaya.* Ghaziabad: Prakashan, 1984. Collection of articles by different critics addressing Markandaya's handling of themes such as social change and East-West confrontation and the development of her work's structure and narrative technique. Provides an overview of her work.

Ramamurthi, K.S. "The Women Novelists." *The Rise of the Indian Novel in English.* New Delhi: Sterling Publishers, 1987. 66–111. Discusses the Indian women writers who pioneered writing in English and who are the direct forerunners of post-1947 writers like Markandaya. Illustrates the similarities of concerns and the shared pressures on their feminine sensibilities, by pointing to the common thematic preoccupations such as the exploration of feminine identity and struggle toward self awareness.

Williams, H.M. "Victims and Virgins: Some Characters in Markandaya's Novels." *Perspectives on Kamala Markandaya.* Ghaziabad: Prakashan, 1984. Sees Markandaya's female characters as victims of fate and the malice of others. Views Markandaya basically as an angry writer who has a particular interest in analyzing women characters in detail.

—RAMĀ JHA

Nayantara Sahgal

Nayantara Sahgal was born in Allahabad, India, 10 May 1927. Her parents and a number of relatives, including India's first Prime Minister, Pandit Jawahar Lal Nehru, her uncle, were actively engaged in India's struggle for Independence. She grew up along with her two sisters in the traditional joint family home; thus politics entered her life very early, and she accepted many unusual happenings as a matter of normal occurrence. The visits of police, the imprisonment of her parents, the hectic political activity followed by long periods of silence—all were accepted as everyday events.

After attending school in India, she was sent to the United States, where she majored in history at Wellesley College, graduating in 1947 (the year of Indian Independence). She married Gautum Sahgal in 1949, but they were divorced in 1967; they have three children. She remarried in 1979.

Sahgal, known for both fiction and journalism, has been a political journalist and columnist for Indian, American, and British newspapers. Although her political writings are important, it is as a novelist that she has been able to project a comprehensive view of life in modern India. Her novels reflect her involvement with politics but also offer an incisive study of human relationships.

She has won several national and international awards including the Commonwealth Writers Prize, the Sinclair Prize, and the Sahitya Academy Award. In 1978 she served as a member of the Indian delegation to the United Nations General Assembly. She is a frequent visitor to the United States where she has been writer-in-residence at various places, including Radcliffe Institute, Southern Methodist University, University of Colorado, the Woodrow Wilson International Center, and the National Humanities Center. Sahgal lives in Dehra Dun, India.

POLITICS AND PERSONAL RELATIONSHIPS

The eight novels that Nayantara Sahgal has written so far revolve around dual themes: first, the political one, that India is passing through a transitional period and Indians must adjust themselves to the changing times; second, that the lack of communication between people, especially between husband and wife, results in unhappiness and prevents human fulfillment. The novelist herself makes it clear that each novel "more or less reflects the political era we are passing through" (Jain *Sahgal* 143). But along with the political themes, she also portrays the modern Indian woman's search for individual freedom and self-realization. She delineates both the political and personal motif in a subtle manner, highlighted by an intricate and polished writing style.

Liberal in her outlook, Sahgal believes in the new humanism and new morality, according to which a woman is not to be taken as "a sex object and glamour girl, fed on fake dreams of perpetual youth, lulled into a passive role that requires no individuality" (Sahgal "Women" 12), but as man's equal and honored partner. There is a happy blend of two sensibilities in her work—the sensibility of an artist and that of a humanist. As a humanist she stands for an unfettered freedom and "pleads for the new marital morality, based on mutual trust, consideration, generosity, and absence of pretence, selfishness and self-centredness" (Asnani *Critical Response* 123). She is intensely moral in her artistic vision and has great respect for the affirmative values of life, suggesting in *A Time to Be Happy* that "The world is in need of a universal culture, universal language, if not in literal terms, at least in terms of thought and values" (152).

Her first novel, *A Time to Be Happy,* is primarily concerned with the sociopolitical life of the turbulent period of Indian history just before the advent of Independence. It throws broad hints about the novelist's advocacy of women's individual freedom, which becomes the central motif in the later novels. Maya, one of the major personages in the novel, emerges as Sahgal's first woman to struggle to free herself from marital bondage.

There are two kinds of characters in the novel: those brought up in the traditionally conservative mold who are suspicious of all change and the others who must make some kind of immediate adjustment to a pattern of living that is slowly evolving as the established values are in flux and give place to the new. For example, the "Englishness" that once had been a matter of pride is ending because Indians are becoming conscious of their freedom or lack of it. Sanand, for one, in spite of his Western education has developed a profound respect for his Indianness. No longer an Anglicized puppet but acutely aware of political and social forces, he drifts into the spate of nationalism, learns Hindi and spinning, and even contemplates switching over to the dhoti-Kurta style of dress. His employer, Mr. Trent, notices all these activities and warns Sanand, who boldly informs Mr. Trent that nothing is wrong with his activities and the steps he has been taking are only to familiarize himself with his own country. He feels unhappy and bewildered at having been so alienated by his upbringing:

> "It is a strange feeling to be midway between two worlds, not completely belonging to either. I don't belong entirely to India. I can't. My education, my upbringing and my sense of values have all combined to make me un-Indian. What do I have in common with most of my countrymen? and of course there can be no question of my belonging to another country." (151)

After his marriage to Kusum, who comes from a Nationalist background, Sanand's inner conflict about his rootlessness and unreal existence surfaces more often, and this impels him to be more of an Indian and less of a "carbon copy of an Englishman." After Independence he wants to resign from the English factory where he has been working. The main theme of the novel thus emerges as the awakening of Sanand to the social and political realities of a newly Independent India.

The title of Sahgal's second novel, *The Time of Morning*, obviously suggests the "Morning of National Freedom." In the morning after Independence, the men at the helm of affairs had to plan the course of action, programs, and strategies to realize the new goals set for the people's security, peace, and prosperity. The life depicted in this novel has been described as "shot through and through with politics . . . and sex, an eating, drinking, merrymaking, hugging, kissing, dancing and copulating world, with conferences, committees, public meetings, get-togethers, discussions, seminars, processions, demonstrations, protests, boycotts, interspersed with parties and club socials" (Asnani "The Novels" 43).

The plot resembles a web constructed of variegated and complex threads, one being the Kailas-Rashmi-Rakesh story. Kailas renounces his law practice, defies British Government, and joins in the service of his Motherland. His devoted wife belongs to the old generation of Indian womanhood. Their only daughter, Rashmi, married to a foreign service bureaucrat, is at home with her parents; alienated and distraught, she contemplates separation from her husband. Rakesh, another member of the Indian Foreign Service, had nostalgic longings for Rashmi when she married six years earlier. His longing still intense, he immediately senses that something is amiss when he meets her and rightly infers that "it was marriage, that had altered her, made her a moth trapped in cement" (108).

The novel brims with these fractured people: Saleem and Saira whose relationship is troubled; Nita who dreads the shadow of marriage; Neil Berensen, an architect with the Peace Institute, who philanders while his family remains in Norway; Leela who has found freedom in her American life but cannot discard her upbringing and commits suicide when she becomes pregnant; Arjun and Uma whose unhappy marriage leads Uma to drinking and indiscriminate sexual affairs. Sahgal, speaking neither for tradition nor modernity, appears to choose the better aspects of each. According to one critic, Sahgal's female characters have a single passion: "It is the longing to be free, freedom from all restraint in work and deed. . . . They want to be fully alive and themselves" (Malhotra 224). As an example, Rashmi's divorce and sexual relationship with the architect do not become a "'tasteless parody of transplanted modernity' but [represent] an inner need for communication and involvement which remains unsatisfied. Sex is only of secondary importance" (Jain "Aesthetics" 43). Nita, on the other hand, grumbles when she is not allowed to smoke and hates the idea of getting married but gives herself to Kalyan and acknowledges her debt to him: ". . . the freedom to be myself. I'd never have known it but for you" (18).

Throughout, Sahgal reinterprets the rigid concept of morality by studying the aesthetics of the situation and projects "a new morality which discards conventions and upholds the freedom of individuals to work towards self-realisation and involvement. Morality ceases to be isolated from the rest of human life and becomes a growing part of life" (Jain "Aesthetics" 47-48). In so doing, Sahgal ruthlessly attacks the age-old wrongs that Indian society has inflicted on its women and pleads for an honored place of equality so that every marriage can become a give and take partnership; she sees lack of communication as the main cause of marital discord, a problem that can be overcome if what she calls the "oxygen of understanding" (*Storm* 220) is let loose in an atmosphere of freedom.

The third novel, *Storm in Chandigarh*, depicts the actual situation in the 1960s of the separation of the Punjab and Haryana with Chandigarh as their common capital, which each claims exclusively as its own. While violence is the theme of the novel, it is not only political but takes an invisible, more subtle form as well: the infliction of one person's will on another, the kind of emotional violence that husbands and wives practice in their relationships. Sahgal has not only depicted the desire to gain control over another's mind but has also tapped deeper layers of human behavior by analyzing the fearsome jungle of male-female relationships.

Through the political upheavals, she reflects the emotional crises in the marital relations of the various characters. For example, Vishal's marriage to Leela remained an unsuccessful search for communication, but in Saroj's company Vishal feels fulfilled and redeemed, six years after the death of his wife, because they are able to communicate with each other. In another of the tangled relationships portrayed, a temperamental incompatibility separates Saroj and Inder; Saroj has been brought up in a liberal atmosphere, whereas Inder is a conformist whose traditional values remain stagnant, exemplied by his obsessive concern over Saroj's loss of virginity before her marriage. For Inder the sex act is complete in itself, but for Saroj emotional involvement is more important, her anguish and distress conveyed in the remark: "I am alone even when Inder is here" (22). While Inder treats Saroj brutally for her premarital affair, he indulges in an extramarital relationship. Sahgal seems appalled by the fact that there are still "people like Inder who believe in two codes of conduct—one for men and the other for women" (Asnani "The Novels" 58).

In her treatment of sex, Sahgal is aware that it cannot be ignored or suppressed and is a part of the male-female relationship, but she relates it to the feelings behind the act, the involvement or indifference with which it is beset. The attitude that governs one's approach to sex, she shows through her characters' responses, goes a long way toward establishing its morality or immorality. As one critic has pointed out, in Sahgal's world "Sex in or outside marriage is not an unrelated or self-contained act. It is to be viewed with reference to a situation and an attitude and no single rule can help to judge it" (Jain "Aesthetics" 47).

The novel that follows, *The Day in Shadow*, can be read as a sequel to *Storm in Chandigarh*. It not only re-enacts the theme of marital disharmony but also reflects the same sustained moral vision as it delineates the emotional and economic strains of divorce on a woman. The narrative focuses on Som and Simrit, who seemingly got on well during the first few years of marriage; but Som's inability to understand his wife, to consider her as anything more than an object fit for physical pleasure and enjoyment, compels Simrit to seek human communication outside marriage. She confides to Raj: "If I'd known you well before my divorce, there might not have been any divorce. Knowing you would have taken care of one need and my marriage another" (159). Treated by Som as a possession, Simrit is not only the victim of his attitude but also of a system that says a wife is her husband's property and has no individuality outside of marriage.

Som's closing of an arms deal depresses his wife further, and she finds herself unable to respond to his physical demands, becoming "separate, excluded and rebellious" (62). Finally, Som tells her either to get on with a normal life or to finish their farce of a marriage, so she is left with no option but to seek divorce. She innocently signs the "Consent Terms," in which she has been given money in trust for their son; but she cannot use this money and is supposed to pay taxes on it. Thus "the divorce settlement is a continuation of their marriage; it pins her down to the role of a victim and attempts to crush her desire to be free in a positive way" (Jain *Sahgal* 59).

Simrit is a victim of her husband's subtle and inhuman form of exploitation—a sort of beating where "blood and bruises don't show," as Sahgal put it in an article titled "Of Divorce and Hindu Women" (11). In a bid to build a new life for herself, Simrit encounters Raj, a liberal thinker, who not only makes her understand the enormity of the "Consent Terms" she has signed but also helps her to regain her lost mooring, emotional as well as intellectual. In part, Sahgal fiercely attacks, through the revelation of Simrit's financial arrangements, the prevalent notion of a man using a woman for tax purposes even after divorce. For Simrit, divorce does not bring freedom but confrontation with all that is orthodox in a male-centered society. Out of this struggle, though, is born a new Simrit, one who makes choices and decisions, becomes aware of herself as a person, her mind and body opening up to new responses through her relationship with Raj.

Yet Sahgal's handling of divorce is not intended to mean that marriage has failed as a social institution or that it has outlived its utility. Rather, it means that there is the need for a mature approach to marriage, one nurtured with love, care, and candor. In Sahgal's world the act of living is in no way an ascetic one, for her characters inhabit a world full of desires and emotions. But these characters do not always abide by the conventions of society. While many contemporary Indian writers treat sex outside marriage as promiscuous and the woman who indulges in it as immoral, Sahgal proceeds to do something different. According to her view, adultery or asceticism is neither good nor bad in itself. Raj and Simrit are in love, about to be married, and the world that Sahgal prescribes as the only sane and sensitive alternative to power and greed is a personal one grounded in understanding and communication—and a world that contains meaningful sexual relations rather than bestial sensuality.

A Situation in New Delhi, the next novel, portrays the aftermath of Jawahar Nehru's death, the Naxalite movement, and student unrest. There is no cleavage between the political and private world, for the main actors in both are the same. Devi is the central figure; according to her lover Usman her "animation was not of talk or gesture. It radiated from within, through her skin and her eyes, from the source of her being. She was a golden creature, composed of layers of light" (22). Although he had known her as "a brain, an ability, an attractiveness" (29), it was only after the death of her husband when he had gone to console her and had taken her in his arms that he knew her as a woman: "The act of love had never been so simple, fulfilling an unconscious yearning in himself to know her better, deeply, as alone man and woman can know each other. And he knew beyond any doubt that the feel of her breasts under his hand and his seeking mouth, was in some way setting her free" (29). In all respects, Sahgal wants women to become aware of their equal status. Her concern with politics is an integral part of this larger concern, because each of her explorations into political life "reveals her newer and deeper insight into the human psyche" (Asnani *Critical Response* 120).

Plans for Departure, which appeared next, is different from the earlier novels in that Sahgal has not only cast her net wider, but she has also made a non-Indian and non-Hindu character the central protagonist during the time of the Raj. Anna Hansen, a young, intelligent, pretty Danish girl, visits India before she marries. There she works as an assistant to Sir Nitin Basu, an elderly researcher in the fictional town called Himapur and is introduced to Henry, the District Magistrate of the town, and Marlowe Croft, the missionary wanting to establish a church and to preach Christianity to the so-called heathen. It is through Anna, the central consciousness of the novel, that we are given a glimpse into the private lives of these two British men and their wives.

Henry and his wife Stella are portrayed as a couple whose lives are distraught because of their temperamental differences; in the words of Henry, "their differences had been political. Stella was a soldier's daughter and grand-daughter and had been brought up on Mutiny legend and lore" (177). She believes in pomp and show, the smugness and superiority characteristic of the British colonizers, whereas Henry is liberal and sympathetic to the Indian subjects. In this novel, Sahgal has changed her focus. Rather than protesting against female subjugation in a male dominated society, she stresses that for a marriage to be successful both must be sincere, frank, and willing to sacrifice. Despite Henry's compassionate temperament, his marital life becomes embittered and frustrated, ending finally in divorce, because Stella does not return the love and care he has extended her. The relationship of the other pair, Marlowe and Lulu, is also ruined for the same reasons: lack of understanding and communication. Both have been secretive and insincere with each other, but both expect the other to be tolerant and accommodating even though Marlow has married Lulu "not for love" (146) but to make use of her in his missionary effort. She attempts to leave Himapur but dies from an accidental fall; there are sufficient hints in the novel to suggest that her husband had murdered her, notwithstanding the impression of immense sorrow he creates on the mourners. In opposition to these two discordant couples, Anna and Nicholas enter into a happy and harmonious marriage, knowing and accepting each other's inadequacies and follies. Anna's grandmother had once told her that among life's mysteries "Why and whom one loved was the most ineffable" (212).

The title of the novel suggests the significant differences in the departures of the three female characters. Lulu's plans were foiled by her husband and led to death, while Stella brazenly leaves with another man, and Anna enters into a happy marriage.

Rich Like Us, which followed, portrays Sahgal's unconventional and feminist view that the entire social structure in India supports male domination and that women are exploited and victimized on all occasions: in marriage, in sexual relationships, in childbirth, even in adultery. The novel tells the story of Ram, an Indian businessman who visits London and meets a British woman named Rose, who becomes the central figure in the novel. Charmed by her exquisite beauty and elegance, Ram makes an unsuccessful bid "to coax her, bully or trick her into bed" (40). Eventually he proposes to her and they get married, much against the wishes of Rose's parents and with Rose's knowledge that he is already married to Mona, a traditional Hindu wife with a son. Regardless, their marriage is performed according to Hindu rites. On their return to India, Rose insists on Ram divorcing his first wife, but she is advised sanctimoniously that "There is no divorce. Hindu marriage is not a contract. It's a sacrament" (61). As the years go by, the three of them learn to live under the same roof and accept each other; then, yet another woman walks into Ram's life and creates turbulence in the otherwise calm and placid world the two women had built. Mona had earlier attempted suicide but was saved by Rose, and an intimacy developed between them. Together they brought up the son of Mona and Ram, even selecting his bride, and on her deathbed Mona makes Rose promise that she will look after their daughter-in-law.

The two women form an interesting contrast. One is a Hindu wife, bound to the shackles of tradition and conformity, docility and acquiescence, the other a liberal and nonconformist Christian believing in instincts. But both are exploited by male domination. Both love Ram passionately. Even though they suffer humiliation and self-abnegation time and again, they do not leave him. In a conversation with a friend, Rose reveals that the only thing she "could not bear in any circumstances would be a divorce—I could never bear to lose Ram" (216). Emotional and sensitive, both are victims at the hands of the self-centered Ram.

Mistaken Identity, Sahgal's latest novel, once again develops two parallel themes: the first political, the condition of the Indians under the rule of Empire; the other, male-female relationships in a masculinist society.

The narrator-protagonist is the playboy Bhushan Singh, known as "Jumbo," the son of the Raja of Vijaygarh. He is arrested while on a train journey home after months of travel abroad, and is jailed with other prisoners also charged with treason, even though they have not committed any political crimes. But it is 1929 and the country is torn by strife, so the jittery government sees sedition everywhere.

While in jail, Bhushan tells his cellmates stories of his colorful past. He not only reveals his own life history but that of his mother as well, who had been "pledged at five, delivered at menstruation" (27). She had a twin sister and both were married to his father, but one died. In fact, Bhushan is not even sure which one was actually his mother, a circumstance that stresses the condition of women in a time when female children were often strangled at birth. He tells how the woman he thought to be his mother suffered until she left with her lover and gained freedom. He also reveals his own love life, in particular his adolescent affair with a Muslim girl, which resulted in murderous communal riots and led to his banishment abroad.

But what is most fascinating in the novel is the portrayal of Bhushan's mother through his reminiscences. He recalls that ever since she was twenty-two she had been "sentenced to that greenish light of unfilfilled desire" (194). Then he tells how she—ill-treated and despised by her husband—leaves the family palace, hesitating for a second at the entrance and holding her breath before she walks out to star in the most sensational scandal of the generation—the elopement with Yusuf, her communist lover. Unorthodox, unconventional, and rebellious, this woman signals female emancipation. Such an ending Sahgal has never attempted before, but it provides a much needed dimension to her aesthetic and ethical vision.

Through Sahgal's eight novels there has been a visible progression in her vision. In the earlier work the female characters have vaguely craved freedom and attempted to shake off orthodox conventions and moribund tradition, whereas in the later novels the women have freed themselves from bondage and regained their identity. Moreover, their freedom is no longer restricted to the superficial aspects, such as matters of dress, eating habits, smoking, drinking but has enlarged to encompass the whole individual.

WORKS CITED

Asnani, Shyam M. *Critical Response to Indian English Fiction.* Delhi: Mittal Publications, 1985.
———. "The Novels of Nayantara Sahgal." *Indian Literature* 16 (1973): 36–69.
Jain, Jasbir. "The Aesthetics of Morality: Sexual Relations in the Novels of Nayantara Sahgal." *Journal of Indian Writing in English* 6 (1978): 40–56.
———. *Nayantara Sahgal.* Delhi: Heinemann, 1978.
Malhotra, M.L.. *Bridges of Literature.* Ajmer: Sunanda Publications, 1971.
Sahgal, Nayantara. *The Day in Shadow.* Delhi: Vikas, 1971.
———. *Mistaken Identity.* London: Heinemann, 1988.
———. "Of Divorce and Hindu Woman." *Hindustan Times* 12 December 1971: 11.
———. *Plans for Departure.* London: Penguin, 1986.
———. *Rich Like Us.* London: Heinemann, 1985.
———. *A Situation in New Delhi.* Delhi: Penguin, 1977.
———. *Storm in Chandigarh.* Delhi: Hind Pocket Books, 1969.
———. *A Time to Be Happy.* Delhi: Sterling Publishers, 1975.
———. "Women: Persons or Possessions?" *Hindustan Times* 19 July 1970: 12.

NAYANTARA SAHGAL'S PUBLISHED WORK

Novels

A Time to Be Happy, 1957
This Time of Morning, 1965
Storm in Chandigarh, 1969
The Day in Shadow, 1971
A Situation in New Delhi, 1977
Plans for Departure, 1985
Rich Like Us, 1987
Mistaken Identity, 1988

Autobiographies

Prison and Chocolate Cake, 1954
From Fear Set Free, 1962

History

The Freedom Movement in India, 1970
A Voice of Freedom, 1977
Indira Gandhi's Emergence and Style, 1978 (Revised and published in U.S. as *Indira Gandhi: Her Road to Power,* 1982)

SELECTED CRITICAL READINGS

Although the work of Nayatara Sahgal is published abroad and reviewed widely, most of the criticism thus far has come from India. But there it has not gained much attention recently after a burst of interest in the 1970s. Still, the variety of her writing—both fiction and nonfiction—will undoubtedly draw more international attention in the future. In particular, her revolutionary handling of Indian women in a traditionally masculinist society should attract feminist critics as they veer from the British-American canon. As well, Sahgal provides a fictional account, along with her historical writing, of India's Independence movement and its aftermath. Even though Sahgal has not gained the wide attention of such other women writers from India as Anita Desai and Ruth Prawer Jhabvala, her work has earned her a secure place in international literature in English and will eventually be fully recognized.

Asnani, Shyam M. "The Novels of Nayantara Sahgal." *Indian Literature* 16 (1973): 36–69. Provides a detailed analysis of the novels through *The Day in Shadow.* Seeks to examine the twin themes against the background of the national freedom struggle as well as the author's upbringing and family environment.

———. "Portrayal of Man-Woman Relationship in the Novels of Nayantara Sahgal." *Kakatiya Journal of English Studies* 3 (1978): 151–68. Establishes Sahgal as a champion of the new morality according to which a harmonious marital relationship is possible on the basis of mutual trust and understanding.

———. "Contemporary Politics: Its Portrayal in the Novels of Nayantara Sahgal." *Criticism and Research* 7 (1984-85): 147–62. Offers an incisive interpretation of the variegated aspects of political life in Sahgal's first five novels and emphasizes the humanistic values the author upholds.

Jain, Jasbir. *Nayantara Sahgal.* Delhi: Heinemann, 1978. Offers an integrated study of the major themes of her work, covering its historical, social, and religious aspects. Sees her as an important Indian novelist who espouses a humanistic view of life. Provides a useful look at Sahgal's ideas on Hinduism.

———. "The Politics of Hinduism in the Novels of Nayantara Sahgal." *Littcrit* 2.2 (1976): 45–47. Brief but interesting look at the Hindu background governing the novels' characters and conflict.

———. "Sexual Relations in the Novels of Sahgal." *Journal of Indian Writing in English* 6 (1978): 41–47. Examines the dichotomy in Hinduism that allows women to be exploited at various levels.

Jussawalla, Feroza. "Of Cabbages and Kings: *This Time of Morning* and *Storm in Chandigarh.*" *Journal of Indian Writing in English* 5 (1977): 43-50. Explores the twin theme against the backdrop of the early morning of a new nation's life and the disorder prevalent in private as well as public lives.

Kohli, Suresh. *Nayantara Sahgal and the Craft of Fiction.* Delhi: Vikas, 1972. Discusses her work in general, her stylistic and narrative techniques in particular.

Rao, A.V. Krishna. *Nayantara Sahgal—A Study of Her Fiction and Non-Fiction.* Madras: Seshachalam, 1976. Provides a close look at the development of the novels, along with a discussion of the nonfiction, stressing in both the role of Indian history in Sahgal's writing.

Sarma, M.N. "Nayantara Sahgal's Novels." *Journal of Indian Writing in English* 4 (1976): 35–45. Analyzes the marital tension in the lives of Sahgal's protagonists.

Sarma, S. Krishna. "Positive Living: A Brief Examination of Some Features of Nayantara Sahgal's *Storm in Chandigarh* and *The Day in Shadow.*" *Kakatiya Journal of English Studies* 3 (1978): 166–76. Draws on the autobiographical elements and explores the symbolic dimensions in the two novels.

Thomas, T.K. "The Hindu Ethos—A Novelist's Perspectives." *Religion and Society* 20.4 (1973): 54–71. Considers the first four novels in the perspective of religious beliefs in Hindu society.

—RAMESH CHADHA

Bapsi Sidhwa

Bapsi Sidhwa was born in Karachi, India, 11 August 1938, to a Parsee family but grew up in post-Partition Lahore, Pakistan. As a child of two, she contracted polio, with the result that until age fourteen she received no formal schooling. Regarding her illness, she has commented: "This left me with a problem until my middle teens, when I had a few operations and it more or less vanished. But it affected my entire life." To while away the time of a lonely, albeit privileged, childhood, Sidhwa developed the lifelong habit of voracious reading, which helped pave the way to her becoming a writer.

Becoming a writer and getting published, however, was an uphill battle for Sidhwa, who was raised in the conservative Parsee milieu of Lahore. She was married at nineteen, had three children shortly thereafter and spent the following years living the life of an upper-class Pakistani housewife. It was on a family vacation to the North-west tribal areas of Pakistan that Sidhwa heard the story of a young girl, married against her will, who tried to run away, only to be tracked down and killed; the daring of this unfortunate girl caught Sidhwa's imagination in such a way that she felt compelled to tell the story. Most of the writing, she admits, had to be done in secret unless her friends be offended by her "pretentiousness": "After all, I was only a businessman's wife."

Once the novel was completed, appropriately called *The Bride*, she found the courage to show it to a few friends, who liked it enormously; an American friend helped her to place it with an agent. "Then the period of frustration began," Sidhwa recalls. "I went through seven years of rejection slips. I then wrote *The Crow-Eaters*—and the same thing happened. I was told that Pakistan was too remote in time and place for Americans or the British to identify with." But *The Crow-Eaters*— a boisterously humorous look at the Parsee community of the sub-continent—was finally picked up by Jonathan Cape in England. Publication of *The Bride* followed shortly thereafter.

Although *The Crow-Eaters* came under heavy fire by the Parsee community in Pakistan and India, it received favorable reviews in both England and the United States. So did *The Bride*, which is to be made into a movie by Merchant-Ivory films. Favorable reviews have continued with the third novel, *Ice-Candy-Man*.

Clearly Sidhwa has arrived as a writer of international standing. Her novels and short stories have been translated into Russian, German, French, and Urdu. One of the first Pakistanis to be published internationally, she has helped to pave the way for future Pakistani writers. The David Higham award, given to *The Crow-Eaters* for best first novel in 1980, was withheld because Pakistan was no longer part of the British Commonwealth.

Sidhwa now divides her time between Pakistan and the United States. She has taught creative writing at Columbia University, the University of Houston, and Rice University, Houston. She was awarded the Bunting Fellowship at Radcliffe in 1986, and won the Pakistan Academy's National Award for English Literature in 1985.

WOMEN IN HISTORY

Bapsi Sidhwa's *The Bride* and *Ice-Candy-Man* both portray history through the lens of female characters, and in so doing pose a challenge to the ideologies of Patriarchy and War.

Sidhwa's second published novel, *The Bride*, challenges the patriarchal culture and values of Indian-Pakistani society, for the heroine Zaitoon refuses to submit to the system and to accept the status quo. Thus, Sidhwa's ideological stance functions simultaneously as a strategy for challenging "the system" dominated by men and as a strategy of "liberation" for the female self that remains marginalized within that system. In contrast to the attitude of conservative paternalism, which is the hallmark of so many male writers of the subcontinent, such as Ahmed Ali, Sidhwa's attitude toward "the system" in place in post-Partition Muslim Pakistan is much more challenging. For instance, her vocabulary in this description of the *zenana* (in this case, the female quarters in which women of the urban lower middle classes live in the inner city of Lahore) exudes none of the aura of mystique that Ahmed Ali's accounts of the *zenana* in his novel *Twilight in Delhi* (1940) convey:

> The untidy row of buildings that crowded together along their street contained a claustrophobic warren of screened quarters. Rooms with windows open to the street were allotted to the men: the dim maze of inner rooms to the women—a domain given over to procreation, female odours and the interminable care of children. Smells of urine, stale food and cooking hung in the unventilated air, churning slowly, room to room, permeating wood, brick and mortar. Generations of babies had wet mattresses . . . and wiped hands on ragged curtains; and just in case the smells should fade, armies of new-born infants went on arriving to ensure the odours were perpetuated. . . . Redolent of an easy-going hospitality, the benign squalor in the women's quarters inexorably drew Zaitoon, as it did all its inmates, into the mindless, velvet vortex of the womb. (56)

That these quarters are described as "claustrophobic" and the residents as "inmates" (as though of a prison), who are sucked into the squalid atmosphere of this "womb-like," "mindless" enclave, reveals Sidhwa's ideological position to be far different from that of male Indian writers like Ali. Her image of the *zenana* is not of a secluded haven where "hothouse beauties" can be raised in virtue, as portrayed in Ali's work; rather it is a prison where women are forever tied to the mindless pursuit of raising "armies" of children for the perpetuation of a patriarchal system. Thus, it is easy for her to point out the one fact that male idealization of the zenana seeks to conceal—that the protection of female virtue is for the benefit of the male ego: "Proud husbands, fathers and brothers, they were the providers. Zealous guardians of family honour and virtue, they sat, when in their homes, like pampered patriarchs" (56).

That women embrace the very system that oppresses them is, of course, the supreme irony. So we have Zaitoon, the young girl who was snatched from the jaws of death by Gasim during the carnage of Partition; raised on a diet of romantic stories about Qasim's life in the north-west regions of Pakistan, Zaitoon grows up to believe in them:

> Years slipped by. Qasim, nostalgic for the cool mountains, wove such fascination into reminiscences of his life among them, that Zaitoon longed to see what she considered her native land. Her young, romantic imagination flowered into fantasies of a region where men were heroic, proud and incorruptible, ruled by a code of honour that banned all injustice and evil. These men, tall and light-skinned, were gods—free to roam the mountains as their fancies led. Their women, beautiful as houris, and their bright, rosey-cheeked children, lived beside crystal torrents of melted snow. (90)

Needless to say, it is these romantic fantasies of Zaitoon in particular and those of women in general that Sidhwa wishes to destroy. For it is adherence to such fantasies that leads to female subservience by promoting images of men as heroic gods, and women as their beautiful possessions. Little wonder then that Zaitoon, having happily acquiesced to a marriage with a tribal stranger, which was arranged by her adopted father, feels numb and void of feeling when she discovers the unpleasant reality behind the romantic facade of marriage:

> She also grew immune to the tyrranical, animal-trainer treatment meted out by Sakhi. In his presence, she drifted into a stupor, until nothing really hurt her. He beat her on the slightest pretext. She no longer thought of marriage with any sense of romance. She now lived only to placate him, keeping her head averted unless it was to listen to a command. Then her eyes were anxious and obsequious like those of Hamida. (174)

Unlike Hamida (her mother-in-law) and the other tribal women, Zaitoon possesses a courage and an instinct for self-preservation, which prevents her from completely acquiescing to a life of blame and humiliation: "Zaitoon's instinct for self-preservation alone kept her going" (174). That is what gave her the courage to try to escape the confines of a system that would have kept her a prisoner of her husband and of the mountains. Her attempt to get away reveals to Hamida the irony surrounding the concepts of "honor" and "virtue" on which patriarchy is built; she, like countless women before and after her, continue to be subjected to the myths of the system:

Honour! she thought bitterly. Everything for honour—and another life lost! Her loved ones dead and now the girl she was beginning to hold so dear sacrificed. She knew the infallibility of the mountain huntsman.

The old woman was overcome by the memory of her three dead sons. . . . In each grief, a nameless dread: how many more lives would the dead one claim? The set faces of the men, their faces burning with hate and a lust for revenge, their old make-shift guns forever loved and polished. . . .

Men and honor. And now the girl. . . .

Visions floated confusedly in her mind. She, who had been so proud and valiant and wholeheartedly subservient to the ruthless code of her forebears, now loathed it with all her heart. (190-91)

Thus Sidhwa, contrary to writers like Ali, does not romanticize a system that makes a virtue of defending the honor of women—where a woman may be killed if she is suspected of even imaginary infidelities or of exhibiting the slightest desire for independence, as in Zaitoon's case. It is interesting to note that Ali's heroine in *Twilight in Delhi* "chooses" death as a means to freedom and that in her passive resignation to her fate lies the secret of her attractiveness. She acquiesces, she accepts, and is therefore no threat to the system—hence her heroic stature. Zaitoon, on the other hand, refuses to acquiesce, and it is this spirit of defiance that Sidhwa finds admirable and intends the reader to do so as well. That she endorses the young woman's resolution and, by analogy, endorses a challenge to the strictures of patriarchy is revealed through the ending she chooses for the novel: Zaitoon survives. According to Sidhwa, in the original story as told to her many years earlier, the girl on whom Zaitoon is modeled was killed by her husband and his gang. "But," said Sidhwa, "after all that she had been through, I just couldn't allow her to die like that."

In *The Bride*, Sidhwa does not offer any radical solutions to the dilemma of being a woman in a patriarchal culture. Zaitoon survives but only to be taken up and protected by a man who hopefully loves her and will not treat her as cruelly as the comparatively uncivilized tribal husband did. Thus, Zaitoon, despite her heroism, must remain an object in a culture whose history continues to marginalize women. It is important to note, however, that Sidhwa's stance on the idealization of patriarchal culture and history is clearly one of challenge.

In her third novel, *Ice-Candy-Man*, Sidhwa still depicts women as little more than objects in history but moves away from seeing women solely as victims to describing them as emotional pillars of strength who can, through the power of compassion, effect good for others. In this world gone awry, where friend betrays friend, the women suffer the most; yet, ironically, only the women can offer any hope for the salvation of humanity.

Ice-Candy-Man is a novel about the Partition of India into Hindu India and Muslim Pakistan on the eve of the 1947 departure of Britain from one of its most treasured colonies. The story is told through the eyes of a young Parsee girl growing up in the culturally diverse, smelly, raucous city of Lahore. As the story unfolds, we witness the horrifying events leading up to Partition and become privy to the pain and bewilderment of the young, limping Lenny, who sees her world being torn apart, literally and figuratively.

The novel begins, quite modestly, by introducing the reader through Lenny's voice to her domestic world, which comprises a fascinating medley of relatives, friends, and servants: the charming, slightly distant mother; the gruff, tight-fisted but well-meaning father; Electric-Aunt and her over-sexed adolescent son who Lenny refers to fondly as "Cousin"; Lenny's Godmother (on whom Lenny dotes) and her long-suffering Slavesister; a younger brother called Adi; and an assortment of neighbors and servants, the most important of whom is the young and attractive "Ayah," Lennie's nursemaid.

Right from the beginning, we see that Lenny and her Ayah form a bond that symbolically resists attempts by an outside, male world to subjugate them. When a sprightly Englishman sees Lenny being pushed in a pram, he immediately reprimands both Ayah and her: "'Let her walk. Shame, shame! Such a big girl in a pram! She's at least four!'" What he does not realize is that Lenny has a polio-afflicted leg:

> "She not walk much . . . she get tired," drawls Ayah. And simultaneously I raise my trouser cuff to reveal the leather straps and wicked steel callipers harnessing my right boot.
> Confronted by Ayah's liquid eyes and prim gloating, and the triumphant revelation of my callipers, the Englishman withers. (2)

Thus Lenny and her Ayah triumph over the man who knows better.

This kind of bonding also exists between Lenny and her Godmother—and it is significant that Lenny describes her relationship with her godmother as in some way rivaling and bettering male-female relationships:

> Flying forward I fling myself at Godmother and she lifts me onto her lap and gathers me to her bosom. I kiss her, insatiably and excessively, and she hugs me. She is childless. The bond that ties her strength to my weakness, my fierce demands to her nurturing . . . is stronger than the bond of motherhood. More satisfying than the ties between men and women. (4)

It is through watching her Ayah surrounded by a constant throng of male admirers, who range from the Government-house gardener, the local butcher, the handsome masseur, the knife-sharpener, the Chinaman, to the chameleon-like ice-candy-man (who becomes a bird-seller during the winter months and a religious mystic on occasion), that Lenny learns about male-female relationships: "Things love to crawl beneath Ayah's sari. Ladybirds, glowworms, Ice-candy-man's toes. She dusts them off with impartial nonchalance" (19). What Lenny also learns is that Ayah's warm and magnetic personality exerts a generous and taming influence on her many male admirers; that is what keeps them flocking to her side without engendering bitterness or hatred: "I learn also to detect the subtle exchange of signals and some of the complex rites by which Ayah's admirer's coexist. Dusting the grass from their clothes they slip away before dark, leaving the one luck, or the lady favours" (19).

Thus it is that we witness a series of meetings between Ayah and Lenny and her coterie of friends and admirers, through whose conversations we learn a great deal. So does Lenny: "I learn fast. I gain Ayah's goodwill and complicity by accommodating her need to meet friends and relatives. She takes me to fairs, cheap restaurants and slaughter-houses" (20).

It is at these places and through the conversations there that we are apprised of the impending doom of Partition. The ethnic and religious rivalries between Hindus, Muslims, and Sikhs that surface during talks of Partition between political leaders spill over and poison the general atmosphere as well. Lenny realizes, sadly, that her bucolic trips to the Queen's Garden with Ayah and company have also become tinged with the poison of prejudice:

> I can't seem to put my finger on it—but there is a subtle change in the Queen's Garden. Sitting on Ayah's crossed legs, leaning against her chocolate softness, again the unease at the back of my mind surfaces.
>
> I fidget restlessly on Ayah's lap and she asks: "What is it, Lenny? You want to do soo-soo?" I nod, for want of a better explanation. "I'll take her," offers Masseur, getting up. . . . Massuer gropes for my hand, but I twist and slip away and run to the boy and he, pretending to be a steam engine. . . leads me romping to his group.
>
> The Sikh women pull me to their laps and ask the name of my religion.
>
> "I'm Parsee," I say.
>
> "Okee? What's that?" they ask: scandalised to discover a religion they've never heard of.
>
> That's when I realize what's changed. The Sikhs . . . are keeping mostly to themselves.
>
> Masseur leans into the group and placing a firm hand on my arm drags me away. We walk past a Muslim family. With their burka-clad women, they too sit apart. . . . A group of smooth-skinned Brahmins and their pampered male-offspring form a tight circle of supercilious exclusivity near ours. (97)

In this atmosphere of growing ethnic and religious divisiveness, Lenny notices that "Only the group around Ayah remains unchanged. Hindu, Muslim, Sikh, Parsee are, as always, unified around her" (97). It is into her symbolically unified lap that Lenny dives for comfort.

The horror of Partition makes itself known to both the reader and Lenny through the symbolic and real rift in the unity of this motley crew, which culminates in the betrayal of the beloved Ayah. It is interesting to note that the racial and religious ugliness begins to manifest itself within the microcosm of Lenny's household through the violent behavior of its male servants. Hari, the Hindu gardener, becomes the obvious target of the cruel playfulness of the Muslim servants, who wish to humiliate him for his uncircumcised penis:

Yousaf is twirling his [Hari's] plume of hair and tugging at it as if he's trying to lift him. I feel a great swell of fear for Hari: and a surge of loathing for his bodhi. Why must he persist in growing it? and flaunt his Hinduism? and invite ridicule? . . . My dread assuming a violent and cruel shape, I tear away from Ayah and fling myself on the human tangle and fight to claw at Hari's dhoti . . . and, suddenly, it's off!

Like a withered tree frozen in a winter landscape, Hari stands isolated in the bleak center of our violence: prickly with goose-bumps, sooty genitals on display. (117-18)

It is to Sidhwa's credit that she does not absolve the female from the impulse to violence: Witness Lenny's behavior. However, it seems safe to say that Sidhwa more often sees women as ultimately the bulwarks of resistance against violence, as symbols of love and rehabilitation in a hate-filled, destructive world.

Thus, in the midst of an atmosphere of hate and mistrust that begins to envelop the village folk of Pir Pindo when threatening groups of militant Sikhs start to converge on the previously peaceful cohabitation of Muslims and Sikhs, the only "happy" note consists of a little boy's memory of visits to his favorite aunt:

Before dusk Dost Mohammed's younger brother, Iqbal, joins us. He has bought some land in a village four miles west of Pir Pindo. . . . His wife is Ranna's favourite aunt. He loves going to their village . . . and to be spoilt by his Noni chachi [aunt]. She always has something for him to eat or wear, he tells me. His uncle tosses a knitted skull-cap into Ranna's lap, saying, "Here's something from Noni chachi, pahailwan!" (108)

Then he is told that he should leave before dark, advice that "turned the heaviness in Ranna's heart into a stab of fear." Ranna's fears are not ill-founded, as shortly afterwards, once the Partition of India has been announced, droves of militant Sikhs raid the villages of the Punjab, slaughtering and raping; Ranna witnesses the brutal murders of his entire family and is the only one of his village who miraculously survives.

Contrary to both the participation in violence or the resigned acceptance of it, symbolized by the Sikh "granthi" of Ranna's village, the major women characters of the novel try to counter such impulses through some kind of life-affirming action. Ayah, as we have seen, through her very presence served as the cement that held together Hindu, Muslim, Sikh, Parsee, Christian. However, when the mindless cruelty of religious strife claims her as a victim, the circumstances of her betrayal as well as its aftermath serve to underscore Sidhwa's stance on male-female relationships as well as to point to women's capacity for compassionate action as the only hope for humankind's redemption.

When, at the height of ethnic and religious strife, a band of marauding "goondas" comprised largely of Muslim men enters the compound of Lenny's parents' house, everyone instinctively senses trouble for Ayah, who is Hindu. She is immediately sent to hide indoors, while Imam Din, as the oldest male servant, confronts the crowd and tells it to disperse. The description of Lenny's mother, who thus far has been a somewhat shadowy presence, is noteworthy:

> The men's eyes, lined with black antimony, rake us. . . . A hesitancy sparks in their brash eyes when they look at our mother. Flanked by her cubs, her hands resting on our heads, she is the noble embodiment of theatrical motherhood. Undaunted. Endearing. Her cut-crystal lips set in a defiant pucker beneath her tinted glasses and her cropped, waved hair. (179)

Whereas the mother can resist the onslaught of the male gaze, the young Lenny cannot. Though Imam Din, aided by the mother's presence, has told the crazed mob that Ayah is no longer on the premises, Lenny is cajoled by the Ice-candy-man's hypnotic, reassuring eyes into revealing Ayah's whereabouts. He has, after all, been one of Ayah's most fervent admirers, and consequently someone Lenny trusts. Imagine her horror, then, at his betrayal:

> Ice-candy-man is crouched before me. "Don't be scared, Lenny baby," he says. "I'm here." And putting his arms around me he whispers, so that only I can hear; "I'll protect Ayah with my life! You know I will. . . . I know she's here. Where is she?" (182)

Lenny tells him, realizing immediately: "I know I have betrayed Ayah." It is only a matter of minutes before Ayah is dragged out and carried away by the shameless mob, while the household watches helplessly:

> The last thing I noticed was Ayah, her mouth slack and piteously gaping, her dishevelled hair flying into her kidnappers's faces, staring at us as if she wanted to leave behind her wide open and terrified eyes. (184)

After Ayah's disappearance, Lenny, inconsolable, tries to discover her whereabouts and the means to rescue her. In this attempt, we are made privy to a number of facts, which, though they underscore the victimization of women in war, also show us women banding together to help other women, and as such, becoming symbols of empowerment. First of all, we learn that the house next door to Lenny's, abandoned earlier by its Hindu tenants who have fled to India, has become a haven for "fallen women": those women who have been raped and assaulted and can never return to their families because their honor has been stained. Many a night Lenny wakes to hear their wails and screams of terror and desperation; finally she acquires an ayah whom she recognizes as one of those women, on whom she spied occasionally from the roof of her house. Although this ayah is a hopeless figure, one who accepts her role as a victim of fate's cruelty, Lenny rebels against this image of her as well as the kind of resignation she represents. Awakened one night by the wails and laments from next door, Lenny questions Hamida, the new ayah, about the women:

> "Poor fate-smitten woman," says Hamida, sighing. "What can a sorrowing woman do but wail?"
>
> "Who are those women?" I ask.
>
> "God knows," says Hamida. "Go to sleep . . . there is nothing we can do."
>
> My heart is wrung with pity and horror. I want to leap out of my bed and soothe the wailing woman and slay her tormentors. I've seen Ayah carried away—and it had less to do with fate than with the will of men. (214)

The point that Sidhwa makes through Lenny is, of course, that there is something that can be done to rectify men's misdeeds and mistakes; that the very concept of "fate" must be challenged—and challenged by women, who for centuries have accepted persecution at the hands of men masquerading under the guise of "fate."

Lenny's mother, who earlier in the novel seemed to play the role of submissive wife, now comes into her own as a woman of substance: She not only risks her life by storing and supplying petrol to families wishing to flee persecution, regardless of religion, she also becomes actively involved in the rehabilitation of the forsaken women, even employing one of them in her own household.

It is Lenny's Godmother, however, who emerges as a true savior-figure and the moral conscience of the novel. Frustrated by her attempts to locate Ayah, Lenny turns to Godmother for help, whose power and desire to assist the unfortunate seems boundless to Lenny:

> And this is the source of her immense power: this reservoir of random knowledge, and her knowledge of ancient lore and wisdom and herbal remedy. You cannot be near her without feeling her uncanny strength. People bring to her their joys and woes. Show her their sores and swollen joints. Distilling the right herbs, adroitly instilling the right word in the right ear, she secures wishes, smoothes relationships, cures illnesses, battles wrongs, solaces griefs, and prevents mistakes. (211)

How then can Godmother fail to lend a sympathetic ear to Lenny or to right the wrong done to Ayah? Through her tentacles of knowledge, Godmother discovers that Ayah, once abducted, was taken to "Hira Mandi"—the diamond market—and turned into a dancing girl/prostitute. After several months, Ice-candy-man married her, and she now lives, in abject humiliation, with him. Ice-candy-man is summoned to Godmother's house, where Lenny witnesses the following exchange between them:

> Knowing her as I do I can tell by the hooded droop of her wrinkled lids . . . that she is in a cold rage: and God help Ice-candy-man

. . . . [He] is visibly shaken. His hazel eyes dart frantically. . . . I see him now as Godmother sees him. Treacherous, dangerous, contemptible. A destructive force that must be annihilated. (248)

Indeed the dénouement of the novel consists in the figurative annihilation of Ice-candy-man, through the "rescue" of Ayah from his clutches, effected so sympathetically by Godmother. Ayah's own decision to leave the "Mandi" and the relative material comfort and security now provided by a guilt-stricken and lovelorn Ice-candy-man, symbolizes the anti-victim stance that Sidhwa advocates for women throughout the novel. Rather than succumb to her "fate-as-victim," Ayah, given the help of other women like Godmother and Lenny, chooses to fight for acceptance back into her family and society. In allowing for such an open-ended conclusion, Sidhwa not only provides the possibility for Ayah to become mistress of her own fate but also presents female bonding and feminine empathy as antidotes to the violence and corruption wrought by centuries of male dominance in religion and politics.

I conclude by quoting an excerpt from Gerda Lerner's article, "The Challenge of Women's History," because it seems that, above all, Sidhwa's work to date provides a uniquely female perspective on the socio-political context of recent Indian-Pakistani history:

> Women have been left out of history not because of the evil conspiracies of men in general nor male historians in particular, but because we have considered history only in male-centered terms. We have missed women and their activities, because we have asked questions of history which are inappropriate to women. To rectify this, and to light up areas of historical darkness we must, for a time, focus on a woman-centered inquiry, considering the possibility of the existence of a female culture shared by men and women. History must include an account of the female experience over time and should include the development of feminist consciousness as an essential aspect of women's past. This is the primary task of women's history. The central question it raises is: What would history be like if it were seen through the eyes of women and ordered by the values they define? (quoted in Abel: 28)

Sidhwa's *The Bride* and *Ice-Candy-Man* record from a female perspective the bloody history of the Indian-Pakistani Partition as well as the subsequent history of male-dominated Pakistan. Surely, had this history—or any history—been defined or were it to be defined in the future by the kind of values that women like Godmother and Ayah stand for, then the world might well be a less violent place.

WORKS CITED

Sidhwa, Bapsi. *The Bride*. New York: St. Martin's Press, 1983.
———. *Ice-Candy-Man*. London: Heinemann, 1988.

Lerner, Gerder. "The Challenge of Women's History." Quoted in: Abel, Elizabeth, editor. *Writing and Sexual Difference*. Chicago: Chicago UP, 1983.

Quotations from Bapsi Sidhwa, cited in the biography and essay, from a conversation with the author in Lahore, Pakistan, 1988.

BAPSI SIDHWA'S PUBLISHED WORK

The Crow-Eaters, 1981
The Bride, 1983
Ice-Candy-Man, 1988

SELECTED CRITICAL READINGS

Sometimes it seems an unofficial "canon" of international writers in English receives the most critical attention, and Bapsi Sidhwa's work has not yet achieved this status. So the foregoing essay may well be the first full discussion of this interesting body of fiction but will not likely be the last. Her work has been reviewed widely and favorably, so it is probable that it will begin to receive fuller critical attention. The critical readings are therefore limited at this point to selected reviews and one article that includes a discussion of *The Bride*.

Ross, Robert. "The Emerging Myth: Partition in the Indian and Pakistani Novel." *ACLALS Bulletin* 7 (1986): 63–69. Proposes that the events of Partition have started to form myth from which novelists draw. Discusses *The Bride* alongside Nahal's *Azidi*, Singh's *Train to Pakistan*, Rushdie's *Midnight's Children*, and Malgonkar's *A Bend in the Ganges*.

Reviews

Ice-Candy-Man
World Literature Today 62. (1988): 732.
Times Literary Supplement 1 April 1988: 363.
New Statesman 26 Feb. 1988: 23.
London Review of Books 15 Sept. 1988: 19.

The Bride
World Literature Today 58 (1984): 667.
Library Journal 15 Nov. 1983: 2172.
Punch 16 Feb. 1983: 41.
London Review of Books 19 May 1983: 22.

The Crow-Eaters
Times Literary Supplement 26 Sept. 1980: 1057.
New Statesman 19 Sept. 1980: 23.
Observer 14 Sept. 1980: 29.

— FAWZIA AFZAL-KHAN

Buchi Emecheta

Born in Lagos, Nigeria, 21 July 1944, to Ibo parents, who had moved there from Ibuza in Eastern Nigeria, Buchi Emecheta entered a divided, multilingual world, in which she and her group were, if not foreigners, then at least a visiting minority whose customs and language were not the dominant ones. She was thus born into an exile condition, and strategies for survival in that situation remain the main theme in her work.

Despite their adherence to Christianity, Emecheta's parents clung to the traditional ways of Ibo life, and it is to the storytelling of her "big mother" that Buchi Emecheta traces her own desire to tell stories. Another feature of Ibo tradition affected her greatly: the preference for boys and the concomitant low value put on girls and women. Already as a child Emecheta showed unusual tenacity and a spirit of rebellion, thus gaining for herself an education normally given only to the boys in the family.

She left school when she was sixteen in order to get married, and when her husband went to London to study two years later, she accompanied him with their first two children. In London they encountered racial prejudice and lived in appalling slum conditions. Emecheta had three more children, and, as her husband was studying and refused to work, she became the breadwinner of the family, working in libraries and trying to look after the children at the same time.

The marriage broke up, and at age twenty-two Emecheta found herself alone in London with five young children. While looking after them, she took a degree in sociology and wrote fiction. In 1972 the *New Statesman* accepted her stories and launched her on her writing career. Since then, she has lived and worked in London, interrupted by spells in Nigeria. She now supports herself entirely with her writing.

Unorthodox Fictions about African Women

Buchi Emecheta is to date the most important African woman writer. Not only the extent of her output but also the centrality of her subject matter—the role of women in present day Africa—has put her in this position. In her treatment of her subject, she shows courage in challenging traditional male attitudes to gender roles; anger and iconoclastic contempt for unjust institutions, no matter how time honored or revered they are; and a willingness to seek new ways to subvert what she sees as the unjust subjugation of women in the name of tradition.

The starting point and earliest source of inspiration for Emecheta's work was her own life, and her autobiographical novels about her experiences of growing up in

Lagos and living as an immigrant in London's slums hold the key to most of her ideas. While the first two books, *In the Ditch* and *Second-Class Citizen*, describe her childhood in Lagos, her marriage to a student, and their subsequent move to England, they concentrate on her struggle to support and bring up her five children in London. Although *In the Ditch* is Emecheta's first book, it begins at the point in her life when she has left her husband and is living on her own with her five children in a London slum, supporting them by working in a library. The book is a collection of "observations" that Buchi Emecheta sent to the *New Statesman*, which published them and thereby effectively launched her on her writing career.

The story follows the writer's slightly fictionalized self, Adah, as she descends into the "Ditch," which means living on the dole in a council housing estate set aside for problem families. Despite the predictably negative framework set by the appalling conditions, the book hovers between acceptance and rejection of the slum world. Problem families are defined by officialdom as single-parent and possibly colored families, so the world of the council housing estate, Pussy Cat Mansions, is very much a woman's world. They live on the dole and scratch around for whatever warmth life might offer with as much dignity as they can salvage. Emecheta moves her middle-class self into these circumstances and feels both compassion for and solidarity with the women, but she can not identify with them. Her pride is hurt by the charity she is forced to accept, and she has an ambivalent attitude both towards the authorities and her fellow dwellers "in the ditch." She survives racial prejudice by reminding herself of her superior education, her studies, and her former civil service job. The novel's emphasis increasingly falls on the values of initiative and determination, qualities that eventually help Adah to climb out of the ditch.

A woman's personal achievement through hard work becomes the central value in Emecheta's universe, and this alienates her from her traditional Ibo background, where women have ascribed roles as daughters, wives, and mothers. The sentiments she expressed when *In the Ditch* was published define this attitude clearly—and show how well she fitted into the Western bourgeoisie tradition: "I had come a long way, and only people who have set their hearts on achieving something and eventually getting it will realize how one feels at a time like this" (*Head Above Water* 74).

Anger at what she considered unjust criticism in some reviews of *In the Ditch* spurred Emecheta to enlarge on the background of the first novel, so *Second-Class Citizen* is a more in-depth treatment of Adah's life and difficulties. The book also outlines a dilemma in Emecheta's authorship: It celebrates Adah's achievement by outlining the difficulties she has successfully overcome, and it describes the living conditions of the poor in London with the anger and fervor of a socially committed writer. Again, Emecheta is caught between, on the one hand, anger and pity, and on the other hand, her belief that "whatever you want to do in this world, if you set your heart on it, you will always get it" (*Head Above Water* 81).

Second-Class Citizen portrays the young Adah as an unusually determined little girl whose mind is firmly set on getting a Western education, from which she was effectively barred because she was "only a girl." This sets the basic theme that runs through the entire book: an intense anger over the sexual discrimination at the core of her culture and a concomitant contempt for the men who perpetrate it. In England Adah is oppressed on all three scores of sex, race, and class, but the aspect of discrimination that she found most difficult to overcome was the sexual discrimination embedded in her marriage. She is her husband's property and he treats her as such. The injustice is spelled out: She supports them and is responsible for the children while he studies and keeps failing his exams. The book narrows to a battle between the two, centered on domestic issues that are vital to the survival and self-preservation of the woman: sex, motherhood, birth control, economic independence, and a sense of personal value. Through painful experience Adah works out her own solutions to the problems. Marital sex is increasingly equated with rape, and motherhood becomes the focus of Adah's emotional attachment. The birth of each child alienates her further from her husband but strengthens her ties with English society and its value system and hardens her determination to succeed. Her desire for birth control is seen by her husband, Francis, as an attempt to steal control over her body from him, so he beats her severely. The final blow, this one metaphorical, comes when he burns the manuscript of a book she has written. Once she leaves him, there is a strong sense of relief, and the move represents an increasing self-awareness and growing maturity on the part of Adah. She experiences moments of loneliness and longing for affection, but she emerges victorious, vindicated in her belief that success is a matter of will power.

Emecheta's autobiography was updated in 1986 with *Head Above Water*, which describes the continued struggle to bring up her family as a single parent, gain a degree in sociology, find jobs, and to write. It ends with the achievement of two major goals: purchasing a house of her own and settling down to become a full-time writer. In between, the book explores social conditions in black London and sheds interesting light on Emecheta's development as a writer, as it describes her involvement with each of the novels as they emerged.

It comes as no surprise that the manuscript burned by Francis in *Second-Class Citizen* surfaces as Emecheta's next book, *The Bride Price*. With this novel Emecheta departs from her own life story and moves into broader issues. The third novel is set in the early 1950s in Lagos and Ibuza. Despite this radical shift in content, *The Bride Price* is a logical development of Emecheta's writing. She continues to explore the injustices of caste, her main concern in the first two books but the emphasis is somewhat different. Whereas in her autobiographical books Emecheta stresses the possibility of overcoming the restrictions of caste or caste-like conditions through personal initiative, in *The Bride Price* and the following novels set in Nigeria, she stresses the destructive potential of rigid caste structure, which persists in the otherwise rapidly changing Ibo society. And her preoccupation continues to be the role of women. The central character of the novel is Aku-nna, whose name, significantly, means "father's wealth." Thirteen when her father dies, she is forced to move from Lagos with her mother and brother back to their village. Her desire to continue school is frowned upon but accepted, because educated girls fetch higher bride prices. Aku-nna is alienated from the village youth and falls in love with her school teacher. He, however, is the victim of another caste structure, for he is a descendant of slaves and thus not allowed to marry a freeborn. But true love runs its course: They elope under dramatic circumstances, get married, and settle down to a good life, supported by the oil boom, education, and Western values. Then tradition takes its revenge. The bride price has not been paid, and according to tradition the bride must die in childbirth—which is exactly what Aku-nna does. The explanation given for her death hovers uneasily between the psychological and the medical. The book thus ends with the defeat of progressive forces. Such apparent defeatism is somewhat surprising from an author who so far has celebrated achievement.

In *Head Above Water*, Emecheta sheds some light on the question of Aku-nna's death: "Guilt for going against her mother and her uncle killed her," she declares (165), then elaborates by saying that "Aku-nna died the death I ought to have died" (165). The explanation for such a statement lies in Emecheta's persistent feelings of guilt at having chosen her own husband who did not pay any bride price for her. In this matter, she may have chosen Western ways, but the conflict highlights the great cost of changing cultures, even if one is successful in the new culture. Emecheta shares this predicament with other immigrant writers, and it puts her in the tradition of writers like Salman Rushdie, Timothy Mo, and Joan Riley, all of whom try to give meaning to the intercultural state of the immigrant.

In her next novel, Emecheta continues exploring the injustices of Ibo traditions. In *The Slave Girl* she departs completely from her own life and relies partly on the life story of her mother and partly on research. The book is a criticism of Ibo domestic slavery, but in a characteristic, ambiguous way, Emecheta ties Western notions of marriage to Ibo notions of slavery. The central character, Objeta, is sold into slavery when her parents die in the 1916 influenza epidemic in Eastern Nigeria and becomes a domestic slave with no rights whatsoever over her own person. Much of the book describes this kind of slavery, which persisted long after slavery was outlawed. Because this approach necessitates both historical and ethnographical explanations, *The Slave Girl* is closer to the "village novels" of Chinua Achebe, T.M. Aluko, and others; but the ideological content remains very different from those books. Domestic slavery is seen as an integral part of the society, and it is described as unjust and cruel but with certain ameliorating features: Objeta's move from the village to the thriving market town ushers her into the modern world, and as a slave she is among the first to be sent to the missionaries to become a Christian and to learn to read and write. This marks a reversal of the usual pattern of "village novels," because going "from tradition to church" is considered a positive move, not a destructive one. Objeta eventually marries an educated man who sets her free by repaying her former owner the amount originally paid for her. She is now free—free, that is, to belong to her husband. The parallel between domestic slavery and marriage is stated very explicitly: "Slave, obey your master, wife, honour your husband." As a wife Objeta has no more power over her person than she did as a slave. She has simply, as the last line of the novel says, changed masters. Progress has eliminated one caste structure but kept another.

The theme of the slave-like conditions of marriage for a woman is further developed in *Joys of Motherhood*, Emecheta's most accomplished book to date. It is set in a period of Nigerian history, from the thirties to just before Independence, during which enormous changes took place, both political and economic. Yet the Ibo immigrant society in Lagos, the subject of the book, refused to make any allowances for change; in fact as the men experience defeat and humiliations in the new society, they cling even more tenaciously to the power they have over the women and children within their group. The final sufferers become the women who, like Nnu Ego, are caught between economic necessity on the one hand and cultural taboos and aspirations on the other. Nnu Ego struggles hard against terrible poverty and a cruel, irresponsible husband to give her sons an education and to marry off her daughters so that their bride price can help toward the boys' school fees. She achieves her goal but dies a lonely and disillusioned woman. The moral is obvious: By clinging to her traditional role as wife, or first wife, after her husband inherits a second wife from his deceased brother, she is destroyed and, in turn, tries to destroy her daughters' chances for a happier life. In contrast to this, her co-wife Adaku leaves the home and sets up as a prostitute in order to give her daughters the education denied to them within the traditional family structure. The prostitute appears to have Emecheta's blessing, and the novel stands as a testimony to the author's growing radicalization and willingness to consider unorthodox means of change.

This development continues in *Double Yoke*. Emecheta spent a term as writer in residence at the University of Calabar, and the novel is the result of her observations of the relationships between the sexes on the campus. It ties in with one of Emecheta's earliest preoccupations—education for girls and attitudes toward educated women. In *Double Yoke* Emecheta directly confronts the prejudices against educated women in Nigeria, and aims her scorn at Nigerian men. The central character Nko sets out with the intention of being "an academician and a quiet, nice and obedient wife." The latter part of her wish is also what her boy friend wants, but as a result of her experiences, Nko changes her mind. After having faced her boy friend's scorn because she has allowed him to make love to her and after having been forced into a choice of prostituting herself to her professor or not getting her degree, the obedience has worn thin. At the conclusion of the novel, she is pregnant by the professor, but her boy friend is beginning to accept her point of view, by at last "growing up," as Emecheta mercilessly suggests. In Nigeria, according to Emecheta, the relationship between the sexes resembles most of all a war, and independence for women demands that they fight to overcome that tradition.

The role of women continues to be Emecheta's main subject, but within this unity of subject matter two of her novels depart stylistically and conceptually from the main body of work. Emecheta has described *Destination Biafra* and *The Rape of Shavi* as "imaginary works, based on ideas and ideals" (*Head Above Water* 1). As the subject matter of *Destination Biafra* is war, the imaginative backdrop of the book is on a larger scale than her previous, mainly domestic settings. Emecheta tries to cope with army movements, war atrocities, and political deliberations and deceptions. The result is a mixed success. With regard to plot, the novel follows the build-up and the actual events of the war so closely that it is easy to identify all the main agents, despite their fictional names. Into this framework is inserted the story of Debbie, the English educated daughter of a rich Nigerian businessman, who was killed when the civilian government was overthrown in 1966. Debbie, who might be called

Emecheta's ideal woman, chooses to join the Federal army, not because she is bloodthirsty, but because such an action represents yet another unorthodox way of breaking out of the female role of passive suffering.

The main burden of the book, though, is to sort out the confusing ideologies of the war, but it does not quite succeed. In the foreword, Emecheta states: "Yet it is time to forgive, though only a fool will forget." The ambiguity of this statement permeates the novel. Debbie is "a neutral Itsekiri woman" with personal ties to the leaders on both sides of the war. She seems to believe both in a united Nigeria and in the ideals for which Biafra stands, so her self-declared neutrality seems more like a contradiction. There are, however, some clear ideological goals: One is to criticize the role of the British in the war, and the other is to bring to the world's attention the plight of the region successively occupied by Biafran and Nigerian troops, where both sides carried out widespread killings of civilians. The description of this somewhat neglected aspect of the war constitutes the most convincing part of the book.

With *The Rape of Shavi*, Emecheta leaps into fantasy but keeps a firm grip on the didactic purpose that runs through all her work. An allegory about the relationship between Europe and Africa, the novel begins in an unknown place some time in the future after a rumored nuclear holocaust, but in the course of events the action moves very much into the present and into known localities. It also sums up the history of the European conquest of Africa. In one part, a small group of Englishmen flee the threat of a nuclear war in a homemade airplane and crash in an unknown spot in the middle of a desert, where they are surprised to find a thriving community of cattle-rearing desert people. Shavian society has had no contact with the West, and the Shavians live a pre-lapsarian life of peace, justice, dignity, and hospitality, the latter their downfall. They take in the group of refugees, who represent the contradictions and greed of Western civilization. Before long, one of them rapes the prince's future bride. They also discover stones that resemble diamonds. When they have repaired their plane, they take the stones and the Shavian prince with them back to England. The Shavian time of innocence ends, when the prince returns with guns and knowledge, then starts plundering neighboring desert communities, while the whites no longer need the stones and the people starve. Soon Shavian society is devastated by war, drought, and famine, and the surviving heir apparent is faced with the task of picking up the tattered remains. The idealization of pre-contact African society is a countercurrent in Emecheta's writing. In her previous books, the emphasis has been on the negative aspects of traditional African (Ibo) culture, gender roles, and slavery in particular, and Britain, despite its racism, was seen as offering the freedom of social mobility through individual initiative and effort. *The Rape of Shavi* cannot be said to moderate this view, as it is in too sharp a contrast to it. Emecheta seems to be searching for the best values in the world views of her two civilizations, but as they appear stubbornly incompatible, she lands, so to speak, in mid-culture.

Mid-culture is also the center of *Gwendolen*, but in this novel, which represents a return to the social realism of the earlier books, Emecheta tackles the problems of converging and conflicting values in a much more direct manner and with a clearer vision of her own position. *Gwendolen* is set in the black immigrant milieu of

London, which Emecheta knows so well, but for the first time the main character is not a Nigerian but a West Indian. The theme is incest, and although this is new in Emecheta's work it lends itself to the now-familiar scenario of girls and women oppressed by men and fighting for self-respect and what Emecheta refers to as "an identity." The book starts off in Jamaica, where Gwendolen is left behind with her grandmother as first her father, and later her mother, leave for "Moder Kontry" and settle in London. While in her grandmother's care, Gwendolen is molested sexually by Uncle Johnny, who misuses his position as an old family friend and supporter of grandmother in difficult times. This is an important aspect of the concept of incest, for it shows the vulnerability of children in adult relationships. Although the grownups in the village condemn Uncle Johnny when Gwendolen finally tells her secret, her grandmother is annoyed at losing his support, and the village casts Gwendolen, here called June, as a wicked girl. She is given a second chance when her family sends for her, not entirely out of love, but to help look after the three younger children, born in London. Her arrival there gives Emecheta the opportunity to describe immigrant slum conditions through Gwendolen's eyes, which are innocent of the social meaning of her observation. Slowly these observations situate the family at the very bottom of the social scale, illiterate and unable to cope with the complexities of British society, like getting a council flat, but surviving and gaining pleasure and support from a primitive church community.

Her grandmother dies and her mother goes back to Jamaica. During her mother's absence her father starts an incestuous relationship with Gwendolen, who at sixteen has stopped going to school and is looking after her brothers and sister. She becomes pregnant, but at the same time she meets a white boy, another departure in Emecheta's work; she starts a sexual relationship with him, much to her father's relief, as he hopes that the boy friend can take the blame for the baby.

On her return, her mother harbors uneasy but unspoken feelings, which evolve into hatred toward Gwendolen who leaves home and is taken into care after a brief spell in a mental hospital. The outcome is optimistic, if slightly confusing. The father commits suicide, the mother is forced to acknowledge the paternity of the baby when she is confronted with it—it is black, not colored, and looks like her husband—and she turns her anger toward her husband, still not completely reconciling with her daughter. Gwendolen lives with the baby in a council flat and is happy, and her boy friend remains a friend in spite of the shame of the baby's paternity. This ending is seen as "modern": A new set of relationships emerges, formed on the basis of personal choice in opposition to blind adherence to the inherited patterns of race and family relationships. There seems to be an implicit suggestion that this alternative social organization might prevent a repetition of Gwendolen's experiences.

This willingness to search for new ways of social and sexual organization and to change views when social circumstances alter, combined with forthright anger, makes Emecheta a controversial writer. Her criticism of aspects of African tradition invites the charge of traitor to her culture; and her feminism, which viewed through Western eyes is mild (she refuses to be called a "feminist"), has enraged critics— mainly African and male—who have made vitriolic attacks on her books, claiming that they misrepresent Ibo society. Some of that criticism makes one suspect that her books are indeed true and of vital importance.

Insisting on education and middle-class values as the means of female emancipation, Emecheta has summed up her philosophy in an interview in *West Africa*: "I believe in power of the Will, with the help of that man upstairs, of course, but one can always achieve one's goal, if one is determined enough." As a role model for her sisters—black and white—Buchi Emecheta is an important figure. At the same time, her writing represents a vigorous and significant departure in fiction about African women.

Buchi Emecheta's Published Work

Novels

In the Ditch, 1972
Second-Class Citizen, 1974
The Bride Price, 1976
The Slave Girl, 1977
The Joys of Motherhood, 1979
Destination Biafra, 1982
Double Yoke, 1982
The Rape of Shavi, 1983
Gwendolen, 1989

Children's Books

Titch the Cat, 1979
Nowhere to Play, 1980
The Moonlight Bride, 1980
The Wrestling Match, 1980

Autobiography

Head Above Water: An Autobiography, 1986

Other Work

Our Own Freedom (photographs by Maggie Murray; introduction and commentary by Buchi Emecheta), 1981

Article

"Feminist with a small 'f.'" *Criticism and Ideology*. Ed. Kirsten Holst Petersen. Uppsala: Scandinavian Institute of African Studies, 1988. 173–85. Emecheta talks about her background and her writing. Discusses her ambiguous attitude toward Western feminism, to sex, and to polygamy. Concludes that women bear some of the guilt for their marginalization but also stresses the strength of women.

Selected Critical Readings

Buchi Emecheta's writing has inspired numerous but similar articles but, as yet, no full-length study. Criticism is very polemical, divided between critical African male writers and admiring African and Western women. The area most hotly debated is Emecheta's male characters, whom the African male critics see as unjust representations.

Brown, Lloyd W. "Buchi Emecheta." *Women Writers in Black Africa*. Westport: Greenwood Press, 1981. 35–60. Discusses the first four novels and is critical of the acceptance of Eurocentric, middle-class standards in *In the Ditch* and *Second-Class Citizen*. Accuses these novels of ideological fuzziness and finds the negative view of African men exaggerated. Sees a steady improvement in the writing of *The Bride Price* and *The Slave Girl*, which are viewed as sophisticated protest novels, discussing both outer social and inner psychological forms of oppression.

Frank, Katherine. "The Death of the Slave Girl: African Womanhood in the Novels of Buchi Emecheta." *World Literature Written in English* 21 (1982): 476–97. Deals with the first five novels and praises them for their historical and social breadth as well as for their unique portrayals of African women. Describes Emecheta as a feminist and sees her heroines as caught between accepting their Africanness and remaining oppressed, or becoming liberated and renouncing their Africanness. Sees *The Slave Girl* as the focal point of her *oeuvre* because of the many possible ramifications of the slave status. Discusses *The Bride Price* as a contrast to male writers' celebration of traditional African life and, for African literature, its unusual theme of romantic love. The main theme in *Joys of Motherhood* is seen to be the clash between traditional and Western values; the downgrading of motherhood is regarded as heresy.

Palmer, Eustace. "The Feminine Point of View: Buchi Emecheta's *The Joys of Motherhood*." *African Literature Today* No. 13 (1983): 38–55. Discusses *Joys of Motherhood* as a female answer to the social order and happiness in Achebe's novels and concentrates on the discussion of polygamy, where he finds Emecheta unfair. He also finds that her view of African men is exaggerated to the point of unreality. Criticizes her for bias and unashamed presentation of the woman's point of view. Discusses Nnu Ego as a flawed character, wanting modern ways but not having the strength to see them through. Sees Adaku as a forerunner of women's liberation. Concludes that the book is controversial and cannot stand up to sociological scrutiny, but has artistry.

Petersen, Kirsten Holst. "Unpopular Opinions: Some African Women Writers." *Kunapipi* 7.2-3. (1985): 107–20. Starts with a brief discussion of stereotypes of the ideal woman in male writing. Continues with discussion of four African women writers in terms of their attitudes toward feminism (the biological and marital aspects of women's lives and their economic status) and cultural nationalism. Compares Emecheta with other writers, especially Flora Nwapa.

Taiwo, Olade. *Female Novelists in Modern Africa*. London: Heinemann, 1984. Taiwo is slightly uncomfortable with the notion of female writers, finds that they concentrate too much on women and would prefer them to uphold some of the traditions they attack (polygamy, for example). Ama Ata Aidoo's comment on Taiwo's attitude is that "he virtually treats those African women writers whose novels he discusses as though they were his co-wives to whom he dishes out his whimsical favours."

Solberg, Rolf. "The Woman of Black Africa, Buchi Emecheta: The Woman's Voice in the New Nigerian Novel." *English Studies* 64 (1983): 247–61. Discusses briefly the changing role of women in Africa. Includes an analysis of Emecheta's first five novels but concentrates on the images of women in the novels set in Africa. Finds Emecheta's attitude to tradition and feminism ambiguous but her denunciation of male chauvinism clear.

Umeh, Marie Linton. "Reintegration with the Lost Self: A Study of Buchi Emecheta's *Double Yoke.*" *Ngambika: Studies of Women in African Literature.* Trenton: Africa World Press, 1986. 173–80. Describes the novel as a love story with tragic implications. Endorses Emecheta's view of male double standards and finds that the novel captures the core of female discrimination but states Nko's use of sex for her advancement is out of character. Discusses the novel in feminist terms and finds that it shows that gender is a learned quality. Finds the ending unconvincing, too modern to be realistic.

Interviews

With James Adeola. *In Their Own Voices: African Women Writers Talk.* Portsmouth, NH: Heinemann, 1990. 35–45.

With Kirsten Holst Petersen. *African Voices. Interviews with Thirteen African Writers.* Coventry: Dangaroo Press, 1989. 16–20.

—KIRSTEN HOLST PETERSEN

Margaret Laurence

When Margaret Laurence died on 5 January 1987, she had published sixteen books, along with many poems, addressees, and articles in journals, magazines, and newspapers.

Jean Margaret was born in Neepawa, Canada, 18 July 1926, to Robert Wemyss, an attorney, and Verna, a pianist and music teacher. After her mother died when she was four, her mother's sister, a teacher of English, came to care for Margaret and eventually became her stepmother. With her, Margaret Laurence's literary career had its beginnings for they read many books and talked about literature, especially about Canadian literature long before it was a subject taught in Canadian universities and schools.

A line in one of her college poems sums up Laurence's perception of "A world which gave me my own lifework to do." After graduating with a B.A. in English in 1947, she worked for *The Winnipeg Citizen*. Her writing career flowered after her marriage in 1948 to Jack Laurence. Time spent in Somalia and Ghana with her engineer husband inspired both fiction and criticism. Her translations and commentary on Somali oral literature, her fiction with an African setting, and her criticism of literature in English by Nigerians were well received at the time of their publication and are still highly regarded. While they were in Africa, they had two children.

Returning to Canada in 1957, Laurence started using her native country as a setting in the work known as the Manawaka novels. Laurence lived in England for several years after she separated from her husband. Much of the Canadian fiction was written in England, from which she returned in 1969 to become Writer-in Residence at Massey Graduate College, University of Toronto, and at two other Ontario universities.

From 1981-83, she was Chancellor of Trent University, Peterborough, Ontario. Interim chairman during the founding of the Writers' Union of Canada, she received eleven honorary degrees between 1970-1981 and refused many others. She was also active in public life, especially speaking out on nuclear disarmament and censorship. Laurence was presented with the Governor-General's Award in 1967 and again in 1975. In 1971, she received the highest award available to a Canadian citizen when she was made a Companion of the Order of Canada.

THE CREATION OF WOMEN PROTAGONISTS

Margaret Laurence is regarded as a writer of enormous stature, who came out of the Canadian west at a time when a female prairie author was hardly recognized. Ironically, though, the catalyst for her literary career was her experience in the

African nations of Somalia and Ghana. While her engineer husband built projects in the desert, she set out to learn about the Somalis' values, language, ways, and culture; from this interest came her first book, *A Tree for Poverty*, a collection of Somali oral literature in translation with commentary, published in 1954 by the Somali Government. Laurence was never able to write fiction in Somalia, though, because she did not feel able to get "within" the people. She realized early on that novelists require an eye for detail and imaginative sympathy to feel their way into the character; this was still her concern many years later, which she expresses in her memoir.

While living in Ghana, she wrote the first of her six novels, *This Side Jordan*, set in Ghana. Once back in Canada, however, she gained a new perspective and rewrote the book. Told through a straightforward third-person narration, the novel alternates chapters to convey the differences between the African traditional view and the British European imperialist point of view. The central character, Nathaniel Amegbe, teaches African history while inwardly rejecting his Ashanti drummer-father's past. Torn between his Christian training and his traditional wife and despised by whites, he succumbs to bribes of expensive gifts from pupils he recommends to work for a European firm; and he simply endures his humiliation and disgrace. He is set in opposition to the British imperialist Johnnie Kestoe, one of those colonial misfits Laurence sees as doubly alienated because they get along neither in their home country nor in Africa. Africans have always commented on "a certain authenticity" in the novel's African chapters, as they did about the African stories in *The To-morrow-Tamer*. The European chapters also stand up well, though Laurence hardly sympathized with the colonial view.

Africa forced Laurence to think of exile, alienation, conflict of cultures, communication, self-knowledge, freedom and survival, the plight of women, and of the gaining and maintaining of "an independence which was both political and inner." While in Africa, then back in Canada, Laurence examined her early life and realized that she knew her own background best and could not escape it; moreover, she discovered the resources to express the emotional riches of the Canadian prairies to the world. She thought that novelists must be politically and socially engaged, not with abstractions but with particulars of place, speech, and ideas; and she believed that writers must come to terms with their roots and ancestors.

Laurence also realized that Africa and Canada shared the heritage of colonialism. Her African stories and novel had grown out of the conflicts arising when one country colonizes and dominates the other, so that people assessed their lives by means of imperial standards imposed from without. The colonialism in Canada was much less overt, yet, as she pointed out: "Correctness and validity and excellence were still largely derived from external and imposed values, . . . from two other cultures' definitions of us" ("Ivory Tower or Grassroots" 22-23). Most importantly, though, colonialism and the surge of political independence that she witnessed during her years in Africa led Laurence to her central theme concerning the role of women. For to her another kind of colonialism was embedded within the submissiveness and powerlessness of women: their tendency to accept male definitions, to be self-deprecating and uncertain, and "to rage inwardly" ("Ivory Tower or Grassroots" 24).

Further, Laurence felt that women portrayed in literature were rarely like women as they are in their inner and outer reality, rarely like the woman she considered herself to be. So she chose to portray decolonized women interacting honestly with their families, neighbors, and friends; they would remember and tell about their childhood, grandparents, parents, siblings, school, puberty, and boyfriends. She knew she wanted to portray women as they are in life: yearning to care for someone, to be loved and to love in return; knowing who they are before, in, outside, or after marriage. So Laurence explored the plight of women in twentieth-century Canada by writing a fictional history of their condition through four generations: from Hagar to Morag's daughter, Pique. Without consciously setting out to be one, Laurence is a feminist writer. Even though never faulted for portraying men authentically, after a few early stories, Laurence chose women for her protagonists.

In her first novel set in Canada, *The Stone Angel*, Laurence created Hagar who begins the line of her Canadian women protagonists. Considering that Laurence was only thirty-five when she started *The Stone Angel*, her depiction of ninety-year-old Hagar Currie Shipley is all the more remarkable. Laurence has said that she was convinced of the authenticity of Hagar's voice because she felt she knew Hagar, who had come from her grandparents' generation. Further, she was writing about people from her own background, whose idiom she knew, whose lives were familiar to her, and whose world view she understood. To convey Hagar's unvoiced thoughts and her rage against her fate, Laurence chose the first-person narrative to allow this rigid character, living largely in her past, to recall episodes from her life and the stories told her, and at the same time to reveal more about herself than she intended.

Years later, speaking of *The Stone Angel*, in her memoir, *Dance on the Earth*, Laurence recalls:

> That book meant an enormous amount to me. It was the novel into which I had invested my life, my heart, and my spirit. It was the novel that had finally made me feel it was necessary to leave my marriage. I never expected the novel to justify what I had done. . . . Twenty-two years later, as I write this in 1986, the old lady is still helping me. I'm told that it has in fact sold more copies in the New Canadian Library edition than any other of their titles. It is in print in paperback editions in Canada, the States, and England. It has been translated into French, Norwegian, and Swedish, and is being translated into Danish, Dutch, and Italian. It has been used in geriatrics courses in Canadian hospitals to teach young nurses about the reality of old people. I must have received, over the years, thousands of letters from readers and from students, letters that have been a mainstay of my life. (165–66)

Laurence also notes that the international reviews of *The Stone Angel* were in sharp contrast as they emphasized different aspects of the central character:

> When the book came out, I recall one English reviewer commenting, "This is the most telling argument for euthanasia I have ever

read," which amused me greatly. It was interesting that the novel was reviewed in England as a study of an old person and in America as the story of a strong pioneer woman—but in Canada, Hagar was, and still is, seen as everybody's grandmother or great-grandmother. (166)

Laurence's next two novels are *A Jest of God* and *The Fire-Dwellers*. The interrelationships between these books are found in symbolic and structural ties, such as titles, epigraphs, nursery rhymes, names, and settings. Schoolteacher spinster Rachel Cameron in *A Jest of God* has no children except her pupils to keep her mind drawn to the present. Living above a funeral home with her mother, Rachel suffers from a stifling inner vacillation and anger that drives the voices of her desires, duties, conscience, responses, and imaginings. Her greatest horror is that she might speak out spontaneously. She finds some comfort in the sensual release she experiences in a short affair with Nick Kazlik, but she is caught in her ancestral connections, for the Scots half of Manawaka does not have much to do with the Ukrainian half. She then suffers through what seems her "pregnancy," which is actually a benign tumor.

The narrower range of Rachel's view of life is best expressed in the first person and present tense but without flashbacks. Laurence explains that the first person conveyed Rachel's pain and her determined efforts to survive, just as her fantasies were necessary to show her yearnings for love. The outer narrative is from Rachel's point of view; the inner monologues represent different voices: her conscience, her desires, her fantasies, her inner commentary, her thoughts, some of her memories, and her judgments. The story of this inward-looking woman records a tortuous struggle to free herself.

Stacey in *The Fire-Dwellers* is a high-school drop-out married to the colorless and ordinary "Mac" MacAindra. Living in a suburb of Vancouver, Stacey is not even aware of a male-oriented chauvinistic society. She never considers getting a job and having someone else care for her four children or her house, for her identity she finds only in relation to the home and the men around her—her husband, his bosses, her father-in-law and his friends. She does wonder what life holds when she fails to communicate with her husband, neighbors, and children, particularly the teenage daughter and the silent two-year-old. At one point, she goes to the seashore and there engages in an affair with Luke Venturi, who becomes a kind of catalyst to her awakening as she talks out her ideas, feelings, and life story. After their affair, Stacey is more aware and begins to show concern over her children, the future they will have, and her husband's presence. Further, Stacey casts aside the self-reproach left over from her Presbyterian upbringing, and affirms love and hope in her own life. As woman-mother-wife-daughter-friend-lover-neighbor, she finds that she now wants a future for herself and her family. As well as Stacey's discovery that she has no real life of her own after many years of marriage, other interlocking themes emerge, including relationships between generations and the sense of anguish and fear Stacey faces, as Laurence puts it, "in bringing up her kids in a world on fire" in a process of life that is "irreversible" ("Gadgetry" 87).

The narrative method in *The Fire-Dwellers* is the most complex of that in any of the novels so far, described as "a fast-shuttering, multiscreen camera and soundtrack technique . . . 'orchestrating' the whirling, kaleidoscopic facets of Stacey's mind and imagination" (Thomas 124). Four levels of consciousness are set in different printed styles to show that the forward-moving narration is frequently in contrast with Stacey's inner commentary, and to point up that what she is thinking differs from what she is saying. The memories are set to one side of the page in an attempt to clarify that they are flashing in and out of her mind while she is doing other things; the dreams and fantasies are identified by italics. Characters' speeches are not enclosed in quotation marks to add to the sense of everything happening at once within the flow of talk and events, as in life; rather than indicators or names, the voice indicates who is speaking. Altogether, each level of consciousness helps to convey the jagged quality of Stacey's life. Laurence's "voices and pictures" succeed, for each has its shape on the page, thereby making, as Laurence has noted, the descriptions "sharp and instantaneous as possible, and always brief" as "life is perceived, in short sharp visual images which leap away from us even as we look at them" ("Gadgetry" 87).

In the fourth novel, *A Bird in the House*, all eight stories are set in Manawaka, during the mid-thirties to the mid-forties when the central character Vanessa left to go to the university in Winnipeg. The stories take place in two homes—the houses of Grandmother McLeod and of Grandfather and Grandmother Connor. Vanessa, as all those around her, is trapped within the walls of family pride and social convention, symbolized by the grandparents' houses. Although *A Bird in the House* comprises eight separate stories, when read together, they give the effect of a novel. Bruce Stoval has noted that the stories carry a "concentrated intensity" and "recapitulate each other and resonate among themselves, telling in the end a single, developing tale" (90). Each story has the same point of view and narrative voice, showing Vanessa in a relationship with another character and carrying her through a series of events until she reaches the final moment of recognition.

The last story, "Jericho's Brick Battlements," brings together most of the characters in the rest of the narrative pieces. Enclosing the others with the first story, the two end stories demonstrate a progression of which the fourth, "A Bird in the House," is pivotal, for in it Vanessa is determined to struggle against her lack of freedom. When she sits in her grandfather's car she remembers how she drove down the streets with him when she was four and how she wrote stories in the car, then later in the loft. Suddenly the twenty-two-year-old Vanessa realizes how much the car must have meant to her grandfather who had walked from Winnipeg to Manawaka with hardly a cent in his pockets, and she can now sympathize with the man whom she had once disliked. After this story Laurence expands the breadth of time covered so that the adult forty-year-old Vanessa with two children looks back over thirty-six years since she rode with her grandfather. By this point, Vanessa has set her house in order and understands her life.

All of the Manawaka novels are memoirs of female protagonists, recalling their childhood, teen years, family lives, other relationships; for Laurence believed that "Fiction becomes a matter of the individual characters moving within a history which includes past, present, and future" ("Ivory Tower or Grassroots" 17). Each book develops the themes of alienation, death, and survival, the struggle of decent, recognizable people groping for understanding of themselves and others, the pain of lost innocence, and finally a gaining of wisdom that can lead to an acceptance of a unique, often humble place in the world.

Laurence's final novel, *The Diviners*, is a *Künstlerroman* that draws upon the author's own experiences, even though all of her work depends on autobiographical material. The protagonist as writer is introduced in *A Bird in the House* but more fully developed in *The Diviners*, whose central character Morag, in her forties, is writing her fifth novel in a cabin by the river where her neighbors are water diviners. Carrying several familiar themes—overcoming alienation, affirming life, accepting death, the novel permits Morag to achieve a fuller understanding than that gained by the earlier women. In *The Diviners*, too, all of Laurence's previous work comes together: uniting characters, incidents, symbols, and themes; combining most of the earlier narrative techniques; and adding new ones to display multi-levels of consciousness, as well as the outer reality and the imagined world, which is achieved in part through using the novels Morag writes and discusses.

By making Morag an orphan at an early age, Laurence presents a character free from a family past, from those customs and values she would have learned. Instead her past has been created for her by her foster father Christie, who tells her tales of the Highland Scots who came to Manitoba led by Piper Gunn. As she learned more history she sifted historical fact from imaginative details while still enjoying Christie's tales of Piper Gunn, his experiences in the First World War, and those he told of Manawaka residents from "reading the garbage." Morag adds to all these tales of Scots and Manawakans the mythology of the Metis revealed to her by Jules "Skinner" Tonnerre who lives nearby. As she grew older, she became more adept at separating myth from historical reality in the two sets of tales about the early settlement of Scots and Metis.

After Morag completes college, she marries Brooke Skelton from a family of British imperialists—thus becoming colonized both as a Canadian and as a woman. Eventually she leaves her English professor husband and the colonialism of marriage and settles along a river in Ontario to write, drawing from the rich history she had gained from Christie's tales of the Scots, Jules' tales of the Metis, and her own memories of Manawaka. Secure in her designated role as writer, mother, and neighbor, she had come a long way from her Manawaka life on the wrong side of the tracks.

Laurence's last book, *Dance on the Earth, A Memoir*, published posthumously, provides insights into a life entwined with art, reveals her feelings about her vocation as a writer, shows concern with the future of her children, and reaffirms her humanity. She structured the memoir around the most influential women in her life, her mothers—her biological mother who died when she was four, her aunt who became her loving stepmother and intellectual mentor, and her novelist mother-in-law who was so supportive of her writing. Edited by her daughter, the book also includes material on the issues that greatly concerned Laurence: nuclear disarmament, pollution of the environment, and pro-choice abortion legislation. Another of Laurence's basic ideas that pervades the book is that women have always done more than their society conditions them to do. And an awareness of that irony by women constitutes Laurence's hope for the future.

WORKS CITED

Laurence, Margaret. *Dance on the Earth, A Memoir.* Toronto: McClelland & Stewart, 1989.
———. "Gadgetry or Growing: Form and Voice in the Novel." *A Place to Stand On: Essays by and About Margaret Laurence.* Edmonton: NeWest Press, 1983. 80–92.
———. "Ivory Tower or Grassroots." *A Political Art: Essays in Honour of George Woodcock.* Vancouver: U of British Columbia, 1978. 15–25.
Stoval, Bruce. "Coherence in *A Bird in the House.*" *Margaret Laurence, Essays.* Brandon: U of Brandon P, 1990. 89–121.
Thomas, Clara. *The Manawaka World of Margaret Laurence.* Toronto: McClelland & Stewart, 1976.

MARGARET LAURENCE'S PUBLISHED WORK

Novels

This Side Jordan, 1960
The Stone Angel, 1964
A Jest of God, 1966
The Fire-Dwellers, 1969
A Bird in the House, 1970
The Diviners, 1974

Short Story Collection

The Tomorrow-Tamer, 1963

Juvenilia and Fantasy

Jason's Quest, 1970
The Olden Days Coat, 1979
Six Darn Cows, 1979
The Christmas Birthday Story, 1982

Memoir

Dance on the Earth, A Memoir, 1989

Criticism and Essays

Long Drums and Cannons: Nigerian Novelists and Dramatists, 1952-1966, 1968
Heart of a Stranger, 1976

Travel

The Prophet's Camel-Bell, 1964

Anthology

A Tree for Poverty, Somali Poetry and Prose, 1954

SELECTED CRITICAL READINGS

Margaret Laurence and her writings continue to be the subject of many articles, dissertations, and books in Canada and other countries. Future studies could take the comparative approach and examine the theme of aging and death, the concern with women's perception, and the use of oral and imaging techniques as well as literary myths.

Blaikie, John, editor. *Margaret Laurence, Essays*. Brandon: U of Brandon P, 1990. Includes papers by North American, Japanese, and European participants at the conference "Margaret Laurence: Her Life and Works," 1988. Offers international perspectives, including problems of translation.

Bowen, Deborah. "In Camera: The Developed Photographs of Margaret Laurence and Alice Munro." *Studies in Canadian Literature* 13 (1988): 20–33. Compares Laurence's use of photographic techniques with that of Alice Munro.

Brady, Elizabeth, and Clara Thomas, editors. *Canadian Women's Studies* 8.3 (1987). Special Laurence issue, titled "Margaret Laurence: A Celebration." Contributions are critical, creative, and memorative in nature, including work by Timothy Findley, Rudy Wiebe, and Margaret Atwood.

Buss, Helen M. "Margaret Laurence's Dark Lovers: Sexual Metaphor, and The Movement Toward Individualization, Heriogamy and Mythic Narrative in Four Manawaka Books." *Atlantis* 11 (1986): 97–107. Presents a thorough discussion of the way Laurence uses sexual metaphor.

———. *Mother and Daughter Relationships in the Manawaka Works of Margaret Laurence*. ELS Monograph Series. Victoria, B.C.: U of Victoria, 1985. Compelling study of the Demeter and Kore myth as prototype for the mother archetype used in complex and wide-ranging ways in the novels.

Coger, Greta. "Margaret Laurence's Manawaka: A Canadian Yoknapatawpha." *Crosscurrent* 1 (1986): 22–36. (Reprinted in Nicolson, *Critical Approaches to the Fiction of Margaret Laurence*) Compares Laurence's world with that created by Faulkner in his novels.

Gunnars, Kristjana. *Crossing the River: Essays in Honour of Margaret Laurence*. Winnipeg: Turnstone, 1988. Shows international interest in West Germany and Norway; discusses Laurence's view of Christianity, balance between her humanism and feminism. Essays take varied approaches: autobiographical, textual, feminist, and semantic.

Holland, Patrick. "Water and Clay: Maurice Shadbolt's *A Touch of Clay* and Margaret Laurence's *The Diviners*." *World Literature Written in English* 21 (1982): 268–74. Discusses the treatment of artist figures, writer and potter, in the two works.

Kertzer, J.M. *Margaret Laurence and Her Works*. Toronto: ECW Press, 1987. Presents biographical background and places Laurence in the Canadian literary tradition; reviews criticism; discusses fiction, especially the narrative voice so essential to the style and content of each female protagonist's story.

Morley, Patricia. *Margaret Laurence*. Boston: Twayne, 1981. Compares and integrates African and Canadian writings as a quest—a "psychic journey towards inner freedom and spiritual maturity"—contributing to an epic vision of tradition and development, native and foreign, family and stranger, and mother and daughter relationships.

Nicolson, Colin, editor. *Critical Approaches to the Fiction of Margaret Laurence*. London: Macmillan, 1989. Critics from Europe, United States, and Canada offer a wide range of approaches—historical, feminist, descriptive, and thematic—to stress the significance of Laurence's work.

Schofield, Mary Ann. "Culinary Revelations: Self-Exploration and Food in Margaret Laurence's *The Stone Angel.*" *Literary Gastronomy.* Amsterdam: Rodopi, 1988: 85–92. Discusses Hagar's attitude toward food and the way food is used to explore her character.

Sorfleet, John R., editor. *Journal of Canadian Fiction* No. 27 (1980). Special issue titled "The Works of Margaret Laurence." Includes four Laurence stories and two of her commentaries, along with discussions of continuity between African and Canadian writings and common themes in the Manawaka novels.

Thieme, John. "Acknowledging Myths: The Image of Europe in Margaret Laurence's *The Diviners* and Jack Hodgins's *The Invention of the World.*" *Commonwealth Essays and Studies* 10 (1987): 15-21. Explores the way the two writers perceive and treat Europe.

Thomas, Clara. *The Manawaka World of Margaret Laurence.* Toronto: McLelland & Stewart, 1976. Incorporates earlier book on Laurence. Thomas is Laurence's official biographer and provides excellent background details on the writing as well as a perceptive discussion of the work.

————. "The Short Stories of Margaret Laurence." *World Literature Written in English* 2 (1972): 25-33. Sees the African stories as told from the point of view of the ironist who grasps the contradictions of both cultures; sees Vanessa's stories in *A Bird in the House* as depicting an outsider observing the world around her, noting also that these stories portray vividly the Canadian depression and drought of the 1930s.

Verduyn, Christl, editor. *Margaret Laurence: An Appreciation.* Peterborough, Ontario: Broadview Press, 1988. Includes articles taking various critical approaches, overviews of the writing, updated biography and bibliography.

Woodcock, George, editor. *A Place to Stand on; Essays by and About Margaret Laurence. Western Canadian Literary Documents.* Vol. 4. Edmonton: NeWest Press, 1983. Includes several of Laurence's speeches and critical analyses, along with interviews. Essays focus on topics such as craftsmanship, the "African apprenticeship," and the Manawaka novels.

York, Lorraine M. *"The Other Side of Dailiness": Photography in the Works of Alice Munro, Timothy Findley, Michael Ondaatje and Margaret Laurence.* Toronto: ECW Press, 1988. Relates Barthes, Eco, and Sontag to the writer using photographic metaphors and structures to portray consciousness, past and present.

— GRETA McCORMICK COGER

Alice Munro

Alice Munro's reputation has grown considerably since 1968 when the Toronto *Globe & Mail* announced that a "shy housewife" had won the Governor-General's Award for her first book, *Dance of the Happy Shades*, and another newspaper headline proclaimed that a "Mother of Three" had received Canada's highest literary prize. Since then she has won this prize twice more and has acquired an international readership and critical acclaim from those who recognize that her portrait of the domestic or local is crucial to what is, nevertheless, a larger fiction.

Munro was born in Wingham, Ontario, Canada, 10 July 1931, the daughter of Robert and Ann Laidlaw. Of her childhood she has said, "We didn't live in town and we didn't live in the country. We lived in this kind of little ghetto where all the bootleggers and prostitutes and hangers-on lived. Those were the people I knew. It was a community of outcasts" (Twigg 18). She began writing intensely romantic stories at the age of fifteen but kept these to herself. In 1949 she left Wingham for the University of Western Ontario in London, where she was an English major for two years. She published three stories in the university literary magazine, but it was not until after her 1951 marriage to James Munro and their subsequent move to Vancouver that she began to write fiction based upon her home region. Her influences then and through subsequent years, as she has indicated, were Katherine Mansfield, James Agee, Edna O'Brien, but most of all writers of the American South, particularly Eudora Welty and Flannery O'Connor.

In Vancouver she lived a split existence that she herself defined as the "life of appearances" and "the real and absolutely solitary life [of writing]" (Ross 296). After twelve years, she and her husband moved to Victoria where they started a successful bookstore. Meanwhile Munro's short stories had appeared in various popular magazines and literary journals in Canada and the U.S. between 1953 and 1968. Eleven of the fifteen stories in her first book were previously published, and this record has continued, as nearly all of the stories in her last two collections were published beforehand, ten alone in *The New Yorker.*

In 1972, after her marriage broke up, Munro returned, with two of her three daughters, to London, Ontario, and in 1974–75 to her alma mater where she became writer-in-residence. Since 1976 she has been married to Gerald Fremlin, a cartographer, and has lived in Clinton, Ontario, not far from Wingham. While never a recluse, she has become a somewhat reluctant public figure as a reader of her work and as a spokesperson on such issues as literary censorship especially when *Lives of Girls and Women* was banned by an Ontario county schoolboard because of its explicit sexual passages.

THE GATE IN HER HEAD

Alice Munro has said, "I think that the kind of writing I do is almost anachronistic, because it's so rooted in one place" (Gibson 248). Although there are exceptions, that place is essentially southwestern Ontario, in towns with fictional names such as Jubilee, Hanratty, Dalgleish, and Logan. Munro writes of small communities and their people, of social territory she calls "absolutely Gothic" and about which she emphasizes, "You can't get it all down" (Gibson 248). From the beginning of her career she has not been concerned with merely describing places, people, and incidents but with the creation of probing, self-conscious, female narrative voices that treat the telling of any story as significant as the tangible details of the story itself. Such voices speak from the point of view of third-person omniscience as well as through limited, first-person utterance; thus Munro consistently emphasizes that the relationship between her own stories and those of her protagonists is one of process as the perceiving consciousness shapes and defines the world. She is especially concerned with the articulation of paradox—those oppositions within character and event that complicate and enrich existence because they must be lived with rather than resolved. The ordinary world in Munro's stories is replete with contradictions, with people and circumstances that refuse to be contained within safe and predictable patterns of voice and experience. Munro's narrators learn to include in their visions both the ridiculous and the sublime, sudden shifts in familiar ways of doing and seeing, life that is, according to one protagonist, "dull, simple, amazing and unfathomable—deep caves paved with kitchen linoleum."

In *Dance of the Happy Shades*, two stories in particular reveal the enlarging of a young girl's perceptions of her family. In "Walker Brothers Cowboy," which Munro has referred to as "personal material cast in the form of a recollection of childhood," a girl and her younger brother are taken by their salesman father to the farmhouse of his former lover. Although she is too young to comprehend the sexual tension between her father and this woman, the girl knows that the world is a different place because she sees him drink whiskey for the first time and refuse to dance with the woman for no apparent reason. Although this story is told in the present tense, seemingly as events unfold, from the beginning the tone and substance of the girl's language and perception indicate that it is a purposely limited recollection on the part of her older self. Thus the storytelling is consistently foregrounded, although on one level the girl's response to what is going on around her is made to seem spontaneous and even naive. In the end she views her father's "kindly, ordinary, and familiar" life as "something [she] will never know," replete "with all kinds of weathers, and distances you cannot imagine."

In "Images," the narrator looks back at an incident in her childhood when she accompanies her father on the checking of his traplines and meets someone he knows from a threatening, unpredictable part of the adult world. Many adults would call Old Joe Phippen a madman, but the narrator recalls being wary of him while recognizing his hovel in a field "as the sort of place I would like to live in myself." As in "Walker Brothers Cowboy," there is a final epiphany of awareness that breaks down polarities and accepts paradox as a foundation for present and future vision.

However, like so many of Munro's protagonists, this girl cannot necessarily communicate such awareness to others.

In this first collection of stories, Munro's concern with what one critic has perceptively described as "contextual revelations of women's [girls'] bodies, ego boundaries and social status" (Irvine 110) is also foregrounded. The narrator of "Boys and Girls" remembers how her mother and father responded to her in gender-specific ways. From her mother she gained a sense of her past but could not depend upon her for support as her mother acceded to a patriarchal view of role-playing in the family. She gradually came to realize that a *girl* was not only what she was in terms of her father's assumptions, but what she "had to become." Told to close a farm gate to prevent a mare, bound for slaughter, from escaping, she chose to open it as wide as she could. When this was discovered, she cried, and her father responded by announcing, "Never mind. . . . She's only a girl." However, while male power dominates the childhood situation, the woman telling the story, shaping it in something other than her father's image, has a power of her own, a voice that, by speaking, releases itself to overcome rather than extend the gap between past and present.

In "Red Dress, 1946" Munro looks closely at the shaping of female consciousness by those social forces that also shape other members of the family. The narrator of this story recalls her early high school days when life's "urgency and brightness" were brought about by "the tension and excitement of sexual competition." She reads magazine articles that tell her to "be gay" and let her eyes sparkle so that boys will ask her to dance, while her mother contributes to such role-playing by tailoring her own inadequate memories of courtship and hopes for her daughter's patterned future into a red velvet dress. Spurned at a school dance, the narrator meets an older girl, Mary Fortune, who announces that she is "not boy-crazy," a state of mind that, much to the narrator's surprise, contains both energy and self-respect. Munro's women learn, throughout her fiction, that it is possible, indeed necessary at times, to live without men, or, at the very least, not to depend on one man to fulfill their physical, emotional, and intellectual needs. Mary offers the narrator genuine female companionship without male chains. However, a boy does intervene, claiming the narrator for a dance and making her one of the "chosen," thus bringing her "from Mary Fortune's territory into the ordinary world." The demand of this ordinary patriarchal world that girls/women have a "mysterious and oppressive obligation to be happy" is resisted by an increasing number of Munro females in later fiction.

The story where Munro "first tackled personal material" is "The Peace of Utrecht," written in 1959. Munro has said that this tale is "the most important" (Struthers 21) in *Dance of the Happy Shades*, and it is vitally so because it reveals for the first time the female, first-person narrator who, through looking back at her earlier experiences, attempts to come to some terms with her present life. This is also the first Munro story to be set in Jubilee, the small town home of Del Jordan, the protagonist of a groundbreaking novel that is one of the most significant works in Canadian literature.

This novel, *Lives of Girls and Women*, is a *Bildungsroman*, but rather than being one unbroken tale of Del Jordan's growth from childhood through adolescence, it is presented in the form of eight connected stories, each focusing on a particularly important set of experiences in her young life. These stories are related in the past tense by an older Del who, it becomes clear, has written the book we are reading. Of course, Munro has written Del's novel, but that fact only underlines Del's creative accomplishment. When asked in an interview whether the book was autobiographical, Munro replied,

> . . . in incident—no . . . in emotion—completely. I suppose it could be called an autobiographical novel . . . most of the incidents are changed versions of real incidents. Some are completely invented, but the emotional reality, the girl's feeling for her mother, for men, for life is all . . . solidly autobiographical. (Metcalf 58)

Del shapes her recollections of the past very much according to her relationships with her parents, especially her mother; with other adults who are not always family members; and with those girls and boys she knew in her Jubilee adolescence. In so doing, she tells the story of herself as a girl who does not have to become a woman according to male expectations, despite the strong patriarchal filtering of her perceptions. The older Del articulates the paradoxes at the heart of female-male ways of being in the world that her younger self could only sense. This younger self seeks out, in particular, the power of the male grotesque that does not have to explain itself as it imposes itself willy-nilly on the lives of girls and women. With her Uncle Benny (really just a friend of her father), oppositions of character and event seem to be essentially benign. However, while as a young girl, Del can remain at a reasonably safe distance from Benny, the final expansion of her vision includes the narrowing of a gap based on age and education, but most of all on gender difference as perceived by social conditioning: "So lying alongside our world was Uncle Benny's world like a troubling, distorted reflection, the same but never at all the same. . . . gigantic and unpredictable . . . [where] anything might happen. . . . It was his triumph, that he couldn't know about, to make us see."

Years later, as a teenager fascinated by sex, Del mistakenly feels that the gender gap can be bridged through knowledge of the "magical, bestial act." When she is approached by Mr. Chamberlain for sexual favors, she acquiesces, allowing the domination of parts of her body so that the "world of decent [female] appearances" in which she feels trapped can be altered. However, it is not only, or even, her body that Mr. Chamberlain wants, but her mind, as he masturbates before her. Although Del is able to objectify this man, to see "all the stubborn puzzle and dark turns" of his male force and threat, and to reject his control, she does not yet reject the aggressive and ego-centered way in which he behaves. His apparent power to do what he wants is something she is still determined to have.

There are different forces at work around and within Del that suggest alternatives to such power. Trying to get "revelation" from her mother, she views her repeated, failed attempts to meet the male world head on, her desperate hurling of encyclopediac facts against patriarchal bastions combined with the romantic gushings of her *nom de plume*, "Princess Ida." Yet her mother is also a storyteller who teaches her daughter the glory and wonder of being "absurd and unassailable" as she shapes for her in language glimpses of a female life.

Against the "straight lines" of her mother's movement is the "nimble malice" of her Aunts Elspeth and Grace, who, though they respect the work of their brother Craig, also laugh at it. The paradox here is that their opposition must be essentially silent before Craig's unquestioning assumption that he must be cared for so that he can get on with his rational discourse, a listing of everything in the history of Wawanash County. There is also Miss Farris, a spinster-teacher who organizes the yearly operettas at Del's public school. However much Del and her friend Naomi want to categorize Miss Farris as frustrated and flirtatious, they have to admit that "Whatever she was after . . . could hardly even be men." Indeed, Del recognizes that she is moved by what Miss Farris conjures up each year through the use of costumes, makeup, and her own intensity, precisely because she brings young females and males together in role-playing that has not the supposed truth and necessity of divisive roles acted out in daily life. If, several years later, Miss Farris's death by drowning in the Wawanash River seems to the town to be an act of suicide or else murder by a man, it is taken by Del as something that could not be contained in Uncle Craig's logical discourse: "a mystery, presented without explanation . . . in all insolence. . . . No revelation here." The revelation is elsewhere, in Miss Farris's triumphant transcendence of what seems to be, on the surface, mere surrender to her fate: "She sent those operettas up like bubbles, shaped with quivering, exhausting effort, then almost casually set free, to fade and fade, but hold trapped forever our transformed childish selves, her undefeated, unrequited love."

Inevitably Del must grow older and enter into relationships with boys. She reads the assertion of a famous New York psychiatrist that when a boy and girl look together at the full moon the boy is thinking of the immensity of the universe and the girl that she must wash her hair. Del has difficulty in treating this concept entirely as male propaganda because she wants both to be loved by men and to think of the universe when she looks at the moon. To satisfy the former urge she goes with Naomi to a local dance hall where they are picked up by two older boys and taken back to a hotel room. What she senses there, through a liquor-induced haze, is the demand that she be normal by getting hold of a man and setting out on the road to marriage. She escapes but only to become involved with the one male in her school who can match or surpass her intellectually. Jerry Storey seeks to dominate her by viewing her reasoning powers and capacity for abstract thought as weak and by pretending to admire her "feminine" capabilities with language. When she and Jerry make an attempt to pull body into his closed circle of perception, there can only be a comedy of errors that must be left behind.

In her subsequent relationship with Garnet French, Del, insisting that "words were our enemies," surrenders to sex. But she does so self-consciously, giving herself over to Garnet's instincts, never to the same old set of assumptions that govern them. If she and Garnet, making love, are persons engaged in "an act of pure faith," able to discover "freedom in [equally shared] humility," sex has always been the means to an end for Garnet, and he inevitably attempts to "baptize" Del into his private church of conquest. She is amazed that he feels he has any power over her and fights for her life in the waters of that same Wawanash River where Miss Farris drowned. Del surfaces to embrace the paradox of having to deal with loss that promotes gain in life and is able to speak the world paradoxically from this point on "with absolute sincerity, absolute irony."

Finally in *Lives of Girls and Women* Munro emphasizes the creative, shaping voice of the older Del Jordan looking back at her days in Jubilee. The concern here is a play upon that unfortunate opposition between female and male that has been stressed throughout—the storyteller must not choose between what are called fictions and facts (labels easily seen as patriarchal), inscribing either entirely what Uncle Craig would call the "real" or what Del, while still in Jubilee, calls "true," the "black fable" in her head that transforms entirely the town and its people. During the time and in the place in which Del was growing up, the female *Bildungsroman* was a fable, completely separate from the supposed history of a young girl's existence. Years later, Del can write what is real and true and that which is, in its utterance, a bridging of the gender gap through assertion of female difference.

The major stories in *Something I've Been Meaning To Tell You* focus on the expression of the real and the true by their female narrators, but Munro's refusal to become a formula writer is shown in two stories in particular when the struggle of the woman to discover and nurture a self separate from that of the man is not always successful. The narrator of "Material" tells of her relationship with her ex-husband, Hugo, in whom she did not believe as a writer. Yet years later, when she reads a story of his in an anthology, she is "moved by magic" and must admit that the woman Hugo has fictionalized "had passed into Art." Her instinct is to praise him and to apologize for her underestimating his abilities, and her independence is compromised when she can only add, "It's not enough," meaning that the extraordinary combination of the real and the true in Hugo's story cannot replace or make up for the absence of such a combination in their previous relationship.

The self-portrait of the woman in "Tell Me Yes Or No" is ambiguous, but the complexities inherent in the acquisition and declaration of the female creative voice are clear. The narrator sleeps once with a man she had met years before, then they both return to their homes in different cities and strike up a correspondence. He is married, she is divorced, and there seems no chance of their ever being together on a permanent basis. The man seems satisfied with this rather light arrangement of long-distance love, but clearly the woman is involved in another kind of need—the link between her love for the man and her past means that there is a wholeness to her life, that it "did not altogether fall away in separate pieces, lost." Her identity seems to be entirely bound up in her fragile relationship by letters, and when the letters stop she is faced with a choice: either keep waiting and hoping for contact or attempt to construct an identity without the man. When she reads of his death in a newspaper report, the choice seems to be made for her. However, from the beginning of the story Munro foregrounds the ambiguities surrounding this "death."

The first words the narrator says are "I persistently imagine you dead." Thus, when in an attempt to put his ghost to rest she visits the city where the man has lived she may well be trying to deal with a living ghost. She is well aware of how women "deceive themselves and uselessly suffer" because of their dependence on men. She describes her meeting with the man's wife who gives her a bag of old love letters, but when she reads them they are from another lover. This meeting and these letters may or may not be real, but they are true for the narrator who must find a way of combining real and true and let go of the man. She creates a story in which her own voice cries freedom from the restrictive relationship for the first time and on her terms: "I invented you, as far as my purposes go. I invented loving you and I invented your death. I have my tricks and my trap doors, too. I don't understand their workings at the present moment, but . . . I won't speak against them."

Munro has admitted elsewhere that there are more than traces of the autobiographical in "Winter Wind" and "The Ottawa Valley," so the female voices speaking in them doubly emphasize the attempt to find a language equal to woman's place in the world. Such a language is found only in the articulation of its own failure, and, significantly, it speaks to the relationship of women with women. In "Winter Wind," the narrator tells her grandmother's story and then says that though there is no tangible proof for any of what she has said. In "The Ottawa Valley," the narrator has been trying to deal with the memory of her mother, "To mark her off, to describe, illumine, celebrate, to get rid of her; and it did not work. . . . Which means she has stuck to me as close as ever and refused to fall away." In both instances the female protagonists discover their being in a language that is not afraid to admit its limitations, that seeks in the end not to control but to release its subject matter.

Munro won her second Governor-General's Award for *Who Do You Think You Are?* Like *Lives of Girls and Women,* the text consists of interrelated stories about the same female protagonist, Rose. The story of Rose emerges very much as that of Del Jordan did—out of a focus on important experiences separated by both small and large periods of time that are themselves given little if any description. The setting is again small-town Ontario, Hanratty rather than Jubilee. However, Rose's adult life, especially as it has been influenced by her childhood and adolescence, is given much attention, and her story is told from a third-person, limited-omniscient point of view.

Munro's use of paradox is heightened in this book, especially as it relates to the ways in which different characters speak publicly and privately and to the familiar oppositions between female and male voices. In "Royal Beatings" Rose's father beats her because she has offended her stepmother, Flo, though it is clear that she and Flo are victims in female roles that cannot be rejected. In contrast, her father "is acting and he means it." Rose must therefore deal with male "treachery [on] the other side of dailiness." But paradox is multiple as she has already heard that quotidian father speak in the shed where he works alone: "'Macaroni, pepperoni, Botticelli, beans'. . . . The person who spoke these words and the person who spoke to her as her father were not the same." Rose herself joins in such clear and nonsensical utterance when she and her brother taunt Flo with a schoolyard chant. It is the initial innocence of words yielding the "tumble of reason . . . the spark and spit of craziness" that Rose cannot ever resist, even though she knows it will collide with her father's public role and result in her beating.

While her father's expansive language only spills forth in private, Flo's uncontained voice is communal in her storytelling. She delights in entertaining Rose with tales of herself and others that elevate the grotesque to the level of local myth and that usually end with one word that binds her to her listeners—"Imagine." Flo is the embodiment of Rose's father's belief that "Women's minds are different," but not in the limited, sexist way that he assumes. Her stories are rebellions against the ordinary, an altering of the usual surface order of things to reveal nosebleeds "whipping out of [people] like streamers" and illegitimate babies served up as lamb chops by the town butcher. Rose is simultaneously fascinated by and ashamed of Flo's versions of the real and the true, and, caught in this paradoxical relationship with her stepmother, both bring home to Flo wild tales of high-school sex and protests that "Katherine Mansfield had no relatives who said *yez.*" The result is that Rose is bound for life to Hanratty through Flo's voice. As an adult she imitates her stepmother in a mocking way before friends and strangers in an attempt to control such influence, not recognizing for a long time that such mimicry is an ultimate form of tribute to a woman whose spirited chronicles "were all a hard life had to offer."

If not exactly a moveable feast for Rose, Hanratty goes with her to the university where she meets her future husband, Patrick. Her knowledge that there are different ways of seeing and being in the world combats Patrick's insistent view of her as someone capable of "milky surrender, the helplessness and gratitude" of a beggar maid. Faced with the wealth and hauteur of Patrick's family, Rose presents her credentials in the form of some of Flo's stories and discovers in doing so "a layer of loyalty and protectiveness"; however, Munro complicates matters by having Rose return to Patrick after having told him that she does not want to get married, precisely because she can imagine herself going back. Within the bounds of childhood and Hanratty, Flo offered alternatives, not multiple perspectives. The latter is no basis for a marriage: Though Rose and Patrick are together for ten years and have a child, their parting is inevitable.

Even after Patrick, it is clear that Rose relies too much on men and is, like Del, in danger of drowning in such dependence. However, she is saved not through a blatant exercise of male power but through having to swim precisely because a man refuses to baptize her. She spends one night with Simon, a university teacher, whose ability to assume roles seems both playful and based on deadly serious childhood experiences in wartime Europe. She assumes that she has met the man "who will change everything" and tells him so; the result is that he does not return. When this happens Rose feels that the disappointments and the "dazzling alteration[s]" of love amount to the same thing for a woman—absence of power. Seeking power, she leaves, driving west to a new life, or so she thinks. Munro never deals in simple solutions because there are no simple problems in her fiction. Rose learns a year later that Simon had cancer and has died; she also learns that it is the very absence of power that women share with men, and her sense of why this is so draws her, unknowingly, closer to Flo who, even in her senility, waits for a shared voicing with Rose.

In the final, title story of this collection, the question "who do you think you are?," which Rose remembers being asked by a public-school teacher, is writ large across her adult consciousness. She remembers a town "character" whom outsiders would call the "village idiot," Milton Homer. Milton marched to his own tune in parades, mimicking those in authority, and, at one time, was allowed to perform a speech of Christian sentiment over newborn babies. His voice and actions remain clarion for Rose through the years, but her imitation of them rings hollow until she admits that it is not Milton she recalls so much as a boy who could "do" him perfectly, Ralph Gillespie. Then she meets a much older Ralph in the Hanratty Legion, expecting a familiar exchange patterned like kitchen linoleum. What Rose learns is that, though role-playing will never close the distance between women and men, they can find a strength through the mutual acceptance that each will always have "something further, a tone, a depth, a light" that the other will never be able to know or possess. Ironically Rose feels closer to Ralph Gillespie than to any of the men she has loved, though his life is, paradoxically, "one slot over from her own." It is a deep cave of recognitions in which she at last appears to be comfortable.

Munro does not repeat herself in her next two collections of stories, even though she continues to work within what some would mistakenly call a restricted genre. Female narrators still look back at their youth, but in *The Moons of Jupiter* adolescence for a number of women does not hold the key to personal revelation and development. Many of Munro's later protagonists, like their creator, are older, concerned with getting on with their present lives, and have teenage children of their own who complicate considerations about family and heritage.

Munro seems increasingly interested in providing multiple points of view within single stories. In "Labour Day Dinner" we are given the thoughts of Roberta and her second husband, George, as well as part of the journals of Roberta's eldest daughter. In "Accident," although the main part of the story is told from Frances's perspective, we also learn what her lover Ted thinks and even a little of the feelings of his wife, Greta. These thoughts and feelings are often contradictory and provide a gloss on individual vision that is mostly absent in previous works. As a result, the competition between the separate voices of women and men is still foregrounded, but the emphasis is on a community of utterance that forgives "in time . . . all our natural, and particular mistakes."

In the final story of *The Progress of Love*, entitled "White Dump," Munro clearly indicates that she is not prepared to stand still as a writer of short fiction and, at the same time draws together the major themes and structures of what has gone before. For one thing, this story is forty-seven pages in length and provides a complex interplay of narrative and event on its own, an interplay that has previously resulted primarily from combinations of related tales. The story is set, like quite a number of others, in the Ottawa Valley, and is told in the third person from the point of view of three women, representing three generations in a family—grandmother Sophie, mother Isabel, and daughter Denise. Each woman has, of course, different reactions to shared experiences and experiences of her own that invariably contribute to the collective condition of the family. Munro moves her readers back and forth among numerous layers of time ranging from a birthday in 1969 to several years later, when Isabel and a grown-up Denise discuss the aftermath of divorce, and further on to when Sophie has been dead for awhile. Despite the layering, there is no confusion. The central paradox arises clearly out of the fragmentary matter around a still vital family nucleus. If one of the central issues is yet very much sexual politics, it is, perhaps more than ever before, a politics between and among women that determines both female difference and the qualities of the gender gap. As we should expect by now, there are no resolutions, for they are like the white dump of this story, a pile of sweetness of which children's dreams are made.

Friend of My Youth is Munro's most recent work. There is a marked bittersweet quality to several of the ten stories, but most emphasize the price paid and the vision gained by women for having intimate relationships with men. As in previous Munro collections, the necessity of such relationships is socially predetermined and then psychologically sustained on an individual level by some female protagonists. In "Hold Me Fast, Don't Let Me Pass," a widow, Hazel, considers the paradoxical emotional chains that bind and distinguish women and men. Referring to a love-triangle in which the man seems to have the upper hand, Hazel thinks of how the man gives the two women "something to concentrate on. A hard limit that you might someday get past in a man, a knot in his mind you might undo, a stillness in him you might jolt, or an absence you might make him regret—that sort of thing will make you pay attention, even when you think you've taught yourself not to." She asks herself if such concentration can make a woman happy and senses that, regardless, a man's happiness depends upon "something quite different." If gender division appears to govern here, there is the apparent hope that getting past the "hard limit" in a man will provide mutual benefits. However, we should realize by now that Hazel's hope is not necessarily Munro's firm belief.

It is in "Meneseteung" (the name of a river that flows into Lake Huron) that Munro provides one of her most telling portraits to date of a woman who attempts to move beyond gender divisions of happiness. Munro's ironic narrative in this story is the saving grace of nineteenth-century poetess Almeda Roth for whom price paid and vision gained are terribly intertwined. The language and poetic form Almeda has been given contain her even as she creatively proclaims herself out of a position of servitude as her father's housekeeper. When he dies, the people of her town, led by newspaper gossip columns, expect her, suitably, to turn to another male authority figure. She seems primed to do so until one night when she witnesses the beating of a woman by her man. With some echoes of Rose in "Royal Beatings" in *our* ears, Almeda hears the woman partake in her own degradation: "She keeps crying 'Kill me! Kill me!' and sometimes her mouth seems choked with blood. Yet there is something taunting and triumphant about her cry. There is something theatrical about it." The woman does not die this time, but Almeda chooses to live by turning away from the proffered hand/fist of her suitor. In doing so, she breaks those chains that bind and distinguish primarily in terms of a power struggle that men will always win if women continue only to "pay attention." Conventional opinion has it that this "lady of talent and refinement" goes mad, but "she knows that she is sane." Almeda Roth is an ancestor for women of Munro's century, for Del Jordan and all the others who would live and create in a world that is both real and true.

WORKS CITED

Gibson, Graeme. *Eleven Canadian Novelists (Interviewed by Graeme Gibson)*. Toronto: Anansi, 1973. 237–65.

Irvine, Lorna. "Changing Is the Word I Want." *Probable Fictions: Alice Munro's Narrative Acts*. Toronto: ECW Press, 1983. 99–126.

Metcalf, John. "A Conversation with Alice Munro." *Journal of Canadian Fiction* 1.4 (1972): 54–62.

Ross, Catherine Sheldrick. "Alice Munro." *Dictionary of Literary Biography*. 53 (Canadian Writers Since 1960). Detroit: Bruccoli-Clark Ltd., 1986. 295–307.

Struthers, J.R. (Tim). "The Real Material: An Interview with Alice Munro." *Probable Fictions*. Toronto: ECW Press, 1983. 5–36.

Twigg, Alan. *For Openers: Conversations with 24 Canadian Writers*. Madeira Park, B.C.: Harbour Publishing, 1981. 13–20.

ALICE MUNRO'S PUBLISHED WORK

Dance of the Happy Shades, 1968
Lives of Girls and Women, 1971
Something I've Been Meaning to Tell You, 1974
Who Do You Think You Are?, 1978 (U.S. title *The Beggar Maid*, 1978)
The Moons of Jupiter, 1982
The Progress of Love, 1986
Friend of My Youth, 1990.

SELECTED CRITICAL READINGS

Munro had been a major figure in Canadian literature for at least fifteen years before any book on her writing was published. Even in a major literary journal like *Canadian Literature*, only two articles on her fiction appeared between 1968 and 1984. Fortunately, critical response to Munro is at last beginning to reflect her importance and the complexity of her writing. Since 1983 two collections of essays have been published and a full-length study of her work as well as a great number of essays. A feminist consideration of Munro appeared in 1990, and other scholars are preparing manuscripts and producing articles, both in Canada and abroad.

Cam, Heather. "Learning From the Teacher: Alice Munro's Reworking of Eudora Welty's 'June Recital.'" *Journal of the South Pacific Association for Commonwealth Literature and Language Studies.* No. 25 (1987): 16–30. Deals with direct connections between *Lives of Girls and Women* and a major Welty story.

Kamboureli, Smaro. "The Body as Audience and Performance in the Writing of Alice Munro." *A Mazing Space: Writing Canadian Women Writing*. Edmonton: Longspoon Press, 1986. 31–38. Argues that dialogic discourse in *Lives of Girls and Women* and *The Moons of Jupiter* utters the plurality of female body and does not imitate monologic, male articulation of that body.

MacKendrick, Louis K., editor. *Probable Fictions: Alice Munro's Narrative Acts.* Toronto: ECW Press, 1983. Ten essays (and an interview with Munro) that examine narrative perspective, structural patterns and disarrangements, complexities of language usage (notably linguistic paradox), and the disruption of a neat art-life reflection in Munro's writing. A purposeful movement "behind" basic thematic approaches to a consideration of her "fictionality."

Martin, W.R. *Paradox and Parallel.* Edmonton: U of Alberta P, 1987. Full-length discussion of the narrative techniques, themes, and patterns of language and experience in Munro's fiction. Begins with consideration of her early, uncollected stories and provides analysis of virtually every story in Munro's six collections to date. By the author's admission, "a straightforward" approach and "old-fashioned critical method" are employed for the benefit of the "common reader."

Miller, Judith, editor. *The Art of Alice Munro: Saying the Unsayable.* Waterloo, Ontario: U of Waterloo P, 1984. A collection of nine critical papers on Munro's work presented at the Waterloo Conference on Munro and an interview with her. Essays deal with voices, patterns of imagery, aspects of metafiction, psychological complexities, double worlds and paradox in Munro's stories. Also strong emphasis on literary influences and on connections between Munro's fiction and that of Canadian and American writers.

Redekop, Magdalene. *Alice Munro's Carnival of Mothers*. London: Routledge, 1990. Argues that Munro confronts our desire to idealize and essentialize the mother. Since the real mother cannot be reproduced, the representation becomes a caricature—a mock mother. In her treatment of both female and male mock mothers in her fiction, Munro radically investigates our assumptions about mimesis.

Wallace, Bronwen. "Women's Lives: Alice Munro." *The Human Elements: Critical Essays*. Ottawa: Oberon Press, 1978. 52–67. Del Jordan in *Lives of Girls and Women* and many of the women in *Something I've Been Meaning To Tell You* recognize the strengths of their many contradictory selves.

York, Lorraine M. "The Rival Bards: Alice Munro's *Lives of Girls and Women* and Victorian Poetry." *Canadian Literature* No. 112 (1987): 211–16. Del rejects "the unreal Tennysonian image of the female" in *The Princess* and turns instead to poetry that encourages her to become much more than a "half-woman" in a male world—Browning's *Men and Women*.

—J.A. WAINWRIGHT

Henry Handel Richardson

Henry Handel Richardson was the pseudonym of Ethel Florence Lindesay Robertson, who was born in Melbourne, Australia, 3 January 1870, the elder of two daughters of Walter Lindesay and Mary Bailey Richardson. Her father, a Dublin-born physician of Protestant-Irish stock, had come to Australia to make his fortune in the goldfields of Ballarat; her mother, the daughter of a Leicester solicitor, had likewise emigrated to Australia to improve her prospects. *The Fortunes of Richard Mahony* is based, to a large extent, on her parents' tragic life together. Her father died in 1879 at the age of fifty-three, financially ruined and insane from what is now thought to have been syphilis.

After her husband's death, Mary Richardson, a woman of great strength and courage, supported her family as a postmistress, an unusual step for a woman of her class. In 1882 she was able to send Ethel to the Presbyterian Ladies' College in Melbourne, one of the first schools of its time to give women an academic education. Richardson's fictionalized, rather negative, account of her years there in *The Getting of Wisdom* angered school officials to such an extent that they would not let the author visit the College when she toured Australia on her only trip back in 1912.

After her graduation in 1888, the family went to Leipzig so that Ethel and Lillian, a talented pianist and violinist, respectively, could study at the Conservatorium there. The experiences in Germany profoundly influenced her writing, giving her the background material for her first and last novels, *Maurice Guest* and *The Young Cosima*, and a grounding in continental literature that was to affect strongly the content and approach of her fiction. It was in Leipzig, too, that she met John George Robertson, a Scottish student of German language and literature, who was to become one of Europe's leading experts on modern German literature. Robertson guided her study of European classics, and when stage fright made a concert career impossible for her, Robertson encouraged her to be a translator and then a writer, meticulously editing her writing, and probably exerting a considerable influence on its style.

They married in 1895 and settled in Strasbourg where Robertson was Professor of English literature at the University. They moved to London in 1903 when he received the first chair of German at the University of London and continued to live quietly until Robertson's death in 1933.

Richardson scrupulously avoided publicity and literary society, even when she became something of a celebrity after the publication of *Ultima Thule* in 1929. Her final years were spent in Hastings with her companion/secretary, Olga Roncoroni. She died there of cancer in 1946, after surviving the worst bombings of World War

II. Her last years are beautifully captured in Roncoroni's essay, included in the collection she compiled with Edna Purdie in 1957, *Henry Handel Richardson: Some Personal Impressions.*

A MORE FORTUNATE READING STRATEGY

Critical reception to the writings of Henry Handel Richardson has been curiously divided. A transcript of it might even read like a courtroom drama, with the prosecution and defense lining up witnesses, from the texts or the Academy, to prove that she was or was not: imaginative, self-centered, a realist, a naturalist, a writer in the Australian tradition, literal minded, a genius, second-rate. Thus one approaches her work gingerly, feeling the need to take sides in an ongoing debate that has, at times, served to obscure rather than enlighten.

On the frontispiece of the 1948 issue of *Southerly* is a striking photo of a middle-aged woman, dark-haired, long-nosed, thin-lipped, with heavy eyelids and fashionably thin eyebrows, a "manly" face, one might say if one were to ascribe to her those traditional attributes of the feminine, dainty features, small nose, full lips: Johanna and Ephie, Laura and Pin, Polly and—who but the Mary she becomes, the ugly duckling turned swan. One does not have to look far to find the source of these contrasting figures. In *Myself When Young*, Richardson goes on at length about her sister suddenly gaining the limelight, becoming the center of attention on the ship to Europe: "'E. [Ettie, short for Ethel] is very well, but Lil is a beauty'" their Irish relatives tell them when they land (82). It is interesting to note the images Richardson transported from life to art, and how many came straight out of her troubled childhood. This is certainly of interest. She had a fascinating childhood—emigrant parents who took part in the colonizing of Australia; a "brilliant" father who went mad; a proper Victorian mother who broke with her class to become a postmistress; and the girls themselves, Ethel and Lillian, musical prodigies who went to Leipzig to study, returning to Australia only once, and then briefly. It is ripe material for literature, and Richardson used it again and again in her fiction as source material. Knowing the biographical background of Richardson's preoccupations does tell us about her life and helps us guess her intentions. But it places the focus on biography and leads us away from her texts.

The same can be said for another major approach to Richardson's work, the tracing of literary influence. Much fine detective work has been done to uncover the structure and characters in Richardson's fiction that were derived from works of nineteenth-century European literature. In "The Art of Henry Handel Richardson," her husband, J.G. Robertson, reveals his wife's reading interests during the time she wrote her major fiction, and investigative analyses have been performed by Nettie Palmer, Dorothy Green, Brian Kiernan, A.D. Hope, and recently Karen McLeod, among others, showing how writers such as Nietzsche, Jakobsen, Björnson, Flaubert, Stendhal, Turgenev, and Dostoyevsky "influenced" her. These critics tell us much about Richardson's interests during the time she wrote her novels and point out strains, movements, motifs utilized by the writer in the service of her fiction. But while we learn about the literary milieu of Richardson's time, the emphasis on ever elusive influence again draws attention from the works themselves.

Similarly misleading are the variety of formalistic approaches to Richardson's works in which they are viewed in terms of a literary structure. For example, often labeled a naturalist, she then has been accused of being too tied to naturalism for her characters ever to be convincing; moreover, her critical neglect on an international scale has been ascribed to her continuing reliance on that "archaic" form while her fellow writers in Europe were launching modernism: "For her contemporaries, [*Maurice*] arrives too late," writes A.G. van Kranendonk, "as the strangely delayed after-flower of a genre against which not only a justified reaction had emerged, but also a highly unjustified prejudice and slander" (239-40). The problem with these approaches is that they promote a simplistic reading in which her work is analyzed only in terms of the chosen form. Rather than discovering form within the work, these readings construct the works to fit the model.

A thoroughgoing reappraisal of Richardson's fiction is certainly in order, and, because of its radical social vision, I strongly suspect this reappraisal will occur within a feminist framework. The texts all focus on enculteration, particularly how major social and political institutions, like education, courtship, marriage, family, and health, become gendered. All her fiction and especially her three major works, *Maurice Guest, The Getting of Wisdom,* and *The Fortunes of Richard Mahony,* focus on enculteration as it intersects with gender and class. What I intend to do in this essay is to explore some new strategies for reading Richardson—and suggest how these strategies can be applied to the above novels. An analysis of the gendering of certain attributes and values in these works—and subsequent utilization of such gendered values and attributes by the Victorian hegemony within them—will reveal a much more subversive vision of gender and class than has been ascribed to Richardson previously.

An examination of binary codes, those hierarchical oppositions inscribed by the patriarchal hegemony with positive and negative values, has provided a useful feminist strategy for uncovering the phallocentric subtext within works of literature (Cixous 63-132). These oppositions, or polarities, center around the fundamental masculine/feminine dichotomy and include such polarities as self/other, active/ passive, head/heart, all of which can be traced back to the male/female paradigm in which the male-identified term is given greater value. Those undervalued or in some cases erased sides of the polarity are encoded as female. Such polarities are found in our discourse and reflect the value system adopted by the speaker or character within a work of fiction. Richardson foregrounds certain binary oppositions, using them as subversive substructure in her fiction, and many of her critics have stressed these oppositions by structuring their thematic explications of her texts around them; thus we see articles with titles such as "*The Fortunes of Richard Mahony*: Dream and Nightmare" (Elizabeth Loder); and "Convention and Freedom: A Study of *Maurice Guest*" (William S. New) reflecting this critical practice. A feminist analysis of binary polarities, however, is not concerned with the oppositional categories as themes but as ways of understanding the logical system or world view behind themes and structures produced by the gendering of values. By exploring these polarities in Richardson's work we can appreciate the irony at its core.

For example, a major dichotomy in *Maurice Guest* seems to be between genius and mediocrity, the musical genius of Schilsky and sexual genius of Louise seen against the utter failure of Maurice to live up to their standards. Many other themes in the novel are subsumed under this critical designation: love and hate; sophistication and provinciality; insider and outsider; rich and poor; powerful and powerless. That genius is a male province in nineteenth-century German music circles is an historic fact to which Richardson alludes throughout the novel, creating the embodiment of the oppressed German *hausfrau* in the figure of Frau Furst, the self-abnegating mother of Richard's tutor Franz Furst, as a comic variation of the Patient Griselda:

> This hard-working, careworn woman, who was seldom to be seen but in petticoat, bed-jacket, and heelless, felt shoes; who, her whole life long, had been little better than a domestic servant; in her there existed a devotion to art which had never wavered. (61)

Frau Furst's belief that women can never do original work, but only "reproduce what someone else has thought or felt" (61), mirrors dogma prevalent in its extreme form in nineteenth-century Germany. She is only an exaggerated, somewhat bathetic version of Louise Dufreyer, the stereotypical female as masochist; within Louise's (and Frau Furst's) social context, masochism and passivity are virtues, and Louise's wealth and beauty give these qualities particular allure. To excel in them, as Louise does, is highly valued. "Some women have a genius for loving. . . . A special talent is needed for that kind of thing; an unlimited capacity for suffering; an entire renunciation of what is commonly called happiness," says Heinz Krafft, a fellow music student, and only one of many who appreciate Louise for her female charms (500). Into this heady atmosphere of masculine domination steps, almost god-like, the premier music student, Schilsky: "Although so great a violinist, he could play almost every other instrument with ease; his memory had become as by-word; his compositions were already famous" (24). Not only talented musically, his power over women is legend. "Not a girl, young or old, but peddled for a word or a look from him; and he was only too prodigal of insolently expressive glances, whispered greetings, and warm pressures of the hand" (67).

Richardson seems to be setting up a pretty straightforward polarity between genius and mediocrity, pitting the Nietszchean Schilsky against the hapless Maurice, who dominates neither the musical nor amatory scene. At the same time, she has opposed the traditional male form of genius as inscribed in Schilsky, one which is active and creative, to the female form of genius, possessed by Louise, which is passive and appreciative. This analysis has been advanced by a number of critics who accept the above stereotype of genius and, accordingly, see Maurice's failure as that of mediocrity: "Louise has the genius for love. Maurice has not. Schilsky has the genius for music. Maurice has not. What the book is about is what Maurice does not possess and cannot attain," writes A.D. Hope (192). A feminist analysis, however, would deconstruct this essentialist view of genius, question the author's point of view, which is clearly ironic, and, I believe, conclude that, although much examined in the novel, genius is not at issue. What is really being explored is success and failure, or, more specifically, what makes for success and failure in late nineteenth-century European society. One could, for example, analyze the part money plays in the novel, and how success and power are purchased. One might also see the novel as an attack on the gendering of the artistic concept of genius and Maurice's failure as a refusal to take on the powerful, sadistic role of his gender. Maurice does not fail because he lacks talent; he never really works at his music. He fails because he is passive and masochistic, that is, because he acts like a woman. By looking at the polarity between Schilsky and Louise, Schilsky and Maurice, we begin to identify this phallocentric vision that has rewarded male aggression and female passivity—and has made the kitchen and bedroom the locus of creativity for the woman artist.

In *The Fortunes of Richard Mahony*, the oppositions of civilization and wilderness, colonizer and colonized, sanity and madness—the primary literary images of the postcolonial project—predominate. Kay Schaffer's convincing argument calling the land in *Richard Mahony* a "revengeful mother, denying man his goal" is a useful starting point for any exploration of binary polarities in the novel, for Schaffer discusses Richardson's ironic vision of male culture as the colonizer, vulnerable to the Mother's revenge, but more powerful and destructive than she (104). In this world Richard is defeated and forgiven, absorbed back into the "rich and kindly earth" (*Richard Mahony* 948), because, like Maurice, he is unable to cope with the world as he finds it. His romantic sensibility—to music, poetry, mysticism—is offended by the prosaic demands of daily life, and he fails both in Australia and at "Home" in England. He is contrasted with, among others, his wife Mary and his friend Purdy, who have managed to adapt successfully to postcolonial life. In the trilogy, as in *Maurice Guest*, failure is again imaged by role reversal and its consequences; the father cannot father, the doctor can no longer doctor: "'Papa... with his head hanging down and his mouth wide open, making funny noises [is] not like a grown up gentleman anymore'" (904), observes his son, Cuffy. Decisions are made by Mary who becomes the breadwinner, and Purdy lies to Richard's children, telling them their father was not a real "man" but instead a coward whose fear led to Purdy's becoming lame. In one way he is telling the truth; Mahony's manliness, in colonial terms, has disappeared with his ability to make and manage money. His madness a visible sign of his inability to survive, he is de/civilized by his loss; for what is civilization in the colonial world if not the control of money:

> This dream it was, of vast wealth got without exertion, which had decoyed the strange, motley crowd, in which peers and churchmen rubbed shoulders with the scum of Norfolk Island, to exile in this outlandish region. And the intention of all alike had been: to snatch a golden fortune from the earth, and then, hey, presto! for the old world again. (10)

So writes Richardson in the much-analyzed Proem to *Richard Mahony*. To miss the irony of the Proem is to miss the gist of the trilogy. Richard's madness must be seen in relation to this ironic vision of civilization. The fact that this "ancient, barbaric country they had so lightly invaded" is female, holding them "captive—without chains; ensorcelled—without witchcraft" (11) genders the enterprise of colonialism as it damns it.

The image of Australia in the Proem is female sexuality incarnate, "lying stretched in the sun like some primeval monster, her breasts freely bared, she watched, with a malignant eye, the efforts made by these puny mortals to tear their lips away" (11). She is the prostitute, the symbol of lust and ruin for the middle-class male—and one from whom he must be protected or die. In contrast to Home/England, Australia is primitive nature, or "the Primitive," that is, the indigenous Australian so completely absent from the trilogy but a formidable presence in her absence. As Cleo McNelly writes in discussing the polarities produced by the postcolonial discourse:

> Home represents civilization, but also order, constraint, sterility, pain and *ennui*, while native culture, the far pole of the myth, represents nature, chaos, fecundity, power and joy. The home culture is, moreover, associated always with the ability to understand by seeing, abstractly, while the other culture is associated with black, with the sense of touch, the ability to know by feeling, from within. The far pole of the tropical journey is indeed the *heart* of darkness. (9)

The lack of any discussion of the indigenous Australian in any but metaphysical terms in Richardson's work is a ripe topic for study, considering Richardson's concern with other marginal groups. What may be called a social feminist critique of Richardson's novels (that is, a critique utilizing feminist methodologies and materials from such areas as history, science, new ethnography, psychology, sociology) would then be particularly productive in understanding the intersections of gender, class, and race in her work—in terms of presences and absences, in terms of the colonial hegemony and its control over ideology and public policy, and where stereotypes in the works mimic or contradict prevailing ideas about gender within the historical context to reveal her subversive attitude towards Victorian society.

In *Sexual Science*, Cynthia Eagle Russett writes of the role played by science during Victorian times to construct the female gender in such a way that it correlated with the society's need to quiet the feminist challenge for equal rights:

> Scientists responded to this unrest with a detailed and sustained examination of the differences between men and women that justified their differing social roles. Anatomy and psychology, and sociology evolved comprehensive theories of sexual difference. . . . These theories were utilized and adapted to explain how and why men and women differed from each other and, often enough, what these differences signified for social policy, and conclusions drawn from them display such a remarkable degree of uniformity that it is fair to say that a genuine scientific consensus emerged by the turn of the century. (10)

Consensus regarding such issues as women's intellectual ability, their moral development, their independence was reached; policies concerning such subjects as labor, education, artistic talent, divorce, child custody, inheritance, religious, social, and political leadership resulted, and social practice was imposed. Richardson was raised in this period, and it is this period that she created in her writing. Her works are filled with debate about gender and certain burning issues of the time found their way into her work in direct and indirect ways, such as suffrage, the education of children, the use of anesthesia and Caesarian section in childbirth. If the character of Johanna in *Maurice Guest* is created partially to show the bitterness and frustration experienced by an intellectual woman who is not allowed to further her education, the character of Louise can be said to express, through her attitudes and actions, the reality of woman's sexual desire—a lesser or even absent drive according to Victorian theorists who claimed that women's sexuality, at least middle-class women's sexuality, was confined, in the main, to her reproductive function, and that sexual passion was a trait of the lower orders of females and of males who were expected to "contain" their desire if they were gentlemen. As Leonore Davidoff explains in her study of Victorian morality, male sexuality, the containing of which was a major goal of Victorian society, was class bound:

> This was a gentility reserved for middle-class men. The working class and native blacks supposedly allowed their sexuality to spill out over their total lives, diverting them from the goal of achievement through work, wasting their energies and draining their vital forces. (20–21)

What is remarkable about Richardson's portrayal of Louise is that it not only flies in the face of Victorian stereotypes of the middle-class woman as a "desexualized Madonna" (21), but it also attacks Victorian mores that demanded punishment for female sexual passion. Allusive of the many Victorian maidens in literature who pay for sexual desire with their lives (Tess D'Urberville, Maggie Tulliver, Catherine Earnshaw), Louise not only evades punishment but is also apparently unscathed and unrepentant, and, we see at the conclusion of the book, a continuing source of sexual stimulation, however vicarious, for succeeding generations of music students.

The question of women's right to institutional wisdom was much debated at the time Richardson's second book, *The Getting of Wisdom*, is set, for aside from basic literacy instruction, an academic education was not readily available to women until the last part of the nineteenth century. How many women, like Virginia Woolf, Beatrice Webb, Sylvia Townsend Warner, were self-educated within their father's libraries rather than in formal academic settings, and how many more, lacking these voluminous libraries, had to make do with a few books and male conversation? Academies for middle-class ladies specialized in training women for life in the home and gave them instruction in art, music, and needlework. The Presbyterian Ladies' College, on which the school in *The Getting of Wisdom* is based, was one of the first institutions of its kind in Australia to offer women an academic education and in that way can be seen as progressive. Yet, as it is portrayed in the novel—with its emphasis on etiquette and appearance, instruction through rote memory, rewarding of hypocrisy and conformity—it hardly offers women the kind of education they required to compete intellectually with men. It is, however, the education a woman *needed* to take her place as a wife in middle-class Australian Victorian society. As

Anne Summers reports in her study of women in Australia, even the progressive C.H. Pearson, first headmaster of Presbyterian Ladies' College, believed most women at his institution would and *should* marry and that after they married, they should not work:

> Being the 19th century gentleman, Pearson could not conceive of any woman actually choosing an independent path in preference to marriage; nor was he prepared to allow that it might be desirable for a woman to do both. (321)

Thus, most "higher" education during that time, she tells us, was geared towards educating girls for marriage and motherhood.

The Getting of Wisdom is, in a sense, about a descent into the world of women, a barely disguised allegory that begins in the Edenic garden of Laura's rural home and follows her journey to the underworld, the school where, on first entering, Laura remarks: "It must be like this to be dead" (221). This is the intellectual world relegated to women: not a mirror of the world above, the world of men, but a living hell for a girl like Laura with an independent and creative spirit, a world totally contingent on males, who "doggedly" guard the entrance to the free world outside: Mr. Strachey, the Principal, to whom even the feared headmistress, Mrs. Gurley, defers; the curate, Mr. Shepherd, to whom sister and wife dedicate their lives; and, of course, the male Christian god, and the phallocentric discourse of theology through which female subservience receives its justifications. Here women are brought to learn their theological and biological destinies, their inferiority on the moral and evolutionary scale. For example, a teacher at the school, Miss Hicks, says to a schoolmate of the eleven-year-old Laura:

> "You're blessed with a real woman's brain; vague, slippery, inexact, interested only in the personal aspect of a thing. You can't concentrate on your thoughts, and worst of all, you've no curiosity—about anything that really matters. You take all the great facts of existence on trust—just as a hen does." (10)

She is only reflecting ideas about a woman's intellectual capacity prevalent in Victorian society, ideas like those advanced by Charles Darwin who, in his extremely influential book on gender, *The Descent of Man, and Selection in Relation to Sex,* theorized, on the basis of his observations of animal life, that:

> The chief distinction in the intellectual powers of the two sexes is shewn by man's attaining to a higher eminence, in whatever he takes up than can woman—whether requiring deep thought, reason, or imagination, or merely the uses of the senses and hands. . . . We may also infer from the law of the deviation from averages . . . that if men are capable of a decided pre-eminence over women in many subjects the average of mental power in man must be above that of woman. (564)

Darwin's "proof" consists of lists of those historical figures who have attained greatness—all male.

The patriarchal spirit of the school is captured brilliantly in the scene in which Laura takes her final history exam, the exam which will decide whether or not she will graduate. She passes it by cheating, but the author's sympathy lies with her, and her cheating is seen as the proper response of one who has been persistently degraded and marginalized. It is during this exam that her (male) history examiner, Dr. Pughson, derides Laura's computational skills while patronizing her musical talent: "How like a woman that is!" he says, "Playing at concerts when she can't add two and two together" (220). Moreover, the test is predictably Eurocentric, a reflection of the school's general curriculum. Why hadn't they been questioned on "Bourke and Wills, or the Eureka stockade, or the voyages of Captain Cook? . . . something about one's own country, that one had heard hundreds of times and was really interested in," Laura wonders (221), questioning a curriculum that did not include the study of Australian culture until the 1970s. Like Dickens's Gradgrind, who tells his class, "In this life we want nothing but facts, sir; nothing but facts!" (*Hard Times* 12), the instructors at the school teach the girls to memorize and recite, and that they must never create:

> By dint of close attention, of pondering both the questions asked by Miss Hicks, and the replies made by the cleverest pupils, she began to see more clearly where true knowledge lay. It was facts that were wanted of her; facts that were the real test of learning; facts she was expected to know. Stories, pictures of things, would not help her an inch along the road. (77)

Unlike Dickens, however, Richardson has revealed the gendering of wisdom and ignorance and the negative role this played in women's lives; the getting of wisdom, the learning of the "facts" of life, is really the learning of the rules, rules which, Laura discovers, are *Man*-made.

The Getting of Wisdom is much less subtle in its critique of masculinist society than *Maurice Guest* and much less complex than *The Fortunes of Richard Mahony*. It is an angry book, where satire flavors characterization, making sympathy with any one character difficult. A social feminist approach would question the educational principles articulated in the book and explore the historical precedents for them; it would deconstruct the socio-psychological model of femininity and masculinity and show where public policy was influenced by these models; it would expose the sociopolitical context of such gendered concepts as wisdom and ignorance so as to allow the reader to appreciate the depth of Richardson's ironic vision.

In *The Empire Writes Back*, the authors compare women with "the colonized" in terms of a shared experience of otherness:

> They share with colonized races and peoples an intimate experience of the politics of oppression and repression, and like them they have been forced to articulate their experiences in the language of their oppressors. (Ashcroft 175)

The position of otherness experienced by women and other marginalized groups is a recurrent theme in Richardson's novels in which her main characters are almost always positioned outside the discourse of the dominant hegemony. Otherness is experienced by Maurice Guest, as an Englishman in Germany, but even more, as a male who will not assume his gender role, and by Laura as an unformed, female child in a patriarchal culture. But it is within the character of Richard Mahony that the colonial dilemma is ultimately inscribed. While colonialism as a mirror of the female predicament is suggested in *The Getting of Wisdom*, it remains one of the major themes of *Richard Mahony*.

As an Anglo-Irishman, Richard is the ultimate misfit, neither English nor Irish, rejected by both for being too much the other. With no community of class or nationality behind him, people do not know who he is. He is even isolated within his profession. Having studied medicine in Scotland, where he received the most progressive education of his time, he has difficulty relating to his more conservative colleagues in Australia. Making Richard a physician gives Richardson a chance to present her skeptical view of this profession in its Australian manifestation. It appears that doctors in colonial Australia are incompetent, lazy, ignorant, poorly trained, and often drunk; they are also exploiters, the worst being gynecologists, who are contemptuous of women and uninterested in learning about their medical needs. Dr. Rogers, who attends Polly in her first delivery, argues with Richard about the use of chloroform in childbirth:

> He cited such hoary objections to the use of the new anaesthetic in maternity cases, as Mahony had never expected to hear again: the therapeutic value of pain; the moral danger the patient ran in yielding up her will . . . and the impious folly of interfering with the action of a creative law. (157)

Rogers's reluctance to give Polly anesthesia in a timely fashion is probably responsible for the baby's death. In that light, Mahony is seen as enlightened and competent. He is a good man, a cultured man, more a victim of greed and political oppression than a perpetrator of it, but a perpetrator nonetheless. He benefits from colonialism—his fortunes rise and he is able to retire because of his investments in a goldmining company. It is only when he becomes greedy and wants to make even more money that his fortunes fall, and with his financial disgrace follows mental collapse.

As implied above, Richard's madness can be looked at as a metaphor for the collapse of his fortunes, and as a punishment, not for exploitation but for failure and bad business sense; accordingly, his incarceration in an insane asylum is what Michel Foucault might call "a gigantic moral imprisonment" (274), because, like Maurice Guest, Richard is unwilling to play the role outlined for him by the society. Richard's experiences in the two insane asylums exemplify the author's ironic attitude toward class divisions in colonial Australia. In the colonial world, external attributes—the right decorum, clothes, linens, dishes—what people can see, hear, and touch, achieve an exaggerated importance as class markers since there is no history or tradition of class affiliation. Many scenes in *Richard Mahony* contain spoofs of the newly rich (former convicts and greengrocers) affecting the trimmings of the middle and upper classes, quite successfully, since class in the new world is purchased, not inherited. However, the trimmings are all Richard has left and when he is first placed in an expensive hospital for the insane his only concern is that he still have his "clean collars" and "hankchiefs [sic]" (906). When Mary's money runs out, she is forced to send him to an institution where the poor send their insane; the place is no longer called a "hospital" but an "asylum" and he is now called a "lunatic." At the asylum he is not treated according to his former station, for he cannot pay for it; he is now a prisoner, with a "warder," who is "a coarse, strongly built man with a low forehead and the under-jaw of a prizefighter" (920), a man whose position in society is emblemized by seemingly simian features. He gives Richard his meals on "tin plates," and it is this fact, and not his mental condition, that convinces Mary that he must be cared for at home; with the right external markers he can again be a gentleman.

Richardson's preoccupation with power relationships, particularly relationships concerning class and gender, is apparent throughout the trilogy. Her depriviledging of the European perspective and her identification of Richard with marginal characters is persistent. While critics have attacked her fiction over the years, claiming it was too shackled by realism or naturalism to be really convincing, I suspect she is manipulating genre rather than being manipulated by it, surprising the reader by upsetting expectations, subverting Victorian ideology as she seems to agree with it. Seen within the androcentric framework of genre the trilogy can, indeed, be said to fail, for Richard's death is foreordained and thus there is no room for character development. However, as I have suggested, Richardson's ironic point of view consistently unsettles the reader; the works, and particularly *Richard Mahony*, ask the reader to judge the nineteenth-century European world that perpetrated colonialism. After all, the anti-colonial motifs introduced in the Proem continue throughout the trilogy and are echoed at the novel's end, with Richard's burial. This is a novel about colonialism and the encoding of the values of imperialism. The trajectory of Richard's fortunes must be seen as ironic rather than tragic, for his death is only tragic if we see colonialism as positive and worthy of success.

The fact that Henry Handel Richardson began her writing at a time when modernism was emerging—and completed the bulk of *The Fortunes of Richard Mahony* when it already had been introduced and was carrying the day—has seemed to bias critics, many of whom explored the book as a nineteenth-century relic and missed the extraordinary challenge of her feminist and colonialist critique. Frequently ironic, her works present a skeptical view of the concepts of gender and class constructed by Victorian society. What I have tried to do is present some approaches to reading Richardson so that her radical vision, so long obscured, can emerge. Viewing Richardson's work through a feminist lens should allow us to appreciate her subversive qualities, especially apparent when seen alongside the current postcolonialist debate. Consistently in dialogue with social issues, the theory informing her approach to these issues is, consciously or unconsciously, activist.

WORKS CITED

Ashcroft, William, Gareth Griffiths, and Helen Tiffin. *The Empire Writes Back: Theory and Practice in Post-colonial Literature.* London: Routledge, 1989.

Cixous, Helene, and Catherine Clement. "Sorties: Out and Out: Attacks/Ways Out/Forays." *The Newly Born Woman.* Minneapolis: U of Minnesota P, 1986.

Darwin, Charles. *The Descent of Man, and Selection in Relation to Sex.* New Edition, Revised & Augmented. New York: D. Appleton, 1896.

Davidoff, Leonore. "Class and Gender in Victorian England." *Sex and Class in Women's History.* London: Routledge and Kegan Paul, 1983. 17–71.

Dickens, Charles. *Hard Times.* New York: New American Library, 1961.

Foucault, Michel. *Madness and Civilization: A History of Insanity in the Age of Reason.* London: Tavistock, 1971.

Hope, A.D. "Henry Handel Richardson's *Maurice Guest.*" *Meanjin Quarterly* 14 (1955): 186–89.

Loder, Elizabeth. "The Fortunes of Richard Mahony: Dream and Nightmare." *Southerly* 25 (1965): 251–63.

McNelly, Cleo. "Natives, Women and Claude Levi-Strauss: A Reading of *Tristes Tropiques* as Myth." *Massachusetts Review* 16 (1975): 7–29.

New, William S. "Convention and Freedom: A Study of *Maurice Guest.*" *English Studies* Anglo-American Supplement (1969): lxii–lxviii.

Richardson, Henry Handel. *The Fortunes of Richard Mahony.* New York: The Press of the Readers Club, 1941.

———. *The Getting of Wisdom.* New York: Dial Press, 1981.

———. *Maurice Guest.* New York: Dial Press, 1981.

———. *Myself When Young.* Melbourne: Heinemann, 1964.

Rossing, Karl-Johan, editor. *Letters of Henry Handel Richardson to Nettie Palmer.* Uppsala: Lundequistska, 1953.

Russett, Cynthia Eagle. *Sexual Science.* Cambridge: Harvard UP, 1989.

HENRY HANDEL RICHARDSON'S PUBLISHED WORK

Novels

Maurice Guest, 1908
The Getting of Wisdom, 1910, rev. 1931
The Fortunes of Richard Mahony, trilogy: *Australia Felix*, 1917; *The Way Home*, 1925; *Ultima Thule*, 1939
The Young Cosima, 1939

Short Story Collections

Two Studies, 1931
The End of a Childhood, 1934

Autobiography

Myself When Young, 1948

SELECTED CRITICAL READINGS

The major response to Henry Handel Richardson's works has issued from within Australia. Several books have come out, including the exhaustive critical biography by Dorothy Green, and numerous articles on her major novels appear regularly in scholarly journals. In the main, critical approaches have explored three central issues: European influence, particularly of the school of naturalism, on her work; influence of Australian literature and culture on her writing; and the degree to which the author's reliance on factual detail, especially autobiographical elements, affects her writing. International recognition, however, has not kept pace with the Australian response. While a few critical books have appeared during the past 15 years, Richardson's work is rarely studied in journals and magazines, and she is rarely included in the canon of twentieth-century literature in English. Moreover, she has rarely been considered within the context of feminist literature, an aspect of her work that needs more study. It is probable that the opening of her papers and manuscripts, housed at the National Library in Canberra, Australia, in 1996, will inspire more aggressive critical attention.

Bird, Delys. "Towards an Aesthetics of Australian Women's Fiction: *My Brilliant Career* and *The Getting of Wisdom.*" *Australian Literary Studies* 11 (1983): 171–81. Attempts to apply Elaine Showalter's theory of gynocriticism to fiction by Australian women writers, using Richardson's *The Getting of Wisdom* and Miles Franklin's *My Brilliant Career* as paradigms. Views both works as subversive in trying to "assert a place for a growing girl in a society which disallows her one except in its own reductive terms."

Buckley, Vincent. *Henry Handel Richardson.* 2nd ed. Melbourne: Oxford UP, 1970. Regards Richardson an "impressive failure," one whose importance comes more from her place in the development of Australia's literature than for actual greatness. Contends that while *The Getting of Wisdom* and *Ultima Thule* are praiseworthy, the rest of her work is too often marked by "simpleminded naturalism" and melodrama.

Butcher, Margaret K. "From *Maurice Guest* to *Martha Quest*: The Female *Bildungsroman* in Commonwealth Literature." *World Literature Written in English* 21 (1982): 254–62. Discusses *Maurice Guest* as a colonial female *Bildungsroman*. Of necessity, the three women in Maurice's life all gain their education in untraditional ways and emerge strong, although Louise needs to be "paired" to Schilsky to realize her destiny. The fact that the novel does not focus on women makes it transitional in the development of the female *Bildungsroman*, while *The Getting of Wisdom*, in focusing on Laura completely, is a more fully developed example of the form, which reaches true fruition in Doris Lessing's *Martha Quest* (1962) and Margaret Laurence's *The Diviners* (1974).

Eldershaw, M. Barnard. "Two Women Novelists." *Essays in Australian Fiction.* Melbourne: Melbourne UP, 1938. 1–23. Considers Richardson's critical reputation, including an analysis of why she is not better known. Calls *The Fortunes of Richard Mahony* a great work because of the detailed characterization; sees *Maurice Guest* and *The Getting of Wisdom* as less successful.

Elliott, William D. *Henry Handel Richardson.* Boston: Twayne, 1975. Thorough examination of Richardson's life and works, focusing on her as the first Australian writer "to develop a multidimensional single character in an extended work of fiction."

Green, Dorothy. "Power-games in the Novels of Henry Handel Richardson." *Who Is She?* New York: St. Martin's Press, 1983. 84–97. Argues that Richardson was aware of different roles women could play and even planned her women characters as types, being especially interested in "power games" between the sexes. Sees *The Fortunes of Richard Mahony*, in particular, abounding with analyses of Victorian relationships.

———. *Ulysses Bound: Henry Handel Richardson and Her Fiction.* Canberra: Australian National UP, 1973. Probably the most thorough and influential book on Richardson to date. According to Green, it was written because of "a profound disagreement" with the critics, who have complained of Richardson's literal mindedness. Focuses on a psychological analysis of Richardson's work, and often relies on diaries, essays, and other personal documents.

Hope, A.D. "Henry Handel Richardson's *Maurice Guest.*" *Meanjin Quarterly* 14 (1955): 186–89. Influential early article by the important Australian poet. Asserts that *Maurice Guest* is not about love, as many critics have written, but about genius and was much inspired by Nietszche in character and themes.

Jeffares, A. Norman. "Richard Mahony, Exile." *Journal of Commonwealth Literature* 6 (1969): 106–19. Comprehensive introductory analysis of *The Fortunes of Richard Mahony* demonstrating the epic quality of the trilogy. Puts the motifs of exile and return, hunter and hunted, flight and freedom in a classic context and compares the work with *The Dubliners* in this aspect and in the reception they received from critics in their native lands.

Kiernan, Brian. "The Fortunes of Richard Mahony." *Southerly* 29 (1969): 199–209. Argues that *Richard Mahony* has great weaknesses: Much of the imagery is obvious; the style often sentimental and cliché ridden; the author lacks an ironic distance that obscures her point of view. But Kiernan's psychological analyses of Richard's and Mary's relationship and of Richard's psychological deterioration are excellent.

Kramer, Leonie. *Henry Handel Richardson.* Melbourne: Melbourne UP, 1967. Psychological study of Richardson and her work. Believes she was not a writer of the "very highest order" because she was "skilled in reconstruction rather than in creation. Her mind was exceedingly literal, and the respect for accuracy which makes her so reliable a writer also filters her imagination."

Kranendonk, A.G. "A Neglected Masterpiece." Translated with an introduction by Noel Macainsh. *Southerly* 37 (1977): 231–40. Originally published in the Dutch periodical *De Stem* in 1928. Kranendonk argues that *Maurice Guest* is on a level with the best continental realist and naturalist writers and second only to the work of Thomas Hardy. Concludes that the book is unknown because it came out too late, it was "too difficult" for the average reader, and not experimental enough for the avant garde readership of the time.

Loder, Elizabeth. "Maurice Guest: Some 19th Century Progenitors." *Southerly* 26 (1966): 94–105. Useful background article demonstrating in great detail the influence continental writers exerted on *Maurice Guest*, particularly Flaubert in *Madame Bovary*, Dostoyevsky in *Crime and Punishment*, Freud in *Interpretation of Dreams*, the German romantics Goethe and E.T.A. Hoffman, and Nietzsche.

McFarlane, Brian. "Power in Dark Places: *The Fortunes of Richard Mahony.*" *Southerly* 37 (1977): 211–28. Comprehensive analysis of the three volumes of the trilogy, showing that, while the prose style of the trilogy is decidedly weak, *Ultima Thule* is extremely moving, indeed reaching greatness and power.

McLeod, Karen. *Henry Handel Richardson.* Cambridge: Cambridge UP, 1985. Detailed examination of Richardson as a major writer deserving more status and attention that she has received.

Believes Richardson's great strength is her characterization, especially her depiction of intimate relationships. Proposes that her affiliation with the European realistic tradition places her outside the modern English tradition, which probably accounts for her critical obscurity.

Mann, Maureen. "The Genesis of *The Young Cosima*: Henry Handel Richardson's Most Neglected Novel." *World Literature Written in English* 17 (1978): 96–105. Describes *Young Cosima* as "a book of considerable merit" deserving "more serious attention that it has received to date." The largely biographical analysis concludes that the novel is weakened by its commitment to fact, from which the book had its genesis and on which the book relies.

Moore, T. Inglis. *The Misfortunes of Henry Handel Richardson*. Canberra: Canberra University College, 1957. Asserts that Richardson's works, while greatly praised in her day, have not survived because, despite great strengths in characterization, construction, and objectivity, they are lacking in imagination and passion, sympathy and altruism, and a moral and a spiritual center. Believes her work reflects the writer herself, who was known to be self-centered and depressed.

Palmer, Nettie. *Henry Handel Richardson: A Study*. Sydney: Angus & Robertson, 1950. First complete study of Richardson's life and work. Gives a close reading of the novels and stories, and analyzes them in terms of the author's life and times. Establishes the terms of Richardson criticism today, especially in her discussion of the tendency to sculpt fiction from factual material.

Purdie, Edna, and Olga M. Roncoroni. *Henry Handel Richardson: Some Personal Impressions*. Sydney: Angus & Robertson, 1957. Nine essays by persons intimate with Richardson, including close personal friends, neighbors, her editor at Heinemann, her nephew, and Australian critic Nettie Palmer. The editor, Edna Purdie, was John Robertson's colleague at the University of London, and Olga Roncoroni was Richardson's devoted companion-secretary for over 25 years.

Riemer, A.P. "*Young Cosima*: A Reconsideration." *Southerly* 40 (1980): 190–203. Finds *The Young Cosima* a "disturbing" and "evasive" work that avoids controversial subject matter (such as Cosima Wagner's anti-semitism) while succeeding in expressing the "persistent contradiction" of the main characters. Argues that by presenting domestic and everyday details the work succeeds in demythologizing the Wagner myth.

Robertson, J.G. "The Art of Henry Handel Richardson." In *Myself When Young* by Henry Handel Richardson. New York: Norton, 1948. Close analysis of *Maurice Guest*, *The Getting of Wisdom*, and *The Fortunes of Richard Mahony*, written in 1928–29, by the distinguished literary scholar (and Richardson's husband). Puts works in the context of European literary movements, citing specific influences on the author's style and approach.

— MARIAN ARKIN

III. Decolonizing Boundaries

The workings of colonialism set up boundaries—geographical, cultural, histori-cal, artistic, and personal. Always at the Center loomed the Seat of Empire—London, the Metropolis—always superior and smug. Those outside the Center's geographical boundaries were considered—and often considered themselves—second rate: their place of birth not their true home, their indigenous or colonial culture inferior, their history invented, their art either "primitive" or a copy of the real thing. Once the Empire crumbled, the then fading boundaries were decolonized. And the effect was sometimes good, sometimes bad, as the writers exploring this theme would show.

For Shirley Hazzard, a world without boundaries has created a "literary no-man's land," thus a challenge to contemporary novelists who find themselves caught within a "dislocation" that brings about an "unprecedented loss of geographical, to some extent, national and even social, sense of belonging." This theme of personal and geographical exile Horst Priessnitz traces through Hazzard's writing. Dislocation is the central theme, too, of Salman Rushdie's fiction. Fawzia Afzal-Khan, discussing this Asian-born writer living in London, concludes that all his work leads to the destruction of "old ideologies, old forms, old oppositional structures and rigid definitions," that is, the erasure of traditional boundaries. Taking up "religion as a colonizing power" in Rushdie's *The Satanic Verses*, Afzal-Khan draws parallels between colonial and religious containment, both of which set limits on personal territory. Unlike Hazzard, who recognizes a sadness in life without boundaries, Rushdie believes that the decolonization process will invent regeneration.

Malcolm Lowry, a Briton, might be said to have become an international writer in English accidentally by ending up in Canada where he did most of his work; Canada now claims him. Sherrill Grace speaks of Lowry's attraction "to the metaphor of the voyage and to the idea that his art, like his life, was a constant voyage of change and discovery." By setting all idea of boundaries aside, Lowry, according to Grace, portrayed "this century's most intransigent problems" through an "apocalyptic" vision that "balances the horror of final destruction with the revelation of hope through renewed voyaging." Like Lowry, Elizabeth Jolley was born and grew up in England, but by crossing boundaries is now an Australian writer. A.P. Riemer examines Jolley's unlikely career in which an immigrant forged an international reputation from the remotest part of a remote country. Finding in her work recurrent "images and concerns," Riemer sees them as relevant "to the dilemma of the artist in exile." The kind of dislocation that Hazzard's men and women encounter in a world without boundaries occurs as well in Jolley's work, for Riemer describes her characters as experiencing "a sense of disorientation and alienation," then adds that this is "a familiar aspect of the migrant experience."

But Ruth Prawer Jhabvala's decolonization of boundaries far exceeds that of the writers discussed so far. A Jewish refugee from Germany, Jhabvala came to England with her family when she was twelve. Ten or so years later she left Britain to go to India, where she lived for 25 years, the wife of an Indian and a writer who captured the Indian scene so totally that she was long thought a native. As Yasmine Gooneratne's essay title indicates, Jhabvala has "returned to the West," yet remains what Gooneratne calls "that contemporary phenomenon, the unhoused itinerant author who writes . . . out of a 'free' and unhoused state." Although Jhabvala's recent work encompasses "three continents," all of it carries the qualities Gooneratne describes as "the helplessness of the refugee, the discontented and alienated sensibility of the expatriate, the exile's longing for home." Unhoused, marginalized as well, Jhabvala resembles another of the international writers in English, Doris Lessing, who was born in Persia, reared in Africa, and has lived most of her adult life in England. Calling Lessing a writer on the margin who creates untried "maps of new worlds," Lois Marchino stresses the importance of Lessing's colonial experience in forming her "way of seeing," hence her "overriding theme": the "urgency of expanding individual consciousness and seeing ourselves in relation to others in new ways, the imperative of creating new maps." These maps, charting life in Africa, then in England, at times in the imagined future, aim to break down the false boundaries imprisoning self.

Well into the twentieth century some guardians of Australian letters set boundaries, asserting that for the literature to be truly Australian it must draw from the country's landscape—the bush in particular; from its people—mainly those who lived in the bush; and from its history—that is, heroic pioneers struggling against hardship, a struggle often lost. On the surface it would seem that Peter Carey has stayed more or less within those boundaries. But as Helen Daniel points out, he explores "the mythopoeic history of Australia" not the actual. Nor does he extol the virtues of pioneer tenacity but rather subverts "those levels of national identity that have been infiltrated and colonized by the past"; therefore, Daniel says, "His is at once a vision of postcolonial society on the cusp of the future and a profound dialogue with Australian history and with ancestral murmurs deep within the national consciousness." Although Ray Willbanks describes Randolph Stow as "most Australian," he also finds him to be "among the least Australian" of the country's writers. On one hand, Willbanks explains, Stow has recorded with precision the landscape and the people, but on the other he has crossed the boundaries of literary realism, ignoring economic and social conflicts to explore the "internal, spiritual, metaphysical" and using the Australian landscape to signify the inward state.

For another Australian novelist, Thomas Keneally, there literally exist no boundaries when it comes to fictional settings and times. While some of his early work takes Australia as its locale, the Antarctica, Europe, Africa, the United States have served as well, whether in the fifteenth century or the present. Thomas Coakley proposes that this diversity of space and time remains essential to Keneally's world view, which "constructs a reeenactment of the present in the past," for always there emerge "the backgrounds of desolation, suffering, and death." So Keneally's characters, Coakley notes, move without boundaries across the same desolate stage no matter the place or time. In contrast to Keneally's departure from Australia, the poet Les Murray remains faithful to his homeland, so much so that at first reading his poetry may appear parochial. Paul Kane, however, argues otherwise, maintaining that Murray "wishes to mediate between rival claims in Australian (and Western) culture and to negotiate a settlement within an economy of absolute values, whereby the local becomes, in the end, the universal." Murray's "poetic project," Kane stresses, hopes to break down the divisions—the boundaries—that separate one human from another, taking as his metaphor the "triadic division" of postcolonial Australian society: those disjunctions among "the Aboriginal, the urban, and the rural."

Hena Maes-Jelinek, in her use of Wilson Harris's own term, "the universal imagination," apologizes for the word "universal," which she fears has fallen into critical disrepute being "seen as the major instrument of Euro-American centered discourse" on the literature of the formerly colonized. Without exercising the dreaded "cultural hegemony," she explores Harris's densely structured fiction in light of the author's assertion that the "universal imagination," the "re-visionary strategies," and "other texts" work "to create a multi-textual dialogue." Maes-Jelinek shows how this idea has informed his writing as a whole: its narrative strategies, characterization, and imagery. She also notes how he has decolonized artistically the boundaries of his West Indian heritage, "[Wilson Harris] has always dissociated himself from any clearly defined and, even more, from any militant notion of national or racial identity."

In contrast, James Gibbs places the 1986 Nobel Laureate, Wole Soyinka, firmly within the African milieu—Soyinka's native Nigeria in particular. Gibbs traces a long and distinguished career that has blended political activisim and art, that has managed the unlikely marriage of "earth to heaven"—as the essay's title suggests. Citing the artist-activist hero of Soyinka's novel, *Season of Anomy*, Gibbs finds reflections of Soyinka himself, the artist and the activist struggling "to reconcile the two aspects of his projects to express a wholeness of vision, to come to terms with past and present, with the indigenous and the imported, with the passing show and the eternal values." Although a formidable writer of essays, poetry, and fiction, Soyinka has excelled, according to Gibbs, as a dramatist, his plays decolonizing the artistic boundaries between African and Western tradition; his drama makes an "engagement with other models, both African and European," a "creative interaction . . . in which neither partner is dominant, and from which emerges a sturdy hybrid."

As boundaries disintegrated and decolonized themselves, a new kind of character entered international English literature: the immigrant. Although portrayed earlier by Anita Desai (*Bye Bye Blackbird*), Buchi Emecheta (*In the Ditch* and others), and Kamala Markandaya (*The Nowhere Man*), those who move from the former colonies to their late colonizer's home have not yet received a full share of attention; perhaps immigration will evolve into a major theme. In fact two of the younger writers, Timothy Mo and Bharati Mukherjee, have already lent the immigrant novel new dimensions. Victor Ramraj sees Mo—born in Hong Kong of Chinese-British parentage and living in London—as "fascinated by the amorphous world that exists at the meeting point of different cultures." Mo's work so far has examined the dual heritage of a Cantonese-Portuguese man living in Hong Kong and the cultural conflict between the British and Americans and the Chinese during the opium wars. But it is his novel, *Sour Sweet*, about a Hong Kong family in London, which serves as germinative for immigrant fiction through what Ramraj calls its "complex exploration of individuals encumbered with cultural duality." Mukherjee, born and reared in India, like Mo is an immigrant but to the United States not England. And she proudly calls herself an "immigrant writer," determined to decolonize boundaries, as she has announced in her manifesto, "Immigrant Writing: Give Us Your Maximalists." Liew-Geok Leong notes how Mukherjee "scours the complex multicultural worlds of her foreigners, the new Americans, to portray their displacement and adaptation." As Leong stresses, Mukherjee apprehends sadness but not defeat in a world without boundaries; she depicts that world, albeit "relegated to marginal status by mainstream North America," as "throbbing, exuberant and dynamic with the energy and passions of 'aliens' determined to survive, succeed and, ultimately, belong."

The act and art of decolonizing boundaries remains central to international literature in English, destructive of past separateness, constructive of future oneness.

Shirley Hazzard

S hirley Hazzard was born in Sydney, Australia, 30 January 1931, where she grew up and received her education at the Queenswood School. Because of her father's employment in the Australian government service, she lived in Hong Kong and in New Zealand, and traveled to England and to the United States.

In 1952 she joined the United Nations Secretariat in New York. While serving on the UN headquarters staff, she traveled in Europe and worked during 1957 in Naples. Her decade of experience with the UN inspired two of her books, the collection of satirical short stories, *People in Glass Houses*, and her nonfiction work, *Defeat of An Ideal: A Study of the Self-Destruction of the United Nations*. Since 1960, when she began to write fiction—some of her stories appeared first in *The New Yorker*—her time has been divided between New York and Italy.

In 1961 she retired from the United Nations to devote herself to writing. Two years later she married the American scholar and biographer Francis Steegmuller, whom she met at a party given by Muriel Spark, and in the same year published a collection of short stories, *Cliffs of Fall*. In addition to fiction, she has also written numerous articles on literature and international affairs. Her novel *The Transit of Venus* received the National Critics Circle Award in the United States and the PEN Faulkner Award for Fiction in 1980. In 1982 she was elected to the American Academy and Institute of Arts and Letters. She has been a guest lecturer at New York, Columbia, and Princeton Universities. She is now a citizen of the United States.

After an absence of over twenty years from her native country, she began to visit Australia again in the 1970s. Following her participation in Writers Week at the Adelaide Festival of Arts, she published in *The New Yorker* a study of changes in Australian intellectual life since the post-war years. In 1984 she was invited by the Australian Broadcasting Corporation to give the annual Boyer Lectures. In these four radio talks, which were published as *Coming of Age in Australia*, she described and commented on the change in Australia's cultural climate. While she had to go abroad to achieve artistic freedom and to develop her talent as a writer, the Australia of today, she argued, has changed radically in that its people have enlarged their ideas, their tolerance, imagination, and curiosity: "Experience is there, and humanity, character, and conscience. Only the realisation is awaited, and the inspired acceptance."

Glimpses of Paradise

In 1979 Shirley Hazzard pinpointed what was for her one of the greatest thematic challenges facing the contemporary writer:

No-man's land or at any rate literary no-man's land might be the title of this talk, since one of the greatest challenges faced by contemporary novelists is an unprecedented loss of geographical and, to some extent, national and even social, sense of belonging. . . . In the past most communities and persons could regard themselves as existing, however precariously, within some form of continuity. Departures were made from a recognisable home, afflictions were suffered under recognisable injustice or duress. . . . In the past half century a great dislocation has blown this state of affairs—humanly and culturally—to smithereens. And it's these smithereens that new novelists today must begin to assemble and identify as best they can. ("Problems" 179–80)

Loss of a sense of place, whether geographical, social, or national, is, according to Hazzard, an experience not confined to people whom circumstances oblige to live in all the various corners of the earth or to travel from one country to the next: It is an alienation felt by anyone who observes the changes in his or her own local environment. For Hazzard, as for Edward Said and others, this is a central, if not the central experience of modern man—one to which the millions of refugees, of exiles, and of emigrants in every continent of the world bear vivid testimony. In Hazzard's stories and novels, motifs of travel and flight, of emigration and exile play an important role—but in order to understand these we must first distinguish between the chief characteristics of these various states.

Exile has its origin in the ancient practice of banishing the politically unacceptable to a life on foreign shores, there to be marked with the inescapable stigma of the outsider. Outward homelessness is merely the sign of inner, spiritual absence. Refugees, on the other hand, are a phenomenon of the twentieth century, one that does not exist in the singular, for it refers generally to the great numbers of innocent people who in the face of war, catastrophe, persecution, or extreme need—whether spiritual or material—abandon their homes and seek the solace of whatever international aid is available. The refugee, like the exile, is a political figure born of the force of external events. The emigrant, on the other hand, has recourse to inner, private motives and to his own free will: Personal development, career prospects, marriage, friendship, chance, sheer curiosity, or the yearning for change can all play a role here (Said 166–67). What is, however, common to all three groups is the break with home and history, the transplantation into a new and often strange environment along with the resultant physical as well as spiritual deracination. It is this situation that determines the search for new bearings, for a new identity and a new home. Shelter and safety may be found in identification with a particular geographical and political *locus*, but the more powerful the role played by inner, personal motives in leaving one's home, the deeper will the new spiritual roots be cast. People who have left their inherited land voluntarily behind them will look not for a new nation or a new country but rather for a sense of belonging independent of geography or politics; one for which these will often provide no more than a public, symbolic delineation.

Hazzard's travelers, exiles, and emigrants are searching for an ideal; her emigrants in particular are men and women with a vacuum in their souls, which they are intent on filling, and for this purpose they constantly pause, on the lookout for forms and structures that might serve as home and so determine the end of their journey. Their experience in this respect is like Hazzard's own, who to the question "Do you have a paradise you can define?" gave the answer: "*Et in Arcadia ego*—and luckily often. Many glimpses of paradise, through place and art, through love" (Kavanagh 214). For her (generally female) protagonists, as for the author herself, paradise is something temporally defined: a happiness that, though complete as only love can make it, does not indicate the end but merely a temporary resting point on the journey. In contrast to the sojourner herself stand the patriot and nationalist figures who create the conditions of her stay, figures rooted fast in the cultural heritage of their land and in the values of its people. It is through their initiation into and their loss of this transient happiness that Hazzard's travelers undergo spiritual growth.

Hazzard's novels and stories can be divided into two groups. The first is predominantly negative in the life situations it portrays; the imperfections of men and the inhumanity of their world conspire to make even passing glimpses of the lost paradise impossible. But in the second group women and men are able from time to time to experience complete happiness. The first group comprises the short story collections *Cliffs of Fall, People in Glass Houses,* and the critique of the United Nations, *Defeat of an Ideal.* Hazzard does not hesitate to use satire to unmask the conditions that enslave people and repress their humanity. She appeals here to Pope:

> Satire, ridicule is only honorable, I think, when used by the helpless against the powerful, when used *not* from emotion but from courage and principle. I agree with Pope, that it is a "sacred weapon"—"O sacred weapon, left for Truth's defense,/Sole dread of folly, vice and insolence." (Danvers 43)

The powers on which Hazzard deploys the weapon of satire in *People in Glass Houses,* a series of stories connected by their recurrent figures, are the representatives of a Kafkaesque global organization easily identifiable with the UN. Its victims are the tortured captives of a mammoth bureaucracy, who manage somehow to maintain the remnants of human dignity in their hopeless battle against a conformism that has become an end in itself. Whether they are called Swoboda, Tong, Ismet, Choudhury, Rodriguez-O'Hearn, or Artmole-Brown, they are displaced persons: In the glass walls of their prison they have an occupation, but no home. The ideals of the organization, right in themselves, have been swamped in meaningless regulations, and only if these are disregarded can they come to life. They do so, for instance, in the figure of Algie from "Nothing in Excess": a person who so far has managed to withstand the pressures of the bureaucracy but, as a consequence, faces dismissal. He is warned by his conformist friend Jaspersen to take to heart the policy of the organization, hallowed by antiquity, of "moderation in all things" (*People* 25); but Algie refused and counters that dictum with his own *credo* of a spontaneous and authentic humanity:

"Nothing in excess," Algie repeated. "But one has to understand the meaning of excess. Why should it be taken, as it seems to be these days, to refer simply to self-indulgence, or violence—or enjoyment? . . . At the other end of that temple, there was a second inscription—'Know Thyself.' . . . Meant we should understand ourselves in order to be free." . . . "No thanks old boy, really. Fact is, I'm not suited to it here, and from that point of view these chaps are right. You tell me to get inside their minds—but if I did that I might never find my way out again." (25-26)

The field worker in "The Meeting" experiences a similar disillusionment for, after he has succeeded in improving the miserable condition of the people of El Attare, he discovers that his report has fallen on deaf ears because he has failed to couch it in the bizarre statistical language of the mandarins.

All of the stories are variations on the same theme, as one critic has pointed out:

. . . in the stultifying atmosphere of the building that houses the Organization, conversations and directives are reduced to gobble-dygook, personal relationships are nonexistent, hypocrisy is so prevalent that the term becomes meaningless, and individuality is so alien that it is taken not for eccentricity but for subversiveness. (Wellein 393)

With its message that conformity imposed from above is the death of individuality and of humanity, the book is reminiscent of Huxley, Orwell, and Waugh. What detracts from one's enjoyment as a reader is the varying quality of the stories and above all their wearisome repetitiveness, though this is redeemed by Hazzard's ability to capture the dehumanized world of her satire in the mirror of language: ". . . as an anatomist or pathologist, she used a keen scalpel to dissect a good netful of those multi-specied fish gathered in international waters and confined in that great glass tank on the East River" (Granat 10).

People in Glass Houses can be read as a first draft of Hazzard's critical account of the United Nations, *Defeat of an Ideal.* In almost ten years working for the secretariat of the UN, Hazzard had been able to gather enough material to provide the factual basis for her fictional critique. Along with many of her contemporaries, she was repelled by the fear the organization showed when confronted by the real problems of the day, Biafra and Vietnam, by the weakness of the first secretary general Trygve Lie, who allowed the FBI inside the UN building to spy on employees, and by the complacency of Dag Hammarskjöld, who failed to stop these develop-ments and failed equally to prevent the organization from becoming a top-heavy bureaucracy indebted as much to multinational business as it was to the real needs of its member states. Hazzard arraigns the leading figures of the organization for turning a blind eye to the qualities of integrity, conviction, and competence, which the UN charter demands, and for thereby contributing to the perversion of the ideals on which the United Nations was founded.

As a global organization, she argues, it is far too large to be competent, too Americanized to be unbiased, too much of a caste system to be credible. Hazzard's suggestion that the organization should be moved to a smaller country elicited from Australian writer Kylie Tennant the comment that this ". . . sounds mighty like advertising the removal of a lady of easy virtue from a Park Avenue flat paid for by a millionaire into a mod con, paid for by a committee of spinsters" (26). Hazzard's critique met with a varied response: Keith Kyle reproached her for poor style, intellectual frivolity, and hysterical exaggeration (556-57), but she defended herself publicly in a letter to the editor of the *Times Literary Supplement* (4 May 1973), observing that she had simply called for a corrective to what were glaring abuses, and others took her side. She had already anticipated her critics in the foreword to the book, when she asserted:

> It is precisely the predicament of the present body that produces, for the first time, an opportunity for a revitalized and radically different United Nations. Anyone who makes, as does the present author, the assertion that this must come about . . . will be accused—by those he holds responsible—of disrespect to the United Nations Idea. (xiv)

This plea should be listened to. In the final sentence of the foreword Hazzard expresses her motives, motives that have unfortunately been largely overlooked by those to whom her words are principally addressed:

> He [any critic] might bear in mind the response of Igor Stravinsky to persons who, long ago, accused him, in his *Pulcinella* transposition, of disrespect to the genius of Pergolesi: *"You respect. I love."* (xiv)

If the dominant motif of *People in Glass Houses* is the external forces that repress the instincts of humanity, in *Cliffs of Fall,* a collection of stories published in 1963, the repressive forces are internal to the men and women whose vision of paradise they impede. The protagonists of *People in Glass Houses* were the prisoners of a giant organization; the voyagers and emigrants in *Cliffs of Fall* are imprisoned by their own inadequacy. The stories are set in hotels, pensions, street cafes, and railway stations, and their common theme is man's inability to love. The travelers are on a sort of odyssey, both inner and outer, which has as its goal an alliance of love, but one that it never attains. The two lovers in "The Party" fail each other because one of them is unwilling to be the home that the other seeks. In "A Place in the Country" half-heartedness and dishonesty are the destructive principles. Vittorio, who in the story that bears his name falls in love with an English woman passing through his town, is rewarded with the admonition that they belong to incompatible cultural codes. Miranda, estranged from her husband and courted by an admirer ten years younger than herself, is, in "In One's Own House," in a condition of emotional flight; and in "Villa Adriana" the fleeting encounter of the two anonymous protagonists takes place during a sightseeing tour.

These cursory relations, like the momentary act of emancipation of the young poet in "Harold," when he reads his poems to the guests in an Italian pension, take place almost always in Italy. As such they point the way forward to *The Evening of the Holiday* and *Bay of Noon*. The Italy of these stories is both a geographical and a symbolic entity, a catalyst for the inner processes it witnesses. A French guest in the pension describes the particular flair of the place:

> "I simply mean that in our countries one must still be prepared for a few surprises, but here all experience is repetition, and that gives one an outrageous sense of proportion. That's why we feel so comfortable—why we find it so attractive to come here." (*Cliffs* 159)

The English travelers experience a sky that seems to invite the restoral of human harmony in a mutually given and received ecstasy:

> . . . but then there was that sky. He had never experienced such a sky. In England, where heaven is a low-hung, personal affair, thoroughly identified with the King James Version, a sky such as this would not have been tolerated for a moment. It was a high, pagan explosion of a sky, promising indulgence for all kinds of offenses to which he had not the slightest inclination. (178)

The story "Cliffs of Fall," whose title comes from a poem by Gerard Manley Hopkins, illustrates with particular clearness both the book's common theme and the symbolic function of place. Here, too, the travelers are in a state of flight, seeking in a relation of love for a way out of their inner crisis but seeking in vain. The landscape becomes a psychograph reflecting at one moment a memory of lost harmony, at another the torment of a distraught soul. It is not yet, as it will become in the novels, an active element in the plot. Thus the Swiss Alps impress Elizabeth as a mirror-image of her jagged emotional state:

> "The mountains bother me more—I mean, the look of them."
> "The drama," he said. "Yes. Because they have something analogous to our emotions. They look like a graph of one's experience. Isn't that it?"
> "I suppose so," she agreed, "There's a poem,—
>
> *'O the mind, mind has mountains; cliffs of fall*
> *Frightful, sheer, no-man-fathomed. Hold them cheap*
> *May who ne'er hung there.'* " (126–27)

Cliffs of Fall anticipates the corpus of themes and figures developed by the novels. Despite the transitoriness of the happiness that Hazzard's travelers here, too, experience, the novels in contrast to the stories depict phases and degrees of paradisaical bliss within the maze of human waywardness, a bliss in whose genesis love, art, and the right place play a decisive role.

The title of *The Evening of the Holiday* (1966) is taken from a poem by Giacomo Leopardi; it already indicates the thematic division of the novel into the elements of departure, associated with evening, autumn, and winter, from a season of fulfilment, a festal summer and spring. The two leading participants in this holiday and in its end come from two different cultural backgrounds: Sophie, half English, half Italian, belongs properly to neither world. She feels like a traveler on the deck of a ship in a foreign port, a prey always to "the solitary pang of the expatriate" (*Evening* 42). In Italy, where she meets the architect Tancredi, she is also, at least at first, a foreigner:

> She felt like an outsider at a family feast. She wondered: What am I doing here, on this road, with this man, these sights, this language? She wished she were an authentic tourist—an Englishman come to flaunt his reticence, an American secretly hankering for gift wrapping and matching towels. She did not really know where she most belonged. Even those places to which she felt most drawn were mere approximations of home. (43)

Tancredi, on the other hand, is a "patriot," a Sicilian, knit to the culture and the history of his home, from which he draws his strength and his identity. Sophie feels the strangeness of the Tuscan landscape, Tancredi its oneness with his soul. His house possesses a garden, the age-old symbol of human dreams and longings, and in it is an ancient fountain, the embodiment of Tancredi's immemorial cultural roots. At her first encounter with Tancredi, Sophie dips her hand into the waters of this fountain, and the golden bracelet falls from her wrist, a talisman of the relation she is to form both with him and with his country.

To the restless Sophie, Tancredi offers himself as refuge and as home: "'Think of me—as another possibility, along with the letters and the walks. A sort of aunt perhaps'" (37)—an offer that Sophie is able only hesitantly to accept. Then, however, a relationship develops between them of a love that is at once, as Hazzard several times suggests, complete, fateful, and transitory. The song of the nightingales in the darkening garden evokes for Sophie Keats's "Ode to a Nightingale," and the whole scene illustrates the mood that runs through the first stanza of that poem, whose exact wording Sophie cannot for the time being remember. Surrounded by the Tuscan landscape she experiences at Tancredi's side a sense of happiness that turns what had been an alien environment into home:

> She wanted to go on for ever—but wanted it intensely, as if it were a possibility—and wondered whether she had ever been as happy as this. . . . She withdrew her hand and replaced it at his side. "I don't ever want to arrive." (72)

Sophie loves with an entire disregard for social conventions and consequences and with an almost unearthly perfection: "The earth might be uninhabited, from the way she behaved" (101). She has found her paradise; but Tancredi feels unable to share with conviction in that fullness:

> Her love is perfect, he thought. What one always hears about—perfect love. Then he told himself, with relief and a certain satisfaction: I am not worthy of that. Not up to it at all. I am an ordinary person—a fallible, inconsistent, mortal man. (102)

Although she does not at first admit it, Sophie too knows that this degree of happiness cannot last, and the evening of the holiday becomes a leavetaking from paradise, and one that demands of them more than they can give. This leavetaking is anticipated, long before it actually takes place, in the storm that lays waste the garden, a desolation consummated after the lovers' separation. The fountain dries up, and the dominant mood of the last chapters is one of winter, death, and war. Both partners seek a new direction in their lives, and the novel reveals itself, as Leonie Kramer has observed, to be one of untaken chances, of inconclusiveness:

> If one is left with any single sensation after closing the book, it is of opportunities missed, both in life and death, of the inconclusiveness of human actions, of the suspension of possibilities. Love is sacrificed, death is unimpressive, human relationships are incomplete. There is a pervasive sense of anti-climax, summarised in the last paragraph in the words, "The song never reaches its conclusion." (44)

With *The Bay of Noon*, Hazzard, as the critics have remarked, moved into Henry James and E.M. Forster country. Henry James's Paris is her Naples. Like *The Evening of the Holiday*, *The Bay of Noon* is "almost a study of the interpenetration between person and place, between actors and their setting" (117). The crack through which the storyteller allows us a glimpse into the spiritual vacuum of her protagonists is slowly widening. At the end of *The Bay of Noon*, Jenny, the novel's principal character, summarizes her life history:

> We are like those early explorers of Australia who died of thirst on expeditions to the dead centre of a continent, always thinking they must come ultimately to water—to an inland sea, to a lake, a river, a cascade. Deceived by salt deposits, by rivers that flow inland, by the fossils of seashells, they were driven on by incredulity as well—by disbelief that one could come so far without drawing nearer to what one sought. (154)

The Bay of Noon differs from the earlier novel in the unattainability of its imaginative goals. There an at least temporary sojourn in the paradise of perfect love was understood to be possible; here the novelist confines herself to the presentation of two forms of mutually irreconcilable attraction.

Jenny, an English woman working in Italy, is in a state of freely chosen emigration. She has left her home in order to escape from an incestuous love relationship with her brother. Naples is only one stop of her journey, albeit up till now the most important one, for it is here that she meets Gianni and Gioconda as well as the

Scottish scientist Justin P. Tulloch. Gianni and Gioconda become a stable focus in Jenny's life, the embodiment of beauty and culture, stasis and rootedness. Their life, their manners, their very speech fill Jenny with homesickness (93–94); particularly Gianni, who, like Tancredi, is described as a patriot, is the personification of a somewhat exalted southern urbanity whose authentic human value Jenny only gradually learns to appreciate. Gianni's cultivated being is mirrored in his very environment:

> The beauty of this flat of Gianni's was the most troubling of his inconsistencies. It reflected not only an unfeignable degree of intellect and feeling, but even—for its main impression was of clear surfaces, of space without ornament—a certain austerity of temperament: qualities that one must exclude from Gianni's composition in order to make his daily self comprehensible. (92)

His relationship with Gioconda breaks down when Gioconda begins to feel herself a stranger in that familiar world; she leaves him, only to discover that the loss of home is often the simplest way of retaining one's love for it.

Gionconda sets off on a tour of Europe in search of herself; Jenny, meanwhile, is in the throes of her own spiritual crisis, from which she is rescued by Gianni's responsive interest in her. The love relationship between them is, however, short-lived, as Gianni is waiting for Gioconda to return and Jenny is confronted with the alternative of Justin P. Tulloch, the "nationalist" and forerunner of Ted Tice in *The Transit of Venus*. Italian warmth, romanticism, and openness in the person of Gianni meet in Tulloch's Scottish reserve and down-to-earthness. Like Gianni, Tulloch is a man with strong roots, one who can remain true to himself and his cherished ideals even in a foreign land. Like the artist whom Gioconda had met in her youth, he belongs to that category of persons to whom Hazzard ascribes the power of independent human action, the precondition for the status of genuine individuality.

Tulloch's attitude to love differs from Gianni's in that it is not concerned with harmony and the giving of oneself to another, but with "mountains of the mind" and with plumbing of the "cliffs of fall/Frightful, sheer, no-man-fathomed":

> "All that which you deplore—the blind obsession, the unequal sacrifice, the punishment invited and inflicted—that is love. Believe me. It's pointless to call upon perfect harmonies and deathless romance. For love, you must look closer to home." (76)

Such love, however, is only possible when the lovers have filled their own spiritual vacuum and discovered their identity. Jenny has to agree with Tulloch's diagnosis: "'We are both, to be explicit, at a loss. Isn't that it? Have been deprived of something and are in a state of abeyance. Can afford to be fastidious, having insufficient courage, at present, to be otherwise'" (77). That Tulloch's definition and diagnosis are declarations of love is something Jenny only realizes when she hears of his death in a plane crash.

Jenny undergoes a process of change and maturation, which is, once again, not by chance set in Italy. Italy and Naples are less the symbolic Eden, the place of harmony, than the arena of this inner growth. Both Gianni and Tulloch emphasize the anthropomorphic qualities of the landscape: "'Here you could practically say it's an indoor landscape. It's Nature with beautiful manners—no, that's too tame. Rather, it's as if Nature were capable of thought, of joy'" (144). When Jenny finally leaves Italy, it is to find a home in the new world. But, in her "search . . . closer to home" (146), Italy will still in her memory be the place where consciousness awoke: "Like the dye they had injected into my veins, the country coloured my essence, illuminated the reaction to everything else. Here, literally, I had come to my senses" (145). The motto of the novel, derived from W.H. Auden's poem "Goodbye to the Mezzogiorno," makes sense in the light of Jenny's development; Italy becomes her home inasmuch as it is there that she gains maturity, there that she puts behind her the stages of childhood and youth (119): "I felt knowledge, as I say, coursing in my body, making everything different" (122). If *The Evening of the Holiday* was a temporary stay in paradise, *The Bay of Noon* marks the loss of paradise through the eating of the fruit of the tree of knowledge. The motto reminds us of this paradise that once was and has now gone:

> To bless this region, its vendages, and those
> Who call it home: though one cannot always
> Remember exactly why one has been happy,
> There is no forgetting that one was.

If Hazzard had written only *The Transit of Venus*, she would have been sure of a place in international English literature. The novel exemplifies almost perfectly Hazzard's themes and her technical accomplishment. The symbolism of names, the art of premonition, the choice of place, the choreography of the figures, the reinterpretation of the antipodean myth—these things alone would make of the novel a successful work. The author herself disputes the concept of development in her *oeuvre* ("Author's Statement" 206), but *The Transit of Venus* marks an artistic highpoint. Thematically it is a continuation of *The Bay of Noon* with the principal characters, Caro Bell and Ted Tice as two more wanderers in search of their lost paradise, a paradise that, if only for a brief moment, they find in the existence of a love transmuted and refined by suffering.

Despite its complexity, *The Transit of Venus* is so constructed that Caro's life history stands in contrast to those of her half-sister Dora and her sister Grace, and that her most important relationships, those with Paul Ivory, Adam Vail, and Ted Tice, are at the same time stages in a process of mental and emotional ripening.

Dora, Grace, and Caro, with their varying attitudes to life, represent different approaches to physical and spiritual exile. All three are Australians cast up on the coasts of Europe and America, but only for Grace and Caro does the journey to Europe become "A mystical passage to another life, from which no one returned the same" (37). In contrast to Dora, who personifies an everyday existence devoid of growth and change and as such spreads chaos and misery around her, Caro and Grace are for all their differences both capable of development. Their very appearance—"dark she, fair she" (9)—signals their contrasting personalities: "In looks, Caro was as yet unfinished, lacking some revelation that might simply be her own awareness; unlike Grace, who was completed if not complete" (9). In Europe their ways part. Grace, charming as well as beautiful, the embodiment of stillness and adaptability but at the same time in search of these qualities, marries the indescribably boring Christian Thrale and withers at his side: "Grace knew perfectly how the practised conformity of her days gratified her own desires. Yet one might cling to security and still be bored by it" (196). From this dismal round she is briefly saved by her romance with the doctor Angus Dance; but Dance withdraws in order not to compromise either "Perfect Grace" (282) or his career, and Grace, "a navigator, who seeks land in a horizon deceitful with vapours" (285-86), who seeks "sacred and profane love" (287) in one, is broken on the rocks of a perfect, unrequited love. Capable of loving unconditionally, she catches a glimpse of paradise but is forbidden to set foot there. Caro, however, unlike her more passive sister, is driven by hope and expectation and above all by the active will to shape her life for herself. And that life, like her persona, is full of dynamism. At the very beginning of the novel we are told: "Caro would decide at which table she belonged. She was young to have grasped the need for this" (9-10). The quest for true love will determine her life, although she does not yet understand that truth has its own life; and in this quest Paul Ivory, Adam Vail, and Ted Tice will in their own ways help her.

First she falls for Paul Ivory, an attractive and successful writer engaged to a beautiful young aristocrat, Tertia Drage. As yet she is deaf to the advances of the less striking Ted Tice as well as to his warning about Ivory's character: "'His faults aren't those of youth. He has no growth, merely automatic transmission'" (74). In the sacred ring of the Avebury circle, Caro gives herself to Paul in the belief that she has found the fulfillment of her desires although her infallible sense of truth in the person she loves leads her to suspect that that person is in this instance a criminal on the run. Her love for Paul marks the first stage in her development: "From ignorance she had gone, in one hour, to this superiority of common knowledge" (100).

Like Grace, Caro experiences a bitter disappointment, for with his marriage Paul, in spite of all his promises, pushes her out of his life: "He had not merely left her, but left her behind" (125–26). They meet again in London a few months later, and Paul takes advantage of the absence of his wife to relaunch his adventure with the deeply injured but still loving Caro. Her will to truth, however, wins against his seductive arts:

> "There must be an end somewhere to deception. Ultimately there must be the truth."
> "And do you think the human need to deceive is not also part of truth?"
> "Of reality, not truth." (152)

Plunged by the separation into a physical and emotional crisis, Caro is confronted with the proof of Paul's simple inhumanity when he sees her sick and in need and does nothing for her. Their relationship deteriorates into a state of war: "They were converging from extremes, two opposing commanders who meet while their forces slaughter, not to make peace but to exchange a high, knowing, egoistic sadness before resuming battle: two minutes' silence, their brief armistice" (170). Their final meeting is her moment of disillusionment. Paul's admission that he is homosexual, that he has a man's life on his conscience, and that his love for Caro was an act of revenge against the hated rival, Tice, does nothing to restore his integrity. On the contrary, it deepens one's sense of his baseness. Like Dorian Gray he has paid for his success with a full cup of moral depravity. Caro's world breaks into pieces: "She had wanted knowledge, but not to know this. Knowledge had become a fearful current in which a man might drown" (310).

She is saved from her crisis by the "American Adam" Vail who, like Paul's father the poet Rex Ivory, like the South American poet Ramón Tregeár, and like Ted Tice, possesses the humanity that gives rise to acts of selfless love. Adam publicly opposes his country's aggressive policies in Latin American and is unconcerned at the rage of the government press. He takes up the cause of Tregeár, who has been practically condemned to death and whose idea of "solidarity" comes very close to Caro's understanding of truth: "'The only proper solidarity is with the truth, if one can discover it'" (249). Vail turns out to be the savior who prepares Caro for her last meeting with Tice.

Taught by her encounters with Paul Ivory, Adam Vail, and Ramón Tregeár, Caro can see now into Ted's true nature and is able for a short time to enter into a love absolute in its unearthly perfection. Tice is one of the few scientists in literature with any depth. A professional astronomer, he is endowed with a strong will to truth and with an openness to genuine human feeling. In contrast to the professor of literature Wadding and the careerist Paul Ivory, he stands for the ideals that Rex Ivory, Adam Vail, and Ramón Tregeár have lived and suffered for. The quest for truth is more important than visible external success. Long before he is called Edmund Le Gentil (160), he has identified himself with the fate of Guillaume Legentil, an early astronomer who journeyed to India to take observations of Venus but arrived too late and, having waited eight years for a new sighting, was unable to record anything because visibility on that day was so poor: "'His story has such nobility you can scarcely call it unsuccessful.' Ted was honouring the faith, not the failure" (16).

For Paul, Caro was just a conquest, but Ted respects her individuality. He knows of Paul's crimes but does not use this knowledge against him because he sees that Caro loves his rival; on the other hand, he does not cease loving Caro when she marries Adam Vail: "'What I have done has been for hope of her. What I do now will be for lack of her. . . . Do you call it freedom?'" (198). After Adam's death he, now himself married, meets Caro again. Paul's confession has opened her eyes and this former lover has become "everything shoddy, derelict; the torn kite unstuck from the sky" (310); and Ted's nobility and moral integrity have become all the more visible: "In Caroline Vail's own life and thought, Ted Tice had become supreme" (324). Ted embodies not only the will to absolute truth but the power to absolute love. Shortly before her death, Caro realizes that the grail she seeks also lies beyond all human limitations:

She tried to see how it had come about, and only knew she had
been seeking some extreme. That extreme might be the force, pure
and terrible, of a man's attested strength of will. It was as if Ted Tice
had created this event in her through the cosmic power of love.
(325)

Their last meeting, overshadowed by subtle premonitions of tragic parting, takes
place in a geographically definable locality but at the same time outside all
measurable dimensions: "They were moving in the light of a past or other world"
(331). Their declarations of love in the face of certain death possess a degree of
absoluteness, which, despite—or perhaps because of—the approaching tragedy,
seems like a glimpse of paradise regained, a place of supraterrestrial happiness: "They
were natural and supernatural, in that blank place, like amorous figures from
mythology" (336).

David Rowbotham must speak for many readers when he affirms of *The Transit
of Venus*:

> It is (I repeat) a great novel—of love, pain, hope, humanity, and of
> destinies and destinations—a novel which shall last, preserving
> language as well as wisdom, and forever placed among its peers.
> (24)

WORKS CITED

Danvers, Dennis. "A Conversation with Shirley Hazzard." *Antipodes* 1 (1987): 40–43.
Granat, Robert. "Organization Cake." *Book World, Washington Post* 5 Nov. 1967: 10.
Hazzard, Shirley. "Author's Statement: Shirley Hazzard." *Australian Literary Studies* 10 (1981): 204–08.
———. *The Bay of Noon.* Ringwood: Melbourne: Penguin Australia, 1973.
———. *Defeat of an Ideal: A Study of Self-Destruction of the United Nations.* New York: Macmillan, 1973.
———. *The Evening of the Holiday.* Melbourne: Penguin Australia, 1983.
———. *People in Glass Houses.* Melbourne: Penguin Australia, 1983.
———. "Problems Facing Contemporary Novelists." *Australian Literary Studies* 9 (1979): 179–81.
———. *The Transit of Venus.* Melbourne: Penguin Australia, 1983.
Kavanagh, Paul. "Astronomer of Souls: An Interview." *Southerly* 45 (1985): 209–14.
Kramer, Leonie. "The Light in the Piazza." *The Bulletin* 10 Sept. 1966: 44–45.
Kyle, Keith. "The Quality of the 38th Floor." *The Listener* 26 April 1973: 556–57.
Rowbotham, David. Review, *The Transit of Venus. The Courier-Mail* 29 Nov. 1980: 24.
Said, Edward. "Reflections on Exile." *Granta* 13 (1984): 159–72.
Sissman, C.L.E. "Books." *The New Yorker* 13 June 1970: 117–18.
Tennant, Kylie. "Decline and Fall of the United Nations." *Sydney Morning Herald* 30 June 1973: 26.
Wellein, Lawrence. Review, *People in Glass Houses. Studies in Short Fiction* 5 (1967–68): 392–94.

SHIRLEY HAZZARD'S PUBLISHED WORK

Novels

The Evening of the Holiday, 1966
The Bay of Noon, 1970
The Transit of Venus, 1980

Short Story Collections

Cliffs of Fall, 1963
People in Glass Houses, 1967

History

Defeat of an Ideal: A Study of the Self-Destruction of the United Nations, 1973

Selected Articles

"Problems Facing Contemporary Novelists." *Australian Literary Studies* 9 (1979): 179–88.
> Points out that the novelist lives in a "no-man's land," having lost a sense of geographical, even social and national identity. This loss has sent the novelist on an inward journey from which he returns obsessed with his own emotions and opinions; sees this as an unfortunate development and cites Patrick White as an example of a writer who has managed to overcome these problems.

"We Need Silence to Find Out What We Think." *New York Times Book Review* 14 Nov. 1982: 11, 28–29.
> Sees the novelist's and poet's task as "to convey states of mind and of being as immediately as possible, through language." In order to avoid evasion and to write fearlessly, the writer must think fearlessly, and for this, Hazzard argues, citing Orwell as an example, it is necessary to have an independent mind.

SELECTED CRITICAL READINGS

Literary critics have long focused their interest mainly on the ideological and aesthetic qualities of *The Transit of Venus*, devoting little attention to its overall artistic development. It would therefore be interesting to investigate the varied treatment of the quest motif, the concept of love, the narrative style, the effects wrought by change of setting and character development, the symbolic use of names and locations, and the employment of irony in the delineation of character in the complete work. An examination of the influence of literary prototypes and the function of intertextual references also needs to be undertaken. Similarly, the role of Hazzard's nonliterary writings should be more seriously considered, as these could shed light on further central motifs in her work.

Baym, Nina. "Artifice and Romance in Shirley Hazzard's Fiction." *Texas Studies in Language and Literature* 25 (1983): 222–48. Sees *The Transit of Venus*—and Hazzard's other fiction—as traditional in structure, but argues that its "conspicuous passion for literary art" places it alongside the "most radical experimental novel." Discusses all of the fiction in the light of contemporary literary theory, which Baym admits Hazzard's book defies. (Annotation source: *Australian Literary Criticism—1945–1988* by Robert Ross)

Bird, Delys. "Text Production and Reception: Shirley Hazzard's *The Transit of Venus*." *Westerly* 30.1 (1985): 38–51. Questions whether a literary work succeeds because of its packaging and promotion, then examines *The Transit of Venus* in this light, determining that its warm reception resulted from the kind of presentation accorded to it. (Annotation source: *Australian Literary Criticism*)

Capone, Giovanna. "Shirley Hazzard: *Transit* and *The Bay of Noon*." *Australian Literary Studies* 13 (1987): 172-83. Treats *The Bay of Noon*, set in Italy, as another "transit" story that involves special ways of looking at experience and of facing a sense of geographical and personal dislocation.

Colmer, John. "Patterns and Preoccupations of Love: The Novels of Shirley Hazzard." *Meanjin* 29 (1970): 461–67. Argues that Hazzard's stories and novels are centrally concerned with the theme of love. Discusses her work in the light of this theme and its ironic variations.

———. "Shirley Hazzard's *The Transit of Venus.*" *Journal of Commonwealth Literature* 19.1 (1984): 10–21. Sees Hazzard as a disciple of Flaubert and other major European writers; examines her style, complexity of design, characterization, and her "ironic scrutiny" of human relationships.

Lehmann, Geoffrey. "The Novels of Shirley Hazzard: An Affirmation of Venus." *Quadrant* 25.3 (1981): 33–36. Discusses the nexus between the theme of love and "the immateriality of the material world of outcomes and facts," which is seen as one of the recurrent themes in Hazzard's fiction; arrives at the conclusion that in her early novels the act of love is terminated by withdrawal and departure, whereas in her later novels love is presented as an absolute state of being.

Levy, Bronwen. "Constructing the Woman Writer: The Reception of Hazzard's *The Transit of Venus.*" *Gender, Politics and Fiction: Twentieth Century Australian Women's Novels.* St. Lucia: U of Queensland P, 1985: 179–99. Examines the reviewing of fiction written by women, focusing on Hazzard's novel and comparing its reviews to criticism of work by other women writers. Suggests that Hazzard's approach to women stems from "bourgeois American liberalism," hence the favorable reviews by "establishment" critics and the lack of attention by feminists. Proposes that traditional critical approaches to women's writing need to be assessed in the light of the "feminist socialist" viewpoint. (Annotation source: *Australian Literary Criticism*)

Moon, E.B. "Fate, Individual Action, and the Shape of Life in Shirley Hazzard's *The Transit of Venus.*" *Southerly* 43 (1983): 332–44. Argues that *The Bay of Noon* and *The Transit of Venus* are linked by the key theme of search and that both novels have as partial subjects an explanation of the forces that give impetus and direction to human life; shows how these forces shape individual experience, and illustrates the extent to which the future is accessible or within control of the individual.

———. "'Indispensable Humanity': Saviours and Destroyers, and Major and Minor Characters in Shirley Hazzard's *The Transit of Venus.*" *Southerly* 45 (1985): 94–108. Argues that Hazzard contrasts her characters in terms of their essential humanity and that one of the criteria for differentiation is the extent to which these characters might be regarded as saviors or destroyers. Sees another patterned contrast in that between the astronomer/scientist and the writer/artist, which extends the motif of saviors and destroyers to include, in a provocative opposition to the idea of destroyers, the notion of creators.

Negri, Alegrina. "Ripening in the Sun: Shirley Hazzard's Heroines in Italy." *Westerly* 28.4 (1983): 37–42. Shows that not only Hazzard's English women but also her Italian women are appreciative of the special qualities of the Italian landscape and that the influence of place upon characters forms a major thematic structure in her work.

Rainwater, Catherine, and William J. Scheick. "'Some Godlike Grammar': An Introduction to the Writings of Hazzard, Ozick, and Redmon." *Texas Studies in Language and Literature* 25 (1983): 181–211. Discusses the writings of Hazzard, Cynthia Ozick, and Anne Redmon, arguing that each seeks some "goldlike grammar" to describe and reconcile the unmanageable chaos of human existence. For each the ordered and meaningful exploration of chaos involves essential questions about memory, the past, free will, fate, language, and art.

Sellick, Robert. "Shirley Hazzard: Dislocation and Continuity." *Australian Literary Studies* 9 (1979): 182–88. Stresses the importance of the loss of a geographical, national, and social sense of belonging and shows that war, no-man's land, and the need for a sense of belonging are some of the central strands that thread through the novels and stories.

Taylor, Nancy Dew. "An Introduction to Shirley Hazzard's *The Transit of Venus*." *World Literature Written in English* 24 (1984): 287–95. Shows how astronomical and mythological references, setting, metaphors, symbols, allusions, ironies, and ambiguities work together to emphasize presentiment. Argues that because Hazzard wanted the whole to seem "preordained" and "fated" her use of foreshadowing is an important element in her novel.

Wieland, James. "'Antipodean Eyes': Ways of Seeing in Shirley Hazzard's *The Transit of Venus*." *Kunapipi* 5.2 (1983): 36–49. Reveals that "antipodean" in Hazzard's world suggests a positive inversion of the geographical and philosophical implications of the age-old myth of the Antipodes. "European eyes" perceive only the accepted and prevailing views, whereas "antipodean eyes" are able to see beneath the surface appearances; characters with "antipodean eyes" are capable of conscious acts of independent humanity.

———. "Going Through with Things: Men and Women in *The Transit of Venus*." *Commonwealth Novel in English* 3 (1984): 1–20. Examines the novel's war motif, considering it essential to an understanding of the moral values represented by Hazzard's characters. Argues that what distinguishes one character from another is "the willingness or reluctance to signal a difference from the established power elite." Sees two sets of characters opposing each other: on the one hand the individuals who refuse to join the mass society and to adapt to its moral standards, on the other the bureaucrats who conform and reduce others to their own level.

Interviews

With Dennis Danvers. *Antipodes* 1 (1987): 40–43.
With Paul Kavanagh. *Southerly* 45 (1985): 209–19.
With Catherine Rainwater and William J. Scheick. *Texas Studies in Language and Literature* 25 (1983): 213–21.

— HORST PRIESSNITZ

Salman Rushdie

Salman Rushdie was born 19 June 1947 in Bombay, just before India won its independence from Great Britain and the subcontinent was divided into India and Pakistan. Reared in a Muslim household where both English and Urdu were spoken, Rushdie recalls his childhood as being "uneventfully happy" and occurring in "an atmosphere of books." His father, a Cambridge-educated businessman, read serial fairy tales to his son and three daughters, and Rushdie recalls his mother as the "keeper of the family stories." No wonder, then, that by the time Rushdie was five years old he wanted to be a writer.

In 1961, at age fourteen, Rushdie was sent to Rugby, the elite English public school. There he was subjected by some classmates to "minor persecutions and racist attacks," memories which partly explain his reluctance to return to Cambridge University in 1965. Another major reason behind Rushdie's desire to stay in the Pakistani city of Karachi, where his parents had moved in 1964, was the Indian-Pakistani war then raging; the psychological and emotional impact of the war between his "native" and his "adopted" country was such as to "partially derange" him, much as it would the main character in *Midnight's Children.*

On the insistence of his parents, however, Rushdie did return to England, and at Cambridge was pleasantly surprised to find that persecution by his peers was a thing of the past. Majoring in history, Rushdie received his M.A. degree with honors in 1968 and then spent a year working as an actor for a multi-media theater in a south London working-class neighborhood. Leaving the stage (having "discovered his mediocrity"), Rushdie worked for another year as a copywriter before turning his hand to fiction.

His first published novel, *Grimus,* was a commercial failure but received favorable attention, especially from science fiction buffs. His second novel, *Midnight's Children,* which took five years to write, was first published in the United States in 1981, where it received rave reviews and later went on to win the prestigious James Tait Memorial Prize in England as well as the Booker Prize. Translated into twelve languages, the novel is a serio-comic epic that allegorically chronicles the history of India through the lives of the 1001 children born during the midnight hour of 15 August 1947—the day India gained its independence. In 1983, Rushdie's third novel, *Shame,* appeared; it takes up the shame, honor, and political violence so deeply embedded in the moral and political consciousness of Pakistani society. Because its central thread is a scathing retelling of the late President Zia-ul-Haz's downfall and the execution of Prime Minister Zulfiqar Ali Bhutto, Rushdie was surprised that *Shame,* though banned in Pakistan, nevertheless received reviews in the English-language press in that country that were as glowing as those in England and the United States.

The Satanic Verses is Rushdie's most controversial novel. Viewed by the Islamic world as a blasphemous attack on their religion and on the prophet Mohammed, the book has incited riots worldwide. The perceived blasphemy also led to the issuance of a death threat against its author by Ayatollah Khomeini of Iran, which has not been rescinded even after the Ayatollah's death. Rushdie continues to live in London under the protection of Great Britain's government. Twice married and divorced, Rushdie has one son, Zafar.

RELIGION AS A COLONIZING POWER

In *The Satanic Verses*, Salman Rushdie draws religion into the orbit of his colonial critique, seeing it as yet another insidious element of containment. For religion has been a colonizing power, too, one that has enslaved humankind's thinking. It is this capacity to control human thought that religion shares with the rule of Empire—the subject of *Midnight's Children* and *Shame*. And it is toward the destruction of any such power that Rushdie's fictive strategies are always aimed.

The complex, somewhat uneven action of the novel revolves around the bizarre transformation of the only two survivors of an airplane hijacking: Gibreel Farishta and Saladdin Chamcha who miraculously escape the disaster by falling leisurely through the atmosphere and landing on the shores of England. Once Gibreel acquires a halo and Saladdin develops horns and hooves, the classic struggle between good and evil begins. But the crucial question arises: Which one is good, which evil? After all, from the outset Farishta (a Persian word meaning "angel") behaves far from angelically. For one thing, he watches silently as policemen come into the house, where the men are recovering, and whisk his friend Saladdin off to jail. To ensure that the boundaries between the concepts of good and evil remain fuzzy, Rushdie provides a fabulous description of the two survivors intertwined during the course of their fall from the heavens:

> Hybrid cloud-creatures pressed in on upon them, gigantic flowers with human breasts dangling from fleshy stalks, winged cats, centaurs, and Chamcha in his semi-consciousness was seized by the notion that he too had acquired the quality of cloudiness, becoming metamorphic, hybrid, as if he were growing into the person [Gibreel] whose head nestled now between his legs and whose legs were wrapped around his long, patrician neck. (7)

The quality of being "metamorphic," a "hybrid," is one with which the real Saladdin Chamcha is most familiar. As an Indian-born immigrant who desperately wants to be an Englishman, Chamcha smacks of the "brown Englishman," an outsider more English than the English, the Fanonian native who abandons his own race in favor of his oppressor's. Yet he fails to realize this, for Chamcha (from an Urdu word meaning "spoon," but connoting "bootlicking") believes he has succeeded in transforming himself from an Indian into an Englishman. Consequently, his humiliating treatment at the hands of the British police and immigration officers dumbfounds him, and he pleads: "Don't you see? I'm Maxim. Maxim Alien." This is a reference to his former job as an actor and voice-over artist on British television. The irony, of course, is that even then he had played an alien, and his supplication to the police and immigration officers now hauling him away only serves to alienate him further from them.

Just as this episode illustrates the absurdity of the kind of containment engendered by colonialism—showing how falsely people judge one another as they categorize in terms of "us" and "them," "self" and "other," "British" and "Indian," so the rest of the book exposes the dangers of placing vast and complex concepts like "Good" and "Evil" into neat boxes, frames, or categories.

Enter: genus—*religion*, species—*Islam*.

A central question asked often in the book is raised for the first time by the female terrorist aboard the jetliner that crashed as she addresses the terrified passengers:

> "When a great idea comes into the world, a great cause, certain crucial questions are asked of it," she murmured. "History asks us: what manner of cause are we? Are we uncompromising, absolute, strong, or will we show ourselves to be time-servers, who compromise, trim and yield?" Her body had provided her answer. (81)

Chamcha's response to this question and to the woman's answer is, I would argue, Rushdie's own response to what is good and what is evil within the context of Islam—that same dichotomy posed by all religions:

> The enclosed, boiling circumstances of his captivity . . . made Saladdin Chamcha want to argue with the woman, unbendingness can also be monomania, he wanted to say, it can be tyranny, and also it can be brittle, whereas what is flexible can also be humane, strong enough to last. (81)

The controversy over good and evil in Islam begins with the fundamental question of faith: Muslims are asked to accept unconditionally the Quran as the revealed word of God, the archangel Gabriel (Gibreel in Arabic) as the instrument of revelation, and Mohammed as the holy prophet unto whom the Book was revealed in an unbroken and untrammelled continuum.

To accept these tenets on faith and without doubt is clearly "good" within the framework of the Islamic belief system. "Evil" in this value system would be to raise questions or cast aspersions on the authenticity of these tenets of orthodox Islam. What Rushdie sets out to do in the sections of the novel entitled "Mahound" and "Return to Jahilia" is then "evil" within this religious framework. Undoubtedly, Rushdie intends to debunk the myths of Islam: Not only are the epic revelations of the Archangel Gabriel reduced to the banal level of hallucinations experienced by an aging movie star on the brink of insanity, but the prophet Mohammed himself is now a Mahound, a devilish creature. Part of what makes Mahound devilish is what one of his former disciples, Salman the Scribe, refers to as the "convenience" of his revelations and the compromising nature of his beliefs, his "idea."

For instance, when Mahound, businessman turned prophet of Jahilia, is approached in the early years of his religion by the idolatrous Grandee of Jahilia, who promises converts in return for compromise, Mahound agrees. His three faithful disciples are angered and shocked by their prophet's decision to compromise on what they consider to be a fundamental tenet of belief: the monotheistic nature of God. The exchange between disciples and prophet illustrates the pragmatic motives of Mahound:

> "Or it's a different trap," Salman persists. "How long have we been reciting the creed you brought us? There is no god but God. What are we if we abandon it now? This weakens us, renders us absurd. We cease to be dangerous. Nobody will ever take us seriously again."
>
> Mahound laughs, genuinely amused. "Maybe you haven't been here long enough," he says kindly. "Haven't you noticed? The people do not take us seriously. Never more than fifty in the audience when I speak, and half of those are tourists. Don't you read the lampoons that Baal pins up all over town? . . . They mock us everywhere, and you call us dangerous," he cried. (106)

The conflicting approaches of the disciples and their prophet to the solution of a problem at hand illustrate the polar tensions implicit in the question, "What kind of idea are you?"—raised first by the terrorist woman, later by Mahound himself, and in another episode by another "seer," a woman named Ayesha. For an idea to be "true," to be worthy of belief, does it necessarily have to be unyielding, fixed, beyond compromise? That certainly seems to be the answer the disciples want to hear. But Mahound/Mohammed holds to a different viewpoint. "Sometimes," he says, "I think I must make it easier for the people to believe" (106).

What he means, of course, is that in the face of numerous obstacles to the spread of his faith, including a strong unwillingness of a polytheistic society to accept overnight a monotheistic religion, why not compromise a little. What harm could it do to accept the Grandee's offer of a wholesale conversion of Jahilia in return for a declaration from the prophet that the three favorite goddesses of Jahilia are granted angelic status in Islam? As Mahound asks himself in a tormenting bout of self-questioning: "The souls of the city, of the world, surely they are worth three angels? Is Allah so unbending that that he will not embrace three more to save the human race?" (111). Needless to say, Mahound rules in favor of inclusion, rather than exclusion. However, this time, his gamble does not pay off. He discovers shortly that he has been duped by the Grandee and his wife Hind. As Hind says, "If you are for Allah, I am for Al-Lat. And she doesn't believe your God when he recognizes her. Her opposition to him is implacable, irrevocable, engulfing" (121). So much for compromise. Yet Mahound, ever the pragmatist, does manage to win back the trust and favor of his disciples by now declaring his previous declaration the work of Shaitan, that is verses dictated by Satan, not God.

The defection of Salman the Scribe occurs when the latter, as official scribe of the book, realizes the convenient nature of some of the revelations. He begins to notice "how useful and well-timed the angel's revelations tended to be, so that when the faithful were disputing Mahound's views on any subject . . . the angel would turn up with an answer, and he always supported Mahound" (364). This, coupled with the fact that Mahound does not recognize (at least, not initially) Salman's alterations of the holy text, drives Rushdie's namesake into the camp of the nonbelievers.

Is this "blaspheming" of the central character and tenets of Islam then meant to ridicule both? Should such an impulse be seen as evil? I think not. For, if we recall Chamcha's response to the question, "What manner of cause are we?", it is in favor of compromise: "Unbendingness . . . can be tyranny, whereas what is flexible can also be humane, and strong enough to last" (81). Clearly, Mahound's flexibility, his willingness to compromise and to mold his needs to the situation, as well as his demonstration of managerial skills in converting, then keeping his sheep within the fold, attest to the strength and wisdom of a man through whose efforts a religion has endured.

What emerges from the analysis so far, then, is that form and content, mirroring each other, bespeak a need for mixing up, for shattering all neat divisions and oppositions such as those that exist between formal concepts like "realism" or "myth," or between moral ones like "good" or "evil," which have engendered the Manichean oppositions of colonialism: black/white, self/other, us/them, insider/outsider. In other words, the point of view that emerges is not anti-Islam, but anti-closure, opposed in principle to any fixed way of looking at things. Framed in such a way, Rushdie's impulse toward blasphemy becomes in truth an impulse toward regeneration: renewal born of a destruction of fixed ways of seeing and understanding. The evil of blasphemy therefore becomes a virtue, as lines blur between the sacred and the profane, between reality and illusion. Is what we are reading an enactment of real events from Islamic history, or merely the delusions of a crazed, aging Indian movie star? Is Mahound prophet or devil, man or saint? Must we always think in terms of such binary oppositions?

What Rushdie goes on to say in the rest of this nonlinear novel is that it is precisely the impulse to categorize, to divide, classify, and contain the world, its inhabitants, and its events that has led to misunderstanding, exploitation, hatred, and violence. The conflict in which both Chamcha and Farishta find themselves embroiled is not just their private quarrel, a betrayal of the former by the latter that Chamcha tries to avenge, but a conflict between the forces of good and evil; it is a universal conflict of epic dimensions that in the world of the novel takes the shape of an apocalyptic battle between the colonizers and the colonized, those who *belong* and those who do not, between the white Englishmen and the intruding black immigrants. When Chamcha is finally released from the custody of the British police and immigration officials, he finds a refuge in—of all places—an Indian restaurant owner's boarding house. The very culture and people he has spent his entire life running away from embrace him in his moment of need. As Abu Sufyan, owner of the establishment, puts it: "Where else would you go to heal your disfigurements and recover your normal health? Where else but here, with us, among your own people, your own kind?" To which, Chamcha, alone in the attic room, makes the ungrateful response: "I'm not your kind. . . . You're not my people. I've spent half my life trying to get away from you" (253). Yet, if we find Chamcha's response ungracious and alienated, surely the terms of Sufyan's query are just as unsettling. Within the Rushdean universe, there is something unhealthy, something destructive and violent that leads to and will ensue in the conflict created by categorizing, by dividing the world into opposing camps: Us against Them, Black against White, Believers against Nonbelievers, Good against Evil.

And this is precisely what happens.

In the chapter "The Angel Azraeel," we are given a surrealistic and horrifying picture of race relations in Great Britain. Brickhall, known for its concentration of Asian and Black residents, becomes the scene of an apocalypse in the wake of the race riots that break out following the death in jail of one Dr. Uhuru Simba. Dr. Simba, revolutionary symbol of the Brickhall immigrants, conveyer of their grievances and demands for better treatment to those in power, is unjustly accused of being a murderer, and while in jail dies mysteriously. The bizarre official explanation of his death—that he died because of a nightmare—does not go down well with his people. In fact, the whole atmosphere of Brickhall becomes increasingly grim, one in which a violent confrontation becomes inevitable:

> "I want you to understand," Mrs. Roberts [Simba's mother] declaimed to the sizeable crowd that had gathered angrily outside the High Street police station, "that these people are gambling with our lives. They are laying odds on our chances of survival. I want you all to consider what that means in terms of their respect for us as human beings." And Hanif Johnson, as Uhuru Simba's solicitor, added . . . that in an age of extreme overcrowding in the country's lock-ups it was unusual, to say the least, that the other bunk should have been unoccupied, ensuring that there were no witnesses . . . and that a nightmare was by no means the only possible explanation for the screams of a black man in the hands of custodial authority. In his concluding remarks, afterwards termed "inflammatory and unprofessional" by Inspector Kinch, Hanif linked the community liaison officer's words to those of the notorious racist John Kingsley Read, who had once responded to the news of a black man's death with the slogan, "one down; one million to go." The crowd murmured and bubbled. . . . "Stay hot," Simba's brother Walcott cried out to the assembly. "Don't anybody cool off. Maintain your rage." (450)

Walcott's advice, born of rage, impotence, and a desire for revenge against centuries-old discrimination, is, nevertheless, unsound. For hatred, once again a result of categorizing and containing others in order to maintain power over them, leads to a violence that cannot be similarly contained. The dream, the desire for revenge, must ultimately turn into a nightmare that destroys not just the hated but the hater as well.

So it is only fitting that the role of destroyer should be assigned to the angel of the novel, Gibreel Farishta, who goes out to purchase Azraeel, the legendary trumpet of Destruction of the World, for this express purpose. The necessity of the cleansing mission of destruction slowly becomes clear to Gibreel, and so to the reader:

> He is the Archangel Gibreel, the angel of Recitation, with the power of revelation in his hands. He can reach into the breasts of men and women, pick out the desires of their inmost hearts, and make them real. He is the quencher of desires, the slaker of lusts, the fulfiller of dreams. . . . What desires, what imperatives are in the midnight air? He breathes them in.—And nod, so be it, yes.—Let it be fire . . . Fire, falling fire. "This is the judgement of God in his wrath," Gibreel Farishta proclaims to the riotous night, "that men be granted their hearts' desires, and that they be by them consumed." (461)

In the ensuing debacle, the fire-breathing Gibreel destroys Brickhall with a vengeance. Black, brown, or white, male or female, young or old, no one escapes his fury, except Saladdin Chamcha and some young Asians he rescues, who have assimilated to the degree that they do not retain the old, oppositional structures of belief. In a sense, Saladdin, too, is spared in order to be given a chance to begin anew. At the end of the novel, he returns to India to patch things up with his father whom he has not seen, spoken to, or written to in decades. In his refusal to have anything to do with his past, Chamcha has also been guilty of thinking in terms of oppositions—of categorizing and labeling all that is English as good and worth striving after, and all that is Indian (including a demanding father) as bad or certainly unworthy of his attention and acknowledgment. By showing a Saladdin who can learn and adapt, who can go from being a Salahuddin to a Saladdin and then back to Salahuddin again, Rushdie is once again pointing to the power of endurance inherent in flexibility, whereas an inflexible temperament, a monomaniacal fixation on any idea is a sure recipe for madness and death. And this precisely is what happens to the angel, Gibreel Farishta, who cannot shake off his obsession with retribution. He is stuck forever, it would seem, in his role as Avenger, and it is this role that causes him to kill his mistress and friend in a fit of jealousy:

> I am the angel the god damned angel of god and these days it's the avenging angel Gibreel the avenger always vengeance why (544)

There is no answer to the "why" except that in the end we become the roles we play, we become as contained and boxed in as the frameworks that engulf us, if we accept the conventions of definitions. Gibreel ends up destroying himself, because finally he cannot live according to the definition of himself as an angel. He tells Chamcha at the very end:

"I told you a long time back," Gibreel Farishta quietly said, "that if I thought the sickness [of being, or thinking he is an angel] would never leave me, that it would always return, I would not be able to bear up to it." Then, very quickly, before Salahuddin could move a finger, Gibreel put the barrel of the gun into his own mouth; and pulled the trigger; and was free. (546)

In choosing to let the "angelic" Farishta die, and the "satanic" Chamcha live, Rushdie is surely challenging the conventional definitions of "good" and "evil." He has done this, of course, throughout the novel and ends on a note that suggests only those who are flexible survive (hence Chamcha over Farishta, Mahound over Ayesha) and that all old, inflexible ideologies and definitions of the world and of its peoples must die, be destroyed, if there is to be any hope of renewal, of survival. This is what Chamcha himself acknowledges, as he stands alone, surveying the scenes of his childhood:

He stood at the window of his childhood and looked out at the Arabian Sea . . . moonlight . . . created the illusion of a silver pathway, like a parting in the water's shining hair, like a road to miraculous lands. He shook his head; could no longer believe in fairy-tales. Childhood was over, and the view from this window was no more than an old and sentimental echo. To the devil with it! Let the bulldozers come. If the old refused to die, the new could not be born. (547)

All old ideologies, old forms, old oppositional structures and rigid definitions must be done away with before regeneration can occur. This has been Rushdie's message, both in content and in form, throughout his work. It is only in *The Satanic Verses*, however, that he draws explicit parallels between religion and colonialism as hegemonic strategies of containment. Whereas the latter has tried to contain people within racial and geographical boundaries and definitions, religion has tried to delimit and contain intellectual territory. Both kinds of containment are reprehensible to Rushdie, and the only way out he sees is through destruction and "blasphemy."

WORK CITED

Rushdie, Salman. *The Satanic Verses*. London: Viking, 1988.

SALMAN RUSHDIE'S PUBLISHED WORK

Novels

Grimus, 1975
Midnight's Children, 1981
Shame, 1983
The Satanic Verses, 1988
Haroun and the Sea of Stories, 1990

Travel

The Jaguar Smile: A Nicaraguan Journey, 1987.
> A brilliantly focused and haunting portrait of the people, politics, land, and poetry of Nicaragua. Although sympathetic to the cause of the Sandinistas, Rushdie nevertheless criticizes the flaws of the movement.

Commentary

"In Good Faith." *Newsweek* 12 Feb. 1990: 52–54+.
> Written exactly a year after he was forced to go into hiding, Rushdie defends *The Satanic Verses,* and argues for the right of freedom of expression. In talking about those passages deemed most offensive by Muslim readers, Rushdie insists they have been read out of context, and, furthermore, that their fictionality has been dismissed and distorted.

"Is Nothing Sacred?" *Granta* 31 (1990): 97–110.
> Text of the Herbert Read Memorial Lecture, delivered by Harold Pinter at the Institute of Contemporary Arts, London, 6 Feb. 1990. In it Rushdie, still in hiding after the death threat against him, essentially questions the whole notion of "sacredness." He begins by saying nothing is, or should be considered "sacred" in the postmodern world, because such absoluteness inevitably leads to conflict and war; he then seemingly contradicts himself by insisting on literature as a sacred object of secularism; but finally denies even literature that privilege because he realizes that "We must not become what we oppose." Nevertheless, he does end with a plea that suggests he wishes to be considered on his own terms— which does translate as a call for literature to be accorded a privileged space: "the privilege of being the arena of discourse, the place where the struggle of languages can be acted out."

SELECTED CRITICAL READINGS

Since the publication of his second novel, *Midnight's Children,* Salman Rushdie has received a fair amount of attention both in the western press and academic journals. His work has been likened to that of Sterne, Swift, García Márquez, and Günter Grass. Stylistically, his writing is a mishmash of conflicting genres such as myth, the comic epic, magical realism, and so on, with the result that many reviewers and critics label his fiction as "unclassifiable." With the publication of his controversial novel, *The Satanic Verses,* Rushdie has become the object of intense scrutiny for a worldwide community of scholars; thus the critical responses will certainly mushroom in the future.

Afzal-Khan, Fawzia. "Post-Modernist Strategies of Liberation in the Works of Salman Rushdie." *Journal of South Asian Literature* (1988): 137–45. Discusses *Midnight's Children, Shame,* and *Grimus* as postmodernist works with a twist. Whereas the postmodernist literary movement in the West has been a movement away from the burdens of history, the breakdown of form in Rushdie's work is seen as a paradigmatic third world strategy of liberation from all western formal strategies that have sought to contain other cultures.

Appignanesi, Lisa, and Sara Maitland, editors. *The Rushdie File.* Syracuse: Syracuse UP, 1990. Collection of articles and statements on the controversy surrounding *The Satanic Verses.*

Batty, Nancy. "The Art of Suspense: Rushdie's 1001 (Mid-) Nights." *Ariel* 18.3 (1987): 49–65. Compares the novel to Scheherazade's tales, pointing out that yoking literary dimensions with the historical is desirable as Rushdie has done. He employs suspense not just to amuse but to save the narrative act from absurdity.

Bader, Rudolf. "Indian *Tin Drum.*" *International Fiction Review* 11 (1984): 75–83. Draws comparisons between *Midnight's Children* and Günter Grass's *Tin Drum*, pointing out the historical and narrative similarities.

Brennan, Timothy. *Salman Rushdie and the Third World, Myths of the Nation.* New York: St. Martin's, 1989. Argues that Rushdie's work comprises much more than *The Satanic Verses*, seeing all the writing as an example of "Third World nationalism" and "anti-colonial liberalism." Sets Rushdie's novels into the larger picture of postcolonial and Latin American writing. The analyses focus in part on the use of Hindu and Muslim myth, in part on the treatment of contemporary politics and social conditions. First full-length study of Rushdie's work. Extensive bibliography.

Cronin, Richard. "The Indian English Novel: *Kim* and *Midnight's Children.*" *Modern Fiction Studies* 33 (1987): 201–13. Intriguing comparative study of Kipling's *Kim* and *Midnight's Children* that draws some not so obvious parallels.

Durix, Jean-Pierre. "The Artistic Journey in Salman Rushdie's *Shame.*" *World Literature Written in English* 23 (1984): 451–63. Argues that Rushdie explores the possibility of turning fiction into a dialogue between realism and fantasy, his work insisting on art's ability to hold "irreconcilable positions."

Jussawalla, Feroza. "Resurrecting the Prophet: The Case of Salman, the Otherwise." *Public Culture* (Fall 1989): 106–17. Claims that Rushdie, with the publication of *The Satanic Verses*, has clearly established himself as an Orientalist—one who views the world of Islam and of the Asian and black populations of Britain from the disparaging point of view of the West. Points to Rushdie's adoption of post-Joycean narrative techniques, his use of jokes, and his adoption of a Dantean perspective of the prophet Mohammed as examples of Rushdie's co-option within a western or "Orientalist" ideology.

Leithauser, Brad. "Demoniasis." *New Yorker* 15 May 1989: 124–28. Attempts to shift the discussion of *The Satanic Verses* away from the religious controversy to the book's literary merits and demerits; finds that despite exhibiting some stunning feats of virtuosity, the book is essentially flawed by Rushdie's fondness for "excess."

Parmeswaran, Uma. "Handcuffed to History: Salman Rushdie's Art." *Ariel* 14 (1983): 34–45. Discusses two short stories, "The Prophet's Hair," "The Free Radio," as well as *Grimus* and *Midnight's Children.* Claims that all of Rushdie's work is an attempt to achieve a "fission-fusion" between individual lives and the forces of history, toward which end he employs a number of narrative devices.

Pipes, Daniel. *The Rushdie Affair: The Novel, the Ayatollah and the West.* New York: Birch Lane Press/Carol Publishing Group, 1990. Analyzes the religious issues raised, giving Muslim critics credit for their views, while denouncing censorship.

Riemenschneider, Dieter. "History and the Individual in Anita Desai's *Clear Light of Day* and Salman Rushdie's *Midnight's Children.*" *World Literature Written in English* 23 (1984): 196–207. Argues that both are concerned with humankind's quest for identity, both relate that quest to individual's past lives; notes that the understanding of the past and the role of history differ in the two novels.

Swann, Joseph. "'East Is East and West Is West': Salman Rushdie's *Midnight's Children* as an Indian Novel." *World Literature Written in English* 26 (1986): 353–62. Argues that it is indeed an Indian novel, that the two worlds do meet, for the novel brings them closer.

Wilson, Keith. "*Midnight's Children* and Reader Responsibility." *Critical Quarterly* (1984): 23–37. Treats *Midnight's Children* as a novel that challenges the notion of novelist as mimetic mediator between reader and reality. Argues that *Midnight's Children* acknowledges the inevitable subjectivity of the creative process. Helps to explain Rushdie's resistance to realism as an adequate way to reflect contemporary reality.

Biography

Weatherby, W.J. *Salman Rushdie: Sentenced to Death.* New York: Carroll & Graf Publishers, 1990.

Interview

With Blake Morrison. *Granta* 31 (1990): 113–25.

— FAWZIA AFZAL-KHAN

Malcolm Lowry

Malcolm Lowry was born 28 July 1909 and raised in the Wirral area of Cheshire, England, and he died in 1957 "by misadventure" in Ripe, Sussex. In many ways, the coroner's description of his death also sums up his life, which was a series of misadventures. It is important for his readers to know something of his biography because Lowry was a highly autobiographical writer.

He was the youngest of four sons in an upper middle-class English family. His father, Arthur Lowry, was a successful businessman and a stern, Victorian patriarch, but he did his best to support his wayward son. He sent him to exclusive schools, arranged for him to sail to the Far East in 1927, and sent him to St. Catharine's College, Cambridge (1929–1932), where he received a third-class in the English tripos. By this time, he was already the "black sheep" of the family, drinking heavily, writing, spinning bizarre stories about his own life, and refusing to comply with parental wishes. In 1929 he met the American poet, Conrad Aiken, who was paid by Lowry senior to act as his son's tutor, and Aiken became a major influence on Lowry's art and life.

In 1934 Lowry married his first wife, Jan Gabrial. They went first to New York City, then by stages to Cuernavaca, Mexico, where they lived from 1936 to 1937. By the time Lowry left Mexico in July 1938, his turbulent marriage to Jan was over. He had experienced the torment of the damned, and he had completed two drafts of his masterpiece, *Under the Volcano*, which is set in Mexico and based upon his experiences there.

In 1939 Lowry moved to Vancouver, British Columbia, in Canada where he was joined by Margerie Bonner, his second wife, and this began the longest period of relative calm and productivity that he would ever know. During these years he lived humbly as a remittance man on money sent from his father, and Margerie helped him with his work. The Lowrys left their beloved beach cabin in Dollarton, on the north shore of Burrard Inlet across from Vancouver, in 1954. After an extended trip to Italy and France, where Lowry's drinking increased and his health deteriorated, he entered a hospital in London and gradually regained enough strength to return to writing. When he died on 27 June 1957, after consuming alcohol and barbiturates, he left several unfinished novels in his projected masterwork, *The Voyage That Never Ends.*

AN ARTISTIC VOYAGE

From the beginning of his career as a writer, Malcolm Lowry was drawn to the metaphor of the voyage and to the idea that his art, like his life, was a constant voyage of change and discovery. While the predominance of this image in his work may be attributed to his own personality or temperament, he was also deeply influenced, in the early stages of his career, by other writers and philosophers who articulated similar views, such as Nordahl Grieg, Conrad Aiken, Henri Bergson, and J.W. Dunne, to name only the most significant.

Lowry discovered the work of Aiken before he turned twenty, and a novel called *The Ship Sails On* by the Norwegian Grieg shortly after. From Aiken he learned how to control and exploit the wheeling rhythms of his own prose, and in both Aiken and Grieg he found writers who showed him how to create fiction from the fabric of his own life. But if autobiography is one of the chief characteristics of Lowry's work, philosophical depth is another, and the philosophical thinkers who would always mean the most to Lowry—Bergson, Dunne, William James, Swedenborg, Ortega y Gasset—stressed the romantic values of imagination, religious mysticism, endless voyaging, and the complex ("serial" in Dunne's terms) interconnections among all aspects of creation above either a rationalistic or materialistic explanation of reality. Lowry drew on these influences throughout his life as he formulated what he began to call in the early forties *The Voyage That Never Ends*.

This plan for a series of interconnected novels (Grace 6-12), began as a trilogy, which was to include *Under the Volcano*, *Lunar Caustic*, and "In Ballast to the White Sea." But even before Lowry lost his huge manuscript for "In Ballast" in a fire, he was already beginning to feel confined by the trilogy structure. By 1951 he described his *Voyage* as a sequence of five or six novels "of which the *Volcano* would be one, though not the best one by any means" (*Selected Letters* 267). What he wanted to capture through this sequence was the cyclic movement of a man's life as he experiences repeated challenges, defeats, and renewals and struggles to shape and understand existence through a series of interrelated novels; this, of course, was Lowry's own struggle, and although the *Voyage* protagonist, Sigbjørn Wilderness, is not relentlessly portrayed as a novelist, he is nonetheless an image of man, or of the human consciousness, the creator of his own life story.

At the time of his death, Lowry had only written a small part of the projected *Voyage* and had published even less. *If* he had lived to finish it, and had not changed his plans, it would have looked like this:

> The Ordeal of Sigbjørn Wilderness 1
> Untitled Sea Novel (*Ultramarine*)
> *Lunar Caustic*
> *Under the Volcano*
> *Dark as the Grave Wherein my Friend Is Laid*
> Eridanus (later published as *October Ferry to Gabriola*)
> La Mordida
> The Ordeal of Sigbjørn Wilderness 2

Lowry always intended *Volcano* to have a central position in his *Voyage*, but his protagonist's voyage through life actually begins with his first published novel, *Ultramarine*, continues with the nightmare vision of *Lunar Caustic* and the hell of *Volcano*, then gradually moves towards a hard-won vision of salvation and paradise regained in the last novels. *October Ferry to Gabriola* and the final novella in his collection of related stories, *Hear us O Lord from heaven thy dwelling place*, called "The Forest Path to the Spring," offer exquisite glimpses of the kind of spiritual and psychological happiness Lowry was capable of imagining for humanity.

Ultramarine and *Lunar Caustic* are both extremely interesting works in their own right, quite apart from the role each plays in Lowry's *Voyage*. *Ultramarine*, while clearly a first novel heavily indebted to Aiken, Grieg, and T.S. Eliot, demonstrates the young Lowry's fascination with language and its ability to capture the inner processes of the mind, with themes of guilt, failure, and love, and with his need to portray a ship on a voyage as the quintessential symbol of life. The young hero, Dana Hilliot, at sea for the first time, is rejected, bullied, and abused for being a toff, but he survives this ordeal to reach a new understanding of life and an acceptance of the need to continue voyaging. *Lunar Caustic* is a short *tour de force* set in New York's Bellevue Hospital where the hero, now called William Plantagenet, has gone to seek psychiatric advice and to observe the inmates. As with the sea voyage, Lowry actually spent some time in Bellevue Hospital in 1935, and he turned this experience into an extraordinary vision of society as a madhouse from which escape seems impossible. The only hope in this grim allegory lies with a few meager gestures of human compassion and love and in the certain knowledge that the struggle continues.

In many ways, Lowry's masterpiece, *Under the Volcano*, tells the same story, but it does so on a scale that makes almost all his other work pale by comparison. *Under the Volcano* is one of the great books of this century because of the beauty of its language, the power and importance of its subject—the fall of mankind and the destruction of this world, and the strength of its intricate yet supple structure. Although an Aristotelian notion of character was not his chief concern in the novel, Lowry nevertheless created in his drunken Consul, Geoffrey Firmin, one of the most memorable, tragic figures of modern literature. The other characters, Geoffrey's friend, Jacques Laruelle, his estranged wife, Yvonne, and his half-brother, Hugh, while characters in their own right, are more important as aspects (together with the Consul) of the human consciousness and as symbols in Lowry's modern allegory of the Garden of Eden.

Lowry's prose is dense, his sentences convoluted, his vocabulary demanding, and his style is characterized by a rich allusiveness, an elaborate web of repetition, images, and symbols, and by deliberate, dizzying shifts in perspective. *Volcano*, in short, asks a great deal of its readers, but if we take care, on a second or third reading, to examine his writing, it becomes clear that the rich prose is what creates the sense of fatality in a complex, sinister yet beautiful, and always interrelated world. It is also, through careful modulations of this prose, that Lowry is able to move from descriptions of the Mexican landscape to dialogue taut with strain and failed communication to those wheeling, hallucinatory presentations of the Consul's mescal-fogged memory and mind that force the reader to see the world with his eyes.

Each of the novel's twelve chapters is presented from the point of view of one of the four characters. Thus, chapters three, five, seven, ten, and twelve belong to Geoffrey; chapters two, nine and eleven to Yvonne; chapters four, six, and eight to Hugh, and chapter one to Laruelle. Despite the intricate web of connection established between and among chapters at the level of the language, however, the characters' ability to communicate across chapters or to understand where their lives are headed is thwarted by the restriction of point of view in each individual chapter. Not even love—conjugal, brotherly, or divine—seems strong enough to bridge the gaps that exist between the characters. But as with each of the novels in the *Voyage* cycle, Lowry insisted that there be some hope, and he allowed for hope in the "trochal" or wheel-shaped structure of the narrative. Chapter one takes place on the Mexican Day of the Dead, 1 November in 1939, but the rest of the story unfolds between 7 a.m. and 7 p.m. on the Day of the Dead in 1938, exactly one year before. In other words, we relive the tragic events of 1938 in chapters two through twelve, only to be reminded, when we reach the end, that the wheel of time has turned and that chapter one takes place in the fictional present of 1939; someone has survived to tell this tale, and while there is life there is hope; the voyage never ends.

The subject of *Under the Volcano* can be summed up as a portrayal of the last day in the lives of a drunken British ex-Consul and his estranged wife as they wander around the violent landscape of Mexico beneath the twin volcanoes Popcatapetl and Ixtaccihuatl, arguing, eating, and drinking until he is shot by the local police and she is trampled to death by a horse. (Even John Huston's 1986 film version, however, captured more of the novel than the summary just given.) *Under the Volcano* is set on the eve of the Second World War and just at the end of the Spanish Civil War. Domestic affairs in Mexico are a complex mix of political upheaval and external interference. All of Western history, then, has conspired to create this Day of the Dead as one of momentous importance for the world. The fact that these people cannot learn to forgive and love each other in time but must drive one another to destruction becomes a fable for the times, a lesson in humankind's violence, selfishness, and stupidity, an allegory—as Lowry explained in his famous 2 January 1946 letter to Jonathan Cape—of expulsion from the Garden of Eden of this world. And this theme, perhaps more than all the other qualities of *Volcano*, continues to account for its importance today and its relevance to modern readers. This novel casts an anguished backward glance at human history, a history of conquest, imperialism, savagery, genocide, and greed, and asks us to consider what the future holds. To be sure, Lowry's vision is an apocalyptic one, but it balances the horror of final destruction with the revelation of hope through renewed voyaging. On the last page of the novel we are reminded of this threat and this hope:

> ¿Le gusta este jardín
> Que es suyo?
> ¡Evite que sus hijos lo destruyan!

> (Do you like the garden,
>   which is yours?
> Keep your children from
>   destroying it!)

In *Under the Volcano*, Lowry created a great example of modernist art, a novel that achieves a mythic vision in a tightly unified artistic whole. It is the kind of vision that, like those of Woolf, Joyce, Pound, and Eliot, Lowry could only create in art. Although there are traces, even at this stage, that he wanted to explore a new, more experimental, type of fiction, it was not until the later, unfinished works and some of the stories that what critics increasingly speak of as a "postmodern Lowry" began to emerge. As presently edited and currently available, *Dark as the Grave* and *October Ferry to Gabriola* give only a faint idea of what Lowry was seeking. The first novel is more interesting in its relationship to *Under the Volcano* and it cannot be understood without reference to that book. *October Ferry* is more interesting on its own, as the story of a lawyer and his wife who are on a voyage in search of a new home because they are being evicted from their present beach cabin, but it is only a draft of the complex narrative it would have been had Lowry lived to finish it.

Lowry's collection of eight stories, *Hear us O Lord from heaven thy dwelling place*, however, is a small masterpiece with some of Lowry's very finest as well as his most experimental writing. The stories are ordered to present a metaphysical and symbolic journey from Vancouver south to the Panama Canal and across to the Atlantic, then north to Europe and back to Vancouver again. Together they represent a miniature "voyage that never ends," and they mirror, through motifs, images, symbols, and situations, Lowry's novels. They should, of course, be read as a collection and in sequence, but two of the stories deserve particular attention: "Through the Panama" and "The Forest Path to the Spring."

"Through the Panama" is a novella-length diary of a writer, chronicling Martin Trumbaugh's passage through the canal with his wife. The entries are short and dated, but they gradually swell to include a wide variety of other texts by other people from ship's notices to sections from Martin's reading to long passages from a novel he is writing about a writer who has become enmeshed in the novel he is writing. Part way through the story/diary, the page splits into a main column with marginalia, and these marginalia quickly take over the diary proper. What Lowry has created is a superb metafictional story about the anxieties and challenges faced by a writer and about the very nature of storymaking, whether it is the artist or just the ordinary person who is making the tale. Beyond that, Lowry has commented upon the nature of language itself, on how it can run away and how words grow from other words. Lowry's protagonist is a kind of twentieth-century Ancient Mariner (hence the quotations from Coleridge's poem and the use of marginal glosses) who must tell his tale before he can be released into his continuing voyage. The ordeal of language, of storying, of speaking is an ordeal in communication, and if we are to preserve our humanity, says Lowry, we must communicate.

"The Forest Path to the Spring" is Lowry's meditation upon paradise regained. He had intended to use it as the coda to his *Voyage*, and he set it on the beach at Dollarton where, with Margerie, he had known the happiest years of his life. Structured in eight sections and resembling a musical composition in the use of repetition and motif, it is the first person narrative of a retired jazz composer who is trying to adjust to his new life and recapture not only health and happiness but also his ability to compose. Although he is haunted by past sins, failures, and guilt, the narrator is assisted in his recovery by the rhythms of nature, the tides, the birds, the stars, the sunrises, and the rain until he comes to realize that God's creation has a pattern and a purpose that can include him if he can only live in harmony with these rhythms. His final vision is of the fog lifting, of the wash from a freighter "breaking along the curve of the beach" (285) and of the rain: "Each drop falling into the sea is like a life, I thought, each producing a circle in the ocean, or the medium of life itself, and widening into infinity" (285–86).

Malcolm Lowry was not a prolific writer, but in his relatively short career he produced one of this century's masterpieces, an extraordinary collection of short fictions, and four novels of interest. He also wrote approximately eight hundred letters, many of which rank with his finest prose fiction. His aesthetic development led him from the modernist form of *Volcano* to a highly experimental form of metafiction that is more characteristic of postmodern than modern writing, and his concern for language, historiography, and autobiography links him with a number of major English-language writers from the early modern and the contemporary periods. What perhaps marks Lowry as a writer apart from great modernists such as Joyce, Pound, Woolf, and Eliot is his ability to combine deep personal passion and belief with the portrayal of the century's most intransigent problems. One listens to Lowry's voice with the same fear, trembling, and awe that one listens to William Faulkner, Patrick White, or Keri Hulme.

WORKS CITED:

Grace, Sherrill E. *The Voyage That Never Ends: Malcolm Lowry's Fiction*. Vancouver: U of British Columbia P, 1982.

Lowry, Malcolm. *Hear us O Lord from heaven thy dwelling place*. Harmondsworth: Penguin, 1969.

———. *Selected Letters of Malcolm Lowry*. Edited by Harvey Breit and Margerie Lowry. Philadelphia: J.B. Lippincott, 1965.

———. *Under the Volcano*. Harmondsworth: Penguin, 1963.

MALCOLM LOWRY'S PUBLISHED WORK

Novels

Ultramarine, 1933 (revised edition 1962)
Under the Volcano, 1947
Lunar Caustic (edited by Earle Birney and Margerie Lowry), 1963
Dark as the Grave Wherein my Friend Is Laid (edited by Douglas Day and Margerie Lowry), 1968
October Ferry to Gabriola (edited by Margerie Lowry), 1970

Short Story Collection

Hear us O Lord from heaven thy dwelling place, 1961

Poetry

Selected Poems (edited by Earle Birney), 1962

Letters and Other Writings

Letters between Malcolm Lowry and Jonathan Cape about 'Under the Volcano,' 1962
Selected Letters of Malcolm Lowry, 1965
Malcolm Lowry: Psalms and Songs (edited by Margerie Lowry), 1975
The Letters of Malcolm Lowry and Gerald Noxon, 1940–1952, 1988

SELECTED CRITICAL READINGS

The major collection of Lowry's manuscripts, letters, and other materials is housed in Special Collections of the Main Library at the University of British Columbia. Scholarship in the field is very active, and three major projects are currently underway: a new Lowry biography by Gordon Bowker; a scholarly edition of the collected poems edited by Kathleen Scherf, with annotations by Chris Ackerley; and a scholarly, annotated edition of the collected letters by Sherrill Grace. A new collection of critical essays on Lowry is to be published soon: *Swinging the Maelstrom: New Perspectives on Malcolm Lowry,* edited by Sherrill Grace (McGill-Queens Press). The *Malcolm Lowry Review,* edited by Paul Tiessen at Wilfrid Laurier University, is an invaluable source of current information on Lowry and Lowry studies.

Ackerley, Chris, and Larry J. Clipper. *A Companion to Under the Volcano.* Vancouver: U of British Columbia P, 1984. Useful source of line by line information on references in the novel.

Binns, Ronald. *Malcolm Lowry.* London: Methuen, 1984. General discussion of Lowry's work, stressing *Under the Volcano.*

Bowker, Gordon, editor. *Malcolm Lowry Remembered.* London: Ariel Books, 1985. Collection of reprints of interviews with Lowry's family and friends. Most interesting of these is an interview with Jan Gabrial (Lowry's first wife), in 1975.

Bradbrook, Muriel. *Malcolm Lowry: His Art and Early Life.* Cambridge: Cambridge UP, 1974. Discussion of Lowry's post-*Volcano* work in light of information about his youth in England.

Costa, Richard Hauer. *Malcolm Lowry.* New York: Twayne, 1972. Introductory study of Lowry's work with some biographical information.

Cross, Richard K. *Malcolm Lowry: A Preface to His Fiction.* Chicago: U of Chicago P, 1980. Introductory study.

Day, Douglas. *Malcolm Lowry: A Biography.* New York: Oxford UP, 1973. First full biography of Lowry. Day uses a Freudian approach to the man and his art and provides a fine reading of *Under the Volcano.*

Epstein, Perle. *The Private Labyrinth of Malcolm Lowry: Under the Volcano and the Cabbala.* New York: Rinehart & Winston, 1969. Detailed study of Lowry's debt to the Cabbala, which results in an interesting if reductive reading of the novel.

Grace, Sherrill E. *The Voyage That Never Ends: Malcolm Lowry's Fiction.* Vancouver: U of British Columbia P, 1982. Critical study of Lowry's *oeuvre* putting the novels in the context of Lowry's plans for a series of novels.

Kilgallin, Tony. *Malcolm Lowry.* Erin, Ontario: Press Procépic, 1973. General discussion of *Ultramarine* and *Under the Volcano* with reference to Lowry's life and influences.

Markson, David. *Malcolm Lowry's Volcano: Myth, Symbol, Meaning.* New York: Times Books, 1978. Major study of the novel with close attention to the symbolic texture of the narrative.

New, William H. *Malcolm Lowry: A Reference Guide.* Boston: G. K. Hall, 1978. Annotated bibliography of writing about Lowry up to 1976.

Salloum, Sheryl. *Malcolm Lowry: Vancouver Days.* Vancouver: Harbour Publishing, 1987. Careful and informative discussion of Lowry's life in Vancouver between 1939 and 1954 with useful photographs and maps.

Smith, Anne, editor. *The Art of Malcolm Lowry.* New York: Barnes and Noble, 1978. Collection of important, original essays on all aspects of Lowry's work.

Tiessen, Paul, editor. *A Strange Assembly of Parts.* Metuchen, N.J.: Scarecrow Press, 1990. Collection of critical essays.

Wood, Barry, editor. *Malcolm Lowry: The Writer and his Critics.* Ottawa: Tecumseh Press, 1980. Collection of essays on the critical response to Lowry's work.

Woodcock, George, editor. *Malcolm Lowry: The Man and his Work.* Vancouver: U of British Columbia P, 1971. Collection of essays on various aspects of Lowry's work, most reprinted from earlier publication.

Woolmer, Howard J. *Malcolm Lowry: A Bibliography.* Revere, Penn.: Woolmer/Brotherson, 1983. Full, formal bibliography of all Lowry's publications.

— SHERRILL E. GRACE

Elizabeth Jolley

E lizabeth Jolley was born in Birmingham, England, 4 June 1923, of an English
father and an Austrian mother. After attending a Quaker school, she served as
a nurse in wartime England. In 1959 she immigrated to Western Australia with her
husband Leonard, a librarian.

Until the late 1970s and early 1980s she remained largely unpublished and
pursued a number of occupations—as a nurse, a part-time instructor, an orchardist,
and a farmer. As her writing came to be published, recognition allowed her to devote
more attention to her literary work, though she continues to be involved in teaching,
especially creative writing courses.

She is much sought after for conferences, makes regular appearances at writers'
festivals, and gives public readings of her work. In addition to her novels and short
stories, Jolley has written some poetry, has worked for radio, and has written a
screenplay based on her novel *Milk and Honey*.

She lives in Perth, Western Australia.

New Worlds and Old

Australia itself is isolated from the centers of literary culture, but the isolation of
Western Australia is unimaginable to the inhabitants of Europe and North America.
Perth and its port Fremantle are poised on the edge of nothing: To the east thousands
of miles of desert separate them from the populated areas along Australia's eastern
and southern seaboard; to the west nothing but ocean; to the south Antarctica; and
a long way to the north the countries and cities of Southeast Asia. It was in this
unlikely environment that Elizabeth Jolley forged an international reputation. When
in 1959 she arrived in Perth with her husband and children, the city was yet to
experience that commercial and cultural expansion, which, despite its isolation, has
made it into one of the liveliest places in Australia. Her emergence as a well-known
and much praised writer shadows, in a way, the transformation of Perth from a
sleepy, backward town to a place where some of the most interesting aspects of
Australian life were to occur during the 1970s and 1980s. In 1959 she was
unknown, had published nothing, and must have despaired of ever finding a
publisher. By the end of the 1980s she was a much celebrated writer in her adopted
country and also enjoyed international renown. Her career could well be the subject
matter for a Victorian moral tract: the triumph of perseverance. The publication of
Mr Scobie's Riddle in 1983 by Penguin Books—with all the possibilities of publicity
and distribution offered by a large and respected publishing house—was probably the

single crucial event in her literary career, more important than subsequent awards and accolades. The novel touched a nerve among the Australian reading public, focusing attention on the simultaneously published volume of short stories, *Woman in a Lampshade*, and on several earlier publications, a novel, *The Newspaper of Claremont Street*, and two volumes of short stories, *Five Acre Virgin* and *The Travelling Entertainer*, none of which had penetrated much beyond Western Australia, and also on the then out-of-print novel, *Palomino*.

Jolley has been both extremely reticent and in a way candid about the years prior to her arrival in Perth in 1959. She was born in the English Midlands. Her father's family were Quakers; her mother was Austrian. This odd mixture—in part provincial English Quaker, in part a remnant of the last days of the Hapsburg Empire—accounts for many of the characteristics of her writing. The Quaker side of her heritage is reflected by the frequent concern (some would say near obsession) with matters of personal conscience, with the sense that human beings are under an obligation to live the good life to the extent of their ability—even though, more often than not, they fail or achieve the desired end only partially. It is also mirrored by the obvious impact the Old Testament exerts on her imagination—its phrases resound through many of her works, sometimes by way of direct quotation, sometimes by way of subtle allusion. Her Austrian heritage finds equally important reflections in her novels and stories, most notably, perhaps, in the way so many are colored by monuments of Austrian-German culture, the music of Beethoven, Schubert, Schumann, and even Wagner. More significant, though, is her concern with the bizarre and the grotesque, her interest in curious sexual situations, all of which are contrary to the purity, indeed potential naivete, of the Quaker ethic but reflect instead the emotional, psychological, and sexual ferment of *fin de siècle* Vienna—a Vienna that must have been strong in the mythology of her mother's family.

Few precise details of her life have been revealed. This reticence is characteristic of her public personality. Though much in demand for book-readings, for seminars and symposia, she remains genuinely modest, almost self-effacing, surprised that she should be the center of attention, even of mild adulation. One gains a strong impression of an intensely private person whose life is kept separate from her literary work. And yet it becomes obvious to anyone engaged in even a superficial reading of her books and stories that many personal experiences, often of a very private sort, constitute a base to her many and varied writings. Certain images, preoccupations, even obsessions recur in various guises but always remain striking and recognizable. Of course, great caution is required when a critic begins to discuss such matters. One suspects, nevertheless, that here is an amalgam of the imagined and the experienced that these images and concerns are of immediate relevance to her fictional and literary preoccupations—and to the dilemma of the artist in exile.

The point of reference for a consideration of this aspect of her work is provided, with characteristic oddity, by her latest novel, *My Father's Moon*. It is an essential part of literary folklore that a writer's first novel is the most colored by autobiographical details. This, Jolley's ninth novel, seems from internal and external evidence to offer the most direct and perhaps the most candid evidence about her early years. It is alone among her substantial fictions in having a specifically English setting. It depicts a precise time and place—the Midlands during the war—despite certain passages that span various periods, and one crucial episode that may be set in Australia—where the narrator, Veronic Wright, sees a woman she thinks might be Nurse Ramsden, on whom she had had a crush many years ago. Most of the action is centered on St. Cuthberts, a hospital largely given over to the care of wounded soldiers. Veronica, an awkward, shy girl lacking all confidence, all ability to deal with a perplexing world, observes the near-surrealistic ceremonies and rituals of hospital routine. Some of the best sections of this at times somnambulistic novel record in precise, minute detail the boredom, the discomfort, and the occasional horrors of hospital life along with the curious mixture of cozy comfort and stultifying restrictions. The Quaker boarding school, with its innocent otherworldliness that nevertheless allows room for adolescent crassness and brutality, which Veronica leaves in order to become a trainee nurse at St. Cuthberts, provides another instance where *My Father's Moon* through the inevitable distortions of fiction provides some clues to the personal experiences that helped to form the characteristic—and unique—landscape of Jolley's writings.

Institutions, schools, hospitals, and prisons are the most important locations in Jolley's novels and stories. In such places individuals find themselves in situations where they cannot escape the consequences of proximity and isolation. They are cut off from the outside world by physical distance—as in the bizarre summer school for creative writing in *Foxybaby*—or, as in the case of the elderly inhabitants of St. Christopher and St. Jude in *Mr Scobie's Riddle*, by senility and incontinence. In *Milk and Honey* and in the isolated farmhouses of *Palomino* and *The Well* the restrictions are self-imposed, the products of diffidence, fear, of an irresistible need to exclude the confusing and menacing world of "ordinary" reality. Within these confines the characters may ignore all conventions, engage in practices that the "normal" world would frown upon, or, as in the case of the Heimbachs in *Milk and Honey*, indulge their fantasies of being different, set aside, even special, with at times terrible consequences. Much of Jolley's fictional world is claustrophobic, its "reality" often that of a nightmare. Her characters are compounded of shrewd, acute observations of the quirks and foibles of human behavior and of a stylized artifice, suggesting to some readers the presence of an allegorical intention. Only in these somewhat abnormal settings—the school, the hospital, the prison, the farmhouse, the suburban dwelling tightly quarantined from quotidian reality—is Jolley's singular fictional world capable of existing. Even where such enclosures are not formally established by way of a particular setting, as for instance in Edwin Page's suburban house in *The Sugar Mother*, where there are no physical or psychological barriers, the tendency is, nevertheless, to isolate the characters against intruders, against anything that might impinge on their private, often fantasy-ridden existence.

My Father's Moon provides, in its boarding school and in its hospital, some clues about what experiences and environments contributed to the fashioning of Jolley's fictional world. Nevertheless, these familiar elements fail, on the whole, to achieve the impact of her best writing. Some parts of the novel—nocturnal raids on a secret cache of food in rationed wartime Britain, the clumsy attempts at intimacy by young and by some not-so-young women confined in the artificial enclosure of the hospital—possess the admirable sharpness and controlled eccentricity of Jolley at her best; still, the novel gives the general impression of a dulling of sensibility. The reason may be that the material lies too close to direct experience. It is a recollection, no doubt distorted, of the sights, sounds, occupations of Jolley's youth in the Black Country, establishing a distinct, though not necessarily direct, relationship with personal experience and recollection. For this reason there is a greater concern with what might be described as social reality than elsewhere in Jolley's writing. Veronica Wright is conscious of not merely her awkwardness (a characteristic shared by several of Jolley's protagonists) but also of her social inferiority in the elaborate stratifications of the British caste system. While the novelist is capable of registering such nuances—at least as they existed some 40 years ago—these areas of concern are not where the singular achievement of her work resides. Jolley's best writing emerges when social preoccupations are subsumed within fictional structures— which, while not strictly allegorical, have many of the characteristics of fables, and when the characters fulfill specific roles within stylized, essentially artificial narratives. Reality is transmuted, not reflected, and that transformation is achieved most strikingly in those works written from the perspective of Australia, the country where she lives and the country that claimed her as its own once her literary reputation grew.

Still, very little mention of Australia or specific description of its people, its landscape, its institutions may be found among Jolley's works. Nevertheless, the bulk of it is colored by what is obviously the experience of the newcomer (or the exile) refracted and altered into emblematic fables. Most of Jolley's characters experience a sense of disorientation and alienation. This is, of course, a familiar aspect of the migrant experience, and it is of importance in any account of Australian culture after the late 1940s, because since that time various waves of migration have injected into a hitherto almost uniformly English-speaking population many ethnic, cultural, and religious elements for which the uniformity of "old" Australian society was at times menacing, at others merely perplexing. By the early 1980s, that is by the time that Jolley's reputation was on the point of becoming established, such elements within the Australian population had had time to assimilate, to be, that is, parts of the nation's cultural fabric without becoming totally identified with older and still persisting patterns. It is to such people—but not only to them—that Jolley speaks eloquently in her characteristic concern with the outsider, with those part-alienated creatures whose relationship with a puzzling land and society is disturbing and ambivalent. Two works, a short story and a novella, provide particularly revealing instances of this important aspect of her writing.

Miss Peabody's Inheritance is a wry, economically constructed fable in which this most important preoccupation is very clearly evident. Miss Peabody, a gawky, awkward, middle-aged spinster, lives in a depressing British suburb with her appalling invalid mother. Her life is unrelievedly dull: Between the boredom and petty intrigues of the office and her mother's increasingly strident tyranny, she feels trapped, exploited, and drained of vitality. The one element of her life to sustain her is her correspondence with Diana Templeton, a writer of popular romances, who describes in vivid, loving detail the wonders and beauty of her Western Australian farm. Miss Peabody longs to visit her glamorous friend, to see for herself this earthly paradise. When the opportunity to escape arises, she seizes it, makes the long journey to the other side of the world, only to find that her friend has died in the nursing home where she had spent the years during which she wrote her glowing letters about her farm, its paddocks, creeks, and wildlife. Reality, even if exotic, never corresponds with the images fantasy creates.

The short story "Paper Children" (from the collection *Woman in a Lampshade*) incorporates this theme even more clearly—perhaps too clearly to ensure success. Clara Schultz, retired Director of a woman's clinic, travels from Vienna to visit her daughter Lisa, who had been smuggled out of wartime Vienna and now lives in Australia on her husband's farm. At the end of the story we learn that Clara's voyage was never accomplished, that the several confusing and contradictory reunions recounted in the tale were flashes of fantasy or hallucination experienced by the dying Clara during the last moments of her life in her apartment in the Leharstrasse. These fantasies survey various possibilities of disappointment and alienation. Lisa is, by turns, victim and predator, her husband is now brutal, now cowed. Their farm is impoverished or merely prosaic, the house decayed or commonplace. The reader, like Clara, is perplexed, lacking the key to so puzzling a world. In this manner the migrant's or the exile's experience is transformed and refracted within the story. "Paper Children," though somewhat contrived, nevertheless offers a paradigm not merely of the experience shared by other characters in Jolley's fiction but of the tenor that distinguishes her most compelling writing.

Milk and Honey, a curious and fascinating essay in the "Gothick," is the most elaborate embodiment of this aspect of Jolley's work. The novel was obviously conceived while the sense of cultural and geographical dislocation was still very immediate. That becomes clear in an odd, somewhat clumsy prologue, which may have been a last-minute addition to the published text. It begins with the ominous phrase "A wind blew through Europe"; this wind gathers in itself, all manner of things: soot, dirt, horse manure, brickdust, and thistledown, coming to rest at length in an alien soil where such debris nevertheless attempts to retain its identity. In a large gloomy house somewhere—possibly in Perth—a superficially *gemütlich* family of Austrians attempts to pursue its beloved and traditional way of life: music, food, and sentiment. The external world is kept at arm's length—the family, the Heimbachs, are sufficient unto themselves; what lies beyond is hostile and puzzling, and to be shunned. The narrator Jacob, who lives with the family in order to be provided with a home and with training in music, is at first enchanted and enthralled by this seemingly magic world. His rare excursions into the world outside—to visit the barber, for instance—persuade him of the dull, unattractive ordinariness of all that is not contained within the Heimbachs' magic circle. But age, experience, and ultimately disillusionment convince him all is not as it seems: The Heimbachs' charm, culture, and considerateness merely form a veneer over cruelty, exploitation, and the refusal to acknowledge any standards, any claims but their own. That European heritage that seems so woefully absent from this pragmatic and suburban world (possibly an emblem of how Jolley saw Australia at the time she was writing *Milk and Honey*) is revealed as displaying cruelty and something akin to barbarism.

The individual tone of *Milk and Honey* is unmatched in Jolley's other works, which tend more towards the oblique, the ironic, the grotesque, rather than the "Gothick." The particular intensity of tone in *Milk and Honey* may be the result of Jolley addressing herself directly, though in terms of emblems, perhaps symbols, to her continuing concern with the alienated figure in an unfamiliar, possibly hostile, landscape. The novel does not maintain consistent control over this intensity; but there are compensations: For once there is a boldness of design that many find lacking in Jolley's essentially miniaturist's structures. Nevertheless, the themes and preoccupations that are thrown into such sharp relief in *Milk and Honey* are generally present in more muted and ironic ways in all her fiction.

For many readers, *Mr Scobie's Riddle* remains the most satisfactory and best sustained of the novels. The enclosed world of St. Christopher and St. Jude, an old-age home in a suburb of a large city, provides a memorable and eloquent emblem for Jolley's characteristic concerns and preoccupations—that is, a confined and artificial world. Its inhabitants are restricted and constricted by their own disabilities and by the strictures imposed on them by those in charge: the nurses, the menacing matron Mrs. Price, and the sinister housekeeper Mrs. Rawlings. Yet, restricted though their lives are, the inmates are capable of an intensity of imaginative experience that, although often locked into private and eccentric selves, reveals a curious richness in comparison with the dullness of external, mundane reality. Thus Miss Hailey, the disgraced former Headmistress (who appears in another guise as Arabella Thorne in *Miss Peabody's Inheritance*) may lead a complex existence as the writer of a great, though unpublished and unpublishable novel, and be sustained by fantasies, or perhaps memories, of a golden time when she conducted her favorite pupil on a pilgrimage to the great centers of European culture. Mr. Scobie, the former and equally compromised music teacher, remembers a curiously innocent yet damaging relationship with one of his pupils. On the few occasions that these characters are able to leave—or to escape from—the nursing home, the outside world is dreary and commonplace. St. Christopher and St. Jude, whose name suggests that it harbors the wayfarer and the one beyond hope, is narrow and constricting, but it provides a location for the imagination to soar, no matter in how eccentric a fashion. The theme of cultural displacement is contained here in a most admirable objective correlative.

Other aspects of *Mr Scobie's Riddle* reveal significant parallels with later books—though this may not, of course, reflect the order of composition. The nursing home harbors a sinister netherworld where the staff lead a chaotic life symbolized by the cutthroat game of poker lasting into the small hours of each morning, while, in the trailer in the back garden, Mrs. Price and Mrs. Rawlings watch over a shadowy guest, or prisoner, the husband of the former, consort of the latter. In these images, the fragile world of the inmates—that life of curious emotional and even intellectual intensity—is constantly threatened by dangerous subterranean forces. No convincing explanation is offered about the causes or the purpose of these alarming activities, but they serve to enhance that notable sense of grotesque claustrophobia that is such a marked characteristic of Jolley's writing. The two worlds are in disturbing and perplexing conflict. While it may be going too far to identify this as a specifically Manichean view of life, such notions cannot be excluded entirely from a consideration of these significant aspects of Jolley's fictional imagination.

The below-stairs world of menace and threat makes a memorable contribution to the effect of *Foxybaby*, technically the most accomplished of Jolley's novels. The setting once again is completely isolated: a boarding school somewhere in a sparsely populated countryside, possibly the wheat belt of Western Australia but carrying suggestions of a strangely distorted English rural world. To this remote place comes a collection of ill-assorted people to take part in a residential creative writing course. Alma Porch—a writer of no great accomplishments, one gathers—is to be a tutor, bringing along her nearly finished novel, also called *Foxybaby*. The residents are as eccentric and wayward as the inmates of the nursing home in *Mr Scobie's Riddle*. They enter into an increasingly hectic carnival of folly, a saturnalia or *Walpurgisnacht* that makes parts of the novel resemble a minimalist *The Magic Mountain*. But once more, beneath the daylight world of the school, there is a curious night world of the domestic staff: Miles the caretaker and a witchlike crone, Mrs. Finch, both of whom seem to have stepped out of *Cold Comfort Farm*. While Miss Peycroft, the autocratic principal keeps her guests starved on a diet of lettuce leaves (for the aim of the summer school is to improve the participants' waistlines as much as their minds), Miles serves sumptuous meals at exorbitant prices in his impromptu basement restaurant. His other means of generating income is provided by the carefully arranged accidents in which most of the guests' cars seem to become involved, with Miles being the only person capable of organizing repairs in such an isolated location. Once more, the conflict between inmates and staff, while vague and shadowy, contributes to the surrealistic intensity of the novel.

Clearly, the sense of threat and menace implicit in chaotic forces that are capable of dominating, exploiting, and even tormenting unfortunates who find themselves trapped in some enclosure or institution is a source of much fictional interest for Elizabeth Jolley. One should be chary of assigning specific social, political, or personal significances to this concern. But obviously it is of considerable importance in Jolley's unique and characteristic fictional world. The theme or image surfaces even where the setting and the action are not absolutely confined to such institutionalized isolation, as in *The Well* and *The Sugar Mother*. Both novels, but more importantly the latter, contain memorably bizarre images of how isolation (in both instances self-imposed) makes people prey to predators lurking without.

The Well (like *Palomino*) takes place in an isolated farmhouse occupied by two women, one much younger than the other. They enter a relationship that is a disturbing mixture of sympathy and conflict. Menace lurks outside in the shape of the mysterious man whom the entrapped women kill and throw down the well. With oblique biblical overtones, that attempt to contain the predatory menace of the world outside is frustrated, for at the climax of the novel the well (like that into which Joseph was cast by his brethren or like the tomb in the gospels) seems to be empty. The concern with such predatory incursion is, nevertheless, related more elaborately, and with a greater degree of Jolley's characteristically macabre humor, in *The Sugar Mother*. This novel, together with *Milk and Honey*, is the only instance in Jolley's full-scale fiction where the central character, the organizing consciousness is male.

Edwin Page, an expatriate Englishman who teaches English literature in what is presumably an Australian university, is married to the brilliant Cecilia, a successful gynecologist whose career seems far more glamorous and spectacular than her husband's humdrum academic one. Edwin is marooned in their suburban house, which is very much Cecilia's house, while she attends prestigious meetings and conferences abroad. The vacuum in Edwin's life is gradually filled by the slow inexorable possession of the house, and of himself too, by Leila, an overweight, dull young woman, and by Leila's mother, tenants in the house next door. At first Edwin is suspicious and resentful of these homely and sentimental predators, but eventually he becomes totally captivated. Their control over him is confirmed when Leila gives him the child Cecilia the gynecologist had been unwilling or unable to grant. *The Sugar Mother* was not received with great enthusiasm by initial reviewers, but it will come, I think, to be recognized as one of Jolley's most accomplished novels—not the least for its rich, though dark, comic treatment of such predators as the outrageously passive Leila and her grotesquely suburban mother.

The portrait of women that emerges from *The Sugar Mother*, as well as from other novels and stories is, to say the least, hardly flattering. Nevertheless Jolley has been claimed by sections of the feminist movement as their own. These are difficult waters for a critic—especially a male critic—to enter, yet no account of her work may avoid a consideration of the issues raised by such appropriation. A commonly encountered situation in Jolley's fiction, a source of much literary effect and complication, is the intense relationship between two women, frequently where one is considerably older than the other. Often the relationship involves control and domination; and most frequently the treatment borders on the burlesque. One recurrent image is that of a mature, dominating woman in a position of acknowledged authority who has an intense though clumsily playful relationship with an assistant who tends to be self-effacing and awkwardly reticent.

Josephine Peycroft of *Foxybaby* plays one half of the most extended instance of this relationship. She is a grotesquely bullying monster; her aptly-named offsider, Miss Paisley, is cowed by her friend's and employer's larger-than-life bossiness. And yet there remains, despite the almost gross comedy, something tender about the friendship between the overbearing principal and her timid assistant. That relationship appears again in Diana Templeton's novel, sections of which are reproduced in *Miss Peabody's Inheritance*. Arabella Thorne exerts the same ironhanded influence over her colleagues, yet she is capable of forming sentimental attachments to some of the "gels" under her care. Daphne in *The Sugar Mother* is a similar character, except that lacking a partner or victim—the distinction is not always clear—she remains forlorn and expends her reserves of affection and aggression on dogs. Elsewhere these characters and relationships surface in fleeting references or in minor episodes; for example, in one of the progressive schools where Veronica of *My Father's Moon* finds employment after leaving St. Cuthberts, the headmistress requests that she *never* be disturbed when sharing the bathroom with her assistant.

It is easy, indeed tempting, to see a parody of lesbianism in these relationships. The characters seem to confirm common prejudices about the prevalence of homosexuality in closed institutions like boarding schools and hospitals. Whether the relationships between these domineering women and their mousy assistants or impressionable charges is sexually based remains uncertain. In fact, Jolley's work is unusual by present-day standards for its general avoidance of explicit sexual description. Still, the particular intensity of the relationships makes it difficult to exclude sexual implications. What, then, are we to make of this continuing concern? Does it represent a disapproving attitude towards certain types of lesbian relationships? Is Jolley dissociating herself from the contemporary fashion of attempting to make acceptable those sexual practices once considered perverse and unnatural? Any answer to that conundrum must be tentative, and must, moreover, be based on an individual's assessment and interpretation of an essentially *literary* phenomenon. My own estimate would be that these grotesque elements represent an ambivalent response towards the nature of female homosexuality, especially in the context of present-day liberal attitudes. I suspect that one part of Jolley's artistic temperament finds such relationships unpleasant, alarming, and perhaps even monstrous, for suggestions of predators and victims are too strong for this notion to be dismissed out of hand. Yet there are instances when she deals with such relationships in a more sympathetic manner, and sexual implications are irrelevant.

The extended treatment of these possibilities, however, comprise the least satisfactory part of Jolley's work, as in *Palomino*, which depicts an intense and complicated relationship between two women: Laura, a disgraced middle-aged doctor who has withdrawn into seclusion on an isolated farm after being imprisoned for murder, and Andrea, a deeply disturbed young woman who is carrying her brother's child. Interestingly, *Palomino* also contains the most extended instances of the concern with the pastoral that we see elsewhere in Jolley's work reflected in the distorting mirrors of fantasy or parody—as in the wholly imaginary Antipodean earthly paradise conjured by the crippled Diana Templeton for her naive correspondent, the enthralled Miss Peabody. In *Palomino* such descriptions of rural Australia appear overdone and cloying. Similarly, the isolated life led by the two main characters has a sentimental quality largely absent from Jolley's usually more acid portraits of the emotional bonds that bind women despite differences in age, culture, and temperament. Possibly, *Palomino* did not receive the thorough revision accorded the other novels. Whatever the case, it is significant that this is the one novel where one can suspect an advocacy of so-called "unnatural" relationships.

No such claim may be made for *The Well*, the other book depicting the relationship between an elderly woman and a girl in an isolated farmhouse. What this novel possesses, and *Palomino* lacks to a great extent, are two important distinguishing characteristics of Jolley's fiction: a sense of menace and the shadowy but nonetheless compelling conflict between two people shut away from the world by choice or by the force of circumstances. The strangely disturbing relationship between the elderly and patriarchal Hester Harper and the young waif Katherine is depicted in terms of a nicely-judged series of shifting patterns; the two women perform elaborate variations on the themes of dominance and subservience, now one dominant, almost predatory, now the other. Compared with *Palomino*, Jolley's treatment of this persistent and characteristic preoccupation is finely controlled. It leads to the suggestion that while her work is obviously informed by an awareness of those problems and particular circumstances women face in a society seeming to be male-dominated, her mature fiction transforms such concerns into literary rather than sociological or political constructs.

Something must be said as well about the technical aspects of her work. Even though most of the novels and a number of the stories are experimental in shape and mode, the experimentation confines itself to fairly conventional and traditional bounds. For one thing, there is usually a firm sense of location and of characters within such locations, even when both prove to be the products of fantasy or hallucination. But within these boundaries there remains room for considerable structural ingenuity. For example, *Miss Peabody's Inheritance* and *Foxybaby* both contain sizeable portions of a novel allegedly written by one of the characters. In *Foxybaby* there is the suggestion that the whole of the novel occurs within Miss Porch's dream when she falls into a light sleep aboard the airless bus bearing her to Miss Peycroft's establishment. *My Father's Moon* emerges as the most radical of the novels in its treatment of time and place. While the bulk of the action takes place during World War II in an English hospital, the narrative also reveals Veronica's experiences at boarding school, her unhappy attempts to bring up her illegitimate daughter without financial support from her family, and a vaguely specified and much later time that she may have spent in Australia.

One can argue that Jolley displays a keen interest in the question of the novel, a preoccupation of most contemporary fiction writers. But her experiments—if that is what they are—with the possibilities of the postmodernist novel are prompted by a characteristic of her writing that inevitably puts considerable difficulties in the way of longer structures. For Jolley is essentially a miniaturist. The most memorable aspects of her novels and stories come about when individuals find themselves in characteristic and telling situations, those where a world of possibilities and implications reveals itself by a significant glance or gesture. Even in a generally unsatisfactory work like *My Father's Moon*, there appear any number of these vignettes—a nurse chasing cockroaches with a knitting needle, the formidable matron surrounded by the trimmings of her office, and, best of all, a diminutive refugee from Hitler's Austria clicking around her English hosts' floors on impossible high heels, leaving behind drops of her uncontrollable *monatsfluss.* Nevertheless, the very sharpness and immediacy of these images, their ability to sum up and to evoke economically and vividly a complex of possibilities and experiences, means that the novelist encounters considerable difficulties in achieving those linkages necessary in an extended narrative structure. Yet each of her works, even the least satisfactory, bears the stamp of an imagination both vivid and concrete, and most manage to find a fine accommodation between the commonplace and the macabre—the location of her individual voice.

ELIZABETH JOLLEY'S PUBLISHED WORK

Novels

Palomino, 1980
The Newspaper of Claremont Street, 1981
Mr Scobie's Riddle, 1982
Miss Peabody's Inheritance, 1983
Milk and Honey, 1984
Foxybaby, 1985
The Well, 1986
The Sugar Mother, 1988
My Father's Moon, 1989

Short Story Collections

Five Acre Virgin and Other Stories, 1976
The Traveling Entertainer and Other Stories, 1979
Woman in a Lampshade, 1983
Stories, 1988

Articles

"Author's Statement." *Australian Literary Studies* 11 (1981): 213–15.
"A Child Went Forth." *Australian Book Review* (Nov. 1983): 5–7.
"Who Talks of Victory?" *Meanjin* 46 (1987): 4–15.
> Recalls her life in England and her experiences as a nurse-trainee during the war. Says that her characters do not claim victory, only "hold out."

SELECTED CRITICAL READINGS

The publication of *Mr Scobie's Riddle* in 1982 prompted the beginning of what has proved to be lively critical interest in Jolley's work. In the main, critics have focused on three aspects of her fiction: the sense of alienation (cultural, personal, and psychological); the concern with the act of writing—the question of fiction in general; and the perspective feminist studies provide for the understanding of Jolley's work. No doubt all of these areas but especially the last will continue to attract critics, possibly to the detriment of certain aspects of Jolley's fiction that have not received the attention they deserve, notably her interest in the bizarre and the grotesque.

Daniel, Helen. "Elizabeth Jolley: Variations on a Theme." *Westerly* 31.2 (1986): 50–63. Examines Jolley's fiction as variations on several themes—alienation, displacement, lesbianism, among others—in terms of the postmodernist novel's preoccupation with the play between reality and fiction.

————. *Liars, Australian New Novelists.* Melbourne: Penguin Australia, 1988. Substantial part of this book concerned with the work of several experimental or innovative Australian writers is devoted to Jolley and her relationship with developments in postmodernist fiction.

Garner, Helen. "Elizabeth Jolley: An Appreciation." *Meanjin* 42 (1983): 153–57. Lively, sympathetic response by a well-known Australian writer, written at a time when Jolley's work was on the point of gaining recognition.

Goldsworthy, Kerryn. "Voices in Time: *A Kindness Cup* and *Miss Peabody's Inheritance.*" *Australian Literary Studies* 12 (1986): 471–81. Study of narrative methods employing "deconstructionist" techniques to the work of Jolley and Thea Astley.

Jones, Dorothy. "'Which hend you hev?': Elizabeth Jolley's *Milk and Honey.*" *Westerly* 31.2 (1986): 35–49. Thorough examination of *Milk and Honey*, drawing attention not merely to its themes and preoccupations, but as well to literary, musical, and cultural analogies within its complex fabric of fantasy, "Gothick" horror, and near-allegory.

Kirkby, Joan. "The Nights Belong to Elizabeth Jolley: Modernism and the Sappho-Erotic Imagination in *Miss Peabody's Inheritance.*" *Meanjin* 43 (1984): 484-91. Surveys Jolley's fiction through

Milk and Honey, concentrating on "love between women, the interplay between memory and imagination" as sources of "joyous release" or as preludes to "tragedy."

————. "The Call of the Mother in the Fiction of Elizabeth Jolley." *SPAN* 26 (1988): 46–63. Examines the importance of "gynesis" ("the putting into discourse of 'woman' or 'the feminine' as problematic") in Jolley's work, elaborated with copious references to Julia Kristeva, Toril Moi, Claire Kahane, and others.

Riemer, A.P. "Between Two Worlds—An Approach to Elizabeth Jolley's Fiction." *Southerly* 43 (1983): 239–52. Examines Jolley's work up to *Mr Scobie's Riddle*, concerned with her attempts to find fictional images for the sense of cultural and geographical alienation experienced by the migrant or the "displaced person."

————. "This World, the Next, and Australia—the Emergence of a Literary Commonplace." *Southerly* 44 (1984): 251–70. Examines images of Australia, especially the *topos* of Australia as the land of the living dead, in the work of various British and Australian novelists, with some emphasis on Jolley's work as representing a departure from or modification of older prototypes.

————. "Displaced Persons—Some Preoccupations in Elizabeth Jolley's Fiction." *Westerly* 31.2 (1986): 64–79. Further exploration of the preoccupations examined in an earlier essay, taking into account Jolley's publications after 1983, and concentrating on *Milk and Honey* as a fantasia on the themes of displacement and exile.

Salzman, Paul. "Elizabetlh Jolley: Fiction and Desire." *Meridian* 5 (1986): 53–62. Examines the connection between desire (sexual, aesthetic, cultural) and the craft or art of writing, with emphasis on the various images of writers and writing within Jolley's fiction.

Interviews

With Candida Baker. *Yacker: Australian Writers Talk About Their Work*. Sydney: Pan, 1986. 210–33.
With David Headon. *Meanjin* 44 (1985): 39–46.
With Paul Kavanagh. *Southerly* 49 (1989): 438–51.
With S. Trigg. *Scripsi* 4 (1986): 245–64.
With Ray Willbanks. *Antipodes* 3 (1989): 27–30.

—A.P. RIEMER

Ruth Prawer Jhabvala

I n 1975 Ruth Prawer Jhabvala received the Booker-McConnell Prize for her novel set in India, *Heat and Dust*. Until the Prize brought her international fame, her identity as a European writer had not been generally known. She was born on 7 May 1927 in the German city of Cologne, the younger child and only daughter of a Polish/Jewish lawyer named Marcus Prawer and his wife, Leonora Cohn Prawer. Ruth Prawer initially encountered English at school, but wrote her first stories in German. When the family escaped to Britain from Nazi Germany in 1939, twelve-year-old Ruth rapidly made the transition to a new language.

Loss of their entire social and family circle so darkened the Prawers' early years in Britain that Marcus Prawer took his own life as the news from Nazi Germany of one death after another filtered through to England. Ruth went to school in England and later to the University of London, where she read for a degree in English and made "The Short Story in England, 1700–1750" the subject of an M.A. thesis. In 1951 she married Cyrus Jhabvala, a Parsi architect from Delhi, and left Britain for India.

When Ruth Jhabvala took up residence in New York in 1976, she had lived 25 years in India, brought up three daughters, and published eight novels and four collections of short stories. She had also entered on a successful complementary career as a screenwriter for the films of Merchant-Ivory. In both fiction and film her early work concentrated on Indian characters in Indian settings and after 1966 altered focus to include a series of studies of Westerners in India. Following her move to the United States the area of her literary activity expanded further to include writing screenplays for cinematic versions of novels by other writers, among them Henry James, Jean Rhys, and E.M. Forster. She has published since 1976 two more novels, set for the most part in the United States.

In 1978 Ruth Jhabvala was awarded the Neil Gunn International Fellowship, and in 1984 London University's honorary degree of Doctor of Literature, the Fellowship of Queen Mary College (her former London University college), and a MacArthur Foundation Fellowship for her writing. Also in 1984, the British Film Institute and the Museum of Modern Art (New York) jointly published a book devoted to the Merchant-Ivory-Jhabvala films.

RETURN TO THE WEST

When Ruth Prawer Jhabvala took up residence in 1976 in an apartment on New York's East Side, she left behind her (seemingly for good) the Delhi milieu that had been her home for 25 years and that had provided the settings for every novel she had published during her sojourn in India. India had provided characters and a background, too, for every one of her published short stories: with one exception, the story "A Birthday in London," an intimate glimpse into the lives of Jewish refugees in postwar Britain, which was published in her first collection of short fiction, *Like Birds, Like Fishes.*

Enraptured by India on her first encounter with it in 1951, believing that she understood it well, she had entered with enthusiasm into the role of an Indian wife and mother and as a beginning writer had regarded with delight the complex and colorful life around her. On the first appearance of her work in print, the author's Indian surname and the detail with which she depicted Indian family life had led complimentary reviewers in India and overseas to identify her as an Indian writer. It was an error that she does not seem to have been in any great hurry to correct. She had become, after all, "Indian" by marriage, her children had been born and were growing up in Delhi, and until 1960 (when she revisited England for the first time in nine years) it was the landscape, society, and atmosphere of India that filled her vision and provided the impetus or inspiration for her writing.

Even when, as happened later in her career, her feelings towards the country of her adoption underwent a profound change, it is worth noting that she has chosen neither to revert to her own Polish/German family name of "Prawer" nor to assert her identity as a Westerner by means other than taking up residence in New York, a location that is, incidentally, much more convenient to the pursuit of her interests in filmmaking than the more remote Delhi.

Jhabvala's early work focused on India and Indian characters, which she approached at the start from the vantage point of her European background. It is possible that her experience of life as a displaced and isolated European refugee child in Britain made her sensitively alert to the dilemmas faced by the Punjabi refugees who poured into Delhi, casualties of a newly partitioned independent India. It is possible that such sensitivity had roots that went deeper still, for as a Jewish child at school in a Germany coming increasingly under Nazi influence, she had known what it felt like to be called names by strangers in the streets and to be shunned by schoolfellows and neighbors.

The helplessness of the refugee, the discontented and alienated sensibility of the expatriate, the exile's longing for home: These are aspects of twentieth-century experience that have consistently struck deep notes in Jhabvala's novels. These notes are to be heard in the accounts in her two earliest novels of the lives of Punjabi refugees in Delhi and later in the helpless anger of certain European characters such as Esmond Stillwood of *Esmond in India* and Etta of *A Backward Place,* stranded and longing for "home" in an India that has no place for them.

Alert, even when writing her earliest novels, to the intricacies and complexities of Indian society in general and the extent to which an individual in that society tends to reflect and embody social and cultural norms peculiar to his or her community, Jhabvala seems to have taken care from the first to avoid writing of what she could not observe at first hand. Her experience of Indians in India was limited in her early years there to two communities: the wealthy, English-educated group of Parsi professional families (probably the most sophisticated and Westernized community in India) into which she had married; and the energetic Punjabi community and their extended families with which she came into intimate contact through the household of her architect husband's Punjabi partner.

The Parsis are a self-contained community within Indian society: Of Persian origin, their complexions kept fair and their health somewhat delicate through generations of intermarriage within their own small community, the wealthy Parsi families of Bombay and Delhi incline (with some famous and distinguished exceptions) towards the professions rather than "trade." They tend to keep themselves fastidiously aloof from the lives of their fellow Indians and have maintained, without in any way compromising their patriotism or their feeling for India as "home," a high regard for European culture and English education. Although *To Whom She Will* voices some criticism of a wealthy and effete Indian upper class, the life led by that class was one into which an English-educated European such as Jhabvala would have been able to fit without much difficulty.

The Punjabis, on the other hand, are an energetic, entrepreneurial community, vigorous traders and business people with deep roots in rural India, whose resourcefulness Jhabvala saw amply demonstrated during her early years in Delhi, to which city many Punjabi refugees were drawn after Partition. All India observed the determination and hard work with which they successfully built themselves fortunes from the little they had brought with them.

Wisely shutting peasants and Maharajas, fields and palaces out of her fiction for the moment, the young author concentrated on drawing the Delhi life around her, basing most of her writing on upper-class professionals, public men, and ladies of leisure fashioned on Parsi models, and setting them moving along plotlines derived from the eighteenth-century English comedies of manners with which her British education had made her familiar. The settings she provided for "cultured" (that is, Europeanized) Indian families similarly have much in common with what she knew best in the India she encountered in 1951: the style of living observable in wealthy Parsi households at the upper end of India's social scale. These strategies proved very successful, not only producing lively social comedy but, in retrospect, making an acutely observed point about class divisions within Indian communities. Thus the elegant, well-appointed households of Vazir Dayal Mathur and Tarla in *To Whom She Will* and of Har Dayal and Madhuri in *Esmond in India* are worlds apart, not only from the households of other "Indian" characters in those novels, but from the Bombay suburb inhabited by middle-class Parsis that has been recently drawn so vividly by Rohinton Mistry in his collection of short stories, *Tales from Ferozha Baag* (1988).

For most of her middle-class characters, Jhabvala looked to Punjabi models, achieving striking successes with her portrait of a Punjabi refugee family in her first novel *To Whom She Will* and following this with lively, individualized character-izations of the Punjabi businessman Lalaji and his family in her second, *The Nature of Passion*.

Once it had assimilated, and become accustomed to, the very potent glamor and charm of an oriental society, Jhabvala's eye seems to have been attracted to the inconsistencies and contradictions of Indian life. She possesses a lively sense of comedy, and in *To Whom She Will* she applies the rules of English social comedy to the Indian "arranged marriage." *The Nature of Passion* is an ironic and perceptive study at close range of the family life of an unscrupulous and corrupt Indian businessman. That she does not condemn the arranged marriage outright (as less informed Western writers have often done) and presents Lalaji as endearing and even lovable, although corrupt indicates the range of Jhabvala's intelligence and sympathy as well as the flexibility of the quiet, ironic tone that has become one of the hallmarks of her writing. In an interview with Ramlal Agarwal in 1974 she recalled: "Perhaps I loved [India] then because of my being Jewish. The Indian family life, the humour was closer to the Jewish world I knew than the Anglo-Saxon world" (33). In one of her short stories, "The Aliens," which was first published in the collection *Like Birds Like Fishes*, life as part of her businessman husband's extended Punjabi family offers an insular and conventional young English girl no peace or privacy and few satisfactions. It is notable that Peggy is the object of her creator's amused pity rather than of her sympathy. It would seem that at this stage of her career Jhabvala thought of life in India as something to be savored and enjoyed: In Peggy she drew one of her earliest alienated Westerners, a young woman who lacks the imagination and resilience to enjoy India.

Persons unfamiliar with India, and therefore forced to generalize about its society, might imagine that marriage into an Asian family would most certainly, for a European of Prawer's background, have piled alienation upon alienation. That depends on the outlook of the newcomer and on the status and background of the family. In *A Backward Place*, her sixth novel, Jhabvala created an appealing female character in Judy, a young Englishwoman married to an Indian actor and glad to be living with him and their young family in Delhi. It is possible that she relived through her fictional presentation of Judy's memories of England something of what "escape" from Europe to India had meant to her during her first years there:

> They hadn't led a very interesting life. "We were just ordinary people," she said. Her father had made precision instruments in a factory; her mother cooked and cleaned and kept Judy away from strangers. Her mother didn't trust strangers; these included the neighbours. You were safest if you kept yourself to yourself. So they did, just the three of them, in that tight little house, with the doors and curtains firmly shut to keep the cold and the strangers out. (42)

By the early 1970s, however, Jhabvala's attitude to India had altered. When Agarwal asked her in 1974 whether she would like to be considered an Indian writer, she replied:

> No, how could I be? I'm not, am I? There's no getting away from that fact. I write differently from Indian writers because my birth, background, ancestry, and traditions are different. If I must be considered anything, then let it be as one of those European writers who have written about India. (34)

Jhabvala's struggle with India, which she has herself described with a kind of passionate desperation in an essay "Myself In India" (published as an introduction to her collection of stories, *Out of India*), is now part of contemporary literary history. In this essay she describes the stages of a cycle of experience through which, according to her observation, all sensitive Westerners must pass who spend any appreciable time in India:

> There is a cycle that Europeans—by Europeans I mean all Western-ers, including Americans—tend to pass through. It goes like this: first stage, tremendous enthusiasm—everything Indian is marvel-ous; second stage, everything Indian not so marvelous; third stage, everything Indian abominable. For some people it ends there, for others the cycle renews itself and goes on. I have been through it so many times that now I think of myself as strapped to a wheel that goes round and round and sometimes I'm up and sometimes I'm down. When I meet other Europeans, I can usually tell after a few moments conversation at what stage of the cycle they happen to be. (13)

In strong contrast to the passage quoted earlier from *A Backward Place* is the mood of a short story written many years later and published in the American edition of Jhabvala's 1976 collection, *How I Became A Holy Mother*. In "The English-woman," an English expatriate wife (clearly modeled on her creator's cyclic theory) prepares after many years in India to return to England: "She is eloping, leaving everything behind her—husband, children, grandchildren, thirty years of married life. Her heart is light, and so is her luggage" (22).

It is interesting to trace Jhabvala's complex relationship with India from its beginnings to its end, to arrive at some idea of its intensity, and to study the process by which, in eight novels and numerous short stories, Jhabvala had transmuted her difficulties with India into art. Her move from India to America, and her present way of life—traveling every year in a circle that links her with members of her family in Britain, India, and the United States—are factors that set up an altogether different set of problems and literary concerns for readers of her work. For one thing, she no longer writes as a European isolated in India but as a European who has found herself a home in a Western city of immigrants, many of whom have undergone experiences similar to her own. While still leading by choice a professional life of comparative isolation and quiet, her work in cinema has widened her experience of people and of places. She is no longer the inexperienced young writer who went to India in 1951 but a mature and skilled author who has developed theories and perfected techniques for the pursuit of her art.

Has she developed a theory about Europeans in America that is comparable in any way to her cyclic theory about Europeans in India? So far her own statements have related to what she would *like* to do: for instance, interviewed in London soon after receiving the Booker Prize for *Heat and Dust* in 1975, she said:

> Having assimilated all this Indian experience I don't want to forget it or cast it off; what I want to do is to take it out again as a

> Westerner, enriched by what I have learned there. . . . I can't throw
> away the past twenty-four years, nor do I want to. What I'd really
> like to do is record the journey back. (Rutherford 377)

Eight years passed before Jhabvala published a novel to follow *Heat and Dust,* but during those years she recorded, in several screenplays and short stories, her observations of American life. "That's how I get to know a place, through writing" (18), she had said to John Pym in 1978, and the film "Roseland" (1977) is an interesting example of the way in which she combined her impressions of New York life with her personal interest in the immigrant experience. "Roseland" takes as its subject and setting the Broadway institution of the same name, a live-music dance hall that attracts serious dancers as well as lonely New Yorkers of all races and classes. Three stories about Roseland habitués explore the lives of people who live out their favorite fantasies on the floor of the famous old dance hall: In the third of these an elderly Central European immigrant and retired cook dreams of winning a dance prize before she dies.

Her work on "The Europeans" (1979) and "The Bostonians" (1984) appears to have assisted the process by which she was, during this period, getting to know America by means of writing about its people and places. Writing the screenplay for "The Europeans" gave Jhabvala an opportunity to combine the same elements she had used in "Roseland" in a completely different style, and at a different level, as she retold the story of the sophisticated and somewhat predatory cousins from Europe invading the rigidly conservative domesticities of a Boston family.

But working with the Merchant-Ivory team on film versions of the novels of a major writer such as James, whom she deeply admired, was, of course, an artistic experience in itself that exercised and extended Jhabvala's abilities and skills. Vincent Canby, in a *New York Times* review, found "The Bostonians" "a major achievement . . . a rare delight, a high comedy with tragic undertones, acted to passionate perfection by a cast of the best actors ever assembled by the Merchant-Ivory-Jhabvala team," and ranked the film "among the finest film adaptations of a classic novel that anyone has yet made" (15). There is also to be considered her work on the screenplay for the Merchant-Ivory film "Hullabaloo over Georgie and Bonnie's Pictures" (1978), in which a young American art-collector and the representative of a British museum of fine art struggle for the possession of a Maharaja's famous collection of Indian miniature paintings.

Among the short stories in which Jhabvala brought the America she was exploring into amusing or tragic conflict with the India she knew well are three that hold special interest for the student of her work. In "How I Became A Holy Mother," an American model enters a new phase of her life as a religious charlatan. In two stories published in 1978 Jhabvala presented studies of predators and American victims: "Parasites" is set in an old Manhattan brownstone mansion; "A Summer By The Sea" focuses on a particularly grim holiday spent at a beach house by an American family.

In the third of these, authorial emphasis is not so much on the mysterious "Indian" background of the predatory Hamid, as on the Americans whose psychological weaknesses he exposes and pitilessly exploits. Hamid can be said to lead back to Jhabvala's Indian fiction, in particular to Swamiji, the religious charlatan of her 1972 novel, *A New Dominion*, while his spectacular good looks and callous heart link him with Gopi in the same novel and look forward to the characters of Leo Kellermann in *In Search of Love and Beauty* and Crishi in *Three Continents*. Hamid's victims joyfully open their hearts and homes to the predator as Louise and her friends open theirs to Kellermann in Jhabvala's first "American" novel, and as Lindsay, Michael, and Harriet Wishwell in her second gladly donate their family home "Propinquity" to the Fourth World Movement represented by Crishi.

In the *oeuvre* of Jhabvala the "American" novels occupy, therefore, the position of large works for which a number of minor pieces in various genres have provided experience and trial runs. It is a position comparable to that occupied in the case of her "Indian" fiction by her novels *A New Dominion* and *Heat and Dust*, the publication of the first of which was preceded by several stories involving Indian holy men and Western spiritual self-seekers and the second by the technically innovative screenplay for the film "Autobiography of A Princess."

In Search of Love and Beauty is a novel in which the image of India seems at first sight to be unimportant and peripheral. Instead, it is the "Continental" background Jhabvala wished to explore in her American fiction that seems best represented in the private lives and secret longings of the Sonnenblick family and their circle, German-Jewish refugees who are building new lives for themselves in the United States. Writing this novel gave Jhabvala an opportunity to explore the psychology of European refugees and immigrants, drawing quite probably, especially in her characters, "memories" of the happy lives they had led in pre-war Germany, on hoarded family material that had remained comparatively untouched during her Indian years. Despite the fact that Jhabvala achieves in it, with conspicuous success, her stated intention to combine her "three backgrounds" if she can, reactions to *In Search of Love and Beauty* were mixed and in many cases perplexing to the author, who had been receiving (especially after *A New Dominion* and *Heat and Dust*) a hostile press in India but who had been recognized by most Western critics as a novelist of major importance. "I have never before been so misunderstood, on both sides of the Atlantic," she wrote at this time (letter to author).

A method of approaching Jhabvala's American fiction could certainly be found through a study of her models: the practitioners of the novel whom she regards as masters of the art of fiction. Jhabvala's literary models, recognizable in her early work as including Jane Austen and Henry James, also include European masters of the novel and the short story. Her borrowings are, however, so skillfully submerged in the imaginative creations of her later years that they are virtually unrecognizable as themselves. The part played by Henry James in shaping her responses to America may well have similarities with that played by E.M. Forster in relation to Jhabvala's Indian novels and stories. In *Heat and Dust*, the single novel in which she treats British rule in India, Jhabvala takes Forster as her principal guide, evoking a British Raj of the 1920s and an Indian Raj of the 1970s that are equally destructive of human personality, hypocritical, restrictive, and false. In *A New Dominion*, a novel in which she examines the workings of an Indian chauvinism in independent India, she writes in the shadow and in the spirit of E.M. Forster's *A Passage to India*.

Equally valid in attempting to understand her aims and assess her achievement would be a study of the early novels and stories through which she first "got to know" India. For example, a study of her novel *A New Dominion*, and especially of its characterization of the sinister, smiling "Swamiji" (the most memorable of Jhabvala's portraits of Indian holy men) illuminates the character of Leo Kellermann, the anti-hero of *In Search of Love and Beauty*. Similarly, a study of Jhabvala's fictional methods could not pass over her skilled presentations of unreliable narrators, especially Lee in *A New Dominion* and the unnamed woman narrator of *Heat and Dust*: characters who, interesting in themselves, can now be seen also as preliminary sketches for the full-length portrait of Harriet Wishwell, the naive narrator of *Three Continents*.

A careful consideration of Jhabvala's work as a whole also shows that from 1960 onward, when she wrote her first screenplay for James Ivory and Ismail Merchant, her best work in both genres has sprung from a fusion of fictional and filmic elements. In addition to her European, Indian, and American experience, she draws today in writing her novels and short stories on a dazzling repertoire of cinematic techniques, learned in the process of translating her own fictions and those of other outstanding writers to the screen.

A chronological reading of her novels and stories highlights the extraordinarily comprehensive way in which Jhabvala's writing—of which her "American" fiction forms as yet only a very small part—could be said to represent and exemplify the social and artistic concerns of the twentieth century. Between 1951 and 1976 she provided an example of the displaced expatriate writers who have been so much part of the postwar international scene. She now illustrates that contemporary phenomenon, the unhoused itinerant author who writes out of a "free" and unhoused state.

Works Cited

Agarwal, R. "An Interview With Ruth Prawer Jhabvala." *Quest* 91 (1974): 33–36.

Canby, Vincent. "'Bostonians': A Proper Jamesian adaptation." *New York Times* 5 August 1984: 15.

Jhabvala, Ruth Prawer. *A Backward Place*. London: John Murray, 1965.

———. "The Englishwoman." *How I Became A Holy Mother*. New York: Norton, 1976: 22–38.

———. "Myself In India." Introduction to *Out of India*. New York: William Morrow, 1986: 13–21.

Pym, J. "'Where could I meet other screenwriters?' A Conversation with Ruth Prawer Jhabvala." *Sight and Sound* 48.1 (1978-79): 15–18.

Rutherford, A., and K.H. Petersen. "*Heat and Dust*: Ruth Prawer Jhabvala's Experience of India." *World Literature Written in English* 15 (1976): 371–77.

Ruth Prawer Jhabvala's Published Work

Novels

To Whom She Will, 1955 (U.S. title: *Amrita*, 1956)
The Nature of Passion, 1956
Esmond in India, 1958
The Householder, 1960
Get Ready for Battle, 1962
A Backward Place, 1965
A New Dominion, 1972 (U.S. title: *Travelers*, 1973)
Heat and Dust, 1975
In Search of Love and Beauty, 1983
Three Continents, 1987

Short Story Collections

Like Birds, Like Fishes and Other Stories, 1963
An Experience of India, 1966
A Stronger Climate, 1968
How I Became A Holy Mother and Other Stories, 1976
Out of India, 1986

Screenplays

Shakespearewalla, 1973
Autobiography of a Princess, 1975

SELECTED CRITICAL READINGS

Ruth Prawer Jhabvala's early novels attracted enthusiastic praise from reviewers in India and overseas who took her to be an Indian-born author, partly because her books focused with intimate particularity on the Indian scene, partly because she has consistently published her work under her Indian husband's family name of "Jhabvala." After the publication of "Myself In India," Indian criticism has become increasingly condemnatory of what it deems Jhabvala's unsympathetic treatment of India and Indians in her fiction, although a select group of critics and reviewers, East and West, have continued to recognize that the subtleties of Jhabvala's ironic treatment of character range freely across divisions of race, nation, and class. Jhabvala's efforts, after moving West, to bring together in her fiction her European, Indian, and American experience, her increasing stature as a writer for the screen, the skill with which she draws upon her cinematic experience in writing her latest novels, and the process of her development from "regionality" to the position of an "immigrant" or "expatriate" writer and thence to her present status as an internationally acclaimed yet essentially "unhoused" writer are areas deserving of close critical attention.

Blackwell, Fritz. "Perception of the Guru in the Fiction of Ruth Prawer Jhabvala." *Journal of Indian Writing in English* 5 (1977): 6–13. Traces the frequent appearance of the "guru" or "swami" figure in Jhabvala's work.

Bradbury, Nicola. "Filming James." *Essays in Criticism* 29 (1979): 293–301. Examines the treatment of Henry James's novel *The Europeans* in the film version made by Merchant and Ivory in 1979.

Gooneratne, Yasmine. "Apollo, Krishna, Superman: The Image of India in Ruth Prawer Jhabvala's *In Search of Love and Beauty.*" *Ariel* 15.2 (1984): 110–17. Examines Jhabvala's utilization of Indian elements in the first of her "American" novels.

———. "Film into Fiction: The Influence upon Ruth Prawer Jhabvala's Fiction of Her Work for the Cinema, 1960–1976." *World Literature Written in English* 18 (1979): 368–86. Explores cinematic techniques used in novels (especially *A New Dominion* and *Heat and Dust*) and examines thematic and technical interaction between novels, screenplays, and films, among them the satiric intentions that link "Bombay Talkie" with Austen's *Northanger Abbey*, and the adaptations of flashback and verbal irony that link "Autobiography of a Princess" with *Heat and Dust*.

———. *Silence, Exile and Cunning. The Fiction of Ruth Prawer Jhabvala.* Delhi: Orient Longman, 1983; 1990. Critical study of Jhabvala's fiction and screenplay writing from 1951 to 1989. A separate chapter on each novel; chapters on the short stories and on writing for the cinema, which comparatively examine a number of selected texts and indicate the nature of their relationship, in matters of theme and technique, to Jhabvala's novels. Introduction, notes and index, bibliography. Illustrated with stills from Merchant-Ivory films.

———. "The Expatriate Experience: The Novels of Ruth Prawer Jhabvala and Paul Scott." *The British and Irish Novel Since 1960.* London: Macmillan, 1990. Compares the approaches taken by Jhabvala and Paul Scott (both winners of the Booker Prize for novels dealing with India) towards depicting Westerners in India.

———. "'The proper accoutrements of style and sensibility': Eighteenth century influences on the fiction of Ruth Prawer Jhabvala." *Language and Literature in Multi-Cultural Contexts* (1983): 141–68. Traces thematic and structural connections between Jhabvala's fiction and films and the novels of Austen and Burney.

Ivory, James. *Autobiography of a Princess: Also Being the Adventures of an American Film Director in the Land of the Maharajas.* London: Murray, 1975. Richly illustrated, invaluable first-hand account of the making of Merchant-Ivory films in India. Includes Jhabvala's screenplay for the film *Autobiography of a Princess.*

Williams, Haydn Moore. "Strangers in a Backward Place: Modern India in the Fiction of Ruth Prawer Jhabvala." *Journal of Commonwealth Literature* 6.1 (1971): 53–64. Examines Jhabvala as a novelist of contemporary Indian life.

———. "The Yogi and the Babbitt: Themes and Characters of the New India in the Novels of R. Prawer Jhabvala." *Twentieth Century Literature* 15.2 (1969): 81–90. Perceptive analysis of Jhabvala's Indian novels in terms of conflicting symbols of materialism and spirituality.

—YASMINE GOONERATNE

Doris Lessing

D oris May Lessing was born in Kermanshah, Persia (later Iran), on 22 October 1919. Her parents, Alfred Cook Taylor and Emily Maude McVeagh, an English bank clerk and his wartime nurse, emigrated to Persia shortly after World War I and in 1925 moved to a farm in Southern Rhodesia (later Zimbabwe). A brother, Harry, was born two years after Doris. The father, whose leg had been amputated following a war wound, had no previous experience with farming, and the family was always poor. He was a dreamer who became a cynic; Lessing's mother was domineering but ineffectual. On their African farm they were socially and physically isolated, surrounded by the open veld. Lessing attended a Catholic convent school in Salsbury but left when she was fourteen, saying she had eye problems; however, she continued reading voraciously.

In 1938 Lessing moved to Salsbury to work in various jobs, mostly clerical, and began writing fiction. She married a minor civil servant, Frank Charles Wisdom, in 1939, and had a son, John, and a daughter, Jean. She divorced in 1943 and two years later married a German-Jewish refugee, Gottfried Lessing. She had a son, Peter, in 1947, and divorced in 1949. She has said, "I do not think marriage is one of my talents. I've been happier unmarried than married" (*A Small Personal Voice* 46).

In 1949 Lessing emigrated to England, settling in London, and in 1950 published her first novel, *The Grass Is Singing.* Since then she has continued to live in London and to make her living as a professional writer, writing reviews, media scripts, and nonfiction in addition to her novels, short stories, plays, and a book of poems. During the early sixties she worked in the theater, helping to establish Centre 42, a populist art program, and writing her own plays.

Lessing's interest in politics began with a Marxist group in Rhodesia, and in England she was briefly a member of the Communist Party, leaving it officially in 1956. In the late 1950s she participated in mass demonstrations for nuclear disarmament and was a speaker at the first Aldermaston march in 1958.

In the late 1960s Lessing's thinking was heavily influenced by the mystical teachings of Indries Shah and Sufism, which emphasizes conscious evolution of the mind in harmony with self and others. Although for many years Lessing resisted the role of public persona, since the mid-1980s she has made numerous public appearances.

Her awards include the Somerset Maugham Award, the German Shakespeare Prize, the Austrian Prize for European Literature, and the French Prix Médicis for Foreigners.

MAPS OF NEW WORLDS

Doris Lessing has spent forty years attracting readers. Since 1950, with the publication of *The Grass Is Singing,* the year after she emigrated from Southern Rhodesia to England and settled in London, she has given an increasingly worldwide audience a remarkable literary production. Her writing is multi-genred, varied, often experimental in form and structure, and powerful in themes and moral commitment. Her works are widely translated (though at different times in different countries), and she has long had a serious audience. The United States has provided her earliest and staunchest readership as well as the bulk of Lessing criticism. Her work is treated in virtually all books on contemporary novelists, women's literature, and twentieth-century fiction, and virtually all survey anthologies of short fiction include her short stories, which probably represent her most enduring art. But it is her novels that have reflected and in many cases created her readers' ways of looking at the world. For it is in the novels that Lessing describes, analyzes, and questions the great issues of the times. The novels map the worlds, mixing realism and fantasy as they chart contemporary life. Their territory covers detailed views of the individual consciousness and expands to the outer space of the cosmos.

Lessing's fictional maps are multiple, multi-dimensional, and overlapping, suggesting no one map is adequate or complete. She constantly reminds her readers that the map is not the territory. Her encompassing and overriding theme is the urgency of expanding individual consciousness and seeing ourselves in relation to others in new ways, the imperative of creating new maps.

The continuity of themes throughout all Lessing's works establishes a loyal audience and intrigues critics, especially since subgenres of her novels vary widely, including social realism, naturalism, science fiction/space fiction, inner space/outer space, utopian/dystopian, futurist/visionary, fantasy, fable, transcultural postmodern, and combinations of these in experimental ways. She widens her readership too by her sweeping scope of topics and interests: gender relationships, sexuality, motherhood, politics, psychoanalysis, racism, ageism, mysticism. Critic Mona Knapp refers to Lessing's variety as "an overwhelming medley of ideas, themes, fictional techniques, and perspectives," adding, "The very heterogeneity of the *oeuvre* makes it a fitting illustration of its foremost premise: that truth and substance cannot be smoothly compartmentalized and labeled, but are in constant flux" (180).

Lessing is never afraid to be didactic, and her positions are clear on all her wide range of subjects. As one commentator notes, "There are few subjects she has not written about and few positions she has taken that do not alienate someone" (Fishburn 10). Certainly different readers prefer different books, but many continue to read them all, if only to disagree with them. American critics have tended to dislike her space fiction series *Canopus in Argos,* for example, but they are interested in Lessing's ability to switch fictional directions. South Africans read her novels with African settings to complain that her racial views are biased. Science fiction and younger readers consider her fantasy and space fiction underrated and her realism rather tedious. Certain reviewers disagree with her attitudes toward freeing women's roles and grumble that she makes "insensitive male" almost redundant. Others criticize her style, finding it sometimes "repetitive, prolix, didactic, and trivial" (Schlueter 293). But the readership continues to grow.

What enables Lessing to map such a close analysis of self with a sweeping analysis of global sociology, politics, and metaphysics? Perhaps one should merely remember that genius can appear anywhere. Or perhaps one can leave it assumed, as Lessing does with her Martha Quest, introduced in the first of the *Children of Violence* series as an adolescent who "repudiates the colour bar" and "dislikes racial prejudice in all its forms, including anti-Semitism" (*Martha Quest* 43), her liberal credentials already established. Martha, whose background so closely parallels Lessing's, is an avid and eclectic reader, but she finds no accurate representation of herself in the past. She sees herself as a product of her age, the historical times, and her heritage—"British, and therefore uneasy and defensive" (8). Martha is a detached observer who can focus a dispassionate eye on her own isolation, guilt, and sense of responsibility; she is already a writer (keeping a diary) lured by the power and rhythm of words. And when this young Martha's thoughts "swam in a mazed and unfed way through her mind" she has "her familiar daydream" of a fabulous and ancient four-gated city whose smiling, beautiful citizens live harmoniously (11). At age sixteen the essential Martha Quest *is*.

In considering this question of Lessing as social interpreter and social critic, most who have written about her works have looked to Lessing's situation as exile, as an outsider to her own culture.

Katherine Fishburn, for example, traces Lessing's "alienation" to both of her parents. Their attitudes and situation made Lessing a thoughtful and often critical outsider, her critical habit of mind a response to the clash of temperaments and the complicated emotional states of her parents. This enabled Lessing to separate from other whites and their ideas of racial superiority. Added to this alienation was the physical environment of the veld, where Lessing learned to become at one with nature and the community at large, "a concept given concrete form in the natives' mud huts, which after serving their usefulness would be reclaimed by the bush" (Fishburn 8).

Mona Knapp, in "This Business of Being an Exile," uses houses as the image that best illustrates Lessing's outlook, especially her distrust of compartmentalizing, and quotes Lessing in *Going Home*: "I don't live anywhere; I never have since I left that first house on the kopje. I suspect more people are in this predicament than they know" (7). Knapp explains Lessing as "an outsider in principle, in voluntary self-exile from all the collectives and movements" (2). From this separation follows Lessing's insistence on an alternative way of viewing life, "a new vista open to anyone willing to take off the blinders of collectivism and seek it" (Knapp 184), whether it is Martha Quest finding another geographic and psychic country, Charles Watkins in *Briefing for a Descent into Hell* drifting through sea space, the narrator in *Memoirs of a Survivor* stepping through the wall, or Planet 8's Representative achieving another form of being.

Ruth Whittaker sees colonialism as crucial to Lessing's work, noting that Africa not only provided settings for much of her fiction but also provided Lessing a way of seeing. Lessing belongs to neither the natives nor to the veneer the white colonials imposed on them, "and it is this marginality which enables her to act as an observer, and gives an additional clarity to that detachment which is an essential prerequisite of the artist" (Whittaker 4). When Lessing moved to England, "her colonial, expatriate eye makes strange the familiar, and her readers are thus reintroduced to what they thought they already knew, from a different perspective. In her later fiction she is perfectly able to view this planet from afar since she has always stood at a distance from her material. . . . Her own sense of displacement, of not belonging, enables her to work on the borders of our consciousness: charting, mapping, delineating an unknown country, acting in fact like a new colonial, pioneering and appropriating new territory" (Whittaker 5).

Lessing herself summarizes the importance of her African years in the Preface to *African Stories*, including her sense of waking "every morning with one's eyes on a fresh evidence of inhumanity" (viii): "I believe that the chief gift from Africa to writers, white and black, is the continent itself. . . . This is not a place to visit unless one chooses to be an exile ever afterwards from an inexplicable majestic silence lying just over the border of memory or of thought. Africa gives you the knowledge that man is a small creature, among other creatures, in a large landscape" (viii).

Lessing's most purely realistic novels are those set in Africa. With few exceptions, the novels whose settings are elsewhere combine realism and fantasy or go to other planets altogether. One exception is *Retreat to Innocence*, Lessing's first novel set in England. It is a novel she disavows, and it has only briefly been in print. Lessing says she did not do the theme or the material justice, and she will not permit its reissue (Kaplan and Rose 38). Its failure is in part a result of the central character's retreat as signified by the title, of her refusal to see, for Julia Barr is politically naive and fails to develop her own values.

After Lessing had written three realistic volumes about Martha Quest set in Africa (*Martha Quest, A Proper Marriage, A Ripple from the Storm*), numerous short stories set in Africa, and various nonfictional commentaries about both Africa and England, she again created a realistic London for her monumental achievement, *The Golden Notebook*. But in this pivotal metafictional novel Lessing expands the boundaries not only through her complex structural and stylistic technique but because Anna Wulf goes through layers of madness acknowledged in herself and in others, questioning the idea of "reality" itself.

From *The Golden Notebook* on, except for the finishing volume of Martha Quest in Africa, *Landlocked*, Lessing blurs the lines between what is commonly regarded as realism with other forms, pioneering a version of magic realism—a merging and converging of real and unreal, using words and form to invent and continuously reinvent the world.

When Lessing brings Martha Quest to London in *The Four-Gated City*, Martha deliberately challenges the boundaries of her mind to achieve new states of awareness:

> a state, then, that had been in fact the surprise of her being in London, its real gift to her. She had learned that if she walked long enough, slept lightly enough to be conscious of her dreams, ate at random, was struck by new experiences throughout the day, then her whole self cleared, lightened, and she became alive and light and aware. (36)

Later Martha experiments further with Lynda Coldridge and alone, developing psychic powers, which she uses as the novel itself moves from present time to the late 1990s after some unspecified worldwide catastrophe.

Lessing's subsequent fiction becomes more and more concerned with alternate states of reality. Lessing's point is that our definitions of reality have been reductive and limiting and that readers should recognize a wider span of what reality includes. Along with this emphasis on connections and wholeness rather than on a limited, narrowed reality, Lessing moves her characters to outer space or other planets (*Briefing for a Descent into Hell*, most of *Canopus in Argos*), to other realms or dimensions (*The Memoirs of a Survivor, The Marriages Between Zones Three, Four, and Five*), or at least to other countries as a tourist (*The Summer Before the Dark*). *The Diary of a Good Neighbor* and *If the Old Could . . .*, while set in a realistic London, were first published under a pseudonym, as though in part Lessing was unsure of using the realistic technique again, and in fact here too, especially in *The Diary of a Good Neighbor*, Lessing undercuts the realism by inserting into Jane Somer's diary an overlapping of her various fictional versions of the life of Jane's friend Maudie Fowler, based on Maudie's stories, much as she did with Anna Wulf's notebooks in *The Golden Notebook*.

It is as though once Lessing moved her characters out of Africa she could no longer accept conventional fictional representations of reality to describe them. The only two real exceptions, *Retreat to Innocence* and *The Good Terrorist* are unsuccessful novels, which show how inadequate this form is for both characters and narrator. *The Good Terrorist* shows stupid and unsympathetic would-be revolutionary terrorists running around cities in England; the dominant image of the central character is of her emptying hundreds of odorous chamberpots that have collected in an old house whose bathrooms are clogged, indicating the futility of her revolutionary pretensions.

The Fifth Child is especially interesting because the novel appears to present an accurate record of a recognizable English family, but to other readers it is a fantasy, a tale of an alien being born to this family. The novel hovers on some point that embraces both categories. It mimics those pictures where foreground and background flicker and reverse. Or, like a rotating yin/yang circle, apparently opposing concepts are instead together, inseparable. As critic Betsy Draine reminds us, "Lessing has always produced her most exciting work when struggling to integrate seemingly incompatible perceptions, ideologies, and styles (143).

This merging and interweaving clearly relates to the mapping of worlds and consciousness for which Lessing is most noted. Few twentieth-century writers have been more conspicuous in their concern with the quest motif. All Lessing's fiction concerns the discovery of self in relation to others, the understanding of sexual and self-identity, and the search for a comprehensive attitude toward humanity that would allow us to live together more harmoniously. Martha Quest is the quintessential Lessing protagonist-as-seeker. Throughout *Children of Violence* Martha spends long hours with psychiatrists and psychoanalysts of differing philosophies. She analyzes her dreams and her writings. She takes part in political movements and social causes. She uses sexual intimacy as a means of understanding herself and reaching planes of heightened awareness. She reads widely and talks endlessly with a wide variety of people. By the end of the series, Martha has explored the major paths to knowledge in the Western world.

It is useful to compare this quest with Lessing's way of presenting many of the same ideas in *Shikasta*, the first of the *Canopus in Argos* series. After the only gap in Lessing's long publication career, the five years between 1974 and 1979, she moved to an explicitly science fiction mode. Characters from other planets concern themselves with the progress of our own, here named Shikasta, and human understanding of these outer space creatures and forces is imperative for human survival. Put another way, Martha's quest has become cosmic quest. In the introduction to Shikasta, Lessing speaks of "the exhilaration that comes from being set free into a larger scope": "I had made—or found—a new world for myself, a realm where the petty fates of planets, let alone individuals, are only aspects of cosmic evolution. . . . I feel I have been set free to be as experimental as I like, and as traditional" (*Shikasta* ix).

Although many readers are attracted by the nonrealistic framework, in *Shikasta* the ploy of having the galactic empires Canopus and Sirius in rivalry with the Empire Puttiora and its criminal planet Shammat fighting over the fate of Shikasta is cumbersome and distracting. The full title of the book, *Canopus in Argos: Archives. Re: Colonised Planet 5. Shikasta: Personal, Psychological. Historical Documents Relating to Visit by Johor (George Sherban). Emissary (Grade 9). 87th of the Period of the Last Days*, is not only hopelessly unwieldy but also misleadingly indicates the report of a single individual, Johor, while in fact the novel presents a series of reports and commentaries by many different space creatures observing Shikasta over a long period. Some of these beings have assumed human forms either to assist or to hinder human development, and most of the book consists of their messages to each other. This plurality of alien speakers is confusing, although it again allows Lessing to present opposing views and a variety of ideas. These ideas are for the most part expressions of the standard Lessing themes: the individual versus the collective, political systems and their interference with racial and sexual equality, the interconnectedness of all life, and the need for a more enlightened individual consciousness.

In *Shikasta* Lessing assumes her former readers are still with her, as indicated for example by the inclusion of reports by Lynda Coldridge, last seen in *The Four-Gated City*. Lynda talks about Martha Quest and other characters from the earlier book. Yet there are no characters to care about in *Shikasta*; typical of science fiction conventions the characters are underdeveloped, and most often referred to in classes or by functional designations such as servant, worker, or old man. Whether Shiskastans or aliens, they lack description and are merely ideological mouthpieces. Referring in an interview to these characters, Lessing asks her interviewer: "But the relationship between these sort of stylized men and women—that doesn't strike you as even somewhat comic? Which was my intention, slightly" (Bikman 24). The interviewer replies "No." The stylized characters are not comic, and merely leave the ideas of the novel undramatized and more heavy-handed than in Lessing's earlier works.

The ideas in *Shiskasta* lack subtlety. As Francine Du Plessix Gray says in a review,

Lessing has "laudable passion but leaden rhetoric as she launches into annoyingly simplistic attacks on the all too obvious evils of white racism, exploitative ecology, and Western imperialism" (Gray 70). The tone of the novel is overly moralistic and quasi-religious, with "evil forces at work in this galaxy of ours," as Johor says (*Shikasta* 43). Good planet Canopus emanates a power flow called the substance-of-we feeling, SOWF for short, but an unpredictable alteration in the cosmic force fields breaks Earth's lock with SOWF and the planet degenerates. Earth's name is therefore changed from Rohanda, "which means fruitful, thriving" (*Shikasta* 14) to Shikasta, "the hurt, the damaged, the wounded one" (*Shikasta* 24). Bad planet Shammat spreads its evil influences. As one reviewer notes, "There is something unsatisfying about a vision of history that suggests humans could not, after all, help making the messes they have, that their blunders were all ordained by a small tic in the cosmos" (Paul Gray 102).

Yet by contrast, the future of Shikasta still demands immense individual human responsibility, with or without the substance-of-we fix. The highly vaunted telepathic power shared by some of the characters is mundane with no explanation of why these powers are presupposed beneficial, since they could be equally adaptable for evil purposes. Worse yet, the Providers and Benevolences from outer space seem to be "paternalistic, imperialist, authoritarian, and male supremacist" (Le Guinn 32). Yet that sense of individual responsibility is the reader's basic guideline—that same Lessing message of the need for an expanded consciousness that would let us know how to follow the Cosmic Will, the "voluntary submission to the great Whole" (*Shikasta* 26).

Well, Lessing suggests, maybe there actually are intelligent beings in space who so thoroughly understand the interrelatedness of all life that they interest themselves in the destiny of Earthlings. Perhaps that possibility is our great hope and our great fear. The tension between the two readings—fantasy and possible reality—mirrors the jarring tension between the fictional frame and the realistic assessment of problems on Shikasta.

The quests in *Canopus in Argos* are thus the same as Martha's, though embedded in cosmic space as well as Earth. Lessing ultimately tells the same message over and over, but in a variety of forms so that the message might be heard in a way that makes it a part of our lives. It is this persistent narrative persona— Lessing's creative imagination—that remains fascinating, even though some of the individual novels are not. Lessing's narrative voice is that of an intense spirit who explores, who maps, whose ultimate sense of human life is that the individual is meant to quest, to go beyond mere observation to struggle with the visions of what could be.

As Johor comments on the first page of the *Canopus* series, "This is a catastrophic universe, always; and subject to sudden reversals, changes, cataclysms, with joy never anything but the song of substance under pressure forced into new forms and shapes. . . . Things change. That is all we may be sure of" (Shikasta 3). Lessing clearly values the exploration of change, and her novels insist that changes in the ways we view ourselves and our worlds are necessary if life on this planet is to survive.

WORKS CITED

Bickman, Minda. "A Talk with Doris Lessing." *New York Times Book Review* 20 March 1980: 24.

Draine, Betsy. *Substance Under Pressure: Artistic Coherence and Evolving Form in the Novels of Doris Lessing.* Madison: U of Wisconsin P, 1983.

Fishburn, Katherine. *Doris Lessing: Life, Work, and Criticism.* Fredrickton, Canada: York Press, 1987.

Gray, Francine Du Plessix. "Crusading Novelists." *Quest* 3.8 (1979): 70.

Gray, Paul. "Visit to a Small Planet." *Time* 21 Apr. 1980: 102.

Kaplan, Carey, and Ellen Cronan Rose. *Doris Lessing: The Alchemy of Survival.* Columbus: Ohio UP, 1988.

Knapp, Mona. *Doris Lessing.* New York: Frederick Ungar, 1984.

Le Guinn, Ursula. "Re: Colonised Planet 5 Shikasta." *New Republic* 13 Oct. 1979: 32.

Lessing, Doris. *The Four-Gated City.* New York: Bantam Books, 1970.

———. *Martha Quest.* New York: Plume Books, 1970.

———. *Shikasta.* New York: Knopf, 1979.

Schlueter, Paul and June, editors. "Doris Lessing." *An Encyclopedia of British Women Writers.* New York: Garland Publishing, 1988. 291–94.

Whittaker, Ruth. *Doris Lessing.* New York: St. Martin's Press, 1988.

DORIS LESSING'S PUBLISHED WORK

Novels

The Grass Is Singing, 1950

Children of Violence (5 volumes): *Martha Quest,* 1952; *A Proper Marriage,* 1954; *A Ripple From the Storm,* 1952; *Landlocked,* 1965; *The Four-Gated City,* 1969

Retreat to Innocence, 1956

The Golden Notebook, 1962

Briefing for a Descent into Hell, 1971

The Summer Before the Dark, 1973

The Memoirs of a Survivor, 1974

The Diaries of Jane Somers, 1984 (originally published as *The Diary of a Good Neighbor,* 1983, and *If the Old Could . . .,* 1984, under the name Jane Somers)

The Good Terrorist, 1985

The Fifth Child, 1988

Science Fiction

Canopus in Argos: Archives (5 volumes): *Shikasta,* 1979; *The Marriages Between Zones Three, Four, and Five,* 1980; *The Sirian Experiments,* 1981; *The Making of the Representative for Planet 8,* 1982; *Documents Relating to the Sentimental Agents in the Volyen Empire,* 1983

Short Fiction

This Was the Old Chief's Country, 1951

Five: Short Novels, 1953

The Habit of Loving, 1957

A Man and Two Women, 1963

African Stories, 1968

The Temptation of Jack Orkney and Other Stories, 1972 (British title: *The Story of a Non-Marrying Man and Other Stories*)

This Was the Old Chief's Country, Vol. II of Doris Lessing's Collected African Stories, 1973

Sunrise on the Veld, 1975

A Mild Attack of Locusts, 1977

To Room Nineteen/Her Collected Stories, Vol. I, 1978

The Temptation of Jack Orkney/Her Collected Stories, Vol. II, 1978

Stories, 1978

Memoirs

Going Home, 1957
In Pursuit of the English: A Documentary, 1960
Particularly Cats, 1967

Essays

A Small Personal Voice (edited by Paul Schlueter), 1974
Prisons We Choose to Live Inside, 1987
The Wind Blows Away Our Words, 1987

Plays

Each His Own Wilderness (in *New English Dramatists*), 1959
Play with a Tiger, 1962

Poetry

Fourteen Poems, 1959

SELECTED CRITICAL READINGS

Critical commentary on Lessing's works was well under way in the 1960s, and the sheer volume of criticism since then has been extraordinary and is still increasing. In the United States alone, nearly thirty book-length studies focus exclusively on Lessing. In addition to hundreds of articles in various publications, major journals such as *Contemporary Literature* and *Modern Fiction Studies* have devoted special issues to Lessing, and there are special collected issues from such organizations as the Popular Culture Association and the International Association for the Fantastic in the Arts. Lessing's works figure prominently in numerous books on women in literature, contemporary British novels, and twentieth-century fiction. The *Doris Lessing Newsletter* began publication in 1976 and the Doris Lessing Society was formed as an allied organization of the Modern Language Association in 1979. International Lessing criticism is also increasing, particularly European. Lessing's works have been approached from Jungian, archetypal, Marxist, Freudian, reader response, feminist, new critical, semiotic, and deconstructionist critical perspectives— and many combinations of perspectives, which reflect the wide variety of readers and the serious attention Lessing has commanded throughout her writing career.

Bloom, Harold, editor. *Doris Lessing.* New York: Chelsea House, 1986. Brings together useful criticism from 1962 through 1985, arranged in chronological order of original publication. Covers major themes and commentary on the realistic novels including *The Good Terrorist.*

Doris Lessing Newsletter. Published bi-annually since 1976 by the Doris Lessing Society, affiliated since 1979 with the Modern Language Association. Contains reviews, short essays, and exchange of information and ideas about Lessing's works and readings and interviews. Editorship and place of publication change from year to year.

Draine, Betsy. *Substance Under Pressure: Artistic Coherence and Evolving Form in the Novels of Doris Lessing.* Madison: U of Wisconsin, 1983. Sees Lessing's themes as related to her narrative strategies, the evolution of form as an imperative pressure on content. Traces historical influences on Lessing's formal choices. Covers novels through the *Canopus in Argos* series.

Fishburn, Katherine. *The Unexpected Universe of Doris Lessing: A Study in Narrative Technique.* Westport, Conn.: Greenwood Press, 1985. Considers Lessing's science fiction from *Briefing for a Descent into Hell* through the *Canopus in Argos* novels. Argues that the science fiction has the purpose of transforming reality, involving the reader in ideas and the intricacies of the texts rather than in characterization.

————. *Doris Lessing: Life, Work, and Criticism.* Fredericton, Canada: York Press, 1987. Brief overview of Lessing, including literary biography, critical response, and annotated bibliography.

Kaplan, Carey, and Ellen Cronan Rose, editors. *Doris Lessing: The Alchemy of Survival.* Columbus: Ohio UP, 1988. Detailed history of Lessing criticism followed by selected original essays by various critics such as Kaplan's "Britain's Imperialist Past in Doris Lessing's Futurist Fiction" and commentary on Doris Lessing interviews.

Knapp, Mona. *Doris Lessing.* New York: Frederick Ungar, 1984. Covers works through Volume V of *Canopus in Argos*, plus material on Lessing's plays, poetry, and nonfiction. Shows relationships in theme and structure throughout Lessing's work.

Pratt, Annis, and L.S. Dembo, editors. *Doris Lessing: Critical Studies.* Madison: U of Wisconsin, 1974. Reprint of Autumn 1973 special issue on Lessing by *Contemporary Literature.* Ten essays on major novels plus Florence Howe's interview, "A Conversation with Doris Lessing" in which Lessing discusses *The Golden Notebook.*

Rose, Ellen Cronan. *The Tree Outside the Window: Doris Lessing's Children of Violence.* Hanover, NH: UP of New England, 1976. Applies Erik Erikson's theory of ego-development to Lessing's *Bildungsroman, Children of Violence* series; shows metaphoric progression of Martha Quest from "the shell" of childhood to "the tree outside the window" in creating herself.

Rubenstein, Roberta. *The Novelistic Vision of Doris Lessing: Breaking the Forms of Consciousness.* Urbana: U of Illinois P, 1979. Shows cyclic design in Lessing's repeated themes, particularly the mind discovering, interpreting, and ultimately shaping its own reality. Comprehensive (through 1978) chronological approach including the relationship between fictional structure and meaning, the purpose of doubling, and the relationship between fiction and reality.

Schlueter, Paul. *The Novels of Doris Lessing.* Carbondale: Southern Illinois UP, 1973. Provides a thematic approach to Lessing's novels through 1972, particularly the appeal of communism to Lessing's liberal mind, the racial problems of southern Africa, the role of "liberated" women in a patriarchal society, and writing as an aspect of self-examination.

Seligman, Dee. *Doris Lessing: An Annotated Bibliography of Criticism.* Westport, Conn.: Greenwood Press, 1981. Comprehensive and well-annotated bibliography through 1978. Incorporated earlier checklists and bibliographies by Selma Burkhom, Burkhom and Margaret Williams, Catherine Ipp, Agate Krouse, Carol Fairbanks Myers, R. S. Roberts, and others. Includes bibliography of research and teaching suggestions, interviews with Lessing, and book reviews.

Singleton, Mary Ann. *The City and the Veld: The Fiction of Doris Lessing.* Lewisburg: Bucknell UP, 1977. Treats novels through *Memoirs of a Survivor.* Argues that Lessing's veld represents Nature, associated with the unconscious, intuition, direct experience, and repetition; the city represents society, ego-consciousness, logical and discursive thought, symbolism, and fragmentation. Uses Jungian psychology, the imagery of alchemy, and the influence of Sufism to show how Lessing reconciles differences.

Sprague, Claire. *Rereading Doris Lessing.* Chapel Hill: U of North Carolina P, 1987. Examines various repetitive patterns including mother and daughters, aging and dying, multiple mirrors, and doubling. Covers novels through *The Sirian Experiments.* Discusses Lessing's major artistic decision to write *The Golden Notebook* after she had published the first three volumes of *Children of Violence,* then returning to volumes IV and V.

Sprague, Claire, and Virginia Tiger, editors. *Critical Essays on Doris Lessing.* Boston: G. K. Hall, 1986. Review essays and various other articles plus general introduction to Lessing and chronology of works. Divided into sections on Politics and Patterns, Female (Other) Space, Inner and Outer Space, and Reception and Reputation.

Steele, M. C. *Children of Violence and Rhodesia: A Study of Doris Lessing as Historical Observer.* Salisbury, Rhodesia: U of Rhodesia Department of History, 1974. Provides historical context for Lessing's novels set in Africa. Claims Lessing overlooked post-World War II improvements in economic and social conditions in Rhodesia and questions the validity of her portrayal of white society. For a response to Steele, see Diane Gage's "The Relevance of History" (*Doris Lessing Newsletter* 2, Winter 1978: 4-5).

Taylor, Jenny, editor. *Notebooks/Memoirs/Archives: Reading and Rereading Doris Lessing.* London: Routledge and Kegan Paul, 1982. Collection of original essays including Taylor's interview with David Gladwell, director of the film *Memoirs of a Survivor.* Other critics cover major novels and such topics as Rebecca Rowe's discussion of Lessing as exile and as woman writer.

Thorpe, Michael. *Doris Lessing's Africa.* London: Evans Brothers, 1978. Sees Lessing as essentially African and all her writings from her position as African exile, the isolate, the outsider. Covers novels through 1969. Earlier book, *Doris Lessing* (1973), also concentrates on African subject matter.

Whittaker, Ruth. *Doris Lessing.* New York: St. Martin's Press, 1988. Overview study of Lessing's novels, including chapter on colonial, expatriate stance and the influence of the concepts of colonialism not only on Lessing's settings and characterization but also on her way of viewing the world.

— LOIS A. MARCHINO

Peter Carey

P eter Carey was born in 1943 in Bacchus Marsh, a country town in the
Australian state of Victoria, into a family of aviators and used car salesmen. He
was educated at the local school and for seven years at a leading private school,
Geelong Grammar. He later studied science for one year at Monash University in
Melbourne, attracted by the alchemy of organic chemistry. At age nineteen he joined
an advertising agency and lived in Melbourne until 1967. In 1968 he lived in
London, then returned to Sydney where he became involved in another advertising
agency. After a period in a Queensland commune and several years in Sydney, Carey
now lives in New York City. He is married to Alison Summers. They have one son.

His first book of stories, *The Fat Man in History*, was published in 1974 and
favorably received in Australia, England, and the United States. His second collection
of stories, *War Crimes* (1979), won the New South Wales Premier's Literary Award
in 1980, an award he won again in 1982 for his first novel, *Bliss*, which also received
the Miles Franklin Award and the National Book Council Award. *Illywhacker* won
the Victorian Premier's Award and *The Age* Book of the Year Award and was
shortlisted for the Booker Prize. *Oscar & Lucinda* won the Miles Franklin Award and
the National Book Council Award and in 1988 the prestigious Booker Prize.

In 1990 Carey was artist in residence at New York University, where he taught
and completed his fourth novel.

THE RIVALRIES OF THE FICTIONS

The work of Peter Carey has a luminous energy—full of invention, vitality,
exuberance. All his work is baroque, built on contradiction and paradox, on rival
versions of things, rival visions, rival worlds to explore contestant possibilities going
on underneath the surface. With a profound dismay at many of the impulses and
forces of Australian culture yet with a perverse delight in the very paradoxes and
contradictions he uncovers, Carey searches for new constructions of contemporary
consciousness. While he explores many aspects of Australian identity, he is
essentially confronting those levels of national identity infiltrated and colonized by
the past. His is at once a vision of postcolonial society on the cusp of the future and
a profound dialogue with Australian history and with ancestral murmurs deep within
the national consciousness.

In an exploration of the mythopoeic history of Australia, Carey reflects the
colonizing of the imagination with stories and storytelling inherited from Europe and
transported to the Australian landscape. In *Oscar & Lucinda*, Christian stories "lay

across the harsh landscapes like sheets of newspaper on a polished floor. They slid, slipped, did not connect to anything beneath them" (307). This is the central concern of all Carey's work, the slippage and sliding across the surface of landscape and the search for the connections, the stories, the images, which hold between a people and its landscape. All Carey's work is about stories, those we fabricate ourselves and those thrust upon us, dislodging our own. Through an exploration of the myths imposed from without rather than composed from within, his work turns on notions of truth and lie, across tessellations of people and place, landscape and time.

Carey's work has a literary kinship with the work of Borges, Fowles, Vonnegut, and García Márquez and is in the tradition of Sterne's *Tristram Shandy* in a fabulous blend of arch realism with stubborn and corroborative immediacy, with splendid fabrication and narrative ambiguity. In the 1970s and 1980s, a period of extraordinary growth in Australian fiction, Carey has been a major force among Australian writers exploring modes of the fabulous and the surreal, often postmodernist, often with a subversive image of Australian history and often with a quantum logic of contradiction and uncertainty. Much recent Australian fiction by writers such as Peter Mathers, Frank Moorhouse, Murray Bail, David Foster, David Ireland, Rodney Hall, and Elizabeth Jolley explores paradoxes of space and time and change, often with a prismatic play of mind, ludic and absurdist, a fabric of hazard, paradox, and instability, in which writer and reader are accomplices and collaborators.

Carey's major novels, *Illywhacker* and *Oscar & Lucinda*, play out contradictions of time and space through a dialogue with the past, revisiting and revising aspects of Australian history. In his first works, the short story collections, *The Fat Man in History* and *War Crimes*, Carey writes in a speculative mode, elaborating and embellishing a central paradox, sometimes a trap of consciousness, sometimes a proposition, which he pushes into startling new dimensions. Many stories sustain contrary worlds as they blur into each other, smudged across the fantastic and the absurdist into new territories of the real. In some, there is a grim vision of contemporary capitalist society, together with the ambiguous lure of American dreams, colonizing contemporary Australia even as Australia extricates itself from the legacy of British colonialism. Politically and culturally, Carey's fiction explores the shaping of contemporary Australian consciousness through its heritage of myths and dreams and stories.

Much of his short fiction, which is speculative and fabulous, turns on a disturbing vision of the unknown and nightmarish lurking within the familiar. In several stories, there is a Kafkaesque dilemma of entrapment and dislocation, his characters bereft of categories of orientation. In the title story of his first collection, the fat men are greedy oppressors in a cycle of revolution and stasis, running on as if in perpetuity. In "American Dreams," a small Australian town becomes its own spectator when a model of it is built, a replica reality through which the artifice and the real are drawn into disturbing symmetry. The town is stilled on the knife-edge of self-consciousness, inhabiting the dream of American life—America being a talismanic image.

Many of Carey's short stories create extravagant worlds that refract fantastic mirror images of reality. In "Crabs," there is the nightmarish vision in a drive-in theatre, where the Karboys prowl and plunder, and where Crabs himself is stranded, being stripped of hope as relentlessly as his car is stripped of parts. Outside there is only a waste land where ultimately Crabs is stranded, a displaced outsider beyond the theater boundaries. In "Peeling," the narrator anticipates and contemplates the unhurried exploration of the woman, Nile. He finds first the other marginal selves she contains until all veneers are peeled back to reveal the fragments of a small white doll without features. Underneath the surface layers of the world, there is only an image stripped of features, only absence.

In "Do You Love Me?" Carey begins with the fabulous notion that parts of the country are becoming less real, heralding the beginning of dematerialization, first of the neglected nether regions of the land, then buildings, and finally people. The caretaker of a building about to dematerialize claimed to see "other worlds, layer upon layer, through the fabric of here and now" (*The Fat Man in History* 22). Throughout Carey's short fiction, he peels back layers, some dark and disturbing, some fine and diaphanous. In *Bliss*, too, Harry Joy discovers "there were many different worlds, layer upon layer, as thin as filo pastry" (8), as if rival worlds hover in the margins of the present, impatient to break through the fabric of presence and absence.

While *Bliss* develops some of the preoccupations of Carey's short stories by exploring levels and layers of reality, it also represents a turning point in Carey's work with the elaboration of the theme of the cultural origins of stories—the provenance of stories and myths that collectively define and confine national identity. This theme, which underlies Carey's major novels, *Illywhacker* and *Oscar & Lucinda*, is one of the dialogues running beneath the surface of *Bliss*: a negotiation between inherited stories and the composition of both private and collective myth. Harry Joy dies at the start of *Bliss* and as he slides between the spaces in the air, he recognizes "the worlds of pleasure and pain, bliss and punishment, Heaven and Hell" (8). These familiar polarities mark out the territory of the novel, within which Carey maps new landmarks and evolves new myths. Early in the novel, there is a gathering of myths of innocence and purity, myths religious, social, political, national, myths of Harry Joy's time. The opening of the novel is closely tied to narrative and storytelling, to the stories of good and evil he inherited from childhood. When Harry himself becomes the storyteller, passing on his heritage to his family, he transmits the stories imperfectly and they take on different meanings. In a novel that is post-Christian, Harry tries to conceive new myths, a new eschatology, a new god, a post-Christian quest for salvation in a world where salvation and damnation are not untrammelled opposites but chameleon, the distinctions sliding.

Trapped in a Hell he has himself constructed, Harry Joy becomes a cartographer, surveying and mapping this unknown world, classifying anew its creatures. He recognizes the horrors of the business and commercial world as well as the truth of Bettina's infidelity and his children's incestuous commerce. In the central section that takes place in the hospital, with a mix of absurdity and existential horror, Harry experiences loss of identity and is stripped down to a residual self. The center of his private gravity shifts and his determinations are no longer his own but invaded by Alex Duval in a nightmare of dispossession. Alex and Harry carry out an absurd struggle for identity, impersonating each other, so that identities slide between them just as Heaven and Hell have been impersonating each other, sliding to and fro throughout the novel like all the other polarities of Harry's world. Throughout *Bliss*, there are talismanic images of New York; and Vance's stories contain apocalyptic images of New York, "the most beautiful and terrible city on earth. All good, all evil exists there" (18). Dreaming of New York and subscribing to the articles of American faith, Bettina feels marooned, stranded in an outpost of the American Empire. The United States, as in the story "American Dreams," is an ambiguous lure, at once attracting and repelling.

Bliss explores the myths by which we live, those that have failed us, the myths we have lost. It explores the existential horror lying just below the surface of the ordinary life of a Good Bloke. Yet, as the novel flips from heaven to hell, from freedom to captivity, from nightmare to bliss, it is a work of contrary energy and affirmation. Harry Joy is not finally trapped in his own infernal vision, but can discover and explore new territories within the layers of the world. Through storytelling and the ritual retelling of myths, Harry Joy regains and revitalizes his lost heritage in the idyllic Bog Onion Road community with Honey Barbara, a community hungry for ceremony and story.

From *Bliss*, Carey turned to the past in search of origins and explanations, in his two major novels, *Illywhacker* and *Oscar & Lucinda*. *Illywhacker* is a magical family saga that dances across time and pitches into the future, full of tales on trajectories that intersect, as if more and more stories wait on the periphery, impatient to be told, while more and more characters importune. Constantly disrupting its own forward movement, *Illywhacker* explores history as an intricate configuration of stories, a construction as architecturally bizarre as the Pet Emporium with which the novel ends. In this magical family saga, running from the gold-mining days in the nineteenth century into the beginning of the new millennium, Carey explores themes of national identity and mythology within a legacy of inherited myths of England amid the intrusion of American myths. In *Illywhacker*, history—real or invented, lies or truth—is storytelling.

Like an American *Illywhacker*, Allan Gurganus's *Oldest Living Confederate Widow Tells All* (1989) explores the nature of tales and their passage through time, the way tales accrete meaning as inherited histories retouched by memory and embossed by time and teller. Spiralling through 150 years of American history, the novel is narrated by 99-year-old Lucy Marsden, born one year before Carey's Herbert Badgery, whose story spirals through Australian history. Lucy Marsden tells all in a quicksilver voice, mirthful and acerb, meditative and slangy, skittish and crackling with an irrepressible delight in her myriad tales and variant histories. Much of the novel upsets old rivalries, both national and private: polarities of race and politics, war and peace, past and present, self and gender. Turning on a sense of hidden continuities between past and present, like *Illywhacker*, *Oldest Living Confederate Widow Tells All* is no linear narrative on a family biographical run through history but circular, a beaded necklace of tales and memories, which Lucy keeps polishing. In this intricate construction of truth and history and talespinning, all the tales open out of each other, the beginnings of one the middle of a myriad others, the tip of tales untold.

In *Illywhacker* too, the narrative is circular, looping back and forth through history, but Carey takes us beyond the mirage lines of truth and invention into a deliberate and sustained ambiguity, with the opening proclamation that Herbert Badgery, the narrator of *Illywhacker*—conman, spieler, salesman—is also a liar. Lying is the manner of Herbert Badgery's narration and lying is his subject, the theme of his version of Australian history, his specialty "The role of lies in popular perceptions of the Australian political fabric" (488). From the start, the narrative is set on the sharp edge of the liar's paradox, which violates accepted categories of the true and false, the real and invented. It is accompanied by the ambiguous *caveat* to the reader. The liar's paradox is also the paradox of the dupe—the believer, the reader—the contradiction of belief and disbelief that is at once the literary core of the novel and at the same time the national and cultural core of Carey's version of Australian history.

Spinner of tales and webs, illywhacker and spieler, trickster and quandong, conman, fabricator: Such is the protagonist and narrator on whose angle of vision the readers, the believers, the self-deceivers will always depend. And, in case the reader's trust is restored by the very energy and power of the writing, Herbert's proclamation reappears at different points, once so ambiguously that even the reader most determined to believe is thrown into deliberate confusion. This is the point where Leah Goldstein accuses Herbert:

> A hundred things come to me, things that amused me at the time, touched me—and now I see they were only excuses to thieve things from me. And even then you have not done me the honour of thieving things whole but have taken a bit here, a bit there, snipped, altered and so on. You have stolen like a barbarian, slashing a bunch of grapes from the middle of a canvas. (549)

A liar, a spieler, a thief who steals like a barbarian, a salesman and a showman who urges us not to waste time trying to "pull apart the strands of lies and truth, but to relax and enjoy the show": This is the narrator of *Illywhacker*. With a "salesman's sense of history," Herbert's narration is the spiel to persuade the reader to buy this version of Australian history.

Herbert is 139 years old, born in 1886, and so the novel opens in the year 2025—unless Herbert is lying, which he is, playing with time and fiction and the reader's trust, trafficking throughout in twentieth-century Australian history, from the era immediately after the First World War back to late nineteenth century and through to the putative future where Australia is a pet shop. The narrative begins in November 1919 when Herbert, aged thirty-three, lands in a paddock in Balliang East, in the middle of the lives of the McGrath family, with whom he swaps lies for free accommodation:

> I was an Aviator. That was my value to them. I set to work to reinforce this value. I propped it up and embellished it a little. God damn, I danced around it like a bloody bower-bird putting on a display. I added silver to it. I put small bluestones around it. (33)

Tenuous, in need of constant embellishment, a lie is also an invention of the self, a means of inhabiting other guises of the self. To Jack McGrath, dreamer and visionary, Herbert delivers value: Jack is his straight man, his willing customer, the believer.

Inside his own history, Herbert plays many roles and dons many guises. He is *inter alia* an aviator, used car salesman, thespian, nomad, bigamist, architect, prisoner, student, writer, and the 139-year-old androgynous patriarch of the Badgery family. Taking in the shearers' strike of the 1890s, the rise of aviation, the 1930s Depression, the Second World War and the influx of Americans, the 1950s and on to the 1970s, from there to the putative future, *Illywhacker* comprises the Badgery family saga. From Herbert's childhood to his marriage to Phoebe, his nomadic life with Sonia and Charles, his thespian life with Leah Goldstein and the American entrepreneur, Nathan Schick, his period in the Rankin Downs prison, there mastering literacy and graduating by correspondence with new inklings of political lies, the center of gravity shifts to Charles and Emma and thrusts forward to the pet shop in Sydney, where Hissao ultimately takes charge of the Badgery family fortunes.

As *Illywhacker* sprawls through time and space, it spirals through decades, with characters who come and go, slipping off the edge of narrative only to reappear later. Herbert keeps interrupting his own narrative to anticipate, darting ahead to hint at exciting developments, or to retrace, dashing back to an earlier episode, so that the narrative proliferates sideways and backwards as well as running ahead. With a sense that behind every yarn, every thread, every tale, there are more and more stories waiting to be told, the narrative seems conical or cuneiform, with only the tip showing. It slithers in complex traces across the page, inside skins likely to be sloughed off at any moment. Like the snakes actually slithering through the novel, the narrative itself is serpentine and sinuous, uncoiling as if never-ending, until it tapers and finally reveals the sub-caudal scales at the very tip of the tail.

Amid all the images of pets and animals in *Illywhacker*, the narrative sheds a succession of opaque skins, until we glimpse the future. A splendid architectural vision, the Pet Emporium is ever more bizarre and absurd, as its residents inhabit their private visions, and Australia becomes a human museum, its caged exhibits an endangered species: Australians, shearers, manufacturers, inventors, bushmen, Aborigines, artists, writers, and Herbert Badgery himself, the 139-year-old exhibit, all exhibits of political and national lies, which Australians, willing dupes and self-deceivers, believed.

Through this magical family saga, which abounds with fantastic vignettes and bizarre happenings, the family legacy of lies is bequeathed through generations. "Spawned by lies, suckled on dreams, infested with dragons" (359), this family history is the Australian history of lies and self-deception, a web of historical lies: lies about settlement and Aborigines, lies about English colonization, the lies about whole eras, lies that cling and entrap. And Herbert knows the soft allure of lies, the comfort of believing. Always embellishing and dancing in fabulous display, Herbert's telling is in the true illywhacker style, darting off at tangents, doubling back, teasing out tangles and knots of narrative.

With its extraordinary blend of comic vignettes, absurdist notions, zany fictions, and convincing images of time and place, which are constantly challenged by the artifice of the novel, *Illywhacker* turns on contradictions and rivalries not only of narration, but of history as well. Behind Herbert's narration is Carey's own version of Australian history and the lies on which it has turned. Through Herbert, Carey explores the national comfort, the collective soft allure, the freedom and the entrapment of lies. From the outset, there is a play on truth and fiction, across lies political, national and historical, and personal lies that are guises and disguises of the self. Through calibrations of the lie—some lies beautiful and noble, some subsistence lies, some mean and ignoble, sniveling things, Carey explores calibrations of truth. In *Illywhacker*, Carey himself is the writer as liar, forever pitching us between belief and disbelief through a fabulous web of lies at once personal and collective, familial and cultural.

While *Illywhacker* spreads tentacles into the future, *Oscar & Lucinda* revisits the 1860s, and the rivalries here become a shimmering play of light and dark—the shiny mysteries of glass and the nightmarish images of darkness and hell. In this baroque vision of spire and shaft, the Reverend Oscar Hopkins and Lucinda Leplastrier are two noble gamblers looking for a game, on an arc across hemispheres. *Oscar & Lucinda* is a contemporary dialogue with the past and an exploration of the shadows of myths and Christian stories across the Australian landscape. It is also an exploration of nineteenth-century literary shadows. Like John Fowles in *A Maggot* (1980) and John Irving in *A Prayer for Owen Meany* (1989), Carey draws on nineteenth-century forms and modes to explore the themes of faith, dissent, and risk that brood over the twentieth century.

Because the novel's narrator, the great-grandson of the Reverend Oscar Hopkins, is writing in the present, he holds in his left hand a Prince Rupert's drop "not the fabled glass stone of the alchemists, but something almost as magical" (132). Formed by dropping molten glass into water, a Prince Rupert's drop seems unbreakable, but if the slender tail is nipped with pliers it bursts into a myriad fragments: a spectacular moment of "Fireworks made of glass. An explosion of dew. Crescendo. Diminuendo. Silence" (135). The novel is Carey's Prince Rupert's drop in which he grips the tail of the past and in one dazzling movement all the slivers of time and chance and a vast array of characters are spread out before us in an explosion of word and image. The delightful Wardley-Fish with his awkward kindness and enduring love for Oscar recognizes Oscar as a man of "holy profligacy" and "one of those trick drawings in *Punch* which have the contradiction built in so that what seems to be a spire one moment is a deep shaft the next" (184). This is the *trompe l'oeil* of Oscar and of the novel, the spire soaring up into the light and the shaft reaching down into darkness and hell.

The early part of the novel draws on Edmund Gosse's *Father and Son*, as Oscar grapples with a fundamentalist upbringing. An angular, ungainly creature with wild red hair, a neat triangular face, and flapping hands, Oscar has a reedy, fluting voice and a nervous scuttling gait. He is a moving figure from the start in Hennacombe in England where he is trapped in his own bewilderment and grief. For Oscar, a man who lacerates himself with his paradoxes of self and God, the toss of the tor in the hopscotch game is a revelation of divine will commanding him to leave Theophilus and become Anglican, just as later it will command him to emigrate to Australia. He receives Wardley-Fish into his life as a spiritual messenger, a divine agent sent to reveal the wonders of the racetrack and the proper religious activity of gambling. In the spiritual conundrum of the novel, Oscar sees his passion for gambling as vile but his notebooks of betting data as diaries of his communion with God.

Giddy with fear of water, Oscar's journey to Australia on the *Leviathan* is a nightmare demanded of him by the hopscotch will of God. While up above there is phosphorescence, a luminescent sea of globes of fire, Oscar is exiled below, a creature of dark. Searching for a game, Lucinda Leplastrier prowls through the gargantuan ship. In a triumph of contingency, the two lives come together through the joyous conjunction of a game. When they meet, Oscar articulates the Dostoevskian notion on which the novel turns: that gambling is noble, part of the divine design. Religious faith is a wager, a bet on the existence of God in which we stake our lives on a structure of fancies. For Oscar and Lucinda, existence is gloriously random, life the play of chance, the roll of the dice—and the dividend, "We are alive . . . on the very brink of eternity" (419). Spurning all the structures of safe passage through life, they choose the knife-edge of risk.

In colonial New South Wales, Lucinda spurns the vouchsafed conventional life and pits herself against the male voodoo, determined to manufacture her dreams at Prince Rupert's Glassworks in Sydney. Lucinda discovers the wonder of glass as a child: "glass is a thing in disguise, an actor . . . invisible, solid, in short, a joyous and paradoxical thing, as good a material as any to build a life from" (135). Entranced by the mysteries of glass, Lucinda dreams of building a structure of glass, a pyramid, a tower, an arcade of glass spun like a web, until she conceives the fabulous image of a glass church. When the lives of Oscar and Lucinda lock together, Oscar, too, becomes entranced with glass and the image of the glass church, seeing glass as the material closest to the soul, light and spectra free of imperfection. Together they spin dreams of glass, life, God, and gamble everything, staking all on a dream. At the Prince Rupert Glassworks in Sydney, glass and gambling become one with the bet on the glass church. Both are betting their inheritance, Lucinda her fortune, Oscar his faith. As the expedition leaves, Lucinda feels the absurdity of the venture, not the crystalline image of her dreams but a heavy folly. The passage of the church across unmapped territory is a dark emblem of the cost of their dream, the journey up the river a hellish journey into the heart of darkness. Adrift and desolate inside a laudanum nightmare, Oscar is trapped under the tyranny of Jeffris and during the massacre of the Aborigines he becomes a horrified witness, haunted thereafter by his complicity. Out of all the patterning of light and dark, the novel ends with darkness. Drifting up the river inside the glass church, in the presence of sacred stories more ancient than those he carries in his Bible, he is the black-suited figure inside, until the glass cracks, splintering into ice-knives hanging above Oscar, a consummate image of the incongruity of Christian stories in this ancient landscape.

Oscar himself is a figure created out of slivers of gospel stories: Jonah and the Whale and the parting of the waters are transmuted into the massive ship, the *Leviathan* where Oscar huddles below in the dark. Jesus walking on the water becomes Oscar's terror of water and death in water. The Burning Bush is transmuted into the fiery light as Oscar assembles the glass church. No Lazarus here, only the death of Stratton, the murder of Jeffris, and the massacre of Aborigines. No miracles of driving out demons, only the voracious gambling monster that must be fed. The story of the river that turned to blood, the story of Jesus rising from the dead and ascending to heaven—these shift to the story of Oscar pulled down into the river waters surrounded by bat-winged figures, a sacrifice offered up to the firmament of his own dream. New stories start here, handed down to Kumbaingiri Billy by his aunt, Oscar's Aboriginal Mary Magdalene, on the day Jesus came to Bellingen to construct the glass church and reach Boat Harbor by Good Friday.

Oscar & Lucinda explores the incongruity of inherited Christian stories in a timeless landscape already alive with ancient stories, an incongruity Carey summons up in the splendidly paradoxical image of the glass church moving across an ancient landscape. In this post-Christian novel, the old Christian stories break up and founder, like glass shattering in the face of the ancient landscape. For Australia is not a Christian landscape:

> You could feel it in the still shadows along watercourses. She felt
> ghosts here but not Christian ghosts, not John the Baptist or Jesus
> of Galilee. There were other spirits, other stories, slippery as
> shadows. (163)

Oscar brings Christian stories into the Australian landscape, stories that have disappeared now just as the Gleniffer church has vanished. The narrator, Oscar's great-grandson, hears the echoes of their ghostly presence and searches for an explanation of the vanished stories.

In *Oscar & Lucinda*, there are many literary shadows, which conjure up nine-teenth-century literary kin. In a wry literary joke, Carey even posits a link with George Eliot through Lucinda's mother, a link Lucinda disclaims when she finds Eliot without sympathy. The style is often Dickensian, with wonderfully comic incisive sketches, like Mrs. Stratton walking at an angle for carrying books, thus revealing her donnish nature; or the image of the d'Abbs house, a ball of string and a grand expensive tangle in which the pristine d'Abbs dances; or Bishop Dancer's vision of Sydney as a dressed-up orphan's party, with maids donning tiaras, piemen dressed as gentlemen in this reversal of roles. At once Conradian in its journey into the heart of darkness and Dostoevskian in its reach of dark and light, its themes of faith, risk, and gamble, *Oscar & Lucinda* is an exuberant contemporary work that engages with the literary inheritance of storytelling, across the landscape of time, history, dream.

Throughout his work, Carey's baroque vision turns on rivalries of time, contradictions of truth and lies, bliss and hell, dream and reality, light and dark, all lit by the energy and ebullience of his work, playing across the mythic, the familial, the historical. In his exploration of the mythopoeic landscape of Australia, his work has a richness that lifts it out of time and place to a quest for the constructs of contemporary consciousness. From the futuristic and surreal landscape of his short stories to rivalries of the present in *Bliss*, from *Illywhacker*'s spiral through 150 years of Australian history and tilt into the future, to the nineteenth-century contraries of light and dark in *Oscar & Lucinda*, his work flows across the landscape of imagination towards the future. Spectral images of the future hover over his fictions, emerging from the past in the passage of stories, histories, and lies, with a luminous sense of the way stories are embossed by time and teller. With a profound sense of his era as it tilts towards the new millennium, he explores connections and planes, shadows and mirages, in a tangled hierarchy of time and history and consciousness.

WORKS CITED

Carey, Peter. *The Fat Man in History.* St. Lucia: U of Queensland P, 1974.
———. *Bliss.* Sydney: Picador, 1982.
———. *Illywhacker.* St. Lucia: U of Queensland P, 1985.
———. *Oscar & Lucinda.* St. Lucia: U of Queensland P, 1988.

PETER CAREY'S PUBLISHED WORK

Novels

Bliss, 1982
Illywhacker, 1985
Oscar & Lucinda, 1988

Short Story Collections

The Fat Man in History, 1974
War Crimes, 1979
Exotic Pleasures (selections from *The Fat Man in History* and *War Crimes*), 1981

SELECTED CRITICAL READINGS

Published critical material on the work of Peter Carey is limited at present but likely to increase in the near future. Critical articles might be addressed to Carey's links with both North American and Latin American fiction; his place in contemporary Australian fiction, both historically in terms of its resurgence in the 1970s and 1980s and in terms of its impulses and directions in the 1990s, particularly his links with younger Australian writers such as Tom Flood, author of the first novel *Oceana Fine*, and Nigel Krauth, author of *The Bathing-Machine Called the Twentieth Century*, as well as with established writers such as Rodney Hall and Murray Bail. More generally, such critical approaches might explore Carey's work in terms of the historicizing in contemporary world literature on the eve of the new millennium. Some Australian critics are addressing the political themes in Carey's work, notably his concerns with capitalism and colonialism: for example, some brief sections in the recent survey, *The New Diversity: Australian Fiction 1970-1988* (Melbourne: McPhee Gribble, 1989), by Ken Gelder and Paul Salzman.

Daniel, Helen. "'The Liar's Lump' or 'A Salesman's Sense of History': Peter Carey's *Illywhacker.*" *Southerly* 47 (1986): 157–67. Views the novel as an inventive and comic commentary on Australian political and social lies.

———. "Lies for Sale, Peter Carey." *Liars, Australian New Novelists.* New York: Penguin, 1988. 145–84. Discusses selected short stories and all of Carey's novels to *Oscar & Lucinda*, in terms of the "lie" of fiction, the truth of contradictions, and the paradoxes of quantum logic. Considers Carey in the context of the writer as "Liar" in relation to other contemporary Australian writers.

Dovey, Teresa. "An Infinite Onion: Narrative Structure in Peter Carey's Fiction." *Australian Literary Studies* 11 (1983): 195–204. Explores of the nature of stories and narrative in Carey's work with reference to literary theorists.

Ross, Robert. "'It Cannot *Not* Be There': Borges and Australia's Peter Carey." *Borges and His Successors: The Borgesian Impact on Literature and the Arts.* Columbia: U of Missouri P, 1990: 44–58. Considers Carey as part of international literature, his short fiction breaking away from the once predominant social realism of Australian literature. Discusses the influence of Borges on Carey's short stories and compares their philosophical and fabulist affinities, their handling of time, chance, fate.

Turner, Graeme. "American Dreaming: The Fictions of Peter Carey." *Australian Literary Studies.* 12 (1986): 431–41. Explores some links with Borges and García Márquez as well as North American narrative modes and themes of postcolonialism and the construction of history.

—HELEN DANIEL

Randolph Stow

During the 1950s Randolph Stow was the *Wunderkind* of Australian literature. By the age of twenty-three he had published three novels and a book of poems. He was twice awarded the Gold Medal of the Australian Literature Society and received the prestigious Miles Franklin Award. As with many Australian writers, Stow was published in England and in the United States before he was published at home. Typical of the international attention given to the early work is a statement by Granville Hicks in *The Saturday Review of Literature*, praising Stow's 1958 novel *To the Islands*, "Universal is a large word, but if it can ever be used it can be applied to *To the Islands*."

Central to the early poetry and fiction of Stow is the fairly isolated coastal town of Geraldton, Western Australia, where he was born 28 November 1935. Stow's family had been in Australia for five generations, with the Stows coming from Suffolk and his mother's family—the Sewells—coming from Essex. Stow's father Cedrick was a lawyer, and Randolph Stow first enrolled in Law at the University of Western Australia in Perth. The death of a young friend impressed on Stow the urgent desire to create. At nineteen he began his first novel, *A Haunted Land*, and the Western Australian poems collected as *Act One*. He changed his course of study from Law to Arts and took a B.A. degree in English and French.

Stow was interested in anthropology and language and worked for a time at the Anglican Mission near Wyndham in northwest Australia and in New Guinea, places which were to figure as settings in *To the Islands* and *Visitants*.

Stow has taught in Australia, England, and Denmark. Except for teaching stints and periods of travel, he has lived since 1966 in England in Suffolk and Essex, counties familiar to his ancestors and locales used as settings in his particularly English novels, *The Girl Green as Elderflower* and *The Suburbs of Hell*.

AN AUSTRALIAN ANGST

Randolph Stow is one of the most Australian of his country's novelists; from an equally valid point of view, he is among the least Australian—this joining of opposites in itself a frequent aspect of his fiction. He is like his countrymen in that in his own life as well as in his fiction he has been tremendously influenced by the Western Australian landscape—by its vastness, its emptiness, its beauty, its severity, and perhaps, ultimately, its indifference to man. He has been the Australian writer recording the antipodean experience of season reversal, geographical isolation, cultural dependence. Like many other Australian writers, he has been a careful, realistic observer of this landscape, noting with the precision of a poet its variation and texture, its abundance and lack. With equal precision, he has recorded the vagaries of the land's human inhabitants, both black and white, with careful attention to dialect as well as psychology.

Yet it is in his concern with people that Stow has been from the beginning one of the least characteristic writers in Australia. Unlike the flock of social realists who dominated Australian writing from the beginnings into the 1960s, Stow has not shown interest in characters struggling with economic or physical or societal problems; rather he has concerned himself with characters whose struggle has been internal, spiritual, metaphysical. Like the older writer Patrick White who has written novels of the inward quest, Stow has created characters who are misfits on a variety of levels and whose condition has resulted from a compounding of causes. In Stow's fiction, landscape and an inward state are often made parallel: In *To the Islands*, as Heriot moves into the emptiness of the outback, he moves into the emptiness of his own being; in *Tourmaline* the physical coma of the town equals its spiritual coma and might be extended to Australia's spiritual stasis. From their convict beginnings to the hedonistic present, Australians have never been particularly interested in religion, neither the physical church nor the metaphysical quest. Thus it is not surprising to find that both Stow and White met with critical opposition for their nonpragmatic fiction. As Anthony Hassall notes, Kylie Tennant, herself an Australian novelist, wrote of *Voss,* a novel similar in theme to Stow's *To the Islands* and *Tourmaline,* "when the book strikes off into the deserts of mysticism, I am one of those people who would sooner slink off home" (quoted in Hassal, *Strange Country* 53).

If Stow, as did White, took Australian literature into a new direction, it was not a direction new beyond Australia, for interior exploration had long been the territory of Dostoyevski, Kazantzakis, Joyce, Woolf, Faulkner, Hesse, to name a few. Stow's contribution was the bonding of the Australian experience, particularly the unique geographical experience of the Western Australian, with modern spiritual angst, an angst variously expressed, but expressed in Stow's works in terms of Christianity, nihilism, and Taoism.

Stow wrote his first two novels, *A Haunted Land* and *The Bystander,* while still an undergraduate at the University of Western Australia. Although he now dismisses those novels as juvenilia, one finds in them the sort of central characters who dominate the five novels set in Australia and in *The Visitants,* set in nearby New Guinea. In all the novels the protagonists are introversive, incommunicative, injured by an inability to love or by the absence of a sustained or sustaining love. Malcontent is brought on by geographical isolation, the death or desertion of a loved one, by a physical affliction, by a sense of personal weakness, unworthiness, spiritual bankruptcy, or mental disintegration.

To the Islands, Tourmaline, and *Visitants* are good examples of Stow's particular concern with the interdependency of setting, protagonist, and metaphysical need.

To the Islands won for Stow Australia's most prestigious literary prize, the Miles Franklin Award. Its setting is an Aboriginal mission near Wyndham in northwest Australia, a place where Stow had worked, observed black-white interaction, and learned some of the local Aboriginal language. Heriot, an old man —a stern, wild haired Lear, has come to retirement age as the director of the mission. But he cannot retire, for the mission has been his life and no other place or role is suitable to him. In his old age he is filled with bitterness and anger, anger at the hard life that has killed his wife and family, anger at the unchanging Aborigines for whom patriarchal Christianity has failed, anger at his own guilt: "I believe in nothing," he says, "for years I set myself up as a philanthropist and was really a misanthrope all the time" (41). During a cyclone Heriot throws a stone at Rex, an Aborigine with whom he has quarreled. Thinking he has killed him, Heriot strikes out alone into the Kimberley Mountain wilderness, wandering aimlessly, suicidally. Heriot is followed and supported by Justin, an old black man who loves him and helps him to endure his walkabout until he comes to a kind of self-forgiveness for his misused life and a kind of understanding of the oneness of all things.

Stow is exploring several concerns in this novel. Heriot's agony to a degree represents the loneliness of the European white man in this great, empty landscape, his head filled with lines from Western literature, his imported values and spiritual maxims no match for a land too big for him, for a people whose gods are older, whose spirits are freer. Heriot is filled with the white man's guilt for the genocide committed on the Aborigines at Onmalmeri; he is also troubled by coming to recognize the size of his own ego, the misdirected belief that he can save someone else when he cannot save himself, in fact does not know himself.

During his wanderings Heriot shares food with a blind woman and confesses his sins to an aged man he meets at a deserted mission. No longer in a position of authority, he learns human sympathy in his equal association with his servant Justin; finally, too, he learns to forgive his enemy Rex, and to forgive himself. As Heriot reaches the sea, he finds that the spiritual islands the Aborigines have spoken of, the place to which dead souls go, do not exist. Asking Justin to leave him, Heriot spends his last days alone at the entrance to a cave containing the remains of human skeletons. Beyond the cave and the cliff is the empty sea, and, staring into the endless horizon, Heriot speaks: "'My soul,' he whispered, over the seasurge, 'my soul is a strange country'" (203–04).

Stow writes in his introduction to the novel that the land crossed by Heriot, the north Kimberleys, has been crossed by few white men. The strange country to which Heriot comes on an interior level is also unknown territory; and the recognition that this strange country exists is in itself both a discovery and a starting point.

Stow is then a religious writer who celebrates the mystery inherent in life; but while he makes observations on the mystery, he provides no map. For in the course of his walkabout, Heriot has wavered in both will and acquiesence, in belief and in speculation. At the end of the novel, he achieves neither Christian salvation, Eastern enlightenment, nor the Aboriginal island resting place for the soul. But, with the easing of dogma and his sense of superiority, comes possibility and relief from the fear that has so long gripped this white man: the Australian fear of "the eternal silence of the space" about him (60).

In *Tourmaline* Stow moves the reader into the hinterland of Western Australia, to a dying mining town at the dead end of a road. He writes, "There is no stretch of land on earth more ancient than this. And so it is blunt and red and barren, littered with the fragments of broken mountains, flat, waterless. . . . It is not a ghost town.

It simply lies in a coma. This may never end" (8). The narrator of the novel and one of the four main characters is called the Law. Like Heriot, a lonely man, the Law is imprisoned by age and perception. He is keeping the record and begins his story with a death and an arrival. A corpse is put into a packing-case from Tom Spring's store, a case marked "SPRING PERISHABLE." On the same day a thin blond man, who calls himself Michael Random, is picked up beyond the limits of Tourmaline by the driver of a supply truck. The nearly dead young man is nursed back to life and creates in the town "curious yearnings" (17). Random is the first man to arrive for many years, because the town has ceased to exist for those beyond it. When Random tells the townspeople he is a diviner and that he will find a new source of water to make Tourmaline bloom again, a process of mutual delusion begins: The diviner is imbued by the inhabitants of Tourmaline with Christlike powers and he in turn believes himself a savior.

The Law and most of Tourmaline work themselves into a frenzy of excitement and devotion toward their savior Random, each seeing in him a fulfilment of some personal need. Only two men in Tourmaline stand in forceful opposition to Random: Kestrel, the devil-like pub owner, Random's alter ego; and Tom Spring, a passive man who quietly espouses a Taoist philosophy.

In a climactic divining scene, Random fails, just as the suicidal marks on his body indicate that he has failed in other ways before. Instead of striking water, or life, for a parched land—or true spiritual renewal, he strikes gold, a mineral useless to desert bound Tourmaline. For nothing is known of the world beyond, only that out there "wild beasts are loose" (26). As the novel ends, Random leaves the safety of Tourmaline, apparently to kill himself in the desert; Tom Spring dies with no confirmed realization; and Kestrel returns from the outside world to begin his reign, one thinks, of darkness.

To the east of Geraldton, where Stow grew up, lie the Murchison goldfields and the towns of Cue, Wiluna, Yalgoo, Day Dawn, and Sandstone. A drive through those places would indicate the actuality and authenticity of the setting of Tourmaline— red rock, blowing sheet iron, broken buildings. Stow has written about the importance of place: "The boundary between an individual and his environment is not his skin. It is the point where mind verges on the pure essence of him, that unchanging observer that for the want of a better word we must call the soul" (quoted in Hassall 3). The desert produces thirst, thirst fosters need, need produces solution or mirage. When the soul calls for nourishment, the methods for supply are multiple, as apparently are the suppliers and the inherent risks. *Tourmaline*, grounded in reality but suggestive of myth, is Stow territory. The place is right; the questing characters are there; the spiritual goal is uncertain.

Christianity, nihilism, Taoism—all are offered to the seekers of Tourmaline, but as in the case of the spiritual dilemma of Heriot, Stow points a finger; he does not offer a solution. Nihilism breeds nihilism. Kestrel is cruel, selfish, destructive. Random, the false prophet, full of self-hatred and anger, himself deluded, deludes others who give themselves so carelessly to him. The Christianity that the diviner persuades the town to follow is an aggressive one, binding much of Tourmaline to its leader. Of it, Tom Spring says, "A hundred minds with but a single thought add up to but a single halfwit" (184). At the end of the novel, The Law, commenting on his and the town's mistake, says: "There is no sin but cruelty. Only one. And that original sin, that began when a man first cried to another, in his matted hair: Take charge of my life, I am close to breaking" (221). The alternative to giving the spiritual self to another is represented by Tom Spring, who believes in aloneness, silence, simplicity, a close affinity with the land, both the empty desert surrounding Tourmaline and the far away stars covering it. The Law writes, "His God had names like the nameless, the sum of all, the ground of being. He spoke of the unity of opposites, and of the overwhelming power of inaction. . . . He said, I must become empty in order to be filled, must unlearn everything . . ." (186-87).

What of a nation with a desert in its heart, a town comatose, individuals quickening into life with a hope of deliverance? As usual with Stow there are no answers, only questions. The coffin marked SPRING-PERISHABLE points to the cyclic nature of life; what lies between birth and death or beyond is open to conjecture. "I say we have a bitter heritage," The Law writes at the novel's close. "That is not to run it down" (221). Whatever life is, there is a value in it to the spirit. Of the future of Tourmaline, perhaps of the earth as a whole, The Law writes, "Wild beasts were loose in the world. Terrors would come. But wonders, too, as in the past. Terrors and wonders, as always" (221).

Visitants is another of Stow's novels dealing with characters trapped by an estranging place. It is based in part on his experiences as an assistant to the government anthropologist in Papua, New Guinea, and as a cadet patrol officer in the nearby Trobriand Islands, where he learned the Biga-Kiriwinar language, and contracted malaria. As with the Western Australian novels, place is rendered with careful realism and the Islanders speak at times in words from their own language. The title of the novel reverberates with several levels of meaning. The Prologue describes the sighting of visitants in a disc-shaped space craft over Papua in 1959. These unearthly visitants seen by reliable witnesses hover in the reader's imagination throughout the novel. The immediate story, however, involves the suicide of patrol officer Alistar Cawdor and is told through bits and pieces of personal reminiscence given by whites and blacks at an official inquest into the suicide. Insight into Cawdor's life is also derived from his journal entries and from the memory of various characters, which go beyond the official hearing.

Cawdor has been fascinated by the prospect of visitants from another world, hoping for some sort of communication to relieve his pain of isolation and insecurity. As he grows more and more inward, pulled toward personal madness, he sees himself as alien even to the human race. He is himself an inept visitant; not even a return to his home in Australia would help. As his madness grows toward self-destruction, he sees his own house, that is, his mind, divided, invaded by a destructive, annihilating visitant.

As with Stow's other wounded protagonists, Cawdor has been failed by love—his father has died and his wife has left him. As with Heriot and the Law, he tries to lose himself in his job, and as in their circumstance, his official position and his interpretation of it keeps him away from the nourishment of human contact. As Heriot has a supportive servant in Justin, Cawdor has his houseboy Kailusa, who himself commits suicide on learning of Cawdor's act. But unlike Heriot and the Law, Cawdor has no reprieve, no chance to analyze or repair his house, for his affliction is more severe than theirs. He has lost the power to communicate. The constructive silence that is healing to Tom Spring is destructive to Cawdor, who says, "I couldn't know anybody, I can't know anybody" (71). Even his diary entries become more cryptic and silent until he suffers a mental breakdown. He writes, "My house is echoing with the footsteps of the visitor, and the person who lived there before is dying. That person is bleeding. My house is bleeding to death" (189).

In this the bleakest of Stow's novels, where the emptiness and alienation felt by all his protagonists lead this time to suicide, there is still some metaphysical hope, even if it is projected through the madness of Cawdor. Early in the novel he has expressed Heriot's fear that the universe is only silence and emptiness, so he is eager to meet the spaceship visitants as a sign of shared consciousness. But as he is dying he writes, "Do not be sorry. Everything will be good, yes, everything will be good. . . . I saw. . . . Down the tunnel. My body. Atoms. Stars" (186). Commenting on this passage, Stow said: "He's saying . . . that it doesn't matter if his physical body dies, the elements will re-form and all will be well" (quoted in Hassall 144). But as for life as we know it on this planet, T.A.G. Hungerford, to whom the book is dedicated, suggests Stow's meaning: "I am as distant from you as the stardwellers. We may visit, and perhaps hover, and even exchange friendly signals, but in the end you will never know more about me than I care to reveal" (quoted in Hassall 146).

Clearly, death has always been a way out for the Stow protagonist, and it has been the fate of Heriot, Random, Cawdor, and other characters in earlier novels. Death has been preferable to enduring the loss of love or to sustained geographical and spiritual isolation. The promise of a life after death, some metaphysical certainty, has never been a strong conviction for any of the characters, and even with Cawdor the circumstance of his affirmation must be realized.

Visitants was the last of Stow's novels of alienation. In 1966 he moved to England. Thirteen years later he finished *Visitants*, not able, he says, to finish it until after he had written *The Girl Green as Elderflower*, a novel in which a Cawdor-like character recuperates from a mental illness and learns to affirm life, accepting both the dark and the light, the cycle of growth and decay.

Randolph Stow, that most Australian, least Australian writer seems at home in the English countryside of his ancestors. *The Suburbs of Hell* is an evocation of place (Harwich in England), as were the Australian novels. And the book is filled with death and mystery. But gone is the personal, brooding consciousness that felt so distinctly the isolation and intrusion of Australia, a land alien and far away.

WORKS CITED

Hassall, Anthony J. *Strange Country: A Study of Randolph Stow.* St. Lucia: U of Queensland P, 1986.
Stow, Randolph. *To the Islands.* London: Stecker & Warburg, 1982.
———. *Tourmaline.* London: Macdonald, 1963.
———. *Visitants.* London: Stecker & Warburg, 1979.

RANDOLPH STOW'S PUBLISHED WORK

Novels

The Merry-Go-Round in the Sea, 1965
A Haunted Land, 1956
The Bystander, 1957
To the Islands, 1958, revised 1982
Tourmaline, 1963
Midnite: The Story of a Wild Colonial Boy, 1967
Visitants, 1979
The Girl Green as Elderflower, 1980
The Suburbs of Hell, 1984

Poetry

Act One: Poems, 1957
Outrider, 1962
A Counterfeit Silence: Selected Poems, 1969

Libretti

Eight Songs for a Mad King, 1971
Miss Donnithorne's Maggot, 1977

SELECTED CRITICAL READINGS

Considered one of Australia's most important writers since the 1950s, Randolph Stow has received considerable critical attention, more for his fiction than for his poetry. Early criticism focused on the symbolic, metaphysical nature of his fiction, seeing it as a departure from the usual Australian novel of social realism. Later criticism has concerned itself with Stow's use of narrative structure and language.

Beston, John B. "The Theme of Reconciliation in Stow's *To the Islands*." *Modern Fiction Studies* 27 (1981): 95–107. Looks at Heriot's three sins for which he attempts expiation: being born, racism, hatred. Indicates how sins move from the universal to the personal, then move toward reconciliation.

Dommergues, André. "The Confluence of Three Cultures in Randolph Stow's *To the Islands*." *Commonwealth* 6 (1984): 49–55. Examines the confluence of Australian, European, and Chinese cultures in *To the Islands*. Says Stow unites East and West as well as Aboriginal culture.

Dutton, Geoffrey. "The Search For Permanence: The Novels of Randolph Stow." *Journal of Commonwealth Literature* No. 1 (1965): 135–48. Identifies a theme running throughout Stow's early novels: the need to find permanence through the quest for love and the establishment of religious faith as well as the struggle against physical and mental ruin.

Hassall, Anthony J. *Strange Country: A Study of Randolph Stow*. St. Lucia: U of Queensland P, 1986. Studies each novel and volume of poetry. Sees Stow as a metaphysical writer dealing with themes both specific to Australia and the Australian consciousness as well as problems relative to Western man in general. A major work; includes interviews and extensive bibliography.

Higginbotham, Paul D. "'Honour the Single Soul': Randolph Stow and his Novels." *Southerly* 39 (1979): 378–92. Traces the use of Taoist ideas throughout Stow's novels.

King, Bruce. "Randolph Stow's Novels of Exile." *Antipodes* 1 (1987): 75–78. Shows Stow in his work moving away from Australia toward a kind of spiritual exile. Traces how novels interconnect and illuminate each other. Praises Stow's achievement in the use of language.

Oppen, Alice. "Myth and Reality in Randolph Stow." *Southerly* 27 (1967): 82–94. Focuses on *The Merry-Go Round in the Sea*; explains how cruelty, a haunted atmosphere, the search for identity—themes from the earlier novels—are introduced in this work, then treated more realistically in the later novels.

Wallace, Robyn. "Messiahs and Millennia in Randolph Stow's Novels," *Kunapipi* 3.2 (1981): 56–72. Uses *Tourmaline* and *Visitants* as examples of Stow's millenarian themes. Sees such themes as equivalent to redemption and salvation—significant concerns in the author's work.

Willbanks, Ray. *Randolph Stow.* Boston: Twayne, 1978. Begins with biographical material, then provides a thorough introduction to Stow's fiction and poetry, with discussions of the major works. Bibliography.

———. "Keys to *The Suburbs of Hell:* A Study of Randolph Stow's Novel." *Journal of Commonwealth Literature* 22.1 (1987): 47–54. Considers this novel in view of Stow's earlier work, then explains how it can be read in terms of Dante's *Inferno*, concluding that the novel creates a real world as one well beyond reality.

Interviews

With Anthony J. Hassall. *Australian Literary Studies* 10 (1982): 311–25.
With Richard Kelly Tipping. *Antipodes* 1 (1987): 71–74.

—RAY WILLBANKS

Thomas Keneally

A prolific writer, averaging close to a book a year for the past quarter century, Keneally anchors most of his work in history. Not content simply to reconstruct the past, he uses his novels to show that the present is the fulfilment of history.

Thomas Michael Keneally was born in Wauchope, New South Wales, Australia, 7 October 1935. He attended schools in Sydney and Strathfield, New South Wales, and studied for the Catholic priesthood from 1953 to 1960 but did not take orders. Keneally taught high school in Sydney from 1960 to 1964 when his first novel, *A Place at Whitton*, was published. In 1965 he married Judith Martin. From 1968 to 1970, he was a lecturer in drama at the University of New England, Australia.

He won the Miles Franklin Award for *Bring Larks and Heroes* in 1967 and for *Three Cheers for the Paraclete* in 1968. *The Survivor*, published in 1969, shared the Cook Bicentenary Award. In 1972, Keneally received the Royal Society of Literature Award for *The Chant of Jimmie Blacksmith*, which was made into a film in 1978. *Schindler's Ark* (*Schindler's List* in the United States), which he published in 1982, was awarded the Booker Prize and the *Los Angeles Times* Fiction Prize.

In addition to his novels, Keneally has written several short stories, five plays, a children's book, and a travel book. He received the Order of Australia in 1983 for his service to literature.

Though he still considers Sydney his home, he has in recent years spent considerable time abroad, especially in the United States. He and his wife have two daughters.

CYCLE AND REDEMPTION

A peculiar irony pertains to Thomas Keneally's fiction: So subtle is his artistry that the veneer he creates misleads many critics to judge his work against the standards of a very limited kind of realistic fiction—one that operates strictly on the surface. Unfortunately, to restrict one's attention to the surface of Keneally's work is to miss its soul.

Keneally's fictional world is a broad one in terms of geography, chronology, and diversity of characters. Antarctica, Australia, France, Yugoslavia, the United States, Germany, Poland, Byelorussia, Eritrea—all are within his realm. The Hundred Years War in the fifteenth century, Australia's settlement as a penal colony in the eighteenth century, America's Civil War, Australia's Federation days, the World Wars of the twentieth century and their aftermath have all provided him with the backgrounds of desolation, suffering, and death against which his novels take place. His protagonists have included saints, murderers, priests, soldiers, rebels, explorers, government officials, journalists, and even a foetus. Despite this diversity, Keneally's world sometimes seems cramped. The reader, in moving from one novel to another, begins to sense there is but one stage and one stage manager who deftly transforms today's scene of desolation into tomorrow's different but equally bleak one; that yesterday's "ambiguous" protagonist is today's in a different garb.

Such a perception is consistent with Keneally's transcendent theme: The past is fulfilled in the present. The past, in his words, is "a parable about the present" (quoted in Tiffin 125); if the inhabitants of the present fail to learn from the past, they are likely to repeat it. The historical novelist's function is to "find evidence in earlier events for the kind of society we have now" (Tiffin 125). For Keneally, history is "the present digested and cast up in encapsulated form" (Clemens and Robinson 70).

The cyclic view of time implicit in this theme derives in part from the Christian liturgical year—an overt element in several Keneally novels, most prominently *The Chant of Jimmie Blacksmith.* The liturgical year reenacts the birth, life, death, and resurrection of Christ. The reenactment is both ritualistic and "real": The crucifixion of Christ is remembered *and* re-created. In the Catholic ceremony of the Mass, the priest is the agent of reenactment. And as an author, Keneally constructs a reenactment of the present in the past. He is the agent through which the present is "digested" and "encapsulated," making its tie to the past discernible. That parallel may be part of the reason he sees a connection between his training as a priest and his role as a writer (Beston 53).

An equally important basis for Keneally's cyclic view of time is "the Aboriginal idea of *Tjuparata,* Dreaming" (*To Asmara* 75). Darcy, the journalist who narrates most of *To Asmara*, notes that "the time of *clever men* [ancestors] was circular; or else it was two parallel snakes of time, the past and the present, and they kept on interweaving . . ." (75). This sense of interwoven and interdependent strands of time is most obvious in *Blood Red, Sister Rose*; *A Family Madness*; *The Playmaker*; and *To Asmara*. But the cyclic notion of time is implicit in all of Keneally's fiction. The idea that past and present are linked tends to trivialize change, because yesterday's tragedy is today's tragedy, despite differences in the trappings. The links are both causal and essential. The past, in most cases, is inescapable.

The nature of his theme requires Keneally to maintain what David Daiches calls an "aesthetic distance" between his readers and his characters (63). He must sustain his readers' sense of the big picture: to present a Jimmie Blacksmith as both an interesting character and a kind of "black Everyman" (Daniel 25) requires a skillful balancing of the individual and the universal. If the reader gets too close to Jimmie, the link to the universal will be lost, and he will be little more than an interesting footnote to history. If one is kept at too great a distance from Jimmie, he will become an abstraction, and interest will fade. This balancing act can trouble some readers, especially those who approach Keneally's work expecting to find a more conventional form of "realism." Robert Towers, reviewing *A Family Madness* in *The New York Times Book Review*, writes, "The externalized approach to character . . . might well have been effective, *mutatis mutandis,* in a more expressionist sort of novel." However, Towers continues, in such a "clearly realistic" work, that approach "can only count" as a flaw. "Mr. Keneally," writes Towers, "needed to have been much more exhaustive in his approach, more imaginatively and empathetically involved in his creation, for its fictional—as distinct from its documentary—ambitions to have been achieved" (9). Such a complaint would be valid if Keneally were writing the kind of "documentary" novel Tower suggests. Yet the most frequently voiced complaints—about a lack of "inwardness" in his characters and about his fondness for "abstract formulation" (Tiffin 135)—indicate that Keneally's intentions are more than documentary.

The Chant of Jimmie Blacksmith, besides being one of Keneally's best known novels, offers a clear example of his technique in developing his theme. In this novel, he uses a narrator with limited omniscience to present a modified account of an historical incident, the murderous rampage of Jimmie and Joe Governor—both halfbreeds—in the year 1900. The omniscience is limited in the sense that the narrator seldom penetrates further than the present consciousness of a particular character. Often, the reader can discern an ironic note that seems to transcend the individual consciousness through which a piece of information is filtered. For example, in the aftermath of the first killings, the narrator says the Newby boys are "insatiable for words like monstrous, unpardonable, black butchers" (89); that same irony infects the narrator's comment on the women's view of Mrs. Newby's death: "Her dying was grand; it was royal and saintly, outscaling her weekly cheese-paring in Gilgandra, her bullying of Gilda, to an extent that Jimmie Blacksmith would have considered unjust" (88).

All such violations of the novel's norm move away from individual consciousness rather than beneath it. The only time the author allows the reader to glance beneath the veil of consciousness is when consciousness ceases to function and disjointed fragments from the past (and, presumably, the unconscious or subconscious) bubble to the surface. So it is near the end of the novel when Jimmie, maddened by the pain of a bullet wound, lies on a bed in a convent and juxtaposes memories of his tribal initiation and his mother Dulcie, with the face and voice of one of the convent nuns (173).

Such limited perspective is certainly not unique to Keneally's work. Doris Lessing, for example, uses precisely the same pattern—right down to the irony—in her short story "To Room Nineteen," and yet her reader, in the course of a few pages, comes to know Susan Rawlings much more completely than Keneally's reader knows Jimmie Blacksmith at the end of the novel. The difference is that the reader stays with Susan's consciousness as it moves steadily through an understandable pattern of development. On the other hand, Keneally's reader moves in and out of Jimmie's consciousness, gathering glimpses of his thoughts—segments of the pattern, rather than the whole. As Jimmie hacks at Miss Graf, for example, the reader moves into his thoughts as his consciousness registers a response to the act, but then, almost immediately shifts to Jackie Smolder's thoughts (79-81). In other words, the reader is presented with a series of responses to discrete events rather than a whole pattern. An underlying pattern may be discovered retrospectively, but it is never presented whole. Even when the reader spends an entire chapter hovering about Jimmie, as in Chapter Two, for example, one catches only segmented thoughts, usually responses to dialogue.

Many other writers, such as the American John O'Hara, segment consciousness in much the way Keneally does, without sacrificing the reader's sense of psychological depth, the sense that one has been permitted a glimpse of a character's soul. O'Hara does it by having his characters engage in what might be called "dramatic interior monologues," which leave the reader with the impression of watching the character's thought processes. It is a kind of cleaned up, sorted out version of stream of consciousness. O'Hara reinforces the effect by taking advantage of his often praised ear for the spoken nuance: Within the dramatic interior monologue, the reader hears the character's previously established "voice."

The point of these comparisons is to suggest that Keneally has a number of techniques available that would allow him to segment his characters' consciousness *without* sacrificing the illusion of depth or inwardness. But in *The Chant of Jimmie Blacksmith*, Keneally chooses not to employ such "realistic" techniques. Why?

Why, also, does he show such a fondness for "abstract formulations"—for the very neat symmetries of black and white worlds pervading *The Chant of Jimmie Blacksmith*? He establishes the pattern in the very first sentence of the novel: "In June of 1900 Jimmie Blacksmith's maternal uncle Tabidgi—Jackie Smolders to the white world—was disturbed to get news that Jimmie had married a white girl in the Methodist church at Wallah" (1). Black world, white world; black and white names; black husband and white wife. The parallels continue as the narrator alludes to the black and white doctrines about conception: Although the missionaries would insist that a woman who gives birth to a "pale" child has been "rolled" by white men, Jimmie's mother Dulcie and other members of the Mungindi tribe in which Jimmie has been raised know that their god Emu-Wren, rather than the white man, quickens the child in the womb, whether the child be pale or dark (1-2).

The first chapter of the novel also presents parallel Mungindi and Christian "resurrections." Jimmie's rebirth as a man—his resurrection "out of the chrysalis and out of the lizard's mouth"—coincides with the white man's celebration of Christ's resurrection at Easter, a day when new Christians are baptized or "reborn" (3). The Mungindi appear to be quite open-minded about the relationship of their own myths to those of others: "For the truth of Mr. Neville and the truth of Emu-Wren ran parallel. Mr. Neville had his place, as did the poor-bugger-white-fella-son-of-God-got-nailed" (6). The same chapter alludes also to the long coexistence of the native Australian and European cultures—and parallel barbarisms. Quoting an Aboriginal song about an ancient woman-stealing raid, the narrator observes that the raid "had taken place during the English civil war, two and a half centuries previously" (4).

This careful plotting of symmetries is not limited to showing parallels between the black and white worlds, though. Part of Jimmie's initiation to manhood—his tribal rebirth—involves knocking out a tooth, his "initiation tooth" that Tabidgi carries with him as part of his effort to "save" Jimmie. Late in the novel, after Jimmie has been wounded in the mouth by a pursuer's bullet, his initiation tooth is recalled in his fevered dream: "The pain of his mouth became the pain of tooth-excision at his initiation" (164). In that same dream, Jimmie sees his mother, "a primal Dulcie, greasing her gums and thighs religiously, to aid his cure and birth from the great Lizard" (164). Just in case the careless reader misses the parallel, the narrator alludes to it a few pages later: "He slept and his wound pained on. As any rebirth wound could be expected to" (173). This reference to "rebirth" echoes not only Jimmie's earlier rebirth as a man, but also his attempt to be reborn as a *white* man on the morning after he is arrested for being drunk. As a constable watches Jimmie washing himself with the cold water from a pump, Jimmie is moved to feel pity for the policeman: "Jimmie Blacksmith was baptizing himself a white man, whereas there was nothing the constable could baptize himself" (13). Unfortunately, it is not that easy. By the end of the novel, Jimmie is—in the narrator's words—"lost beyond repair somewhere between the lord God of Hosts and the shrunken cosmogony of his people" (148)—somewhere, that is, between the black world into which he was born and the white world into which he has tried to be reborn.

The word "rebirth" also sets up the novel's ultimate symmetry: Having opened with the Easter of Jimmie's rebirth as a man in 1891, it ends ten years later with another Easter and his death. Unlike Christ, who was nailed to a cross, Jimmie was hanged from a gallows. And, in Jimmie's case, "three days" culminates in his executioner's return to his butcher shop, rather than in a resurrection.

Another "difficulty," besides the lack of inwardness and the apparent obsession with symmetries, is Keneally's curious habit of giving his characters names that they proceed to act out. For instance, no one accustomed to reading Keneally's novels is surprised to find the Kabbels of *A Family Madness* inclined to constant caballing. In *The Chant of Jimmie Blacksmith*, the historical names, Jimmie and Joe Governor, have given way to Jimmie and Mort Blacksmith. The surname lends itself to two readings: "black"-"maker" or "forger"; and "maker" of "blackness" or death. In several senses, Jimmie discovers that, as a black, he can make only blackness—that is, make black offspring (as Newby tells him, "it doesn't matter how many times yer descendants bed down, the'll never get anything that don't have the tarbrush in it" [61])—and manufacture the blackness of death. In fact, he comes to take pride in his ability to *make* death: The narrator observes, "the thorough nature of the punishment he had dealt out continued to soothe and flatter him. Because he had been effective. He had actually *manufactured death and howling dark* [emphasis added] for people who had such pretensions of permanence" (96).

Changing the name of Jimmie's brother from "Joe" to "Mort," with the latter's suggestion of death, is related to another modification of history by Keneally. Joe Governor was a halfbreed, Jimmie's full brother; in the novel, Mort is a full-blooded Aborigine and a half-brother to Jimmie. As Chris Tiffin points out, Keneally's change increases Jimmie's isolation from both the black and white worlds (123). The change also sets up another of those black-white parallels of which Keneally is so fond. The last time Mort appears in the novel, he is, true to his name, dead: "He had been bled in the cowshed and dogs scented the stain of his historic blood on the earth floor, and cattle lowered their slow snouts" (160). As Mort's blood colors the earth at this point in the novel, so, earlier, did the blood of Jack Fisher, a "lovely dead white boy" whose wound Jimmie had seen bleed "plentifully onto the earth floor" of the blacks' camp at Verona (25). As Fisher—murdered by a black—is, in Jimmie's eyes a white "totem" or emblem, so Mort—murdered by a white—becomes, by the end of the novel, the black totem.

In case the name "Jack Fisher" is not explicit enough for the Keneally reader unfamiliar with the work of T.S. Eliot, Jessie L. Weston, or Sir James Frazer, the narrator describes Jack's father, an undertaker, as the "Merriwa Croesus" (37). And, a year after Fisher has been hastily buried near Verona, his bones are resurrected, as the narrator says, "in their remnants of wet flesh"—another impotent Fisher King (42).

"Miss Graf" has a significant role in the personification game, too. Substitute "ph" for the "f" and, without a change in the sound, a character has become a pictorial representation. And that is precisely what Miss Graf becomes by the end of the novel: After describing the press cartoonists' sketch of "the nascent motherland," the female figure "Australia," the narrator notes, "She rather resembled Miss Graf" (177). If Miss Graf somehow represents Australia, it is probably to be taken as significant that Jimmie kills her by chopping her "leisurely between hip and ribs," in other words, by cutting her in half (79). Also significant, perhaps, is the fact that this larger than life Miss Graf/Australia of the press appears shortly after Jimmie's dream of "a primal Dulcie": another white-black pairing, this one of mythic proportions (164).

What, then, do the "externalized approach to character," the "abstract formulations," and the personifications add up to? Brian Kiernan uses the term "historical fable" to justify Keneally's treatment of Jimmie's character; he says it would be impossible to "present from the inside the aboriginal side of Jimmie's nature" (491). That view, though, seems to support Towers' contention that Keneally falls short on imagination and empathy. Kiernan goes on to say, "In the historical fable, the author can win the reader's belief that life could have been like this by simpler means . . . than would be necessary in a novel of contemporary life" (492). Again, the critic seems to be selling Keneally short on imaginative power.

Perhaps the more accurate, though unfashionable, term would be "allegory." Angus Fletcher's description of the troubling surface of allegory sounds very much like an echo of the complaints about Keneally's fiction voiced by some critics (see Porter, for example). Allegory, Fletcher says, makes sense even if read literally; however, its "surface suggests a peculiar doubleness of intention" and the work becomes more interesting after "interpretation" (7). A.C. Charity's definition of "typological allegory" bears a striking resemblance to Keneally's statement about his mode of historical fiction. "Typological allegory," according to Charity, emphasizes the "quasi-symbolic relations which one event may appear to bear to another," particularly the "analogical" relations "between events which are taken to be one another's 'prefiguration' and 'fulfillment'" (quoted in Barney 31). Paraphrasing Keneally's statement in terms of Charity's definition, one would say that Keneally attempts to find an analogical relationship between "earlier events" and the "kind of society we have now"; in terms of *The Chant of Jimmie Blacksmith*, the events of 1900 are the "prefiguration" of the present state of Australian society, which, in turn, becomes the "fulfillment" of history.

Stephen A. Barney's definition of allegory is similar: "The word 'allegory,' 'other-speech,' *alieniloquium*, suggests that allegories present one thing by a customary route, and another thing more deviously" (16). In terms of *The Chant of Jimmie Blacksmith*, the thing presented by "a customary route" is the Governor brothers' killing spree; the thing "more deviously presented" is Keneally's "parable about the present." Read this way, the novel becomes a "psychomachia"—an allegorical battle for a soul.

The soul in question is the soul of Australia—a nation just about to become "a fact" (177). The contenders for that soul are the Aboriginal culture, represented in the novel by Dulcie, Mort, and Tabidgi, and the white culture of Christianity, represented by the Reverend Neville, Miss Graf, and the other whites. Keneally portrays the Aboriginal culture—in its purest form—as dependent upon the land and the cycles of nature and ritual for identity. The white culture is an amalgam of sex, power, and possession—carefully tied together in the conceit of fencing that dominates the first half of the novel; the white culture's tenuous sense of identity is embodied in the shallow figure of Dowie Stead whom the narrator describes as "a national product" (89).

In Jimmie Blacksmith, builder of fences and deputy constable, the white seed has created an instrument for rooting out the blackness that was once the soul of Australia. But Jimmie's inability to root out his own blackness, to be himself accepted as white or to have his offspring accepted, leads to a reaction. The instrument appears to turn on its creator. Ironically, however, even after Jimmie escapes the whites' direct control and begins to wreak havoc in the lives of individual whites, he is still used against black Australia. White society makes him a devil associated with the blackness that must be rooted out.

In the end, Mort—the Aboriginal culture's purest embodiment—is dead and literally drained, and Jimmie and Tabidgi have, before their executions, embraced white Christianity, which even Mr. Neville has come to question (175-78). Like the *tjuringa* stones—the "external capsules of souls"—in the sacred place desecrated by white "footballers," the soul of Australia has been "snapped across the middle"; in Jimmie's words, "It's buggered an' no help fer it" (150). This wound to the continent's soul underlies the bleakness of Keneally's vision. What make that vision bearable are the flashes of human love, idealism, and honesty—the innocent, brotherly love of Jimmie and Mort; McCreadie's breathless efforts to restore the desecrated holy place and to "save" Mort; the Reverend Neville's pained realization that he misled Jimmie in linking "ambition," "industry," and "property" to the "message of Christ" (176). These are the bright spots on Keneally's "darkling plain."

The Chant of Jimmie Blacksmith dramatizes the struggle for the soul of a continent, which, like the human beings who people her, is "between gods" (*Paraclete* 12). Keneally is telling a story far larger than the tale of two blacks who go on a rampage. That historical incident, coinciding as it does with Australia's Federation, is a convenient starting point. A novel of "documentary" realism would not have provided Keneally with a broad enough canvas to tell the story he wanted to tell, to raise the incident above its status as a footnote to history. The points that have brought objections from some critics—"externalized" characters, "abstract formulations," and personifications—are really clues to the existence of a "more deviously" presented story, Keneally's "parable about the present."

The links between past and present continue to be explored in Keneally's most recent fiction. *A Family Madness* offers a twentieth century reenactment of the theme of "original sin" common to Greek tragedy and the Old Testament: The sins of the fathers are visited upon their children. *The Playmaker* shows history collapsing into the present as players reenact the roles they have played in life and a play from an earlier period is translated into terms of the novel's present (which, of course, is "past" for Keneally and his reader). In *To Asmara*, an Australian journalist in Africa finds himself replaying a failed relationship from his past. At the end of the novel, his self-sacrifice purifies his love and he breaks free of the pattern. To the casual reader, his escape is a Pyrrhic victory—he is, after all, apparently dead or captured. Seen through Keneally's lens, though, the journalist's "victory" is probably the only kind possible.

WORKS CITED

Barney, Stephen A. *Allegories of History, Allegories of Love*. Hamden: Archon Books, 1979.

Beston, John B. "An Interview with Thomas Keneally." *World Literature Written in English* 12 (1972): 49–56.

Clemens, Walter, and Carl Robinson. "Giving Life to History: A Prolific Aussie Discovers the Present in the Past," *Newsweek* 31 Mar. 1986: 70.

Daiches, David. *A Study of Literature: For Readers and Critics*. 1948. New York: W.W. Norton, 1964.

Daniel, Helen. "Purpose and the Racial Outsider: *Burn* and *The Chant of Jimmie Blacksmith*." *Southerly* 38 (1978): 25–43.

Fletcher, Angus. *Allegory: The Theory of a Symbolic Mode*. Ithaca: Cornell UP, 1964.

Keneally, Thomas. *To Asmara*. New York: Warner Books, 1989.

———. *The Chant of Jimmie Blacksmith*. Sydney: Angus and Robertson, 1972.

———. *Three Cheers for the Paraclete*. Sydney: Angus and Robertson, 1968.

Kiernan, Brian. "Fable or Novel? The Development of Thomas Keneally." *Meanjin* 31 (1972): 489–93.

Porter, Hal. "Thomas Keneally." *Contemporary Novelists*. London: St. James Press, 1976. 750–52.

Tiffin, Chris. "Victims Black and White: Thomas Keneally's *The Chant of Jimmie Blacksmith*." *Studies in the Recent Australian Novel*. St. Lucia: U of Queensland P, 1978. 121–40.

Towers, Robert. "Breezy, Boozy, and Byelorussian," *New York Times Book Review* 16 Mar. 1986: 9.

THOMAS KENEALLY'S PUBLISHED WORK

Novels

The Place at Whitton, 1964
The Fear, 1965
Bring Larks and Heroes, 1967
Three Cheers for the Paraclete, 1968
The Survivor, 1969
A Dutiful Daughter, 1971
The Chant of Jimmie Blacksmith, 1972
Blood Red, Sister Rose, 1974 (U.S. title: *Blood Red, Sister Rose: A Novel of the Maid of Orleans*)
Gossip from the Forest, 1975
Season in Purgatory, 1976
A Victim of the Aurora, 1977
The Confederates, 1979
Passenger, 1980
The Cut-Rate Kingdom, 1980
Schindler's Ark, 1982 (U.S. title: *Schindler's List*, 1983)
A Family Madness, 1985
The Playmaker, 1987
To Asmara, 1989

Other Books

Moses the Lawgiver, 1975 (Written in conjunction with an English television series)
Ned Kelly and the City of the Bees, 1978 (Children's fantasy)
Outback, 1983 (Travel book)

Article

"The World's Worst End?" *Antipodes* 2 (1988): 5–8.
> Analyzes impact of European cultural assumptions and "cultural cringe"—academic contempt for local literature—on Australian literary activity. Sees contemporary Australian writers receiving "premature canonization," followed by criticism "for failing to be Faulkner after all."

SELECTED CRITICAL READINGS

Until the 1972 publication of *The Chant of Jimmie Blacksmith,* serious attention to the work of Thomas Keneally was generally limited to Australian literary journals such as *Meanjin* and *Southerly.* Since then, international publications like *World Literature Written in English, World Literature Today,* and *Antipodes* have regularly featured reviews as well as broader essays on Keneally. In the United States, popular journals such as *Time* and *Newsweek* have given prominent reviews to each novel since *Schindler's List.* Keneally has also caught the notice of more specialized publications, from the *New Yorker* and the *New Republic* to the *Village Voice.*

Brady, Veronica. "The Most Frightening Rebellion: The Recent Novels of Thomas Keneally." *Meanjin* 38 (1979): 74–86. Maintains that since *The Chant of Jimmie Blacksmith,* Keneally's vision seems increasingly alienated. He appears in subsequent work to be "opting . . . for the melancholy pleasures of disillusionment."

Burns, D. R. "The Way of Extravagance—Randolph Stow and Thomas Keneally." *The Directions of Australian Fiction, 1920–1974.* Melbourne: Cassell Australia, 1975. 207-30. Examines Keneally's novels from *The Place at Whitton* through *Blood Red, Sister Rose.* Sees him exploring "spiritual" territory opened by Patrick White. Praises Keneally's "artistic seriousness, his high sense of calling, his refusal to evade the challenges of his art." Judges him to be "in the first rank of living writers in English."

Clemens, Walter, and Carl Robinson. "Giving Life to History: A Prolific Aussie Discovers the Present in the Past." *Newsweek* 31 Mar. 1986: 70. Provides an overview of the author's life and work and excerpts from an interview.

Cotter, Michael. "The Image of the Aboriginal in Three Modern Australian Novels." *Meanjin* 36 (1977): 582–91. Links *The Chant of Jimmie Blacksmith* with Randolph Stow's *To The Islands* and Patrick White's *Riders in the Chariot* as efforts to dramatize "the two-way dehumanization involved in colonialism." Keneally's novel explores the whites' fears that "the boundary"—"those socio-economic prizes, 'home, hearth, wife, land'"—"will not hold" against "the tribal intentions of the black man." The whites' "poverty of soul" is the basis for their insecurity, which, in turn, necessitates repression. Should Jimmie succeed within the white world, the basis for white supremacy in Australia would be undermined.

Daniel, Helen. "Purpose and the Racial Outsider: *Burn* and *The Chant of Jimmie Blacksmith*." *Southerly* 38 (1978), 25–43. Echoing Richard Wright's claim that "the Negro is America's metaphor," Daniel sees Jimmie Blacksmith "as a kind of black Everyman, as an emblem of the spiritual aridity of white society." He has been led to cast off tribal values and replace them with the values of white society, "the 'holy state' of possession," only to discover that whites are unwilling to allow him to succeed within their context.

Johnson, Manly. "Thomas Keneally's Nightmare of History." *Antipodes* 3 (1989): 101–04. Sees Keneally as one of a group of "contemporary writers of substantial international reputation" (including Christa Wolf, Raja Rao, Benedict Kiely, Bruce Chatwin, and John Berger) who take an "evolutionary" approach to changing "by degrees the nonfictional world so as to make it fit for truly human existence." Argues that Keneally's mixing of history and fiction is "an innovative conjugation that at least constitutes a subgenre to be read on its own terms, and may be pushing the novel itself into a subgenre."

Kiernan, Brian. "Fable or Novel? The Development of Thomas Keneally." *Meanjin* 31 (1972): 489–93. Suggests that in blending fable and history in *The Chant of Jimmie Blacksmith* Keneally has found a way to draw on his real strengths as a writer. In this, his "best integrated novel," Keneally combines the two in a way that allows him to highlight the contrast "between the avowed ideals of Australian nationhood and the actual values manifested in the treatment of the aboriginals."

Krauss, Jennifer. "Outlandish Truths." *The New Republic* 4 Jan. 1988: 40–41. Faults Keneally for writing a novel (*The Playmaker*) "shackled to the straight and narrow, to history." Complains that the novel is little more than a script "played out, and more colorfully, by historians." Suggests Keneally would have been better off to start his novel where history leaves off.

Lardner, Susan. "Two in One." *The New Yorker* 19 May 1986: 118–19. Compares Keneally the author with the narrator of *Victim of the Aurora*: The latter's disillusionment with the twentieth century may reflect the author's "loss of heart, which deadens his new book [*A Family Madness*]."

McGregor, Craig. "Australian Writing Today: Riding Off in All Directions." *New York Times Book Review* 19 May 1985: 3, 40. Characterizes *Schindler's Ark* and Keneally's other works as "historical novels recast to a modern lapsed-Catholic sensibility."

McInherny, Frances. "Women and Myth in Thomas Keneally's Fiction." *Meanjin* 40 (1981): 248–58. Argues that Keneally's portrayal of women is "strongly reactionary." Sees the female as "the essence of Keneally's violent and bloody and chaotic universe, the embodiment of that mythical Other who must be placated or controlled, who is always and forever the dangerous force outside the sentient and intelligent male world." Calls his view of women "distasteful" and "potentially harmful."

Porter, Hal. "Thomas Keneally." *Contemporary Novelists*. London: St. James Press, 1976. 750–52. Offers a very unsympathetic evaluation of Keneally's work through 1975. For example, Porter sees *A Dutiful Daughter* as a "grotesque" and "impure" fantasy, the author's "most aggressive failure as an artist." Finds something lacking in Keneally's work, but "what the lack is is difficult to define."

Ramson, W.S. "*The Chant of Jimmie Blacksmith*: Taking Cognisance of Keneally." *The Australian Experience: Critical Essays on Australian Novels*. Canberra: Australian National UP, 1974. 325–44. Maintains that the novel's concern with Aboriginals is "less an instance of man's inhumanity to man than . . . an aspect of 'the Australian experience,' a chapter in the Australian's progress towards national identity." Sees major thematic and structural flaws in the novel.

Sturm, Terry. "Thomas Keneally and Australian Racism: *The Chant of Jimmie Blacksmith*." *Southerly* 33 (1973): 261–74. Sees the failure of white Australian values as rooted in the inadequacy of the white concept of sexuality. Both Jimmie Blacksmith's violence and the violent responses of white society have their roots in repressed sexuality.

Tiffin, Chris. "Victims Black and White: Thomas Keneally's *The Chant of Jimmie Blacksmith*." *Studies in the Recent Australian Novel*. St. Lucia: U of Queensland, 1978. 121–40. Compares Keneally's novel with his historical sources, especially Frank Clune's *Jimmy Governor*. Sees Jimmie Blacksmith as "the most successfully drawn of Keneally's recurrent sensitive, oppressed, ultimately self-destructive victims."

Towers, Robert. "Breezy, Boozy, and Byelorussian." *New York Times Book Review* 16 Mar. 1986: 9. Charges that Keneally needs to become "more imaginatively and empathetically involved in his creation," that his characters "are curiously lacking in inwardness, in the suggestion of psychological depth."

Walker, Shirley. "Thomas Keneally and 'the special agonies of being a woman.'" *Who Is She?* New York: St. Martin's Press, 1983. 150–62. Like McInherny, Walker finds Keneally's attitude towards women objectionable: "All too often both the violence and the burden of moral justification are inflicted on the female figure." She sees *The Chant of Jimmie Blacksmith* as "not so much concerned with racism as with sexism."

Wills, Garry. "Catholic Faith and Fiction." *New York Times Book Review* 16 Jan. 1972: 1–2+. Sees Keneally as the first in the "first rank" of "a brilliant crew of novelists . . . rendering Catholic experience as never before." Keneally "has built up his vision of a world 'between-gods,' with patience and growing economy."

Interviews

With Candida Baker. *Yacker 2*. Sydney: Pan Books, 1987. 116–42.
With John Beston. *World Literature Written in English* 12 (1972): 49–56.
With Laurie Hergenhan. *Australian Literary Studies* 12 (1986): 453–57.

—THOMAS P. COAKLEY

Les Murray

Les Murray was born 17 October 1938, on the rural north coast of New South Wales, Australia, and brought up on a dairy farm. After attending school in the town of Taree, he went to the University of Sydney in 1957 and stayed until 1960, when he left without a degree; he returned in 1969 to graduate. He also served in the Royal Australian Naval Reserve between 1959 and 1960. In 1962, he married Valerie Morelli; they have five children.

He worked as a translator at the Australian National University, Canberra, from 1963 to 1967. After a year and a half in Europe, he returned to Sydney in 1968 and worked at a number of transient jobs before going to Canberra again, where he took a position in the Prime Minister's Department (during the administration of the Liberal PM John Gorton) in the Economic Development Branch.

Moving to Sydney, he decided to refuse meaningless employment and, in his own words, "Came Out as a flagrant full-time poet in 1971." He has since supported himself with his literary work. Murray served as editor of *Poetry Australia* between 1973 and 1979. In 1986, after almost thirty years away, he and his family moved to a forty-acre farm near where he was born.

Murray, long known as Les A. Murray but recently dropping the middle initial, has received numerous awards and prizes. They include the Australian Literature Society Gold Medal (1984), and the New South Wales Premier's Prize for the best book of poetry in 1983-84. He is a frequent recipient of grants from the Literature Board of the Australia Council.

RELEGATION AND CONVERGENCE

Les Murray describes himself as "more often a meditative than a lyrical poet" (*Persistence* 21). It would be more accurate, perhaps, to say that Murray composes meditative lyrics, sometimes brief, sometimes extended, but all composites of the lyric impulse to celebrate and the meditative desire to describe. What distinguishes Murray from most lyrical poets, however, is that he celebrates not the self but others, and it is this wider concern with "subject matter" that gives his poetry its meditative principle of organization. Murray can seem to turn a subject over in his mind until it is burnished on the page as poetry (as in "The Future" and "Cumulus"), and yet his poems never appear static, never aspire to an autotelic form. At the same time, his poems are never ecstatic, never aspiring to vatic effusion. His is a middle style, one that can appropriate all forms and concerns to itself without ever surrendering a sense of controlling intelligence. What Murray meditates upon is astonishingly diverse; he seems able to write about anything his attention happens to fall upon. But there are a cluster of concerns clearly central to his poetry (involving relations between such broad categories as society and culture, religion and history, family and morality), and what begins to emerge from the poetry is an overriding commitment to what might be called a meditative mediation. That is, Murray, in his meditations, wishes to mediate between rival claims in Australian (and Western) culture and to negotiate a settlement within an economy of absolute values, whereby the local becomes, in the end, the universal.

Two related concepts in this poetic project stand out; the first is "convergence," the second "relegation." Convergence is Murray's word for the hoped-for integration or "fusion" of what he considers Australia's three main cultures, the Aboriginal, the urban, and the rural (*Persistence* 24). Murray is unique in insisting on this triadic division, where Australian white culture is not simply (or only) opposed to Aboriginal black culture but is essentially divided against itself. Indeed, this eventually reduces down to a series of dichotomous (and dualistic) concepts regarding white Australia; yet, such a tendency should not obscure the very real engagement with Aboriginal culture, which, early on at least, is one of the most striking features of Murray's poetry.

In his prose essay, "The Human-Hair Thread," Murray gives an illuminating account of the Aboriginal element in his own poetry. This ranges from passing allusions to place names to full scale deployments of Aboriginal themes and forms. Among the more significant instances of the latter are poems like "The Ballad of Jimmy Governor," "The Conquest," and "Walking to the Cattle Place" (*Vernacular A*). But the best known and most fully articulated example is the long poem, "The Buladelah-Taree Holiday Song Cycle" (*Vernacular B*). Drawing upon a translation of an Arnhem Land Aboriginal poem, *The Moon-Bone Song*, Murray attempts to use an Aboriginal poetic mode to "celebrate" his own "spirit country," a section of the north coast of New South Wales between the towns of Buladelah and Taree, where he grew up. Murray writes of the poem that in it he was after "an enactment of a longed-for fusion of all three cultures, a fusion which, as yet perhaps, can only exist in art, or in blessed moments when power and ideology are absent" (*Persistence* 24). The poem is a brilliant portrayal and evocation of the cyclic return of the "Holiday" experience, when people from the cities arrive to enjoy nature and renew their family ties. It is primarily a vision of harmony and happiness, though it also contains and represents the social tensions that accompany it. The poem is certainly his most successful attempt at imaginative "convergence," and the sense of unity and serenity make it a very attractive poem. Here, for instance, is how he describes the long line of traffic wending its way up the coast at night, alluding both to Aboriginal naming and to the mythic Rainbow Snake:

> It is the season of the Long Narrow City; it has crossed the Myall,
> it has entered the North Coast,
> that big stunning snake; it is looped through the hills, burning all
> night there.

Murray considers the Aboriginal to be the "senior culture," and here it is clearly "setting the tone and controlling the movement of the poem" (*Persistence* 24). Murray speaks of himself as an inheritor of the Jindyworobak movement of the 1930s and 1940s, which sought to integrate Aboriginal themes and materials into Australian literature, making "assimilation a two-way street." He goes on to say that "Convergence is a better word here, though; assimilation carries too deep a stain of conquest, of expecting the Aborigines to make all the accommodations while white people make none. The Jindies represent a creolising impulse in our culture" (*Persistence* 29). Murray, himself, appears to want to carry on this impulse or tradition, but his recent books seem to de-emphasize Aboriginal elements in favor of considerations of white culture, both urban and rural. In part, this occurs because Murray tends to collapse the Aboriginal culture into the rural, since, for him, the Aborigines are "actually part of a larger class of the rural poor, and it is still often more useful to see them in that light than in currently fashionable radical-racialist terms" (*Persistence* 5). What lies behind this submerging of one culture into another is very likely the strong dualistic impulse one finds in Murray, where sharply-drawn antinomies and dichotomies often seem to organize the poetry along foundationalist lines. Thus, the desire for fusion and convergence seems to give way to a preference for drawing distinctions, for defining those issues and values that clash in Australian society. At times this appears a dialectical movement, seeking to resolve or overcome the oppositions, while at other times it seems less a *rapprochement* than an obdurate retrenchment.

The project of convergence, then, begins to modulate into a concern with what he calls "relegation." The two are connected, however, since it is the relegation of one people or class by another that leads to that divisive split requiring a healing convergence. "When I was growing up," writes Murray, "the injustice of urban attitudes was shifting from the black people (feckless, primitive, a doomed, inferior race) to the white rural population (bigoted, conservative, ignorant, despoilers of the environment, a doomed, obsolete group)" (*Persistence* 6). Murray clearly represents the "despised" values of rural culture in opposition to the "imported" or trendy values of the urban (the poem, "Sidere Mens Eadem Mutato," contains the parenthesis that "In times of trend, death comes by relegation"). Many of Murray's best poems, particularly early ones, have urban settings, as in "An Absolutely Ordinary Rainbow" and "The Sydney Highrise Variations," but from the beginning, and more and more so in later years, it is the rural culture that dominates thematically and contextually. And right from the start this presented certain difficulties for Murray, given the critical climate:

> What happened was that I came to Sydney about the same time as critics began saying insistently that Australia should become an urban culture. Literature now had to follow the facts of demography: since most Australians lived in cities, the literature should be about cities; the outback image had to be dismissed to the past as an irrelevance. Well I came with a head full of knowledge about the bush, and my timing was off. But I went on and wrote my things anyway. I just thought all that had to be done was to write them

more deeply and with more sophistication than they'd had in the
past. (Oles 29)

An even more emphatic shift in this direction became evident after 1986, when
Murray and his family moved back to rural Bunyah after almost thirty years away.
This move seems highly symbolic in retrospect, since Murray's polemic against the
urban subsequently intensified. Relegation, it turns out, is almost always what the
urban culture does to the rural (now including the Aboriginal). More broadly still,
Murray sees relegation as what the modern, post-Enlightenment world has done to
ancient, pre-industrial civilizations. Indeed, there is no major poet now writing in
English who is more adamantly opposed to certain current ideologies of interna-
tionalism than Les Murray, though he is by no means a narrow nationalist. For
Murray, much of contemporary culture, particularly in its amoral, aggressive, and
relegating manifestations, is something to be fiercely resisted.

A convenient example of this is the poem, "Sydney and the Bush," which is an
overview, in miniature, of the history of urban and rural cultures in Australia. Where
once there was a dialectical relationship between the two, each one offering
something the other lacked, "When Sydney and the Bush meet now/there is
antipathy" (*Vernacular B*). For Murray, Australia's "indigenous" values are to be
located in the rituals of Bush or country people, but even so, as the poem, "The
Mitchells," suggests, this can be found or relocated in the city as well ("nearly
everything/they say is ritual. Sometimes the scene is an avenue"). Increasingly,
however, there is a sense that the urban culture has lost its way precisely because
it has abandoned the humane and simple values enshrined in the country ethic. In
"Forty Acre Ethno," he writes of his return to rural life:

> Coming home? It was right. And it was time.
> I had been twenty-nine years away
> after books and work and society
> but society vanished into ideology
> and by then I could bring the other two home.
> (*Daylight*)

"Ideology" is Murray's word for radical politics, particularly various Marxisms and
feminisms, which he sees as "imported" and inappropriate to Australia. According
to Murray, true society, a humanist undertaking, has vanished under the corrosive
influence of fashionable left-wing European rhetoric and competitive American
consumerist imperialism. As he writes in "The Emu and the Equalities of Interest"
(elsewhere entitled "Second Essay on Interest: The Emu"):

> Some truths are now called *trivial*, though. Only God
>   approves them
> Some humans who disdain them make a kind of weather
> which, when it grows overt and widespread, we call *war.*
> (*Daylight*)

Opposed to this is the enduring, ingenuous language of rural life; again, from "Forty Acre Ethno":

> Dad speaks of memories, and calls his fire homely:
> when did you last hear that word without scorn
> for something unglossy, or some poor woman?
> Here, where thin is *poor*, and fat is *condition*,
> "homely" is praise and warmth, spoken gratefully.
> (*Daylight*)

This is what Murray calls the "vernacular republic," that intersection of language and value marking the common life of rural people and representing the best hope for a future Australia, a place where democracy is egalitarian and culture integrated. But for this to happen, the urban culture has to be displaced from its dominant position. Indeed, the notion of dominance itself has to be rooted out to make way for a more decentralized and just society. Murray presents this imperative in terms of yet another set of oppositions: "the war between Athens and Boeotia."

In his essay, "On Sitting Back and Thinking About Porter's Boeotia," Murray presents this dichotomy (going back to the time of Hesiod) as "two contrasting models of civilization between which Western man has vacillated." He continues:

> In the past, Athens, the urbanizing, fashion-conscious principle removed from and usually insensitive to natural, cyclic views of the world has won out time and again, though the successes of Boeotia have been far from negligible. Now, I think, there are senses in which we may say that the old perennial struggle is coming to a head, with Australia finding herself, very much to her surprise, to be one of the places in which some sort of synthesis might at last be achieved. (*Peasant* 173)

Here we find, again, a longing for convergence or synthesis, but one that requires the dismantling of predominant modes and mores, since "Athens has recently oppressed Boeotia on a world scale, and has caused the creation all over the world of more or less Westernized native elites which often enthusiastically continue the oppression" (*Peasant* 176). The native, popular, folk, "vernacular" traditions can only survive and flourish in the world if the highly centralized, deracinated urban culture gives up its dream of elitist domination. What Murray argues for, and often holds up for examination in the poems, is a very fundamental shift in consciousness and attitude. In a poem such as "The Quality of Sprawl," Murray defines a Boeotian approach to life by giving multiple examples of it:

> Sprawl is the quality
> of the man who cut down his Rolls-Royce
> into a farm utility truck, and sprawl
> is what the company lacked when it made repeated efforts

to buy the vehicle back and repair its image.
(*Daylight*)

Similarly in "Equanimity," he gives an account of what lies at the heart of "human order," a spiritual quality ("an equanimity") that allows for an inner personal peace and a sense of human commonality:

Quite different from inertia, it's a place
where the churchman's not defensive, the indignant aren't
on the qui vive,
the loser has lost interest, the accountant is truant to remorse,
where the farmer has done enough struggling-to-survive
for one day, and the artist rests from theory—
where all are, in short, off the high comparative horse
of their identity.
(*Vernacular B*)

Or again, in a lighter vein, a Boeotian sensibility surfaces in "The Dream of Wearing Shorts Forever," where all the varieties of shorts are enumerated and accounted for, and a plea made for their general adoption:

Now that everyone who yearned to wear long pants
has essentially achieved them,
long pants, which have themselves been underwear
repeatedly, and underground more than once,
it is time perhaps to cherish the culture of shorts.
(*Daylight*)

But this sense of the possibilities inherent in a cultural shift toward the Boeotian and away from the Athenian gets defined in increasingly stark terms, so that the hope for fusion or convergence is a bleak one from the perspective of the embattled position of those relegated. Murray is not one to mince his words; some later poems have been sharply critical of Western society, such as "The Import of Adult Flavours," where Europe is presented as having "sold scorn of innocence" in order to "snare/cold luxury nestled inside despair." Murray makes large claims for the efficacy of poetry (following a tradition that goes back to Sidney and Shelley), and, in the proliferating dichotomies that structure his polemics, he constructs models that reverse and overturn "Athenian" viewpoints.

Another such paradigm is found in the essay, "Poems and Poesies: How We Form Reality." In characteristic fashion, Murray divides his primary subject (writing) into two elements: "Narrrowspeak" and "Wholespeak," which derives from his sense that "Humans have two main modes of consciousness, one for waking, one we call dreaming." The first corresponds to the realm of discursive thought, "prose exegesis and exhortation," where the "forebrain" dominates; the other involves dream, daydream and reverie and takes place in "the older so-called limbic levels of the brain." Murray sees aesthetic experience, especially poetry, as a harmony of both modes. "It is a fusion of the two," he says, "and delivers us into wholeness of thinking and of life" (3-6). With this distinction in place, he can go on to suggest that such activities as literary criticism and theory are doomed to a fundamental difficulty, since they partake of only the "forebrain" mode and cannot fully comprehend the "wholespeak" of true literature. Where there is not this fusion of dream and reason (as well as other aesthetic elements like rhythm and movement), the result is partial, mere "narrowspeak," or, as he calls it, a *poesy* (as opposed to a *poem*). Poetry here becomes a very broad term, embracing any kind or mode of imaginative fusion, where dream and reason come together (thus he can speak of Marx's dream, Freud's dream, or the "Jewish poem of God"). Indeed, he begins the poem, "Poetry and Religion," by saying:

> Religions are poems. They concert
> our daylight and dreaming mind, our
> emotions, instinct, breath and native gesture
>
> into the only whole thinking: poetry.
> Nothing's said till it's dreamed out in words
> and nothing's true that figures in words only.
> (*Daylight*)

Again, we have here an image of convergence, where a vernacular republic is to be built upon the foundations of an opposition fused into a unity. "Wholespeak" is ranged against "narrowspeak," as poetry is to poesy, or as the rural is opposed to the urban, the Bush to Sydney, Boeotia to Athens, the egalitarian to the elite, equanimity to ideology, and so on through any number of paired terms. But the negotiation of these terms is complex and problematical. It is often difficult to know just how cultures and societies are to move from relegation to convergence, given the incompatibility and incommensurateness of the opposing elements that construct them. As Murray himself notes, such a fusion "as yet perhaps, can only exist in art, or in blessed moments" (*Persistence* 24), which is to say that it depends upon individual moments in the lives of people. Perhaps it is only at the level of the personal that such change is possible, that the hope for a healing change depends upon the aggregation of such renovated lives in a democratic context where they would have a cumulative effect. Hence, the emphasis on the vernacular, the common, the egalitarian, as the basis for convergence, and, in both the poetry and the prose, the concomitant rage against relegation.

Whatever one finally makes of Murray's dichotomies (and there will be many who will want to question them from any number of theoretical and practical positions), there can be no doubt that the very act of formulating them lends his poetry a discernible outline and purpose. Given the extraordinary range of Murray's poetic genius, his mode of cultural criticism is necessarily augmented and intensified, and this concatenation of effects helps explain his appeal.

WORKS CITED

Murray, Les A. *The Peasant Mandarin: Prose Pieces*. St. Lucia: U of Queensland P, 1978.

———. *The Vernacular Republic: Poems 1961–1981*. Sydney: Angus & Robertson, 1982. (Cited as *Vernacular A*)

———. *The Vernacular Republic: Selected Poems*. New York: Persea Books, 1982. (Cited as *Vernacular B*)

———. *Persistence in Folly*. Sydney: Angus & Robertson, 1984.

———. "Poems and Poesies: How we form Reality." *The Age Monthly Review* 6.8 (January 1987): 3–6.

———. *The Daylight Moon and Other Poems*. New York: Persea Books, 1988.

———. "The Import of Adult Flavours." *Antipodes* 3 (Spring 1989): 54.

Oles, Carole. "Les Murray: An Interview." *The American Poetry Review* 152 (March/April 1986): 28–36.

LES MURRAY'S PUBLISHED WORK

Poetry

The Ilex Tree (with Geoffrey Lehmann), 1965
The Weatherboard Cathedral, 1969
Poems Against Economics, 1972
Lunch & Counter Lunch, 1974
Selected Poems: The Vernacular Republic, 1976
Ethnic Radio, 1977
The Boys Who Stole the Funeral (verse novel), 1979
The Vernacular Republic: Poems 1961-1981, 1982
Equanimities, 1982
The People's Otherworld, 1983
The Daylight Moon, 1987

Essays

The Peasant Mandarin: Prose Pieces, 1978
Persistence in Folly: Selected Prose Writings, 1984

Anthologies (editor)

The New Oxford Book of Australian Verse, 1986
Anthology of Australian Religious Poetry, 1986

SELECTED CRITICAL READINGS

Les Murray, now widely considered one of the finest poets writing in English today, is a prolific and ambitious writer, and critics have been quick to appreciate his talent. While as yet there are no full-length published studies of Murray's poetry, he has been the subject of numerous articles and even dissertations. Murray's books are regularly reviewed in Australia and Great Britain, where the audience is widespread, and his work now attracts considerable attention in the United States, where selections of his poems have been published by Persea Press under the titles, *The Vernacular Republic: Selected Poems* and *The Daylight Moon* (though neither volume is fully consistent with the Australian version of the same title). Murray's growing international reputation will likely be cemented whenever a Collected Poems is issued, since readers and critics outside of Australia are largely unaware of the extent of his poetic output. It is already clear from current criticism that a "Murray industry" is developing, and we are likely to see major studies in the near future. Among the sort of work we can expect is a close look at Murray's religious concerns as they compare with those of other important poets, such as Yeats, Eliot, Auden, and Lowell.

Barnie, John. "The Poetry of Les Murray." *Australian Literary Studies* 12 (1985): 22–34. Sensitive and useful look at the thematic concerns found in *The People's Otherworld* and *Persistence in Folly* (both published in 1984). The focus is on how Murray has constructed his genuinely distinctive poetic voice. Gives a fair and balanced account.

Birkerts, Sven. "The Rococo of His Own Still Centre." *Parnassus: Poetry in Review* 15.2 (1989): 31–48. Serious and empathetic appreciation of Murray's poetry. Highlights those poems most appropriate for inclusion in the Murray "canon."

Bourke, Lawrence. "The Rapture of Place: From Immanence to Transcendence in the Poetry of Les A. Murray." *Westerly* 33.1 (1988): 41–51. Traces the movement in Murray's poetry from a concern with place and community to an increasing interest in religious and transcendent ideas. Finds a constant element, however, in the central concern with the bardic voice, a representation of the poetic imagination.

Hart, Kevin. "'Interest' in Les A. Murray." *Australian Literary Studies* 14 (1989): 147–59. Careful and rigorous account of the philosophic and ideological suppositions that lie behind much of Murray's thought and poetry. High point in Murray criticism. Ends with an illuminating comparison with the English poet, Geoffrey Hill.

Kane, Paul. "Sydney and the Bush: The Poetry of Les A. Murray." *From Outback to City: Changing Preoccupations in Australian Literature of the Twentieth Century*. New York: American Association of Australian Literary Studies, 1988. 15–22. Considers the dialectical relationship between the rural and urban elements in Murray's poetry. Finds a synthesis of the two at the level of style.

Pollnitz, Christopher. "The Bardic Pose: A Survey of Les A. Murray's Poetry." *Southerly* 40 (1980): 367–87; 41 (1981): 52–74 & 188–210. Three-part extended survey of Murray's career through his first seven books. Excellent introduction that makes a solid case for Murray as a "major" poet. Part three gives a sympathetic account of the verse novel, *The Boys Who Stole the Funeral*. (Pollnitz is the author of a forthcoming book-length study of Murray's work.)

Porter, Peter. "Les Murray: An Appreciation." *Journal of Commonwealth Literature* 17.1 (1982): 45–52. Brief but inclusive look at the poetry by an expatriate Australian poet. Personal appreciation but incisive. Puts the poetry in a wide context.

Taylor, Andrew. "The Past Imperfect of Les A. Murray." *Reading Australian Poetry*. St. Lucia: U of Queensland P, 1987. 189–97. Examines Murray's sense of time, past and present, and argues that the absence of the female in his poetry stems from the early loss of his mother. Uses some deconstructive critical strategies.

Trigg, Stephanie. "Les A. Murray: Boeotian Count." *Scripsi* 2.4 (1984): 139–48. Reviews *The Vernacular Republic* and *The People's Otherworld*, showing how the concerns shift and change from the pastoral to the supernatural. Concise and intelligent.

Zwicky, Fay. "Language or Speech? A Colonial Dilemma." *Overland* 98 (1985): 42–46. Critical, at times acerb, review of *The People's Otherworld*. Discusses Murray's poetry in general and questions some of his aesthetic and political stances.

Interviews

With Lawrence Bourke. *Journal of Commonwealth Literature* 21.1 (1986): 167–87.
With Carole Oles. *American Poetry Review* 15.2 (1986): 28–36.
With Barbara Williams. *Poetry Canada Review* 7.2 (1985–86): 47–48.

—PAUL KANE

Wilson Harris

Wilson Harris is a poet, novelist, and critic of Guyanese origin. He was born in New Amsterdam, 24 March 1921, in what was then British Guiana. He was educated at Queen's College, Georgetown, and became a government surveyor in the 1940s. He then led many expeditions into the interior to do mapping and geomorphological research.

Although he began to write as a young man and had close connections with a group of writers in Guyana whose work appeared in the magazine *Kijk-Over-Al*, his explorations into the interior and in coastal areas had a tremendous impact on his imagination and affected his vision of landscapes and peoples, to which he first gave expression in the "Guiana Quartet." He explained it himself as "the shock of great rapids, vast forests and savannahs —playing through memory to involve perspectives of imperilled community and creativity reaching back into the Pre-Columbian mists of time" (*Contemporary Novelists* 563). He discarded several novels before he felt satisfied with the form of *Palace of the Peacock*, published in 1960.

Harris emigrated to England in 1959 and lived in London until a few years ago when he moved to Essex. He is married to Margaret Whitaker, a poet and playwright. He is now the author of eighteen novels and two volumes of novellas. In 1967 he started giving talks and writing essays that are most profitably read in conjunction with his fiction and vice versa since they are mutually illuminating. Most of them express his intense concern for the future of civilization and the regenerating role of the imagination. He has been a visiting professor and writer-in-residence in many universities—West Indies, Toronto, Leeds, Aarhus, Yale, Mysore, Newcastle in Australia, California, and for a number of years he regularly spent a few months at the University of Texas at Austin in both capacities. He was Commonwealth Fellow at the University of Leeds in 1971 and received a Guggenheim Fellowship in 1973 as well as a Southern Arts Writer's Fellowship in 1976. He received an honorary doctorate from the University of the West Indies in 1984 and the University of Kent at Canterbury in 1988. He was the first recipient of the Guyana Prize for fiction (1985–87).

SEEKING THE MYSTERY OF THE "UNIVERSAL IMAGINATION"

The universal imagination—if it has any meaning or value—has its roots in subconscious and unconscious strata that disclose themselves profoundly within re-visionary strategies through intuitive clues that appear in a text one creates. That text moves or works in concert with other texts to create a multi-textual dialogue.
—Wilson Harris, "Validation of Fiction"

At a time when the claim to universality has become very suspicious in post-colonial writing and criticism, because it is seen as the major instrument of Euro-American centered discourse to maintain its cultural hegemony over formerly colonized worlds, Wilson Harris asserts the power of what he calls the "universal imagination" to stimulate genuine creativity. As a matter of fact, from his earliest writings he has always dissociated himself from any clearly defined and, even more, from any militant notion of national or racial identity and, in this respect, his work differs markedly from most West Indian writing. My purpose in this essay is to attempt to show that the "universal imagination" informs his work as a whole—the shape of his narratives, characterization, and use of imagery—whose striking originality is not just the expression of his idiosyncratic approach to fiction but offers an unusually deep analysis of Old and New World civilizations as well as a vision of their potential renewal. What Harris means by "universal imagination" is not an easily definable concept, and most of his essays are basically reflections on the creative process itself, born of the need to explore its essential nature *after* being immersed in it while writing fiction.

In the poetry he wrote before moving on to fiction, Harris gave the name of Greek gods and heroes to his Guyanese personae. The effect then of this association between Guyanese and classical Greek worlds seemed mainly to give his characters an immediately recognizable mythical dimension while pointing to the significance for the community of the deprived figures he was thus elevating to a heroic or divine status. In retrospect, however, it also appears that the elements from Greek or other European mythologies in both poetry and early fiction belong, in his view, with New World pre-Columbian myths and coexist in a "universal unconscious," which assumes very different expressions as they are apprehended by artists of different backgrounds. For example, Harris himself has drawn attention to a parallel between Blake's "Tyger tyger burning bright/In the forests of the night," the tiger imagery represented on the Aztec calendar, and the tigerish stripes perceptible in natural Guyanese sceneries like striped reflections in a waterfall ("Validation" 42–43), while the tiger-imagery in *The Whole Armour* can be read as variations and a reworking of the tiger image in Blake's and Eliot's poetry.

This brief allusion to the importance Harris gives to strata of experience buried in the unconscious and what they have in common with a different kind of experience and its interpretation in other parts of the world is only meant to emphasize a major feature in his fiction, namely that, from *Palace of the Peacock* to his latest novel, Harris explores *intuitively* these deeper strata in order to unearth the eclipsed, buried, or repressed species of otherness ignored in centuries of so-called Caribbean historylessness. "Otherness" in Wilson Harris's fiction is also mysterious to the perceptive consciousness. It certainly includes those he has called the "uninitiate," the victims of history or of present-day exploitation in *The Guyana Quartet*—that is, the vanished and vanishing Amerindians in *Palace of the Peacock*, the poor East Indian laborers in *The Far Journey of Oudin*, or the descendants of runaway slaves in *The Secret Ladder*. In the eyes of the victims, however, the "other" is the feared conquistador, like Donne in *Palace of the Peacock*, or the invader, like Fenwick, the apparently menacing though well-intentioned technologist in *The Secret Ladder*. Otherness can take on the form of god and man, the sacred and the profane, of social, historical, spiritual and psychological phenomena, and even the visible yet never wholly penetrated forms of the natural world. Harris approaches this mysterious reality at once with extraordinary audacity and the tentativeness of exploration. But except in a very momentary apotheosis of vision in *Palace of the Peacock*, the quest for it remains incomplete in his work, which is why, for all their variety in subject and setting, his novels can be regarded as successive stages in one unfinished quest. Nevertheless, whatever it represents, the "other" remains throughout the mainspring of creation.

Palace of the Peacock, the first part of the "Guiana Quartet," remains today the most widely read of his considerable work and, for many, his masterpiece, though Harris never stopped developing and some of his later novels, particularly *Carnival*, receive now as much attention. *Palace of the Peacock* is a landmark not just in Caribbean fiction but in fiction in English generally, exploding as it does all conventional approaches to narrative and modifying them far more radically than the early twentieth-century modernists had done, rejecting also much more critically the realistic mode of writing from which even the most experimental of these writers never broke completely away, and initiating a "species of fiction" uniquely his own. Harris's work is steeped in Guyanese history, which he regards as an indelible component of the Guyanese psyche and a ghostly presence or reality pervading the country's varied landscapes. He has a special interest in local myths, some of which he has rewritten in two collections of stories (*The Sleepers of Roraima* and *The Age of the Rainmakers*). But his mind and imagination have been nourished by Western art, literature, philosophy, and anthropology. So that in addition to his visionary perception of the human condition, it is this striking alchemy of the impact of history on landscape and people, Old and New World myths, "re-visions" of Western cultural legacies together with his bold stylistic innovations, which accounts for much of his originality.

Palace of the Peacock recreates quintessentially the repeated invasion of Guyana after the Renaissance, the abortive meeting between the conquerors and the Amerindian folk and, symbolically, the exploitation of land and people from time immemorial. It is a re-creation of all such expeditions initiated out of a misconceived idealism and thirst for power. Donne leads a multiracial crew on a nameless river into the interior in search of cheap labor for his plantation and of the legendary El Dorado. But as they meet one obstacle after another both on the river and in their conflicting relationships with one another, their pursuit of the folk turns into a struggle for survival and a quest for salvation. Through this simple narrative line Harris nevertheless disrupts most fictional precedents and deliberately eschews any pretense to a supposedly objective historical reconstruction, though his subject is history or rather its traumas, whose deeper psychological effects he explores on the border between consciousness and the unconscious, or of life and death, like the reconstruction of Donne's death in chapter five. Not only do outer and inner psychological landscapes coincide and real landscape features spatialize inner states of mind, the concrete and the intangible often overlap as again and again the surface reality is breached to reveal the tormenting obsessions of the crew with power or wealth, with Mariella, the native woman (at once sexual object, symbol of the land and spirit of the place, and ambivalent muse), to reveal also the mixture of terror and beauty they experience in their journey towards death and rebirth. Here are a few examples:

> The outboard engine and propeller still revolved and flashed with mental silent horror now that its roar had been drowned in other wilder unnatural voices whose violent din rose from beneath our feet in the waters. (24–25)

> I stifled my words and leaned over the ground to confirm the musing footfall and image I had seen and heard in my mind in the immortal chase of love on the brittle earth. (31)

> Something had freed them [the crew] and lifted them out of the deeps, a blessing and a curse, a reverberating clap of thunder and still music and song. The sound was jubilant and obscure and tremulous in their ear like a dreaming sword that had cut them from the womb. (55)

The narrative is largely told by a nameless first-person narrator who mostly "dreams" the seven-day reconstruction of their journey at several levels of perception even at the very beginning of the novel when his opening vision of the shot horseman immediately afterwards shifts to a vision within a dream: "I dreamt I awoke" (19). Though perceived as separate individuals since the narrator sees Donne, his brother, outside himself, they make one, sharing "one dead seeing eye and one living closed eye" (19), but they also contain the multiracial crew who embody various aspects of their community of being, just as the crew Fenwick leads into the Canje in *The Secret Ladder* are so many selves equally sprung from "one complex womb" (*Palace* 39). Keeping in mind that the crew belong to all the races to be found in contemporary Guyana, this phrase clearly shows that they are both victimizers of the folk they pursue and victims themselves of the historical circumstances that brought them or their ancestors to Guyana. This suggests that there is no going back on history as indeed the crew realize in a moment of vision: "They saw the naked unequivocal flowing peril and beauty and soul of the pursuer and the pursued together, and they knew they would perish if they dreamed to turn back" (*Palace of the Peacock* 62). That they should also be part of Donne, the skipper with the English Renaissance name, whose imagination benumbed by will-to-power revives after acknowledging his own egotism and the folk's existence, emphasizes their heterogeneous and human, rather than national, identity. The novel as a whole is an imaginative "re-vision" of the expedition, which progresses through intuitive thrusts as the narrator allows people or phenomena formerly ignored or taken for granted to impinge upon his consciousness:

> I saw—rising out of the grave of my blindness—the nucleus of that
> bodily crew of labouring men I had looked for in vain in his
> [Donne's] republic and kingdom. They had all come to me at last in
> a flash to fulfil one self-same early desire and need in all of us. (27)

The effect of the narrator's intuitions and glimpses of what he calls "the true substance of life . . . the substance of the folk" (52), together with the violent ordeals on the river and in his mind—as depicted at the beginning of chapter six—is to crumble the crew's hard carapace of prejudice and polarized thinking, making possible the apprehension of that third nameless dimension (or "otherness"), which all the protagonists in Harris's fiction approach from different angles in their attempt to achieve what proves to be the real purpose of their quest: the genesis or regeneration of the imagination. In *Palace of the Peacock*, Harris initiates the process in which most of his characters were to be involved: the disruption of their self-sufficient personality until a terrifying void is reached, similar to the psychological void suffered by conquered Amerindians and transported slaves, which Donne experiences in chapter ten and from which the construction of his new vision can begin. In addition to his personal experience, the void is also the so-called "historylessness" of the Caribbean, typical of a condition of "invisibility" anywhere (also represented in *Black Marsden*) because the people concerned are unseen or eclipsed. Harris considers that the experience of those who have been "forgotten" by history is as much part of a country's (and the world's) heritage as the recorded or celebrated feats of acknowledged heroes. This experience is the unseen face of tradition, which must be explored and brought to the surface to modify the consolidated plane of tradition that alone is usually recognized (*Tradition* 28–29). He therefore links the self-assertion or indifference of those who ignore eclipsed people(s) with what he regards as the uniform and authoritarian character of realism, its predominantly one-dimensional representation of reality, whereas the apprehension of the unseen is for him the prime mover of a "heterogeneous complex of the imagination" ("Interview" 70). The unseen source of inspiration in *Palace of the Peacock* is the invisible fugitive folk eventually constellated into stars in the peacock's tail while the reborn crew appear at the windows of the palace, even though "the inseparable moment . . . of all fulfilment and understanding" (116) is an evanescent vision.

A major example of the way in which the realistic texture of experience is altered in *Palace of the Peacock* occurs in Part III, "The Second Death," when the body of the crew begin to disintegrate through the sacrificial death of Carroll, the youngest among them. In another context Harris has suggested that the "second [death] is a psychical design to fissure inner paralysis" (*Womb* 47). As the crew approach dangerous rapids, their ears are stopped as were Ulysses' crew when he navigated past the island of the Sirens while Ulysses himself, bound to the mast, could hear their enchanting song. Here, however, the Siren is among the crew in the shape of the old Arawak woman made prisoner by Donne, who is momentarily transfigured into a young enchantress (the youthful Mariella). The crew are also momentarily blinded as they silently accuse one another of wishing to rape her. But Harris reverses our expectations of the significance of the myth for she is a victim, even if an ambivalent one—both daemon and saving muse. Perhaps only Carroll can hear her song as he stands up to help his companions and disappears silently into the water, arousing compassion in the crew, unsealing their eyes of the cloud of "cruelty and self-oppression" and unstopping their ears. Carroll's death is immediately followed by the temporary rescue of the crew, and the old woman who all this time made one with the roaring rapids of the river ("Her crumpled bosom and river grew agitated with desire. . . . The ruffles in the water were her dress rolling and rising to embrace the crew." 62) now recovers her wrinkled appearance. But from then on the pursuing crew begin to perceive formerly neglected possibilities of fulfilment in their relationship with their respective "Mariella" or native woman. Thus Harris gives new life and a moral significance in a Guyanese context to a Western myth, which he was to "rewrite" in a more complex way in *The Waiting Room*, using it metaphorically through the novel to render the condition of poise when the exploring consciousness surrenders the self without allowing itself to be engulfed by the other: "he dared to lean as never before (without actually falling) upon the abyss of invention and confront the . . . hollow within which she stood" (*The Waiting Room* 52).

All Harris's fictions bridge continents imaginatively and show that the catastrophic encounters between peoples could have led to a fruitful dialogue between cultures instead of destruction, oppression, and a never wholly digested enmity. As he has himself pointed out, "catastrophe is part-and-parcel of genuine change and of the difficult transformation of habits of power and fixtures of greed" (*Explorations* 98). We have just seen that his "translation" of a Western myth breaks down an apparently fateful actual event, the rape of the Amerindian folk, which another novelist might have been presented realistically. Through most of his fiction there is also a conjunction of myths from different cultures or a revival of ancient gods in contemporary circumstances, such as the Norse god Odin in *The Far Journey of Oudin* or Poseidon in *The Secret Ladder*, who heralds "a new divine promise born of an underworld of half-forgotten sympathies" (379). In Cristo, the protagonist of *The Whole Armour*, merge a shamanistic experience and a re-enactment of Christ's sacrifice. Rebirth in *The Secret Ladder* takes place through the experience of Guyanese Perseus and Andromeda (Bryant and Catalena), while Fenwick slays the head of the Gorgon (Jordan, the representative of adamant, misplaced authority), whose terrifying mask is being "translated" and metamorphosed through *Tumatumari*. In *Companions of the Day and Night*, which largely takes place in Mexico, the dateless days of the Mexican Calendar convey the timeless dimension into which the Aztecs and their civilization have fallen, though here, too, pre-Columbian layers of civilization and the instrument of their eclipse, the Spanish conquering Christ, yield to a Mexican Christ whose susceptibility to the accumulation of trials imposed on the Mexican people creates in him "a combination of levels . . . that gave him the magic of universality" (31). In his latest novel, *The Infinite Rehearsal*, Harris "rewrites" the myth of Faust, which lends itself particularly well to an evocation of

European will-to-power but is here associated to the pre-Columbian myth of Quetzalcoatl. This novel further explores the nameless condition first actualized in *Palace of the Peacock*, then personified in "Idiot Nameless" in *The Eye of the Scarecrow* and *Companions of the Day and Night* and now in Ghost, the character in whom the void or hollowness is again presented as "the ground of creative conscience and value" (*The Infinite Rehearsal* 51).

I have already suggested that Harris's protagonists are not limited to the self-sufficient, clear-cut personality of characters in realistic fiction. At the end of *Heartland* Stevenson, the major character, sees that the ordinary social self is but a "self-created prison-[house] of subsistence" yet also "the confusing measure of vicarious hollow and original substance" (90). This phrase points again to the void as an essential stage in the creative process and the perception of "original substance." It also helps us understand Harris's approach to characterization. The void is both a state that the character reaches before or as he becomes more sensitive to the reality of others (comparable to Keats's notion of "negative capability") and the state of those others, an apparent *tabula rasa* from which they are being retrieved, as Harris shows so well in *Ascent to Omai* and *Black Marsden*. Therefore characterization in his fiction largely proceeds through the protagonists's perceptions or failure to perceive what is essential in others. So that vision and understanding become moral criteria replacing the often limiting codes of a given society. It must be emphasized, however, that Harris's concern with vision in depth goes together with a sensuous rendering of the characters' experience and does not deny the natural world. Rather vision is reached *through* that world as in the opening scene of *Ascent to Omai*, in which a sunbeam pierces the mists and the "rain-sodden atmosphere" to reveal "the figure of the scarecrow, ruined porcknocker," a ghostly "faceless face," partly real, partly envisioned by the protagonist who ascends an actual mountain in the Guyanese interior.

The increasing self-reflexiveness in Harris's novels is also a major aspect of his method of characterization, almost inevitably so since his characters are involved, as indicated above, in a genesis or rebirth of the imagination. In the so-called London novels (*Da Silva da Silva's Cultivated Wilderness, The Tree of the Sun, The Angel at the Gate*) visionary self-reflexiveness merges with sensuousness into the painting metaphor. Da Silva da Silva, a major character in two of these novels, is an actual painter who keeps "revising" his paintings and discerns in "a uniform cloak of paint" a mutation of history, "the mutation, born of the arousal of suppressed cultures, suppressed tones of feeling" (*Da Silva da Silva* 10). In his earlier novels and some of his own posterior comments on his conception of fiction, Harris saw his protagonists involved in a "trial" of self-judgment (see *Heartland* and *Ascent to Omai*) or in a "drama of consciousness," a phrase which explains his frequent use of terms related to drama like "play of the soul," "theatre of arousal," "comedy," or "infinite rehearsal"—the title of his latest published novel in which the hero's aunt stages plays "revising the histories of the world" (35). Da Silva's revisions of his paintings are a kind of "infinite rehearsal," by which Harris means the necessarily repeated, deeper, and multiple approaches to given experiences. They are necessary because any single approach is partial and limited, so that the quest for truth and wholeness is by its very nature infinite and unfinished. Hence the constant revision and "infinite rehearsal" by which the protagonist constantly "revises" his own positions while, at a further remove, Harris himself constantly "revises" his own fictions and sometimes other writers' (like Dante's *Divine Comedy* in *Carnival* and Goethe's *Faust* in *The Infinite Rehearsal*). Da Silva da Silva eloquently sums up this process:

> Each ancient frame becomes a vacancy to sustain many canvases, many incarnations, unpredictable densities, that appear and disappear to reappear in order to immerse one in a new and just dialogue between what is apparently strong and what is apparently weak. I am apparently weak. I am afflicted by recurring voices. I hear them at the heart of this great city, the regional accent of birds and bells, the voices of the past, the voices of the present. (10–11)

The actualization of the revisionary process in the texture of Harris's narratives occurs through his protean metaphors or what he himself recently called "convertible imageries" (*The Guyana Quartet* 10). His rewriting of the myth of Ulysses and the Sirens discussed earlier is not only a "rehearsal" and reinterpretation of that myth, the evolutionary use of the water imagery in this episode and the chapter as a whole is "convertible imagery." So is the sun metaphor in *Palace of the Peacock*, whose changing effect from blinding disk to shattered fragments of light to visionary stars and organs of vision conveys the development of Donne's consciousness. It is not just that the meaning of metaphors develop and that one kind of reality is transformed into another; they express the extraordinary contrasts and variety of the visible world, like the "wilderness" metaphor in *Da Silva da Silva's Cultivated Wilderness*. But, as already mentioned, the world of the senses they evoke is a gateway *through* which other densities are reached. The word "through" is a frequent pivot in the narrative, which suggests the possibility of conversion. Again, when Da Silva "paints" his way around the Commonwealth Institute in London and circumnavigates the globe imaginatively, he gropes "into an abyss . . . confronting the half-human status of man . . . a gulf of animal losses . . . as though that gulf were an opportunity for, and an expedition into, illuminations one needed to find" (68). Similarly, the "Carnival" metaphor in the novel by that title evokes a universal "carnival of history," while the repeated penetration of the outward masks of reality leads to the discovery of partial truths or of other realities, themselves of a dual or even more complex nature.

The coexistence of opposites in any phenomenon, natural or human, and the possible conversion of one kind of reality into another are expressions of a fundamental irony in the heart of all life, a creative irony that Harris sees as part of the "Universal Imagination" and that runs through his fiction. It implies a capacity to discriminate between "like yet unlike forces," which assume an infinite number of shapes in his narratives. In *The Infinite Rehearsal*, for instance, Faust is an ambivalent character, both tempter and guide for the I-narrator who acquires a capacity "to mirror yet repudiate and breach" conventional and automatic behaviors. First of all, there is irony in the fact that what seems most obvious, conventional, or taken for granted in appearances, actions, or thought, can be the very doorway through which the protagonist has access to another dimension of being. There is also irony in "like yet unlike forces" in that, depending on the intention behind them, apparently similar forms of behavior can have different effects or their effects can be modified in the course of action.

As a conclusion, I shall quote one example among many of the ways in which this stimulating irony functions in a limited passage to transform a character's understanding. It occurs in *The Angel at the Gate* when the heroine feels separated from her alter-ego by a rising wall:

> Her obsession with "the wall" was a way . . . of identifying sexual nightmares and racial, class-fixated, economic riddles. It was a way of identifying hardened inferiority complexes, hardened superiority complexes, dogmas of inequality. Equally, it was a revelation of doomed lives, doomed graces or non-graces, on either side of the wall that needed to be re-interpreted as an epitaph of the imagination through which to resume a conception of universal, endangered cradle in imagination. . . .
>
> It was a wall she felt . . . she must herself have composed within layers and layers of self, and through which she must seek a door into what lay uncannily close at hand, uncannily far away, and beyond. In certain senses it was less a divide between herself and others and more the paradox of space that divided yet enclosed— enclosed yet released—its inmates . . . forever. *Forever* was itself a crack, a flute, a trumpet, an echo of blood and sea, bone and ice, sky and flight, wheel within wheel shaping itself into gesture, radical gesture of hope. (52–53)

WORKS CITED

Harris, Wilson. "Validation of Fiction: A Personal View of Imaginative Truth." *Tibisiri*. Aarhus: Dangaroo Press, 1989. 40–51.

———. *Tradition, the Writer and Society*. London: New Beacon Books, 1967.

———. *The Womb of Space, the Cross-Cultural Imagination*. Westport, Conn.: Greenwood Press, 1983.

———. *Explorations*. Aarhus: Dangaroo Press, 1981.

Munro, Ian, and Reinhard Sander. "Interview with Wilson Harris." *Kas-Kas*. Austin: University of Texas, 1972.

WILSON HARRIS'S PUBLISHED WORK

Poetry

Fetish, 1951
Eternity to Season, 1954

Fiction

Palace of the Peacock, 1960
The Far Journey of Oudin, 1961
The Whole Armour, 1962
The Secret Ladder, 1963
> (The novels above form the "Guiana Quartet." They were reprinted with minor changes in one volume as *The Guyana Quartet*, with a "Note on the Genesis of *The Guyana Quartet*" by the author, 1985. This edition was used in the essay.)

Heartland, 1964
The Eye of the Scarecrow, 1965
The Waiting Room, 1967
Tumatumari, 1968
Ascent to Omai, 1970
The Sleepers of Roraima, A Carib Trilogy, 1970
The Age of the Rainmakers, 1971
Black Marsden, 1972
Companions of the Day and Night, 1975
Da Silva da Silva's Cultivated Wilderness, 1977
Genesis of the Clowns, 1977
The Tree of the Sun, 1978
The Angel at the Gate, 1982
Carnival, 1985
The Infinite Rehearsal, 1987
The Four Banks of the River of Space, 1990
   (This novel forms a trilogy with the two previous ones.)

Criticism

Tradition, the Writer and Society. London: New Beacon Books,1967. Rpt. 1973.
   First basic formulation of Harris's conception of fiction, his rejection of realism, his personal view of tradition, of the role of myth, particularly in Caribbean society and in literature. Critical assessment of West Indian writers. Very useful to anyone approaching Harris's work for the first time.
Explorations, A Selection of Talks and Articles, 1966–1981. Edited with Introduction by Hena Maes-Jelinek. Aarhus: Dangaroo Press, 1981.
   Contains fourteen essays and covers Harris's critical development over fifteen years. Further explores the respective roles of myth and history, the "making" of tradition and initiates his continuing inquiry into the nature of imagination. Also contains essays on Guyanese Poetry, Janet Frame, Patrick White, Wole Soyinka, Jean Rhys, and Joseph Conrad.
The Womb of Space, The Cross-Cultural Imagination. Westport, Conn.: Greenwood Press, 1983.
   A more complex investigation into cultural heterogeneity, the cross-cultural sources of imagination, its functioning and multifarious expressions, particularly through an analysis in depth of fiction by William Faulkner, Edgar Allan Poe, Jean Toomer, Paule Marshall, Juan Rulfo, Patrick White, and Ralph Ellison.

SELECTED CRITICAL READINGS

This list of studies is very selective but attempts to cover most of Harris's novels as well as major aspects of his work. Except for pioneers like Michael Gilkes and Kenneth Ramchand, West Indian critics were rather slow to respond to his fiction though they are now doing so (see, among others, Marc McWatt and Jeffrey Robinson in *The Journal of West Indian Literature,* which started publication in 1986). Harris, it seems obvious, is an artist ahead of his time and has a reputation for "difficulty"—both stylistic and in the concepts he devises because they are not, or not exclusively, rational. However, any new novel of his now arouses considerable attention in Europe, in the West Indies, and in the rest of the English-speaking world. It is not just his fiction that elicits commentary; critics interested in literary theory are discussing his concepts and personal critical approaches to fiction and their relevance to postcolonial criticism. However, all aspects of Harris's work are closely interrelated. Now that exegeses of most novels to date have been published and their most striking features commented upon, what is needed at this stage is an overall study showing the link between those features and Harris's use of language, his idiosyncratic style. Also, in spite of a very few essays on the "prophetic" or "shamanistic" side of his writing, most critics have been shy of discussing those aspects that cannot be explained rationally.

Adler, Joyce. "*Tumatumari* and the Imagination of Wilson Harris." *Journal of Commonwealth Literature* 7 (July 1969): 20–31. Perceptive analysis of *Tumatumari.* Raises fundamental questions implicit in Harris's fiction.

Drake, Sandra. *Wilson Harris and the Modern Tradition. A New Architecture of the World.* Westport, Conn.: Greenwood Press, 1986. Discusses Harris in connection with the modern tradition and argues that he is a third-world modernist. Offers perceptive analysis of four novels: *Palace of Peacock, Tumatumari, Ascent to Omai,* and *Genesis of the Clowns.*

Durix, Jean-Pierre. "Crossing the Arawak Horizon." *Literary Half-Yearly* 20 (1979): 83–92. An excellent study of the formal aspects of "Arawak Horizon."

———, editor. *Symposium on Wilson Harris.* Special issue of *World Literature Written in English* 22 (1983). Apart from Harris's own essay on Faulkner's *Intruder in the Dust* and an interview, contains articles on his poetry and early writings, on *Palace of the Peacock, The Eye of the Scarecrow, Ascent to Omai, The Tree of the Sun,* and on "Structure and Vision in the Novels of Wilson Harris." A stimulating collection analyzing major phases in the author's development.

Gilkes, Michael, editor. *The Literate Imagination: Essays on the Novels of Wilson Harris.* London: Macmillan, 1989. Apart from Wilson Harris's own essay on "Literacy and the Imagination" contains eleven essays by different authors on his work approached from various perspectives and grouped under three headings: "Phenomenal Space," "Language and Perception," and "The Dialectical Imagination." Extremely useful.

———. *Wilson Harris and the Caribbean Novel.* London: Longman, 1975. Very good introduction to Harris's novels up to *Black Marsden.* Places Harris's work in its Caribbean context and gives special emphasis to theme of psychic reintegration.

Howard, W.J. "Wilson Harris's *Guiana Quartet*: from Personal Myth to National Identity." *Ariel* 1 (1970): 46-60. Reprinted in *Readings in Commonwealth Literature.* Edited by William Walsh. London: Oxford UP, 1973: 314–28. Places Guiana Quartet in symbolist tradition and points to affinity with Blake and Yeats. Harris transforms history into myth.

James, C.L.R. *Wilson Harris—A Philosophical Approach.* Trinidad: University of the West Indies, 1965. Relates Harris's thought to existentialism, particularly Heidegger.

Lacovia, R.M. *Landscapes, Maps and Parangles.* Toronto: Black Images, 1975. Presents numerous extracts from Harris's work to demonstrate that he creates a "reticulum of resonance" by superimposing images.

Mackey, Nathaniel, editor. *Hambone* 6 (Fall 1986). Issue with a special focus on Wilson Harris. Apart from Harris's contribution ("Character and Philosophic Myth"), contains essays by Jerome Klinkowitz, Hena Maes-Jelinek, Jean-Pierre Durix, and Joyce Adler on *The Angel at the Gate*, intertextuality and "The Art of Translation," *Carnival*, and "Female Figures and Imagery in Wilson Harris's Novels."

————. "The Unruly Pivot: Wilson Harris's *The Eye of the Scarecrow*." *Texas Studies in Literature and Language* 20 (1978): 633–59. Perceptive study of the form of *The Eye*. Insists on the increasingly self-reflexive nature of Harris's fiction.

Maes-Jelinek, Hena. "'Inimitable Painting': New Developments in Wilson Harris's Latest Fiction." *Ariel* 8.2 (1977): 63-80. Concentrates on painting as an exploratory metaphor and on notion of tradition in *Da Silva da Silva's Cultivated Wilderness* and *Genesis of the Clowns*.

————. *The Naked Design. A Reading of Palace of the Peacock*. Aarhus: Dangaroo Press, 1976. General introduction to Harris's fiction and detailed study of the language and imagery in *Palace of the Peacock*.

————. *Wilson Harris*. Boston: G.K. Hall, 1982. Traces the development of Harris's fiction from *Palace of the Peacock* to *The Tree of the Sun* through a detailed analysis of each novel up to *Black Marsden*, which initiates a new phase illustrating Harris's notion of "The Novel as Painting." The novellas and five novels in that phase are discussed in one last chapter.

————. "Wilson Harris." *West Indian Literature*. London: Macmillan, 1979. 179–95. General introduction to Harris's work in the context of fiction in English. Traces his major development through major phases.

————. "The Wisdom of Uncertainty: Re-visionary Strategies in Wilson Harris's *The Infinite Rehearsal*." *Semper aliquid novi. Littérature comparée et littératures d'Afrique*. Tübingen: Gunter Narr Verlag, 1990. An analysis of Harris's latest novel, which throws light on the concepts mentioned in the title, i.e. "revisionary strategies" and "infinite rehearsal," and explains how these function in his fiction.

McDougall, Russell. "Wilson Harris and the Art of *Carnival* Revolution." *Commonwealth* 10 (1987): 77–90. A sensitive and excellent Bakhtinian interpretation of *Carnival*, drawing parallels between different forms of art (painting, music) and analyzing in detail the formal aspects of the novel.

Petersen, Kirsten Holst, and Anna Rutherford, editors. *Enigma of Values: an Introduction*. Aarhus: Dangaroo Press, 1975. Apart from Harris's essay on Melville's "Benito Cereno," contains a very useful introduction by the editors to many of his basic concepts. Also includes essays on *Palace of the Peacock* and *Tumatumari* as well as discussions of Conrad's *Heart of Darkness*, Jean Rhys's *Wide Sargasso Sea*, and Golding's *The Inheritors* in the light of Harris's ideas.

Ramchand, Kenneth. "*The Secret Ladder*." *An Introduction to the Study of West Indian Literature*. Jamaica: Nelson Caribbean, 1976. Extremely good and illuminating detailed study of this novel, written specially for students but useful to all readers.

Slemon, Stephen. "'*Carnival*' and the Canon." Ariel 19.3 (1988): 59–75. As in previous article on *Carnival* (*Kunapipi* 9.3) discusses allegory in this novel but explores this aspect in greater depth and uses a more theoretical approach.

Interviews

With Michel Fabre. *World Literature Written in English* 22 (1983): 2–17.
With Kalu Ogba. *Caribbean Quarterly* 29.2 (1983): 54–62.
With Stephen Slemon. *Ariel* 19.3 (1988): 47–56.
With Jane Wilkinson. *Kunapipi* 8.2 (1986): 30–45.

— **Hena Maes-Jelinek**

Wole Soyinka

Born into an educated and Christian family in Nigeria on 13 July 1934, Wole Soyinka went to school in Abeokuta and Ibadan. After undergraduate studies in Arts at University College, Ibadan, and in English at the University of Leeds, he graduated in 1957, then began graduate study. However, when the opportunity came to work at the Royal Court Theatre, London, he neglected his studies and concentrated on writing, broadcasting, and gaining practical experience in the theater.

He returned to Nigeria and to a research post at University College, Ibadan, at the beginning of 1960, the year in which the country gained Independence. He quickly became involved in the literary, theatrical, and political life of Nigeria: writing for the press, the stage, radio, and television; helping to found a theater company, directing plays, and acting; participating in a human rights organization and making his position on the issues confronting the country widely known. Circumstances have changed and over the past three decades he has moved within the academic world and spent extended periods outside Nigeria. But at a fundamental level he has followed the pattern of activities he established in the early sixties and has remained true to the vision that informed some of his earliest work.

Since Independence in 1960, Nigeria has lived through a period of civilian misgovernment, a series of coups, a civil war, an oil boom, a second period of corrupt civilian rule, more coups and attempted coups. Soyinka has responded to each of these changes in a decisive and idiosyncratic way, ensuring that his position, however unpopular, is widely known. Between 1960 and the end of the eighties, he was arrested twice and on one occasion held in detention for a period of more than 27 months. When in Nigeria he has been deeply involved in politics, on rare and brief occasions working with the regime in power, more often adopting an anti-establishment position, always combative and outspoken.

Although primarily committed to Africa and to Nigeria, he has lived on a large map since the sixties: His plays have been widely performed, sometimes under his direction, and his novels and poems have been translated into many languages. His book of prison notes, *The Man Died*, and his autobiography, *Ake*, have been particularly admired abroad. He has received numerous international awards, including, in 1986, the Nobel Prize for Literature. Since that award Soyinka has found it easier to get across his views on issues affecting Africa and human rights, and he has continued to write and publish. Despite having opportunities to live and work in the United States, it is clear that Nigeria remains his home and that he feels a primary responsibility to combat racism and to fight for the human rights of Africans.

"MARRYING EARTH TO HEAVEN"—
A NOBEL LAUREATE AT THE END OF THE EIGHTIES

Wole Soyinka is still writing, being awarded honors, and embarking on new ventures. The preceding biographical sketch and the primary bibliography that follows this essay—and are essential reading for it—do not do justice either to the complexity of his life or to his creativity. They do, however, provide indications of some of the changes that the passage of years have brought and draw attention to his continuing concerns. In the paragraphs that follow, I fill in some of the sketch in the note and the bibliography and justify some of the items included. I indicate his attempts to find consistency and to reconcile disparate elements and suggest a basis on which recent work can be assessed. The conclusion consists of a response to a recently published poem entitled "Cremation of a Wormy Caryatid."

First, a note on sources. Many of the details of Soyinka's recent life incorporated into the biographical note have been gleaned from *West Africa,* a London publication that draws extensively on Nigerian newspapers and now regards Soyinka as someone whose words and deeds are of interest to its readers. Such a source is generally reliable but occasionally the newspapers on which it relies make mistakes, and sometimes Soyinka descends on those who have got hold of inaccurate information. He has compared the delight he takes in correcting such people to the satisfaction of squashing a troublesome mosquito. Biography has rarely been a more dangerous occupation; but Soyinka has put so much of his genius into his life and drawn so effectively on his own experience for his creative writing that forays into it must be risked.

In a sense Soyinka cannot escape blame for the interest the press now shows in his private life and in his family. He has often made use of his own life in his writing, and the inclusion of "Cor Teach" in the autobiographical section of the bibliography draws attention to a relevant early piece. The essay dates from his time in London at the end of the fifties and grew out of his employment as a supply teacher. While modest in scale, it approaches the immodest in tone: Soyinka is at the center of the action and has all the best lines. "Cor Teach" is not, however, his earliest surviving autobiographical work; at present I think that honor belongs to one of his broadcasts for the BBC during the late fifties. As was the case for many other British and international English writers, the BBC provided an important source of early employment and experience. The Corporation's archives contain abundant evidence of Soyinka's early determination to earn a living as a writer.

In 1981 the amount of information about Soyinka's childhood was immensely extended by the publication of his evocative and readable *Ake: The Years of Childhood.* It contains an abundance of family details, descriptions of formative experiences, and clues to the development of a complex personality. Authors' claims to total recall should not be taken seriously since elements of fiction inevitably intrude into any autobiography, and *Ake* is no exception. It is the product of a selective process that reflects tendentious purposes. In the preceding biographical sketch, I mention Soyinka's parents but not his children. This was because the marriage of his parents, "Essay" and "Wild Christian," presented in *Ake,* appears to have been a remarkable coming together of different personalities, forces even, which provided an image that Soyinka has drawn on repeatedly. *Isara: A Voyage Around "Essay,"* published in 1989, explores the world in which Soyinka's father lived and the values he stood for. It provides opportunities for homage and self-projection, for re-creation and celebration. Essay and Soyinka's outgoing mother are now both dead, but they continue to influence his apprehension of forces present in society and have profoundly affected his writing. The same cannot be said for other members of his family.

The vivid and frequently dramatic account of his first eleven years won Soyinka many new admirers. It was undoubtedly influential in swaying the people who more than any others affected his reputation during the eighties—the members of the Swedish Academy—forcing his life into the public arena and providing a magic ring of visibility he can turn whenever he wants to ensure attention for himself or a cause. In *Kongi's Harvest,* one of the characters suggests that a new system of dating should be used to indicate the significance of the harvest: In Soyinka's life the Nobel Prize was so significant for his public profile that one might suggest, only a little facetiously, two periods: "Pre Nobel" and "Post Nobel."

Preparing the biographical note is made difficult by the way Soyinka sometimes plays hide and seek with public attention. One such game was played on 15 October 1965 when, as part of a protest against rigged elections, he held up the radio station at Ibadan. In the days and weeks that followed, he was first "wanted" and then tried; he held the center of the national stage and attracted a certain amount of international attention. It must be pointed out that he pleaded not guilty to the charges against him and that he was acquitted, but the trial and the way Soyinka writes about the whole episode in his partly autobiographical prison notes, *The Man Died,* do not convince me of his innocence.

Another period of particular interest in Soyinka's life is August 1967: a tense time in the Nigerian Civil War. Did Soyinka, as Olusegun Obasanjo suggested in the reference to a "celebrated playwright" in his book about the Civil War, bring pressure to bear on the future head of state? Though happy to fuel speculation about his ability to ring Obasanjo on a normally silent telephone line, Soyinka has recently stated that Obasanjo misrepresented their exchange. His side of this story, already presented to an audience at the time of the launching of Obasanjo's book, *My Command,* is promised in a forthcoming volume of essays entitled *Continuity and Amnesia: A Selection for the "Newbreed" Republic.* There, it seems, he refers to Obasanjo as "affectedly patronising in his factionalist narrative" and proclaims that "history does not forgive the distorting tricks of memory." Another talkative mosquito reduced to a smear of blood! The publication promises to make accessible a substantial amount of Soyinka's writing for the Nigerian press—a too often neglected area of self-expression and one that shows how deeply he is involved with the political life of his native Nigeria. Until it is published and examined by historians and political scientists, Soyinka's role in this area, as in other matters, will continue to be the subject of speculation.

Many of his published essays indicate his longstanding involvement in national affairs, including his concern about road safety. It is typical of Soyinka that he should follow words with deeds, and in the years since he wrote *The Road* and his poem for a friend killed in a car crash, "In Memory of Segun Awolowo," he has devoted a very considerable amount of time and energy to road safety campaigns, working with uniformed agents employed to reduce the dangers for Nigerian travelers. There is every indication that his participation in Nigerian public life will continue to be intense as his country enters the nineties and begins an ambitious experiment with a two-party political system.

While regularly involved in Nigerian domestic politics, Soyinka's appearances on the international scene tend to have some of the qualities of a Black Pimpernel. When, on 16 October 1986, the new age was introduced with the announcement that he had won the Nobel Prize for Literature, a posse of journalists immediately set out on his trail. They found him in Paris and for a brief period his presence in, or absence from, a particular place at a particular time was not a matter for debate. But for those with a continuing concern about the life and work of the often elusive writer, what he was doing immediately before and soon after the announcement became of considerable interest. It transpired that he was in Paris on 16 October partly to follow a theater group from Martinique to Limoges where they were to perform his production of *La Metamorphose de Frere Jero*. Had it not been for the announcement of the prize, it is quite possible that many would have remained ignorant of his work with the Caribbean group—which I shall return to. After giving the media his reaction to the award—broadly that he regarded it as recognition of African creativity, Soyinka took flight to Nigeria. It seems he was anxious to escape from the international press corps and wanted to be in Nigeria to share his news with his compatriots. Within hours of his arrival in Lagos, the editor of an investigative Nigerian journal was killed by a letter bomb, and Soyinka used his higher-than-ever profile to demand a thorough investigation. This call was widely reported. The whole sequence shows that Soyinka often works in comparative obscurity in the theater and uses his renown to work for justice. He is deeply aware of the obligations that come with access to the media; the ring of visibility is a ring of power and responsibility.

Unlike productions and political protests, writing by a world famous author, so long as it reaches a final form, must eventually become available to all interested readers. In preparing the primary bibliography, judgments have had to be made about work that may have been completed or may be "in progress." At a ceremony in Nigeria towards the end of 1989, he launched three titles: one *"Mandela's Earth" and Other Poems*, had already appeared in the United States and the United Kingdom. Another, *Isara: A Voyage Around "Essay,"* has already been mentioned, and the third, *The Search*, is a selection of extracts from *Isara* for young readers. The decision to publish *The Search* prompts the comment that, despite being regularly attacked as a "difficult" and elitist writer, Soyinka has produced works that have been enjoyed by young people. These include stories such as "Keffi's Treat," poems such as "Telephone Conversation," and plays such as "Childe Internationale."

The collection of essays promised for the new decade and the last two titles share a Nigerian publisher. The decision to choose a Nigerian publishing house is not unprecedented; for example, he was involved in founding Orisun Publications in Ibadan, which issued *Before the Blackout*, and he published his long poem *Ogun Abibiman* in Ibadan. He now appears to have made an increasing commitment to Nigerian publishers. This may spring from a determination to swim against the neo-colonialist current that treats Africa as a source of raw materials rather than finished products. It may also be part of an attempt to extricate himself from the contradictions of being a committed Pan-Africanist whose work seems to be directed primarily at a Western readership by virtue of the fact that it first appears in Great Britain and the United States.

It is right that the plays should stand first in the bibliography. Though Soyinka is deliberately a man of many parts who expresses himself in various forms, and though *Ake* and *Isara* show him mining a rewarding vein in prose, his reputation is primarily that of a dramatist. His achievements as a playwright are certainly remarkable: He first showed precocious talent, then demonstrated that he could work in an extraordinary variety of styles and bring together disparate elements. *The Lion and the Jewel*, in which both media attention—at its most basic—and marriage are significant themes, made a delightfully amusing contribution to the debate about the direction Africa should take as more and more nations achieved a degree of independence. *The Trials of Brother Jero* developed a deft narrative-theatrical style to create a fast-moving farce, which has delighted audiences in many countries and cultures and which encodes a warning about gullibility. *A Dance of the Forests* was over ambitious, but its very daring, its attempt to draw dialogue drama and festival theater together, and its presentation, through Demoke the carver and Ogun his deity, of beings in whom creativity and destruction are interlocked makes it worth dozens of more modest successes. *The Strong Breed* drew masterfully on Nigerian purification rituals and on the facilities available in the modern theater to explore the nature of responsibility and sacrifice. In the plays of the mid sixties, *Kongi's Harvest* and *The Road*, Soyinka is present as an assured playwright in control of two traditions: exploring the frontiers of drama, confidently manipulating his dual inheritance, bringing together metaphysics and satire, combining festival theater with the traditional drama. The play that came howling and groaning from his experience during the Nigerian Civil War, *Madmen and Specialists*, is more forbidding but shows a similar concern with form and shape, with molding theatrical traditions to communicate a vision.

While away from Nigeria during the early seventies, Soyinka wrote *Jero's Metamorphosis* and *Death and the King's Horseman*. The first revealed a determination to use the stage to contribute to debates about events in his homeland, in this instance the public execution of those found guilty of armed robbery. The second embodied a reflective and deeply moving examination of the Yoruba world with its sense of continuity and the impact on it of a fragmented, rootless but well-armed colonial presence. It contains some of Soyinka's most powerful dramatic verse, and represents a grappling with the theme of responsibility, which lies close to the roots of his creative consciousness. *Horseman*'s ability to carry the weight of Soyinka's ideas is indicated by the fact that he has returned to it repeatedly; he has directed three productions, one in Ife, two in the United States. It is central to his work.

The plays of the mid-seventies and eighties show a determination to comment directly and forcefully on Nigerian and African politics. This trend, which was anticipated in the early and unpublished satire on South Africa, "The Invention," and which took on a more radical complexion in the post-Civil War period, is exemplified by the unpublished agit-prop sketches, "Before the Blow-out." A very successful record of political songs, "Unlimited Liability Company," an attack on the government of Shehu Shagari in the early eighties, should also be mentioned, not least because it draws attention to Soyinka as musician, singer, and composer, facets of his many-sided creative personality that help to explain his interest in "total theater."

The heavy-handed manner of "The Invention" may account for the author's decision to "try to bury it." Certainly, in his major works of the sixties, the metaphors were taken further and the individuals were transformed into species: Kongi can be Banda as well as Nkrumah, and in performance Soyinka has tried to link him with Nigerian military leaders and Mobutu. There was a change of attitude in the eighties, for in order to appreciate *Opera Wonyosi* the audience needs to be well informed about a considerable number of Nigerian scandals and outrages; and a familiarity with the reputations of African heads of state is a prerequisite for following the satirical shafts loosed in *A Play of Giants*. This is a more obviously engaged and political drama, more clearly attractive to the radical critics who had emerged in Nigeria and whom Soyinka has dubbed "Leftocrats." His attacks on "vulgar Marxists" during this period should not be taken as evidence that he is unmoved by the claims of the left. They should rather be seen as evidence of his determination to establish precise boundaries and exact lines of demarcation. But the changing mood in politics, in literature, and in literary politics clearly left its mark on Soyinka's work during the seventies. The plays became more occasional and more limited in appeal and have dated quickly; the essays have become more intemperate.

Beginning with his version of *The Bacchae* by Euripides, which was commissioned by the National Theatre in London, Soyinka has acknowledged in the most obvious way the impact of other writers. In addition to Euripides, influential figures include John Gay and Bertolt Brecht, for *Opera Wonyosi*, and Jonathan Swift, whose writing assisted in the birth of *Die Still, Rev. Dr. Godspeak*, the radio play that grew into *Requiem for a Futurologist*. The influence of Jean Genet on *A Play of Giants* introduces another author with whom Soyinka can interact. During 1987 he worked on an adaptation of the French writer's *Balcony* for the Royal Shakespeare Company. Scheduled to open in October, the adaptation did not satisfy Soyinka, so the production failed to take place and the project remains a straw in the wind.

Soyinka's recent interest in adaptation is illuminating. It reveals, I suspect, that the overwhelming desire to write original plays has weakened through the years. This is neither surprising nor is it uncommon, since, to some extent, playwriting is a young man's activity. For every dramatist who writes deep into middle age, there are many who, in their mature years, use the skills they have cultivated to prepare adaptations and, nowadays, film scripts. The patterns of creativity associated with the names of John Arden, Arnold Wesker, and Harold Pinter have features in common with Soyinka's and are more typical than those linked with the names of Sophocles, Shakespeare, and Ibsen.

Observers who have rushed to the conclusion that Soyinka is exhausted as an original playwright should be aware that the recent published works are never mere adaptations; they always add new perspectives and represent a radical reworking. The interest in adaptation draws attention to aspects of other work, which have sometimes been overlooked, particularly the extent to which the early plays, such as *The Lion and the Jewel* and *The Trials of Brother Jero*, represent an artistic engagement with other models, both African and European. In those two plays Soyinka responded to the Yoruba masquerade and folk narrative traditions and to the work of Joyce Cary and Bertolt Brecht. In *A Dance of the Forests* purification ceremonies and possession rituals were brought together with a multitude of European influences, including such unlikely bedfellows as Capek and J.B. Priestley. Soyinka has always been eclectic and has often been creatively reactive; he responds, sometimes in admiration, often in anger, to other writers' work, and his own position is frequently defined by the use made of borrowed elements and the differences established with existing texts. I have little expectation that Nigerian critics who follow the cultural nationalist line as defined by Chinweizu will recognize the subtlety of this creative interaction, this kind of marriage in which neither partner is dominant, and from which emerges a sturdy hybrid.

It should be pointed out in the context of a discussion of Soyinka's productivity that his theatrical output, in a broad sense, has not diminished as much as appears from a glance at the titles and dates in the bibliography. This is because he has found creative expression in productions, theater-linked activities, and a film, "Blues for the Prodigal." Perhaps because of his proximity to a vital oral tradition in which improvisation within limits is encouraged, perhaps because he is an actor, a dancer, and a director as well as a writer, Soyinka has always put great emphasis on plays in performance. Each of his productions of his own plays has been different, shaped for a particular audience in a particular place at a particular time. On occasions, as with his one and only production of *Opera Wonyosi*, he has even been prepared to introduce new elements in mid-run in order to ensure topicality and relevance. The 1986 Caribbean production of *Jero's Metamorphosis* was, I think, the first time he had staged that play, and the fact that it was performed in French was only one aspect of the way it differed from his original text. In several ways it was a new play. For example, for a world grown accustomed to the activities of Islamic fundamentalists, an ending was provided involving the arrival of representatives of a militant Islamic sect. One of them drew a gun while the other demanded "a summit conference" with the "desk general."

In recent years, Soyinka has been involved in major productions. Some of these have been in the United States and have involved considerable new thought to cope with problems of communication from one culture to another. In the production of *Death and the King's Horseman* at the Vivian Beaumont Theater in New York during the early months of 1987, a new character, a Babalawo, was introduced into the first scene in order to help the audience appreciate that tension was increasing and the future troubled. Before any final judgment is made about the current state of Soyinka's theatrical creativity, the new productions of these old plays have to be taken into consideration.

Soyinka made an early impact as a poet and has continued to write poetry. *"Mandela's Earth" and Other Poems*, which contains verses composed over a fourteen-year period, is the most recent publication. It illustrates trends that can be observed in his work in other forms over this period: For example, there is the concern with African politics, with African heads of state, with corruption in Nigeria, with American values, and, in the poems, which comprise the section entitled

"Mandela's Earth" and make an appearance in the title, with South Africa. Soyinka is present in several characteristically different roles, as, for example, celebrant and satirist, but the manner is frequently public, reflecting the increased demand for public performances and for statements on issues. On occasions the choice of subject suggests that Soyinka is filling a role as poet laureate of Anglophone Africa, a performance that will not surprise readers who recall his response to the news that he had been awarded the Nobel Prize. The wit is stretched thin on occasions, as in the play on "Mengele" and "Mandela" in "Like Rudolf Hess, The Man Said," but there is evidence that Soyinka is still as capable as ever of engaging with events and of thinking through images in energetic language. His genius is abundantly seen in "Cremation of a Wormy Caryatid."

The caryatid of the title is an elaborate wooden carving, the work of a long dead Demoke, which depicted a variety of scenes including a procession of "sages, warriors, lords" and a palanquin, a "middle dais" of "lords and warriors, harem,/ Diviners," and a "base podium" on which there is a row of kneeling slaves. "The cyclic symmetry"—or wholeness of vision—"that ruled the carver's world" also incorporated "Birds of swirling plumage" and animals. The carving stood, Soyinka writes, in his "gallery," but it had been "a host/To woodworms," which had "probed . . . outward piety" and "aired hidden/Histories through a million perforations." The "tell-tale signs" had been regularly cleaned away by the "untutored dusters" of those who did not recognize the evidence of destructive forces at work. The poet mourned: "Alas, the mites have punctured hoards of lust,/Left mere form, and scooped the substance." So he decided to burn the caryatid on the grounds that "To save the grove, we isolate the tree." A conflagration was arranged at evening, which was a particularly appropriate time since "twilight/Is the favourite hour of ancestral parting." In a passage that draws on Yoruba verse forms and is partly in Yoruba, Soyinka pulls together the two traditions carried by the two languages. The Yoruba allusions are matched by half-echoes of lines about mutability and mortality, about dust and ashes, which are familiar to students of English literature. The Yoruba-English interlude is followed by a precise and measured description of the bonfire:

> The cinders of past epochs sink—but slowly.
> Lack of substance clings tenaciously
> To form. Pillars rise in flames of conquest,
> Peel, incandescent.

The poet watched—as who has not?—the unfolding drama of burning wood. In this instance the symbolism rises as effortlessly as smoke from the cremation of the carved record of a world that has already gone—"the borers," the poet observed had "worked well."

In a reversal of the sequence alluded to in the title of James Baldwin's *The Fire Next Time*, the heavens opened and "rain [came] as arbiter." It drew "a curtain of discretion on the altar hearth." The poet suggests that this may have been "to forestall a second,/Third or fourth idolatry? Urn Fetishism?" He plays with this idea before moving towards a conclusion that hints at some of the ambiguities in the scene:

A pottage of ash and cinders marks the spot,
A loathsome mound, pocked by drum throbs
Pressing from the skies . . . Yes, these stubborn
Scepters, exorcised, yet marrying earth to heaven!

In an early script for a documentary film, Soyinka expressed his delight in the process by which Igbo artists constructed and embellished clay mbari houses. They worked knowing that as soon as their task was finished the process of erosion and destruction would begin, and that before long a different artist would be charged with the responsibility of reconstruction to reflect a changing reality and a new apprehension. In the richly allusive "Cremation of a Wormy Caryatid," Soyinka shows his familiarity with the ways in which African art has been destroyed and exploited, burnt and sold, by representatives of alien religions and of new commercial interests. The poem stands as a transformation of a work of art from one form into another: The conflagration is an occasion for mourning, but a poem has risen from the ashes. The combination of thought and event, and the fusion of image and idea in this poem show Soyinka at his finest.

The poet's insistence on the lack of substance in the procession of the palanquin above the row of kneeling slaves does not mean that all from the past is corrupt and eroded. The continued vitality and expressiveness of the African world is recognized, incorporated into the fabric of the poem by the use of Yoruba. The wormy caryatid is specific, resonant, suggestive, not allegorical.

Soyinka continues his attempt to drive a consistent course through the mass of contradictions that make up the writer's lot in a country such as Nigeria. He also endeavors to do this through his verse, his plays, his productions, by his work in film, his involvement as a road safety marshal, through a multitude of activities such as workshops and conferences, and the fulfillment of his obligations as a professor at the University of Ife and as President of the International Theatre Institute. These last two roles have now been cast off, but equally demanding responsibilities have been taken on, including the construction of an unusual house—to his own design—near Abeokuta, and the establishment of a foundation named in honor of his father.

The bibliography also includes translations and fiction, which bear witness to Soyinka's longstanding interest in these genres. *The Forest of a Thousand Daemons* did not emerge from a vacuum but was part of his concern with the work of D.O. Fagunwa, which had already resulted in publications. His current interest in translation includes attempts to monitor the quality of the translations of his own works and time-consuming efforts to advance the cause of Swahili translations of African writing.

Although *The Interpreters* was his first extended work of fiction, it was preceded by a significant number of short stories, two of which bore the title, "A Tale of Two Cities," possibly because a volume with that title was envisaged. He moved into the novel form with authority, but in certain respects the novels give the feeling of being substitutes for work in other genres: drama in the case of *The Interpreters* and film in the case of *Season of Anomy.*

A comparison of the novels brings home a theme that runs through this essay: the different moods of the decades in which they were written and the importance of the Civil War, which separated the sixties from the seventies. The political and economic situation in Nigeria inevitably affected sensitive artists and the expansive, ebullient, Africanist sixties, gave way to the narrower focus of the seventies in which ideological issues moved to the fore. Ofeyi, the artist and activist at the center of the second novel, struggles to reconcile the two aspects of his projects to express a wholeness of vision, to come to terms with past and present, with the indigenous and the imported, with the passing show and the eternal values; he tries to make a marriage between earth and heaven.

WOLE SOYINKA'S PUBLISHED WORK

Drama

The Swamp Dwellers, 1958
The Lion and the Jewel, 1959
The Invention, 1959
Camwood on the Leaves, 1960
A Dance of the Forests, 1960
The Trials of Brother Jero, 1960
The House of Banigeji (Act 2), 1962
The Strong Breed, 1962
The Road, 1965
Kongi's Harvest, 1965
Before the Blackout, 1965
The Detainee, 1965
Madmen and Specialists, 1971
The Bacchae of Euripides: A Communion Rite, 1973
Jero's Metamorphosis, 1973
Death and the King's Horseman, 1975
Opera Wonyosi, 1977
Die Still, Rev. Dr. Godspeak, (radio version of *Requiem for a Futurologist,* 1982), 1983
Requiem for a Futurologist, 1983
A Play of Giants, 1984

Poetry

First Rites of the Harmattan Solstice, 1966
"Idanre" and Other Poems, 1967
Poems from Prison, 1969
A Shuttle in the Crypt, 1970
Ogun Abibiman, 1976
"Mandela's Earth" and Other Poems, 1988

Novels

The Interpreters, 1965
Season of Anomy, 1973

Translations (from work by D.O. Fagunwa)

"Agbako," 1964
"Kako," 1966
The Forest of a Thousand Daemons: A Hunter's Saga, 1968

Autobiography and Essays

"Cor Teach." *Ibadan* 7 (Nov. 1959): 26–27.
>   Account of experiences as a school teacher in London, 1959.

The Man Died: Prison Notes of Wole Soyinka, 1973
>   The "Prison Notes" include not only autobiographical material but also poems and speculation on various topics.

Myth, Literature and the African World, 1976
>   A series of lectures given at Cambridge; includes literary criticism and cultural analysis. "The Fourth Stage: Through the Mysteries of Ogun to the Origin of African Tragedy" is included as an Appendix.

Ake: The Years of Childhood, 1981
>   Recounts Soyinka's first eleven years.

Art, Dialogue and Outrage: Essays on Literature and Art, 1988
>   This collection of essays, lectures, addresses, papers, and interviews, written since the early sixties, brings together important statements on cultural issues.

Isara: A Voyage around "Essay", 1989
>   Reconstructs part of the life of Soyinka's father.

The Search, 1989
>   Excerpts from *Isara* for younger readers.

Continuity and Amnesia: A Selection for the "Newbreed" Republic.
>   The forthcoming volume will include articles, statements, addresses, etc., on Nigerian politics, society, and history.

SELECTED CRITICAL READINGS

Criticism on Wole Soyinka's writing has long been abundant. In the Post Nobel era it has become even more so. And it is unlikely that it will diminish as international critics from Ibadan to Ithaca examine the varied dimensions of this multi-faceted work.

Adelugba, Dapo, editor. *Before Our Very Eyes: Tribute to Wole Soyinka, Winner of the Nobel Prize for Literature.* Ibadan: Spectrum, 1987. Tributes from varied perspectives and recollections of friends provide a picture of Soyinka's life and a discussion of his work.

Asanga, Siga, editor. *African Theatre Review* 1.3 (1987). Brings together articles on Soyinka's role in Mbari, his religious convictions, his plays in performance, their ritualistic and satirical aspects, the tragic elements in his comedy, and the parallels between his work and that produced in Ireland some 80 years ago.

Chinweizu, Owuchewka Jemie, and Ihechukwu Madubuike. "Towards the Decolonisation of African Literature." *Okike* 6 (1974): 11–27. Early contribution to a controversy that still rumbles on about Soyinka's relationship with Africa. Soyinka has replied to this trio of critics, whom he has dubbed "the troika" and "Neo-Tarzanists" on a number of occasions.

Coger, Greta, compiler. *Index of Subjects, Proverbs and Themes in the Writings of Wole Soyinka.* New York: Greenwood, 1988. Helpful reference work, described by its title.

Galle, Etienne. *L'homme vivant de Wole Soyinka.* Paris: Silex, 1987. First full-length study in French devoted to Soyinka; evidence of increasing French interest.

Gates, Henry Louis, Jr., editor. "Soyinka Issue, Part 1." *Black American Literature Forum* 22 (1988). Contains articles on British and Nigerian responses to the Nobel Prize, on the critical reception of Soyinka in Sweden, on Soyinka and social responsibility, the literary aesthetic of African socialism, social vision, the problem of authenticity, ritual and satire.

Gibbs, James, editor. *Critical Perspectives on Wole Soyinka.* London: Heinemann, 1980; Washington, D.C.: Three Continents, 1980. Includes introduction, bibliography, and essays concerning Soyinka as poet, playwright, and novelist.

————. "Soyinka Issue." *The Literary Half-Yearly* 28 (1987). Contains articles on the Nobel Prize events, on the critical reception of Soyinka in Sweden, Nigeria, and Italy, on his autobiographical writing, prose style, use of the Ogun myth in poetry and drama, on "Telephone Conversation," reception of *The Road* in India, and the problem of authenticity.

————. "Soyinka Issue." *Research in African Literatures* 14.1 (1983). Includes articles on Soyinka's journalism, the form of his drama, "Four Archetypes," his version of *The Bacchae*, and on *Death and the King's Horseman.*

Gibbs, James. *Wole Soyinka.* London: Macmillan Modern Dramatists Series, 1986. Considers the plays in theatrical, biographical, and political contexts.

Gibbs, James, Ketu H. Katrak, and Henry Louis Gates, Jr., compilers. *Wole Soyinka: A Bibliography of Primary and Secondary Sources.* Westport: Greenwood, 1986. Covers the period up to 1984; subsequent research has inevitably revealed gaps.

Jeyifo, Biodun. *Soyinka Demythologised: Notes on a Materialist Reading of 'A Dance of the Forests', 'The Road', and 'Kongi's Harvest'.* Ife: Ife Monographs on Literature and Criticism, 1983-84. Offers commentary by the most significant of the left-wing Nigerian critics.

—————. *The Truthful Lie: Essays in the Sociology of African Literature.* London: New Beacon, 1985. Contains a radical critique of Soyinka's work.

Jones, Eldred Durosimi. *The Writing of Wole Soyinka.* London: Heinemann, 1983. Second edition of a standard and invaluable introduction to Soyinka's work.

Katrak, Ketu H. *Wole Soyinka and Modern Tragedy: A Study of Dramatic Theory and Practice.* New York: Greenwood, 1986. Contains extensive reference to Soyinka's writing about tragedy as well as to his tragedies.

Maduakor, Obi. *Wole Soyinka: An Introduction to His Writing.* New York: Garland Publishing, 1987. Considers Soyinka's poetry, fictional and autobiographical prose, metaphysical plays, and literary criticism.

Moore, Gerald. *Wole Soyinka.* London: Evans, 1978. Comprehensive critical account; revised edition.

Nouvelles du sud 2 (1985-86). Includes papers on *The Bacchae, Brother Jero,* other plays, Soyinka's universalism, his female characters, and links with Genet. Contains several contributions by Etienne Galle, Soyinka's trusted French translator.

Ogunba, Oyin. *The Movement of Transition: A Study of the Plays of Wole Soyinka.* Ibadan: Ibadan UP, 1975. Examination of the plays by a critic with a background in Yoruba life and Nigerian politics.

Ogunba, Oyin, and Abiola Irele, editors. *Theatre in Africa.* Ibadan: Ibadan University Press, 1978. Includes essays drawing attention to some of the current issues in African theater.

Ogunbiyi, Yemi. *Drama and Theatre in Nigeria: A Critical Source Book.* Lagos: Nigeria Magazine Special Publication, 1981. Contains an important collection of background documents.

Olney, James. "Wole Soyinka's Portait of the Artist as a Very Young Man." *Southern Review* 23 (1987): 527–540. Olney's article on *Ake* is the centerpiece of an issue with a substantial section on Soyinka and poems by him.

Ricard, Alain. *Theatre et nationalisme: Wole Soyinka et Leroi Jones.* Paris: Presence Africaine, 1972. Published in English by the U of Ife P, 1983. Draws interesting comparisons between the two playwrights.

—JAMES GIBBS

Timothy Mo

With just three novels so far, Timothy Mo already has established himself as one of the prominent writers in international English literature. He has won several literary awards. Two of his novels, *Sour Sweet* and *An Insular Possession* were shortlisted for the Booker Prize, Britain's most prestigious literary award. *Sour Sweet* was also shortlisted for the Whitbread Prize in 1982 and won the Hawthornden Prize that year. His first novel, *The Monkey King,* was awarded the Geoffrey Faber Memorial Prize in 1979.

Mo, the son of an English mother and a Cantonese father, was born in 1950, in Hong Kong, where he was raised and educated until the age of ten. Many of his experiences in Hong Kong, such as anticipating typhoons, swimming in Repulse Bay, and traveling to the New Territories, have made their way into *The Monkey King.* Mo subsequently moved to Britain and later attended Oxford where he studied history, a discipline that manifests itself in his historical novel, *An Insular Possession.* On graduation, he worked as a reviewer for the *Times Educational Supplement* and the *New Statesman* and as a part-time journalist for the *Boxing News.* Mo himself is a former bantamweight boxer, a pursuit that in *Sour Sweet* informs his portrayal of Lily's early training in temple boxing. Mo now resides in London but returns regularly to Hong Kong. He made an extended research trip to China while working on *An Insular Possession,* on which he spent five years.

The serio-comic style of his portrait of traditional Chinese families in *The Monkey King* and *Sour Sweet* has evoked comparison of these novels with V.S. Naipaul's early works and *A House for Mr. Biswas.* Mo is flattered by the comparison with Naipaul, one of the novelists, including Doris Lessing and Thomas Mann, whom he admires.

THE INTERSTICES AND OVERLAPS OF CULTURES

Like many writers with colonial backgrounds, Timothy Mo, who is of English and Cantonese parentage, is fascinated by the amorphous world that exists at the meeting point of different cultures, which, in his case, are those of China and Britain. He has made this his fictional world. His first two novels are scintillating portraits of individuals caught between two traditions. In *The Monkey King*, Chinese youths struggle to reconcile Western and Chinese values. *Sour Sweet* is about Chinese immigrants in Britain who cope with problems of assimilation. In both novels, Mo's deft comic touch is evident, though in *Sour Sweet* it is tempered by the author's consciousness of the pain as well as the humor in the immigrants' emotional and social adjustment to their new environment. Though Mo is capable of telling irony, he never dismisses or mocks these inhabitants of the interstices and overlaps of different cultures. *An Insular Possession* marks a break from the early novels in form and conception. Unlike *The Monkey King* and *Sour Sweet*, which employ the traditional nineteenth-century narrative form, this novel is postmodernist in structure. It has a historical theme—the founding of British Hong Kong—and focuses not so much on individuals as on historical forces and developments. Nevertheless, in its depiction of the encounter of the British and Chinese on the early nineteenth-century South China coast and in its attempt to integrate Western and Chinese conceptions of the novel form, the work evinces Mo's abiding interest in the interaction of cultures.

The Monkey King, set in Hong Kong of the 1950s, presents a portrait of Wallace Nolasco, a youth of Cantonese and Portuguese descent, who tries to come to grips with the often antithetical values and customs of his dual heritage. Schooled in Western values by his father, he is initially critical of Chinese society, but at the end of the novel he succeeds in reconciling himself to his two cultures, adopting the virtues of the one to temper the shortcomings of the other. His cultural and ethical enlightenment parallels his maturation as a family man and a man of affairs. He evolves from an immature youth, dependent on his in-laws, into a responsible adult, respected by his family and community. Mo's novel then is a study of both the complex culture of a particular group of people caught between two worlds and the maturation of an individual in such a society.

The narrative through which Mo explores these ideas is a traditional one: The exile returns home a wiser and better person. The novel begins with Wallace's arranged marriage to May Ling, the daughter of Mr. Poon, a rich but miserly, tyrannical Hong Kong merchant, who expects his son-in-law to join the other members of the extended Poon family in submitting to his authority. The Westernized Wallace, skeptical of this traditional family hierarchy, is unwilling to do so, though he finds that he must temporize with his father-in-law because of his financial dependence on him. Forced to flee Hong Kong because of his illegal use of government documents at Mr. Poon's instigation, Wallace escapes with his wife to a remote village in the New Territories, where he is exposed to traditional Chinese ways of life. He develops into a resourceful individual, whose knowledge of both Chinese and Western practices enables him to become a leader in the village. The novel concludes with his returning to take charge of the family's business and domestic affairs on the death of Mr. Poon.

Mo quickly establishes in the opening paragraphs the duality of Macao society, Wallace's home before his marriage. Like his father, also of Portuguese and Chinese ancestry, Wallace perceives himself as Portuguese and denies his Chinese ancestry. But he finds it impossible to suppress one half of his psyche and identify himself uniculturally. As a child he is conscious of the lines of demarcation between the Portuguese and the Chinese that negate intimate dealings with each other. Yet he recognizes that both groups are colonials and have a common bond as "prisoners together in a long chain-gang" (3). He himself speaks impeccable Cantonese yet affects not to understand it, dismissing it as a vulgar dialect. He shares his father's snobbishness towards the Chinese though he is reluctant to accept his uncritical admiration of the British. His father prominently displays in his home a photograph of Victorian English soldiers standing imperiously with the severed heads of Chinese pirates at their feet. Wallace has to refrain from tauntingly reminding him of the Japanese domination of the British during the Occupation.

In relating Wallace's initial experiences with the Poon family, Mo emphasizes the power Mr. Poon wields over every member of his extended family. Bound by tradition and economically dependent on him, they all heed his dictates. Through Wallace's irreverent and skeptical comments—which contribute immensely to the humorous tone of the novel—Mo censures the Chinese patriarchs' abuse of their position in the traditional family structure. However, Mo suggests recurrently that there are many parallels between Chinese and Western societies and that one is not necessarily better than the other. Wallace's father acknowledges this commonness in an injunction to his son: "Understand the English," he advises him, "and you will understand the Chinese, too" (3). And though his father appears not to be conscious of it, Wallace is alert to the common brutality of both peoples implicit in the painting of the English soldiers and the Chinese pirates. Mo's dramatic account of Mr. Poon's physical abuse of his adult son with a golf club anticipates the incident in the Tiger Balm Gardens where the Englishman, Mr. Allardyce, beats with a stick some Chinese children who are provoking a caged monkey—a parallel that points up the similarity between Mr. Poon's tyranny and European imperialism.

Mo's depiction of Wallace's early married life questions the structure of the extended family that works against husbands and wives developing as nuclear units. Wallace is frustrated by the lack of any exclusivity in his relationship with his wife. In the Poon household, his filial relationship with Mr. Poon, however tenuous, is expected to take precedence over his marital ties with May Ling. Wallace resists this traditional priority, unlike Ah Lung, Mr. Poon's son, whose submission to his father ruins his relationship with his wife and sons. May Ling and Wallace's exile in the New Territories, away from Mr. Poon, allows both to develop their individuality and at the same time draws them closer together as husband and wife.

Mo clearly acknowledges the shortcomings of the Chinese family structure, particularly its frustration of any bonding between husband and wife, but he is heedful of the redeeming virtues of the extended family. He is aware, like Wallace, that it provides security and support for the individual when it is informed by tolerance and concern rather than by domination and tyranny. Despite their happy stay in their village retreat, both Wallace and May Ling yearn to return to the family fold. Wallace realizes "with awe" that he is "homesick . . . for the Poons!" (168). Mo sanctions the merits of the extended family by ending the novel with Wallace, secure in his relationship with his wife, returning to take charge of the Poon family on the death of Mr. Poon. Wallace distances himself from Mr. Poon's harsh dictatorial patriarchy. The members of the family are happy to have him succeed Mr. Poon. For his part, Wallace discourages their "deference" to him, which he views as "a burden" (214). He urges his relatives to think for themselves, reiterating his comments to his nephews when he first arrived at the Poon mansion that they should develop initiative and always ask the "reason for doing anything, like we Portuguese boys did" (70). He advises them to become like the Monkey King of Chinese legends, which, though its master tries to deprive it of its independence by encircling its head with an iron band, manages through ingenuity, courage, and a degree of mischief to thwart its master. That Wallace's era will be different from Mr. Poon's is affirmed in the concluding chapters by traditional images of rebirth—the New Year, spring, and dawn—and by the birth of Wallace's son. The final incident of the novel is Wallace's nightmare about his having to eat at a traditional dinner ceremony the brain of a live monkey. The images of rebirth remain dominant in the last chapter, but in introducing this nightmare in the final paragraph, the novelist concludes with a warning that Wallace must guard against reverting to the worst aspects of tradition.

One of the metaphors Mo uses to describe the transition in the Poon household from Mr. Poon's to Wallace's stewardship is that of "evolving" (214). He likewise presents Wallace's reconciliation with his dual heritage in terms of a metamorphosis. Before his exile, Wallace urges May Ling to adopt the Western style of their friend Mabel Yip. Like Pippy DaSilva, a Chinese girl who yearns to make England her home, and Major, a Chinese youth who perceives himself as British, Mabel is simply a mimic of Western ways. Mo employs her as a foil to both May Ling, who is reluctant to associate with her, and Wallace, who, though himself a devotee of Western culture, comes to acknowledge the important to his psyche of his Chinese ancestry. Mo conveys effectively Wallace's receptiveness to his Chinese culture in the incident that tells of Wallace's unintentionally descecrating an ancestral burial ground and, persuaded by May Ling, symbolically offering as an act of atonement his Western watch. This incident occurs just after they take up residence in the New Territories, and it marks the beginning of Wallace's involvement with activities in the traditional village, where he adopts and modifies Western practices to cope with such natural and human problems as typhoons and village rivalries.

Mo employs a traditional chronological structure and linear narrative in this first novel. His unfamiliar setting, which he presents convincingly from within, is enough to impart freshness to the novel without the aid of experimental and innovative forms or techniques, which he attempts later in *An Insular Possession.* In his portrayal of the meeting point of Chinese and Western culture in Hong Kong, Mo provides rich details of everyday life and customs. But these are not intended as exotic or decorative. In a work where the protagonist struggles to establish himself as an individual untrammelled by constricting customs, such customs by necessity have to be evoked vividly and immediately. Many of the particulars of Chinese traditions, such as the legend of the Monkey King, the dinner rituals, or burial practices, function symbolically and integrally.

The novel has a pervasive comic tone, but it is seldom if ever sardonic. In fact, many scenes—especially those based on cultural misunderstandings—lean towards farce rather than satire. Mo's humor enables him to achieve a necessary measure of esthetic distancing and detachment as he sympathetically writes from within the lives of individuals who struggle to accommodate themselves to their antithetical cultures.

Sour Sweet is an even more complex study of such individuals. With the very first sentence, Mo situates the novel at the conjunction of cultures: "The Chens had been living in the UK for four years, which was long enough to have lost their place in the society from which they had emigrated but not long enough to feel comfortable

TIMOTHY MO

in the new" (1). In Wallace's struggle to reconcile himself to his two cultures, he is sustained by an environment that—however influenced by the West—is still predominantly Chinese. On the other hand, the Chens, who live in what they perceive as an alien society, lack such cultural support and are subject to intense conflict within and among themselves. Mo suggests in *Sour Sweet* that for the Chens and other tradition-minded Chinese immigrants to the West, there are three possible ways of coping with the duality of their world: They could adhere adamantly to their ancestral way of life that sets them apart from their new society; they could abandon traditions and assimilate into the new culture; or they could try to reconcile the two cultures—the most challenging of the three options which can be realized, as Lily says, only by "*yin* cancelling *yang*" (278), that is, by finding the point of "equilibrium" between the two cultures.

In *Sour Sweet*, Mo examines these possibilities in a paradigmatic form. The three prominent members of the Chen household represent the three ways of coping with the alien culture: Lily, the protagonist of the novel, tries to achieve a cultural equilibrium; her husband, Chen, adheres inflexibly to tradition; and Mui, Lily's sister, readily assimilates Western culture. It is not until the end of the novel that Lily comes to see the merits of a reconciliatory position. In the rest of the novel, she is as tradition bound—though not as inflexible—as her husband, and Mo portrays her as a foil to Mui. Both sisters are involved in a significant struggle to influence the growth of Chen and Lily's son, Man Kee, who evidently represents the future of the Chinese immigrants in the West.

Chen regards himself in Britain as an "interloper" and "gatecrasher" (1) and makes no attempt to understand his new society. He is hobbled by tradition even in his relation with his wife, with whom he develops no intimacy. Unlike Wallace, who comes to welcome May Ling's initiatives, he is disquieted by his wife's resourcefulness and determination. He would like her to conform to the traditional role of the passive wife. Even her face, he concludes, has "too much character" (16), which is not consonant with his Cantonese idea of female beauty, but which, he discovers, "Westerners . . . found attractive, though" (17). Comparing him with his son, the narrator observes that "Man Kee, happy child, was getting a fresh start. He had no history, no heritage to live up to, no goal to fulfill, no ancient burden to carry" (111). Chen's brief involvement with the Triad, the Chinese secret criminal organization, is allegorically significant to the theme of cultural alienation. The members of the Triad, who, steeped in tradition, see themselves as representatives of "the old and true way, a way which has all but vanished" (71), relentlessly hunt down Chen, whom they wrongly believe has misappropriated packages of their illegal drugs and eventually murder him—a death that is perhaps more significant allegorically than literally.

The allegorical implication of Chen's death is stronger at the end of the novel. Just as the members of the Triad, the self-proclaimed enforcers of Chinese traditional life, haunted Chen when he was alive, they relentlessly intrude on Lily's life through the money they remit to her anonymously each month with clockwork regularity to compensate for their error in killing Chen. Lily, unaware that Chen has been murdered, believes that the money comes from Chen, though she cannot fathom why he has left her. The mysterious remittance never lets her forget her husband.

It evidently parallels her sense of tradition that remains lodged in her psyche constantly tugging at her no matter how much she tries to adapt to life in the West. Her decision at the end of the novel to maintain an equilibrium between the two cultures is a major step for someone who from birth was brought up in a strictly traditional way by her father. Wanting a son, he brought her up as a boy, exposing her to the severe training of traditional temple boxing and expecting her to be aggressive and defiant. Mui, her sister four years her senior, conversely was brought up as a girl to be "uncomplaining, compliant, dutiful . . . submissive" (10).

Despite her passive upbringing, however, Mui does not unthinkingly gravitate towards assimilation of her new culture. Mo does not portray her simply as a mimic, like Mabel Yip, Pippy DaSilva, and Major of *The Monkey King*, who ape Western habits. When Mui comes to Britain to assist the Chens after the birth of Man Kee, she is intimidated at first by her alien environment and seldom ventures outside their home. She spends hours before the television set, which provides her with a form of escapism but also teaches her about British life. She undergoes a dramatic change and begins to adapt to her new environment much faster than Lily right after the incident in which she breaks Man Kee's fall from a window ledge, saving him from possible death. Lily observes that "from this point on she seemed to grow in confidence" (18). Mo's emphasis on this incident as the turning point in Mui's behavior points up the allegorical dimension of the novel. From here on, the sisters' contrasting responses to their environment are recurringly indicated and clearly underscored in the roles they play in Man Kee's upbringing.

Lily believes that the British education Man Kee receives will turn him into a "foreign devil boy" (236), and initially she and Chen consider sending him to be educated in Hong Kong to imbue him "with correct Chinese qualities, veneration for parents, for instance" (167). Realizing the impracticality of this plan, however, she decides to counter his British education by sending him to supplementary Chinese classes. Mui believes that these classes will complicate his young life and have a negative effect on his ability to adjust to his new environment. Lily dismisses Mui's view as eccentric but she admits that Mui "has his best interest at heart" (236). When Man Kee is assaulted by a school bully, Mui and Lily are at odds as well over Lily's decision to pass on to him the training in temple boxing she received from her father. Mui feels that this would only make him aggressive and work against him in school. She accuses Lily of teaching the boy "wicked things" and of "foolish interference" (234) in Man Kee's formal education. She encourages him instead to be receptive to British manners and customs, which she herself is assimilating. She urges Lily and Chen to be similarly receptive and not to garrison themselves against an imagined enemy. She befriends such Chinese as Mrs. Law, who "started a new life in England at the age of fifty-five" (43) and later marries an assimilationist Chinese—after an unfortunate but significant affair with an unidentified lover of "Western ancestry" (275) that produced an illegitimate child. This child and Man Kee, Mo suggests, represent the new generation of Chinese immigrants who will be more amenable to reconciling themselves to their environment. He concludes the novel with Lily's preoccupation with Man Kee's future and her reluctant admission that she cannot keep him away from Mui. Once resentful of Mui's "seriously distorted values" (203) and dismissive of her as "having lost her bearings" (276), she recognizes that Man Kee must be exposed to Mui and her husband to save him from "growing up in an unbalanced home" (277).

The paradigmatic and allegorical structure of *Sour Sweet* notwithstanding, the novel is a remarkably realistic and vivid re-creation of life in the Chinese immigrant community. Mo captures the odors, sights, and sounds of the various environments, enriching his work with details of the daily activities of cooking, gardening, commuting, socializing, and working, and with evocation of the immigrants' fears, joys, biases, and aspirations. In Lily, he creates a memorable female character, who, husbandless at the end of the novel, stands with spirit unbroken ready to cope with her new world. Mo's detailed recounting of the activities and conversations of the Triad members has a documentary exactness, which anticipates the numerous newspaper reports that comprise a major portion of *An Insular Possession*. He acknowledges as sources for his chapters on the Triad such sociological studies as Gustave Schlegel's *Thian Thi Hui, the Hung League* (1866) and W.P. Morgan's *Triad Societies in Hong Kong* (1960). In the first two-thirds of the novel, Mo alternates chapters on the Triad and on the Chen family—a structural device that, besides creating narrative suspense over Chen's fate, points up the intrusive nature of inexorable traditions on the lives of the protagonists. As Lily becomes less possessed by traditions, Mo foregrounds her experiences, no longer alternating chapters on her family and on the Triad.

Mo treats both Lily and Mui sympathetically without sanctioning the one's interaction with the new culture over the other's. He suggests that the individual psyche, which is "the product of upbringing rather than of any innate traits of personality" (10), dictates the path to be taken. For Mui, who unlike Lily escapes her father's rigid adherence to ancestral ways, assimilation comes fairly easily. Lily reluctantly agrees to reshape her world but on her own terms, which categorically excludes abandoning her heritage. Chen's blind allegiance to tradition is clearly not sanctioned. It leads to destruction, as Mo indicates by his unattractive portrayal of the members of the Triad as criminals who declare themselves as the upholders of tradition. Mo's emphasis on the long shadow cast by the Triad on the protagonists' lives, together with his moving account of their impoverished lives, inner tensions, and family conflicts, renders this novel—despite its humorous scenes occasioned by cultural faux pas and misunderstanding—a more serious and complex exploration of individuals encumbered with cultural duality than *The Monkey King*.

In *An Insular Possession*, Mo returns to Hong Kong and its vicinity, but it is now Hong Kong of the early nineteenth century. In this vast, expansive, epic novel, he relates the circumstances that led to the founding of British Hong Kong at the end of the First Opium War. Once again, Mo is absorbed with the clash of Western— particularly British—and Chinese cultures. The complexity of the conjunction of cultures is emphasized in the very opening of the novel, where, describing the Pearl River, in whose estuary lies Hong Kong, Mo observes: "The river succours and impedes native and foreigner alike: it limits and it enables, it isolates and it joins" (1). In exploring this meeting of cultures on the South China coast, Mo focuses not so much on personal, individual experiences, as in his early novels, but on the collective and the historical. Whatever individual portraits he sketches are of public figures, which—like his use of the present tense throughout—serves but to authenticate and render immediate the historical realities. The individuals, though rendered alive and engaging, are subservient to the historical theme. In this regard the novel can be compared with such historically based novels as, say *War and Peace*, where the unfolding history provides a backdrop that heightens the protagonists' experiences.

The First Opium War was fought between the British and the Chinese over the British importation of opium into China, which was prohibited by Chinese law. Britain, because of a trade imbalance with China created by the increasing market in Europe for Chinese tea and silk, decided to rectify this by deliberately promoting the consumption of opium in China, which they supplied the Chinese from the British East India Company's fields in India. At the beginning of the war, the British, using two gunboats, powered by innovative steam engines and armed with new Congreve rockets, destroyed a Chinese fleet of twenty-nine outdated sailing ships— a victory that set the course of the war, which ended with the Chinese allowing European traders in the South China ports and ceding Hong Kong island to the British.

Mo uses numerous points of view, voices, and forms that impart a sense of authenticity and inclusiveness to his historical study. A scholarly narrative voice provides historical commentaries with the ring of academic essays. An example is the long treatise on the similarity between the West Indian triangular trade in slaves, sugar, and metal items and the East Indian triangular trade in teas, opium, and woven clothing. "Both," the narrator comments, "are of an extraordinary, a classic simplicity, Cartesian almost in their ruthlessness and clarity" (22). At one point, adopting the eighteenth-century novelistic style, the narrator intrudes to provide a transition to his essay on the history and geography of Macao: "How different are Canton and Macao (to which our story and heroes now pass)" (48).

Mo complements the historian-narrator's voice by including a variety of fictional documents, simulating the primary sources commonly consulted by historians. There is quite a large number of these documents—some loosely based on actual ones—such as newspaper reports, correspondence, official records, court transcripts, diaries, journals, and memoirs, which together constitute more than half the novel. The most frequently used sources are the reports, essays, and commentaries— written in a sonorous Victorian style—in the two rival newspapers, the *Canton Monitor*, the conservative organ of the European traders, and *The Lin Tin Bulletin and River Bee*, founded by two young Americans who vehemently opposed the opium trade. The contents of these two newspapers not only advance the historical narrative, they serve primarily to raise and examine the issues related to the opium trade and to create a feel of time and place. The lines are clearly drawn between the newspapers: While one attacks the emperor's "arbitrary, excessive, and irrational" (29) levies and trade restrictions, the other reprimands the British missionaries who "*go up the coast in opium-clippers and distribute Bibles with the drug!*" (248); while one considers the Chinese expendable, the other sympathizes with their lot; while one features formal portraits of officers and merchants, the other offers moving sketches of the impoverished, who are "*regarded but never seen*" (305).

Mo further explores the historical theme through the consciousness of two young Americans, Gideon Chase and Walter Eastman, who work initially for an American trading company in the European community of Canton but later found *The Lin Tin*

Bulletin and River Bee to crusade against the immoral opium trade and the British involvement in the First Opium War. The two, as idealistic youths and as Americans with no vested interest in the opium trade, straddle the Western and Chinese worlds and function as interpreters and intermediaries between the two societies. Chase, who significantly becomes versed in Chinese, is the translator for the Chinese and the British. Mo imparts an individuality and distinctiveness to the two: Eastman, who develops an interest in the innovative daguerreotype, is witty and temperamental; Chase, a writer and scholar, is high minded and considerate. Mo's interest in them, however, is less in their personal development than in their ideas and observations on the players in the opium trade and in their value as eyewitnesses to the historical occurrences and the daily life of that period. In addition to their newspaper reports and commentaries, the two, as men of ideas, are constantly discussing between themselves and with others the issues of the day. Both are present at many of the major incidents and battles. Both provide details of the social activities of the European expatriates—such as boating parties, attendance at operas, and visits to brothels—and the daily life of the Chinese. Eastman, for instance, sketches graphically the death of a Chinese bitten by a cobra—an activity Chase describes as "a ghoul's work" (139). Such eyewitness accounts are an additional primary source for the historian and supplement the information provided in the numerous documents that constitute the major portion of the novel.

As important as Mo's historical account of the circumstances that led to the establishment of British Hong Kong is his sustained examination throughout the novel of the different ways the artist gives shape to experience. Mo explicitly examines the relative merits of various antithetical approaches, forms, and techniques that he himself employs in his attempt to come to grips with the historical realities of which he writes. He counters the scientific and representational with the imaginative and impressionistic, the statistical with the imagist, the conversational with the formal, the expository with the narrative, the personal with the official. A recurring discussion between Eastman and a fellow artist concerns the impressionistic and the representational functions respectively of painting and the early form of photography, the daguerreotype, the exact nature of which Mo provides an extended explanation, as he does of many other technical processes including those of the Congreve rocket, heliogravure, and steam engines.

The most significant antithetical pairing of the various modes of shaping reality relates to the difference between the Chinese and the Western perceptions of the novel. In an essay on Chinese literary modes published in *The Lin Tin Bulletin and River Bee*, the anonymous writer, who is most likely Chase, points out that the Western novel addresses the experiences of the individual as hero or heroine while Chinese prose romances—the equivalent of Western novels—relate the life of the group, particularly the family, of which "the individual personages are mere parts of the whole, with no intrinsic importance in themselves" (318). In his portrayal of Chase, Eastman, and their friends and antagonists, Mo adheres to this injunction, rendering the study of the individual secondary to that of the nations and peoples involved.

There is yet another crucial difference between the two novel forms: While the Western novel tends to be "*linear,*" proceeding, even though it may ramble, "along a course of cause and effects, each contributing to the movement as a whole," the Chinese prose romance is "*circular*," made up of separate episodes joined by "the loosest of threads"; it stresses "incident, character, and language" rather than narrative progression and contains "long passages or extracts of poetry, fable, song, and essays, lists of goods, recipes, formulas for patent medicines, and even spells" that are introduced and "exist *for their own sake*!" The difference between the two narrative structures is underscored by metaphors: One is "a river . . . pushing to the sea," the other is "a still lake" (316). Mo evidently combines both structures in *An Insular Possession*, which created difficulties for some reviewers who complained about the static quality of the novel (Lee 24; Scott 25).

Combining these two structures posed the problem of closure for Mo. In the last chapter, as Chase and Eastman discuss their future and that of their crusading newspaper after the British triumph over the Chinese, Eastman observes that there is "no blank end, only . . . the succession of moments leading on to something else," and he accuses Chase of belonging to the category of individuals who "will have things in the round" and "love an end, causes, the balance sheet drawn and equalled" (575). Mo manages to end and not end his novel by including two appendices, "A Gazetteer of Place Names and Biographies Relative to the Early China Coast" and an extract from Chase's unfinished and unpublished autobiography, both fictional documents. Though the novel ends with Chase abandoning his newspaper and conceding defeat in his fight against the opium trade, the appendices reopen the narrative, indicating that Chase goes on to become a distinguished academic in Chinese studies and implying that Britain eventually renounces the opium trade.

Mo's novel is not a polemic against imperialism or Westerners. He is capable of wilting irony against exploiters, but he finds them on both sides of the conflict. As an old Chinese saying, quoted by Chase, states: "The PEOPLE fear the mandarins; the MANDARINS fear the foreigners; the FOREIGNERS fear the PEOPLE" (257). Mo lets Chase observe that under "the different veneers of varying laws, institutions, and civilizations . . . the Old Adam is the same. His nature contains the same admixture of bad and good . . . whether . . . subsumed under an integument which is yellow, black, red, white, coffee, or any combination of known fleshly tints" (257). Such a belief in the commonness of all peoples underlies Mo's balanced account of those involved in the clash of cultures in *An Insular Possession* as well as his sympathetic portrayal of individuals like Wallace of *The Monkey King* and Lily and Mui of *Sour Sweet*, who find themselves in the interstices and overlaps of cultures.

WORKS CITED

Gorra, Michael. Rev. of *Sour Sweet*. *Hudson Review* 38 (1986): 670-72.

Larson, Charles R. Rev. of *The Monkey King*. *World Literature Today* 53 (1979): 626.

Lee, Hermione. "Saga of the Opium Wars." Rev. of *An Insular Possession*. *The Observer* 11 May 1986: 24.

Lewis, Peter. "Hong Kong London." Rev. of *Sour Sweet*. *Times Literary Supplement* 7 May 1982: 502.

Mo, Timothy. *An Insular Possession*. London: Chatto & Windus, 1986.

———. *The Monkey King*. London: Abacus, 1984.

———. *Sour Sweet*. London: Abacus, 1983.

Scott, Rivers. "Eastern Eye." Rev. of *An Insular Possession*. *The Listener* 8 May 1986: 25.

Timothy Mo's Published Work

The Monkey King, 1978
Sour Sweet, 1982
An Insular Possession, 1986

Selected Critical Readings

Very little critical material exists on Timothy Mo's work. So far only two journal articles by the same author, one on *The Monkey King,* the other on *Sour Sweet,* have been published. However, there are numerous reviews of his books in some of the most prestigious journals and newspapers on both sides of the Atlantic. Many of them are substantial reviews, and they are in the main favorable. Several consider Mo to be a major talent and have compared him with V.S. Naipaul and Salman Rushdie. *An Insular Possession* in particular has been widely reviewed and has earned high praise. Mo has mentioned that he has supplemented his personal knowledge of Chinese society with such sociological and anthropological studies as H.D.R. Baker's *A Chinese Lineage Village,* James L. Watson's *Emigration and the Chinese Lineage,* and William Stanton's *The Triad Society*—interesting avenues to investigate. Given Mo's impressive achievement in all three novels, it should not be long before they attract substantial critical attention.

Articles

Rothfork, John. "Confucianism in Timothy Mo's *The Monkey King.*" *Tamkang Review* 18 (1987–88): 403–21. Perceives *The Monkey King* as a fictional critique of neo-Confucian ethics particularly its sanctioning of authoritarianism, which frustrates creativity and initiative, as Wallace struggles with Mr. Poon, the embodiment of these destructive values.

———. "Confucianism in Timothy Mo's *Sour Sweet.*" *Journal of Commonwealth Literature* 24.1 (1989): 49–64. Examines *Sour Sweet* as a study of the Confucian state of *Tao,* in which the individual acquires a whole, integrated personality by balancing antithetical forces; sees Lily at the end of the novel as on the road to achieving *Tao.*

Reviews

The Monkey King
Larson, Charles R. *World Literature Today* 53 (1979): 626.

Sour Sweet
Gorra, Michael. *Hudson Review* 38 (1986): 670-72.
Lewis, Peter. *Times Literary Supplement* 7 May 1982: 502.
Yardley, Jonathan. *Washington Post* 31 Mar. 1985: 3, 8.

An Insular Possession
Buruma, Ian. *New Republic* 11 May 1987: 39-41.
Enright, D.J. *Times Literary Supplement* 9 May 1986: 498.
Lee, Hermione. *The Observer* 11 May 1986: 24.
Martin, Brian. *The Spectator* 10 May 1986: 36-37.
Scott, Rivers. *The Listener* 8 May 1986: 25.
Wilce, Gillian. *New Statesman* 9 May 1986: 27.
Winks, Robin W. *New York Times Book Review* 19 April 1987: 2.

—Victor J. Ramraj

Bharati Mukherjee

Bharati Mukherjee was born on 27 July 1940 in Ballyunge, a middle-class neighborhood of Calcutta, India. Her parents were Bengali Brahmins. The second of three girls, Mukherjee lived the first eight years of her life in a typical joint family of between 40-45 members, comprising aunts, uncles, cousins, and servants, all under one roof, and attended an Anglicized Bengali school in the area.

Her father, Sudhir Lal, was a chemist who owned a pharmaceutical company in partnership with a Jewish immigrant from the Middle East. He left the business shortly after her eighth birthday and took his family to England and Switzerland where he worked on his research projects and sent his children to schools there. On their return to Calcutta after three years abroad, they moved to "fashionable Chowringhee," and Mukherjee was enrolled in Loreto House, an elite school for girls run by Irish nuns who followed a heavily British and European curriculum. As a result, Mukherjee lived an Anglicized life in school and a Bengali one at home.

After receiving a bachelor's degree from the University of Calcutta, and a master's degree from the University of Baroda, Mukherjee left India in 1961 on a scholarship to the University of Iowa Writers' Workshop. There, she met American-born Canadian author, Clark Blaise, and married him during a lunch break two years later. After obtaining her MFA in creative writing at Iowa, she then completed a doctorate in English and comparative literature there.

Before settling in Canada in 1966 with Blaise and their two sons, and taking Canadian citizenship, Mukherjee taught English at Marquette University in Milwaukee and the University of Wisconsin at Madison. In Canada, Mukherjee and Blaise held three or four jobs a year in order to support themselves and their family, writing during weekends and in the small hours of the night. According to Mukherjee, she was brought up "spectacularly rich—in the Third World sense" but has been "spectacularly poor" almost all her adult life.

In 1981, Mukherjee moved to the United States with her family and has lived there since, becoming an American citizen. She has taught creative writing at Columbia University, New York University, Queens College, and the University of California, Berkeley.

She remembers always having wanted to be a writer and writing her first novel, never finished, at age eight. In her writing, she has been sustained by the momentum of a work-in-progress: "There's not a single moment when I'm not thinking stories in my head. Sometimes endings will come to me in dreams." Mukherjee's fiction is gaining increasing recognition from critics, reviewers, and the public. Her short story, "Isolated Incidents," won first prize in 1980 from the Periodical Distribution

Association; another, "The World According to Hsu," has also won a Canadian journalism award. *The Middleman and Other Stories* received the U.S. 1988 National Book Critics Circle Award in Fiction.

EXPATRIATES AND IMMIGRANTS, DISPLACEMENT AND AMERICANIZATION

In an era where air travel has made the distant close, the remote accessible, and rich and poor mobile, the migration of an underclass to more privileged countries is a commonplace. Individual movements across national and ethnic boundaries, and the consequences borne by their participants, comprise the core of Bharati Mukherjee's stories. With few exceptions, the motley, restive group of refugees, emigrants, fugitives, mercenaries, professionals, and others populate the territories explored by three novels and two collections of short stories. Without exception, the international and contemporaneous perspectives of her work are readily perceived.

Her characters are moving, about to move, recently moved or already moved. Mostly immigrants who seek a better life in the United States and Canada or would-be emigrants dreaming of futures in the West from homes in less developed Asian countries, their odysseys, together with their physical and emotional passion for survival in alien quarters, are the stuff of Mukherjee's narratives. She scours the complex multicultural worlds of her foreigners, the new North Americans, to portray their displacement and adaptation, those of whom she speaks in her article on immigrant writing: "They have all shed past lives and languages, and have traveled half the world in every direction to come here and begin again" ("Immigrant Writing" 28). Mukherjee's immigrants may be divided into those whose experience of the discontinuities of displacement are such that they either cannot re-place their reality or develop a tragically misplaced one and those, who in their determination to see America as their home, exuberantly will themselves to become Americans over and above their original nationalities.

Mukherjee distinguishes between "the aloofness of expatriation" and the "exuberance of immigration" (Introd. to *Darkness* 3); in the former, the newcomer resists adaptation and assimilation into the host ethos, thus maintaining his own ethnicity, whereas the immigrant prefers to be influenced and adopted by his host country. A corresponding dichotomy operates on the aesthetic level, where the expatriate writer who is an exile is unwilling and unable to identify with the society in which he or she lives, and whose expatriation Mukherjee regards as "the great temptation, even the enemy, of the ex-colonial, once-third-world author." In the exuberant essay, "Immigrant Writing: Give Us Your Maximalists!," she writes that the exiled or expatriate writer's position can lead to isolation, for "the native society marches onward and perhaps downward; the exiled writer preserves her image of it in prose increasingly mannered and self-referential. . . . the deeply rooted exile can end up . . . talking only to herself and her biographer." Mukherjee believes that "Lacking a country, avoiding all the messiness of rebirth as an immigrant eventually harms the finest sensibility" (29).

Although her fiction has shown a discernible movement towards Americanization in style as well as in protagonists' acceptance of a country that invites them to make their own rules, free from the rigid and feudalistic traditions of their native past, Mukherjee's first work, *The Tiger's Daughter*, pursues an opposite direction with the return to India of Tara Lal Banerjee, twenty-two year old daughter of a wealthy and prominent Bengali Brahmin. Vassar-educated Tara has married an American and has been away from home for seven years. Although she has always regarded herself as an Indian, she discovers, more as outsider than native, the complex and confusing web of politics, poverty, privilege, and hierarchies of power and class in India through Calcutta, her hometown. Tara has dreamed for years of this return but now finds herself imbued with a certain "foreignness of spirit," attributable not only to her American domicile but also to her early education in Calcutta, at a private school run by Belgian nuns.

She feels alienated and irritated by the trivial and trivializing passions and attitudes of the well-heeled, mainly English-speaking Bengalis with whom she socializes in the Catelli-Continental Hotel, an enclave from the disorderly world outside. These westernized friends yet disapprove of a western husband; for one of her friends, being an American immigrant is inadequate compensation for the loss of class power and privilege as an Indian. Tara's state is comparable to, though not identical with, that of an expatriate who stands apart from the emotional and spiritual tenor of the country in which she resides—a country which was once her own. So dislocated by her homecoming is she that she comes to visualize her husband's face, not fully and whole, but in "bits and pieces in precise detail." The psychologiocal, social, and cultural displacement that she suffers makes her nervous and excitable; at a picnic, for instance, Tara becomes hysterical over a harmless water snake, expecting tragedy where there is none.

The aimlessness and diffuseness of her return are underpinned by the number of journeys—beginning with the train journey from Bombay to Calcutta, which criss-cross the novel—and are suggestive of a heroine in search of some knowledge or revelation that proves elusive. A new friend, Joyonto Roy Choudhury, takes her out to see the funeral pyres on the Ganges; friends organize a picnic in her honor; she visits the hill resort of Darjeeling, then the new township of Nayapur. During a tour of Choudhury's compound, where a squatter settlement has established itself, Tara is assaulted by a little girl in apparent jealousy over her sari. She realizes, however, that there was no single crisis she could point to later and say that she had then become a totally different person.

The "relentless anticlimaxes" Tara suffers also affect the tenor of *The Tiger's Daughter*, by giving it an anti-climactic feel, unlike Mulkherjee's subsequent, more focused and forceful work. Relatively plotless, episodic, and leisurely, the novel is chronologically structured to follow the processes of Tara's personal and emotional displacement and disenchantment, which are also bound up with the industrialist and politician, P.K. Tutunwala, whom Tara first meets on her train journey to Calcutta. It is at Nayapur, which Tara visits with her friends, that Tutunwala exploits what he perceives as her liberated status, the result of her American education and marriage to a "mleccha." He seduces her in his room, an act that makes a surprisingly passive Tara cynical about him, and to a certain extent, disillusioned about India.

Of her first novel, Mukherjee recalls: "I used the omnisicient point of view and plenty of irony. This was because my concept of language and notions of how a novel was constructed were based on British models" (Carb 619). Despite the narrative omniscience that allows the author complete accessibility to character and scene, Mukherjee's ironic strategy (an example of which is Tara's observation that from Calcutta, New York appears exotic in its violence, this being made before her remote, then close, encounters with Marxist-inspired Naxalite demonstrators) distances the heroine from audience; a certain authorial detachment is palpable. Further, uneven in pace and texture, *The Tiger's Daughter* lacks the assurance of style and incisiveness of voice that have become definitive of Mukherjee's work. In its portrayal of the experience of exile that marks the return of the native, ill at ease in his or her own country, it not only anticipates Mukherjee's own discovery of her "immigrant" self, after the year she spent in India in 1973 had forced her to view herself "more as an immigrant than an exile" (*Days and Nights* 284), but may also explain her fictive relocation after *The Tiger's Daughter* in other countries, especially North America.

Wife, Mukherjee's second novel, is also about displacement and alienation, for it reveals the psychological destructiveness of that condition in Dimple Dasgupta, immigrant to the New World, "A young Bengali wife who was sensitive enough to feel the pain, but not intelligent enough to make sense out of her situation and break out" (*Days and Nights* 268). Where *The Tiger's Daughter* shows a certain ambivalence by the protagonist towards both India and America, among Mukherjee's works, *Wife* takes the psychology and geography of displacement as far as possible in its terse pursuit of disaster. Unlike Tara's entrapment in Calcutta by a claustrophobic circle of family and friends, Dimple's predicament is bombardment by tensions between American culture and society and the traditional constraints surrounding an Indian wife, between a feminist desire to be assertive and independent and the Indian need to be submissive and self-effacing. No resolution emerges from the subversion exercised by the values, ideals of freedom, and individuality identified with America, and the cultural identity—Dimple's—that they undermine and unravel.

Already, Dimple feels that it is impossible to be modern and intelligent and still be heroic, that is, to be like Sita of the *Ramayana*, the model of wifely endurance and loyalty. She finds herself unable to opt for one or the other. Dimple's problems with adaptation lie far more deeply than the temporary culture shock diagnosed by a rather obtuse husband. As has been noted, "Even while in Calcutta, Dimple is an escapist and lost in her private world of fantasy" (Jain 16), like setting her heart on marrying a neurosurgeon, a most unrealistic goal for one who does not complete her university education, is no beauty, and comes from a respectable but not distinguished family. Dimple's more sensible parents select an engineer, Amit Basu, for their daughter instead.

A few months after marriage, the couple emigrate to the United States and stay with Jyoti and Meena Sen in Queens, where the Indian community has set up its little India. Dimple's confinement, in this crucial "settlement" period, to the Indian community in Queens does not facilitate adaptation to the host country. Neither does her husband's veto of her desire to work. Even as Jyoti advises her not to restrict herself to fellow Bengalis but also to befriend Punjabis, Gujaratis, and South Indians, all expatriates who could be united as Indians abroad, where they were often communal in India, Amit Basu forbids his wife to work for Vinnod Khanna, whom he distrusts, "as all Punjabis were lecherous, dirty and uncultured." Amit believes, "With so many Indians around and a television and a child [the Sen child], a woman shouldn't have any time to get crazy ideas" (69).

Ironically, it is through her addiction to American television that Dimple's "crazy ideas" are formed. Through it she acquires her understanding of American home life; through *Better Homes and Gardens* numerous recipes and romantic notions of American housekeeping. As a result of television, Dimple's ideas about America are tied to questions of love and death:

> . . . everything she saw on TV was about love; even murder and death were love gone awry. But all she read in the newspapers was about death, the scary, ugly kind of death, random and poorly timed. (73)

As television insidiously erodes an already warped sense of reality, Dimple finds increasing difficulty in distinguishing between what she has seen on television and what she has imagined; her husband, too, becomes indistinguishable from some of the men on television.

Dimple's resentment towards Amit sporadically erupts into little acts of rebellion as when she starts talking back or challenging him or in her growing awareness of sexuality. While Amit's schedule is determined by his job as a boiler maintenance engineer, no such pattern of routine is imposed upon Dimple. When the Basus move out of the Sens' apartment to look after the Mookerjis' apartment during their sabbatical, Dimple's sense of relief at being on her own is not accompanied by any constructive organization of free time. Unwilling to brave the world outside, yet bored, frustrated, and ignorant of actual patterns of social intercourse in America, she retreats into an entropic state of inertia, exhaustion, and endless indecisiveness. Her sudden forays into the world beyond the apartment—dressed in Marsha Mookerji's clothes, trying to resolve her displacement through the assumption of another's personality—prove abortive. Trying another "American" way, Dimple has an affair with Milt Glasser, Marsha's brother, but continues to weave fantasies of sex and death in her imaginary life.

As Dimple's frustration deepens with paranoia about burglars and monsters on the prowl, she is filled on occasion with "an insane desire to hurt," once even lunging at Amit with a paring knife, thinking him an intruder. The predisposition towards violence has already been demonstrated in India with her vicious killing of a mouse and her self-induced abortion by skipping rope in the bathroom to discontinue a pregnancy that would have "cluttered up the preparation for going abroad." Her obsession in America with death is certain indication that all is not well; in the failure of adaptation, in the extent of displacement, she is the complete resident alien. The intimations of death, which come from her nightmares of decapitation and murder, contrast sharply with her earlier visions of the cozy homes inspired by *Better Homes and Gardens*, thinking that "In America, anything is possible. . . . You can be raped and killed on any floor" (129).

Thus in the final surreal sequence, Amit and Dimple are in bed, watching a discussion about suicide on the Johnny Carson show, when Dimple is transfixed by an episode in which a baby face in a birdcage is poked at until it turns into a "mangled bleeding mass," then wrapped in newspaper, from which silk scarves, rabbits and a wispy bra are extracted. Hallucination or reality? The incident makes no impression on Amit, Mukherjee's emphasis is on Dimple's consciousness and perception of reality. But this, and the succeeding scene, in which Amit's toe bleeds from a needle in the rug, are the prelude to the wife's murder of her husband, whom she stabs seven times, symbolically, in apparent repudiation of the Hindu marriage bond signified by the ritual seven steps taken by the newly married couple (Sivaramkrishna 81). As Amit's decapitated head "stayed upright on the counter top, still with its eyes averted from her face," Dimple's displacement comes to a tragic end (213).

Wife was succeeded by *Darkness* and *The Middleman and Other Stories*, two collections of short stories that, in their variety and resourcefulness, gritty optimism, and vernacular registers, prepared the way for Mukherjee's most recent work, *Jasmine*, where identity is defined by circumstance, its fluidity a requisite of survival. *Jasmine* bears out Mukherjee's earlier statement that "instead of seeing my Indianness as a fragile identity to be preserved against obliteration, . . . I see it now as a set of fluid identities to be celebrated" (Introd. *Darkness* 3). Instead of the alienation present in *The Tiger's Daughter* and *Wife*, *Jasmine* presents a protagonist whose first instinct is survival, realized through multiple identities in different places.

Arguably, had Dimple shown more *sense* about her situation, or remained within the Indian community at Queens, or had a more supportive husband, she would have suffered the usual culture shock instead of incapacitating estrangement. Whereas her attempts at wearing Marsha's clothes suggest the borrowing of an American identity, Jasmine Vijh is a mistress of identity change. She does not borrow; she becomes. She is also more American in temperament and spirit, more action-oriented than Dimple and Tara. Departing from these educated, city-bred Bengali women with upper-caste or middle-class backgrounds, Mukherjee chooses a feisty, resourceful, semi-educated Punjabi country girl to do battle with the rigors of immigrant experience; and she has used a narrative structure full of jagged time shifts to relate Jasmine's history.

Jasmine uses a first-person point of view, unlike the third-person narrative strategies of its predecessors. It is a measure of Mukherjee's confidence as an American writer, a process she traces to *Darkness* and her adoption of American English as her language, that whereas *Wife* skillfully reproduces the cadences and reveals the ironies of Indian-English speech, *Jasmine* revels in the American idiom. Jasmine discovers her flair for English at the village school in Hasnapur, where she was born. She grows up haunted by a prophecy from an astrologer that she would suffer the misfortune of widowhood on her wedding night.

A natural fighter and adapter, Jyoti (Light), as she is first called, escapes marriage at thirteen to a widower with three children but falls in love with the voice of Prakash Vijh before she sets eyes on him. Jyoti's love for him must be attributed in part to his knowledge of English, just as her ability to survive, if not thrive, in the English-speaking New World must be attributed in part to her linguistic allegiance converted into a prerequisite in a spouse. For Jasmine says: "I couldn't marry a man who didn't speak English, or at least one who didn't want to speak English. To want English was to want more than you had been given at birth, it was to want the world" (68).

In an attempt to "make me a new kind of city woman" (77), Prakesh renames his wife Jasmine. When he is killed by a bomb intended for Jasmine shortly before he is to leave for Florida as a foreign student, an avenging widow phantoms her way there, forged papers taking her through the Middle East, Hamburg, and Amsterdam before she arrives in Florida by boat under cover of darkness. Jasmine eventually makes her way to New York, where she finds "an archipelago seething with aliens" (140). For five months, she stays with Prakash's former teacher and his family, until the restrictions of an Indian household and the chaste behavior expected of a widow prove too much for her. "In this apartment of artificially maintained Indianness," she says, "I wanted to distance myself from everything Indian, everything Jyoti-like." Too young for widowhood, too intrigued "by the city and the land beyond the rivers," Jasmine chooses mainstream America (145).

The Americanization of Jasmine begins with her first job of looking after the daughter of Taylor and Wylie Hayes for two years. They become *her* family, and she strives to become the person they think she is: "humorous, intelligent, refined, affectionate. Not illegal, not murderer, not widowed, raped, destitute, fearful" (171). Her self-motivated transformation from alien to immigrant, a process accompanied by an increasing possession of her own desires and self-worth, differentiates her from the uncertainties of Tara and the insecurities of Dimple.

Unlike her Bengali predecessors, Jasmine is Punjabi-tough. On her first night in America, she finds herself murdering the captain of the boat, who has raped her, and escaping from the motel. While in the Hayes's employ, she accidentally comes across the murderer of her husband operating a hot dog stand in New York; to escape what she feels can be her fate, she flees—all the way to Iowa—where she meets Bud Ripplemeyer, the local banker and lives another life as his girlfriend and future wife, Jane.

Their life together is radically changed after Bud is crippled in a shooting incident, and Jane has to be a full-time nurse to him. Yet she decides to carry his child by getting herself pregnant artificially. Bravely putting up with her fate, she is also stifled by Bud's dependence on her until an opportunity for yet another life presents itself with the appearance of Taylor Hayes and his daughter at her doorstep. Taylor fell in love with Jasmine in New York and is now wifeless, Wylie having left him for another man. The still pregnant Jasmine decisively chooses "the promise of America" over "old-world dutifulness." It may be said in mitigation that Jane knows that Bud's former wife still cares for him and tells her that on the telephone before she embarks on another frontier journey to "re-position the stars" (240).

In *Jasmine*, the imaginative and fantastical fuse and the transformations bestowed upon the heroine are reminiscent of the reincarnations integral to Hindu cosmology: "I have had a husband for each of the women I have been. Prakash for Jasmine, Taylor for Jase, Bud for Jane. Half-Face for Kali" (197). Her multiple names (and rebirths)—Jyoti-Jasmine-Jassy-Jane-Jase—attest to her resilience. The novel's energetic shuttling between past and present, present and future, dramatizes not only the presence of the past (and the pastness of the present) but also the dynamic consciousness and individuality of the heroine as she blooms "from a diffident alien with forged documents into adventurous Jase" (186). Lifetimes of experience are crammed into relatively few years; Jasmine is put through the most gruelling confrontations with death (Prakash), murder (Half-Face), suicide (Darrel, her neighbor in Iowa); she is for a while, adoptive mother to Du, a Vietnamese refugee, and is expecting the child of a man whom she leaves for another. The picaresque, surrealistic, and no-holds-barred ethos of *Jasmine* more than occasionally strains reader credibility and recalls Mukherjee's resolution in her Epilogue to *Days and Nights in Calcutta*: "Even more than other writers, I must learn to astonish, to shock" (287). The voice of Jasmine, surprisingly articulate and assured, is not always believable, given her background and circumstances; it is her creator's voice that takes over and speaks for her, the result perhaps of too close an identification with the subject.

"Voice" in fact has a special place in Mukherjee's aesthetics. "To me there are no Indian themes, American themes or English themes. What I'm trying to produce is a voice perhaps" (Quoted in Sivaramkrishna 72). Passionate and intense, riveting, urgent, and incisive at its best—at its worst, Mukherjee's voice is too taut and brittle to sustain credibility. Notwithstanding the importance she places on voice and the consequent belittlement of thematic identity, Mulkherjee does see herself today as an American writer influenced and inspired by the melting pot of her adoptive country:

> I see myself as an American writer in the tradition of other American writers whose parents or grandparents had passed through Ellis Island; Indianness is now a metaphor, a particular way of partially comprehending the world. . . . I see most of these as stories of broken identities and discarded languages, and the will to bond oneself to a new community against the everpresent fear of failure and betrayal. (Introd. *Darkness* 3)

The expatriate and immigrant voices speaking out from *Darkness* and *The Middleman and Other Stories* belong to men and women of different nationalities, not confined to Indian women in their twenties as in her novels but men and women of varying ages, from teenagers to the middle-aged and older. Of the dozen stories in *Darkness*, two are set in Canada, eight in the United States, one in Madagascar, and one is a virtuoso interpretation of a Moghul painting. In one way or another, they all concern relationships between white Americans and American society, and black or colored immigrants. Whether as wives of professionals, illegal Indians, teenage children, or working men and women, they are united by their darkness of skin. The latter's association in nonimmigrant minds with unknown and unfamiliar worlds and the suspicion with which they are often regarded probably account for the collective title of the volume.

There is no desire to return to the country of origin, but the new country, while guaranteeing a better livelihood than at home, does not necessarily guarantee happiness. A good number of stories have violent endings or focus on sex. The nostalgia for home present in several stories is often viewed by Mukherjee as a temporary antidote for alienation and displacement. What is common to most of the characters is their need to survive. Take the eponymous teenage narrator of "Angela," who had her nipples cut off by soldiers in Bangladesh when she was six. Adopted by an American Christian family in Iowa, Angela is compelled to assimilate. Her tight declaration, "The name I was born with is lost to me, the past is lost to me" (13), evokes an emotional ambivalence towards her adoptive country. Angela is finishing high school but is being courted by the earnest and middle-aged Indian from Goa, Dr. Menezies; consequently, Angela is torn between the modern and American pursuit of a college education that would equip her for a career and the traditional Asian security of marriage.

While cultural displacement seems not to have affected Angela, another Muslim narrator, Nafeesa Hafeez, married to a professional, is conscious that she is a "not-quite's" wife, thus exemplifying the estrangement the colored man feels in a white man's land. The rootlessness of a peripatetic life has made the cynical lady from Lucknow feel "at home everywhere because she is never at home anywhere" (31). When her affair with an elderly American immunologist is discovered by his wife, the latter's calm and brisk dismissal of Nafeesa is sufficiently devastating to expose the brittle fragility of Nafeesa's sense of self. Once imagining herself too fascinating to be resistible, she now regards herself as "just another involvement of a white man in a pokey little outpost" (33).

In Mukherjee's fiction, a woman's sexual involvement often functions as a measure of detachment from native mores and, correspondingly, of her assimilation and Americanization. Sexual openness is seen as part of the freedom from tradition America offers. Although Leelah, narrator of "Hindus," points to the inescapable obstacle posed by the past in the process of assimilation in her remark, "No matter how passionately we link our bodies with our new countries, we never escape the early days" (139), the seduction exercised by a more open and anarchic environment and the liberation of sensibility, if only partial at times, are particularly evident in Mukherjee's women. But with their more conservative backgrounds, South Asian men and women react in different ways: women, by expressing their sexual needs more candidly; men, by believing their countrywomen are freer in America than in their native land or are more uninhibited and self-sufficient than they have been brought up to be.

In "Nostalgia," Dr. Manny Patel, psychiatric resident at a hospital in Queens, is blackmailed for a half-night stand with a young Indian woman whom he imagines to be an Indian goddess; whose apparent forthrightness he mistakes for a "bold sign of honest assimilation" (112). An accomplice, purportedly her uncle, demands money and claims a professional favor from the victim. Another immigrant, Vinita in "Visitors," wanting all along to exchange India for a foreign country, discovers in her accountant husband's expensive condominium that she is in "a new country with no rules" (167). Vinita is put off, as well as pleased, by the bold compliments of an Indian graduate student who, against Indian custom, enters her apartment when she is alone, mistaking her willingness to allow him in for sexual interest. The exchange with Rajiv Khanna marks a sexual initiation of sorts for the married Vinita, by creating in her an excitement about the forbidden and unknown. She feels that night "an irresistible force" to steal out of her husband's bed and "run off into the alien American night" (176).

Half the stories in *Darkness* are about women and their responses to North America. One of the most radically liberated women in Mukherjee's short fiction is Bombay-born Babli Bhowmick in "A Father." She is an American-trained engineer and feminist, whose father is an avid devotee of Kali, patron goddess of his family. When Mr. Bhowmick discovers his unmarried daughter's pregnancy, his shock gives way to delight at the prospect of becoming a grandfather, but such modernity is shortlived and ends in violence. He attacks his daughter when she reveals she has resorted to the "bottle and syringe" method of conception, her feminist freedom of choice proving too much for him.

On the other hand, two stories set in Toronto portray the tensions between immigrants and their society. In "The World According to Hsü," Ratna, the only character in Mukherjee's fiction with a "secondhand interest in the English language and a decided aversion to British institutions," is reluctant to move from Montreal to Toronto. Of Indian and Czech parentage, Ratna knows that whereas Montreal classifies her as English, in race-conscious Toronto, she would not even be Indian, but a "Paki." "And for Pakistanis, Toronto was hell" (41). "Tamurlane" is set in Toronto, in the world of Indian cooks and kitchen hands who work at the Mumtaz Bar B-Q. It has been suggested that the title refers to "Timur the Lame" (Nazareth 185), the tandoori chef who, thrown in front of a train by Canadian racists, survives but is later shot in a raid on illegal aliens by the Mounties, ironically holding his bona fide Canadian passport in front of his face. The hostility shown towards Canada in both stories is probably the result of Mukherjee's unhappy experience there in the seventies, a country she found dismal for race relations. During this time, she wrote, felt, and was made to feel expatriate rather than immigrant.

A less pessimistic view of immigrant experience is presented in Mukherjee's second cycle of stories, *The Middleman and Other Stories*, which has a wider circle of participants. Besides South Indians, she uses Middle Eastern, Vietnamese, Filipino, Italian, and Afghan characters. The survivalist mentality, code, and ethic are more evident here than in *Darkness*; so are sexual relationships between men and women and immigrant encounters with white America. Taken in all, the stories reflect the changing America she sees from the "influx of the last 10 or 15 years of people from Asia, Latin America and the Middle East"; they "celebrate the new America and the new immigrants who are pushing the frontier back inch by inch" (Melwani 36). Her geographical purview is also extended to locations outside North America in several stories. In an adroit mixture of narrative voices, male and female, young and old, Mukherjee expresses the resourcefulness of her resident aliens.

The man in the title story is Alfie Judah, a hustler of Middle Eastern Jewish descent who makes "a living from things that fall" (3). Alfie currently supplies guns to guerrillas in Mayan country; his dealings "can't stand too much investigation" (5). When his client is shot dead by the latter's girlfriend, Alfie is spared as a result of his having earlier made love to her. Survivor to the end, Alfie plans to beat a hasty retreat for the nearest town, possibly to sell information about the guerrillas. Another merchant of opportunity, Danny Sahib in "Danny's Girls," makes a living from marriageable Indian girls whom he sells to Indian grooms with the guarantee of Permanent Resident status through marriage to American citizens. Both men are pragmatists, not overly concerned with ethics, without difficulties in adaptation insofar as both opportunistically make the system work for them.

The Middleman continues Mukherjee's portrayal of attempts by women to break free from tradition in a liberating environment. At the innocuous level, Panna Bhatt in "A Wife's Story" has left home to make something of her life. She has come to New York to study for a Ph.D. in special education, a degree she admits she will never use in India. Panna befriends a Hungarian immigrant, and, in a gesture of liberation from Indian mores governing the conduct of women, goes to the theater with her friend, whose wife and family are still in Hungary. Panna has a past; she has suffered riots, uprootings, separation, her son's death. She pretends that nothing has changed when her husband visits her. Suppressing the Americanization of her identity, she assumes the old Indian front and plays the pliant wife but, having tasted freedom in America, refuses to accompany her husband home, citing her unfinished course as the reason.

The original (prototypical) Jasmine (Vassanji), finding Trinidad too tiny for a girl with ambition, in the story "Jasmine," enters America as an illegal immigrant, like her widowed successor, Jasmine Vijh. Finding her work at the Plantations Motel in Detroit too dull and uninspiring, she takes off for Ann Arbor and secures a job as a mother's helper with the Moffits. Before long, Bill Moffit has fallen in love with her and seduces "the flower of Ann Arbor, not Trinidad" (138). With looks and drive but no official documents and papers, Jasmine is left with only what she "wanted to invent and tell" (138); her resourcefulness and inventiveness, like Jasmine Vijh's, are indispensable tools for survival and success.

A number of intense and action-oriented stories defy the bounds of credibility with their singleminded focus on violence or sex. "The Tenant" is Maya Sanyal, a Brahmin who is divorced from her white American husband. With a Ph.D. in comparative literature, Maya has come to Cedar Falls, Iowa, to teach. As her surprising secret sex life is revealed, her bizarre behavior is blamed on her divorce. As a result of it, "she lost her moral sense, her judgement, her power to distinguish" (107). Maya's seemingly compulsive and casual sexual liaisons are metaphors for her rootlessness, loneliness, and loss of bearing, but the rationale provided by Mukherjee does not provide a sufficient explanation for them.

By and large, the stories show few continuities with the cultural and historical pasts of her characters; there is little looking back, but the presence of the past may sometimes require the Indian to negotiate between her native and adoptive worlds. The younger she is, the less likely is she disposed to do so. Existentially too, she may flutter between the two, as Mrs. Bhave in "The Management of Grief" does between spirit and reality, India and Canada, after her family dies in a devastating airplane explosion. The management of the past is vividly realized in Jase's predicament in "Fathering" of understanding his Vietnamese daughter's belief in spirits and her attempts to appease them. Similarly, "Loose Ends" tests the responses of white Americans to immigrants. Marshall is hurt when his Filipino girlfriend, Blanquita, leaves him but quickly takes another woman to assuage his loneliness. When Blanquita has a change of heart, Marshall is prepared to take her back. Marshall's acceptance of Blanquita's foreignness and his feelings for her surmount the cultural gap between them; equally, despite Jase's incomprehension of Eng's Vietnamese ways, he is aware that he never felt for his children (by an earlier marriage) what he feels for her; he chooses Eng rather than his American girlfriend.

In the movement from immigrant subcultures to mainstream culture that *The Middleman* represents, "Orbiting" is striking for the very Americanizing process it celebrates, through an improvisatory Thanksgiving, which is an initiation rite for Roashan, a refugee from Kabul. In his three months in the New World, the newest comer has acquired a girlfriend, Rindy (Renata) Marcos, an American of Italian parentage. Rindy's sister is married to an Amish American; her father was born in the United States of Italian parents; her mother came as a Spanish immigrant. In the American melting pot of culture and ethnicity, the pot-luck Thanksgiving dinner held on a makeshift table in Rindy's apartment is also an initiation for Rindy's parents, who meet Roashan for the first time. Rindy is determined to teach him to walk like an American, to dress and fill up a room "instead of melting and blending but sticking out in the Afghan way" (74–75). But it is Roashan (whose name Mr. Marcos promptly Americanizes to "Roy") who elegantly carves the turkey with his Afghan dagger, and who has already picked up some American ways, like bringing flowers and presenting them to Mrs. Marcos.

For Mukherjee, ". . . there are people born to be Americans. By American I mean an intensity of spirit and a quality of desire. I feel American in a very fundamental way, whether Americans see me that way or not" (Quoted in Steinberg 47). In the challenges posed by America to her expatriates and immigrants, Mukherjee shows that, inevitably, it is America that is affecting them in varied ways; so far only in a few stories is immigration handled from the mainstream culture's point of view. Her abundant imagination brings the tensions and forces within the multicultural and multiethnic spheres of her new Americans to vivid life. Mukherjee recreates their world—more often than not relegated to marginal status by mainstream North America—throbbing, exuberant, and dynamic with the energy and passions of "aliens" determined to survive, succeed, and, ultimately, belong.

Works Cited

Carb, Alison B. "An Interview with Bharati Mukherjee." *Massachusetts Review* 29 (1988): 647–54.

Jain, Jasbir. "Foreignness of Spirit: The World of Bharati Mukherjee's Novels." *Journal of Indian Writing in English* 13.2 (1985): 12–19.

Melwani, Lavina. "The Best of Two Worlds." *Asia Magazine* 8-10 Dec. 1989: 34–36.

Mukherjee, Bharati. *Darkness*. New York: Penguin, 1985.

———. *Days and Nights in Calcutta*. New York: Doubleday, 1977.

———. "Immigrant Writing: Give Us Your Maximalists!" *New York Times Book Review* 28 August 1988: 1, 28–29.

———. *Jasmine*. New York: Grove Weidenfeld, 1989.

———. *The Middleman and Other Stories*. Boston: Houghton Mifflin, 1988.

———. *Wife*. Boston: Houghton Mifflin, 1975.

———. *The Tiger's Daughter*. Boston: Houghton Mifflin, 1972.

Nazareth, Peter. "Total Vision." *Canadian Literature* 110 (1986): 184–91.

Sivaramkrishna, M. "Bharati Mukherjee." *Indian English Novelists*. New Delhi: Sterling Publishers, 1982. 71–86.

Steinberg, Sybil. "Immigrant Author Looks at U.S. Society." *Publishers Weekly* 25 Aug. 1989: 46–47.

BHARATI MUKHERJEE'S PUBLISHED WORK

Novels

The Tiger's Daughter, 1971
Wife, 1975
Jasmine, 1989

Short Story Collections

Darkness, 1985
The Middleman and Other Stories, 1988

History

Kautilya's Concept of Diplomacy: A New Interpretation. Calcutta: Minera, 1976.
>   A study of Kautilya (Canakya; Chanakya), Hindu statesman and philosopher, who lived around 300 B.C.

Memoir

Days and Nights in Calcutta. New York: Doubleday, 1977.
>   An "accidental autobiography," co-written with Clark Blaise; an account of a year in Calcutta. First half is Blaise's response to his experience of India; second, Mukherjee's, which relates her childhood in the opening chapters. Book closes with two epilogues, Mukherjee's identifiably a writer's manifesto. (Mukherjee is writing the screenplay for the film version of the book.)

Commentary

The Sorrow and the Terror: The Haunting Legacy of the Air India Tragedy. Ontario: Penguin, 1987.
>   Co-written with Clark Blaise. About the 1985 explosion and destruction of an Air India plane traveling from Toronto to Bombay, over Ireland and the Irish Sea. The crash killed 329 people, mostly Canadians of Indian descent. The authors argue that the Canadian government mistook the tragic event for an Indian disaster rather than regarding it as their concern.
"Immigrant Writing: Give Us Your Maximalists." *New York Times Book Review* 28 August 1988: 1, 28–9.
>   An essay about the richness and density of the immigrant world in the United States, and its abundant creative possibilities. Argues for a fictive tradition of minority immigrant voices.

SELECTED CRITICAL READINGS

There is little material available on Bharati Mukherjee's work at this point, apart from the interviews she has given and the good number of mostly favorable book reviews (some of which are listed here in lieu of extensive critical articles). It is certain that time will catch up quickly with her work, and the time lag between publication and criticism made good. As she gains prominence not only as an Indian woman novelist but also an American one, critical studies are likely to acquire a growing momentum. Given the modernity of her fiction and its substantial relevance to contemporary life, research and criticism on Mukherjee will be neither narrow in scope nor limited in number. Her work opens itself to many critical possibilities, possibly multidimensional in perspective. The changes in her style and her voice are fruitful areas of research and linguistic analysis. Her Indianness, Americanness, and feminism are potential subjects. Mukherjee readily invites comparison with writers like Maxine Hong Kingston or Ruth Prawer Jhabvala; her immigrants may be compared to Kingston's; her expatriates in America to Jhabvala's in India. Then, too, her alienation from

Canada may be related to her absorption with the United States. Yet another critical possibility lies in comparing Mukherjee with European-based expatriate writers like Kamala Markandaya, V.S. Naipual, Salman Rushdie, Timothy Mo, and Kazuo Ishiguro.

Articles

Jain, Jasbir. "Foreignness of Spirit: The World of Bharati Mukherjee's Novels." *Journal of Indian Writing in English* 13.2 (1985): 12–19. Discussion of *The Tiger's Daughter* and *Wife*, which are compared. Tara Banerjee and Dimple Dasgupta seen as "immigrants both in place and mind." Stresses "foreignness of spirit" in both women.

Melwani, Lavina. "The Best of Two Worlds." *Asia Magazine* (Hong Kong) 8–10 Dec. 1989: 34–36. General but useful article on Mukherjee's present and past life, her writings, and literary influences. Includes interview.

Rustomji-Kerns, Roshni. "Expatriates, Immigrants and Literature: Three South Asian Woman Writers." *Massachusetts Review* 29 (1988): 654–65. Discussion of Santha Rama Rau, Bharati Mukherjee (*The Tiger's Daughter, Wife, Days and Nights in Calcutta, Darkness*) and Kamala Markandaya.

Sivaramkrishna, M. "Bharati Mukherjee." *Indian English Novelists.* New Delhi: Sterling Publishers, 1982. 71–86. *The Tiger's Daughter* and *Wife* separately discussed, and compared. Argues that Mukherjee's protagonists "are neither typically Indian nor exotically westernised . . . [but] essentially human, basically feminine in their sensibility . . . struggling to find modes of authentic communication."

Steinberg, Sybil. "Immigrant Author Looks at U.S. Society." *Publishers Weekly* 25 August 1989: 46–47. Overview of Mukherjee's work, interspersed with comments from an interview with her. Ends with *Jasmine* and with Mukherjee's definition of her Americanness.

Reviews

Coles, Don. Rev. of *Days and Nights in Calcutta. Canadian Forum* 57 (April 1977): 38.

Kakutani, Michiko. "Refugees from the Third World and Elsewhere, Rootless in the United States." Rev. of *Jasmine. New York Times* 19 Sept. 1989: A16.

Leong, Russell. "Still the Golden Door." Rev. of *The Middleman and Other Stories. Far Eastern Economic Review* 4 May 1989: 67.

Levin, Martin. "New and Novel." Rev. of *Wife. New York Times Book Review* 8 June 1975: 17, 20.

Nazareth, Peter. "Total Vision." Rev. of *Darkness. Canadian Literature* 110 (1986): 184–91. (Comprehensive discussion)

"Oh, Calcutta." Rev. of *The Tiger's Daughter. Times Literary Supplement* 29 June 1973: 736.

Parameswaran, Uma. Rev. of *Darkness. World Literature Today* 60 (1986): 520–21.

Interview

With Alison B. Carb. *Massachusetts Review* 29 (1988): 647–54.

— LIEW-GEOK LEONG

IV. Decolonizing Self

How a colonial society, then postcolonial, affects the individual it begets has long been a theme essential to international writing in English. (It is ironic that sometimes the writer has questioned a borrowed identity in a borrowed language and literary form.) The acts of decolonization already discussed prepare for this journey of self and suggest that gradually self will be decolonized as the remnants of colonialism fade: the history rewritten, the patriarchy restructured, the boundaries broken down. Still, this quest goes far beyond the facts of colonial history, decolonization, and postcolonialism, as it reaches into the amorphous state of self in the modern world.

One of the great voices recording this real and metaphorical journey has been that of Patrick White, the Australian who received the Nobel Prize for Literature in 1973. Carolyn Bliss sees his work "structured by the controlling metaphor of spiritual quest." In spite of what is described as his sometimes "bleak assessments of human worth and potential," Bliss draws from his "vision and visions" an "overall tenor" that is "astonishingly optimistic, especially when viewed as a product of our terrorized and terrified age." Bliss also mentions that White, although writing in the European tradition, has placed his work firmly in Australia, whose present and past—the colonial and postcolonial states—serve as his metaphor for the larger "spiritual quest."

Another major writer who handles the theme in both its phases most forcefully is the West Indian born V.S. Naipaul, whose work comprises a series of journeys. Peggy Nightingale notes that he "has constantly attempted to mediate history, both his personal history and that of various colonial experiences"; and through an impressive body of fiction and nonfiction, he has carried out his assertion "that the task of a writer is to impose order, to try to make sense of the chaos of reality." Concluding a discussion of novels, travel books, and essays that embrace most of the postcolonial world, Nightingale turns to Naipaul's last novel, *The Enigma of Arrival*, seeing in it the possibility—but not the absolute assurance—that his "personal tension between individual assimilation into the dominant English tradition and his political consciousness of the legacy of imperialism have been resolved." Nightingale then adds that the dominant culture cannot help but change as it is infused by those emigrating from the formerly subordinate cultures; hence, assimilation and decolonization work in both directions so that what Naipaul expects when he arrives at his destination might in the long run be vastly different from what he actually discovers.

Jean Rhys is another of those writers of dual identity, with both England and the West Indies claiming her. Pierrette Frickey's essay does not try to determine literary loyalty but analyzes how Rhys's "divided self"—a West Indian heritage and a long European residence—informs her masterpiece, *Wide Sargasso Sea*, which depicts the sojourn between the inward and outward states, the colony and the center. Frickey concludes that the novel comprises "a vision of a future in which the differences and incomprehensions setting men and women apart have no place." So it would seem that through creating a fiction, Rhys, who thought writing a self-centered act—"a necessary catharsis," decolonized herself and others.

Much the same could be said of New Zealand's Janet Frame, whose "voyage between self and society" Nancy Potter traces. Described by Potter as an "experimental" novelist, Frame sets much of her work in postcolonial New Zealand cities, then links them with what she calls mirror cities in England and the United States, a technique tending to mark the same division between the dominant cultures and the subordinate that Naipaul and Rhys confront. But Frame, the most unlikely of the international writers and one whose work redefines postmodernism, seems to display little interest in the reality of colonialism, "post" or otherwise. Instead, she sees the decolonization process in highly personal terms, for, as Potter concludes, Frame's work continues "to construct bridges" between a richly furnished imagination and "the external world of mirror cities around the globe."

Craig MacKenzie's essay on Bessie Head, the South African who eventually moved to Botswana, describes yet another act of self-decolonization by recounting the sojourn of "alienation, breakdown, and renewal" in Head's work, which MacKenzie considers an "idiosyncratic divergence" in African literature. He praises her ability "to break out of narrow traditionalistic modes of perception" and to discover "the possibility of interracial cooperation and friendship." Relying in part on a biographical approach, MacKenzie also reveals how the act of writing helped to free the writer, as it had done for Rhys and Frame.

The Indian novelist Anita Desai has also focused sharply on the state of self in a postcolonial society, and, according to Florence Libert's discussion, introduced the psychological novel into Indian literature. Concentrating on the "discrepancy" between the inner and outer worlds as recorded in Desai's *Fire on the Mountain*, Libert creates a paradigm that serves to elucidate all of Desai's subtly constructed fiction, which takes up the quest of the Indian in a society still reeling from its long colonial experience. Interestingly, in her latest novel, *Baumgartner's Bombay*, Desai turns tables and depicts a European immigrant in India.

Finding a vision in Timothy Findley's work that is both post "holocaust" and "colonial," Diana Brydon enlarges the project of decolonizing self that occupies the other writers. This Canadian novelist, Brydon says, "creates moral parables that explore the contemporary meaning of horror" in the hope that the reader might be regenerated through "the fictional witnessing of texts like his." Robert Ross discovers much the same kind of dark vision in the fiction of Thea Astley, who calls her native Australia the "parish" and who extends the truth drawn therein through metaphors that unfold into spiritual journeys toward an elusive center. Unlike Findley, though, Astley beholds little possibility for regeneration and limits in her work the state of grace to rare visionaries.

The decolonization of self engaging these writers—and the others in international literature—constitutes a journey, which always played an integral part in colonial life. But the sea voyage of the past has evolved into a metaphor for self-exploration, for self-decolonization; no longer is its purpose the conquest and settlement of new lands.

Patrick White

P atrick Victor Martindale White was born in London, 28 May 1912, to patrician Australian parents. Because their class still thought of England as "Home," they had elected to reside there for a portion of their two-year wedding trip through Europe and the Middle East. Victor White, Patrick's father, was a third-generation Australian whose grazier family had large landholdings in the Hunter Valley near Sydney. His mother, Ruth Whithycombe White, had arrived in Australia as an infant with her British parents. When the White's son was six months old, the couple returned to Australia where "Paddy's" only sibling, Suzanne, was born in 1915.

White was a precocious child, having "flipped through most of Shakespeare" by age nine (*Flaws* 7), and he always felt himself a stranger in his family, a sort of "cuckoo" hatched by unsuspecting birds of another breed (*Flaws* 10). Yet despite this sense of estrangement, he did not applaud his parents' decision to send him to school in England in 1925. In fact, his stint at Cheltenham College seemed a four-year sentence of exile from which he gladly escaped in 1929 to return to Australia and work as a jackeroo on sheep stations in the Monaro district and near Walgett. While so employed, he tried his hand at fiction but nothing from this period survives.

The year 1932 saw him once again in England, this time to begin a happier stay at King's College, Cambridge, where he took a degree in modern languages, traveling often to the Continent to improve his command of French and German. Leaving the university in 1935, he established himself in London to pursue a career in the theater. These hopes were disappointed, but with other projects he had more success, publishing his first novel in 1939 and beginning the second that same year during a visit to the United States. He wrote ten other novels, as well as plays, poems, short stories, a memoir, and other nonfiction.

With the outbreak of World War II, White joined the RAF intelligence forces, subsequently serving in the Middle East and Greece. He chose to return to Australia after the war, bringing with him Manoly Lascaris, a Greek friend who would become his lifelong companion. The two settled first at Castle Hill on the outskirts of Sydney, but in the mid sixties, they moved to a house near Sydney's Centennial Park and have remained there except for occasional trips abroad.

Always a private and quiet man, unequipped for self-promotion and reluctant to discuss his work with interviewers, White was more unsettled than gratified by the 1973 award of the Nobel Prize for literature. He did not go to Stockholm to accept the honor and diverted the prize money into a fund to recognize and assist other Australian writers.

Threats to his beloved Centennial Park, the rise and fall of the Whitlam government, Australia's involvement in the Vietnam War, ecologically disastrous mining schemes, injustices to the Aborigines, and the horrifying prospect of nuclear war made the White of the seventies and eighties more visible and vocal than before. Yet he continued to cherish his privacy, shrug off lionizers, and suspect his own accomplishments. In his autobiographical memoir, *Flaws in the Glass*, he remarked, "What is seen as success, my own included, has often filled me with disgust" (151). For half a century his work has rejected received formulas for success and sought instead to feed the "hunger after spirituality," which he long ago surprised in a secular world (White "Old Man" 13).

Patrick White died 30 September 1990 in Sydney.

VISION AND VISIONS

Arguably the finest writer Australia has yet produced and the sole Australian to be awarded the Nobel Prize for Literature, Patrick White is now numbered in the first ranks of international writers in English. World acclaim has come for a number of reasons. One of these, although surely the least compelling, is the impressive volume and variety of his work. During a writing career spanning fifty years, he has published twelve novels, eight plays, two collections of poetry, three books of short stories and/or short novels, the occasional uncollected poem or story, a screenplay, an autobiographical memoir, and enough other nonfiction to fill a recently released anthology. His standing in the international community, though, is largely due to his novels, which will be the focus of attention here.

Also of clear but secondary importance in accounting for his international stature is White's use of specifically Australian locales, characters, history, and preoccupations. Although the Swedish Academy lauded him in part for "introduc[ing] a new continent into literature," a remark that rankled some in Australia, White is far from a local colorist. He has made no secret of the fact that concern, as well as love for his native land drew him back to it after education in England, travel in Europe and the United States, and service in World War II, which took him to Greece and the Middle East. What he loved was the pure and elemental landscape, the memories of childhood, and the sense of belonging in Australia; what he feared was "the Great Australian Emptiness," an emptiness not of unsettled territory, but of unexplored souls and unchallenged assumptions (White "Prodigal Son" 157).

After a seven-year hiatus following the 1948 publication of *The Aunt's Story*, it was this Emptiness, in which he saw material prosperity and intellectual vacuity exalted, that prompted him to write *The Tree of Man*, where he treated the lives of "an ordinary [Australian] man and woman" whose consciousness touches "the mystery and the poetry" available to heightened perceptions. Through this and later efforts, he hoped to help "people . . . a barely inhabited country with a race possessed of understanding" ("Prodigal Son" 157-58). This has remained an imperative project for White, and nearly all of his subsequent work has had Australian settings, both historical and contemporary. Yet, like all great writers, White speaks finally to concerns that transcend both parish and period.

Thus, in accounting for White's importance, other remarks made by the Swedish Academy are more apposite. The Nobel Prize citation, for example, noticed both genre and style in White's work, describing his fiction as "epic and psychological narrative" and commending him for "wrestling with the language in order to extract all its power and all its nuances, to the verge of the unattainable." Here we are on firmer evaluative grounds, since stylistic and formal accomplishments certainly *are* among the most persuasive reasons for White's reputation.

Formally, his major novels tend to be hybrids, successfully meshing features of nineteenth-century realism with twentieth-century modernism and postmodernism, while simultaneously incorporating archetypes of character and form as old as literature itself. For the most part, the novels are structured by the controlling metaphor of spiritual quest. Their protagonists are thus eligible for epic stature but such an assessment can be made only at the end of the novels and from an extramundane perspective. Judged by the standards of this world, the characters often appear to be shabby, confused, and ineffectual.

The paradox is implicit in Peter Wolfe's description of Whitean protagonists as "saints of failure" (231). These are people whose failures to do or be what they demand of themselves goad them toward the further efforts that clarify their sense of mission. Eventually, their struggle may elevate them to a plane of understanding on which worldly success or failure becomes meaningless.

Examples abound in White's fiction. There is Theodora Goodman of *The Aunt's Story* who breaks faith with her discipline of self-destruction and is permitted to enclose, though never to efface, the antitheses that have torn her apart. There is Voss, whose quest for apotheosis turns instead into one for recovered "human status" (*Voss* 390), in the pursuit of which he learns that love and humility draw man closest to deity. There is Hurtle Duffield of *The Vivisector*, the artist urged by what he sees as repeated artistic failures toward continued efforts to realize the phenomenal world and approach the unnameable Indigod. There is Ellen Roxburgh of *A Fringe of Leaves* whose jungle odyssey brings her knowledge of the true dimensions of human evil. Final examples are Himmelfarb of *Riders in the Chariot* and Elizabeth Hunter of *The Eye of the Storm*, who function most redemptively in others' lives when they cease their respective attempts to redeem or direct those others. White's understanding of the nature, inevitability, and efficacy of failure is most plainly stated by the character of Le Mesurier in *Voss*, who reflects that "The mystery of life is not solved by success, which is an end in itself, but in failure, in perpetual struggle, in becoming" (269).

White's handling of the theme of fortunate and liberating failure has precedents reaching at least as far back as the Bible. Adam and Eve's failure to obey the rules condemned them to further choices and a quest for the moral maturity such choices construct. Their death sentences also made necessary a reciprocal promise of everlasting life, achieved through Christ, Himself the paramount example of worldly defeat transcended and transmuted into otherworldly victory.

Thus White's contemporary fiction flowers from ancient, mythic roots. But his work also strikes the reader as nearly Victorian in its massive scope and ambition and in its creation of fully-fleshed characters with fully articulated worlds in which to move. Dickensian casts of supporting characters often gather around the lead actors, and White's intricate and contrapuntal plots have been termed "Jamesian" (Steiner 111). His works also portray extraordinary people, often in extraordinary circumstances and states of consciousness. It is not surprising, then, that White has sometimes claimed derivation from a nineteenth-century tradition, and to the list of British authors of the period by whom his work has been influenced has added the names of Stendhal, Flaubert, Tolstoy, and Dostoyevsky.

But perhaps we should not be so quick to place him, for White's novels also penetrate character to achieve a degree of multidimensional psychological depth that recalls Joseph Conrad and later moderns like William Faulkner. White also holds additional modernist credentials: his early use of Lawrentian imagery and Joycean interior monologue, and his later preference for the more mediated narrative voice adopted by Virginia Woolf. A willingness to breach realistic-naturalistic conventions in startling and ambiguous ways further separates him from his nineteenth-century predecessors. Examples are the oneiric visions that allow Voss and Laura Trevelyan not only to know precisely what is happening to each other while separated by thousands of miles but to be together, ease each other's burdens, and consummate their love through visions in which flesh and spirit also merge. A similar sort of instinctual telepathy links the four protagonists of *Riders in the Chariot* and the Brothers Brown of *The Solid Mandala*. In these and other novels, such as *The Eye of the Storm* and *A Fringe of Leaves*, characters often assume allegorical roles as fragments of a single, severed being who longs for reconciliation.

This allegorical strain in White's work again complicates decisions as to genre assignment and period affinities. Further confusing matters is his increasing preoccupation with such postmodern concerns as the artist's role and liabilities and the patent artificiality of art. Strictly speaking, some of these concerns have been with White from the outset. An uneasiness with the murky morality of art as it imposes arbitrary form and coherence on human complexity was first expressed in the 1947 play *The Ham Funeral* and exhaustively explored in later works, particularly *The Vivisector* (1970), *Flaws in the Glass* (1981), *Memoirs of Many in One* (1986), and *Three Uneasy Pieces* (1987). His fiction, nonfiction, and drama contemplate both the possible irrelevancy of art and its potential for harmfulness, leading White to conclude, "My pursuit of that razor-blade truth has made me a slasher" (*Flaws* 155), and to worry that "Art can be almost a worse crime than living" (*Memoirs* 157).

White also shares with postmodernists a radical distrust of language. Having once hoped for a career either in painting or music, he has always been dissatisfied with the opacity of "grey, bronchial prose" (*Flaws* 150) and disturbed by the indeterminancy and weakness of words. Arthur Brown of *The Solid Mandala* states the problem with matchless simplicity: "words are not what make you see" (51). Yet, like his characters, White finds that failures provoke renewed attempts, in his case, the attempt to create "completely fresh forms out of the rocks and sticks of words" ("Prodigal Son" 158) and thereby to "come close to the core of reality, the structure of reality" (White quoted in McGregor 219).

The search for new approaches with which to render "the structure of reality" is certainly on the postmodern agenda and has long been on White's. Relatively new, however, is White the patent metafictionist. Self-conscious examination of his own enterprise as a writer is pronounced in both *Memoirs of Many in One* and *Three Uneasy Pieces*, his most recent works. In the first, White himself appears as a character who is a writer serving as editor of a deceased friend's journals; and in "The Age of a Wart" from the story collection, the unnamed first-person narrator is a writer to whom international acclaim and prestigious literary awards have not delivered a sense of self-worth.

By mirroring an extratextual self in his last fictions, White may have signaled some new, more transparently confessional directions. But such tactics again forestall decisions as to the kind of fiction he wrote. By turns archetypal, allegorical, epic and intimate, realistic and symbolic, Victorian, modern, and postmodern, the Whitean vehicle may be unmistakable, but it is also unclassifiable.

Stylistically, too, White's fiction seems to demand a category unto itself. Richly nuanced, marked by suggestive omissions and equivocal, double-edged metaphor, fond of the conjectural and conditional, frequently shifting point of view, forever juxtaposing different realms of being and apprehension, and nearly always offering the option of ironic reading, style in White's work poses the greatest challenge his critics still have to face.

Granted, we have come some distance from the days when the Australian poet A. D. Hope could dismiss Whitean prose as "pretentious and illiterate verbal sludge" (15). In fact, a 1989 book by Rodney Edgecombe argues convincingly for a "continuity of vision and style" in White's best novels (159), which "mediates meaning with a subtlety that a discursive mode, no matter how lucid and accessible, would necessarily have . . . to forgo" (xi). Recent studies by Karin Hansson and David Tacey also begin to address the problem of style in White's work, but in ways so mutually exclusive they suggest that no critical agreement has yet been reached even on how to describe the style, let alone how to assess it. Obviously, much work remains to be done on this aspect of White's achievement.

White's work thus commands international attention for a variety of reasons: because of its volume and diversity, because of its committed and provocative Australianness, because its form intrigues and its style engages. But I want to focus here on what I advance as an even more important reason: in the field of contemporary English-language literature, White is something of a philosophical anomaly.

In some ways, of course, he is a man of his age. Far from anomalous is his satiric perspective on contemporary society, most pointed in his plays and in such novels as *Riders in the Chariot*, *The Vivisector*, and *The Twyborn Affair*. Modern readers have come to expect that humankind in the aggregate will be seen as petty, grasping, and preoccupied with the material and trivial. Thus we are not surprised when White furnishes just such sorts of human beings. Nor are we surprised that special people in his novels and plays should be allowed to transcend the limitations of herd mentality and progress in individually formulated directions. Pariahs, outsiders, megalomaniacs, and geniuses of various stripe are the darlings of twentieth-century literature. Neither White's irony nor his characters sprout from unfamiliar soil.

Thus we must look elsewhere for White's oddity. We can begin to account for it by noticing that he openly and insistently espouses belief in what he calls a "Divine Presence" ("Credo" 111) with a crucial though not omnipotent role in human affairs.

He has gone so far as to say that religion, as he conceives it, is behind all his work. Such an affirmation does not, however, constitute the whole of his distinction. Religious faith as an aspect of artistic vision may be unusual in contemporary writers, but it is not unprecedented, as examples like Graham Greene and Flannery O'Connor attest. Rather, the Whitean apostasy from contemporary creeds consists most centrally in the way such belief is embodied in his fiction.

Rodney Edgecombe has remarked as a "recurring theme" in White "the opening up of selfhood to the divine" (xii). Focus upon such a theme is peculiar enough in an emphatically secular age, but even stranger is White's manner of handling it. Put simply, he provides his characters with visions. The opening of self, in a moment characteristically portrayed as a paradox of giving and receiving, diminution and expansion, sometimes allows the character to glimpse the very countenance of God.

Whitean visions tend to share certain features, among which is their precondition. Characters usually approach visionary moments from the perceived state of moral or spiritual failure discussed above. For example, Stan Parker of *The Tree of Man* is granted his vision only after having admitted his failures to connect with others, whether the wife who deceived him, the children who deserted him, or the old man in the flood whom he could not or would not save. He also acknowledges his failure to connect with the divine, an inadequacy shared and eventually mourned by Voss, Hurtle Duffield, Elizabeth Hunter, Ellen Roxburgh, Himmelfarb, and other of White's characters.

Also characteristic of Whitean vision is its placement at a climactic moment, often at or near the protagonist's death. If embedded within an ongoing life, as is the case for Elizabeth Hunter, the vision nonetheless crystalizes that life into a meaningful pattern, thereby offering a paradigm of what existence informed by vision might become.

Moments of vision inhabit an ontological sphere, which is fundamentally apart from everyday life. Thus they are never described unambiguously. In fact, as White's writing career progresses, he grows increasingly vague about these experiences, increasingly cognizant of the collapse of language under the pressure of such immensity. Nonetheless, the imagery in which he clothes the visions does manage to convey their quintessential nature: transcendent and transpersonal.

In undergoing vision, the character typically relinquishes the will and permits a greater force to take control. He or she cannot compel vision because its bestowal is an act of pure grace, unearned and often undeserved by the recipient, who acknowledges unworthiness by abandoning the self. The illuminate then feels self melt away. Imagery of dissolution proliferates. But as the self dissolves, it is also amplified toward coincidence with the infinite. The motion is that produced by ripples radiating from a stone dropped in a pool. In this process, the self comes finally to embrace the whole and somehow to acquire it as well. Through such acquisition it may be reconstituted: full, perfect, and serene. In terms of the related Christian paradox, the visionary finds life by losing it. He/she becomes most essentially him/herself when least purposefully and deliberately so. A case in point is Hurtle Duffield, whose masterpieces are painted when he is not artist but passive medium and is "being painted with, and through, and on" (*Vivisector* 600).

The experience of Le Mesurier of *Voss* bears most of the hallmarks of the Whitean vision: absence of human will or control, ambiguity, images of dissolution and centrifugal enlargement, the merging of self and world, and the eventual reconstitution of self as other and better. Sent on an errand by the expedition's leader, Le Mesurier rides into a desert thunderstorm:

> At once his matted hair began to stream out, and as the wind encircled the pale upper half of his forehead, he seemed to be relieved of some of the responsibility of human personality. The wind was filling his mouth and running down through the acceptant funnel of his throat, till he was completely possessed by it; his heart was thunder, and the jagged nerves of lightning were radiating from his own body.
>
> But it was not until the farther side of the ridge, going down, and he was singing the storm up out of him, that the rain came, first with a few whips, then with the release of cold, grey light and solid water, and he was immersed in the mystery of it, he was dissolved, he was running into crannies, and sucked into the mouths of the earth, and disputed, and distributed, but again and again, for some purpose, was made one by the strength of a will not his own. . . .
>
> Riding down the other side, the young man conceived a poem, in which the silky seed that fell in milky rain from the Moon was raised up by the Sun's laying his hands upon it. His flat hands, with their conspicuously swollen knuckles, were creative, it was proved, if one dared accept their blessing. One did dare, and at once it was seen that the world of fire and the world of ice were the same world of light. (247–49)

This vision, like many in White's work, admits the character to an apprehension of the essential unity, beauty, beneficence, and power pervading creation and incorporating its creatures.

In part, Whitean visions are recognizable as such because they *do* resemble each other. But they also differ, not only in structural details but, more significantly, in their import. What the vision teaches the illuminate does not stay constant throughout White's career. In its shifts, however, visionary experience marks the several stations of a spiritual pilgrimage on which White sends his protagonists and to which he invites his readers. In their entirety, the visions thus map the landmarks of the Whitean moral universe. They further suggest that this universe is to be apprehended and negotiated in four stages, through which the fiction itself also progresses.

In White's early work, the message of vision is oneness: oneness of character with others, with the natural world, and by the time of *The Tree of Man*, with whatever Force or Being has authorized both. It is important to note that the vision here advocates not a oneness of bland homogeneity but rather a circumscription within dialectical tension of the dichotomies that plague and define earthly experience: self and others, pleasure and pain, real and unreal, victim and victimizer, success and failure, sacred and profane. Limitlessness is the leitmotif of vision in the early fiction, and its mode is the abrogation of category. Through visionary experience, characters are brought to awareness of the web of responsibility and culpability that connects their lives to others, a "mystery of unity" (*Happy Valley* 162) imbued with "an infinity of purpose" (*Living and the Dead* 13, 382). With *The Tree of Man*, the novel that first reflected White's renewed religious faith, infinity has been made to stretch even further. From this point on, purpose will be grounded in a transcendent force that subsumes individual goals within its grand design.

Although White's first two novels, *Happy Valley* and *The Living and the Dead*, are generally agreed to be apprentice works, embryonic forms of the Whitean vision are nevertheless central to their meaning. Holding a letter from Oliver Halliday, the lover who has left her, Alys Browne of *Happy Valley* feels its implications expand in a "circle of light that receded, without circumference . . ." (289). Those implications are clarified in Oliver's parallel epiphanies in the course of which he accepts the discipline of suffering for himself and extends his healing pity to a whole human world that "find[s] . . . its expression in cleavage and pain" (162).

Similarly, Eliot Standish of *The Living and the Dead* is awakened to the linkages between his and others' lives and the obligations such connections carry. The end of the novel shows him affirming an accumulation of shared experiences and expressing the desire to "touch . . . into life" the many who, like him, have drugged themselves into a stupor of self-absorption (383). Both novels admit their protagonists to a postlapsarian world of knowledge and moral accountability, but in neither is it quite clear whether admission is given or earned. Vision, in other words, has not yet assumed the aspect of revelation it will take on in later work.

A vastly enlarged understanding of selfhood is at the heart of Theodora Goodman's vision in *The Aunt's Story*, as it is for Eliot Standish of the previous novel. But significant differences emerge here as well. For one thing, the ontological status of the visionary experience is more clearly marked in *The Aunt's Story*. The knowledge Theodora gains comes from beyond the self; it is not arrived at through some complicity of memory and reverie, as seemed to be the case for Oliver, Alys, and Eliot. To Theodora, knowledge comes as a gift of grace. Granted, the role, which in later fiction will be played by divine agency, is here taken by Holstius, an imaginary being projected out of Theodora's own fragile and fragmented personality. Still the otherness of this oracular figure is essential. As the price of knowledge he demands the surrender of willful self, a condition which for Theodora and for later illuminates becomes prerequisite to the realization of full selfhood.

Other demands made by Holstius reflect further advances in White's developing concept of vision. Not only is the antithesis of self and other to be acknowledged as delusion, so that eventually Holstius himself may be reincorporated, but *all* antitheses are to be recognized as shifting mirror images of each other. Reality is revealed as an ongoing flux of opposites, "true permanence" as "a state of multiplication and division" (286). Therefore, Holstius tells Theodora:

> I expect you to accept the two irreconcilable halves. . . .
>   You cannot reconcile joy and sorrow. . . . Or flesh and marble, or illusion and reality, or life and death. For this reason, Theodora Goodman, you must accept. And you have already found that one

constantly deludes the other into taking fresh shapes, so that there is sometimes little to choose between the reality of illusion and the illusion of reality. Each of your several lives is evidence of this. (280)

In a later illumination, Theodora further accepts her many lives or selves:

In the peace that Holstius spread throughout her body and the speckled shade of surrounding trees, there was no end to the lives of Theodora Goodman. These met and parted, met and parted, movingly. They entered into each other . . . And in the same way that the created lives of Theodora Goodman were interchangeable, the lives into which she had entered, making them momentarily dependent for . . . this portion of their fluctuating personalities, these were the lives of Theodora Goodman, these too. (286–87)

Theodora, who began the novel longing to annihilate the self, here becomes a virtual encyclopedia of selfhood.

The state of flux that Holstius forces Theodora to recognize and even celebrate is stabilized in White's next novel within a circumscribing scheme of divine origin. In his "self-portrait," *Flaws in the Glass*, White recounts the circumstances surrounding what was less the recovery of tepid childhood belief than a leap into a new faith, founded on a conception of God as Absolute Antonym: the opposite of human frailty, egomania, and general ridiculousness (143–48). The incident that brought him to this perception, an ignominious fall in the mud while loaded down with dog dishes, occurred between the writing of *The Aunt's Story* and *The Tree of Man;* and it is this notion of divinity as otherness that informs the later novel and provides the goal of protagonist Stan Parker's quest.

Throughout the novel Stan endures inklings of transcendence, especially insistent in natural excesses such as fire, flood, drought, and gale. He sees how impotent he is before such forces and also realizes his impotence in human relationships. At the same time, he senses within himself the potential to approach the powers that unman him; and in part because his inquiry persists, his spiritual hungers are finally appeased.

Stan Parker's moment of illumination, which descends on him as he sits in his overgrown garden, heralds his approaching death. In its emphasis on pattern, the vision thus imposes meaningful final shape on a life that, like the garden, has harbored noxious weeds and sprawled beyond control:

Out there at the back, the grass, you could hardly call it a lawn, had formed a circle in the shrubs and trees which the old woman had not so much planted as stuck in during her lifetime. There was little of design in the garden originally, though one had formed out of the wilderness. It was perfectly obvious that the man was seated at the heart of it, and from this heart the trees radiated, with grave movements of life, and beyond them the sweep of a vegetable garden, which had gone to weed during the months of the man's illness, presented the austere skeletons of cabbages and the wands of onion seed. All was circumference to the centre, and beyond that the worlds of other circles, whether crescent of purple villas or the bare patches of earth, on which rabbits sat and observed some abstract spectacle for minutes on end, in a paddock not yet built upon. The last circle but one was the cold and golden bowl of winter, enclosing all that was visible and material, and at which the man would blink from time to time, out of his watery eyes, unequal to the effort of realizing he was the centre of it. (504–05)

By juxtaposing imagery of birth, life, and death, White suggests in this passage that reality is for Stan what it was for Theodora: cyclical growth, decay, and renewal. At the same time, however, the superimposed design of concentric circles not only refers the entire process to Stan, who sits at its hub, but embraces all change within constancy. The constancy is that of the ultimate circle, which is also the Ultimate Other, the God of constancy who administers but is very much immanent within the inconstant world. It is therefore appropriate that Stan should inform the young evangelist who intrudes upon him that God is in the humblest of matter, even a gob of spittle, and should receive in response to a prayer the revelation that "One, and no other figure, is the answer to all sums" (508).

Vision in White's early fiction thus conveys a sense of unity and wholeness, the integration of the many in the context of the One. This fundamental tenet of the Whitean metaphysic is retained in his fiction; but in the subsequent four novels, the emphasis shifts to the states and experiences that enable vision. In *Voss, Riders in the Chariot, The Solid Mandala,* and *The Vivisector,* White stresses the necessary humiliation of the spiritual seeker, the need to give up all pretense of managing one's destiny and to admit instead to failure, weakness, and unworthiness.

Although only the last of these four novels focuses reader attention on a single protagonist, each features at least one central character who is afflicted with megalomania or hypertrophied complacency. Voss believes he can conquer and reign over the heart of Australia and the hearts of those he will make his subjects. Laura Trevelyan takes smug pride in her humility and self-abasement. Himmelfarb hopes that his own sacrifice will redeem humanity and history. Ruth Godbold uses militant love like a cudgel. Waldo Brown decides that preservation of an imagined core of artistic potential justifies betrayal of his twin brother. Hurtle Duffield lives by the precept that all moral obligations are nullified by the demands of art.

In three of these four novels, a life capped by visionary experience disabuses the protagonists of faith in their delusions. Both Voss and Laura come to realize the arrogance of their assumptions. Although access to Voss's vision is denied the reader, Laura reports its message, the "true knowledge" that "only comes of death by torture in the country of the mind" (443). This is the knowledge that "When man is truly humbled, when he has learned that he is not God, then he is nearest to becoming so. In the end, he may ascend" (384). When vision comes to Himmelfarb, he is undergoing precisely the process Laura has described. "Truly humbled" at last and dying of the mental and physical tortures he has suffered, he acknowledges that "it had not been accorded to him to expiate the sins of the world" (*Riders in the Chariot*

459). This admission opens him to his God, who is approached both in a moment of "stillness and clarity" amidst the raucous confusion of the mock crucifixion (454) and later in a deathbed dream of spiritual union (472–73).

Death also brings vision to Hurtle Duffield, who has earlier been "stroked by God" into an embryonic state of incipient rebirth (*Vivisector* 599). Subsequently, he relinquishes artistic agency to divine direction. He also begins at last to love and affirm the chaotic, anarchic reality of his experience, the world of *Dreck* symbolized in the novel by Rhoda, his deformed adoptive sister, and previously rejected in favor of the ordered serenity of art. He starts work on his ultimate painting, one that will express his conception of God as the "otherwise unnameable I-N-D-I-G-O" (602) but is of course denied this blasphemous closure and consummation. Instead, he is "stroked" again and dies; yet the novel seems to leave him in the presence of the "indi-ggoddd" his final works and words invoke (603).

Things are somewhat different in *The Solid Mandala*. In the case of Waldo Brown, insularity hardens to the point that it is impermeable to visionary experience. On the other hand, Waldo's twin Arthur, the holy idiot whose innocence has always left him open, inhabits a state of grace more or less uninterruptedly and communes with vision on an almost daily basis. To be open, however, is to be vulnerable, and Arthur's vulnerability is deepened by the fact that he embodies the unrealized spiritual potential of the whole, healed personality into which he and his brother ought to merge. When even Arthur's love is unable to reclaim his brother, Waldo dies and Arthur is brutally severed in two. Yet Arthur's efforts are not entirely futile. Personally enfeebled, he nonetheless functions as a powerful redemptive agent in the lives of the other two factions of his hoped-for mandalic quaternity: Dulcie Feinstein and Mrs. Poulter. To Mrs. Poulter, he comes to stand for that aspect of God human and threatened enough to compel belief and pity.

Vision in the novels of the late fifties and sixties thus emphasizes the strength that comes of weakness and the fact that simplicity, humility, and the renunciation of self are critical to spiritual progress. But other qualities are also requisite. White's next two novels focus our attention on one of these: sheer tenacity.

In *The Eye of the Storm*, the protagonist's tenacity seems the most salient aspect of her character, except perhaps for rapaciousness. Although she is eighty-six and has suffered a stroke, Elizabeth Hunter keeps a death grip on life. She is also unrelenting in the control she exercises over her satellites, including her adult children who spend the whole of the novel and have apparently spent the whole of their lives in fruitless attempts to elude her influence. None of this is especially praiseworthy. But as the novel continually circles—through allusion, prolepsis, and memory—the moment granted Elizabeth Hunter in the eye of the storm, White suggests that what seems obstinacy in Elizabeth may more accurately be described as a sometimes perverted resolve. In other words, her behavior can often be explained by reference to the vision: her determination to recover it, her desire to rediscover the self she became at that moment, and the perhaps unconscious wish to push others toward similar encounters with the self.

The actual vision has also prioritized endurance. It comes as a temporary respite from a raging hurricane, offering her a momentary suspension of but not exemption from life's exigencies. The moment's profound peace tempts Elizabeth toward an ecstatic death, but "some force not her absent will" directs her ears to the scream of a gull impaled by the wind on a tree branch (*Eye of the Storm* 382). "At least the death cry of the insignificant sooty gull gave her back her significance," says White (382). The significance is that of life itself of which "she had not experienced enough . . ." (382). This realization sends her in search of shelter as the Eye turns away. God's last demand of her is that she go on.

White's next novel, *A Fringe of Leaves*, harks back to earlier fiction in its insistence on the need for empathetic identification with fellow sufferers. It also offers a kind of inversion of *Voss*, in that where Voss had to discover his potential for human goodness and gentleness, Ellen Roxburgh must confront her capacity for evil and cruelty. But the message of vision to Ellen is most simply what is was for Elizabeth Hunter: that she must persist in living, despite or because of her several "betrayals" of love and trust (390).

The moment of "peace" and "beatitude" that Ellen experiences in Pilcher's rude chapel, built as an act of penance for his own multitudinous sins, comforts her with the knowledge that only God is pure love and that all human attempts at love must consequently be mere approximations (391). The grief that gives rise to her tears in the chapel seems to cleanse her, and her new understanding to strengthen her in the effort to love again. Her first act upon leaving the chapel is to resume what is imaged as a life sentence to be served amid humanity, and the close of the novel describes the tentative beginnings of her service in the form of a love for the merchant Jevons. Chastened and "ineluctably earthbound" (402) but still "smouldering" with the fires of life (404), Ellen exits the novel rededicated to life and its perpetuation.

Having pursued through four decades of fiction the apprehension of oneness that may open to those who cultivate humility and self-abnegation and who persevere in the quest, the visionary of White's most recent works is finally ready for the last phase of spiritual initiation, in which he or she seeks and may even find forgiveness, reunion, and a fellowship of man. This difficult territory—the Whitean equivalent of Beulah land—is entered tentatively and with protective self-mockery. But in the latest work, it is occupied with confidence and quiet joy.

The imperative of reconciliation is a primary theme of *The Twyborn Affair*. It is felt as a desperate desire by sexually and culturally disoriented Eddie Twyborn, who spends two-thirds of the novel in female clothes and female identities, in foreign climes and among foreign peoples. Eddie needs to be reconciled to self, family, past, and homeland. But in this sometimes cynical, often discouraged and discouraging novel, the extent to which his needs are met remains uncertain.

In the novel's final pages, two visions are granted: one to Eudoxia/Eddie/Eadith and the other to his/her mother Eadie. Eddie's occurs as he lies bleeding to death on a London street after having been injured by one of the bombs that signaled the onslaught of the Blitz. The vision is atypical in White, in that an atmosphere of apocalyptic chaos replaces the usual ambiance of ecstasy and serenity:

> In a moment it seemed to Eddie Twyborn as though his own share
> in time was snatched away, as though every house he had ever lived
> in was torn open, the sawdust pouring out of all the dolls in all the

rooms, furniture whether honest or pretentious still shuddering from its brush with destruction, a few broken bars of a Chabrier waltz scattered from the burst piano, . . . all contained in the ruins of this great unstable temporal house, all but Eddie and Eadith, unless echoes of their voices threading pandemonium. (429)

Although White's imagery in this passage does imply totality, it does not so much enclose the whole as explode it. In addition, the fact that the protagonist continues to function here as Eddie *and* Eadith, male and female, suggests that the duality of his/her nature is unresolved, perhaps irreducible. On the other hand, White's last few phrases imply that Eddie/Eadith may have escaped the general ruin of time, having groped his/her way out of pandemonium as Theseus threaded the maze of the Minotaur. Has Eddie/Eadith been received out of time and anarchy or not? The author refuses to say.

The implications of Eadie's visionary moment are far less equivocal. Waiting in her London hotel for Eddie/Eadith's visit, she is given a moment White later described as one of "grace" (*Flaws* 257). Temporarily shielded from the cataclysms of the present, Eadie is returned to the calm atemporality of her Sydney garden, where she finds "harmony at last" in contemplation of an achieved reconciliation with her child (432). Wounds to Eddie's body have just killed him, but his lacerated spirit seems healed by Eadie's forgiving love, a love that restores her son/daughter to self, family, and home. White leaves to the reader the task of reconciling Eddie/Eadith's vision with Eadie's and reclaiming a wholeness for the book analogous to that which Eadie's vision seems to have provided her child.

Doubled and counterpointed visions are also a feature of *Memoirs of Many in One*, in which the onerous job of editing a dead friend's memoirs starts "editor" Patrick White reluctantly off on a quest eventually parallel to that of Alex Gray. Alex spends the whole novel in one fantastic guise after another, always in search of an authentic self. Her increasingly frantic and unlikely essays into selfhood are occasionally blessed with illuminations, most strikingly in the passage describing her desert vision of a dark "miraculous Being" who bathes her spirit in a "stream of understanding" (139). In the vision, the highest good inheres in coming together, in union through understanding.

The project of arranging and annotating Alex's memoirs forces the editor into a position vis-à-vis his subject, which finally resembles that of the miraculous Being. Although he wants to maintain a scholarly distance, he succumbs to the temptation to understand. After Alex's death, he and her officious daughter undertake a sort of pilgrimage intended to recapitulate her life in the places she lived it and to "lay a few ghosts" (184). But the ghosts of Alex's many selves refuse to be laid. Patrick encounters her in the form of a Greek nun, an Italian guerrilla, and most importantly, the corpse of Santa Chiara who appears to him as Alex on her deathbed. This final vision, among other things, convinces him that he and Alex will "never [be] quit of each other" (192). They are now two registers of the same first-person voice, two faces of one "great creative ego" (192). By the end of the novel, Patrick has very nearly *become* Alex, living in her house, sleeping in her bed, bullied by her daughter, and aware of the reciprocal roles he and Alex have exercised within each other's lives and arts.

Of course, this sort of reconciliation is not altogether positive. The novel leaves us wondering whether Alex and Patrick have not usurped as much as embraced each other's essential natures. But no such mixed emotions are aroused by "The Age of a Wart," the last of the short stories collected in *Three Uneasy Pieces.* In the story's final passage, the narrator celebrates a reunion with a long-absent spiritual twin, whose selfless service to others has acted as life-long ironic commentary on the narrator's service to his possibly irrelevant art. Differences are overcome, however, and irony eradicated, when the twin rejoins the narrator in a deathbed vision:

> He has come. He is holding my hands in his. I who was once the reason for the world's existence am no longer this sterile end-all. As the world darkens, the evil in me is dying. I understand. Along with the prisoners, sufferers, survivors. It is no longer I it is we.
> It is *we* who hold the secret of existence
> *we* who control the world
> WE

(58–59)

In its emphasis on understanding, the passage recalls the challenges issued to Eadie Twyborn and "editor" White. Even more importantly, in its institution of an empathetic brotherhood of sufferers, the vision comes full circle, returning us to *Happy Valley* and its consanguinity of pain.

One final point to make about this moment is that it empowers: We hold the secret; we have the strength; we can achieve the vision. In other words, while some tenets of the Whitean philosophy may strike us as rather bleak assessments of human worth and potential, visions like this one prove that the overall tenor of his metaphysic is astonishingly optimistic, especially when viewed as a product of our terrorized and terrifying age. White sees human beings, at least some human beings, as capable of the task he sets them.

Moreover, this vision speaks to us out of a most audacious fictional form. In a time characterized by artistic retrenching, a time of writers who have lost the confidence of the great moderns, writers whose daring often extends only in the direction of formal ingenuity, and whose obsession with their own processes sometimes derives from a fear of impotence before larger concerns, White not only tackles the oldest, grandest themes but defends and preserves the linkages between text and world. He seems to believe that literature, indeed art of all sorts, still matters in the most profound of ways. The spiritual journeys chronicled in his novels—through failure and humiliation to humility, renunciation, empathy, integrity, and union—are open to his readers as well. It may be that only the heroic can complete such journeys, but it is also true that only an heroic artist could have conceived them. It is finally this heroism that marks White as one of the century's most significant writers.

WORKS CITED

Björksten, Ingmar. "A Day with Patrick White." Trans. John Martin. *Nation Review* 21-27 June 1974: 1179.

Edgecombe, Rodney Stenning. *Vision and Style in Patrick White: A Study of Five Novels.* Tuscaloosa: U of Alabama P, 1989.

Hope, A. D. "The Bunyip Stages a Comeback." Rev. of *The Tree of Man*, by Patrick White. *Sydney Morning Herald* 16 June 1956: 15.

Mackenzie, Manfred. "Patrick White's Later Novels: A Generic Reading." *Southern Review* 1 (1965): 5–18.

McGregor, Craig, editor. *In the Making.* Melbourne: Nelson, 1969.

Sharman, Jim. "A Very Literary Luncheon." *National Times* 30 June 1979: 26-27, 30–31.

Steiner, George. "Carnal Knowledge." Rev. of *The Eye of the Storm*, by Patrick White. *New Yorker* 4 Mar. 1974: 109–13.

White, Patrick. *The Aunt's Story.* 1948. New York: Avon, 1975.

———. "Bitter old man prays for the failed, the deranged, the poor." *Sydney Morning Herald* 22 July 1988: 13.

———. "A Conversation with Patrick White." *Southerly* 33 (1973): 132–43.

———. "Credo." *Overland* No. 111 (1988): 16.

———. *The Eye of the Storm.* 1973. New York: Avon, 1975.

———. *Flaws in the Glass: A Self-Portrait.* New York: Viking, 1981.

———. *A Fringe of Leaves.* 1976. New York: Viking, 1977.

———. *Happy Valley.* 1939. New York: Viking, 1940.

———. *The Living and the Dead.* New York: Viking, 1941.

———. *Memoirs of Many in One, by Alex Xenophon Demirjian Gray.* New York: Viking, 1986.

———. "The Prodigal Son." *Australian Letters* 1.3 (1958): 37–40.

———. *Riders in the Chariot.* 1961. New York: Avon, 1975.

———. *The Solid Mandala.* 1966. New York: Avon, 1975.

———. *Three Uneasy Pieces.* Fairfield, Australia: Pascoe, 1987.

———. *The Tree of Man.* 1955. New York: Avon, 1975.

———. *The Twyborn Affair.* London: Jonathan Cape, 1979.

———. *The Vivisector.* 1970. New York, Avon, 1975.

———. *Voss.* 1957. New York: Avon, 1975.

Wolfe, Peter. *Laden Choirs: The Fiction of Patrick White.* Lexington: UP of Kentucky, 1983.

PATRICK WHITE'S PUBLISHED WORK

Novels

Happy Valley, 1939
The Living and the Dead, 1941
The Aunt's Story, 1948
The Tree of Man, 1955
Voss, 1957
Riders in the Chariot, 1961
The Solid Mandala, 1966
The Vivisector, 1970
The Eye of the Storm, 1973
A Fringe of Leaves, 1976
The Twyborn Affair, 1979
Memoirs of Many in One, by Alex Xenophon Demirjian Gray, 1986

Short Fiction

The Burnt Ones, 1964
The Cockatoos: Shorter Novels and Stories, 1974
Three Uneasy Pieces, 1987

Plays and Screenplay

(Production dates in parentheses)
The Ham Funeral, 1965 (written 1947; produced 1961)
The Season at Sarsaparilla, 1965 (1962)
A Cheery Soul, 1965 (1963)
Night on Bald Mountain, 1965 (1964)
Four Plays, 1965 (contains the above plays)
Big Toys, 1978 (1977)
The Night the Prowler: Short Story and Screenplay, 1978
Signal Driver, 1983 (1982)
Netherwood, 1983 (1983)
"Shepherd on the Rocks" (1987)

Poetry

Thirteen Poems, 1930 (?)
The Ploughman and Other Poems, 1935

Memoir

Flaws in the Glass: A Self-Portrait. New York: Viking, 1981.
> A sometimes rancorous, always illuminating "self-portrait" rather than chronological autobiography. Includes sections on periods of his life and on his travels (mainly in Greece and the Greek islands), as well as sketches of episodes, friends, and enemies. Comments on his "sexual ambivalence" and describes the genesis of many of his novels.

Commentary

"The Prodigal Son." *Australian Letters* 1.3 (1958): 37–40. (Reprinted in *The Vital Decade: Ten Years of Australian Art and Letters*. Melbourne: Sun Books, 1968. 156–58).
> Defends and explains White's decision to return to Australia after World War II, rather than remain an expatriate. Source of several much-quoted remarks, such as those on the "nostalgia of desert landscapes," "stimulus of time remembered," "Great Australian Emptiness," Australian critics as "dingoes . . . howling unmercifully," and his determination "to prove that the Australian novel is not necessarily the dreary, dun-coloured offspring of journalistic realism."

From *In the Making*. Edited by Craig McGregor. Melbourne: Nelson, 1969. 218–22.
> White discusses his use of religious themes, his writing processes, the centrality of character to his fiction, and some literary influences.

"A Conversation with Patrick White." *Southerly* 33 (1973): 132–43.
> Describes his early life, the beginnings of his writing career, and the recovery of his belief in a divine being. Answers questions about recurring themes and preoccupations in his work and his ironic handling of character.

"Patrick White Speaks on Factual Writing and Fiction." *Australian Literary Studies* 10 (1981): 99–101.
> Text of an address given for the National Book Council Awards, 1980. Treats the genesis of his "self-portrait" (see above) and calls such a project "the most difficult kind of factual writing."

"Patrick White." *Imagining the Real*. Sydney: Australian Broadcasting Corporation, 1987. 15–18.
> The political White at his most acerb in a talk for a 1986 symposium held in Canberra by Writers Against Nuclear Arms. White is particularly hard on Ronald Reagan but also chastizes Australians for "complacency" about the arms race and other atrocities.

Patrick White: His Life and Work. Sydney: Australian Broadcasting Corporation, 1988.
> Consists of five audiocassettes of programs broadcast on ABC radio in 1987. Traces White's life and career, includes lengthy passages from his work read or dramatized by actors, and provides excerpts spoken by White himself from interviews and from *Flaws in the Glass*.

"Bitter old man prays for the failed, the deranged, the poor." *Sydney Morning Herald* 22 July 1988: 13.
    Edited text of a 1988 speech given at La Trobe University, Melbourne. Makes a plea for honesty
    and "integrity" in the personal and political lives of Australians, particularly of the Bicentennial,
    which he calls "the great Australian lie." Avows that true nationhood "is born of suffering" and
    calls for "a civilization based on humanity."

Patrick White Speaks. Leichhardt, New South Wales: Primavera Press, 1989.
    Collection of White's nonfiction including major interviews, speeches, and some material either
    previously unpublished or very difficult to find. Provides a bibliography of editions of White's
    books in English and other languages.

SELECTED CRITICAL READINGS

The volume of work on Patrick White, both by Australian and overseas critics, dwarfs
that devoted to other postwar Australian writers. At present, there are better than
twenty-five book-length studies of his achievements in fiction and drama as well as
hundreds of shorter pieces: articles, reviews, monographs, theses and dissertations,
special journal issues, book chapters, symposium proceedings, and the like. Until the
seventies, books on White tended to be synoptic and introductory, but, particularly
since he won the Nobel Prize for Literature in 1973, increased international
attention and the growing estimation of his worth within Australia have generated
more specialized studies of his themes, imagery, anti-realist techniques, and most
recently, style. Heated arguments persist about the wellsprings of his work: whether
religious or secular, the product of intuition, the unconscious, or a more or less
coherent philosophy. Full response to his style remains a challenge to today's White
critics, and comparative perspectives on his work are still too few. The list that
follows emphasizes books, and especially recent entries, as more likely to offer
comprehensive treatments of White and to be informed by earlier criticism.

Akerholt, May-Brit. *Patrick White.* Australian Playwrights Series 2. Amsterdam: Rodopi, 1988. Only the
    second book-length study of White as a dramatist. Discusses all eight of his plays chronologically,
    with special attention to characterization, staging devices, and the way in which White's satire
    "expos[es] Australia to . . . Australians."

Beatson, Peter. *The Eye in the Mandala, Patrick White: A Vision of Man and God.* New York: Harper
    & Row, 1976. A relatively early (and influential) thematic study of White's writing as "an attempt
    to revivify certain theological clichés and to reveal their contemporary human relevance" (2).
    Treats the *ouevre* through *The Cockatoos* (1974) as the expression of a single, coherent vision,
    rather than tracing shifts and developments. Sees three interpenetrating "worlds" in White's
    fiction: those of ultimate being, self, and nature.

Berg, Mari-Ann. *Aspects of Time, Ageing and Old Age in the Novels of Patrick White, 1939–1979.*
    Goteborg, Sweden: ACTA Universitatis Gothoburgensis, 1983. Focuses attention on the themes
    of time and time's passage in White's novels. Especially concerned with the role of memory in
    directing narrative.

Bliss, Carolyn. *Patrick White's Fiction: The Paradox of Fortunate Failure.* New York: St. Martin's, 1986.
    Explores what the author identifies as a major thematic paradox: that the failures so often
    experienced by characters can lead to their successful redemption. Links this approach to style

and genre by showing how White imposes failure on himself, a discipline that gives rise to distinctive features of his work. Treats all the fiction through *The Twyborn Affair.*

Björksten, Ingmar. *Patrick White: A General Introduction.* 1973. Translated by Stanley Gerson. St. Lucia: U of Queensland P, 1976. First published in Swedish in the year White won the Nobel Prize for literature and translated thereafter into German, Norwegian, and English, this book was influential in shaping European response to White. Argues that suffering is the "path to insight" in his work, and covers his early poetry, first volume of short fiction, and first four plays, as well as novels through The Eye *of the Storm.*

Colmer, John. *Patrick White.* Contemporary Writers Series. New York: Methuen, 1984. Most recent and among the briefest of the general introductions. Treats the fiction chronologically (through *The Twyborn Affair*) and devotes one chapter to the plays and short stories. Notes a "new vision of . . . potential reconciliation" between the individual and group and a "more compassionate view of human nature" emerging in recent work.

Dyce, J.R. *Patrick White as Playwright.* St Lucia: U of Queensland P, 1974. First book-length study of White as a dramatist. Treats the four plays he had then published: *The Ham Funeral, The Season at Sarsaparilla, A Cheery Soul,* and *Night on Bald Mountain.* Considers whether White's plays measure up to his novels and the ways in which, for good or ill, they differ from the fiction.

Edgecombe, Rodney Stenning. *Vision and Style in Patrick White: A Study of Five Novels.* Tuscaloosa: U of Alabama P, 1989. Concentrates attention on *Voss, Riders in the Chariot, The Solid Mandala, The Vivisector,* and *The Eye of the Storm* to mount an argument for a "continuity of vision and style" in White's best novels. Advances the work from *The Tree of Man* to *The Eye of the Storm* as "a canon of great novels" and sees those before as flawed stylistically and those after as marred by a restricted, even self-satirizing vision. Provides close and exhaustive stylistic analysis of the works under consideration.

Hansson, Karin. *The Warped Universe: A Study of Imagery and Structure in Seven Novels by Patrick White.* Barometern, Kalmar: CWK Gleerup, Lund, 1984. Analyzes the novels from *The Aunt's Story* to *The Eye of the Storm* (with a note on *A Fringe of Leaves*), focusing on imagery and structure as well as metaphysical affinities between White and Jung, Blake, and Schopenhauer. Finds a "system of structures and symbols" underlying the organization of these middle novels but also identifies "development within the series." Argues finally that White's philosophical universe is "warped" because "only the chosen few" are deemed worthy of admittance to its apprehension.

Kiernan, Brian. *Patrick White.* London: Macmillan, 1980. General introduction to White by an Australian and choosing to concentrate on the works' "historical, cultural context" and "local and temporal, as well as universal, aspects." Discussion begins with White's early poetry and continues with novels, stories, and plays through *Big Toys.* Interested throughout in White's treatment of Australian society.

McCulloch. A. M. *A Tragic Vision: The Novels of Patrick White.* St. Lucia: U of Queensland P, 1983. Largely Nietzschean reading of White, covering all his novels through *The Twyborn Affair.* Views his work as "the expression of the tragic vision of an artist in the modern world." Sees *The Twyborn*

Affair as a successful "post-modernist tragedy" and the culmination of White's search for an adequate vehicle of tragic vision.

Morley, Patricia A. *The Mystery of Unity: Theme and Technique in the Novels of Patrick White.* Montreal: McGill-Queen's UP, 1972. Among the first book-length studies of White to go beyond synoptic treatments towards a focus on underlying themes. Prioritizes the approaches of archetypal criticism to find that the author's theme is the "mystery of unity about the world," a phrase taken from *Happy Valley.* Argues that his apprehension of this unity places him in the great tradition of Western religious writing. Covers novels through *The Vivisector.*

Myers, David. *The Peacocks and the Bourgeoisie: Ironic Vision in Patrick White's Shorter Fiction.* Adelaide: Adelaide University Union Press, 1978. To date, the only book to be exclusively concerned with White's short fiction. Identifies an omnipresent, "dualistic" irony in the short fiction, which rewards suffering with "epiphany" and undercuts epiphany with "anti-climax." Also likens White's preoccupations to those of Kafka and includes a chapter on narrative technique in the shorter fiction.

Shepherd, R., and K. Singh, editors. *Patrick White: A Critical Symposium.* Adelaide: Centre for Research in the New Literatures in English, 1978. Collection of papers presented at a 1978 symposium on White, which John Barnes describes as an attempt to ascertain why White's work "matters so much" to Australians. Papers range from assessment of White's overall achievement, to debates about the religious dimensions of his work, to analyses of individual texts, to questions of White's "Australianness" and whether his novels are Victorian or twentieth century.

Steven, Laurence. *Dissociation and Wholeness in Patrick White's Fiction.* Waterloo, Ontario: Wilfrid Laurier UP, 1989. As late as 1989, finds it necessary to demonstrate that "White is a major writer" and does so by arguing that within his work a "wholeness" located in a world of human relationships opposes the duality or "dissociation" produced by the Whitean longing for the ideal in an imperfect world of flux and impermanence.

Tacey, David J. *Patrick White: Fiction and the Unconscious.* Melbourne: Oxford UP, 1988. Probably the most controversial book published on White to date. Using Jungian concepts, argues that White's fiction is the product of his unconscious, which is mired in an unresolved mother complex. Therefore, sees White's questers seeking not self-realization but "self-immolation" in the "maternal source." Contends that with *The Solid Mandala* White's own battle for psychic liberation is lost and his focus must shift henceforth from the son to the symbolic mother figure who dominates later novels. Treats the fiction through *Memoirs of Many in One.*

Texas Studies in Literature and Language 21.2 (1979). Special issue devoted entirely to White. Gathers critics of several nationalities who take a variety of approaches. Includes a bibliography and Alan Lawson's well-known essay on problems in White criticism.

Walsh, William. *Patrick White's Fiction.* Totowa, New Jersey: Rowman & Littlefield, 1977. Introduces readers to White's novels through *A Fringe of Leaves* as well as his first four plays and first two collections of short fiction. Finds in White "the qualities of largeness, uninhibited confidence, and potent creative energy" the author identifies in much current international literature in English.

Weigel, John A. *Patrick White*. Boston: Twayne, 1983. Opens with a biographical chapter, drawing much of its material from *Flaws in the Glass*. Treats White's poetry, fiction, and drama from *Thirteen Poems* to *The Twyborn Affair*. Distrusts summary statements about any aspect of White's work or thought and characterizes him as "a visionary with a sense of humor."

Wilkes, G. A., editor. *Ten Essays on Patrick White*. Sydney: Angus & Robertson, 1970. Collects essays on White from the Australian literary journal *Southerly* (1964–67) and arranges them under the headings "Novels," "Some Reconsiderations," and "Plays and Short Stories." Includes helpful essays on *The Aunt's Story*, *The Tree of Man*, *Voss*, *Riders in the Chariot*, and *The Solid Mandala*.

Wolfe, Peter. *Laden Choirs: The Fiction of Patrick White*. Lexington: UP of Kentucky, 1983. First and final chapters provide overviews of the major issues engaging readers and critics of White. Interim chapters individually treat the novels through *The Twyborn Affair*. Conveys throughout the richness and complexity of White's "art of the copious" and the difficulties that attend his attempt to "court the ineffable."

Biography

Marr, David. *Patrick White—A Life*. New York: Knopf, 1991.

— CAROLYN BLISS

V.S. Naipaul

S ir Vidiadhar Surajprasad Naipaul received his knighthood in the Queen's New Year List, 1990. The honor recognizes Naipaul's contribution to literature over more than thirty years.

In those thirty years Naipaul has wrestled with the ambiguity inherent in being an East Indian West Indian who identifies most strongly with the traditions and culture of England. He was born on 17 August 1932 in Chaguanas, central Trinidad. His grandfather was one of many Indians transported to Trinidad as indentured laborers to replace black slaves in the cane fields of the West Indies. While some members of his family mixed Hindi with English throughout their lives, others, most importantly his father who struggled to become a journalist and writer of short stories in English and who introduced his son to English literature at an early age, moved rapidly away from the family's Hindu background. Naipaul has commented that his late brother, Shiva, thirteen years younger and also a writer, knew little of the Hindu tradition that was dying during his own boyhood.

While his father, Seepersad, was certainly the strongest influence on Naipaul's life, his mother's family, the Capildeos, also figures in his work. The Capildeos were a prominent family in Trinidad and active in Trinidadian politics; an uncle, Rudranath, was leader of the Indian Democratic Labour Party. Trinidadian politics are dealt with satirically in early novels (especially *The Mystic Masseur* and *The Suffrage of Elvira*) and provide the source for more serious treatments in later work (especially *The Mimic Men* and *Guerrillas*).

After beginning his education at Chaguanas Government School, Naipaul attended Tranquillity Boys' School for four years and then entered the most prestigious secondary institution of Trinidad, Queens Royal College, where he was a scholarship student specializing in French and Spanish. He won a special scholarship to University College, Oxford, in 1950, where he read English.

After Oxford, he became a British Broadcasting Corporation freelance writer and editor of the program "Caribbean Voices." It was in the BBC's freelancers' room that he wrote his first stories that were collected in *Miguel Street*. (These stories were not published until 1959, after his first two novels appeared.) In this early period he also wrote many reviews for *New Statesman*.

A House for Mr. Biswas, a novel based on his father's life, confirmed Naipaul's reputation. From then on, he was able to gain commissions for nonfictional writing as well as a market for his fiction. While maintaining his base in England, he has traveled through former colonies recording their efforts to establish themselves as independent nations; this material often appears as articles in the *New York Review of Books* or leading London newspapers' Sunday editions before it is collected into a volume, such as *India, A Wounded Civilization* or *The Return of Eva Perón.*

Besides the knighthood, Naipaul has been honored with many prizes; among them are the Llewellyn Rhys Memorial Prize (*The Mystic Masseur*), the Somerset Maugham Award (*Miguel Street*), the Hawthornden Prize (*Mr. Stone and the Knights Companion*), the W.H. Smith Prize (*The Mimic Men*), the Booker Prize (*In a Free State*), and a Phoenix Trust Award.

His career has not, however, been without controversy, for many critics and reviewers bitterly condemn his comments on various postcolonial societies, which he has invariably characterized as impoverished by their history as colonies and unlikely to break free of the past to establish a strong independent presence in the world.

FINDING THE PRESENT IN THE PAST

"How can the history of this futility be written?" As a young writer Naipaul asked this question in *The Middle Passage* when he tried to portray the outcome of colonialism in various Caribbean countries. It is a question that has haunted him throughout his career. First, he has been repeatedly condemned for the "patronizing," "superior," or "racist" attitude many critics believe he adopts toward Third World societies, and this line is often quoted as an example. Second, answering his own question, Naipaul has himself turned historian and written a highly unusual history of Trinidad (*The Loss of El Dorado*). Third, he has, in his journalism, tried to capture events and to portray his personal interpretation of the legacy of colonialism in such a way that historians may add his views to others to gain the type of picture that is often lost in historical accounts. Finally, through his fiction, Naipaul has constantly attempted to mediate history, both his personal history and that of various colonial experiences, in order to capture insights that transcend simply knowing what happened.

In a television interview subsequent to publication of *The Enigma of Arrival* ("The South Bank Show" 8 March 1987), Naipaul asserted that the difference between history and fiction is that fiction must be logical. Real events, he said, rarely make any sense at all; if a novel recorded events as they are, it would be condemned as implausible. He was speaking specifically of the relation between his journalistic accounts of three murders in Trinidad ("Michael X and the Black Power Killings in Trinidad") and the novel closely based on the murders, *Guerrillas*. The murderer was a Trinidadian of mixed race, Michael de Freitas (alias Michael Abdul Malik alias Michael X), who achieved a small following in London by preaching Black Power. He returned to Trinidad accompanied by another self-proclaimed leader of the Black Power Movement and a white woman. In the novel, Michael Abdul Malik is Jimmy Ahmed; one of the victims was the woman, Gale Benson, who becomes Jane.

The long feature articles attempt to portray the conditions and events that made it possible for Abdul Malik to gain patronage from white English people, press coverage, and so on, but the articles focus on the individual's story, and the power of the journalism is achieved through the portrayal of a tormented and insecure human. The portrait does not flatter Abdul Malik but it does inspire compassion for him. On the other hand, those individuals who take him up are treated with some contempt, and so are both societies contributing to the Abdul Malik phenomenon. Naipaul's hypothesis, expressed in other nonfictional writing of this period, is that a society reveals itself in the quality of its interpersonal relationships—an idea developed, for instance, in articles on Argentina and Uruguay collected in *The Return of Eva Perón*. Consequently, where personal interaction ends in violence, we should expect to find an exploitative and inhumane setting.

In the fiction, *Guerrillas*, the physical setting receives much more attention than in the nonfiction,"The Killings in Trinidad." Details, such as backyard shacks, swarms of children, burning rubbish, carrion *corbeaux*, abandoned factories, pariah dogs, the scarred countryside reflect the political disarray of the island. There is an attempt to find the logic, the explanations for events that in the nonfiction seem quite bizarre. Naipaul suggests a colonial past that explains how a mixed society was thrown together to form a community without common standards or goals. Jimmy Ahmed tells the story of the foundation of the Sablich family fortune and seems to recognize in its opportunism and exploitation the seeds of present corruption under the veneer of respectability. Harry de Tunja is also aware of his family heritage of impermanence: ". . . the surname I carry is really the name of a town in South America. . . . When we were in Tunja we were called de Cordoba. And I suppose in Cordoba it was Ben-something-or-other. Always the last place you run from" (130). The introduction of a South African white campaigner for equal rights—also, as it transpires, a man on the run from his own vulnerability—broadens the horizons of the novel to suggest a global perspective beyond the specific West Indian experience of the aftermath of colonialism. The attempt to portray political action based on race does not, however, result in any suggestion of solutions for the specific or global ills resulting from colonial history. In Naipaul's view the past has doomed this society never to achieve a viable political or economic identity independent of the colonial master.

From early in his career, Naipaul asserted that the task of a writer is to impose order, to try to make sense of the chaos of reality. Any of his books may be approached from this perspective, but a brief consideration of *A House for Mr. Biswas* will show how the novelist's imagination orders the raw material of his boyhood and his father's biography. The image of the title, Mr. Biswas's attempts to acquire his own house, controls the structure of the novel. Except for a brief introductory section, which starts the story where it will eventually end, the novel moves chronologically through the story of Mohan Biswas, for whom Naipaul's father, Seepersad, was the model. In his attempts to gain independence from his wife's family, Mr. Biswas becomes the archetypal victim of colonization, economically dependent and lacking in status unless he remains associated with the family's power. At the same time, though, within their Trinidadian setting, the Tulsi family are themselves becoming deracinated and dislocated as they lose their Hindu identity.

The final challenge both to individual and to group when they are transplanted from their original homes, as were the Indians in Trinidad, is to establish an alternative way of life that builds on the strengths of the old and draws on the best qualities of the new. Both the Tulsis and Mr. Biswas fail to meet that challenge, but

Mr. Biswas does manage to free himself of his dependence on the Tulsis and establish his wife and children in a home of their own. He suffers pain and humiliation in gaining his goal, and his house is far from sound, but clearly we are to see his achievement as heroic. His son Anand, narrator of the story, takes a step further away from his Hindu origins and, like Naipaul himself, gains a scholarship to study in England.

So individuals seem able to gain some measure of success, at least as it is measured by the standards of the dominant culture. But the society within which their personal stories are told is portrayed by Naipaul as small and impoverished, in several senses of both words. In other writings, such as *The Middle Passage*, Naipaul explains what he believes to be the cultural failure of the society by stating that those who claimed the colony in the first place were profoundly second rate and incapable of creating anything like a New World; his opinion is that all they did was to set up a hollow imitation of the metropolitan culture, so the transported Negroes and Indians imitated an imitation as they were stripped of their own cultures.

A later novel, probably his masterpiece, *The Mimic Men,* turns to much of this material again, but in this case the treatment of it is much less grounded in actual events and the construction of the novel is much less linear. Through Ralph Singh who is drawn briefly into a political life, Naipaul reveals not just a personal history but also the political story of a West Indian island struggling to find its cultural identity in a myriad of borrowed and imported fragments. Isabella, the island, is a fictional compilation of elements from Trinidad, Jamaica, and Guyana.

While, despite the narrator's introspection, *The Mimic Men* offers a more political and outward-looking perspective than *A House for Mr. Biswas,* like all of Naipaul's novels, it focuses on the individual within the society. Ralph Singh tells his own story, and because he discovers the story by telling it, Anand's chronological organization of Biswas's story is impossible for him. Singh shares an obsession with many of Naipaul's characters and their real-life prototypes: He writes in order to discover, possibly to establish his personal reality. When Singh finds a huge log washed up on the shore of Isabella, he has "thoughts, too alarming to pursue, about things existing only when seen" (128). There is a suggestion that for much of the "Old World," the Third World exists only when it forces itself into consciousness.

The Mimic Men abounds in images that underline the colonial's struggle to maintain a grip on reality: Singh's writing, Singh's naming games in London and his changes to his own name, the houses of characters from various backgrounds in Isabella, and most powerful of all, the image of shipwreck. In Singh's eyes, and in Naipaul's, the arrival of people from a wide variety of backgrounds, and their loss of cultural identities, parallels the experience of shipwreck—being lost without the necessities of life. When Singh writes about a family outing of his boyhood, he tells of driving through a village where the mulatto residents are referred to as Spaniards and through a "Carib" village where the residents are more Negro than indigenous Indians:

> . . . it was like being in an area of legend. The scale was small in time, numbers and area; and here, just for a moment, the rise and fall and extinction of peoples, a concept so big and alarming, was

concrete and close. Slaves and runaways, hunters and hunted, rulers and ruled: they had no romance for me. Their message was only that nothing was secure. (136)

The shipwrecked people of Isabella cling to the fragments of their disappearing pasts, fail to establish a vital new culture, and long to become a part of the powerful metropolitan culture of the colonial master. Hence, Singh retreats to London to try to write his personal history and in doing so to gain understanding of what it means to be a postcolonial. Selwyn Cudjoe argues that Singh and Naipual actually fail to move from being colonial subjects to postcolonial persons, because they never cease to identify themselves with the mother country; they never believe that a separate and autonomous national identity is possible for an independent former colony.

While readers must be wary of assuming that Singh always represents Naipaul's own views, the character and the author are very closely identified. One of the strongest links is Singh's interest in history. Singh sees in the attempt to write history an opportunity to discover calm and order; eventually he decides that he is "too much a victim of that restlessness which was to have been my subject" (39), and abandons the attempt to write a history of empire; but Naipaul pursued Singh's dream. Anyone tracing the chronology of Naipaul's writing will not be surprised that his next work was the history of Trinidad's colonial period, *The Loss of El Dorado*. Nor is it surprising that this book identifies the origins of many traits Naipaul condemns in his nonfictional accounts of Third World societies.

Naipaul's history of Trinidad attempts to rediscover the past behind the legends of school textbooks. In writing of the Congo ("A New King for the Congo: Mobutu and the Nihilism of Africa"), Naipaul has said that where history of the Congo is known only through Belgian textbooks, African history has disappeared. Similarly, in *A Bend in the River*, which draws on this nonfiction and was written after *The Loss of El Dorado*, he expresses distrust of history, saying that one can never be sure what the real story was because historians are so selective in what they offer. He tries to stop this happening to Trinidad by recreating, among many others, Sir Walter Ralegh (who passed through Trinidad on his quests for El Dorado) and Antonio de Berrio (the Spaniard who founded the first European settlement in Trinidad), Picton (the first British governor of Trinidad who tortured runaway slaves), and Francisco Miranda (who used Trinidad as a staging post for the revolution in Venezuela). Naipaul returns the heroic legends to human scale by showing the lies and half-truths that drove and that were perpetuated by these figures, and that eventually formed the legends. He also discovers some of the totally unknown victims of the past: Luisa Calderón, a mulatto tortured in Picton's prison; Jacquet, a slave and poisoner of other slaves and of his master's infant son, whose own death remains a mystery—suicide? poisoned by another slave?; but the Carib and Arawak Indians are erased completely.

Many readers find it strange that Naipaul does not continue his investigation of the history of Trinidad into the time of the arrival of indentured Indians to replace freed Negroes in the cane fields. He comments only briefly that "It was a new human dereliction in the pattern of what had gone before" (*Loss of El Dorado* 374), and for him the pattern that has been established is that the indentured Indians will become an anonymous aspect of a colony whose history abounds in lies, delusions, failures, corruption, brutality, absurdity, and futility. These words recur constantly in Naipaul's work—both fiction and nonfiction. It is characteristic of a writer who seeks to impose order that he documents patterns and parallels from the past to the present and from one postcolonial society to another, and in so doing he repeats words and images, often emphasizing dereliction and loss. Recent critical approaches to Naipaul's work have emphasized its debt to Hindu philosophy and literature; the emphasis on cycles and predetermination in his historical work may be seen as an aspect of this debt. The almost obsessive search for parallels, repetitions, and patterns may also be considered the greatest weakness in Naipaul's work. While he is capable of drawing unforgettable word portraits of people and places he has visited, he still interprets each new experience from the perspective of his earlier work.

Having established some of the themes running through Naipaul's writing, it is necessary to confront the genuinely problematic aspect of his career. In those works already discussed and in the rest of his fiction and nonfiction, Naipaul clearly demonstrates a political consciousness of imperialism's deprivation of subjugated people's cultural identities. However, there is something lacking in his discussions of the Third World, something Selwyn Cudjoe addresses fully in his critical work. He identifies the problem as one grounded in Naipaul's racism and his filial relation with the culture of the metropolis and states that Naipaul fails to explore fully the West Indian or any other Third World scene because he is incapable of penetrating and appreciating different cultural styles and structures. According to Cudjoe, Naipaul's reality is Western, particularly European, and specifically British. Thus, in *The Loss of El Dorado*, Naipaul turns to written European sources but neglects oral traditions or scholarship that might have helped him understand better the Negro slave society he virtually ignores. Or in discussing Indian writers' autobiographies in *India, A Wounded Civilization*, Naipaul judges them from a Western perspective, failing to recognize that someone from a totally different cultural background will have different personal goals and not seek the objectivity preferred by Westerners.

The Enigma of Arrival establishes once and for all that Naipaul himself identifies with the metropolitan culture, that he has become an assimilated migrant in England. Ralph Singh asks himself repeatedly, "Why, recognizing the enemy, did you not kill him swiftly?" In effect, many who condemn Naipaul for his judgments of former colonies are asking the same question. What many of them fail to acknowledge is that Naipaul has recognized and described the enemy, imperialism and those colonizers who trampled roughshod through so much of the world. Therefore, I cannot read *The Loss of El Dorado* as Naipaul's "final historical-political justification for his condemnation of his society" (Cudjoe 118). Rather I see it as his final attempt to place the blame for the suffering, dislocation, and loss of colonial people everywhere. But I accept Cudjoe's point that Naipaul has not progressed in understanding past his articulation of the cultural deprivation inflicted by imperialism. Naipaul's personal and artistic dilemma seems to be that he knows his own cultural identity is that of the enemy—an identity established by his schooling under primarily British expatriate masters, his father's reading of Conrad and Dickens to him, his childhood and youth in a British-dominated colony where his people were losing their grip on their Hindu past.

Helen Tiffin in a recent article emphasizes how different are the two kinds of postcolonial circumstance: The indigenous peoples of some places, such as India, Africa, and the South Pacific, have alternative metaphysical systems with which to challenge European perspectives; but Caribbean people and the nonindigenous people of Canada, Australia, and New Zealand have no such formulated systems other than those borrowed from colonizers. Wilson Harris and George Lamming "interrogate the inscribed system" (Tiffin 173), but Naipaul cannot seem to bear taking that position. It appears that he cannot appreciate how powerful the alternatives to European culture can be in places where the European way was only a veneer added to existing ways of thinking and believing. So he interprets Africa or India as if they were Trinidad. But Africa and India are different. In addition, Naipaul certainly underestimates the vitality, richness, and individuality of developments in the cultural traditions of the Caribbean and other developing postcolonial societies.

Naipaul's most recent books include *Finding the Center* and *India, A Million Mutinies Now,* in which he seems to come to terms with his personal past and with colonial realities better than ever before, and, paradoxically, *The Enigma of Arrival,* in which he pretends to fictionalize through a narrative persona his personal experience of finally entering into the rhythms of the English countryside. In *The Mimic Men* a character of French ancestry tells Ralph Singh, who longs for the Himalayas, of his grandfather's pictures:

> "But where you are born is a funny thing. My great-grandfather and
> even my grandfather, they always talked about going back for good.
> They went. But they came back. You know, you are born in a place
> and you grow up there. You get to know the trees and the plants.
> You will never know any other trees and plants like that." (204)

Landscape completely dominates *The Enigma of Arrival* as the author/narrator chronicles getting to know the trees and his gradual adaptation to seasonal change in his adopted home.

If one were to believe *The Enigma of Arrival,* it would seem that Naipaul's personal tension between individual assimilation into the dominant English tradition and his political consciousness of the legacy of imperialism have been resolved. However, *The Enigma of Arrival* can be taken as a challenge to the conventions of the traditional English novel: There is no plot, virtually no characterization except for the narrator's introspection, and though the author claims it is a novel, it is almost entirely fact rather than fiction. In that sense, could this "faction" stand as a challenge to the political and personal authority of British tradition, even though it seems to say the narrator/author is assimilated? After all, there is in Wiltshire, dominated as it is by the image of Stonehenge, a past that long precedes the current Euro-American hegemony; and it is Naipaul's uncharacteristic sympathy with the mystical in Africa that surprised readers of *Finding the Center.* Giving the Keynote Address at a 1989 conference on the role of the migrant in postcolonial literature, West Indian writer and scholar, Edward Baugh, reminded his audience that cultures are not fixed, that they constantly change, and migrants within any culture contribute to that change even as they are being "assimilated."

At this time one may only raise the possibility that the center Naipaul is finding is not exactly the center we (or he) might expect.

WORKS CITED

Baugh, Edward. "Keynote Address. A Change of Skies: The Literature of Migration." Conference of the Post-Colonial Literatures and Language Research Centre, Macquarie University, Sydney, Australia, October 1989.

Bragg, Melvyn, Interviewer. "The South Bank Show—V.S. Naipaul." London Weekend Television. 8 March 1987.

Cudjoe, Selwyn. *V.S. Naipaul: A Materialist Reading.* Amherst: U of Massachusetts P, 1988.

Naipaul, V.S. *Guerrillas.* New York: Vintage, 1980.

———. *The Loss of El Dorado.* New York: Penguin, 1981.

———. *The Mimic Men.* New York: Vintage, 1980.

Tiffin, Helen. "Post-Colonialism, Post-Modernism and the Rehabilitation of Post-Colonial History." *Journal of Commonwealth Literature* 23 (1988): 169–81.

V.S. NAIPAUL'S PUBLISHED WORK

Novels

The Mystic Masseur, 1957
The Suffrage of Elvira, 1958
A House for Mr. Biswas, 1961
Mr. Stone and the Knights Companion, 1963
The Mimic Men, 1967
A Flag on the Island, 1967
In a Free State, 1971
Guerrillas, 1975
A Bend in the River, 1979
The Enigma of Arrival, 1987

Short Story Collection

Miguel Street, 1959

History, Travel, Personal Essays

The Middle Passage, 1962
An Area of Darkness, 1964
The Loss of El Dorado, 1969
The Overcrowded Barracoon, 1972
India, A Wounded Civilization, 1977
The Return of Eva Perón with *The Killings in Trinidad,* 1980
A Congo Diary, 1980
Among the Believers, 1982
Finding the Center, 1984
A Turn in the South, 1989
India, A Million Mutinies Now, 1990

SELECTED CRITICAL READINGS

Much analysis of Naipaul's work has appeared in critical journals, both obscure and accessible, in books devoted to his works alone, and in volumes covering several other writers. The following bibliography gives preference to books and tries to represent both early critical responses and later publications, favorable views and less appreciative, specialist reading, and background materials.

Cudjoe, Selwyn. *V.S. Naipaul: A Materialist Reading.* Amherst: U of Massachusetts P, 1988. Reveals how "Indian" much of Naipaul's early work actually is. Takes a strong political stance in revealing (in Cudjoe's assessment) Naipaul's lack of sympathy with and understanding of the Third World. Psychoanalytical readings are less convincing than the political.

Dabydeen, David, and Brinsley Samaroo. *India in the Caribbean.* London: Hansib Publishing, 1988. Collection of essays, poems, and prose by scholars and writers on the history and culture of Indians in the Caribbean. Helps provide a context for Naipaul's work.

Griffiths, Gareth. *A Double Exile: African and West Indian Writing Between Two Cultures.* London: Marion Boyars, 1978. Will assist the reader who wants to place Naipaul's work in a wider context. Griffiths is not one of Naipaul's admirers but he offers a balanced appraisal.

Hamner, Robert. *V.S. Naipaul.* New York: Twayne, 1973. Provides a solid survey of the earlier works.

———, editor. *Critical Perspectives on V.S. Naipaul.* Washington, DC: Three Continents Press, 1977. Includes reprints of some of the most influential early articles on Naipaul's work: R.H. Lee, "The Novels of V.S. Naipaul"; Gordon Rohlehr, "Character and Rebellion in *A House for Mr. Biswas*"; Maureen Warner-Lewis, "Cultural Confrontation in *A House for Mr. Biswas*"; V.S. Pritchett, "Climacteric"; Karl Miller, "V.S. Naipaul and the New Order"; Victor Ramraj, "The All-Embracing Christlike Vision"; Peter Nazareth, "*The Mimic Men* as a Study of Corruption"; John Updike, "Fool's Gold"; David Ormerod, "In a Derelict Land"; Gordon Rohlehr, "The Ironic Approach"; A.C. Derrick, "Naipaul's Technique as a Novelist"; Robert Hamner, "Character and Setting"; Bruce MacDonald, "Symbolic Action"; Francis Wyndham, "Services Rendered." Also includes articles by Naipaul.

Luis, William, editor. *Voices from Under: The Black Narrative in Latin America and the Caribbean.* Westport, Conn: Greenwood, 1984. Includes "V.S. Naipaul and the Question of Identity" by Selwyn Cudjoe. Another text that helps place Naipaul and his contribution to international writing.

McWatt, Mark, editor. *West Indian Literature and Its Social Context: Proceedings of the Fourth Annual Conference on West Indian Literature.* Cave Hill: U of the West Indies, 1985. Includes: Elaine Fido, "Psycho-Sexual Aspects of the Woman in V.S.Naipaul's Fiction"; Cheryl Griffith, "The Woman as Whore in the Novels of V.S. Naipaul"; Gloria Lyn, "Naipaul's *Guerrillas*: Fiction and Its Social Context"; Jeffery Robinson, "V.S. Naipaul and the Sexuality of Power"; John Small, "Sexuality and Cultural Aesthetic in the Novels of V.S. Naipaul."

Morris, Robert K. *Paradoxes of Order: Some Perspectives on the Fiction of V.S. Naipaul.* Columbia: U of Missouri P, 1975. Not an easy book to read, but many of the insights are valuable. Morris discusses Naipaul's attempts to impose order on the chaos of reality through his fictional writing.

Nightingale, Peggy. "V.S. Naipaul as Historian: Combating Chaos." *Southern Review* 13 (1980): 239-50. Emphasis on *The Loss of El Dorado.* Considers Naipaul's approach to history as revealed there and in some other works. (Elaborates some of the points touched on in the present essay)

———. *Journey Through Darkness: The Writing of V.S. Naipaul.* St. Lucia: U of Queensland P, 1987. Covers both fiction and nonfiction through 1984 in a chronological account of the development of major themes and interests. Emphasizes the interrelationships between fiction and nonfiction, stressing the way the nonfiction reveals the fantastic element in reality, while the fiction strives to find ordering principles.

Ramchand, Kenneth. *An Introduction to the Study of West Indian Literature.* Kingston, Jamaica: Nelson Caribbean, 1976. Offers insights for readers who wish to gain more perspective on Naipaul's work and early West Indian responses to it.

Rutherford, Anna, editor. *Common Wealth.* Aarhus, Denmark: Akademist Boghandel, 1972. Includes: Sam Selvon, "Note on Dialect"; Victor Ramraj, "The All-Embracing Christlike Vision: Tone and Attitude in *The Mimic Men*"; Shiva Naipaul (V.S.N's brother), "The Writer Without a Society."

"A Symposium of New Approaches to Commonwealth Literature." *Journal of Commonwealth Literature* 23 (1988): 144–81. Three essays on critical approaches to Commonwealth literature, with references to Naipaul's work: Viney Kirpal, "What Is the Modern Third World Novel?"; Stephen Slemon, "Post-Colonial Allegory and the Transformation of History"; Helen Tiffin, "Post-Colonialism, Post-Modernism and the Rehabilitation of Post-Colonial History."

Thieme, John. *The Web of Tradition: Uses of Allusion in V.S. Naipaul's Fiction.* London: Hansib Publishing, 1988. Considers major novels from the perspective of their relation to Western literary traditions and to Indian traditions.

Walsh, William. *V.S. Naipaul.* New York: Barnes and Noble, 1973. A very early appreciation of Naipaul's first books; typical of the criticism that provoked a backlash from Third World critics.

White, Landeg. *V.S. Naipaul: A Critical Introduction.* London: Macmillan, 1975. Though now somewhat out of date, still one of the best studies of Naipaul's work through *The Mimic Men.* Acknowledges some of the reservations about Naipaul's perspectives, but White is an admirer of his writing.

— PEGGY NIGHTINGALE

Jean Rhys

England and the West Indies claim Jean Rhys as their own, placing her respectively in the rank of their foremost writers. While acknowledged in *The New York Times Book Review* in 1974 as "the best living English novelist," she is also recognized as one of the major Caribbean writers. In the words of a fellow West Indian writer, her novel, *Wide Sargasso Sea*, is "a touchstone against which to assay West Indian literature before and after it" (Hearne 323–24).

The 1966 publication of *Wide Sargasso Sea* attracted attention to Jean Rhys, whose first four novels had fallen with their author into oblivion. Suddenly the almost forgotten Rhys, whom many thought dead, received the W.H. Smith Literary Award and the Heinemann Award of the Royal Society of Literature, and one year before her death in 1979, she was invited to Buckingham Palace by the Queen to receive the prestigious Council of Great Britain Award for Writers.

In addition to five novels, Rhys wrote three books of short stories and an autobiography, *Smile Please*, published posthumously. Twelve books, a two-hundred page bibliography, numerous interviews, and an increasing number each year of quality articles written about her works all attest to the extent of her international acclaim. Wilson Harris's comment on Rhys, "Her imaginative insights are 'white' and 'black'" (142), most appropriately explains why Jean Rhys, a writer who straddles two continents, best captures the alienation of man at odds with the norms of his society, the outsider, whether it be in Europe or in the West Indies. Praised by writers such as V.S. Naipaul, John Updike, Joyce Carol Oates, Shirley Hazzard, and many others, Rhys is now one of the most studied contemporary women writers.

Until she was seventeen years old, Rhys remained in Dominica, an island in the Lesser Antilles where she was born in 1890 of a Welsh father, who had come there to practice medicine, and a white Creole mother from a family of planters. She spent the rest of her life, except for a brief visit in 1936 to Dominica, in Great Britain and in Paris. Having to interrupt her studies at the Royal Academy of Dramatic Arts in London because of her father's death, she worked for a short time as a chorus girl and a model, drifting through England in a culture alien to her, existing on a meager income.

She married a Dutch-French songwriter, journalist, and minor writer, Jan Lenglet (Edward de Nèves—pen name), who was later imprisoned for financial irregularities. She lost a son soon after his birth, had a daughter, Maryvonne, and subsequently divorced Lenglet. Rhys then married a publisher's reader, Leslie Tilden-Smith, who died in 1945. Her third husband, a retired naval officer, died in Cheriton-Fitzpaine, the small village in Devonshire where Rhys spent the last years of her life and where she completed her masterpiece, *Wide Sargasso Sea*, as well as her autobiography, which was published in its unfinished form soon after her death in 1979.

THE DIVIDED SELF

> If you look into your mind, which one are you, Don Quixote or Sancho Panza? Almost certainly you are both.
>
> —George Orwell

The complexity of Jean Rhys's fiction has eluded many readers and critics. The apparent simplicity of her plots and the easily recognizable themes unifying her fiction are in part responsible for this oversight. Ford Madox Ford's preface to *The Left Bank and Other Stories*, labeling Rhys as the writer who could best plead the case of the underdog, marked the beginning of a trend that dominates most of the criticism on Rhys. Although new trends show increased attention to Rhys's use of language and style, until recently attention has been primarily directed to Rhys's treatment of the female victim of a society ruled by power, men, and money and of the exile living in a world alien to her.

It is generally agreed that the five novels of Jean Rhys, although having differently named women as central characters, are about one woman, namely Jean Rhys herself, a central consciousness through which experience is sifted. Her five novels tell the story of a woman's passage through life, beginning with the arrival in England of a seventeen-year old white Creole from Dominica, Anna Morgan in *Voyage in the Dark*, whose desperate attempts to find love, companionship, and security fail. She grows older and drifts penniless from one hotel room to another, moving from void to void as V.S. Naipaul remarks. Whether called Anna, Marya, Julia, or Sasha, in *Voyage in the Dark*, *Quartet*, *After Leaving Mr. Mackenzie*, and *Good Morning, Midnight*, she is a lonely and misunderstood stranger never quite fitting the norms of the society in which she lives and defined as the sort of oddity better left alone for anyone's comfort. Yet, in spite of her much commented upon passivity, she manages to overcome physically and mentally life's more serious blows. A helpless victim she is not; she is a survivor: "Going from room to room in this cold dark country, England, I never knew what it was that spurred me on and gave me an absolute certainty that there would be something else for me before long" (*Smile Please* 111–12).

Jean Rhys admittedly wrote about her own experience because she believed that writing must begin with the truth and the only truth she knew was herself. She considered writing a necessary catharsis. Since most of her interviews make this clear, there is the temptation to take her pronouncements too literally and to interpret her fiction as the true account of her life. This is ignoring her comment about readers, who ". . . believe the lies far more than they believe the truth" (Vreeland 229). Facts in Rhys's novels are romanticized when, as she says, "you . . . push onto reality what you feel" (Vreeland 230). This persistent reliance on Rhys's autobiographical material also ignores her belief that writing is more important than the writer, "Only the writing matters. . . . I used to think that all writing should be anonymous" (*Letters* 190). It also fails to take into account what

Jean Rhys means about the truth. She once said to her amanuensis, David Plante, "You see I am a pen, nothing but a pen. . . . It's only then that I know I am writing well. It's only then that I know my writing is true. Not really true, not as fact. But true as writing" (Plante 257).

Furthermore, American and European criticism of Jean Rhys tends to ignore the West Indian character of her fiction. In fact it was not until the publication of Wally Look Lai's and Kenneth Ramchand's pioneer articles on *Wide Sargasso Sea,* in 1968 and 1970, respectively, that she was acknowledged as a West Indian writer by her Caribbean peers. Thereafter, the Rhys criticism became polarized between American and European criticism on one hand and West Indian on the other, the latter treating almost exclusively issues pertaining to the West Indianness of Rhys's fiction and in particular *Wide Sargasso Sea.* Ramchand attributes this division to the difficulty non-West Indians may have in perceiving the nuances that make a novel West Indian— aspects of the landscape, the language, and the history, for instance. He further contends that "This kind of difference between readers of [*Wide Sargasso Sea*] exists for the fictional characters too" (102), since essentially the novel is about the dissonance of points of view between Rochester, the British groom, and Antoinette, his white Creole bride. With the exception of Teresa O'Connor's study of Rhys's novels as West Indian, that aspect of Jean Rhys's fiction still remains largely the domain of West Indian criticism.

In calling attention to the "mutual incomprehension" between Antoinette and Rochester, and between European and West Indian readers of *Wide Sargasso Sea,* Ramchand raises an important issue. And so does Teresa O'Connor's statement "that the island and England symbolize in Rhys's novel the underlying and eventually mutually destructive differences between Antoinette and Rochester" (149). The issue is the duality of Rhys's own consciousness reflected in *Wide Sargasso Sea* by the marriage of Antoinette and Rochester. It seems fitting to consider Rhys's last novel as the work of a writer who straddles two worlds, a work that incorporates both nuances, European and West Indian, and therefore one that calls for the joint interpretation of critics from both sides of the Wide Sargasso Sea. It is through the analysis of such consciousness that one acquires an insight into the kind of historical, social, and cultural imperatives responsible for the differences separating Antoinette from Rochester and the readers of Rhys's fiction.

With *Wide Sargasso Sea,* Rhys produced not only a masterpiece of West Indian fiction, but most importantly a novel uniting the contradictory voices within the self, the voices controlling her writings when, as she would often say, "The Book is in control of me" (*Letters* 274). *Wide Sargasso Sea* effects a final return home and with it the symbolic journey within the self. The novel represents a dialogue between the two forces dividing Rhys's consciousness, closing with a vision of unity made possible by the final identification with one of the elements of this duality. Such interpretation requires close examination of the relationship between structure, characterization, images, and language in Rhys's last and major work of fiction.

This consideration makes possible the view of Rhys's entire *oeuvre* as a circular journey of self-discovery, beginning with *Voyage in the Dark,* the voyage within the darkness of the self. It marks Rhys's own departure from the island of her birth, the place where she identified with conflicting worlds and their values: that of the white

Creole descendants of planters and that of the black islanders. The three novels usually referred to as Rhys's European works, because of their European setting, *Quartet, After Leaving Mr. Mackenzie,* and *Good Morning, Midnight,* correspond to the initiation phase during which the heroine experiences Europe, her father's land. Rhys's final novel, *Wide Sargasso Sea,* brings the heroine back home to Dominica, where she confronts for the last time the conflicting realities of her childhood world, Europe, and the West Indies, symbolized by Rochester and Antoinette. The incarceration of Antoinette in the tower of Rochester's English estate at the end of the novel stands as a reminder of the Rhysian heroine's European saga; Antoinette's isolation in the tower at Thornfield parallels the lonely and deprived existence of the Rhysian heroine during her exile in a world as unreceptive and as cold as that of the stone tower. But unlike the closure of the preceding novels, *Wide Sargasso Sea* ends with a solution to the identity crisis given symbolic representation in Rhys's fiction. The solution is implicit in the action prefigured by Antoinette's dream at the end of the novel. Through her plunge to death from Rochester's tower toward Tia, the West Indian black friend whose reflection she sees in the pool below, Antoinette achieves for Rhys the ultimate freedom, that of the self. Tia and Antoinette, the black and white counterparts within Rhys's consciousness, have achieved unity through the existential leap from the world of Rochester toward that of Tia, whose image appears in a pool reminiscent of the one at the Dominican family retreat at Granbois.

In returning to the West Indies, Rhys established, therefore, a final and necessary connection with the place of her birth and the origin of her consciousness. It is only through this journey that she could make a last attempt at answering Rochester's question about Antoinette's identity, "Creole of pure English descent she may be, but they are not English or European either" (67). Born from a Welsh father and a white Creole mother, Rhys spent the most critical years of her psychic development on the island of Dominica, where she internalized the contrary values of her Victorian home setting and of the dominant black culture surrounding her. No passage better illustrates this than the following, where the young Rhys finds herself looking at both worlds, being emotionally distant from one and socially removed from the other: "The life surged up to us stiff and well behaved, looking on . . . [the Blacks] were more alive, more a part of the place than we were. . . . I used to long fiercely to be black and to dance, too, in the sun" (*Smile Please* 50-53). At an age where the child's identity is formed, such experience could have but traumatic consequences, as indicated by her own comment in *Smile Please,* "I would never be part of anything. I would never really belong anywhere, and I knew it" (124). In Rhys's last novel, past and present, Europe and the West Indies, meet in a final confrontation, allowing her an insight into the conflicting realities that shaped her consciousness and her writings.

In his discussion, "The Path of Ambivalence," Robert Rogers notes that an individual who suffers from internal conflicts is likely to attempt to cope with his contrary impulses by developing "personality constellations" represented in literature by characters symbolic of these different drives (109). In *Wide Sargasso Sea,* Rhys stages her own inner drama, using Antoinette and Rochester as symbolic representation of her divided consciousness. She endows Antoinette and Rochester with characteristics of her own so that the thread connecting the two to each other and to Rhys is fairly apparent. For instance, in one passage of the novel, Rochester reminds himself of the danger of succumbing to passion with Antoinette, using words similar to those employed by Rhys to describe herself. He notes, "It was not a safe game to play. Desire, Hatred, Life, Death come very close in darkness" (94). Rhys's words to the prosecutor during the imaginary court scene in which she puts herself on trial at the end of *Smile Please* are similar: "It is in myself . . . All. Good, evil, love, hate, life, death, beauty, ugliness" (161). The paradoxical nature of Rhys's consciousness is transferred to Antoinette, Rhys's double, and identified by Rochester, Rhys's prosecutor or superego. Freud argues that the formation of the conscience is made possible by the ego's capacity to split itself off and to pass judgment on itself (40, 41). Rhys is "All"; she incorporates this fearful symmetry. To reckon with it would be "a dangerous game," warns the omniscient voice of Rochester. Rhys also reminds herself in the autobiography written a few years before her death that any attempt to pry into the web of one's consciousness can indeed be a dangerous game. Her make-believe trial ends with the prosecutor's observation about her writing, ". . . it is dangerous under the circumstance" (163).

Rhys's imagery in *Wide Sargasso Sea* also allows for a symbolic interpretation of Rhys's final voyage into the darkness of the self, a place characterized by André Gide as a "shaggy undergrowth . . . wild darkness" (641). The prevailing atmosphere of the work is mysterious and paradoxical; things are often not what they appear to be; the unknown looms threatening, as the reader is made aware that the very mystery that attracts Rochester to Antoinette and to her island also destroys him. In a 1959 letter to Francis Wyndham, Rhys said, referring to the writing of the novel, ". . . it fascinates me more than anything else I've ever tried to write and it is more elusive" (*Letters* 178). In 1964 she said of Antoinette, "The girl becomes the symbol of the elusive place" (*Letters* 281). And assuming that *Wide Sargasso Sea* is the symbolic representation of Rhys's inner self, that place is Rhys's own consciousness. In the novel, Grace Pool, the objective narrator whose distancing allows for greater objectivity, refers to Antoinette as "the girl who lives in her own darkness" (178).

In reality, both Rochester and Antoinette live in their respective darkness, symbolic of the confused consciousness of which they are a part, Rhys's own. The landscape of *Wide Sargasso Sea*, with its tangled vegetation and its concealing darkness, symbolizes the threatening unknown of the subconscious. Antoinette describes the garden at Coulibri in terms of opposites, "beautiful," yet "it had gone wild. The paths were overgrown and a smell of dead flowers mixed with the fresh living smell" (19). It incorporates life and death, as Rhys does, "dead flowers" and "living smell." It stands for evil and goodness, as indicated by the implied oxymoron: "Snaky looking" orchids, "wonderful to see" are giving a "scent . . . very sweet and strong." Evil and danger, thus, lurk in tantalizing appearance. "I never went near it," says Antoinette (19). Similarly, in the convent where Antoinette is sent after the burning of Coulibri, "everything was brightness, or dark. . . . the nun's habits were bright, but their veils, the Crucifix hanging from their waists, the shadow of the trees, were black. That was how it was, light and dark, sun and shadow, Heaven and Hell" (57).

Rochester's perception of the island is similar to Antoinette's view of the West Indian landscape. Alike, yet distinct, the two contrasting elements dividing Rhys's consciousness, Antoinette and Rochester, mirror one another; the island's mysterious quality eludes both Antoinette's Britishness, the Rochester within her, and Rochester himself. Rochester sees the Dominican honeymoon retreat of Granbois as Antoinette did the garden at Coulibri, "a beautiful place—wild, untouched, . . . with an alien, disturbing, secret loveliness" (87). For Antoinette, Coulibri is "wild" and "beautiful"; for Rochester, the garden is "wild" and "lovely." In another description reminiscent of Antoinette's view of the convent where life and death cohabit, Rochester describes the forest surrounding Granbois as "hostile"; the path is "overgrown." Yet it leads to a paradisiacal garden with "rose trees that had grown to an incredible height . . . a wild orange tree covered with fruits. . . . A beautiful place" (104). It is a place where love (the rose), the tree of life (the orange tree), and fertility (covered with fruits) contrast with the evil darkness of the forest surrounding it.

In her autobiography, Rhys uses the same contrasting technique to describe places in Dominica, thus merging past and present, impressions of yesterday and today. For instance, she speaks of Morgan Rest, her family's mountain retreat as "a very beautiful place. . . . It was alive," yet "there was something austere, sad, lost" (*Smile Please* 82). The sea is beautiful, "blue," but also "treacherous" (*Smile Please* 87). Bonavista, one of the family's vacation places, is "wild, remote, and lonely" (*Smile Please* 21), and the playground of the old Quarantine Station was a "bland self-satisfying place, and yet something lurked in the sunlight" (*Smile Please* 25). And, too, the garden of the Geneva plantation seen from Rochester's, Antoinette's, and Rhys's vantage point is the same, a garden of Eden symbolic of Rhys's own dualism. *Smile Please* also contains images of life and death, beauty and ugliness, safety and danger, as in this example: "In the sunniest part of the garden grew roses and the 'English flowers.' But in the shadow the Sensitive Plant which shut its leaves and pretended to die when you touched it." (34).

Rhys's impressionistic mastery allows the reader to establish a connection between landscape and characters, between inner consciousness and its content. If the setting of *Wide Sargasso Sea* reflects Rhys's inner dualism, so do the myths Antoinette and Rochester respectively represent. Antoinette embodies the mystical quality of the West Indies, for which Rochester thirsts, "I was thirsty for her, but that is not love," a comment he reiterates later, ". . . she belonged to the magic and the loveliness. She had left me thirsty and all my life would be a thirst and longing for what I had lost before I found it" (172). Similarly Rochester represents the mystery of Europe that Antoinette must identify. The desire to assuage this symbolic thirst with the help of Christophine's love potion parallels Rochester's. To Christophine's comment, "If the man don't love you, I can't make him love you," Antoinette replies, "Yes, you can. That is what I wish and that is why I came here. You can make people love and hate" (112). Rhys's voyage from one side of the Sargasso Sea to the other is symbolic of that dangerous but necessary quest for an understanding of the mutually exclusive and incomprehensive elements dividing the self. Without it, self-coherence cannot be achieved.

The ambivalence generated by an inner emotional split and a confusion about identity is often responsible for the adoption of myths as ways of coping with one's inner tension (Rogers 6). Antoinette's premonition of what England is really about stems from a dream prefiguring her exile there. In it myth and reality are set in contrast: England is "rosy pink in the geography book map. . . . They say that frost makes flower patterns on the window panes." And although she questions this assumption in light of what she knows to be true, "I must know more than I know already. For I know that house where I will be cold and not belonging," she dismisses the thought and chooses to believe in the myth: "but my dream had nothing to do with England and I must not think like this. I must remember about chandeliers and dancing, about swans and roses and snow" (111). Similarly, Rochester is aware that everything that he had imagined true turned out false (178), and like Antoinette he realizes that "only the magic and the dream are true—all the rest's a lie" (178). Faced with uncertainty, the lie might be preferable to truth; if only palliative, it prevents having to probe further into a mystery better left untouched.

At the beginning of *Voyage in the Dark*, Anna Morgan remarks, "Sometimes it was as if I were back in [Dominica] and as if England were a dream. At other times England was the real thing and out there was the dream, but I could never fit them together" (8-9). And later as she tries to describe the island flowers to Walter, she remarks, ". . . when I began to talk about the flowers out there I got the feeling of a dream, of two things I couldn't fit together" (101). At the onset of that symbolic introspective journey, dream and reality are confused. Identities are blurred. *Wide Sargasso Sea* brings the voyage to a conclusion. Confined by Rochester to the solitary tower symbolic of the dark and inescapable inner realm of the self, Rhys through Antoinette is impelled to take final action. The vastness of the continent in which Rhys spent most of her life is reduced to the restricted space of an English tower in the novel, symbolic of her journey through life. And on this narrow stage where, as Antoinette remarks, "time has no meaning," the last scene of a long drama is acted (184-85). It must give Charlotte Brontë's mad Creole a different destiny: "Her end— I want it in a way triumphant," Rhys announced in a letter written in 1958 (*Letters* 156). The triumph is Antoinette's liberation from Rochester and her symbolic return home. At a deeper level, it represents Rhys's personal victory in her struggle to achieve identification and to do so with self-coherence. In this sense the conclusion of *Wide Sargasso Sea* signifies a beginning, not an end, Antoinette's last dream prefiguring her death but also a new life.

The progression of the novel leads to this conclusion through Antoinette's three dreams, the last of which brings her story to closure. The first and second are almost identical. In both, Antoinette is alone in a forest with a man, a terrifying stranger, whom she describes as hateful. She is afraid and screams. Also, in both is the suggestion of a sexual experience. The significant differences between the two dreams are Antoinette's struggle against the man in the first and her passive surrender to him in the second. In them are symbolically represented the stages through which Antoinette (Rhys) must go in order to achieve selfhood: resistance; submission to what cannot be otherwise, as Antoinette says, "this must happen" (59); and final triumph with the achievement of self-coherence. The earliest of the dreams took place at Coulibri estate: "I dreamed that I was walking in a forest. Not alone. Someone who hated me was with me, out of sight. . . . and though I struggled and screamed I could not move. I woke crying. The covering sheet was on the floor and my mother was looking down at me" (26–27). The following one occurs while Antoinette is at the convent school, soon before her pre-arranged wedding to a man she does not know, Rochester:

> It is still night and I am walking towards the forest. . . . I walk with difficulty following the man who is with me. . . . I follow him sick with fear but I make no effort to save myself; if anyone were to try to save me, I would refuse. This must happen. . . . He turns and looks at me, his face black with hatred. . . . I touch a tree and my arm holds on to it. . . . the tree sways and jerks as if it is to throw me off. Still I cling and the seconds pass and each one is a thousand years. "Here, here," a strange voice said, and the tree stopped swaying and jerking. (59–60)

According to Homeric concept, man has a double existence, one visible and another invisible and set free only by death. In the soul dwells a stranger, according to Erwin Rohde, "a weaker double, whose realm is the world of dream" (quoted in Rank 60). Hence, in recounting his dream, the narrator records a dialogue between the self and its doubles. Rycroft similarly proposes that "Dreaming is . . . a reflexive mental activity in which the self becomes twofold, one part observing the other, arguing with, reflecting upon and resisting implications of ideas presented to it by the other" (45). And Jung proposes that characters in a dream are "personified figures of the dreamer's personality" (52). As such, Rochester represents one of the elements of Rhys's inner consciousness, the rejected one, the hateful stranger. Rochester stands as everything British, everything foreign to her personality, which is closer in sensitivity to blacks than to whites: "I wanted to be black. I always wanted to be black. . . . Being black is warm and gay, being white is cold and sad" (*Voyage* 27).

Antoinette's third and final dream marks the end of the struggle between the two opposites within Rhys's consciousness. If *Voyage in the Dark* is symbolic of the inner darkness and confusion within the divided self, *Wide Sargasso Sea* represents the final exploration of a duality, symbolized by the relationship of Antoinette and Rochester. Ramchand sees the novel as an exploration of the differences in order to bring harmony to the divided self of modern man. He sees Antoinette and Rochester as standing for two distinct sets of human values, which in combination achieve wholeness (102–03). One can argue, however, that wholeness in Rhys's last journey into the self comes rather with the identification with one of the elements of that duality. It is realized with Antoinette's choice to join the world of Tia in an act of symbolic rebirth.

In the dream, death is the metaphor for a new beginning of life. The West Indian flamboyant tree giving life to the soul buried under it and the flames consuming Rochester's European estate merge symbolically: "If you are buried under a flamboyant tree . . . your soul is lifted up when it flowers"; then, as Antoinette turns to look at the tower in flame, just before she leaps from its embattlements, the sky assumes the color of the flamboyant tree that unites life and death, "I turned round and saw the sky. It was red and all my life was in it" (185). Also, Antoinette's jump from the burning tower presupposes a death symbolic of a rebirth since by severing permanently her ties with Rochester and the world he represents, she can freely claim her West Indian identity. Her existential leap is away from Rochester and from the identity he had forced upon her toward the reflection of Tia, her black childhood friend, whose reflection appears in a pool at Coulibri, the Jamaican estate where she was born: "But when I looked over the edge I saw the pool at Coulibri. Tia was there. She beckoned to me and when I hesitated, she laughed. I heard her say, you frightened? And I heard the man's voice, Bertha! Bertha! . . . And the sky was red. . . . I called 'Tia!' and jumped and woke" (190).

Following this account of the dream, Rhys ends *Wide Sargasso Sea* with Antoinette's realization, "Now at last I know why I was brought here and what I have to do" (189). Antoinette now sees the real burning of Thornfield Hall. Thus ends the journey into the darkness of the inner self where confused voices called and where Antoinette must reckon with a paradoxical identity—Antoinette/Bertha (West Indian/British). It is no accident that Rhys should conclude with a scene foreshadowed in the beginning of the novel. In it, Antoinette, who has just seen the fire consume Coulibri, the symbol of European colonialism and its symbol of misguided power paralleling Rochester's, turns to see Tia. At that moment, Tia hurls a stone at Antoinette. In this action is recorded the most tragic consequence of humankind's misunderstanding of one another: "When I was close I saw the jagged stone in her hand but did not see her throw it. I did not feel it either, only something wet running down my face. I looked at her and I saw her face crumpled up as she began to cry. We stared at each other, blood on my face, tears on hers. It was as if I saw myself. Like in a looking glass" (45). In *The Double in Literature*, Robert Rogers points to the widely held belief in ancient culture that reflections were the same as souls or responsible for the well-being of the body (7). Antoinette's reflection in the looking glass is Tia, her soul or double. The pain is reciprocal as the blood of one is the tears of the other.

Wide Sargasso Sea is a vision of a future in which the differences and imcomprehensions setting men and women apart have no place. Antoinette achieved what Rochester could not, wholeness. Rhys's fictional journey through the darkness of the self represents the contemporary search for harmony in a fragmented world. Here lies Antoinette's and Rhys's greatest triumph.

WORKS CITED

Harris, Wilson. "Carnival of Psyche: Jean Rhys's *Wide Sargasso Sea*." *Kunapipi* 2.2 (1980): 142–50.

Hearne, John. "The Wide Sargasso Sea: A West Indian Reflection." *Cornhill Magazine* No. 1080 (1974): 323–33.

Jung, C.G. *Dreams*. Princeton: Princeton UP, 1974.

Look Lai, Wally. "The Road to Thornfield Hall: An Analysis of Jean Rhys's *Wide Sargasso Sea*." *New Beacon Reviews: Collection One*. London: New Beacon Books, 1968. 38–52.

O'Connor, Teresa F. *Jean Rhys: The West Indian Novels*. New York: New York UP, 1987.

Ramchand, Kenneth. "Wide Sargasso Sea." *An Introduction to West Indian Literature*. Sunburry-on-Thames: Nelson Caribbean, 1976. 91–107.

Rhys, Jean. *Smile Please*. London: André Deutsch, 1979.

———. *Voyage in the Dark*. Harmondsworth: Penguin Books, 1982.

———. *Wide Sargasso Sea*. London: André Deutsch, 1977.

Rogers, Robert. *The Double in Literature*. Detroit: Wayne State UP, 1970.

Rank, Otto. *The Double*. Trans. Harry Tucker, Jr. New York: New American Library, 1979.

Rycroft, Charles. *The Innocence of Dreams*. New York: Pantheon, 1979.

Wyndham, Francis, and Diana Melly, editors. *The Letters of Jean Rhys*. New York: Viking, 1984.

JEAN RHYS'S PUBLISHED WORK

Novels

Postures, 1928 (U.S. title, *Quartet: a Novel*, 1929; published later as *Quartet*)

After Leaving Mr. Mackenzie, 1931

Voyage in the Dark, 1934

Good Morning, Midnight, 1939

Wide Sargasso Sea, 1966

Jean Rhys: The Complete Novels, 1985

Short Story Collections

The Left Bank and Other Stories, 1927

Winter's Tales, 1960

Voices, 1963

Tigers Are Better-Looking, with a Selection from The Left Bank, 1968

Penguin Modern Stories, 1969

Sleep It Off, Lady, 1976

Memoir and Letters

Smile Please, an Unfinished Autobiography, 1979

The Letters of Jean Rhys (1931-1966), 1984

SELECTED CRITICAL READINGS

Only after the publication of *Wide Sargasso Sea* was Jean Rhys recognized as a Caribbean writer by her West Indian compatriots. Kenneth Ramchand's pioneer article on the novel places her in their rank by defining *Wide Sargasso Sea* as a West Indian novel. Generally West Indian critics of Jean Rhys write about the alienation of the white minority in the period of post-emancipation, the West Indian setting and Rhys's sensitivity to it, the language and symbols that make *Wide Sargasso Sea* a truly West Indian work. European and American critics, on the other hand, have traditionally ignored the West Indian character of Rhys's fiction, turning their attention instead to Rhys's treatment of the female social outcast, whose consciousness is central to all her novels, and to the autobiographical nature of her books. Recently, however, there appears to be a trend toward a study of Rhys's writing technique, to what can be considered the Rhysian aesthetic. Scores of articles on Rhys's work have appeared in major American, West Indian, and European journals. Mellown's annotated bibliography, listed below, provides an extensive listing of articles to the early 1980's, but now needs to be updated, for the articles continue to appear. This list is limited to the books that have been published so far.

Angier, Carole. *Jean Rhys.* Harmondsworth: Penguin, 1985. An interpretation of Rhys's work as autobiographical, the book follows her journey into the self through writing.

Davidson, Arnold E. *Jean Rhys.* New York: Ungar, 1985. Explores the marginality of Rhys's central characters, showing how it reflects the alienation of modern men and women, defined by the society in which they live.

Frickey, Pierrette, editor. *Critical Perspectives on Jean Rhys.* Washington: Three Continents Press, 1991. Collection of essays by international critics on various aspects of Rhys's work. Extensive bibliography

Gardiner, Judith Kegan. *Rhys, Stead, Lessing, and the Politics of Empathy.* Bloomington: Indiana UP, 1989. Shows the progression in Rhys's writing from the description of the duality between gender, classes, and races in her early works to the more subtle and complex handling of her characters, perceived in an everchanging historical and social context.

Harrison, Nancy. *Jean Rhys and the Novel as Women's Text.* Chapel Hill: U of North Carolina P, 1988. A feminist critical and theoretical description of Rhys's work pointing to the qualities that make a woman's novel different from a man's and to women's responses to Rhys's writing.

Hemmerechts, Kristien. *A Plausible Story and a Plausible Way of Telling It: A Structuralist Analysis of Jean Rhys's Novels* (Series 14, Vol. 163). New York: European University Studies, 1986. A structuralist analysis showing the patterns of dependence characteristic of the relations among the women in Rhys's novels and their lovers and husbands. An examination of Rhys's narrative techniques.

James, Louis. *Jean Rhys.* London: Longman, 1978. Places Jean Rhys within the tradition of Caribbean authors. Valuable source of information on her West Indian background and its effect on her entire fiction.

Kloepfer, Deborah Kelly. *The Unspeakable Mother: Forbidden Discourse in Jean Rhys and H.D.* Ithaca: Cornell UP, 1989. Examines Rhys's thematic and stylistic handling of maternal loss and rejection through the analysis of Rhys's repeated references to dead mothers, dying mothers, abortions, miscarriages, and infant death.

Mellown, Elgin W. *Jean Rhys: A Descriptive and Annotated Bibliography of Works and Criticism.* New York: Garland, 1984. Useful reference book, citing articles into the early 1980s.

Nebeker, Helen. *Jean Rhys, Woman in Passage: A Critical Study of the Novels of Jean Rhys.* Montreal: Eden Press Women's Publications, 1981. Exploration of the Freudian symbols and Jungian archetypes in Jean Rhys's novels.

O'Connor, Teresa F. *Jean Rhys: The West Indian Novels.* New York: New York UP, 1987. Shows the influence of Rhys's childhood in Dominica on her writings.

Staley, Thomas. *Jean Rhys: A Critical Study.* Austin: U of Texas P, 1979. Pioneer study of Rhys's writing, analyzing the modernism in her fiction.

Wolfe, Peter. *Jean Rhys*. Boston: Twayne, 1980. Chronological study of Rhys's work, centering on her development throughout the work of an archetypcal woman who is dispossessed, lacks ideas, and falls prey to men in a male-dominated society.

Interviews

With Marcelle Bernstein. *Observer Magazine* (London) 1 June 1969: 40–42, 49–50.
With Peter Burton. *Transatlantic Review* 36 (1970): 105–09.
With Elaine Campbell. *Kunapipi* 2 (1980): 152–57.
With Hanna Carter. *Guardian* 8 August 1968: 5.
With Judy Froshaug. *Nova* Sept. 1967: 45.
With Barry Pree. *Observer Magazine* (London) 3 Oct. 1976: 8–9.
With Ned Thomas. *Planet* 33 (1976): 29–31.
With Elizabeth Vreeland. *Paris Review* 21 (1979): 219–37.

—PIERRETTE FRICKEY

Janet Frame

J anet Frame has characterized the New Zealand society of her youth as a house with neither basement nor attic. This metaphor illuminates only one aspect of her complicated background. More substantial details of Frame's life are treated impressionistically in her three-volume autobiography, particularly the enduring poverty of the Depression, tragic accidents, and a series of misfortunes that haunted her early years.

She was born in Dunedin, in 1924, and grew up in Oamaru, the child of an itinerant railway engineer father and a mother who yearned to be a writer. Of the five children, the one son was early diagnosed as epileptic, and two of the four daughters drowned in coincidentally similar accidents ten years apart. Janet Frame left the University of Otago for a brief teaching career but spent eight years of her early adulthood in mental hospitals, under the mistaken diagnosis of schizophrenia. She endured a series of electric shock treatments and narrowly escaped a lobotomy. Suffering isolation and insecurity, she found comfort in close reading of writers from Shakespeare to Rilke and Virginia Woolf.

After leaving the hospital, she was befriended by the short story writer Frank Sargeson, and her fortunes and confidence began to improve. Although she has lived abroad for periods of time in England, France, and the United States, she has always returned to New Zealand, settling in various towns before resuming her travels. She held the Robert Burns Fellowship at the University of Otago in 1965, the Winn-Menton Scholarship in 1974, and has been a fellow of Yaddo and the MacDowell Colony. She was awarded the 1989 Commonwealth Writers Prize for *The Carpathians.* In 1973, she changed her surname to Clutha, the name of the river that flows south of Oamaru, but she continues to be published as Janet Frame. Since Frame has given almost no lectures and few interviews, her reflections on her work and the influences of reading, childhood, education, family life, and travel are best derived from her three volume autobiography.

The Voyage between Self and Society

For Janet Frame writing has been not only vocation and art but a life- and mind-saving act as well. While not being linked conventionally, her works possess a remarkable organic unity; they retell similar stories with systematic variation in kaleidoscopic patterns. Her fiction continues to investigate ultimate questions: the nature of reality, art, sanity, memory, truth, life, and death.

Born nearly forty years after Katherine Mansfield, Frame began to publish following World War II. Her fictional world bears occasional resemblance to that of

Iris Murdoch, Patrick White, Chistina Stead, and Elizabeth Jolley, and her language reveals that, like Lawrence Durrell, she is also a poet. Fundamentally skeptical of institutions and disdainful of the comfortably unexamined life, she creates fiction that extends the traditional limits of genre and form. The discoveries her characters make are not always easily transmitted to a public arena, nor do their discoveries make them happier or more loving human beings. They learn personal courage and inner wisdom by disregarding the world's deceptive order and unity.

Frame remains difficult to categorize as futuristic, experimental, fabulist, illusionist, or trickster. Her reader must practice patience and avoid reaching neat conclusions or rushing to parables. The reader, like some of the characters, may be initially struck by one symbol: a burning snowman, a nightmare garden, the town rubbish dump, a field of toy soldiers, or the legendary Memory Flower. But Frame and her various narrators prefer indirection and enjoy the possibilities of satire and irony. An example of this capacity for wit occurs in *Scented Gardens for the Blind*. Both the title and epigraph of this novel suggest a form of communication: that the sightless might experience their surroundings by smelling the flowers. The initial narrator Vera Glace tries to fulfill the possibility of her name by willing her silent daughter into lucidity and clear speech. But the daughter prefers to take her philosophic instruction from a congenial teacher named Uncle Black Beetle, who discourses from the windowsill on death and the futility of materialism. The reader is instructed (and warned) by a literary cousin of Uncle Black Beetle who dwells in the dictionary between the words *trichotomy* and *trick*.

In selecting names of characters and places and even titles, Frame often sets up one expectation and demolishes it with systematic brilliance. Some of the choices have enduring significance, as in the cases of the Withers, Livingston, and Rainbird families. Others tempt and tease, like Malfred Signal, Ciss Everest, Miss Float, Colin Monk, and Turnlung. Some choices invite association of Frame's story and intention with familiar myths. So it is with Daphne Withers, Thora Pattern, and Istina Mavet. From childhood, Frame read appreciatively from classic mythology through Shakespeare and the Brontës and Hardy; she mixes well-known tales with her characters' private discoveries, as they hold up not a mirror but a prism to experience. The grand sweep of legendary heroes has been reduced in the late twentieth century. Godfrey Rainbird, awakened from his coma and back at his job in the Dunedin Tourist Bureau (in *The Rainbirds*), envies the original Lazarus and thinks his grave could be merchandised as a minor attraction.

Frame employs all the fictional furniture—titles, names, language, climate, and seasons—to enlarge and intensify her theme. In *The Adaptable Man*, one of her most traditional works, she uses (and parodies) the traditional English novel. Later novels suggest more cosmopolitan influences. Although Frame can never be accused of being a conventional realist, she can describe arrestingly much twentieth-century malaise at the edges of her landscapes, from urban squalor to the threat of nuclear disaster. Since Frame has been an intelligent tourist or pilgrim throughout much of her life, the settings of her fiction convey the atmosphere of various places and the sense of dislocation. Many of the first stories of *The Lagoon* and *The Reservoir* are set in a childhood world, threatened by adulthood, a world that can be associated with some of the landscape and situations of Frame's own youth. Her first three novels reflect the disappointments in leaving childhood, in such a town as Waimaru, for the nightmares of mental hospitals like Cliffhaven, Treecroft, and Lawn Lodge, or for the ritual voyage "home" to England undertaken by Toby Withers, afflicted by the Overseas Dream, via the *S.S. Matua* to London.

As Frame has moved around the world, her settings have also: *Scented Gardens for the Blind* links England and New Zealand; *The Adaptable Man* is entirely rooted in the town of Little Burgelstatham deep in the Suffolk countryside; *A State of Siege* is set in the far north of New Zealand; *The Rainbirds* brings an English family to Dunedin. The dominant images of *Intensive Care* derive from the Great War; the action moves between a Recovery Unit in a converted English great house, Culin Hall, and the increasingly surreal Waipori City with its cement factory and slaughterhouse. More recently, Frame's settings have linked the United States and New Zealand. *Daughter Buffalo* moves from such Manhattan scenes as the Natural History Museum and the Central Park Zoo to a geriatric hospital in New Zealand. The protagonist of *Living in the Maniototo* never does visit the desolate Maniototo plains in Otago, but she lives intensely, if briefly, in three contrasting locations: Blenheim, an upscale new Auckland suburb; Baltimore, portrayed as Poe might have experienced it; and Berkeley, California, Blenheim's "sister city." The mountain range for which *The Carpathians* is named appears only during an incidental dream; that novel is set in New York City and on Kawai Street in the North Island town of Puamahara, where the lifelong New Yorker Mattina Brecon settles temporarily.

Of course, Frame is also a poet, and scattered throughout what might be classified as her prose are poetic passages from lyric songs to complex meditations. Centrally concerned as she is with communicating from inside the mind and imagination, she presents characters who inhabit those risky situations at the borders of language, as the title *The Edge of the Alphabet* suggests. Such characters live on this dangerous fringe as Daphne Withers in her "dead room" or the silent Erlene Glace or Decima James, the institutionalized autistic of *The Carpathians*. Even the artist Malfred Signal leaves her home to settle in a lonely storm-battered cottage and finally retreats into a miniature room in her mind. On the other hand, attempted communication can be disappointing; for example, Mattina Brecon, whose career has been spent in publishing, realizes the limits of language in the patter of the astronauts describing their moon walk.

Like many experimental novelists, Frame attempts to test not only the limits of language as communication but the validity of witness and memory. Toward that end, she presents various entertaining and distracting techniques and voices, such as notebook entries, dreams, fantasies, and letters. Tricks and coincidences abound in her work; the supposed dead emerge from coma or earthquake. Others die in bizarre circumstances, under a falling chandelier or in a swirl of household detergent, for example. Often the identity of the narrator is in question. The epilogue of *Daughter Buffalo*, a novel set exclusively in America, reveals the real author as the geriatric Turnlung, who has never left New Zealand. It is not entirely certain who narrates *Living in the Maniototo*—Mavis Furness Barwell Halleton or her alter egos Alice Thumb, novelist, or Violet Pansy Proudlock, ventriloquist. Similarly the conclusions of *Scented Gardens for the Blind* and *The Carpathians* cast doubt on the originally announced narrators.

The internalized and experimental language along with the complex and somewhat ambiguous themes of Frame's fiction may be better understood by considering closely her autobiography. After publishing ten novels and four books of short stories and poems and having reached her sixtieth year, she undertook to interpret her past in three volumes: *To the Is-land, An Angel at My Table,* and *The Envoy from Mirror City.* These three books treat her first forty years—1924 to 1963, that is, her childhood, education, sickness, recovery, and first trip overseas. Without denying the final relativity of individual observation, the autobiography reveals the process of transforming intense personal experience into art. The first volume, in a chapter called "Imagination," describes Frame's struggle with "true personal history," its dates and years, either stretching out horizontally or arranged in neat vertical piles. She concludes that ". . . the memories do not arrange themselves to be observed and written about, they whirl, propelled by a force beneath, with different memories rising to the surface at different times and thus denying the existence of a 'pure' autobiography" (*Is-land* 235). The process of remembering, therefore, creates a sort of whirlpool, ". . . a dance of dust or sunbeams or bacteria" (236).

Few readers had expected a neatly reconstructed chronicle of dates and facts. Several critics have suggested that Frame has reclaimed her own life through the autobiography into an interior mirror city, into which the reader may gaze. She has also provided a personal history of an international English writer from a transitional generation. The New Zealand writers in the generation immediately before hers included Frank Sargeson (1903-1982), Sylvia Ashton-Warner (1908-1984), and Robin Hyde (Iris Wilkinson) (1906-1939). These writers frequently described their struggles against provincialism, conformity, and cultural isolation. Frame is of the generation of the poet James K. Baxter—a generation that broke away from the provincial and was less traumatized by philistinism than disappointed by the failure to attain an ideal society in the Happy Islands.

For Frame it was necessary to measure her national literature (or its absence) in relation to that of the rest of the world. Appropriately, her autobiography is marked, or framed, by journeys: Volume One ends on the Sunday slow train to Dunedin; Volume Two leaves her on the deck of a passenger ship bound from Wellington on her first trip to England; at the end of Volume Three she is returning on another ship to New Zealand. The three volumes are in themselves messengers, intermediaries, between their events—death, disappointment, illness, and exile—and her interior life. As the title of Volume Three indicates, Frame has successfully set out on pilgrimages to Mirror City, an amalgam of those yearned-for, exotic, ever-larger cities from Dunedin to London to New York. She had become a citizen of these places; it was irresponsible to stare passively at them as a tourist: "What use is there in returning only with a mirrorful of me? . . . The self must be the container of the treasures of Mirror City, the Envoy as it were, and when the time comes to arrange and list those treasures for shaping into words, the self must be the worker, the bearer of the burden, the chooser, place and polisher" (*Envoy* 140–41). She concludes sternly that collecting images is travel writing, not worthy of fiction; her trips to the mirror cities have been apprenticeships in the politics of use. The creative self is an Orpheus or Envoy figure who has taken on some of the traits of Rilke's Angel, the presence invoked by the title of her second volume.

Interestingly, Frame seems less hostile to both environments (New Zealand and the various mirror cities) in her autobiography than in her fiction. She does emphasize consistently her isolation and her perception of the stigma of being poor, then different, and, finally, mentally ill: "It was best for me to escape from a country where, since my student days, a difference which was only myself, and even my ambition to write, had been looked on as evidence of abnormality" (*Angel* 190). All three volumes provide a selection of sharp impressions of a Depression childhood as glimpsed from 56 Eden Street in Oamaru, a place that might have been under other circumstances "a kingdom by the sea." There was the usual mix of Saturday movie matinees and the growing discovery of real literature, balanced by the liabilities of rotting teeth and dirty clothes. The misery was probably more dense than in usual childhoods, although Frame seems to deny her singular experiences, at least originally. Speaking of one sister's death, she says, "Somehow Myrtle's death did not really 'qualify'; it was too much within me and a part of me, and I could not look at it and say *dreamily, poetically,* 'Ah, there's a tragedy. All poets have tragic lives.' My brother's illness did not 'qualify' either; it was too present" (*Is-land* 166). Many of the events in *To the Is-land* are described with more distance and cooler emotion than evident in their original appearance in fiction. For example, it is possible to compare the short story "The Bull Calf" (*The Reservoir* 63–73) with the episode as recounted in Chapter 23, "Scrapers and Bluey," of *To the Is-land.* Both describe a child's discovery that the family's bull calf has been castrated. In the autobiography Frame rather casually narrates the incident, concluding with the observation that she was infuriated by the adults' secretive attitude. The story concentrates on the maturation of its heroine, Olive, intensifies her sense of betrayal, and concludes with a tearful scene in which Olive begins to comprehend priorities or compromises in adult life.

Generally the mood of *To the Is-land* is remarkably cheerful, as if the disappointments and tragedies have been distanced. *Owls Do Cry* is a far more terrifying book. The four Withers children fear the complete collapse, not only of their house but of their entire world, as if they had been trapped inside a squirrel cage. The death of Francie Withers in the volcanic fury of the dump fire may be compared with the restrained account of Myrtle's drowning in the town baths. Some aspects of the real story, too coincidental or poignant for fiction—like Myrtle's disappearance from a family photograph, had been excised from *Owls Do Cry*; they were either too painful or too unrealistic for fiction. On the whole, the autobiography in its first volume emphasizes nostalgia, produced by the inevitable loss of innocence. The first chapter of *An Angel at My Table* describes how the future constructs itself over the past. "The future accumulates like a weight upon the past. The weight upon the earliest years is easier to remove to let that time spring up like grass that has been crushed" (*Angel* 13).

From age 24 to 32 Janet Frame moved in and out of mental hospitals, and she has frequently drawn directly and indirectly upon this buried life for her fiction. In *Angel at My Table* she indicates that she put on a mask, dissolved herself into a sense of doomed eternity and that, subsequently, in her fiction she deliberately understated the squalor and inhumanity of those years: ". . . were I to rewrite *Faces in the Water* I would include much that I omitted because I did not want a record by a former patient to appear to be over-dramatic" (*Angel* 102). It is not an analytical explanation of her mental collapse that engages her; aside from the strains of poverty and the shock of loss when her sisters drowned, she refused to dwell on causes for her breakdown. Almost from childhood and adolescence she disappeared for about a decade, missing post-war affluence, labor strikes, McCarthyism, and the culture of the times, emerging into a strange world. "I knew only of Prospero, Caliban, King Lear, and Rilke, these for me, being occasions of the past decade" (*Angel* 139). She suggests the difficulty of identifying herself, even in terms of the correct pronoun: "My previous community had been my family. In *To the Is-land*, I constantly use the first person plural—we, not I. My time as a student was an I-time. Now as a Seacliff patient, I was again part of a group. . . . I became 'she,' one of 'them'" (*Angel* 73).

She adopted a classification provided by Frank Sargeson as a "sane, mad person." The autobiography suggests that she accepted this distinction as a protection. From her earliest marking as "so original" by a patronizing teacher, she assumed the "distorted privilege" of mental illness. By the time she reached the university, she was sitting in the Dunedin Public Library reading case histories of Van Gogh, Hugo Wolf, or Schumann and identifying with them. "My place was set, then, at the terrible feast. I had no illusions about 'greatness' but at least I could endow my work and—when necessary—my life with the mark of my schizophrenia" (*Angel* 82). The really remarkable journey of this autobiography into self reclamation is expressed in the second and third volumes as she releases herself from that dubious distinction of such classification:

> Although I was still inclined to cherish the distorted "privilege" of having schizophrenia because it allied me with the great artists more readily than my attempts to produce works of art might have done, I suspected that my published writing might destroy that tenuous alliance, for I could not people, everlastingly, my novels with characters suffering from "the Ophelia syndrome" with details drawn from my observations in hospital. (*Envoy* 93)

This identification with that gray and mysterious and private world set her apart. The circumstance qualified her for special consideration and distanced her sharply from her readers. It also provided additional problems in the writing of a candid autobiography. "The fact that, invariably, I was forced to go to such lengths to uncover my 'secret, true' self, to find the answers to questions that, had I the confidence and serenity of being myself 'in the world' could have been asked directly, was evidence to me of a certain unhealthy self-burial" (*Envoy* 99).

Her early life was constructed on compensatory strategies. At school she might have been awkward, badly dressed, obviously poor, and socially unacceptable, but she compensated by becoming the prizewinning pupil, the teacher's favorite, the obliging and uncomplaining good girl. In a sad bargain she gave up identity and resigned herself to an apparently lifelong residence in the hospital: "I had woven myself into a trap, remembering that a trap is also a refuge" (*Angel* 99). Freed of the temptations or requirements of so-called "normal" society, she was free to cultivate an interior life seen by nightmare vision, which she repeatedly encapsulated in a literary figure as "the room two inches behind the eyes" (*Angel* 99). This is an identical construction of Malfred Signal's refuge in *A State of Siege*. Even after her release from the hospital, Frame describes herself as maintaining the submissive role; she continues to deliver herself to various protectors. The autobiography allows her to name and describe her behavior: ". . . at its best it is the role of the queen bee surrounded by her attendants; at its worst it is that of a victim without power or possessions, and in both cases there is no ownership of one's self" (*Angel* 189). In selecting a public role that was so circumscribed, she established social and perhaps literary limits. She finds it significant that she refused to explore the second story of a house in which she lived on the Balearic Islands. She seems to have fled from demanding relationships while accepting the attentions of protectors whom she scorned. These episodes are awkwardly described; it is obviously difficult for a sixty-year-old writer to re-create her clumsy attempts of almost thirty years before to make up for a tragically lost decade.

But the most unsettling discovery revealed in the autobiography was her learning in the winter of 1957 that she had never been a schizophrenic at all. More sophisticated medical evaluation at Maudsley Hospital in London clarified that a tragic error in diagnosis had been made. She was both vindicated and confused; the revelation swept away excuses and explanation. The discovery was what she described as "the official plunder of my self-esteem" (*Envoy* 103). Painful as the discovery was, it attended the most intensely productive period of her life. She was able to announce her confirmation as an artist: "I can erase myself completely and live through the feelings of others" (*Envoy* 81).

This statement of self confidence did not mark a dramatic change in the tone, techniques, and voice of Frame's work. She has continued to refine her craft consistently and to construct bridges between her complicated retreat in that richly furnished mind and the external world of mirror cities around the globe. She tells us that writing actually saved her life; as in her fiction, the purpose of her writing the autobiography was to connect the events and myths of her two worlds, inner and outer.

Works Cited

Frame, Janet. *An Angel at My Table*. New York: Braziller, 1984.
———. *The Envoy from Mirror City*. New York: Braziller, 1985.
———. *To the Is-land*. New York: Braziller, 1982.

Janet Frame's Published Work

Novels

Owls Do Cry, 1957
Faces in the Water, 1961
The Edge of the Alphabet, 1962
Scented Gardens for the Blind, 1963

The Adaptable Man, 1965
A State of Siege, 1966
The Rainbirds, 1969 (U.S. title, *Yellow Flowers in the Antipodean Room*)
Intensive Care, 1970
Daughter Buffalo, 1972
Living in the Maniototo, 1979
The Carpathians, 1988

Short Story Collections

The Lagoon, 1951
The Reservoir, 1963
Snowman, Snowman, 1963

Poetry

The Pocket Mirror, 1967

Children's Book

Mona Minim and the Smell of the Sun, 1969

Autobiography

To the Is-land, 1982
An Angel at My Table, 1984
The Envoy from Mirror City, 1985

SELECTED CRITICAL READINGS

From 1970 to the present, Janet Frame's work has been energetically reviewed and discussed, at first in New Zealand, then increasingly overseas. Although her novels are often experimental, demanding, and frequently bleak in outlook, critics have been attracted by her individual vision and voice as well as her control of language. The organic nature of her work has permitted tracing particular themes throughout the body of fiction. The publication of her autobiography has encouraged comparisons between her life and art. The next stages of criticism may approach the work comparatively and from such perspectives as feminism and postmodernism.

Alcock, Peter. "On the Edge: New Zealanders as Displaced Persons." *World Literature Written in English* 16 (1977): 127–42. Discusses isolation and alienation expressed by four New Zealand writers: Mansfield, Mulgan, Sargeson, and Frame. Places Frame in context.

Ashcroft, W.D. "Beyond the Alphabet: Janet Frame's *Owls Do Cry*." *Journal of Commonwealth Literature* 12 (1977): 12–23. Emphasizes journey motif in the novel as escape from limitations of modern society.

Delbaere-Garant, Jeanne. "The Divided Worlds of Emily Brontë, Virginia Woolf and Janet Frame." *English Studies* 60 (1979): 699–711. Compares Frame with Brontë and Woolf, emphasizing Frame's visionary capability.

Evans, Patrick. "'Farthest from the Heart': The Autobiographical Parables of Janet Frame." *Modern Fiction Studies* 27 (1987): 31–40. Parallels themes, techniques, and metaphors in Frame's early short stories with those of later novels.

——. *Janet Frame.* Boston: Twayne, 1977. Provides essential and comprehensive information on all aspects of Frame's life and work, including critical perspectives.

——. "Janet Frame and the Art of Life." *Meanjin* 44 (1985): 375–83. Treats several novels as integrated in theme, suggesting that autobiography is the most congenial genre for Frame, permitting great artistic freedom.

Hankin, Cherry. "Language as Theme in *Owls Do Cry.*" *Critical Essays on the New Zealand Novel.* Auckland: Heinemann, 1976. 88–104. Explicates *Owls Do Cry* through a complete analysis of its linguistic elements.

Hyman, Stanley Edgar. "Reason in Madness." *Standards: A Chronicle of Books for Our Time.* New York: Horizon Books, 1966. 239–43. Discusses *Scented Gardens for the Blind* with early admiration.

Jones, Lawrence. "The One Story, Two Ways of Telling, Three Perspectives: Recent New Zealand Literary Autobiography." *Ariel* 16 (1985): 127–150. Investigates differing approaches to their life stories in the autobiographies of Sargeson, Brasch, Ashton-Warner, and Frame.

——. "No Cowslip's Bell in Waimaru: The Personal Vision of *Owls Do Cry.*" *Landfall* 24 (1970): 280–96. Analyzes novel comprehensively, emphasizing rejection of middle-class values and retreat into madness.

MacLennan, Carol. "Dichotomous Values in the Novels of Janet Frame." *Journal of Commonwealth Literature* 22 (1987): 179–89. Contends that Frame's characters consistently and articulately resist mainstream values.

Mercer, Gina. "Exploring the Secret Caves of Language: Janet Frame's Poetry." *Meanjin* 44 (1985): 384–90. Explores major themes and attitudes toward language and the power of words in Frame's poetry and relates these to her prose.

Robertson, Robert T. "Bird, Hawk, Bogie: Janet Frame, 1952–1962." *Studies in the Novel* 4 (1972): 186–99. Connects early stories with *Owls Do Cry.* Establishes first three novels as trilogy and discusses provincialism and regionalism in her work.

Ross, Robert. "Linguistic Transformation and Reflection in Janet Frame's *Living in the Maniototo.*" *World Literature Written in English* 27 (1987): 320-26. Discusses Frame's language as illustrating transformation and reflection within the novel and explicates the unreliable elements of this work.

Rutherford, Anna. "Janet Frame's Divided and Distinguished Worlds." *World Literature Written in English* 14 (1975): 51–68. Analyzes various thematic dichotomies in several novels and concludes that Frame is persistently pessimistic about resolving alienation.

Stead, C.K. "Janet Frame: Language is the Hawk." *In the Glass Case: Essays on New Zealand Literature.* Auckland: Oxford UP, 1981. 130–36. Concentrates on *Living in the Maniototo* as a successful demonstration of Frame's talent, and emphasizes wit and irony within the novel's language and situations.

Stein, Karen F. "The Dark Laughter of Janet Frame." *Pacific Quarterly* (*Moana*) 9 (1985): 41–47. Focuses on satire, humor, paradox, and wit in Frame's novels as enhancing artistic techniques and as coping mechanisms.

—NANCY POTTER

Bessie Head

Bessie Head was born on 6 July 1937 in Pietermaritzburg, South Africa. Her mother, Bessie Amelia Emery, was a member of a wealthy landowning family of Scottish descent, her father a black stablehand who cared for the family's race horses. This liaison resulted in Bessie Amelia Emery being placed in a mental hospital, where the young Bessie (named after her mother) was born. Her mother died in 1943, having never emerged from psychiatric custody.

Bessie remained in foster care until 1950 when she was placed in an Anglican mission orphanage. Here she completed her schooling and in 1955 gained a Natal Teachers' Senior Certificate. During this period she read voraciously, mainly in the Asian literature section of the Durban City Library. She worked as a teacher for two years, and thereafter as a journalist in Johannesburg for a newspaper in the DRUM stable, *Golden City Post*, writing articles for teenagers in the *Home Post* supplement from 1958 to 1960.

In 1960 she moved to Cape Town, where she met and married a newspaper reporter, Harold Head. They had a son, Howard. After the breakup of the marriage, Head applied unsuccessfully for a passport to take up a teaching post in Botswana and in March 1964 left South Africa on an exit permit, which prohibited re-entry to the country. Upon arrival in Botswana, she taught for a while as a primary school teacher in Serowe, but when this position was terminated she was registered as a refugee.

In 1969 she experienced the onset of mental illness, which occurred in the form of sporadic attacks spread over a period of two years. Her novel *A Question of Power*, which was ranked eighth of fifteen "most influential books for the decade" by *The Black Scholar*, describes in graphic and disturbing detail the harrowing process of her mental breakdown. Towards the end of 1970 she emerged, however, with a reconstituted sense of self, a new resolve, and a firmer grip on the world.

In 1979, having once had her application refused, she was granted Botswanan citizenship. In 1982 she was invited to Gaborone to give a special lecture and to participate in a booksigning at an official exhibit on "Writers of Botswana." Her long hard battle for acceptance appeared to have been won. Ultimately, however, she remained a woman with a crippling legacy of loneliness and rejection, eking out an existence in a quiet corner of Africa. After being in a coma for several days, she died in Serowe on 17 April 1986.

ALIENATION, BREAKDOWN, AND RENEWAL

Bessie Head's novels are intensely private, remarkable works. They are charged with an honesty and power that arise from deep experience with the issues explored. One of their most intriguing features is their idiosyncratic divergence from other African novels in terms of treatment of theme and authorial perspective. In *When Rain Clouds Gather*, which deals with the conflict between modernity and tradition (the stock-in-trade of much African fiction since the appearance of Achebe's classic *Things Fall Apart* in 1958), Head inverts the customary story line of this genre, which in Southern Africa typically focuses on the passage of the protagonist from his rural village to the bright lights of the city (as in Peter Abrahams's 1946 novel, *Mine Boy*), and eschews a simplistic paradigm of racial conflict by constructing, in fictional terms, the possibility of interracial cooperation and friendship. Her second novel, *Maru*, further establishes her uniqueness in Africa by its incisive probing into the racism that exists in traditional African societies and by its dramatic inversion of the social pyramid in Botswana: A despised Masarwa (Bushman) woman, considered the lowest of the low, marries a future paramount chief of the dominant tribe of the region and with this single act throws time-honored prejudices into disarray. And, finally, in her concern with women and madness in *A Question of Power*, claims one critic, Head "has almost single-handedly brought about the inward turning of the African novel" (Larson 521).

The above examples should serve to illustrate Head's unique status in the field of African literature. Her novels have gained her an international reputation: Their "inclusivity," their insistence on universal human values and concerns, and, in *A Question of Power* particularly, their desire to break out of narrow traditionalistic modes of perception to embrace diverse religious and mythological systems have made Head accessible to an international readership. For this reason the present essay will focus principally on the novels and conclude with a brief synopsis of the later short stories and social histories that constitute a new orientation in Head's life and work.

Arthur Ravenscroft has remarked that Head's novels form a trilogy of sorts. He observes that "each novel both strikes out anew, and also re-shoulders the same burden" (175). In each case the central issue is the struggle of the protagonist to resolve his or her inner crisis by an effective engagement with the outer world. A pattern emerges: The interior torments of the characters are set in a concrete, historically specific context; they work through the psychological stress created by this disjunction to a reconciliation of interior and exterior, private and social.

The stress becomes progressively more interior and also more personal. As the focus narrows from a broader, external one to an inner psychic one, so the issues approximate more closely the personal experiences of the author. The problems displayed on a flat Botswanan landscape in *Rain Clouds* are embodied by individual characters in *Maru* and are finally internalized completely in *A Question of Power*. This progression traces the sequence of events in the author's life: from deracination in Francistown, to alienation and, finally, mental breakdown in Serowe. With a writer as honest as Head, the correlation between personal experience and its embodiment in fiction is profound. And it is this path that is most fruitful to follow in a critical appraisal of her novels.

In *When Rain Clouds Gather*, Makhaya, a young black South African political refugee, flees across the border to Botswana. His exile is provoked by the iniquities of the South African political system, which he felt impelled to resist; but his resistance led to a two-year jail sentence. The disintegration of self that came as a result of his experience of black urban ghetto life in South Africa he carries with him on his flight to Botswana. The novel, therefore, is a record of a South African political exile's determination to take root in a foreign land. Makhaya's reasons for leaving are fundamentally political, yet his exile is not an overt political strategy:

> I just want to step on free ground. I don't care about people. I don't
> care about anything, not even the white man. I want to feel what
> it is like to live in a free country and then maybe some of the evils
> in my life will correct themselves. (10)

Makhaya's quest is for "peace of mind," and this he opposes to the road that leads to "fame and importance" (20). This polarity is typical of Head: "I would deliberately create heroes and show their extreme willingness to abdicate from positions of power and absorb themselves in activities which would be of immense benefit to people" ("A Note" 27). Indeed, similar choices are made by characters in her later novels. She is clearly sceptical of political activism or party politics, and her characters instead seem bent upon pursuit of personal fulfilment.

Golema Mmidi, the village in which Makhaya seeks refuge, is full of individuals who have fled there to "escape the tragedies of life" (22). Their harsh circumstances have forced these villagers to become progressive, to break with traditional tribal agriculture through not having any traditionally acquired wealth. Head is interested in this sort of people: They represent possibilities for a new life—something she herself was desperately trying to reconstruct. The villagers pose a threat to Matenge, their arch-conservative, tribalistic chief who uses servants as personal slaves and enforces the rigid class distinction between royalty and commoner. Flanked by the semi-literate Pan-Africanist, Joas Tsepe, Matenge becomes a force for evil in the novel.

Pitted against this unholy alliance between die-hard traditionalism and opportunistic black nationalism are the progressive characters in *When Rain Clouds Gather*. Gilbert Balfour, a young English agronomist; Dinorego, who first meets Makhaya and brings him to the village; and Paulina Sebeso, a passionate and lonely widow exiled from her home in Northern Botswana. Maria, Dinorego's daughter and Mma-Millipede, with her quaint blend of Christianity and Setswana custom, are two lesser characters who join the four protagonists in their bid to oppose Matenge and the weight of tradition behind him. It is to the spirit of cautious progressiveness in the villagers of Golema Mmidi that Gilbert appeals. Joined by Makhaya, they work for the cooperative development of Botswana's resources. In this regard, Gilbert is the spokesman for small-scale capitalist development:

> Golema Mmidi has the exact amount of rainfall of a certain area in
> southern Africa where Turkish tobacco is grown very successfully.
> It's a very good cash crop too, and if everyone in Golema Mmidi

grows a bit and we market it co-operatively—why, we'll all be rich
in no time. (59)

Head's support for capitalist development is evident in this passage and, indeed, runs
as a theme throughout the novel. The precise nature of this development and path
to general prosperity is, however, ill-defined. The key to this indeterminacy lies in
Head's conceptual orientation: She does not work from a preconceived political
ideology and apply it to the issue at hand. With Head, abstract moral principles have
much more weight and are by their very nature less easily translated into political
and social practice. For her, generosity, courtesy, and respect for the common person
are the touchstones to positive social, political, and economic strategies. This
orientation is what provokes Arthur Ravenscroft's reservations about the novel:

> The precise relationship between individual freedom and political
> independence, and between a guarded core of privacy and an
> unbudding towards others, may seem rather elusive, perhaps even
> mystical . . . and I see it as one of the weaknesses of *When Rain
> Clouds Gather.* (178-79)

Makhaya Maseko's quest is to find inner peace by a constructive engagement with
the social world. In the ideal world of Golema Mmidi both of these desires are offered
fulfilment. His involvement in cooperative farming is matched by cooperation at an
emotional human level. In Golema Mmidi he finds people willing to share their
goods, both material and spiritual. The "feeling of great goodness" (184) that
permeates the life of the village translates itself into both practical activity and human
cooperation.

This "feeling of goodness" is the element that is crucial to the success of Head's
fictive world. It is also the unexamined "given" from which she is able to construct
a tenuous link between the public and the private. The weakness of this link is
revealed in the attitudes that Paulina and Mma-Millipede have towards the
cooperatives. They do not enter the project with an awareness of what it stands for—
what it means to the economic life of the subsistence dwellers of Golema Mmidi.
Their motivations are personal. When Gilbert anxiously asks Mma-Millipede to
recommend a woman who will start cooperative tobacco farming under Makhaya's
supervision, she sees this as an opportunity for matching Paulina off with Makhaya.
The link between the personal and the social thus becomes fortuitous, indetermi-
nate. This indeed is an example of the whole tone of the novel: Everything positive
develops by happy accident. This is why it has been accused of being excessively
romantic (Ravenscroft 179). The introduction of the "God with no shoes" (185) at
the end of the novel is an attempt to make events less arbitrary—to supply the causal
connection between events that is lacking.

One is immediately aware, when reading *Maru,* that it and *Rain Clouds* belong
to different orders of fiction. *Maru* has different rules for its own internal coherence
and also for its interpretation by the reader. The first few pages are an epilogue to
the events that unfold through the rest of the novel. Ravenscroft calls them "a species
of sealed orders for the reader" (179). The invitation, therefore, is to read more

deeply into already-known events, to dwell more seriously on the wider social and metaphysical significance of the human drama.

Maru is at one level a story of rival lovers competing for the affections of the same woman. The drama is heightened by the fact that they are both in line for chieftaincy of their tribe and that the woman who commands their love is a "Masarwa" (Bushman)—a social outcast. The rivalry of Maru and Moleka is that of two powerful personalities vying for supremacy. Maru is portrayed as being manipulative and perceptive, Moleka as bright, passionate and energetic. Through most of the story it is Maru who has the upper hand; he has "creative imagination" (58), whereas Moleka has energy without the imagination to direct it: "They were kings of opposing kingdoms. It was Moleka's kingdom that was unfathomable, as though shut behind a heavy iron door. There had been no such door for Maru. He dwelt everywhere" (34). Maru's godlike omniscience gives him ascendancy, but this is threatened by the love that Margaret awakens in Moleka. Moleka's power is latent: It is an unknown quantity that Maru fears. With the awakening of his love for Margaret, Moleka's energy becomes channeled, and he experiences an indefinable surge of power. Maru's calculations are momentarily unbalanced, but he deftly averts this threat to his supremacy by engineering the marriage of Moleka to his sister and, ultimately, his own marriage to Margaret. He abdicates political responsibility and moves away from Dilepe village, leaving tribal authority in the hands of Moleka. The social implications of Maru's marriage are profound: Margaret comes from a race of untouchables.

It is clear when reading *Maru* that individual characters are meant to stand for something else, that individual actions and events are a way of expressing things that go beyond the confines of narrative realism. The logic of these actions and events is therefore not one of externally observable cause and effect. What gives coherence to events in *Maru* are the inner workings of the minds of the characters. The drama becomes internal; the subjects enter into a relationship with each other at a psychic level.

The psychic plane—or in Head's terms, the realm of the soul—is accessible only to Maru, Moleka, and Margaret. The novel therefore becomes a three-sided struggle in the realm of the soul. Maru's quest is to attain the realm of the inner self, the being in touch with the secret pulse of the universe. He moves from the alienation of his tribal, exterior identity to his inner identity as a "king of heaven" (35). Similarly, Margaret's journey from alienation to wholeness is a passage from her racially ascribed identity to her true inner identity. Through the union of two equal souls, Maru and Margaret defy the prejudiced world and anticipate a new world of true racial equality.

If one takes seriously Head's claim to write "didactic" novels ("Some Notes" 30), it is clear that what she is "preaching against" in *Maru* is racial prejudice. Her moral condemnation of this iniquity is unequivocal. What is not clear is what alternative is projected. *Maru* is offered on one level as a way to end racial antagonism: There is a real sense that Head is concerned to engage with the real world, institute change, put an end to prejudice and reactionary codes of behavior, establish genuine equality between the races and the sexes. On another level she seeks the liberation of the pure, creative, individual soul. These ideals are in conflict in *Maru*. Maru, at the highest rung in Botswanan society, is ideally placed to institute reform, yet in doing so he alienates himself from the people of his society. He achieves change at the expense of leadership of his tribe.

The point is that Head is unable to affirm the values of African tribal socialism because of her alienation from this world. Her ideal is the fulfilment of individual desires, yet her context *is* African, and so she divides one character into two—each part of which plays a different yet equally necessary role. Ravenscroft recognizes the ambiguity that this tension in her thought engenders: ". . . are we sure, at the end, that the two chief male characters, Maru and Moleka . . . are indeed two separate fictional characters, or that they are symbolic extensions of contending character-traits within the same man?" (179). This raises the question of how we are to interpret *Maru.* Is it to be read as realism or allegorical fable? On a realistic level the novel simply does not work: It is highly unlikely that two socially attractive, eligible men would compete for the affections of an outcast. And if we are to interpret the novel as a piece of realism, what does one make of a character like Ranko, who appears and disappears like Prospero's Ariel in Shakespeare's *The Tempest?* The novel is equally impossible as a description of the outcome of racial antagonism. The ending—the fairy-tale marriage of the prince to the misprized princess—is fanciful, to say the least.

Maru reads better as a sort of parable, a moral discourse on the evils of racial prejudice. Indeed, the power of the novel can be felt in the richly evoked social tension of the village of Dilepe, where racial prejudice is a tangible presence— perhaps an authentic reworking of the author's own experience. But the power of love, the magnetism between personalities, the communication between souls on a psychic level, the inexorable forces operating beneath the events of the workaday world are all aspects of human experience captured with vitality by Head. And it is here that the real power of the novel lies. *Maru* succeeds as a personal, almost mystical vindication of the power of love over evil—not that this is a reading without its share of problems.

Head seemed to be aware of the complexities and ambiguities that the text produces:

> With all my South African experience I longed to write an enduring novel on the hideousness of racial prejudice. But I also wanted the book to be so beautiful and so magical that I, as the writer, would long to read and re-read it. ("Social and Political Pressures" 23)

The dual intention suggested here foreshadows the duality in the novel itself: the real, historically specific problem of racism and the method of its eradication and the fairy-tale, magical, allegorical dimension. *Maru's* ostensible aim is to preach against racism; what it finally comes to deal with is the liberation of the individual soul. This inconsistency reflects Head's status as an exile as well as an artist in the context of the subsistence life of the Botswanan peasants. As an exile she is alien, as an artist she is apart. She affirms, finally, what she knows to be an inner truth—her "otherness," her loneliness, the afflictions she shares with Margaret: "In the distance, a village proceeded with its own life but she [Margaret] knew not what it was. . . . She was not a part of it and belonged nowhere" (93).

In *A Question of Power* the identification of author and protagonist is at its closest. Head in fact describes *A Question of Power* as "totally autobiographical" ("Head Interview" 25), and one of the reasons that the novel is so inaccessible is that it is so intensely private: "Elizabeth and I are one" ("Head Interview" 26). The novel explores Head's early childhood, her life with her foster parents and at the orphanage, her marriage and eventual departure for Botswana to teach at a primary school there. This is the "real world," which contains the primary interests of the novel, which is the journey of the soul through the realms of universal good and evil. It comprises a very small part of the novel (15-21), and despite further allusions to her early life and also to her contemporary life in the village of Serowe—her vegetable gardening, her involvement in cooperatives, the activities of her little son, everyday events in the village—greater urgency is given to her inner struggle to attain a sense of, in Head's terms, true human values with which she can once more engage positively with the real world.

It is difficult to construct a logical, coherent way through the lurid dream sequences of the novel, but the issues that emerge clearly, and with which the dream personae Sello and Dan and other figures challenge her, are those specifically related to her experiences as an underprivileged Colored growing up in South Africa. These anxieties are common in the race-obsessed social system of South Africa: a sense of personal worth (a Colored child is considered to be the product of an immoral alliance between black and white), an inability to identify with Black Consciousness and Pan-Africanist groups, and an anxiety that one is abandoning one's fellow-downtrodden by elevating oneself socially and materially.

The issue that ultimately emerges from this disquiet is the question of personal power and how to use it for the betterment of humankind—hence, of course, the novel's title. Elizabeth expresses this as the underlying motivation for her "soul-exploration":

> She was talking to a monk [Sello] who had used an unnatural establishment to express a thousand and one basic principles as the ideal life because, in the heat of living, no one had come to terms with their own powers and at the same time made allowance for the powers of others. (35)

Elizabeth considers her powers to be used positively when they are used on the basis of love for all people: "an awakening of her own powers corresponded to an awakening love of mankind" (35). This is the affirmation that occurs again at the end of the novel: "She [Elizabeth] had fallen from the very beginning into the warm embrace of the brotherhood of man, because when a people wanted everyone to be ordinary it was just another way of saying man loved man" (206).

Elizabeth's inner struggle is induced, like Makhaya's and Margaret's, by her dual alienation from South Africa and Botswana, for Head's characters are, like her, isolated. Thus Elizabeth's affirmation of good is not made on behalf of society in general. She is unable to assert, in a partisan way, the superiority of one culture, or society, or political system over another and comes instead to ground her arguments upon the soul of the solitary individual, the basic unit of humankind. Her lodestar, in other words, is her commitment to the ordinary person.

The real world of the novel centers on Elizabeth's involvement in communal gardening. Food production on a cooperative basis incorporates all of her aspirations: sharing with the community, coming to terms with the harsh environment, and creating, in Head's own words, "new worlds out of nothing" ("Preface to 'Witchcraft'" 72). In the phrase "Cape Gooseberry," all of these aspects are brought into a symbolic focus:

> The work had a melody like that—a complete stranger like the
> Cape Gooseberry settled down and became a part of the village life
> of Motabeng. It loved the hot, dry Botswana summers as they were
> a replica of the Mediterranean summers of its home in the Cape.
> (153)

The "Cape Gooseberry" (which becomes Elizabeth's nickname) is of course a symbol of Head's own exile and successful resettlement. It also symbolizes the progressiveness of the multi-national Motabeng community and also the Batswana themselves—their willingness to try something new to break the stranglehold the semi-desert environment has on rural Botswana. In all this there is resilience, a sense of commitment, of determination to take root, which suggests that Bessie Head is reshouldering the issues dealt with in *Rain Clouds*.

In *Rain Clouds*, Makhaya's struggle is to reconcile his material existence with his inner life. His life is conceived to be channeled by his experience in these two dimensions. He acts in the real world, and the world, in turn, provokes an inner reaction. The two realms are finally brought into accord. With *Maru*, the stress is more upon the inner self. Yet Maru succeeds in his ideals only when he has brought the outside world into harmony with his inward desires. In *A Question of Power* the relationship between inner and outer is at its most tenuous. There is virtually no causal connection between reality and Elizabeth's nightmares. At one point in the novel she questions this disjunction: "How did it all happen here, in so unsuspecting a climate, these silent, tortured, universal questions of power and love; of loss and sacrifice?" (97–98). Yet the novel ends on an affirmative note: "Maybe, the work she and Sello had done together had introduced a softness and tenderness into mankind's history. . . . They had perfected together the ideal of sharing everything and then perfectly shared everything with all mankind" (202). In broad terms this is a similar kind of affirmation to those made in the earlier novels. The "ideal of sharing everything" is at the basis of Head's moral perspective. And she sees this principle as applying to every aspect of human life: Thus in the economic sphere, for example, co-operatives are the expression of this communal spirit. Elizabeth's mental breakdown occurs in the process of testing these ideals. But she has withstood the assaults upon her sense of human value and has emerged revitalized: "from the degradation and destruction of her life had arisen a still, lofty serenity of soul nothing could shake" (202).

It was asserted at the outset that one of the ways in which sense could be made of Head's novels is by recognizing the close relation between lived experience and its artistic expression. This is especially true of *A Question of Power*. The language of the text—its rich but puzzling metaphors, unpredictable shifts in tense and in the context of the action—indicates that *what* is communicated is so private and internal that it prescribes *how* it is to be communicated.

Elizabeth's dreams possess a certain narratological authority: they are, in fact, the very "stuff" of the text, the locus of the real life of the novel. A key to the phantasmagoria of *A Question of Power* seems to lie in a remark that comes just before Elizabeth plunges into insanity:

> In many ways, her slowly unfolding internal drama was far more absorbing and demanding than any drama she could encounter in Motabeng village. The insights, perceptions, fleeting images and impressions required more concentration, reflection and brooding than any other work she had ever undertaken. (29)

This describes the mental events that unfold in the novel. But what is peculiar (and should therefore sound a warning to the alert reader) is the palpable sense one has when reading the above passage that, in introducing the drama to follow, Head seems at the same time to be talking about her own activity of writing: that the author, in other words, so closely identifies with her protagonist she is unable to exploit the customary distance between author and character that underpins the workings of a more conventional, realistic novel.

It is true that some of these imponderables were present in *Maru*. Indeed, the narrative style of *Maru* in some ways anticipates the later novel, especially where the author deals with the "realm of the soul" in which the spiritual struggle between Maru, Margaret, and Moleka takes place. In *Maru*, however, the author does finally attempt (unsatisfactorily, it was argued) to knit the "real world" and the "realm of the soul" together into a cohesive whole. In *A Question of Power*, there is no such attempt at unity: What Head attempts through Elizabeth is an exploration of the experiences of her life and an investigation into what they signify in the greater context of an Africa in transition. The novel calls upon the reader to abandon conventional expectations in order to strike directly towards its heart. The invitation, in other words, is to plunge into the nightmare reality of Elizabeth's consciousness, to experience at a narrative level the real struggle of the protagonist, and to emerge finally, with her, exhausted but spiritually renewed.

The second phase of Head's output represents a major break with what came before. *A Question of Power* proved to be a turning point, and Head was able from this point on to explore more objectively her country of exile. Her work of this phase evinces few of the disconcerting anomalies that flaw her novels. *The Collector of Treasures* and *Serowe: Village of the Rain Wind*, particularly, have a symmetry and harmoniousness of form that testify to the author's new sense of allegiance to Botswana, and of course, to Serowe.

The Collector of Treasures is a collection of thirteen stories dealing with the issues that emerge in Botswanan village life: tribal history, the missionaries, religious conflict, witchcraft, rising illegitimacy, and, throughout, problems that women in the society encounter. Each of these issues is central to a particular story. Yet each story is also deftly allusive and evokes vividly and richly the sense of a real, living, bustling village struggling to cope with the intrusion of new forces into its traditional social fabric. Head transcribes oral sources—village history, gossip, and folklore—into literature, reshaping the spoken to suit the new medium of the written, the guiding intention being to explain a village in its own terms.

Serowe: Village of the Rain Wind is a documentary companion to the stories of *The Collector of Treasures*. It is composed of a series of transcribed interviews edited and prefaced by the author to constitute a portrait of Serowe village. The primary historians are, in this case, the people themselves. Bessie Head introduces the village by a general description, and the interview material is then shaped and arranged into historical and thematic groupings, principally around the lives of three men who had a profound effect on the region: Khama the Great, Tshekedi Khama (Khama's son), and Patrick van Rensburg, a former South African diplomat who became involved in educational and self-help schemes in Serowe. In *Serowe* the author sets the record straight, for the book reinterprets from a fresh perspective events that make up the history of this remarkable village. "Africa," Head observes in her Introduction, "was never 'the dark continent' to African people" (xiv).

A Bewitched Crossroad, Head's last published work, demonstrates her sustained interest in the history of Botswana and constitutes, in effect, an extension of the appendix to *Serowe*, "The Founding of the British Bechuanaland Protectorate, 1885-1895." *A Bewitched Crossroad*, with its bold mingling of fact and fiction, was Head's most ambitious project. In 1981 she had already published extracts from it prefaced by a description of the work as "my major obsession, the Khama novel" ("A Bewitched Crossroad" 5).

This essay has attempted to trace the autobiographical strain that surfaces persistently in Head's novels without neglecting other critical coordinates germane to more orthodox literary-critical practice. It has been argued that Bessie Head's novels show an increasing interiority of perspective. This interiority culminates in the cathartic *A Question of Power*, which signals an end to an "inwardly-directed" phase in the author's life. *The Collector of Treasures* goes on to explore in a more outward reaching way the life of Head's adoptive village. The short story as a genre—particularly in Head's use of it—seems singularly able to cope with the material yielded by the author's more objective interest in episodes of village life. It is a genre, moreover, that is appropriate to a new phase in the author's life. *Serowe: Village of the Rain Wind* naturally has different dimensions to the collection of stories but is nevertheless a companion volume, and part of the same community-directed project. Both volumes are, in their different ways, remarkably well suited to the author's new intentions, and they evince a symmetry and balance absent in the novels. *A Bewitched Crossroad* represents in some ways a return to the novel genre, and yet its importance—and, indeed, area of competence—is more impressively demonstrated in its reinterpretation of Southern African history. In different ways Head's last three works show a capacity to explore the lives of the Botswanan people. The new direction she takes in these works involves a surmounting of the problems of isolation and alienation that characterized her earlier phase and a new commitment to Botswana and, particularly, the people of Serowe. For it was in Botswana, in the quiet rhythm of its daily life and, most important, its continuity with the past, that Bessie Head was able to carve out a spiritual as well as physical home and work out in creative terms political alternatives for a more hopeful African future.

WORKS CITED

Larson, Charles R. "Anglophone Writing from Africa." *Books Abroad* 48 (1974): 520–21.

Head, Bessie. "Bessie Head interviewed by Michelle Adler, Susan Gardner, Tobeka Mda and Patricia Sandler, Serowe, 5 January 1983." *Between the Lines: Interviews with Bessie Head, Sheila Roberts, Ellen Kuzwayo, Miriam Tlali.* Eds. Craig MacKenzie and Cherry Clayton. Grahamstown: National English Literary Museum, 1989. 5–30.

———. "A Bewitched Crossroad." *The Bloody Horse* 3 (1981): 5–11.

———. *Maru.* London: Heinemann, 1972.

———. "A Note on *Rain Clouds.*" *Gar* 33 (1979): 27.

———. "Preface to 'Witchcraft.'" *Ms.* 4 (1975): 72–73.

———. *A Question of Power.* London: Heinemann, 1974.

———. *Serowe: Village of the Rain Wind.* London: Heinemann, 1981.

———. "Social and Political Pressures that Shape Literature in Southern Africa." *World Literature Written in English* 18 (1979): 20–26.

———. "Some Notes on Novel Writing." *New Classic* No. 5 (1978): 30–32.

———. *When Rain Clouds Gather.* London: Heinemann, 1972.

Ravenscroft, Arthur. "The Novels of Bessie Head." *Aspects of South African Literature.* Ed. Christopher Heywood. London: Heinemann, 1976. 174–86.

BESSIE HEAD'S PUBLISHED WORK

Novels

When Rain Clouds Gather, 1969
Maru, 1971
A Question of Power, 1974
A Bewitched Crossroad: An African Saga, 1984

Short Story Collections

The Collector of Treasures and Other Botswana Village Tales, 1977
Tales of Tenderness and Power, 1989

Social History

Serowe: Village of the Rain Wind, 1981

SELECTED CRITICAL READINGS

With few exceptions, critics were initially slow to recognize the significance of Bessie Head's writing, and it was only with her death in 1986 that research gained momentum. The publication of *Bessie Head: A Bibliography* (Susan Gardner and Patricia E. Scott, Grahamstown: National English Literary Museum, 1986) coincided with her death and appears to have fulfilled the function of generating further research while serving at the same time as an index of the gathering pace of Head scholarship. For example, it lists some 250 items of which 35 are critical articles on her work appearing between 1972 and 1985. In the three years following the appearance of the *Bibliography* the number of critical articles on Head has more than tripled. In addition, at least six dissertations and several other full-length studies of her work are underway, confirming Bessie Head's status as a major African writer.

Beard, Linda Susan. "Bessie Head's *A Question of Power*: The Journey Through Disintegration to Wholeness." *Colby Library Quarterly* 15.4 (1979): 267–74. Offers a clear, incisive perspective on Head's most difficult novel. Isolates the major religious coordinates of the novel (Judaism, Christianity, Buddhism, Hinduism, and classical mythology) and attempts an explanation that will resolve the novel's many intractable paradoxes and polarities.

Clayton, Cherry. "'A World Elsewhere': Bessie Head as Historian." *English in Africa* 15.1 (1988): 55–70. Establishes the interrelations between *Serowe: Village of the Rain Wind* and *A Bewitched Crossroad* and examines the contributions of both histories to the overturning of colonial myths about the African hinterland.

Johnson, Joyce. "Metaphor, Myth and Meaning in Bessie Head's *A Question of Power*." *World Literature Written in English* 25 (1985): 198–211. Examines the novel by careful consideration of its structure and its central concerns and motifs. Offers a reading that attempts to render comprehensible the events of the novel and the key concepts that the author employs.

Johnson, J. "Bessie Head and the Oral Tradition: The Structure of *Maru*." *Wasafiri* 3 (1985): 5–8. Examines *Maru* in relation to African myths, legends, and folktales. A rich insight into the mythological and universal resonances of a novel that appears to yield limitless levels of signification.

MacKenzie, Craig. "Short Fiction in the Making: The Case of Bessie Head." *English in Africa* 16.1 (1989): 17–28. Explores the area of contiguity between the stories of *The Collector of Treasures* and the milieu of informal gossip and tales that characterizes contemporary village life in Botswana.

————. *Bessie Head: An Introduction*. Grahamstown: National English Literary Museum, 1989. Contains four sections (interspersed with photographs): Chronology, Biographical Note, Critical Note on Texts, Select Bibliography. Attempts to convey in an introductory but accurate vein the contours of Head's life and work.

Marquard, Jean. "Bessie Head: Exile and Community in Southern Africa." *London Magazine* 18.9–10 (1978–79): 48–61. (Extracts reprinted in *Contemporary Literary Criticism* 25, 1983: 237–38) Consideration of Head's novels and unpublished (at that point) social history of Serowe, interspersed with extracts from an interview. Offers a vivid picture of the writer's early life in South Africa and her day-to-day life in Serowe. Provides a useful introduction to a writer poised midway in her career.

Nkosi, Lewis. "Southern Africa: Protest and Commitment." *Tasks and Masks: Themes and Styles of African Literature*. Essex: Longman, 1981. 76–106. Nkosi discusses Head's first three novels alongside writing by other Southern African authors, notably Lessing and Mphahlele, in a chapter devoted to an examination of the dynamic of protest and commitment in Southern African writing in the 1950s and 1960s. Offers an informed critic's assessment of the respective merits and demerits of Head's novels.

Ogungbesan, Kolawole. "The Cape Gooseberry Also Grows in Botswana: Alienation and Commitment in the Writings of Bessie Head." *Presence Africaine* 109 (1979): 92–106. (Reprinted in *Journal of African Studies* 6: 1979 206–12) Explores the dynamic of alienation and commitment in Head's novels and collected and uncollected stories. Contrasts her with fellow South African exiles and reveals that her apolitical outlook, her willingness to take root in a neighboring African state, and her commitment to ordinary village life mark her off from her South African contemporaries.

Ravenscroft, Arthur. "The Novels of Bessie Head." *Aspects of South African Literature.* Ed. Christopher Heywood. London: Heinemann, 1976. 174–86. (Extracts reprinted in *Contemporary Literary Criticism* 25, 1983: 233–35) Seminal article that places Head's novels in a new category of the South African novel by virtue of their vision for a future South Africa based on the models of independent African states. Argues that the novels reflect an increasing interiority of perspective, that each novel returns to the central issues of personal contentment and political power, and that each tries to resolve these issues in different ways. Points to the author's unusual toughness of mind and realistic perspective on African politics and society.

Taiwo, Oladele. "Bessie Head." *Female Novelists of Modern Africa.* London: Macmillan, 1984. 185–214. Useful general introduction to Head's novels, short stories (*The Collector of Treasures*) and social history (*Serowe: Village of the Rain Wind*). Discusses each of the works separately and in order of appearance.

Wilhelm, Cherry. "Bessie Head: The Face of Africa." *English in Africa* 10.1 (1983): 1–13. Densely allusive reading of Head's novels which evokes the texture of Head's fictive world as well as its greater socio-historical resonance. Argues that the novels share a basic quest pattern in which the protagonist struggles to attain a sense of belonging in both a geographical as well as an existential sense.

— CRAIG MACKENZIE

Anita Desai

Anita Desai was born on 24 June 1937 in the northern part of India, a region whose climate has exerted a strong influence on her; she has said: "I really think those summers of the north make me whatever I am."

Of mixed parentage—her mother Toni Nimé was German and her father D.N. Mazumdar was Bengali, she was educated at Queen Mary's School, Delhi, and completed her B.A. in English literature at the University of Delhi in 1957. She worked for a year in Calcutta and there married Ashvin Desai in 1958. They have four children.

Desai started writing at the age of seven and began to publish pieces in children's magazines; her first story appeared when she was nine. She has received the Winifred Holtby Prize for Regional Literature of the Royal Society of Literature, London; the Sahitya Akademi (India's National Academy of Letters) Award for English; and the Federation of Indian Publishers and Author's Guild of India Award for Excellence in Writing. *Village by the Sea* earned the Guardian Award for Children's Fiction in 1982. Desai was a member of the Advisory Board for English of the Sahitya Akademi for a number of years and in 1978 was elected Fellow of the Royal Society of Literature, London.

She has lived in Calcutta, Bombay, Chandigarh, Delhi, and Poona. For the past three years she has taught in the English Department of Mount Holyoke College. She now divides her time between Massachusetts and Delhi.

DISCREPANCY BETWEEN THE INNER BEING
AND THE OUTSIDE WORLD

Like most of Anita Desai's work, *Fire on the Mountain,* her fifth novel, addresses the problem of isolation and the lack of communication between individuals. This time the recurrent theme is developed through the story of Nanda Kaul, an elderly woman who leads a secluded life in the small village of Kasauli high in the Himalayas. Like much of Desai's fiction, the novel revolves around female characters: Nanda Kaul, the protagonist; her great-granddaughter, Raka; and an old friend of Nanda Kaul's, Ila Das.

In *Fire on the Mountain,* as in most of Desai's work, atmosphere and landscape are intricately linked. These two elements are used symbolically and are associated with human emotions and sensations, thus enabling the reader to form a more complete picture of the characters because the world around them is directly connected both to their inner being and actions. Kasauli's atmosphere holds an emblematic quality for those who meet there, each perceiving the place and its atmosphere differently and each seeking solace in it: Nanda Kaul attracted by the barrenness and silence; Raka, her great-granddaughter, drawn to its wilderness; Ila Das enthralled because it is "a little bit of the past come alive" (132).

The novel's first words help to situate the central character in her familiar setting: "Nanda Kaul paused under the pine trees to take in their scented sibilance and listen to the cicadas fiddling invisibly under the mesh of pine needles" (3). The quietness and beauty of her surroundings are rendered all the more acute by the recurrent use of "s" alliterations and repetitions of "i" sounds, which resound like the wind whispering in the trees and the birds twittering. Nanda Kaul immediately reveals a strong affinity for the place where she lives: "Everything she wanted was here, at Carignano [the name of her house]" (3). While the setting is barren, it tends to symbolize the woman's loneliness and seclusion, corresponding exactly to "the place . . . that she had wanted and prepared for all her life" (3). As the wife of a university vice-chancellor and the mother of many children, Nanda Kaul had once led a busy life entertaining her husband's colleagues and students and taking care of her household. Now rejecting all these duties, she wants to escape from that past. As the novel progresses, she is seen evolving in this barren place, which appears ideal for her personal exploration.

A natural element towards which Nanda Kaul feels attracted throughout *Fire on the Mountain* is the tree, a symbol of loneliness and withdrawal. Her identification with trees is enhanced by her desire for absolute tranquility and peace: "She would lie still, still—she would be a charred tree trunk in the forest" (23). Not only does the protagonist long to be a tree, but she wants to be a particular kind as well, a tree that has been burned by a fire and of which only a "charred trunk" remains. Fire, the central symbol of the novel—as the title suggests, embodies the internal conflict that consumes Nanda Kaul. Her emotional life is troubled by the two antagonistic feelings within her: a desire to care for others and a strong need for isolation. Wanting to do away with the past, she has chosen to live on her own, that desire for freedom and privacy symbolized in part by her identification with a bird of prey, the eagle. But she feels her freedom is not going to last, fears it has been threatened by the news of her great-granddaughter's arrival; then she is reminded of the sense of duty by the call of another bird, the cuckoo, a symbol of domesticity that calls her back to reality. Even though she was determined not to allow anyone or anything spoil her privacy, she answers to the call of the cuckoo with an "ironic bow," the same "ironic bow to duty that no one had noticed or defined" (19) when she was responsible for her household. Yet another bird reflects Nanda Kaul's feelings, this time the parrots, which disturb the quietness Nanda seeks, their quarreling representative of her inner strife.

After the life of silent suffering Nanda Kaul has endured, she has at last reached a stage where she has obliterated a past full of obedience and rejected totally her marital and matriarchal role. So she resents any approach from another human as an encroachment upon her personal freedom. Having just received news that her great-granddaughter is coming to stay with her, she fears that she will have to take care of the girl in the same way as she had her children, and this idea disturbs her—the emotion revealed once more by a bird, the hoopoe feeding its nestling.

But far from being an "unwelcome intrusion," Raka turns out to be an independent sort who does not invade Nanda Kaul's privacy. A strange girl, Raka comes from a broken home with an alcoholic father and a mother who suffers from nervous breakdowns. She has also been weakened by typhoid, and for this reason has been sent to the mountains to recover. On her arrival, her senses are immediately aroused by the surroundings, and she is drawn to the animal life in particular. Unable to endure enclosed spaces, she feels stifled and imprisoned like a bird in a cage when left alone in her bedroom. Her feelings and thoughts, however, are not described directly; rather they are alluded to by her actions, her odd behavior indicating the nature of her feelings. When she is mentioned, it is mainly from the point of view of Nanda Kaul or Ila Das. For the most part, then, it is their apprehension of Raka's actions along with the conversations between Raka and Rama Lal, the cook, by which her character is revealed.

A solitary child, Raka is cautious and mistrustful of other people, for her parents have caused her so much suffering that she beholds their cruelty in all human beings. So it is in nature that she seeks what humans cannot give her, her furtive, shy actions bringing the others to liken her to "a secretive bird." As she takes her solitary walks in the mountains, she is not attracted by nature's gentle, beautiful side but by its desolate and destructive aspects. This fascination with the wilder part of nature is first suggested by the image of the cuckoos:

> No one ever came here but Raka and the cuckoos that sang and sang invisibly. These were not the dutiful domestic birds that called Nanda Kaul to attention at Carignano. They were the demented birds that raved and beckoned Raka on to a land where there was no sound, only silence, no light, only shade, and skeletons kept in beds of ash on which the footprints of jackals flowered in grey. (94)

Raka's response to this part of her surroundings hints at the final scene in *Fire on the Mountain*, for her solitary wanderings always lead her to the burned houses and ruins. Drawn to them and fascinated by fire, she feels a need to destroy, a need that surfaces when she sets the forest ablaze at the end of the novel.

One of her walks leads her into a traumatic experience: She observes a dance club at night and finds the scene appalling, because it reminds her of the perverse and nightmarish life with her parents. She recalls the image of her drunken father acting violently toward her helpless, emotionally unstable mother. Wanting in the past to escape from such childhood memories, Raka is now forced to face up to those experiences, a burden she had never really admitted to herself.

Raka resembles her grandmother, both of them solitary, both of them sorting out their past. Although they live together, each follows her own path in trying to form an identity. Yet they inhabit different worlds, even their desire for independence stemming from distinct motives. For Nanda Kaul solitude is a self-imposed effort, a means to take revenge on life; for Raka it is an innate need. Ironically, Nanda Kaul finds it difficult to acknowledge that the personal solitude she strives to attain at such great cost comes so spontaneously to a child. Further, she realizes that Raka's childhood has led her to apprehend life in a realistic manner, quite the opposite from her own understanding.

Nanda Kaul, in spite of herself, is bothered by the child's indifference and resents the relationship developing between Raka and the cook Ram Lal, who acts as an agent between the girl and the woman. Obsessed with the supernatural, he mesmerizes Raka with strange stories. This angers Nanda Kaul who resents the fact that Raka should spend time with the cook and remain aloof from her grandmother, the reaction bringing to light one of Nanda Kaul's weaknesses, jealousy. But the more Raka rejects her, the more Nanda Kaul is attracted to this great-grandchild who manages to keep to herself so unconsciously and effortlessly.

Several times Nanda Kaul attempts to communicate, the first occasion being an offer to go for a walk to Monkey Point. The venture, though, turns out to be a failure, for both are so aware of the other's presence that their reactions are unnatural. Raka finds Nanda Kaul's company a hindrance to her exploration of nature, and she has no wish to share her experience with the old woman. Raka, blending so perfectly with the landscape that she is compared to "a seed" or "a blade of grass," feels at Monkey Point that she could fly like an eagle. Earlier the eagle's image had been used to represent Nanda Kaul's longing, but now it symbolizes Raka's need for freedom and privacy. Later, Nanda Kaul tries once more to gain the girl's attention by telling her stories of her own childhood, in a "musical voice that did not sound as if it belonged to her" (82). While Raka shows enthusiasm at first, she soon becomes suspicious of the truth in the stories and loses all interest.

Although any attempt to communicate proves disastrous, their living together has helped both to gain self-confidence and a kind of self-realization. Nanda has learned that by putting on airs she will not gain the love of the child, who is in fact a younger version of herself. Raka becomes "the finished, perfected model of what Nanda Kaul herself was merely a brave, flawed experiment" (47).

Then another arrival threatens Nanda Kaul's privacy: Her old friend Ila Das telephones and wants to visit. This character is introduced into the narrative through an unusual device—her voice. Nanda Kaul, after all these years, had still not gotten accustomed to Ila Das's irritating voice, which had always affected her adversely. Even as she hears Ila Das speaking on the telephone, she finds herself disgusted and wants to escape the sound of her speaking.

The section in which Ila Das actually appears is entitled "Ila Das leaves Carignano." For it is after returning home from a short visit at Nanda Kaul's house that Ila Das will meet her death. When she arrives at Carignano, the children insult and assault her, which prefigures the prey-and-predator tragedy in which Ila Das will play the victim. She turns out, as her story unfolds, to be a pitiful character, even though everything about her, from her voice to her everyday life, is treated in a tragi-comic light.

Although very different, Nanda Kaul and Ila Das are alike in that both endure old age with difficulty and try to find an escape from it: Nanda by living a life of contemplative seclusion, Ila by fighting against injustice. Once Ila Das starts reminiscing about the days long gone, Nanda Kaul feels even more uncomfortable, for she has been trying to flee from this very past. Ila Das, in truth, is deceiving herself by recalling and recounting scenes from her life that she creates as she speaks. At times she does awaken unpleasant memories in Nanda Kaul, especially that of her husband's lengthy affair with another woman. Although Nanda Kaul has done everything to break free from her past physically and mentally, she cannot escape it. Ila Das becomes the symbol of Nanda Kaul's own self-delusion, and her very presence causes Nanda Kaul great turmoil. Still, even as Raka and Ila Das upset her, they inadvertently help her to gather the strength to face her life—past and present—honestly and truthfully, something she had never done before.

In the last pages of the novel, the hitherto slow-paced narrative gains momentum as it describes the rape and murder of Ila Das. This event triggers a humiliating confession from Nanda Kaul, who unleashes a torrent of revelations. Immediately after the visitor's departure, though, Nanda Kaul feels relieved and slightly guilty over not inviting the woman to stay for the night, but that soon vanishes. The narrative then turns to a description of Ila Das on her way home, the creation of suspense achieved very deftly. Although she departs in a comic manner, the opening sentence of chapter 11 prefigures the tragedy that is to beset her: "Ila Das did not take the Garkhal road that led down the hillside to her village, no" (135). The emphasis through negation at the end of the sentence suggests the danger that lies in store and projects the ominous mood that is to be created. Then Ila Das's passage through the bazaar leads her to the grainseller who warns her that she should not walk alone at night, even though he does not disclose what he knows of the impending danger: that is, that Preet Singh, a villager, had come to see him that very day and had spoken ill of Ila Das because she was trying to prevent him from marrying off his young daughter to a wealthy old man from whom he would get a sizable dowry. Again, the presence of danger is hinted at: "He [the grainseller] frowned with uneasiness. It was growing dark" (138). Although she pretends not to be afraid, "Ila Das hurried out of the bazaar . . . in a kind of panic" (138). The intense atmosphere is built up by repetition and short, simple sentences, some of them narrated in reported thought: "The way was full of hazards, full of hazards. The grainseller was right. She trembled" (139).

Ila Das will never reach her home. The path will lead her to death. At the last detour, darkness has brought coolness and Ila shivers, everything, all the natural elements warning her of danger and forming a sinister atmosphere. At the very moment that the reader feels relieved on learning, "Now at last she came to the final fold of the hill. Once around it, she would be home" (141), the action shifts abruptly:

> Just then a black shape detached itself from the jagged pile of the rock, that last rock between her and the hamlet, and sprang soundlessly at her. She staggered under its weight with a gasp that ripped through her chest. It had her by the throat. She struggled, choking, trying to stretch and stretch and stretch that gasp till it became a shout, a shout that the villagers would hear, the red dog would hear, a shout for help. But the fingers tightened. Now she tore her mouth open for breath, now she opened her eyes till they boggled, and popped, and stood out of her head as she saw, in the cold shadow, that it was Preet Singh, his lips lifted back from his teeth, his eyes blazing down at her in rage, in a passion of rage. She

lifted her hands to dislodge his from her throat and she did dislodge them. They fell away, but only to tear at the cotton scarf that hung about his neck, only to wrap that about her throat, tighter, tighter, tighter, so that the last gasp rattled and was still. Her eyes still swivelled in their sockets, two alarmed marbles of black and white, and quickly he left the ends of the scarf, tore at her clothes, tore them off her, in long, screeching rips, till he came to her, to the dry, shrivelled, starved stick inside the wrappings, and raped her, pinned her down into the dust and the goat droppings, and raped her. Crushed back, crushed down into the earth, she lay raped, broken, still and finished. Now it was dark. (142–43)

Preet Singh's act is one of revenge executed under passion. Ila Das, by trying to prevent him from marrying off his young daughter, has called into question the condition of women in India, with its tradition of male dominance and female submission. By questioning this dominance and submission, Ila Das challenged Preet Singh's ego and virility, which so infuriates him that he wants to assert his power and superiority over her. This he can do by raping her, thus violating her womanhood, something that murder alone would not have accomplished.

It is sadly ironic that Ila Das, a woman who has strived to live a just, fair, and honest life should meet with such an end. Years earlier, as a senior teacher—she had been appointed thanks to Nanda Kaul's influence on her husband—Ila Das had not tolerated the nomination of a junior teacher for the post of principal when it should rightfully have been hers. To show her disagreement with this unfairness, she had resigned. Jobless, she took up several insignificant posts, then became a social worker on Nanda Kaul's advice. Receiving a pittance for her efforts, she had had to visit the most squalid places to try to re-establish justice where it had long been absent. Finally, it was Ila Das's refusal to accept unfairness that led to her horrible death.

Following the description of the rape scene, the final chapter opens with "the sharp, long sliver of the telephone's call" (143). Any intrusion from the outside world infuriates Nanda Kaul, the sound of the telephone angering her especially. It is with irony that Nanda Kaul hopes that the person ringing her is not Ila Das. She decides not to answer. But the cook does, and calls her to the phone, where the voice of a police officer coldly informs her of Ila Das's rape and murder. Nanda Kaul's immediate reaction is one of helplessness and disbelief, reflected by hysterical cries: "No, no, it is a lie! No, it cannot be. It was all a lie—Ila was not raped, not dead. It was all a lie, all" (145). Then a flood of revelations is released, their complexity conveyed with remarkable verbal economy:

She had lied to Raka, lied about everything. Her father had never been to Tibet—he had bought the little Buddha from a travelling peddler. They had not had bears and leopards in their home, nothing but overfed dogs and bad-tempered parrots. Nor had her husband loved and cherished her and kept her like a queen—he had only done enough to keep her quiet while he carried on a lifelong affair with Miss David, the mathematics mistress, whom he had not married because she was a Christian but whom he had loved, all his life loved. And her children—the children were all alien to her nature. She neither understood nor loved them. She did not live here alone by choice—she lived here alone because that was what she was forced to do, reduced to nothing. All those graces and glories with which she had tried to captivate Raka were only a fabrication: they helped her to sleep at night, they were tranquillizers, pills. She had lied to Raka. And Ila had lied too. Ila, too, had lied, had tried. No, she wanted to cry, but could not make a sound. (145)

The harsh reality of Ila's end with all that it implies makes Nanda Kaul realize and acknowledge that she must relinquish her life of fantasy. At once her illusions, which have helped her deal with her life and with the burden of her past, are destroyed. Nanda Kaul's life had been so mundane that she had wanted to make it livelier by pretending to Raka—and to some extent to herself—that she had had a dreamlike childhood. The past had been so overwhelmingly present that in order to escape from it, she had had to create her own world inhabited with illusions and fantasy. Images from the past jostled against each other in her mind as she recalled a most painful event that had decisively marked her existence and created her bitterness: namely, her husband's unfaithfulness, the knowledge of which she had had to live with while pretending she knew nothing about it. All she had imagined about her marriage had only been that for which she had longed.

Nanda Kaul's realization is made all the more vivid by the device of accumulation. The stream-of-consciousness technique is highly effective in rendering the breathless emotion of this revelatory scene. But the experience does enable Nanda Kaul to come to terms with her husband's infidelity and to surmount the feeling that she has been cheated in life. As the passage progresses, it grows in intensity, for Nanda Kaul has finally dropped her mask, at last recognizing the importance of being truthful to herself and the futility of evading reality. She even accepts the fact that her roles as wife and mother were failures. Learning about the rape and murder enables her to face what she had so painfully concealed, what had undermined her faith in life. As Nanda Kaul recognizes the truth of her past, there seems to be an echo of Raka's earlier moment of discovery when she witnessed the scene at the club. For just as Raka's world of pretense was shattered when she faced the truth about her childhood, Nanda's world of illusions crumbles.

Ironically, then, with Ila Das's tragic end comes the beginning of a new, true life for Nanda Kaul, and not, as commonly seen by critics, her death. It is most likely the description of Nanda Kaul that has led to an interpretation of the novel asserting her death: "She twisted her head, then hung it down, down, let it hang. . . . Nanda Kaul on the stool with her head hanging, the black telephone hanging, the long wire dangling" (145). Although one must acknowledge that the climax of the novel is ambiguous, nothing in the text actually says that Nanda Kaul dies.

Instead, Ila Das's death, which leads to the destruction of Nanda Kaul's life of illusions, is what lends the novel its meaning. Not only would Nanda Kaul's death add little to the narrative, it would diminish its momentum. A second death, especially that of the main character, would seem false, contrived, and anti-climactic. Moreover, Nanda Kaul's discovery of the futility of a life of fantasy would not have carried such significance if it had simply been a revelation coming to her just before dying. Nanda Kaul must live after the discovery in order to struggle toward a new life based on truth—not an easy matter. Further, at this moment she becomes more aware of Raka's dependence on her, realizing that Raka would have to return to a miserable life with her parents. Finally, two deaths would have concluded the novel on far too pessimistic a note, as if life were both hopeless and meaningless.

The novel culminates with the forest burning. Although surprising in some ways, it is clear, in retrospect, that the event has been foreshadowed throughout, beginning with the title, *Fire on the Mountain*. Both Nanda Kaul and Raka have been obsessed with the element of fire, Nanda Kaul first showing Raka the ruins from previous fires, then Raka being drawn back to them again and again. The fire alluded to in the middle of the novel, which then seemed unreal—"It was far away. . . . It was like a fire in a dream—silent, swift and threatening" (74)—has now been brought close and into reality. Raka, who stole a box of matches from the kitchen and set ablaze the forest around Carignano, calls at the window to her great-grandmother: "'Look, Nani, I have set the forest on fire. Look, Nani—look the forest is on fire'" (145).

By starting the fire, she destroys in a symbolic way the illusions with which Nanda Kaul has lived; she burns the life of dreams that Nanda Kaul had built up around her to make her life bearable and to avoid facing reality. But once the fantasies are reduced to ashes, truth survives. It is apt that Raka should be the agent of destruction, for earlier when Nanda Kaul talked about her childhood, the girl detected that the old lady was making up the stories. And when Nanda Kaul and Ila Das dredged up the past as they imagined it, Raka became restless and bored, again aware of their lies. Thus, Raka's act cannot be regarded as one of gratuitous violence and destruction, but one powerfully symbolic.

Through the characters of Nanda Kaul, Raka, and Ila Das, each experiencing a different kind of alienation, Anita Desai explores, with the subtlety and artistry that have become the hallmarks of her work, those themes constituting her fictional preoccupations: lack of human communication and the devastating effect of spiritual isolation. And she grafts on yet another human conflict, one that dominates her work: the discrepancy between the inner being and the outer world.

WORK CITED

Desai, Anita. *Fire on the Mountain.* New York: Penguin, 1986.

ANITA DESAI'S PUBLISHED WORK

Novels

Cry, the Peacock, 1963
Voices in the City, 1965
Bye-Bye Blackbird, 1971
Where Shall We Go This Summer?, 1975
Fire on the Mountain, 1977
Clear Light of Day, 1980

In Custody, 1984
Baumgartner's Bombay, 1988

Short Story Collection

Games at Twilight, 1978

Children's Books

The Peacock Garden, 1974
Cat on a Houseboat, 1976
The Village by the Sea, 1982

Articles

"Indian Fiction Today." *Daedalus* 118 (1989): 207–31.
> States that the unity of the scene is a common feature in Indian writing. Sees a new confidence in young writers whose work is characterized by reproduction of the spoken language.

"Indian Women Writers." *The Eye of the Beholder. Indian Writing in English.* London: Commonwealth Institute, 1983. 54–58.
> Notes that Indian women writers lean toward poetry and short stories rather than the novel; Indian fiction by women tends to explore feminine identity.

"The Indian Writer's Problems." *Modern Indo-English Fiction.* Delhi: Bahri Publications, 1982. 222–26.
> Explores status of Indian literature written in English; considers English an adequate tool for Indian writers.

SELECTED CRITICAL READINGS

Most Indian writers in English have taken the political life of the country as their main theme; Anita Desai, however, has set a new trend among these writers by focusing her attention on the self. Consequently, she is widely regarded as the pioneer of the psychological novel in Indian literature in English. With her exploration of the internal landscape and her mastery of the writer's craft—she has been called a "poet in prose." This remarkably sensitive writer has received wide acclaim both at home and abroad. Still, although reviewed widely outside of India, most of the critical work thus far has originated there. In her latest novel, *Baumgartner's Bombay,* she has taken a new direction, choosing to have a European male as the protagonist against the backdrop of the Second World War, in contrast to her previous work where the main characters have most often been Indian women trying to find inner peace. This approach deserves critical attention, in that it shows a new stage of development in Desai's fiction. Another novel that has not received much critical notice is *Bye-Bye Blackbird,* which examines the Indian immigrant's plight in England.

Amanuddin, Syed. "Anita Desai's Technique." *The Fiction of Anita Desai.* Delhi: Bahri, 1989. 154–64.
> Existentialist analysis of *Fire on the Mountain, Clear Light of Day,* and *In Custody;* sees the fiction as a process of discovery and Desai as "a describer rather than an explainer."

Bande, Usha. *The Novels of Anita Desai. A Study in Character and Conflict.* Delhi: Prestige Books, 1988.
> Examines characters from most of the novels in the light of Third Force Psychology—how they become alienated from their real selves and how they manage, if at all, to regain their equilibrium.

Belliappa, Meena. *Anita Desai. A Study of Her Fiction.* Calcutta: Writer's Workshop, 1971. Sees Desai's fiction bringing about a new trend in Indian writing in English: the shift from the external world to the inner world of the individual.

Dhawan, R.K., editor. *The Fiction of Anita Desai.* Delhi: Bahri, 1989. Collection of critical essays discussing themes and techniques of all of Desai's fiction.

Jain, Jasbir. "Anita Desai." *Indian English Novelists. An Anthology of Critical Studies.* Delhi: Sterling, 1982. 24–50. Sees Desai's work focusing on the absurdity of life and the existential search for meaning; stressing that in her fiction Reason is inadequate in itself, so humans turn to Unreason.

———. *Stairs to the Attic. The Novels of Anita Desai.* Jaipur: Printwell, 1987. Explores the role of the unconscious and of the importance of place in Desai's fiction. (Includes an interview with Desai)

Jena, Seema. *Voice and Vision of Anita Desai.* Delhi: Ashish, 1989. Argues that as Desai places more importance on characters than on other aspects, she has established the psychological novel in Indian literature in English.

Kanwar, Asha. *Virginia Woolf and Anita Desai. A Comparative Study.* Delhi: Prestige Books, 1989. Points out the similarities of the two writers: concept of time; depiction of female characters; influence of characters' past on their consciousness; use of nostalgia and memory.

Krishna, Francine E. "Anita Desai: *Fire on the Mountain.*" *Indian Literature* 25.5 (1982): 158–69. Stresses importance of landscape as an extension of the characters' inner selves. Sees the characters as victims.

Maini, Darshan Singh. "The Achievement of Anita Desai." *Indo-English Literature. A Collection of Critical Essays.* Ghaziabad: Vimal Prakashan, 1977. 216–29. Considers Desai a more powerful prose stylist than a novelist.

Nandakumar, Prema. "Sombre the Shadows and Sudden the Lights: A Study of Anita Desai's Novels." *Perspectives on Indian Fiction in English.* Delhi: Abhinav, 1985. 174–99. Sees Desai's fiction as an attempt to come to terms with loneliness, symbolized by the contrast between darkness and light.

Prasad, Madhusudan. *Anita Desai: The Novelist.* Allahabad: New Horizon, 1981. Comprehensive study of the novels to date, with emphasis on the existentialist concerns.

Rao, Ramachandra B. *The Novels of Mrs Anita Desai. A Study.* Delhi: Kalyani, 1977. Believes that the strength of her fiction derives from the limitation of the world she depicts, a world of characters in conflict with their inner selves. Presents an interesting discussion of the problems of Indian writing in English.

Sharma, R.S., editor. *Anita Desai.* Delhi: Heinemann, 1981. Critical articles on *Cry, the Peacock, Voices in the City, Bye-Bye Blackbird, Where Shall We Go This Summer?, Games at Twilight, Clear Light of Day,* addressing a particular thematic aspect of each work.

Srivastava, Ramesh K., editor. *Perspectives on Anita Desai.* Ghaziabad: Vimal Prakashan, 1984. Critical articles and introduction, with an account of the novelist's life and theory of fiction. Discussion of works as psychological novels; analyses of themes, symbolism, characterization, and narrative technnique. (Includes an interview with Desai)

———. "The Psychological Novel and Desai's *Cry, the Peacock.*" *Six Indian Novelists in English.* Amritsar: Guru Nanak University, 1987. 275–98. Argues that subject matter, characterization, narrative technique, symbolism, images, and the disturbed time scheme all work together to make *Cry, the Peacock* a psychological novel with sustained poetic prose.

Interviews

With Corrine Bliss. *Massachusetts Review* 29 (1988): 521–37.
With Yashodara Dalmia. *The Times of India* 29 April 1979: 13.
With Florence Libert. *World Literature Written in English* 30 (1990): 47–55.
With Kirsten Holst Petersen. *Kunapipi* 6.3 (1984): 83–85.
With Atma Ram. *World Literature Written in English* 16 (1977): 95–103.
With Pascale Seguet. *Commonwealth Essays & Studies* 10.2 (1988): 43–50.

—FLORENCE LIBERT

Timothy Findley

With the publication of *The Wars* in 1977, Timothy Findley emerged as one of Canada's most important post-war novelists. His troubling moral parables are couched in a mannered style that owes much to the bizarre stories of the American John Cheever and to the moral concerns of his mentor, Thornton Wilder. But his narrative innovations and subversive questioning of Western society's "master narratives" mark him as undeniably a Canadian, postcolonial writer.

Although he began to write seriously in 1956, for twenty years he had been best known as an actor in radio, television, and theater. This experience informs his fiction, which is noted for its heightened dramatic moments, its highly visual appeal, and its use of cinematic techniques.

Born in Toronto, 30 October 1930, Findley, a stockbroker's son, studied with a private tutor after a year's bout with glandular fever interrupted his secondary education in 1945. He later abandoned his studies to apprentice in repertory theatre, before landing a position in the company assembled to open the Shakespeare festival at Stratford, Ontario, in 1953. After this season, he moved to England to attend London's Central School of Speech and Drama, graduating in 1954. He played several parts in England, then joined a U.S. company and moved to the United States, working for eighteen months in Los Angeles and living in Topanga Beach, before returning to Toronto.

In 1964 Findley moved with William Whitehead, a Canadian Broadcasting Corporation writer and producer, to Stone Orchard, a farm near Cannington, Ontario, outside Toronto, where they have made their permanent home. Together they have collaborated on several award-winning scripts for radio and television. Findley won the 1971 Armstrong Award (radio) for *The Journey* and the 1975 ACTRA Award (television, best documentary writer) for his adaptation, in collaboration with Whitehead, of Pierre Berton's history of the building of the Canadian Pacific Railway, *The National Dream*. Findley was the first writer-in-residence at the National Arts Centre in Ottawa in 1975, where he wrote *Can You See Me Yet?*, first presented at the NAC in 1976. During 1977-1978 Findley served as Chairman of the Writer's Union of Canada and during 1978-1979 he was writer-in-residence at the University of Toronto.

Findley's third novel, *The Wars*, won the Governor General's Award (Canada's most prestigious national literary prize) and the City of Toronto Book Award in 1978. During 1980-81 he worked on the screenplay for the film of *The Wars*. In 1985 *Not Wanted on the Voyage* won the Canadian Authors Association Literary Award. Findley was made an officer of the Order of Canada in 1986. He also won the

Canada/Australia Literary Award in 1986, traveling to Australia and New Zealand to read. His adaptation of *Famous Last Words* was broadcast by CBC radio in 1988.

A POST-HOLOCAUST, POST-COLONIAL VISION

"Make Peace With Nature, Now," the title of Donald Cameron's 1973 interview with Timothy Findley, conveys the content and urgency of all Findley's fiction. He cannot forget the impact of his first childhood experiences watching newsreels of the Second World War as his Uncle Tiff, his namesake, lay slowly dying from injuries sustained in the First World War, nor can he really forgive his father for joining the air force in 1939, when Findley was eight, without telling his son. The far-reaching impact of war on those left behind remains a recurrent theme, perhaps most memorably evoked in his 1988 short story collection, *Stones*. In "Stones," the title story of the volume, the psychic violence of Dieppe overshadows the physical and survives into times of official peace. In "Dreams," the murderous nightmares of schizophrenic patient and empathetic psychiatrist invade one another, drenching the dreamers in blood and highlighting current tolerance of the violence of everyday life in the post-Bomb age.

For with the dropping of the atomic bomb on Hiroshima and Nagasaki, Findley believes that "our moral concept of horror was altered forever" (Aitken 88). The impact of that altering generates the drama of all his writing. He creates moral parables that explore the contemporary meaning of horror and the implications of one of his favorite words—forever.

That moment, when "our moral concept of horror was altered forever," is symbolically recaptured in *Not Wanted on the Voyage* through the parodic rewriting of the Biblical story of Noah's Ark and the Flood that destroyed a world. It is also the key to the mystery behind *The Telling of Lies*. The answer to the classic detective story question, "Who Killed Calder Maddox?", derives paradoxically from the past, when Vanessa Van Horne and her fellow prisoners of war were liberated into a world "where the Bomb had not fallen just on Hiroshima and Nagasaki—but on all of us. Forever" (339). Findley's readers learn with Vanessa that Maddox's murderous life and his eventual murder are the logical consequences of that first decision to destroy a whole people. It would seem that genocide, once legitimated so publicly, has moved from the realm of the unthinkable, or least the unsayable, into the realm of standard government policy. The now documented CIA-funded psychological experiments performed without their knowledge on Canadian patients during the 1950s and 1960s in Montreal provide in *The Telling of Lies* a graphic illustration of our new tolerance for horror. They also show the changing face of imperial/colonial relations in the latter half of this century, for Findley's vision is conditioned as much by his location in space as by his location in time. As a Canadian writer, his perspective is influenced by his double sense of living at once at the center of his own country's experience but also on the margins of empires, between the declining British and the ascendant United States.

The horror of organized, technological violence, directed against other human beings, against animals, and against the rest of the natural world, recurs throughout Findley's fiction. His concerns are thus with the most widely debated issues of contemporary times—the surviving legacy of fascism, the nature of progress, the role of technology, eugenics, ecology—but his approach to these problems may seem unusual to some readers because it comes from a postcolonial rather than an imperial position. Findley's work questions the assumptions of the dominating world view and investigates instead the perspectives of the dominated.

His central characters are all in some sense or another marginalized figures. Hooker Winslow in *The Last of the Crazy People* is a child, shut out from full understanding of the adult dilemmas swirling around him. In *Can You See Me Yet?*, Cassandra Wakelin, like her namesake a prophet unheeded by her contemporaries, lives and dies in a mental asylum. The Damarosch family in *The Butterfly Plague* feel themselves to be isolated from the rest of humanity by virtue of their inherited hemophilia. Robert Ross of *The Wars* cannot participate in the militaristic orgy of violence that is consuming his civilization; his beloved encephalitic sister Rowena symbolizes his difference. In *Famous Last Words*, Hugh Selwyn Mauberly is marked as an outsider by his name, borrowed from Ezra Pound's poem of that title, by his vocation as a poet, and by his father's suicide in the opening scene of the novel. *Not Wanted on the Voyage* is peopled by the dominated, symbolically relegated by Noah to the lower decks of the ark. Most daringly, perhaps, Mottyl, one of the novel's chief centers of consciousness, is a cat. She is joined by Mrs. Noyes, the gin-drinking, hymn-singing, long-suffering wife of the patriarchal tyrant, Noah. Ham, her sensitive, scientifically curious son, forms a liaison with "Lucy," who is Lucifer in drag, in flight from God's intolerant perfection of a heaven. Emma, through her relationship with Lotte, one of the "ape children" also rejected by God and his representatives as imperfect, completes this register of the dispossesed. Finally, in *The Telling of Lies*, Vanessa Van Horne has been permanently marked by her experiences as prisoner of war, particularly by witnessing her father's murder on the order of the Japanese Commandant. In a parallel fashion, her best friend, Meg Riches, has been altered by witnessing the destruction of her husband Michael by the illegal but officially condoned psychological experiments performed in Montreal.

Findley's writing always begins with such people. He talks of characters coming to him and demanding that their story be told, that they be released from his head into the world outside. Their humanity is paramount. The stories and ideas flow from their experiences and dilemmas, taking shape around his sense of who they are, where they have come from, and what they must say. Perhaps his training as an actor gives special force to his sense of each character as a living person, not just an embodied idea or a function of the plot. Certainly he hopes that after reading his work people will come away with "A sense of having been somewhere with real people, and a sense that they've been moved to struggle with the same dilemmas that I'm struggling with" (Meyer and O'Riordan 54). These dilemmas concern the "ethical role of the imaginative writer in the latter part of the twentieth century" (Irvine 16) and the necessity, not just to expose but also to resist "the discursive strategies of older and contemporary imperialisms" (Tiffin 54). Such resistance is embodied textually, in the stories Findley chooses to tell and in the narrators who tell them, as well as dramatized through the compelling characters he creates.

These marginalized central characters of Findley's witness the horrors of the age, and each acts to the best of his or her ability to resist. Collectively, they represent the fragile forces of love, the power of the imagination to dream otherwise, and the willingness, not only to speak out and bear witness but also to strike back in violence against the exercise of evil. The meaning of their own implications in violence remains the most problematic dimension of Findley's aesthetic. Findley does not shy away from loaded terms like evil, but he does refuse to place them in the simplified system of a polarized universe. His moral fables provide no easy answers; rather, like Vanessa Van Horne's idea of all art, they "record bewilderment" (27). In Findley's hands, this recording of bewilderment becomes the most powerful indictment of all.

Only *Famous Last Words* and *The Butterfly Plague* deal explicitly with the Fascism dominant during the Second World War, but all his work returns to the moral questions that fascism forces us to confront, and to the insistence that fascist forces were not defeated in the war but survive today in different guises. *The Telling of Lies* is his most chilling documentation of the parallels to be drawn between the Japanese concentration camps of the Second World War and contemporary North America, which Findley portrays as metaphorically a concentration camp with ideologically constructed walls, which only become visible when an unforeseen crisis occurs.

This novel begins with its narrator, Vanessa Van Horne, musing that "Something I wanted to save has been destroyed behind my back" (1). The elegant old hotel that is being closed down to make way for a condominium complex comes to represent the humane orientation toward the world that is being lost to more arrogant assumptions of power. The ignorance, apathy, and complacency that allow such shifts without protest are shown to be the allies of evil, yet how to act for the good in such a brutalized world is far from clear. Meg is not condemned for her murder of Maddox, the man responsible for the development of the drugs that destroyed her husband's mind and body, but neither is her act seen as in any way sufficient.

The book's conclusion remains enigmatic. Vanessa, the witness to these events, has been politicized. She decides to remain passive no longer but recognizes that this resolve in some ways links her to her enemies: "I admit I have joined my enemies. I admit that I am prepared to do what they have done: even to use their weapons. I do not admit that this is wrong. I would ask whoever questions this to tell me what is right" (359). She concludes that "Someone sold us out—but only when we ceased to pay attention" (359). Her final act is to "pull the shade" (359), which would seem to represent a retreat from the outside world into inner resources, yet the concluding words of the novel add, "And the shade is green" (359). Green the color of the natural world. Green the liturgical color of hope. Is this a reorientation of personal priorities to effect a new alliance with the forces of nature and morality, a retreat to focus the powers of concentration before resuming engagement? Findley leaves to his readers the responsibility to decide.

Not Wanted on the Voyage comes to a similarly problematic ending, managing at once to combine the sense of ending that comes with a momentous decision with the undecidability of a radical open-endedness. Mrs. Noyes has always known how to say "Yes" to life. What she needs to learn is how to say "No" to Noah, with his life-denying edicts and his fear of difference. At the conclusion of the novel she does say "No" to Noah's vision of the future. Her praying for rain moves her away from Noah's God toward an alliance with Nature, and it would seem toward a commitment to the voyage that never ends rather than to Noah's tyrannical vision of "another world and more cats to blind" (352). Yet to pray for rain in an already flooded world seems a futile gesture.

The ambiguous gesture that defies both interpretation and final judgement lies at the heart of all Findley's writing. It shapes his first novel, *The Last of the Crazy People* as well as his best known work, *The Wars*. Both novels indict adult society, questioning its equation of brutalization with maturity and of madness with dissent. Findley told Cameron that "There's always someone who must do insane things in order to clarify what . . . is bright and good. Hooker had to murder in order to achieve peace for those people, in order to demonstrate his love for them" (55). Such a contention remains highly questionable and is not convincingly realized in this first novel. It is more successfully presented in *The Wars*, where Robert's freeing of the horses and murder of his commanding officer puts Findley's questioning of established values in a much clearer light. This novel questions society's need for wars, the value of unquestioning obedience to authority and blind belief in progress, and humanity's subordination of animals to human purposes. Like Hooker, Robert Ross retains his childhood innocence and compassion. These qualities render them misfits in a brutalized world, and, in Findley's view, render their actions heroic.

These characters are not presented as isolated individuals, but as people within a community at a certain historical moment. In a statement much like Vanessa Van Horne's conclusion quoted above, Findley suggests that "Hooker has a lot to do with the Kennedy thing and also with the urgency with which we must wipe out the old order. We must destroy what is destroying us. We must kill what is killing us. We must violate the violators . . ." (Cameron, 62). *The Last of the Crazy People*, *The Wars*, and *The Telling of Lies* expose the bankruptcy of the Canadian ruling elite, "the dead end of the Family Compact" (Gibson 139) but in such a way as to comment symbolically on the need for change everywhere.

The Butterfly Plague, *Famous Last Words*, and *Not Wanted on the Voyage*, set respectively in Hollywood, Europe, and the world of the imagination, are clearly symbolic texts that on the surface would appear to have little to do with Canada, yet the Canadian perspective that privileges the bystander or witness above the actor and that values the community above the individual clearly directs these works. In *Not Wanted on the Voyage*, Findley shows the myth of origins established in the Biblical Genesis to be the site of a power struggle. The voices excluded from Genesis have their say in Findley's narrative. Women, children, workers (here called "the lower orders"), animals, and creatures from folklore (Lucifer, fairies, and unicorns) all speak as interested participants in Noah's attempt at establishing his version of events and his control as dominant. These characters contest the way the Noah myth establishes its patriarchal authority by condensing God and Noah into a single term and by refusing to "see" their difference (as with the fairies) or to acknowledge their equal right to self-determination (as with the women and the animals). The novel may be read as a parable challenging the imperialist version of colonization as well as a warning against fascist eugenics and the impossible fascist quest for purity of any kind. Indeed it suggests that such activities are related, sharing fundamental assumptions that are dangerous to our continued survival on earth as a humane civilization.

Noah's rewriting of history to justify his version of events points to one of the most discussed aspects of Findley's imaginative project: his postmodernist awareness of the interestedness of all historical writing. Linda Hutcheon discusses *The Wars* and *Famous Last Words* as "historiographic metafiction," works that examine the relationship between fiction and history in a self-conscious manner that recognizes both are human constructions rather than simplistic givens. *Famous Last Words* records what Mauberley terms "the temper of the times and the motto we had adopted: the truth is in our hands now" (177). "Truth" becomes a relative, strategically changeable concept to be manipulated by the powerful and the power-hungry. This fluctuating reality is juxtaposed against the continuing certainty that Mauberly reads in the handprint in the cave at Altamira: "I knew I was sitting at the heart of the human race—which is its will to say I am" (173). The handprint records an ancient urge to survive the imminent holocaust of an ice age through the testament of art and the memory of its witnesses. That handprint is repeated in Mauberley's wall-writing and Findley's novel. Each asks for our attention.

This call for attention rings throughout Findley's fiction. With no one to attend, the moment is forever lost, history may unwittingly repeat itself, and the tale yields to silence. Findley's stories always assert, with the epigraph to *Stones* that "we are tomorrow's past"; we are responsible to future generations, responsible for our lapses in attention as well as for our sins of commission.

In his introduction to *Dinner Along the Amazon*, Findley writes that "the pursuit of an obsession through the act of writing is not so much a question of repetition as it is of regeneration" (x). The characteristic obsessions arising out of the intersection of the postcolonial and post-holocaust experiences that recur throughout Findley's work continually renew themselves through the compellingly individual sitings of each new work. Findley repeats the moment of choice preceding holocaust through re-citings (that alter through re-siting) of Biblical myth, the history of two world wars, the murder of a family, the new ice age (signalled by the arrival of the iceberg at the end of *Famous Last Words* and the beginning of *The Telling of Lies*).

These repetitions incorporate contradictory tendencies in Findley's work: his fear that given a second chance, humanity would make the same mistakes again, and his hope that perhaps we could act differently, to create a better world, given our attention to the fictional witnessing of texts like his. His fictions therefore often parodically repeat earlier texts to introduce the difference of his own perspective. Most memorably, *Not Wanted on the Voyage* writes back against Genesis, *Famous Last Words* against Pound's "Hugh Selwyn Mauberly" and *The Telling of Lies* against Thomas Mann's *Death in Venice*. Each repetition replaces similitude with difference, arguing through the achieved regeneration of the intertextual play of the imagination for the possible regeneration of humanity as a whole. Findley hopes, with Mrs. Noyes, that "Cruelty was fear in disguise and nothing more. . . . that fear itself was nothing more than a failure of the imagination" (252). Through creating imaginative worlds that his readers can enter to experience their own world as refracted through his decentered imaginative perspective, Findley challenges his readers to join him in that process of regeneration.

WORKS CITED

Aitken, Johan. "'Long Live the Dead': An Interview with Timothy Findley." *Journal of Canadian Fiction* 33 (1981–82): 79–83.

Cameron, Donald. "Timothy Findley: Make Peace With Nature, Now." *Conversations with Canadian Novelists.* Vol. I. Toronto: Macmillan, 1973. 49–63.

Findley, Timothy. *The Butterfly Plague.* Rev. Markham: Penguin, 1986.

———. *Dinner Along the Amazon.* Markham: Penguin, 1984.

———. *Famous Last Words.* Toronto: Clarke Irwin, 1981.

———. *The Last of the Crazy People.* Toronto: Macmillan, 1977.

———. *Not Wanted on the Voyage.* Markham: Penguin, 1985.

———. *Stones.* Markham: Viking, 1988.

———. *The Telling of Lies.* Markham: Viking, 1986.

———. *The Wars.* Markham: Penguin, 1978.

Gibson, Graeme. "Timothy Findley." *Eleven Canadian Novelists.* Toronto: Anansi. 1973. 115–49.

Hutcheon, Linda. "Canadian Historiographic Metafiction." *Essays in Canadian Writing* 30 (1984–85): 228–38.

Irvine, Lorna. "Crises of the Legitimate: Matt Cohen and Timothy Findley." *The American Review of Canadian Studies* 19 (1989): 15–23.

Meyer, Bruce, and Brian O'Riordan. "Timothy Findley: The Marvel of Reality." *In Their Words: Interviews with Fourteen Canadian Writers.* Toronto: Anansi, 1984. 44–54.

Tiffin, Helen. "*Not Wanted on the Voyage*: Textual Imperialism and Post-colonial Resistance." *Australian-Canadian Studies* 6.2 (1989): 47–56.

TIMOTHY FINDLEY'S PUBLISHED WORK

Novels

The Last of the Crazy People, 1967
The Butterfly Plague, 1969 (Revised edition, 1986)
The Wars, 1978
Famous Last Words, 1981
Not Wanted on the Voyage, 1984
The Telling of Lies, 1986

Plays

Can You See Me Yet?, 1977
"The Journey: A Montage for Radio." *Canadian Drama* 10.1 (1984): 116–40.
"The Paper People: A Television Play." *Canadian Drama/L'art dramatique canadienne* 9. 1 (1983): 62–164.

Short Story Collections

Dinner Along the Amazon, 1984
Stones, 1988

Article

"Legends." *Landfall* 40 (1986): 327-32.
 Recollections of encounters with the legendary figures of Patrick White and Janet Frame.

SELECTED CRITICAL READINGS

The bibliography to consult is: Carol Roberts and Lynne Macdonald, *Timothy Findley: An Annotated Bibliography* (Toronto: ECW Press, 1989). Although there are no full-length studies of Findley in print as of January 1990, at least three such manuscripts on his work have been completed but are not yet published. Findley has received remarkably little attention to date for a writer of his stature. Most critical commentary focuses on *The Wars* and *Famous Last Words*.

Benson, Eugene. "'Whispers of Chaos': Famous Last Words." *World Literature Written in English* 21 (1982): 599–606. Argues that "Findley's theme is violence, examined usually within a political context" (600). Discusses all the work before *Famous Last Words*, analyzing the handling of violence and the fictionalization of history.

Brydon, Diana. "'A Devotion to Fragility': Timothy Findley's *The Wars*." *World Literature Written in English* 26 (1986): 75–84. Argues that "the fragility of beauty in all its forms—of the human mind and body, of reason and passion, and above all of their highest achievement, civilization—shapes the design of *The Wars*" (75). Findley's devotion to fragility appears to depend on a sense of the primacy of violence, a primacy that at once fascinates and appals him. This aesthetic philosophy places him in the company of other Canadian writers like Leonard Cohen, Michael Ondaatje, and Phyllis Webb.

———. "'It could not be told': Making Meaning in Timothy Findley's *The Wars*." *Journal of Commonwealth Literature* 21.1 (1986): 62–79. Focuses on the unresolved and unresolvable contradictions in *The Wars*, to describe the text's problematizing of how human beings make meaning when telling a story, reading a text, and writing history. Argues that *The Wars* writes against the established conventions of the war novel genre to question binary oppositions and to create a postcolonial perspective on European civilization.

Cude, Wilfred. "Timothy Findley." *Profiles in Canadian Literature 4*. Toronto: Dundurn, 1982. 77–84. Straightforward reading of *The Wars* that denies its meaning is at all complex. Argues that the novel infuses "beauty and hope into one of the world's most traumatic experiences" (82) and that those who see ambiguity in *The Wars* have had their perceptions clouded by "the logic of the death-seeker" (81).

Duffy, Dennis. "Let us Compare Histories: Meaning and Mythology in Findley's *Famous Last Words*." *Essays on Canadian Writing* 30 (1984-85): 187–205. Argues that *Famous Last Words* "deals with the beholder's response to the spectacular corruption of a figure who ought to have been a hero" while chronicling "the European bourgeois order's final collapse before the seductions of the radical right" (189). Analyzes the novel's narrative practice of blurring the distinctions between fiction and fact and between history and mythology to argue that the novel both deconstructs myth as lie and affirms myth as symbolic structure.

Howells, Coral Ann. "'History as She Is Never Writ': *The Wars* and *Famous Last Words*." *Kunapipi* 6.1 (1984): 49–56. Argues that *The Wars* and *Famous Last Words* are stories about writing and reading that problematize history. Focusing on the literariness of Findley's fictions, it treats the novels as psychobiographies in which the most important referents are the names of their protagonists. Examines the homosexual subtext of *The Wars* and the modernist intertext of *Famous Last Words* to argue that in Findley's blurring of fact and fiction the focus falls on interpretation rather than truth.

———. "''Tis Sixty Years Since': Timothy Findley's *The Wars* and Roger Macdonald's *1915*." *World Literature Written in English* 23 (1984): 129–36. Comparative study focusing on the postcolonial problem of redefining the relation of the colony-turned-nation to Britain and on the postmodernist problem of articulating the relation of history to myth.

Hulcoop, John. "'Look! Listen! Mark My Words!': Paying Attention to Timothy Findley's Fictions." *Canadian Literature* 91 (1981): 22–47. Argues that Findley is a stylist who is perfecting "a style that is unmistakably his own—a marvellous mixture of the lyric and dramatic that can be put to narrative purposes" (41). Analyzes the distinguishing characteristics of that style, including its focus on the element of fire, its stress on looking and paying attention, its involvement of the reader, and its dramatic elements.

Hutcheon, Linda. "Canadian Historiographic Metafiction." *Essays in Canadian Writing* 30 (1984-85): 228–38. Places *Famous Last Words* in the contemporary context of historiographic metafiction, which signals these writers' "need to investigate both the ontological nature and the function of their literary products and of the processes that created them and keep them alive" (236).

Irvine, Lorna. "Crises of the Legitimate: Matt Cohen and Timothy Findley." *The American Review of Canadian Studies* 19 (1989): 15–23. Argues that Findley employs gynesis to subversive ends, using the emerging voices of women to rethink narrative, challenge master narratives, and explore the meaning of Canadian and female marginality.

Klovan, Peter. "'Bright and Good': Timothy Findley's *The Wars.*" *Canadian Literature* 91 (1981): 58–69. Analyzes *The Wars* to argue that Robert's life is presented "as a tragic journey marked by his progressive refinement and destruction by the basic elements: earth, water, air, and fire" (59).

Kroller, Eva-Marie. "The Exploding Frame: Uses of Photography in Timothy Findley's *The Wars.*" *Journal of Canadian Studies* 16 (1981): 68–74. Analyzes how photography is both a metaphor and an aspect of the narrative technique of *The Wars*.

McKenzie, M.L. "Memories of the Great War: Graves, Sassoon, and Findley." *University of Toronto Quarterly* 55 (1986): 395–411. Places *The Wars* within the context of British literature of the First World War to describe both Findley's debt and his contribution to that tradition. Argues that the British writers "seek to understand the past and its effects on the present," whereas Findley's novel "points strenuously towards the future" (396).

Miller, Mary Jane. "An Analysis of 'The Paper People.'" *Canadian Drama* 9.1 (1983): 49–59. Analyzes the reception, timing, major themes and techniques of Findley's astringent television drama "The Paper People."

Murray, Don. "Seeing and Surviving in Timothy Findley's Short Stories." *Studies in Canadian Literature* 13 (1988): 200–22. Analyzes the various functions of sight in the stories included in *Dinner Along the Amazon* to stress the importance of looking as a mode of characterization in Findley's work.

Ricou, Laurie. "'Obscured by Violence': Timothy Findley's *The Wars.*" *Violence in the Canadian Novel Since 1960.* St. John's Memorial University (Canada), n.d. 125–37. Explores the difficulties that Robert and the narrator of *The Wars* experience when confronted by violence and analyzes the novel as a collage about storytelling.

Scobie, Stephen. "Eye-Deep in Hell: Ezra Pound, Timothy Findley, and Hugh Selwyn Mauberly." *Essays on Canadian Writing* 30 (1984-5): 206–27. Analyzes the complexity of Findley's references to Pound's poem to argue that what distinguishes Findley's Mauberly is the "heroism of his bearing witness" (209). Sees the central question of the novel as "that of the 'truth' of Mauberly's testament" (212), with literal truth subordinated to moral truth and political analysis subordinated to psychological presentation. The "doubling effect of the mirror image" structures the novel (218).

Shields, E.F. "Mauberly's Lies: Fact and Fiction in Timothy Findley's *Famous Last Words.*" *Journal of Canadian Studies* 22.4 (1987–88): 44–59. Argues that while recognizing the fiction inherent in much that is presented as fact, Findley does not deny the existence of objective reality but continues to insist on the necessity for responsiblity and guilt.

Tiffin, Helen. "Not Wanted on the Voyage: Textual Imperialism and Post-colonial Resistance." *Australian-Canadian Studies* 6.2 (1989): 47–56. Detailed analysis of *Not Wanted on the Voyage* as a postcolonial text that exposes the discursive strategies of imperialism and deconstructs them as an act of resistance.

Vauthier, Simone. "The Dubious Battle of Story-Telling: Narrative Strategies in Timothy Findley's *The Wars.*" *Gaining Ground: European Critics on Canadian Literature.* Edmonton: NeWest, 1985. Detailed, theoretically informed analysis of the narrative strategies by which "authority is achieved and/or undermined" in *The Wars* (11).

Woodcock, George. "Timothy Findley's Gnostic Parable." *Canadian Literature* 111 (1986): 232–37. Argues that *Not Wanted on the Voyage* "performs the same kind of bold and illuminating outrages on revealed religion as *Famous Last Words* performed on history" (233). Examines the parallels between Gnostic doctrine and Findley's text.

York, Lorraine M. "'A Shout of Recognition': 'Likeness' and the Art of the Simile in Timothy Findley's *The Wars.*" *English Studies in Canada* 11 (1985): 223–30. Examines the function of similes to familiarize the otherwise untellable horrors of war in *The Wars*.

———. "'Violent Stillness': Timothy Findley's Use of Photography." *The Other Side of Dailiness: Photography in the Works of Alice Munro, Timothy Findley, Michael Ondaatje, and Margaret Laurence.* Toronto: ECW, 1988. 51-92. Argues that the function of the photograph changes over the course of Findley's writing from being a symbol of stasis and death to becoming "the guardian of the human imagination under siege" (92), a mode of remembering.

Interviews

With Eugene Benson. *World Literature Written in English* 26 (1986): 107–15.
With Donald Cameron. *Conversations with Canadian Novelists*, Vol. I. Toronto: Macmillan, 1973. 49–63.
With Graeme Gibson. *Eleven Canadian Novelists.* Toronto: Anansi, 1973. 115–49.
With Terry Goldie. *Kunapipi* 6.1 (1984): 55–67.
With Bruce Meyer and Brian O'Riordan. *In Their Words: Interviews with Fourteen Canadian Writers.* Toronto: Anansi, 1984. 44–54.
With Alison Summers. *Canadian Literature* 91 (1981): 49–55.

—DIANA BRYDON

Thea Astley

Born in Brisbane, Australia, 25 August 1925, Thea Astley was brought up in a family of journalists and was educated at convent schools in Brisbane, where she early on displayed interest and ability in literature and music. Her Roman Catholic upbringing and education figure prominently in her writing. Australia's tropical state Queensland, of which Brisbane is the capital, serves as the setting for most of Astley's fiction—the far northern part in particular. In 1958 she published her first novel, *Girl with a Monkey*. Since then she has published ten more novels and a collection of short fiction as well as numerous uncollected stories and essays.

After studying arts at the University of Queensland, Astley taught in Queensland country schools for several years. Those experiences serve as the basis for her early novels. In 1948, she married Jack Gregson, a musician and administrator in the New South Wales school system, and moved to Sydney. They have one son. She continued teaching in high school until 1967 when she joined the faculty of Sydney's Macquarie University, where she taught Australian literature. Until her retirement from Macquarie in 1980, Astley combined writing with teaching and family responsibilities; she has commented that she never had time to participate in Sydney's fashionable literary society.

Since their retirement, she and her husband lived first near Cairns in Northern Queensland, but now live south of Sydney along the ocean, where she devotes her time to writing. They have traveled extensively during the last few years, especially in the United States. Astley has served as a guest lecturer at the University of Aarhus in Denmark and at Memphis State University.

Although Astley's work has never enjoyed a wide popular or academic reception in Australia, it has often been honored by literary prizes. For three of her novels Astley received the Miles Franklin Award—one of Australia's most distinguished prizes, and for *Beachmasters* she earned the Australian Society of Literature's Gold Medal. *A Kindness Cup* was named Book of the Year by *The Age*, a Melbourne newspaper. In 1989, she received the Patrick White Prize, which is given each year to an Australian writer who has made a notable contribution to the country's literature but has not received full recognition. Nobel Laureate Patrick White created the trust for the Prize from his own Nobel award. In 1988 Astley's alma mater, the University of Queensland, granted her an honorary doctorate.

While the publication in 1967 of *The Slow Natives* marked Astley's debut in the United States, her American reputation has grown steadily since the appearance of *Beachmasters* in 1985. Her work also now receives more attention in Australia.

WRITING THE PARISH AND EXTENDING THE METAPHOR

Thea Astley has said that "the parish is the heart of the world," that "literary truth is derived from the parish, and if it is truth it will be universal." In the same essay, she discusses a poem about Queensland and notes that "it is the manner in which these things are seen and interpreted that creates the truth and the poem—not the thing itself" ("Being a Queenslander" 255, 257).

That Astley's fiction comes from her own parish—meaning in the most general sense "near the house"—might mark her for some a provincial writer who most often dwells in and on Northern Queensland. Yet Australian critics and readers have at times admonished Astley for realizing the parish untruthfully: drawing the folk with too acerb an edge, scarifying honored traditions in Australian culture, even attacking the Roman Catholic church. Further, that Astley's rendition of the parish has been "seen and interpreted" in such a way as to create "the truth and the poem—not the thing itself" has often led to criticism of her writing style as too dense, too contrived, too symbol laden.

Astley's work has long run a course of its own far outside the mainstream of Australian writing. Astley has never been exact enough in her representation, mundane enough in her prose, to fit the school of realism that still dominated Australian fiction when she started writing. Nor has she taken up popular causes, such as Marxism, feminism, or nationalism, which have at times shaped some Australian storytelling. Neither has she relied on warmed-over metafictional techniques, now so self-consciously fashionable in much Australian work. Instead, Astley's writing stands by itself, as surely as that of Patrick White and Randolph Stowe, as that of Judith Wright, all of whom in the 1950s beheld Australia in a new way: wrote the parish—the Australian landscape, people, experience, history—and extended into metaphysical dimensions the metaphors they discovered.

Just as Astley's individualistic and original body of work adds to the possibilities of Australian literature, it also belongs fully to international writing in English. After all, a prime characteristic of the fiction emanating from the defunct Empire is its adherence to the parish, whether it be Africa or Canada or India or New Zealand, or wherever the English and their language spread; and the exotic locale has long been part of the literature's appeal. Still, no matter how farflung the parish or how exacting its representation, fiction based solely on distance and faithful rendering constitutes little more than rarefied regionalism, a limitation from which the body of writing once called colonial literature sometimes suffered. In such instances, the writers failed to extend the metaphor when making fictions out of the preoccupations that characterize international literature in English, whether from the colonial or postcolonial era.

In the past those preoccupations have been the multiple dilemmas created by colonialism itself, the response to an alien landscape, the evolutionary process of language, and the quest for the center. Now that the word colonialism most often carries a prefix, usually "neo" or "post," the controlling subjects have shifted but not changed altogether. For the imperial residue yet lingers, the landscape continues to intrigue, the English language keeps on evolving. And, most importantly, the center still beckons: In the past it was "Home," the metropolis, England; then the "heart of darkness" in the new land; finally a grasp of self in a postcolonial setting. Such is the stuff from which a writer like Thea Astley extends her metaphors when writing the parish of her Australia.

Now let us examine the novels, in order of their publication, to discover in each the nature of the parish and the controlling metaphor as well as their relationship one to the other and their overall development.

Astley's first novel, *Girl with a Monkey*, records the last day a country school-teacher named Elsie spends in a dusty Queensland town, a parish to recur in subsequent work. As Elsie waits for the train, her life during the past few months unfolds through memory. This device, employed unobtrusively, displays Astley's skillful shifting of time even in her first novel, a technique perfected as her writing progresses. The book is about loneliness brought on by isolation, both physical and spiritual—"some nausea of spirit" (31), Elsie names it, thereby defining the metaphor that controls the narrative. As the novel closes, she leaves the bleak town that has been her parish to travel toward another center where she may or may not find answers. In one form or another Elsie appears again and again in the later fiction, as though her departure were in some way representative of Astley's own start on a fictional journey.

The next book, *A Descant for Gossips*, also takes as its parish a Queensland town, no less dusty and dreary than the one Elsie left behind. Again schoolteachers figure prominently, this time a man and woman whose love affair provides the "descant for gossips." But the main character is Vinny Lalor, who is first seen "moving through the motionless morning to her personal crucifixion at the town's heart" (2). Here, then, is the metaphor that the story of a lonely, rejected, ridiculed schoolgirl extends. At the end Vinny contemplates suicide—or maybe carries out her intention, a finality the novel leaves open. As she holds the poison, she thinks to herself that "It might hurt a bit, . . . but she would never have to be hurt again" (259). Vinny is the first of a long line of misfits, outsiders, who appear in Astley's novels; unlike the crucifiers, the victim glimpses truth, arrives at the periphery of the sought-after parish of the mind, perhaps gains admission to its center through death.

The parish expands in the third novel, *The Well Dressed Explorer*, to encompass several Australian towns and Sydney, in particular. George Brewster, a journalist, is the well-dressed explorer, the title serving as the metaphor. But he turns out to be an ineffectual, timorous, pompous explorer whose quest for the center leads him into a stale marriage, failed love affairs, and a mediocre journalistic career, where he masters the cliché and aphorism. A fruitless conversion to Catholicism—"he staggered spiritually like a God-drunk into the dusk" (74)—counts as his most singular attempt to explore and failure, even if his enthusiasm at first knows no bounds:

> Through eyes of stained glass George must regard the world. His breath was liturgical. In those days clerical collars thrilled him almost as much as plunging necklines. A peasant simplicity regulated his attitude to prayer. . . . His entire seriousness took him regularly through temporal obligations to religion, and he made Lenten resolutions of ambitious sinlessness. (105)

Although the first two novels employ Christian symbols in odd ways, such as men lighting "votive cigarettes" (*Girl* 77), this passage introduces a strain running through future novels in which the rites and dogma of Catholicism are carnivalized. Too, the novel brims with wit, often directed at Brewster, whom the narrator undercuts throughout; perfected here, the ironic handling of character dominates the books to come as those in the tale reveal their flaws at the merciless hand of the teller.

The next novel, *The Slow Natives*, moves to the tropical city of Brisbane and draws a sympathetic picture of a teenage boy named Keith; it is the adults who suffer the narrator's scorn— their corruption, altogether petty and trivial in nature, is set against the boy's innocence. Amid the trials of growing up, especially with bored and philandering parents, Keith gropes for some kind of center that will ensure stability in what promises to be a world of "slow natives," moaning "through the guilt of . . . satisfaction" (105), flopping "amid the failed prayers," struggling against "thorns of failure, the dead twigs" (85). A kind of traditional *Bildungsroman*, certainly a simple enough story on the surface, *The Slow Natives* turns out to be the densest of the novels so far and introduces several types who will figure variously in later works: the sensitive but failed artist; the older woman obsessed with sex; the innocent among the corrupt; the priest "with his vocation askew" (75); even a slightly mad nun ("God's call girls" nuns are dubbed in the next novel); and the older homosexual who suffers humiliation as penance for his often thwarted seduction of youth.

A group of "slow natives"—some introduced in the previous work, others new— take a trip in *A Boat Load of Home Folk*, whose parish is a South Sea Island but not a tropical paradise, a place where it rains "hammers of wet" (14), where "There are far too many palms" (1), where "The flies hovered in clouds" (35). The vacationers and the bedraggled colonials who stayed on after Empire reveal their tortured selves, literally and figuratively dwelling on the rim of a volcano—"And in the centre of it all, like the red heart of a monstrous volcanic cone, his own blazoned guilt" (212). Then a hurricane strikes the island and establishes the metaphor that patterns this study of humankind's guilt and sin and futile striving for the redemptive center. A short novel but immensely complex in its structure, *A Boat Load of Home Folk* introduces numerous characters, setting them in their immediacy as they dodge the storm's destruction—"In the morning, only the bar-rail was left" (170), and tracing the past that has generated their spiritual turmoil—"the sore fruit that was his [their] soul[s]" (175). Most survive, but none reach the eye of the storm, the quiet center of the hurricane. That longed-for refuge becomes a mockery, reinforced by the ersatz celebration of the Eucharist, where bits of cardboard in a sauce replace the Host, administered by a crone named Miss Paradise—"he took his communion from priestess Paradise who watched, spooning herself, her punishment shared about" (182). In contrast, the novel ends with a legitimate mass so that those "troubled by disaster" would be "mollified by ritual" (218).

The Acolyte, appearing four years later, might well be Astley's finest novel, certainly her most sophisticated and perhaps her most difficult. Once more set in the Queensland parish—at first in the now-familiar country towns, then along the vast state's spectacular southern coast with scenes in famed Surfer's Paradise, the book follows the career of a blind Australian composer named Holberg for whom the first-person narrator sees: an "acolyte" to the sightless priest of art. That is the metaphor the narrator extends in this *tour de force*, which satirizes most aspects of contemporary Australian life, art and the artist in a postcolonial society, and at times the novel form itself. The cast of quirky characters, sifted through the narrator's sharp eye, represent the vulgarity, pretensions, provincialism, and a number of other unsavory qualities Astley sees dominating postcolonial Australia, a society that has too long been a kind of acolyte to England. The artist—whether a novelist, painter, composer—finds such a secondary place inhospitable, for again he or she is considered an acolyte to "real" artists from Europe; to enlarge on this point, the narrator (Astley's persona?) heaps ridicule on local music critics, Australian audiences, and "arty" hangers-on. The form of the narrative is such that it pokes fun at its own pretensions, and overspills with puns, symbols, elaborate and self-conscious prose; on occasion the narrator stands back and marvels at his own virtuosity, which is admirable, as this passage on artistic use of Freudian symbolism illustrates:

> I've never been one of your symbol hunters. It's only since I've been absorbed by the arty parasites that nudge their tiny proboscises into the skin of Holberg's talent that I realize my deficiency in a whole world of experience. . . . I simply don't see trees as dicks thrusting into the gaping uterus of the sky. I see them as trees. I need help. Here's a whole acre of people who live in a world of phalli, . . . of gulping labia, of fourth-form interpretations of cars, whales, telegraph poles and mammalian light-bulbs. . . . It makes eating an ice-cream cone difficult. You take my point, doc? (199)

Astley has said that she wrote the novel partially in reaction to the harsh criticism on her previous work, especially of the symbolism and prose style that had been called "precious" and "overwrought," thus intending to ridicule her own art. She has long felt that the woman Australian novelist, especially during the 1950s and 1960s, has been treated harshly by Australian critics unless she remained an acolyte, writing "female literature" and avoiding any originality and experimentation.

Yet this richly textured work transcends its satire, its dubious purpose as a reply to critics, even its perceptive view of the artist in a postcolonial society. Once more the search for a spiritual center emerges, however subtly, suggesting that the greatest work of art is, after all, salvation of the soul. Not that any of the characters succeed. The acolyte abruptly stops his account of their twisted lives, wondering: "Where will it all end?" (287).

While Astley seemingly traces a single theme, consistently satirizes Australian society along with humankind's universal absurdity, and forever shapes language so that at times it is grotesque and inverted, then elegant and perfected, she has written no two novels alike. *A Kindness Cup*, which follows *The Acolyte*, has straight, spare lines as it reconstructs an actual event in Australian colonial history. Yet indignant as Astley appears to be over the colonists' treatment of Aborigines, her story constitutes far more than a polemic on imperialistic misdeeds. The extended metaphor is the very cruelty and guiltlessness of much-admired pioneers who took others' land as their own; in one way, this novel treads familiar postcolonial literary ground by recounting the old story of the usurper and the usurped. Necessarily, Astley forsakes as her parish modern Australia's brassy California/Miami-like Gold Coast she had so skewered in the previous novel and moves back in time to one of those forsaken towns she relishes, a place where "Coastal scrub has thinned out its scraggy imprecision and has become the scraggier, scrubbier buildings" (21). In the limited third person—mainly through the eyes of the visitor Dorahy, the narrative supports a double time frame, first a reunion of townspeople in the present, then a massacre of Aborigines twenty or so years earlier. Ostensibly, the occasion marks a jubilee of the town's settlement, but Dorahy, searching for "a kindness cup" amid prevailing hypocrisy, turns time back to the white settlers' act that forced Aborigines off a cliff to death. He attempts in vain to instill guilt, the failure preordained when he walks into a tea shop shortly after his arrival and finds the waitress

> . . . sluicing out the evening before. Rinsing the last stains of it, a thin girl has been doing penance with mop and bucket. She couldn't care less about this elderly man with his thin face and thinner voice demanding tea. She isn't forgiving anybody, refuses the credit of his smile, while slinging her bile across one table surface after the other with a rancid grey rag.
> But he tries. (22)

The scene set, Dorahy's experiences at the "jubilee" unfold, intertwined with accounts of his earlier teaching days in the town and the bloody event itself. Determined to be a martyr, tireless and at times tiresome in his self-appointed role as harbinger of guilt and punishment and redemption, Dorahy finally falls victim to the townspeople's inherent violence: ". . . so tired he accepts the fleshly damage of his enemies like some peculiar blessing, lying on the rain-wet grass, his lips curled in the smile of pain" (135). No place, then, for the prophet, who lies reveling in his agony outside the hall where those he tried to save sing in ironic background "Should auld acquaintances be forgot," a familiar Robert Burns poem containing the line "We'll tak' a cup o' kindness yet."

But the prophet in the writer Astley rises from the "rain-wet grass" and continues, for the next novel, *An Item from the Late News*, might well carry her darkest view of humankind's folly: the parish again a forlorn country town called Allbut; the metaphor a precious stone (the holy grail?) found by a wanderer simply named Wafer (a Christ figure?). An emotionally unstable narrator—guilt-ridden by her betrayal of Wafer—tells the story of his fall that took place "those two months ten years ago now when the town prepared for and then dismissed its barbaric Christmas" (1). That Christmas is remembered as "barbaric" profanes and contradicts the holy day celebrated mid-summer in Allbut with ". . . the beer-gut belchings and the rattle of schooner glasses that always discover the Christmas crib and soothe the infant with whack yoicks" (1). One of the characters says "God certainly comes into the picture sometimes" (137), and in this most obviously parabolic of her novels Astley brings God squarely into the picture, namely with the "mad saint" Wafer, who at the hands of the townspeople dies in a mockery of crucifixion. One thinks of another outsider turned into martyr, albeit a simpler one, Vinny Lalor in *A Descant for Gossips*.

"It is time to storian" (2). So ends the prologue to *Beachmasters*, the novel that follows. The reader has just been presented on the first page a litany and directed to pray "in three tongues: in Seaspeak, in English, in French; for there are three ways of praying" (a suggestion of the trinity?). From a technical standpoint, this novel is the most accomplished since *The Acolyte*: deft in its balancing of complex events and time shifts—"So quick to tell. So long in the happening" (27); exact with its representation of numerous characters—"They breathe, those searchers, the shallow air of dreams, walking the frail crust of longing" (14); and lucid in the integration of English and French with the pidgin form of both called Seaspeak. As in *A Boat Load of Home Folk*, the parish is a south sea island, an outpost of colonialism, "where there was no weather, only hot and hotter with rampaging wets in the monsoon months, quick sunsets and sudden daylights as the world cracked open like an egg and everywhere this spinach green, this straining blue" (16). The metaphor taken is a native revolution against latter day imperialism, the story derived from an actual event and familiar enough as postcolonial subject matter:

> How could he speak honestly of the criminality of colonialism, the banditry of planters and trading empires, of the fools of men who strutted on the red carpets of tradition, sustained by a bit of coloured rag, centuries of acute distinction and a belief in their own godhead? (160)

Still, Astley's preoccupation with "the sore fruit" of the soul finally overshadows the revolution's native leader—based on a real person—and the ensuing action, although both are faithfully and sympathetically treated. At the end, the revolution has crumbled, the leader jailed and humiliated, and the motley assortment of colonials (a homosexual priest, feckless administrators and their bitter wives, an aging prostitute, among others) stay on in their corrupted Eden, far from either the imperial center, or the spiritual. Only innocence in the person of young Gavi finds redemption, not through death this time, but through recognition, which "trembles at the edge of his mind" (185).

It's Raining in Mango returns to the familiar parish of Northern Queensland and adopts for its metaphor the family history, long a favored subject among Australian realists, often urbanites, who gloried in the hardships of bush life and basked in the heroism of sturdy colonialists who conquered the land or were conquered by it. But Astley, a fabulist not a realist, subverts the form, neither glorying nor basking. Instead the novel blends the nineteenth with the twentieth century, the dead with the living, proving that not much differs from time to time: "As it was. Is" (15).

The novel stands as a kind of metaphysical and metafictional—and likely more lasting—version of Colleen McCullough's popular Australian family history, *The Thorn Birds* (1977). For Astley it has never been what the characters do that matters, never a literal record that she intends; it is rather what does not happen that interests her, and the reader. So it seems natural for her work to move even further from reality, where it never dwelt long anyway, and go in the direction of the fabulous, the fantastic. In absorbing the heritage left by Borges and García Márquez and others, though, Astley proves herself no slavish imitator, but an innovator as she continues on a fictional journey to the center, all the while a recognition of sin, guilt, and redemption trembling at the edge of the fictions themselves.

The latest novel, *Reaching Tin River*, opens three times, Belle, the first-person narrator, concluding after her attempts that "I cannot invent reality." She has just tried, and failed:

> I am looking for a one-storey town
>   with trees
>   river
>   hills
>   and a population of under two thousand
>   one of whom must be called Gaden Lockyer.
> Or
>   Mother was a drummer in her own all-women's group, a throbber
>   of a lady with midlife zest and an off-center smile.
> Or
>   I have decided to make a list of all the convent girls who learnt
>   to play "The rustle of Spring" by Christian Sinding between 1945
>   and 1960. (7)

She tries three more times to begin the story, once about her life on the family property called "Perjury Plains," next about a tropical vacation when she finds her husband "trying to hump the house girl. I say *trying.*" Finally she offers: "Tin River is a townlet of terminal attractiveness. Tin River is a state of mind" (8). If it is left up to the reader to choose, let us take the latter: "Tin River is a state of mind." Here is the parish—the perennial Northern Queensland town—and the metaphor—at last blended into a state of mind.

When the first novel, *Girl with a Monkey*, ends, Elsie has just set off on a journey. Over three decades later, we meet her modern counterpart—infinitely more sophisticated, often equally annoying in her self-absorption, still suffering from what Elsie called "some nausea of spirit." To reach Tin River, Belle, too, journeys. And what a trip it becomes: across Australia's landscape (or "eyescape" as Belle calls it), with side trips into the Northern Hemisphere's cities, San Diego and New York, all the while meeting those oddball characters that always people the novels. One of the most striking parts of Belle's reaching is her obsession with a nineteenth-century empire builder, the Gaden Lockyer mentioned at the outset. Trying to enter his life first through blown-up photographs, then his journals, Belle eventually takes up residence in the Tin River nursing home where the once admired Lockyer died a disgraced and lonely old man. The journey over, Belle, who has emerged finally from her state of fantasy, admits that she is beginning to find "absorption *outside* . . . rather than *within,*" and draws a perfect circle, placing the smallest of points beyond it; this she describes as herself: "The center lost outside its own perimeter" (223).

From so cursory a survey of a thirty-some-year imaginative journey, perhaps we can conclude that Thea Astley has sought to write the parish and extend the metaphor into the elusive center of being; that her characters with the "sore fruit" of their souls will—except rarely—remain outsiders outside the truth, "the smallest of points" beyond the redemptive circle.

WORKS CITED

Astley, Thea. *The Acolyte.* In *Two by Astley.* New York: G.P. Putnam's Sons, 1988.

———. *Beachmasters.* New York: Penguin, 1985.

———. "Being a Queenslander: A Form of Literary and Geographical Conceit." *Southerly* 36 (1976): 252–64.

———. *A Boat Load of Home Folk.* New York: Penguin, 1983.

———. *A Descant for Gossips.* St. Lucia: U of Queensland P, 1984.

———. *Girl with a Monkey.* New York: Penguin, 1987.

———. *An Item from the Late News.* St. Lucia: U of Queensland P, 1982.

———. *A Kindness Cup.* In *Two by Astley.* New York: G.P. Putnam's Sons, 1988.

———. *It's Raining in Mango.* New York: G.P. Putnam's Sons, 1987.

———. *Reaching Tin River.* New York: G.P. Putnam's Sons, 1990.

———. *The Slow Natives.* Sydney: Angus & Robertson, 1976.

———. *The Well Dressed Explorer.* Sydney: Angus & Robertson, 1962.

THEA ASTLEY'S PUBLISHED WORK

Novels

Girl with a Monkey, 1958
A Descant for Gossips, 1960
The Well Dressed Explorer, 1962
The Slow Natives, 1965
A Boat Load of Home Folk, 1968
The Acolyte, 1972
A Kindness Cup, 1974
An Item from the Late News, 1982
Beachmasters, 1985
It's Raining in Mango, 1987
Reaching Tin River, 1990

Short Story Collection

Hunting the Wild Pineapple, 1979

Collection

Two by Astley (*The Acolyte* and *A Kindness Cup*), 1988

SELECTED CRITICAL READINGS

Even though Thea Astley's books have consistently won awards in Australia, they have not until recently received much critical attention there. Her work is now widely reviewed in major North American publications. It is also at last being discovered in Australia, and favorable reviews are replacing the formerly negative ones. So additional full-fledged critical articles will probably begin to appear, both in Australia and abroad. Already her work has been approached comparatively, certainly a rich field that should be explored more fully. Consideration of language, religious symbolism, and structure also offer unlimited possibilities.

Clancy, Laurie. "The Fiction of Thea Astley." *Meridian* 5 (1986): 43–52. As the title suggests, the article surveys what is considered a substantial accomplishment.

Goldsworthy, Kerryn. "Thea Astley's Writing, Magnetic North." *Meanjin* 42 (1983): 478–85. Offers a biographical account of Astley, along with a general discussion of her fiction.

———. "Voices in Time: *A Kindness Cup* and *Miss Peabody's Inheritance*." *Australian Literary Studies* 12 (1986): 471–81. Concludes that Astley and Elizabeth Jolley employ a linguistic playfulness that makes their narrative techniques difficult to define. Discusses the narrative chronology in *A Kindness Cup*, the actual narrative act in *Miss Peabody's Inheritance*.

Matthews, Brian. "Life in the Eye of the Hurricane: The Novels of Thea Astley." *Southern Review* 6 (1973): 148–73. This first serious discussion covers the fiction through *The Acolyte*, seeing the novels as a chronicle of those who move within a self-created storm and sometimes succumb to it. Notes that the work transcends its Australian context.

Miner, Valerie. "The Brilliant Career of Thea Astley." *Los Angeles Times Book Review* 7 August 1988: 11. Recalls a meeting with Astley in Australia and offers a general discussion of her life and work.

Perkins, Elizabeth. "A Life of its Own: A Deconstructive Reading of Astley's *A Kindness Cup*." *Hecate* 11 (1985): 11–17. Heavy with theory and terminology, the article argues that the text fails as it tries to break into a "masculinist world of writing," but this self-imposed failure reveals a "'feminine'" awareness. Argues that traditional critical treatment of Astley's novels is inadequate, but "deconstructive" readings place her alongside great women writers.

Ross, Robert. "Mavis Gallant and Thea Astley on Home Truths, Home Folk." *Ariel* 19.1 (1988): 83–89. Draws comparisons between Astley's *A Boat Load of Home Folk* and Gallant's *Home Truths*, showing how they allow their characters to glimpse truth rarely and briefly.

———. "The Shape of Language in Thea Astley's Work." *World Literature Written in English* 28 (1988): 260–65. Focuses on *An Item from the Late News* to illustrate how Astley subverts language and Christian symbolism to sustain her preoccupation with guilt and redemption.

Smith, Graeme Kinross. "Thea Astley." *Kunapipi* 4.1 (1982): 20–37. Talks about Astley's life and surveys her work. Includes an interview.

Tareha, Nicola Jane. *The Legend of the Leap*. Townsville: Foundation for Australian Literary Studies, 1986. Explains variations of the legend used in *A Kindness Cup*, focusing on the version Astley followed. Notes the legend's archetypal elements, discusses the novel, and includes relevant historical documents.

Interviews

With Candida Baker. *Yacker, Australian Writers Talk About Their Work*. Sydney: Pan Books, 1986. 29–53.
With Jennifer Ellison. *Rooms of Their Own*. Melbourne: Penguin Australia, 1986. 50–69.
With Robert Ross. *World Literature Written in English* 26 (1986). 264–69.
With Ray Willbanks. *Antipodes* 2 (1988). 107–08.

— ROBERT L. ROSS

V. Decolonizing Art

W hen those who had ventured into the territory of Empire first began to write, they faithfully adhered to the artistic dictates of the center. Indigenous writers, then educated for the most part in mission schools, did much the same. They exercised care over diction, always fearful that they would not be understood if they used native words; they also avoided introducing the dramatic changes that characterized local English usage. If the writer dared to break these rules, then the book probably included a glossary or was even rendered into so-called standard English before being published abroad. That is no longer the case; today Urdu or Tagalog words, slang peculiar to the Australian outback, or bits of traditional African poetry appear without explanation in the English text. And the "correct" English once ordered by the center has often been replaced by Caribbean or Samoan dialects. Anita Desai, one of the most traditional stylists, observed recently that the Indian novel in English now reflects the linguistic characteristics of the English spoken on the sub-continent instead of the formal style that was long preferred.

Bharati Mukherjee admitted that she relied on nineteenth-century British novelistic techniques in her early fiction because that was all she had learned from the Western education she received in Calcutta. Through emphasis on an official literature—British, that is—the center dictated in one more way and assured that its literary forms would not be diluted by, say, the oral traditions of African or Australian Aboriginal poetry or the dissonance of the East that Kamala Markandaya talks about. In another respect, Judith Wright calls on poets to use indigenous materials—the flora and fauna of their immediate environment, not the skylarks and daffodils on the other side of the world.

The writers represented in this collection of essays have all acted to decolonize the art of writing, and many of the critics talk about the way the work is written even as they concentrate on theme, thereby adhering to the obvious literary precept that form and matter cannot be separated. The essays' authors in some instances have focused primarily on technique.

For one, Temple Hauptfleisch in examining the work of the South African playwright, Athol Fugard, decides to forego a discussion of Fugard's anti-apartheid stance, believing that his international acclaim stems too often from "what he writes *about*, rather than on how he sets about it." Hauptfleisch proposes that Fugard's singular ability to place "the image, the word, and the 'carnal reality' . . . in the little pool of light called the stage" comes largely from circumstances determined by the playwright's South African milieu and experience. T.G. Bishop explores another strand of the colonial-center artistic dilemma in his discussion of the Australian poet,

Gwen Harwood. He wonders why some continue to believe that the artist must be at "the center of things" in order to be taken seriously, just as Hauptfleisch questions whether Fugard's perceived politics of the local have brought him fame rather than his theatrical originality. Can true literary art come from faraway places? Or must it originate in the metropolis, then spread outward? According to Bishop, "the work of Gwen Harwood ignores the boundaries drawn by insistence on the cosmopolitan international." Instead it displays sophistication "without relinquishing a precise and local eye and ear" in its analysis and integration of "a complex dialectic of passion and intellect, loss and salvage, parish and globe."

Rodney Edgecombe approaches in a like manner the writing of J.M. Coetzee, the South African novelist who has not addressed apartheid directly but whose work has often been read abroad as though he did. Edgecombe places Coetzee into the larger tradition and treats his work from an intertextual standpoint: a logical approach considering that Coetzee restructured *Robinson Crusoe* into his novel *Foe*. Apprehending "the notion of oracularity" as central to the novels, Edgecombe explains how the "oracular elements" are first manifested in the formulation of the texts, then in their "ambiguity and ambivalence." Similarly, Robert Darling takes the poetry of A.D. Hope far afield from the poet's Australian homeland and examines it as a continuing statement on "the role of myth in the everyday psychic life of individuals." Removing Hope's work from colonial margins and relating it to the center, Darling concludes that as a poet "Hope is able to take his place in the international brotherhood of humans striving to elicit the music of the world."

The lingering belief that art outside the center lacks originality affects the way audiences view David Williamson's plays both at home and abroad. Beyond Australia they are often praised not so much for their artistic accomplishment as for their comic picture of what others think Australians are like. And at home they are usually taken as satires on contemporary Australian life. Brian Kiernan corrects this over-simplified view by arguing that the plays, while highly "accessible" on any level, exceed both satire and comedy and combine the two forms into an original drama with a rare "human dimension."

Patrick Morrow examines the art of one of the earliest international writers to gain recognition, Katherine Mansfield. Most of her short life was actually spent in Europe not in her birthplace New Zealand. Yet what many consider her best fiction is set in her homeland. And the questions Morrow indirectly raises are: Would her writing have been the same had it not been for her early New Zealand experience? Could she have experimented so successfully "with the idea of the perfect short story, trying to capture perfection over and over"? Morrow says not, as he introduces her work in the light of a notebook Mansfield kept during a camping tour in New Zealand; he calls this notebook a synthesis of "her external world to suit the needs of her internal disposition," that which formed the basis of her fictional achievement.

So far this discussion has taken up writers who descended from the predominantly Anglo-Saxon settler societies in South Africa, Australia, and New Zealand. But such is not the case with Nick Joaquin from the Philippines and Ediriwira Sarachchandra from Sri Lanka. Both are pioneer figures in the English language literature of their native countries and served to establish a literature not purely English in tradition but one that blends the dual cultures they inherited as former colonial subjects. Leonard

Casper notes that Joaquin's generation learned "to accommodate themselves not only to American ways but to revel in the remnants of what Spain left behind." (It is worthy to note that the imperialism Joaquin knew was American not British.) According to Casper, the blending of the Filipino's several heritages—"the many Manilas"—provides the impetus for Joaquin, who considered himself a "third-party mediator and healer" whose work was "devoted to reconciliation, the sifting and winnowing of all aspects of the Philippine experience."

Recording the "virtuosity and vision" of Sarachchandra, the preeminent Sri Lankan writer, Lakshmi de Silva pictures him as a beneficiary of the colonial system in which he was reared. She proposes that the dual heritage "sharpened and refined his cognizance of the palpable or tenuous barriers that separate cultures as well as the ineluctable forces that govern men in whatever culture they be born or bred." No colonial lackey but a truly decolonized artist when Sri Lanka was still called Ceylon, Sarachchandra early on rebelled against his purely Westernized education and took up as well the study of Sri Lankan literature and languages, then merged the two traditions in his drama, fiction, and scholarship. He is credited with establishing modern Sinhalese drama, has written fiction in Sinhalese and in English, and has published philosophical and critical works in both languages.

Robert Hamner examines the work of Derek Walcott, the important West Indian poet and playwright. Focusing for the most part on the way Walcott blends the pictorial arts with writing, Hamner discusses how the poet-playwright has used the tool of "chiaroscuro" to create dramatic contrasts—namely those between the two cultures that had "divided to the vein" Walcott's life from the outset. Hamner concludes that "The legacy of empire and consequently of Walcott's poetry is black Caliban confronting the white world in its own realm."

The role of the artist in a postcolonial society has been examined in numerous works of fiction, such as Patrick White's *The Vivisector*, Thea Astley's *The Acolyte*, Wole Soyinka's *Season of Anomy*, Margaret Laurence's *The Diviners*, Janet Frame's *Living in the Maniototo*. But the one writer who has addressed this subject over his entire career is Robertson Davies. In discussing Davies' nine novels dealing with the Canadian artist, Thomas Tausky traces the work moving from a period marked by "the disabilities of a colonized existence" to a time when "Canada is shown to be capable of shedding her colonial clogs."

Much the same could be said of the other countries represented in this collection of essays—and of their writers who helped to bring about the change.

Athol Fugard

Considered South Africa's premier and most contentious playwright since the late 1960s and even on occasion described as "the greatest active playwright in English"—as a *Time* magazine profile called him (7 August 1989)—Athol Fugard has always seen himself and his work as firmly rooted in South Africa. It is his relationship with life in that strife-torn region of the world that informs his work and serves both as its material and as its inspiration.

Fugard was born in South Africa on 11 June 1932 in the Karoo town of Middelburg; his mother was an Afrikaner and his father an English-speaking South African, descended from what he has described as Anglo-Irish stock. In 1935 the family moved to the predominantly English-speaking city of Port Elizabeth, where Fugard grew up, went to school, and was basically to spend the rest of his life. Here his mother first ran a boarding house and later the St. George's Park Tearoom.

A scholarship allowed Fugard to attend the University of Cape Town for a B.A. in philosophy. However, before taking his finals, he left the university and hitchhiked up Africa to spend a year working his way around the world on ships. On his return he took various jobs, including that of reporter for a local newspaper and later for the South Africa Broadcasting Corporation, clerk in the Fordsburg Native Commissioner's Court—Johannesburg, and stage manager for the state-funded National Theatre Organisation. In this period he also met and married Sheila Meiring, an actress who was herself to become a distinguished author. Under her influence, he began a period of intense amateur theater involvement with the Circle Players in Cape Town and the African Theatre Workshop in Johannesburg and wrote and produced his first two plays. After another sojourn in England and Belgium, trying to break into theater, the Fugards returned to South Africa in December 1960 to settle permanently in Port Elizabeth, where their daughter Lisa was born the following year.

From here on Fugard has worked professionally as full-time playwright, actor, and director, largely acting in and directing only his own work, though he has been closely involved with a variety of black and alternative companies—notably the Serpent Players in Port Elizabeth, The Space in Cape Town, and the Market Theatre in Johannesburg. Although Fugard has often been at odds with government and its agencies on political grounds, his influence has spread throughout the South African theatrical system, revitalizing and markedly influencing both its form and its direction.

As his international reputation grew, Fugard began to accept invitations to work in other countries and in other media (notably film and television) but always on a temporary basis. The most profitable such arrangement seems to have been the recent period of involvement with the Yale Repertory Theatre, where he has workshopped and premiered a number of his recent plays, before producing them in South Africa and elsewhere. However, he always returns to one of his two homes in the Eastern Cape Province to revitalize himself and to begin another exploration of the world about him.

THE IMAGE, THE WORD, AND THE "CARNAL REALITY"

One of the reasons, I suppose, why I write for the stage—beyond, or before, all the spoken words there is the possibility of this code— the Carnal Reality of the actor in space and time. Only a fraction of my truth is in the words. (Athol Fugard, *Notebooks* 171)

Athol Fugard's status as South Africa's best known playwright and his reputation as writer of international acclaim have, it seems, largely been based on what he writes *about* rather than on how he sets about it. He has risen to prominence for his intense and lifelong opposition to apartheid, becoming to a large extent a symbol of the artist against oppression (along with such writers as Alan Paton, Nadine Gordimer, Mongane Serote, André Brink, Es'kia Mphahlele, and Breyten Breytenbach). However, the majority of critics are divided on this aspect, many finding his works rooted in, yet transcendent of, the merely local. Others argue that his politics are naive and based on an outmoded form of liberalism, or that he is so irrevocably tied to his own position as a bourgeois white South African that his works are inevitably counterproductive of the political aims of the majority. In fact, these and similar issues quickly became and remain a major area of debate in Fugard studies.

Of course the matter is immensely complex and in the long term certainly cannot be reduced to a simple either/or issue concerned with where Fugard stands in terms of the South African liberation struggle. Even the most critical commentators are uncomfortably aware of this complexity. Because of the controversy generated, though, the debate has tended to obscure Fugard's equal, if not more important, long-term contribution to contemporary world theater. Since the political issue is extensively dealt with elsewhere (as noted in the "Selected Critical Readings"), this essay will focus on certain formal aspects of Fugard's dramaturgy.

Athol Fugard is a prime example of the play*wright*, the constructor of plays in physical, theatrical space—and he himself has always striven consciously to define his artistry in this fashion as his published *Notebooks* and a variety of interviews attest. This quality almost certainly derives from the extensive personal involvement he exercises in the process of theater-making, functioning not only as writer but also often as scribe, teacher, actor, designer, stage manager, and director. He is not and has never been a study-bound writer of "literary" playtexts, but a practical craftsman whose workshop is the stage. Every Fugard play has, at least in part, been shaped in rehearsal and has had its first production under his personal direction; often he has cast himself in one of the roles as well. It is a way of working that apparently evolved from his early days of "poor theater"—in both the financial sense and in the more theoretical Grotowskian one—when he worked with amateur black actors in the badly equipped halls and rooms of the townships of Johannesburg and Port Elizabeth—experimenting, improvising, learning, teaching. And the basic process evolved there has since become the only way he can and will work; and the eventual advantages are obvious to anyone confronted with the complex and tightly woven texture of his best plays in performance, for they become moments of total theatrical communication in which images, words, sounds, gestures, and actions become one indelible statement.

This approach has caused him to evolve a very personal style of theater in order to utilize the particular—that is, the details and realistic surface of life about him—to probe fundamental human reactions to specific but generally encountered existential problems. Despite Russel Vandenbroucke's disclaimer that "Fugard cannot be considered either a stylistic or thematic innovator" (264), the form in which Fugard has chosen to cast his thoughts has been as influential as the content of his works has been. The impact of his theater-making processes on a generation of writers, performers, and audiences raised on a colonial heritage of British drama (Shakespeare to Shaw) was profound and contributed significantly to the evolution of the thoroughly distinctive forms and styles associated with contemporary South African theater. At the same time Fugard's own discoveries in theater-making have enabled theatergoers the world over to identify with and enjoy his explorations of his "region" and have provided the international canon of English plays with a few immensely performable works that appear set to become true twentieth-century classics. Even if they possess no utterly new inventions, they do constitute excellent examples of how the existing conventions, forms, and styles may be integrated and reinterpreted in the service of the performance.

Two elements constantly recur in some way or another as specific concepts in both Fugard's writing and in his thinking about writing. They are *the image* and *the word.* The way in which he has struggled with and sought to integrate, utilize, and give physical, theatrical life to these two concepts has to a great extent shaped his own distinctive form of theater and his presentation of characters and the world in which they live.

Let us first examine *the image.*

Boesman and Lena opens on an empty stage. A man appears, heavily burdened, followed after a few moments by a woman, similarly burdened. They carry their total worldly possessions on their backs, including their shack, which they set about assembling on stage. When the play ends after two acts, the house has been smashed, so they pick it up and walk off in the same way, everything on their backs, and the stage is empty once more.

It is a visual image as strong as any in the canon of contemporary theater. Of course the echoes of similar images from Samuel Beckett (*Waiting for Godot*) and Bertolt Brecht (*Mother Courage*) are obvious and indeed useful. But the image itself is actually a very personal one for Fugard, with its roots in two generative images that Fugard describes in an often quoted passage from his *Notebooks* (166). The fuller version, quoted here and containing the crucial last line, comes from Fugard's introduction to *Boesman and Lena and Other Plays:*

> [I] realized that the genesis of the play lies possibly in an image from over ten years ago—Coloured man and woman, burdened with all their belongings, whom I passed somewhere on the road near Laingsburg. It was sunset and they were miles from the nearest town. Then of course, also the old woman near Cradock on the drive back from Norman's trial. 'Put your life on your head and walk.' (xxi)

Fugard is immensely aware of his reliance on the *image* in his playwriting—and he defines the concept for himself by paraphrasing Ezra Pound: ". . . the presentation of a psychological and emotional complex in an instant in time" (*Notebooks* 77). In his case it is very often a *visual* image that serves as a generating point for the plays. Thus there is the studio photograph of a man sitting with a cigarette in one hand and a pipe in the other, which was used as the basis for the improvisation of *Sizwe Bansi is Dead*. The main "story" of the play starts and ends with the Man (Sizwe Bansi) striking precisely that pose: the pose of a man with a dream. The play explores the dream and the forces that threaten it. *Statements after an Arrest under the Immorality Act* also arises from a photographic image: a set of six photographs in a police file taken during the arrest of a couple contravening the Act that prohibits any sexual relationship across racial barriers. The re-enacted "photographs" of the two people, trying to hide their nakedness as the lights flash on them, becomes a stunning visual correlative for and preamble to the verbal "exposure" they are subjected to in their "statements" that follow.

The *image* may be as simple as a photograph or an old coat, or it may be more complex, more verbal, as we have seen in the discussion of *Boesman and Lena*. The generative image Fugard supplies for *People Are Living There* is a case in point: "One image has resurrected an old complex of ideas: Milly's panic when she realizes late at night that she has spent the whole day in her dressing gown" (Introduction to *Statements* xii). Just that. But it becomes the central image with which the eventual play opens:

> An arm comes up. The light goes on. We see *Milly*. About fifty years old, dressed in an old candlewick dressing gown, her hair disordered, her face swollen with sleep. She waits expectantly, as if the light and chimes might evoke some response in the silent house.

And the play then explores that existential panic, as Milly tries to get something from the few hours of the day that remain, something that will make sense of her life, which she does by creating an image of her own, an image of "having fun," a party with cake, cold drinks, and party hats.

In this way, as each play develops, Fugard gradually refines and then extends the original image into a network of related or complementary images. Yet the original, generative image remains virtually unaltered at the core of the play, must in fact remain unaltered for it to remain the same play, as Dennis Walder has shown in his study (4). Thus for example, according to Fugard, *Hello and Goodbye* originated from two very disparate images he had noted in his *Notebooks*, the first a memory of his crippled father crying out in the dark from pain (ix-x) and the second a face from his youth, a man standing motionless on a street corner in Port Elizabeth (xiii). Unlike some of those used in other plays, neither one of these images becomes a direct physical presentation on stage, though Johnny does narrate his father's pain and eventually his own solitary vigils on the street watching the prostitutes. Yet they permeate the whole complex of images Fugard created in the eventual play, including Johnny taking up his father's crutches at the end to become his father (a "resurrection" long awaited by the man at the crossroads?), Hester tearing open the boxes, spilling their contents on the floor in search of the "compensation" her father had received after his accident—and in search of her life.

Not all the images are equally successful, of course, as one might see from some of the early plays (*No-Good Friday, Nongogo*). Some images are rather belabored and obvious, not quite intrinsic to the action of the particular play, and others are slightly out of focus, perhaps not worked through well enough. *A Lesson from Aloes*, while in some ways exceptionally well conceived in terms of the world Fugard is trying to examine, sets up the images in a somewhat set-piece fashion, while *A Place with the Pigs* loses impact and focus through unspecific references and images.

Certainly Fugard's latest play, *My Children, My Africa*, lacks the impact of a strong central image or an integrated set of images—at least in the first version that premiered in 1989. The uncharacteristic episodic and chronological structure Fugard used reduces the play itself to the form of his opening metaphor: a debate between the opposing parties, across racial, sexual, and generational divides. Like so much of the angry *agitprop* theater of the early eighties in South Africa, the play becomes dependent on a series of narrative addresses to the audience for its exposition of character, and thus far more obviously verbal, far more overtly—even uncomfortably—cerebral, than is usual in Fugard.

Nevertheless in the best of his work such images are completely transformed into a potent, wholly theatrical mode of expression. As Walder points out, the image expresses "the climax of a shifting pattern of emotions of gradually increasing strength, a moment of revelation"—the "living moment" Fugard is constantly seeking (4). One such moment occurs in *"Master Harold" . . . and the boys*, when Hally turns and spits in Sam's face. No words can express the impact this action carries in a theater. Another superb theatrical image occurs in *The Road to Mecca* when the candles are lit in the living room of Helen's home. Here is a magic moment that forms part of and provides a lyrical setting for Helen's long and decisive exposition of her journey and of her "Mecca." It is an image that delineates and enhances the meaning of the words, while the words in their turn help to define the image of light driving back the darkness. It is sheer theater.

Let us now examine *the word.*

Despite his frequent insistence that the words of the play are only a part of his "truth" or meaning, Fugard is extremely fond of words and they are fundamental to his thinking and his writing. His dialogue, for instance, is colorful and expansive, and his very individual use of regional dialects has become an important and distinctive attribute of his writing. It clearly links up with his interest in the "texture" of things and his view of himself as a "regional writer." Surface realism is a tool he constantly uses to seduce his audiences into joining him in an exploration of his far from mundane themes, and the sounds and rhythms of language varieties are superbly useful in simulating such realism.

The plays often also contain inordinately long speeches, which is one of the most obvious markers of the didacticism that underlies much of Fugard's writing—and indeed that of most serious writers in South Africa. Furthermore, while the language is made to seem sparse and tight, it remains very self-consciously "language": rhythmical, symbolic, image-laden, and *aware of the meaning of words and their power.* The last-mentioned attribute is particularly interesting in terms of Fugard's dramatic form. To illustrate, let us return to *Boesman and Lena* for a moment. At a point early in the second act, Boesman describes the bulldozing of the squatter camp, as well as his own emotional reaction to the destruction of their "pondok" (shack, lean-to). He is talking to Lena on a bare stage, with their personal belongings—a few pots, pans, bottles, and the makings of a lean-to—piled about them. The excited description is pure narrative, enhanced by the gestures and mocking physical impersonations of Lena and the other squatters reacting to the event. In the midst of this, Boesman turns to Lena and forcibly demands her attention. "Listen now." he says, "*I'm going to use a word*" [my emphasis].

The word in this case is *Freedom,* and the play has been structured around that concept and the possible nuances of meaning it—and its antithesis—may have. But the word, and the concept itself, have their roots in the generative visual image described above: two people carrying their lives on their backs. Thus "Freedom" for Boesman and Lena becomes a Thoreauesque desire for casting off the coils of possession, of shedding the load of the past and even of one's life, of the self. "Heavy" is the word most often on Lena's lips, and it is applied to herself, her physical body, and to her own life.

This is a concept mirrored exactly in the images Fugard supplies in his play. The empty stage, the burdened actors, the description of the razing of the shacks. But Boesman, the uneducated castout, seeks to define that image, that thought, by encapsulating it in a word: the one, single, defining, and final word. By giving the thought a name—*Freedom*—that image and word become one.

Every single play Fugard has written contains this idea of *the word* in some form or another—even the plays workshopped under his guidance (from *The Coat* to *The Island*). It is the word as a means of coming to terms with, defining, explaining, gaining control of a reality the characters have difficulty comprehending. Not that the word is the same in each case, or even a single word, though certain words— Freedom, the Future, Truth—do reoccur often enough to become thematic. It can also be a phrase, a thought, or a verbal game of some kind. Whatever form it takes, the word derives from the theme that derives from the original generating image. But once set, it signals the key scenes in the play, becomes in a sense the verbalized image of the play's fundamental focus and the issues surrounding it. Basically this concept of *the word* appears in two guises in the plays: as *the word/idea/thought* and as *a name.*

In the first case, a character will consciously use a word, a single word, often prefacing it with the warning that the word is to be used, or with some indication of the importance the word has for the situation or for the character's own thinking. Thus for example:

That's a big word. . . . Money. It could mean security. . . (*Nongogo*)

. . . independent. A big word isn't it? (*No Good Friday*)

That's a word, hey! Brothers! . . . (*The Blood Knot*)

There's a word—beer does it in the dark—Brewing! (*Hello and Goodbye*)

What's the word? Birth. Death. Both. Jesus did it in the Bible. (PAUSE) Resurrection. (*Hello and Goodbye*)

I used to think the right word for me was numb. There wasn't any Feeling. (*People Are Living There*)

Remember your words when we jumped off. . . . Heavy words, Winston. . . . 'Farewell Africa.' (*The Island*)

I'm proud! . . . I teach my children how to spell that word. (*Statements After an Arrest Under the Immorality Act*)

Caring. Not the most exciting of words, is it? Almost as humble as a tool. But that is the Alchemist's Stone of human endeavour. . . (*Dimetos*)

You know what the really big word is, Helen? . . . I used to think it was 'love.'. . . But there's an even bigger one. Trust. (*The Road to Mecca*)

Home? Don't use that word. I don't know what it means anymore. (*A Place with the Pigs*)

. . . my head was trying to deal with that one word: the Future! . . . what does he really mean? (*My Children, My Africa*)

On occasion the word is used on its own, without preamble, but with the same purpose. In such cases the word is often marked out for special emphasis in the printed text, usually with a capital letter—and is intended to be *played* that way in performance, with emphasis, as something strange and new and significant.

In *People Are Living There* Milly recalls: "Every time, every chance—falling stars, black cats, white horses—every wish was Happiness! . . . I had it. That night I mean . . . Happiness." That then is what her party is about: a situation in which she tries to discover/recapture a brief moment of Happiness—or just to understand what the word means. In *A Place with the Pigs* Pavel rages at the pigs who have eaten the butterfly: "This is my punishment Praskovya . . . to watch brutes devour Beauty and then fart . . . to watch them gobble down Innocence and turn it into shit." In *My Children, My Africa* the intellectual Mr. M. also talks in capital letters: "I've been Sweating . . . Because of those animals, the one called Hope, has broken loose and is looking for food. . . . It is as dangerous as Hate and Despair."

Elsewhere the word is on occasion introduced as a "thought" or an "idea," as in *The Blood Knot*:

I like the thought of this little white girl . . . better than our future, . . . It's a warm thought for a man in winter. It's the best thought I ever had and I'm keeping it. . . . Ja, there's a thought there. What about you Morrie? You never had it before? . . . that thought?"

Alongside this word/thought/idea pattern, Fugard also has another phrasing for the concept. It is found in "naming." Virtually each play carries a reference to names in it, and some plays are even structured around the concept, such as *Nongogo* and *Sizwe Bansi Is Dead.* Again, by putting a name to something, by being able to call it something, one gains a modicum of understanding of and control over it. The characters often define themselves, their lives and their world in this way. Like Sophia in *Dimetos:* "If I'm not a servant what am I? Mother? Sister? . . . There's also 'friend' 'companion'. . . if the others are too personal. How do you see me Dimetos? Who am I?" To Dimetos the answer is simple, initially at least, yet somehow it remains complex, even unfathomable. It lies in a name: Sophia. Later in the play Sophia finds herself redefined in terms of another name:

> DIMETOS: I have no argument left, Sophia. . . least of all with my fate.
> SOPHIA: So I've finally got an identity. Not mother, sister, companion or friend . . . but your fate.
> DIMETOS: Part of it.

Knowing your name—or the name for what you are—has ontological status, becomes an insight into a fundamental truth. "Where do I begin?" asks the former prostitute Queeny in *Nongogo,* and Johnny replies that "there is a name for everything." So she comes up with a name: "Nongogo. A woman for two and six." It is who she is, what life has made her. Admitting that she was a prostitute becomes the crucial moment in the play. It becomes "Acceptance" to use a Fugard-like formulation.

In *Sizwe Bansi Is Dead* the questions surrounding identity and a name gain a physical dimension in the structure and presentation of the play itself, as Sizwe Bansi switches passbooks—and accordingly identities, lives, status—with a dead man, Robert Zwelinzima, so that he may have access to a job in the city. And it frightens him: "I don't want to lose my name, Buntu. . . . Don't make jokes, Buntu. Robert . . . Sizwe . . . I'm all mixed up. Who am I?" His new friend, Buntu, is more practical: "Look, if someone was to offer me the things I wanted most in my life, the things that would make me, my wife, and my child happy, in exchange for the name Buntu . . . You think I wouldn't swop?" What's in a name after all? Nothing but a (new) life. Perhaps.

Names and naming abound in *"Master Harold" . . . and the boys.* Thus when the crisis arises in the relationship between Sam and Hally/Master Harold, it is physically shown in a number of images—Sam dropping his trousers and Hally spitting in his face, for example; but it is given its most telling verbal form in Hally's insistence that Sam change his mode of address:

> HALLY: (Pause as Hally looks for something to say) To begin with, why don't you also start calling me Master Harold, like Willie.
> . . .
> SAM: (Quietly and very carefully) If you make me say it once, I'll never call you anything else again.
> HALLY: So? (The boy confronts the man.) Is that meant to be a threat?

The attitudes provoked by the names people are called in the course of the action roar through the play like a wildfire thereafter, turning it into one of Fugard's most effective attacks on hypocrisy and racism.

An interesting and more extended form of naming occurs in what may be called the "naming game." Found in many of the plays, it is normally used to prepare the way for the central theme or to reinforce it. In *"Master Harold" . . . and the boys*, for example, the naming game involves the names of heroes, that is, possible role models for a confused and impressionable Hally. Sam constitutes such a model for both Hally and Willie, and the play explores the pressures brought to bear on that delicate relationship by psychological and social forces raging within and around the three characters. The physical equivalent of the naming game is the dancing lesson Willie receives from Sam. It is another image to be carried through and worked out in the rest of the play.

In *Nongogo*, when Sam facetiously tries to help Patrick select a name for his soon to be born child, it also turns into a game. They try out and discard a number of names, for as Patrick says, a name is "all I'm ever likely to give it." As the question of the name crops up at various points further on in the play, it begins to accumulate more and more weight, until it climaxes in Queeny's single-word admission of her previous life/occupation: "Nongogo." The game establishes and reinforces the central image of the play—a woman for two and six—and sets up the moment of revelation and acceptance, when Queenie reappears in the final scene: dressed to kill.

The game has a slightly different function in the opening scenes of *Hello and Goodbye*. Johnny is shown counting off the seconds, naming the items surrounding him, and planning his moves for the next day, in an effort to retain his sanity, to grasp some kind of reality with which to ward off or at least make manageable the unknown, unexplored, and threatening world looming outside the walls of the room. The detailed reality of his memories is in marked contrast to the slight, almost impressionistic set described for the play. Into this naming exercise comes the one name he has forgotten: that of his sister, Hester. She arrives like an alien, a threatening and disruptive influence in the narrow but known world he has managed to create so far.

Lena plays a similar cataloguing game in *Boesman and Lena* when she tries to name all their stops on their road to the place they find themselves now. As if by understanding that and being able to name every place in the right order, she would understand her life. It is possibly futile, as Lena learns when Boesman recites the correct sequence:

> LENA: (pause . . . she is loaded). Is that the way it was? How I got
> here? . . . It doesn't explain anything.
> BOESMAN: I know.
> LENA: Anyway, somebody saw a little bit. Dog and a dead man.
> (They are ready to go.)

Knowing where you came from does not necessarily show you what you have on
your back. All you can do is carry it—say the words, the names, and the images.

Now let us examine *the carnal reality of the stage.*

We have so far seen the word and the image to be inextricably linked in the
texture of Fugard's work. It is around and through this nexus of word/image that
Fugard structures the action of his play—by supporting them with and even
converting them into, individual actions by his characters. In other words by turning
the abstract image/word into the "carnal reality" of an actor in a physical space. It
is clear that, despite the often almost mundanely "realistic" and conventional
seeming surface of the works, Fugard's theater is far from being purely representational
in the popular sense. There is a sparseness, a condensation of time and space, and
a concern with the existential, even amid the seeming trivia of the sets and the
"ordinariness" of the characters, which goes far beyond the surface of the "story."
Yet, unlike his mentor Samuel Beckett (Vandenbroucke 269–70), Fugard deliberately moves into and *uses* the surface of regional realism in parable fashion, making
it a *medium* by which to get his audience to come to grips with issues beyond the
individual, the personal, and the parochial. For to Fugard playwriting is a process of
structuring and exploring a series of intensely laden images and concepts rather than
merely displaying or narrating a conventional story in the usual causal sequence.

What makes this approach work eventually *in the theater* and what has given
Fugard's work the stamina to endure and indeed gain popularity over the course of
three decades is the simple fact with which I began this essay: Fugard is a play*wright,*
a maker of plays who works with living actors to create moments of theater in living
time and space. For him the whole process of writing/making a play is focused on
one thing only: that highlighted moment when the performer moves out into the
three-dimensional space before an audience and lets the image happen: that moment
when the word, the image, and all else takes on physical life, becomes another
human experience to be witnessed, thought through, lived through.

Fugard calls this the "living moment," for which he admits to having a fascination.
He describes it as:

> . . . the actual, the real, the immediate, there before our eyes, even
> if it shares in the transient fate of all living monuments. I suppose
> the theatre uses more of the actual substance of life than any other
> art. What comes anywhere near theatre in this respect except
> possibly the painter using old bus tickets, or the sculptor using junk
> iron and driftwood? The theatre uses flesh and blood, sweat, the
> human voice, real pain, real time. (*Notebooks* 89)

Let us end this discussion then by taking a final look at how a craftsman integrates the image, the word and the actor-in-space-and-time into a "living moment" of theater.

Hello and Goodbye takes place in a set consisting of a pool of light, within which a few pieces of furniture suggest a room. The edge of the light suggests the walls of the room. But the set also suggests that it may all be dream, or like a dream. People appear and disappear randomly, and time and space is in truth fluid—despite the solid furnishings. Hester has given up her hopes of finding the "compensation," realizing it was never there. There is only life. So she moves to the edge of the light, greets Johnny, and leaves. He is lying on the ground, where he had fallen when she had pulled the crutches from under his arms as he revealed the fact of his father's death.

> (Johnnie makes a move as to get up, then sees the crutches some distance away from him on the floor. He stares at them for a few seconds then very laboriously drags himself along the floor to them. With equal effort he holds them upright and goes onto them. He stands still, on one leg for a few seconds, then realizes he is standing on the wrong leg and changes over.)

> JOHNNIE: Why not? It solves problems. Let's face it, a man on his own two legs is a shaky proposition. She said it was all mine. All of it—my inheritance. These, seeds . . . and memories. . . . I've got a reason. I'm a man with a story. . . . What's the word? Birth. Death. Both. Jesus did it in the Bible. (Pause.) Resurrection. (Pause.)
> CURTAIN

By becoming his father, by assuming his crutches—and hence his past—Johnny turns into someone else, far different from the nervous, desperate figure in the opening scene. Taking up the crutches becomes a symbol for taking up the burden of his father's whole life, the trivia of which now lie spread around him in the contents of the boxes. The actual assumption of the burden is not simply verbalized, it is shown, in the image of the man on the crutches; and it is a conscious decision, as both the words and the actions suggest—the subtle touch of switching from one leg to the other, for example. But then the whole event is given another dimension by the introduction of one word with resounding significance in the narrow world Johnny occupies: "Resurrection." As words, images, and actions come together in the little pool of light called the stage, and one is confronted once again with that ultimate Biblical irony whereby to gain eternal life a man must first die, a man on crutches becomes a man resurrected: Johnny's first miracle.

WORKS CITED

Fugard, Athol. *Boesman and Lena and Other Plays.* Cape Town: Oxford UP, 1980.

———. *Notebooks: 1960–1977.* Johannesburg: Ad. Donker, 1983.

———, John Kani, and Winston Ntshona. *Statements. Three Plays.* London: Oxford UP, 1974.

Vandenbroucke, Russel. *Truths the Hand Can Touch: The Theatre of Athol Fugard.* Johannesburg: Ad. Donker, 1986.

Walder, Dennis. *Athol Fugard.* London: Macmillan, 1984.

ATHOL FUGARD'S PUBLISHED WORK

Plays

(First production dates in parentheses)
No-Good Friday (1958), 1977
Nongogo (1959), 1977
The Blood Knot (1961), 1963; revised version, 1987
Hello and Goodbye (1965), 1966
The Coat (1966), 1971
People Are Living There (1968), 1969
Boesman and Lena (1969), 1969
Orestes (1971), 1978
Statements after an Arrest under the Immorality Act (1972), 1974
Sizwe Bansi is Dead (with John Kani and Winston Ntshona) (1972), 1974
The Island (with John Kani and Winston Ntshona) (1973), 1974
Dimetos (1975), 1977
A Lesson from Aloes (1978), 1981
"Master Harold" . . . and the boys (1982), 1982
The Road to Mecca (1984), 1985
A Place with the Pigs (1987), 1988

Unpublished plays

The Drummer (1980)
My Children, My Africa (1989)

Film Scripts

The Occupation: A Script for Camera, 1968
Mille Miglia (broadcast, 1968)
The Guest: An Episodes in the Life of Eugene Marais (broadcast, 1977), 1977
Boesman and Lena (released, 1973)
Marigolds in August (with Ross Devenish) (released, 1980), 1982

Novel

Tsotsi, 1980

Memoir

Notebooks: 1960-1977 (edited by Mary Benson), 1983

SELECTED CRITICAL READINGS

For almost two decades Athol Fugard has held center stage in critical studies of South African drama and theater. Internationally he has been seen as a solitary genius, towering above his South African contemporaries, and it has taken a long time for that mistaken assumption to be rectified by scholars prepared to go beyond the confines of published plays and plays produced in English alone. Today he is more properly viewed as one of the prime catalysts—and one of the crowning glories—of an evolving theatrical tradition that had its roots in the mid-1950s. Both inside the country and beyond its borders, the interest in Fugard has escalated remarkably over the past ten years, with postgraduate studies of his work proliferating all over the world, especially in South Africa, England, Australia, and the United States.

However, only two book-length studies have been published to date, neither of them by a South African scholar. Perhaps the most obvious problem for all scholars, and certainly a major point of debate all along, has been Fugard's political position and the role his works have played (or have not played) in advancing the struggle for a just society in South Africa. It is a dilemma demonstrated by the bibliography provided here.

Durbach, Errol. "*'Master Harold' . . . and the boys*: Athol Fugard and the Psychology of Apartheid." *Modern Drama* 30 (1987): 505–13. Sees Fugard's "confessional" play as the record of "a rite of passage clumsily negotiated," one which addresses the actual psychopathology of apartheid, not the temporary and superficial political symptoms represented by the laws and follies of the current regime.

English in Africa 9.2 (1982). Special number dedicated to Fugard on his fiftieth birthday. Contains an interview, two articles on Fugard's work by Margaret Munro and Sheila Roberts, and a discussion of the Fugard Collection in the National English Literary Museum.

Gray, Stephen, editor. *Athol Fugard.* Johannesburg: McGraw-Hill, 1982. Provides a useful introduction to Fugard through a wide-ranging collection of articles, interviews, and reviews—many of them difficult to obtain elsewhere. Includes a chronology, biography, bibliography as well as critical articles by ten major Fugard scholars.

Green, Michael. "'The Politics of Loving'—Fugard and the Metropolis." *World Literature Written in English* 27 (1987): 5–17. Discusses the debate around Fugard studies, and Fugard's acceptance inside and outside South Africa. Stresses the need perhaps to redefine the parameters of criticism and the criteria used in approaching the work.

Gussow, Mel. "Witness." *The New Yorker* 20 Dec. 1982: 47–94. Detailed portrait of Fugard and the way he works, based on in-depth interviews and a sensitive insight into the works of the playwright.

Hauptfleisch, Temple, and Ian Steadman. *South African Theatre: Four Plays and an Introduction.* Pretoria: De Jager-HAUM Educational, 1984. Seeks to place the work of Fugard within the wider context of South African theater in general. Sees him as part of an evolving tradition rather than as a solitary phenomenon in a barren cultural landscape. Contains the text of *Hello and Goodbye* as well as a critical assessment of the author's place in the evolution of the tradition.

Kavanagh, Robert. *Theatre and Cultural Struggle in South Africa.* London: Zed Books, 1985. Contends that the true history of South African theater lies in the "Majority Theatre," which arose in the black townships of the country from the late 1950s onward in reaction to political dominance by whites. Places Fugard's early work in this context, concentrating on *No-Good Friday*, and finds his work supportive of the dominant ideology in the country.

Orkin, Martin. "Body and State in *Blood Knot/ The Blood Knot.*" *South African Theatre Journal* 2 (1988): 17–34. Compares the original and the revised texts of the seminal Fugard play. Goes beyond the usual ("political/universal") dichotomy, to look at how the physical "body" and attitudes toward it function in the relationship between the brothers as well as how the state— as outside force —interpellates and subjects that body.

Theatre Quarterly 7 (Winter 1977–78): 44–95. Features a survey of the theater in South Africa, edited by Russel Vandenbroucke. Besides important contextual material (a chronology and select bibliography; articles on Afrikaans, English, and Black theater), contains an interview with Mary Benson and comments on Fugard by a variety of performers and directors.

Vandenbroucke, Russel. *Truths the Hand Can Touch: The Theatre of Athol Fugard.* New York: Theatre Communications Group, 1985. Stresses the "universal" qualities of Fugard's writing, beyond the parochially political, in a detailed analysis of all the plays, scripts, and other writings. A thorough study, with a solid biographical base, providing an important portrait of Fugard as a complete man of the theater.

Walder, Dennis. *Athol Fugard.* London: Macmillan, 1984. (New York: Grove Press, 1985) Introduction to Fugard and his works that stresses the sociopolitical background heavily. An overriding criterion in discussing each play is the extent to which it (consciously or unconsciously) appears to reflect and even has the potential to subvert the evils of apartheid.

Wertheim, Albert. "The Prison as Theatre and the Theatre as Prison." *The Theatrical Space, Themes in Drama 9.* Cambridge: Cambridge UP, 1987. Looks at Fugard's use of the physical stage itself to explore the ramifications of the central image of "imprisonment"—and hence also of "freedom," a favorite theme in much of Fugard's work. A number of the playwright's dramaturgical techniques are illustrated in the analysis.

Wortham, Chris. "A Sense of Place: Home and Homelessness in the Plays of Athol Fugard." *Olive Schreiner and After.* Cape Town: David Philip, 1983. Focuses on the so-called Port Elizabeth plays to illustrate the ways in which Fugard uses the local and the regional as essential material through which to explore a metaphysical and even transcendental search for self in each of his characters.

—TEMPLE HAUPTFLEISCH

Gwen Harwood

Gwen Harwood was born Gwen Foster in Brisbane, Australia, 8 June 1920, and spent "early years of great happiness" with her younger brother, parents, and grandmother in a household full of music and verse. After leaving school she studied piano and composition under a well-known musician and Handel scholar. On his advice she decided against a concert career, instead working for and obtaining her teacher's diplomas in music. While teaching as his associate, she was also appointed organist at All-Saints' Church in Brisbane. In these years, she explored music, theology, and philosophy with friends and visitors. She was an accompanist in lieder and very active in the musical life of Brisbane. This life the Second World War abruptly halted.

In 1945, Gwen Foster married Bill Harwood, whom she had met through a mutual friend, and left Brisbane to move to Hobart, where her husband was taking up an appointment in the English department at the University of Tasmania. She recalls feeling "an anguish I had never known" as she stepped from the plane to confront the cool, moist landscape of a Tasmanian summer. Her activity as a practicing musician was arrested and domestic responsibilities supervened.

At this time, through her husband, she first encountered the work of Wittgenstein, which became the major focus of her philosophical interests and later an important point of departure for her poetry. They had four children and "from a kind of domestic slumber" she began to write and publish poetry under her own name and several pseudonyms. Her first book was published in 1963, by which time she had returned to work as a medical secretary and was beginning to involve herself actively in music again. Four more books, including a *Selected Poems*, have followed. Beginning with "The Fall of the House of Usher" for composer Larry Sitsky in 1965, Harwood has also written texts for several Australian composers in opera, cantata, choral symphony, and other forms.

Gwen Harwood has received numerous awards for her work, including the *Meanjin* Poetry Prize in 1958 and 1959, the Robert Frost Award in 1977, the Patrick White Award in 1978, and a Literature Board of the Australia Council Fellowship, 1973-1976. After her husband's retirement, they spent ten years on a bush property of five acres at Oyster Cove. They currently live in Hobart, Tasmania.

LIFE SENTENCES

Members of modern intellectual and artistic avant-gardes often regard it as a necessity for serious consideration that one be "at the center of things," at or close by some vital, creative, and usually very urban place. Remote from such cynosures, colonial writers of the past often suffered through versions of this notion, and so do their successors at times. Yet there is no reason, other than for fashion's sake, why originality should be thus gregarious. The work of Gwen Harwood ignores the boundaries drawn by insistence on the cosmopolitan and international. Harwood lives in Hobart, Tasmania, and has for nearly thirty years written poetry that engages the work of Blake, Heine, and Wittgenstein, that ponders music and quantum physics, without relinquishing a precise and local eye and ear. As much a familiar figure at the Hobart Public Library, scanning the latest issue of *Mind*, as in her dinghy, watching for the twitch on her fishing-line, she has produced a body of work governed by the desire at once to analyze and integrate a complex dialectic of passion and intellect, loss and salvage, parish and globe.

A series of renunciations brought Gwen Harwood at last to poetry. By the time she came to writing as an active vocation (though with roots that stretch back to earliest childhood love for lyric, hymn, and rhyme) she had already absorbed or relinquished a number of lives: a concert career, the heady intellectual excitement of the late 1930s, the tropical landscape and climate of Brisbane. Perhaps many others could offer a similar tale of that time, but for Gwen Harwood these dislocations seem to have formed a pattern of echoing loss and recompense that has organized much of her poetry. But though drawn to the elegiac mode, by both history and temperament, Harwood has always chastened elegy from sentimentality through the very strength of the hunger for recovery that first set it in motion. "Recovery" here must be understood to contain two equal vectors, often in tension with one another: the return of the lost through some figurative translation (into dream, memory, talisman, or haunting), and the repair of the elegist. But since recovery in the former sense is very likely the occasion of relapse in the latter, a continuous dialectic or cycle is sketched out. An early poem published in 1949, "The Fire-Scarred Hillside," shows these elements present from the first. An acute eye for particulars of color, movement, and line is coupled with a strong sense of life at once resilient and intensely fragile, as painful as persistent:

> Rocks are held in the air
> torn up with the twisting never-relaxing roots,
> carried by the ram's horn buckle and fast held coil
>   from where the thin grass shoots
> to mark with an eyelash fringe the hollow gouge in the soil.
> . . .
>   Creatures here are small;
> rock-coloured spiders, lizards in restless sleep
> hide in the stones—oh, but the birds are bright—
>   see in a flickering sweep
> the airboned finches, the dear flamebreasted robin alight.

There is at once stillness and surprising motion here, as of something beginning to stir, even if this means a return from one pain to another in the thrusting forth of "new leaves (fantastic spears) to the rain or the wind's shock." "All here is tense," says another stanza, and tension becomes both mood and method. Despite some rhythmical sponginess, a link to Hopkins emerges clearly (especially the Hopkins of "Pied Beauty"), in the shared sense of pain and regeneration as sacramental counterparts. It is very much a trial poem, and a poem of coming *through* trial, but in the burnt Australian slope the poet already has a moving trope for her own combination of earliness and lateness, the particular burden of her own "new leaves." In stubbornness and serenity, the "dark, inflexible trees" reach down deep beneath the scarring, as their branches hold "in a crooked frame" the landscape "clean-pencilled, lovely in line and fold." There is a whole poetics here, uniting roots and leaves, pain and poetry.

Despite this budding, it was not until around 1960 that Harwood's work began to appear regularly in Australian journals. Andrew Taylor has described her appearance at this time on the scene of Australian poetry as "a period of excitement and also of bewilderment." The latter response stems from Harwood's use of several pseudonyms, both then and later, so that tracking her work became something of a puzzle for readers: Was this a single poet, or a remarkable new school "of virtuoso technical accomplishment, wit and insight?" (Taylor 73). Some of these pseudonyms were tactical—her work was at one point banned from *The Bulletin*, because of an acrostic poem of which the editors, when they noticed it too late, disapproved. Jennifer Strauss has suggested that the various names were used "in order to get an unprejudiced hearing" (335), though there is no evidence that this was a motive. But in fact Harwood's use of pen names predates these incidents, which only served to reinforce an impulse towards shape-shifting already in play. Rather the pseudonyms are a ludic device by which the poet projects divisions from within her work onto the level of authorial ascription. The pen name "Miriam Stone" offers an example of this impulse to mask: Stone's poems treat especially the frustration and despair of women locked in domesticity to the stagnation of their other needs. Clearly a version of Harwood's experience in Hobart haunts such poems as "Suburban Sonnet" or "Burning Sappho," but their ascription to the emblematic "Miriam Stone" allows bitterness to emerge as one aspect of a composite poetic sensibility, elements of which can be distinguished by giving them separate names. The impulse to follow out and analyze the tensions within an image or situation, as in "Fire-Scarred Hillside," reappears at another level. The use of pseudonyms is in this way consistent with Harwood's method elsewhere in her earlier poems, and it should not be surprising, in retrospect, that a poet as committed to dialectical tension as Harwood should experiment in this way with alter egos. Indeed the opening poem of her first book carries this very title, "Alter Ego," and imagines, through the structure of Mozart's music, the possibility of multiple historical selves being subsumed synchronically "beyond/Time's desolating drift" if only the right light or mode of consciousness could be found to glimpse them in.

This deliberate heightening of ambivalences in search of the point where they can be not merely contained but synthesized is a fundamental method of Gwen Harwood's poetry of the 1960s. The poems are in general tightly organized in formal units (stanzas, sonnets), and yet emotional disputes and intellectual contradictions struggle within them. Such strain functions, paradoxically, at once to complicate and to clarify, serving the operation of a careful moral intelligence, which weaves its judgments through its registration of details. These can be details of diction, image, rhythm, sometimes all three. In the sonnet "In the Park," for example, a woman first discusses her joy in her children with a chance-met former lover. But then alone, "nursing/The youngest child, [she] sits staring at her feet/To the wind she says, 'They have eaten me alive.'" It is a powerful evocation of despair at potential denied and self violated. But even this conclusion is not embraced in isolation from larger concerns, and the dialectical turn of Harwood's moral intelligence appears in a rhythmic detail that uncovers a latent commentary. The careful enjambment after "nursing" moves the iconic image of the despairing woman towards a famous Blakean "Proverb of Hell": "Sooner murder an infant in its cradle than nurse unacted desires." Sympathy for the woman is not thereby erased, far from it, but her dilemma begins to be integrated with general moral questions of the kind Blake opens. Measured against Blake's counter proposition, she becomes a parabolic figure for a certain trapped apprehension of experience—no longer an object either of easy sentiment or equally easy rage. At the same time Harwood displays and interprets her own relation to Blakean models, making explicit the female figures of both frustration and rebellion in the proverb.

More complex instances of this shifting play of ironic framings are provided by the closing sequence of Harwood's first book, featuring Professor Eisenbart, illustrious descendant of the doctor-hero of a German comic song, an ancestor he might disdain in public but privately welcome. Eisenbart's discomforts and discomfitures are arrayed about the ambivalences that attend the aging of this eminent physicist and sensualist in his sexual relationships first with a beautiful young woman, then with an adolescent boy. Harwood's poems attempt to render Eisenbart's delicate calculus between, on the one hand, the theatricality of his language and self-performance, and, on the other, the pain and need they attempt self-consciously to publish. At the zoo with his youthful mistress, for example, aging Eisenbart finds the stares of the public (who also stare at an ape) disconcerting—too close to a reminder of his own ridiculous vulnerability. Aggression, anxiety, disdain, and impotence play through one another in his retort, which both his own rhythmic anticlimax and his mistress's mock approbation deftly puncture:

> "Glutted with leisure
> dull-coupled citizens and their buoyant young
> gape at your elegant freedom, and my face
> closed round the cares of power, see with mean pleasure
> age scaling massive temples overhung
> with silver mists of hair—that handspan space
>
> corners their destiny at my word they'll bear
> acerebrate hybrid monsters. Fiat nox!
> Let the dark beast whose cat-light footpads scour
> my cortex barren leap from its cage and tear
> their feathers out!"
> His mistress said, "What shocks

await the bourgeois!" ("Panther and Peacock")

The poem patterns its emblems—panther, peacock, ape, lovers—in complex and ironic dialectic. Eisenbart's assurance and his anxiety emerge as siamese twins: transformed to the vain peacock in his dream, he is himself ripped apart by the panther. Dream and poem leave him in a shadowy middle state as "His mind . . . groped worldwards," balanced between terror and comfort, life and death, frozen by a premonition of mortality into the attitude of a *pietà*, over which his mistress bends as the Virgin. The aggressively ironic detachment Eisenbart so carefully cultivates is thus revealed, over the course of the sequence, to be the agony of a between-state that can achieve no uncontaminated consummation of either desire or aggression. Despite his vision of himself as an eagle of sexual rapine, his Aschenbach-like encounter with the boy in "Ganymede" ends in impotence and derisive laughter. In the final poem, "Group from Tartarus," his concluding motto, straddling pathos and melodrama, becomes "Too old to love, too young to die."

The intellectual sensibility, which generates these balanced analytic discriminations, suggests at times also the tradition of philosophical lyric that springs from the seventeenth century and includes Donne's love poetry and Marvell's dialogues of soul and body, a line reappearing more recently in Yeats, echoes of whom are also to be found in Harwood's work. These poems seek to address and analyze experience by arguing several competing perspectives on it against one another. As the dialogues stage a debate before an audience of interested readers, so these poets move into the realm of public utterance, inviting the readers to follow a specific topic or proposition through its back-and-forth progress. It is their various practice of such poetic dialectic that brings these poets together with Blake and Hopkins into Harwood's work. In her poems confrontations are frequently staged not only between parties, but also between levels of style. As in older dialogic poems in this tradition, often the jostle of forces emerges into explicit personifications. "I Am the Captain of My Soul" offers its title as a metaphor that at once generates a series of heuristic personfications around the "topic" of its epigraph:

"The human body is the best picture of the human soul."
—Wittgenstein
But the Captain is drunk, and the crew
hauling hard on his windlass of fury are whipped
by his know-nothing rage. Their terror
troubles the sunlight. "Now tell me,"
the Captain says, as his drunkenness
drifts into tears, "what's to keep me
at ease in this harbour?"

The Captain's pain, a generalized grief, is closely related to the impulse to elegy already noted in Harwood's work. The "crew" are Hands, Eyes, and Body, and each tries in turn to mollify or chasten the Captain, "I," as he rages and "gulps/from his flagon of grief," by offering palliatives or sublimations. The Captain, however, will not be comforted with such evasions and sticks to his grief like an old wino, stubborn and incapable. The ancient allegorical figure of the ship of life is tensed into a small philosophical drama on the subject of pain, its corrosiveness, inevitability, and secret metamorphoses:

> "We'll tell you,"
> say Hands, "in our headlong chase through a fugue
>
> for three voices, you heard a fourth voice naming
> divisions of silence. We'll summon
> that voice once again, it may tell you
> of marvels wrung from sorrow endured."
> "We have seen," says Eyes, "how in Venice
> the steps of churches open and close
> like marble fans under water."

> "You can rot in your sockets," the Captain cries.

The poem's analytic distinctions turn towards the violent in the abrupt leap from the mannered aestheticism of Hands' Venice (probably derived from Ruskin) to the Captain's piratical cursing. Argument threatens to turn into quarrel, and diction to break out of the restraining frame of the allegory. But the allegory, the variety of diction, the formal process of the dialogue all maintain the air of a public performance, even of an intensely private existential dilemma.

Harwood's first book often runs contrasts of diction forcibly into one another, running the risk of damage to a reader's momentum: Simple syntax can be juxtaposed against weighty polysyllable, or homely against grotesque image. The result is to increase the sense of the containment of powerful contraries but not in some mysterious intrapsychic space of the poet's poetical ego. Rather these questions are to be shared by a community of inquirers out of the fact of their common experience of pain, love, grief, terror. The stretching for a language at once precise and heightened occasionally leads to strange effects, as for example in "Clair de Lune":

> Let us walk with this cone of light
> lying seaward. It points where earth's ashen
> impoverished fragment importunes
> all oceans and lovers and poets,
> whose waxing has made and whose waning
> unmade you, whose wall-scaling tinsel
> has captured your visored city.

Though the risk such work runs is of eroding clarity, its rewards are a richly energetic and baroque texture of complex modulations.

Less disintegrative but employing a similar strategy of allegoresis to discern multiple levels of response is "Triste, Triste," a post-coital meditation around the philosophy of human sexual experience. Here the discrete elements, "spirit," "heart," "body" each seek release into a paradise, but their needs interfere with one another. Some brief reconciliation is achieved only in the marginal and passive space of sleep:

> In the space between love and sleep
> when heart mourns in its prison
> eyes against shoulder keep
> their blood-black curtains tight.
> Body rolls back like a stone, and risen
> spirit walks to Easter light;
>
> away from its tomb of bone,
> away from the guardian tents
> of eyesight, walking alone
> to unbearable light with angelic
> gestures. The fallen instruments
> of its passion lie in the relic
>
> darkness of sleep and love.
> And heart from its prison cries
> to the spirit walking above:
> "I was with you in agony.
> Remember your promise of paradise,"
> and hammers and hammers, "Remember me."
>
> So the loved other is held
> for mortal comfort, and taken,
> and the spirit's light dispelled
> as it falls from its dream to the deep
> to harrow heart's prison so heart may waken
> to peace in the paradise of sleep.

What could be more ordinary, even banal, than sleep after sex? The problem here is to find language to convey the deep import of that banality, its vital crosscurrents. The language is typical of Gwen Harwood's solution to this problem in her first book. Meter and diction are at once precise and evocative. The scene and mood of the love poem and the reworking of the Passion are digested together into the formulation of a purely human Redemption, which provides a means of talking about "the ordinary" in a way that catches the crucial interest and mystery of that category of experience. Intellectual abstraction and the use of the familiar archetypal narrative afford language cool enough to clarify a sentiment that might otherwise cloy. Hence again the lack of any sense of the egoistic "confessional" or the self-dramatizing about the poem: It speaks in public of private experience in an attempt to find a language adequate to the complex texture of an experience no less compelling for being ordinary. This is the "ordinary" understood in a fuller sense than a description of the mundane event or a limitation to the chronicle. It is revealed to contain modes of knowledge and feeling in themselves philosophical or containing philosophy if scrutinized. Here the results of Harwood's extensive meditation on Wittgenstein begin to be felt most originally. It is as though to the gnomic beginning of his *Tractatus*, "The world is everything that is the case," Harwood were responding by attempting to explore and coordinate some of the many cases into which the world can be declined. How many cases has "desire," for example? Does each of them decline, or accept, the world differently? "Ordinary" experience would then become a category of immense import, and the world be opened to philosophy and poetry in far-reaching ways. In the exploration of what languages will transfigure the ordinariness of the most powerful emotions (by which I do not mean their triviality) are also to be found the traces of Harwood's extensive reading in American poetry, in Emily Dickinson, in Robert Frost, and especially in Robert Penn Warren, with whom in particular she has expressed a deep affinity.

Pain is a complex and ordinary experience of just this kind. Harwood's poems are full of pain: physical, emotional, spiritual, intellectual, dreamed, suffered, inflicted, resolved, or even sharpened, by the precision of the language found for it. "At the Water's Edge," "Daybreak," "Group from Tartarus," "Iris" imagine pain as the stabbing of a beak—something that strikes from above, from the realm of those weirdly figurative beings, birds, that sing like us but are not part of "our" mammal world. Fastening on this most personal and yet most ineffable of experience of events, Harwood takes it as opening onto the fundamentally mysterious mapping between language and the world, as it did also for Wittgenstein because it poses most urgently the question of adequate communication. As pain becomes more complex, so too must the modes of describing and accounting for it. Perspectives multiply and compete. Two people, or two versions of the same person—say, sleeping and waking, or present and past—may require different languages to describe their experience of it. Nor may these languages be easily separable but may speak through one another, if one is, for example, telling the story of a nightmare from which one has just awakened. "Fido's Paw Is Bleeding," written with the mock simplicity of a childhood rhyme, addresses the problem of languages for pain through four exemplary figures, each with a particular version of "language-use."

> Fido's paw is bleeding.
> Fido's master finds the cut,
> puts a nice clean bandage on,
> gives his pet a slice of meat.
>
> Fido's paw is hurting.
> Fido cannot offer proof.
> Fido's master tries to ease it
> when his dog begins to whimper
> how could he withhold belief?
>
> Master's heart is broken.
> Master's mistress left his roof.
> Did she find his house oppressive?
> Who can tell—she would not speak,

> Simply packed her gear and left.
> Polly screeches, "Shut your beak!"
> Polly isn't talking sense. . . .

Philosophical jokes abound here about the relation of linguistic behavior to experienced states and in what way the former can be said to index or express the latter. Later, Fido will begin faking pain to gain attention as Master turns to poetry to measure out his grief. Each instance comments tacitly on the others: Polly's rote on Master's metrical sorrow, Fido's silent pain on Polly's mechanism, and so on.

"Fido's Paw" is one of the last of Harwood's poems to use the allegorical method of argument: Its comic success is in part the result of a sense of the mechanical about the procedure itself. In its place have come poems less discursively intellectual, with the look of personal anecdotes (even when they are not in fact so). In fact such poems are not a new development, being present as early as "A Postcard" from the poet's first book. But beginning with the "New Poems" section of the *Selected Poems*, with poems such as "Dust to Dust" and "Father and Child," they have become more urgent as they answer a growing need to spell experience as directly as possible into a language of parable. Hence the turn of recent work more and more to memory, elegy, and dream.

Consider the title poem of *The Lion's Bride* for example. The parabolic nature of this sonnet is at once apparent and, though based immediately on Schumann, its true forebear is the Blake of the *Songs of Experience*, who seems an urgent presence early in the volume:

> I loved her softness, her warm human smell,
> her dark mane flowing loose. Sometimes stirred by
> rank longing laid my muzzle on her thigh.
> Her father, faithful keeper, fed me well,
> but she came daily with our special bowl
> barefoot into my cage, and set it down:
> our love feast. We became the talk of the town,
> brute king and tender woman, soul to soul.
>
> Until today: an icy spectre sheathed
> in silk minced to my side on pointed feet.
> I ripped the scented veil from its unreal
> head and engorged the painted lips that breathed
> our secret names. A ghost has bones, and meat!
> Come soon my love, my bride, and share this meal.

As Shakespeare's Pyramus would put it: "Lion vile hath here deflowered his dear." Norman Talbot has discussed a fourfold generic pattern he finds in the poem, whereby the lion is at once hero, saint, victim, and fool. However this may be, the "brute" lion is clearly a literalist of the emotions, with no tolerance for the mediation of the figurative imagined in the bridal veil. His understanding of love, heroic but limited, is glossed by his ingestion of his love as a meal, turning the figurative incantations of marriage ("and they shall be one flesh") into a grisly reality. His vigor and sensuality rebel against any attempt at symbolic abstraction. No nobility of tone is lost thereby—the lion is not conscious of anything amiss—but something is certainly lost—the possibility of figurative transcendence by deferral represented in the veil. The poem is another version—with a different outcome—of "Triste, Triste." "Human" life is not to be satisfied with the literal only—it smells of mortality. It is the figure that gives life.

A similar point appears in a later poem of the same volume, "A Valediction," and allows us to see the continuum between the "biographical" poems and others not directly so. The occasion of the poem appears to be the death of a former love. It is therefore a work of mourning—as so many of Harwood's more recent poems are—whose principal task is to rescue what it can from mortality for the living through the work of the figurative. In this case Donne, or more particularly, the history of Harwood's own interactions with Donne, provides the saving mediation. Donne is revealed to have been figurative of Harwood's experience from the very first. The words of "his" text have become inextricably sedimented with "her" history, which they both represent and transfigure. Donne's poetry can console not only because it speaks itself of valediction, but because it bears in its very words the history it is being asked to farewell. Having troped the mourner's experience, once, it can do so again:

> As always after parting. I
> get from its place the Oxford Donne,
> inked in with aches from adolescence.
>
> Who needs drugs if she has enough
> uppers and downers in her head?
> Though names are not engraved herein,
>
> who can be literally dead
> if he leaps from an underlining
> into my flesh at *The Sunne Rising*?

The latter question insists on the miraculous conservation performed by the plasticity of language, its fostering of human meanings that resist time's erasure. The underlinings in Donne are at once part and not part of Donne, and now part and not part of the death of her friend. The words of the dead may be modified in the guts of the living, as Auden insisted, but they also modify those guts in their turn. Here the fact that reading and writing have their own history not of the body allows Harwood to assert the failure of death through the hermetic and magical traces of her own adolescent responses to Donne. Language is always a life sentence.

The consistency of Harwood's interest in what might otherwise seem a miscellany of matters—memory, music, dreams, analytic philosophy, quantum physics—becomes explicable when viewed from the perspective of her concern for the interpenetration of contraries. Quantum physics insists on the undecideability of certain questions about the presence or absence of phenomena, just as memory's traces maintain a constant, often painful presence-in-absence for the past, no more to be dismissed as "mere illusion" than the vexations of dreaming. Music, memory, and dream share the ability to collapse the diachronic into the synchronic (and to reverse this process), and to transfigure divergent ideas and images through one another. Music is here a kind of dreaming, memory a kind of lifelong music, linguistic philosophy a creative power, as Vincent Buckley has remarked. So in *Bone Scan*, Harwood's most recent book, a poem to a dead pet cat can be followed by one on a famous modern quantum physics thought-experiment and share more with it than a feline protagonist. Lines such as "In shade a royal presence/watches the sunlit lawn/and the unsuspecting doves" ("A Feline Requiem") have their direct counterparts in:

> ". . . Verily all will not be well
>
> if, to the peril of your souls,
> you think me gone. Know that this house
> is mine, that kittens by mouse-holes
> wait, who have never seen a mouse."
> ("Schrödinger's Cat Preaches to the Mice")

It is contemporary physics' insistence, sometimes an uncanny one, that true absence is an impossibility that makes it attractive to Harwood's imagination, since it translates into an abstract, if paradoxical, system her own interest in the figurative accommodations necessary to continue living in one's own language and memory in a world of mutability. Just as the marks in the Donne volume refute the death of a friend, so the mere existence of doves or mice supports the presence of the spectral cat.

As these latter poems suggest, elegy has formed an increasing part of Harwood's output in her more recent volumes. This newer work is rich with memory, memory that saturates all levels of experience, both sleeping and waking. Even works that are not directed to mourning specific people are colored with the impulse to revise, revisit, and reconcile. The opening poems of *Bone Scan* return to the "Class of 1927" in Harwood's Brisbane primary school and record various events there in which the poet learned or failed to learn lessons of pain and pity. Memory, now become "morbid, chronic/nostalgia," develops into fable before the reader's, and the poet's, eyes. The sense of others' pain and our helpless responsibility for it intensifies with each clearly recalled detail, "in the easiest and most convincing terms, as if this 'shape' were there in the events themselves and they had only to be narrated for it to shine forth" (Malouf 18). Harwood's vocabulary has simplified a great deal in this latest book, relying on direct and evocative monosyllables that begin to carry their own metaphysical charge, without the wrestling that marked the earlier style: clean, clear, light, breath, walk, earth, lapse, change, feast, water, safe. Even as the objects around her in the world have become more directly invocable in the poetry, they have emerged as more direct in their meanings. Allegory appears in these poems less like an inflection of an intellectual stance than as the mode through which objects present themselves in the first place to the gaze. Hence *Bone Scan* concludes with a series of nine poems designated "Pastorals," not only because they are set in and treat the natural world, but because they revive a sense of the mutual reflection and interdependence of world and language on which the pastoral relies, "tuning its pipe unto the waters' fall." The exploration of the landscape of pain is not suspended however, but moves out onto another plane, taking the natural world as its occasion and emblem. If nature itself has no memories, consciousness can find versions of its own structures everywhere embedded in it in ways that at once sharpen and console:

> Two worlds meet in the mirror
>   of the quiet dam. The trees
> lift stem and crown above
>   their own calm images.
>
> Rest, in the heart's dry season,
>   where the green reeds stitch light
> to light, where water levels
>   unendingly the bright
>
> ripple of leaf or wind-breath:
>   inverts the bowl of the sky
> to a cup of deep enchantment,
>   as if some perfect eye
>
> saw memory and substance
>   as one and could restore
> in depth, in flawless detail,
>   time as it was before.
>
> Why does the body harbour
>   no memory of pain,
> while a word, a name unspoken
>   in the mind cuts to the bone?
>
> When time is turned to anguish,
>   lastborn of nature, rest,
> where shade and water offer
>   solace to all who thirst.
> ("Reflections")

The object of attention here is the reflective surface, delicate and tender partition between substance and shadow, and hence between world and mind, flesh and word. The activity of the human is located somewhere along this membrane, in the repairing stitches of inner and outer light, in some impossible unity of trace and presence imagined as a painless language, or perhaps a redeemed body. The pastoral landscape responds to this ideal of integration by providing the eye of anguish with a direct responsive allegory both of its desire ("a perfect eye") and of the impossibility of that desire. Reflection is after all an already alienated state, and only an eye not itself the surface of the water can catch the doubling the mirror performs. Hence the retirement into the saving shade is all that can be offered—in the end not a repair, but a palliation.

In this recent poem, much that was present in "The Fire-Scarred Hillside" can still be discerned: the registration of physical detail, the discovery of the natural emblem, the appropriation of detail and emblem into a complex argument, the diagnosis and transmutation of pain, the use of oppositional pairs of elements. Harwood's poetry belongs to the type that does not undertake a dramatic revision of its fundamental direction over time, but rather becomes more and more the thing it was through assimilating new postures and materials to an established set of procedures. The fire has long receded from "Reflections," but this does not mean that the poetry must suffer a decline in intensity or vigor. On the contrary, the implication of that early poem is that mature growth of foliage is more and more to be expected, that the bed of ashes will continue to fertilize—awaiting some more refining fire to come:

> . . . I hold
> in my unhoused continuing self
> the memory that is wisdom's price
> for what survives and grows beneath
> old skies, old stars.
>
> Fresh mornings rim
> the carapace of night with gold.
> The sandgrains shine, the rockpools brim
> with tides that bear and wash away
> new healing images of day.
> ("Carapace")

WORKS CITED

Buckley, Vincent. "Gwen Harwood: Notes on the Dream." *Gwen Harwood*. Adelaide: Centre for Research in the New Literatures in English, 1987. 65–72.

Malouf, David. "Some Volumes of Selected Poems of the 1970s." *Australian Literary Studies* 10 (1981): 13–21.

Strauss, Jennifer. "The Poetry of Dobson, Harwood and Wright: 'Within the Bounds of Feminine Sensibility'?" *Meanjin* 38 (1979): 334–49.

Taylor, Andrew. "Gwen Harwood: The Golden Child Aloft on Discourse." *Gwen Harwood*. Adelaide: CRNLE, 1987. 73–91

Talbot, Norman. "*The Lion's Bride*: Gwen Harwood's *Liebestod*." *Quadrant* 17.4 (1983): 90–92.

GWEN HARWOOD'S PUBLISHED WORK

Poetry

Poems, 1963
Poems/Volume Two, 1968
Selected Poems, 1975
The Lion's Bride, 1981
Bone Scan, 1988

Libretti

The Fall of the House of Usher (with composer Larry Sitsky), 1974

Memoirs/Childhood Stories/Other Work

"Lamplit Presences." *Southerly* 40 (1980): 247–54.
"Among the Roses." No. 4 *Westerly* (1981): 5–8.
"The Glass Boy." *The Bulletin* 13 Apr. 1982: 77–79.
"Gemini." *Overland* No. 88 (1982): 2–4.
"The Seventh House." *Overland* No. 101 (1985): 13–14.
"Memoirs of a Dutiful Librettist" and "Time Beyond Reason. *Gwen Harwood*. Adelaide: CRNLE, 1987: 1–12 & 13–22.
> Unpublished libretti and words for music include "Lenz; Voices in Limbo," "Fiery Tales," "The Golem," "De Profundis," with Larry Sitsky; "Commentaries on Living," "Symphony No. 8 'Choral,'" with composer James Pemberthy; "Sea Changes," with composer Ian Cugley; "The Waking of the World," "The Golden Crane" (for children), "Northward the Strait," with composer Don Kay.

Letters

Blessed City: Letters to Thomas Riddle, 1943. Sydney: Angus & Robertson, 1990.
> Familiar letters describing the writer's work and life in wartime Brisbane.

SELECTED CRITICAL READINGS

Gwen Harwood is still comparatively neglected in accounts of Australian literature. Though well known within Australia, her work still needs introduction outside it. Extended critical work is sparse, can be difficult to obtain, and often covers the same ground. In part this may be due to Harwood's never having announced a poetic program or engaged in the aesthetic polemics that might position her as an "aspect" of Australian writing. Commentary has yet to explore in detail such questions as the poetry's development over time, its relation to various lyric traditions—English and American as well as Australian, or its use of philosophy and music as medium and metaphor. Future work in these areas is desirable.

Brissenden, R.F. "A Fire-Talented Tongue: Some Notes on the Poetry of Gwen Harwood." *Southerly* 38 (1978): 3–20. Surveys general characteristics and development of the poetry, arguing for a growing simplification of poetic means sustaining a consistent set of concerns. Good introduction.

Buckley, Vincent. "Gwen Harwood: Notes on the Dream." *Gwen Harwood*. Adelaide: CRNLE, 1987. 65–72. Examines the depiction and role of dreams and dream-narratives in Harwood's poems. Explores the complex relations between dreaming, writing, memory, nostalgia, imagination.

Douglas, Dennis. "Gwen Harwood: The Poet as Doppelgänger." *Quadrant* 13.2 (1969): 15–19. Argues for "tension," "balance," and "dual awareness" as crucial terms for and in the poetry. Draws attention to the violence implied in many poems, at both a thematic and dictional level. (Drew reply from A.D. Hope; see citation below).

———. "A Prodigious Dilemma: Gwen Harwood's Professor Eisenbart and the Vices of the Intellect." *Australian Literary Studies* 6 (1973): 77–82. Response to Hope's attack on his earlier piece, defending and extending his position on Harwood's "Professor Eisenbart" sequence.

Hoddinott, Alison. "Gwen Harwood and the Philosophers." *Southerly* 41 (1981): 272-87. Explores Harwood's use of analytic philosophers such as Wittgenstein and Gilbert Ryle as points of departure in her poems. Bases her observations in part on personal knowledge of Harwood and her husband and their intellectual interests.

Hope, A.D. "Gwen Harwood and the Professors." *Australian Literary Studies* 5 (1972): 227–32. (Reprinted in *Native Companions*, Sydney: Angus & Robertson, 1974: 197-203) Draws attention to the sophistication of Harwood's ironies, which he claims Douglas (see above) missed. Demonstrates in detailed reading of "Panther and Peacock."

Lawson, Elizabeth. "Towards the Heart's True Speech: Voice-conflict in the Poetry of Gwen Harwood." *Southerly* 43 (1983): 45–72. Identifies competing "voices," lyric and satiric, in the earlier poems that destabilize one another. Argues that these develop toward a synthesis in the poems about the pianist "Kröte."

O'Sullivan, Vincent. "Voices from the Mirror: Approaching Gwen Harwood." *Gwen Harwood*. Adelaide: CRNLE,1987. 23–40. General, personal introduction. Quotes widely and draws thematic parallels but is somewhat impressionist in approach. Pays some attention to the use of formal structures.

Sellick, Robert, editor. *Gwen Harwood*. Adelaide: CRNLE, 1987. Contains two memoirs and a poem sequence by Harwood, critical essays by O'Sullivan, Talbot, Buckley, and Taylor, and an extensive checklist of works by and on Harwood.

Strauss, Jennifer. "The Poetry of Dobson, Harwood and Wright: 'Within the Bounds of Feminine Sensibility'?" *Meanjin* 38 (1979): 334–49. Discusses these poets as test-cases for the existence of "feminine sensibility," and as viable precursors for an Australian feminist poetry. Decides in the negative on both issues.

Talbot, Norman. ". . . Truth Beyond the Language Game: The Poetry of Gwen Harwood." *Australian Literary Studies* 7 (1976): 241–58. Develops a critical schema for describing recurrent thematic and mythographic patterns in the poetry. Compares this schema with the work of Blake and Stevens.

———. "Boxing the Compass and Squaring the Circle: Quaternary Form in Gwen Harwood's Poems." *Gwen Harwood*. Adelaide: CRNLE, 1987. 41-58. Less about "formal" issues than about "four" as an analytic tool of the imagination. Sees this as a recurrent typological strategy in the poetry, in the shaping of roles such as artist, intellectual, lover, and victim.

Taylor, Andrew. "Gwen Harwood: The Golden Child Aloft on Discourse." *Gwen Harwood*. Adelaide: CRNLE, 1987. 73–91. Uses various post-structuralist positions to undermine the notion of "identity" in some Harwood poems.

—T.G. BISHOP

J.M. Coetzee

J. M. Coetzee was born in Cape Town in 1940 and graduated from the University of Cape Town with two consecutive honors degrees, one in English and one in mathematics. While working as a systems programmer for IBM, he obtained his M.A.; then, after a further spell as systems programmer with International Computers (when he was sent to the Cambridge Mathematical Laboratory), he went to the University of Texas at Austin, where he obtained a doctorate in 1969. After teaching at the State University of New York in Buffalo, he returned to the University of Cape Town in 1972, where he has lectured in the English department on American literature, linguistic criticism, and the eighteenth-century novel.

In 1984 he was appointed Professor of General Literature and is primarily responsible for a postgraduate course in literary studies. The academic distinctions conferred on him are too numerous to list, but he has, among other things, been Butler Professor at the State University of New York and Hinkley Professor at Johns Hopkins. He also holds an honorary doctorate from the University of Strathclyde, a Life Fellowship from his own university, and is a Chevalier dans l'Ordre des Arts et des Lettres and a Fellow of the Royal Society of Literature.

Although a portion of *Dusklands* was written in America, Coetzee has produced the greater part of his fiction in the spare time allowed him by his teaching and research. His novels have received numerous awards: the CNA Prize (twice), the Geoffrey Faber Memorial Prize, the James Tait Black, the Booker, the Prix Estranger Femina, and the Jerusalem prizes.

THE ORACULAR VOICE

At the age of nineteen, J. M. Coetzee published a poem in a student journal at the University of Cape Town. That the piece, "Truth lies sunken," is uneven almost goes without saying, but the comparative immaturity of the poet did not bar him from writing passages of real beauty, passages that adumbrate themes of future novels and murmur with pre-echoes of his strange and haunting voice. Here is the first verse of the poem:

> Truth lies sunken in a well,
> Giving forth two echoes when we call.
> Call, now, call.

Watch the shivering of the image on the water;
Stand, and if you do not breathe,
Watch, and it will follow you,
Though at the bottom of a well,
Copying the frieze of your repose.
So these symbols shine to you,
Reflecting your greater light;
So, as our faces lie upon the water, I call,
And wait to hear the echoes of my call
Collect among our wanderings. (25)

Here access to truth—and even this is not guaranteed—depends on perfect composure, that collectedness and patience in the face of the inscrutable that we witness, say, in *Waiting for the Barbarians*, or *The Life and Times of Michael K.* It is true that in each of the novels, with the exception of *In the Heart of the Country*, there *is* a journey, an anabasis in search of the Truth that stands on a hill, but in every case the active quest for meaning yields to a contemplative inwardness, to the attempted reformation of the image disturbed by the very effort of search, as the sound waves that have fractured the surface of the water in "Truth lies sunken" die away into the silence that might or might not disclose a meaning. This ambivalence, the ambivalence of the "two echoes," is of course a central part of any Coetzee novel and is the locus of some of its dark power. Consulting Truth in this way, the poet-speaker is giving her the status of an oracle and seeking clarity in the midst of confusion; yet his answer is only an echo, a mocking replication of his question in a question. This ought not to surprise us—oracles have traditionally trafficked in frustrating obscurity. We have only to think of the Cumaean sibyl in the sixth book of the *Aeneid*—"obscuris vera involvens"—or of Plutarch's justification in *Moralia* for the verse formerly issued by the pythia at Delphi—"[the god] . . . is not unwilling to keep the truth unrevealed, but he caused the manifestation of it to be deflected, like a ray of light, in the medium of poetry, where it submits to many reflections and undergoes subdivisions." In the Coetzee poem Truth gives forth two echoes. The exact status of that plural is not decided. There are two callers, and, by extension, there might be as many echoes as there are consultants. On the other hand Truth might be the vector of two *contradictory* echoes, and mock the seekers with her own unverifiability. In either case there can be no resolution, and Truth, far from being the simple entity of Plutarch's discourse, becomes a specter of relativity at her very source, in her Democritan well. But, even in the face of this apparently cynical conception of truth that evades detection, the poet enjoins his audience to make the call, knowing in advance that the quest is likely to be defeated, and that truth will finally provide only an echo of its questioning, mimetically rendered in the *inclusion* that frames the adverb "now" in the act of calling. This early poem offers itself as an epigraph for the later novels: It insists on the effort of the quest even in the face of certain and often foreknown defeat. The reason that E. R. Dodds adduces for the popularity of oracles in Ancient Greece can be adduced also for the desperate—the heroically desperate—quest of Coetzee's characters: "The crushing sense of human ignorance and human insecurity, the dread of divine *phthonos*, the dread of *mi-*

asma—the accumulated burden of these things would have been unendurable without the assurance which such an omniscient divine counsellor could give, the assurance that behind the seeming chaos there was knowledge and purpose" (Dodds 75). The knowledge and purpose that ancient oracles seemed to affirm, however, were given the saving form of statement—ambiguous statement, granted, but one that completed the upward rhythm of question with the downward one of answer.

By contrast, the notions of an infinite regression of echoes, or of a sinister silence that teases the inquirer out of thought—these constitute an altogether bleaker proposition, and it is the proposition that Coetzee's fiction often, and his critical writing sometimes, makes. In his introduction to *White Writing*, for example, he projects the South African landscape as a sort of oracle withholding its truth from the poet who consults it:

> . . . the lone poet in empty space is by no means a peripheral figure in South African writing. In the words he throws out to the landscape, in the echoes he listens for, he is seeking dialogue with Africa. . . . What response do rocks and stones make to the poet who urges them to utter their true names? As we might expect, it is silence. Indeed, so self-evidently foredoomed is the quest that we may ask why it persists so long. (8-9)

Clearly, then, the notion of oracularity is central to Coetzee's novels, and it manifests itself in two major ways. In the first place it engenders the works themselves, since it is through the often frustrated quest for meaning that the texts are formulated, and the coordinates of the characters' dilemmas set down; and, in the second, it characterizes the authorial stance behind them, one marked by oracular ambiguity and ambivalence and even silence, one that refuses to dispense sureties, one that offers the irresolute trail of the ellipsis rather than purposive, summary disclosure. What we encounter in such works as *Foe* is not so much the *incidental* polysemy that attends on any nonreferential discourse as the construction of a matrix designed to sustain manifold readings of the fictional design. Some of Coetzee's commentators—Hena Maes-Jelinek and Teresa Dovey among them—have described his fiction in terms of allegory; but I would suggest that a more precise generic classification might be that of the open parable. Here there is no hierarchy of significances, applied as in allegory upon the bedrock of the narrative stratum by stratum, and requiring of the author an articulated, albeit encoded, intention. Rather, the novelist's cryptic withdrawal facilitates a series of "coequal" readings whose plausibility, as in some perceptual puzzles, depends entirely on aspect, on the reader's position vis-à-vis the material. Which is not to say that the novels admit of a hermeneutic free-for-all in the way a Rorschach blot might be construed. Virgil C. Aldrich has said of the duck-rabbit and lampshade-lopped pyramid pictures that although "a condition of what you see is what you have in mind, the aspect is not just a thought or even just a subjective image; it is an object of perception of some sort. The figure objectively accommodates the various aspects" (20). This stress on "objective accommodation returns us to the notion of oracularity, to the fact that while the reader/consultant might be mystified, it is a mystification controlled by the *conscious* ambiguity of the oracle, its readiness to concede that truth is too problematic a term for simple relay, that it must submit, as Plutarch saw it *must* submit, to many reflections and undergo subdivision.

Without questions, there would be no oracles, and it is in a pregnant, often existential, question that the generative seed of Coetzee's novels is to be found. Teresa Dovey has remarked apropos of his first book, *Dusklands*, that "'I have high hopes of finding whose fault I am' . . . may be regarded as the ontological query around which the novel as a whole is articulated" (71). Since the novel is a diptych, both "wings" of which are cast in the first person, we have no authorial guarantee of solution, only the personal records of two men to a greater or lesser degree psychopathic. The meaning that emerges from their juxtaposition is as ambiguous in its nonverbality as pictorial art itself. Eugene Dawn in fact says of the photographs that will accompany his analysis of the Vietnam War, "I respond to pictures as I do not to print" (it is presumably their inscrutable open-endedness that supplies an "electric impuse" to his imagination), and he then proceeds impassively to describe one of them. It is of an American soldier in the act of copulating with a frail Vietnamese woman, "possibly even a child":

> He smiles broadly; she turns a sleepy, foolish face on the unknown
> photographer. Behind them a blank television screen winks back
> the flash of the bulb. I have given the picture the provisional title
> "Father Makes Merry with Children." (*Dusklands* 14)

That smile, for all its broadness, is an archaic smile, inscrutable, susceptible of many readings. Does it betoken pride in sexual prowess? Does it mask shame? Is it a smile of callous *Schadenfreude* at the violation of innocence? It might be all of these things, and it might be none of them. The "unknown photographer," himself a type of the *auctor absconditus*, has simply automated the transcription with his camera button. So, too, the television screen, which blankly echoes the flash of the camera. Dawn's inscription is provisional not only in its being kept under threat of substitution by another, but also by its very nature. Any title must admit to being indefinitive, and like the present one, lie open, with Delphic irony, to alternative constructions: the security and decency of the suburban paterfamilias jangling against the violence of the imperial rapist. The multiplicity of the echoes that Truth gives forth from her well can be read also into the alternative accounts of Clawer's death in the second part of the novel, a feature that Jonathan Crewe ascribes to its metafictive impulse (91), but which suggests not so much a Nabokovian play with illusion as the irrecoverability of the objective facts as they are ingested by the consciousness that renders them. It is Peter Knox-Shaw's mistake to assume that the absence of overt authorial judgment in *Dusklands* amounts to vicarious sadism, a mistake implicit in his repeated description of the novel as something "bifurcated," as though the halves of the novel, far from being detached and thrown forth like the sybil's leaves, are conjoined in the presence of the author. Knox-Shaw claims that had an "economic motive" been supplied for the conduct of the Dutch explorer, it would in some way have become meaningful; that whereas Le Vaillant "shrewdly identifies an economic motive behind the wholesale denigration, . . . the violence of *Dusklands* is made to appear comparatively gratuitous" (28)—which is to say that Joseph Conrad's Kurtz somehow becomes comprehensible in terms of his ivory hoard. The fact of the matter is that both Conrad and Coetzee are documenting the psychopathic states that colonialism and crypto-colonialism necessarily foster, and neither author need billboard his intention. Indeed the illusive nature of *Heart of Darkness* seems to have provided part of the inspiration for the novelist's procedure of *Dusklands*—one recalls the little parable of fog and casket in E. M. Forster's *Aspects of the Novel.* Just as Truth in the early poem echoes her interrogators, so Eugene Dawn in *Dusklands* claims to have discovered all the "truths" in his Vietnam report by introspection (15), and later notes: "My true ideal (I really believe this) is of an endless discourse of character, the self reading the self to the self in all infinity" (40).

Nothing can be verified because everything is caught up in the solipsistic cycle of the narrative recessed endlessly upon itself. Dawn projects the same monologic indeterminacy upon Patrick White and Saul Bellow, whom he describes as performing tricks to give their monologues "the air of the real world" (38). He forgets, however, that both *Voss* and *Herzog* are third person omniscient in their narrative vantage, and that the convention there is a guarantee of a finality and reliability unavailable to first person accounts, the form that Coetzee favors for all his novels with the exception of *Michael K,* which is not without a first person inset— the pharmacist's monologue.

The problem of authorial endorsement is equally acute in work that follows *Dusklands,* for Magda in *In the Heart of the Country,* from the very start, gives us the statutory "two answers" of truth, and her opening statement about the plumed horse is, if not retracted, then forced into a multiple choice format that allows the story no ontological stability: "They came clip-clop across the flats in a dog-cart drawn by a horse with an ostrich-plume waving on its forehead. . . . Or perhaps they were drawn by two plumed donkeys, that is also possible" (*In the Heart of the Country* 1). Possible, perhaps, but surreal—plumes and horses, yes, but plumes and *donkeys?* The reader's dilemma is intensified later on in the novel (36-37), for example, where the anaphoric phrase "Or perhaps" has the effect of splicing several retakes of the same situation, rather in the manner of William Burroughs, though what is merely the prurient slow motion of pornography in the case of that author is here a desperate and poignant and futile attempt at teasing out the babel of echoes that issue from the well of Truth. At the end of the book, Magda's deranged attempts to communicate with capsules projected by her imagination are directly continuous with that "innocent" substitution of two donkeys for a horse in its opening.

Waiting for the Barbarians is, like its predecessor, a novel stocked with oracular motifs, inscrutable data, and frustrated construction. We see it in its most obvious form in the scrambling of the geographic information, its topography constructed, like the composite maiden of Zeuxis, from a multitude of contradictory sources. There can be no doubting that the South African border is among the many that waveringly come into and go out of focus, but it is also the border of the Roman Empire at the time of the Antonines, and many other borders besides. The Magistrate relates his story in what some critics have described as the historic present; however, the historic present can be marked only by modulation from a more traditional preterite and back again. The tense of *Waiting for the Barbarians*, as of much of the earlier writing, is better viewed as the tense traditionally employed in critical writing, a variant of the gnomic present that seems to affirm the eternal renewability of the experience at hand. It is the tense of interpretation, the tense that runs and reruns its data through the mind's eye. The material is more irrefutably there than it is in Magda's narrative—the Magistrate's marginal position in the Empire after his expedition invests him with the moral authority of a dissident—but that in itself gives no assurance of a final exegesis of the facts. For the narrator is not only concerned to make sense of a senseless situation, but also to retrieve a cultural past that the Empire has all but effaced. The wooden slips he recovers from the desert never in fact yield their meaning, pore over them as he might, but they do offer him the occasion for solidarity with the Barbarians when, during his interrogation, he projects a false, apparently subversive, interpretation onto them. A kind of truth does echo off the inscrutable surface here. Elsewhere, however, we are made aware that memory and other modes of subjectivity supervene upon the reality they mediate and slowly dissolve its certitudes:

> This is the last time to look on her clearly face to face, to scrutinize the motions of my heart, to try to understand who she really is: hereafter, I know, I will begin to reform her out of my repertoire of memories according to my questionable desires. (*Barbarians* 73)

There is a nice ambiguity to be found in the phrase "questionable desires," suggesting as it does both objective opprobrium and the subjective impulse to question.

Waiting for the Barbarians is a massive reply in the mind of the Magistrate, but it also contains within itself the technique of retake so desperately applied by Magda in *In the Heart of the Country*. This is manifest in a recurrent and in some sense incremental dream. Dreams, as much as oracles, have been honored as vehicles of divination, but like oracles, they seldom prove definitive. One has only to recall that, in *Aeneid* VI, "sunt gemini somni portae," one emitting true, the other false visions. The Magistrate himself never construes his dream; he merely relays it. It is sometimes presented without a dream framework, so that it becomes continuous with the narrative, which, in view of the strange slow motion of its tense, also has an oneiric feel. At first the nightmare centers on images of sterility and evanescence (the snow fort that the girl is building seems to offer itself as possible metaphor for the life-denying militarism and illegitimacy of the Empire), but in its final form it transmutes the snow castle into an oven, from which emerges the salvific offering of daily bread (109). (One senses the influence of Patrick White's *Voss* on these episodes, for in that novel, too, dreams become a cryptic vehicle of meaning, also laced with images of kilns and sacraments.) The leaves upon which the sibyl transcribes her puzzling messages seem furthermore to be glimpsed in the metaphor that attends the dream's final mutation, which is summoned from a range of options as if by an effort of will: "So I lie . . . and fall into a second sleep, into a confusion of images among which I search out one in particular, brushing aside the others that fly at me like leaves" (*Barbarians* 109). Yet, despite the irremissive drive towards clarification, the writer finally acknowledges that his own narrative has no finality. The wooden slips have proved impermeable to his search for significance; his own story is already beginning to slip and slide: "For a long while I stare at the pleas I have written. It would be disappointing to know that the poplar slips I have spent so much time on contain a message as devious, as equivocal, as reprehensible as this" (*Barbarians* 154).

Michael K differs from the Magistrate in having reached a state not dissimilar to the "animal tranquillity and decay" of Wordsworth's Old Man. The restive quest for meaning is not his primary concern, and, for the first time in the fiction of Coetzee, the task of construing data is delegated to the third person narrator. Every now and again the narrative gives promise of oracular revelation—"he tried to listen to the great silence about him" (90), and Michael is rewarded with rudimentary epiphanies that plot his relation to the universe. Paradoxically, though, they are epiphanies of non-meaning, confirming only a blind existential urge: "He thought of himself as a termite boring its way through a rock. There seemed nothing to do but live" (91). Truth finally proves to be as evasive with him as with his more articulate and self-aware counterpart in *Waiting for the Barbarians*: "Always, when he tried to explain himself to himself, there remained a gap, a hole, a darkness before which his understanding baulked, into which it was useless to pour words. His was always a story with a hole in it: a wrong story, always wrong" (150-51).

It is symptomatic of the mysterious power of Coetzee's fiction that it should be able retrospectively to make so confident and complacent a novel as *Robinson Crusoe* a "wrong story," a story that, having initially no hole, has had one drilled into it by the queries and ambivalences of *Foe*. And *Foe* itself does not resolve its own mysteriousness. In the climactic vision of Friday in the wreck, the power of revelatory speech that seems momentarily to be promised is subverted as a stream of water indistinguishable from the element into which it is emitted.

Works about the oracular tend themselves to become Delphic and oblique from the very sense of imponderabilities that they have tried to explore. One thinks of the endless niceties of nuance in the late work of Henry James; one thinks of the chiastic utterance of John Keats's urn, repelling with its arched verbal sufficiency any effort to break it open. J. M. Coetzee's novels are in this respect their honorable successors.

WORKS CITED

Aldrich, Virgil C. *Philosophy of Art*. Englewood Cliffs, NJ: Prentice-Hall, 1963.

Coetzee, John. "Truth lies sunken." In *Groote Schuur: Literary Annual* (University of Cape Town, 1959): 25–27.

Coetzee, J.M. *Dusklands*. Johannesburg: Ravan Press, 1974.

———. *In the Heart of the Country*. Johannesburg: Ravan Press, 1978.

———. *The Life and Times of Michael K*. Johannesburg: Ravan Press, 1983.

———. *Waiting for the Barbarians*. Johannesburg: Ravan Press, 1981.

———. *White Writing: On the Culture of Letters in South Africa*. New Haven: Yale UP, 1988.

Crewe, Jonathan. "*Dusklands*." *Contrast* 34 (1974): 90–95.

Dodds, E.R. *The Greeks and the Irrational*. Berkeley: U of California P, 1951.

Dovey, Teresa. *The Novels of J.M. Coetzee: Lacanian Allegories*. Johannesburg: AD. Donker, 1988.

J.M. COETZEE'S PUBLISHED WORK

Novels

Dusklands, 1974
In the Heart of the Country, 1976
Waiting for the Barbarians, 1980
The Life and Times of Michael K, 1983
Foe, 1986
Age of Iron, 1990

Anthology

A Land Apart: A South African Reader (edited with André Brink), 1986

Criticism

White Writing: On the Culture of Letters in South Africa. New Haven: Yale UP, 1988. Arguably the
finest work of criticism ever to emerge from South Africa, the book collects most of Coetzee's
writing on South African literature.

SELECTED CRITICAL READINGS

J.M. Coetzee's reputation as a novelist was at first restricted largely to South Africa.
International recognition came with the publication of *Waiting for the Barbarians*,
which received coverage in the popular media from such figures as Bernard Levin.
The Booker Prize, awarded for his fourth novel, *The Life and Times of Michael K*,
brought him still greater prestige, and sparked a lively retrospective interest in the
earlier novels, which, together with their successors, have all been issued by Penguin
in international editions. *In the Heart of the Country* has also been filmed as *Dust*.
It is difficult to distinguish major schools or trends in a corpus of critical writing that
is in some respects still in its beginning stage though no doubt set for rapid growth.
The open-endedness of Coetzee's fictions has tended to attract critics with
deconstructionist leanings, ever alert to such aporias as the "presence of absence,"
while, those on the other extreme of the critical spectrum, commentators of a
Marxist cast, have examined his anatomies of colonialism and racial oppression with
greater or lesser degrees of sympathy.

Crewe, Jonathan. "*Dusklands.*" *Contrast* 34 (1974): 90–95. A substantial early review that examines
the structure of the novel.

Dovey, Teresa. *The Novels of J M Coetzee: Lacanian Allegories.* Johannesburg: AD. Donker, 1988.
This is so far the only book on the author, immensely detailed and painstaking, but informed with
assumptions and arguments that, to a non-Lacanian, are not always compelling: for example,
Dusklands becomes a tract about the erect phallus; *In the Heart of the Country* a discourse on
the vagina.

———. "John Coetzee and His Critics: The Case of *Dusklands.*" *English in Africa* 14 (1987): 15–30.
A spirited defense of Coetzee against his detractors.

du Plessis, Menan. "Towards a True Materialism." *Contrast* 52 (1981): 77–87. Defends the subtlety and obliquity of *Waiting for the Barbarians* against Marxist attacks on its being insufficiently *engage.*

Gillmer, Joan. "The Motif of the Damaged Child in the Work of J.M. Coetzee." *Momentum: On Recent South African Writing.* Pietermaritzburg: U of Natal P, 1984. Compilation of child imagery in the first three novels.

Gordimer, Nadine. "The Idea of Gardening." *New York Review of Books* 2 Feb. 1984: 3, 6. Makes some problematical assumptions about allegory and ascribes to Coetzee a "revulsion against all political and revolutionary solutions."

Harvey, C.J.D. *"Waiting for the Barbarians."* *Standpunte* 154.4 (1981): 3–8. Straightforward and enthusiastic appraisal of the novel, relating it to the Leavisite "great tradition."

Knox-Shaw, Peter. "*Dusklands*: A Metaphysics of Violence." *Contrast* 53 (1982): 26–38. Interesting approach, but makes one or two untenable statements as a result of a seeming blindness to important features in Coetzee's art.

Maes-Jelinek, Hena. "Ambivalent Clio: J.M. Coetzee's *In the Heart of the Country* and Wilson Harris's *Carnival.*" *Journal of Commonwealth Literature* 22 (1987): 87–98 & 15–30. Suggests, among other things, that *In the Heart of the Country* is an allegory of South Africa's international isolation, though the supporting argument is not developed fully enough to win universal assent.

Martin, Richard G. "Narrative, History and Ideology: A Study of *Waiting for the Barbarians* and *Burger's Daughter.*" *Ariel* 17.3 (1986): 3–21. Plays novels of radically different procedure against each other and concludes that "*Waiting for the Barbarians* is a tragedy in which the significance of events is their lack of significance." Intelligent and interesting analysis, partially based on deconstructionist precepts.

Muller, Helen. "Who Is Michael K?" *Standpunte* 175.1 (1985): 41–43. Summary allegorical reading of the novel that has a field day with proper nouns.

Olsen, Lance. "The Presence of Absence: Coetzee's *Waiting for the Barbarians.*" *Ariel* 16.2 (1985): 47-56. One of the first deconstructionist readings of Coetzee; engaging and suggestive.

Penner, Dick. "Sight, Blindness and Double-Thought in J.M. Coetzee's *Waiting for the Barbarians.*" *World Literature Written in English* 26 (1986): 34–45. Tabulation of the imagery of eyes and spectacles and the bearing this has on the central vision of the novel.

Rich, Paul. "Apartheid and the Decline of Civilization Idea: An Essay on Nadine Gordimer's *July's People* and J.M. Coetzee's *Waiting for the Barbarians.*" *Research in African Literatures* 15 (1984): 365–89. Discusses how colonizers have attempted to justify their enterprise in the name of civilization. Attacks *Waiting for the Barbarians* for its incomplete understanding of historical forces.

Sandbank, Shimon. "The Other Barbarian." *Ariel* 69 (1987): 85–88. Brief but notable account of the novels that shows them "deeply ambivalent about the part we assign to the other."

Watson, Stephen. "Colonialism and the Novels of J.M. Coetzee." *Research in African Literatures* 17 (1986): 370–92. Sympathetic examination of the first four novels in which Watson projects Coetzee as a variant of Albert Memmi's "dissenting coloniser."

Williams, Paul. "*Foe*: The Story of Silence." *English Studies in Africa* 31 (1988): 33–39. An incisive placing of the novel as a work concerned with "the self-enclosed text, or more accurately, the text-enclosed self."

Interview

With Stephen Watson *Speak* 1 (1978): 21–24.

— RODNEY EDGECOMBE

A.D. Hope

Although A.D. Hope did not publish his first book of poetry until he was nearly fifty, he has for the last three decades been the dominant figure in Australian poetry.

Alec Derwent Hope was born in Cooma, New South Wales, Australia, 21 July 1907, the first son of a Presbyterian minister. The father, Percival Hope, moved to a rural area of Tasmania when Hope was four. Hope's first few years of education took place at home, and he exhibited a poetic instinct at an early age. By the time he was eight he had composed a rhyme of fifty-two stanzas, one for each week of the year, exhorting his mother to do her Christian duty. Hope later wrote that his mother "gently suggested that I might perhaps consider improving my own conduct rather than hers" (*Native Companions* 5).

At the age of fourteen, Hope was sent to the Australian mainland to complete his education, first to Bathurst, then to Sydney. He then entered St. Andrew's College of the University of Sydney, where he distinguished himself as a student of philosophy and won a scholarship for further study at Oxford.

After a mediocre performance that brought him a third-class degree, Hope returned to Sydney in 1930 during the worst of the Depression. He worked for several years as a public school teacher and vocational psychologist before obtaining positions at Sydney Teachers' College, the University of Sydney, and at the University of Melbourne. In 1951 Hope became Professor of English at what is now the Australian National University and published his first collection of poetry four years later. In 1969 he became a Library Fellow and in 1972 Professor Emeritus.

His many awards include the Encyclopaedia Britannica Award for Literature, the Age Book of the Year Award, the Robert Frost Award, Companion of the Order of Australia, the Grace Levin Prize, the Arts Council of Great Britain Award, the Myer Award, the Levinson Prize, and the Ingram Merrill Award. Hope was made O.B.E. in 1972 and A.C. in 1981. These honors were followed by his election as Ashby Visiting Fellow of Clare Hall, Cambridge, and Honorary Fellow of University College, Oxford, in 1985. He and his wife still reside in Canberra.

THE MYTHOLOGY OF THE ACTUAL

Halfway through "A Letter from Rome," a conversational long poem written in both the form and style of Byron's *Don Juan*, A.D. Hope writes of one event during his visit to Italy with a seriousness not found in the rest of the poem. That moment of special importance was when Hope retraced Byron's steps to Nemi, site of the rituals revolving around the Golden Bough. His visit united him in intent with Byron—"I like to think/What drew him then is what has drawn me now/To stand in time upon that timeless brink"—and compelled him to pour a libation on the face of the water before wading out into the lake. The poet admits he was "possessed, and what possessed me there/Was Europe's oldest ritual of prayer." Although Hope's persona in the poem shrugs off the experience, "Well, let it pass: I have no views about it," he does allow that he "sensed some final frontier passed" before returning to the brisker manner of the poem.

This is a very telling incident in Hope's work, and it is most appropriate that he stands at the threshold of the numenous by retracing the steps of an artist back to a source of western myth. Throughout Hope's career, a remarkably consistent commitment to art, and especially the art of poetry, as a handmaiden of myth has been apparent in his work.

In *Native Companions* Hope noted how central to the individual is this connection between myth and poetry. He remarked that in early childhood

> . . . we create our myth of the world and our own dance of language which expresses and celebrates the myth. By "myth of the world" I mean that picture of the way things and people are which differs from every other person's picture, and both reflects and helps to form what we call an individual, a unique person or personality. All art, and poetry more than other arts, is the product of this personality and the expression of its individual myth. (8)

Leonie Kramer, writing of Hope's book, *A Midsummer Eve's Dream*, noted: "His whole argument in the book depends on accepting the notion that poetry is . . . the repository of mythological stories which have deep psychological relevance to the everyday life of human beings." Probably the poem in which Hope most explicitly and most thoroughly examines the role of myth in the everyday psychic life of individuals is that central but flawed work "An Epistle from Holofernes." (It is sometimes the case with Hope's work that the poems most explicitly giving voice to Hope's beliefs, and thereby most convenient for the critic, are not among his stronger efforts poetically.)

The speaker in the poem, supposedly the ghost of Holofernes, recognizes that myth no longer has the immediate power it once had, and such a condition is our loss: "Myths formed the rituals by which ancient men/Groped towards the dayspring and were born again." And Nemi is symbolic of the dayspring. Despite our general loss of the rites of myth as sustenance for our spiritual lives, the mythic still has its value, even in this age of unbelief: "Yet myth has other uses: it confirms/The heart's conjectures and approves its terms" and "speak[s] to us the truth of what we are."

But these myths must be remade for modern man who is sinking ever lower in the swamp of cynicism. The natural remaker of myths is, of course, the poet:

> Yet the myths will not fit us ready made.
> It is the meaning of the poet's trade

To re-create the fables and revive
In men the energies by which they live,
To reap the ancient harvests, plant again
And gather in the visionary grain,
And to transform the same unchanging seed
Into the gospel-bread on which they feed.
("An Epistle from Holofernes")

The mythic fosters a sense of community; the individual existence is given validity because it partakes of a higher reality. Myth is universal, and the community of artists forms an international brotherhood. This fact, coupled with Hope's impressive linguistic abilities, accounts for the amount of effort Hope has put into translation in the last decades of his poetic career. For myth to have continuing meaning for man, it must not be static. The mythic has validity because new myths are continually reshaping themselves or are being reshaped in ways that speak to the contemporary predicament. Most modern myths have narrowed to some extent, the cosmological having given way to the nationalistic. Almost our only grand myths left are those of science.

Hope has frequently transformed the familiar myths, as David Kalstone has pointed out: "His skill is partly one of reinterpretation. The literary scene is one we know, but the characters have been assigned new positions on stage" (620). In "The End of a Journey," the poem Hope places first when he makes a selection of his poetry, Ulysses has come back to Ithaca, but finds his triumphant return to a life of peace, a life of administration rather than heroism, hollow. Although the poem covers ground usurped by Tennyson, Hope's is still a fine treatment of the theme. Ithaca becomes the hero's worst banishment. It is worth noting that Hope began this poem at about the time he worked on the first drafts of his poem "Australia." Just having returned home from England, Hope must have found in Ulysses a personal myth.

This identification with Ulysses is sustained over the years: The concluding poem of his book, *A Late Picking,* published in 1975, was "Spatlese," the last verse of which reads:

Old men should be adventurous. On the whole
I think that's what old age is really for:
Tolstoy at Astapovo finds his soul;
    Ulysses hefts his oar.

In Hope's old age, Ulysses is no longer moping at the shore but is ready for new odysseys. It is also more than coincidence that Hope here places a mythic hero and a writer so closely together in the same poem; after all, they deal with the same material.

Many other myths with which Hope does not identify in quite as personal a manner are even more substantially altered. Circe becomes a victim of her own spells; Prometheus' gift of fire destroys mankind; Faustus finds his soul has been taken from him before his death without his knowing it when the bureaucracy of

Hell converts to the principles of high finance; Persephone comes to love Dis just as she leaves him. The license that Hope takes with these myths is the privilege of the poet. For myth is universal because it is rooted in common experience, and a poet is, in many ways, a mythologist.

In his poem "Romancero," Hope outlines how myth grows from the ordinary to the extraordinary. Einhard, in his *Life of Charlemagne*, reports that a baggage train was ambushed in the Pyrenees; in time, however, this rather mundane incident grows into legend as "Romancero" unfolds: "Three centuries pass. A poet retells the tale;/Roland's disaster, riding home from Spain,/Becomes more glorious than most victories." The speaker remarks: "History gives way to epic, as it should;/Heroic deeds from commonplace facts are born." The poem examines further the transition of epic into high romance: how a small band of Basque bandits gives way to a "countless Saracen host," how Roland's sword Durandal became a "valiant Knight/ Who fell at Roncesvalles beside his lord." But then the mythologizing process is reversed as the poet gives way to the scholar and the historian, leaving us with "sober History." And Hope states there is another kind of truth:

> Truth, as they say, is great and shall prevail.
> I have no quarrel with that; but what of Rhyme
> Whose truth is vision, whose task to guard the pass
> With Roland or seek with Galahad the Grail?
> For those who gaze in her enchanted glass
> Time has an end whose end is not in time.
> ("Romancero")

Hope is not pleading here for an obscurantism that ignores the modern world in order to return a sense of meaning and mystery to existence; it is worth noting that meaning and mystery ultimately appear to be inextricably linked. What he does plead for is recognition of another sort of truth, an enchantment, that is not contrary to history and science but springs from them as legend springs from historical event. Myth must be grounded in fact as the language of poetry is grounded in the language of the shopkeeper. Ultimately, Hope realizes, for a modern myth to be created the artist must not ignore the quotidian world but must transform it. And nowhere does the presence of the factual so assert itself as in the sphere of science.

Science and poetry are rarely seen as intellectual partners in this century. The range of empirical knowledge has expanded to such a degree that not even a scientist can grasp many of the latest findings in the other sciences. Each field has developed its own terminology so that every pursuit seems to require a new language. The essential concerns of the scientific and the poetic often seem at loggerheads; the former is supremely empirical, the latter anything but empirical in common practice today. The poet has turned inward, more concerned with his own moods than with order in the universe and, Hope would argue, has thereby lost the world. Indeed, Hope has claimed that the "treasures of knowledge, the vast new resources for the poetic imagination that lie in the discoveries of science, remain practically untouched by creative writers" (*Cave* 92). He is more outspoken in *The New Cratylus*: Poets "have simply failed to keep up with the transformation of the whole universe which science has achieved in the last century" (168). But the task of the poet is, obviously, not to chronicle the progress of science as would a textbook but to "elicit its proper music, to make us feel the power and delight of what this knowledge adds to our concept of the world and of human life in it" (168-69).

Although this sounds reasonable in theory, it still seems rather vague. Hope both expands and refines the idea in the central metaphor of the essay, "Day-time and Night-time Vision," in which he states that the poet is "concerned not with analytic knowledge but with eliciting what the medieval philosophers called the *quidditas*, the *whatness* of things." While Hope does acknowledge that "Daylight vision is infinitely superior, more exact and precise" than nighttime vision, he immediately adds, "But it has one limitation":

> Had the human race grown up in a world continually illuminated
> by the sun it would have considered the earth, the sun and the
> moon to be the whole universe. . . . I believe that the poets, that
> artists in general, have another kind of vision, that the imagination
> is an instrument of seeing and apprehending, and that its function
> is constantly to be enlarging the scope of the scientists' vision.
> (182-83)

This vision is not composed solely of information, raw data to fuel the latest scientific formulation. It is a different kind of knowledge, but it is not to be separated from the scientific sphere in the way that poetry is cut off today. Rather, it is the complement of the scientific, just as night is the complement of day. It is an extraction of music, the music of myth, from the same materials from which the scientist extracts data. Poets have by and large shirked the challenge this age of science has presented them, as Hope has pointed out:

> It seemed to many in the nineteenth century that not only religion
> but the whole field of mythology, the pasture of poets, was being
> destroyed by the discoveries of science. The poets of a later age have
> had to find another view in which the mysterious bow of God's
> covenant with man remains valid for the imagination and is not
> touched by what the sciences of optics and meteorology tell us.
> (*Answers* 34)

But how does one create a mythology from a scientific context that seems most unmythological? From the wonderment of not knowing and the striving to discover. The universe, despite all the advances of science, seems ultimately unknowable, perhaps more so now than ever before; it is this unknown that fosters myth, myth that is not only a celebration of the unknown but a tribute to the artist and scientist who attempt, and fail, to fathom it. Probably in no one poem by Hope are the dual adventures of science and art seen as more of a tandem than in "On an Engraving by Casserius." Hope is nowhere more successful at drawing the mythic from the actual than in this poem.

The poem begins with the seekers, those who give their lives to asking questions, in what seems like a global waste land "set on this bubble of dead stone and sand,/ Lapped by its frail balloon of lifeless air,/Alone in the inanimate void." These scientists and artists are termed "clots of thinking molecules," hardly a picture one would usually draw in praising creation—but Hope is here insisting that the material world be accurately observed with its "night of nescience and death." The reader would expect more imagery of the waste land to follow, but immediately the speaker shares his admiration of those who attempt to overcome their limited sphere: "This of all human images takes my breath;/Of all the joys in being a man at all,/This folds my spirit in its quickening flame."

The speaker then alerts the reader that the occasion for the poem is the persona's perusal of a book of scientific prints, a book of anatomy. Calling the book's makers "great cosmographers,/Surgeon adventurers," the poet sums up their goal as reaching "towards the central mystery/Of whence our being drawn and what we are." The book is from the university library at Padua, then as now a leading center for the study of medicine. The makers of the particular illustration that so attracts the speaker are baldly identified: "Casserio and Spiegel made this page." The poem is as relentless in its rendering of fact as is the science with which it is concerned. Our particular time is contrasted with the time of Casserio and Spiegel, ours being an "age in which all sense of the unique,/And singular dissolves . . . In diagrams, statistics, tables, maps." But the speaker indicates immediately that our modern sense of abstraction had not yet corrupted their concerns:

> Not here! The graver's tool in this design
> Aims still to give not general truth alone,
> Blue-print of science or data's formal line:
> Here in its singularity he has shown
> The image of an individual soul;
> Bodied in this one woman, he makes us see
> The shadow of his anatomical laws.
> An artist's vision animates the whole,
> Shines through the scientist's detailed scrutiny
> And links the person with the abstract cause.

The particular is not yet lost in the general; it is clearly intimated that a major part of the reason for this is that an "artist's vision animates the whole." The general laws are but a shadow that still allow for the unique, the individual, that which cannot be placed in "diagrams, statistics, tables, maps."

We are then made aware that the central subject matter of the engraving is a corpse of a pregnant woman. Hope ponders her life and notes her transformation beyond the temporal frame through the joint effort of art and science. It is at this point that the mythologizer's eye begins to play but only after an unblinking look at cold, objective fact. This nameless girl, this "corpse none cared, or dared perhaps to claim" with her unborn child might easily have been totally forgotten, "passed, momentary as a shooting star,/Quenched like the misery of her personal life," had she not been dissected and drawn by Guilio Casserio. Now, however, "still in the abundance of her grace,/She stands among the monuments of time." The actual dissection is described sensually:

> And with a feminine delicacy displays
> His elegant dissection: the sublime
> Shaft of her body opens like a flower
> Whose petals, folded back expose the womb,
> Cord and placenta and the sleeping child.

The womb, cord, placenta, and embryo take on mythic qualities; they are described as being like ". . . instruments of music in a room/Left when her grieving Orpheus left his tower/Forever, for the desert and the wild." The poet describes the corpse's pose as a "sibylline stance" and then attempts an even more daring metaphor; he first compares the woman to Eve in that she "holds the fruit/Plucked, though not tasted, of the Fatal Tree." She then seems like the second Eve, Mary, in her "Offering of her child in death to be/Love's victim and her flesh its mystic rose." Here we have affirmation, a heavenly vision in the midst of human tragedy.

The image is almost too much. Hope senses this and grounds it immediately in a way that will still elicit the same music:

> No figure with wings of fire and back-swept hair
> Swoops down with his: Blessed among Women!; no sword
> Of the spirit cleaves or quickens her; yet there
> She too was overshadowed by the Word,
> Was chosen, and by her humble gift of death
> The lowly and the poor in heart give tongue,
> Wisdom puts down the mighty from their seat;
> The vile rejoice and rising, hear beneath
> Scalpel and forceps, tortured into song,
> Her body utter their magnificat.

The language here is somewhere between that of High Mass and a Celtic Rite. Of course, such verse demands an act of assent from the reader, much as that of Hopkins often does. If this is merely a corpse being cut apart, the poem has degenerated into the worst kind of "poetizing." But poets always leave themselves open to such a charge any time they attempt to elevate the actual beyond the material, any time they assist in the creation of myth. The man who returns to Plato's cave is thought mad, but, to borrow Seamus Heaney's phrase, he sings "close to the music of what happens."

After the beatification of the corpse, Hope considers how four centuries of science since Casserio have still not found that for which he was seeking, that though the "patient, probing knife/Cut towards its answer" for four hundred years "yet we stand in doubt." All our theories in the end prove insufficient when faced with the central reality: "The universals we thought to conjure with/Pass: there remain the mother and the child." There at the center of the question are the mother and her child; and the corpse and foetus become a "Loadstone, loadstar." The scientific exploration, the autopsy, revealed new physical truths but left the mystery unanswered. It did not destroy or compromise the mystery, for the explanation deepened the mystery all the more for being unable to solve it. Science fails to reveal the "mask beyond the mask beyond the mask." One is left with the same silent awe before the incomprehensibility of the numenous that the poet sensed at Nemi. Hope ends the poem with an imagined speech that might be given by the mother and child in which it is stated that "all man's intellectual quest/Was but the stirrings of a foetal sleep" and heralds a new birth, a new nature when the "deep/Dawns with that unimaginable day." Certainly the first seers of that "unimaginable day," the new shepherds minding their flocks, will be the poets whose concerns are those of the heart and mind. The scientist adds knowledge. The poet adds something more, Hope believes:

> Poets, at any rate in this age, which is all we can be asked to answer for, are not called on to be polymaths, just to be poets, to keep and tend the delicate, inexorably extending edge of human awareness. As knowledge increases in range and complexity, making more and more demands on human abilities, consciousness must, in turn, continually extend its scope and range, and this is the physical task of poetry and the other arts, the task of "adding to being." (*Cratylus* 172)

The nature of being is such that the spiritual crouches within the physical and arises from it. The mundane facts of our existence are transformed by the very nature of matter itself.

In "An Epistle: Edward Sackville to Venetia Digby," Hope notes that nature, while it "makes each member to one end" still can "give it powers which transcend/Its first and fruitful purpose." He then cites the example of the tongue; as it was created for the taste of a "speechless manlike brute," how could one "have conceived the improbable tale, the long/Strange fable of the Speaking Tongue?" The tongue, originally an instrument for animal taste, becomes the creator of poetry, and poetry gives birth to myth. We see the doubleness of physical nature as a continuous reality: The hand made for plucking fruit can hold a violin bow. Science and poetry, physical matter and mythology are partners in the dance of spirit. In "A Mu'Allaqat at Murray's Corner," Hope writes:

> Come, friend, we must be going. We thought to share
> The last of the wine, but the wine will always be there;
> From that unbelievable, necessary part
> Of life that is not part of living its fountains start.
> Nothing is lost, though brightness should fall from the air.

The "unbelievable, necessary part/Of life that is not part of living" might seem tortuous phrasing, but it is probably as close as one can come to this sense of that numenous something that less scientific ages could call God. It can be defined specifically only in terms of what it is not; like the failings of scientific research or the openings in a Henry Moore sculpture, it is an absence from which presence drinks its shape. Yet for all its unbelievability, it is overwhelmingly there and a necessary part of the design.

All science, all art, all human endeavor, become a shared experience. What poetry adds to the scientific adventure is a sense of the individual; the dead mother and her child seen through the eye of the scientist who was also an artist ceased to be a slab of meat on a surgery table and became almost totemic beings. Yet this recognition of the individuality brings with it an awareness of being a member of the community of strivers, of artists. In "Vivaldi, Bird and Angel" Hope states: "Somewhere beyond this frame of natural laws,/Moving in time on its predestined grooves,/I hear another music to which it moves." He then adds:

> Wherever I go, whatever I do, I seem
> To step in time to that resistless stream
> And though, I trust, a rational man, I vow
> I heard it as a child, I hear it now;
> With every year I live, it sounds more clear,
> More vast, more jubilant to the inward ear;
> Beyond my power to imagine or invent
> That choir of being, or this sole instrument
> Of my response to that invisible world.
> Gift? or delusion? or defect unfurled
> From genes that I inherit? I cannot tell;
> I only know I hear it and, as well
> That when I hear them humbly, as I do,
> I know with pride, the masters heard it too.

This sense of something shared comes close to religion. Science, the arts, and religion reveal part of the mystery, and each has its community of believers.

The sense of the universal rooted in the individual is the essence of the mythological process. As a poet, A.D. Hope is able to take his place in the international brotherhood of humans striving to elicit the music of the world. Conversely, he is able to take part in this adventure because he is a particular man in a particular place, for myth must be localized. As Hope notes in the final stanza of "Beyond Khancoban":

> Man is made by all that has made the history of man,
> But here the Monaro claims me; I recognise
> Beyond Khancoban the place where a mind began
> Able to offer itself to the galaxies.

WORKS CITED

Hope, A.D. *Antechinus*. Sydney: Angus & Robertson, 1981.
———. *A Book of Answers*. Sydney: Angus & Robertson, 1978.
———. *The Cave and the Spring*. Chicago: U of Chicago P, 1970.
———. *Collected Poems 1930–1965*. New York: Viking, 1976.

————. "Day-time and Night-time Vision." *Australian Voices: Poetry and Prose of the 1970s.* Canberra: Australian National UP, 1975. 181–83.

————. *Native Companions: Essays and Comments on Australian Literature 1936–1966.* Sydney: Angus & Robertson, 1974.

————. *The New Cratylus.* Melbourne: Oxford UP, 1979.

————. *New Poems 1965–1969.* New York: Viking, 1970.

————. *Selected Poems.* Manchester: Carcanet, 1986.

Kalstone, David. "Two Poets." *Partisan Review* (1967): 619–25.

Kramer, Leonie. *A.D. Hope.* Melbourne: Oxford UP, 1979.

A.D. HOPE'S PUBLISHED WORK

Poetry

The Wandering Islands, 1955
Poems, 1960
Selected Poems, 1963
New Poems, 1965–1969, 1969
Dunciad Minor: An Heroik Poem, 1970
Collected Poems 1930–1970, 1972
Selected Poems, 1973
A Late Picking: Poems 1965–1974, 1975
A Book of Answers, 1978
Antechinus, 1981
The Age of Reason, 1985
Selected Poems, 1986

Drama

The Tragical History of Doctor Faustus by Christopher Marlowe (purged and amended by A.D. Hope),1982
Ladies from the Sea, 1987

Criticism

Australian Literature 1950–1962, 1963
　　　　Brief overview of Australian poetry, fiction, and drama of the 1950s and early 60s.
The Cave and the Spring: Essays on Poetry, 1965
　　　　Collection of essays dealing with various aspects of poetry and the poetic process. Of particular note are "The Discursive Mode," dealing with the erosion of poetic forms through ecological analogies, and "Free Verse: A Post- Mortem," Hope's most detailed assault on free verse.
A Midsummer Eve's Dream: Variations on a theme by William Dunbar, 1970
　　　　Book of meditations on the poetic process, the effect of culture on the creative work, and an in-depth consideration of medieval Scottish culture loosely clustered around an analysis of Dunbar's poem "The Tretis of the Tua Mariit Women and the Wedo."
Native Companions: Essays and Comments on Australian Literature 1936–1966, 1974
　　　　Collection of essays dealing with Australian writers, often from a personal and anecdotal basis. Of particular interest is the first essay, "Meet Nurse!," which is concerned with Hope's own youth and development as a poet.
Judith Wright, 1975
　　　　Examination of his fellow Australian poet's work.
The Pack of Autolycus, 1978
　　　　Series of essays dealing with literature in general, beginning with *Beowulf* and concluding with D.H. Lawrence. There is no necessary thread connecting the essays except as subjects that attracted Hope's interest.

The New Cratylus, 1979

    Hope's most comprehensive statement on poetry and the poetic process. Book is both personal and theoretical and the best source in which to find Hope's critical perspectives on poetry.

Selected Critical Readings

Despite the fact that A.D. Hope is widely discussed and reviewed, especially in Australia, there is at the time of this writing no book-length study of his work yet published. Indeed, there is a noticeable shortage of any critical survey of Hope outside Australia, an odd circumstance for an important poet who has been an established international figure for over three decades. One possible reason is that the direction of poetry from the 1950s through the early 80s was inimical to Hope's work. Most of the substantial criticism also pre-dates Hope's turn to narrative verse.

Brissenden, R.F. "Review of *New Poems*, by A. D. Hope." *Southerly* 30 (1970): 83–96. One of the most extensive reviews of any individual volume of Hope's poetry and a good general commentary on his development as a poet to that point.

Buckley, Vincent. *Essays in Poetry: Mainly Australian.* Melbourne: Melbourne UP, 1957. First in-depth analysis of Hope's work and still one of the best, though limited, of course, to his early poetry. Buckley is especially insightful in his observations as to the tactile nature of much of Hope's verse. First to term Hope a "classical poet whose material is Romantic."

Gwynn, R.S. "A.D. Hope." *Critical Survey of Poetry: Supplement.* Englewood Heights, N.J.: Salem Press, 1987. 184–192. Excellent overview of Hope's poetic career. Gwynn places particular emphasis on Hope's craftsmanship. Interesting as well for being one of the latest entries on Hope, and one of the few by an American in recent years.

Heseltine, Harry. "Australian Image: The Literary Heritage." *Oxford Anthology of Australian Literature.* Melbourne: Oxford UP, 1985. 298–312. Heseltine is particularly good in his discussion of the element of horror and cruelty in Australian literature. Though Hope is only mentioned in part of the essay, the entire piece is invaluable in approaching Hope's earlier poetry and seeing its Australian roots, roots not always easily discernable.

Kramer, Leonie. *A.D. Hope.* Melbourne: Oxford UP, 1979. The longest published consideration of Hope's work. Though written before Hope's discursive, narrative poetry of the 1980s, this study is the most thorough critical introduction to Hope's work for the newcomer.

McAuley, James. *A Map of Australian Verse.* Melbourne: Oxford UP, 1975. The best analysis of the dualities of Hope's earlier work. McAuley divides the verse into three basic categories, the Apollonian, Dionysian, and the Orphic.

Mezger, Ross. "Alienation and Prophecy: The Grotesque in the Poetry of A.D. Hope." *Southerly* 36 (1976): 268–83. Perceptive handling of Hope's use of the grotesque and Gothic before 1960. Mezger makes the point that Hope's use of the grotesque is ultimately redeemed by his contrasting images of reason, that the grotesque calls attention "to the norm, standard, attitude or value from which the grotesque is a deviation."

Wallace-Crabbe, Chris. "Three Faces of Hope." *Meanjin* 26 (1967): 396–407. Stresses the dualistic nature of Hope's poetry to mid-career. Comments that Hope is capable of lucid heights because the murky depths are so well explored. Stresses the operatic nature of many of Hope's monologues and is particularly good in his discussion of the unexpected ending of Hope's tribute to Yeats.

Walsh, William. *A Manifold Voice: Studies in Commonwealth Literature.* London: Chatto & Windus, 1970. Good general survey of Hope through mid-career. Puts Hope in general context of international literature in English rather than portraying him as an isolated phenomenon or an Englishman marooned in Australia.

Interview

With Peter Kuch and Paul Kavanagh. *Southerly* 47 (1986): 221–31.

—ROBERT DARLING

David Williamson

David Keith Williamson was born in Melbourne, Australia, 24 February 1942, the elder son of Keith Williamson, a bank employee, and his wife Elvie. His early years were spent in a Melbourne suburb and his adolescence in the country town of Bairndale, where he attended high school.

Williamson studied mechanical engineering at the Universities of Melbourne and Monash. While an undergraduate he was involved in scripting and producing revues and developed an interest in becoming a writer. After graduating from Monash, he worked for a year as an assistant project engineer at General Motors Holden before becoming a lecturer in Mechanical Engineering at Swinburne College of Technology, Melbourne.

Williamson married Carol Cranby in 1965 and around the same time became actively involved in opposition to the Vietnam War. While lecturing at Swinburne, Williamson studied psychology part-time at the University of Melbourne and was later appointed to a lectureship in psychology at Swinburne. He was continuing to write, and in 1968 his first full-length play (the unpublished "The Indecent Exposure of Anthony East") was produced.

The simultaneous success of *The Removalists* and *Don's Party* in the early 1970s allowed Williamson to write full-time for the stage, film, and television. He was divorced in 1972, and in 1974 married journalist Kristin Green. They live in Sydney.

Williamson was a foundation member of the Australia Council, the national arts-funding body, and later a member of its Theatre Board. For a brief period he was a commissioner of the Australian Broadcasting Commission before resigning in protest at political interference. He has long served as president of the Australian Writers Guild and been a prominent spokesman for the arts. As well as innumerable awards for his scripts, Williamson has received the Order of Australia for his services to theater and an honorary doctorate from the University of Sydney.

SATIRIC COMEDIES

Drama has often been described as the most social of the arts. The plays of David Williamson certainly reflect many of the social, cultural, and political changes that have occurred in Australia over the past twenty years—to the extent that he is frequently quoted as a sociological observer and perceived as the "chronicler" of the middle class. At the same time, his phenomenally successful career as a professional writer, unprecedented in his own country, has involved him directly with many of the individuals, institutions, and movements instrumental in the development of Australian theater and cinema over the same period.

Williamson first came into prominence in Melbourne's alternative theater at the beginning of the 1970s. A manifestation of the counter culture of this time, the alternative theater movement combined interests in formal and stylistic experimentation with social critique. Ray Lawler's *Summer of the Seventeenth Doll* (1955), the most successful of earlier Australian plays, provided the movement with its *bête noir*. Lawler's play was seen as moribund "bourgeois naturalism" in its conventions and as sentimental in its evocation of the national code of mateship. Younger generations, inspired by contemporary American "off-off-Broadway" and English "fringe" theater, were seeking their own appropriate forms and styles to satirize contemporary Australian society, particularly its male chauvinism, xenophobia, and materialism.

Williamson's first full-length success in the alternative theater, *The Coming of Stork* in 1970, bears some similarities to the quasi-naturalistic satires of other Australian new wave writers, most notably Jack Hibberd and Alex Buzo. The play is structured in a series of scenes—a carryover from Williamson's experience writing for revues—rather than conventional acts and presents the conflicts over values, particularly sexual values, in a household of young technology college graduates. Mateship and male chauvinism are exposed but more comically than in satires by his contemporaries. Following its initial success at Melbourne's La Mama Theatre, Williamson adapted it for the screen and, as "Stork," it became one of the revived Australian film industry's first commercial successes. Later the play was to have a long run in Los Angeles.

The next year saw overlapping productions of two new Williamson plays in Melbourne's leading alternative theaters. *The Removalists*, which presented troubled relationships between the police and the public and between the sexes, premiered at La Mama. A black comedy, that started as stereotyped social satire, *The Removalists* moved increasingly into absurdism and the theater of cruelty. Its situation, in which a pair of policemen interfere in a domestic dispute, develops through a theatrically brilliant sequence of moves that arouses, then reverses the audience's expectations, bewildering them as to what is real and disturbing and what, with comic relief, they can recognize as ritualized bluff and dissembling—until the coda in which the two policemen turn to pummelling each other, now that there is no one else left to pummel. The subtextual revelations of how authoritarianism and insecurity, and sexuality and violence, are intertangled produces a play that is not only quasi-naturalistic in its socially accurate observations but also a play with distinctly absurdist overtones.

Before *The Removalists* had finished its run (with the playwright himself in the role of the removalist—or furniture mover, though this translation into American English misses the grim pun in the title), *Don's Party* had opened around the corner in the Australian Performing Group's Pram Factory. Like many other new wave plays by Williamson's contemporaries, *Don's Party* uses the found form of a familiar social ritual. In this instance, the ritual is that of the election night party, which provides an occasion for presenting the bored, frustrated lives of early middle-aged suburban couples—the beneficiaries, like the playwright himself, of post-war affluence and the expansion of educational opportunities.

Immediately after establishing the normal relationships between its various professional couples, the play proceeds to vary these in an elaborate carnival game of sexual politics—a game in which each male tries to take another's place without losing his own. The theatrical formality of farce is at least as important to this play's development as the accuracy of its social observations. As in *The Coming of Stork*, the entrance of a zany sort disrupts the others' strained efforts to repress their marital tensions and to observe the social norms. Here the zany is the lecherous Cooley, with his much younger and sexually "liberated" girl friend. But in contrast to the earlier play, the frenetic pace of the farce and the incessant gagging in *Don's Party* are integrated into a satiric presentation of contemporary mores to achieve a wider set of socially significant implications. The party's rise to bacchanalian euphoria and its subsequent collapse into hung-over depression subtly relate its course to the waxing and waning of the guests' hopes for a new life politically and personally.

Both *The Removalists* and *Don's Party* would prove the conspicuous successes of the "new wave" of writing emerging in the alternative theater. Not overtly experimental—though *Don's Party*, with its large cast and continuously shifting interactions presented the director and actors with challenges, both plays confronted audiences with social types and situations they could readily identify or identify with. The language rang true, even if—at a time when Australian idioms were still unfamiliar on the stage or screen—some found the verisimilitude shocking. Reviewers and audiences alike were beguiled by Williamson's "naturalism," and the playwright identified himself as a naturalist, by which he meant that he wrote from experience and direct observation not in imitation of Brecht, Beckett, or other influences on some of his contemporaries. Naturalism, however, hardly assisted identification of the combination of realism, comedy, and satire that distinguished his style and tone from that of his more ostentatiously experimental contemporaries. A polemical preference for experimentation over so-called naturalism was long to confuse the critical reception of Williamson's comic-realistic satires. His subsequent descriptions of himself as a satirist, combined with the widening range of Australian theater through the 1970s and revivals of his earlier plays, would assist later recognition of Williamson as an essentially comic writer.

The production of *The Removalists* at Sydney's equivalent to Melbourne's alternative theaters late in 1971 launched Williamson's national career and led shortly after to the establishment of his international reputation when he received the George Devine Award for most promising playwright from London's Royal Court. By then Williamson was working on a commission from the Melbourne Theatre Company and, following a sensationally successful Sydney production of *Don's Party* in 1972, he was commissioned to write another new play for that company's inaugural season at Sydney's Opera House.

Jugglers Three, Williamson's play for the MTC and his debut in the mainstream theater, was produced in 1972 and was a hit with the public and critics, though it has since proved to be one of the more ephemeral of his plays. Conceived originally as a black comedy revealing the corrupting moral effects of the Vietnam War on Australian society, the draft submitted to the state-subsidized MTC encountered objections and was restructured. The original script's flashback scenes to Vietnam were replaced by a farcical subplot, new characters were introduced, and a set of domestic and sexual imbroglios substituted for the wider range of moral implications intended in the earlier version.

What If You Died Tomorrow, produced in 1973 as part of the inaugural Opera House season was another critical and commercial success. The production transferred to London and, through revival, the play itself has proved more durable than *Jugglers Three*. In its drawing on personal experience, *What If You Died Tomorrow* is more blatantly an "autobiographical" play than its predecessor. It problematizes the success of a doctor turned novelist who, like the playwright himself at that time, was in a new personal relationship. But Williamson's skills in rapid pacing, multiple interactions, and conflicting levels of dialogue detach the comedy from the purely personal and elevate its concerns to a more general and existential search for values.

The Department, his next play, marked the first of the "institutional" plays as distinct from the "personal" plays. It initially confused critics who were expecting more rambunctious behavior and verbal fireworks from the author of *The Removalists*, *Don's Party*, and *Jugglers Three*. Clearly drawing on Williamson's memories of teaching in the mechanical engineering department at Swinburne, *The Department* was a comparatively low-keyed but subtly constructed satire of institutions of any kind, including the political. Ideals and principles are the first casualities in Robby's battle to maintain and increase his power as the head of department; he invokes them merely for tactical defenses in his strategy to outwit at any cost his rival in the physics department. Instead of pursuing the real enough educational issues themselves, Williamson allows the farcical possibilities inherent in Robby's manipulation of them to emerge—thus implicitly inviting extension to other issues and institutions. As the play traveled across the country, critics came to discover new virtues in it and a new, less crudely naturalistic playwright; however, the metaphoric as well as the satiric implications they discerned in *The Department* could with hindsight be discerned in Williamson's earlier plays as well and had perhaps been obscured by both the assumptions of naturalism and the style of productions they had received.

Paradoxically, Williamson's next play, *A Handful of Friends*, is his most naturalistic in the historical or Ibsenite sense of that term. A comedy of professional and sexual manners, it involves its set of highly articulate and self-conscious characters— a filmmaker and his actress wife, an academic, his wife, and his journalist sister— in an acrimonious release of revelations about the past. In contrast to the use of real time in *The Removalists* and its successors, the events in *A Handful of Friends* take place over a longer period. As well, there is a more obvious metaphoric patterning of the language. While *A Handful of Friends* has not proved one of Williamson's widely traveled and frequently revived works, it showed that he was experimenting technically, even if still within the broad conventions of realism.

The Club, first produced in 1977, has proved through constant revivals the most popular of Williamson's plays. Although set in the committee room of one of Melbourne's Australian Rules football clubs, it was readily perceived as a satire of institutions of any kind and the self-serving motives of individuals. The deals and duplicity exposed in the pre-committee meeting are the stuff of basic politicking in any apparently democratic institution, whether a football club of any code or the government of the day. The question running throughout *The Club*, of where power lies ultimately, is resolved finally in favor of democracy. But such optimism is qualified ironically—by a reversal that might remind us of *The Department* and the confusion of ends and means in that institution. The players resolve to do what they ought to have been doing all along—playing to win—and so bring the club's supporters to their aid in thwarting the committee's plans for their replacement. With its found form of a meeting, the structure is reminiscent of *The Department*'s, while its more pronounced farcical overtones— especially the elaborate deception of Jock the villain—are reminders of what by this time had come to seem vintage Williamson. The Sydney production of *The Club* transferred to London, then retitled *Players*, the play enjoyed good runs in Washington, D.C., and on Broadway. Later it was filmed.

While the critics' perception of Williamson was shifting away from seeing him as simply a naturalist observer with an uncannily acute ear for the vernacular and psychologist's eye for contradictory behavior, his next play would confuse their new appraisal of him as a satirist. *Travelling North*, first produced in 1979, was both assertively innovative in its fluent use of cinematic techniques and also emotionally involving for audiences. Perhaps influenced by his adaptation of *King Lear* for school students and certainly drawing on personal memory and observation, Williamson's new play embraced not only the lifestyles of different generations and subcultures but also the grand Shakespearean themes of love and marriage, life and death —and resurrection.

The play has an obvious socio-historical specificity. Opening around the time in which *Don's Party* is set, when hopes for an end to two decades of conservative rule in Australia were dashed, the play ends on the eve of the Whitlam Labor government's coming to power. But clearly a wider view than the political is being told through the story of Frank, the lifelong humanitarian and former Communist, and Frances, the grandmother with whom he falls in love toward the end of his life. The constant scene changes show them together and apart, as lovers and parents, in wintry Melbourne and the paradisaical North, not only placing them in a variety of situations and relationships to reveal them as humans but also to suggest a pattern to life. It is a pattern that is unpredictable, ironically given Frank's Lear-like intentions to put aside all cares for his remaining years, but it is a pattern that assumes inevitability as he approaches death. At the end there is a sense of life as mysterious but ultimately fulfilling. The dialogue does not attempt to explicate this, except for asserting Frances's belief that there is a god, a moral order, and some ultimate significance to life against Frank's agnosticism and sardonic rationalism. Characteristically, the dialogue is composed of brief exchanges spiced with jests rather than extended passages of heightened language. But the music (Vivaldi, Bach, Mozart, Beethoven, Schubert) specified as part of the play's total structure in performance invokes a dimension beyond the everyday. Similarly, the stage direction at the end that Frank is to rise from the chair in which he has just died and join the rest of the cast to take the curtain call is, as a stage direction, completely prosaic. In performance though it suggests a sense of regeneration and the continuance of life that an audience could associate with Shakespeare and his late comedies. *Travelling*

North was high comedy, and if writing for the screen had inspired the play's rapid changes of time and scene, then it is appropriate that the film version provides the definitive performance to date.

The Perfectionist in 1982 developed further the fluent scene and time shifts found in *Travelling North* for a comic-satiric examination of marriage. More than in any previous Williamson play the issues—the impact of the women's movement on middle-class, two career marriages, but beyond that the perennial clashing of idealism and pragmatism—are fully on the surface, consciously present in the minds of mature, intelligent, articulate characters who engage with them openly and wittily. While the battle of the wits is couched in contemporary idioms, the play is at least as much a formal comedy and traditional battle of the sexes as a slice of life. By implication, the playwright who presents these conflicts and the audiences who observe them cannot offer any resolution but can only recognize the existential and comic accuracy of Barbara's realization that "There aren't any easy solutions—you just have to hope there are enough good moments to make the whole hassle worthwhile."

When *Sons of Cain* premiered in 1985, it seemed implicitly to address those of Williamson's critics who were asking what had happened to the confronting style of the early plays with their clash of various sub-cultures and levels of language and their engagement with socio-political issues rather than the gently satirized "pseudo problems" of the bourgeoisie. The new play confronted the scandals then linking politicians and police to drug trafficking and corruption that were preoccupying the Australian press—and raised the social-moral question: If this is how we live now what is to be done? *Sons of Cain* combined elements reminiscent of Williamson's earlier plays for the alternative theater with others familiar from his more recent comedies of manners. Something of the comic strip stereotyping of the early plays enters into the characterizing of public figures, and Kevin Cassidy, the investigative editor and the play's central figure, seems in part a throwback to Williamson's earlier larrikins. At the same time, the battle between the sexes in the newspaper office has a formal symmetry reminiscent of *The Perfectionist.*

By this time, Williamson had written over a wide range of comedy—from the low and farcical, as in *The Coming of Stork*, to the high and serious, as in *Travelling North*—and had re-combined the stylistic elements of comedy, satire, and realism within successive plays. The intervals between his plays had been increasing as he became more involved in his parallel career of writing for the screen. He adapted most of his plays for film or television and accepted and initiated commissions for those media. His original script for Peter Weir's film *Gallipoli* (1981) and his adaptation of C.J. Koch's novel for the same director's *The Year of Living Dangerously* (1983) brought him international prominence as a screenwriter and numerous offers from Hollywood.

In 1980 he had been commissioned to write a play to celebrate the Sydney Nimrod Company's tenth year, and he burlesqued the local film industry in a light-hearted satiric farce. *Celluloid Heroes*, though, failed to gain the mounting acclaim that had greeted his preceding plays, perhaps because of expectations that the latest Williamson would not only amuse but also reveal through satire some significant aspect of how we live now. In *Emerald City*, produced in 1987, Williamson again satirized the film industry but in the mode of *The Perfectionist's* sophisticated comedy of manners rather than that of *Celluloid Heroes'* farce. Combining the presentation of personal, moral, and sexual conflicts with satire of the industry, *Emerald City* again showed Williamson's characteristic ability to create, with an air of detachment, significant comedy out of immediate experience. The screenwriter in the play, Colin, is clearly a comic version of Williamson himself and Colin's conflicts between his artistic integrity and the lure of fame and fortune a projection from critical reactions to Williamson's recent works. Elegantly articulate and with its allusions to *The Wizard of Oz* even literary in comparison with Williamson's earlier plays, *Emerald City* could still accommodate the philistine Mike McCord, Colin's rival, his alter ego, and—like Kevin Cassidy in *Sons of Cain*—a throwback to the larrikins of *The Coming of Stork* and *Don's Party*. A wickedly incisive analysis of the film industry, the play also entertains through comedy questions of personal and professional integrity that have more than local or topical application.

So far, this account has been concerned with the appearance of Williamson's plays in the Australian theatrical context, the successive entry of different styles and techniques into his work, and the predominantly local critical responses. As the dominant writer for the Australian stage and cinema for the past two decades, Williamson has seen a succession of Australian and English reviewers praise his plays for their "sociological" acuity or damn them for condoning the vulgarity of the society they present. Fascination with his naturalism—the social mimesis of the plays—has predominated over stylistic and technical considerations. However, by now many of Williamson's plays have been produced around the world, whether in English or in translation, and have been adapted for internationally distributed films. This suggests that as plays, rather than as merely entertaining observations of the local and the topical, his satiric comedies offer directors and actors satisfying pieces for performance—and offer audiences far beyond Australia the satisfactions of engaging, intelligent, and amusing theater.

Like *Sons of Cain*, *Top Silk*, produced in 1989, poses questions of how government and the law can address the drug problem, but this time in a family rather than in an institutional setting, and the questions of moral responsibility are raised in more personal terms. While *Top Silk* was panned by the critics as implausible, even melodramatic, the public responded enthusiastically. This invites two related general observations: Williamson is a popular entertainer, closer to his public than to his critics; and audiences share his ethical concerns while enjoying his humor. A new play, *Siren*, was produced in 1990. This play also engages with a current public issue, the corruption associated with land development and with the more perennial personal theme of sexual fidelity but in the mode of sophisticated bedroom farce.

To see Williamson as a satirist is to assume that he implies ethical norms: The police should not take the law into their own hands; institutions like an engineering department or a football club should not lose sight of their purpose in petty rivalries and ambitions; newspapers and politicians should defend the public good; spouses should be faithful, friends loyal, and so on. Such norms are commonplace or commonsensical. Yet people being what they are shown to be, nothing is quite so simple. Williamson's recognition of the disparities between how people ought to behave and how in fact they do generates his satire—but also his comic amusement and ambivalence. His frequently observed compassion for his characters—even his monsters of egoism—made his early plays seem more ambiguous or gave them a more human dimension than the satires by his contemporaries in the alternative theater. Since then, he has engaged with a wide range of public and personal issues, not in any dogmatic or didactic way but with a resignedly tolerant, comic acceptance of the fact that, human nature being what it is, life is likely to muddle on in much the same inconsistent way. If this suggests that in his work there is some conflict between the comic and the satiric, then his re-engagements with it in so many different plays also suggest it continues to stimulate strong and—to use his own word—"accessible" drama.

DAVID WILLIAMSON'S PUBLISHED WORK

Plays (First production dates in parentheses)

The Removalists (1971), 1972
Don's Party (1971), 1973
Three Plays (*The Coming of Stork*, 1970; *Jugglers Three*, 1972; *What If You Died Tomorrow*, 1973), 1974
The Department (1974), 1975
A Handful of Friends (1976), 1976
The Club (1977), 1978
Travelling North (1979), 1980
The Perfectionist (1982), 1983
Sons of Cain (1985), 1985
Collected Plays (*The Removalists*, *Don's Party*, titles in *Three Plays*), 1986
Emerald City (1987), 1987
Top Silk (1989), 1990

Screenplay

Gallipoli: The Screenplay (In *The Story of Gallipoli*), 1981

SELECTED CRITICAL READINGS

While Williamson's works have generated a prodigious amount of newsprint, critical appraisal beyond reviews is limited to a couple of books and a few articles. Interest has concentrated on the social attitudes presented in his work rather than on the manner of its presentation. The proven effectiveness of Williamson's styles and techniques in the theater invites equal critical consideration.

Fitzpatrick, Peter. *Williamson*. Sydney: Methuen Australia, 1987. Calls Williamson a "storyteller to the tribe" and "a shaper of cultural images." Provides a critical study of the plays to *The Perfectionist*.

Holloway, Peter, editor. *Contemporary Australian Drama*. Rev. Ed. Sydney: Currency Press, 1987. Includes a previously unpublished article: Peter Fitzpatrick's "Styles of Love: Williamson in the Eighties"; reprints David Williamson's "*The Removalists*: A Conjunction of Limitations" from *Meanjin* 4 (1974); Brian Kiernan's "The Games People Play"; two general surveys of contemporary Australian drama—Margaret Williams's "Mask and Cage" from *Meanjin* 2 (1973), and Roslyn Arnold's "Aggressive Vernacular," *Southerly* 4 (1975).

Kiernan, Brian. "An Australian Playwright Goes to Washington." *Antipodes* 3 (1989): 105–07. Discusses Williamson's debut as a playwright in the United States.

———. *David Williamson: A Writer's Career.* Melbourne: William Heinemann, 1990. Critical biography.

———. "The Games People Play: The Development of David Williamson." *Southerly* 35 (1975): 315–29. Argues that Williamson explores patterns of social interaction rather than character and theme. Maintains that the work is not naturalistic but absurdist in spite of its apparent realism.

———. "Comic-Satiric-Realism: David Williamson's Plays since *The Department.*" *Southerly* 46 (1986): 3–18. Suggests that critics have missed the comic-satiric dimensions of the later plays, which show the difference between how people behave and how they ought to behave, thereby generating universal satire.

McCallum, John. "A New Map of Australia: The Plays of David Williamson." *Australian Literary Studies* 11 (1984): 342–54. Examines the creation of a world recognizable to audiences, the objective and naturalistic style of the plays, and the autobiographical quality. Considers the plays a map that graphs the Australian social chronicle from the late 1960s.

Ross, Robert. "David Williamson." *Critical Survey of Drama.* Englewood Cliffs: Salem Press, 1985: 2085-94. Provides biographical information; surveys the plays—their technique and themes.

Zuber-Skerritt, Ortrun, editor. *David Williamson.* Amsterdam: Rodopi, 1988. Includes selected talks and articles by, and interviews with, Williamson; extensive bibliography of newspaper and magazine articles and reviews.

Interviews

With Candida Baker. *Yacker.* Sydney: Pan Books, 1986. 290–315.
With Paul Kavanagh and Peter Kuch. *Southerly* 47 (1986): 131–41.
With Ray Willbanks. *Antipodes* 2 (1988): 104–06.

—BRIAN KIERNAN

Katherine Mansfield

Kathleen Mansfield Beauchamp—later to become Katherine Mansfield—was born on 14 October 1888 in Wellington, New Zealand. Her father was a successful businessman, her mother a Victorian lady who left to others the rearing of their four daughters and one son.

Mansfield was sent with her sisters to a finishing school in London in 1903. When she got back to New Zealand in 1908, she persuaded her father to let her return to England on a yearly allowance of 100 pounds. Arriving in London shortly before her twentieth birthday, she entered one of the most disordered times of her life, and there is scant information about this period. She did become pregnant and traveled to Bavaria where she miscarried—and where she wrote *In a German Pension*, her first collection of short stories.

Mansfield met John Middleton Murry in 1911, and there began a stormy relationship that continued throughout her life. They married in 1918.

Experiencing intense periods of creativity, Mansfield established a solid reputation as a writer. Yet her short life was plagued with personal problems, depression, then illness, which was diagnosed as tuberculosis in 1917. Once she recognized that her death was only a matter of time she began both to write incessantly and to search frantically for a cure. Moving restlessly from place to place, sometimes accompanied by Murry, sometimes by her longtime friend Ida Baker, Mansfield wrote some of her best work during this time.

In October 1922 she joined the Gurdjieff Institute near Paris in a last desperate attempt for a cure. At the end of December, she wrote to Murry asking him to visit her. She died a few hours after he arrived, on 9 January 1923.

The Idea of the Perfect Short Story

While it is undeniably true that Katherine Mansfield's major contribution to literature has been and will continue to be regarded as her five volumes of carefully and innovatively complex short fiction, she did a good deal of other writing as well. Mainly through the connections and support of her husband, editor John Middleton Murry, Mansfield produced a considerable number of literary essays and reviews. Besides loving to perform dramas, she also wrote a number of her own theatrical *jeu d'esprits*. Motivated by rage and the desire for experimentation with language and form, Mansfield over her tragically few creative years wrote a surprisingly substantial amount of poetry. According to Cherry A. Hankin, who edited the moving and extensive *Letters Between Katherine Mansfield and John Middleton Murry*, this correspondence "In a sense . . . is the novel she never wrote" (2). In addition, Mansfield produced that anomaly of prose called *The Urewera Journal.* Because the *Journal* has no obvious place in the corpus of Mansfield's literature and because it is formally problematic, this slender volume of observations, sketches, notes, and letters exists somewhat as a thematic antecedent for her later work and as a cross index to her stylistic preoccupations.

The *Journal* is a log Mansfield kept during a month-long camping tour on the North Island of New Zealand in 1907, in which she records encounters with Maoris; her impressions of the landscape, of the weather, of the Maoris, the campfires, her companions; records of her illnesses, her clothes, and her place in the rugged Urewera bush. Thus her account of the journey is not simply a recapitulation of the sights and events nor a rhapsody of her enjoyment nor a repudiation of her several displeasures, but rather a rethinking of her travel and the notion of traveling so that neither retains meaning on its own, so that they are resonances of each other. Mansfield is, in a very real and measurable way, trying to reinvent epistemology. Thus what we have here with *The Urewera Journal* is an outrageous pun—an epistolary epistemology.

The *Journal,* carefully constructed from the Turnbull Library's Mansfield materials, is a celebration of formal problems. Some of the entries are coherent, complete declarative sentences, some are merely descriptive or attributive phrases strung together along a common theme. Some entries, while resembling diary entries, contain none of the effusive language endemic to that form but convey terse estimations of the party's progress through the countryside. Other entries are letters to various relatives.

None of this would be very interesting if Mansfield did not insist always on synthesizing her external world to suit the needs of her internal disposition, which probably was not so tortured as *suspicious.* Every detail of the journey she chose to record forms part of a textual scheme that relies on the succession of entries (some of which are out of order) to tell a story. The notion of going There and returning back Here is framework enough to sustain any necessary conflicts and achieve Plot.

Insofar as all the entries are addressed to some reader, even if that reader is only Mansfield, they are letters; and epistolary writing harbors some formidable magical properties. First, letters obviate their writers; the writers disappear, die into the text. The text is everything. Second, the letter accentuates the reader; other forms imply the reader, but the epistolary demands its reader. So while we always have Mansfield's unmistakable personal voice, there is no quantifiable characterization of her or anyone else. They are all displaced. But the narrative does not refute people; it only replaces them, reconstructs them in a more fluid medium, one that reveals substantive relationships between writer and narrative without reflexivity and not at the expense of the reader's relationship to the actual events of the story.

Thus, Mansfield fuses textual problems in the *Journal.* The effect is a self-generative maintenance program that insures the form a workable if not wholly equitable place between performer and her audience. Whether Mansfield is writing in the lyrical mode or penning pedestrian commentaries in the margins, she is forever acting out all our fantasies of increase, of making art out of doodles. Who can accuse her of gratuitous overwriting when, at the end of the first entry, we read: "How we play inside the house while Life sits on the front step and Death mounts guard at the back" (25).

The Urewera Journal, then, can be seen as the introduction to Mansfield's art, which in essence was experimentation with the idea of the perfect short story, an attempt to capture perfection over and over again, and to do it differently each time. Mansfield composed with language, played music and painted pictures with her words, then crushed the art with the real. Mansfield demands, then almost abuses, the active reader; the author's words are beautiful, but their meaning cuts and leaves one cold.

Because Mansfield's stories are so very complex, one cannot afford to ignore any aspect of their meaning but must examine the patterns that develop character and theme, patterns that appear repeatedly: experiences of the family, communication gaps in marriage and in romantic relationships, class distinctions, the male as simultaneously domineering and weak, the female as victim but deserving of her punishment because she allows herself to be victimized, and the idea of lying. While these patterns relate closely to Mansfield's life, they are not simply illustrations of her life. Those thoughts and feelings, coming from her experiences, gave her the material with which to work, but she created the stories. Thus to hone in on one character as representing the author ignores the fact that Mansfield the author created all her characters and their thoughts.

Even though themes reoccur, the stories are never alike. For this reason, some critics hold that the constant experimentation kept her from developing a particular style. She did have a style, one that was never stagnant but forever guided by her prevailing ambition: to create the perfect short story.

Let us examine some representative Mansfield stories, one example per book, then make a full encounter with "Prelude," the short story she worked on over the years.

"The Modern Soul" (*In a German Pension*) opens with the female narrator sitting with Herr Professor while he favors her with his conversation and far superior knowledge. The two Godowska women approach, and after a brief conversation all four return to the pension for the evening recital in which Sonia and the Professor perform separate acts. Sonia invites the narrator to an evening walk that ends abruptly when Sonia dramatically faints outside the hairdresser's shop. Naturally, the Professor runs to her aid. The next morning the female narrator learns at breakfast that the Professor and Sonia are spending the day in the woods.

There is a sharp contrast between appearance and reality in this story. The Professor and Sonia represent the world of appearance. For instance, the Professor requests that the narrator not leave when the Godowskas approach because he is afraid of how the situation might appear to the two women. His confrontation with reality, however, is that he must pay for his late-night milk. In comparison, Sonia spends her whole life pretending to be what she is not, an actress. In one subtle instance, her conflict with reality is revealed when her mother thoughtfully points out a visible safety pin in her skirt. Although Sonia is labeled a "modern soul" by the Professor, it is the Professor who acts as the real "sole" upon which Sonia walks all over through her grand performance. The narrator sees through Sonia when she leaves her after the fainting spell, knowing that Sonia was in no real danger. The narrator also notes that "modern souls oughtn't to wear this [stays]" (7), an observation that also strengthens the point that Sonia tries to *appear* to be a modern soul but in actuality is not.

The story is filled with sexual images and allusions. The professor proudly stating the fact that he has eaten such a quantity of fruit can be taken as representing the number of women he has seduced. Sonia adorns herself with flowers that represent spring and the season of fertility. Even in her performance, she extends a sensuous invitation of going into the woods "as lightly draped as possible, and bed among the pine needles." Another obvious allusion to sexuality occurs when the Professor must loosen Sonia's stays, which he willingly does, or so the reader assumes. The Professor, at the beginning of the story, had emerged from the woods only to return to nature, at the end of the story, for enjoyment with Sonia.

Raoul Duquette, the speaker of Mansfield's confessional monologue, "Je ne parle pas français" (*Bliss and Other Stories*) sits in a Parisian cafe and wanders mentally through his past, vacillating between fantasy and actuality. The reader can immediately distinguish between Mansfield's impressionism, "thin, dark girls with silver rings in their ears and market baskets on their arms" (351), and Raoul's superficial ideas, "people are like portmanteaux" (350). Once again, Mansfield has set up a double viewpoint: She states the true nature of things, while Duquette tells how things appear. For example, although Raoul describes himself as "a gentleman, a writer, serious, young, and extremely interested in modern English literature," he reveals himself as a pimp, a neurotic, an effeminate character who can marvel at a woman's suffering and while watching her in tears think of the scene's literary possibilities. The distaste the reader feels for Raoul is increased by his actions in his Madame Butterfly relationship with Dick, a tweedy English writer, who leaves Raoul after a strange friendship, only to return with Mouse, a stereotypical Englishwoman with a cape and a craving for tea, who announces her helplessness and naivete to Raoul with the statement "Je ne parle pas français." Dick, in turn, deserts Mouse to return to his mother. Eventually, Mouse is deserted as well by Raoul, who recognizes that his shallow nature would not allow him to play the noble protector for very long. So Mouse is left completely alone in France, unable to speak the language and unable to go home because her friends think she is married.

This complex story, one of Mansfield's longest, should be approached with several particulars in mind. The themes of loneliness, homelessness, and abandoned love are dealt with in connection with each major character. Raoul says that he has no family, and he severs all human relationships, preferring to observe cafe patrons rather than developing a serious friendship with someone like Mouse. Dick is emotionally unable to continue relationships; he isolates himself from Raoul and Mouse until he is as lonely as the man of the song who sought a dinner. Dick is dependent on his mother, and this extreme dependence kills his relationship with Mouse who loves him. Mouse is Madame Butterfly, much more so than Raoul, although he likes to picture himself in such a way. At the end, Mouse becomes the true victim, the personification of loneliness, homelessness, and abandoned love.

The limited scope of the characters is important to notice, for the characters in the story are treated as stereotypes—not so much by Mansfield as by one another. The story's title itself, "Je ne parle pas français," sums up the lack of understanding among the characters. Further supporting this idea of isolation, Mansfield names the characters with specific qualities in mind for each of them. "Raoul" is a name the French associate with homosexuality and cannibalism; also, it is the name used to describe a cultured man who behaves foolishly. Raoul's surname "Duquette" suggests "coquette" and Raoul's duplicity—what he calls himself in contrast to what he shows himself to be. Needless to say, "Mouse," a common nickname for women, carries unpleasant connotations, suggesting as it does submission. Dick's personality is limited because he isolates himself and will not play any role for any length of time other than that of his mother's son.

Mansfield's abilities to manipulate a story and leave the reader with a disturbing impression at the end are striking. Here, for example, she shows the familiar plight of loneliness and homelessness in several different lights, for the impressions one forms about Raoul, about the cafe Madame, and about Mouse and Dick are all quite different, even as each character is equally isolated outside the circle of human warmth. Mansfield transforms "Je ne parle pas français" from a stale little phrase into an overwhelming statement of loneliness.

In "The Young Girl" (*The Garden Party and Other Stories*), Mrs. Raddick, her attractive seventeen-year-old daughter, and her young son Hennie are Londoners visiting the French Riviera. The seemingly bored young girl and her mother leave Hennie with a friend of Mrs. Raddick's, a Frenchman, while they go to gamble. The girl soon returns, too young to be admitted to the casino. She reluctantly accompanies her brother and the anonymous narrator to a cafe. Initially declaring lack of appetite, she nonchalantly echoes Hennie's orders of hot chocolate, pastries, and ice cream, then powders her nose. An elderly man, whom she either fails to notice or ignores, stares at her. Mrs. Raddick does not meet them at the promised time, and the young girl, close to tears, insists on waiting alone for her mother.

The moods in "The Young Girl" are made up of the tension between maturity and immaturity—both psychological and physical—and of frustration as illusion is confronted with bitter reality. The young girl, in a period of transition between childhood and adulthood, struggles to establish her identity. That she is reaching physical maturity is evident in the narrator's perception of her as well as in the stares of the men in the cafe. In contrast, though, the casino refused to grant her the status of an adult. Still, the young girl feigns indifference to and disdain for both the casino and the cafe and acts as she believes a mature woman would—casually powdering her nose, disinterested in and mentally distant from all that goes on around her. Her illusions of maturity, represented in her performance, were undermined first in her rejection by the casino, then on having to wait, humiliated, for her negligent mother. While men's appreciative stares invite her to enter the mature world in the role of the stereotypical female admired and devoured by males, her mother and the casino have rejected her as a member of that world. Still, she no longer wishes to identify with Hennie's "childish" world. The result of her predicament is isolation. Childhood is no longer carefree but becomes characterized by anxiety, trauma, and repression.

"When dear old Mrs. Hay went back to town after staying with the Burnells she sent the children a doll's house" (570). The house stood in the Burnell courtyard, reeking of paint, oily green with a yellow front door and porch and two red and white chimneys. Thus begins "The Doll's House" (*The Dove's Nest and Other Stories*). The Burnell children, Isabel, Lottie, and Kezia, were overwhelmed, especially with the toys that seemed real. Kezia, in particular, looking for a special kind of realness in the house, spotted a tiny oil lamp on the dining-room table. The next day at school Isabel got to brag about the doll's house because she was the oldest, but Kezia managed to tell about the wonderful lamp. The girls at school wanted to be Isabel's friend that day, because she was the one to pick who would get to come and see the doll's house first. It was finally decided that the girls would come each day in pairs, going into the courtyard only, of course, so they wouldn't disturb the grownups.

The day soon came when all the girls at school had seen the doll's house except for the Kelveys, and no one expected them to be asked, because Lil and Else Kelvey were the daughters of a washerwoman and came to school dressed in scraps; no one knew where their father was—probably in prison. The teacher treated the Kelveys differently from her other pupils, and the girls never played with them. That day when everyone had seen the doll's house but the Kelveys, the lunchtime conversation lagged, so the children made some fun out of taunting the common girls. Their cruelty was exhilarating: "The little girls rushed away in a body, deeply, deeply excited, wild with joy" (575). It seemed that everyone knew how to treat the Kelveys except Kezia, who saw them walking home that afternoon and took them to visit the doll's house. They even got to see the lamp before Kezia's Aunt Beryl discovered the outcasts in the courtyard and chased them away. After all, Beryl's afternoon had been dreadful: "A letter had come from Willie Brent, a terrifying, threatening letter, saying if she did not meet him that night in Pulman's Bush, he'd come to the front door and ask the reason why! But now that she had frightened those little rats of Kelveys and given Kezia a good scolding, her heart felt lighter. That ghastly pressure was gone. She went back to the house humming" (577).

Mansfield draws some very disturbing comparisons in this story and delivers one prickling point after another; the reader is caught in the parallel between the teacher's subtle smiles, the little girls' outright exclusion of the Kelveys, and Beryl's treatment of them. Once again Mansfield demands an active reader, one who will see the parallel between the schoolgirls' glee and Beryl's humming after they abuse the Kelveys. Certainly, Mansfield, who came from a wealthy family, knew how class distinctions work whether among children or adults. (Of course, the cruelty of class distinctions serves as the basis for Mansfield's most widely known story, "The Garden Party.") When the reader connects with the emotions in "The Doll's House," that is the moment when Mansfield takes control. She can be cutting in her manipulation of her reader, but this story has a brightening at the end, which is unusual for Mansfield. The brightness lies in the "rare smile" of one of the Kelvey girls, who says, "'I seen the little lamp'" (577).

"The Tiredness of Rosabel" (*Something Childish and Other Stories*) tells of an evening in the life of a young London milliner named Rosabel. Tired from a hard day's work, she goes home on the bus after forsaking dinner in order to buy violets. A girl nearby is reading a romance novel, as Rosabel daydreams. Having reached her dreary room, she reflects on the day's events, including her experiences with a rich and handsome young couple, recalling that when the woman left the man to pay for the hat, he had suggestively complimented her. From this experience, she constructs her own fairy-tale romance with him, in which she possesses all the luxury and beauty she could never have in reality. Her fatigue sends her to bed, still optimistic and smiling in the gloom and grime of her existence. The dichotomy between the rich young woman and Rosabel, that between the "haves" and "have nots," is obvious. The fact that both women are exploited is perhaps less apparent. Although Rosabel's fantasy of wealth seems to sustain her in her poverty, its effect is not positive but self-destructive in its perpetuation of repressive societal norms and stereotypes for women, regardless of social status. Rosabel's fatigue contributes to her willingness to engage in utopic fantasy, and while her feelings of discontent are momentarily pacified, Rosabel subconsciously validates the status quo and her continued exploitation by fantasizing herself among those who are responsible for her present condition. At issue, however, is not social class alone but gender as well. Just as violets are objects of beauty to be possessed, so are women represented in both Rosabel's real and fantasized lives. Mansfield's bitter irony succeeds in portraying the evils of romantic "opiates," those which oppressors use to intoxicate and thereby control others. This exploration of the female consciousness and of women's roles in society demonstrates the enlightened view that Mansfield held.

"Prelude" (*Bliss and Other Stories*), Mansfield's longest short story, was a lifelong project, which has been surrounded by much controversy since her death. Mansfield began writing the story, which was finally published as "Prelude," when she was about sixteen and, although she submitted a copy of the story to Leonard and Virginia Woolf's Hogarth Press for publication, she continued working on it intermittently throughout her life. The development of her working copy, a much longer story called *The Aloe*, can be compared to the development of Mozart's *Requiem*, which was also left unfinished. Perhaps Mansfield identified with Mozart, who also died from tuberculosis and a sexually transmitted disease and never completed "Prelude" because she, like the great composer, felt that completing her major work would hasten her death. Vincent O'Sullivan, however, suggests that (regardless of her fears that her life was intertwined with the completion of the story) she felt compelled to write it, supporting his idea with a line from one of Mansfield's letters: "If I do not write this book I shall die" (Murry *Letters* 162).

O'Sullivan has produced an excellent edition of *The Aloe* and "Prelude" in which Mansfield's manuscripts of *The Aloe* (including passages she later crossed out) are compared page by page with the published text of "Prelude." O'Sullivan's introduction provides important information about Mansfield's progress on the work, publication of "Prelude" by Hogarth Press, and John Middleton Murry's posthumous publication of *The Aloe* in 1930. O'Sullivan does not directly criticize Murry's treatment of Mansfield's work; however, he does contend that Murry's publication of *The Aloe* contained "the stylistic impositions of another hand." O'Sullivan's introduction is cautious, and he carefully supports his assertions about Mansfield's work with quotations from her letters and journals, but, like many of Mansfield's critics, he concentrates too much on the details of Mansfield's life and the history of the text and fails to deal with the content itself.

But O'Sullivan does make one very important point about the stories. He quotes Mansfield's desire in her early twenties to write a "sketch, hardly that, more a psychological study" (15), and suggests that *The Aloe* and "Prelude" are examples of this "new way to tell a story," which is "not so much a narrative about events shared by several people, but as one where several temperaments unfold in the slantings of perspective, in the tilting gradations of time" (17). His point provides a valid explanation for the development in "Prelude." Although the experiences of the characters are centered around the move from Wellington to the country, Mansfield's focus is not on the move itself but how each character reacts to it. The children perceive the move as an adventure, yet Linda Burnell seems listless and indifferent. Her sister, Beryl Fairfield, on the other hand, views it as an end to her chances for freedom through marriage and subsequent financial independence from her brother-in-law. Stanley Burnell, despite the inconvenient distance from town, is proud of his acquisition. His mother-in-law looks forward to the bounty of the country home's gardens.

It is easy to avoid the hidden agendas in Mansfield's work by reading the stories on a superficial level, and this is especially true of "Prelude." Details that seem at first to be contradictory or inadequately developed become frighteningly clear upon a second or third reading. For example, Beryl Fairfield appears to be a beautiful woman desirous of a husband, yet she remains inexplicably alone. Upon more careful examination, however, the reader begins to question her attractiveness, for she admits to acting (even when she is alone), playing flirtatious games (even with her sister's husband), and lying in her letters to friends. These confessions make her testimony suspect at best; perhaps she is also lying about her personal charm as well. Beryl, like Rosabel in "The Tiredness of Rosabel," continually escapes from the reality of her situation by fantasizing about the man who will rescue her. This is just one instance of the subtleties that fill "Prelude," in which Mansfield, working on the broader canvas of a longer story, addresses several of the themes that usually occur separately in her shorter works—male dominance and insensitivity, female oppression and reinforcement of their own oppression, and lonely, unwanted children.

Stanley, like Daddy in "Six Years After," is a childishly vain man, proud of his material possessions, insistent on being pampered and having his own way. He expects his mother-in-law to get his slippers for him and demands constant reassurance from his wife Linda that he will not get fat. On the surface, his relationship with Linda appears to be a mutually happy one. Stanley cannot wait to return home from work and see her at the end of the day; Linda curls up in bed with him and urges him, "yes, clasp me" (230), as they fall asleep. Yet the idea of the couple's happiness is undercut, for Linda's thoughts as she walks through the yard ultimately reveal Stanley as a source of anger and resentment. Her attitude towards her children, which has been apparent from the beginning of the story when she says "we shall simply have to cast them off" (219), suggests a problem made brutally clear as she thinks about her feelings during sexual intercourse: "When she had just not screamed at the top of her voice: 'You are killing me. . . .' For all her love and respect and admiration she hated him" (258). She does not want the children she has or those Stanley will force her to have in the future, and she hates him for continuing to impregnate her despite her poor health. While Stanley's treatment of Linda is inexcusable, her refusal to assert herself encourages his thoughtless behavior and reinforces her situation. Linda's festering resentment, which she is unwilling or unable to direct towards her husband, unfortunately, manifests itself in her inattention to her children, behavior as inexcusable as her husband's behavior towards her.

That Mansfield never completed "Prelude" leaves her open to the criticism that she attempted to write a novel and failed; however, "Prelude" stands on its own as a short story, and a careful reader will see the eloquence of the work and realize that a novel is not necessary to legitimize Mansfield's success as a writer. "Prelude" serves not only as an example of Mansfield's ability as an innovative fiction writer but also as an excellent example of her insightful and precocious feminist perspective. She possessed an uncanny ability to cut to the heart of issues and understood, perhaps more fully than many contemporary feminists, that male oppression is not only the fault of sexist, insensitive males but also the fault of women who allow themselves to be dominated.

"Prelude" is noticeably incomplete, and the text of *The Aloe* as well as letters and journals provide insight into Mansfield's plans for "Prelude." Nevertheless, Mansfield herself prepared "Prelude" for the 1918 publication by Hogarth Press, and in this form it is a powerful story that shows her responsiveness to human conflicts, dedication to form, and commitment to social comment.

WORKS CITED

Gordon, Ian, editor. *The Urewera Journal.* London: Oxford UP, 1977.

Hankin, C.A., editor. *Letters Between Katherine Mansfield and John Middleton Murry.* London: Virago Press, 1988.

Mansfield, Katherine. *The Short Stories of Katherine Mansfield.* New York: Ecco Press, 1983.

Murry, John Middleton, editor. *The Letters of Katherine Mansfield.* New York: Alfred A. Knopf, 1929.

O'Sullivan, Vincent, and Margaret Scott, editors. *The Aloe with Prelude.* Wellington: Port Nichelson Press, 1982.

KATHERINE MANSFIELD'S PUBLISHED WORK

Short Fiction

In a German Pension, 1911
Prelude, 1918
Je ne parle pas français, 1920
Bliss and Other Stories, 1920
The Garden Party and Other Stories, 1922
The Doves' Nest and Other Stories (edited by J.M. Murry), 1923
Something Childish and Other Stories (edited by J.M. Murry), 1924
The Aloe (edited by J.M. Murry), 1930

Poetry

Poems (edited by J.M. Murry), 1924
The Poems of Katherine Mansfield (edited by Vincent O'Sullivan), 1989

Drama

Katherine Mansfield: Dramatic Sketches (edited by David Dowling), 1988

Journals

The Journal of Katherine Mansfield (edited by J.M. Murry), 1927

Journal of Katherine Mansfield, "Definitive Edition" (edited by J.M. Murry), 1954
The Urewera Journal (edited by Ian Gordon), 1977

Letters

The Letters of Katherine Mansfield (edited by J.M. Murry), 1928, 1929
Katherine Mansfield's Letters to John Middleton Murry, 1913–1922 (edited by J.M. Murry), 1951
Letters Between Katherine Mansfield and John Middleton Murry (edited by C.A. Hankin), 1988

SELECTED CRITICAL READINGS

With Mansfield's seemingly endless masques, lies, remarkable relationships with so many remarkable people, her wildly individual combination of colonialism and European experiences, plus her unusual reactions to her severe health crises, a great deal of attention has been paid to her biography. True, she led an extraordinarily creative and fascinating life, sometimes scandalous. But what a Mansfield bibliography quickly reveals is the sketchy amount of understanding and explication of her literary work. While Mansfield's life has been pretty thoroughly explored in relation to her writing, there is still much to say about the writing itself.

Alcock, Peter. "'An Aloe in the Garden: Something Essentially New Zealand in Miss Mansfield.'" *Journal of Commonwealth Literature* 11.3 (1977): 58–64. Incorporating other critics and their works, proposes that Mansfield's work conveys a deep, troubled, loving concern for her home country and its escape and growth from the Old World to the new capitalist world.

Alpers, Antony. *The Life of Katherine Mansfield.* New York: Viking, 1980. Alpers says that this book "replaces" his 1953 study, *Katherine Mansfield: A Biography,* drawing on materials previously unavailable and taking advantage of the passing of time. Provides a full-scale, frank treatment of Mansfield's life and interprets the work generally from a biographical standpoint. Includes extensive bibliography of secondary materials.

Beachcroft, T.O. "Katherine Mansfield's Encounter with Theocritus." *English* 23 (1974): 13–19. Compares Mansfield with Theocritus and discusses with references to "Carnation," "Stay Laces," and "Pictures," how his mime form probably influenced Mansfield.

Brown, Constance A. "Dissection and Nostalgia: Katherine Mansfield's Response to World War I." *The Centennial Review* 7 (1979): 329–45. With qualifications from stories set during the war in England and France, claims that WWI caused Mansfield's writing to take two separate but parallel paths after 1915: her loathing of the corrupt European world and her longing for New Zealand and her peaceful, pastoral childhood. Includes her brother's death in the war and its great effect upon her writing and life.

Burgan, Mary. "Childbirth Trauma in Katherine Mansfield's Early Stories." *Modern Fiction Studies* 24 (1978): 395–412. Focuses on "Prelude" and "At the Bay" and especially the character Linda whom Mansfield used to express her feelings toward the pain and toil of motherhood and her anger at woman's isolation and vulnerability suffered during pregnancy.

Fullbrook, Kate. *Katherine Mansfield.* Great Britain: Harvester Press, 1986. Describes her own view of feminist literature and how it should and should not be applied to Mansfield. Employing feminist critical techniques, criticizes and defends Mansfield's work, including her life, letters, journal, and stories, especially "Prelude."

Hankin, Cherry. "Fantasy and the Sense of an Ending in the Work of Katherine Mansfield." *Modern Fiction Studies* 24 (1978): 465–74. Examines Mansfield's use of fantasy and reality to bring her stories to a close and shows how this knowledge will further the reader's understanding of the short story form and Mansfield's "artistic practice." Uses many stories to illustrate the way characters psychologically move from fantasy to reality or vice-versa.

———. *Katherine Mansfield and Her Confessional Stories*. New York: St. Martin's Press, 1983. Provides a biography of Mansfield, including examples of her work, notes from her journal, and excerpts from her letters. Discusses Mansfield's "lifelong quest for psychological understanding" and its effect on her life and work.

Hanson, Clare, and Andrew Gurr. *Katherine Mansfield*. New York: St. Martin's Press, 1986. Stresses Mansfield's life in France, and neatly ties her later development to her years in New Zealand.

Kleine, Don W. "Mansfield and the Orphans of Time." *Modern Fiction Studies* 24 (1978): 423–38. Examines "The Daughters of the Late Colonel" and its outward structure of time and space along with its stylistic and "psychic textures," which together produce a "comic stasis . . . a comedy of fragmented time."

McLaughlin, Ann L. "The Same Job: The Shared Writing Aims of Katherine Mansfield and Virginia Woolf." *Modern Fiction Studies* 24 (1978): 369–82. Addresses Mansfield's and Woolf's similarities in their stories' interests and how acknowledging these similarities somewhat disturbed their own concepts of uniqueness and led Woolf to feelings of rivalry and jealousy toward Mansfield.

Maxwell-Mahon, W.D. "The Art of Katherine Mansfield." *UNISA English Studies* 16-17 (1979): 45–52. Discusses who influenced Mansfield and her creative ability, disclaiming Murry's ideas. Examines Mansfield's shifts in time-sequencing, grammatical usage, dialogues, and spaces in five of her stories.

Stead, C.K. "Katherine Mansfield and the Art of Fiction." *The New Review* 4 (1977): 27–34. Discusses, while correcting some of Murry's mistakes concerning dates and the reasoning behind Mansfield's work, how and why her techniques and genius developed and their effect on the short story in general.

Webby, Elizabeth. "Katherine Mansfield: Everything and Nothing." *Meanjin* 41 (1982): 236–43. Criticizes and/or praises Mansfield's biographers, such as J.M. Murry, Antony Alpers, Sylvia Berkman, Margaret Scott, Jeffrey Meyers, and C.K. Stead. Emphasizes the need for a critical biography that focuses on Mansfield's work rather than on her life.

Zinman, Toby S. "The Snail Under the Leaf: Katherine Mansfield's Imagery." *Modern Fiction Studies* 24 (1978): 457–64. Asserts that through patterns of imagery, as with animals, Mansfield illustrates that humans are victims of life and the only way to endure is through irony. Supports this view through examples from numerous stories.

—PATRICK MORROW

Nick Joaquin

When Nick Joaquin was offered the National Artist Award for 1976 by Ferdinand Marcos, he negotiated first for the release of another Filipino writer then being detained under martial law. His self-assurance—based on a longstanding reputation as journalist, playwright, novelist, short story writer, poet, and biographer—made him immune to political manipulation. He had already received the Stonehill Award for the Novel (1960) and the Republic Cultural Heritage Award for 1961.

Nick (Nicomedes) Joaquin was born 4 May 1917 in Paco, Manila. His mother, Salome Márquez, was a graduate of the normal school system under Spain and one of the first teachers in the American public schools in the Philippines. His father, Leocadio, was a colonel during the Revolution of 1896 and, later under the Americans, both a lawyer and businessman. After his father's death when Nick was thirteen, he left high school and educated himself with books from his father's personal library and from the National Library. His closest encounters with modern literature came from American magazines.

His 1943 essay, *La Naval de Manila*, describing the miraculous seventeenth-century defense of the city against the Dutch, won him both an Associate in Arts certificate from the University of Santo Tomas and a 1947 scholarship to the Dominican monastery in Hong Kong. He returned to Manila in 1950 to work as stage manager for the acting troupe of his sister-in-law Sarah, with whom he had lived during the Japanese Occupation.

That same year he became a proofreader for the *Philippines Free Press*, then rose to the rank of contributing editor, famous for his essays under the anagrammatic name "Quijano de Manila." In 1970, because of labor problems at the *Free Press*, he joined Gregorio Brillantes at the *Asia-Philippines Leader*, until martial law closed that periodical in 1972. By then he was already famous as historian of the foreshortened Golden Age of Spain in the Philippines, the folk-Catholicism of his short stories, his nostalgic play on Spanish honor endangered by corruption in wartime Manila, and his novel of the multi-layered, often self-conflicting heritage of the modern Filipino.

A Rockefeller grant had taken him to the United States, Mexico, and Spain in the early postwar years. Later he was invited as a cultural representative to Taiwan, Cuba, and the Peoples Republic of China. He now lives quietly in San Juan, a Manila suburb, yet feels comfortable with each new wave of writers, perhaps because they have been influenced by him towards a higher regard for their national history as well as for the country's land- and city-scapes.

THE MANY MANILAS

Despite the pseudonym, "Quijano de Manila" (Manila Old-Timer), associated with his years at the *Philippines Free Press*, Nick Joaquin has refused to be identified exclusively with the centuries of Spanish dominion over the city of his birth. The Manila of his early childhood still considered Spanish the language of the elite and held itself remote from the folk culture and regional vernaculars of *provincianos*. Only gradually did it become a genuinely national capital, with massive immigration from the rice and sugar lands, north and south. English was already flourishing as the language of instruction in the greatly expanded public school system, and writers as well as bureaucrats adapted as rapidly to the sounds of American words as they did to the new democratic ways. The zarzuela coexisted with ragtime, the Kahirup debutantes with gangs of *kanto*-boys.

Joaquin's generation therefore had a choice. It could either suffer from customs seemingly torn between convent rigidity and Hollywood casualness or, as in his own case, try to adapt each to the other and both to indigenous Malayan practices as well as to demands made by the tropics on these intruders from the temperate zone. Just as Filipinos had learned for purposes of ventilation to pierce the solid walls of Spanish colonial churches and houses, so did those early in the twentieth century learn to accommodate themselves not only to American ways but to revel in the remnants of what Spain left behind when it took its official departure. Joaquin was one of those.

No Filipino has yet matched the virtuosity of Nick Joaquin's response to this plenitude of riches, visible in the numerous genres summoned by him particularly to dramatize Manila's growth, after the Second World War, into a metropolitan magnet for people from all over the Philippine archipelago. Manila Bay had always made the islands an inviting place for international trade; in the 1940s it quickly became even more, a cosmopolitan nucleus for multinational industries and mercantilism. Just as, centuries earlier, Manila had been an *entrepôt* for the galleon trade between Mexico and China, so does it remain today in Joaquin's eyes a crossroad culture whose unique mixtures he delights in describing. Where a geologist, intent on reconstructing otherwise inaccessible history, might tend to see the Philippines in successive stratified layers of time, Joaquin as anthropologist has regard for its conglomerate rather than sedimentary nature. Society as he sees it is more a matter of mutual encroachments than simple juxtaposition. Its description requires all the versatility he can provide.

Joaquin's interest in Spain, whose influence on Manila's food and architectural facades impressed itself on him daily as a boy, was further piqued by the disturbing fact that other young writers, along with their characters, seemed to be "without grandfathers." In *La Naval de Manila* he mocks such Filipinos for arguing that Spain contributed nothing of value "except, perhaps" religion and national unity. He writes of "the pre-Spanish drift of totem-and-taboo tribes" and speaks of the revolution of 1896 against Spain as "our violent birth": separation from the motherland. Similarly he describes the development of theater in the Philippines as having to "go through the same tortuous development as, say, the English drama, which, originating in religious and morality plays, passed through a blood-and-thunder phase, similar to our *moro-moro* period, that culminated in the Elizabethan drama." Unfortunately, he has said, the development of Philippine literature in Spanish was hindered by the coming of the Americans. But that is no reason to pretend it never existed or that its influence has not survived.

His fiction, in fact, is quick to acknowledge everywhere the coexistence of past and present, the mingling of Christian and pagan, folk and colonial values, and a mix-mix of languages. In *Prose and Poems* embroidered tales such as "The Mass of St. Sylvestre," "The Legend of the Virgin's Jewel," and "The Legend of the Dying Wanton" waver between appeals to superstition and to faith in divine intervention. "May Day Eve" compels belief in fantasy, by the evocation of a future husband in an enchanted mirror; and "The Summer Solstice" invokes the figure of Salome raised above John the Baptist, whose religious festival she has appropriated. The same perception of primitive beliefs as possible sources for primal mystical rites recurs in stories in *Tropical Gothic.* "Candido's Apocalypse" presents a young boy who can see inside the flesh and bones of others to their very essence. "The Order of Melkizedek" studies a timeless ambiguous figure, part priest, part devil. The legend of "Doña Jeronima," saintly recluse secretly visited by the prelate of Manila, later becomes the central enigma in an otherwise political novel, *Cave and Shadows,* about student revolts against the Marcoses.

In *La Naval de Manila,* Joaquin writes that, because three and a half centuries of Spanish rule ended in revolt, Filipinos tend to exaggerate the enmity between themselves and the past and, in effect, attempt to disinherit the future from much that already had been accommodated to their own daily way of life. He suggests that this separation leading to self-deprivation, in the name of self-identification, is not an abnormal relationship between sons and fathers. A variation on the age-old problem of finding one's self among options available from the past is dramatized in his short story, "Three Generations." A would-be seminarian identifies more with his lusty, loving grandfather than with the brutally confining chastity of his father. All the conflicts in religious conventions that deny the body's existence and its claims are presented through the troubled loyalties of the son's search for significances beyond mere piety.

With a change in gender, this same theme of a generation gap in need of healing is repeated and elaborated in Joaquin's often-staged play, *A Portrait of the Artist as Filipino.* The Second World War has destroyed the old Spanish churches in Manila's Intramuros but not the memory of what those churches still represent: fulfilment of the Old Testament through the New and redemption of the world of tempestuous nature by a benevolent God made flesh. All this is embodied in Don Lorenzo Marasigan, despite the fact that he never appears, although, at the final curtain, his arrival (to view the Naval de Manila procession) is triumphantly anticipated. The play centers on the Marasigan daughters' readiness to be seduced by misdirected hopes of preserving the family from the most extreme deprivations brought on by war. They are tempted to sell Don Lorenzo's portrait of Aeneas bearing his father Anchises and the household gods from burning Troy, en route to founding Rome. At the last moment they renounce that dishonorable act and confirm the family values that are their true inheritance. The fact that the painting remains as invisible as Don

Marasigan not only unites them as equivalent moral instruments but reinforces the spiritual ever-presence of ancient verities, in Joaquin's perception of what remains constant in history amid dynamic changes.

The difficulty of reconciling the Filipino's several heritages is more complexly treated in *The Woman Who Had Two Navels* (first published as a novella in *Partisan Review*, 1953, at half its later length). Connie de Vidal's obsession with what she considers her two navels would be merely hysterical were it not also symbolic of the interplay between the divinely oriented Spanish past and the pragmatic American-influenced present, as well as the daily intersection of time and eternity, or the unity of body and soul. For better or for worse, these seeming opposites combine, as the author's reliance on mirror images implies. Bandleader Paco Texeira, said to resemble his wife Mary as closely as a twin, is caught between the passions of the two sister-sirens, Concha de Vidal and her daughter Connie. Similarly Macho, a former love of Concha's, has been wished onto unwilling Connie as her husband. Connie rejects Macho when she discovers his former letters to Concha, and he, in turn, shoots her mother in futile revenge.

That terrible tragedy to which they have all contributed becomes the turning point, away from despair, for Connie. In Hong Kong she meets old rebel Monson, who has lived in exile rather than face post-Revolutionary life at home, and they recognize in each other how they have refused to confront life-as-it-is, guided by life-as-it-ought-to-be. Through moral memory and collective experience, both essentials to Philippine culture, Joaquin portrays the possibility of a living tradition in which future as well as past must participate. Concha says that Monson once was "my conscience walking around in elegant clothes." It is the recovery of conscience that allows the surviving characters courage enough to continue.

So elegant is Nick Joaquin's fiction that he has sometimes been accused of lacking the very social conscience—that sense of collective consideration of and care for others, that he requires of his characters. Such criticism acknowledges that his concern for general working conditions did lead to his leaving the *Philippines Free Press* after twenty years' tenure there and that he accepted the National Artist Award, despite his distaste for the Marcoses, only on condition that fellow writer Pete Lacaba be freed from detention. These concessions notwithstanding, critics have tended to misunderstand his writing, especially where it involves Spanish times, and call it a refusal to engage ongoing reality. Such a view not only misses the subtleties of his notion of culture as organic—the many pasts are constant pressures shaping the present—but ignores the more direct contact with the commonplace he has consistently provided for his readers, particularly through essays contributed to the *Free Press* from 1950 to 1970 and partially reprinted in a series of paperbacks in the late seventies. Most of these deal with well-known personages such as General MacArthur, Carlos Romulo, Eisenhower, Aguinaldo, Marcos, Ponce Enrile; but more often he provides special insight into the lives of movie stars, Huks, a ballet dancer wed to a Yugoslav refugee, the Filipino who married a Miss Universe from Finland, a boxer, archaeologists, spiritists, the Muslim minority, fellow writers, and artist friends. No reporter has equaled his ability to say things succinctly and gracefully. But his greatest pride has been that nothing Filipino is alien to him and, furthermore, that he can provide a fresh perspective on the ordinary person as well as on those well-known. He has even written *Stories for Groovy Kids* without patronizing and included poems for children in his *Collected Verse*.

The breadth of his interests clearly is breathtaking, although it took considerable urging to have him cull his reportage finally for reprinting. He was torn between inherent modesty and the right of the people to reread whatever has proven enduring from his many years as commentator on life in Manila's alleys as well as on its avenues.

His identification with common things—though described in an uncommon way—is his principal attribute and explains why, in an essay entitled "The Way We Were" in *Writers and Their Milieu* (1986), he expresses his embarrassment as a young writer with the literature of others who wrote as if Philippine history began with the fall of Manila to Commodore Dewey. He himself could never write without noticing all the concentric circles, in space and time, surrounding any object on which his focus falls. Consequently, although he felt closer to the working class and street people than many so-called committed writers, he never sought to be called a "proletarian writer," because such labels were limiting and, in any case, borrowed from other countries. The thoroughness of his penetrating interviews and extensive research has been enough to authorize his independence and to assure those capable of recognizing it that in his studied way he has long been a genuine liberal, though a stranger at the public barricades in the seventies.

Marxist radicals, especially, were upset by his collection of essays, *A Question of Heroes* (previously serialized in the *Free Press*), documenting the services to the 1896 Revolution of not only the underprivileged described in Teodoro Agoncillo's *The Revolt of the Masses* (1956) but also those from the middle and upper classes who risked everything by turning on the Spaniards who originally had empowered them. His portraits of such men as Antonio Luna, Jose Burgos, Marcelo del Pilar, and Graciano Lopez-Jaena emphasize the role of the *ilustrados* during the last three decades of the nineteenth century. His argument is that the entire period—from the Propaganda Movement initiated by Filipinos in Spain, to the Philippine-American War—constitutes a single event, still unfinished.

The same critics, bent on excluding Joaquin from the liberation movement, were surprised therefore when, with martial law only nominally ended due to Pope John Paul II's visit in 1981, he dared to release *The Aquinos of Tarlac* in 1983. It traces in vivid detail the life of Benigno Aquino from his exploits as a young reporter in Korea, through his marriage to wealthy Corazon Cojuangco and his enlightened treatment of their sugar plantation tenants, his political rise as mayor and governor, to his senatorship. Although it stops short of the imprisonment of Aquino by Marcos during the very first hours of martial law, everyone realized the implications of the book: Marcos had invented charges against Aquino because he feared him as a popular rival for the Presidency. Further inferences were drawn by the appearance of the biography the same year that Aquino, returning from the United States after heart surgery, was assassinated in Manila's international airport. Although Joaquin had reluctantly accepted the National Heroes Award, he never let himself be used by the Marcoses for their political advantage. When the Revolution of 1986 occurred and the people, having bravely defended the ballot boxes against Marcos forces, peacefully and en masse ejected the dictator and his family, Joaquin's *The Quartet of the Tiger Moon* was one of the first books to report, with evident pleasure, the regime's last days. Finally he had achieved credibility even among his critics as a participant in the struggle towards democracy and not merely as a detached observer.

To those who had followed Joaquin's career with more sensitivity, however, the seriousness of his concern had always been evident. The same year that his biography of the Aquinos was released, he published his second novel, *Cave and Shadows*. Here he attempts to recapitulate all the themes from his earlier work, while providing special relevance to the period of martial law. The novel's narrative line dwells on the mysterious death of a young mestiza in a hermit cell, long the place of religious rites by both Christians and pagans. The accidental cause of death is finally solved. However, the more profound mystery evoked by Joaquin involves the creative tension, which his work regularly has dramatized, between the sacred and the profane, here in the figures of the Catholic recluse La Hermana and the folk spiritist Ginoong Ina. Are these women, from different periods of history, essentially the same person, just as the author provides the possibility of a series of male reincarnations in his earlier story, "The Order of Melkizedek"? Joaquin's recurring proposition seems to be that folk Catholicism, with its mixture of animism and monotheism, may be closer to the natural relation of spirit and body than those conventional Western doctrines that once polarized body and soul. His novel offers a picture of the Filipino, even one immersed in the cosmopolitanism of Manila, as having umbilicals connecting him with multiple worlds. This is the author's philosophical/psychological equivalent of that tradition of tropical exuberance that has often been identified with Filipino art, which, like nature itself, abhors a vacuum.

The Platonic reference in the novel's title suggests that human vision is always too limited to rule out such cosmic possibilities of interconnectedness. All things ultimately may be reconcilable, just as Joaquin implies that every Filipino has to come to terms with all historic precedents, including the folk culture so often neglected. But there is a secondary layer to the title's reminder that nothing is ever quite what it seems. The action in the novel, which includes student demonstrations similar to what has become known as the First Quarter Storm, on the barricades of the University of the Philippines, occurs just prior to the 1972 declaration of martial law. In part, therefore, the novel must be read as a concealed indictment of Ferdinand Marcos's violation of human rights under "constitutional authoritarianism," when "safe houses" in fact became places of torture, the "New Society" simply meant transfer of power and wealth from one crony elite to another, and the public assassination of Senator Aquino was staged so that his apparent killer could be murdered immediately in order to mask a military conspiracy. In this novel, as throughout the body of his work, Joaquin demonstrates that nothing can safely be considered irrelevant to complete self-knowledge, to a nation's crisis of identity, or to the question of who, in what capacity and when, contributed to the death of the spiritual deliverer who returned to assist his people. Joaquin has always been fascinated by such allegories of collusion or communion, within the vortex of Manila, the "city of man."

Above all, he has seen himself in the role, so necessary according to the culture of the Philippines, as third-party mediator and healer. His commentary on the two novels of national martyr Jose Rizal, in *La Naval de Manila*, tries to rescue those works from idolatry. He asks that they be "read simply for pleasure—as all good books should be." However, his treatment of Rizal later in *A Question of Heroes* is serious, if deliberately short of sanctifying, and the previous year, 1976, he presented his countrymen with *The Complete Poems and Plays of Jose Rizal*, in translation from the Spanish. The connection between Rizal and Joaquin lies in more than their shared versatility. (Rizal was a skilled eye doctor as well as a distinguished author of political fiction and poetry.) Rizal had joined the Propaganda Movement in Spain in anticipation that the Peninsular liberals would make Filipinos in the island first-class citizens, with representation in Madrid. He was a reformist, not a separatist. Ironically, however, his novels were blamed for subsequent uprisings in Manila, and he was summarily executed by a firing squad. The further irony is that his death helped inspire the revolution that he had sought to prevent. Like Rizal, Joaquin is devoted to reconciliation, the sifting and winnowing of all aspects of the Philippine experience, the choosing of those elements that are compatible and essential to the ongoing momentum of the Philippine character.

NICK JOAQUIN'S PUBLISHED WORK

Novels

The Woman Who Had Two Navels, 1961
Cave and Shadows, 1983

Short Story Collections

Selected Stories, 1962
Tropical Gothic, 1972
Stories for Groovy Kids, 1979

Plays

A Portrait of the Artist as Filipino, 1966
Tropical Baroque, 1979

Poetry

The Ballad of the Five Battles, 1981
Collected Verse, 1987

Collection

Prose and Poems, 1952

Biography

The Aquinos of Tarlac: An Essay on History as Three Generations, 1983

Reprints from *Philippines Free Press* articles

Reportage on Crime, 1977
Reportage on Lovers, 1977
Nora Aunor and Other Profiles, 1977
Ronnie Poe and Other Silhouettes, 1977

Amalia Fuentes and Other Etchings, 1977
Gloria Diaz and Other Delineations, 1977
Doveglion and Other Cameos, 1977
Manila: Sin City and Other Chronicles, 1980
Language of the Streets and Other Essays, 1980
Reportage on the Marcoses, 1981

Essay Collections

La Naval de Manila and Other Essays, 1964
> Tribute to Spanish heritage; the miraculous defeat of a Dutch armada off Manila, 1646; comments on zarzuelas and moro-moros, and the novels of Rizal.
A Question of Heroes, 1977
> A defense of those *ilustrados*/aristocrats who fought for the Malolos Republic against Spain in 1896; a retort to Agoncillo's Marxist argument in *The Revolt of the Masses.*
Almanac for Manileños, 1979
The Quartet of the Tiger Moon, 1986
> Covers the Revolution of 1986.

Translations

The Complete Poems and Plays of Jose Rizal, 1976
A Spaniard in Aguinaldo's Army: The Military Journal of Telesforo Carrasco y Perez, 1986

SELECTED CRITICAL READINGS

In his introductory essay to *Writers and Their Milieu,* Nick Joaquin rather wryly admits his irritation with certain critics' oversimplified classifications of his work. The anticlerical have attacked him for being a "Catholic writer"; the pious, for being too "pagan." He prefers to be seen as someone interested in the whole of creation, and, as a Filipino, he wants credit only for having helped his fellow writers open their pages to all that immediately surrounds them: both as substance and as mystery. So far, the largeness of his world view can be approximated only through a composite of critical assessments, before these become fixed clichés obscuring the complex reality of his achievements.

Abad, Gemino H., and Edna Z. Manlapaz, editors. *Man of Earth: An Anthology of Filipino Poetry and Verse from English, 1905 to the Mid-50s.* Quezon City: Ateneo UP, 1989. 227–34; 384–85. A sampling of Joaquin's earlier poetry, with extensive biographical data.

Alegre, Edilberto N., and Doreen G. Fernandez, editors. *Writers and Their Milieu.* Manila: De La Salle UP, 1987. Contains Nick Joaquin's "The Way We Were" (1–9); a rare self-evaluation in which he separates himself from critical misreadings.

Bernad, Miguel A. "Haunted Intensity." *Bamboo and the Greenwood Tree.* Manila: Bookmark, 1961. 53–67. Confuses the conflict of values within characters with Joaquin's failure to provide Christian attitudes in stories that Catholic doctrine should dominate.

Casper, Leonard. "Nick Joaquin." *New Writing from the Philippines: A Critique and Anthology.* Syracuse: Syracuse UP, 1966. 137–45; 311–82. Discusses Joaquin's fiction and poetry as an intermingling of Christian and pagan values.

————. "Beyond the Mind's Mirage." *Firewalkers: Literary Concelebrations 1964–1984.* Quezon City: New Day, 1987. 168–71. Addresses the motif of timelessness and its relevance to folk-Catholicism in *Tropical Gothic.*

Galdon, Joseph A., editor. *Philippine Fiction.* Quezon City: Ateneo UP, 1972. 1–73. Contains essays devoted to various works by Joaquin in terms of Spanish traditions, excesses of style, and the metaphysical quest in the first novel: Furay, "The Power and Greatness of Nick Joaquin"; Constantino, "Illusion and Reality in Nick Joaquin"; Garcia-Groyon, "Joaquin's Connie Escobar: Rise and Fall"; Lacaba, "Winter After Summer Solstice: The Later Joaquin"; Pablo, "The Spanish Tradition in Nick Joaquin."

Lumbera, Bienvenido, and Cynthia Nograles Lumbera, editors. *Philippine Literature: A History and Anthology.* Manila: National Book Store, 1982. 244–45. Discusses recognition by Joaquin of problems of both personal and national identity, finally decided by choice as one "sifts through history and the present."

Mojares, Resil B. *Origins and Rise of the Filipino Novel: A Generic Study of the Novel until 1940.* Quezon City: U of the Philippines P, 1983. 337, 353. Comments on Joaquin's suggestion that the English language offered a *visual* dimension to pre-print literatures otherwise oriented towards an *oral* culture.

Roseburg, Arturo G. *Pathways to Philippine Literature in English.* Quezon City: Phoenix Press, 1958. 172–235. Sees Joaquin as a "frustrated priest" concerned with struggles between good and evil, writing with "mystical intensity" and with sympathy for sinners.

San Juan, Jr., E. *Subversions of Desire: Prolegomena to Nick Joaquin.* Quezon City: Ateneo UP, 1988. A Marxist critic, who once called Joaquin an agent of American imperialism, here describes Joaquin's contradictions as reflections of flaws in Philippine society at large. First full-length commentary on Joaquin.

— LEONARD CASPER

Ediriwira Sarachchandra

E diriwira Sarachchandra was born 3 June 1914 in what was then known as Ceylon, now Sri Lanka. His father was a postmaster, his mother a teacher.

When he attended the University of Ceylon, consciousness of cultural deracination—due to British rule in a country where the middle class spoke English rather than Sinhalese or Tamil—inspired him to read Sanskrit, Pali, and Sinhalese. He graduated with honors in 1936.

In 1939 he studied Indian philosophy and music at Tagore's Institute, Shantiniketan, India. From 1942-44 he was sub-editor of the Sinhalese dictionary. He then gained a postgraduate degree in Indian philosophy as an external student of the University of London and was appointed Lecturer in Pali at the University of Ceylon. In 1947 he entered the University of London, studied Western philosophy, and in 1949 received a doctorate, having written a dissertation on Buddhism, later published as *Buddhist Psychology of Perception*.

Appointed Professor of Pali at the University of Ceylon, he became Professor of Modern Sinhalese Literature, published *The Folk Drama of Ceylon* and in 1955 received a Rockefeller Foundation award to study drama. His work took him to India, the United States, and Japan. Earlier experimentation with adaptations of Western drama had convinced him that Sri Lanka, with its recorded history of verse and prose literature reaching back to the eighth and thirteenth centuries, respectively, yet lacking any native form of theater, needed a mode akin to Eastern traditions. In 1956 when he presented *Maname*, converting the folk-drama style known as "Nadagama" to an intensely powerful stylized art, the form fired the enthusiasm of audiences, critics, and playwrights; and a Sinhalese theater was born. *Maname* was staged recently in London.

Acknowledged as the Island's supreme playwright, he also won Arts Council awards for the Best Novel of the Year with *The Dead* (in Sinhalese, 1959) and *With the Begging Bowl* (in English, 1984).

After 1965 he taught at Denison University, Ohio, and Earlham College, Indiana. From 1974-77 he was appointed Ambassador to France, accredited to Switzerland and the Vatican, and was a delegate to UNESCO. He next served as Research Professor at the East-West Center, Honolulu.

Sarachchandra has received numerous honors and awards. The University of Jaffna and The University of Peradeniya conferred on him the degree of Doctor of Literature in 1982. In 1983 he was awarded the Kumaran Asan World Prize, by the State of Kerala, India, and he won the Ramon Magsaysay Award for Literature in 1988.

Now Professor Emeritus, Sarachchandra lives in Sri Lanka.

VIRTUOSITY AND VISION

To many Eastern writers, the colonial heritage may mean a garnered richness of reading, response, and resource—an easy and equal familiarity with the dramatic techniques of Shakespeare or the Shakuntala of Kalidasa and the epics that relate the combats of heroes who set out to avenge the abduction of Sita or Helen. To Ediriwira Sarachchandra, born in 1914 and experiencing colonial rule to the full before the Island gained its independence in 1947, it was a factor that sharpened and refined his cognizance of the palpable or tenuous barriers that separate cultures as well as the ineluctable forces that govern men in whatever culture they may be born or bred. It is this keenness of cultural and psychological perception and discrimination that is apparent in his novels; yet the response of foreign reviewers to *Foam Upon the Stream* proves that the effect of his fiction is not limited by cultural boundaries.

As a boy Sarachchandra belonged to an era where a child could be fined five cents for speaking a word of Sinhala or Tamil in school. In a recent letter, he recalls:

> At school I learned only English literature and heard only of English writers. I remember reading and enjoying English poets like Keats, Swinburne, Wordsworth, Robert Burns. . . . It was about that time that I started to write English poetry.

So the urge to write germinated in boyhood, just as a dawning interest in folk-drama made him soon scour the villages in the valley below his home, watching performances of folk-plays and learning folk music.

If the Colonial educational system equipped him with fluency in English, it also had less predictable results:

> I think the reaction to the Westernized atmosphere was that nationalistic feelings were stirred within me as within so many young people. . . . At school I matriculated with English, Latin and Science subjects . . . but when it came to entering the University for higher studies, I felt I ought to study Sinhalese and Pali which were more relevant to our lives than Latin and English. (Letter)

It was a decision that was to lead to Sarachchandra's gaining a reputation as an English novelist by the most circuitous of routes: he won the Arts Council Award in 1959 for the Best Novel of the Year in Sinhalese, with the first novel he wrote, *Malagiya Attho* (The Dead); a little less than three decades later in 1984 he won the same organization's award for the Best Novel of the Year in English, *With the Begging Bowl.*

Sarachchandra's instantaneous success as an English novelist is hardly surprising, since he had previously proved his preeminence in so many other fields—philosophy, literary criticism, research, dramaturgy. Each had claimed his energy, his passion, his meticulous, loving precision, and every one of these disciplines finally converged to enrich his vision as well as his technique as a novelist. Few save scholars specifically concerned with the more abstruse aspects of Buddhism or Indian

Philosophy are likely to dip into his *The Buddhist Psychology of Perception*. Yet it indicates the nature of his preoccupations.

His work as a literary scholar and critic, when he was Professor of Modern Sinhalese at the University of Ceylon, reveals a very different Sarachchandra, a downright slashing critic, as quick with a cudgel as rapier against hidebound conventionality and irrational adherence to tradition. He is evidently an ardent lover of the grace and skill, responsive to every nuance of suggestion, whether emotive or descriptive, in a literature dating back to the eighth century yet quick to advocate departure from tradition in the interests of creating a literature flexible and frank enough to mirror the complex realities of the twentieth century. *Modern Sinhalese Fiction* did much in the 1940s and 1950s to improve standards of judgment among readers. Just as his critical work benefited the reading public, his close study of the texts he analyzed necessarily profited him as a writer and alerted him to the dangers that may dog the less wary author.

It is true that Sarachchandra's power as a novelist need not be attributed to anything other than innate ability; still, as Alexander Pope stressed, "True ease in writing comes from art, not chance." So Sarachchandra's unerring skill in guiding the responses of his readers may in part be accounted for by his previous experience as a dramatist. We must keep in mind that his career as a novelist, in Sinhala to begin with, commenced two years after his dazzling success as a dramatist, when *Maname* moved the emotions of a nation in 1956. Drama was his first love; when he listened to the gramophone records of Tower Hall performers from the days of gaslight and glitter or watched village rituals through the night, a spark was kindled. It glowed into active flame when a few undergraduates gathered to talk and sing in their mother tongue at a time when the last feeble flickers of Sinhala theater in the form of the stiff melodramas of the Minerva Players with modern backgrounds belied by bombastic declamation and ill-timed (if appealing) bursts of melody died out when "bioscope" caught the fancy of the populace. It was left to the bilingual intelligentsia, stimulated by Professor E.F.C. Ludowyk's productions of Shakespeare, Brecht, and Pirandello, to dream of a Sinhalese theater. Its foundations they believed could only be laid by assimilating the best of European drama. As Sarachchandra worked as both translator and producer of adaptations of Moliere, Wilde, and Chekhov, he may have unconsciously absorbed much that would develop his own abilities, but if so, no traces are visible. The potency of Sarachchandra's poetic dramas is more easily experienced than described, because he handles language with such sensitivity, such dazzling virtuosity, employing all the resources of wordstock to achieve a range that embraces poignance, irony, subtlety, and strength. Above all, his art is something he has grown from the roots. It was to discover these roots that he turned to research.

He had to pursue his research with some difficulty because of practical problems. A passage from the preface to *The Folk Drama of Ceylon*, which mentions these difficulties, also throws considerable light on the conditions in which the folk drama operates:

> I must mention that I was able to undertake a systematic study of the Sinhalese folk-play only after the University of Ceylon granted me a sum of a thousand rupees to meet the initial expenses. This

grant, though small, enabled me to make a beginning in earnest by
. . . having special performances arranged for my benefit. The
performance of a folk-play, however, is rather costly as a large
number of actors take part, besides drummers and accompanying
singers and most of them are scattered in various professions and
have to be trained specially for the occasion. . . . A ceremony like
a Gara Yakuma or a Gam Maduwa can never be arranged for the
special purpose of studying it, as folk priests do not like to perform
such ceremonies unless a genuine occasion has arisen. (ix)

He studied the varied forms of drama in different regions:

Certain types of entertainment are found only in certain villages and
unknown in others . . . in addition there exists a broad division of
the arts into those of the Pata Rata (the plains) and those of the Uda
Rata (the hill country). (vii)

After observing and recording the full range of such performances he came to the
conclusion that

The drama is only a by-product of activities seriously directed
towards the sustenance of the entire life of the community, namely
the propitiation of Gods and Demons and the performance of
magical rites which are calculated to prevent diseases, ward off evil,
bring plentiful crops and confer general prosperity on the village.
(vii-vii)

He points out that "The Sinhalese folk-play as it exists in the villages today is. . .
closely associated with the ritualistic practices of the folk religion" (1), which
survived even after the triumph of Buddhism around 250 B.C., for Buddhism, an
austere system of thought concerned with spiritual liberation and ethics, offered no
immediate help in the material sphere. Hence the people still turned to the gods and
demons, invoking them to avert sickness and disaster or to ensure prosperity. He
comments that

Many of the plays are still in a rudimentary stage in which dance has
not yet become drama . . . some of the plays at any rate are so similar
to the ritual dances that it is very easy to see the process of
evolution. At one end are the elaborate ceremonies, connected with
the worship and propitiation . . . at the other end are the plays
approximating, in varying degrees, to drama. Between these we
have a number of short interludes of a dramatic nature . . . these
interludes are meant to provide comic relief when . . . the all-night
sitters begin to nod. (1)

Here we see the transition from exorcism to entertainment just as the rituals show basic elements of drama such as impersonation, dialogue, and costume. For example Thovil or "Devil Dances" are held to cure diseases by exorcising the demon who afflicted the sufferer. Dancers elaborately masked as "demons who represent various diseases, and whose appearance is described as being similar to the appearance of the people who are affected by these diseases" (25) or as ferocious fanged ogres with protruding eyeballs make spectacular entrances, leaping into the arena with eerie hooting, whirling flaring torches, and dancing wildly to a frenzied drumbeat. Apart from the masks, they are dressed alike in garments of leaves worn at the waist and a shaggy fur wrap for the upper part of the body. A dialogue takes place, with occasional humorous or ribald lines to provoke laughter, but the purpose is more utilitarian than entertainment. Here is a typical exchange:

> Demon: Why did you invite me?
> Priest: You have been inflicting a disease upon a certain person.
> That is why we called you here.
> Demon: I admit these are diseases inflicted by me. What will you
> give me if I cure them? (37)

The demon, having been denied the human sacrifice, that he demands at first or even an animal sacrifice, finally agrees to depart and accepts the offerings that must be handed over by the patient himself.

The research that culminated in the publication of *The Sinhalese Folk Play*, which was saluted by the *Times Literary Supplement* as being of "so wide a scope that it must surely interest all who wish to trace the development of dramatic forms," had other consequences as well: it developed the power of acute observation that characterizes Sarachchandra's novels and short stories; above all, the material that claimed the searching, questioning eye of the observer simultaneously activated latent creative powers. Regarding his quest, Sarachchandra recalls:

> At that time there was nothing that could be called a Sinhalese theatre. Actually although the Sinhalese possess a literature that goes back to about the 8th century A.D. (this includes the verses on the "Mirror Wall" of Sigiriya) no dramatic literature has been handed down to us from the written tradition. What survives today is the folk tradition. . . . I was concerned about this situation and wanted to do something about it. In my researches into the folk theatre, the idea growing in my mind was that what would draw audiences to the theatre was a form of theatre that would have its roots in the style of the folk plays, which I thought had an idiom of their own, although they lacked a literary framework in which the relationship of the characters to one another was worked out to its logical or artistic culmination. (Letter)

The result was *Maname*:

It has often been said that through *Maname*, Professor Sarachchandra was able to appeal successfully to every class of theatregoer and to bring a new audience into the Sinhala theatre. . . . Partly influenced by his familiarity with Japanese theatre, he transformed the traditional *nadagama* with its rigid conventions and limitations into a rich and flexible form of stylized drama that could serve to convey complexities of character and theme.

Reggie Siriwardene's comment on the play, here conjoined with mine, shows how fully Sarachchandra realized his aims and how the writing of *Maname* led him to discover abilities of which he had been unaware. But the most immediate effect that *The Sinhalese Folk Play* had on the gestation of the novels was that it secured him a Rockefeller Foundation Fellowship, which enabled him to spend a period in Japan studying drama. The impressions and experiences of this period resulted in his first novel in Sinhalese, *Malagiya Attho (The Dead)*. The book was later translated, along with its sequel into Japanese by Tadashi Noguchi; these two books formed the basis of his third English novel, *Foam upon the Stream: A Japanese Elegy*.

The first of his English works released for publication, however, was "Of a Queen and a Courtesan," a novella that appeared in 1970 in *Solidarity*, a magazine edited in Manila by Sionil José. The story centers on the dividing line between life and art, which the artist by the nature of his occupation tends to find blurred and confusing. The novella falls naturally into two parts. In the first, appropriately the period of rehearsals, while Virasena, a director with an established reputation for excellence is molding his cast to present a stylized poetic drama, we see the dominance of the irrational in the form of unexplained obstructions and ugliness and the natural intrusions of ill-health and uncertainty. The second part presents the flowering of art and the transfiguration of the real: "Yes, the Queen, for she was not Gunavati anymore . . . transcending the limits of space and time . . . to emerge in the fullest radiance, the highest dignity of the human spirit." And Virasena experiences the exultation of the successful artist:

> As he sat watching it, he thought he could almost hear the heartbeat of the audience, and it was in tune with the rhythm on the stage. There were great moments too when he experienced the rapture of being able to communicate almost perfectly and to have the evidence of such communication presented directly to his senses. (22)

"Almost perfectly"—the qualification brings in the necessary touch of objectivity, highlighting the sense of limitation that life invariably imposes on the artist and prevents him from totally transcending the barriers between mind and reality.

Life and art merge disastrously in Virasena's obsession, which springs from a consciousness of his own power rather than Gunavati's, despite her triumph:

> Virasena . . . found himself slipping into the auditorium as the lights dimmed and when the drums beat their rhythm and the queen

> emerged from the darkness into the gleaming circle of light, it became to him an experience he had never known before, something unique in his entire life in the theatre. It was never the same on two consecutive nights, so that he felt impelled to go again and again. She seemed to be creating her role afresh on every occasion so that he was never tired of watching her. . . . After a while he began to feel that he constituted an integral element in any night's performance. She could give of her best because of his presence among the audience. She must first establish rapport with him, before she could establish rapport with the rest and he thought now as she entered the stage her eyes ran among the audience looking for him as if to get the cue from him like at rehearsals, and that it was only after they sought him out . . . and rested on him a moment that she was able to enter her role and perform her part. And he could almost see the faint light that flashed across her face when this secret rapport was established. (32)

The illusion falls apart when he discovers that she is in love with a fellow actor, and briefly the artist is submerged as Virasena indulges in the crude weaponry of calumny, denigrating the young man and spreading rumors concerning Gunavati's health, in a desperate effort to possess the queen he has created, a conflict that is resolved when the young couple announce their marriage and pay homage to him.

A striking feature of Sarachchandra's three novels is their diversity: *Curfew and a Full Moon*, set against the grimness of the abortive youth insurrection of 1971, is written with a chilling restraint, in striking contrast to *With the Begging Bowl*, a harsh, yet hilarious satire; both contrast with the delicate poignance of the Japanese romance, *Foam upon the Stream*. The only common element, virtuosity apart, is a penetrating ironic vision.

Curfew and a Full Moon has a three-part structure, which can be seen as corresponding to Amaradasa's stubborn preservation of the illusion of the tranquil innocence of Peradeniya, the journey to Polonnaruwa that brings a confrontation with reality, and his return to Peradeniya to live with this new knowledge. The novel is permeated by the horror and guilt that shook the ease and complacency of the Sri-Lankan middle class on realizing that the system that maintained them in moderate comfort had driven others to the point of desperation and to the gun; these emotions must have pricked with a persistent immediacy in the case of those professors whose ignorance of the impending tragedy presented evidence of their failure to gain the confidence of the students. To Professor Amaradasa, with his deep and spontaneous fondness for the students, the fault and responsibility seems his:

> He had wasted his years studying ancient civilizations which did not help him to understand the problems around him. There was nothing he could communicate to his students which was worthwhile in the context of the lives they led or was relevant to their needs. (6)

Sarachchandra, however, supplies sufficient evidence that it is circumstances rather than a choice of discipline that makes him powerless to aid or even dissuade them. As Professor of Archaeology, Amaradasa conducts a group of students on a study tour of the Ruined Cities and waxes lyrical in his lectures on such monuments as King Nissanka's stone Vine-Bower, the Palace, and Audience Hall: "From the palace terraces the laughter of noble ladies playing ball-games floated out . . . in the cool water of the pond young maidens lay . . . breasts vying with the lotus buds" (93). But one of the students, Nandasena, in angry rhetoric argues that such ancient monuments are symbols of feudal oppression; valuing them binds people to the past and prevents them from liberating themselves, so it would be better to break them and utilize the bricks to shelter the living. The excursion is cut short by the outbreak of the insurgency; it is only when they are back at Peradeniya that Amaradasa learns that Nandasena has died in a gun battle with the Army and is told: "He's a very poor boy, Sir. . . . They live in a little thatched hut. . . . His father does nothing, only parades up and down the road all day. His mother sits by a kerosene lamp and rolls coir [coconut fiber] into rope till morning. They live on whatever she earns. . . . There are eight in the family. . . . I don't know how they eat" (131).

The novel, however, centers not around the insurgency but around the protagonist's unwilling involvement and the impulses that prompt him. Episodes in the dilapidated faculty club and at meetings convened by the Vice-Chancellor present sketches of some professors as parlor pinks and/or indefatigable manipulators of political patronage for personal profit, while the scholarly Amaradasa's weakness is a desire to relate more closely to his students, an impulse that places him at risk and does not ensure their safety. His response, in the Prologue, to the familiar face and voice that urges "Join us Sir" parallels and is parodied by the exuberant dream that follows the return from the nightmare excursion: "'You must join us Sir. We knew you'd never turn your back on us.' They lift him up and carry him round and round the bus . . . with the others . . . singing 'Hail, Comrade Amaradas! Hero of Peradeniya!'" (129–30). This is an ironic comment on the fact that Munasinha and Wijesiri, constant welcome visitors at his house, do not confide that they are Guevarists and set out on the excursion with rebel uniforms in their bags; nonetheless, their trust brings them to the back door of his bungalow when the defeated rebels are hiding. Though timid enough to deny subscribing to the students' revolutionary organ and to burn Isaiah Berlin's *Karl Marx* for fear of being suspected of revolutionary tendencies, Amaradasa is prompt to receive the two young men. Yet are courage and concern summoned up only in response to the demand of the moment? When a student in jail writes begging for a visit, he ignores the warning of his more callous (or cautious) colleague, Randhusena, and goes at once, risking suspicion and police surveillance in response to his own judgment that it would be despicable not to answer Somaratna's call. Yet, when asked to come another day and to follow a complicated and tedious procedure, he does not return. Finally, *Curfew and a Full Moon* not only delineates a period of violence and despair but also the gap between aspiration and performance in a man of intellect and basic decency.

With the Begging Bowl depicts a group of Sri Lankan Embassy personnel with a humor reminiscent of Daumier's scarifying caricatures. Keertiratna, the unassuming and idealistic Ambassador believes he has been rewarded for helping to bring Mrs. Bandaranaike to power by his eloquence at the elections; the more worldly-wise gossip that he has been rewarded for less honorable service of which he remains ignorant. The Ambassador's wife is an efficient homemaker and hostess but a willful and unpredictable woman. The Embassy functions in a state of grinding poverty; if the staff, as Sarvan points out, are prone to pettiness, intrigue, and mean and joyless economies, it is due to "having to keep up appearances in expensive Europe on their Third World salaries and allowances. . . . Much of their character and conduct arises from economic realities back home" (440). Mistaken identities, reversals of expectations, sheer visual comedy in the depiction of everyone down from the Ambassador caught in a St. Vitus' frenzy of rhythm and Keertiratna's noneventful dalliance are all the stuff of farce; but there is a solid base of political history and also a darker streak as the Ambassador founders under the pressure of domestic infelicity and the threat to his prestige leveled by the overbearing and deceitful First Secretary. Yet Keertiratna, as Goonetilleke comments, is not only a victim. He also has a positive side as he tries to improve the Embassy and serve his country. Here irony plays on the juxtaposition of dreams and fact; seeking to project the national identity Keertiratna finds that Sri Lanka's batiks are derived from Indonesia, her brasswork from India; its national costume imitates the North Indian *sherwani* or South Indian *verti*. He dreams of offering Sri Lanka's greatest gift, Buddhism, to the French President, unaware that the latter regards it as the enervating cause of Asia's poverty.

Foam upon the Stream has five parts. Part I is narrated by Dharmasena ("Daruma San"), a Sri Lankan academic on an American Foundation Fellowship intended to help creative writing, whose wife and daughter have returned to Sri Lanka. Japan enchants him because of its undisturbed Asian identity and the atmosphere inspires him to attempt his first novel; but inspiration wilts, then sprouts again as Noriko, a quiet guileless girl who works at a bar but shares his taste for Kabuki, begins to frequent his room, cooks, tidies, and washes for him, and finally accepts his pressing invitations to go out with him. But the exquisite tranquility he enjoys is disturbed on hearing she has a date with a Japanese man: "I was a foreigner and couldn't enter wholly into her life; we could never express to each other our innermost feelings" (37). The core of the situation is more complex; the lack of contact and communication between two people deeply in love yet divided less by the barrier of unrelated cultures, of circumstances—such as his obligations to his wife, or disparity of background and character—than by the insurmountable loneliness of the human condition.

Part I, written on a note of lyric intensity, records Daruma San's delight in the company of Noriko, through whom he gains a growing intimacy with Japan—its art, landscape, life. Part II bridges the period between his departure for Sri Lanka and his return to Japan. As in Part IV, which performs the same function, the omniscient narrator presents Dharmasena's alienation from country and family; his environment jars on his senses, and he cuts himself off from his wife Ramya, save in company, speaking briefly only on family matters: "He would lie with her half-heartedly more out of a sense of duty than anything else" (68). He is conscious of his "cold cruelty" (71); and he envies the ease with which his German friend gets divorced and marries again—a solution he (like his Indian friend) finds unthinkable in terms of suggesting it to a wife and disrupting a familiar circle. Moreover, would Noriko out of her Japanese context be happy or be Noriko?

The novel reverts to Dharmasena's voice. Returning, he finds Noriko cold. Aware of the need to adjust, he nonetheless seeks to recapture memories by revisiting their haunts, particularly La Poupee. The concreteness of description does not reduce the wistful hunger of the quest—or its pain. A new building has replaced La Poupee. The deep-seated sense of impermanence and the sorrow of change pervades the novel with a delicate melancholy and emerges as its theme; its title is taken from a verse in *The Hoka Priests* from Arthur Waley's *Noh Plays of Japan*:

> We who pass through a world
> Changeful as the dews of evening
> Uncertain as the skies of summer
> We that are as foam upon the stream.

Here the lines embody a basic concept of Buddhism—Anitya, Transience.

An overdose of sleeping pills, taken to dull his despair or give effect to his constant thoughts of suicide as a certain source of happiness, makes Noriko thaw: They sleep together for the first time. He departs, then returns, separated from his wife; yet his hesitation, his seeming reluctance on the verge of marriage exasperates Noriko who throws a tantrum and leaves. Her absence for a night enables him to put his solution into practice, so that the passage of time and experience will not alter their love.

The novel is written with an economy that gives it power as well as delicacy. Part V, related by Noriko, dwells on the immediate pressures of life, its practical problems, physical needs and discomforts, in a manner which not only underlines her simple domesticated approach to love in contrast to Dharmasena's intensity and tendency to indulge his emotions but also emphasizes the difference between the poetry of love and its prose.

In his fictional studies of people, particularly those temporarily uprooted from their own cultures and brought into contact with others, Sarachchandra broadens the reader's apprehension of ways of life and ways of thought—those factors affecting the framework of human existence and contributing to the interplay of the conscious and unconscious impulses that determine the individual's course of action. Ultimately, the writer's sensitivity to such distinctions and his ability to project them, like his technical virtuosity, serve to express the complexity and clarity of his perceptions. His is a disenchanted vision, bleak, yet poignantly conscious of the possibilities of a life invariably and tragically thwarted by time, change, and the vulnerability of reason.

WORKS CITED

Goonetilleke, D.C.R.A. "Sri Lanka." *Journal of Commonwealth Literature* 22 (1987): 90–93.
Sarachchandra, Ediriwira. *The Folk Drama of Ceylon.* Colombo: Department of Cultural Affairs, 1966.
———. *Curfew and a Full Moon.* Hong Kong: Heinemann, 1978.
———. *Foam upon the Stream—A Japanese Elegy.* Singapore: Heinemann, 1987.
———. "Of a Queen and a Courtesan." *Solidarity* , Feb. 1970: 20–50.

———. *With the Begging Bowl*. Delhi: B.R. Publishing Corporation, 1986.

———. Letter to the author, November 1989.

Sarvan, Charles P. "*With the Begging Bowl*: The Politics of Poverty." *World Literature Today* 63 (1989): 439–43.

EDIRIWIRA SARACHCHANDRA'S PUBLISHED WORK IN ENGLISH

Novels

Curfew and a Full Moon, 1978
With the Begging Bowl, 1986
Foam upon the Stream—A Japanese Elegy, 1987

Short Stories

"Of a Queen and a Courtesan," 1970
"The Death of His Oldest Friend," in *An Anthology of Modern Writing from Sri Lanka*, 1981

Philosophy

Buddhist Psychology of Perception, 1958

> An attempt to interpret in terms intelligible to the reader familiar with Western philosophy the Buddhist view of mind as expressed in Pali literature of the early period, the sermons, and of the later period, the Abhidamma (Metaphysics).

Literary History

The Sinhalese Folk Play and The Modern Stage, 1952; *The Folk Drama of Ceylon*, revised and expanded, 1966

> Presents the results of many years of observation and study of rituals to exorcise demons of disease or propitiate gods, both seen as forces affecting earthier concerns than the higher religions followed by the villagers, such as Buddhism, Hinduism, Christianity. Describes the rituals associated with different areas. Of anthropological interest in particular.

Criticism

Modern Sinhalese Fiction, 1943

> Pioneer attempt to assess the work of contemporary novelists, it was Sarachchandra's first work as a critic. Written in English, it was later revised with substantial additions that broadened its scope.

The Sinhalese Novel, 1950.

> Revised and expanded version of the 1943 work, this book maintains the necessity of applying purely literary criteria to a new form borrowed from the West rather than looking to Sanskrit literary conventions or following the earlier tendency to judge the novels on the strength of their moral values.

SELECTED CRITICAL READINGS

Critical notice of Sarachchandra's novels both in Sri Lanka and overseas has currently been confined to the examination of individual novels either in isolation or in comparison with the works of other Sri Lankan novelists. It is likely that more attention will be directed to the novels as viewed together for purposes of analysis and evaluation. The two original short stories will repay study, particularly if examined in conjunction with Ranjini Obevsekere's and Ashley Halpe's translations.

de Silva, D.M. "*Pemato Javati Soko* and Its Context." *Ediriwira Sarachchandra Festschrift*. Sri Lanka National Commission for UNESCO, 1988: 28–48. Examines Sarachchandra's place as playwright in the context of the period and this play in relation to his other dramas.

de Silva, Lakshmi. "The Poetic Dramas—Text and Technique." *Ediriwira Sarachchandra Festschrift.* Sri Lanka National Commission for UNESCO, 1988: 23–27. Focuses on the complex interplay of psychological and social forces in the text as revealed obliquely through poetic suggestion.

Gooneratne, Yasmine. "Ediriwira Sarachchandra: An Asian Writer and His Milieu." *Ediriwira Sarachchandra Festschrift.* Sri Lanka National Commission for UNESCO, 1988: 5–8. Notes that Brahmins and Buddhist monks were once the guardians of literature but respect swung to the English educated and led to the neglect of classic work. Sarachchandra attempted to recover and reassert a national unity by returning to earlier traditions and techniques.

———. "Choosing a Setting: Review Article." *New Ceylon Writing* 4 (1979): 99–107. Examines translations and *Curfew and a Full Moon,* seeing the novel's bare language as a way of expressing an objective view of the 1971 Insurgency in Sri Lanka.

Goonetilleke, D.C.R.A. "Sri Lanka—Annual Bibliography of Commonwealth Literature." *Journal of Commonwealth Literature.* Comments on *Curfew and a Full Moon* (Vol. 14, 1979); on *With the Begging Bowl* (Vol. 22, 1987); on *Foam upon the Stream* (Vol. 23, 1988).

———. "Ediriwira Sarachchandra, *Curfew and a Full Moon.*" *Navasilu* 3 (1979): 115–16. Rates the novel as rewarding for its depiction of the liberal but ineffectual don and the portrayal of the insurgents as callow yet genuinely idealistic. Argues that the documentary texture of the first two parts raises unfulfilled expectations in that the role of the rebel leaders is not assessed.

Halpe, Ashley. "The Novels of 1978–1987." *Ediriwira Sarachchandra Festschrift.* Sri Lanka National Commission for UNESCO, 1988: 72–79. Focuses on the novelist's technique by enumerating the variety of communicative modes employed in *Curfew and a Full Moon* and the sophisticated awareness of form and tonal nuance evident in *With the Begging Bowl* and *Foam upon the Stream.*

———. "Sri Lankan Literature in English and Its Context." *New Literature Review* (1982): 3–15. Surveys the full field of Sri Lankan creative writing in English. States that *Curfew and a Full Moon* is a subtle and sensitive book with language characterized by controlled expressiveness.

Moores, Alan. "A Romantic Tug-of-war." *Asiaweek* 19 July 1987: 69. Assesses *Foam upon the Stream* as a compelling, authentic novel; judges the format of the book appropriate to show the complexities of cultural differences.

Paniker, Ayappa. "Sinhabahu and the Theatre of the Roots." *Ediriwira Sarachchandra Festschrift.* Sri Lanka National Commission for UNESCO, 1988: 65–67. Recognizes Sarachchandra as a pioneer in the process of cultural decolonization, noting that his experiments return to the nonillusionistic poetic drama of pre-colonial times.

Ramachandra, Ragini. "*Foam upon the Stream.*" *Literary Criterion* 22 (1987): 90–92. Identifies the novel's theme as the consequence of inaction and the elusive and ephemeral nature of human happiness.

Reynolds, C.H.B. "Too Deep for Tears." *Ediriwira Sarachchandra Festschrift.* Sri Lanka National Commission for UNESCO, 1988: 1–4. Rates the two Sinhalese novels that are the basis of *Foam upon the Stream* very highly.

Sarvan, Charles P. "*With the Begging Bowl:* The Politics of Poverty." *World Literature Today* 63 (1989): 439–443. Points out that Sarachchandra courageously uses harsh comedy as an instrument because it is the nature of satire to exaggerate. Suggests that the aim of the work is to dispel rhetoric and the aura of the past in order to prompt an honest examination of the island's present.

—LAKSHMI DE SILVA

Derek Walcott

Derek Alton Walcott is not only an outstanding poet and dramatist from the West Indies, he is arguably one of the best writers in the English language today. He was born to Warwick and Alix Walcott in Castries, capital of St. Lucia, West Indies, 23 January 1930. Taking up his calling at an early age, he had his *25 Poems* privately printed in 1948. *Henri Christophe*, the play he claims as his first, was produced in 1950, by the St. Lucia Arts Guild, the company founded by Walcott and his twin brother Rodney.

After completing his B.A. degree at the University of the West Indies in Jamaica in 1953, he taught briefly in St. Lucia, Grenada, and Jamaica. A Rockefeller grant allowed him to study theater in New York in 1957-58. Then he settled in Trinidad in 1959 to found the Trinidad Theatre Workshop and write for *The Trinidad Guardian*. Following seventeen years of writing, directing, and producing with mounting success on the international scene, he resigned from the Workshop and eventually moved to the United States in the late 1970s. At present he teaches at Boston University and travels frequently to write and supervise productions of his plays in the Caribbean, England, and other parts of the United States.

Walcott's fourteen books of poetry and four volumes of plays have earned him numerous awards—among them: Guinness Poetry Award, 1961; Royal Society of Literature Heinemann Award, 1966; Fellow of the Royal Society of Literature, 1966; Cholmondeley Award, 1969; Obie Award for *Dream on Monkey Mountain*, 1971; Jock Campbell New Statesman Award, 1973; Order of the British Empire, 1972; Member of the American Academy and Institute of Arts, 1979; Welsh Arts Council International Writers Prize, 1980; MacArthur Foundation Award, 1981.

THE ART OF CHIAROSCURO—
CALIBAN CONFRONTS THE WHITE WORLD

Derek Walcott is more than a poet and dramatist; he exhibits the vision of the painter as well, utilizing three rather than just two artistic forms of expression. Beyond obvious allusions to movements, periods, styles, and names of famous pictorial artists, the visual arts enter all that he writes. The painterly aspects of specific works have been ably covered: Edward Baugh devotes a book, *Derek Walcott: Memory as Vision: Another Life* (1980), and a major article, "Painters and Painting in *Another Life*" (1978), to this aspect of Walcott's autobiographical poem; and Robert Bensen's analysis of *Midsummer* is entitled "The Painter as Poet: Derek

Walcott's *Midsummer* "(1986). Beyond the poetry, there are Walcott's years as arts editor for the *Trinidad Guardian*. Victor Questel itemizes eighty-one articles devoted to architecture, painting, and sculpture in "Walcott's Hack's Hired Prose" (1978).

Suffice it to say, the explicit connections between the pictorial arts and Walcott's poetry have been made. His drama, however, remains virtually untouched, and the more subtle influences of the visual arts throughout his work remain to be explored. That aspect of painting, which is most pervasive, is his manipulation of light and shadow: chiaroscuro in its fullest application. Chiaroscuro goes beyond contrasts and potential conflict; it is essential for representing the third dimension, physical and spiritual depth. Describing the device in the works of Rembrandt, Robert Wallace argues that it creates "an atmosphere that half conceals and half discloses both the tangible and intangible, in exactly that region where a glimpse of the 'soul' may be caught" (135). On both counts, this simple device is indispensable to Walcott. It serves as a touchstone for understanding not only the primary subject matter of his poetry and drama but also the evolution of his writing style.

Although the full exploitation of chiaroscuro in Walcott's plays is not realized until the 1983 version of *The Last Carnival*, the interplay of light and dark elements figures in even the earliest works. Traditionally, stagecraft has depended on conflict for sustained interest. Walcott's is no exception. It gains poignancy, however, when the playwright is transforming established theatrical form into an indigenous vehicle for a black, third world community. There are given racial, cultural, linguistic, and geographical differences. Encompassing these differences alone requires a layering of effects that casts shadows, both physical and emotional. Perhaps the earliest successful adaptation of Walcott's brand of chiaroscuro to theater is the divided psyche of Corporal Lestrade in the internationally acclaimed *Dream on Monkey Mountain*.

Prior to this he had composed docudramas such as *Henri Christophe* and *Drums and Colours*, which depict Caribbean history through a European filter, or portrayed vivid West Indian characters in local-color plays like *The Sea at Dauphin* and *Ti-Jean and his Brothers*. Christophe and Ti-Jean are black men struggling against white institutions—seeking independence from France or from the plantation system, respectively. Cultural and color differences play off each other in each play, but Walcott aptly summarizes the central irony of Henri Christophe's "fustian" style: There is a "contradiction of being white in mind and black in body . . . yet the Jacobean style, its cynical, aristocratic flourish came naturally to this first play—the corruption of slaves into tyrants ("What" 12-13).

By the late 1960s Walcott had sufficiently mastered the dichotomy between his native culture and the formal demands of theater to achieve a tentative synthesis. *Dream on Monkey Mountain* demonstrates this in two ways. Through the example of Bertolt Brecht he learned enough about classical oriental theater to capitalize on Trinidad's carnival tradition—incorporating dance, masks, mime, music, and folk symbolism within a controlled story line ("Meanings"). Second, the European/ Apollonian mind and the Dionysian/African soul are not cast as dialectic opposites.

The resolution rests on two characters. Makak, the protagonist, reconciles disparate forces within himself by sinking roots in his native soil. An equally significant portrayal of the central dilemma occurs in the person of the half-white, half-black mulatto Lestrade. From mechanical adherence to the white man's law at the first of the play to fanatic enforcement of black revenge at the end, Lestrade, as his name suggests, straddles two cultures. Since he insists on blindly following one racial ethic or the other, he becomes an integer with no personal identity. Makak's advantage is that he reclaims his African heritage in a positive way, not as vengeance against an external antagonist. The action rises to a violent scene wherein Makak beheads the white apparition who had inspired him to embrace blackness and the past; however, the nightmare is complemented with the final scene in the morning mist. There Makak delivers a paean to his native, mountain home: not European or African, but West Indian.

Conflict in these early plays depends heavily on the interplay of color. Since Walcott was born in a culture educated to disparage everything local by European standards, it is natural that his subject matter should depend on the contrasts between two world views. It is a simple extension of this practice of opposing one thing against another to account for the thematic importance of all Walcott's dichotomies. For example, his translation of Tirso de Molina's *El Burlador de Sevilla, The Joker of Seville*, dramatizes the idea that the Old World corruption of the New World results from the individual's subservience to societal taboos. A similar message emerges in Walcott's treatment of Jamaica's Rastafarian community in *O Babylon!* In this case, the protagonist (like Makak) deviates from his non-conformist subculture to make individual peace with the land.

White and black, light and dark are so ingrained in the social background it could be argued that what I am calling Walcott's aesthetic choices are contextual prerequisites. The broader implications of his reliance on chiaroscuro, however, become unavoidable in *The Last Carnival*, the published version of a play from the 1970s previously entitled "In a Fine Castle." Whereas the earlier incarnation focuses on the futile attempts of a mulatto reporter to live between the worlds of his Black-power girlfriend and the withdrawing colonialist values of the De La Fontaines, by 1983, the reporter, Brown, has become a minor character. In transition, the pervasive atmosphere of the play becomes *fin de siècle* rococo, and the central characters are an English governess, Agatha Willett, and the declining French creole family of Victor and Oswald De La Fontaine.

Tonal qualities of chiaroscuro appear in the first scene when Agatha, newly arrived in Trinidad, is struck by the aroma of cocoa and the astonishing light of the tropics: "So clear! All this. It's as if the world were making a fresh start" (6). Victor's response, "Damned hard to paint," reveals his obsession. He is an effete impressionist, who eventually assumes the identity of Watteau. In scene two, Victor has costumed everyone to replicate Watteau's *Embarkation to Cythera*. He even projects the painting on a screen and observes that Watteau painted his whole culture in sunset hues, "an elegy to the light" (17). Scene five is set at dusk; translucent panels are used for a shadow play that degenerates from Victor's artistic moment into burlesque. To close the scene, Victor is shown in silhouette as he upbraids villagers for reducing his Cythera into Calypsos.

Victor's last scene comes at a cricket match on Independence Day in 1962. For him the moment is a *fête champêtre*, thoroughly Manet. Unfortunately, art and life fail to satisfy his inner needs. Sometime thereafter he commits suicide, thus following

Watteau in an early death. Act two takes place in 1970, in the De La Fontaine's Port of Spain townhouse. Victor's spirit lives on in his unfinished imitation of Watteau's *Embarkation*. The painting on the wall and the carnival season thematically unify the two acts.

The nostalgic decadence of Watteau's eighteenth-century contemporaries is echoed in the decline of the De La Fontaines. Victor's son Tony uses the painting to comment on the stasis of the creole aristocracy as rebels hide in the hills and national troops assert their new power:

> With this light like the fire, orange, and silks, the sunset, I see the moment of stillness Victor wanted. Because here we are, we can't move. Just like these people in the painting. Motionless. (91)

The De La Fontaines are anachronistic, watching their last carnival. The natives, to whom Agatha has been teaching self-reliance, are reveling in their independence, full of action in spite of the fact that they have no sense of direction. The future and the past coalesce in the last act, on the docks once again as Agatha prepares to depart with Victor's daughter Clodia. As she is forced to leave the land of her birth, Clodia admonishes Brown, the cynically detached reporter, to find a cause for which he could die.

White gives way literally to black in *The Last Carnival*, and Walcott paints the shifting play of light as though it were one of the cast. The pastel costumes, the glow of sunlight, pale moonbeams, shadows, and references to eighteenth-century period pieces intermingle with jokes, calypso music, and the emotional expressions of characters to create a living tableau. The mental as well as physical complexion flows from the palette. The result is most evident in *The Last Carnival*, but Walcott the artist always visualizes his plays, drafting set and costume designs in watercolors during the writing and production of each one ("Meanings" 48).

Flexible as the utilization of chiaroscuro may be in the drama, Walcott's inventiveness reaches new dimensions in his poetry. This is not evident in his early verse because by his own admission he sought to prolong "the mighty line of Marlowe, of Milton" ("What" 31) and as with his plays his poems conform to established patterns. Drawing examples from his *Collected Poems: 1948-1984*, it is apparent that his first three volumes—*Poems, In a Green Night, Selected Poems*—are heavily indebted to the past. Tension continually arises as background and foreground are set against each other. From *Poems*, "As John to Patmos" employs a simile between his home and the Apostle John's biblical isle of exile, then the persona vows to praise his local environment. "Prelude" bemoans the loss of childhood and refers to Dante. "A City's Death by Fire" commemorates a major conflagration in Castries, but the imagery and syntax are vintage Dylan Thomas.

Similar cross references underscore Walcott's eye for vivid detail, color, and connections between matter and form. He does not strive to bring out the uniqueness of his islands or his own style. The only piece reprinted from *Selected Poems*, "Origins," focuses on the Caribbean in light of the various cultural strands leading to the present. The Greek and African heritage, Christian ceremonies,

Columbus, are part of an oceanic exodus. In a sewing image that recurs in different guises elsewhere, the speaker describes two worlds stitched together by caravels, "Like the whirr of my mother's machine . . . /Like needles of cicadas stitching the afternoon's shroud" (14). Afternoon and shroud serve the bitterness of a poem ending with the "birth of white cities . . . /And the annihilation of races" (16).

As he has done with the plays, Walcott seems to need a point of comparison to achieve his more vivid effects. The contrasts provided figuratively by chiaroscuro in *In a Green Night* assume a more impressive context through allusion. Another parallel with the drama is the fact that he continues to avoid categorical imperatives. Light and dark, good and bad, old and new are interdependent. This is explicit in two of the best known poems from *In a Green Night*. "Ruins of a Great House" extends Donne's "For Whom the Bell Tolls" to the descendant of slaves as he realizes that England, too, was once a neglected colony. The moment arises because wind borne ash stirs the ember of his mind and burns his eyes with "the ashen prose of Donne." "A Far Cry from Africa" asks "Where shall I turn, divided to the vein? . . . /Between this Africa and the English tongue I love?" (18). Not only is there contrast, but the dimensions of the poem are deepened spatially and temporally.

Although Walcott writes with one eye on Western tradition, his poetry depends so heavily on specific details from his immediate surroundings that this phase of his development might be labeled his sensuous period. The ruins in "The Ruins of a Great House" stand over the unmarked graves of slaves. The man in "A Far Cry from Africa" feels "poisoned with the blood" of two races. Less dramatically, in "Two Poems on the Passing of an Empire," the appearance of a heron on a stump is enough to complete a landscape and its call underlines the silence. Swallows stitch together opposing eves in "Orient and Immortal Wheat;" masts thread archipelagoes like Odysseus' in "A Sea-Chantey." Poem after poem comments on the quality of the light, which may be emerald, vaporous, Egyptian, summery, blue, lemon, or varied according to the sun, moon, or lamps. An outstanding example appears in the sonnet sequence entitled "Tales of the Islands." His exact description of Bernini's *The Ecstasy of St. Teresa* links her "nest of light" with black bathers who need "the strength to reach/Above the navel." Light, which is physically reflected off their wet bodies, must be internalized as a higher faculty.

With a humorous twist, another pair of these sonnets depicts a Catholic priest indulging in savage rites while nearby a beach party is in full swing. The speaker picks up on the irony sardonically, "Great stuff, old boy; sacrifice, moments of truth." One of the revelers is a "Black writer chap, one of them Oxbridge guys." In his alternating casually between dialect and standard English, there is more than wit; another form of juxtaposition captures the local atmosphere. In "Islands," among the last selections from *In a Green Night*, Walcott argues that a climate seeks its own style. At this point in his career, he defines his ideal in typically sensual terms:

> Verse crisp as sand, clear as sunlight,
> Cold as the curled wave, ordinary
> As a tumbler of island water.

Contrary to such aims, the style does not become any more transparent as Walcott continues to develop many of the themes and devices introduced in his first three collections.

Since part of *Selected Poems* is reproduced in *The Castaway and Other Poems*, they have much in common; yet the latter puts more emphasis on the bitterness of exile. Three poems printed in both books retain the sensuality of earlier verses and add what seems to be a more philosophical strain. The cost of exile is explored throughout *The Castaway* but "Missing the Sea," "A Map of Europe," and "Coral" bring out the values of positive and negative space. The first of these makes the distant sea palpable through the absence of its familiar sound. Citing the examples of Leonardo, Canaletto, Chardin, and Vermeer, the second poem uses synaesthesia to assert that

> The light creates its stillness. In its ring
> Everything IS. . . .
> . . .
> . . . Only the gift
> To see things as they are, halved by a darkness
> From which they cannot shift.

Apparently the mere differentiation that makes an object what it is simultaneously fixes its isolation permanently. Sensuality and philosophy combine with equal finality in "Coral." Recalling the shape, texture, even the pores of his lover's anatomy, the poet inverts Archimedes' discovery: "Bodies in absence displace their weight" (73)

The ultimate castaway appears in "Crusoe's Journal," a poem which is reprinted in *The Gulf and Other Poems*. Speaking through Daniel Defoe's Robinson Crusoe allows Walcott a recognizable literary reference point and, more importantly, allows a modicum of distance from which to speak. After allusions to the Bible, Eden, a second Adam, and a man conscious of his shadow in prayer, the poet enters the scene himself, vacationing on Crusoe's island of Tobago. Unobtrusively the two merge and in the final segment a group of little black girls—"Friday's progeny"— becomes the center of a light-flooded scene. Hearing the call to vespers and watching the children's crinolines ignite with the setting sun, he realizes,

> nothing I can learn
> from art or loneliness
> Can bless them as the bell's
> Transfiguring tongue can bless.

The speaker judges himself and his profession against literary precursors and the efficacy of his writing.

What I am calling the philosophical aspect of Walcott's use of chiaroscuro becomes increasingly apparent in the "Gulf" section of *The Gulf and Other Poems*. The title poem itself includes one of the new physical devices that symbolizes detached observation. In spite of its transparency, glass presents a barrier between a viewer and his subject. In "The Gulf," the speaker looks down on the earth through the window of a trans-Texas airliner. He is conscious of the pane of glass itself, but it becomes both a rhyming word and a metaphor for the "pain" of life, then for a "plain" style of writing. Next, after he notes how the face of a loved one becomes plainer under glass, he muses that from on high the earth appears to heal its scars and renew itself. There follows a catalog of disasters—wars, slaughter, his status as a secondary citizen, all gulfs that divide mankind—until he pronounces his epitaph on the violence, "age after age, the uninstructing dead." Evidence that Walcott is never disengaged, even when he purposely establishes a distant perspective, is readily available in several other poems and in the fact that the observer in "The Gulf" exhibits profound concern.

As the angle of vision acquires greater value for Walcott in *The Gulf and Other Poems*, it is significant that chiaroscuro also establishes itself for the first time as an overt literary device. After "Che" and "Negatives," two otherwise minor poems, the whiteness or blackness of an object can no longer be dismissed as incidental or innocent fact. When Walcott commemorates the fallen revolutionary leader Che Guevara, he evokes the name of Baroque master Caravaggio to emphasize the stark relief of a grainy black and white news photograph. Guevara's corpse glares from the funeral slab, transforming itself into marble, white iron, in the fear and doubt of his enemy. "Negatives," too, derives from a news clipping, this time of Biafran bodies on a white road. A single name, Christopher Okigbo is recalled, but within the description of the unidentified, white commentator who "illuminates the news behind the news, . . . /with, perhaps, pity" anger simmers. Based on the content of this poem, the title takes on three levels of meaning, each dependent on the contrasts of light and dark. The photograph itself was first a negative black and white reversal of its "positive" image in the paper, but more to the point here is the doubly negative fact that black Hausas had executed black Ibos; furthermore, the sardonic tone of the poem itself compounds the negativity.

By the end of *The Gulf and other Poems*, Walcott turns his perspective on his own accomplishments. In "Nearing Forty" and "The Walk," he considers the encroachments of middle age, the prospect of losing his creative edge, the discovery that his meteoric ambition may be only a damp match. As always, the immediate foreground is measured against a foil: youth's "false dawn" dwindles to the "fireless and average." He asks in "The Walk," "When was your work more like a housemaid's novel,/some drenched soap opera which gets/closer than yours to life?" The modest pose conveniently brings together Walcott's sensuous imagery and the contemplative quality that reflects his maturation process.

Although the conclusion of *The Gulf and Other Poems* may appear to reflect self-doubt, it actually suggests confidence, the poet's assurance to verbalize his deepest misgivings. This is not the first instance of Walcott's confessional tendency, yet it foreshadows the third phase of his development. His next volume, the autobiographical *Another Life* is a virtual "Portrait of the Artist as a Young West Indian." Together with *Sea Grapes* and *The Star-Apple Kingdom*, Walcott turns his personal life into the primary vehicle of poetic expression.

Painting as opposed to writing and art versus life are two of the central metaphorical contrasts in *Another Life*; therefore, lighting effects are prominent throughout the book. In the twilight of the opening scene, a mesmerizing sun bathes the inlet with amber until the sky "grew drunk with light." Literally and metaphorically, the black child considers himself "a prodigy of the wrong age and colour." He in his poetry, and his friend Gregorias in painting, strive to record their experiences of the immediate present and of the imported "romantic taxidermy" of the past. As colonials, they are divided children who doubt which is the true light, noon or twilight; yet, they swear,

> never [to] leave the island
> until [they] had put down, in paint, in words,
> as palmists learn the network of a hand,
> all of its sunken, leaf-choked ravines,
> every neglected, self-pitying inlet
> muttering in brackish dialect.

Noble as the goal may sound, embedded in the oath is the possibility of leaving eventually. The location and size of the island conspire to make emigration seem inevitable. For this reason, the youth swears further to "make of my heart an ark" (250), to carry the island within when he departs.

As has been the case with the plays, Walcott continues to deal with the conflicts between imported and local influences. Regardless of the contradictions, choosing to record the island does not preclude the inclusion of all that western tradition bequeathed to the New World. The result in one instance is to have thoughts drift from "Italianate cabbage palms" in old landscapes to the problem of his complexion:

> How often didn't you hesitate
> between rose-flesh and sepia,
> your blood like a serpent whispering
> of a race incapable of subtler shadow,
> of music, architecture, and a complex thought.

Embedded even among these complaints about racial stereotyping is reference to the difficulty of portraying the modeling shadows of chiaroscuro on dark skin.

Concerns of the artist continue to assert themselves in disparate contexts in *Another Life*. He senses betrayal in his need to leave St. Lucia to pursue his calling. Worse yet, he realizes that his impulse to make poetry of his love for Anna is to break faith with the woman and the emotion itself. At the end of the poem he has left Anna, Gregorias, and the island but given them immortality through his record. Ultimately, the "other life" of the title, the life of the imagination, becomes the illumination of his reality.

The next two books comprising this personal phase of Walcott's evolution, *Sea Grapes* and *The Star-Apple Kingdom*, also draw from his life; the only element missing is continuous autobiographical linkage. For example, the centerpiece of *Sea Grapes*, "Sainte Lucie," is a bilingual *tour de force* in creole and English on facing pages. This paean to his birthplace centers on a mural painted by his friend Dunstan St. Omer, the "Gregorias" of *Another Life*. The title poem *Sea Grapes* may or may not suggest that Walcott has committed adultery, but by now his thematic tensions are very familiar. As the adulterer heads home, he identifies his predicament with that of a mythological unfaithful husband: Odysseus from another place and time. Both of them suffer "The ancient war/between obsession and responsibility." Having made his comparison with this Mediterranean predecessor, once again, he poses art against life to conclude, "The classics can console. But not enough" (297).

By the end of *Sea Grapes*, the middle-aged poet has reconciled himself to the process of growing old. In "Dark August," he learns to appreciate the medicinal bitterness of dark days when in the past he had loved only the sun and bright days. "Sea Cranes" and "The Morning Moon" contribute to the mood given voice in "To Return to the Trees," new found respect for the color grey. The promise and vigor of youth yield to the strength of verse that takes root like a durable almond tree,

> going under the sand
> with this language, slowly,
> by sand grains, by centuries.

In essence, the speaker discloses the subtler values of gradations between black and white, youth and age.

Selections from *The Star-Apple Kingdom* in *Collected Poems* present several vivid personae, in particular, Shabine of "The Schooner *Flight*" and the Jamaican politician in the title poem. Shabine, like Walcott, is a poet of mixed ancestry, and like the speaker in "Sea Grapes" he is torn between duty (to wife and home) and passion for Maria (the woman he loves). When the power shifts from the white to the black race in the West Indies, he is left without a party. The title poem picks up the political theme with an added personal element; the central figure in the poem is modeled after Walcott's former classmate at the University of the West Indies, Michael Manley, Prime Minister of Jamaica (Thomas 44–45).

The main character's preoccupation is with the fortunes that have placed him in the great house that slaves would have viewed from the outside in days gone by. In an old photograph, he is struck by the dark skinned servants who are forced to the periphery of the picture. Out of their mouths a silent scream carries reverberations from their epoch to his own, leading to the conclusion that silence transforms itself into a "creak of light . . . between/the noises of" the polarized world. As might be expected, those divisions are the contrasts that have dominated Walcott's poetry: rich and poor, North and South, white and black, two Americas, and the separate people of Jamaica's parishes.

There is nothing remarkable about Walcott's chiaroscuro in "The Star-Apple Kingdom," except a hint of surrealism in that extended, silent scream of light. Significantly, there is innovative manipulation of light and dark in a shorter poem, "Forest of Europe," which adds a new dimension to his poetry. The first stanza is an extended simile with synaesthesia in the leaves falling like piano notes from the bare trees' music stands. Through the first four lines, the description of dark woods against a winter landscape is standard fare. Then in the fifth verse, the lines of trees are "ruled on these scattered manuscripts of snow," and suddenly the chiaroscuro, by double-entendre, applies both to the image and to the lines of poetry on the page as well.

This legerdemain certainly has little bearing on the larger meaning of "The Forest of Europe"; nevertheless, it is one more device by which Walcott asserts his personal hand. The imagery is as sensual as ever; the setting creates a tone of quiet contemplation, and the two figures in the poem are Walcott and his close friend, Joseph Brodsky. On the one hand, "The Forest of Europe" culminates Walcott's mature style in *The Star-Apple Kingdom*. On the other hand, it introduces a surrealistic dimension wherein poems occasionally draw attention to their existence as textual matter.

This tendency does not constitute a new style, but by 1979, through gradual increments, Walcott begins to cultivate an existential facet. The three volumes in the 1980s, *The Fortunate Traveller*, *Midsummer*—both of which are excerpted in *The Collected Poems*—and *The Arkansas Testament*, bring together all of Walcott's accumulated themes and writing techniques. Although no single approach to representative poems in his later work covers his varied performance, a brief look at his expanded use of chiaroscuro is revealing.

From *The Fortunate Traveller*, "Piano Practice" laments the predicament of a poet who grew up in only one climate, and it takes up the surrealism of "The Forest of Europe" with musical "scales skittering like minnows across the sea." "Jean Rhys" makes use of old photographs mottled with chemicals and age. The figures and spaces turn shades of brown and white. One "V of Chinese white" represents a sea gull, but beyond the context of the photograph, Walcott reads in it "the white hush between two sentences." The synaesthesia of sight and sound once again punctuates the multileveled chiaroscuro of poetic description and the act of writing. The appropriateness of this ambiguous reference is increased when at the end of the poem Walcott describes a young Jean Rhys staring at a white candle, a copy of *Jane Eyre* in one hand. Since this novel became the source of Rhys's famous *Wide Sargasso Sea*, Walcott's picture of the writer telescopes the whiteness of the light into her wedding dress of white paper.

The immediacy of composing "The Hotel Normandy Pool" is explicit when the poet refers to the shadow of his pen on the page and to the fact "that this page's surface would unmist/after my breath as pools and mirrors do." The poem turns confessional when the pool and mirrors bring his children and the disfigurations of divorce to mind. As may be expected of Walcott, his feeling of abandonment eventually assumes classical overtones with references to Ovid who endured his seaside exile in the ancient past. Painting, too, enters in colorful simile:

> At dusk, the sky is loaded like watercolour paper
> with an orange wash in which every edge frays—
> a painting with no memory of the painter—.

Juxtapositions such as these of past and present, age and youth, immediate and universal, modern and classic, night and day, writing and thinking, life and art flow on through *Midsummer*. This one season is traced through time and space to imperial Rome, eighteenth- and nineteenth-century France, England, Walcott's residences in Trinidad and Boston, and Joseph Brodsky's Russia. For Chardin and the Impressionists, light "was the best that time offered" because "everything becomes/

its idea to the painter." That is to say, meaning resides in the eye of the beholder. In this case, the terms of existence appear impartial. Another passage captures the heat of racial unrest in Warwickshire and the obstacles to artistic comity:

> I was there to add some colour to the British theatre.
> "But the blacks can't do Shakespeare, they have no experience."
> . . .
> Praise had bled my lines white of any more anger,
> and snow had inducted me into white fellowships,
> while Calibans howled down the barred streets of an empire
> that began with Caedmon's raceless dew, and is ending
> in the alleys of Brixton, burning like Turner's ships.

The legacy of empire and consequently of Walcott's poetry is black Caliban confronting the white world in its own realm.

A single poem in *The Arkansas Testament* epitomizes the value of chiaroscuro in Walcott's verbal portraiture. "The Light of the World" takes its inspiration from a peasant girl who suggests to the poet a black Delacroix's *Liberty Leading the People*. The ridges and planes of her face, the lines of her profile flicker before him as the rural transport is caught in passing headlights. Amid passengers boarding and descending, he recalls the constraints of the life he had abandoned long ago. Overwhelmed by his people's quiet strength and his irretrievable loss, he concludes, "There was nothing they wanted, nothing I could give them/but this thing I have called 'The Light of the World.'" With these words, the woman's beauty that inspired the poem and the act of writing the poem become one. Literal chiaroscuro brings out the highlights and shadows of the girl's features, elicits a whole plane of existence. In Walcott's writing, chiaroscuro also dramatizes the salient points where art and life intersect.

From the beginning, I have contended that chiaroscuro is never merely an exchange between black and white. Along with linear and ariel perspective, it creates the illusion of bulk and depth for three dimensional objects in a two dimensional plane. It suggests a fixed source of light, illuminating surfaces or obscuring mysterious depths, playing on faces to betray moods and psychological states. For artists since the Renaissance and the Baroque periods, it has also been an effective tool for creating dramatic contrasts. In the poetry and plays of Derek Walcott, who was "divided to the vein" from birth, chiaroscuro is as inevitable as night and day.

WORKS CITED

Baugh, Edward. *Memory as Vision: Another Life*. London: Longman, 1978.
———. "Painters and Painting in *Another Life*." *Caribbean Quarterly* 26.1–2 (1980): 83–93.
Bensen, Robert. "The Painter as Poet: Derek Walcott's *Midsummer*." *The Literary Review* 29 (1986): 257–68.
Questel, Victor. "Walcott's Hack's Hired Prose." *Kairi* (1978): 64–67.
Thomas, Ned. "Derek Walcott." *Kunapipi* 3.2 (1981): 42–47.
Walcott, Derek. *The Arkansas Testament*. New York: Farrar, Straus and Giroux, 1987.

———. *Collected Poems: 1948–1984.* New York: Farrar, Straus and Giroux, 1986.

———. *The Last Carnival.* In *Three Plays.* New York: Farrar, Straus and Giroux, 1986.

———. "Meanings." *Savacou* 2 (1970): 45-51.

———. "What the Twilight Says: An Overture." Introduction to *Dream on Monkey Mountain and Other Plays.* New York: Farrar, Straus and Giroux, 1971. 1-40.

Wallace, Robert. *The World of Rembrandt: 1606-69.* New York: Time-Life, 1965.

DEREK WALCOTT'S PUBLISHED WORK

Poetry

25 Poems, 1948
Epitaph for the Young, 1949
Poems, 1951
In a Green Light: Poems 1948-1960, 1962
Selected Poems, 1964
The Castaway and Other Poems, 1965
The Gulf and Other Poems, 1969
The Gulf, 1970
Another Life, 1973
Sea Grapes, 1976
The Star-Apple Kingdom, 1979
Remembrance and Pantomime, 1980
The Fortunate Traveller, 1981
Midsummer, 1984
Collected Poems, 1986
The Arkansas Testament, 1987
Omeros, 1989

Plays

Henri Christophe, 1950
Harry Dernier, 1952
Ione, 1957
Dream on Monkey Mountain and Other Plays (Includes in addition to title play: *The Sea at Dauphin, Ti-Jean and His Brothers,* and *Malcochon*), 1970
The Joker of Seville and O Babylon!, 1978
Three Plays (Includes: *The Last Carnival, Beef, No Chicken,* and *A Branch of the Blue Nile*), 1986

Selected Articles

"Leaving School." *London Magazine* 5.6 (1965): 4–14.
    Rich autobiographical detail of early life; discusses influential names, events, reading matter.
"The Muse of History: An Essay." *Is Massa Day Dead?* Edited by Orde Coombs. Garden City, NY: Doubleday, 1974. 1–28.
    Discusses the aesthetic of the colonial poet who masters history, language. Elated with potential in the West Indies. Topics covered include burden of history, Adamic poet as opposed to polemic revolutionaries, language, race, "imitation" as creative act, the folk.
"The Caribbean: Culture or Mimicry?" *Journal of Interamerican Studies and World Affairs* 16.1 (1974): 3–13.
    Claims that West Indian identity is dependent on more encompassing American geography; that West Indian politicians defraud people with mimicry of power politics.
"A Colonial's-Eye View of the Empire." *Triquarterly* 65 (1986): 73–84.
    As disinterested outsider, the colonial realizes empires die and art survives. No power monopolizes civilization.

SELECTED CRITICAL WORKS

Walcott began as something of a West Indian prodigy, praised at home and abroad for escaping the usual romanticism expected of the region's poets. Robert Graves placed him above most of his English-born contemporaries. From the beginning, critics recognized Walcott's debt to Western tradition—Elizabethans, metaphysicals, Dylan Thomas, then Robert Lowell, W. H. Auden, and Joseph Brodsky in poetry; the Jacobeans, Bertolt Brecht, and even classical Oriental sources in drama. During the late sixties and early seventies, he resisted pressures to act the "people's poet," yet he incorporated folk and postcolonial issues into some of his best poetry and plays. Major articles are now focused on the aesthetic as well as the social aspects of his work. Given the cross-currents of international cultures in his writing and the growing reflexive self-consciousness of his style, deconstruction of his intertextuality should prove to be highly enlightening.

Ashaolu, Albert Olu. "Allegory in *Ti-Jean and His Brothers*." *World Literature Written in English* 16 (1977): 203–11. Examines six levels of allegory: artistic, historical, political, moral, Christian, social.

Baugh, Edward. *Derek Walcott: Memory as Vision: Another Life*. London: Longman, 1978. Traces impact of memory (history), influence of childhood friends and tradition. Substantiates factual world underlying poem. Finds rich variety of moods, masterful handling of ideal and ordinary.

———. "Painters and Painting in *Another Life*." *Caribbean Quarterly* 26.1–2 (1980): 83–93. Argues that art imagery complements historical allusions, significant in complex subject and texture of this layered poem.

———. "Ripening With Walcott." *Caribbean Quarterly* 23.2–3 (1977): 84–90. Sees the breadth of vision in *Sea Grapes* as rooted in personal experience.

Bensen, Robert. "The Painter as Poet: Derek Walcott's *Midsummer*." *The Literary Review* 29 (1986): 257–68. Discusses painting as subject, source of imagery, governing use of light and color, range of themes.

Breslow, Stephen P. "Trinidadian Heteroglossia: A Bakhtinian View of Derek Walcott's Play *A Branch of the Blue Nile*." *World Literature Today* 63 (1989): 36–39. Shows how the play draws from African, patois, French, English, classical Latin legacy and experience of St. Lucia, Trinidad, and the United States; play "reverberates with reflexive consciousness of itself."

Brown, Lloyd. "Caribbean Castaway New World Odyssey: Derek Walcott's Poetry." *Journal of Commonwealth Literature* 11.2 (1976): 149–59. Discusses the New World as dream and corrupted reality, and the poet's role in it.

Burton, Richard D. E. "Derek Walcott and the Medusa of History." *Caliban* 3 (1980): 3–48. Discusses how the creation of a creole culture rehumanizes in wake of plantation society, and shows how Walcott's poetry is neither popular nor populist but avoids propaganda.

Fabre, Michel. "'Adam's Task of Giving Things Their Name': The Poetry of Derek Walcott." *New Letters* 41.1 (1974): 91–107. Discusses the dialectical development of folk and traditional elements in poetry.

Fox, Robert Elliot. "Big Night Music: Derek Walcott's *Dream on Monkey Mountain* and 'The Splendours of Imagination.'" *Journal of Commonwealth Literature* 17.1 (1982): 16–27. Sees Makak as mythological—his dream, the work, and the world merging at crossroads of the imagination.

Goldstraw, Irma E. *Derek Walcott: An Annotated Bibliography of His Works.* New York: Garland, 1984. Thorough listing of primary publications to 1984.

Hamner, Robert D. *Derek Walcott.* Boston: Twayne, 1981. Assesses career to 1980.

Ismond, Patricia. "Walcott versus Brathwaite." *Caribbean Quarterly* 17.3–4 (1971): 54–71. Provides exposition of relative positions; Brathwaite as folk poet and Walcott as Eurocentric traditionalist—and a superior craftsman.

Morris, Mervyn. "Walcott and the Audience for Poetry." *Caribbean Quarterly* 14.1–2 (1968): 7–24. Notes that in spite of artistic sophistication, Walcott communicates with people. Shows that this skill is in part the result of his range of linguistic levels.

Ramchand, Kenneth. "Derek Walcott." *An Introduction to the West Indian Literature.* London: Thomas Nelson and Sons, 1976. 108–26. Surveys evolving career and makes connections between the poems and Walcott's life and the landscape.

Taylor, Patrick. "Myth and Reality in Caribbean Narrative: Derek Walcott's *Pantomime.*" *World Literature Written in English* 26 (1986): 169–77. Distinguishes between mythological and liberating narrative, arguing that *Pantomime* recreates myth of Crusoe/Friday as liberating narrative.

Thomas, Ned. *Derek Walcott: Poet of the Islands.* Welsh Arts Council, 1980. Takes up particularity of place and voice in Walcott. Analysis of three representative poems: "Ruins of a Great House," chapters 21–22 of *Another Life*, and "The Star-Apple Kingdom."

Interview

With Sharon L. Ciccarelli. In *Chant of Saints.* Urbana: U of Illinois P, 1979. 296–309.

—ROBERT D. HAMNER

Robertson Davies

A prolific writer in a variety of genres, Robertson Davies learned his trade at an early age: "It [writing] just seemed to be something which I naturally did. Growing up in the family I did. . . . We all wrote things" (Davis 11). His father, Rupert Davies, arrived in Canada from Wales in the 1890s and prospered as a newspaper publisher, ultimately becoming a member of the Canadian Senate; his mother, Florence McKay, occasionally took a turn as a reporter and was very well-read.

Robertson Davies was born in the small community of Thamesville, Ontario, 28 August 1913. When he was six, the family moved to a larger town, Renfrew, where he was victimized by school bullies. To Davies, the family was "always on the move" and this contributed to "a sort of rootlessness" he felt (Davis 127). By the time he was a teenager, the family was in the city of Kingston, and two years later Davies was sent to a private boys' school, Upper Canada College ("Colborne College" in his novels). University education at Queen's University ("Waverly") and Balliol College, Oxford, followed. At all three educational institutions, Davies was able to pursue the passion for theater that he had felt from early boyhood. He spent a season working for Tyrone Guthrie at the Old Vic but realized that he could not have a career as a professional actor and in 1940 returned to live permanently in Canada.

Davies served as editor and then publisher of the *Peterborough Examiner*, an Ontario newspaper owned by his father, from 1942 to 1963. The Samuel Marchbanks sketches were originally written for *The Examiner*. Davies began his connection with the University of Toronto in 1960 as a visiting professor and in 1961 was appointed the first Master of Massey College, a residence for graduate students and Senior Fellows within the University of Toronto. He served with distinction in that capacity until 1981.

Davies has received many honorary degrees. A winner of the Governor General's Award for Fiction, he is a fellow of the Royal Society of Canada, a companion of the Order of Canada, and the first Canadian to be elected an honorary member of the American Academy and Institute of Arts and Letters.

Davies divides his time between Toronto and a country home in Caledon, Ontario. In his late seventies, he is still publishing novels and gaining ever wider recognition.

THE CANADIAN ARTIST

Robertson Davies has been a trenchant commentator on Canadian literary and social life, an important contributor to the development of modern theater in Canada, a witty personal essayist, and in his more serious essays an impassioned advocate of a life of introspection and cultivation. It is not possible in a brief essay even to touch on all aspects of this extraordinary literary production, so I will concentrate on the nine novels widely regarded as his finest achievements.

The first of Davies' three trilogies, the Salterton trilogy, takes its name from the imagined community of Salterton, which is very closely modeled on Kingston, a small but historic city in Eastern Ontario. The city's commercial life has been stagnant since the mid-nineteenth century, and it retained an overwhelmingly British character until and beyond the time Davies wrote his novels about it.

It is the spirit of charming but backward-looking provinciality that Davies has accurately captured in the Salterton trilogy. Though these novels have remained popular, they have not been given the critical respect accorded his more recent fiction, since some have argued from the time of their appearance that they idealize a colonial existence. Davies has maintained, however, and with justice, that his aim was to record rather than glorify "a sort of delayed cultural tradition":

> About the period that I was working on the Salterton novels . . .
> there were still people living in places like Salterton whose tradition
> was directly Edwardian, and who saw nothing wrong with that.
> (Davis 74)

The first two novels of the trilogy, *Tempest-Tost* and *Leaven of Malice*, have in common a concentration upon the Salterton setting whereas the third novel, *A Mixture of Frailties*, takes its protagonist away from Salterton and explores more ambitious themes. Yet the first two books, circumscribed as they are in comparison with Davies' later work, nevertheless have a distinctive character of their own that effectively combines light comedy with an underlying seriousness.

The amateurishness of amateur theater is not seen in an attractive light in *Tempest-Tost*. Central to the book's structure is a production of *The Tempest*, performed by Salterton amateurs and directed by a professional, a Salterton native who has found success in New York. Davies is unequivocal in his support of the two characters whom he defines explicitly as professionals (330), the director Valentine Rich and the musical director and church organist Humphrey Cobbler. Both these characters are said to have abilities the others lack, but more importantly they are utterly dedicated to their art—Rich admits she is still "stage-struck" (81), and Cobbler contends that "the one thing which is more important than peace is music" (183). Despite the artistic passion that unites them, Davies' two professionals are in an important respect opposites: Valentine wins popularity for herself and brings out the best in others because "she never sought or demanded anything for herself" (174); the flamboyant Cobbler, who proudly asserts that "the unthinkable has always been rather in my line" (240), gains no applause in a conservative community for his Bohemianism. These two models of creativity—the collaborator and the individualist—will reappear in novel after novel.

The amateurs are always being distracted from their artistic efforts by motives that weigh more with them than the theater and their failings are compounded by low expectations of themselves. After the dress rehearsal, everyone except the director expects the worst because "nothing appeals so strongly to the heart of the amateur actor as a thoroughly depressing estimate of his work" (321). One character, who seems to be speaking for Davies, sees this outburst of masochism as a national characteristic: "We [Canadians] flog ourselves endlessly, as a kind of spiritual purification" (332).

Davies' treatment of one of the disastrous amateurs, Hector Mackilwraith, shows his ability to combine farce with a sensitive portrayal of the redeeming side of an unlovable character. Like many of Davies' subsequent protagonists, Mackilwraith is a middle-aged man faced with the painful task of self-examination. In love for the first time, he finds that he must discard "his whole concept of life," founded upon rigid principles of planning and common sense (204). We find out about Hector by means of two strategies Davies borrowed from his earlier writing: Brisk dialogue resembling that of a play exposes Hector's worldly innocence while authorial ruminations in the manner of an essayist peer into his soul. Davies originally thought of *Tempest-Tost* as a play (Davis 19), and he has never entirely abandoned the impulse to use the narrator as an essayist.

The same fictional methods are prominent in *Leaven of Malice*, but they are enlisted in the service of a darker imaginative vision. In accordance with the novel's title, Davies shows Salterton to be consumed by ill-will, and if events turn out happily it is only after several obsessed characters do their utmost to destroy any opposition to Salterton's continued cultural stagnation.

More explicitly than in *Tempst-Tost*, Davies in *Leaven of Malice* associates individual nastiness with a collective will on the part of the "brave rearguard" (171) to perpetuate in Salterton the values of another time or place. Walter Vambrace and Louisa Bridgetower, consciously sworn enemies, are similar in this respect: Vambrace convinces himself that his vicious rage is justified because he belongs to an "aristocratic tradition" (123) and possesses the Celtic soul (116), while Mrs. Bridgetower, "a captain among those forces in Salterton which sought to resist social change" (171), had initiated her Thursday At Home gathering before the First World War. Laura Pottinger, whose venom is principally directed against Cobbler, thinks of herself as a "soldier's daughter," and her father, who almost made it to the Boer War, stood for the principles of "Victorian Anglicanism" (65). Bevill Higgin, the lower-class Irishman who is ultimately unmasked as the author of the false engagement notice that drives the plot, is viewed by Solly Bridgetower as a sorry representative of the "British heritage" (192).

The characters who struggle to promote a more genuinely civilized Salterton are often shown to be timid, embattled, or at odds with one another. Dean Knapp, the Anglican cleric who is Cobbler's chief supporter at the Cathedral, cannot defend himself against Vambrace's bullying. Gloster Ridley as a newspaper editor is a model of good sense, but for much of the novel he cannot exorcise the bitter memories of his past. He gives an eloquent defense of the element of "old-time roguery" in journalism, which is "its fascination" (158), but it soon turns out that "the genuine raffishness of Humphrey Cobbler disturbed him" (161). Cobbler, the author's darling for the second novel in succession, is in perpetual danger throughout this book because of the determined assaults of his enemies.

In the novel's climactic scene, Matthew Snelgrove, yet another cultural dinosaur—a Tory lawyer who models himself upon the "lawyer-squire of the eighteenth [century]" (82)—accuses Cobbler of inserting the mischievous engagement notice and more generally of being a "shameless rowdy" (291). It is left to Dean Knapp to draw Davies' pessimistic conclusion that malice does not confine itself to Higgin's feeble practical joke and is a common ingredient in human nature. This view is not entirely dissipated by the positive consequences of Higgin's action—the genuine engagement of the two persons wrongly said to be engaged and Ridley's positive, if limited, self-examination. The final revelations, with the gathering of nearly all the characters in one location and suspicion shifting from a false suspect to the true villain, recall the conventions of the detective story, a genre previously invoked by Professor Vambrace's ludicrous efforts to unravel the mystery by playing private detective and imagining himself as a disciple of the School of Intellect rather than the School of Force (140).

Davies draws on more exalted literary traditions in *A Mixture of Frailties*, an important transitional work that takes its protagonist away from Salterton in her quest for a career as a singer. In its exceptionally detailed account of a musical education, Monica Gall's story in some ways follows the pattern of the *Künstlerroman*. It is crucial, however, that the site of Monica's training in art and exploration of life is England. As Davies has an American remark, "we've been living in a kind of Henry James climate" (195): Like the heroine in a novel by James, the North American innocent encounters evil as well as sophistication when she ventures abroad. Finally, in the section of the novel devoted to Salterton, we see in clever contrast to Monica's destiny, a kind of anti-*Bildungsroman*, attractive characters locked in the frustration of failed development.

Monica's mentors—the voice coach Murtagh Molloy, the conductor Sir Benedict Domdaniel (modeled, Davies has said, on Sir Adrian Boult [Davis 49]), the composer Giles Revelstoke—form another pattern of telling contrasts. Monica is the disciple of Molloy and on a grander scale of Sir Benedict in her acquisition of interpretive skills. To be a true interpreter, Sir Benedict assures her, Monica must seek to perform a work as a composer would have wished it performed (240) and to be able to do that, he insists, interpretive artists must learn how to feel, and how to "recapture those feelings and transform them into something which we can offer to the world in our performances" (214). The validity of these principles is demonstrated negatively by Revelstoke, who has the willful passion of the creator rather than the distilled wisdom of the interpreter and is consequently a disaster in both his personal life and his effort to conduct his own work.

Monica is given much practice in her task of "broaden[ing]" her "range of feeling" (213). Molloy attempts unsuccessfully to rape her; Revelstoke claims her as his mistress; after Revelstoke's sordid death, Sir Benedict woos and wins her. England offers little comfort in the way of making the rough emotional places plain. Revelstoke, based as Michael Peterman has shown (107) upon the composer Peter Warlock, is mean-spirited at the best of times and often savage. Monica's outburst, "I hate you damned superior Englishmen. . . . and I hate your rotten little Ye Olde Antique Shoppe of a country" (213), is shown to have cause. Yet the union of Monica and Domdaniel is Davies' sanction of the principle that an artist's training can best be gained where art is best cultivated (the same principle, one presumes, that informed his own apprenticeship in the English theater). Tempting as it is to label Davies' view as colonized, we must also remember that the Canada of the 1950s did not offer the artistic opportunities that are available thirty years later. The interplay of Monica Gall's character and the themes of the *Künstlerroman* and the Jamesian international romance provide difficult challenges for Davies. Not only as an interpreter rather than a creator but also as a "bardic" rather than "sexual singer" (107), Monica has a temperament that is subdued in itself and downright meek when compared to the forceful personalities of her teachers. Yet she is not always passive: In using diverted funds to finance Revelstoke's compositions, she shows determination and even that artistic unscrupulousness Davies finds so fascinating. Davies insists on her strength of character by linking her repeatedly through the narrator's comments with her domineering mother and by having her take an unorthodox part in the deaths of her mother and of Revelstoke. Her strong doses of enlarged feeling are purchased at the expense of some skepticism on the part of the reader.

While Monica expands, Solomon Bridgetower contracts. The tyrannical parent, a perennial figure in Davies' novels, is here represented by Louisa Bridgetower and Ada Gall. Mrs. Bridgetower's will, which provides for Monica's education at the expense of her own son, nearly destroys Solly while it enables Monica to free herself from the potentially fatal clutches of "Ma" Gall. The image of Solly's imprisonment within the parental home that by the terms of the will he is bound to maintain is compelling.

Fifth Business, the first novel of the second trilogy, brought Davies much wider recognition. Though links between the two trilogies have been convincingly demonstrated, the wider scope, powerful incidents, and intriguing characterization of the Deptford Trilogy has ensured its continuing popular and critical success.

Davies has called attention to the fact that the trilogy deals with "universal" psychological traits that nevertheless have a "Made in Canada mark":

> All the three principal characters are Canadians, one of whom has been shaped by Canada's unquestioned virtues, but also by its want of spiritual self-recognition; the second, exposed to the same virtues, yields to Canada's allurements of glossy success; the third feels the lash of Canada's cruelty, which is the shadow side of its virtues, and arises from Canada's lack of self-knowledge. (Lawrence 11–12)

In these portraits, we recognize in order Dunstan Ramsay, Boy Staunton, and Paul Dempster, the three characters whose lives take their direction from an errant snowball thrown in the small southwestern Ontario town of Deptford (in reality, Davies' birthplace, Thamesville).

Davies' mixed evaluation of Canada, as shown in the preceding quotation, is consistent with the images of Deptford and of Toronto provided in these novels. Dunstan Ramsay is on occasion Deptford's apologist, while Paul Dempster is its accuser. Boy Staunton, characteristically, "did not like to be reminded of Deptford, except as a joke" (210). For Ramsay, "if it had sins and follies and roughnesses, it also had much to show of virtue, dignity, and even of nobility" (10). Yet on the whole we see more of the limitations of provinciality in Deptford than of its generosity.

Davies has remarked that he first thought of the theme of *Fifth Business* as revenge, but later, in working out the implications of the snowball incident, came to understand that its more fundamental theme was guilt (Lawrence 8). Though innocent of any wrongdoing, Dunstan is haunted by guilt arising from his being the intended target of the snowball that instead hits and permanently damages Paul Dempster's mother.

Yet, licensed by Davies' own inclination to find a "theme" for his book, one may find other themes that seem equally fundamental both to *Fifth Business* and to the entire trilogy. Important in all three books is the characteristic Davies theme of the need for self-knowledge, a responsibility that he views as essential to the middle years of life. It is in their dedication to this task that Dunstan and David Staunton of *The Manticore* distinguish themselves.

Central to the imaginative vision of the trilogy is the concept of a "world of wonders." This is not only the title of the third volume but also an idea of life introduced early in *Fifth Business*, in Dunstan's account of his childhood attraction to magic: "it had seemed to me to be a splendid extension of life, a creation of a world of wonders" (43). Dunstan's magical experiments are fiercely opposed by his mother and by Paul Dempster's father: It is a defining and limiting characteristic of Deptford that it values pragmatism and conventional piety above the claims of the imagination. Dunstan's later absorption with saints is another manifestation of a willingness to dwell in the world of the marvelous, as his friend Liesl remarks when she enlists him as Dempster's biographer.

Dunstan is neither a saint nor a magician, but as a hagiographer and the inventor of a magician's fictional "autobiography," he participates creatively in the experiences he contemplates. Both magic and sainthood are shown to be founded upon illusion, but it is this kind of illusion that sustains Dunstan and makes him more than the "amusingly eccentric" (230) schoolmaster patronized by Boy Staunton. As a writer who evokes and cherishes wonders, Dunstan in his creative occupation is a counterpart of his own creator, who defines himself as a writer of "romances" (Davis 267).

The romance Dunstan creates for Paul Dempster (or Magnus Eisengrim, as he has chosen to call himself) begins with his birth as "a child of the steppes" (254). This is an absolute fabrication, but it does recognize Eisengrim's determination to rid himself of the traces of Deptford, and it reflects both his bitter isolation and the "wolfishness" that Paul admits is in his character (347). *Fifth Business* is essentially

Dunstan's book, while Boy Staunton is a dominating presence in *The Manticore. World of Wonders* is devoted to the influences that shaped Eisengrim and the claims of his art.

The final volume of this trilogy is, therefore, a *Künstlerroman* and shares that attribute with the third volume of the Salterton trilogy. One can hardly imagine two characters more different than Monica Gall, the bardic singer, and Magnus Eisengrim, the conjuror with a "Magian World View" (323). Yet the apprenticeship the two artists experience constitutes a link between them: Both undergo the testing experiences Davies regards as crucial for the artist's formation, and both find teachers who are acutely aware of the need for artistic interpretation as well as technical excellence.

Monica Gall's adventures in England, lurid as they are, seem tame in comparison with the harrowing course of Paul Dempster's early life. After years of alienation as the son of the village madwoman, Paul escapes to a carnival, Wanless's World of Wonders, where he is immediately raped by the troupe's magician, Willard. An unimaginative sadist with one talent, Willard is pure evil and brings out evil in Paul; the story of Paul's ultimate triumph, aided by Willard's morphine addiction, is one of the most gripping, as well as most disturbing, episodes in all of Davies' fiction.

Yet Willard, like Molloy in *A Mixture of Frailties*, can provide the technical instruction that is the necessary, though not sufficient, condition for artistic excellence. Paul's tutor in artistic performance, the counterpart to Sir Benedict Domdaniel, is Sir John Tresize, the star actor in a British traveling company, which brings a repertory of old-fashioned melodramas to Canada. Whereas Domdaniel believed in subordinating his personality to the intentions of the composer, Tresize is an "egoist" who "was wholly devoted to an ideal of theatrical art that was contained . . . within himself" (192–93). So whereas Monica Gall learns artistic humility, Paul Dempster learns artistic egoism. As an apprentice magician, he is "Nobody" (59), ensconced as a necessary part of Willard's deception for hours inside a monstrous contrivance named Abdullah. As an apprentice in the theater, he is also essential to deception, in that he plays Tresize's double; nevertheless, whereas the carnival is based on the principle of the "gaff" (66), cheating the audience, Tresize's performance, Eisengrim later recalls, "refreshes dry places in the spirit."

As an egoist who pays respect to his audience, Eisengrim follows in Tresize's footsteps, though he returns to his childhood pursuit of magic. The bond with an audience therefore is vital to Eisengrim's self-esteem, his rebirth (202) as man and artist. So Tresize's theatrical romance is presented with much sympathy through Eisengrim's roles as narrator and as successful protégé. Yet Davies did not forget that the Canadian audience for Tresize was the same in its values as the members of the Salterton "brave rearguard." So even if it is a discredited character who remarks that Tresize's productions were "soothing syrup in aid of a dying colonialism" (262), the accusation has its impact in the novel; in a less polemical way, Eisengrim himself acknowledges that the melodramas Tresize staged appealed to "a core of loneliness and deprivation in these Canadians of which they were only faintly aware" (292).

Eisengrim and Tresize are only two among many artist figures who populate the pages of *World of Wonders*. The international cast includes the dour and metaphysical Swedish filmmaker Lind, who believes in "artistic truth"; his cameraman

Kinghovn, who is another example of the artist as technologist; the British producer and novelist Ingestree, who champions "the theatre of ideas" (261). These characters are gathered to produce a work of art, a film about Robert-Houdin, in which Eisengrim returns to the egoism of the actor. They also assemble to hear Eisengrim's autobiographical subtext for his performance.

The notion of the subtext is, if taken literally, a very flimsy contrivance. It can be regarded more sympathetically, however, as the medium by which Eisengrim expresses himself at the "confessional moment" (15; 345–46) of his life. The narrative strategy Davies adopts for each of the novels in the Deptford Trilogy is essentially the same, though it manifests itself in different artistic forms. In each novel, a reserved but passionate character dares to reveal himself through an exploration of his past. Dunstan Ramsay, in *Fifth Business*, is driven by indignation at being patronized to write a confessional letter to his Headmaster; David Staunton, feeling himself to be at the point of mental breakdown, opens himself up to Jungian analysis in *The Manticore*. The latter novel, not as powerful a work as the other two, and also the least concerned with the definition of the artist's life, nevertheless is in its own way an absorbing study of professional and personal development; David Staunton is a mainstream Davies protagonist in his effort to find a vocation—in his case the law—which will shelter him from the emotional ravages of a domineering parent.

The third of Davies' trilogies, the Cornish Trilogy, is the only one to be named for a man rather than a place, but places continue to matter greatly in this extension of Davies' fictional world. The place that matters most in the two outer volumes of the trilogy is the University of Toronto, Davies' academic and spiritual home for the past twenty-five years and the university that for many years dominated the intellectual life of Canada. As one character justly remarks in *The Rebel Angels*, the first novel of the trilogy, the University of Toronto is "like an Empire" (187); the two "realms" with which Davies is concerned are Trinity College ("Spook") and Massey College ("Ploughwright"). Davies, the Master of Massey College for decades, has the Warden of "Ploughwright" remark that the university "is a city of wisdom" (186), and the Deputy Warden comments that Guest Nights at Ploughwright are "one of civilization's triumphs over barbarism" (168).

Davies shows us that academics have the passions, the egotism, and at times the creativity of artists. A Renaissance historian given to temper tantrums admits he wants a Rabelais manuscript more than he ever wanted a woman (266). This man, Clement Hollier, is one of the three "Rebel Angels" of the title; he and a classicist-priest Simon Darcourt are, according to their graduate student disciple Maria Theodoky, like two Rebel Angels in the Apocrypha who taught men "everything" after their banishment from Heaven (257); a third character, John Parlabane, is a philosophical skeptic, a rebellious monk, and a failed novelist who is linked with the most well-publicized Rebel Angel, Lucifer.

Maria with her youthful idealism and Darcourt with his middle-aged wisdom share the tasks of narrating the story and upholding the best values of the academy. Hollier's obsessiveness, Parlabane's evil, and the sneaky nastiness of a third academic, Urky McVarish, constitute a subtext or an ironic counterpoint that qualifies, though it does not entirely undermine, the explicit assertion that "the scholar's life is a good life" (168).

It is when Maria becomes most divided in her allegiances—between her aspirations as a scholar and her consciousness of her Gypsy heritage—that she becomes most interesting. Like Monica Gall, she is an attractive pupil who finds that offers of love and sex are part of her teachers' education. Like Monica, she has to ponder whether her true allegiance lies with her non-intellectual origins or her acquired intellectual discipline ("root" or "crown" in the imagery of the later novel). Maria's gypsy family is presented with great warmth (as compared to the crude satire to which the Gall family is subjected), and Davies seems to share the otherwise unreliable Parlabane's view that root as well as crown needs to be preserved.

The Rebel Angels shows Davies' awareness of the sophistication of contemporary Canada; his apprentice no longer needs to go abroad to find enlightenment. *What's Bred in the Bone* returns to an earlier, cruder Canada, "Canada the wide-eyed farmboy" (411), which offers the protagonist, Francis Cornish, little intellectual stimulation. Cornish's undergraduate years at "Spook" take up little more than a page, whereas his time at Oxford is treated much more extensively.

Cornish spends his childhood years in Blairlogie, a version of the town of Renfrew, northeast of Ottawa, in which Davies spent several boyhood years. Blairlogie is beset by racial and religious tensions, and its prevailing atmosphere of mean-spiritedness, seen at its worst in the sadistic humiliation of a dwarf, makes it even less attractive as a community than Deptford. Raised by adherents of competing religions and tormented by schoolboy bullies, Cornish finds the basis for "lifelong misanthropy" (72) by the time he reaches kindergarten.

Yet Blairlogie also provides Cornish with the material for his single great achievement, a painting of the Marriage at Cana in which the figures are drawn from the world of his childhood. In this novel, yet another *Künstlerroman,* the protagonist succeeds in the vital task prescribed for him by his mentor: "Find your legend. Find your personal myth" (227). Cornish uses the religious and stylistic vocabulary of Renaissance painting, but equally essential to the creativity of the work is the assimilation of his personal, Canadian experience.

The categories of artistic development first elaborated in *A Mixture of Frailties* are still applicable, though in a somewhat modified way, to this much later novel. Cornish's only instruction that is exclusively technical is provided by a Paris artist who advises him about color (255-56). Much more important as a teacher of technique but also Cornish's "father in art" (398) is Tancred Saraceni, a restorer of old paintings under whom Cornish works for several years. Saraceni, who defines himself as a "fine craftsman" (223), restores art in the same spirit with which Domdaniel conducted music, respecting the intentions of the original creator and seeking "to play the assistant to the dead master" (225). In producing a work that is seriously considered to be an older masterpiece, Cornish surpasses his teacher and becomes what he always wished to be, "a painter rather than a craftsman" (280), a genuine "Meister" (290; 398) in his own right.

Yet Cornish's triumph is undiscovered in his own lifetime. Since *The Marriage at Cana* is a byproduct of an elaborate scheme to hoodwink the Nazis into buying inferior paintings, Saraceni and his pupil have repainted rather than restored and consequently Cornish can never claim credit for his masterwork. In this aspect, *What's Bred in the Bone* is the most sustained treatment Davies gives to a theme that haunts his later work: the intrinsic trickery of art. Eisenstein's magic illusions, the modifications Maria Theodoky's mother and uncle make to old stringed instruments before selling them, Saraceni's "tarting up these four-hundred-year-old dullards" (293): Each of these enterprises involves equal parts of deception and artistry. In the mythic dimension so pervasive in Davies' fiction, Mercury is the astrological influence (312, 435) upon Cornish that inspires the fusion of art and guile. Cornish's self-questioning, his affinity with the past, and his uneasiness with a contemporary idiom that has lost interest in religion and myth make him a fictional surrogate for Davies himself.

The reinterpretation of Cornish's masterpiece forms one of the plots in the final novel of the trilogy, *The Lyre of Orpheus.* We are led to the same conclusions about the painting as in the previous novel, but we see the evidence as it is uncovered by Simon Darcourt, Cornish's biographer. Davies uses this opportunity to explore with skill and knowledge yet another craft, the art of biography, but more importantly Darcourt's work as a biographer expands his idea of himself: He ceases to consider himself an "Abbé," a clerical "educated upper servant" (9)—in the vocabulary of an earlier trilogy, a "Fifth Business"—and comes to regard himself, in the vocabulary of the Tarot pack, as a "Fool of God" (287–89; 296–97).

Darcourt is to be counted among the several characters engaged in that crucial task in Davies' fiction, finding one's soul (380). An artistic performance is once again the challenge that prompts self-examination. Arthur Cornish, the enthusiastic backer for an opera based on notes left behind by the Romantic composer E.T.A. Hoffman, comes to learn what it means to be a vital but undervalued patron. The opera, *King Arthur, or the Magnanimous Cuckold,* becomes a painful reminder to him of the role he plays as the betrayed husband of Maria, who has had one tryst with Geraint Powell, the opera's director and Arthur's best friend. By the end of the novel he has come to terms with the defeats he has suffered and is as magnanimous in love as the mythical Arthur is said to be in the finale to the opera. Maria and Powell, linked directly and frequently to their counterparts in the Arthurian story (Maria is associated with both Guinevere and Elaine), have to come to new understandings of their relationships with Arthur and of their private and professional selves.

The most interesting characters in the varied cast of professors, musicians, and theater people are that familiar pair, an apprentice musical artist and her teacher. As an "offensive little brat" (11), Hulda Schnakenburg seems different from Gall, Dempster, and Cornish; however, "Schnak" displays the conspicuous talent, the uncongenial upbringing, the need for instruction in life as well as art, and the tendency to develop an emotional attachment for her teacher, which are the hallmarks of the *Davieskünstler.* Her mentor, a Swedish composer-conductor named Gunilla Dahl-Soot, has already found her firm soul, thus providing a useful contrast to the vulnerable and mutable personalities that surround her.

The vale for all this soul-making is the academic and theatrical landscape of Toronto and Stratford, Ontario, the home of the Stratford Shakespearean Festival. Though there is much talk in the novel of Hoffman's "Kater Murr" (the spirit of

Philistinism), anti-intellectual forces are kept at bay; and the novel suggests very clearly that it is feasible to lead a harmonious, cultured, and productive existence in the Canada of the 1980s. Much of the serenity of this novel derives from that assessment.

Taken together, Davies' novels constitute an extraordinarily rich and permanently valuable impression of Canadian life. Readers outside of Canada may see this national life, particularly in the early novels, as an example of the disabilities of a colonized existence. In the later novels, Canada is shown to be capable of shedding her colonial clogs; at the same time, the subtle and brilliantly imagined exploration of the artistic character in the last two trilogies will captivate anyone inclined to take an interest in the complex relations between the artist and the society he represents, cherishes, and scorns.

WORKS CITED

Davies, Robertson. *Fifth Business*. Toronto: Macmillan, 1970.
————. *Leaven of Malice*. Toronto: Clarke Irwin, 1954.
————. *The Lyre of Orpheus*. Toronto: Macmillan, 1988.
————. *The Manticore*. Toronto: Macmillan, 1972.
————. *A Mixture of Frailties*. Toronto: Clarke Irwin, 1958.
————. *The Rebel Angels*. Toronto: Macmillan, 1981.
————. *Tempest-Tost*. Toronto: Clarke Irwin, 1951.
————. *What's Bred in the Bone*. Toronto: Macmillan, 1985.
————. *World of Wonders*. Toronto: Macmillan, 1975.
Davis, J. Madison, editor. *Conversations with Robertson Davies*. Jackson: UP of Mississippi, 1989.
Lawrence, Robert G. "Canadian Theatre in Robertson Davies' *World of Wonders*." *Studies in Robertson Davies' Deptford Trilogy*. Victoria, B.C.: U of Victoria, 1980. 114–23.
Peterman, Michael. *Robertson Davies*. Boston: Twayne, 1986.

ROBERTSON DAVIES' PUBLISHED WORK

Novels

Tempest-Tost, 1951
Leaven of Malice, 1954
A Mixture of Frailties, 1958
Fifth Business, 1970
The Manticore, 1972.
World of Wonders, 1975
The Rebel Angels, 1981
What's Bred in the Bone, 1985
The Lyre of Orpheus, 1988

Plays

Overlaid: A Comedy, 1948
Eros at Breakfast and Other Plays, 1949
Fortune, My Foe, 1949
At My Heart's Core, 1950
A Jig for the Gypsy, 1954
Hunting Stuart and Other Plays, 1972
Question Time, 1975

Fictional Sketches

The Diary of Samuel Marchbanks, 1947
The Table Talk of Samuel Marchbanks, 1949
Marchbanks' Almanack, 1967
High Spirits, 1982

Criticism and Essays

A Voice from the Attic. New York: Knopf, 1960
> Essays on "the world of books," with sections on books dealing with religion and psychology, sex, "the well of the past," theater, humor, pornography, and writing. Addressed to "the clerisy": "those who love books, but do not live by books."

Stephen Leacock. Toronto: McClelland & Stewart. 1970
> A rewarding monograph on the earlier Canadian satirist, with some application to Davies' own work.

One Half of Robertson Davies. Provocative Pronouncements on a Wide Range of Topics. Toronto: Macmillan, 1977.
> A collection of Davies' speeches on a variety of light and serious topics. The "Thoughts about Writing" and "Masks of Satan" sections are of particular interest, as is the final item, "The Canada of Myth and Reality."

The Enthusiasms of Robertson Davies. Edited by Judith Skelton Grant. Toronto: Macmillan, 1979.
> A collection of Davies' journalism, drawn mainly from the 1940s, 1950s, and 1960s. Divided into three sections: Characters (short profiles, mainly of writers); Books; Robertson Davies (autobiographical essays).

The Well-Tempered Critic: One Man's View of Theatre and Letters in Canada. Edited by Judith Skelton Grant. Toronto: Macmillan, 1981.
> Essays from a variety of newspaper and magazine sources on Canadian theater (many reviews of Stratford Festival productions) and on books by important Canadian writers.

"Signing Away Canada's Soul: Culture, Identity and the Free-Trade Agreement." *Harper's* Jan. 1989: 43–47.
> A passionate denunciation of the Canada-U.S. Free Trade Agreement then being debated in Canada, with interesting general comparisons between the two countries.

SELECTED CRITICAL READINGS

Davies' work has been widely available and very favorably reviewed outside of Canada for the past two decades. Extended critical consideration is still, however, largely confined to Canada. On the whole, Davies has been well served by his critics. Three full-length books have been published on his work, and there have been several monographs, two special issues of journals, and many critical essays. His fiction lends itself to a wide variety of approaches, and many of these directions have been explored. His ideas have been traced; the formal elements in his writing have been analyzed; relationships within each trilogy and from one trilogy to another have been described; issues such as the place of Jung in his work have been debated. An engagement with theory is more evident in recent articles.

Benson, Eugene, editor. "Robertson Davies, Dramatist." *Canadian Drama* 7.2 (1981). A special issue devoted to Davies' work in the theater. Includes seven essays, some making connections with Davies' fiction; an interview by Ann Saddlemyer, and the text of the dramatization of *Leaven of Malice.*

Buitenhuis, Elspeth [Cameron]. *Robertson Davies.* Toronto: Forum House, 1972. An early monograph that discusses Davies' work up to *Fifth Business.* Analyzes satiric and romance elements in the fiction, Davies' voices, and recurrent character types.

Cude, Wilfred. *A Due Sense of Difference: An Evaluative Approach to Canadian Literature.* Lanham, Md.: UP of America, 1980. 69–132. Three chapters on *Fifth Business* discuss such topics as the significance of the Headmaster and Padre Blazon, *Huckleberry Finn* as a context for Davies' novel, and the devil inside Dunstan Ramsay.

Davis, J. Madison, editor. *Conversations with Robertson Davies.* Jackson: UP of Mississippi, 1989. An invaluable collection of twenty-eight interviews recorded between 1963 and 1988. Davies' strong personality and opinions always come through, and there are many important comments on his early life and on individual works. Includes a previously unpublished, lengthy, and stimulating interview with Gordon Roper (9–61).

Godard, Barbara. "World of Wonders: Robertson Davies' Carnival." *Essays in Canadian Writing* 30 (1984): 239–86. An intriguing Bakhtinian reading of Davies' canon, emphasizing the "carnival spirit" of his fiction, though Davies "has a much darker view of carnival" than Bakhtin. Rituals involving pagan ceremony, food, alcohol, music, and magic are noted.

Grant, Judith Skelton. *Robertson Davies.* Toronto: McClelland & Stewart, 1978. A fifty-page monograph that intelligently surveys Davies' work up to *World of Wonders.* Comments on the more optimistic tone that enters Davies' work with *A Mixture of Frailties*; discusses the "self-revelation" of the natural and moral philosophy of the Deptford trilogy.

Heintzman, Ralph H., editor. *Journal of Canadian Studies* 12.1 (1977). A special issue on the Deptford trilogy, including essays by Cude, Neufeld, and Thomas, and Robert Cluett's computer-assisted study of Davies' diction.

Keith, W.J. "The Roots of Fantasy: Document and Invention in Robertson Davies, Fiction." *Journal of Canadian Studies* 20.1 (1985): 109–19. Investigates the interconnection of realism and fantasy in Davies' fiction. The Salterton trilogy contains many romance conventions despite its apparent realism. Comments on Borges-like qualities in Davies' work.

Koster, Patricia. "'Promptings Stronger' than 'Strict Prohibitions': New Forms of Natural Religion in the Novels of Robertson Davies." *Canadian Literature* 111 (1986): 68–82. Observes that a wide variety of Davies' characters "under extraordinary stress" behave "in accordance with some deep, but normally unrecognized, religious promptings." Distinguishes between morality, based on self-knowledge, and religion, based on a deep-seated impulse, in Davies' fiction.

Lawrence, Robert G., and Samuel L. Macey, editors. *Studies in Robertson Davies' Deptford Trilogy.* English Literary Studies Monograph Series 20. Victoria, B.C.: U of Victoria, 1980. An excellent collection of nine essays on the Deptford Trilogy. Subjects investigated include the relationship of the Deptford Trilogy to the Salterton Trilogy; the folkloric background; clockwork; public figures; autobiography; Jung; the law; archeological background; the state of Canadian theater. Includes a valuable essay by Davies on "The Deptford Trilogy in Retrospect."

Lennox, John Watt. "Manawaka and Deptford: Place and Voice." *Journal of Canadian Studies* 13.3 (1978): 23–30. Compares Davies' use of the Deptford setting with the presentation of a small prairie town in the work of another distinguished Canadian novelist, Margaret Laurence.

Monk, Patricia. *The Smaller Infinity: The Jungian Self in the Novels of Robertson Davies.* Toronto: U of Toronto P, 1982. A full-length study that explores Davies' early work as well as the Deptford Trilogy in the light of Davies' absorption with the work of Jung.

Morley, Patricia. *Robertson Davies.* Profiles in Canadian Drama. Toronto: Gage, 1977. A monograph dealing with all of Davies' drama. Investigates patterns of irony, romance, and melodrama.

Neufeld, James. "Structural Unity in 'The Deptford Trilogy': Robertson Davies as Egoist" (Heintzman 68–74). Examines unifying factors in the trilogy: Deptford and Sorgenfrei as "points of reference"; framing devices; the concept of egoism. Argues that David Staunton is "the key to the trilogy's thematic unity."

Owen, Ivon. "The Salterton Novels." *Tamarack Review* 9 (1958): 56–63. Argues that Davies' first trilogy goes beyond light comedy in exploring "the shadows of Salterton." Concentrates on *A Mixture of Frailties*, which is regarded as more ambitious and rewarding, though flawed, than its two predecessors.

Peterman, Michael. *Robertson Davies.* Boston: Twayne, 1986. An outstanding work of criticism. Much original information in the biographical section; detailed and incisive commentary on the Marchbanks books and on Davies' work as a dramatist; stimulating essays with a strong awareness of autobiographical elements and the Canadian cultural background on each of the novels up to and including *The Rebel Angels*.

Roper, Gordon. "Robertson Davies, Fifth Business and That Old Fantastical Duke of Dark Corners, C.G. Jung." *Journal of Canadian Fiction* 1 (1972): 33–39. A pioneering article pointing out the relevance of Jung to Davies' novel. Outlines Jung's theories, and claims that the structure of *Fifth Business* is indebted to Jung's concept of "individuation," the growth of the individual personality towards wholeness.

Ryrie, John. "Robertson Davies: An Annotated Bibliography." *Annotated Bibliography of Canada's Major Authors.* Toronto: ECW, 1981. 3: 57–279. A comprehensive and well-presented bibliography of Davies' writings and the critical response to them.

Thomas, Clara. "The Two Voices of *A Mixture of Frailties*" (Heintzman 82–91). Concludes that the narration of *A Mixture of Frailties* is divided between a "social-satirist" voice in the account of Salterton and a voice "warm with human understanding and sympathy" to relate Monica Gall's story.

Williams, David. "The Confessions of a Self-Made Man: Forms of Autobiography in *Fifth Business*." *Journal of Canadian Studies* 24 (1989): 81–102. Uses current autobiographical theory as the basis for a skeptical view of Dunstan Ramsay's "self-justifying" confessions. Suggests that Dunstan suppresses and distorts his mother's role in his life and idealizes Mary Dempster for psychological reasons. Argues against a Jungian interpretation of the novel.

—THOMAS E. TAUSKY

General Bibliography

The emphasis here is on materials that are reasonably accessible to the reader who wants more information on various aspects of international literature in English. Assistance with this bibliography was provided by Nan Bowman Albinski (New Zealand), Robert Hamner (Caribbean), and Thomas Tausky (Canada).

PART ONE: INTERNATIONAL MATERIALS

Journals

The following journals, with the exception of *World Literature Today*, are devoted exclusively to international literature in English. (*WLT* regularly includes such material and reviews, along with its coverage of literature in several languages.) The articles are varied: focusing on writers from any one of the countries where English is a literary language; taking a comparative approach; tracing literary movements; formulating critical theory; providing bibliographical material. The country of publication is given in parentheses.

ACLALS Bulletin (published by the Association of Commonwealth Literature and Language Studies; publication place varies with ACLALS Headquarters)

Ariel—A Review of International English Literature (Canada)

Australian and New Zealand Studies in Canada (Canada)

Commonwealth (France)

Journal of Commonwealth Literature (Great Britain)

Kunapipi (Denmark)

Literary Criterion (India)

Literary Half-Yearly (India)

New Literature Review (Australia)

SPAN (Australia)

World Literature Today (U.S.A.)

World Literature Written in English (Canada)

Bibliography

Journal of Commonwealth Literature publishes a yearly bibliography of literary and critical works from the various regions.

Critical Theory

Ariel (special journal issue)—Articles on Post-Colonialism and Post-Modernism (Vol. 20.4, 1989).

Ashcroft, Bill, Gareth Griffiths, and Helen Tiffin. *The Empire Writes Back.* New York: Routledge, 1989.

Durix, Jean-Pierre. *The Writer Written: The Artist and Creation in the New Literatures in English.* Westport, Conn.: Greenwood, 1987.

Harris, Wilson. *The Womb of Space; The Cross-Cultural Imagination.* Westport, Conn.: Greenwood, 1983.

Zach, Wolfgang, editor. *Literature(s) in English, New Perspectives.* New York: Lang, 1990.

Histories. Surveys

Commonwealth Literature. Introduction by William Walsh. London: Macmillan, 1979. (Collection of bio-bibliographical materials on individual writers)

Ferres, John H., and Martin Tucker, editors. *Modern Commonwealth Literature* (A Library of Literary Criticism). New York: Ungar, 1977.

Goldie, Terry. *Fear and Temptation: The Image of the Indigine in Canadian, Australian and New Zealand Literature.* Kingston: McGill-Queen's UP, 1989.

Gurr, Andrew. *Writers in Exile, The Creative Use of Home in Modern Literature.* Atlantic Highlands, N.J.: 1981.

King, Bruce. *The New Literatures in English—Cultural Nationalism in a Changing World.* New York: St. Martin's, 1980.

Kirkpatrick, D.L., editor. *Contemporary Novelists.* 4th Ed. New York: St. Martin's, 1986. (Not devoted exclusively to international literature in English, but includes many major figures)

Larson, Charles R. *The Novel in the Third World.* Washingtdon, D.C.: Inscape, 1976.

Nightingale, Peggy, editor. *A Sense of Place in the New Literatures in English.* St. Lucia: U of Queensland P, 1986.

Singh, Kirpal, editor. *The Writer's Sense of the Past (Essays on Southeast Asian and Australasian Literature).* Singapore: Singapore UP, 1988.

Walsh, William. *Commonwealth Literature.* New York: Oxford UP, 1973.

PART TWO: NATIONAL MATERIALS

AFRICA

Journals

African Literature Today (Sierra Leone)

African Studies Review (U.S.A.)

English in Africa (South Africa)

Research in African Literatures (U.S.A.)

Bibliographies

Berria, Brenda F. *Bibliography of African Women Writers and Journalists (Ancient Egypt—1984).* Washington, D.C.: Three Continents Press, 1985.

Lindfors, Bernth. *Black African Literature in English: A Guide to Information Sources.* Detroit: Gale, 1979.

———. *Black African Literature in English, 1977–1981, Supplement.* New York: Africana Publishing, 1986.

———. *Black African Literature in English, 1982–1986.* New York: Hans Zell, 1989.

Critical Theory

Amuta, Chici. *The Theory of African Literature.* London: Zed Books, 1989.

Chinweizu, Onwucheka Jemie, and Ihechukwa Madubuike. *Towards the Decolonisation of African Litera-*

ture. Washington, D.C.: Howard University Press, 1983.

JanMohammed, Abdul. *Manichaean Aesthetics: The Politics of Literature in Colonial Africa.* Amherst: U of Massachusetts P, 1983.

Ngugi wa Thiong'o. *Decolonising the Mind: The Politics of Language in African Literature.* London: Currey, 1986.

Research in African Literatures (special journal issue)—Articles on Critical Approaches to African Literature (Vol. 21.1, 1990).

Histories, Surveys

Coetzee, J.M. *White Writing, On the Culture of Letters in South Africa.* New Haven: Yale UP, 1988.

Gray, Stephen. *Southern African Literature.* London: Rex Collins, 1979.

Gikandi, Simon. *Reading the African Novel.* London: James Currey, 1987.

Klein, Leonard S., general editor. *African Literatures in the 20th Century, A Guide.* New York: Ungar, 1986.

Obiechina, Emmanuel, editor. *Language and Theme: Essays on African Literature.* Washington, D.C.: Howard University Press, 1990.

AUSTRALIA

Journals

Antipodes—A North American Journal of Australian Literature (U.S.A.)

Australasian Drama Studies (Australia) (Includes materials on the South Pacific and Southeast Asia)

Australian Literary Studies (Australia)

Meanjin (Australia)

Southerly (Australia)

Westerly (Australia) (Includes materials on the South Pacific and Southeast Asia)

Bibliographies

Andrews, Barry G., and William H. Wilde. *Australian Literature to 1900: A Guide to Information Sources.* Detroit: Gale, 1980.

Day, A. Grove. *Modern Australian Prose, 1901–1975: A Guide to Information Sources.* Detroit: Gale, 1980.

Jaffa, Herbert C. *Modern Australian Poetry, 1920–1970: A Guide to Information Sources.* Detroit: Gale, 1979.

Ross, Robert L. *Australian Literary Criticism—1945–1988, An Annotated Bibliography.* New York: Garland, 1989.

Critical Theory

Docker, John. *In a Critical Condition: Reading Australian Literature.* Melbourne: Penguin Australia, 1984.

Gibson, Ross. *The Diminishing Paradise: Changing Literary Perceptions of Australia.* Sydney: Angus & Robertson, 1984.

Hope, A.D. "A.D. Hope Reflects on the Advent of an Australian Literature." *London Review of Books.* 4 Sept. 1986: 10–11.

Histories, Surveys

Goodwin, Ken. *A History of Australian Literature.* London: Macmillan, 1986.

Green, H.M. *A History of Australian Literature.* 2 vols. Sydney: Angus & Robertson, 1961. Rev. by Dorothy Green, 1984.

Hergenhan, Laurie, editor. *The Penguin New Literary History of Australia.* Melbourne: Penguin Australia, 1988.

Kramer, Leonie, editor. *The Oxford History of Australian Literature.* Melbourne: Oxford UP, 1981.

Wilde, William H., Joy Hooton, and Barry Andrews. *The Oxford Companion to Australian Literature.* Melbourne: Oxford UP, 1985.

CANADA

Journals

American Review of Canadian Studies (U.S.A.)

Atlantis: A Women's Studies Journal (Canada)

Books in Canada (Canada)

British Journal of Canadian Studies (Scotland)

Canadian Literature (Canada)

Canadian Poetry: Studies, Documents, Reviews (Canada)

Essays in Canadian Writing (Canada)

Studies in Canadian Literature (Canada)

Bibliographies

Fee, Margery, and Ruth Cawker. *Canadian Fiction: An Annotated Bibliography.* Toronto: Peter Martin Associates, 1976.

Gnarowski, Michael. *A Concise Bibliography of English-Canadian Literature.* 2nd ed. Toronto: McClelland & Stewart, 1978.

Lecker, Robert, and Jack David. *The Annotated Bibliography of Canada's Major Authors.* 7 vols. to date; four authors per volume. Toronto: ECW Press.

Moyles, R.S. *English-Canadian Literature to 1900: A Guide to Information Sources.* Detroit: Gale, 1976.

Watters, R.E., and Iglis Freeman Bell. *On Canadian Literature 1806–1960.* Toronto: U of Toronto P, 1966.

Critical Theory

Moss, John, editor. *Future Indicative: Literary Theory and Canadian Literature.* Ottawa: U of Ottawa P, 1987.

Histories, Surveys

Keith, W.J. *Canadian Literature in English.* New York: Longman, 1985.

Klinck, Carl F., editor. *Literary History of Canada.* 2nd ed. 3 vols. Toronto: U of Toronto P, 1976. W.H. New, editor, Vol. 4. Toronto: U of Toronto P, 1990.

Lecker, Robert, Jack David, and Ellen Quigley. *Canadian Writers and Their Works.* 14 vols to date; monographs on four or five writers in each volume. Toronto: ECW Press.

Moss, John, editor. *The Canadian Novel: A Critical Anthology.* 4 vols. subtitled *Beginnings, Modern Times, Present Tense, Here and Now.* Toronto: NC Press, 1980–85.

New, W.H. *A History of Canadian Literature.* London: Macmillan, 1989.

———, editor. *Dictionary of Literary Biography.* Vol. 53: *Canadian Writers Since 1960, First Series.* Vol.

60: *Canadian Writers Since 1960, Second Series.* Vol. 68: *Canadian Writers, 1920–1959, First Series.* Vol. 88: *Canadian Writers, 1920–1959, Second Series.* Vol. 92: *Canadian Writers, 1890–1920.* Detroit: Gale, 1986–1990.

Reappraisals: Canadian Writers. Proceedings of an annual conference. 14 vols to date. Ottawa: U of Ottawa P.

Toye, William, editor. *The Oxford Companion to Canadian Literature.* Toronto: Oxford UP, 1983.

CARIBBEAN

Journals

Caribbean Quarterly (Jamaica)

Caribbean Review (U.S.A.)

Journal of Caribbean Studies (U.S.A.)

Journal of West Indian Literature (Barbados)

Bibliographies

Allis, Jeannette B., editor. *West Indian Literature: An Index to Criticism, 1930–1975.* Boston: G.K. Hall, 1981.

Dance, Daryl Cumber, editor. *Fifty Caribbean Writers: A Bio-Bibliographical Critical Sourcebook.* New York: Greenwood Press, 1986.

Critical Theory

Baugh, Edward, editor. *Critics on Caribbean Literature.* London: Allen and Unwin, 1978. (Four divisions: "Contexts for Criticism"; "From Colonialism to Independence"; "Relationships: Individual, Community, Mankind"; "A Language of One's Own")

Smilowitz, Erika Sollish, and Roberta Quarles Knowles, editors. *Critical Issues in West Indian Literature.* Parkersburg, Iowa: Caribbean Books, 1984.

Histories, Surveys

Brown, Lloyd W. *West Indian Poetry.* New York: G.K. Hall, 1978.

Burnett, Paula, editor. *The Penguin Book of Caribbean Verse in English.* Harmondsworth: Penguin, 1986.

Gilkes, Michael. *The West Indian Novel.* Boston: Twayne, 1981.

Herdeck, Donald, editor. *Caribbean Writers: A Bio-Bibliographical-Critical Encyclopedia.* Washington, DC: Three Continents Press, 1979.

James, Louis, editor. *The Islands in Between: Essays in West Indian Literature.* London: Oxford UP, 1968.

King, Bruce, editor. *West Indian Literature.* London: Macmillan, 1979.

McWatt, Mark, editor. *West Indian Literature and Its Social Context.* Cave Hill, Barbados: Proceedings of the Fourth Annual Conference on West Indian Literature, 1985.

Ramchand, Kenneth. *An Introduction to the Study of West Indian Literature.* London: Thomas Nelson & Sons, 1976.

———. *The West Indian Novel and Its Background.* New York: Barnes and Noble, 1970.

Van Sertima, Ivan, editor. *Caribbean Writers.* London: New Beacon, 1968.

INDIA

Journals

Journal of Indian Writing in English (India)

Literary Endeavour (India)

South Asian Review (U.S.A.)

Kakatiya Journal of English Studies (India)

Bibliography

Singh, Amritjit, Rajiva Verma, and Irene M. Joshi. *Indian Literature in English, 1827–1979: A Guide to Information Sources.* Detroit: Gale Research, 1981.

Critical Theory

Iyengar, K.R. Srinivasa. *The Adventure of Criticism.* Bombay: Asia Publishing House, 1963.

Jussawalla, Feroza. *Family Quarrels: Towards a Criticism of Indian Writing in English.* New York: Lang, 1985.

Histories, Surveys

Butcher, Maggie, editor. *The Eye of the Beholder: Indian Writing in English.* London: Commonwealth Institute, 1983.

Kachru, Braj B. *The Indianization of English: The English Language in India.* Delhi: Oxford UP, 1983.

Mukherjee, Meenakshi. *The Twice Born Fiction: Themes and Techniques of the Indian Novel in English.* New Delhi: Heinemann Educational Books, 1971.

Naik, M.K. *A History of Indian Writing in English.* New Delhi: Sahitya Akademi, 1981.

Naik, M.K., editor. *Dimensions of Indian Literature in English.* Delhi: Sterling, 1984.

Srinivasa, Iyengar, K.R. *Indian Writing in English.* 4th ed. Delhi: Sterling, 1984.

NEW ZEALAND

Journals

Journal of New Zealand Literature (New Zealand)

Landfall (New Zealand)

Histories, Surveys

Beatson, Peter. *The Healing Tongue, Themes in Contemporary Maori Literature.* Palmerston North: Massey U Studies in New Zealand Art & Society 1, 1989.

Evans, Patrick. *The Penguin History of New Zealand Literature.* Auckland: Penguin, 1990.

Hankin, Cherry, editor. *Critical Essays on the New Zeland Novel.* Auckland: Heinemann, 1976.

————, editor. *Critical Essays on the New Zealand Short Story.* Auckland: Heinemann, 1982.

Jones, Lawrence, editor. *Barbed Wire and Mirrors.* Otago: U of Otago P, 1987.

Stead, C.K. *In the Glass Case, Essays on New Zealand Literature.* Auckland: Auckland UP, 1981.

Williams, Mark. *Leaving the Highway, Six Contemporary New Zealand Novelists.* Auckland: Auckland UP, 1990.

Sturm, Terry, editor. *The Oxford History of New Zealand Literature in English.* Forthcoming.

SOUTH PACIFIC, SINGAPORE, MALAYSIA

Histories, Surveys

Fernando, Lloyd. *Cultures in Conflict.* Singapore: Grahame Brash, 1986.

Hyland, L. *Discharging the Canon: Cross Cultural Readings in Literature.* Singapore: Singapore University Press, 1986.

Simms, Norman. *Silence and Invisibility: A Study of the Literatures of the Pacific, Australia and New Zealand.* Washington, DC: Three Continents Press, 1986.

Subramani. *South Pacific Literature: From Myth to Fabulation.* Suva: University of the South Pacific Press, 1985.

Yap, Arthur. *A Brief Critical Survey of Prose Writings in Singapore and Malaysia.* Singapore: Educational Publications Bureau, 1972.

Index

A

G

Contributors

Cecil A. Abrahams *was born in South Africa. Opposing apartheid, he left there in the 1960s to do graduate work in Canada. Since then he has taught at universities in Canada, Africa, and the Caribbean. He is now Professor of English at Brock University, Canada. A pioneer in the field of African literature, he has published numerous articles and critical books, including one on Alex La Guma, and has edited several collections of essays. He is the personal and literary biographer of two South African writers, Alex La Guma and Peter Abrahams.*

Fawzia Afzal-Khan *was born in Pakistan, and grew up there and in Africa. Receiving her Ph.D. from Tufts University in 1986, she is now an Assistant Professor of World Literature at Montclair State College in New Jersey. She has published articles on several Asian writers and her book,* Cultural Imperialism, *is forthcoming from Princeton University Press.*

Nan Bowman Albinski *is an Australian teaching in the English Department at Pennsylvania State University. She has published extensively on Australian/New Zealand literature and utopian fiction, including* Women's Utopias in British and American Fiction *(1989). She is currently working on a biography of the Victorian feminist writer, Lady Florence Dixie, and on a series of annotated bibliographies for the Australian/New Zealand Studies Center at PSU.*

Marian Arkin, *Professor of English at City University of New York, LaGuardia, is co-editor of the* Longman Anthology of World Literature by Women *(1988) and author of several articles and books on pedagogy. She is managing editor of* Antipodes *(A North American Journal of Australian Literature) and on the editorial advisory board of* Ariel.

Shyam Asnani, *Associate Professor of English at Himachal Pradesh University in Shimla, India, is the author of* Critical Response to the Indian English Novel *(1985) and* New Dimensions of the Indian English Novel *(1987). He was the guest editor of* Literary Endeavour's *special issue on Patrick White (1986) and has published numerous articles on Indian writing in English.*

Rudolf Bader, *Switzerland, has published widely in the field of international literature, particularly Australian, and has been associated with universities in*

Singapore, Australia, and Canada. He is currently at the University of Wuppertal in Germany. His book, Images of Europe in Australian Literature, *is forthcoming.*

Bruce Bennett *is Associate Professor of English and Director of the Centre for Studies in Australian Literature at the University of Western Australia in Perth. He edits the literary quarterly* Westerly, *and is the editor of several books, including* A Sense of Exile: Essays in the Literature of the Asia-Pacific Region *(1988),* European Relations *(1985),* Place, Region and Community *(1985), and* The Literature of Western Australia *(1979). He has also published many articles on Australian literature.*

T.G. Bishop *is an Australian who received his Ph.D. from Yale University recently and is an Assistant Professor of English at Case Western Reserve University. He teaches Renaissance literature but maintains a lively interest in the writing from his homeland, especially the poetry.*

Carolyn Bliss *is the author of* Patrick White's Fiction: The Paradox of Fortunate Failure *(1986), as well as numerous articles on White and Australian literature in general. She teaches in the Humanities Division of the University of Utah and is the editor of the* Newsletter *of the American Association of Australian Literary Studies. In 1988 she was invited to Australia by the Australian government for a familiarization tour of the country.*

Diana Brydon *teaches at Guelph University, Canada, where she edits* World Literature Written in English. *Her interests range across international literature in English and recently she has focused in particular on critical theory as it pertains to the formation of postcolonial discourse. She is the author of* Christina Stead *(1987).*

Leonard Casper, *Professor of English, Boston College, is the author-editor of six volumes on Philippine literature, and since 1969 has been involved with the* Encyclopedia Americana *entry on the Philippines, where he has twice been a Fulbright lecturer.*

Ramesh Chadha *teaches at Himachal Pradesh University, Shimla, India, and is the author of* Cross-Cultural Interaction in Indian English Fiction *(1988). She has contributed numerous articles and reviews to Indian journals.*

Thomas P. Coakley *is a Professor of English at the United States Air Force Academy and a Lieutenant Colonel. In addition to articles on American and Australian literature, he is the author of* War in the Information Age: Command, Control, and Technology.

Greta McCormick Coger *was born in Canada, but now teaches at Northwest Mississippi College. She is the founder of the Margaret Laurence Society and editor of its* Newsletter. *Among her publications are several articles on*

Laurence's work, as well as Index to Subjects, Proverbs, and Theme in the Writings of Wole Soyinka *(1988).*

Rosemary Colmer, *who was born in the Sudan, is a Lecturer in English at Macquarie University, Sydney, where she is involved with the Post-Colonial Literatures and Language Research Centre. She has written extensively on West African fiction and is currently editing a collection of essays,* A Change of Skies: The Literature of Migration.

Helen Daniel *is a book dealer in Melbourne and writes on contemporary Australian fiction. She is the author of* Double Agent: David Ireland and His Work *(1982),* Liars: Australian New Novelists *(1988), and numerous articles, especially on postmodernism. She has recently edited* Expressway, *a collection of short stories by Australian writers, and compiled* The Good Reading Guide *(1989), a book that selects the favorite Australian fiction from 1968-88.*

Robert Darling *recently completed a Ph.D. dissertation on the poetry of A.D. Hope, at the University of Rhode Island; he is now an Assistant Professor of English at Keuka College, New York. In addition to reviewing and writing about poetry, he regularly publishes poems in American, British, and Australian magazines.*

Reed Way Dasenbrock, *Professor of English at New Mexico State University, is the author of* PMLA*'s first article on international literature in English (102.1, 1987). He has published extensively on the work of James Joyce, comparative literature, literary theory, and the writing of various figures from Africa and the Caribbean.*

Lakshmi de Silva, *Senior Lecturer in English at University of Kelaniya, Sri Lanka, specializes in drama and has translated into English the Sinhalese work of Martin Wickramasinghe and Ediriwira Sarachchandra.*

Jean-Pierre Durix, *Professor of English at the University of Burgundy, France, edits* Commonwealth, *an international journal. He is the author of numerous articles and* The Writer Written, The Artist and Creation in the New Literatures in English *(1987). He has also translated into French novels by Wilson Harris and Witi Ihimaera.*

Phyllis Fahrie Edelson, *Professor of English at Pace University, New York, is editing an anthology of Australian literature, to be published soon by Ballantine. Having published several articles on Australian writing, she is also the book review editor for* Antipodes *and the author of* A Guide to Australian Masterworks.

Rodney Edgecombe *recently published* Vision and Style in Patrick White *(1989). A Senior Lecturer at the University of Cape Town, South Africa, he is* *the author of a book on George Herbert and is currently writing one on the American poet Richard Wilbur.*

Margery Fee, *Director of the Strathy Language Unit at Queen's University, Canada, has published articles on Keri Hulme as well as on Canadian writers, criticism, literary nationalism, and English usage in Canada.*

Pierrette Frickey *was born in France and now teaches comparative literature at West Georgia College. Developing an interest in West Indian literature during recent years, she has just completed editing a book of essays,* Critical Perspectives on Jean Rhys.

James Gibbs *teaches at the University of Liege, Belgium, and has published extensively on Wole Soyinka, including a book on his drama,* Wole Soyinka *(1986). He also assisted in preparing* Wole Soyinka: A Bibliography of Primary and Secondary Sources *(1984) and edited the special "Soyinka Issue" for* Research in African Literatures *(14.1, 1983) as well as* Critical Perspectives on Wole Soyinka *(1980).*

Yasmine Gooneratne, *who was born in Sri Lanka, is the Director of Macquarie University's Post-Colonial Literatures and Language Research Centre (Sydney). Her varied books include critical studies of Alexander Pope, Jane Austen, Ruth Prawer Jhabvala (*Silence, Exile and Cunning, *1983, 1990), and nineteenth-century Sri Lankan writing. She has also published poetry and fiction, as well as Sri Lankan history, and is the editor of* New Ceylon Writing. *Professor Gooneratne was recently awarded the Order of Australia for her distinguished contribution to literature and education.*

Sherrill E. Grace *is Professor of English at the University of British Columbia. She has published widely on modern literature, including books on Margaret Atwood and Malcolm Lowry. Her most recent book is* Regression and Apocalypse: Studies in North American Literary Expressionism *(1989). She is currently preparing a scholarly, annotated edition of* The Collected Letters of Malcolm Lowry.

Robert Hamner, *Professor of English and Humanities at Hardin-Simmons University, Texas, has served as Fulbright Professor at the University of Guyana and has published numerous articles on West Indian literature. His books include* V.S. Naipaul *(1973),* Critical Perspectives on V.S. Naipaul *(1977),* Derek Walcott *(1981), and* Third World Perspectives on Joseph Conrad *(1989).*

Anthony J. Hassall *is Professor of English at James Cook University of North Queensland, Australia, where he is also Director of the Foundation for Australian Literary Studies. He has published many articles on Australian fiction and on eighteenth-century English literature. His books include* Henry Fielding's

Tom Jones *(1979)*, Strange Country: A Study of Randolph Stow *(1986, 1990), and* The Making of Xavier Herbert's "Poor Fellow My Country" *(1988). He edited the Randolph Stow volume for the Australian Authors Series (1990), and is General Editor of the University of Queensland Press's Studies in Australian Literature Series. He is currently writing a book on Peter Carey's work.*

Temple Hauptfleisch *is Lecturer in Theatre Studies at the University of Stellenbosch, South Africa, where he also heads the Theatre Research Project. Founder and co-editor of the* South African Theatre Journal, *he has also published extensively on South African theater, including a bibliographical study of Athol Fugard and, with Ian Steadman,* South African Theatre: Four Plays and an Introduction *(1985). He is the author of twelve plays and editor of several one-act play collections.*

J.J. Healy, *Professor of English at Carleton University, Canada, is a pioneer critic of Australian Aboriginal literature. He has published numerous articles on both the way Anglo-Celtic writers in Australia have treated Aborigines in fiction and the writing of Aborigines. His* Literature and the Aborigine in Australia, *first published in 1979, was recently released in a revised edition.*

Ramā Jha *is both a professor and publisher, teaching at the University of Delhi and working with Chanakya Publications, which specializes in scholarly books on all aspects of Indian art and society. She is the author of* Gandhian Thought and Indo-Anglian Novelists *(1983) and numerous articles on Indian writers. Actively involved in the women's movement in India, she also regularly contributes to national newspapers as a reviewer and commentator.*

Feroza Jussawalla, *who was born and grew up in India, is Associate Professor of English at the University of Texas, El Paso, where she founded the Asian and African Studies Program. She is the author of* Family Quarrels: Towards a Criticism of Indian Writing in English *(1985) as well as articles on Indian fiction in English.*

Paul Kane, *Assistant Professor of English at Vassar College, has published several essays on Australian poetry and is the poetry editor of* Antipodes. *During 1984 he was a Fulbright Scholar in Australia. His own book of poems,* The Farther Shore, *appeared in 1989.*

Brian Kiernan, *Associate Professor of English at the University of Sydney, has published extensively on Australian literature, his books and articles ranging from Henry Handel Richardson to Patrick White. He has also edited a collection of Henry Lawson's work and an anthology of contemporary Australian short stories. His most recent book is* David Williamson: A Writer's Career *(1990), a critical biography of Australia's leading playwright.*

G.D. Killam, *Professor of English at Guelph University, Canada, edited* World Literature Written in English *for many years. Long a critic of African literature, he has published and edited books on various writers, including Achebe and Ngugi. He is one of the general editors for* The Routledge Encyclopaedia of Commonwealth Literature, *scheduled for publication in 1992.*

Liew-Geok Leong *is a Senior Lecturer at National University of Singapore. Her research interests include the relations between history and literature and she is currently working on a series of essays focusing on the literature emerging from the Pacific War in Singapore and Malaysia. Her first volume of poetry appeared in 1990.*

Florence Libert *recently completed graduate work at the University of Nice in France, where she wrote on Anita Desai's work. A native of France, she teaches in the Foreign Language Department at the University of Texas, Austin, and is currently translating Desai's short stories into French.*

Craig MacKenzie *is a researcher at the National English Literary Museum in Grahamstown, South Africa. Completing a thesis in 1985 at the University of Natal on the writings of Bessie Head, he has published several articles on her work as well as* Bessie Head: An Introduction *(1989). He is co-editor of* Between the Lines *(1989), which includes an interview with Head.*

Hena Maes-Jelinek *is Professor of English and Commonwealth Literature at the University of Liege, Belgium, and president of its Centre for Commonwealth Studies. Her books include* Criticism of Society in the English Novel between the Wars *(1970),* The Naked Design *(1976), and* Wilson Harris *(1982). She has edited* Commonwealth Literature and the Modern World *(1975) and with others* Multiple Worlds: Multiple Words *(1987),* A Shaping of Connections—Commonwealth Literature Then and Now *(1989), and* Crisis and Creativity in the New Literatures in English *(1990). She is also one of the editors for a new series published by Rodopi of Amsterdam, "Cross/Cultures, Readings in the Post-Colonial Literatures in English."*

Lois A. Marchino *wrote one of the earliest dissertations on Doris Lessing, and since then has continued reading and writing about her work and that of other contemporary women novelists. She teaches at the University of Texas, El Paso.*

Gerald Monsman, *Professor of English at the University of Arizona, has written several books on nineteenth-century British figures, including* Confessions of a Prosaic Dreamer: Charles Lamb's Art of Autobiography *(1984),* Walter Pater's Art of Autobiography *(1980),* Walter Pater *(1977), and* Pater's Portraits *(1967). He has published essays on Olive Schreiner, Gerard Manley Hopkins, Romanticism, and the Victorian period.*

Patrick Morrow, *Professor of English at Auburn University, has published articles and books on Bret Harte and the Western frontier, but in recent years has turned his attention to the literature of the South Pacific about which he has published several articles. In 1981 he was a Fulbright Professor in New Zealand and in 1989 was awarded a Fulbright grant to do research in New Guinea.*

Peggy Nightingale *is a Senior Lecturer at the University of New South Wales, Sydney, and is the author of* Journey Through Dartkness: The Writing of V.S. Naipaul. *She edited* A Sense of Place in the New Literatures in English *and has published articles on South Pacific and West Indian literature.*

Jonathan Paton *is a Senior Lecturer in Education at the University of the Witwatersrand, South Africa. He edited with Marcia Leveson an anthology of South African poetry,* Voices of the Land *(1985), and published in 1990* The Land and People of South Africa.

Kirsten Holst Petersen, *who teaches at the University of Aarhus, Denmark, has published widely in the field of postcolonial studies, including work on African women writers and the African poet John Pepper Clark. From 1983 to 1986 she was the Danish Research Scholar at the Scandinavian Institute for African Studies. She has also co-edited several books of essays on African literature and is one of the editors of* Kunapipi, *a journal of international literature in English.*

Nancy Potter, *Professor of English at the University of Rhode Island, has long been involved in the study of international literature in English and has been a Fulbright Professor in New Zealand. A fiction writer herself, she has published two volumes of short stories,* We Have Seen the Best of Our Times *and* Legacies.

Horst Priessnitz, *a Professor at the University of Wuppertal, Germany, has published extensively on Australian literature, both in English and German, focusing in particular on the reception, modification, and adaptation of Anglo-European literature in Australia. Other areas of interest include British and American poetry. He is the co-founder of the Society for Australian Studies in Germany.*

A.P. Riemer, *Associate Professor of English at the University of Sydney, has written extensively on Renaissance literature, including two books on Shakespeare and critical editions of four of his plays. In recent years he has directed his attention toward Australian literature and has published studies on the works of Patrick White, Christina Stead, and Elizabeth Jolley.*

Victor J. Ramraj *is Professor of English at the University of Calgary, Canada. He is the author of* Mordecai Richler *(1983) and of numerous articles on several areas of international English literature, particularly Caribbean and Canadian.*

He is co-editor of West Indian Short Stories: An Anthology, 1900-1980 *(1990) and is the editor of* Ariel: A Review of International English Literature.

Robert L. Ross *is editor of* Antipodes *and the author of* Australian Literary Criticism, 1945-1988 *(1989). He has published extensively on Australian writers as well as on other figures from international literature in English. He is a Research Associate at The Edward A. Clark Center for Australian Studies, University of Texas at Austin.*

Rowland Smith *is McCulloch Professor at Dalhousie University, Canada, and Dean of Arts and Social Sciences. Former Director of Dalhousie's Centre for African Studies, he has written widely on modern British literature and international English literature. His publications include* Lyric and Polemic: The Literary Personality of Roy Campbell *(1972), and, as editor,* Exile and Tradition: Studies in African and Caribbean Literature *(1976) and* Critical Essays on Nadine Gordimer *(1990).*

Thomas E. Tausky, *Professor of English at the University of Western Ontario, Canada, edited Sarah Jeannette Duncan's* The Simple Adventures of a Memsahib *(1986). He has also published articles on Canadian literature and is editor of the journal* Australian and New Zealand Studies in Canada.

J.A. Wainwright *is a Professor of English at Dalhousie University, Canada. He has published numerous articles on modern Canadian literature, as well as a literary biography of the Canadian poet-novelist Charles Bruce. In addition he has published four books of poetry.*

Ray Willbanks, *Professor of English at Memphis State University, is the author of* Randolph Stow *(1978), as well as articles on Stow's work. His book of interviews with Australian writers,* Australian Voices *was published by the University of Texas Press in 1991. He is fiction editor for* Antipodes.

Sharon R. Wilson *is Professor of English and Women's Studies at the University of Northern Colorado, Greeley. Founding Co-President of the Margaret Atwood Society, she has published extensively on Atwood, including the first articles on her visual art. She has also published articles on Doris Lessing and Samuel Beckett.*